1 CORINTHIANS

Baker Exegetical Commentary on the New Testament

ROBERT W. YARBROUGH AND ROBERT H. STEIN, EDITORS

Volumes now available

Luke	*Darrell L. Bock*
Romans	*Thomas R. Schreiner*
1 Corinthians	*David E. Garland*
Revelation	*Grant R. Osborne*

David E. Garland (Ph.D., The Southern Baptist Theological Seminary) is professor of New Testament at Truett Theological Seminary, Baylor University. In addition to his other publications, he has written commentaries on Mark and Colossians/Philemon and is the New Testament editor for the revision of the Expositor's Bible Commentary.

1 CORINTHIANS

DAVID E. GARLAND

Baker Exegetical Commentary on the New Testament

Baker Academic

A Division of Baker Book House Co
Grand Rapids, Michigan 49516

©2003 by David E. Garland

Published by Baker Academic
a division of Baker Book House Company
P.O. Box 6287, Grand Rapids, MI 49516–6287
www.bakeracademic.com

Printed in the United States of America

Library of Congress Cataloging-in-Publication Data

Garland, David E.
    1 Corinthians / David E. Garland.
       p. cm. — (Baker exegetical commentary on the New Testament)
    Includes bibliographical references (p.) and indexes.
    ISBN 0–8010–2630-X (cloth)
    1. Bible. N.T. Corinthians, 1st—Commentaries. I. Title: First Corinthians. II. Title.
III. Series.
BS2675.53.G37 2003
227′.2077—dc21   2003041852

To John and Sarah

Contents

Series Preface

The chief concern of the Baker Exegetical Commentary on the New Testament (BECNT) is to provide, within the framework of informed evangelical thought, commentaries that blend scholarly depth with readability, exegetical detail with sensitivity to the whole, and attention to critical problems with theological awareness. We hope thereby to attract the interest of a fairly wide audience, from the scholar who is looking for a thoughtful and independent examination of the text to the motivated lay Christian who craves a solid but accessible exposition.

Nevertheless, a major purpose is to address the needs of pastors and others involved in the preaching and exposition of the Scriptures as the uniquely inspired Word of God. This consideration affects directly the parameters of the series. For example, serious biblical expositors cannot afford to depend on a superficial treatment that avoids the difficult questions, but neither are they interested in encyclopedic commentaries that seek to cover every conceivable issue that may arise. Our aim, therefore, is to focus on those problems that have a direct bearing on the meaning of the text (although selected technical details are treated in the additional notes).

Similarly, a special effort is made to avoid treating exegetical questions for their own sake, that is, in relative isolation from the thrust of the argument as a whole. This effort may involve (at the discretion of the individual contributors) abandoning the verse-by-verse approach in favor of an exposition that focuses on the paragraph as the main unit of thought. In all cases, however, the commentaries will stress the development of the argument and explicitly relate each passage to what precedes and follows it so as to identify its function in context as clearly as possible.

We believe, moreover, that a responsible exegetical commentary must take fully into account the latest scholarly research, regardless of its source. The attempt to do this in the context of a conservative theological tradition presents certain challenges, and in the past the results have not always been commendable. In some cases, evangelicals appear to make use of critical scholarship not for the purpose of genuine interaction but only to dismiss it. In other cases, the interaction glides over into assimilation, theological distinctives are ignored or suppressed, and the end product cannot be differentiated from works that arise from a fundamentally different starting point.

The contributors to this series attempt to avoid these pitfalls. On the one hand, they do not consider traditional opinions to be sacrosanct, and they are certainly committed to do justice to the biblical text whether or not it supports such opinions. On the other hand, they will not quickly abandon a long-standing view, if there is persuasive evidence in its favor, for the sake of fashionable theories. What is more important, the contributors share a belief in the trustworthiness and essential unity of Scripture. They also consider that the historic formulations of Christian doctrine, such as the ecumenical creeds and many of the documents originating in the sixteenth-century Reformation, arose from a legitimate reading of Scripture, thus providing a proper framework for its further interpretation. No doubt, the use of such a starting point sometimes results in the imposition of a foreign construct on the text, but we deny that it must necessarily do so or that the writers who claim to approach the text without prejudices are invulnerable to the same danger.

Accordingly, we do not consider theological assumptions—from which, in any case, no commentator is free—to be obstacles to biblical interpretation. On the contrary, an exegete who hopes to understand the apostle Paul in a theological vacuum might just as easily try to interpret Aristotle without regard for the philosophical framework of his whole work or without having recourse to those subsequent philosophical categories that make possible a meaningful contextualization of his thought. It must be emphasized, however, that the contributors to the present series come from a variety of theological traditions and that they do not all have identical views with regard to the proper implementation of these general principles. In the end, all that really matters is whether the series succeeds in representing the original text accurately, clearly, and meaningfully to the contemporary reader.

Shading has been used to assist the reader in locating the introductory comments for each section. Textual variants in the Greek text are signaled in the author's translation by means of half-brackets around the relevant word or phrase (e.g., ⌜Gerasenes⌝), thereby alerting the reader to turn to the additional notes at the end of each exegetical unit for a discussion of the textual problem. The documentation uses the author-date method, in which the basic reference consists of author's surname + year + page number(s): Fitzmyer 1981: 297. The only exceptions to this system are well-known reference works (e.g., BDAG, LSJ, *TDNT*). Full publication data and a complete set of indexes can be found at the end of the volume.

Robert Yarbrough
Robert H. Stein

Author's Preface

I am grateful to many people for helping this commentary come to fruition. It is an interesting exercise to come to 1 Corinthians after first writing on 2 Corinthians in another series, and I thank Moisés Silva for offering me this opportunity to contribute to the BECNT series. Jim Kinney and Wells Turner from Baker Academic have been very supportive and patient, and Robert Yarbrough proved to be a careful and constructive editor. I am thankful to those students who have read the manuscript in various stages: Anni Judkins, Andy Arterbury, Derek Dodson, Adam English, James Edward Ellis, Justin T. Pankow, and Kris Pratt. I owe the greatest gratitude to Scott Bertrand, who read the entire manuscript and made invaluable comments. Diana, my wife and partner in the gospel, has always been a tower of strength and a model of the love Paul describes in 1 Corinthians 13. I am also in the debt of the many who have wrestled with this letter in various commentaries, monographs, and articles. They have become my teachers and debate partners. The contemporary relevance of this letter written to a Christian community situated in a city dominated by a worldview, aspirations, impulses, conventions, and symbolism that were antithetical to the cross of Christ was driven home to me in every section. Humanity has not changed its sinful ways since Paul wrote to the Corinthians, and only the gospel of the cross he proclaimed offers redemption.

David E. Garland

Abbreviations

Bibliographic and General

ABD   *The Anchor Bible Dictionary,* edited by D. N. Freedman et al., 6 vols. (New York: Doubleday, 1992)

BAGD   *A Greek-English Lexicon of the New Testament and Other Early Christian Literature,* by W. Bauer, W. F. Arndt, F. W. Gingrich, and F. W. Danker, 2d ed. (Chicago: University of Chicago Press, 1979)

BDAG   *A Greek-English Lexicon of the New Testament and Other Early Christian Literature,* by W. Bauer, F. W. Danker, W. F. Arndt, and F. W. Gingrich, 3d ed. (Chicago: University of Chicago Press, 2000)

BDF   *A Greek Grammar of the New Testament and Other Early Christian Literature,* by F. Blass, A. Debrunner, and R. W. Funk (Chicago: University of Chicago Press, 1961)

BGU   *Aegyptische Urkunden aus den Königlichen Staatlichen Museen zu Berlin, Griechische Urkunden,* 15 vols. (Berlin, 1895–1983)

CIL   *Corpus inscriptionum latinarum*

DBSup   *Dictionnaire de la Bible: Supplément,* edited by L. Pirot and A. Robert (Paris, 1928–)

DPL   *Dictionary of Paul and His Letters,* edited by G. F. Hawthorne and R. P. Martin (Downers Grove, Ill.: InterVarsity, 1993)

IG   *Inscriptiones graecae,* editio minor (Berlin, 1924–)

IGR   *Inscriptiones Graecae ad res Romanas pertinentes,* edited by R. Cagnat et al. (Rome: L'Erma, 1964)

JB   Jerusalem Bible

KJV   King James Version

LSJ   *A Greek-English Lexicon,* by H. G. Liddell, R. Scott, and H. S. Jones, 9th ed. (Oxford: Clarendon, 1968)

LXX   Septuagint

MM   *The Vocabulary of the Greek Testament: Illustrated from the Papyri and Other Non-literary Sources,* by J. H. Moulton and G. Milligan (reprinted Grand Rapids: Eerdmans, 1976)

MS(S)   manuscript(s)

MT   Masoretic Text

NA[27]   *Novum Testamentum Graece,* 27th rev. ed., edited by [E. and E. Nestle,] B. Aland, K. Aland, J. Karavidopoulos, C. M. Martini, and B. M. Metzger (Stuttgart: Deutsche Bibelgesellschaft, 1993)

NAB   New American Bible

NASB   New American Standard Bible

NEB   New English Bible

NIDNTT   *The New International Dictionary of New Testament Theology,* edited by L. Coenen, E. Beyreuther, and H. Bietenhard; English translation edited by C. Brown, 4 vols. (Grand Rapids: Zondervan, 1975–86)

NIV   New International Version

NJB	New Jerusalem Bible
NKJV	New King James Version
NRSV	New Revised Standard Version
NT	New Testament
OCD	*Oxford Classical Dictionary*, edited by S. Hornblower and A. Spawforth, 3d ed. (Oxford: Oxford University Press, 1996)
OT	Old Testament
OTP	*The Old Testament Pseudepigrapha*, edited by J. H. Charlesworth, 2 vols. (Garden City, N.Y.: Doubleday, 1983–85)
P. Oxy.	Papyrus Oxyrhynchus
Rab.	*Rabbah*
REB	Revised English Bible
RSV	Revised Standard Version
SB	*Kommentar zum Neuen Testament aus Talmud und Midrasch*, by H. L. Strack and P. Billerbeck, 6 vols. (Munich: Beck, 1922–61)
SEG	Supplementum epigraphicum graecum
SIG	*Sylloge inscriptionum graecarum*, edited by W. Dittenberger, 3d ed., 4 vols. (Leipzig, 1915–24)
TDNT	*Theological Dictionary of the New Testament*, edited by G. Kittel and G. Friedrich; translated and edited by G. W. Bromiley, 10 vols. (Grand Rapids: Eerdmans, 1964–76)
TEV	Today's English Version
TLNT	*Theological Lexicon of the New Testament*, by C. Spicq; translated and edited by J. D. Ernest, 3 vols. (Peabody, Mass.: Hendrickson, 1994)
UBS[4]	*The Greek New Testament*, 4th rev. ed., edited by B. Aland, K. Aland, J. Karavidopoulos, C. M. Martini, and B. M. Metzger (Stuttgart: Deutsche Bibelgesellschaft/United Bible Societies, 1993)

Hebrew Bible

Gen.	Genesis	2 Chron.	2 Chronicles	Dan.	Daniel
Exod.	Exodus	Ezra	Ezra	Hos.	Hosea
Lev.	Leviticus	Neh.	Nehemiah	Joel	Joel
Num.	Numbers	Esth.	Esther	Amos	Amos
Deut.	Deuteronomy	Job	Job	Obad.	Obadiah
Josh.	Joshua	Ps.	Psalms	Jon.	Jonah
Judg.	Judges	Prov.	Proverbs	Mic.	Micah
Ruth	Ruth	Eccles.	Ecclesiastes	Nah.	Nahum
1 Sam.	1 Samuel	Song	Song of Songs	Hab.	Habakkuk
2 Sam.	2 Samuel	Isa.	Isaiah	Zeph.	Zephaniah
1 Kings	1 Kings	Jer.	Jeremiah	Hag.	Haggai
2 Kings	2 Kings	Lam.	Lamentations	Zech.	Zechariah
1 Chron.	1 Chronicles	Ezek.	Ezekiel	Mal.	Malachi

Greek Testament

Matt.	Matthew	Eph.	Ephesians	Heb.	Hebrews
Mark	Mark	Phil.	Philippians	James	James
Luke	Luke	Col.	Colossians	1 Pet.	1 Peter
John	John	1 Thess.	1 Thessalonians	2 Pet.	2 Peter
Acts	Acts	2 Thess.	2 Thessalonians	1 John	1 John
Rom.	Romans	1 Tim.	1 Timothy	2 John	2 John
1 Cor.	1 Corinthians	2 Tim.	2 Timothy	3 John	3 John
2 Cor.	2 Corinthians	Titus	Titus	Jude	Jude
Gal.	Galatians	Philem.	Philemon	Rev.	Revelation

Other Jewish and Christian Writings

Adam and Eve	Books of Adam and Eve
Add. Esth.	Additions to Esther
Apol.	Tertullian, *Apologeticus* (*Apology*)
1–2 Apol.	Justin Martyr, *First and Second Apology*
As. Mos.	Assumption of Moses
Bar.	Baruch
2 Bar.	2 (Syriac Apocalypse of) Baruch
Barn.	Barnabas
Bel	Bel and the Dragon
Bib. Ant.	Pseudo-Philo, *Biblical Antiquities*
Cels.	Origen, *Contra Celsum* (*Against Celsus*)
1–2 Clem.	1–2 Clement
Dial.	Justin Martyr, *Dialogus cum Tryphone* (*Dialogue with Trypho*)
Did.	Didache
Diogn.	Diognetus
1 Enoch	1 (Ethiopic) Enoch
2 Enoch	2 (Slavonic) Enoch
1 Esdr.	1 Esdras
2 Esdr.	2 Esdras (4 Ezra)
Herm. Man.	Shepherd of Hermas, *Mandate(s)*
Herm. Sim.	Shepherd of Hermas, *Similitude(s)*
Herm. Vis.	Shepherd of Hermas, *Vision(s)*
Hom. 1 Cor.	John Chrysostom, *Homiliae in epistulam i ad Corinthios*
Hom. Rom.	John Chrysostom, *Homiliae in epistulam ad Romanos*

Ign. Eph.	Ignatius, *Letter to the Ephesians*
Ign. Magn.	Ignatius, *Letter to the Magnesians*
Ign. Pol.	Ignatius, *Letter to Polycarp*
Ign. Rom.	Ignatius, *Letter to the Romans*
Jdt.	Judith
Jos. As.	Joseph and Aseneth
Jov.	Jerome, *Adversus Jovinianum libri II*
Jub.	Jubilees
Let. Arist.	Letter of Aristeas
Let. Jer.	Letter of Jeremiah
1–4 Macc.	1–4 Maccabees
Marc.	Tertullian, *Adversus Marcionem* (*Against Marcion*)
Mart. Isa.	Martyrdom and Ascension of Isaiah
Mart. Pol.	Martyrdom of Polycarp
Odes Sol.	Odes of Solomon
Pol. Phil.	Polycarp, *Letter to the Philippians*
Ps.-Phoc.	Pseudo-Phocylides
Ps. Sol.	Psalms of Solomon
Sib. Or.	Sibylline Oracles
Sir.	Sirach (Ecclesiasticus)
T. Abr.	Testament of Abraham
T. Gad	Testament of Gad
T. Isaac	Testament of Isaac
T. Iss.	Testament of Issachar
T. Jacob	Testament of Jacob
T. Job	Testament of Job
T. Jos.	Testament of Joseph
T. Levi	Testament of Levi
T. Naph.	Testament of Naphtali

T. Reub.	Testament of Reuben	Tob.	Tobit
T. Sim.	Testament of Simeon	Wis.	Wisdom of Solomon
T. Sol.	Testament of Solomon		

Josephus and Philo

Abr.	On Abraham	Jos.	On Joseph
Ag. Ap.	Against Apion	J.W.	The Jewish War
Alleg. Interp.	Allegorical Interpretation	Life	The Life of Josephus
Ant.	Jewish Antiquities	Migr. Abr.	On the Migration of Abraham
Chang. Nam.	On the Change of Names	Mos.	On the Life of Moses
Cher.	On the Cherubim	Plant.	On Noah's Work as a Planter
Cont. Life	On the Contemplative Life		
		Post. Cain	On the Posterity and Exile of Cain
Creat.	On the Creation		
Decal.	On the Decalogue	Quest. Gen.	Questions and Answers on Genesis
Dreams	On Dreams		
Drunk.	On Drunkenness	Rewards	On Rewards and Punishments/On Curses
Flight	On Flight and Finding		
Gaius	On the Embassy to Gaius	Sacr.	On the Sacrifices of Abel and Cain
Good Free	Every Good Person Is Free	Sobr.	On Sobriety
		Spec. Laws	On the Special Laws
Heir	Who Is the Heir of Divine Things?	Unchang.	On the Unchangeableness of God
Husb.	On Husbandry	Virt.	On the Virtues
Hypoth.	Hypothetica/Apology for the Jews	Worse Att. Bet.	The Worse Attacks the Better

Rabbinic Tractates

The abbreviations below are used for the names of tractates in the Babylonian Talmud (indicated by a prefixed *b.*), Palestinian Jerusalem Talmud (*y.*), Mishnah (*m.*), and Tosefta (*t.*).

ʿAbod. Zar.	ʿAbodah Zarah	Ketub.	Ketubbot
ʾAbot	ʾAbot	Mak.	Makkot
ʿArak.	ʿArakin	Meg.	Megillah
B. Bat.	Baba Batra	Ned.	Nedarim
B. Meṣiʿa	Baba Meṣiʿa	Qidd.	Qidduŝin
B. Qam.	Baba Qamma	Šabb.	Šabbat
Ber.	Berakot	Sanh.	Sanhedrin
Bik.	Bikkurim	Soṭah	Soṭah
ʿErub.	ʿErubin	Sukkah	Sukkah
Giṭ.	Giṭṭin	Yebam.	Yebamot
Ḥul.	Ḥullin	Yoma	Yoma
Ker.	Kerithot	Zebaḥ.	Zebaḥim

Qumran / Dead Sea Scrolls

1QH	Thanksgiving Hymns/Psalms (*Hôdāyôt*)
1QM	War Scroll (*Milḥāmâ*)
1QpHab	Commentary (*Pesher*) on Habakkuk
1QS	Manual of Discipline (*Serek Hayyaḥad*, Rule/Order of the Community)
1QSa	Rule of the Congregation (1Q28a, appendix A to 1QS)
4Q416	Instruction[b] (formerly, Sap. Work A[b])
CD	Damascus Document

Classical Writers

Descr.	Pausanias, *Graeciae description* (*Description of Greece*)
Diatr.	Epictetus, *Diatribai/Dissertationes*
Eloc.	Demetrius, *De elocutione* (*Style*)
Ep.	various authors, *Epistulae* (*Epistles*)
Eth. nic.	Aristotle, *Ethica nicomachea* (*Nicomachean Ethics*)
Geogr.	Strabo, *Geographica* (*Geography*)
Inst.	Quintilian, *Institutio oratoria*
Leuc. Clit.	Achilles Tatius, *Leucippe et Clitophon* (*The Adventures of Leucippe and Cleitophon*)
Lives	Diogenes Laertius, *Lives of Eminent Philosophers*
Mem.	Xenophon, *Memorabilia*
Metam.	Apuleius, *Metamorphoses* (*The Golden Ass*)
Mor.	Plutarch, *Moralia*
Or.	various authors, *Orationes* (*Discourses*)
Rhet.	Aristotle, *Rhetorica* (*Rhetoric*)
Sat.	various authors, *Satirae* (*Satires*)
Satyr.	Petronius, *Satyricon*

Greek Transliteration

α	a	ζ	z	λ	l	π	p	φ	ph
β	b	η	ē	μ	m	ρ	r	χ	ch
γ	g (n)	θ	th	ν	n	σ ς	s	ψ	ps
δ	d	ι	i	ξ	x	τ	t	ω	ō
ε	e	κ	k	ο	o	υ	y (u)	ʽ	h

Notes on the transliteration of Greek
1. Accents, lenis (smooth breathing), and *iota* subscript are not shown in transliteration.
2. The transliteration of asper (rough breathing) precedes a vowel or diphthong (e.g., ἁ = *ha*; αἱ = *hai*) and follows ρ (i.e., ῥ = *rh*).
3. *Gamma* is transliterated *n* only when it precedes γ, κ, ξ, or χ.
4. *Upsilon* is transliterated *u* only when it is part of a diphthong (e.g., αυ, ευ, ου, υι).

Hebrew Transliteration

א	ʾ	בָ	ā	qāmeṣ
ב	b	בַ	a	pataḥ
ג	g	חַ	a	furtive pataḥ
ד	d	בֶ	e	sĕgôl
ה	h	בֵ	ē	ṣērê
ו	w	בִ	i	short ḥîreq
ז	z	בִ	ī	long ḥîreq written defectively
ח	ḥ	בָ	o	qāmeṣ ḥāṭûp
ט	ṭ	בוֹ	ô	ḥôlem written fully
י	y	בֹ	ō	ḥôlem written defectively
כ ך	k	בוּ	û	šûreq
ל	l	בֻ	u	short qibbûṣ
מ ם	m	בֻ	ū	long qibbûṣ written defectively
נ ן	n	בָה	â	final qāmeṣ hēʾ (בָה = āh)
ס	s	בֵי	ê	sĕgôl yôd (בֵ = êy)
ע	ʿ	בֶי	e	ṣĕrê yôd (בֶ = ôy)
פ ף	p	בִי	î	ḥîreq yôd (בִ = îy)
צ ץ	ṣ	בֲ	ă	ḥāṭēp pataḥ
ק	q	בֱ	ĕ	ḥāṭēp sĕgôl
ר	r	בֳ	ŏ	ḥāṭēp qāmeṣ
שׂ	ś	בְ	ĕ	vocal šĕwāʾ
שׁ	š	בְ	–	silent šĕwāʾ
ת	t			

Notes on the transliteration of Hebrew
1. Accents are not shown in transliteration.
2. Silent *šĕwāʾ* is not indicated in transliteration.
3. The unaspirated forms of בגדכפת are not specially indicated in transliteration.
4. *Dāgeš forte* is indicated by doubling the consonant. *Dāgeš* present for euphonious reasons is not indicated in transliteration.
5. *Maqqēp* is represented by a hyphen.

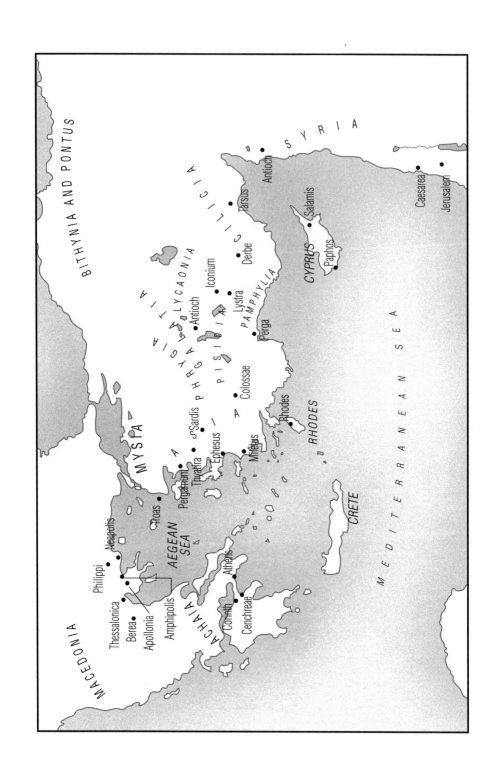

Introduction to 1 Corinthians

Roman Corinth

The city of Corinth was ideally situated on the narrow land bridge between Peloponnesus and mainland Greece. Strabo (*Geogr.* 8.6.20) attributes the city's wealth to the fortune of being "the master of two harbors." Cenchreae, about six miles to the east on the Saronic Gulf, led straight to Asia, and Lechaeum, about two miles to the north on the Corinthian Gulf, led straight to Italy. A four-mile rock-cut track (*diolkos,* built ca. 625–585 B.C.) connected the two ports, enabling cargo and even small ships to be hauled across the isthmus to the other gulf, and thus allowed transporters to avoid the treacherous sea journey around the cape of the Peloponnese (cf. Acts 27). Corinth was a natural crossroad for land and sea travel.

Corinth had aroused Rome's wrath as the chief city of the Achaean league, which revolted rather than submit to Rome's demands to dissolve the league (cf. Cicero, *De lege agraria* 1.5; Strabo, *Geogr.* 8.4.8; 8.6.23; Pausanias, *Descr.* 2.1.2). The Roman military machine's superior numbers and prowess led to the league's inevitable defeat and the demolition of its leading city in 146 B.C. Lucius Mummius, the Roman general, sacked and burned the city. Reportedly, the male population was killed, the women and children were sold into slavery (Cicero, *Tusculanae disputationes* 3.53–54; Strabo, *Geogr.* 8.6.23; 10.5.4; Pausanias, *Descr.* 2.1.2), and the city's treasures were plundered. The extent of the destruction of the city may have been exaggerated by the ancient sources (Wiseman 1979: 494), but 146 B.C. marks its end as a normally functioning city.

Strabo (*Geogr.* 8.6.23) asserts that the town remained desolated and largely uninhabited for 102 years after this defeat. Its old shrines became a curiosity for tourists, and the ruins provided shelter to squatters and visitors to the Isthmian games now under the control of Sicyon (C. Williams 1987: 26; Stansbury 1990: 134).[1] In 44 B.C., shortly before his assassination, Julius Caesar decided to establish a Roman colony on the site with the official name *Colonia Laus Iulia Corinthiensis* (Colony of Corinth in Honor of Julius).[2] Rome established colonies to solve over-

---

1. For a general discussion of the history of Corinth during this time period, see Wiseman (1979).

2. Gebhard (1993) presents evidence that the pan-Hellenic Isthmian festival returned to Corinth's control almost immediately after the colony was founded. The emperor Nero visited Corinth in A.D. 66 and participated in the games (and, not surprisingly, won).

crowding in the city and to promulgate Roman civilization across the world. This resettlement created a new Roman heritage for Corinth and gave it a different appearance from its Greek period. The new city was laid out with a new grid on top of the former Greek city (see Romano 1993). Many of the existing Greek buildings were utilized in the design, but the Romans imposed a city plan, architecture, political organization, and ethos different from the Greek predecessor.[3]

Strabo (*Geogr.* 8.6.23; 17.3.15) recounts that Julius Caesar colonized the city with persons predominately belonging to the "freedman class." Rome needed to export the swelling ranks of the poor and settle its potentially restless army veterans. The city's Roman identity was guaranteed by the immigration of a Roman population. Hopkins (1978: 66) estimates that during the years 88–80 B.C., "Roughly half of the free adult males in Italy left their farms and went to Italian towns or were settled by the state on new farms in Italy or the provinces." A portion of these must have resettled in Corinth. Crinagoras (*Greek Anthology* 9.284) acidly refers to the Corinthian settlers as "those often sold, unstable or disreputable slaves." Appian alleges that the first colonists were desperate and out of options, and Strabo's (*Geogr.* 8.6.23) claim that they looted the Greek tombs and established a market for necrocorinthian ware suggests that these first colonists were strapped for cash (Lanci 1997: 26–27). The city, however, was soon transformed from ruin to riches. The denizens of Corinth in Paul's day were known for their wealth and ostentation. The new city allowed many aggressive freedmen and their heirs, who would have been freeborn, the chance to acquire wealth through commercial ventures. Without an entrenched aristocracy, the citizens of Corinth were not fated "to remain in their allotted position on the social scale" but had a real opportunity for upward social mobility, primarily by attaining wealth and buying friendships and clients (Carter 1997: 53). The favorable economic climate attracted settlers from all over the empire who could work their way up the social ladder. Stansbury (1990: 120–21) makes it clear, however, that this society was not egalitarian. It was an oligarchy that was "hierarchic and elitist, and therefore safe" from a Roman point of view. De Vos (1999: 189) notes that the elite "used a number of social control mechanisms to restrict access to their group, including wealth, marriage, and social ties." Despite the city's prosperity, poverty afflicted many inhabitants. Alciphron (*Epistles* 3.60), a second-century writer, explained why he did not go to Corinth: "I learned in a short time the nauseating behavior of the rich

---

3. Willis (1991) argues that the character of Corinth continued to be Hellenistic and that its Roman character should not be overemphasized at the expense of its Greek past. Gill (1993) disputes his conclusions and contends that scholarship should continue to read the correspondence against the background of a Roman city (cf. also De Vos 1999: 182–83; Winter 2001: 7–25).

and the misery of the poor." Murphy-O'Connor (1984: 148) interprets the proverb "Not for every man is the voyage to Corinth" (Strabo, *Geogr.* 8.6.20; Horace, *Ep.* 1.17.36) to mean that only "the tough survived there." Winter (1989) points to evidence of grain shortages after Paul left Corinth that resulted in famines worsening the divide between rich and poor.

In Paul's time, Corinth had a mixed ethnic population of Roman freedmen, indigenous Greeks, and immigrants from far and wide. De Vos (1999: 187–88) argues that it is conceivable that Jews were included among the original colonists and that a strong Jewish community was "well integrated and on good terms with the wider community." Despite this diversity, Corinth was heavily influenced by Rome, and C. Williams (1987: 31) argues that its population "felt themselves to be Roman." Pausanius's claim that the city was basically Greek has been reevaluated. Winter (2001: 16) remarks, "While Pausanius provides important information on the topography and religious sites of Corinth from a later era, his rereading of Corinth from the fashionable perspective of the Greek Classical revival in the Rome of his day does not provide hard background evidence of the culture of the mid-first century." Stansbury (1990: 116) concludes, "The Greek Corinth of old would live on in folk memory and literature, reinforced by the traditions of the Isthmian festival." But everything was given a Roman stamp. When Paul visited, the city was geographically in Greece but culturally in Rome.

In what follows, I highlight two factors from this urban context—social relations and religious/philosophical influences—that I believe have a direct bearing on the Corinthians' behavior and their misinterpretation of the Christian faith that Paul is compelled to address.

Social Relations

This letter should be read against the background of Corinth as a city imbued with Roman cultural values (Gill 1993: 328). Aulus Gellius (*Noctes atticae* [*Attic Nights*] 16.13.9) claimed that colonies were "miniatures" of Rome. They were established to foster the majesty of Roman culture, religion, and values. The original freedmen settlers were still under obligation to their former masters in Italy, and they may have acted as their business agents (De Vos 1999: 190). The official language of Latin predominates in the extant public inscriptions prior to the time of Hadrian (101 of 104 [Kent 1966: 19]), and the inscriptions on the coinage minted by the magistrates were in Latin.[4] The religious focal point of the Corinthian forum was the temple at the west end dedicated

---

4. Eight of the seventeen names associated with Corinth in the NT are Latin: Fortunatus (1 Cor. 16:17), Lucius (Rom. 16:21), Tertius (Rom. 16:22), Gaius and Quartus (Rom. 16:23), Aquila and Priscilla (Acts 18:2), and Titius Justus (Acts 18:7).

to the imperial family (designated Temple E). It was of Roman construction and towered over all other temples as an ever present symbol of the dominant imperial presence.[5] Upon entering the forum, one could not help but direct an eye to this temple, and the construction of the long line of buildings blocked the view of the grand archaic temple to the north.

When Paul came to Corinth to begin his missionary activity, the city teemed with commerce as the vital link between Rome and its eastern provinces, attracting traders from everywhere in the empire (C. Williams 1993). Throngs attended the Isthmian games. A building boom occurred between the reigns of Augustus and Nero, making Corinth "arguably the most dazzling and modern of Greek cities" (Savage 1996: 36). Many inhabitants were so affluent that "wealth and ostentatious display became the hallmark of Corinth" (Betz 1985: 53), which contrasted with the relative poverty of the surrounding countryside of Achaia. Betz (1985: 53) attests that while "Greeks tried as best they could to preserve their traditional culture, the Corinthians indulged new attitudes and ways of life fueled by the new wealth and unbridled by ancestral tradition. Thus, the province and its capital were in many respects worlds apart." Corinth rose in status as a Roman colony while the surrounding areas tied to the Greek past decreased in status. Spawforth (1994: 407) calls attention to grievances raised against Corinth by people of Argos who grumbled that the Corinthians were proud of their privileged position with Rome and had turned their backs on their Greek heritage and the other cities in the old Achaean league (see Winter 2001: 4–5, 19–20).

This letter also should be read against the background of a mercantile society, as "the core community and core tradition of the city culture were those of trade, business, entrepreneurial pragmatism in the pursuit of success" (Thiselton 2000: 4). These values fed the zeal to attain public status, to promote one's own honor, and to secure power. According to Savage (1996: 35), "Perhaps no city in the Empire offered so congenial an atmosphere for individual and corporate advancement." B. Peterson (1998: 61) asserts that Corinth "seems to have been a city designed for those who were preoccupied with the marks of social status"—that is, "the value which others place on one's goods and achievements" (Barclay 1992: 56). Horace's (*Sat.* 1.6.16–17) mockery of the Roman populace as "absurd slaves to fame, who are stupefied by titles and masks" could apply to Corinth. Meeks (1983: 54) argues that an individual's status was tied to a variety of factors: "occupational prestige, income or wealth, education and knowledge, religious purity, family and ethnic group position, and local-community sta-

---

5. It is probably the Temple of Octavia, which Pausanius (*Descr.* 2.3.1) mentions as above the marketplace (cf. C. Williams 1989).

tus." They do not all carry the same weight, and their relative value in the equation depends on who is doing the weighing. Meeks (1983: 54) explains, "Most individuals tend to measure themselves by the standards of some group that is very important to them—their reference group, whether or not they belong to it—rather than by the standards of the whole society." One could possess high status according to certain markers but low status when it came to others, creating a status dissonance that fed an internal restlessness and a greater desire to achieve the *dignitas* that one believed was one's due. Stansbury (1990: 278) contends that a "shortage of reasonable avenues of honor at the top of the political structure" existed. The scramble for scarce honor was as intense as the scramble for scarce wealth. The result was that many well-to-do sought honor wherever they could get it. Stansbury (1990: 278) lists the available options as "sponsoring private entertainment, games and festivals, patronage of new cults or *collegia*, demonstration of rhetorical skill or philosophical acumen, sponsorship or receipt of an approved honorary statue with appropriate epigraph, and socially conspicuous displays of a private retinue of slaves and freedmen." In this social climate, one could only increase one's standing via a "combination of patronage, marriage, wealth, and patient cultivation of connections" (Stansbury 1990: 87; cf. Chow 1992). MacMullen (1974: 106–7) argues that a key measure of one's standing in Roman societal structure was the size of philanthropic gifts and the number of clients. Crucial for any success and status in this culture was attaining the patronage of powerful persons and bestowing benefaction on others to establish an array of influential friends and clients, exerting political enmity to ostracize opponents, and employing skillful oratory to persuade others in any assembly. To use terms from American culture: schmoozing, massaging a superior's ego, rubbing shoulders with the powerful, pulling strings, scratching each other's back, and dragging rivals' names through the mud—all describe what was required to attain success in this society. Persons also wanted to accumulate wealth and "then display or distribute it in a way that would bring individual honor" (Stansbury 1990: 76). Possessing wealth cleared a path for social climbing because it enabled one to buy friends and clients through extravagant spending and win the esteem accorded benefactors.

The implications of this backdrop for understanding the problems that beset the Corinthian church should not be underestimated. Few Christians could have been unaffected by the dominant culture surrounding them, even if they assimilated its values only subliminally. Most, if not all, of the problems that Paul addresses were hatched from the influence of this setting. Values that were antithetical to the message of the cross—particularly those related to honor and status so basic to the Greco-Roman social system, in which power manifesting itself in ruthlessness and self-advancement is thought to be the only sensible course—percolated into the church, destroying its fellowship and its Christian witness as some members sought to balance civic norms with Christian norms. Secular wisdom—which reflected the code of conduct of the social elites, who jostled one another for power, prestige, and popularity—had its hold on members of the church. Its values played havoc on Paul's attempt to build a community based on love, selflessness, and the equal worth of every member. Corinthian society was riddled by competitive individualism, and this ethos spilled over into the relationships in the church as wealthier members competed for followers. Socially pretentious and self-important individuals appear to have dominated the church. It is likely that they flaunted their symbols of status, wisdom, influence, and family pedigree and looked down on others of lesser status. They appear to have wanted to preserve the social barriers of class and status that permeated their social world but were nullified in the cross of Christ. For some, the Christian community had become simply another arena to compete for status according to the societal norms.

Drawing on Mary Douglas's anthropological studies and grid and group matrix, Carter (1997: 51) thinks that this church's culture fits the model of a "highly egocentric, individualistic and competitive society, dominated by the 'Big Man,' who imposes himself as a leader, and who derives prestige and power from the size of his following." He goes on to describe this culture as "highly materialistic and egocentric: any sense of relationship or mutual obligation rests purely on a fiscal basis: where there is no interchange of goods or services there is only suspicion, hostility and the risk of warfare." Although this sociological model may not fit the Corinthian church precisely, it does help to make sense of internal power struggles that were tearing the church apart. The recent trend is to trace the problem in Corinth back to "personality centred politics" (Clarke 1993: 93; see also M. Mitchell 1993: 67; Welborn 1997). The discordant factions within the community did not revolve around fine points of theological interpretation but developed between rival leading figures who may have been the hosts of different house churches. Paul does not address specifically the theology of the factions but condemns the fact that Corinthians were aligning themselves along party lines and around specific persons, who apparently developed and encouraged personality cults. These unnamed individuals in the church were likely to be wealthier and influential and were unduly influenced by worldly wisdom.[6] Those who provided homes for worship are most likely the culprits. They could exert more influence in their home than

6. Some in the church apparently enjoyed the privileges of the well-off (see Judge 1960; Theissen 1987: 69–110; 2001; Meeks 1983: 51–73; D. Martin 2001). They had property and the means to travel. The named persons associated with Corinth who fit this description are Crispus (Acts 18:8; 1 Cor. 1:14), Titius Justus (Acts 18:7), Stephanas (1 Cor. 1:16; 16:15–17), Erastus (Rom. 16:23), Gaius (1 Cor. 1:14; Rom. 16:23), and possibly Chloe (1 Cor. 1:11), if she was a Christian and resided in Corinth and not Ephesus (cf. Phoebe [Rom. 16:1–2]).

in a neutral meeting place. Because they ranked higher socially and because the group met on their turf, they could control worship practices, the distribution of honors, organization patterns, and even doctrine, and they would be looked upon by others as examples to follow.

The "spirit of the world" (2:12) is synonymous with the "wisdom of the world" (1:20; 3:19; cf. "wisdom of this age," 2:6), and Pickett (1997: 63) contends, "The latter phrase demystifies the former in that it shows that to be under the influence of the 'spirit of the world' is to be guided by the values which constitute its wisdom." It makes clear that the conflict pits God and God's ways, exhibited in the weakness of the cross, against the world and its ways, exhibited by its fascination with displays of status and power. Pickett (1997: 64) continues, "Thus the world which stands in opposition to God is a real social world, and the 'spirit of the world' refers, in some sense at least, to the values which govern the attitudes, judgments and behaviour of the people in that world." It is the baneful influence of this secular wisdom on members in the church rather than some overarching theological misconception that lies behind most of the problems that Paul addresses in the letter (cf. Winter 2001 for a similar approach). It, not some imagined theological dispute swirling around Peter, Apollos, Paul, or the elusive Christ party, sparked off the rivalries ripping apart the fellowship. It is behind the Corinthians' attraction to flashy displays of knowledge, wisdom, and spiritual gifts. It throws light on why someone pursued a lawsuit against a brother Christian (6:1–11), why some sought to justify eating food sacrificed to idols so that they could participate fully in their society (8:1–11:1), why the issue of headdress during worship became a problem (11:2–16), and why some wished to vaunt their spiritual gifts above others (12:1–14:40). Paul pictures the church as divided into "haves" and "have-nots" (11:22). Since one needed to affirm one's wealth and social status to confirm one's identity in this culture, the "haves" show no qualms about humiliating the "have-nots" at the Lord's Supper, widening the division in the camp (11:17–34). The cultural values may shed light on aspects of the man living with his father's wife and the church's incriminating silence (5:1–8).

Barclay (1992) offers an important entrée into understanding the social roots of the problems in Corinth by noting a stark contrast between the issues Paul addresses in 1 Thessalonians and those in 1 Corinthians. Though the two churches were founded within months of each other, "these sibling communities developed remarkably different interpretations of the Christian faith" (Barclay 1992: 50). Barclay isolates one neglected factor that may explain this phenomenon: the social relations with outsiders. One discerns in 1 Thessalonians evidence of painful conflict with outsiders (1 Thess. 1:6; 2:2, 14–16; 3:3) and a sense of alienation from society and hostility toward it (1 Thess. 4:5, 13; 5:7). By contrast, no reference to the Corinthian church's experience of social alienation appears in 1 or 2 Corinthians (Barclay 1992: 57). Instead, Paul contrasts the affliction and dishonor of apostles with the Corinthians' relative tranquility (1 Cor. 4:9–13; 15:30–32; 16:9). The Corinthians appear to be getting on quite well in their community (De Vos 1999: 206–14). Paul can envision certain ones participating in feasts in the dining rooms of pagan temples (8:10) and being invited to share meals in the homes of unbelievers (10:27). Unbelievers drop into worship gatherings (14:24–25). Some members of the church make use of the civil court system to bring suit against other believers (6:1–8). Apparently, they have no religious scruples about being well integrated into a pagan society that is inherently hostile to the wisdom of the cross. In Corinth, no countercultural impact, so central to the preaching of the cross (1:18–25), is evident. Their faith appears not to have created any significant social and moral realignment of their lives. They face little or no social ostracism, and the lack of external pressure contributes to their internal dissension.

Paul thinks that it is fine to have contact with unbelievers to witness to the gospel (9:19–23; 10:32–33), but he views the world with "dark apocalyptic spectacles" (Barclay 1992: 60) and declares that "bad company ruins good morals" (15:33). His insistence throughout the letter that the church is set apart (cf. 1:2) from a world doomed to be destroyed would not have been necessary in Thessalonica, according to Barclay (1992: 59). Barclay's (1992: 71) conclusion about the Corinthians' attitude toward their faith and the nature of the church unveils the root of Paul's grievances against them:

> The church is not a cohesive community but a club, whose meetings provide important moments of spiritual insight and exaltation, but do not have global implications of moral and social change. The Corinthians could gladly participate in this church as one segment of their lives. But the segment, however important, is not the whole and the centre. Their perception of their church and of the significance of their faith could correlate well with a lifestyle which remained fully integrated in Corinthian society.

In this letter, Paul addresses the issue of the church's identity over against its cultural surroundings and seeks to stake out firm boundaries. The problem was not that the church was in Corinth but that too much of Corinth was in the church (Fee 1987: 4). He seeks to disarm the warring factions, to bolster the sense of their common union in Christ, and to widen the boundaries between the church and its surrounding culture. Paul seeks to reform their values so that they live in a manner congruent with the cross and to make them aware that only God's measure of judgment at the end of the ages has any consequence.

He shows how he has abandoned his concern for status because the message of the cross he preaches makes it contemptible in the eyes of God. In fact, God has already made that judgment known in the cross and resurrection of Christ, with the result that the world can be divided up into those who are being saved and those who are perishing (1:18; 2 Cor. 2:15).

Religious Influences

As a cosmopolitan city, Corinth was a religious melting pot with older and newer religions flourishing side by side. De Vos (1999: 192) identifies the gods and cults celebrated by the Corinthians as "Apollo, Aphrodite/Venus, Asclepius, Athena, Athena Chalinitus, Demeter and Kore, Dionysus, Ephesian Artemis, Hera Acraea, Hermes/Mercury, Jupiter Capitolinus, Poseidon/Neptune, Tyche, Fortuna, and Zeus." Egyptian mystery cults, such as the worship of Isis, also were practiced.[7] Never to be forgotten was the ubiquitous attraction of magic. The imperial cult, an "alliance of throne and altar" forged by Augustus, was virulent and expansive during this time and was extremely influential in a Roman colony. Broneer (1971: 170) asserts, "Scholars' penchant for orderly exposition and clear definition can be misleading for an understanding of the religious life of a given period because they pretend to make clear what was anything but clear to the ancients." Most persons could accommodate all gods and goddesses into their religious behavior, and they could choose from a great cafeteria line of religious practices. Many believed that there was safety in numbers: the more gods that one appeased and had on one's side, the better. The temple of Demeter in Pergamum, for example, also had altars to the gods Hermes, Helios, Zeus, Asclepius, and Heracles. Angus (1925: 192) cites the private chapel of the emperor Alexander Severus (third century) as containing shrines to Orpheus, Abraham, Apollonius of Tyana, and Jesus. In one papyrus fragment the writer says, "I pray to all gods" (P. Oxy. 1766 [18]), and an inscription announces, "We magnify every God" (*SIG* 1153). Some welcomed the religious stimulus that strange new gods provided (cf. Acts 17:18–21), since they offered new ways of experimenting with religion and worship. Roman officials did not police private associations and became upset with religious behavior only when it was perceived as disturbing the peace and security they so zealously guarded. The Roman senate did take action against groups suspected of gross immorality, subverting good order, and drawing people away from expected civic loyalty.

---

7. Apuleius (*Metam.* 11) gives a full description of his initiation into the Isis cult in Corinth.

Paul's opening comments in Rom. 1:18–32 may provide us with impressions that match Corinth's religious and ethical milieu. The plethora of idols in the city illustrated his point that humans had exchanged the true God for false gods and honored the creature rather than the Creator, and that the human mind was a perpetual factory of idols. They did not see fit to have God in their knowledge, so God gave them up to their unfit minds (Rom. 1:28). The unfit mind is so corrupted that it no longer can think straight and becomes a totally untrustworthy guide in moral decisions. The city's rampant immorality was living proof of this principle. The breakdown of morals leads to the breakup of society, as cataloged in Rom. 1:29–32. It results in a religion based on falsehoods, a body that is defiled, and a society in which hate and war are at home. The inevitable price of having one's way with God is spiritual poverty and in the end moral abasement.

Paul's statements in Rom. 1:18–32 imply that Christians and Jews were different from the dominant pagan culture because of their religious intolerance of other gods and their rigorous standards regarding sexual conduct. As a result of the former, they were labeled "atheists" because they did not believe in the traditional gods—only their one God. Apuleius (*Metam.* 9.14) describes a certain baker's wife in his novel as "an enemy of faith and chastity" because she is a "despiser of all the gods whom others did honor." Christians were labeled "misanthropes," haters of humankind, because they refused to join in the worship and sacrificial meals offered to local, traditional gods and in their great festivals that quickened local pride or to help polish a city's image as loyal to the emperor by taking part in the imperial cult. Their detachment rankled their neighbors as an impious disparagement of sources of civic vanity. Since the gods were also deemed to be the ones who preserved the state and social order, to reject them opened up the city to divine disfavor and catastrophe. Christians may also have been deemed strange because they themselves had no temples or national temple. They met in private homes (or rented assembly halls) at night, greeted each other with a holy kiss, and partook of the body and blood of one who was crucified by Roman authorities in a provincial backwater. Christians also had no particular national identity and consequently had no established political ties with the Romans. Any repudiation of the imperial cult would have made them particularly vulnerable and politically suspect.

The most important religious influence in Corinth at this time was the imperial cult, which worshiped political power as divine. The emperor cult pervaded public space. Wink (1992: 300) observes that empires "cannot exist for a moment without the spiritual undergirding of a persuasive ideology." Stansbury (1990: 260) notes, "Religious ceremony and political authority were inseparable." The Romans in the first century did not worship the seated emperor but only his "genius," which, as Wink (1992: 300) contends, is "his inspiration, the daemon or god or spirituality that animated the incumbent ruler by virtue of his being incumbent. His 'genius' is the totality of impersonal power located in an office of surpassing might." Winter (2001: 270–71) comments, "The imperial cult grew more spectacularly throughout the empire during the Julio-Claudian and Flavian period than the early Christian movement ever did, and the establishment of a federal cult in Corinth was a matter of great political, social, and financial importance for the colony." The cult was the incarnation of Roman ideology on Greek soil and tended to raise the prestige of the city. In addition to the quadrennial and the biennial Isthmian games, which became connected to the imperial cult, the federal imperial cult celebrated the reigning emperor's birthday every year. It required an overt display of reverence for the imperial house and the performing of sacrifices and conducting of festivals and feasts (see *IGR* 4:1068c [cited by Winter 2001: 275]). Winter notes evidence that householders sacrificed on altars outside their homes as the cult procession passed by (citing Price 1984: 112).

Paul's proclamation that Jesus alone is Lord (8:5–6) directly challenged the imperial cult. "Lord Jesus" was a different kind of "emperor," "savior," and "son of God" than Caesar. The problem for some was that this Lord offered no actual political favors in this worldly realm. S. Mitchell's (1993: 10 [cited by Winter 1995: 176]) reflections about the imperial cult in Anatolia are applicable to Corinth:

> One cannot avoid the impression that the obstacle which stood in the way of the progress of Christianity, and the force which would have drawn new adherents back to conformity with the prevailing paganism, was the public worship of the emperors. . . . It was not a change of heart that might win a Christian convert back to paganism, but the overwhelming pressure to conform imposed by the institutions of his city and the activities of his neighbours.

At a later time and in a different place, Pliny the Younger (*Ep.* 96) used the imperial cult to determine whether persons were Christians or not: if they were willing to deny their Lord and sacrifice incense to a statue of a living emperor, they were not Christians.

This raises the question of how someone like Erastus, whom Paul identifies in Rom. 16:23 as the city's οἰκονόμος (*oikonomos*, which may be equivalent to "aedile"), coped with the pagan trappings of his office (Stansbury 1990: 323). Most assume that he was the same Erastus who paid for paving the plaza adjoining the theater to fulfill an election pledge and publicized this benefaction with an inscription. With the abbreviations spelled out in brackets, it reads: [——] *Erastus pro aedilit[at]e s[ua] p[ecunia] stravit*. Kent (1966: no. 232) translates it: [——] "Erastus in return for his aedileship laid [the pavement] at his own expense." The cognomen is unusual and does not occur elsewhere in Corinthian evidence. Its rarity does not demand that these two mentions of Erastus point to one and the same person, but its rarity in Corinth strengthens the likelihood that they are (see Gill 1989; Clarke 1993: 46–56). Since the inscription fits the general time frame of Paul's letters, it is unlikely that two different persons with this uncommon name held office in Corinth.[8] Bartchy (*ABD* 6:67) thinks it highly probable that Erastus "had to sell himself to the city (as a form of bonding) in order to secure this responsible position" (cf. Cadbury 1931; Theissen 1982: 75–83; Fox 1986: 293; D. Martin 1990: 15–16, 174–76). But Kent (1966: no. 232) interprets the lack of a patronymic in the inscription as suggesting that he was a freedman "who had acquired considerable wealth in commercial activities." Since it is unusual for Paul to mention someone's office, Erastus must have had a reasonably high standing (De Vos 1999: 200 n. 83). Stansbury (1990: 332), however, argues that aedile was an annual office, and it would only be by chance that Paul wrote to the Romans the year that Erastus held that office. Paul probably used *oikonomos* "in a generic sense of one with responsibilities in the running of the city, that is, a decurion." Stansbury (1990: 383) surmises,

> Possibly Paul uses the term in a general sense that would be understood of a class of local offices below those held by the top four magistrates. More likely he meant a specific minor office, although one worthy of some respect to the general populace. Since Corinth apparently lacked the office of quaestor, a subordinate of the aedile likely took on many functions of that financial office. Paul's phrase probably describes a minor office of this sort.

This conclusion does not dismiss the significance of Erastus. He is likely to have succeeded in business, and Paul and others may have found his shipping contacts useful (Stansbury 1990: 323–24).

The question is, How could someone with this role have carried out his civic duties and maintained his social and political connections as a practicing Christian? The wealthier members of the Corinthian church would have faced enormous social pressure to conform to religious expectations, particularly those related to the imperial cult, if they were to advance or to preserve their place in society. This problem was the source of much of the tension between Paul and the wealthier members. This backdrop may shed light on Paul's discussion of the issue of food

---

8. What was the relationship between the Erastus of Rom. 16:23 and the Erastus of Acts 19:22? Were they the same person? Or were they father and son, or brothers, sharing the same cognomen? Or were they unrelated? Erastus is also named in 2 Tim. 4:20, where Paul says he remained in Corinth.

sacrificed to idols and why it would have been so problematic for many in the church.

Misinterpretation of the Christian Faith

Since Paul reacts to what the Corinthians are saying, it seems imperative to try to reconstruct what they were thinking so as to understand better his responses. The method used, mirror-reading—reading what Paul says as in some measure mirroring what the Corinthians have said—is fraught with the danger of making mistakes, as the reasoning is necessarily circular (see Barclay 1987). When such reading is carried out injudiciously, the text can become the servant of preconceived impressions. The interpreter can read too much into what Paul says, read in his or her own biases, and misread Paul's argumentation in a particular passage. Too often in the interpretation of this letter mirror-reading has been used incautiously and overconfidently. The forces shaping the Corinthians' thoughts and actions have been attributed to a particular theological aberration rooted in Gnosticism, Jewish wisdom theology, or an "over-realized eschatology." One theological misconception, however, is unlikely to explain the sundry problems Paul addresses in the letter. If Paul thought that a misrepresentation of the gospel he first preached to them lay behind their problems, then, Pickett (1997: 44–45) reasonably asks, "Why did he not provide them with a more explicitly theological corrective as he does, for example, in Galatians?" It is far more likely that the influences on them were more amorphous and that their behavior was swayed by culturally ingrained habits from their pagan past and by values instilled by a popularized secular ethics. It is imaginable that some of the prominent members thought "in a Stoicizing manner," having been given a token education in this philosophy in their youth (Paige 1992). This body of opinions would have endorsed exalting the individual wise person at the expense of the community and would have permitted the wise to do whatever was right in his own judgment (Paige 1992: 189, 190).

The prominence of the references to the Spirit in this letter suggests that the Corinthians have misinterpreted their experience of the Spirit in some way. They may have understood the Spirit to be the inrush of heavenly power into their lives that granted them a new status and conferred upon them knowledge and great spiritual gifts. It could have fed their pride so that it grew to dangerous levels. They became "puffed up" and "arrogant" and fancied themselves to be "spiritual ones" (3:1; cf. 2:13, 15; 9:11; 12:1; 14:37), "mature" (2:6), and "wise" (3:18; 4:10). Spiritual gifts apparently were compared and some were judged more or less spiritual and more or less valuable according to the same criteria employed in secular culture. Certain gifts were championed over others, and certain persons displaying those gifts were championed over others

(3:21; 4:6–7). Paul cannot deny their spiritual experiences (2:4), nor does he want to denigrate them. But he will not address them as spiritual ones; they instead are fleshly (3:1), too much caught up in this world and its values. Everything occurring at Corinth proved his case: the power factions, the shocking case of incest, suing one another in pagan courts in order to get advantage over the other. Barclay (1992: 71) also reasons that "the more the Corinthians understood their faith as a special endowment of knowledge and a special acquisition of spiritual skills, the less they would expect to embrace hostility: any intimations of conflict would be resolved or minimized."

Another problem that seems to have stunted their spiritual growth was their apparent misunderstanding of the end times and the last judgment. Some label the problem "over-realized eschatology" (Thiselton 1977–78) that took literally Paul's assertion "Behold, now is the day of salvation" (2 Cor. 6:2) and created an overheated, spiritualistic illusion that they were already living in the kingdom come as if the day of the Lord had arrived (cf. 2 Thess. 2:2). I think that "over-realized eschatology" has been overplayed by interpreters. The Corinthians' problems are more attributable to a *lack* of a clear eschatological vision of the defeat of the powers of this age and the final judgment of God looming on the horizon. They did not view this world as decisively evil and consequently were ready to make compromises with it. Barclay (1992: 71) opines, "The apocalyptic notes in Paul's theology which harmonized so well with the Thessalonians' experience failed to resonate with the Corinthians."

Paul's Response

Pickett (1997: 29) states, "As an organizer of Christian communities who wrote letters to sustain and build up those communities, Paul's main concern was with praxis, that is, with how members of the community lived out their faith convictions." This letter, in particular, would corroborate that conclusion with its concerns for practical problems of Christian behavior and church administration. Paul's response, however, is profoundly theological. He is interested in the Corinthians' social, moral, spiritual, and theological development, since, for him, these things are all tied together. Grindheim (2002: 690) observes: "For Paul, sociology is indicative of theology." Correct living is rooted in correct thinking about the significance of the cross, the belief in one God, the work of the Spirit, and the hope of the resurrection, to name only a few theological issues in the letter.

1. Paul seeks to thwart personal rivalries and quash elitist splinter groups to build up a harmonious community. M. Mitchell (1993) argues exhaustively that the letter has one central theme. It is a "unified and coherent appeal for unity and cessation of factionalism," and M. Mitchell

finds this theme in every unit. Paul urges the Corinthians no longer to be driven by self-interest but to work together for the common good. The letter is laced with imagery of building up (3:9, 16; 6:19; 8:1; 10:23; 14:3–5, 12, 17, 26) as opposed to tearing down. The imagery of each member as a vital part of the body (12:12–28) drives home the point. God gives the Spirit to the church for one purpose, namely, to build up a harmonious community—not so that some Christians could claim superiority over other Christians.

2. Paul seeks to subvert the societal values antithetical to the wisdom of the cross that have infiltrated the church so that they will live cruciform lives modeled after Christ and his apostles. Paul clashes with and challenges the culture's customary assessment of shame and honor "by promoting himself and Jesus Christ as figures of shame" (Stansbury 1990: 472). He revels in the "foolishness" of the cross as judged by the truly foolish wisdom of the world that dooms it to destruction. Paul expects submission to the cross to quash egoism and to lead all Christians to serve one another. Barrett (1968: 64) comments,

> Of all the epistles, those to the Corinthians are most full of Christian paradox—of strength that is made perfect in weakness, of poor men who make many rich, of married men who are as if they had no wives, of those who have nothing but possess all things, who are the scum of the earth but lead it to salvation, who die and yet live; and the heart of the paradox is the preaching of the feeble and stupid message of the crucified Christ, which nevertheless proves to have a power and a wisdom no human eloquence possesses, since it is the power and wisdom of God himself.

One aspect of Paul's response to the problem of egotism in the church is to shore up those on the lower end of the social scale. He reminds the Corinthians at the outset that God uses the weak, the low and despised in the world, and the things that are not to bring about change in the wise, the strong, and the things that are (A. Mitchell 1993: 570). His description of the social profile of the community in 1:26–31 should cause them to reevaluate the meaning of high, worldly status and to knock the props out from all human boasting. They must reassess what truly counts before God and rely on their status in Christ rather than their social status (Fee 1987: 84).

Paul also seeks to undermine the self-aggrandizement of the leading figures in the church by casting himself and Apollos as field hands, building contractors, and servants, and he identifies apostles as those who are indistinguishable from the dregs of society (4:10–13). He explains how becoming a slave to serve others and to gain them for Christ is integral to his understanding of his apostolic calling (9:19). He wants those leaders in the church who parade their status and look down on others to do as he does, to lower themselves and accept a servile role that emulates Christ and himself. The basic principle is expounded in 10:32–11:1: "Be without blame with respect to Jews, Greeks, and the church of God just as I myself seek to please everyone in all things, not seeking my own advantage but that of the many in order that they be saved. Become imitators of me just as I am of Christ."

Regarding the Corinthians' interpretation of the Spirit, it seems that they believed the work of the Spirit was most apparent in unusual and impressive manifestations such as speaking in tongues. For Paul, the spiritual life of the church is not to be found in the visible things alone—healings, glossolalia, eloquent preaching. These are only things that the Corinthians use to show off. He writes, "We did not receive the spirit of the world but the Spirit who is from God, that we might know the things which have been freely given to us by God" (2:12). The most central work of the Spirit is something that is unexpected. It leads believers to the crucified Christ (2:2) and to the glory that awaits the end of the age (2:9–10). In 2:4, he states that the Spirit was behind his first preaching to the Corinthians. In 2:13, he maintains that he spoke about God's gracious acts toward them "not in words taught by human wisdom, but in words taught by the Spirit, fitting spiritual things to spiritual expression." The key result of the Spirit is communication about God and Christ that others can understand and that builds up the community of faith (14:1–5).

3. Paul's opening prayer in 1:8 that they be "blameless on the day of our Lord Jesus Christ" broaches the issue of eschatology that the Corinthians appear to have neglected or misunderstood. He believes that the world is passing away and, in a certain sense, has already reached its end, and he "draws the corresponding consequences for anthropology and ethics" (Schrage 1964: 139). Doughty (1975: 69) contends that the eschatological language in the letter "functions to raise up a particular understanding of Christian existence." He maintains, "Paul's understanding of Christian existence is based on the recognition that 'the present time' (ὁ νῦν καιρός, ho nyn kairos) has been decisively qualified by God's salvation deed in Christ (Rom 3:26)." Paul understands Christians to be living in the intersection of two ages, "the present evil age" and "the age to come." As Soards (1999: 13) defines it, "The 'present evil age' is the world of mundane realities in which human beings live; the 'age to come' is the supernatural realm of the power of God." This present age is marked by the rule of Satan, the god of this world (2 Cor. 4:4). Its overlords are minions of Satan and as such are ignorant of God's purposes and are doomed to perish (1 Cor. 2:6, 8). Its wisdom is faulty because it glorifies itself and not God (1:20; 2:6; 3:18). All who live according to its standards will meet with disaster on the day of the Lord Jesus Christ, which brings wrath and destruction for those who are not

in Christ. The day brings judgment through fire even for Christians (3:13).

Paul proclaims that the cross of Christ (1:17–18) and his resurrection have inaugurated the end of this age and its thralldom over humanity (10:11; cf. 2 Cor. 5:17). It has inaugurated the proleptic defeat of sin and death (15:54–57) and the reversal of the law's curse and judgment. Christians have a foretaste of the age to come through the Spirit, but it is only a foretaste. They are destined for glory, but that final glory awaits the resurrection. Christ is Lord, and his rule must be evident in the way Christians live. Doughty (1975: 86) notes that baptism into Christ makes obedience possible: "That which makes obedience necessary and gives it meaning, however, is that the Christian continues to live in a world under the power of sin."

Paul plays the eschatological card in every issue he addresses in the letter except the one concerning headdress in 11:2–16. It appears in the discussion of factions (2:6–8; 3:10–15, 16–17), incest (5:5), lawsuits (6:2–3, 9–10), sexual immorality (6:14), marriage (7:29–31), idol food (9:25; 10:11–13), the Lord's Supper (11:26, 32), and spiritual gifts (13:8, 12). This theme reaches its climax with the long discussion of the resurrection, and it stamps his parting words: "If anyone does not love the Lord, let him be accursed. *Maranatha* [our Lord, come]!" (16:22).

The cross, its wisdom or its effect, is also pivotal in every issue except the one concerning headdress. It is central to his discussion of factions (1:18–31; 4:8–13) but also appears in his discussion of incest (5:7–8, "Cleanse out the old leaven, in order that you might be a new lump, just as you are unleavened. For Christ, our Passover, was sacrificed"), lawsuits (6:7, "Why not rather be wronged? Why not rather be defrauded?"), sexual immorality (6:20, "For you were bought with a price; therefore glorify God in your body"), marriage (7:23, "You were bought for a price; do not become slaves of humans"), idol meat (8:11, "the brother for whose sake Christ died"), the Lord's Supper (11:26, "you proclaim the Lord's death until he comes"), spiritual gifts (13:1–13, the principle of love), and the resurrection (15:3, "For I delivered to you among the first things, what I also received, that Christ died on behalf of our sins according to the Scriptures").

Paul's Ministry in Corinth

Acts 18:11 reports that Paul stayed in Corinth for eighteen months (cf. Gal. 1:18; 2:1; Acts 19:10). Engels (1990: 112) suggests three reasons for the long stay. First, "as a major destination for traders, travelers, and tourists in the eastern Mediterranean, Corinth was an ideal location from which to spread word of a new religion." Dio Chrysostom (*Or.* 8.9), in the guise of the philosopher Diogenes, describes the swarm attending the Isthmian games in this way:

That was the time, too, when one could hear crowds of wretched sophists around Poseidon's temple shouting and reviling one another, and
their disciples, as they were called, fighting with one another, many
writers reading aloud their stupid works, many poets reciting their poems while others applauded them, many jugglers showing their tricks,
many fortune-tellers interpreting fortunes, lawyers innumerable perverting judgment, and peddlers not a few peddling whatever they happened to have.

Some of those who visited or immigrated to Corinth would be open to
hearing the good news Paul preached.

Second, the city provided Paul an opportunity for some measure of
economic independence. He could "practice his own trade as tentmaker
since there was probably a high demand for his products: tents for sheltering visitors to the spring games, awnings for the retailers in the forum, and perhaps sails for merchant ships" (Engels 1990: 112).

Third, immigration (slaves and free) resulted in a population more
open to something new like the gospel and its offer of new attachments,
since they had severed their local ties and were living anonymously in a
big city.

Acts 18:2 refers to the expulsion of Jews from Rome by the emperor
Claudius, and Paul met in Corinth two of these Jewish refugees, Prisca
and Aquila, who were Christians and fellow tentmakers. The decree has
been dated to A.D. 49. Acts 18:12–17 also refers to Gallio as the proconsul
of Achaia, and an inscription fragment dates his tenure in office from
July 1, A.D. 51, to June 30, A.D. 52 (see Murphy-O'Connor 1983: 149–60,
178–82; Riesner 1998: 203–7).

Paul is hauled up on charges near the end of his stay and the beginning of Gallio's taking office (Haacker, *ABD* 2:902). Gallio probably
shared the anti-Jewish sentiments of his brother, Seneca, and the Jews'
expulsion from Rome may have caused him to be negatively disposed to
them (Riesner 1998: 209). These dates suggest the founding of the
church by Paul sometime in February/March A.D. 50 (Riesner 1998:
210). The accession of Gallio as proconsul seems to have brought Paul's
successful activity in the city to an end (Riesner 1998: 210), and Paul
leaves Corinth around September A.D. 51 for Ephesus. He then travels to
Jerusalem before revisiting the Galatian churches (Acts 18:19–22) and
establishing a base in Ephesus (Acts 19:8–10). After Paul left Corinth,
the newly converted Apollos arrived for substantial work (Acts 18:27–
19:1; 1 Cor. 3:6; 16:12), and Paul had to carry on his work in Corinth in
absentia.

The church Paul founded was diverse and socially stratified. It would
have had a Jewish component (7:18) along with Gentile proselytes and
God-fearers partial to Judaism (see Trebilco 1991: 145–66), and former
devotees of idols and folk religion (8:7). Some may have been Roman

citizens. Some were better off, while others belonged to the disenfranchised (foreigners and slaves). Acts 18:6–7 records Paul's ministry in Corinth resulting in Crispus, the ruler of the synagogue, and Titius Justus breaking away from the synagogue to join him.[9] De Vos (1999: 203–5) estimates that the church membership was on the order of one hundred, similar to the membership in many *collegia* (cf. Chow 1992: 204; Witherington 1995: 30–31, 114–15). De Vos thinks that with such large numbers they could have "met together monthly in a purpose-built club room," which may have been provided by Gaius (Rom. 16:23). This makes the most sense of the reference to outsiders dropping into the church's worship meetings. De Vos (1999: 205) thinks it unlikely that they would have dropped in uninvited to the house of someone who was an elite. They probably met weekly in different house churches, which may have been the hothouses for the rivalries that tore the church asunder.

The Nature of Paul's Letter to the Corinthians

First Corinthians is a private letter. It contains things one expects to find in private correspondence: specific information such as travel plans (16:5–9), proper names of individuals (1:14, 16; 16:10, 12, 17), and references to specific events (1:14–16; 2:1–4).[10] Much of the information and allusions that stump later interpreters would have been obvious to the original correspondents. As a private letter, it serves a particular purpose in a particular moment in time when a particular decision had to be made. Anderson (1999) raises a serious challenge to the recent trend to interpret the letter using ancient rhetorical theory. There is a danger that a method that is a useful accessory to interpretation can become all-embracing, overelaborate, and rigidly applied. Anderson (1999: 264–65) argues against M. Mitchell (1993) that the letter cannot be "analysed in terms of sustained rhetorical argumentation," because it "bears little resemblance to a rhetorical speech." Paul's letter writing was informal. He used rhetorical devices but was not constrained by the rules of formal rhetoric. Demetrius's comments on epistolary style continued to govern the practice of formal letter writing. He allowed that the letter was like a dialogue except it is not extemporary utterance. It

---

9. The departure of such prominent figures could only have been perceived by other Jews as a humiliating loss. They may also have been concerned that this messianic sect would arrogate to themselves unique privileges and exemptions accorded the Jewish religious tradition (see Winter 1999). They attempted to rectify this slight to their honor through the courts by bringing the case before Gallio (Acts 18:12–17).

10. Paul mentions fourteen persons by name: Sosthenes (1:1), Apollos (1:12; 3:4, 5, 6, 22; 4:6; 16:12), Timothy (4:17; 16:10), Barnabas (9:6), Cephas (1:12; 3:22; 9:5; 15:5), James (15:7), Chloe (1:11), Crispus (1:14), Gaius (1:14), Stephanas (1:16; 16:15, 17), Fortunatus (16:17), Achaicus (16:17), and Aquila and Priscilla (16:19).

is "committed to writing and is (in a way) sent as a gift" (*Eloc.* 224) and is not "a speech for the law courts" (*Eloc.* 229). Demetrius (*Eloc.* 228) also advises that the length of a letter should be "kept within bounds." The length of 1 Corinthians certainly exceeds those bounds, and some have claimed that it consists of more than one piece of correspondence (see Sellin 1987: 2964–82; 1991). The various and sundry partition theories have been satisfactorily refuted by Merklein (1984), Belleville (1987), and M. Mitchell (1993), and need not occupy us. Suffice it to say that Paul cannot be circumscribed by rhetorical or epistolary straitjackets (see L. Alexander 1989). He often sets off on his own path.

Occasion

Paul writes this letter from Ephesus before Pentecost (16:8), probably in the spring of 54 or 55 (Schrage 1991: 36; Thiselton 2000: 31–32). He is trying to keep up a long-distance relationship with this church without the benefit of the modern communication technology to which we are accustomed. The letter serves as his substitute presence. He has written a previous letter to the Corinthians that included the admonition not to associate with the sexually immoral (5:9). What precipitated that letter is unclear, and despite attempts of some scholars to find remnants of it embedded in the extant letters, it remains lost to us. The existence of this previous letter and Paul's comments about it in 5:9–11 reveal two things. First, it means that 1 Corinthians should not be read as if it were a series of essays on different themes. It is the continuation of an ongoing conversation between Paul and the church. Second, his comments reveal that he is acutely aware that he could be misunderstood. He is painfully conscious of this fact when he carefully qualifies what he says, for example, in 4:14; 9:15; and 10:19. The problem is that written correspondence is susceptible to misinterpretation even when the bearer of the letter is deputized to interpret what it means and particularly if a reader/auditor is ill-disposed to receive what is being said. Since Paul directly challenges the behavior of those who are likely to be powerful figures in the church, the potential is ever present for the targets of his ethical shafts to twist and distort his remarks. Not only must Paul persuade the culprits to change their behavior, but also he must garner the support of the entire community for them to exert moral suasion and authority over the miscreants.

This second letter to Corinth has been prompted by oral reports from Chloe's people about the factional infighting in the church (1:11). Paul also has gotten wind of the case of incest (5:1), the factions at the Lord's Supper (11:18, "I hear there are factions among you"), and their confusion over the concept of the resurrection of the dead (15:12, "some among you are saying"). We cannot exclude the possibility that he also got an earful from Stephanas and his companions about the situation in Corinth and possibly also from Apollos, but he does not name them as sources. The Corinthians have also sent him a letter (7:1), probably carried by Stephanas, with various queries. In response, Paul alternates between reactions to the oral reports and answers to the Corinthian letter (Terry 1995: 43):

Oral reports (1:10–4:17 / 4:18–6:20)
   Corinthian letter (7:1–40 / 8:1–11:1)
Oral reports (11:2–34)
   Corinthian letter (12:1–14:40)
Oral reports (15:1–58)
   Corinthian letter (16:1–12)

The relationship between Paul and the church has not yet deteriorated to the stage it is in when he writes 2 Corinthians, and the situation that this later letter depicts *should not* be read into the interpretation of 1 Corinthians. Paul is not on the defensive in this letter as he is in 2 Corinthians.

Overall, the letter may be summed up as a warning against various perils to which the Corinthians imagine themselves to be immune or are simply oblivious. He warns against the perils of cliques and power factions that rip the fabric of the church's unity (1:10–4:21), of sexual immorality (5:1–7:40), of idolatry (8:1–11:1), of cliques and power factions that sabotage the church's worship (11:2–14:40), and of denying the resurrection of the dead (15:1–58). To prevent them from plummeting into an abyss, he brings them back to his first preaching of the cross and his first preaching of the resurrection. Goulder (2001: 230) describes the letter as a "masterpiece, hard to fault: it is fair-minded, diplomatic, straightforward, dignified, principled, vigorous, fatherly, conciliatory." I find this description of the letter hard to fault.

  I. Letter opening (1:1–3)
 II. Thanksgiving for God's grace given to them (1:4–9)
III. Factions and dissension in the church (1:10–4:21)
    A. The report of their factions (1:10–17)
    B. The foolish wisdom of the cross (1:18–25)
    C. God's choice of the foolish (1:26–31)
    D. Human wisdom versus the Spirit and power of God (2:1–5)
    E. The Spirit's revelation of God's wisdom (2:6–16)
    F. Evaluating the work of God's servants (3:1–17)
    G. How to regard oneself; how to regard others (3:18–4:5)
    H. The apostles as models of the wisdom of the cross (4:6–13)
    I. Appeal to imitate their father Paul (4:14–21)

IV. Incest, lawsuits, and prostitution (5:1–6:20)
- A. The case of incest (5:1–8)
- B. Renewed warnings about tolerance of sin in the church (5:9–13)
- C. Admonition against lawsuits (6:1–11)
- D. Admonition against visiting prostitutes (6:12–20)

V. Instructions about sexual relations, divorce, and marriage (7:1–40)
- A. Sexual relations within marriage (7:1–5)
- B. Celibacy or marriage for the unmarried and widows (7:6–9)
- C. Instructions about divorce for those married to Christians and for those married to non-Christians (7:10–16)
- D. Guiding principle underlying the discussion: remain as you are (7:17–24)
- E. The advisability of marriage for the betrothed and for widows (7:25–40)

VI. The dispute over food sacrificed to idols (8:1–11:1)
- A. Introduction of the issue of idol food (8:1–6)
- B. Refutation of their practice because of its danger to fellow Christians (8:7–13)
- C. Paul's own example to undergird his counsel (9:1–27)
  - 1. Paul's right as an apostle to receive support (9:1–14)
  - 2. Paul's freedom used to spread the gospel (9:15–23)
  - 3. Paul's self-discipline: an example from the world of athletics (9:24–27)
- D. Refutation of their practice from the negative example of the history of Israel in the wilderness (10:1–13)
- E. Refutation of their practice from the example of the Lord's Supper (10:14–22)
- F. Practical advice for dealing with the issue of idol food in pagan settings (10:23–11:1)

VII. Headdress in public worship (11:2–16)

VIII. Divisions at the Lord's Supper (11:17–34)

IX. The use of spiritual gifts in public worship (12:1–14:40)
- A. Introduction of the topic of spiritual gifts (12:1–3)
- B. Variety and unity of spiritual gifts (12:4–11)
- C. The diversity and interdependence of members of the body (12:12–31)
- D. Love: a more excellent way (13:1–13)
- E. The comparison between tongues and prophecy (14:1–19)
- F. The preference for prophecy (14:20–25)
- G. Regulations for worship and concluding instructions on spiritual gifts (14:26–40)

I. Letter Opening (1:1–3)

Conventional Hellenistic letters opened with a simple basic formula, "A to B, greetings" (χαίρειν, *chairein*), or "To B from A, greetings," followed by a wish for good health (see Exler 1923: 60–66; J. L. White 1986: 198–200). Paul's christological convictions lead him to modify this standard greeting. He is not an ordinary correspondent but one who writes with apostolic authority from God. He has been chosen by God and addresses the Corinthian congregation as God's representative. The recipients are not ordinary people but a society established and set apart by God. The greetings are not ordinary good wishes but blessings of grace and peace that reflect the spiritual reality brought about through God's act in the death and resurrection of Christ. When the greetings in Paul's letters are compared synoptically, the slight variations reveal some of the concerns that occupy him in writing the letter. In this letter, Paul emphasizes the unity of the one church of God, which is set apart as holy and integrally bound to all across the world who call upon the name of the Lord Jesus Christ. Corinth is a Roman colony established to spread Roman ideology, but the church in Corinth is God's. By identifying Jesus as Lord, he subtly denies this title to Caesar.

Exegesis and Exposition

¹Paul, called [to be] an apostle of Christ Jesus through the will of God, and Sosthenes the brother. ²To the church of God that is in Corinth, sanctified in Christ Jesus, called [to be] saints together with all those who call upon the name of our Lord Jesus Christ in every place, theirs and ours. ³Grace to you and peace from God our Father and the Lord Jesus Christ.

1:1 Paul identifies himself as an apostle of Jesus Christ by God's call (cf. 2 Cor. 1:1; Eph. 1:1; Col. 1:1; 2 Tim. 1:1). As an apostle *called by God* and not by the church, he is beholden to no one congregation. God's will alone determines his calling and life, and God alone is the ultimate appraiser of all that he does (Danker 1989: 29; cf. 4:3–4). We need not jump to the conclusion that he intends to pull rank on them and establish his authority over them from the outset (cf. 1 Cor. 12:28–29; 2 Cor. 10:8; 13:10). He does not write to issue pronouncements but to inform, instruct, clarify, persuade (10:15), and interpret (7:10–16). Nor does he write to defend his apostleship (contra Fee 1987: 28–30; cf. the introduction to 9:1–27 below). Thiselton (2000: 45) corrects this common misinterpretation: "Paul sees his apostleship not as an instrument of power but as a call to become a transparent agency through whom the crucified and raised Christ becomes portrayed through lifestyle, thought, and utterance."

The title "apostle of Jesus Christ" encompasses a matrix of ideas. The term is connected to the Hebrew *šālîaḥ*, "sent man" (Agnew 1986: 83). In the NT, apostles are witnesses to Christ's resurrection (9:1; 15:3–9), though not all witnesses to the resurrection are apostles. The key phrase is "called through the will of God." It conveys that Paul did not choose this ministry as a promising career path nor was he nominated for it by human authorities (Gal. 1:1). He was captured and constrained by God's sovereign call, which makes him into something he was not (Gal. 1:15–16; 2 Cor. 5:14). He interprets this beckoning as an outpouring of God's grace because of his unworthiness for the role as one who previously persecuted the church (15:9–10). The verbal idea in apostle (ἀποστέλλω, *apostellō*) implies being sent out by Jesus Christ. As Edwards (1885: 2) aptly puts it, Paul was "called out of the world to be sent to the world." The call confers on him a missionary commission to carry the gospel to the Gentiles (Gal. 1:16; 2:7; Rom. 11:13; 2 Cor. 10:13–16; Eph. 3:1–2), which determines both the direction of his ministry, from Jerusalem to Illyricum to Rome to Spain (Rom. 15:19, 24), and the recipients of his ministry (Gal. 2:8). He understands himself to be sent by Christ to speak authoritatively the full truth of the gospel (1:17), to placard Christ crucified (Gal. 3:1; Litfin 1994. 196), and to establish churches. He and his team were "the first to come all the way to you with the good news of Christ" (2 Cor. 10:13–14), and he performed the signs of a true apostle (2 Cor. 12:12). Their founding as a church is the seal of his apostleship (9:2; 2 Cor. 3:2–3), and he remains responsible for them as their father in the faith (4:14–21).

Paul passed on to them the traditions about Jesus (11:23; 15:3), and he continues to interpret for them the meaning of these traditions (7:10–16) as one who has received mercy from God to be a trustworthy interpreter (7:25), guided by the Spirit of God (7:40), and having insights into the mystery of God (2:7–13; Eph. 3:5) and the mind of Christ (2:16). The statement of Jesus in John 13:16, "the messenger [ἀπόστολος] is not greater than the one who sent him," recalls this maxim: "The one whom a man sends is like the man himself." Paul understands that being Christ's emissary requires him to imitate Christ and to be imitated himself by others (4:16; 11:1) as he becomes a living paradigm of the gospel and the scandal of the cross. He incarnates the weakness of the cross as one exhibited as last of all, as one sentenced to death, and as a spectacle to the world (4:9). He makes himself a slave to all so that he might win others to Christ (9:19), which is why apostles are both first (12:28) and last (4:9; 15:8; Thiselton 2000: 66).

With the exception of Romans, Paul always mentions co-senders in his salutation—an unusual feature compared with other extant letters from this period. Prior (1989: 39–42) contends that Sosthenes was the scribe who wrote the letter, but why would a scribe insert his name in the salutation as a co-sender (cf. Tertius, who identifies himself as the writer of the letter in Rom. 16:22)? Murphy-O'Connor (1993: 562–79) infers from the use of "we" in 1:18–31 and 2:6–16 that Sosthenes had a more extensive hand in the writing of the letter than the average scribe. Thiselton (2000: 69), however, offers the most convincing explanation for Paul's inclusion of Sosthenes in the greeting: "Paul does not perceive himself as commissioned to lead or to minister as an isolated individual, without collaboration with co-workers." He is not a maverick apostle but part of a ministry team.[1]

Sosthenes must have been known to the Corinthians, since Paul identifies him only as "the brother."[2] We cannot prove that he is the same Sosthenes named in Acts 18:17 as the "ruler of the synagogue." After the case against Paul before the governor Gallio collapsed, Acts reports that "all" beat Sosthenes but does not specify which group did this or why. Was it the Jews irate over his mismanagement of the case or his sympathies with Paul, or the Greeks taking advantage of a Jew out of favor with the authorities (Barrett 1968: 875)? Acts does not report his conversion as it does that of Crispus, another ruler of the synagogue (Acts 18:8), and Paul does not list Sosthenes as one of those he baptized in Corinth as he does Crispus (1 Cor. 1:14). His name, however, may have been remembered and cited in the Acts narrative because he was known to have become a Christian.[3] The evidence does not allow us to say much more.

1:2 Corinth was no ordinary city as a Roman colony, but in contrast to secular letters that lauded the fame and status of the recipients' locale, Paul pays no compliments to the city. The important thing about Corinth is the recipients of this letter. They are not ordinary people but a consecrated society established by God, called by God, and set apart as God's people in Corinth. Paul's use of the phrase "church of God" (ἐκκλησία τοῦ θεοῦ, *ekklēsia tou theou*), inherited from Scripture, has

---

1. Apollos (16:12) appears to be independent of Paul, which may explain why he is not named as a co-sender.

2. "Brother" becomes a title for Christians (cf. 2 Cor. 1:1; 8:18, 22; Philem. 1), which conveys that they are "all sons and daughters of the one Father" (Barrett 1968: 31; cf. Matt. 23:9).

3. Myrou (1999) makes an interesting but unprovable claim that Crispus and Sosthenes are the same person and that Crispus was renamed Sosthenes by Paul. Crispus can mean "curly" or "unsteady," and Sosthenes means "steady in strength." Paul made the change in the same way he made a play on the meaning of the name of Onesimus (useless/useful) in Philem. 11. Crispus is not unsteady but steady.

three implications. First, Schrage (1991: 102) contends that in Greek usage ἐκκλησία refers predominantly to a political assembly (cf. 14:28, 34). Thiselton (2000: 75) claims, "The words stress the call *to assemble together as a congregation* in God's presence." The Corinthians' assembly is, then, distinguished from all other assemblies that might gather in Corinth as one that belongs to God (10:32; 11:16, 22; 15:9) and confesses Jesus Christ as Lord. The possessive τοῦ θεοῦ (*tou theou*, of God) clarifies that the church is not some "man-made organization" created to preserve and promulgate particular religious traditions (Bornkamm 1971: 178–79) or a society of like-minded persons governed by human aspirations and values.[4] The church of God makes claims to exclusive truth in contrast to voluntary associations that "were typically more concerned with fellowship and good times than with claims of salvation" (McCready 1996: 62). In the political assembly, the art of elegant rhetorical persuasion is paramount; in the assembly of God, the proclamation of Christ crucified, delivered in weakness, fear, and trembling, and the demonstration of the Spirit's power are utmost.

Second, Paul's use of the singular "church" (cf. 1 Thess. 1:1; 2 Thess. 1:1) differs from the plural he tends to use in other letters, which refer to "all God's beloved" (Rom. 1:7) or "to all the saints" (Phil. 1:1; Eph. 1:1; Col. 1:2). There probably was more than one house church in Corinth, but by addressing them as one church the emphasis falls on their unity as the people of God, a chord that is struck throughout the letter (cf. 3:9, 16, 23; 10:17; 12:12–13, 27; Belleville 1987: 17).

Third, the term was used in the LXX for the people of Israel. Applied to the church at Corinth, it underscores their continuity with God's people of old (cf. 10:1).

· This one church is composed of the sanctified (ἡγιασμένοι, *hēgiasmenoi*; 1:30; 6:11), who are called to be saints (ἅγιοι, *hagioi*). Voluntary associations in this era never used the epithet ἅγιοι to identify themselves, yet it marks the fundamental identity of the Christian assembly. This epithet recalls Lev. 19:2: "Speak to all the congregation of the people of Israel and say to them: You shall be holy, for I the LORD your God am holy" (NRSV). O. Evans (1974–75: 197) delineates the Jewish background of the word "sanctified" as an eschatological concept describing "the true Israel, the Elect People of God, consecrated to serve his righteous cause in battle against his enemies and destined to share in the glories of his kingdom." Designating them as "saints" has at least four implications. First, they are "saints" by God's call (as Paul is an apostle by God's call). The translation "called to be saints" may imply that this is some goal they must attain, but the Corinthians already

---

4. Paul may be subtly cautioning the church's patrons that though the assembly might gather in their house and be aided by their patronage, it is not their church.

are "saints" in the same way that Paul already is an apostle. As Paul did not achieve his apostleship, so they do not achieve holiness but receive it (Conzelmann 1975: 21). Second, belonging to the holy people of God qualifies them as saints set apart to serve God's purposes, not their own. All Christians are equally holy so that none is to be regarded "saintlier" (in the modern sense) than others. Third, they are called to a particular lifestyle and are bound by moral strictures and standards of behavior because God is holy (Lev. 19:1–2; Exod. 19:5–6; 22:31; 1 Cor. 3:17; cf. 1 Thess. 4:3; 5:23). They are to embody values that are radically different from those in their surrounding culture. Fourth, the term "saints" has corporate significance, as O. Evans (1974–75: 198) recognizes, "'The saints' are not an aggregate of individuals who are characterized by a special quality of holiness; they are a holy community." They are not set apart from the world as lone saints but set apart with others as a community of saints with obligations to one another as well as to God. One of the hallmarks of holiness is *wholeness,* and Paul wants this church to be whole and without divisions to represent God's holiness to the world.

The phrase σὺν πᾶσιν (*syn pasin*) is not to be taken with τῇ ἐκκλησίᾳ τοῦ θεοῦ (*tē ekklēsia tou theou*), as if Paul were addressing all Christians along with the Corinthians (Robertson and Plummer 1914: 2). Paul simply wishes to remind them that the church of God extends beyond Corinth. They were called to be saints *together with* all those who "call upon the name of the Lord in every place." "Every place" may reflect Jewish usage referring to their meeting-places (see Lietzmann 1949: 5; Conzelmann 1975: 23 n. 40 for the synagogue inscriptions), which Paul could apply to Christian meeting-places (cf. 1 Thess. 1:8; 1 Tim. 2:8). When Paul describes himself as being led in a triumphal procession that causes the fragrance of knowing Christ to spread to "every place" (2 Cor. 2:14), however, he connects it to the church's worldwide mission (so Conzelmann 1975: 23 n. 40; M. Mitchell 1993: 194). "Every place" may allude instead to the dispersal of Christians throughout the world (Belleville 1987: 18). "The church of God that is in Corinth" is not the center of God's witness in the world but simply a constituent part of that witness. The phrase "theirs and ours" is somewhat confusing. It could refer to "their *place* and ours" (Edwards 1885: 4) or "their *Lord* and ours" since all Christians share a common Lord (Godet 1886: 47). Paul intends the latter (cf. Rom. 10:12, "the same is Lord of all"), which thematically prepares the way for his question "Is Christ divided?" (1:13).

In Paul's greetings, we usually find a remark that anticipates one of the main topics to be discussed in the balance of the epistle (O. Evans 1982: 192–93). Here, he notes their calling to sanctity that bonds them to others. As a Roman colony, Corinth was the center of Roman presence and influence in the province of Achaia. The surrounding Achaean neighbors were tied to the Greek past and had become their social inferiors. The letter betrays that an attitude of superiority had crept into the church at Corinth and was destroying their solidarity. By linking them with "all those who call upon the Lord in every place" and underscoring that it is "their [Lord] and ours," Paul sounds a universal note that undermines their independent streak and egotism.[5] As Thiselton (2000: 74) remarks, "They are not the only pebble on the beach." They do not "possess Christ for themselves alone" (Robertson and Plummer 1914: 3). This universalizing reference does two other things as well. It sets up Paul's appeals to the practice in all the churches as a guide for the Corinthians' conduct (7:17; 11:16; 14:33, 36), and it lays the foundation for his later request for them to make a charitable contribution to Christians in Jerusalem (16:1–4).

Those who call upon the name of the Lord are converted and believe in his name (cf. Acts 2:21; Rom. 10:12–14; cf. 1 Cor. 6:11), proclaim his name, offer prayer and devotion to him in worship (cf. 16:22; Acts 9:14, 21; 22:16), and are prepared to suffer for him (Cullmann 1964: 12).[6] Dunn (1998: 247) comments that the title "Lord" denotes "dominance and the right of disposal of superior over inferior—whether simply master over slave, king over subject, or, by extension, God over worshiper. To confess someone as one's 'lord' expresses an attitude of subserviency and a sense of belonging or devotion to the one so named." Calling upon the Lord acknowledges that he is master and we are his slaves (6:19–20). Since "Lord" appears frequently in the LXX for Yahweh, to call upon Christ as Lord intimately connects him to God as a divine figure. Thiselton (2000: 79) comments that to call upon the Lord is "not to invoke some shadowy, unknown deity, but to commit oneself in trust to the one whose nature and character have been disclosed as worthy of this trust." The confession binds them to the one Lord (8:5–6) and to all other believers. It also severs them from those who insist that Caesar is the world's lord. Paul names Jesus as Christ three times in this brief salutation. N. Wright (1992: 41–49) claims that Paul understands the term "Christ" specifically to mean the Messiah, the king of Israel, and takes for granted that Israel's king, who accomplishes God's purposes on earth, is the world's king (cf. Ps. 72:8; Isa. 11:10; 1 Cor. 15:25–28). Paul wants to bind the Corinthian Christians to other believers across the world, however remote, and to cut them off from any deleterious allegiances to their unbelieving neighbors closer at hand.

"Grace and peace" are not simply the ordinary good wishes of a greeting. Many assume that Paul christianized the secular epistolary greet-   **1:3**

---

5. Weiss (1910: xli, 4) is wrong to attribute this universalizing note to a later editor.
6. The middle voice (ἐπικαλουμένοις, *epikaloumenois*) intensifies the calling.

ing χαίρειν (*chairein*, hail; Acts 15:23; James 1:1) by changing it to χάρις (*charis*, grace) and combining it with the Jewish greeting of שָׁלוֹם (*šā-lôm*, peace; cf. Dan. 4:1 LXX; 2 Bar. 78:2; *b. Sanh.* 11b).[7] S. Porter (*DPL* 698) contends, however, "There is little substantive evidence from Greek Jewish letters of the time that superscriptions with 'peace' were used as a convention that Paul might have borrowed."[8] S. Porter thinks that it was created by Paul "to emphasize the comprehensive work of God: it is one of gracious giving and forgiveness for previous hostility" (cf. Rom. 5:1; 15:13; Eph. 2:14; Col. 1:20). It is a "wish-prayer" (Lindemann 2000: 28, who argues that the optative copula "may be" is to be supplied) and not just a perfunctory greeting, because Paul expands it to include the agent who fulfills the prayer: "from God our Father and the Lord Jesus Christ" (Thiselton 2000: 81). Paul does not offer them his own greetings but those of God and Christ, who stand intimately together, because he does not write simply as a friend but as God's and Christ's apostle. Through this letter, he wishes to establish their presence in the community, not just his own, and extends to them the peace Jesus bestowed on his disciples (John 20:21). "Grace and peace" express his deep theological convictions about what God had accomplished in Christ: "grace" is the source of Christian life, and "peace" is its consummation (Edwards 1885: 5).

Again, this greeting is subversive. The peace offered by God through Jesus Christ rivals that of the peace established and propagated by the emperor, who is passed off as the world's great savior and benefactor. Tacitus (*Agricola* 30.5) has the British general Calgacus attempt to rally his troops before battle with the Romans by saying, "To plunder, butcher, steal these things they misname empire: they make a desolation and call it peace" (cited by Wengst 1987: 52).

---

7. Cf. the discussions in Lohmeyer (1927), Friedrich (1956), and Berger (1974).

8. "Peace" appears in all the greetings of letters attributed to Paul (Rom. 1:7; 2 Cor. 1:2; Gal. 1:3; Eph. 1:2; Phil. 1:2; Col. 1:2; 1 Thess. 1:1; 2 Thess. 1:2; 1 Tim. 1:2; 2 Tim. 1:2; Titus 1:4; Philem. 4) and in many of the closing benedictions (Rom. 16:20; 2 Cor. 13:11; Gal. 6:16; Eph. 6:23; 2 Thess. 3:16; cf. Phil. 4:9).

II. Thanksgiving for God's Grace Given to Them (1:4–9)

The thanksgiving periods in Paul's letters have been assumed to take the place of the *captatio benevolentiae* in ancient speeches except that they are addressed to God (Findlay 1910: 759). To be sure, Paul intends to gain the audience's goodwill in this opening section, but not through rhetorical artifice (Thiselton 2000: 85, 93–94; cf. Pogoloff 1992: 99–128). He does not praise the Corinthians (contrast Phil. 1:5; Col. 1:4; 1 Thess. 1:3, 6–8; 2 Thess. 1:3–4; Philem. 5, 7) but pays tribute for what God has done, is doing, and will do in their midst through Christ. Three conjunctions—ὅτι (*hoti*, because, 1:5), καθώς (*kathōs*, since, 1:6), and ὥστε (*hōste*, so that, 1:7)—introduce clauses outlining the evidence of God's grace. In comparison to the thanksgiving periods in his letters to other churches, it is noteworthy that Paul singles out the Corinthians' gifts of speech and knowledge and that they do not fall short in any grace-gift (χάρισμα, *charisma*), but he omits any mention of their love (contrast Phil. 1:9; Col. 1:4; 1 Thess. 1:3; 2 Thess. 1:3; Philem. 5) or work (contrast Phil. 1:6; Col. 1:10; 1 Thess. 1:3; 2 Thess. 1:11).[1] Both appear to be wanting in the Corinthian church. Paul will seek to correct this problem by exalting love over both knowledge (8:1; 13:2, 8–13) and speech (13:1, 8–13). In the conclusion he exhorts them to do all things in love (16:14). He intends for this letter to have the effect of bringing their work (praxis) "up to the same standards as their 'eloquence and knowledge'" (Betz 1986: 33).

Most secular letters included some description of the sender's state and a wish for health for the recipient. Paul rarely mentions what has happened to him and instead focuses entirely on how God's grace has worked itself out in the lives of the recipients and interprets their present situation in light of God's promised future (Thiselton 2000: 87). The thanksgiving section also serves as a prelude that introduces some of the concerns and themes of the letter. Paul briefly broaches the topic of gifts (ἡ χάρις τοῦ θεοῦ ἡ δοθεῖσα ὑμῖν, *hē charis tou theou hē dotheisa hymin*, 1:4; χάρισμα, 1:7). In chapters 12–14 he will discuss grace-gifts in depth. The word χάρισμα refers

---

1. The mention of their love in 2 Cor. 8:7 refers to their love for him, not for one another.

to any concrete expression of grace (Fee, *DPL* 340), and though some of the extraordinary phenomena mentioned in chapters 12–14 loom large in this letter, the term in this context should not be limited to any one particular manifestation.[2] He addresses the issue of "word" (1:5) in 1:10–4:21 and 13:1–14:40 and "knowledge" in 8:1–13 and 13:1–13 (cf. 12:8; 14:6). Paul's preaching to the Corinthians (τὸ μαρ-τύριον, *to martyrion*, 1:6) is the topic in 2:1–16. The day of the Lord Jesus Christ and the judgment when all will be called to account (1:7–8) are addressed throughout the letter (3:13; 4:3, 5; 5:5; 6:2; 11:26; 15:23, 47, 52; 16:22). Mentioning their call to fellowship in Christ (1:9) heralds the corporate nature of the life in Christ that lies at the heart of much of the exhortation in the letter, particularly the call to unity. The thanksgiving section is more than an introduction to some of the concerns that occasioned the letter; it has a parenetic function (Schubert 1939: 89). It calls the readers to reconfirm their faith for which Paul gives thanks.

Exegesis and Exposition

[4]I thank ⌜my⌝ God always concerning you for the grace of God given to you in Christ Jesus. [5]Because in everything you were made rich in him, in all speech and all knowledge, [6]since the testimony borne to Christ was established among you, [7]so that you do not fall short in any grace-gift while eagerly awaiting the revelation of our Lord Jesus Christ, [8]who also will confirm you to the [very] end free of any charge on the day of our Lord Jesus ⌜Christ⌝. [9]God is faithful through whom you were called into common-union with his son Jesus Christ our Lord.

1:4 Paul cultivates a thankful spirit and refers to his regular habit of giving thanks "always," that is, at every opportunity (Thiselton 2000: 89; cf. 15:58), for this church. He did not suddenly think of them when he began to send this letter. After reading the Corinthian correspondence, one might wonder what Paul could find about them for which to give thanks. Many observe that giving thanks that they are enriched with gifts is surprising since this letter reveals that they have misunderstood and perhaps misused them. Fee (1987: 36) corrects views that assume that Paul indulges in sarcasm by noting that he "recognizes that the problem lies not in their gifts, but in their attitudes toward these gifts. Precisely because the gifts come from God, Paul is bound to give thanks for them." The focus of his thanksgiving falls on what God graciously has done among them in Christ, not on their own particular qualities (cf. 4:7). He gives credit where credit is due, to God, the source of these eschatological blessings (Brown 1995: 67 n. 5). This reference to God's

---

2. For example, in 7:7 he applies the noun to the absence of sexual desire that allows for celibacy.

grace *given* to them undercuts any egocentric pride in their spiritual achievements.

Christ Jesus is mentioned four times in the salutation, and Christ or the pronoun referring to him is repeated in every verse of the thanksgiving. Through Christ, God has "given" (1:4), "enriched" (1:5), "confirmed" (1:6), and "called" (1:9); and God will "confirm" them on the day of our Lord Jesus Christ (1:8). The gift of grace comes only to those who are in Christ Jesus and to no others, and Paul reminds them that he too is a recipient of God's grace (3:10; 15:9–10). All Christians are in Christ Jesus together, and none can imagine themselves to be self-sufficient, self-ruling, or detached from other Christians.

The Corinthian believers have been made rich in everything through their close relationship to Christ and acceptance of his loving sacrifice (2 Cor. 8:9). Paul zeroes in on their enrichment in speech (λόγος, *logos*) and knowledge (γνῶσις, *gnōsis*). He also attests to their abundance of gifts in 2 Cor. 8:7: they overflow in everything—in faith, in speech, in knowledge. "Speech" could refer to their eloquence, which gives expression to their knowledge. The ancient world placed a premium on rhetorical skills. As B. Peterson (1998: 59) describes it,

1:5

> In Hellenistic society the practice and expectations of rhetorical eloquence were pervasive. Not only were political leaders expected to speak persuasively and eloquently, but so also those who claimed authority in philosophy and religion. Among such people there was great competition, and success depended upon one's ability to express the power of the divine in his or her performance—not only through miracles, but also through rhetorical performances [see also Litfin 1994: 14].

As a spiritual gift, however, "speech" more likely refers to spiritual speech such as tongues and prophecy (12:10, 28; 13:1–2).

Paul will make a distinction between rhetorical eloquence, glossolalia, and prophecy (forth-telling). The first he depreciates. He did not proclaim the mystery of God to them in lofty words of wisdom, yet his preaching was effective (2:1–4). His words were not instructed by human wisdom but by the Spirit because he was interpreting spiritual things (2:13) and because the kingdom of God depends not on talk but on power (4:20). The act of speaking in the tongues of mortals or of angels, when it is not suffused with love, Paul discounts as loud clanging (13:1). Silence is sometimes preferable (14:28). Prophecy is the most valuable because it builds up the church rather than just the individual (14:1–12) and can lead others to faith (14:20–25).

"Knowledge" refers to their spiritual insight—the knowledge to understand all mysteries (13:2), their objective knowledge about idols (8:1–6). Paul values such things because it allows him to appeal to their judgment. But knowledge does not top the list of what he thinks is most important for the upbuilding of the community (8:1–3). Like "speech," this gift can be misused to cause division. Some in Corinth appear to come off as know-it-alls, and they could even misapply their knowledge to destroy another believer who has a weak conscience (8:11). Knowledge, like speech, also needs to be leavened with love (8:1; 13:2). Paul also will remind them that they know only in part and see only dimly (13:9, 12) and will ask them eleven times in the letter, "Do you not know?" (3:16; 5:6; 6:2, 3, 9, 15, 16, 19; 9:13, 24; 12:2), implying that their knowledge is yet imperfect, particularly when it comes to moral issues.

Brown (1995: 71) comments, "The Corinthians' greatest liabilities and greatest strengths lie in their gifts." This paradox is created by their misinterpreting the significance of their enrichment by God. As material riches can inspire poisonous, self-destructive attitudes and behaviors, so can spiritual riches. But we know this only from having read through the entire letter. Paul is not being sarcastic but genuinely affirming the particular gifts from God that they prize the most.

1:6–9 The καθώς (kathōs) has a causal sense (since, insofar as; cf. 1 Thess. 1:5) and affirms that their enrichment was established by their response to Paul's testimony borne to Christ (objective genitive). He proclaimed Christ crucified and resurrected, and they believed (1:23; 2:1–4; 15:3–5, 11). His testimony awakened their faith, which created the church of God in Corinth.

The verb ὑστερεῖσθαι (hystereisthai) in 1:7 can mean "to lack," "to miss out"; but followed by the preposition ἐν (en), it may have the nuance "to come short of" (Thiselton 2000: 97). With a deft swipe at their undue pride, Paul affirms their own self-understanding as "gifted" but does so in a backhanded way. Instead of congratulating them for their abundant spiritual endowment, he says that they do not fall short in this area. He will instruct them in the letter what this giftedness means. The gifts come from God for the upbuilding of the community. They can take no credit for them, and their gifts do not lift them above others. All Christians are gifted, and no one gift makes one greater than another.

Being enriched with grace-gifts does not mean that they have arrived (Fee 1987: 36). He intimates that more is to come in Christ. Now they await (ἀπεκδέχομαι, apekdechomai, used of the end time in Rom. 8:19, 23, 25; Gal. 5:5; Phil. 3:20) the revelation of Jesus Christ. The goal of the adventure to which God has called them still lies in the future (11:26), when tongues will cease and knowledge will become outmoded (13:8). Those who are being saved can expect salvation; those who are perishing, wrath (4:5; 15:23; 1 Thess. 1:10). The period of waiting in a world whose foundations and structures are crumbling (7:31) is marked by cries of "Lord, come!" (16:22). Waiting requires purifying the purposes of the heart so that church members will not be exposed as frauds on the day of judgment (4:5) and will be braced to face the shame of public vilification (4:11–12) and the dangers from formidable foes (15:30–31). Instead of standing on their dignity as those enriched with speech and knowledge, they should be standing on tiptoe in anticipation of what is to come when God will establish or confirm them as blameless on the day of the Lord. The time of waiting is placed under the shield of God's faithfulness (1:9; cf. 10:13; 1 Thess. 5:24).

Paul subtly reminds them of three things. First, the day of the Lord (1:9; cf. Joel 2:31; Amos 5:18–20), when the king reclaims his kingdom, brings judgment (3:13; 5:5; 2 Cor. 1:14). But God has already acquitted those who are in Christ (1:30; 6:11; cf. Rom. 3:21–26; 5:17–21). Those who were originally blameworthy become free from any charge (ἀνεγκλήτος, *anengklētos*; cf. Rom. 8:1). Conzelmann (*TDNT* 9:395) notes, "The power of grace [1:3] is displayed in its work, the overcoming of sin (R[om]. 5:20f)." This statement discloses that the goal of their Christian calling is to live blamelessly before God.

Second, their confirmation of the gospel (1:6: τὸ μαρτύριον τοῦ Χριστοῦ ἐβεβαιώθη ἐν ὑμῖν, *to martyrion tou christou ebebaiōthē en hymin*) will lead to their confirmation by God (1:8: ὃς καὶ βεβαιώσει ὑμᾶς, *hos kai bebaiōsei hymas*).[3] The passive voice ἐβεβαιώθη points to God establishing the gospel in their midst. The future tense of βεβαιώσει, however, implies that God's saving work is not yet finished. Paul exudes confidence that what God establishes will endure and that God will preserve this splintered congregation. Christian existence depends entirely on God's faithfulness (cf. Phil. 1:6), not on individual giftedness. "Faithful" (πιστός, *pistos*) is placed first in the clause in 1:9 for emphasis. Paul stresses the faithfulness of God in 10:13 in the context of recalling the wilderness traditions. God tested the people so that they would learn to rely only on God (Deut. 8:2), but these traditions reveal "that the human situation was hopeless if the one who first chose the Israelites did not remain faithful to them" (P. Gardner 1994: 154). It is an implicit warning against any false security; their boast can be only in God (1:31; 2 Cor. 10:17). Everything in their lives depends on God's faithfulness and Christ's lordship.

Third, the Christian life is a calling with the goal of fellowship in which believers become one people under Christ's lordship. I have translated κοινωνία (*koinōnia*) as "common-union" because it highlights many of the issues Paul addresses in the letter. Paul has in mind their sharing in Christ (objective genitive), which means far more than merely being together as a fellowship of friendly faces: it signifies sharing "the status of being-in-Christ and of being shareholders in a sonship

---

3. The antecedent of ὅς could be God or Christ, but the syntax is less redundant if "God" confirms them "in the day of our Lord Jesus Christ."

derived from the sonship of Christ" (Thiselton 2000: 104). Common-union with Christ creates common-union with other Christians and precludes common-union with idols (10:14–22).

Additional Notes

1:4. The omission of μου in א*, B, eth is best explained as accidental. The phrase "my God" in Rom. 1:8 and Phil. 1:3 may have led a scribe to insert "my" into the text by assimilation. This insertion would have had to have been universal (Fee 1987: 35 n. 1). It is more likely that these passages represent Paul's normal pattern.

1:8. Both 𝔓[46] and B omit Χριστοῦ. Paul refers to "the day of [our] Lord Jesus" in 2 Cor. 1:14. Widespread support for its inclusion, Paul's consistent reference to "Christ" in this unit, and the possible error of transcription caused by the use of *nomina sacra* (ΙΥΧΥ—uncial abbreviation for Ἰησοῦ Χριστοῦ) make it more likely that Χριστοῦ is original.

III. Factions and Dissension in the Church (1:10–4:21)

Paul's discussion of the Corinthian factions in these opening chapters leads most interpreters to assume that the church was divided into coalitions that claim allegiance to Paul, Apollos, Cephas, or Christ. They were at loggerheads with one another, all vying for greater status. F. C. Baur (1831) argues that the division was caused by conflicting theologies: Pauline Christianity, represented by the Paul and Apollos parties, and Petrine Jewish Christianity, represented by the Cephas and Christ parties.[1] Munck (1959a) argues that false doctrine was not at issue. Others assume that the problem centered only around Apollos.[2] The question is this: Is the community at odds with Paul or with one another, or are they at odds with both Paul and one another? N. Dahl (1977: 322) claims that the other slogans "are to be understood as declarations of independence from Paul."[3] Others assume that Paul intends to reestablish his authority as well as put an end to their divisions and that he does not write as a "disinterested umpire" (Ker 2000: 75, 79). He does seem to be on the defensive in 4.2–5, 18–21, but chapters 1–4 are not written in the style of an apologetic letter (contrast Gal. 1–2; 2 Cor. 10–13).[4] Paul is just as critical of his supporters as he is of any possible critics.

The use of mirror-reading to interpret this section has been misleading (cf. M. Mitchell 1993: 54–55). Baird (1990: 119) comments,

> The preoccupation with opponents has encouraged exegetes to embrace a methodology whereby texts are read as antithetical responses to that which hypothetical opponents are supposed to have said. If Paul denies something, the opponents must have affirmed it. If Paul affirms something, the opponents must have denied it. This method of "mirror reading" has imposed on the interpretation of the epistles an oppressive

---

1. Goulder (2001) revives and updates this view, arguing that behind this letter lies the conflict between two competing missions, Paul's and that of the Jerusalem "pillar" apostles. See also Manson 1962 and Barrett 1982: 28–39.

2. See Hurd (1965: 96–107) and Jewett (1971: 32–40) for a survey of older views.

3. N. Dahl (1977: 61 n. 50) later retracts his thesis.

4. Beardslee (1994: 23) notes that the "I" of Paul keeps appearing with more and more insistence and comments: "Yet Paul brings in his personal vocation precisely as a testimony to faith in the cross with its rebuke of pride, while at the same time showing an immense confidence in the rightness and authority of his claims."

rigidity. A fresh reading of 1 Corinthians is needed—a reading open to a more flexible analysis of the conflict within the Corinthian congregation.

Van Unnik (1993: 144) concurs and regards it as a "wrong historical method" "to reconstruct the unknown ideas of the Christians there by reverting Paul's words to the opposite and by thinking that everything the apostle wrote was prompted by the necessity of contradicting very explicitly ideas that were held by these enthusiasts in the Corinthian ecclesia and which were leading the sheep astray." The key word in this statement is "everything." Paul does write to correct Corinthian error, but not everything he writes is a correction of some specific Corinthian statement.

This section does not deal with an opposition's conflict with Paul in which he offers a defense. It deals with internal rivalries within the community. Lanci's (1997: 63) comments are on target: Before Paul addresses specific points raised by them in their letter and by oral reports, "he attempts first to convince them that they are in trouble. As he sees it, they are divided. Paul here enumerates the symptoms of dissension: quarreling, allegiance to different teachers or leaders, boasting, and claiming special wisdom or knowledge." He wants to reform their outlook and to get them to adopt his own cruciform lifestyle (4:16). Litfin (1994: 181) claims that the preeminence Paul gives to the matter of divisiveness suggests that "the most prominent difficulty in the Corinthian congregation was not theological but interpersonal." Paul seeks to awaken theological thoughtfulness that results in a cross-centered community no longer torn apart by petty bickering and political infighting.

Furnish's (1999: 45) comments are apropos: "Since those who are being saved from perishing have been formed into a community that lives from the cross, they are also summoned to be informed, both individually and corporately, by the mind of the crucified Christ." The power and wisdom of God are manifest in God sending his Son, allowing him to be crucified, proclaiming this message through apostles regarded by the world as weak and foolish, calling into being a church made up of those the world regards as nobodies, and uniting them to Christ, who becomes their righteousness, sanctification, and redemption. God's power and wisdom shame and bring to naught the wise and mighty of this world and teach that humans can find their identity and security in God alone.

In developing his argument in these chapters, Paul takes up a concluding affirmation in one unit and then amplifies it in the next unit. He concludes the thanksgiving section in 1:9 by asserting that God called them into the fellowship of his Son, Jesus Christ our Lord. In the next unit (1:10–17) he criticizes them for allowing divisions to arise in the church. The conclusion in 1:17 that he does not preach with eloquent wisdom so as to empty the cross of Christ of its power becomes the subject of the next unit in 1:18–25 about the foolishness of the cross versus human wisdom. The theme of the foolishness and weakness of God (1:25) is developed in 1:26–31 in God's choice of the foolish and weak. Its conclusion that one can boast only in the Lord (1:31) is developed in 2:1–5, where Paul recalls his first preaching to them in weakness, fear and trembling, and with unadorned speech; yet the power of God created their faith. The concluding contrast between human wisdom and the power of God (2:5) is developed in 2:6–16 with the contrast between the discernment of the spiritual and unspiritual persons. In 3:1–4, Paul characterizes the Corinthians as carnal rather than spiritual people and cites the party slogans ("I belong to Paul" and "I belong to Apollos"), derided in 1:12, as proof that they are carnal. This leads into his comparison between himself and Apollos as servants of God, and he uses three metaphors to characterize the church: God's field (3:5–9a), God's building (3:9b–15), and God's temple (3:16–17).

In 3:18–23, he recaps his argument about the foolishness of the wisdom of the world, which leads to foolish boasting about leaders. This, in turn, leads to his exhortation on how properly to appraise apostles. They are only servants of Christ. Paul summarizes his argument in 4:6–13 and concludes in 4:14–21 with an exhortation for them to imitate the cruciform existence of apostles. The entire section (1:10–4:21) is set off by the phrase "I exhort you" (1:10; 4:16). They are to bring their rivalries under the rule of the cross so that they live in unity. These chapters comprise a warning against the foolishness and destructiveness of human arrogance and an exposition of how God expects those in Christ to live a cruciform life.

A. The Report of Their Factions (1:10–17)

In 1:10–17, Paul develops the idea of fellowship introduced in 1:9. The Corinthians were called into fellowship in Christ but instead have divided up the body of Christ into competing cliques. Paul knows this through reports from Chloe's people. It is not an open rebellion against Paul's leadership but an internal squabble among the bigwigs in the church scrambling for position. The rifts are between themselves and not with Paul. He writes this letter assuming that they still regard him highly as their founding father in the faith and Christ's apostle sent to them by God. In this passage, he launches his censure of their infighting by reducing their disputes to absurdist comedy that would divide up Christ into lifeless fragments.

Exegesis and Exposition

[10]But I exhort you, brothers and sisters, through the name of our Lord Jesus Christ, that you all may agree and that there may not be rifts among you, but that you may be refurbished in the same mind and in the same purpose. [11]For it was made clear to me concerning you, my brothers and sisters, by Chloe's people, that there are dissensions among you. [12]I mean this: that each one of you is saying, "I belong to Paul"; "I belong to Apollos"; or "I belong to Cephas"; but "I belong to Christ." [13]⌐Has Christ been divided?⌐ Paul was not crucified for your sake, was he? You were not baptized in the name of Paul, were you? [14]I give thanks ⌐to God⌐ that I baptized none of you except Crispus and Gaius [15]so that no one might say that he or she was baptized in my name. [16]I also baptized the household of Stephanas. In addition to that I do not know if I baptized anyone else. [17]For Christ did not send me to baptize but to preach the gospel, not with rhetorically sophisticated speech, so that the cross of Christ might not be emptied [of its effect].

1:10 This verse marks the transition from the thanksgiving period to the body of the letter and contains the thesis statement for the first four chapters (M. Mitchell 1993: 198–99; Schrage 1991: 134–35; Witherington 1995: 94; Vos 1996: 87; cf. Aristotle, *Rhet.* 3.12.13; Quintilian, *Inst.* 4.4.2–5.28). Paul's exhortation solemnly urging "concord in a divided church" (M. Mitchell 1993: 198–99) assumes that the Corinthians are rent by divisions, which is evidenced by their vaunting certain ones over others and allowing worldly wisdom to overshadow the wisdom of the cross.

The verb παρακαλῶ (*parakalō*, I exhort) appears in the final unit (4:14–21) of this section (4:16), so that his appeal to the Corinthians brackets 1:10–4:21 (cf. 16:15). Thiselton (2000: 111–12, 114–15) cites Bjerkelund's 1967 study of the form and function of παρακαλῶ clauses to challenge the view that it introduces a rhetorical argument (contra M. Mitchell 1993: 1; Witherington 1995: 94–95). According to Thiselton (2000: 114), the request *"draws its force from a relationship of friendship, trust, or official status between the writer and the addressee(s)"* (italics in the original). Paul makes this appeal to brothers and sisters who stand together as equals under the Lord (see J. L. White 1986: 219). The masculine ἀδελφοί (*adelphoi*, brothers) is gender inclusive and includes sisters (ἀδελφαί, *adelphai*; cf. Phil. 4:1–2). Paul uses the latter word only when he refers specifically to women (7:15; 9:5). Ἀδελφοί is his standard term for Christians, yet 29 percent of the word's appearances in the Pauline corpus occur in 1 Corinthians.[1] In a split community, Paul wishes to emphasize their familial relationship. Though he introduces himself as an apostle commissioned by God, he speaks to them as their sibling.[2] Consequently, his appeal comes in the name of the Lord Jesus Christ (cf. 5:4; 6:11) and not solely on the basis of his apostolic authority (R. Collins 1999: 68; contra Fee 1987: 52). The name of Jesus Christ is the name in which they were baptized and recalls the mercies of God (Rom. 12:1) showered upon them. It may also recall Christ's meekness and gentleness (2 Cor. 10:1). At the conclusion of this section, he beseeches them as their father in the faith imploring his beloved children (4:14–21). Apostolic exhortation can be both brotherly (Schrage 1991: 137) and fatherly. It is not the lordly demand of a tyrant who bludgeons underlings into submission.

Lightfoot (1895: 151) notes the marked classical coloring of the exhortations that follow. "That you all say the same" (τὸ αὐτὸ λέγητε πάντες, *to auto legēte pantes*), that is, "agree," was "used of political communities which are free from factions" and means "to be at peace" or "to make up differences" (Lightfoot 1895: 151). M. Mitchell (1993: 68) identifies it as a stock phrase that describes "the opposite of factionalism": "Those who 'say the same thing' are allies, compatriots, even copartisans. Simply put, they agree with one another." To speak with one

---

1. The plural occurs 27 times and the singular 12 times in this letter, representing 39 of the 133 uses in the Pauline corpus. The percentage jumps higher if some letters are excluded as non-Pauline.

2. In the LXX, the word "brothers" was applied to fellow members of the covenant, kindred Jews (cf. Exod. 2:11; Deut. 3:18; Isa. 66:20; Neh. 5:1; Tob. 1:3; 2 Macc. 1:1), but never non-Jews. Winter (2001: 70) states that no Roman would have called another person "brother" except one who shared the same parentage or who had been formally adopted into the family. Christians understand themselves to be the adopted children of their heavenly Father (Gal. 4:4–6) and therefore also understand themselves to be brothers and sisters.

voice denotes a state of unity as opposed to being torn apart by cantankerous party zeal that leads to a war of words. Robertson and Plummer (1914: 10) offer the helpful analogy that a difference exists between harmony and dull unison. They are to be like a chorus singing from the same page of music, not like a cat's concert with each howling his or her own cacophonous tune.

The church is divided, and most conclude that the rifts (σχίσματα, *schismata*) were caused by rivalry among spiritual groups within the church (Schrage 1991: 138–39; Thiselton 2000: 119). We should be cautious not to allow the modern associations of the word "schism" with splits created by differing doctrinal interpretations to influence our reading of the Corinthian situation. Polhill (1983: 325) claims that factions usually form around ideas, which he thinks surface in the Corinthians' pet watchwords and sloganlike creedal declarations. M. Mitchell (1993: 71) demonstrates, however, that the term σχίσματα need not mean "'parties' with fixed membership, ideologies, and structures, as in the modern sense of the term." They need not have "specific theological or doctrinal positions." Paul's specific reference to their σχίσματα in 11:18 refers to divisions between the "haves" and the "have-nots" that have no doctrinal roots. What triggers Paul's dismay is the report that believers are forming alliances over against fellow believers and creating strife.

Oster (1995: 50) observes, "Party spirit was a common fact of ancient city life and it was commented upon and lamented by more than one pagan author contemporary with early Christianity." The proclivity toward factiousness was present in Corinth long before Paul appeared, and the new converts apparently continued to manifest this competitive spirit in their interactions with their fellow believers after their conversion. Several factors contributed to a party-minded spirit: social stratification, personal patronage, philosopher/student loyalty, and party loyalties fostered by urban alienation (Oster 1995: 50). The rips in the fabric of their unity (cf. 12:25) could have been caused by any number of things and should not be attributed solely to theological differences (see Munck 1959a: 135–39; Koester 1971: 149; Baird 1990: 130).[3] Munck's (1959a) argument that the ruptures were attributable to the influence of the sophistic movement did not convince many, because it was assumed that the second sophistic movement had not begun by the middle of the first century. Since then, Winter (1997d) appeals to Dio Chrysostom, a letter of the student Neilus [P. Oxy. 2190], Favorinus, Herodes Atticus, Plutarch, and Epictetus for evidence of a budding of

---

3. Baird (1990: 123–24, 128) shows that the word σχίσμα can be used "to describe cliques in a cultic association." A papyrus reporting rules of one such association reads, "It shall not be permissible for any . . . to make factions (σχίσματα) or to leave the brotherhood" (Baird 1990: 124).

the second sophistic movement in Philo's and Paul's era in both Alexandria and Corinth. Both Philo and Paul, he claims, contended in their respective settings with a professional guild of "virtuoso orators" who attracted large public followings and who were drawn from wealthy families. They were influential leaders with high social status who were courted by officials, students, and whole communities (Winter 1997d: 55). Winter (1997d: 180–202; 2001: 31–43) claims that the factions stemmed from the secular elitist educational model of the Sophists, with its allegiance to individual teacher and its competitive spirit, which spilled over into the church as the Corinthians lauded their own mentor while lampooning a rival's. Paul chooses not to address individuals caught up in the fray but exhorts all in the church to put partisanship aside and become unified (M. Mitchell 1993: 71).

The phrase "you may be refurbished" (ἦτε κατηρτισμένοι, ēte katērtismenoi) is a perfect passive periphrastic that means to be "put in order or proper condition," to be "restored." It was used as a surgical term for setting bones and as a metaphor for "resetting" broken relationships and reconciling factions (Lightfoot 1895: 47; M. Mitchell 1993: 74–75). Its appearance in 2 Cor. 13:11, where Paul exhorts them, "Put things in order [καταρτίζεσθε], listen to my appeal, have the same mind, live in peace," reveals its connection to living together in peace and harmony. It also reveals that the problem of rivalries is not quickly solved. When he writes his fourth letter to them, Paul still sees discord lurking as a threat to the community (see additional note).

To be "in the same mind" (ἐν τῷ αὐτῷ νοΐ, en tō autō noi) refers to a Christian mind-set that may include being able to judge "what distinguishes good and right from what is evil and wrong" (Edwards 1885: 17). To be "in the same purpose" (ἐν τῇ αὐτῇ γνώμῃ, en tē autē gnōmē) refers to having the same goals and opinion about the truth. M. Mitchell (1993: 79–80) notes (citing Dio Chrysostom, *Or.* 39, as a key example) that these terms appear prominently in ancient texts dealing with factionalism. What follows is Paul's recipe for bringing harmony from this discord.

Paul has received word from Chloe's people (literally, "those of Chloe") **1:11** that the church is racked by dissensions (ἔριδες, *erides*, discords, strifes, contentions). The news of them fighting amongst themselves is one of his chief concerns in the letter. Ἔρις refers to "hot dispute, the emotional flame that ignites whenever rivalry becomes intolerable" (Welborn 1997: 3) and was well known as something that makes a group vulnerable to attack from outside. The word appears frequently in Paul's listing of vices (Rom. 1:29; 13:13; 2 Cor. 12:20; Gal. 5:20; 1 Tim. 6:4; Titus 3:9).

We know little about the informers. The name "Chloe" was an epithet (meaning "verdure") for the goddess Demeter, as "Phoebe" was for

Artemis; and such names were often given to slaves. Lightfoot (1895: 152) concludes that Chloe's name reflects her servile origin and suggests that she was a freedwoman. Since Paul does not tell the Corinthians who she is, they must have been acquainted with her, though she need not be a Christian. She may be a Corinthian or an Ephesian with business in Corinth (so Findlay 1910: 763; Fee 1987: 54). The messengers certainly are Christians, possibly based in Corinth or Ephesus. Conzelmann (1975: 32 n. 16) reasons, "If Chloe's people live in Ephesus, then we can also understand why Paul quotes them for this embarrassing news, and not the delegation from Corinth" (an argument that also serves to counter attempts to partition the letter; see Belleville 1987: 33). "Those of Chloe" may describe members of her family (relatives or children; cf. John 21:2), her retainers, or her slaves (cf. Rom. 16:10, 11; Phil. 4:22).[4] Whoever they were, Paul regards them as reliable witnesses and assumes that the Corinthians would recognize that their testimony carried weight and could not be lightly dismissed.

1:12 Paul gently chides them for lionizing various leaders. Reading "I belong to Paul"; or "I to Apollos"; or "I to Cephas"; or "I to Christ" as party slogans suggests that the Corinthians have divided into four camps, each centered around a particular figure to whom they pay special homage.[5] According to Welborn (1997: 16), these rallying cries bear a striking resemblance to the sloganeering of political factions gathered around personal alliances (see also Conzelmann 1975: 33).[6] Clarke (1993: 93) contends that the Corinthians were influenced by a secular model of leadership that was personality-centered, and they associated themselves with certain high-profile figures.[7] Factions may have clustered around these individuals, but it is unclear what these so-called slogans meant. How do Paul, Apollos, Cephas, and Christ factor in the dispute?

Paul group. The Paul group is assumed to be composed of loyalists to Paul who formed to counter the developments of other groups that tended to denigrate him. They affirmed his special role as father, planter, and builder of the community. If it consisted only of those baptized by Paul, it would have been comparatively small, though presumably comprising the leading households. If such a group exists, Paul is

4. Theissen (1982: 92–94) thinks they are slaves or dependent workers. Had they been freedmen belonging to her household, they would have taken the name of her father.

5. For concise histories of the interpretation of this verse, see Hurd 1965: 96–107; Schmithals 1971: 117–24; Baumann 1968: 49–55; Thiselton 2000: 123–33.

6. Some years later, the author of 1 Clement complains that the Corinthians were being disloyal to the presbyters and likened it to blasphemy. He reminds them of Paul's letter: "With true inspiration he charged you concerning himself and Cephas and Apollos, because even then you had made yourselves partisans" (1 Clem. 47:3).

7. In our age, it may be compared to persons who aspire to self-importance from the slightest association with someone famous. To give an extreme example: "This is so-and-so. His sister-in-law takes her dog to the same veterinarian that movie star X's aunt uses."

not gratified that they champion him. He does not try to strengthen their hand but undercuts supporters and rivals alike.

Apollos group. Apollos (the name is an abbreviation of Apollonius) is described in Acts 18:24–19:1 as a learned Alexandrian Jew. According to Ker (2000: 77), his background was markedly different from Paul's, which made him a more congenial figure to many Corinthians. The description of him as an ἀνὴρ λόγιος (*anēr logios,* Acts 18:24) could mean that he was eloquent or educated, since the two were bound together (Litfin 1994: 123). He was well-versed in the Scriptures (Acts 18:24) and spoke ardently and boldly in the synagogue (Acts 18:25–26). After coming under the tutelage of Prisca and Aquila to correct his incomplete knowledge of the Way, since he knew only the baptism of John (Acts 18:25–26), he went to Corinth and powerfully refuted Jews from his knowledge of the Scripture (Acts 18:28). He is independent of Paul and traveled to Corinth after Paul had left. Why he went is unexplained. Was he sent by those who wrote the letters of recommendation for him (Acts 18:27; cf. 2 Cor. 3:1)?

With his Alexandrian background, Apollos is considered by many (Koester 1971: 149; Pearson 1973: 18; R. Horsley 1978c) to be the likely candidate for the person who introduced Hellenistic Jewish wisdom teaching to the Corinthians. Is it coincidental that Paul's references in this section to baptism (1:14–17; 3:6), rhetorical eloquence (1:17–25; 2:1–4), spirituality (2:6–16), and building on another's foundation (3:10–15) correlate with the description of Apollos in Acts? Ker (2000: 84) contends that the Corinthians esteemed Apollos and Paul differently because they had contrasting approaches and thinks that "Paul sees danger in any approach other than his own." Witherington (1995: 87), however, thinks that Apollos was an "unwitting catalyst of some of these difficulties." It is important to note that Paul does not overtly criticize Apollos but instead takes the Corinthians to task for their wrong estimation of leaders.

Cephas group. Κηφᾶ (*Kēpha*) is a transliteration of Aramaic into Greek; though some have tried to argue otherwise, it refers to Peter. No credible evidence exists that suggests he ever ventured to Corinth. That the Corinthians know that he traveled with his wife (9:5) does not require that he visited there. What this Petrine group would have represented is unclear. From the days of Baur (1831), it has been assumed that it fostered anti-Paulinism. Goulder (1994; 2001) offers an elaborate sketch of the presumed theological tensions between Peter and Paul. Murphy-O'Connor (1996: 277) surmises that the members of this group were Jewish converts who found it difficult to assimilate into a predominantly Gentile community. He conjectures,

> The secular style of Apollos might have contributed to their sense of isolation. From this perspective, "Cephas" functions as a symbol for a type

of Jewish Christian, who, for Paul, is exemplified, not by the consistent James, but by Peter, who surrendered his freedom under pressure. Time had not healed the bitterness of the memory of the incident at Antioch (Gal. 2:11–14).

Christ group. The Christ group is even more mysterious. It supposedly has not formed around a particular church leader but instead unfurls the flag of Christ.[8] But how could Paul "belittle a slogan that pledged loyalty to Christ" (Oster 1995: 53)? Did this group think they had some exclusive relationship to Christ that afforded them a special divine "hot-line" (Thiselton 2000: 133)? Baird (1990: 129) observes, "Strange as it may seem, the party about which we know the least—which may not even be a party—has become the major preoccupation of a large mass of New Testament scholarship." Nearly every problem that surfaces in this letter has been attributed by some commentator to this nebulous group.

My descriptions of these groups are minimal, and my question is Munck's (1959a): Did doctrinal factions and personality cults gathered around these particular figures actually exist in Corinth? Oster (1995: 49) raises two important caveats to take into consideration in discussing this matter. First, he argues that it is "anachronistic . . . to suggest that the division troubling the Corinthian church was similar to the later ecclesiastical fragmentation which has characterized much of church history." The slogans are not akin to self-satisfied swaggering: "I am a Dominican, a Franciscan, a Lutheran, a Calvinist, an Arminian, or a Barthian," and so on (contra P. Lampe 1990: 122; cf. Fee 1987: 155).

Second, it is "equally unfounded to impose a doctrinal framework of orthodoxy/heresy upon this division" (Oster 1995: 49). Pogoloff (1992: 100) contends that commentators "fail to recognize that the smoke of divisions do[es] not necessarily imply the fire of doctrine." Savage (1996: 31) points out that people in the first century were more interested in show than in doctrine ("The bulk of religious people had little or no theology") and cites as evidence the declaration in Petronius (*Satyr.* 44) "No one cares a button for dogma." Nothing in the letter suggests that the Corinthians were being torn apart by doctrinal wrangling. Evidence to help identify doctrinal profiles or practices that distinguish these groups from one another is sparse. This scarcity of data, however, has not stopped commentators from using gossamer-thin filaments of

---

8. Perdelwitz's (1911) argument that a copyist confused Christ for Crispus because of the similar sound of the names in Greek (Χριστός, Κρίσπος) requires that the text was copied from an oral reading. Christian scribes used *nomina sacra,* and there would be no confusing ΧΥ for ΚΡΙΣΠΟΥ. He also argues that κόσμος (*kosmos*) in 3:22 should be changed to Κρίσπος.

evidence to spin elaborate theories about each group (see, for example, Fitch 1971). The results provoke Hurd (1965: 107) to remark that the answers provided by scholars are "determined more by what each scholar has brought to 1 Corinthians than by what he has learned from this letter." Moffatt (1938: 9) attempts to explain this problem away by claiming that Paul was only interested in quashing their quarrelsome spirit rather than offering a critique of their various opinions. Others tend to elevate one of the parties as the chief opponent of Paul, allowing the other rivals to fade into the background. Conzelmann (1975: 34) observes that one can detect "in the Corinthian community tendencies of a pneumatic, enthusiastic, individualistic kind, yet these are to be found in the party system as such, rather than in the peculiarity of the individual groups. Of these groups we know nothing."

The paucity of clues about these groups leads to two more caveats. One should be careful not to read the later developments reflected in 2 Corinthians into the situation of this letter. One also should reject the conclusion of Robertson and Plummer (1914: 12) that the parties at Corinth "are the local results of streams of influence which show themselves at work elsewhere in the N.T." This view presumes that the root of the problem is theological, and it opens the door to reading nearly every problem that appears elsewhere in the NT and beyond into the Corinthian situation. To ascribe differing theological views to the groups rallying under the banner of each of these names has no basis in the immediate context, in the rest of the letter, or in 2 Corinthians, and is unwarranted guesswork.[9] To argue also that the Apollos group criticized Paul because of his lack of rhetorical skill, that the followers of Cephas criticized him because of his refusal to accept support, and that the Christ party asserted their independence from all apostles, as Carter (1997: 56) does, is pure conjecture with little textual support.

M. Mitchell (1993: 83–86) clears the air by questioning whether Paul is citing real slogans at all (contra Welborn 1997: 8–16). She compares them with ancient political texts touting a party affiliation and concludes that they are "more likely caricatures of the Corinthians' behavior which employ, not a common formula of sloganeering in antiquity, but the language of slave ownership and childish dependence" (cf. Isa. 44:5). They match the phrase τῶν Χλόης (*tōn Chloēs*, those belonging to Chloe) in the previous verse (see BDF §162 [7]). M. Mitchell (1993: 84) argues, "To say, 'I support Marcus for aedile' is not the same thing to say 'I belong to Marcus,'" and concludes that "I belong to" is the language of children and reflects the childishness of their rivalries. This perspective corresponds to Paul's slashing remarks in 3:1–4 that they are but infants who must be fed

---

9. The slogans do not appear in the letter after chapter 4 or anywhere in 2 Corinthians.

pabulum instead of solid food because of their jealousy, quarreling, and faction-generating sloganeering. R. Collins (1999: 73) concurs. He thinks that this verse represents

> a forceful piece of rhetoric on the part of Paul rather than a statement about the specific situation at Corinth. The so-called slogans are not slogans used by various groups among the Corinthians. They are caricatures created by Paul. These caricatures implicitly compare the behavior of the Corinthians to that of groups of children who are dependent on their parents or groups of slaves dependent on their masters.[10]

M. Mitchell (1993: 86) characterizes the slogans as "impersonation," displaying the thought of the adversaries as if they were talking themselves (cf. Quintilian, *Inst.* 9.2.30). Paul does *not* say that Chloe's people reported that they were rallying around these names and spouting these slogans. They only reported that the church was riven by dissensions (contra Hays 1997: 22). Paul himself interprets (λέγω δὲ τοῦτο, *legō de touto*, I mean this) what this report implies and exaggerates when he claims "each one" is saying these things.[11] By articulating the divisions in his own words, he "heightens the severity and ludicrousness of the situation" (M. Mitchell 1993: 201). The slogans turn out to be put-downs rather than self-designations. It betrays the individualism that Paul finds so problematic in this community. The "I" is repeated for emphasis to show that they suffer from an "I" disease that is not physical. Why "I" when they are all a part of Christ's body (3:22–23)? R. Collins (1999: 75) contends that "the 'I' points to the root of the problem at Corinth as located in a radical individuality rather than substantive theological differences." This conclusion best explains why in this section Paul addresses not the individual factions but the entire church. It also explains why he never takes on the other teachers but instead emphasizes the good relationship between himself and Apollos.

If Paul recites the names in an ascending scale—Paul, Apollos, Cephas, Christ (so Lightfoot 1895: 154)—then he lists himself first as the least of all the apostles (15:9). But "I belong to Christ" remains puzzling. If this was the rallying cry of a Christ group, then why does the name "Christ" drop out in his later references to the so-called parties?

Paul and Apollos (3:4–5)

Paul, Apollos, and Cephas (3:22)

Paul and Apollos (4:6)

10. So also Murphy-O'Connor 1996: 277.

11. The reference to the ten thousand guardians in Christ (4:15) displays Paul's tendency toward hyperbole.

Does he get "carried away by the rhetorical figure" and cast "his own response in a formula identical with those he attributed to others" (Murphy-O'Connor 1996: 277 n. 104), and declare his own allegiance to Christ, which nullifies all personality cults? Could he be saying, "All this 'I am for this apostle or that' is rubbish: I am for Christ" (Chrysostom, *Hom. 1 Cor.* 3.5; Lake 1914: 127; Hurd 1965: 105; Baumann 1968: 54; M. Mitchell 1993: 82 n. 101; R. Horsley 1998: 45)?[12] The consistent pattern μέν, δέ, δέ, δέ (*men, de, de, de*) seems to dash this suggestion because one expects ἀλλά (*alla*) to mark the contrast (Weiss 1910: 15–16; Fee 1987: 58 n. 54; R. Collins 1999: 72). But what is wrong with saying "I belong to Christ" (cf. Phil. 1:1, "slave of Christ Jesus")? Is this not the confession of every Christian? There is no hint in the text that some Corinthians are claiming a unique relationship to Christ. If there was a Christ party, Paul seems to play into their hands by naming Christ ten times in the previous verses and by declaring that no one can boast except in Christ, who is wisdom from God (1:29–31). In 3:21–22, he rejects boasting in human leaders—Paul, Apollos, Cephas—and follows in 3:23 with an expression corresponding to "I belong to Christ" that he clearly understands in a positive sense and not as a boisterous slogan: "And you [plural] belong to Christ, and Christ belongs to God."

Branick (1982: 260) labels "I belong to Christ" as Pauline sarcasm: "All of you want to belong to particular groups. I belong to Christ!" He thinks that it becomes clear that it is sarcasm only when the reader reaches 3:23. The best explanation of the evidence is that the so-called Christ party did not exist. The declaration "I belong to Christ" is Paul's and prepares for his assertions that he knew only a crucified Christ when he first preached in Corinth (2:2), that he has the mind of Christ (2:16), that he is to be thought of as a servant of Christ (4:1), and that he is a fool for Christ (4:10). His basic argument in these chapters is that no leader has any ultimate significance, and none is to be puffed up in favor of one against another (4:6). "I belong to Christ" ideally describes all believers (3:23; 6:19–20). He wishes to reinforce their common loyalty to Christ and uproot their childish attachment to human leaders. Luther captures the gist of Paul's teaching in his response to learning that the first Protestants were being called Lutherans. He protested,

> What is Luther? The teaching is not mine. Nor was I crucified for anyone. . . . How did I, poor stinking bag of maggots that I am, come to the point where people call the children of Christ by my evil name?

Luther criticized preachers for falling prey to the temptation of vainglory. "May God protect us against the preachers who please all the

---

12. Schrage (1991: 148) considers the phrase to be ironic, reducing the slogan to an absurdity.

people and enjoy a good testimony from everybody," he cried. Faithful preachers should teach only the Word of God and seek only his honor and praise. "Likewise, the hearers should also say: 'I do not believe in my pastor, but he tells me of another Lord whose name is Christ; him he shows me'" (T. George 1988: 53, 72).

What can be concluded about the rivalries in Corinth from these slogans?

1. The rivalries do not revolve around theological issues. Pogoloff (1992: 99–100) notes that Paul normally encourages factions when the opposition teaches a gospel that fundamentally contradicts his (Gal. 1:6–9; 2:11; 5:10–12; 6:12–13; 2 Cor. 11:4, 13–15). He does not compromise theological issues for the sake of unity (cf. 1 Cor. 11:19). In this case, however, not even the so-called Paul group is right. His concern lies elsewhere. It is the "temper of uppishness" (Moffatt 1938: 9), alienating them from one another, that disturbs him. This conclusion does not mean that their theology is not distorted. As Paul evaluates the situation, they have exchanged the wisdom of the cross for delusive, worldly wisdom.

2. None of the persons named lent any support to these so-called parties or encouraged schools to develop around himself. The Corinthians placed too much stock in human leaders, and they may have appealed to these leaders without consciously forming a Pauline, Apolline, or Petrine caucus. It is more likely, however, that Paul utilizes what Fiore (1985) calls "covert allusion" to address the problem. Chrysostom (*Hom. 1 Cor.* 3.4) contends that the Corinthians actually had not been speaking about these figures, and Paul tactfully does not identify by name the real offenders behind the dissension but conceals them "as behind a sort of masks, with the names of the Apostles." D. Hall (1994: 145) thinks that Paul employs good psychological tactics: "There were good reasons for Paul not to attack the party leaders directly. For one thing, his information about the divisions came to him by hearsay from Chloe's household. To name names on hearsay evidence can cause trouble not only for the namer, but also for the informants."

3. It is possible that Fee (1987: 49) is correct in saying that the quarreling over the leaders is not just to champion their favorite "but is decidedly *over against* Paul." It is also possible that they identified with these great leaders to boost their own prestige (Munck 1959a: 157). They may have been trying "to legitimate their power by appealing to renowned figures in the church" (Welborn 1997: 24). I do not think, however, that Paul is on the defensive in this letter as much as Fee believes or that the Corinthians were slinging around party slogans, but I do think that issues of prestige and power were at the heart of the problem. It means that the problems, though localized, were rooted in the universal, sinful desire to seek power and status for oneself.

4. P. Marshall's (1987: ix) contention that the divisions may be rooted in the social situation should not be overlooked. The only other divisions that Paul specifically mentions in this letter center around litigation (6:1–8) and the Lord's Supper (11:18).[13] Both suggest tensions between the richer and the poorer. Paul alludes to their friction when he uses the figure of the body to illustrate the unity of the church: no member can say that it does not belong (12:15–16), and no member can say that it has no need of another (12:21). He might also hint at a division between the glossolalists and the prophets in 14:2–5 (cf. 12:29–30). We do not know how many were in the church but can guess that they were too numerous to meet comfortably in one house and that subgroups of house churches were formed (Murphy-O'Connor 1983: 153–58). Possibly, rivalries sprang up between these house churches and their various leaders (Murphy-O'Connor 1996: 277; Horrell 1996: 117).[14] Filson (1939: 110) notes that "a physically divided church tended almost inevitably to become a mentally divided church." Household loyalty, patron/client relationships, and architectural separation may have been the forces fracturing their unity. From the context, Plutarch's (*Mor.* 788E) statement—"love of contention, love of fame, the desire to be first and greatest, which is a disease most prolific of envy, jealousy, and discord"—may describe the root problem that Paul wishes to eradicate. Clashing egos and selfishness plagued the first Christians (cf. Phil. 1:15, 17; 2:21; 3 John 9) no less than they do Christians today.

Paul attempts to undermine this partisan spirit with three questions. The questions underscore the lunacy of exalting one leader over another when they all have been called into the fellowship of Jesus Christ (1:9). He first asks, "Has Christ been divided?" Unlike the next two questions, prefaced by μή (*mē*), this question does not expect a refutation (so Lightfoot 1895: 154). The answer is yes. It expresses Paul's shock, a tactic he uses elsewhere in the letter (5:2; 6:1; 11:22), and is the equivalent of a statement. "Christ" here represents, by synecdoche (a figure of speech in which a part is used to represent the whole), the church as Christ's body (Schrage 1991: 152; Welborn 1997: 40), an idea that Paul expands upon in 12:12–13, 27. The verb μερίζω (*merizō*) is used to describe disunity in Mark 3:24–26 (cf. Matt. 12:25–26), referring to division in the ranks of Satan, and in Ign. *Magn.* 6:2, referring to a kingdom, city, household, divided against itself. The verb appears to have the same meaning here. Paul uses the verb again in 7:34 to de-

1:13

---

13. I argue that the contention over food sacrificed to idols (8:1–11:1) is not between the "strong" and the "weak" in Corinth but between the know-it-alls and Paul.

14. Klauck (1981: 39–40) conjectures that Paul was hosted by a different house church than Apollos was, which fed the rivalry.

scribe the married man torn apart by his desire to please both the Lord and his wife. The verb depicts Christ being divided into component parts and presents a picture of the church as a divided house. This image is particularly apt if separate house churches are squabbling.

Some interpreters, however, claim that Paul is still thinking about the so-called Christ party; and they take the verb to mean that Christ is divided up and distributed or apportioned only to some, with the Christ party getting the major share (Findlay 1910: 765; Robertson and Plummer 1914: 13; Lindemann 2000: 41). Fee (1987: 60) interprets it as a direct response to the slogan "I belong to Christ": "Absurd! Can Christ be made a party in the same breath as the others?" This interpretation imposes a theory about the various parties, which I reject, based on the meaning of the verb. The question assumes that division in the body of believers divides up Christ (Weiss 1910: 16–17; Conzelmann 1975: 35; Schrage 1991: 153). The vivid imagery of Christ sliced into fragments is Paul's first move decrying the divisions among them.

The answer to the second question, "Was Paul crucified for you?" obviously expects the answer no. Paul was not crucified for their sake (cf. 11:24; 15:3; Rom. 5:8; 8:32; 14:15; 2 Cor. 5:14–15; Gal. 1:4; Col. 1:24), nor did he or any other leader die to expiate their sin. Human leaders are not the source of a believer's redemption. Christ alone is that source, because Christ alone was crucified for them. Paul's subsequent discourse on the wisdom of the cross may imply that their partisan spirit could be attributed, in part, to a "forgetfulness of the crucifixion" (Branick 1982: 268) and the offense attached to it. It is because of Christ's obedience to the point of death on the cross that God highly exalted him and gave him the name that is above every name (Phil. 2:8–9). No human leader can ever be elevated to the same level as Christ. It is through *his* death that God reconciles the world (Col. 1:20) and brings an end to divisions. It is into *his* death that Christians are baptized (Rom. 6:3–6).

Some infer that baptism was a factor in the Corinthians' bickering over leaders. They presume that the Corinthians believed that they had some kind of mystical connection to the one who baptized them. If so, this error might be a carryover from their past involvement in pagan cults in which the initiate remained devoted to the mystagogue who performed the rites (Apuleius, *Metam.* 11; so Wilckens 1959: 16–17; Héring 1962: 7; Conzelmann 1975: 35; R. Horsley 1979: 47; Meeks 1983: 117; Fee 1987: 61; Wolff 1996: 30). Or, they may have derived status vicariously from the one who baptized them (Chrysostom, *Hom. 1 Cor.* 3.6; Soards 1999: 37). If this view was at the root of the problem, it again undermines the case for the "Christ party." Who was their baptizer?

It is more likely that Paul's question "Were you baptized in the name of Paul?" reduces the whole issue to an absurdity, which explains why he need only use his own name without mentioning the others. According to Robertson and Plummer (1914: 13), the phrase εἰς τὸ ὄνομα (*eis to onoma*, Matt. 28:19; Acts 8:16; 19:5) is stronger than other options, ἐπί (Acts 2:38) or ἐν (Acts 10:48), and "implies entrance into fellowship and allegiance." Paul's question assumes that they were baptized into the name of Christ, which signifies a transference from the dominion of this world into God's kingdom, where the believer finds forgiveness, love, sacredness, and fellowship with those who have also renounced the world's values and practices. It also signifies a unique relationship to Christ and all he experienced in his death and resurrection. It means that they now belong only to Christ (3:23) and are one in him. Baptism "into Paul's name" would signify nothing but an idolatrous attachment to a mortal (cf. Acts 14:11–15). The problem is not that the Corinthians failed to understand these truths and that Paul needs to set them straight; the problem is that they have failed to live out the implications of their belief in a crucified Christ and their unity in him.

The mention of baptism seems to distract Paul momentarily from the issue of the community's rivalries. He gives thanks that he baptized none of them except Crispus and Gaius, presumably the first converts, so that so few could ever foolishly claim that they were baptized in his name. He does not disparage baptism as something unimportant but downplays the role of the one who performs the baptism. In the context of his arguments in these opening chapters, he may give thanks for not baptizing many so that the Corinthians could see that ministry was "shared partnership" (Thiselton 2000: 140). Some plant, some water, others harvest. All these workers are interchangeable, but none are interchangeable with Christ or separable from him. **1:14–16**

Crispus is identified in Acts 18:8 as the ruler of the synagogue in Corinth. The inscriptional evidence suggests that this title was honorific, gratefully bestowed on those who were wealthy patrons (including non-Jews) who donated a building or part of one, a mosaic floor, or accoutrements to the synagogue (Murphy-O'Connor 1996: 267; contra Meggitt 1998: 141–43). The *praenomen* Gaius was common (cf. Acts 19:29; 20:4; 3 John 1; Mart. Pol. 22:2). Is he the Titius Justus described in Acts 18:7 as a worshiper of God, whose house was next door to the synagogue and who hosted Paul after irate Jews booted him out for testifying that Jesus was the Messiah? Gaius Titius Justus would be a complete Roman name with *praenomen, nomen gentile,* and *cognomen* (Goodspeed 1950; Bruce 1971: 34; Dunn 1988b: 910). Paul mentions Gaius in Rom. 16:23 as "host to me and the whole church." Murphy-O'Connor (1996: 267) notes that mentioning the "whole" church "is unnecessary if the Corinthian Christians met only as a single group

(1 Cor. 14:23)." It implies the existence of smaller subgroups that met in other house churches (cf. Rom. 16:5; 1 Cor. 16:19; Col. 4:15; Philem. 2). It follows that Gaius was wealthier than the average believer, as he had a house large enough to accommodate the entire church (see Dunn 1988b: 910–11).

Why did Paul baptize so few? Apparently, he did not regard baptism as a sacrament that required "apostolic hands" to administer it (Hays 1997: 24). Perhaps he was aware of the mystical connection between the initiate and the mystagogue administering the secret rites in the mystery cults and deliberately wished to circumvent any possible misconceptions among those coming to faith in Christ from that heritage. If Crispus and Gaius are to be identified with the persons named in Acts, however, then they had roots in Jewish traditions, not some mystery cult. It is unlikely that they would have drawn false conclusions about the significance of the one who baptized them. Murphy-O'Connor (1996: 268) ties Paul's baptism of these comparatively well-to-do men to his mission strategy:

> He had the practical sense to recognize that, while the gospel was offered to all, only those with initiative, leisure, and education could function as effective assistants in the spread of the gospel. Slaves might be model Christians, but they were not their own masters. They could not dispose of their time as they wished. Neither could Prisca and Aquila, who had a living to earn.

I propose another view to explain the inclusion of these two names. Possibly, these two wealthier men were at the root of the controversy as leaders of house churches. It is hard to imagine how persons with their wealth and influence did not have something to do with the disputes. They came from different backgrounds—one Jewish, the other a Gentile God-fearer—and this difference may have fueled strife. By mentioning them by name as those whom he baptized in Corinth, Paul may be reminding these two men of the circumstances of their coming to faith in Christ (cf. Philem. 19). They are both on the same level. He employs a strategy of indirectness to maneuver delicately around sensitive and perhaps bruised egos to avoid causing them to lose face publicly and to promote rapport.

As an afterthought, Paul mentions baptizing the household of Stephanas and does not recall baptizing anyone else. He did not put notches in his Bible to keep a head count of those he had baptized. This memory lapse may imply that Paul dictated his letters without revising them (Lietzmann 1949: 8–9; Barrett 1968: 48). Perhaps Sosthenes or Stephanas himself (Bruce 1971: 340) jogged his memory. On the other hand, since Paul mentions the household of Stephanas again in 16:15 as the firstfruits of Achaia, he hardly could have forgotten them. This omission may not have been a memory lapse but a deliberate gambit to underline how unimportant it is who baptized whom (Hays 1997: 23). I contend that it allows him to place an emphasis on the two key figures in the dispute, Crispus and Gaius.

Paul shifts subjects in this verse to preaching, wisdom of speech, and the cross of Christ and introduces a subthesis (*subpropositio,* Vos 1996: 91). This statement contains the two issues that Paul intends to argue in the rest of chapters 1–4: (1) he is a preacher of the gospel, not a baptizer (1:17a), and (2) human wisdom and the wisdom of the cross are irreconcilable (1:17b). He argues them in reverse order of the way they are stated (Pascuzzi 1997: 31–32). He deals with the wisdom of the cross in 1:18–2:16, and his apostolic role in 3:1–4:13. He is not defending his apostolic status and authority in this section (Pascuzzi 1997: 33) and does not touch directly upon the divisions themselves but addresses "the values which lie behind them" (Pogoloff 1992: 119). **1:17**

Paul attests that his divine calling is not "to perform baptisms" (Thiselton 2000: 143) but to proclaim the gospel (Rom. 1:15; 15:20; Gal. 1:11, 16, 23). God did not call him to be a jack-of-all-ministries. The phrasing ἀπέστειλέν με Χριστὸς . . . εὐαγγελίζεσθαι (*apesteilen me Christos . . . euangelizesthai,* Christ sent me to proclaim the gospel) recalls his apostolic commission (cf. Acts 22:21) and bears a striking resemblance to Mark 3:14, which describes Jesus creating the Twelve ἵνα ἀποστέλλῃ αὐτοὺς κηρύσσειν (*hina apostellē autous kēryssein,* in order that he might send them to preach). Paul discusses his commission to preach again in 9:16–18 and expresses its urgency in the strongest eschatological terms: "Woe to me if I do not proclaim the gospel" (9:16). He may be implying that baptizing converts requires no special gifts compared to preaching.[15] Godet (1886: 84–85) expresses it this way: "To preach the gospel is to cast the net; it is apostolic work. To baptize is to gather the fish now taken and put them into vessels." Salvation does not come without preaching (Rom. 10:14–15; 1 Cor. 15:1–2), and baptism comes only as the sequel to the response of faith after hearing the message.

Paul refines his call to proclaim the gospel further by stating that it is not to preach with a "wisdom of word" (οὐκ ἐν σοφίᾳ λόγου, *ouk en sophia logou*). This phrase can refer to the matter of the speech, with the emphasis on "wisdom." It would refer to a "religious philosophy" (Godet 1886: 87; Lietzmann 1949: 9) that has knowledge of divine matters, or natural philosophy. Pogoloff (1992: 109) objects, "The ordinary usage of *sophia* suggested nothing of philosophical or religious speculation." It had to do with learning that was practically applicable. It is more likely that Paul refers to the form of his speech, with the emphasis

---

15. In Acts 10:48, Peter orders the converts in the household of Cornelius to be baptized but does not do it himself.

on "word." It points to wisdom pertaining to speech or rhetoric and means "not with rhetorical skill" (Litfin 1994: 188–92). Pogoloff (1992: 109) demonstrates that although both words, σοφία and λόγος, have a wide range of possible meanings, "one meaning stands out among the others as the most common and least specialized or esoteric: 'sophisticated speech,'" a product of rhetoric. Pogoloff (1992: 110) contends it was used in particular for "a *speech* delivered in court, assembly, etc." (citing LSJ 1058). In this sense, σοφία λόγου would mean clever, skilled, educated, or rhetorically sophisticated speech. Although it can apply to "cultured speech and cleverness," or "the graces of diction" (Lightfoot 1895: 157), it connotes more than "technical skill at language" (Pogoloff 1992: 113). It is connected to "winning arguments and impressing an audience by rhetorical display rather than content" (Witherington 1995: 103–4).

The λόγος, then, is not just any word, but speech defined by wisdom (2:4)—a wisdom that Paul finds incompatible with the gospel because it relies on manipulative rhetoric (see additional note). He was not called to be a phrasemonger who overwhelms his audience with an eloquence that is an end in itself. He is no oratorical dilettante but a master builder. Why does Paul think that their divisions are churned by human wisdom and are a threat to the theology of the cross (Sellin 1982: 69)? Many commentators assume that Paul raises this point because the Corinthians have criticized him for the lack of rhetorical "pizzazz" in his preaching. Paul's report of their critique in 2 Cor. 10:10—"his speech is contemptible" (cf. 11:6)—would seem to confirm this opinion (so Vos 1996: 96–97). Pogoloff (1992: 113–19), however, shows that a direct connection existed between cleverness in speech and social status and concludes that Paul intends to say that "he did not preach in a status conferring manner." The problem is not simply that manipulative rhetoric causes the cross to "vanish under the weight of rhetorical ornament and dialectic subtlety" (Lightfoot 1895: 157); the problem with this style is that it earns the preacher the crowd's golden opinions. Consequently, Paul is not defending his apostolic power in spite of his speaking deficiencies but attempting to undercut one of the values that has contributed to their divisions: the thirst for honor. Eloquence that elevates the status of the preacher cancels the power of the cross.

Litfin (1994: 130) contends that orators became less concerned about the value of their message than about their approval rating from the audience. To preach the gospel intending to charm and captivate the crowds with clever wordsmithery in order to enhance one's own prestige only empties (κενόω, kenoō) the cross of its effect. Preaching the cross, Paul articulates in 1:18–25, invites derision, not applause. In the cross, God seeks not human ovations but contrition. What is inspired is not the preacher but the word that is preached. Paul finds it contemptible to think that preachers could ever exploit the proclamation of one who was crucified as a means to upgrade their own worldly status. His statement in 1:17 is not a defense of some perceived rhetorical inadequacy on his part but has a paradigmatic function. He mentions himself as an example for the Corinthians to follow (M. Mitchell 1993: 210).

How can rhetorical eloquence threaten to render the cross of no effect? There are three ways.

1. It subverts the dynamic of the persuasive power of the cross by substituting the dynamic of human rhetorical persuasion. Aristotle (*Rhet.* 1.1.1) defines rhetoric "as the faculty of discovering the possible means of persuasion in reference to any subject whatsoever." Litfin (1994: 191–92) argues that the "dynamic of Greco-Roman rhetoric," which prized the speaker's ability to choose and adapt words, arguments, arrangement, and delivery for the greatest impact, places emphasis on the speaker's skill to control an audience's favorable response. The result is that they are swayed by the power of the orator's rhetorical skill rather than converted by the power of the cross. For example, Cicero (*Orator ad M. Brutum* 28.97) praises eloquence, "which rushes along with the roar of a mighty stream, which all look up to and admire, and which they despair of attaining. This eloquence has power to sway men's minds and move them in every possible way. Now it storms the feelings, now it creeps in; it implants new ideas and uproots the old."

One does not preach the cross to win the admiration of the audience. The goal is to have them look up in awe at the cross, which implants new ideas and uproots the old ways of interpreting divine and earthly reality. Thiselton (2000: 145–46) comments, "To treat the gospel of the cross of Christ as a vehicle for promoting self-esteem, self-fulfillment, and self-assertion turns it upside down and 'empties' it of all that it offers and demands." Human brilliance is antithetical to the cross, which jars human sensibilities and subverts all self-promotion by cutting across race, class, gender, and status "to make room for divine grace alone as sheer unconditional gift" (Thiselton 2000: 145). To be full of oneself as a golden-tongued orator is the opposite of emptying oneself (of oneself), which is the paradigm presented by the cross.

2. Sophisticated rhetoric was tied to an educational value system that "enshrined the beautiful and the strong in a position of social power" (Judge 1983: 14). Pogoloff (1992: 120) cites Judge to argue, "What persuades is speech about what is ordinarily unfit for contemplation, not a life which is cultured, wise, and powerful, but one marked by the worst shame and the lowest possible status. Paul's rhetoric of the cross thus opposes the cultural values surrounding eloquence."

3. Clever rhetoric is superficial. It shortcuts the transformation of listeners by simply gaining their assent. It appeals to emotions without

touching the spiritual depths. It may reap numerous baptisms but not many true conversions.

Additional Notes

1:10. According to 1 Clem. 46:5–9, factionalism continued to plague Corinth. The author complains,

> [5]Why are there strife [ἔρεις] and passion [θύμοι] and divisions [διχοστασίαι] and schisms [σχίσματα] and war [πόλεμος] among you? [6]Or have we not one God and one Christ and one Spirit of grace poured out among us? And is there not one calling in Christ? [7]Why do we divide and tear asunder the members of Christ, and raise up strife against our own body and reach such a pitch of madness as to forget that we are members of one another?. . . [9]Your schism has turned aside many, has cast many into discouragement, many to doubt, all of us to grief, and your sedition continues.

1:13. $\mathfrak{P}^{46vid}$, 1912, 1962, syr[p], cop[sa], arm add μή, apparently to make the question "Has Christ been divided?" conform to the following questions and to make sure that this would be read as a question and not as a statement. It would be the earliest commentary on what this question was intended to mean, and Thiselton (2000: 137) considers it to be a textual addition but a valid interpretation.

1:14. The reading τῷ θεῷ is omitted in ℵ*, B, 6, 424[c], 1739, some cop[sa, bo]. Others add μου (A, 33, 81, 326, 330, 436, lat). Omission of thanksgiving "to God" generally is absent in ℵ and B, including in 1:4. Since Paul's general pattern is to include the phrase after εὐχαριστῶ (Rom. 1:8; 1 Cor. 14:18; Phil. 1:3; Col. 1:3; 1 Thess. 1:2; 2:13; Philem. 4), it seems best to regard "to God" as original.

1:17. Since Paul demonstrates rhetorical sophistication in his letters, Pogoloff (1992: 121) concludes that he rejects the cultural values wedded to rhetoric, not rhetoric itself. Litfin's (1994) thesis is that Paul employs rhetoric as his servant, not his master. The result is that Paul "can at once attack rhetoric and employ it in that very attack" (Pogoloff 1992: 120). R. Collins (1999: 76) claims,

> Even Paul's denial that he uses rhetorical technique, lest the cross of Christ be deprived of its power, is a rhetorical device. Ancient rhetors frequently used demurrals and veiled apologies in order to win the goodwill of their audience or disarm their opponents (e.g. Isocrates, *Nicocles*, or *The Cyprians* 45). In any event, the language of the first paragraph in the body of Paul's letter is laced with terms and expression that were commonly used in Hellenistic political rhetoric.

P. W. Gooch (1987b: 49) connects Paul's critique of rhetoric to his critique of worldly wisdom and identifies it as "worldly persuasion" that expresses the speaker's own conceit.

B. The Foolish Wisdom of the Cross (1:18–25)

In 1:18–2:5, Paul sketches how the gospel's message strikes most hearers as foolishness (1:18–25) and how those who respond to the gospel's call are regarded as foolish by the world (1:26–31). He then reminds the Corinthians how his deportment matches the message he preaches (2:1–5) and how that preaching takes effect (2:6–16). In 1:18–25, he reproclaims the message of the cross. It is the power of God to absorb all the blind rage of humanity and to avert its deadly consequences, but humanity, Jew and Greek alike, fails to recognize that truth because it does not fit their categories. Six citations of Scripture appear in 1:18–3:23 (1:19, 31; 2:9, 16; 3:19, 20). All make the point that humans "cannot grasp God's wisdom through their own wisdom" (cf. Gärtner 1967–68: 216).

The argument about God's wisdom versus the world's wisdom may seem to have nothing do with the Corinthian dispute, but Paul is covertly undermining the Corinthian party spirit. P. Lampe (1990: 129) makes the case that Paul uses the rhetorical mode of speech called a *schēma*. It is covert speech that forces the audience to puzzle over the true meaning or application of a statement (cf. Quintilian, *Inst.* 9.2.64–65). P. Lampe (1990: 130) explains that it replaces a thought that might cause an affront with a general thought not necessarily related to the situation. The two main general thoughts in 1:18–2:16 are (1) all human wisdom of this world is bound to perish (1:18–25), and (2) all Christian wisdom is exclusively God's gift through the Spirit (2:6–16). They relate only indirectly to what P. Lampe believes is the specific issue: the Corinthian parties' adoration of the apostles and their wisdom. P. Lampe (1990: 130) concludes,

> Applying both general thoughts to the specific issue, one arrives at the following conclusion: Either the wisdom of the apostles is a human quality and therefore a reason for praising them—but then it is also bound to perish—or the wisdom of the apostles is exclusively a spiritual gift from God, justifying God alone as the object of praise. In both cases the way is obstructed for praising apostles, which sums up the whole thought figure of 1:18–2:16.

P. Lampe contends that Paul basically lulls them into enjoying the derision of Jewish and Greek wisdom before unveiling in 3:18–19 that they are being denounced as well in 1:18–25 for their partisan boasting about their so-called Christian wisdom. Though Paul criticizes Jews and Greeks, his real target is the Corinthians' misbehavior (P. Lampe 1990: 128). P. Lampe (1990: 130) thinks that Paul employs this rhetorical tactic "to avoid stepping openly on the toes of these two other apostles"—Cephas and Apollos. In my opinion, he steps gingerly to avoid offending directly the leaders of the Corinthian factions, who tout their own wisdom. His purpose is to puncture their pride in that vaunted wisdom that leads them into their factionalism. Stansbury's (1990: 475) comments are insightful:

> For those who claim honor on the basis of wisdom, Paul offers the folly (μωρία [mōria]) of the cross. Rather than impressive displays of wisdom, Paul challenges them to proclaim this shameful experience of their master's crucifixion, a divine folly that overturns human wisdom.

The problematic wisdom that Paul censures is not to be conceived solely in terms of its intellectual content. It has a social dimension. The Corinthians tied wisdom to social status (Pogoloff 1992: 8–10). Paul does not reject a counterteaching or ideology, nor does he reject rhetoric per se, but he belittles, instead, the cultural values and high social status attached to so-called wise speech (Pogoloff 1992: 121, 115).

Exegesis and Exposition

[18]For the word, namely, the word of the cross,[1] is foolishness to those who are perishing, but to us who are being saved it is the power of God. [19]For it stands written, "I will destroy the wisdom of the wise and nullify the cleverness of the clever." [20]Where is the wise person? Where is the scribe? Where is the philosopher of this age? Did not God make foolish the world's wisdom? [21]For since in God's wisdom the world did not come to know God through wisdom, it pleased God to save those who believe through the foolishness of preaching. [22]For, indeed, Jews ask for signs and Greeks chase after wisdom. [23]But we preach a crucified Christ: to Jews, a stumbling block; to Greeks, foolishness; [24]but to those who are called, both Jew and Greek, Christ, God's power and God's wisdom. [25]Because the foolishness of God is wiser than human [wisdom], and the weakness of God is stronger than human [strength].

---

1. The repetition of the article in the phrase ὁ λόγος ὁ τοῦ σταυροῦ (*ho logos ho tou staurou*) is used for emphasis and functions as a mild relative pronoun: "the word which is of the cross."

The death of Jesus is one of the foundational symbols that determined **1:18** Paul's vision of the Christian community (Pickett 1997: 29). But Greco-Roman symbols and mythology (see Zanker 1990) competed with the cross to provide a framework for interpreting life. The Corinthians' quarreling reveals that they have absorbed, uncritically, the ideals and values of the pagan world around them, and Paul wants to replace pagan paradigms with the ideals and values exhibited in the cross. When he proclaimed the crucified Christ, however, every hearer from Jerusalem to Illyricum (Rom. 15:19) knew that this so-called Christ had suffered "a particularly cruel and shameful death, which as a rule was reserved for hardened criminals, incorrigible slaves, and rebels against the Roman state" (Hengel 1977: 83). The story behind Jesus' death discloses that he was rejected by the very people he came to save, was deserted by his own disciples, was strung up by the proper authorities, and apparently was powerless to save his own skin. Paul did not sweep the crucifixion under the carpet as an unfortunate episode remedied by the glories of the resurrection. He does not say that he preached the resurrected Christ, but the crucified Christ. Crucifixion and resurrection belong together as part of the gospel story (15:3–5), but the cross was repugnant to ancient sensibilities and assailed the world's self-centeredness and self-destructive ways.[2] It was not yet the "old rugged cross" sentimentalized in hymns, embalmed in stained-glass windows, perched on marble altars, or fashioned into gold charms. Cicero (*Pro Rabirio Perduellionis Reo* 5.16) decries the crucifixion of a Roman citizen, exclaiming, "The very word 'cross' should be far removed not only from the person of a Roman citizen but from his thoughts, his eyes and his ears." To proclaim a crucified Jew from some backwater of the empire as "a divine being sent on earth, God's son, Lord of all and the coming judge of the world, must have been thought by any educated man to be utter 'madness' and presumptiousness" (Hengel 1977: 83). Christianity was cradled in what looks like disastrous defeat, and the unspeakable stigma of the cross exposed the preacher of this message to woeful contempt. Paul, however, did not refer to Jesus' death with embarrassment or skip over the awkward facts. Quite the opposite, it was central to his preaching, because the resurrection disclosed Christ's suffering and death to be God's modus operandi in the world. Since he also argues that the followers of Jesus must share the sufferings of the crucified (Rom. 8:17; Phil. 3:10), the message of the cross is an antidote to human self-glorification. It is "hardly a message for the ambitious" (Stansbury 1990: 476). The gospel transforms the cross as a symbol of Roman terror and political domination into a symbol of God's love and

---

2. Furnish (1999: 39) points out that the cross would have clashed starkly with the appealing religious symbols with which they were familiar, "like a stalk of grain, a basket of fruit, or an erect phallus"—all symbols of fertility, life, or power.

power. It shows that the power of God's love is greater than human love of power.

How could Paul expect anyone to respond to such a message? Litfin (1994: 261) outlines the five steps of persuasion in Greco-Roman rhetoric: (1) attention, (2) comprehension, (3) yielding, (4) retention, and (5) action. Greco-Roman rhetoric stressed step three, getting the audience to yield. Paul, Litfin argues, stressed step two, comprehension. Litfin contends that, in contrast to "sophisticated speech" (1:17), this "word of the cross" was "straightforward and open" and aimed at getting listeners to comprehend the content rather than nod assent after the speaker has proven the case (see also Winter 1997d: 186–94). Paul left the third step, yielding, to the persuasion of the Spirit. Rhetorical strategies designed to manipulate an audience to withdraw its objections empty the cross of its power by putting in its place the orator's artistry and cleverness. I (Garland 1999: 472) write elsewhere, "Paul did not get people to believe by arguing that Christ crucified accords with the common principles of logic or that belief is in the long-term best interests of the hearers. As a herald, he simply announced what God has done in Christ. From his perspective, his job as proclaimer is to make sure that each hears and understands." Paul trusts the power of the cross to convict the audience rather than the power of his eloquence. The Spirit reveals the message's truth to the believer (2:4, 13). The audience is dethroned as the ultimate arbiter of what is true or persuasive (see Litfin 1994: 86), and the message becomes sovereign with the power to save or condemn, depending on the listener's response. Brown (1995: 75–77) makes the case that the word of the cross is a performative word that has the power to change one way of knowing for another: "Through the *logos*, the cross continues to break powerfully into the old world's 'dominant system of convictions' wherever it is proclaimed."

Paul equates the word about the cross with the power of God (just as God's word is tied to God's power in the OT; cf. Jer. 23:29; Wis. 18:14–16). In this case, "power" refers to the effectiveness of the cross to make God known to humankind, to accomplish salvation, to defeat evil, and to transform lives and values. P. Marshall (1987: 387) argues that the word "power" was commonly associated in Hellenistic literature with rhetoric and eloquence (cf. Aristotle, *Rhet.* 1.1.13; 1.2.1; 1.6.14), because eloquence won the powerful orator fame and glory. Pickett (1997: 65) notes,

> This constituted a social definition of power rooted in the values cultivated by those in society who had wealth, status and honour, that is, who were socially powerful; Paul's theological understanding of power, on the other hand, was rooted in the conviction that God's power has been manifested through the weakness of the crucified Christ inasmuch as he has

been made "wisdom," "righteousness," "sanctification," and "redemption" for the believer ([1 Cor.] 1:30).

Since the cross represents painful death and profound humiliation, it calls into question the conventional wisdom about power and the divine. The ancients took for granted that deities possessed power, and the degree of their power determined their ranking in the pyramid of gods. In the cross, that pyramid is turned upside down. The most powerful God appears to be the most powerless. The cross makes hash of all secular and religious attempts based on human wisdom to make sense of God and the world. Victory is won by giving up life, not taking it. Selfish domination of others is discredited. Shame is removed through divine identification with the shamed in a shameful death. God offers a new paradigm that makes the experience of shame the highest path to glory and honor (Stansbury 1990: 472). What makes the story of the cross even more offensive to humans is that it is not simply the foundation of human redemption but is also to become the way of life for believers. They, too, will endure the wounds from slander, mockery, and affliction as they live for others (4:8–10; 2 Cor. 4:7–12; 6:4–10; 11:24–29).

The "word of the cross" brings judgment in its wake and divides humanity into two groups that are not based on the traditional categories of race, gender, and status, but, instead, on their eschatological destiny (cf. 2 Cor. 2:15–16; 4:3; 2 Thess. 2:10). One's response to this message reveals whether a person is headed toward "immortal horrors or everlasting splendours," as C. S. Lewis phrased it. Not surprisingly, the cross looks like the height of folly to those who are self-absorbed. They reject it because it challenges the cherished value of personal gratification, whose currency is wealth, fame, and power. From a human perspective, God's ways look foolish and weak, and no more so than in the crucifixion, where God offers salvation to the world by means it loathes and spurns. The world, however, perishes with its worldly wisdom (cf. Acts 17; 18:15; 26:24).[3] The wisdom of God demonstrated through the ages and quintessentially in the cross of Christ in no way fits ancient, modern, or ultramodern categories of what wisdom is supposed to be. McGrath (*DPL* 194) observes, "It is not simply that God's ways are not our ways; it is that our ways of thinking preclude us from discerning those ways in the first place."

3. The noun μωρία (*mōria*, foolishness) appears in the NT only in 1 Corinthians (1:18, 21, 23; 2:14; 3:19). The adjective μωρός (*mōros*, foolish) occurs in Paul's letters only in 1:25, 27; 3:18; and 4:10, but it occurs 36 times in the LXX, where the fool is skewered for being oblivious to self-destructive behavior. Paul portrays God here as being a wise fool. What seems self-destructive is consciously intended to save others.

Those who respond to the word of the cross with faith regard it as evidence of God's power (Rom. 1:16; 2 Cor. 13:4; Col. 2:12), which requires a radical reversal of human desires and a transformation from conventional ways of living. The participles ἀπολλυμένοις (apollymenois) and σῳζομένοις (sōzomenois) are in the present tense, representing this activity as in process (Fanning 1990: 103). The use of the present tense can also convey the certainty of its future outcome (Schrage 1991: 172).[4] Paul does not question "their basic security 'in Christ'" (Stowers 1990: 261), but he does feel the need to remind the Corinthians that those who are being saved are still on the way and cannot afford to be self-congratulatory. The fullness of salvation awaits "the End" (15:24).

1:19 Paul puts an exclamation point on his argument by citing Isa. 29:14: God destroys the wisdom of the wise. He substitutes "I will nullify" (ἀθετήσω, athetēsō, thwart) in place of the LXX's "I will hide" (κρύψω, krypsō), either under the influence of Ps. 33:10, or because he reads another textual tradition (see R. Collins 1999: 94–96, on Paul's use of the LXX), or because he cites from memory. The ideas, however, are similar. God's actions make the worldly-wise look like blundering fools.

This is not an isolated proof text.[5] The "wisdom of the wise" refers in Isaiah to political shrewdness, and Paul applies it generically to every form of human wisdom that exalts its own cleverness, but the point is the same (Fee 1987: 70; Wilk 1998: 246; R. Collins 1999: 91; Thiselton 2000: 161). All human schemes that fail to take God into account will run aground (Isa. 30:1–2). Isaiah mocks the failed machinations of the worldly-wise Jerusalem politicians who sought to ensure Israel's safety. Their clever statecraft came to nought because their alliance with Egypt so alarmed Assyria that it sparked the invasion they sought to avoid. The prophet reminds them that God is the creator and humans are mere creations, and that God will turn things upside down (Isa. 29:16). God's rescue strategy opts for what appears to be weakness in this situation by allowing Jerusalem to become besieged and crushed before rescuing it. The defeat becomes a new beginning in which the people are "chastened, transformed" (Thiselton 2000: 161).

1:20 The derisive questions "Where is the wise? Where is the scribe? Where is the philosopher of this age?" also echo Isaiah (Isa. 19:12; 33:18). The

---

4. The participles could be middle or passive voice. The indirect middle would make sense in the context, with the subjects acting in what they perceive to be their own interests by either rejecting the message or believing it. It would be translated, "they on their part." Since God is the agent who saves, and salvation cannot be achieved but only received, it is best to read the second participle as a passive.

5. Wuellner (1970: 201) claims that this is the main theme of a previously composed homily—the divine judgment on human wisdom. Whether this theory is correct or not does not affect its meaning in the context (see additional note).

questions are rhetorical.[6] "Wise man" (σοφός, *sophos*), "scribe" (γραμματεύς, *grammateus*), and "debater" (συζητητής, *syzētētēs*) could correspond to the Hebrew חָכָם (*ḥākām*), סוֹפֵר (*sôpēr*), and דּוֹרֵשׁ (*dôrēš*) and an autobiographical reminiscence of Paul's days in the Pharisaic house of study (Hengel 1991: 42); or to the Greek philosopher, Jewish scribe, and a general expression comprehending both roles (Lightfoot 1895: 159; Fee 1987; 70–71); or to three types of tertiary scholars: the rationalistic scholar, the Jewish legal expert, and the rhetorician (Judge 1983: 11). Lautenschlager (1992) questions the usual pejorative translation of the extremely rare term συζητητής as "debater" and argues that it refers to a seeker after philosophical truth (cf. Greeven, *TDNT* 2:893). He translates it "philosopher."

What do these three categories of persons have in common? They are all perceived as professional experts. Paul skewers those who refract their search for truth through the lens of human wisdom and derive their status from their expertise. These who have made it their goal to search for "truth" greet with skepticism anything that does not match their own prejudgment of what truth is. God's truth, revealed in the cross, fails to meet the intellectual elite's criteria, so they reject it and settle for their own humbug. These questions parallel Jesus' thanksgiving to God for hiding "these things" from the wise and learned and revealing them to "babes" (Matt. 11:25). Something about the mentality of those who regard themselves as wise and learned makes them liable to self-deception and inimical to God's revelation. The humble, who count for nothing, on the other hand, are frequently more disposed to being helped and taught. Is this why Christ calls blessed those who are poor, meek, mourning, hungering, and persecuted while the world calls happy those who are rich, exalted, laughing, feasting, and domineering?[7]

The added description of the philosopher as "of this age" modifies the other two categories as well and adds an apocalyptic note that underscores the ephemeral quality of human wisdom. Paul assumes that this age is tottering on its last legs and passing away (7:31). It is "beyond mere reform or correction by 'wisdom' or prophetic word but calls for a new creation" (Thiselton 2000: 165). The wisdom of the cross, by contrast, is the wisdom of the world-to-come.

---

6. Ignatius (*Eph.* 18:1) appears to paraphrase this verse but lists "debater" second, omits "scribe," and adds "Where is the boasting of those called clever [συνετῶν, *synetōn*]?"

7. The "experts" tend to be impatient with and to disdain the common run of humanity. The rabbis tell the story of Rabbi Shammai beating off a doltish prospective proselyte with his builder's cubit (*b. Šabb.* 31a), and Epictetus worries that the philosopher would drive away the inquiring amateur with harsh derision (*Diatr.* 2.12.1–13).

By contriving a means of salvation that is impenetrable to human wisdom and does not meet its criteria of solid evidence and sound reasoning, God made human wisdom useless.[8] As Ruef (1977: 12) aptly states the case, "God makes wisdom foolish by making *foolishness* (the preaching of the cross) into wisdom." What humans think they know about God, who God is, and how God acts and interacts with the world is false because they try to make God reflect their canons of what is wise. Claiming wisdom, they embrace foolishness (cf. Rom. 1:22–23).

We should not jump to the conclusion that Paul denigrates the human faculty of reason or thinks that faith and reason are irreconcilable. Paul, instead, rejects certain traditions of reason, Jewish and Greek, with the focus on "wrong attitudes and behavior in relation to the pursuit of wisdom" (Stowers 1990: 258). The term "wisdom" is vague. He contrasts genuine wisdom from God (1:30; 2:6–3:4; 3:18) with worldly wisdom, but "wisdom as such, or its pursuit, is not condemned" (P. W. Gooch 1987b: 38). Paul scoffs at the wisdom because it is "worldly," not because it is wisdom.

Some take the "wisdom of the world" to refer to a well-defined system of wisdom, which beguiles the Corinthians and infects their Christology. Schmithals (1971: 137–44), Bultmann (*TDNT* 1:708–11), and Wilckens (*TDNT* 7:519–23; 1980) identify it with Gnosticism and a redeemer myth. But R. Wilson (1982: 105) insists, "There are no grounds whatever for seeing any such Sophia myth in the background to 1 Corinthians" (cf. R. Wilson 1972–73). Munck (1959a: 153) identifies it with a mixture of philosophy and sophistry; others tie it to the wisdom tradition reflected in the Hellenistic Judaism of Philo and supposedly introduced into the Corinthian church by Apollos (Pearson 1975: 46; R. Horsley 1977: 237; Davis 1984: 65–74), or with the OT wisdom tradition (Ellis 1978) plus apocalyptic traditions (Scroggs 1967–68). In my view, Paul's critique of wisdom is general and not provoked by specific doctrinal aberrations. Paul's usage empties the word of its normal associations (P. Lampe 1990: 122). "Wisdom" does not refer to a definable set of beliefs or to human reason in itself (see P. W. Gooch 1987b: 16–51) but to an "attitude" characterized by hubris (Conzelmann 1975: 42, 44).[9] The "wisdom of the world" is not a system of thought so much as "a style of life" (Baird 1990: 130), a general way of assessing life that

8. The noun σοφία (wisdom) occurs sixteen times in chapters 1–3 and only nine times elsewhere in Paul. The adjective σοφός (wise) occurs ten times in these chapters and only five times elsewhere in Paul. "Wisdom" is usually modified by a genitive: τοῦ κόσμου (*tou kosmou*, of the world; 1:20; 3:19; cf. 1:27, 28; 2:12; 4:13); τῶν ἀνθρώπων (*tōn anthrōpōn*, of men; 1:25; 2:5); τοῦ αἰῶνος τούτου (*tou aiōnos toutou*, of this age; 2:6; 3:18; cf. 1:20); and τῶν ἀρχόντων τοῦ αἰῶνος τούτου (*tōn archontōn tou aiōnos toutou*, of the rulers of this age; 2:6).

9. This definition of "wisdom" means that Paul is not responding to an accusation that he falls short in this area (contra Vos 1996: 91).

is egocentric. Savage (1996: 77) explains it as "a spirit of the age or an outlook of the time, a habit or fashion of thought which a person might assimilate subconsciously merely by living within a certain society or culture." This spirit is something "the Corinthians would have imbibed as naturally as the air they breathed" (Savage 1996: 77). The wisdom of God is God's saving deed through the cross, which upstages the wisdom of the world. One can know God only according to the cross, not through human wisdom.

Paul denigrates human wisdom that is tied to the human condition, circumscribed, as it is, by partial knowledge, susceptible to self-deceit, and twisted by the proclivity to become infatuated with status. This wisdom fails to comprehend, appreciate, or submit to God's wisdom because it is fatally flawed by egocentrism. Worldly reason is opposed to God because it is blinded by its own conceit and pride. P. W. Gooch (1987b: 41) identifies it as "human intellectual conceit, the puffed-up consciousness of the cocksure, which prevents knowledge of the self as well as God." Its values run counter to the cross because it breeds a competitive and self-serving outlook. It glamorizes self-exaltation and elitism, not self-emptying; comfort and ease, not suffering; personal honor and esteem, not humiliation. Such wisdom is "tantamount to exalting oneself 'in the face of God'" (1:29; Savage 1996: 76), and it lies behind the breakdown of community. This wisdom of the world seeks its own advantage no matter how much it hurts others; the wisdom of the cross serves others with no regard to personal cost (cf. 6:8).

The world has not come to know God through its wisdom, and Paul attributes that failing to God's wisdom. Robertson and Plummer (1914: 21) interpret it as "God's wise dealing with mankind in the history of religion, especially in permitting them to be ignorant (Acts 14:16; 17:30; Rom. 1:24; 11:32)."[10] God was wise enough not to let human wisdom be the key to knowing God.[11] In the cross, God puts *both* Jew and Greek, wise and foolish, trained and untrained, on the same level, canceling out all human enlightenment on the subject of salvation or redemption (cf. Barbour 1979: 63).[12] G. K. Chesterton writes (*Heretics* [1905]), "Carlyle said that men were mostly fools. Christianity, with its

1:21

---

10. See Thiselton (2000: 168–69) for five options defining "God's wisdom."

11. Wedderburn (1973: 134) argues that the phrase ἐν τῇ σοφίᾳ τοῦ θεοῦ (*en tē sophia tou theou*, in God's wisdom) in the first part of the verse is equivalent to εὐδόκησεν ὁ θεός (*eudokēsen ho theos*, it pleased God) in the second and that both point to God's sovereign wisdom "which so orders things that the wisdom of the world is reduced to ultimate futility and its salvation is allowed to lie in the apparent folly of the preaching of the cross and in man's faith, not his wisdom."

12. "Through wisdom" cannot be limited only to a way of life in accord with the Torah, as Goulder (1991) contends. He claims that it is aimed at those who appealed to the authority of Peter. "Wisdom" here embraces both Jewish and Greek wisdom.

surer and more reverent realism, says that they are all fools. This doctrine is sometimes called the doctrine of original sin. It may also be described as the doctrine of the equality of man."

"Knowing God" has nothing to do with abstract, intellectual knowledge about God but, in Scripture, is connected to God's acts of self-revelation (Schmitz, *NIDNTT* 2:395). Knowing God's acts in history and God's promises to act in the future leads one to honor God as the one true God (Rom. 1:21) and to enter into a proper relationship with God based on trust. The problem for the "wise" is that God's acts in history are so unexpected and so enigmatic that they fail to recognize them as God's acts. It may seem as if God deliberately blinds them so that they cannot see (Isa. 29:9–10). But only those who admit that they see through a glass darkly and are open to God's revelation can truly know God and receive God's offer of salvation.

It pleased God to save persons through the foolishness of preaching. In the biblical idiom, when God is said to be "well pleased" (εὐδόκησεν, *eudokēsen*), it refers to God's inscrutable decree, what is otherwise unaccountable, the sovereignty and mystery of God's choice.[13] The "foolishness of preaching" refers both to the content of the preaching ("the word of the cross," 1:18) and its form. Litfin (1994: 195) notes that the terms εὐαγγελίζω (*euangelizō*), κηρύσσω (*kēryssō*), καταγγέλλω (*katangellō*), and μαρτυρέω (*martyreō*) are "decidedly non-rhetorical" terms and play no role in rhetorical literature. Litfin maintains, "No self-respecting orator could have used such verbs to describe his own *modus operandi*." The reason, Litfin (1994: 196) explains, is that the role of the κῆρυξ (*kēryx*, herald) was not "to discover the persuasive probabilities inherent in his subject, or search the τόποι [*topoi*] for arguments that will carry weight with his listeners, much less to package the whole so that the message will be irresistible. . . . That sort of thing belongs to the persuader. The herald's task is not to create a persuasive message at all, but to convey effectively the already articulated message of another." The message is God's, and it is conveyed by means that look weak, foolish, and unimpressive to the world. Carrying a placard announcing the crucified Messiah as the glory of God (Gal. 3:1; 2 Cor. 4:6) in simple unadorned words makes the herald look foolish in the eyes of the world. But such "foolishness" reveals that God, not the messenger, is to be credited for saving those who believe that message. The phrase "those who believe" (τοὺς πιστεύοντας, *tous pisteuontas*) is again in the present tense, which implies continuing trust.

1:22   What the world finds impressive and irresistible are sensory spectacles or demonstrations of irrefutable proof. That is not what God offers in the cross. It confounds both Jews and Greeks. Stowers (1990: 260) com-

---

13. Cf. Mark 1:11; Matt. 17:5; Luke 12:32; Gal. 1:15; Col. 1:19; 2 Pet. 1:17; Eph. 1:5, 9.

ments, "The problem with Jews and Greeks is that they have closed minds blinded by their own traditions of rationality." Jews who demand signs expect God to verify religious claims with compelling proofs, as was done in Israel's past history.[14] The sign they wanted was something "apocalyptic in tone, triumphalistic in character, and the embodiment of one of the 'mighty deeds of deliverance' that God had worked on Israel's behalf in rescuing it from slavery" (Gibson 1990: 53). They get a "sign from above in the cross," but they defame it as blasphemy. The cross does not part the sea for the people to cross in safety and then drown the pursuing enemy. Instead, it splits the temple veil, and only those who see with faith can see the defeat of the enemy. Paul is not attacking Jews as such but a problem endemic to all those who expect God to provide to their satisfaction visible confirmation before they will risk faith. He attacks those who audaciously presume to demand proofs and "then maintain critical distance and draw whatever conclusions from the data that happened to suit their inclinations" (Geddert 1989: 68).

In arguing that the cultural background of Corinth in this era was Roman, Winter (2001: 23–24) considers the word Ἕλληνες (Hellēnes, Greeks) to be ambiguous and a synonym for ἔθνη (ethnē, Gentiles; cf. Isa. 9:12; 2 Macc. 4:10). R. Collins (1999: 106) argues that Paul uses "Greeks" instead of "Gentiles" because they had a "sense of some social superiority" (cf. Rom 1:14, where it appears in contrast to "barbarians"). It is more likely that Paul chooses this word because he regards the chief characteristic of Greek culture to be the search for wisdom. According to Aristotle (Eth. nic. 6.7.2 [1141a]), wisdom is the most perfect of the modes of knowledge. "Seeking" may allude to the groping search of the pagans for God (Acts 17:27; Wis. 13:6). But "wisdom here has more to do with social status and influence than it does with a particular theological position" (Pickett 1997: 54). Paul critiques the social values, honor and power, associated with "wisdom" and not its content (Pickett 1997: 55). To be sure, those riddled with pride will reach false conclusions about God, but Paul's main point is that the message of the cross puts all human pretensions to shame and upends the traditions and cultural values of both Jews and Greeks—and, we might add, of the Romans as well. God's work can be grasped only by faith (1:12; 2:5; 3:5).

Paul preaches something shocking: a crucified Christ.[15] The perfect **1:23** tense ἐσταυρωμένον (estaurōmenon) indicates that he remains the cru-

14. Cf. Matt. 12:38–39; 16:1; Mark 8:11–12; Luke 11:16; John 6:30–31; and Exod. 4:30–31; Judg. 6:36–40; 2 Kings 20:1–11; Josephus, *J.W.* 1.17.4 §§331–32; 6.5.2 §285, §295; *Ant.* 10.2.1 §§28–29; 20.8.6 §§167–70; *Sipre Deut.* 18:19; *b. Sanh.* 98a; 93b; *b. B. Meṣiʿa* 59b; *Exod. Rab.* 9.

15. No definite article appears before "Christ" in the Greek.

cified one. From a Jewish standpoint, a crucified Messiah was an oxymoron, which becomes a major stumbling block (σκάνδαλον, *skandalon*) because Scripture brands anyone hanged on a tree as accursed of God (Deut. 21:23). In Justin Martyr's *Dialogue with Trypho* 31–32, Rabbi Trypho remains unpersuaded by Justin's attempt to prove from Dan. 7 that Jesus was the Messiah and responds, "Sir, these and suchlike passages of scripture compel us to await One who is great and glorious, and takes the everlasting Kingdom from the Ancient of Days as Son of Man. But this your so-called Christ is without honour and glory, so that He has even fallen into the uttermost curse that is in the Law of God, for he was crucified." For those who think that God must be mighty and strong, not weak, the cross is "an affront to God's majesty" (Engberg-Pedersen 1987: 562). It is insulting "to link God with weakness" (P. Lampe 1990: 121).[16] The cross also dashes cherished hopes of temporal triumph and world supremacy.

Gentiles think it folly for God to let his Son die to save others.[17] Paul's preaching not only proclaims that this is what God did but also demands that the listener become joined to Christ in his humiliation and death. What honor or status can accrue from binding oneself to a crucified person? Humans, however, are the fools in thinking that they can "domesticate the sovereign God" and capture God in the images of creatures (Rom. 1:23, 25; P. Lampe 1990: 123–24).

1:24–25 The message trips up some; in others, it trips a recognition of the truth. Chrysostom perceptively comments that the gospel message presents exactly the opposite of what people want and expect, but "that very fact persuades them to accept it in the end." The "called" (οἱ κλητοί, *hoi klētoi*) is parallel to "those who believe" in 1:21 and "us who are being saved" in 1:18. Part of being called is being able to hear God's call and being open to it. "God's Christ" is parallel to the "crucified Christ."

The manifestation of God's power and wisdom is to be seen in God's crucified Christ, who dies to save the foolish and the weak (Schrage 1991: 189). Believers trust that the cross is something that God has done, and since it expresses God's will, it must be an expression of God's wisdom and power. That trust bridges the gap between Jew and Greek, who become one in Christ, and reveals that God's so-called foolishness and weakness are wiser and stronger than the so-called human wisdom that drives wedges between people. The result of God's wisdom does seem quite outlandish. Gentiles respond to the gospel of a cruci-

---

16. The jarring nature of this reality becomes clear in the shift in images from the lion of Judah to the slaughtered lamb in Rev. 5:5–6. A modern advertising slogan uses the expression "ram tough," but no one would ever think to tout a product as "lamb tough."

17. Note the contempt of Lucian (*De morte Peregrini* [*The Passing of Peregrinus*] 13), calling Christ that "crucified sophist" and his believers "poor wretches."

fied Jewish Messiah, preached by a battered and unimpressive Jewish apostle, creating a community in which Jews and Gentiles, slave and free, male and female stand together as equals before God.

Additional Note

1:18–25. The carefully composed material in 1:18–25, reflecting a number of chiastic correspondences and rhythmic constructions (see Bailey 1975), has led some to believe that it was composed prior to the letter and inserted at this point. Branick (1982: 258) regards its poetic density as surprising for the letter form but not for a homiletic form and claims that it was a "coherent unit before its insertion into the letter to the Corinthians," which had only a "general relevance" to the Corinthian situation (Branick 1982: 269). Others agree with this view and try to guess its original purpose. Cerfaux (1931) identifies the material as a scriptural *testimonium*; E. Peterson (1951), as a homily for the day of atonement; Wuellner (1970), as an exegetical homily; and Ellis (1978: 72, 155–56; 213–14), as a set piece of exposition of two independent midrashim. They differ on the extent of the homiletic material included. I judge this approach to be unsuccessful and of little help in understanding Paul's rhetorical strategy.

III. Factions and Dissension in the Church (1:10–4:21)
   B. The Foolish Wisdom of the Cross (1:18–25)
➤ C. God's Choice of the Foolish (1:26–31)
   D. Human Wisdom versus the Spirit and Power of God (2:1–5)

C. God's Choice of the Foolish (1:26–31)

The mention of "the called" in 1:24 provides a segue for Paul's second illustration of God's foolish wisdom: the makeup of the Corinthian community that responded to God's call. The unit is marked off by an inclusio with an allusion to Jer. 9:26 LXX in 1:26 and a citation of it in 1:31. Fee (1987: 79) captures the gist of Paul's argument: God's purpose "in choosing people like them is asserted to have the same design as the cross itself—to save them, but at the same time to 'shame' and 'nullify' the very values in which they are currently boasting." In the context of his denunciations of their divisions, he makes his case: Since all of them were nothing before their conversion, how can any of them think that they have become more special than others when in Christ?

Exegesis and Exposition

[26]Consider your calling, brothers and sisters. Not many of you are wise according to the flesh, not many of you are powerful, not many of you are well-born. [27]But God chose what the world regards as foolish in order to shame the wise, and God chose what the world regards as weak in order to shame the strong. [28]And God chose what the world regards as insignificant and what is despised, the things that are nothing, in order that he might nullify the things that are. [29]So that no flesh might boast before God. [30]From him [and by him] you are in Christ Jesus, who became for us wisdom from God, and righteousness, and sanctification, and redemption, [31]in order that, just as it stands written, "Let the one who boasts boast in the Lord."

1:26   Paul offers empirical evidence of the foolishness of God from his audience's own experience: the founding of the Corinthian church (cf. Gal. 3:1–4). The foolishness and weakness manifested in the cross and its preaching carry over to the kinds of persons who have responded to the preaching. Paul bids them to consider their calling.[1] That calling (cf. 1:1, 2, 9, 24) refers to the circumstances surrounding their coming to faith (Barrett 1968: 57; Fee 1987: 79; Thiselton 2000: 180), not simply their socioeconomic status (contra Witherington 1995: 113). It is shorthand for

---

1. The γάρ introduces a new topic (Thiselton 2000: 179), and the verb βλέπω (*blepō*) followed by the accusative means "consider," "contemplate" (cf. 10:18; 2 Cor. 10:7; Phil. 3:2; Col. 4:17; Mark 4:24).

God's act of calling them purely on the basis of grace (2 Tim. 1:9; cf. Findlay 1910: 771), without regard to their moral worthiness or their status as gauged by human standards. In choosing them, God overlooked their lack of spiritual merit and flouted all worldly measures of human worth (cf. Deut. 7:7). If they were to take stock of themselves and their fellow recruits, they would readily recognize that most, if not all, do not fall into the category of "the cream of society." Becoming Christians also has done nothing to enhance their social estate, which is why the missing copula to be inserted in the litotes should be "are," not "were": "not many of you are wise according to the flesh" (Lindemann 2000: 49).[2] By addressing them as brothers and sisters (ἀδελφοί, adelphoi), Paul allays any impression that he is holding their heritage in contempt. What he says of them applies also to himself as their brother.

The σοφοί (sophoi) are the learned, clever, and experienced. The phrase κατὰ σάρκα (kata sarka, according to the flesh) here means "according to unspiritual, worldly standards." It refers to evaluations made by unregenerate humans employing criteria that are revealed to be bogus in light of God's measures. These worldly norms only factor into the equation those things that can be shown off and admired. They foster boasting and self-reliance, which lead one to spurn God's truth because it challenges all human illusions.

The δυνατοί (dynatoi) are the influential whose wealth gives them the social and political levers of power (Sänger 1985; cf. Acts 25:5; Rev. 6:15). The εὐγενεῖς (eugeneis) are the well-born who have a proud pedigree and belong to the wealthy ruling class, "the blue bloods" (cf. Luke 19:12; Acts 17:11).[3] Philo (Cont. Life 9 §69) uses "good birth," "high character," and "trained in philosophy" as synonymous qualities. Dio Chrysostom's (Or. 15.29–32) attempts to refute the assumption that "it is impossible for anyone to be 'noble' without being 'well-born'" reveal that it was a common bias. Being "well-born"and "noble," he claims, originally applied to persons with respect to "virtue or excellence," not to their parentage (cf. Aristotle, Eth. nic. 4.3.16), but later what he calls the "common run of ignorant men" used the term to refer to "the descendants of families of ancient wealth." Unless something quite exceptional happened to an individual, persons living in this era did not rise up the social ladder but remained within the confines of the social class in which they were born. Prestige belonged only to those of noble parentage. All the terms Paul

2. Wuellner (1973) contends that the ὅτι (hoti) introduces a question: "Were not many of you wise. . . ?" expecting the answer yes (so also O'Day 1990: 263–65, as an example of Pauline irony). R. Collins (1999: 110) counters that Paul does not use an interrogative ὅτι elsewhere, which makes this reading unlikely.

3. In Homer's Iliad 6.123–231, Glaucus and Diomedes first exchange genealogies when they meet. Josephus emphasizes that biblical heroes were "well-born" even where it is not found in the Bible (Feldman 1982: 60).

uses here overlap and refer to the privileged elite as opposed to the plebeians. As Murphy-O'Connor (1998: 10) frames it, "'They' run the economy. 'They' set the standards. 'They' determine who succeeds and who fails." When Paul proclaimed the word of the cross, it did not attract the wise and powerful. They are not excluded (Conzelmann 1975: 50) but tend to exclude themselves by rejecting the wisdom of the cross, which does not honor their achievements but pours contempt on their pride.[4]

O'Day (1990) shows how Paul not only cites but interweaves Jer. 9:22–23 (cf. 1 Sam. 2:10 LXX) into the fabric of his argument in 1:26–31. Jeremiah warns with three parallel statements:

Do not let the wise [σοφός] boast in their wisdom.

Do not let the mighty [ἰσχυρός, *ischyros*] boast in their might.

Do not let the wealthy [πλούσιος, *plousios*] boast in their wealth.

In 1 Sam. 2:10 LXX, a similar warning appears with slightly different vocabulary: φρόνιμος (*phronimos*, wise, prudent), δυνατός (*dynatos*, powerful), and πλούσιος. These things distort an individual's self-identity and a society's character because they deter one from finding identity and security only in "God's steadfast love, justice and righteousness" (O'Day 1990: 261–62). For Christians, the categories "clever," "influential," and "high status" are replaced by "righteousness," "sanctification," and "redemption" in Jesus Christ (1 Cor. 1:30; Thiselton 2000: 178).

MacMullen (1974: 125) identifies the love of status and honor as the motivating force of Greco-Roman culture. It resulted in the well-to-do donating benefactions—large banquets, a variety of public spectacles, temples, and great monuments—to enhance their public reputation. Paul's attention to questions of social identity and status reveal his concern that the values of the culture in which the Corinthians live have inched their way into the church and are creating the divisions. They have become puffed up over against one another (4:6–7). Beacham (1999: 34) observes, "Rome was a highly stratified and therefore immensely self-conscious society characterized by complex systems for defining, signifying, and acknowledging status."[5] Money (*Pecunia*) and

4. In Apuleius's novel (*Metam.* 11.15), Lucius is told by the priest during his initiation into the sacred rites of Isis, "Neither did thy noble lineage, thy dignity, nor neither thy excellent doctrine anything avail thee." This negative evaluation of such things would have struck a chord with many.

5. According to Beacham (1999: 34–35), status and power were in part a function of *dignitas*, "an elusive but pervasive concept whose practical substance . . . consisted of the expectation that an individual's honor and authority enables him to protect and reward his clients, friends, and dependents, from whom in turn he demanded deference, tangible forms of respect for his status, and the assurance that his sense of 'face' would not be slighted, or if it were, that any affront would attract swift and forceful retribution."

Status (*Philotimia*) were worshiped as goddesses (Horace, *Ep.* 1.6.37; Juvenal, *Sat.* 1.113). When Corinth was reestablished as a Roman colony, it was settled by persons of lower social status, freedmen and slaves, but thoroughly imbued with Roman values, with the watchword "Whatever one's rank, it must be maintained" (MacMullen 1974: 106). The church was composed of a cross-section of urban society, excluding the extreme top and bottom (see additional note). The upwardly mobile members were people of "high status inconsistency," that is, "Their achieved status is higher than their attributed status" (Meeks 1983: 73). This inconsistency may have exacerbated the yearning to bask in the glory of others, even if it was only in their reflected glory (see Pogoloff 1992: 188). Murphy-O'Connor (1996: 270) observes, "The sense of insecurity of the successful freedman became a favourite topic in literature." He contends that this insecurity was rooted in "the bitter awareness that one was not recognized for what one had achieved." This was a dyadic society that sought self-definition from others. The pivotal values were honor and shame. People measured their lives by what a delimited group of others thought about them. If someone was an ex-slave, these others could still see that person only as an ex-slave. To compensate, many aspired to increase their social standing in a never-ending pursuit of social honor. Boastful Corinthian Christians are no different from their pagan fellow citizens obsessed with exalting themselves and trying to leapfrog over others to attain honor and prominence. Arrogance and contempt for others were at home in Corinthian society and seem to have a secure place in the church as well.

Murphy-O'Connor (1996: 271) observes, however, that many were attracted to the Christian faith because it "introduced them into a society committed to looking at them primarily as people, all equally valuable and valued. It gave them a space in which they could flourish in freedom." The cross "embodied the paradox they lived" and "made sense of the ambiguity of their lives." Paul's command that they consider their calling suggests that some Corinthian believers may have forgotten their humble estate. Given the values of their culture, they may not have appreciated Paul for reminding them of it.

God's choice (ἐκλέγεσθαι, *eklegesthai*) is reiterated three times for emphasis, and the objects God has chosen are the antithesis of those persons described in 1:26. Godet (1886: 112; cf. Edwards 1885: 37; Thiselton 2000: 184) claims that this choice refers to God's "energetic action" that takes "from the midst of the world . . . those individuals whom no one judged worthy of attention and made them the bearers of His kingdom." Calvin (1960: 44) comments that "in putting the strong and wise and great to shame, God does not exalt the weak and uneducated and worthless, but brings all of them down to one common level." Jesus' parables about wedding guests (Matt. 22:1–14) and banquet guests

1:27–28

(Luke 14:15–24) may illustrate this divine principle in action. Τὰ μωρὰ τοῦ κόσμου (*ta mōra tou kosmou*) literally means "the foolish things of the world." The threefold τοῦ κόσμου means "in the world's estimation" (Barrett 1968: 58). Barrett (1968: 58; cf. Schrage 1991: 211) rightly cautions that translating it as a partitive genitive "implies a world that is partly foolish and partly wise, and it is doubtful whether Paul intended to be as complimentary as this." The context makes clear that "the foolish things" are foolish only in the wrongheaded estimation of those who fail to recognize that they are the real fools (cf. Bar. 3:24–32). I translate the phrase as "what the world regards as foolish."

Paul may use the neuter, "the foolish things," "the weak things," "the insignificant things," and "the despised things," to refer to a class "so little valued that they do not count as individuals" (Godet 1886: 112; cf. Edwards 1885: 37). It would be similar to referring to persons as "the help," "the hired hands," "the gate," or "the body count." Barrett (1968: 58; cf. Lietzmann 1949: 10), however, suggests that Paul generalizes "to spare the Corinthians too blunt a description of themselves, and because he knows that in the next verse he is going to speak of 'things that do not exist.'" Whatever the reason for the neuter, Paul relates the seeming weakness and powerless of the cross to their own weakness and powerlessness and beckons them to see that divine power can work in their social weakness (Engberg-Pedersen 1987: 562).

God did chose the weak not to make them strong, to help them move into the ranks of the upper crust, or to begin a new class struggle but to subvert, invert, and convert human values. God chose the foolish because the wise thought the cross was sheer folly as a means for saving the world, the weak because the strong thought they were powerful enough without God, and the low and despised because the high and mighty did not care to debase themselves by attaching themselves to a crucified God. The foolish, weak, and despised, however, respond more readily to the shame of the cross because they themselves are already shamed. Unlike the powerful, those who are deemed foolish and weak are amenable to receiving the paradox of divine weakness that conveys strength. They respond more readily to the shame of the cross because they themselves belong to the shamed.

The image of shaming or dishonoring would have been vivid in the Corinthian context. Witherington (1995: 8) correctly notes that the worst thing that could happen was "for one's reputation to be publicly tarnished." Shaming was a familiar "public phenomenon" (Thiselton 2000: 186) in spite of Aristotle's (*Rhet.* 2.2.3–6) condemnation of *hybris* as gratuitously doing or saying things to shame another solely for the pleasure of it, because one has the power to do it, or to make oneself feel superior.[6] But Paul does not have in mind a moral-psychological

---

6. See the discussion of hubristic behavior in P. Marshall (1987: 182–94).

shaming as in 2 Cor. 9:4 (Lindemann 2000: 50–51). Instead, the verb "to shame" should be understood in its OT matrix to refer to "coming under God's judgment." God vindicates the faithful and brings the ungodly to shameful ruination (cf. Ps. 6:10; 31:17; 35:4, 26–27; 40:15; 83:16–18; Isa. 41:11; Jer. 2:26). It has "eschatological" connotations: "In choosing the Corinthians God has already begun the final vindication over his enemies" (Fee 1987: 83; cf. Schrage 1990: 211).

The ἀγενῆ (*agenē*, those of mean parentage) are the opposite of the εὐγενεῖς (*eugeneis*, the well-born, 1:26), but the former word is used more frequently to refer to the insignificant or base. It was assumed that the low-born were inherently boorish and morally weak because of their lowly origin. They are defined further as the "despised," "disdained" (τὰ ἐξουθενημένα, *ta exouthenēmena*, 6:4; 16:11). The verb appears in Acts 4:11 to refer to Christ as the stone disdained by the builders, which has now become the cornerstone (Ps. 118:22). They are also identified as τὰ μὴ ὄντα (*ta mē onta*), "the nothings," as opposed to τὰ ὄντα, "the somethings." Godet (1886: 112) and Edwards (1885: 38, citing Winer 1877: 608) distinguish the τὰ μὴ ὄντα, "things that are no better than if they were not," from τὰ οὐκ ὄντα, "things that actually do not exist" (but cf. Lightfoot 1895: 166). It is not that they do not exist, but that they are regarded as if they do not exist.[7] They are without standing in a social hierarchy that may be characterized as "binary": a person was either a one or a zero. The "nothings" were treated as zeroes. By choosing "the things that are nothing," however, God upends the hierarchy and reduces the "somethings" to nothing.[8] The verb καταργεῖν (*katargein*) means "to nullify," "to render inoperative" (2 Cor. 3:7; 13), but it also has an eschatological nuance (Fee 1987: 83; cf. 1 Cor. 2:6; 6:13; 13:8, 10; 15:24, 26) and refers to final destruction.

Throughout the biblical narrative God consistently chooses the most unlikely figures, and Paul maintains that God has continued this pattern in choosing the believers in Corinth. Hays (1997: 32) thinks that Paul's statements parallel Hannah's prayer (1 Sam. 2:1–10) and Mary's song of praise (Luke 1:46–55), which acclaim God, who "raises up the poor from the dust" and "has brought down the powerful from their thrones and lifted up the lowly." Conzelmann (1975: 51) draws a different conclusion: "Paul does not teach that 'the' lowly will be exalted, but that faith becomes the receiver of salvation regardless of worldly standing. He teaches not resentment, but freedom." God's choices disclose

7. The phrase differs from its use in Rom. 4:17–19. There Paul links God's calling "things into existence that do not exist" to God's power to raise the dead and to bring forth a child from Sarah's dead womb (Rom. 4:17, 19).

8. Similar language appears in 2 Bar. 70:3–5, but Baruch regards it as a sign of the end-time confusion that will befall humankind. Paul regards it as part of God's paradoxical means of overthrowing human pride (Schrage 1991: 205).

that the church's creation and success can be attributed only to God's power. P. Lampe (1990: 127) writes, "When the cross is proclaimed and through this act a community is founded, human wisdom and strength do not contribute anything to it. God rejects them as legitimate tools." When this principle is applied to the Corinthian situation, Paul's point is that no apostle, let alone any house-church leader, can receive credit for the creation of the group of redeemed saints in Corinth. All stand empty before God.

1:29   God's ultimate goal in choosing the foolish, weak, and despised was not simply to shame the wise and strong and to nullify the somethings, but to preclude all human boasting. "Flesh" (σάρξ, sarx) is a Hebraism for human beings, and the "all" (πᾶσα, pasa) embraces Jew and Greek. Using the concrete term "flesh" serves notice more forcefully that human beings, as frail, mortal creatures, have no business boasting about themselves in the presence of the immortal God.

    "Boasting" is not a common word in Greek literature, but the practice of praising oneself was quite familiar. The verb καυχάομαι (kauchaomai) and the nouns καύχημα (kauchēma) and καύχησις (kauchēsis) appear predominantly in Paul's letters in the NT, and the majority of those occurrences are in the Corinthian correspondence.[9] "Boasting" can be good or bad, depending on the object of the boast (cf. 9:15–16) or the attitude behind the boasting. It is used in a negative sense of those who boast of their special relationship to God (Rom. 2:17); in the law (Rom. 2:23); in works that they assume earn salvation (Rom. 3:27; 4:2); in human birth or accomplishments according to human standards, which Paul characterizes as "foolishness" (1 Cor. 1:29; 4:7; 13:3; 2 Cor. 10:15–16; 11:12, 16–18; 12:1; Gal. 6:13; Eph. 2:9); in outward appearances (2 Cor. 5:12); and in human leaders (1 Cor. 3:21). It is used in a positive sense of Christians who boast in their future hope (Rom. 5:2); in God, who has saved them (Rom. 5:11; 1 Cor. 1:31; 2 Cor. 10:17); in Christ (Phil. 3:3); in the cross of Christ (Gal. 6:14); in the working of God in oneself (Gal. 6:4; Rom. 15:17) or in fellow Christians, which is closely related to joy (1 Cor. 15:31; 2 Cor. 1:12; 5:12; 7:4, 14; 8:24; 9:2; Phil. 1:26; 1 Thess. 2:19); in sufferings (Rom. 5:3) and weakness (2 Cor. 11:30; 12:5–6, 9); in the salvation of other Christians on the day of the Lord Jesus (2 Cor. 1:14; 9:3; Phil. 2:16); and in authority given by God (2 Cor. 10:8, 13).[10] In the present context, God eliminates

---

9. Thirty-five of thirty-seven occurrences of καυχάομαι occur in Paul's letters and twenty-six of them are in the Corinthian correspondence. Ten of eleven occurrences of καύχημα appear in Paul and six of them are in the Corinthian correspondence. Ten of eleven occurrences of καύχησις appear in Paul and seven of them are in the Corinthian correspondence.

10. On Paul's boasting about preaching for free, see the discussion on 1 Cor. 9:15–16 and Garland (1999: 483–84) on 2 Cor. 11:10.

all human boasting by "conferring his salvation on those who are too foolish, weak, base, and contemptible, and hence too humble, to take any credit for their new exalted position in Christ" (Savage 1996: 58). They have nothing worth boasting about that they did not receive freely from God. Rather than praising themselves, they must humbly await praise from God (4:5). This lesson was difficult to drive home to a congregation enmeshed in a culture in which people were accustomed to tooting their own horns to gain and maintain status.

The phrase ἐξ αὐτοῦ (*ex autou,* of him) expresses both the source and **1:30–31** cause of their being in Christ. Their existence in Christ Jesus is from God (NRSV; cf. Rom. 11:36; 1 Cor. 8:6), and it is also because of him (NIV) that they have this being.[11] This phrase explains what precedes: "If things that were not have now become something, it is due to God alone" (Godet 1886: 115). The emphasis falls on God's gracious act of "election" (Conzelmann 1975: 51), that is, God's pleasure to save them (1:21), call them (1:24, 26), and choose them (1:27–28). The theological meaning of this abbreviated phrase is amplified in Eph. 2:8–9: "For by grace you have been saved through faith, and this not from you [οὐκ ἐξ ὑμῶν, *ouk ex hymōn,* that is, not of your own doing]; [it is] the gift of God [θεοῦ τὸ δῶρον, *theou to dōron*]; not out of works [οὐκ ἐξ ἔργων, *ouk ex ergōn*], lest anyone should boast." All that believers have comes from God, which explains why they can boast only in what God has done for them in Christ and not in themselves. Their identity and security are created by belonging to Christ and being marked by the sign of the cross (Furnish 1999: 43).

Christ became the "wisdom from God *for* us" (dative of advantage).[12] God does not overturn the world's wisdom and pride just for the fun of it but to bring salvation. The crucified Christ became the manifestation of God's wisdom, which here refers to God's long-established plan for the world's salvation (cf. 1:21; 2:7; Eph. 3:10).

The triad of δικαιοσύνη τε καὶ ἁγιασμὸς καὶ ἀπολύτρωσις (*dikaiosynē te kai hagiasmos kai apolytrōsis*)—righteousness, holiness, redemption—is a unit (BDF §444) separate from wisdom (Godet 1886: 117; Edwards 1885: 40). Paul's syntax indicates that the four terms are not treated as coordinate (contra NIV, NKJV). They are the fruit of God's wisdom in Christ. It is not that Christ *is* these things but that believers *have* these things in Christ (Witherington 1995: 117). What did not exist before—righteousness, holiness, and redemption—now exists in Christ (2 Cor. 5:17). These three are not bestowed on believers so that these things now belong to them; they share in these things by virtue of belonging to the crucified Christ (Schrage 1991: 215).

11. Ἐκ is used to express cause in John 6:66.
12. Note that Paul switches from the second person plural to the first person plural.

N. Watson (1983: 387–88) explains why the list of the four things shared by believers (wisdom, righteousness, sanctification, redemption) begins with wisdom rather than righteousness. Unlike the Judaizers, who rely on their works, the Corinthians are tempted to rely on their own wisdom. As in Romans, Paul begins his letter by demolishing false self-reliance. Humans cannot boast before God of their wisdom any more than of their works (Rom. 3:19). N. Watson continues, "In the same way as the cross is the condemnation of the righteousness of man, so it is the condemnation of the wisdom of the world. As it is through the renunciation of righteousness that man attains righteousness, so it is through the surrender of his own wisdom that he receives wisdom. Whoever wishes to be wise in this world must become a fool and thus find wisdom."

The metaphors have been assimilated from the OT but have undergone transformation when refracted through the lens of Paul's Christian faith. He does not discuss what they mean, because he must assume that the Corinthians are already familiar with the concepts. "Righteousness" refers to the state of having been acquitted and sharing Christ's righteous character. When they are arraigned in God's court, God will not judge them on the basis of what they are but as those who are guiltless in Christ Jesus. "Sanctification" refers to the state of holiness, which they have only in Christ Jesus and which allows them into the presence of God. "Redemption" refers to the state of being delivered from sin and its penalty (Rom. 3:24–25; Eph. 1:7, 14; 4:30; Col. 1:14).

To conclude this unit, Paul cites a major theme from the OT that he adapts as a general principle to address the Corinthian problem. The citation "Let the one who boasts boast in the Lord" is loosely recited from Jer. 9:23–24 (cf. 1 Sam. 2:10 LXX; 2 Cor. 10:17). The foolish and ungodly glory in themselves (cf. Ps. 52:1; 49:5–6; 94:3; Judg. 7:2). The wise exult in God (1 Sam. 2:2–3; Ps. 5:11; 34:3; 44:8; Sir. 17:6–8). The Corinthians can boast only in what God has accomplished among them. All other boasting based on comparing themselves favorably to others uses sham, mortal criteria.

Additional Note

1:26. Paul does not intend to provide a social profile of the church, but saying that "not many" are "wise, powerful, or well-born," instead of "no one," implies that some were (cf. Origen, *Cels.* 3.48; Judge 1960: 59; Theissen 1982: 70–72; Gill 1993; Horrell 1996: 95–98; De Vos 1999: 197–203). The Christians in Corinth belonged to a wide range of social strata, but none belonged to the highest orders of Roman society. Just because one was economically prosperous did not mean that one belonged to the social elite.

D. Human Wisdom versus the Spirit and Power of God (2:1–5)

Paul further illustrates God's foolish wisdom by harking back to his foundational preaching of a crucified Christ in Corinth. He came in weakness and in much fear and trembling (2:3). He amplifies his disavowal of wise speech broached in 1:17 to argue, "The messenger is like the message" (Edwards 1895: 43). Preaching is not competitive rhetoric (Thiselton 2000: 107). God's spiritual power overrides and invalidates strategies of manipulative power and self-assertion where the desire to win applause trumps the obligation to speak the truth. Pascuzzi (1997: 32 n. 51) suggests that Paul may have distanced himself "from the seductive rhetoric that only obfuscates, and is moreover inadequate to express, the stark reality of the cross which is God's power forcing upon Christians a whole new order to which they must submit." Friedrich (*TDNT* 3:716) comments, "Christian preaching does not persuade the hearers by beautiful or clever words—otherwise it would only be a matter of words." Attempts to accredit the gospel in a worldly show of wisdom actually discredit the gospel. Paul did not purvey the empty, ephemeral wisdom of this world but disclosed the eternal truth of God's wisdom encapsulated in the cross, and the Corinthians were persuaded because of God's Spirit and power.

Paul's argument can be outlined as follows (Fee 1994: 90):

1. The content of his preaching (2:1–2)
2. The form of his preaching (2:3–4)
3. The reason for both (2:5)

Exegesis and Exposition

[1]And when I came to you, brothers and sisters, I did not come proclaiming to you the ⌜mystery⌝ of God after the manner of one using dignifying speech and wisdom. [2]For I resolved to know nothing among you except Jesus Christ and him crucified. [3]And I was among you in weakness and in much fear and trembling. [4]My speech and my preaching were not with the ⌜persuasive art of wisdom⌝ but with the demonstration of the Spirit and power, [5]in order that your faith might not be based on human wisdom but on the power of God.

2:1–2   Paul employs the first person singular in 1:10–17, switches to the first person plural in 1:18–25, then to the second person plural in 1:26–31, and then back to the first person singular in 2:1–5. Returning to the first person singular in this unit signals to the reader that he is "picking up, as it were, where he left off in 1:17" (Pogoloff 1992: 130). "And when I came . . . proclaiming" recalls his self-identification as an apostle sent by Christ "to preach the gospel" (1:17). He now reminds the Corinthians that his deportment among them matched the message he preached and was centered entirely on Christ and not himself.

The prepositional phrase οὐ καθ᾽ ὑπεροχὴν λόγου ἢ σοφίας (*ou kath' hyperochēn logou ē sophias*) could be connected to his coming or to his proclaiming, but both are integrally connected in Paul's mind. What applies to one applies also to the other. The noun ὑπεροχή means "projection" or "prominence" but is used metaphorically to mean "abundance," "superiority," "preeminence" (cf. 1 Tim. 2:2; BDAG 1034). The phrase ὑπεροχὴ λόγου, "superiority of word," refers not only to elaborate rhetoric (Delling, *TDNT* 8:524; Lightfoot 1895: 170; Wilckens, *TDNT* 7:523) but also to speech that pretends to some superior social status (Findlay 1910: 775; Pogoloff 1992: 131–32; Savage 1996: 72). Paul has in view language that is conducive to self-display. He is saying that he did not put on airs or speak in high-flown language to foist himself off on them as one above the common herd. That posture only turns preaching into an exercise of dominance and triumph. Instead, his demeanor was humble and his speech plain. Lim (1987: 149) contends that Paul was against "that method of preaching which employs literary figures, not as a means to convey better the message of the Gospel, but as ornamentation intended to please and amuse the congregation."[1] If that is correct, then Paul contends that he did not use preaching as a vehicle to exhibit his virtuosity, to win admiration from distinguished persons, or to communicate "I am superior to you."[2] He does not reject rhetoric or wisdom as such, but pompous speech—"the speech of those who are puffed up" (4:19). Savage (1996: 73) connects it to "verbal bullying." Engberg-Pedersen (1987: 563) comments, "Preaching the gospel in ways that exhibit human wisdom would be an expression of self-assertion and would thus go directly against the content of the gospel." The gospel always points beyond humans to God and Christ and becomes garbled whenever humans exploit it instead to headline themselves as its stars. Paul's purpose was simply to give witness to the

---

1. In 1 Cor. 2:1–5, Paul does not reject outright the persuasive methods and arguments of classical oratory. His audience probably was not composed of intellectuals—they were not university professors—and would not have cared about Paul's rejection of classical speech (Savage 1996: 71–72).

2. Thiselton (2000: 207) thinks it may imply "what is above people's heads" and renders it "high-sounding."

gospel message, and witnesses need only give their account in plain, simple language (Lightfoot 1895: 170–71). Everything was to focus on the one preached rather than on the preacher (Schrage 1991: 225). This unaffected manner of speech explains why his preaching did not arouse the curiosity and admiration of the highbrows enthralled by intellectual genius.

The UBS[4] and NA[27] texts opt to read that Paul proclaimed "the mystery of God" rather than "the testimony about God" (or, "borne by God"), and I think that this choice is correct. In the ancient world, "mystery" pertained to something secret, such as arcane religious rites that could not be divulged, or to mystical experiences that allowed one to ascend beyond everyday life to become a temporary, but select, participant in otherworldly bliss (cf. Euripides, *Bacchae* [*Bacchanals*] 64–169). By contrast, Paul uses "mystery" to refer to God's saving purposes in and through Christ. Its content is succinctly described in 2:2 as "Jesus Christ crucified" (Schrage 1991: 227). Those divine purposes are too profound for human ingenuity, no matter how clever, to discover or unravel on its own and can be imparted only by divine revelation. The mystery is truth revealed by God, not truth discovered by human investigation and argument. Humans do not find this truth; it finds them. The mystery goes against all human reason because it is above all human reason, and human cleverness only makes the mystery seem to recede into deeper obscurity. It is particularly impenetrable to those who pride themselves on their wisdom and status because it nullifies that wisdom and status. It reveals that the worldly appearance of status and power is only an illusion.

The mystery, once hidden from eternity past (2:7), has now been revealed in the time of fulfillment, when human experience and history have converged so that it can be comprehended (Matt. 13:11, 17; Rom. 16:25–26). Although Paul's use of the term "mystery" more closely accords with his Jewish heritage, it differs from it in three significant ways. First, in Jewish tradition, the mystery is revealed to "the wise" (cf. Dan. 2:18–23; 4 Ezra [2 Esdr.] 14:26; *Eccles. Rab.* 1.7). By contrast, Paul says that it has been revealed to those whom the world appraises as unwise. The mystery is not reserved for an elite but is open to anyone who chooses to submit to it. Second, the word "mystery" was used in Jewish apocalyptic tradition for God's secret plans for the last days (Rowland 1982: 160–76).[3] Paul does not apply the term to the hidden timing of end-time events but to what God has already done in the person of Christ (Col. 2:3). The heart of the mystery is identified in Christ's death on the cross, which has inaugurated the end time (10:11). Third, Paul

3. Cf., for example, Dan. 2:18, 19, 27, 28, 29, 30, 47; 4:9; 1QpHab 7:4–14; 4 Ezra (2 Esdr.) 14:5; 1 Enoch 104:11–13; 2 Bar. 81:4.

believes that humans cannot know God or God's purposes apart from Christ. Only in Christ do humans have access to unlimited stores of truth, "the deep things of God" (2:10), that otherwise are unattainable to humans. These deep things, which lay bare God's heart, are not hidden from view but can be perceived only though faith in Christ. This is why the gospel is "veiled to those who are perishing" (2 Cor. 4:3–4).

Paul's reminiscence that he resolved to know nothing among them except Jesus Christ, and him crucified (see additional note), does not promote anti-intellectualism but explains his modus operandi. His style was not attributable to some rhetorical ineptitude on his part but to a conscious decision. He intended to proclaim the gospel in ways that were consonant with its message of Jesus Christ crucified and in ways that caused hearers to concentrate on that message and not on the messenger. He deliberately chose to set aside any methods that would showcase his own knowledge and wisdom.[4] Paul is not anti-intellectual, but he does oppose intellectual vanity. He did not come to them as a know-it-all or compose speeches fishing for admiration. On the contrary, he was content to be identified as a know-nothing who preached foolishness: Jesus Christ crucified. But announcing the gospel was his sole focus, and the cross molded his entire message and his whole approach. It was not a new development arising from some previous failure (cf. Acts 17:22–31) but his standard procedure everywhere (cf. 1 Thess. 2:1–10; Gal. 3:1). Jesus Christ can only be preached as the crucified one, and no one can preach Christ crucified to win personal renown. Paul's tacit answer to Job's question "Where shall wisdom be found?" (Job 28:12) is "In the proclamation of Christ crucified" (C. Black 1996: 194).

2:3–5 In the Corinthian correspondence, Paul often reminds the church that God works through weakness. The subject of the preaching, Jesus Christ crucified, was regarded as weak, those who responded to the preaching were regarded as weak (1:27), and the preacher of the gospel came off as weak. How was Paul weak? Fee (1987: 93 n. 21) thinks that Paul refers to some physical illness (cf. Gal. 4:13–14). The adjective ἀσθενεῖς (astheneis) appears in 11:30 to refer to those who have become sick, but the noun ἀσθένεια (astheneia) is not used in the Corinthian correspondence for sickness but for weakness.[5] It is more likely that he has in view something more general: "whatever can detract from the standing and dignity of someone in the estimation of other people" (Calvin 1960: 50). His weakness, then, may include any of the following

4. Hengel (2000: 141–57) makes the case that the earliest missionary proclamation, including Paul's, narrated the story of Jesus' activity and death.

5. Cf. 1 Cor. 15:43; 2 Cor. 11:30; 12:5, 9–10; 13:4; the verb ἀσθενέω (astheneō) appears in 1 Cor. 8:11, 12; 2 Cor. 11:21, 29; 12:10; 13:3, 4, 9.

that made him or others question his sufficiency for the task (2 Cor. 2:16; 3:5): an unimpressive presence, a repellent physical malady, his toiling with his hands, his relative impoverishment, his vulnerability to persecution, his refusal to play to the crowds with silver-tongued oratory. He does not relish being weak but has learned to embrace it as the means by which God's power is revealed in him. Consequently, he identifies himself with the weak of the world (4:10; 9:22) and boasts in his weakness because he has experienced in it the sufficiency of God's grace and the perfection of God's power (2 Cor. 12:5, 9–10). But trying to specify Paul's weakness may sidetrack us from grasping his point, which Weber (1979: 73) appreciates: "It is in the nature of the cross that it cannot be preached elegantly and brilliantly, only in weakness."

"Fear and trembling" elsewhere in the NT refers to the attitude of an obedient slave (Eph. 6:5) or a description of religious awe (Phil. 2:12–13; Heb. 12:20–21). Scholars variously attribute Paul's "fear and trembling" to (1) fear of failure after flopping in Athens (Weiss 1910: 47), (2) jitters about facing new hearers or large crowds (Robertson and Plummer 1914: 31; Hartman 1974: 118), (3) panic from the overwhelming task (Moffatt 1938: 24–25; Fee 1987: 94, citing Acts 18:9–11), (4) apprehension about personal inadequacy (Lightfoot 1895: 171; Bruce 1971: 37; Witherington 1995: 123; Thiselton 2000: 215), and (5) anxiety over personal safety (Calvin 1960: 50; Barrett 1968: 64–65; cf. Acts 18:9; Ps. 55:5). (6) Savage (1996: 73) takes a different tack and argues that, as in the Septuagint, "fear and trembling" depicts a person's "humble response to the awe-inspiring majesty of God." Since Paul was entrusted to preach the word of the cross (1:17–24), his fear and trembling could have been evoked by daily experience of "the power of God and the wisdom of God."[6] (7) Selby (1997) contends that Paul adopts a rhetorical persona to portray himself as an inspired seer in the apocalyptic tradition (cf. Ezek. 1:28; Dan. 7:15; 10:7–9; 1 Enoch 14:14; 4 Ezra [2 Esdr.] 6:36–37; 10:29–30, 55–56) with unique authority to reveal heavenly mysteries. (8) He intends to contrast the haughtiness of speech (2:1), which he rejects as an approach, with his own weakness and profound uneasiness. According to Pogoloff (1992: 131), Paul's "fear and trembling" refers to an affect that was exactly the "opposite of the strength and boldness of a cultured orator." Pogoloff (1992: 135) cites Quintilian's (*Inst.* 12.5.1–5) remarks about the scintillating orator:

> Of all these qualities the highest is that loftiness of soul which fear cannot dismay nor uproar terrify nor the authority of the audience fetter further than the respect which is their due. For although the vices which are

---

6. In the Jewish tradition, however, fear and trembling usually fall upon the enemy because of something God has done (Exod. 15:16; Deut. 2:25; 11:25; Isa. 19:16; Jdt. 2:28; 4 Macc. 4:10).

its opposites, such as arrogance, temerity, impudence and presumption, are all positively obnoxious, still without constancy, confidence and courage, art, study and proficiency will be of no avail. You might as well put weapons in the hands of the unwarlike and the coward. . . . Trachalus appeared to stand out above all his contemporaries, when he was speaking. Such was the effect produced by his lofty stature, the fire of the eye, the dignity of his brow, the excellence of his gesture, coupled with a voice which . . . surpassed the voice of all tragedians that I have ever heard.[7]

As one who projected weakness and fear and trembling, Paul was an "anti-rhetor" (Hartman 1974: 118).[8] He did not come as one who was self-important, competitive, or proud-hearted. The reason for this approach was theological. Brown (1995: 102) recognizes, "To know and to proclaim Jesus Christ crucified is to *show* (demonstrate) the power of the cross by one's own weakness, fear, and trembling." "Stripped of self-reliance" (the real danger, according to Fee 1987: 96), Paul had to cast himself on the mercy and grace of God, and God worked powerfully through him. The Corinthian believers found his message persuasive because of it.

Lightfoot (1895: 172) distinguishes ὁ λόγος (*ho logos*, speech) from τὸ κήρυγμα (*to kērygma*, preaching) in 2:4 by claiming that κήρυγμα refers to the facts of the gospel and λόγος to "the teaching built upon [them], whether in the way of exhortation or of instruction." The two words, however, are interchangeable; and the repetition of synonyms occurs for emphasis (Conzelmann 1975: 54; Thiselton 2000: 217–18). If the reading "not in persuasive art of wisdom" (οὐκ ἐν πειθοῖ σοφίας, *ouk en peithoi sophias*) is original (see the additional notes), Paul would be arguing that the persuasive power of his preaching did not come from wisdom, which is defined in the next verse as "human wisdom" (2:5). Paul uses "wisdom" with a variety of connotations. Here it refers to the skill of persuasion, manipulating arguments and modulating the voice, to beguile the ear and sway an audience. Aristotle (*Eth. nic.* 6.7.1) recognized that "wisdom" was "employed in the arts to denote those men who are the most perfect masters of their art." Paul did not win them over as the perfect master of the art of oratory. Instead, they were confronted with divine proof, "the demonstration of the Spirit and power"

7. Cicero (*De oratore* 1.131–32) regards "bearing and presence" and a resonant and pleasing voice as the keys to splendid oratory.

8. Paul's comments about his weakness are not simply a rhetorical ploy as Pogoloff (1992: 136) suggests, citing Quintilian (*Inst.* 4.1.8–10): "We shall derive some silent support from representing that we are weak, unprepared, and no match for the powerful talents arrayed against us" (cf. Dio Chrysostom, *Or.* 42.3). The scriptural backdrop is more compelling (Snyder 1992: 32; Thiselton 2000: 220). Moses claimed lack of eloquence (Exod. 4:10), Isaiah had unclean lips (Isa. 6:5), and Jeremiah was too young for public speaking (Jer. 1:6).

(ἐν ἀποδείξει πνεύματος καὶ δυνάμεως, *en apodeixei pneumatos kai dy-nameōs*). Ἀπόδειξις is a technical term in rhetoric for "proof" from a verbal demonstration (cf. Quintilian, *Inst.* 5.10.7). But in this case the proof did not come from rhetorical persuasion; it came from God. Faith is based not on how entertaining, informative, or compelling the speaker is but on the power of God transforming the hearts of hearers.

These comments should not be read as Paul's defense against those in Corinth who might have disparaged his deficient rhetorical style in favor of another who was more pleasing. Anderson (1999: 274) correctly notes, "Paul nowhere in these chapters specifically indicates that he is responding to criticism of himself." One needs to read these remarks in the context of his argument's flow (Anderson 1999: 274–75; cf. Witherington 1995: 98). His concern in these chapters is only the party strife shredding their unity (1:10–12). He argues that he proclaimed spiritual truth to them accompanied by demonstrations of the Spirit, and they believed. Their infighting, however, reveals that they are not spiritual persons (3:1) governed by the wisdom of the cross he preached but persons controlled by the foolishness of the world, which jostles for position to gain power and advantage over others. He appeals to his first preaching in Corinth as a model of the wisdom of the cross in action, not as something he must now defend.

The genitives in the phrase ἀποδείξει πνεύματος καὶ δυνάμεως may be objective genitives, "a demonstration of the Spirit and of power" (NRSV, NASB), or genitives of apposition (epexegetical), "a demonstration consisting in Spirit and power." The phrase also may be a hendiadys (using two words to express the same reality), which could be rendered "a demonstration of spiritual power" or "of the Spirit's power."[9] Fee (1994: 92) notes that "for Paul the terms 'Spirit' and 'power' are at times nearly interchangeable; to speak of the Spirit is to speak of power." What is clear is that Paul attributes the Corinthians' conversion to the powerful intervention of the Spirit. He understands God's power, then, to supplant the preacher's weakness. The proof of this power is not the audience's round of applause for the preacher's oratorical art but their changed lives and the formation of a new community. Paul is not talking about "deeds of power" (12:28) or "signs and wonders" attending his preaching (Rom. 15:19; 2 Cor. 12:12), but their conversion (1 Thess. 1:5–6; Fee 1994: 920). Were he referring to miracles, he would have used the plural (Parry 1926: 50). Pogoloff (1992: 138) paraphrases 2:4–5:

Though my speech and my proclamation persuaded you so that you have πίστις [*pistis*, faith] this is not because I used rhetorical methods to sway

---

9. Stephen's preaching in Acts 6:10 is described as speaking with "the wisdom and the Spirit," which "they could not withstand."

you to γνῶσις [gnōsis, knowledge] based on the opinions of those who are usually honored as wise. Rather, your faith is grounded on something far more sure than clever arguments based on opinion. Your faith is as secure as a scientific proof arising from our knowledge of the necessary truths of God's spirit and power.

The gospel calls for faith. Thiselton (2000: 223) describes faith as "'a polymorphous concept' . . . since any attempt at an abstract definition encounters contexts which will not match some *single* meaning or 'essence' of the term." In this context, faith may be defined as "a mind-set which includes both an intellectual conviction of truth," which is a response to proof (ἀπόδειξις), and "a stance of heart and will" that chooses to put "trust in God's salvific act in Christ" rather than in human wisdom "as the basis of life." Faith must always rest in God and is merely self-deception when it rests on human achievements.

Additional Notes

2:1. The reading μυστήριον finds support in important Alexandrian texts (𝔓[46?], ℵ*, A, C, 436, 1912, it[f], syr[p], cop[bo]), and the reading μαρτύριον in mostly Western texts (ℵ[2], B, D, F, G, P, Ψ, 33, 81, 614, it[d, g], syr[h], cop[sa]). If μαρτύριον is original, it could be an objective genitive, "testimony about God" (cf. 1:6, "testimony about Christ" [variant, "about God"]), or a subjective genitive, "testimony borne by God." The word "mystery" occurs twenty other times in the Pauline corpus. The phrase "mystery of God" occurs twice (1 Cor. 4:1; Col. 2:2), while the word "testimony" occurs only five times. The phrase "testimony of God" never appears, only "the testimony of Christ" (1 Cor. 1:6) or "of our Lord" (2 Tim. 1:8). This would make "testimony" the harder reading, and Fee (1987: 88 n. 1) questions why a scribe would substitute the less expected and less colorful "testimony" for the more familiar "mystery" unless it were original (so also Robertson and Plummer 1914: 30; Barrett 1968: 62–63; Wolff 1996: 47). Zuntz (1953: 101) also argues that if Paul had used "mystery" here, it would cause it to "lose much of its force" in 2:7. He thinks that a scribe changed it to "mystery" to assimilate it to 2:7. It is hard, however, to understand how referring to "mystery" in 2:1 causes it to lose its force in 2:7. In each unit so far, Paul employs a word that he will emphasize in the next unit. Proclaiming "the mystery of God" also would not have been inappropriate as the subject of his first preaching, particularly in a synagogue setting. It makes the best sense in the context. The content of the mystery of God is spelled out in the next verse: "Jesus Christ crucified" (2:2). It is the cross that is the "mystery of divine Providence" (Héring 1962: 15). It seems more likely that later scribes, copying when the influence of mystery religions had spread, may have wanted to make the change "to avoid misunderstanding" about Paul's preaching (Thiselton 2000: 207).

2:2. "For I resolved to know nothing" (οὐ γὰρ ἔκρινά τι εἰδέναι) does not match customary word order, in which the negative normally negates the word it precedes (see Lightfoot 1895: 171; R. Collins 1999: 211; Thiselton 2000: 211). Also, the negative for the infinitive should be μή. Moule (1960: 156, 168), however, provides examples of the displacement of the negative and the alteration of οὐ and μή.

2:4. Eleven variant readings with various combinations are represented for this verse. All of the manuscripts read σοφίας and a word from the πειθ- root. Some manuscripts have ἀνθρωπίνης to modify σοφίας; others have some form of λόγος after σοφίας; others have both. The most important readings are:

1. ἐν πειθοῖς σοφίας λόγοις (B, [א*], D, 0150, 33, and split readings among Origen and Chrysostom and other Fathers). The major problem with this reading is that the dative of πειθός as an adjectival form never appears anywhere else in Greek literature. Though no Greek father objected to it, verbal adjectives normally add a -τος suffix. Some argue that the form arose on the analogy of φειδός from φείδομαι, but πιθανός is a widely attested adjective meaning "persuasive" (cf. Col. 2:4), and it was unnecessary for Paul to coin the term (contra Barrett 1968: 218).

2. ἐν πειθοῖς ἀνθρωπίνης σοφίας λόγοις is found in א², A, C, Ψ, Byz.

3. ἐν πειθοῖς σοφίας is found in 𝔓⁴⁶, F, G^gr, Chrysostom^mss.

4. ἐν πειθοῖ σοφίας does not appear in any Greek text but seems to lie behind the Old Latin (it^{f, g}, *persuasione*), and the arguments from intrinsic evidence are strong. It is the shortest reading and can best explain the others (Zuntz 1953: 23–25; so also Weiss 1910: 49; Fee 1987: 88; Pogoloff 1992: 137).

The addition of the final sigma to πειθοῖ (πειθοῖς σοφίας) could be attributable to a simple case of dittography. The ἀνθρωπίνης is an apparent amplification from 2:5 (ἐν σοφία ἀνθρώπων) to clarify which "wisdom" Paul disavows. Were it original, there would have been no reason for a scribe to expunge it. Λόγοις can be explained as a gloss from 1:17 and 2:1. Ἐν πειθοῖ σοφίας best fits the context because "to persuade was the central aim of rhetoric" (Pogoloff 1992: 137), and it balances perfectly its counterpart, "in proof of Spirit and power" (2:5).

2:4. Stowers (1984: 59) makes the case that Paul did not win his converts "by standing on the proverbial soap box and preaching the gospel, often persuasively, to crowds of pagans in public places." Instead, he argues that the center of Paul's preaching activity was open gatherings in private homes rather than in lecture halls or on street corners to whomever happened to pass by, though he also found an audience in the workplace (Acts 19:11–12; Hock 1978). Stowers (1984: 81) comments,

> Public speaking and often the use of public buildings required status, reputation, and recognized roles which Paul did not have. Public speaking, on the one hand, often necessitated some type of legitimation or invitation, or, on the other hand, demanded that the speaker somehow force himself on the audience. Whereas Paul does not fit easily into these typical situations, the private home provided him with a platform where an audience could be obtained and taught without the problems of presenting oneself to be judged by the criteria of public speaking.

The setting may be comparable to Philo's description of a gathering during the feast of Pentecost. When one speaks (in this case, expounding on Scripture), "he has no thought of making a display, for he has no ambition to get a reputation for clever oratory" but to convey clear insight (Philo, *Cont. Life* 10 §75). This statement accords with Paul's aim in preaching the crucified Christ.

III. Factions and Dissension in the Church (1:10–4:21)
    D. Human Wisdom versus the Spirit and Power of God (2:1–5)
➤ E. The Spirit's Revelation of God's Wisdom (2:6–16)
    F. Evaluating the Work of God's Servants (3:1–17)

E. The Spirit's Revelation of God's Wisdom (2:6–16)

The mention of the Spirit leads into the theme of the next discussion. The wisdom of God remains opaque to unspiritual persons with only their natural faculties to guide them, and it can only be discerned by Christians through the assistance of the Spirit. Antitheses expressed in "not/but" statements pervade Paul's argument. What we speak, he writes, is not the wisdom of this age, but the wisdom of God (2:6–7); not what the rulers of this age knew, but what the revelation of God makes known (2:8–9); not what the spirit of this world offers, but what the Spirit of God gives (2:12); not what is taught by human wisdom, but what is taught by the Spirit (2:13); not what the natural human faculties can perceive, but what the Spirit enables one to discern (2:14). The positive statements reveal that this wisdom was foreordained (2:7) and prepared by God (2:9). It is a mystery that is hidden (2:7) but revealed by God (2:10) to the mature (2:6) who love God (2:9) and have received the Spirit (2:12). Only spiritual persons know what has been given to us by God and have the mind of Christ (2:16). Paul asserts that God's wisdom comes through revelation, revelation comes through the Spirit, and only spiritual persons receive this revelation. This revelation points us to the mind of Christ, whose selfless obedience sets the tone for Christian community life. Paul is not on the defensive but offering another argument that exposes the foolishness and wickedness of the Corinthians cliquishness.

This unit addresses the revealed wisdom of the gospel "we speak" (2:6a) over against the wisdom of the world and falls into the following outline:

1. The supernatural origin of the wisdom preached (2:6b–9)
2. The Spirit as the means by which the wisdom is revealed (2:10–13)
3. Spiritual persons as the recipients of this revelation (2:14–16a)
4. The mind of Christ as the outcome of this revelation (2:16b)

Exegesis and Exposition

⁶Yet we do speak wisdom among the mature, but not a wisdom of this age or the rulers of this age, who are being dethroned. ⁷But we speak God's wisdom in a mys-

tery, the hidden wisdom, which God predetermined before the ages for our glory, [8]which none of the rulers of this age comprehended. For if they had comprehended it, they would not have crucified the Lord of glory. [9]But just as it stands written,

What eye has not seen and ear has not heard
and what has not entered the human mind,
things God has prepared for those who love him—

[10]"For" God revealed [these things] to us through the Spirit. For the Spirit searches all things, even the depths of God. [11]For who among humans comprehends the things of a person except the spirit which is in that person? Thus, no one attains knowledge of the things of God except the Spirit of God. [12]But we did not receive the spirit of the world but the Spirit who is from God, so that we might comprehend the things which have been freely given to us by God. [13]These things we speak about, not in words taught by human wisdom, but in words taught by the Spirit, fitting spiritual things to spiritual expression. [14]But the unspiritual person does not receive the things of the Spirit of God, for they are foolishness to him, and he is not able to understand because he is being examined spiritually. [15]But the spiritual person examines all things and is examined by no one. [16]For "Who came to know the mind of God? Who will instruct him?" But we have the mind of Christ.

Paul unequivocally rejects human wisdom (2:5), but he insists that he **2:6** does speak wisdom among the mature.[1] It is a divine wisdom that the unspiritual cannot recognize as wisdom.[2] Paul may use an editorial "we speak" here to refer to his own preaching (Godet 1886: 147; Kaiser 1981: 311; Fee 1987: 101 n. 13) or may refer collectively to his fellow apostles and the unanimity of the apostolic witness (R. Collins 1999: 128).[3] It is more likely, however, that he attests to the unanimity of the Christian witness. Although Paul primarily has his own preaching in mind, all who proclaim the Christian gospel speak this wisdom (Weiss 1910: 53; Lindemann 2000: 61). Héring (1962: 15) wrongly thinks that this wisdom no longer denotes the "pure and simple teaching of the Cross" but involves a "superior stage of Christian teaching . . . reserved for a Christian élite."[4] This interpretation stems from a misreading of

1. Héring (1962: 15) thinks that the verb λαλεῖν (lalein, to speak) denotes private teaching rather than preaching, but the verb is used for proclamation in Rom. 15:18; 2 Cor. 4:13; Phil. 1:14; 1 Thess. 2:2, 4, 16.
2. The repetition of the particle δέ (de) serves to underscore the contrast with human wisdom.
3. In 1:10–3:4, Paul alternates between the first person singular (1:10–17; 2:1–5; 3:1–4) and the first person plural (1:18–25; 2:6–16).
4. This interpretation is so opposed to what Paul argues in this section that Widmann (1979) proposes that 2:6–16 is a gloss introduced by Paul's Corinthian opponents (see also Walker 1992). Murphy-O'Connor's (1986: 81–84) critique of this view is still valid.

the meaning of the phrase "among the mature." Paul did not borrow the term "mature" (τέλειοι, *teleioi*) from the vocabulary of the philosophical tradition to denote those who have attained the pinnacle of wisdom (see Delling, *TDNT* 8:69–72) or from the mystery religions to denote one initiated into esoteric mysteries (see additional note).[5] Its antonym, the "infants" (3:1), shows that he refers to those who are spiritually adult as opposed to the infantile (14:20; cf. 13:11; Phil. 3:15; Eph. 4:13–14; Heb. 5:13–14). Du Plessis (1959: 205) contends that Paul applies the term (like "saints," "beloved," "elect," "called," "faithful") to all Christians.[6] The structure of 2:6–9 reveals that "the mature" are defined in 2:9 simply as "those who love God" (Reiling 1988: 202). They are those who have received the Spirit of God (2:12), who gives them the capacity to understand God's wisdom. Since all Christians have received the Spirit (12:4–11), Paul cannot be referring to some specially favored group (Gärtner 1967–68: 219–20).

Paul does not intend to divide Christians into upper and lower echelons depending on their capacity to apprehend deeper and more mysterious doctrines that go beyond the simpler gospel of the cross.[7] To insinuate that "there are hidden depths of Christian truth" that Paul shared only in the circle of the mature "runs counter not only to the argument as a whole (not to mention this paragraph), but also to the whole of Pauline theology" (Fee 1987: 101, 99–100). The only wisdom he preaches is the wisdom of God revealed in the cross (Robertson and Plummer 1914: 39; Feuillet 1963: 67–68; Schrage 1991: 250; Sandnes 1991: 82–83). The wisdom he speaks among the mature, then, is not a more sophisticated instruction for the gifted few. It is the same wisdom he speaks to all concerning God's redemptive purposes for humankind revealed in the cross (1:18; 2:2). It is spoken to beginning and advanced Christians alike. I disagree with the hypothesis that some Corinthians have complained that he fed them only milk when they, as "mature" Christians (4:8), expected something deeper, and that he now defends his approach by resorting to irony (contra Fee 1987: 103). He is still remonstrating with them about their divisions and is making the case that they disclose a spiritual immaturity that fails to grasp the deep things of God embodied in the cross. Their behavior reveals that they are influenced more by human wisdom than by God's wisdom. Since

5. The term "mature" also does not mean among "the influential," "those in office" (contra Welborn 1997: 34–35).

6. Pearson (1973: 27–30) maintains that Paul's use of the term "mature" is polemical because the Corinthians, influenced by its usage in Hellenistic Judaism as represented by Philo, had applied it to themselves.

7. Such doctrines could include esoteric teaching about eschatological mysteries (Scroggs 1967–68: 34–35, 37, 46).

Paul does not divulge who among them is "mature," the readers must decide for themselves whether they qualify or not.

Paul's use of the terms "mature" and "infants" shows that gradations do exist among Christians (Oster 1995: 81). But the distinction is between juvenile Christians who fail to incarnate the cross by nursing jealousies and stoking rivalries, and the "mature" who accept God's foolishness as wisdom and the world's wisdom as foolishness. Being spiritually adult means recognizing and embracing God's wisdom in the cross and knowing that it invalidates the wisdom of this age. Paul rejects any esoteric wisdom that would sever some believers from other believers who lack this wisdom. The wisdom of this age creates a stratified society of elites and inferiors. By contrast, the wisdom of the cross emphasizes human solidarity. Under the cross, all must stand together.

Commentators divide over whether to take the phrase "the rulers of this age" (οἱ ἄρχοντες τοῦ αἰῶνος τούτου, *hoi archontes tou aiōnos toutou*) as a reference to supernatural powers or earthly powers. Many assume that Paul has in mind angelic or demonic powers that hold the world in their thralldom.[8] Usage of οἱ ἄρχοντες in the NT does not support this view.[9] Paul uses it in Rom. 13:3 to refer unambiguously to earthly rulers (cf. Matt. 20:25). In the sixteen other occurrences of ἄρχοντες in the NT, it signifies earthly leaders and would not have conveyed a demonic sense to the original audience (Carr 1976–77: 23). When the term does have a supernatural dimension, it appears in the singular (Eph. 2:2; John 12:31; Matt. 9:34; 12:24; Mark 3:22; Luke 11:15; cf. 2 Cor. 4:4). The plural term ἀρχαί (*archai*) is used for transcendent powers (Rom. 8:38; Eph. 1:21; 3:10; 6:12; Col. 1:16; 2:10, 15). When it is prefaced by "every," the singular "ruler" (ἀρχή, *archē*) is used, and it is linked with "every authority" (ἐξουσία, *exousia*, 1 Cor. 15:24; Col. 2:10) and "every power" (δύναμις, *dynamis*, Eph. 1:21).

A second view identifies οἱ ἄρχοντες as earthly rulers, the princes of the world (cf. Ps. 2:2; 32:10 LXX; Sir. 10:14; Bar. 3:16).[10] The qualifier "of this age" for rulers is more apt as a description of earthly overlords. Paul attributes the crucifixion to these rulers in 2:8, and humans were plainly responsible for the crucifixion (Luke 23:13, 35; 24:20; 1 Thess. 2:14–15). His statement in 2:8 that had they known the wisdom of God they would not have crucified the Lord of glory seems to point to earthly rulers, not to demonic powers. Christian preaching specifically noted the rulers' ignorance of what God had predestined to take place

---

8. So Origen, *Fragments from a Commentary on 1 Cor.* 9.14–15; Weiss 1910: 53–54; Lietzmann 1949: 12, 170; Bultmann 1951: 173; Wilckens 1959: 61–64; Héring 1962: 16; Barrett 1968: 70; Conzelmann 1975: 61; Schrage 1991: 250, 253–54; R. Collins 1999: 129.

9. The view that they represent the angelic custodians of the nations (Cullmann 1960: 91; Caird 1956: 17) is unpersuasive.

10. Only in later writings are archons referred to as spiritual beings.

in the crucifixion (Acts 3:17; 4:25–28; 13:27). The context also contrasts human wisdom with divine wisdom, and the wisdom of demonic powers seems to be tangential. G. Miller (1972: 525) comments, "The condemnation of the 'rulers of this age' is that, failing to know and acknowledge God through their human wisdom upon which they depended, they ignorantly crucified the 'lord of glory.'" These rulers would be akin to the wise, powerful, and well-born in 1:26–28.[11] The strongest and wisest could not grasp God's plan of salvation. In Roman Corinth, this observation would be a coded denigration of Roman imperial aspirations. The cross was a concrete symbol of Roman power: Dare to challenge us, and we will crucify you. Their arrogant malevolence in this particular crucifixion, however, sowed the seeds of their own undoing.

It is possible to meld the two different views and to understand the rulers of this world order to represent a collective evil that transcends individual humans and their acts. Shadowy forces stand behind the deeds of earthly rulers. Thiselton (2000: 238) argues that "humankind is more than a collection of individual entities or agents, but a corporeity within which evil and evil forces become endemic and structural." In their struggle to establish their own sovereignty over the world, the rulers abet the forces of darkness. As Theissen (1987: 378) reads it, "The *archons* are historical rulers who are heightened symbolically to demonic powers" (cf. Pearson 1973: 33; Wink 1984: 40–45). Paul saw the human drama "played out under the influence of supernatural forces" (R. Collins 1999: 129), and these powers take human wisdom captive and blind it to God's truth. They determine the human situation in the created order, and "no power can be viewed in isolation from the others" (Beker 1980: 189–90). In 2:6–9, Paul emphasizes the superhuman origin of the wisdom he preached, which prevails over the wisdom of all other powers, terrestrial and celestial. In crucifying the Son of God, they all signed their own death warrants, because God chose the cross as the means of their ultimate defeat.

These rulers are "being dethroned" ("abolished," τῶν καταργου-μένων, *tōn katargoumenōn*; cf. 1:28). Hafemann (1996a: 301–13) shows that this verb has an eschatological significance in Paul's letters, expressing the discontinuity between this age and the age to come. What is transitory must give way to what is eternal, and Robertson and Plummer (1914: 37) describe the force of the present tense as "axiomatic." Hafemann (1996b: 288) concludes about the verb,

11. Chrysostom *Hom. 1 Cor.* 7.1; Calvin 1960: 53; Edwards 1885: 52; Godet 1886: 136; Lightfoot 1895: 174–75; Findlay 1910: 778; Robertson and Plummer 1914: 36–37; G. Miller 1972; Carr 1976–77; Fee 1987: 103–4; Clarke 1993: 114–17; Wolff 1996: 53–54; Lindemann 2000: 63.

Its context is consistently eschatological and its meaning is best translated, "to render (something) inoperative, ineffective, powerless," or "to nullify (something) in terms of its effects." Indeed, Paul's use of κα-ταργέω [*katargeō*] warrants its consideration as a Pauline *terminus technicus* to express the significance of the coming and return of Christ for the structures of this world.

The evil that sustains the domination system appears on the surface to be stronger than good. Evil, however, contains the seeds of its own destruction, especially when it unwittingly undoes itself at the moment of what appears to be its greatest triumph, when Jesus is crucified. The cross is the decisive event in a cosmic struggle that unmasks and overthrows the powers of this world. The language Paul uses here parallels the prophecy in 15:24 that Christ will deliver the kingdom to God after dethroning (καταργέω) every ruler, authority, and power, including the last enemy, death. N. Elliott (1997: 176) concludes,

> The crucifixion of Jesus is not for him an instance of official misconduct, a miscarriage of Roman justice. It is an apocalyptic event. It reveals "the rulers of this age," indeed "every rule and authority and power"—procurators, kings, emperors, as well as the supernatural "powers" who stand behind them—as intractably hostile to God and as doomed to be destroyed by the Messiah at "the end."

2:7 The "but" (ἀλλά, *alla*) draws a contrast with what Paul says in 2:1–5: "My speech and my preaching were not with the persuasiveness of wisdom." His wisdom relays God's wisdom, which is cloaked in mystery.[12] That does not mean that it is a mysterious wisdom (contra Wilckens 1959: 64, 65; Scroggs 1967–68: 44–45, 54) or a "Christian theosophy" (contra Héring 1962: 116). The phrase "in mystery" does not modify the verb "we speak." It does not characterize Paul's instruction but the nature of the wisdom of God (Bornkamm, *TDNT* 4:819). Paul does not intend to imply that he imparted esoteric ideas only to a small circle of clever students and kept it from the immature. Kaiser (1981: 312) rightly comments that it is "not something mysterious or a truth humans cannot fathom. Rather, it is a truth or fact which human understanding cannot discover by itself, but which one can adequately grasp once God has revealed it to his prophets or apostles." This mystery is the word of a crucified Christ (2:1–2), which heretofore had been hidden to human inquiry (cf. Eph. 3:9; Col. 1:26).[13] It is the same teaching (see Willis 1989: 116–17) he first spoke to them.

---

12. Θεοῦ σοφία (*theou sophia*) refers to God's wisdom (possessive), not wisdom about God (objective genitive).

13. Pate (2000: 278) notes that in 1 Enoch 2:6–9; 37:2–5; 38:3; 39:4–5; 48:6–7; 62:7, the secrets to be revealed in the last days are associated with wisdom and are known in the present only by the righteous.

This message is hidden mystery because it can be known only through God's revelation. It is now an open secret: open because God has revealed it, and a secret because the revelation both reveals the mystery and obscures it at the same time. The use of the perfect participle (ἀποκεκρυμμένην, *apokekrymmenēn*) expresses Paul's view that it remains hidden (Schrage 1991: 251). It remains veiled only to those who are perishing in their rebellion and unbelief (2 Cor. 4:3), because only the "mature" who love God and who receive the Spirit (2:12) can recognize it as divine wisdom. The wisdom of this age intends "to be openly convincing" (Barrett 1968: 71), to persuade through various means. When the wisdom of this age meets God's wisdom hidden before the ages (Brown 1995: 107) in the cross (Rom. 16:25; Col. 1:26), it finds nothing convincing according to its standards. Instead, it meets disarming weakness, suffering, and the paradox of one identified as the "Lord of glory" enduring the most dishonorable death. It dismisses the cross as consummate folly. Paul's point is that humans cannot unravel the mystery for themselves; it can only be given to them by God. This wisdom can be discerned as wisdom only by those who trust and love God (2:9), not by those who only analyze and debate. In 2:10–13, Paul argues that humans can know it only through the Spirit. Gaffin (1995: 110) concludes, "Believers and unbelievers belong to two different worlds; they exist in not only separate but antithetical 'universes of discourse.'" Consequently, unbelievers will continue to grope in their own darkness and yet think that they see and understand.

One of Paul's firm convictions is that the cross was not plan B; it was decided on beforehand (προώρισεν, *proōrisen*). Paul sweeps across the range of God's plan for human redemption through Christ, moving from "before the ages" to the end of the ages with his reference to "our glory" (Matt. 25:34; 1 Pet. 1:4). "For our glory" points to the Christian's resurrection (15:40–42) and participation in God's end-time salvation, eternal life (Rom. 2:7). Jesus is already the Lord of glory (Phil. 2:9–11), and those who are in Christ are destined to share in his glory. But Paul makes clear in Rom. 8:17 that those who expect to be glorified with Christ (cf. Rom. 8:18, 21; 9:23; 2 Cor. 4:17; 1 Thess. 2:12) must suffer with him. They are "to be conformed to the image of his Son" (Rom. 8:29), which includes "always carrying in the body the death of Jesus, so that the life of Jesus may also be made visible in our bodies" (2 Cor. 4:10; cf. Phil. 3:10–11). This transformation process has already begun as the Christian is made new (2 Cor. 3:18). Christians already experience the glory to come, and will do so in an ever increasing way until they come to the final glory (Fee 1994: 319).

2:8 The wisdom of this world is not simply the skillful marshaling of arguments to persuade others. It is malevolent. It opposes God, and it crucified Christ. N. Wright (1986: 116) observes, "The 'rulers and authorities' of Rome and of Israel—as Caird points out, the best government and the highest religion the world at that time had ever known—conspired to put Jesus on the cross." These rulers did not recognize him to be "the Lord of glory."[14] They also did not even know that the wisdom of God exists as something radically distinct from their own wisdom (Reiling 1988: 203). Their ignorance is nothing new. Those who claim to be in the know have always been clueless about God's ways (cf. Dan. 2:27–28) and always resist any move to oust them from their thrones. But the crucifixion was not an unfortunate case of mistaken identity. Their knee-jerk reaction is to kill, and the rulers knew full well what they were doing. They did not know, however, that they were playing into the hands of God and that their evil butchery would lead to their undoing and humanity's salvation. Evil always bungles things in the end, and the cross exposes its futility and folly. It also reveals that "there is an alternative to the social world as it actually is, there is a possible way of living for humans with each other which is different from the actual one and 'truer' than that, viz. a way of life governed by love only" (Engberg-Pedersen 1987: 565–66).

Paul concludes his first argument in this unit with a scriptural citation introduced by a strong adversative (ἀλλά, *alla*; see Frid 1985). It may highlight the contrast between the rulers of this age who did not know the wisdom of God and "us" to whom it has been revealed. Or, more likely, it stands in parallel to 2:7, ἀλλὰ λαλοῦμεν (*alla laloumen*, but we speak; Schrage 1991: 256; Lindemann 2000: 65). In that case, Paul continues his response to the statement that what he speaks is not the wisdom of this age (2:6). The exact source of this citation is unclear (see additional note), but Paul cites it as Scripture, and it seems to be a paraphrase based on Isa. 64:3 LXX (64:4 MT). The citation does not identify the content of what eye has not seen and ear has not heard but evokes an image of end-time salvation, confirms that God is behind it, and affirms that it can be appropriated only by those who love God. Every possible earthly source of wisdom is excluded, making it impossible for mortals, no matter how creative or innovative, to imagine what God has prepared.

   The eye, ear, and heart are organs of cognition in Semitic imagery. Kaiser (1981: 313) notes that these things did not come from empirical sources (eye has not seen), traditional knowledge passed on in community (ear has not heard), or intuitive insight (heart has not conceived),

2:9

---

14. Paul boldly applies an attribute associated with God—the "God of glory" (Acts 7:2; Eph. 1:17)—to Christ (cf. James 2:1). Cf. 1 Enoch 22:14; 25:3, 7; 27:3, 4; 40:3; 63:2; 75:3. Conzelmann (1975: 63) is mistaken to think that Paul has in mind the myth of a disguised descending redeemer.

nor is it accessible to them.[15] This cognitive equipment may inform human opinions, but it is a useless tool for trying to fathom the heart of God. It is "beyond nature, beyond ideas, beyond the ken of imagination and the reach of merely natural desire" (Edwards 1885: 55).

"What is prepared" may refer to the future blessings of heaven, since the verb ἑτοιμάζω (hetoimazō) is used for heavenly blessing in Matt. 25:34. If the context rules, "what is prepared" is similar to what God foreordained (2:7) to clarify who the "mature" are in 2:6.[16] Holladay (1990: 94) observes that love, not knowledge, "is the sole prerequisite for participating in the divine mystery." This statement could be misunderstood to imply that love is some saving virtue that persons can have apart from knowledge of the gospel. The knowledge Paul opposes is knowledge that leads to self-inflation. Saving knowledge leads to loving God (Exod. 20:6; Deut. 5:10), the greatest of all things commanded (Mark 12:28–30; cf. John 14:23).

2:10–13 Paul shifts his focus to the means by which God reveals heavenly truth that is naturally unknowable. How can something that has no place in the human heart be made known? How do humans cross the divide between the world and God? These can happen only through God's Spirit, who searches all things, even the depths of God. Human creatures do not have access to these things and do not even have the grammar or vocabulary for them until it is graciously bestowed by God's Spirit.

Rather than searching human hearts (Rom. 8:27; Rev. 2:23), the Spirit, as pictured by Paul, penetrates and discloses "the depths of God" (contrast "the depths of Satan," Rev. 2:24). The depths of God refer to what God has foreordained (2:7) and prepared (2:9), the divine plan for human redemption (cf. Rom. 11:33).[17] I agree with Schweizer (*TDNT* 6:426): "The content of the supernatural knowledge is not disclosure of mysteries of the heavenly world but the divine act of love effected at the cross, or the divine sonship granted to the believer thereby." Paul argues from the widely accepted principle "Like is known by like" (Gärtner 1967–68). Since human wisdom does not belong to the same sphere as the divine, it cannot know God (cf. Isa. 55:8; 4 Ezra [2 Esdr.] 4:21). Only God's Spirit apprehends God's plans and purposes, and only God's Spirit can link God and humans together (Gärtner 1967–68: 218).

---

15. The idiom ἀνέβη ἐπὶ καρδίαν (anebē epi kardian, it arose in the heart) is a Semitism meaning to "enter one's mind" (cf. Acts 7:23; Jer. 3:16; 28:50 LXX; BDAG 58).

16. Contrast 1 Clem. 34:8, where the citation more closely corresponds to Isa. 64:4, "for those who wait for him."

17. Wolff (1996: 58–59) notes that the word "depths" is at home in apocalyptic literature (1 Enoch 63:3; 2 Bar. 14:8–9; T. Job 37:6; 1QS 11:18–19). The term's appearance in later Gnostic literature has no bearing on Paul's usage.

What God is doing, only God knows.[18] P. W. Gooch (1987b: 36) explains what Paul means: "It is not simply that just as individuals have private thoughts not known to others, God has private thoughts too, rather, if human things are known only to human knowers, divine things are known only to God's Spirit."[19] Paul's intention "is to draw a thick and heavy line between things human and divine and to place the things of God squarely outside the limits of human knowing." That line is crossed only by the divine Spirit, who works in humans "a likeness of the Lord" (2 Cor. 3:18) and enables the confession "Jesus is Lord" (12:3; Gärtner 1967–68: 221).

The believers' prior reception of the Spirit (3:16; 6:19; 12:13; 2 Cor. 13:5) is foundational to Paul's argument and is taken for granted. Those who receive and experience divine revelation must have already received the Spirit (cf. Eph. 1:17). Spiritual persons are those Christians in whom the Spirit has really become the fundamental power of life (cf. Gal. 6:1). Gaffin (1995: 114) comments that persons are spiritual because they are "indwelt, renewed, enlightened, directed by the Holy Spirit." They are the opposite of persons directed by the spirit of the world (Eph. 2:2). It is that rebellious temper, analogous to the wisdom of the world (1:20; 2:6; 3:19) and compelled by "another spirit" (2 Cor. 11:4), that resists God's Spirit and makes one incapable of recognizing the revelation of God except as foolishness. But Paul's main point is that what derives from this world cannot bridge the gap to apprehend God.

Paul's statement in 2:13 recalls what he argues in 2:4. His preaching "was not with the persuasiveness of wisdom but with the demonstration of the Spirit and power." His teaching was not human invention but "*taught* words from the Spirit." The concluding phrase, πνευματικοῖς πνευματικὰ συγκρίνοντες (*pneumatikois pneumatika synkrinontes*, literally, "combining spiritual with spiritual"), poses a nettlesome problem for interpretation. The πνευματικά (spiritual things; cf. 9:11) is virtually shorthand for the "gospel" (P. Gardner 1994: 138). The gender of πνευματικοῖς, however, could be masculine or neuter, and the verb συγκρίνειν (*synkrinein*) could mean "interpret," "compare," or "combine." The verb is used in the LXX to mean "interpret" (Gen. 40:8, 22; 41:12; Judg. 7:15; Dan. 5:8, 12; cf. Jos. As. 4:10). All of these passages

---

18. Käsemann (1971: 15) makes the valid point that the human spirit does not adequately know itself either: "Generally speaking, we know ourselves least of all." It is only through the revelation of the divine Spirit that we come to true self-understanding.

19. Lightfoot (1895: 179) argues that the first verb, οἶδεν (*oiden*; who of humans knows the things of an individual human?), connotes "direct knowledge," while the second verb, ἔγνωκεν (*egnōken*; comes to know [perfect tense] the things of God), connotes "the idea of a process of attainment." The difference places knowing the things of God "a degree more out of reach" than knowing the things of humans.

refer to one person unlocking spiritual truth revealed by God (usually in a dream) to another person. Paul may understand his preaching analogously as interpreting for untrained ears the message that the Spirit was revealing to their hearts. It makes a plausible reading to take the noun as masculine, parallel to the ψυχικός (*psychikos*, unspiritual person) in 2:14 and the πνευματικοί in 3:1, and to render the phrase "interpreting spiritual things to those who are spiritual" (NRSV). It would return to his thought in 2:6, "We speak wisdom among the mature." Some object that in the LXX this meaning of the verb, "to interpret," is limited to "dreams" (Lightfoot 1895: 181; Robertson and Plummer 1914: 47), and that it strains the classical usage of the verb. In classical usage, it means "to bring two things together fitly," "to combine them."[20] If the noun is taken as masculine, Paul could mean that he combines spiritual things with spiritual persons. If the noun is taken as neuter, however, Paul means that he weds spiritual truths to spiritual expression (Kaiser 1981: 317). The latter makes good sense in the context. Spiritual subjects—namely, the things that God has graciously given, such as Christ's sacrificial death on the cross—require spiritual expression, "words taught by the Spirit." The mode of his teaching matches the nature of the subject matter, like by like. If this is the correct rendering, Paul reiterates his point that the persuasive art of human wisdom is totally inappropriate for expressing divine spiritual truths. Thus, the wisdom he speaks (2:6) is spiritual wisdom.

2:14–15 In 2:14–16a, Paul explains why divine wisdom is not received by the world. God's mysterious revelation exposes the world's helpless blindness when left to its own devices. The ψυχικὸς ἄνθρωπος (*psychikos anthrōpos*) is not a reference to the weak Christian but represents natural, physical existence that is dependent on human faculties without the aid of the Holy Spirit. Schweizer (*TDNT* 9:663) notes that the unbeliever is ψυχικός, while the Christian making no spiritual progress is σαρκικός (*sarkikos*, fleshly, 3:3). The latter incurs censure and admonition because of his or her fleshly orientation; the former is a more neutral term referring to the natural state of a human being apart from the illuminating work of the Holy Spirit.[21] Paul's point: natural reason and intuition are completely unable to receive the divine realities unaided (contrast 1 Thess. 1:6, "you received the word with joy inspired by the Holy Spirit"; cf. 1 Cor. 2:13). Gaffin (1995: 114) cites Calvin's caustic comments: "Faced with God's revelation, the unbeliever is like an ass at a concert." It is completely uninterested in the music and disturbs the concert with an irritating commotion. For example, the Athenian gad-

---

20. Paul uses the verb συγκρίνειν elsewhere only in 2 Cor. 10:12 to mean "compare."

21. The term appears in Jude 19 to describe worldly people who do not have the Spirit and who cause divisions.

flies deemed Paul a "babbler" (Acts 17:18) and scoffed at his preaching of the resurrection (17:32). Gallio regarded the dispute between Paul and the Jews as silly talk (Acts 18:15), and Festus thought Paul to be insane (Acts 26:24). As Grindheim (2002: 697) observes, the "appropriation of divine wisdom requires a special ability. Natural human beings lack this ability (2:14), which is an exclusive attribute of the spirit of God (2:11b)."

The verb ἀνακρίνειν (*anakrinein*) means "to investigate," "to examine" (1 Cor. 10:25, 27), not "to judge" (κρίνειν, *krinein*) or "to discern"(διακρίνειν, *diakrinein*), and is close to ἐραυνᾶν (*eraunan*, to search, 2:10). The natural person analyzes divine truth with his or her limited, earthbound faculties and, not surprisingly, finds this truth wanting (cf. Rom. 1:28). Only one with spiritual perception can examine beyond the visible evidence and attest that the foolishness of God plus the weakness of God equals the power of God. If the message does not come with authenticating signs or sophisticated wisdom (1:22), it whizzes right by those dependent only on natural faculties.

As the Spirit searches all things (2:10), the person guided by the Spirit also can examine all things, particularly God's ways, that were formerly hidden (Fee 1987: 118). Unspiritual persons cannot do this, because they have no help to bridge the knowledge gap and cannot make correct assessments. By saying that the spiritual person is examined by no one (contrast 1 Cor. 14:24), Paul could mean that the unspiritual person, who misjudges the cross as foolishness, also misjudges believers as fools. Their judgments are invalid. It is more likely that this conclusion leads into the next paragraph, in which Paul will admonish the Corinthians for not being spiritual (Fee 1987: 118). If they were truly spiritual in their behavior, he would not be provoked to judge them as *sarkikoi*.

The conclusion to this unit offers scriptural reinforcement to Paul's explanation of why unspiritual persons fail to fathom this wisdom. What human has intellectual mastery over God? Paul cites Isa. 40:13. The Hebrew text of Isa. 40:13 reads, "Who has directed the Spirit [רוּחַ, *rûaḥ*] of the Lord?" but the LXX reads "mind" (νοῦς, *nous*). Lindemann (2000: 74) thinks that "Spirit" would have fit better in Paul's argument and regards this as evidence that Paul was not familiar with the Hebrew text. Silva (*DPL* 633–34) reads the evidence quite differently. Paul argues that the Spirit makes it possible to know God (2:11), and he concludes, "But we have the mind of Christ." Silva deduces that using the word "mind" "links this last comment with the Septuagint quotation, but the Hebrew original, as well as the context of Paul's discussion more generally, makes clear that what the apostle means is, 'We have the Spirit of Christ and therefore we really know Christ.'"

2:16

Paul also substitutes "Christ" for "Lord" (cf. Rom. 11:34, where he cites the passage again and reads "Lord"). In Isaiah's context, the answer to the question "Who knows the mind of the Lord?" is that only God can know these things. For Paul, those who are spiritual, living as they do at the dawn of the new age, have access to the mind of Christ, which in turn gives clearer insight into the mind of God (Dunn 1998: 250).

"The mind of Christ" does not refer to some mystical ecstasy (contra Weiss 1910: 68–69) but is related to "sobriety, watchfulness, faith, hope, and life, not ecstasy" (Willis 1989: 118). According to Willis (1989: 118), it refers "to believers having their outlook shaped by an awareness of Christ." He thinks that Phil. 2:5 provides an important clue for "understanding the meaning of the 'mind of Christ' in 1 Cor. 2:16." This argument shows how Paul's conclusion ties in with the disputes that cause him to entreat them to be of the same mind (1:10). Willis (1989: 119) asserts, "Based upon other Pauline usage and the immediate context, then, the appeal 'to have the mind of Christ' does not mean to think Christ's thoughts after him, nor to have ecstatic experiences, nor to knowing proper dogma. The 'mind of Christ' is not focused upon special wisdom or experiences, but on community life." The "mind of Christ" refers to Christ's obedience, and Paul appeals to it as a paradigm for Christians to follow: "And he died for all, so that those who live might live no longer for themselves, but for him who died and was raised for them" (2 Cor. 5:15). Brown (1995: 145) asserts, "To have 'the mind of Christ' is to have a cruciform mind." It requires putting to death selfish ambitions, humbling oneself, and giving oneself for others. Paul particularly appeals to this mind of Christ when a community is split by dissensions (Phil. 2:2–5; 4:2). The Corinthians' divisions reveal that they are not living the way Christians, taught by the Spirit and endowed with the mind of Christ, should live. They were called into existence by the word of the cross, and they are to embody the word of the cross in all their relationships. Grindheim (2002: 708) summarizes well Paul's point: "To be spiritual . . . is to have apprehended the word of the cross in such a way that it has transformed the entire existence of the believer into its image—to a cruciform life, a life characterized by self-sacrificing love, and where power is manifest through weakness."

Additional Notes

2:6. The search for religio-historical parallels to this passage in Gnosticism or Hellenistic Jewish wisdom speculation has dominated the interpretation of this text. The complaint of Willis (1989: 111) offers a corrective: "Too much of the debate, it seems to me, is more focused upon the background of the terms than the immediate usage in 1 Corinthians." He contends that Paul's "real concern . . . is about conduct more than the reasonings of the Christians in Corinth." Funk's (1966: 301) critique of Wilckens's concentration on words alone in an attempt to spot a gnostic anthropology behind Paul's language is valid. Whether Paul takes Corinthian terminology (so Fee 1987: 102; N. Watson 1992: 22; R. Collins 1999: 124) and fills it with his own content is difficult to prove. Because seventeen of nineteen usages of the word σοφία in undisputed Pauline epistles appear in 1 Corinthians and sixteen in chapters 1–3 (1:17, 19, 20, 21, 22, 24, 30; 2:1, 4, 5, 6, 7, 13; 3:19; cf. Rom. 11:33; 2 Cor. 1:12), most assume that the word is a Corinthian catchword. Thiselton (2000: 230) comments, "Paul wishes to redefine and thus to rescue an important term." Nine other occurrences of the noun, however, are found in Eph. 1:8, 17; 3:10; Col. 1:9, 28; 2:3, 23; 3:16; 4:5. If these letters are authentically Pauline, it undermines the argument that σοφία was only a Corinthian catchword.

2:9. The phrase "as it stands written" suggests a quotation from Scripture, but the precise text cited is obscure. Verheyden (1996) demonstrates that Origen's (in his *Commentary on Matthew* on 27:9) assumption that the quotation was taken from an apocryphal Book of Elijah was attributable to a mistake (contra Weiss 1910: 56). Nordheim (1974) claims that it derives from the Testament of Jacob, but this has been shown false by Hofius (1975) and Sparks (1976). Hofius (1975) claims that the origin of the quotation is unknown, though Berger (1977–78) finds more parallels in apocalyptic Jewish texts. Prigent (1958) thinks that it could derive from the synagogue liturgy; Feuillet (1963) traces it to sapiential traditions (Prov. 30:1–4; Job 28). It is more likely that Paul loosely quotes from the LXX version of Isa. 64:3 (cf. Sparks 1976; Ponsot 1983): ἀπὸ τοῦ αἰῶνος οὐκ ἠκούσαμεν οὐδὲ οἱ ὀφθαλμοὶ ἡμῶν εἶδον θεὸν πλὴν σοῦ καὶ τὰ ἔργα σου ἃ ποιήσεις τοῖς ὑπομένουσιν ἔλεον. This text was interpreted eschatologically in Pseudo-Philo, *Bib. Ant.* 26:13, and Paul may be thinking of it in a loose association with elements of a medley of other passages (Job 28:12–28; Isa. 48:6; 52:15; 65:17; Jer. 3:16; Sir. 1:10).

2:10. The connecting particle δέ has substantial support in ℵ, A, C, D, F, G, Ψ, 33, 1881. Fee (1987: 97 n. 1) argues for γάρ ($\mathfrak{P}^{46}$, B, 6, 88, 181, 326, 365, 1739, 1877, 2127, 2492, sa^ms, bo^ms, Clement) as the more difficult reading, reasoning that a copyist would be more likely to interrupt, deliberately or accidentally, a string of clauses beginning with γάρ with δέ than to create a text with three γάρ clauses in a row (contra Metzger 1994: 481). Fee (1987: 111 n. 57) also contends that the piling up of γάρ is a Pauline stylistic trait (1:17, 18, 19, 21; 3:3, 4; 9:15, 16, 17).

III. Factions and Dissension in the Church (1:10–4:21)
   E. The Spirit's Revelation of God's Wisdom (2:6–16)
➤ F. Evaluating the Work of God's Servants (3:1–17)
   G. How to Regard Oneself; How to Regard Others (3:18–4:5)

F. Evaluating the Work of God's Servants (3:1–17)

In 3:1–4, Paul makes a transition from the first major part of his argument in 1:18–2:16 to the second major part in 3:5–4:5 (Kuck 1992a: 159). In this second stage of his argument his concern about the Corinthians' factions returns to the surface (3:4–5, 21; 4:6) as he zeroes in on how Christian ministers should be evaluated. The issue of wisdom and foolishness resurfaces in 3:18–20. Rather than directly denouncing the guilty parties in Corinth for their misguided behavior, "Paul shows from his own life how someone who has Christian wisdom lives and thereby what Christian wisdom is" (Engberg-Pedersen 1987: 568).

In 3:5–9, he argues that all servants belong to God, their different tasks come from God, and their success comes from God. Consequently, they are all on the same level. By identifying himself and Apollos as mere farmhands, he makes the point that credit for any success belongs only to God, who causes the field to bring forth a crop. The farmhands are interchangeable and replaceable. Leaders in the church are not to use their position to further their own interests and should not expect to accrue acclaim and honor.

In 3:10–15, he changes the image to a building in which God becomes the one who lets out the contract and employs the building inspector to insure that the construction is done correctly and without fraud. In this image, Paul shifts roles from farmhand to head contractor. The competence of each construction worker in carrying out the tasks may vary and the workmanship may vary. God will reward the difference in quality in the final judgment, disbursing rewards for work well done and fines for shoddy work. That appraisal awaits God's final judgment. God alone, not the Corinthians or anyone else, is the ultimate arbiter.

In 3:16–17, he shifts the image from an ordinary building to the temple of God. God will also mete out punishment to any who damage or destroy this temple. Kuck (1992a: 236) captures the gist of the argument: "Paul wants each of his readers to think about his or her relationship to others in the community in the light of the final evaluation and recompense of each before God." The judgment will expose whether they built up the community or subverted it. In the meantime, they can make no special claims for themselves and should seek to serve the good of the community, leaving their rank and status entirely to God.

The passage falls into the following outline:

1. Divisions in the church: Improper evaluation of teachers (3:1–4)
2. The function of teachers: God's field hands (3:5–9)
3. The function of teachers: God's master-builders (3:10–15)
4. The judgment of teachers (3:16–17)

Exposition and Exegesis

[1]And so, brothers and sisters, I was not able to speak to you as spiritual persons but as fleshly, as infants in Christ. [2]I gave you milk to drink, not solid food, for you were not yet able [to digest it]. Indeed, not even now are you able [to digest it], [3]for you are still controlled by selfish impulses. For where jealousy and strife [persist] among you, are you not controlled by selfish impulses and behaving in [all too] human ways? [4]For when someone says, "I belong to Paul," and another, "I belong to Apollos," are you not [mere] humans?

[5]What, then, is Apollos? What, then, is Paul? Servants through whom you came to believe, as the Lord gave to each one. [6]I planted, Apollos watered, but God was giving the growth, [7]so that neither the one who planted is anything nor the one who watered but God who gives the growth. [8]The one who plants and the one who waters are one, but each will receive his own reward according to his own toil. [9]For we are co-workers under God; you are God's cultivation, God's construction.

[10]According to the grace of God given to me, as a skilled master-builder I laid a foundation, and another builds upon it. But let each one take heed how he or she is building upon it. [11]For no one can lay another foundation except that which already has been laid, which is Jesus Christ. [12]But if someone builds upon the foundation with gold, silver, precious stones, timber, hay, straw, [13]the work of each one will become manifest, for the day will make it known, because it reveals itself with fire, and the fire will test the kind of work each one has done. [14]If the work that someone built upon [the foundation] abides, that person will receive a reward. [15]If the work that someone built upon [the foundation] is burned down, the builder will suffer loss but will be saved, yet only in this way, [as one escaping] through fire.

[16]Do you not know that you are the temple of God and that the Spirit of God dwells among you? [17]But if someone destroys the temple of God, God will destroy that person. For the temple of God is holy, and you are that temple.

Paul shifts back to the first person singular, and his wording, "and I, brothers and sisters, was not able to speak," purposely recalls 2:1 (κἀγώ, ἀδελφοί, kagō, adelphoi) and 2:6 (λαλεῖν, lalein), where he gives his account of the message he preached when he first visited Corinth. For   3:1–2 the first time in the letter he criticizes the church directly and sharply, but he cushions his rebuke by addressing them as brothers and sisters (cf. 1:26, 2:1), which conveys solidarity (Kistemaker 1993: 100). The use of maternal imagery of a nursing mother, breast-feeding them milk, also "reinforces the imagery of family" (Gaventa 1996: 102). Gaventa (1996: 103–4) further notes that in contrast to the many other ancient writers who use the image of milk, "Paul speaks of himself as the one supplying the milk." He does not say, "You are still drinking milk and need to be weaned" (contrast Heb. 5:12–14), but "I must still give you milk." Implying that they still require a diet of babies' milk packs a punch for those who think they have advanced far beyond that stage. But the image of "mother Paul," who knows what nourishment they truly need and nurses them (cf. 1 Thess. 2:7; Gal. 4:19), somewhat softens the blow.[1] This image may not convey Paul's "contemptuous attitude toward the intellectuals at Corinth" as Murphy-O'Connor (1998: 18) believes.

He continues the rebuke by saying he was not able to address them as "spiritual persons" because they were in fact "fleshy." Since he also identifies them as "infants in Christ," he must be making some kind of fine distinction: they "are spiritual, but live as if they did not have the Spirit" (Kuck 1992a: 160). Spiritual persons are those in whom the Spirit has really become a fundamental power of life and who have "the mind of Christ" (2:16). As σάρκινοι (sarkinoi, fleshly), they are controlled by natural, human impulses rather than the Spirit. Paul does not use the term ψυχικός (psychikos) from 2:14, because that describes the natural person completely devoid of the Spirit. As Christians, the Corinthians are not ψυχικός (cf. Fee 1987: 123), but their behavior testifies that they are still too much "of the flesh." The term σάρκινος characterizes them as weak and sinful. The contrast becomes clear in Rom. 7:14, where Paul contrasts the law that is spiritual with the person who is of the flesh and sold into slavery under sin. They have not yet been freed from the normative practices of the world. Their adherence to secular attitudes and values belies their baptismal identity (see Pickett 1997: 63). Many interpreters assume that by calling them "infants," Paul intends to emphasize their need to grow (Engberg-Pedersen 1987: 567–68). It is more likely that it is a rebuke for behaving so childishly and unspiritually (Francis 1980: 43). The problem is not that they have failed to progress but that they have failed to comprehend (Francis 1980: 57). While disagreeing with Thiselton's (2000: 291) interpretation that

---

1. Gaventa (1996) thinks that Paul's stunning application of feminine imagery to himself "compromises his own standing as a 'real man,' anticipating the loss of standing that later emerges as he depicts his ministry as that of a planter of someone else's field, a servant of someone else's building, the 'dregs of all things' (4:13)." It throws worldly standards to the wind.

Paul defends himself here against Corinthian criticism of his oratorical shortcomings, I do agree with his assessment in regard to the term "infants" that "the self-centered competitive naiveté which characterizes young children who have not yet learned to respect the interests of the Other will lead to misjudgments about the quality and required methods of Christian proclamation and teaching." The issue is not the criteria they use to judge the role and style of preachers and teachers; it is their failure to appreciate and incarnate the message of the cross, as is evidenced by their wrangling, personal ambition, and arrogance. By calling them "infants," Paul basically challenges their presumption "We all have knowledge" (8:1).

There is double irony in this reproof. If the Corinthians counted themselves among the "mature" and "spiritual," they would have been stunned to find themselves labeled "infants" by Paul. Their behavior reveals that they are not wise and mature but childish and foolish. But there is further irony when this rebuke is read in light of Matt. 11:25–27 and what Paul has said in 1:18–25. Jesus thanked God for hiding "these things" from "the wise and understanding" and revealing them to "infants." The irony is that those regarded as infants (silly and foolish) by the world are the very ones who comprehend the message of the cross. By fancying themselves as wise and mature, the Corinthians cut themselves off from the transforming power of the cross to change their worldly ways.

The contrast between milk (γάλα, gala) and solid food (βρῶμα, brōma) seems to be a transparent metaphor for rudimentary and advanced teaching (cf. Heb. 5:12–14). The metaphor is found in a variety of ancient sources relating to stages of education and development (cf. Philo, *Husb.* 2 §§8–9; *Dreams* 2 §§10–11; *Sobr.* 2–3 §§9–10; *Migr. Abr.* 6 §29; Conzelmann 1975: 72 n. 26; Gaventa 1996: 104–5), but its meaning is to be governed by how Paul uses it in this context. It should not be taken to imply that Paul presented a two-tiered gospel—milk as "the first missionary instruction which declared the facts of the revelation of salvation" and solid food as "the word of wisdom which disclosed its meaning" (Behm, *TDNT* 1:643; cf. Robertson and Plummer 1914: 52–53; Schlier, *TDNT* 1:645; Wilckens 1959: 52–53). Paul's argument here is not that his initial instruction in the gospel (milk) proclaimed the cross and that the Corinthians' immaturity prevented him from moving to more extensive, advanced instruction. I argue above that the "wisdom" he speaks "among the mature" (2:6) is exactly the same message as the word of the cross he preached when he first came to Corinth. To speak of this as "Paul's reserve in disclosing Christian wisdom" (Barrett 1968: 80) or to claim that he kept this wisdom to himself because "as non-pneumatics they were not able to understand it" (Conzelmann 1975: 71) completely misrepresents his intention. He does not divide

Christians into lower-level beginners who need to be fed a diet of theological pabulum and an upper-level elite who can receive advanced, esoteric doctrine, as if Christianity were like the pagan mysteries. Nor does he offer a two-stage wisdom, leading believers to the next stage of more arcane lessons when he thinks they can handle it.[2] In 15:3–7, he reminds them that he delivered to them as of first importance Christ's death, burial, and resurrection. Is there greater Christian truth beyond this message? Did Paul intend to start them off with the message of the cross and then, after they grasped it, advance to deeper things? Did he think that one advanced beyond the simple message of Christ crucified to speaking in tongues, performing healings, and experiencing heavenly visions and revelations (2 Cor. 12:1–10)? What he says about what he learned from his own exceptional, heavenly visions and the ensuing thorn in the flesh suggests not. What was important was not some supernatural communiqué he overheard in the third heaven but the lesson gleaned from the thorn in the flesh here on earth: God's power is made perfect in weakness; whenever one is weak in Christ, then one is strong (2 Cor. 12:8–10). The experience of the thorn in the flesh deepened his spiritual maturity, enabling him to understand, accept, and live out this basic message of the cross.

In the context, Paul believes that the message of the cross exposes the truth about the listeners. Natural humans, left to their own devices apart from the divine Spirit, do not recognize it as the wisdom of God but instead dismiss it as foolishness. The world cannot stomach the cross, and all who reject it demonstrate that they are not "spiritual ones." Spiritual ones are those who hold on to the wisdom of the cross as God's wisdom that makes void worldly wisdom. Hooker's (1966: 20) surmise gets at the truth: "It is possible . . . that the Corinthians' failure to understand the wisdom spoken in a mystery is not due to the fact that Paul is withholding it from them, but is the result of their own inability to digest what he is offering them." The fact is that "his meat does not differ from his milk" (Hooker 1966: 21). The contrast between the two is probably attributable to some Corinthian distinction, which he echoes. Hooker (1966: 21) comments, "Yet while he uses their language, the fundamental contrast in Paul's mind is not between two quite different diets which he has to offer, but between the true food of the Gospel with which he has fed them (whether milk or meat) and the synthetic substitutes which the Corinthians have preferred." They hankered after the more exquisite charms of clever oratory to tickle their ears, which made the simplicity of the word of the cross seem bland

---

2. Such an approach creates a current problem of soft-selling the gospel to draw in seekers and then giving them the message of the cross only if and when someone thinks he or she can handle it. Not surprisingly, many resist the message of the cross because it is so dissonant with all that they have heard before.

and elementary.[3] If Paul's message looks like milk to them, it discloses that they are not as mature or spiritual as they think. In fact, their discord, caused by selfish ambitions that trample the wisdom of the cross, has proved their immaturity. The divisions are incompatible with following Christ because they emulate the world's wisdom. It betokens their party spirit, not the Holy Spirit. Therefore, "they do not need a change of diet but a change of perspective" (Fee 1987: 292). Just as only "the mature" recognize the foolishness of the gospel to be the highest wisdom, so only the mature recognize this "milk" to be solid food.

To conclude, it is not that Paul cannot or does not give them wisdom in the form of solid food; it is that they do not recognize what he gives them to be wisdom. If there is any distinction between the "mature" and the "infants," it is this: "Both the immature and the perfect are affected by the same revelation, but only the perfect penetrate what happens to them and in them" (Theissen 1987: 352).

Paul describes them as still being σαρκικός (*sarkikos*), which is highly **3:3** ironic in a congregation that touted and prized its spiritual giftedness. Some contend that the adjectives σαρκικός and σάρκινος are essentially synonymous (Conzelmann 1975: 72; Schrage 1991: 281–82; Kuck 1992a: 160; Wolff 1996: 64 n. 228; T. Schreiner 1998: 392; R. Collins 1999: 143–44). Others argue that σάρκινος in 3:1 emphasizes the finitude and physical side of their existence versus the spiritual, while σαρκικός has negative ethical overtones (Fee 1987: 124). The -ινος suffix connotes "made of" (cf. 2 Cor. 3:3), while the -ικος suffix connotes "characterized by" (cf. 9:11). In contrast to the adjectives *psychikos*, which describes the unrenewed person, and *sarkinos* (fleshy), which describes the person motivated by natural drives (fallen human nature), the adjective *sarkikos* (fleshly) is a theological evaluation that describes the person who is centered on the self (Thiselton 2000: 289, 292). It refers to an individual's values, attitudes, and judgments, which manifest themselves in self-centeredness, self-indulgence, and arrogant self-sufficiency.

Paul lists jealousy (ζῆλος, *zēlos*) and strife (ἔρις, *eris*) as companion works of the flesh (Gal. 5:20) and as works of darkness, things that gratify the desires of the flesh (Rom. 13:12–14). Treating the church community as an arena in which to maneuver and advance their personal status reveals that they are controlled by human motives (cf. 15:32) and the purely human order of things (κατὰ ἄνθρωπον περιπατεῖτε; *kata anthrōpon peripateite?* literally, "are you not walking

---

3. Soards (1999: 67) comments, "They could not digest the solid food of the message of the cross because they were looking for a wisdom different from God's revealed wisdom."

according to man?"). They act no differently from the rest of Corinthian society (Winter 2001: 40). He exploits a common theme that factionalism is a "human failing" (M. Mitchell 1993: 82), which then testifies to their spiritual deficiency. A divided spiritual community is, for Paul, untenable.

3:4 Paul finally returns to the problem raised in 1:12. P. Lampe (1990: 118) notes the surprising fact that Paul "allots just eight verses (1:10–17) to the party dispute" and does not return to speak about this turmoil until 3:3. It creates suspense. If they are wise and mature, they will see the relevance of the intervening discussion about the word of the cross. Paul puts down all that is merely human and calls them to be more than that (1:2, 30; 6:10–11; 2 Cor. 5:17) as spiritual ones not lacking in any spiritual gift (1:7). But as it stands, the Corinthian ferment reveals a spirit that is all too human and contrary to the ways of Christ.

Paul and Apollos are not leaders of opposing groups as they might be in the world's value system. Paul pronounces that they are only servants of God who have no significance independent of Christ. The reason he does not mention the Cephas or Christ parties (1:12) in the following example (3:5–9) is not because the Corinthians' misplaced loyalty to himself or Apollos is the root of the squabble, nor is it because he did not want to step on the toes of Cephas (contra P. Lampe 1990: 129 n. 15). The reason should be obvious. Only Paul and Apollos had worked in Corinth, and therefore the extended metaphor of the farm and the farmhands could fittingly apply only to them. In fact, he can use this metaphor precisely because he and Apollos are not at the root of the controversy.[4] He can present himself and Apollos as models of the noncompetitive teamwork he wishes them to copy. In the next segment of his argument he shows that those who live cruciform lives understand themselves to be servants working together for God. They understand their success to be entirely dependent upon God but also know that God will inspect and grade their individual stewardship in the judgment.

3:5–9 In these verses Paul makes the point that both he and Apollos are servants who belong to God, whose different tasks come from God, and whose success depends entirely upon God. Though Apollos apparently was not part of Paul's mission team, and Paul is sensitive about breaching another's sphere of labor (2 Cor. 10:12–16; Rom. 15:18–21), he readily acknowledges that Apollos carried forward the work he began

---

4. It is not "a volatile situation" in which open criticism of Apollos could antagonize his supporters, as Ker (2000: 84) contends. It reads too much into what Paul says to conjecture that some in Corinth question the effectiveness of Paul's ministry in comparison to Apollos's work.

in Corinth.[5] He understands their ministries to be complementary under God. They, like all ministers, are to be regarded as equals, though performing different tasks. Kuck (1992a: 164) notes that in four parallel statements Paul places the emphasis on God and the servants' dependence on God:

3.5	Apollos and Paul are servants.	God assigned them the task.
3.6	Paul planted, Apollos watered.	God was giving the growth.
3.7	The planter and the irrigator are nothing.	But God who gives the growth [is everything].
3.8	The planter and irrigator are equal.	[God] will give them their individual reward for their toil.

The conclusion in 3:9 puts "God's" (θεοῦ, *theou*) in the emphatic position to underscore the point. It reads literally, "God's we are co-workers; God's cultivation, God's construction you are."

Paul debunks any misplaced veneration of ministers by deflating the respective roles he and Apollos played in the founding and development of the church at Corinth. They are mere servants (διάκονοι, *diakonoi*) carrying out the varied duties allotted them by their master (cf. 1 Cor. 9:16). They were not called to be party chiefs, because servants cannot become heads "without a breach of trust" (Edwards 1885: 73). The servant image does not stake any claim to authority as God's agents (contra Ker 2000: 85) but lowers their status (D. Martin 1995: 102; Clark 2000: 216–17) in a way that accords with Jesus' view of the disciples' leadership roles (Mark 9:35; 10:42–45; John 13:12–17). Servants who fulfill their assigned duties do not put their masters in their debt but rather are given fresh tasks to carry out (Luke 17:7–10).

Paul lowers their status (τί . . . ἐστιν, *ti estin,* what is) even further by picturing himself and Apollos as humble field hands (the plowboy and the water boy) engaged in manual labor and allows the readers to draw the inference themselves about the status of other ministers whom the Corinthians may have glamorized (Godet 1886: 174–75). The metaphor may have been offensive to them by inverting cultural codes and values attached to their notions about leaders and their stature.

The image of planter and waterer makes several points.[6] First, the labor of one without the other would be useless (Godet 1886: 176); they

---

5. See Murphy-O'Connor (1996: 274–76) for an attempt to reconstruct the activity of Apollos in Corinth.

6. Saying that Apollos "watered" need not be an allusion to his baptizing more Corinthians (cf. 1:14–17). Paul only wants to point to their differing responsibilities.

are interdependent and complementary, contributing "to the same goal" of producing a crop (Kuck 1992a: 166).

Second, though both roles are essential to the task, the laborers are interchangeable. They are "one" (ἕν, *hen*, 3:8), which means either that they are engaged in one total task or that they are to be regarded as one. The value of the labor of one worker cannot be hailed as more important than that of another. What is important is that God is able to make use of their labor. Neither can expect special recognition or allegiance from others.

Third, a rivalry between a planter and a waterer in working a field is absurd. The field is not a battlefield where workers vie with one another for supremacy. It is a farmstead to be brought under cultivation so as to produce fruit (Matt. 21:43). If the farmhands do not work cooperatively, the crop will be ruined.

Fourth, God is the life force who produces the harvest. Planters only scatter the seed supplied to them by God (2 Cor. 9:10) and put it in contact with the soil created by God. Waterers only keep the soil moist for growth by using rainwater supplied by God. Paul uses the aorist tense to sum up the work of the planter and the waterer, but he uses the imperfect (ηὔξανεν, *ēuxanen*) to imply that God is giving growth throughout the planting and watering (Robertson and Plummer 1914: 57; Lindemann 2000: 81). The point is that success does not depend on those who preach, but on God. Against the Corinthians' boasting in their own consequence, Paul argues that every worker is equally insignificant before God. Against their touting one person over another, he argues that every worker is equally indispensable. Against their self-satisfied complacency, Paul argues that each worker will be held accountable to God.

Beyond the grace implicit in workers being given tasks in God's field, Paul affirms that each laborer will receive a separate wage or reward for his or her backbreaking toil.[7] Laborers will be rewarded not according to their success but according to their work (Morris 1958: 66).[8] The idea of rendering to each according to each one's work runs throughout the NT (Matt. 16:27; Rom. 2:6; 2 Cor. 11:15; 2 Tim. 4:14; 1 Pet. 1:17; Rev. 2:23; 20:12–13; 22:12; cf. 1 Enoch 100:7; 2 Enoch 44:5; Pseudo-Philo, *Bib. Ant.* 3:10). Paul will explain more precisely what he means in 3:12–17, certifying that the reward awaits God's final judgment and

---

7. Kuck (1992a: 168–69) notes that κόπος (*kopos*) is a favorite Pauline word "to describe the effort and hardship which the Christian mission necessitates" (cf. 15:10; 16:16), but it is also "an appropriate term in connection with the agricultural metaphor" (Yinger 1999: 214).

8. This idea is prominent in later rabbinic parables (cf. *Sipra* on Lev. 26:9; *Deut. Rab.* 6.7; *Eccles. Rab.* 5.11.5–12; *Midrash Psalms* 26; 37). It contrasts with the scandalous point in Jesus' parable of the vineyard workers (Matt. 20:1–15) that all work earns the same pay.

introducing the possibility of punishment. His intention here is to make clear that the one who hires the laborers, God, determines and distributes the rewards, and not the field, the Corinthians (Yinger 1999: 215).

Paul concludes, "We are God's co-workers." Is he thinking of the relationship between the servants or the relationship between the servants and God? Furnish (1961: 365–67) shows that lexical and grammatical considerations are not decisive, though Paul characteristically uses the noun "to describe the co-operative effort of Christian brethren in the service of the gospel." Many contend that he means they are co-workers together with God.[9] In 9:23, he portrays himself as a partner with the gospel in the common enterprise of winning others. Ker (2000: 87) claims that Paul wishes to stress the "God-given authenticity" of the work.

In the context, it is much more likely that Paul means that they are fellow workers belonging to God.[10] Servants (3:5) are not co-workers with the master. He is not intent on arguing that they are independent partners with God but on showing the unity of their work together, though their functions may differ. He also stresses that workers share an equality of nothingness before God. Each is but a servant of the common gospel, and each stands individually responsible before God (Furnish 1961: 369). The two other occurrences of the emphatic genitive "God's" in this verse convey the idea of possession. Paul's point is that he and Apollos work under God as jointly commissioned by God.

The Corinthians are God's field, but the word γεώργιον (geōrgion) suggests a field under cultivation rather than simply arable land (Godet 1886: 178). The image of the people of God as God's planting has many biblical echoes (Exod. 15:17; Num. 24:5–6; Isa. 5:1–2, 7; 61:3; Jer. 2:21; Amos 9:15). "Building" (οἰκοδομή, oikodomē) was a term widely used for the process of construction on a building site (Judge 1984: 23), and Paul also uses the image of building up the church in 14:3, 5, 12, 26. Both images are passive (Ker 2000: 87): "Whereas the Corinthians might imagine that they are in the position to discriminate between the leaders of their community, Paul implies, for the purpose of this discussion, that they are, in sharp contrast to their leaders, nothing other than the objects of God's work." The images of planting, watering, producing steady growth (3:6), and laying the foundation and building up (3:10) contrast with ideas of instantaneous puffing up (4:19). The images convey that the Corinthians are still a work in progress.

9. So Edwards 1885: 75; Godet 1886: 177; Lightfoot 1895: 188; Weiss 1910: 77–78; Robertson and Plummer 1914: 58–59; Lietzmann 1949: 15; Ker 2000: 87.

10. So Findlay 1910: 789; Héring 1962: 23; Furnish 1961; Barrett 1968: 86; Fee 1987: 133–34; Wolff 1996: 68; Hays 1997: 53; Soards 1999: 71; Thiselton 2000: 306.

Paul shifts the image to that of a building in which God now becomes the one who lets out a contract for a construction project and serves as the building inspector. God inspects to see that it was built correctly, according to specifications, and without fraud and will disburse due rewards and fines. In this image, Paul shifts roles from a farmhand to the head contractor. This second example allows him to introduce another consideration about leaders. The competence of each servant in carrying out the tasks may vary, and God will reward and punish the difference in quality.[11] That appraisal awaits God's final judgment since God alone can properly assess the work. The ultimate evaluations of leaders belong to God, not to those they lead.

3:10–11   As Paul develops the image of the community as God's building, the role of Apollos drops out of the picture. Paul may seem to jumble his images, likening the church first to a field and then a building, but the two images are found together in Jer. 1:10; 18:9; 24:6 (cf. Sir. 49:7; Philo, *Alleg. Interp.* 1.15 §48; Odes Sol. 38:16–22). The building imagery would be quite familiar to any urban dweller, and Paul beckons them to see themselves as a diverse group (some freeborn, some freedmen, some slaves) coming together with many different skills (some highly specialized—masons, carpenters, engravers—others unskilled labor) to construct an edifice.[12] Paul identifies himself as the skilled master-builder (σοφὸς ἀρχιτέκτων, *sophos architektōn*) whose skill and commission both come by the grace of God (cf. 1:4).[13] Though the adjective σοφός means "skilled" in this context, it also relates to the dispute with the "wise in this age" (3:18–20) and his assertion that he speaks "wisdom not of this age" (2:6–16). Shanor (1988: 465) notes that the term appears in temple inscriptions to refer to the supervisor of the day-to-day work of subcontractors. One ancient contract (*IG* VII.3073), which may be regarded as typical, outlines the responsibilities of the contractor: He shall work continually, hire enough skilled craftsmen, and is warned, along with any who take part in the work, against dealing fraudulently. He is also warned about damage to the existing temple or damage to materials and is required to repair anything that is destroyed. Payments and fines are clearly spelled out, and the work must be demonstrated to be worthy.

As the founder of the church (4:15), implied in the idea of the one who planted (3:6), Paul asserts that he "laid a foundation" (cf. Isa.

---

11. Branick's (1982: 263) conjecture that it is a foreign body composed independently from the context fails to appreciate this point.

12. Lanci (1997: 61) finds this picture in Tacitus, *Historiae* 4.53; Plutarch, *Pericles* 12; and Josephus, *Ant.* 8.2.9–3.9 §§58–98. M. Mitchell (1993: 99–105) shows that the image of a building was a common metaphor in the ancient world for political stability and concord.

13. The phrase appears in Isa. 3:3 LXX in a list of skills.

28:16). Though the image of laying a foundation was used for introductory teaching (Philo, *Dreams* 2.2 §8), he would not classify his work among them as simply providing them with the "the rudiments of doctrine" (Conzelmann 1975: 75). The foundation is the gospel, and its footings are anchored firmly in the message of Christ crucified (1:23; 2:2), which can hardly be classified as "rudimentary" or "preparatory." What is crucial for laying the foundation is not the preacher, since there are other apostles, but the one who is preached (Schrage 1991: 298).

That foundational work is completed, and another builds upon it (cf. Rom. 15:20). Paul does not complain about this development, because he expects others to "build up" the church, to add, as it were, flooring, walls, and a roof. A foundation alone without any further construction is pointless (Schrage 1991: 297). He uses indefinite terms throughout this section to describe these other builders (ἄλλος, *allos*, another, 3:10, 11; ἕκαστος, *hekastos*, each one, 3:10, 13; τις, *tis*, anyone, 3:12, 14, 15) and perhaps is "intentionally vague" to allow them to apply what he says to any teacher or leader, since they have "countless guides" (4:15; Kuck 1992a: 172). The present tense of the verb is problematic for those who think he refers to Apollos, since Apollos currently is not present in Corinth (Fee 1987: 138). Ker's (2000: 89) argument that it is a vivid present because Apollos will return (16:12) seems to be special pleading. Paul is not aiming his remarks toward Apollos or any other apostle or their presumed supporters.

"To build upon" refers to preaching and instruction (2 Cor. 10:8; 12:19; 13:10; cf. Eph. 2:19–22), but that task need not be limited to "apostles, prophets, evangelists, pastors and teachers," since they are given "to equip the saints for the work of ministry, for building up the body of Christ" (Eph. 4:11–12; cf. 4:16, 29). Each member has an assignment in this building project (Kuck 1992a: 174), which is confirmed by Paul's concluding exhortation in 15:58 that they "always excel in the work of the Lord." The warning "Let each one take heed how he is building upon it" (3:10; cf. 10:12) expresses the main point of this unit. They can only add what the foundation will bear and "must not exceed the limits, or introduce confusions which would change the character of the building, so as to threaten its eventual collapse" (Derrett 1997: 133). They must use fit materials and follow the plans of the architect (who is God, not Paul) and the building code.

Paul's insistence that there is no foundation other than Christ is not a polemical statement but a general principle. He does not hint that false teachers proclaim another Jesus (2 Cor. 11:4), since they build on the one foundation already firmly in place and not some rival one (Kuck 1992a: 175; Lindemann 2000: 84). He does not allude to any claims by the so-called Cephas supporters that Peter was the rock on which the church is built (Matt. 16:16–18; contra Manson 1962: 194; Barrett 1968: 87–88; Bruce 1971: 43). Kuck (1992a: 172) is correct that Paul is not intent on rooting out some false teaching or different gospel that is not centered on Christ, because he "speaks only of those who build upon the one foundation, not those who lay a different foundation" (cf. Munck 1959a: 141–42). The warning is sweeping and applies to anyone who might build carelessly.

3:12   What is the point of comparison that Paul wishes the reader to catch from the list of building materials? Several suggestions have been offered. (1) The underlying issue may be, What will survive fire? (Schrage 1991: 301; Hollander 1994: 93; Lindemann 2000: 84–85). The first three, "gold, silver, precious stones" (most likely a reference to jewels; cf. 2 Chron. 3:6; Isa. 54:11–12; Rev. 21:18–21; or possibly marble, cf. 1 Chron. 29:2), are inflammable; the second three, "wood, hay, straw," are highly flammable.[14] (2) Weiss (1910: 80) contends that the point of comparison is the different worth and ruggedness of materials, and he divides them into three groups of two: gold and silver denoting costliness and opulence; precious stones and timber less so; and hay and straw much less so (cf. Isa 40:6–8). (3) Others contend that the instructions for building the tabernacle lie in the background and influence what is listed. According to Exod. 31:1–5, God tells Moses that Bezalel has been called to build the tabernacle: "I have filled him with divine spirit, with ability, intelligence, and knowledge in every kind of craft, to devise artistic designs, to work in gold, silver, and bronze, in cutting stones for setting, and in carving wood, in every kind of craft" (cf. Exod. 35:30–36:1). Some of the materials (gold, silver, precious stones, and wood) are mentioned for the building of Solomon's temple (1 Chron. 22:14, 16; 29:2; 2 Chron. 3:6; Hag. 2:8; so Fee 1987: 140–41), which may anticipate Paul's next image of the church as God's temple (3:16–17). This backdrop, however, would not have been obvious to readers, and the inclusion of hay and straw would seem anomalous. (4) Kuck (1992a: 177–78) thinks that Paul has no particular building in mind, because the construction materials are not realistic or consistent and because the emphasis falls on the wide variety of materials the builders use to build on the foundation. The materials represent the quality going into the construction of the building. Some are excellent builders, using materials of exceptional quality; others are less so, using materials of inferior quality. Some materials will en-

---

14. One should not treat the materials as an allegory and interpret them point for point as sound doctrine, good morals, different kinds of hearers, etc. (cf. Findlay 1910: 791).

dure; others will not (Lindemann 2000: 85).[15] This last option best represents Paul's intention. What makes for imperishable building materials for building the church? The wise master-builder laid a solid foundation, and his message of Christ crucified is the standard by which to evaluate all other builders and their materials (Yinger 1999: 216–17). Those attempting to build with human wisdom construct a flimsy house of straw.

Paul takes advantage of the Corinthians' aspirations for reward, status, and praise by reorienting their attention to the future judgment of God, who knows all things (Rom. 2:16) and judges according to divine, not human, standards. He asserts that each individual will have his or her work (not "works," 3:13, 14, 15) assayed in a divine firestorm. In 9:1, he specifically refers to the Corinthians as his "work in the Lord." Whether one's work will endure awaits more than the test of time; it awaits the test of the end time. Each one's workmanship will become "manifest" (φανερὸν γενήσεται, *phaneron genēsetai*), for "the day . . . will make it known" (δηλώσει, *dēlōsei*) as good or bad.[16] "The day" refers to the end-time judgment (cf. Rom. 13:12; 1 Cor. 1:8; 5:5; 2 Cor. 1:14; Phil. 1:6, 10; 2:16; 1 Thess. 5:2, 4; 2 Thess. 2:2).[17] The phrase ὅτι ἐν πυρὶ ἀποκαλύπτεται (*hoti en pyri apokalyptetai*) is ambiguous. The subject of the verb could be "the work," the verb a present passive, and the prepositional phrase ἐν πυρί instrumental, so that Paul says, "it [the work] is revealed by fire." But the subject of the verb is more likely to be "the day" because it stands in closer proximity to the verb. Since "each one's work" is repeated as the subject of the verb in the next clause, it signals that the subject has changed from the previous clause. Also, if "work" were the subject, Paul essentially would be repeating himself. The verb can be read as a present middle with a reflexive sense, which yields this translation: "the day reveals itself in fire" (Fee 1987: 142; Kistemaker 1993: 112–13). This matches the picture of the "revelation of the Lord Jesus from heaven [coming] with his mighty angels in flaming fire, and unleashing vengeance on those who do not know God and on those who do not obey the gospel of our Lord Jesus" (2 Thess. 1:7–8). According to 2 Pet. 3:12, the coming day of God will set ablaze and dissolve the heavens, and the elements will melt with fire. This idea of a fiery

15. Cicero (*Ep. ad Atticum* 14.9) expresses concern about the slipshod construction of his rental property: "Two of my buildings have fallen down, and the rest have large cracks. Not only the tenants, but even the mice have moved out!" (cf. Juvenal, *Sat.* 3.193–202, who complains about a collapsing structure and the danger of fire).

16. Paul describes the man living with his father's wife as doing a "work" (1 Cor. 5:2).

17. Kuck (1992a: 38–149, 229–34) shows that Paul brought together Jewish traditions of postmortem judgment with familiar Greco-Roman traditions in which individuals receive just recompense for their behavior in order to exhort his readers to live up to certain expectations within the group—in this case, the unity of the church.

theophany also appears in Isa. 66:15 ("For the Lord will come in fire, . . . and his rebuke in flames of fire"; cf. Dan. 7:9–10; Mal. 3:1–3; 4:1 [3:19 MT]).[18] This fiery day will "test" (δοκιμάσει, *dokimasei*) each one's work.

The supreme test for a building in a Hellenistic city was fire; the same is true for ministry, except that the fire is a divine fire of eschatological judgment. Its purpose in this context is not to punish (Jude 7; Rev. 18:8; 19:20; 21:8; and many texts in the OT), or to destroy (Matt. 3:10; 13:40, 42, 50; Heb. 10:27), or to refine (Zech. 13:9; 1 Pet. 1:7), but to disclose the quality of the work of Christians (Hollander 1994: 103; Lanci 1997: 67). What is consumed is the building, not the workers as evildoers (see additional note). Paul adapts the traditional motif of testing persons by fire in the final judgment by introducing the various building materials. The fiery test exposes what has lasting value. He then combines this image with the motif of being repaid by God at the final judgment according to one's deeds (Hollander 1994: 103; Kuck 1992a: 181).[19]

Each individual bears responsibility for his or her contribution to the building and will receive a reward or a loss on the basis of the quality of the workmanship (Kuck 1992b: 178). If the building goes up in smoke, the builders discover they have labored in vain (which is Paul's own greatest fear; cf. 15:58; Gal. 2:2; 4:11; Phil. 2:16; 1 Thess. 3:5).[20] If the building stands, the builders will be rewarded for faithful service. The phrase "to receive a reward" means to receive wages for work done (Lanci 1997: 65). Paul is not referring to salvation, as if it were a reward proportional to the work (Spicq, *TLNT* 512). The loss suffered is not the loss of salvation but the loss of a reward (Stumpff, *TDNT* 2:890; cf. 2 John 8), which, in the context, is simply defined as "praise from God" (4:5). Brilliant work does not earn salvation; lackluster work does not lose it. Hollander (1994: 103) articulates Paul's intention:

> Since Paul does not speak of righteous men over against sinners but of two types of builders, both types being Christians, the reward seems to be something additional to salvation and the fine does not imply eternal punishment. Even the unskilled church-builder will be saved. However, he will be saved "as through fire."[21]

Given the world of building contracts that form the backdrop of this image, Paul alludes to a fine for incompetent work. The imprudent worker

---

18. The judgment day is associated with fire in Matt. 3:10; Jub. 9:15; Sib. Or. 2:252–55; 3:72–74; Pseudo-Philo, *Bib. Ant.* 6:16–18; 38:3–4; Vision of Ezra 3–10; T. Isaac 5:21–25.

19. This text does not apply to purgatory (cf. Spicq, *DBSup* 9:560–61; Le Goff 1984).

20. Paul does not broach the issue of those who may be lost forever because of a Christian's careless work.

21. Yinger (1999: 204–36) argues that in 3:5–4:5 Paul's belief in recompense according to deeds is evident and that their salvation is very much endangered by their deeds.

will suffer the humiliation of having the work burned to the ground and with it the prospect of receiving any reward.

The idea of receiving special recognition or reward from God in the judgment (cf. 2 Cor. 5:10) should be read in light of Paul's comments in 1 Thess. 2:19–20. He names the Thessalonians as his hope, joy, and crown of boasting, and his glory and joy (cf. Phil. 2:16; 4:1). His hope is fixed on the return of the Lord, when his work will be appraised, which should produce joy. The "crown" that Paul looks forward to receiving is the blamelessness of the Thessalonian Christians in Christ at his parousia. Paul has a corporate understanding of salvation. He is not interested in insuring his own personal victory and his private entrance into "the pearly gates." It would be a hollow victory if he were the only one there. He links his reward at the judgment to their fidelity to the gospel. His reward will be that his churches will be saved with him. This idea lies behind his comments in 2 Cor. 1:12–14. On the day of the Lord Jesus, when they pass through the judgment together, they will know that his work with them has been accomplished with frankness and godly sincerity, by the grace of God, and that "we are your boast even as you are our boast."[22]

The one whose work is incinerated by the blaze "will be saved [σωθήσεται, sōthēsetai] through fire" (not "by fire")—a colorful picture of a narrow escape (Donfried 1976: 105), reminiscent of Lot escaping Sodom (Gen. 19; cf. 1 Pet. 3:20, in the days of Noah eight persons "were saved through water"). The laborer who used cheap materials and took shortcuts will be pulled out of the flames and the rubble heap in the nick of time (Barrett 1968: 89; Donfried 1976: 106), like a brand snatched from the fire (Amos 4:11; Zech. 3:2). But inept builders are not just pulled from the ashes; "being saved" points to their eternal salvation (1:18, 21; 5:5; 7:16; 9:22; 10:33; 15:2). Even failures will be included in salvation, but they will enter salvation "smelling of smoke," their labor gone up in flames (Fisk 2000: 20). This vivid picture expresses the basic thrust of Paul's warning. It is not that the Corinthians should not judge the work of their leaders before the time but wait for this fiery test and the verdict of a higher court. The main point is found in the explicit command "Take heed how each one of you is building upon the foundation" (3:10).

Paul switches to direct address and a third metaphor that now depicts the church as God's temple. His question "Do you not know that you are the temple of God?" asserts indirectly that they are indeed the tem- **3:16–17**

---

22. In Phil. 1:9–11, Paul prays that on the day of Christ they will be "filled with the fruit of righteousness that comes through Christ Jesus for the glory and praise of God." A surprising reading preserved in $\mathfrak{P}^{46}$ has "and praise to me." This reading accords with the idea of reward expressed here and might be original though it seems anticlimactic and self-serving.

ple of God. The "you" is plural, and Paul speaks of the community gathered in Christ's name—not individuals—as the dwelling of the Holy Spirit. This is one of ten such rhetorical questions in the letter (5:6; 6:2, 3, 9, 15, 16, 19; 9:13, 24), and when it is compared with the way he phrases similar questions to the Thessalonians, "for even as you yourselves know . . ." (1 Thess. 2:1, 5; 3:3, 4; 4:2; 5:2; noted by Fee 1987: 146), it has an accusatory tone. The question introduces a further argument on the preceding subject and can be part of a warning (Yinger 1999: 223; cf. 6:7–9, 15–16).

It is a startling declaration to identify the community in Corinth gathered in their cramped, diminutive house churches as the temple of God. Compared to the grand temples in Corinth and the magnificent temple in Jerusalem, they appear rather ramshackle. But the image of them as God's temple harks back to the foolishness of God and the theme of unity. Paul is not trying to make the case that they are the new spiritualized temple of the last days, replacing the Jerusalem temple (contra Gärtner 1965: 57–58; Héring 1962: 24; Conzelmann 1975: 77). Lanci (1997: 5) shows that both Jews and Gentiles would have understood a temple under construction by diverse persons with diverse talents to be a metaphor for unity. Lanci (1997: 5–6) writes, "For all sorts of people throughout the Mediterranean, some temples functioned as potent images of unity, and an advertisement (to potential adherents) of the deity's influence." Paul cites the Spirit as the epistemological key for understanding the wisdom of the cross in 2:10–16 and now credits the indwelling Spirit as the key to their unity (see Kuck 1992a: 186–87).

Since this community building is the temple of God, where the Spirit of God dwells, Paul introduces a new, more serious threat. While some builders may do a lousy job of building on the foundation and their work will be consumed, some work moves beyond mere shoddiness and becomes destructive. Paul assumes that the community can be destroyed by insiders, not by outsiders. Shanor (1988: 470–71) suggests that Paul does not refer to absolute demolition (διαφθείρειν, *diaphtheirein*, cf. 2 Cor. 4:16), but to some kind of damage, since the word φθείρειν (*phtheirein*) appears in building contracts to refer to damage that might inadvertently occur during construction (so also N. Watson 1992: 34; Lanci 1997: 67–68; citing Burford 1969: 94, 100). Others assume that Paul can only mean "damage," because they understand God's temple to be inherently indestructible. This interpretation fails to appreciate Paul's use of metaphor as he applies it to this local community (see Barrett 1968: 91). It is a severe warning.[23] He has real destruction in mind (Harder, *TDNT* 9:102), and those who destroy God's temple will also be

---

23. Jeremiah's temple sermon (Jer. 7:1–5; 26:1–6) should gainsay any view that God's temple might be indestructible.

destroyed.[24] There is no narrow escape from this sin. Yinger (1999: 220) points out, "The dividing line between poor building and destruction is not clearly marked out, making Paul's initial warning to 'beware how you are building' all the more potent."

Paul does not describe how the temple is destroyed, but it undoubtedly relates in some way to their boastful arrogance, their eagerness to appraise others, and their competitive partisanship—all the things that divide Christ. M. Mitchell (1993: 103) cites the well-known political axiom that "factionalism destroys any political body." Cicero (*De amicitia* 7.23), for example, maintains that no house is so strong, no state so enduring, that it cannot be fundamentally overthrown by animosities and divisions. Paul allows the readers to imagine that their petty jealousies (3:3), boasting (1:29; 3:21; 4:7), arrogance (4:6, 18, 19), and quarrels (1:11; 3:3) might qualify for this bleak judgment. The survival of the church and their salvation is at risk.

Additional Note

3:15. A parallel to Paul's picture of the fiery test appears in T. Abr. 13:11–14 with striking verbal similarities. The archangel Purouel

> tests the work of men through fire. And if the fire burns up the work of anyone, immediately the angel of judgment takes him and carries him away to the place of sinners, a most bitter place of punishment. But if the fire tests the work of anyone and does not touch it, this person is justified and the angel of righteousness takes him and carries him up to be saved in the lot of the righteous. And thus, most righteous Abraham, all things in all people are tested by fire and balance.

The tradition is too late for Paul to depend on it (contra Fishburne 1970–71), and it seems to have been influenced by Christian scribes echoing NT language (E. Sanders, *OTP* 1:878–79; Kuck 1992a: 91). The differences, however, help to highlight Paul's emphasis (Hollander 1994: 99). The scene in the Testament of Abraham depicts the judgment of all creation by Abel; Paul does not refer to the judgment of the righteous over against sinners, but to good and bad builders of the church. In the Testament of Abraham, individuals' works are judged by a balance scale and by fire. If their works weigh enough to balance the "righteousness of God" and if the fire does not touch it, they are saved. By contrast, the reward for Paul is not salvation but something additional to salvation. The loss is not eternal punishment but the loss of this additional reward. In Paul's picture, even the slapdash church-builder will be saved.

---

24. In 2 Cor. 7:2; 11:3, Paul asserts that he has destroyed no one and hints that others have.

III. Factions and Dissension in the Church (1:10–4:21)
    F. Evaluating the Work of God's Servants (3:1–17)
➤ G. How to Regard Oneself; How to Regard Others (3:18–4:5)
    H. The Apostles as Models of the Wisdom of the Cross (4:6–13)

G. How to Regard Oneself; How to Regard Others (3:18–4:5)

Both 3:18–23 and 4:1–5 belong together as a double recapitulation of previous themes, though separated by an unfortunate chapter division (Robertson and Plummer 1914: 68–69). Each begins with a third person singular command: "Let no one be self-deceived" (3:18); "Let each one regard us in this way" (4:1). The first segment (3:18–23) concerns how to regard oneself. It is a "climactic recapitulation" rehearsing the themes from the first major rhetorical unit (1:18–2:16), where Paul connected wisdom and foolishness themes to factions and boasting in leaders (Kuck 1992a: 188). The central motif that the world's wisdom is folly (1:17, 18, 21, 23; 2:1–2) is recalled in 3:18–19. In 3:19–20, the citations from Job 5:12–13 and Ps. 93:11 LXX reiterate the theme that the pretensions of human wisdom stand under God's judgment (1:20, 25, 27, 28). In 3:21–23, he harks back to the factions by recalling the names in 1:12 and 3:4.

The second segment (4:1–5) concerns how to regard God's servants. It rehearses the argument in 2:6–3:17 and reinforces the conclusion that human evaluation is myopic and inherently faulty (2:6–16). Paul applies this specifically to the evaluation of God's servants (3:5–17). He is not defending his role in the community (contra Stowers 1990: 258), but is setting himself up as an example to imitate (4:6, 16). Paul is a servant of God (3:5; 4:1), and so only God can truly evaluate him and all individuals who choose to live out the foolish wisdom of the cross, because only God can fully discern their hearts. No human verdict has any sway with God. That judgment awaits the appointed time, the day of the Lord, when stewards and others will be placed under divine scrutiny to see how they have been faithful in their entrusted task.

Exegesis and Exposition

[18]Let no one be self-deceived. If anyone among you presumes to be wise in this age, let that one become a fool in order to become wise. [19]For the wisdom of this world is foolishness with God. For it stands written, "He catches the wise in their cunning." [20]And again, "The Lord knows the thoughts of the wise, that they are futile." [21]So then, let no one boast in humans. For all things are yours, [22]whether Paul or Apollos or Cephas or the world or life or death or things that

are or things about to be—all things are yours. ²³But you are Christ's, and Christ is God's.

⁴:¹Let a person regard us in this way, as servants of Christ and stewards of God's mysteries. ²Furthermore, it is sought in stewards that they should be found trustworthy. ³Indeed, with me it is a trifling thing that I should be examined by you or on a day appointed by a human court. But I do not even examine myself. ⁴For I am conscious of nothing against myself, but I am not acquitted by this. The one who examines me is the Lord. ⁵So, do not pronounce judgment on anything before the appointed time, until the Lord comes, who also will shed light on the things hidden in darkness and will reveal the purposes of the hearts [of each person]. And then will come to each one the praise from God.

Paul returns to the theme of the wise and the foolish (1:18–25, 26–27; **3:18–21a** 2:14). To be wise, one must be willing to become a fool in the eyes of the world. In his warnings, he continues to address the individual (as in 3:10, 17) instead of the body as a whole.[1] Each person must guard against falling victim to self-deception. The danger is "among you" (ἐν ὑμῖν, *en hymin*) and does not come from outsiders who might deceive them (Eph. 5:6). Presumably, he has in mind those who consider themselves to be "wise" teachers and those who align themselves with these teachers and thereby assume that they, too, are wise. The self-deceived think that they build with gold, when in fact they build with stubble, or that they can get away with destroying God's temple. They may hoodwink themselves and others by posturing as wise according to the faulty standards of this age, but they will not fool God, who sees them as they really are. Paul uses the "if anyone presumes" (εἴ τις δοκεῖ, *ei tis dokei*) clause elsewhere in the letter (8:2; 11:16; 14:37; cf. 10:12; James 1:26) as a gentle reproof. Those who are wise in their own eyes have not yet come to terms with the fact that they still have to reckon with God, who makes human wisdom look foolish. Paul assumes that human judgments are inherently skewed until they are set aright by God's Spirit. Consequently, humans must empty themselves of their own wisdom to be filled with God's wisdom (Calvin 1960: 80).

To make this point, Paul cites two passages from Scripture. The first, from Job 5:13 (see additional note), pictures a hunter stalking prey and capturing it. God catches the crafty with their own craftiness (πανουργία, *panourgia*), a term Paul uses negatively elsewhere (2 Cor. 4:2; 11:3; Eph. 4:14). They are too clever for their own eternal good and always get trapped in their own schemes and ambitions. Ironically, this quotation proves its point, since it comes from Eliphaz, whose "wise" counsel is ultimately discredited. The second quotation, from Psalm

---

1. To be gender neutral, some translations change the third person imperative to a second person plural. This rendering is misleading, and Thiselton (2000: 321) avoids the problem by translating it, "Let no one be self-deceived."

94:11 (93:11 LXX), asserts that the Lord knows our thoughts and that they are futile. Paul adds to the quotation the thoughts "of the wise" (cf. Ps. 94:8). Although God's wisdom is hidden to humans except through revelation (2:16), human thoughts are not hidden to God. Fee (1987: 152) makes the important observation that these verses form a counterpoint to 1:18–25, where Paul declares that what God does looks foolish to the world. Here the tables are turned, and what the clever think and do looks foolish to God. The command "Let no one boast in humans" (3:21a) resonates with the companion motifs that no one is to boast in the presence of God (1:29) and that one can legitimately boast only in the Lord (1:31; cf. Gal. 6:14). Boasting in leaders not only divides and destroys community, but also glorifies oneself before God—a foolhardy thing to do.

3:21b–23 The statement "For all things are yours" mirrors a commonplace in Stoic thinking that was applicable to a variety of situations (R. Collins 1999: 166; Lindemann 2000: 93).[2] The philosophers appealed to it to affirm human self-sufficiency and mastery over all circumstances. Paul uses it to affirm the Christian's complete dependency on God (Soards 1999: 84). Paul put down the Corinthians' pretensions and factions in 1:12 by turning their childish boasts into a burlesque: "I belong to so and so." He now turns that boast upside down by citing the three leading apostolic figures from 1:12—Paul, Apollos, Cephas—and asserting that these renowned servants of God belong to them, not vice versa. Robertson and Plummer (1914: 72) aptly comment, "The church is not the property of the Apostles. Apostles are ministers of the church." The Corinthians were claiming too little, since "all things are yours." They possess all things, however, only because they belong to Christ. Their relationship to apostles and teachers comes under the scope of the lordship of Christ, just as their possession of the world does (Byrne 1987: 85). Christians do not belong to those who passed on and interpreted the foundations of the faith, or to those who founded their community, or to those who baptized them. None of these persons was crucified for them, and they were not baptized in their name (1:13). Consequently, they should not say, "I belong to Paul," but, "Paul belongs to me." That puts teachers in their proper role as servants (4:1). He expands the list beyond ministers, however. They do not belong to life, as if this life were all there is; nor do they belong to death, as if death brought an end to the Christian's life in Christ. Christians are not in bondage to the things that are, or to the things to come (cf. Rom. 8:38). In setting up a chain, he argues that all things belong to them because they belong to Christ and because Christ belongs to God, who is sovereign over all

---

2. Cf. Diogenes Laertius, *Lives* 6.37; cf. 6.72; 7.125; Seneca, *Ep. morales* 109.1; *De beneficiis* 7.2.4–5; 7.3.2–3; 7.4.1; 7.8.1; 7.10.6; 8.3.3; Cicero, *De finibus* 3.22.75; 4.27.74.

things. As Thiselton (2000: 327) explains it, "The Christian shares in the Lordship of Christ whereby creation and the church are restored into cooperative agencies for the well-being of humankind and for the glory of God-in-Christ, set within the providential dimension of the new order in Christ."

By saying that Christ is God's, Paul has no interest in providing fodder for a subordinationist Christology. Byrne (1987: 85) connects "belonging to Christ" with "living for the Lord" (Rom. 14:8; 2 Cor. 5:15) and takes Christ's belonging to God to mean that he "lives to God" (cf. Rom. 6:10), that is, "his whole existence is marked by obedience and directed to the glory of God."[3]

The "thus" (οὕτως, *houtōs*) refers back to 3:21–23 and 3:5–9, which mention servants (διάκονοι, *diakonoi*) and co-workers (συνεργοί, *synergoi*) corresponding to servants (ὑπηρέται, *hypēretai*) and stewards (οἰκονόμοι, *oikonomoi*). It does not refer forward to the following ὡς (*hōs*, as; contra Godet 1886: 204; Robertson and Plummer 1914: 74): "*This* is how people ought to regard us" (Fee 1987: 158–59). The plural "us" is carried over from 3:22 (Fee 1987: 159). Paul does not characterize only his ministry, but that of all Christian ministers. All belong to them, and he reaffirms the basic teaching of Jesus: leaders are servants (Mark 9:35; 10:42–45; Matt. 23:8–12). Although the original meaning of ὑπηρέτης (*hypēretēs*) might have referred to an "under-rower" in a wargalley, it came to mean an assistant, one who receives orders or directions (Spicq, *TLNT* 3:398). Rengstorf (*TDNT* 8:532–33) claims, "The ὑπηρέτης is distinguished from the δοῦλος [*doulos*], always used for slave, by the fact that he is free and can in some cases claim a due reward for his services," and from the διάκονος in that "he willingly learns his task and goal from another who is over him," though without downgrading his personal dignity. He is a subordinate, bound to obey, but he labors as a free person, not as a slave (Rengstorf, *TDNT* 8:534). John (Mark), for example, is identified as the "assistant" of Paul and Barnabas in Acts 13:5. The terminology underlines the fact that ministers work under the orders of their master and have no significance except in relation to their master.

"Stewards" (οἰκονόμοι, *oikonomoi*) is also a servile term, used for "the chief household slave" (R. Collins 1999: 168; contra Reumann 1958) who must give account to the master (cf. Luke 12:42; 16:8–12). Whatever their assignment, they are not freelance operators but are responsible for overseeing operations as they are instructed. To be a stew-

4:1–2

---

3. Fee (1987: 155) notes that this is a "soteriological statement, not a christological one" and observes that when soteriological statements in the NT mention the Father and the Son, they "express subordination" (cf. 15:27–28). He concludes that this statement "has to do with his [Christ's] function as savior, not with his being as God."

ard of God's mysteries implies distributing these mysteries to others and is a major responsibility. But Spicq (*TLNT* 2:574) comments, "No matter how extensive the powers of *oikonomoi*, they are not the owners of the treasures of truth and grace that are entrusted to them; as they administer these treasures they must remain aware of their dependency and of the accounting that they will give." "They go where Christ sends them and deliver what God has given them" (Godet 1886: 205). To use servile language to refer to leaders (cf. 3:5; 9:19; 16:15, 16), instead of using the regular vocabulary of leadership, may have startled Paul's readers (Judge 1974: 196–97; P. Marshall 1987: 134–35), but it reinforces his point. As Clarke (1993: 121) phrases it, "These leaders they are exalting should be perceived as household servants of God." The unity of the ministry enterprise, however, is based on each minister's "servitude and subordination to Christ and to each other" (P. Marshall 1987: 135). Paul's view of Christian leaders as "an inverted pyramid, where leaders are enslaved, belong to the community, and must serve it from below" (Witherington 1995: 145) is radically different from the world's perception of leaders as free, high-status dons bestowing benevolences on those of lesser status.

The word ὧδε (*hōde*) does not indicate "here on earth" (cf. Heb. 13:14) or "in these circumstances" (contra Robertson and Plummer 1914: 75), but with λοιπόν (*loipon*) indicates a further inference ("in this connection, then" [BDAG 603]) to be made from the metaphor of stewardship (Conzelmann 1975: 83; Fee 1987: 160; Kuck 1992a: 198 n. 252). It introduces the chief criterion by which stewards are judged. Since they are in a position of trust, their trustworthiness is crucial. This idea is captured in an ancient document:

> I have empowered you by this document to administer my estate in Arsinoe, and to collect the rents and, if need be, to arrange new leases or to cultivate some land yourself, and to give receipts in my name, and to transact any business connected with stewardship, just as I can transact it when I am present, and to distribute the plots in Karamis, restoring to me what remains over, as to which matter I rely on your good faith, and I confirm whatever you decide about them. (BGU 1:300)

Fee (1987: 160) observes that God seeks of stewards "faithfulness," "not eloquence, nor wisdom (nor 'initiative,' nor 'success'—our standard requirements)." A master does not want a glib talker for a steward, and neither does God. "That they be found faithful" (ἵνα πιστός τις εὑρεθῇ, *hina pistos tis heurethē*) reintroduces the idea of an eventual performance review (3:8, 14–15) by their master. These ministers may belong to them (3:21–22), but they are accountable only to God. The gist of Paul's argument is this: if they are to regard ministers such as Paul, Apollos, and Cephas as menial underlings who belong to them and as

God's household managers whose chief duty is faithfulness, then they also need to regard their local leaders in the same way.

Paul next underscores the incompetence of human judges. Since hu-   **4:3–5**
mans are not all-seeing or all-knowing, their judgments are limited and, more often than not, mistaken. This certainly applies to ministry, since human criteria to measure faithfulness are useless. Paul appears to be on the defensive in declaring, "But with me it is a trifling thing that I should be examined by you." Many assume that he is attempting to deflect their past criticism of him and to preclude them from raising any accusations against him in the future (see N. Dahl 1977: 47–48; Donfried 1976: 105; Theissen 1987: 59; Bassler 1990: 182–83; Ker 2000: 91). They interpret him to be saying a bit audaciously that as God's apostle, he is not accountable to them, fleshly as they are (3:1). Kuck (1992a: 203) counters that Paul's declaration should not "be taken as a proud claim of special apostolic independence and exemption from the congregation's judgment." He contends instead that Paul presents his indifference to being judged by them as an example for them to follow. It bolsters his argument that God's judgment is the only judgment that counts and the only judgment that anybody should care about. Kuck (1992a: 203) describes this statement as "a sober reminder of the way any Christian is to think of himself or herself in relation to the opinions of others." This means that Paul "is not primarily trying to make a point about himself and his relationship to the congregation. Rather, he is setting forth a principle which applies not only to himself, not only to Apollos and Cephas, but also to other teachers and by extension to all who labor in the Gospel, i.e., all believers" (Kuck 1992a: 201; cf. Witherington 1995: 136 n. 1). The use of the first person invites them to share his perspective (as a typical Christian) and reach the same judgments about themselves (Kuck 1992a: 202). He contrasts two incompetent tribunals, humans and human courts (4:3) and one's own consciousness (4:4a), with the only competent, legitimate tribunal, God (4:4b–5; Theissen 1987: 60–61). His point is not that he will not submit to their examination of him, but that the stewards of God's mysteries are accountable only to God (cf. Rom. 14:4), whose test by fire is quite sufficient and not improved by human judgments.

Paul is not grousing because the Corinthians gave him a low fitness report as an apostle or protesting, "Who are you to be judging me?" He is only asserting that no human judgment is final. He does not assume that the examination by the Corinthians will result in a negative fitness report. It also could be positive. His point, however, is that it makes no difference what the conclusion is, whether he is judged to come up short or lauded with praise. Neither verdict carries weight with God; and, consequently, it does not carry weight with him. He hopes that they will learn to share this attitude.

The reference to a human day in court (ἀνθρωπίνης ἡμέρας, *anthrō-pinēs hēmeras*) contrasts with the day of the Lord's judgment (3:13; cf. 5:5; Isa. 13:6; Joel 1:15; Zeph. 1:14) and shows that this is a general warning that humans cannot and do not make the final decision. All human evaluations are premature and inconsequential in light of this judgment, whether it be the appraisal of one's own consciousness, of the Corinthian community, or of a human tribunal. When the Lord comes (cf. 11:26; 16:22), God will inspect the steward's fidelity, penetrating the depths of the human heart, its thoughts and intentions, and exposing the individual's true colors (Luke 16:15; Rev. 2:23). Thiselton (2000: 341) is correct that "Paul does not therefore advocate a thick-skinned indifference to public opinion; his point is a different one, namely, its fallibility, relativity, and limits which make it an unreliable guide on which to depend." Thiselton (2000: 341–42) cites Moltmann's (1967: 23) sage warning that Christians should avoid the despair of assuming failure in advance of the day of the Lord or the presumption of assuming total success in advance of it.

The statement οὐδὲν ἐμαυτῷ σύνοιδα (*ouden emautō synoida*, I am conscious of nothing against myself [dative of disadvantage]; cf. Job 27:6 LXX) is not a defensive statement. Consciousness refers to "self-awareness." Pierce (1955:109) compares it to the "pointer on a dial which registers wrong or clear depending on how the mechanism has been set" (cf. below on 8:7, 10, 12). Paul thinks himself faithful, but that makes no difference. He once regarded himself as "blameless according to the law" and therefore righteous (Phil. 3:6), but he soon learned how terribly wrong he was. If the pointing mechanism is not calibrated correctly, its reading is deceptive. He may acquit himself, but that does not mean he is acquitted. "Acquitted" (δεδικαίωμαι, *dedikaiōmai*) means "justified." We are not justified by our own good opinion of ourselves, because our own opinions may not be justified. A good conscience is a soft pillow—as the proverb has it—but it may be a pillow of self-deception. Deidun (1981: 161) notes that Paul never identifies the promptings of the conscience "with the content of God's demand." Theissen reminds us that the conscious does not have access to the unconscious. "The things hidden in darkness," he argues, refers to "unconscious forces and hidden faults and impulses within us" (see Theissen 1987: 61–65). But "the hidden things of darkness" can also include moral evil that a person consciously hides from others (2 Cor. 4:2; Eph. 5:11–12; John 3:19). As hypocrites, humans camouflage their evil intentions from others with shows of piety (cf. Rom. 2:25–29) to deceive, and often end up deceiving themselves in the process. The "hidden things" could be parallel to "the purposes of human heart," namely, its intentions, wishes, and desires (Schrenk, *TDNT* 1:635). God's inquisition will sustain or overturn our own judgments of ourselves because God is able to examine more than observable deeds. God will bring to light what shrinks from the light, the hidden motives—both good and bad—behind each servant's work (cf. 2 Bar. 83:1–3). Consequently, Paul leaves the evaluation of "his successes and failures with God" (Thiselton 2000: 339), and he reminds the Corinthians that they too will stand or fall before God and that the standard by which they will be judged is the cross of Christ.

Paul now specifies what the reward is that he only alluded to in 3:8 and 3:14. It is praise from God (cf. Rom. 2:29; 1 Pet. 1:7). While some today with more materialistic longings might prefer something tangible, receiving praise was one of the highest goals in the ancient world (Kuck 1992a: 209; cf. DeSilva 2000: 24–27). It helped identify one's place in society. Praise bestows honor; blame heaps dishonor. Kuck (1992a) cites many examples from Greco-Roman literature of persons longing for praise in the afterlife. In the Corinthian context, we may infer that the congregation went to extremes in bestowing praise on individual teachers or leaders for their wisdom while berating others. It resulted in the friction dividing the church. Paul intends to drive home the point that ultimate praise comes from God in the judgment, and it is the only praise that matters.

Additional Note

3:19. The citation from Job does not match the LXX and may be evidence that Paul is quoting from the Hebrew. He also may have combined Job 5:12–13, replacing τῇ φρονήσει βουλην (in the wise counsel) in 5:13 with βουλὰς πανούργων (the counsel of the crafty), resulting in ἐν τῇ πανουργίᾳ αὐτῶν (in their craftiness), which may be nearer the Hebrew (cf. Josh. 9:4; Prov. 1:4). The participle ὁ δρασσόμενος, however, is not found in either verse (διαλλάσσοντα, 5:12; ὁ καταλαμβάνων, 5:13) and is more difficult to explain.

III. Factions and Dissension in the Church (1:10–4:21)
    G. How to Regard Oneself; How to Regard Others (3:18–4:5)
➤ H. The Apostles as Models of the Wisdom of the Cross (4:6–13)
    I. Appeal to Imitate Their Father Paul (4:14–21)

H. The Apostles as Models of the Wisdom of the Cross (4:6–13)

Paul clarifies in 4:6 what he has been driving at in 1:10–4:5. He has not been criticizing Apollos, but "discussing Apollos and himself in order to admonish the Corinthian congregation as a whole" (Kuck 1992a: 210). It is not that the Corinthians "must not exaggerate the importance of such teachers as Paul and Apollos," as Barrett (1968: 105) claims. They must not exaggerate the importance of the teachers and leaders in their midst. The point is this: "If it would be wrong to exalt Paul above Apollos or Apollos above Paul, it would be equally wrong to exalt wisdom-teacher X above wisdom-teachers Y and Z" (D. Hall 1994: 148). Hall compares it to the covert allusion in Jesus' parable of the wicked tenants (Mark 12:1–12) and the story of Elijah and the widow of Zarephath and Naaman's leprosy (Luke 4:24–30): "Paul's statements about himself and Apollos in 3.5–9 were plain statements about real people; but the implied reference was to the various church-builders whose work is analysed in 3.10–20." He uses the relation between himself and Apollos to show how absurd it is in God's church for cliques to form around certain leaders, how inappropriate it is to exalt one leader over another, how foolish their vaunted wisdom looks to God, and how far they have strayed from the message of the cross.[1]

Paul expects them to stay within the limits prescribed by the Scripture texts he has cited in 1:19; 3:19, 20. These texts emphasize the foolishness of human wisdom and boasting and show that perfect wisdom boasts only in the Lord. He also holds up the example of the circumstances of the apostles as models of those who live according to the wisdom of the cross, which the Corinthians should imitate. The contrast between their arrogance and the apostles' humiliation is stark and reveals why the Corinthians are riddled with strife and dissension.

Exegesis and Exposition

[6]With regard to these things, brothers and sisters, I have applied the matter to myself and Apollos for your sake, so that you might learn, ⌜"Not beyond what is written,"⌝ so that you might not be puffed up with arrogance favoring one person

---

1. Fee (1987: 167 n. 10) critiques Fiore (1985: 94–95) for failing to recognize the apologetic element in chapter 4; but Fee, as do many others, overreads the apologetic element into the text.

against another. [7]For who distinguishes you? What do you have that you did not receive? And if you received it, why boast as if you did not receive it? [8]So quickly you have become satiated, already you have become rich, apart from us you have come to reign. Oh, that you did reign that we might reign with you! [9]For I think that God has displayed us apostles as last of all, as near death, because we have become a spectacle to the world, both to angels and to mortals. [10]We are fools because of Christ, but you are sensible in Christ; we are weak, but you are strong; you are esteemed, but we are dishonored. [11]To this present moment, we hunger and thirst, wear tattered clothing, are cuffed about, are homeless, [12]and toil working with our own hands. When reviled, we bless; when persecuted, we endure; [13]when slandered, we speak encouragement. To the present, we have become as the scum of the earth, the off-scouring of all things.

The direct address ἀδελφοί (*adelphoi*) signals a switch in the direction of Paul's argument (cf. 1:10, 26; 2:1; 3:1) as he summarizes his purpose behind what he has written. "These things" could refer to 3:5–4:5 (Weiss 1910: 101; Robertson and Plummer 1914: 80; Kuck 1992a: 210–11), where he explicitly mentions himself and Apollos. This rhetorical unit would then be neatly set off by the introduction in 3:1–4 and the conclusion in 4:6. "These things" also could refer to the whole discourse of 1:10–4:5 (Funk 1966: 286; Fiore 1985: 94; Stowers 1990: 257), or at least it should not be overlooked that 1:18–3:4 lays the foundation for what he says in 3:5–4:5 (Fitzgerald 1988: 120 n. 13; B. Dodd 1999: 45). If so, 4:6 would unlock Paul's intention and strategy in all that precedes. But the lock is difficult to pick open, and this verse has been labeled "a headache for translators" (Legault 1971–72: 227). English translations tend to obscure the difficulty of the phrase τὸ μὴ ὑπὲρ ἃ γέγραπται (*to mē hyper ha gegraptai*, literally, "the not beyond what stands written") by adding a verb ("not to exceed," NASB; "do not go," NIV) to make sense of it. Moffatt (1938: 46–47) abandons any attempt to translate it, calling its meaning "beyond recovery." Fee (1987: 169) concedes that Paul and the Corinthians "were on a wavelength that will probably be forever beyond our ability to pick up." If this verse applies to his argument in 1:10–4:5, then unpacking its meaning is critical for understanding what Paul is doing in the opening section of his letter.

The first task is to ascertain the meaning of the verb μετεσχημάτισα (*meteschēmatisa*). Σχῆμα (*schēma*) means "arrangement" or "formation," and the verb μετασχηματίζειν (*metaschēmatizein*) can mean "to change the form of something" ("transform," Phil. 3:21).[2] D. Hall (1994: 143) notes that many modern commentators are reticent to allow it to have that meaning here and apply the verb to the figures of planting and building in

4:6

---

2. Paul uses the verb in 2 Cor. 11:13, 14, 15 for changing one's appearance: false apostles disguise themselves as apostles of Christ; Satan disguises himself as an angel of light; and Satan's servants disguise themselves as ministers of righteousness.

3:5–17 so that it means "to illustrate," "to exemplify" (Weiss 1910: 101; Colson 1916; Conzelmann 1975: 85–86; Schneider, *TDNT* 7:958; Fee 1987: 167; Vos 1995). Another alternative goes back to Chrysostom (*Hom. 1 Cor.* 12.1), who understands the verb to refer to Paul's use of veiled allusion in discussing their factional unrest. Paul has transferred the figure to himself and Apollos. Though he speaks of community disruption swirling around loyalties to certain apostolic figures—Paul, Apollos, and Cephas (1:12; 3:4–9, 22)—that was not the true cause of the division. There actually were no parties in Corinth rallying around these names (R. Collins 1999: 176). Instead, overzealous allegiance to their own leaders, who go unnamed, has generated the discord. Paul speaks of one reality, the noncompetitive partnership between Apollos and himself, while intending the audience to apply it to another reality, the rivalry among the leaders in Corinth.[3]

One employed figured speech out of deference to the status of the persons charged with faults because they might take offense if overtly accused, but one expected that the allegory would be plain to the listeners.[4] Demetrius (*Eloc.* 289) contends that "veiled language" is a judicious way to censure a despot or ungovernable person for "haughty pride."[5] The advantage is that the censure is "dignified and circumspect" (Demetrius, *Eloc.* 290). By praising individuals who have acted in the opposite way—in this case, Paul and Apollos—"the hearer is admonished without feeling himself censured; he emulates [the one praised], and covets praise for himself" (Demetrius, *Eloc.* 292). Fiore (1985: 95) connects Demetrius's rhetorical tactic of wary censure, which he terms "covert allusion," with what Paul does in these opening chapters (cf. Schrage 1991: 334).[6] P. Lampe (1990: 129 n. 15) defines

3. Chrysostom was followed by Ambrosiaster, Theodoret, Theophylact, Erasmus, Calvin (see Vos 1995: 154 n. 1), and in the modern era by Edwards 1885: 101; Godet 1886: 215–16; Lightfoot 1895: 199; Findlay 1910: 799; Robertson and Plummer 1914: 81; Fitzgerald 1988: 118–19; Clarke 1993: 122; D. Hall 1994: 144; R. Collins 1999: 176; Winter 1997d: 196–201. Fiore (1985: 89) contends that in the rhetorical glossary, σχηματίζειν λόγον (*schēmatizein logon*) means "to compose a speech with veiled meaning."

4. According to Quintilian (*Inst.* 9.2.78), the listener takes delight in detecting the speaker's concealed meaning (though he calls this circuitous method "the refuge of weakness"). Paul's original intent, however, quickly fades from view when other readers, removed from the situation, try to make sense of what he says.

5. Demetrius (*Eloc.* 289–93, 298) describes it as a σχήματος λόγου (*schēmatos logou,* veiled speech) and uses the verb σχηματίζειν (*schēmatizein*) for the employment of "figures" and "covert phrases" and to define "that wary form of language" to be used with potentates.

6. Colson (1916: 384) objects to the misuse of rhetorical terms and modifies it to mean "I changed (by a trope) the names of the party leaders to Paul and Apollos." He imagines that the rhetorical figure would have been described in this way: "When you are obliged to make remarks which may be offensive to the pride of the audience, lead up to them by showing that this depreciation includes yourself." He claims that this "figure" does not appear in lists of ancient rhetoricians because they wrote "for public speakers and public speakers usually avoided depreciatory remarks altogether, and therefore did not need 'figures' to help them."

μετασχηματίζειν (*metaschēmatizein*) as meaning "to hint at something in a disguised speech without saying it *expressis verbis*."

Anderson (1999: 245–50) challenges this interpretation and is correct that Chrysostom does not connect the verb μετασχηματίζειν to any specific rhetorical tactic. He also maintains that one would not expect the verb to mean to "transform *something* by way of a (covert) figure," since the prefix μετα- "implies a *change* of one form to another." Anderson (1999: 249) cites examples in Homer (*Iliad* 2.284–86) and Cyril of Alexandria where the phrase means "to apply these things" or "to transfer these things"—in this case, to Paul and Apollos. Anderson thinks that "these things" refers to the rebuke in 3:5.

What is clear from all of these arguments about the meaning of μετασχηματίζειν is that Paul wishes to avoid upbraiding anyone in Corinth by name. By applying the argument to himself and Apollos, he makes it to be applicable to all leaders in the church. Chrysostom has a better feel for what Paul is doing. Paul assumes that the Corinthians esteem both himself and Apollos, and by using himself and Apollos as examples, he helps them to accept the lesson. Had Paul said, "As for you who deem yourselves so worthy of admiration and examine and judge others," there might have been a knee-jerk resistance to his reprimand. Paul explicitly says in 4:14 that he does not wish to shame them and instead admonishes them as his beloved children. By using aliases rather than fingering the real culprits and by stressing that his depreciation of the role of leaders as servants extends also to himself ("What, then, is Paul?" 3:5), he allays potential resentment and makes it easier for them to swallow the medicine (Chrysostom, *Hom. 1 Cor.* 12.1; cf. D. Hall 1994: 145). Paul has persons other than Apollos in mind when he warns about how other workers build upon the foundation he laid—some using good materials, and others, shoddy (3:10–17). The Corinthians have an example in the harmonious relationship between Paul and Apollos ("in us") and need to adjust their attitudes toward one another accordingly. In sum, he uses the example of himself and Apollos to help them learn how properly to evaluate the stature of leaders in the church.

The second major problem for understanding this verse is ascertaining the meaning of the phrase τὸ μὴ ὑπὲρ ἃ γέγραπται (*to mē hyper ha gegraptai,* literally, "the not above what is written"). Five basic solutions have been proposed. (1) The first assumes that it is completely unintelligible (Conzelmann 1975: 86). This view leads some to regard it as a marginal gloss that has been incorporated into the text by mistake (see additional note). We should treat with caution any putative textual emendations designed to solve an exegetical problem, no matter how ingenious they might be (Ker 2000: 92). No evidence exists that this phrase was not original to the text.

The τό (*to*) is anaphoric, signaling a quotation of something (cf. Rom. 13:9; Gal. 5:14; 6:9), and is equivalent to our "inverted commas" (W. Howard 1921–22: 479; Moule 1960: 110–11).[7] (2) Thus, a second approach is to regard it as a quotation of some proverbial idiom (Lightfoot 1895: 199). The NEB renders it "learn to 'keep within the rules,'" as they say" (cf. NRSV, "so that you may learn through us the meaning of the saying, 'Nothing beyond what is written'"; JB, "remember the maxim: 'Keep to what is written'"). The τό is taken to refer to a recognized principle (P. Wallis 1950). Welborn (1997: 56) thinks that it was "a well-known maxim, with broad cultural currency," but the examples he cites have τὰ γεγραμμένα (*ta gegrammena*) not ἃ γέγραπται. Others take it as a familiar proverb drawn from the experience of children learning to write their letters (Fiore 1985: 322–23 n. 24; Fitzgerald 1988: 124–27; Stowers 1990: 257; Ebner 1991: 33–36; Kuck 1992a: 213; Tyler 1998). To teach penmanship, a teacher would carefully write the letter, word, or sentence, and the pupil would carefully copy it or trace over the lines in the wax tablet.[8] This meaning might fit Paul's reference to them as "infants in Christ" (3:1) and allude to their childish condition. Like maladroit grammar school children, they are writing outside the lines and are admonished to trace their letters correctly. It would mean "do not go above or below the lines." Paul presents Apollos and himself as models of constructive cooperation whom they are to imitate. The problem with this view is that this adage is not found anywhere else, which weakens the argument that it was a well-known cliché.

(3) A third approach treats this phrase as a reference to the terms of a foundational document of the community. Hanges (1998: 288) thinks that the phrase ἃ γέγραπται "refers to some kind of document or legal contract" (cf. Parry 1926: 78). It is akin to cult bylaws that laid out the guidelines and principles necessary for the group's prosperity, and it means not to go beyond the rules. The problem is, What rules are being broken? Why not cite them specifically?

(4) A fourth interpretation regards the phrase as a general warning against immoderate behavior caused by hubris (P. Marshall 1987: 190–95; Pickett 1997: 57–58). The ὑπέρ denotes excessive behavior. "What is written" refers to limits or boundaries that encourage moderation. Paul is warning them against overstepping the boundaries, which leads them to be puffed up on behalf of one over against another.

---

7. We can dismiss the views that it refers to a saying of Jesus (Mark 10:44; Matt. 7:1; so Chrysostom, *Hom. 1 Cor.* 12.2) or to what Paul has written in the previous chapters (Calvin 1960: 90).

8. Tyler cites Seneca, *Ep. morales* 94.51; Plato, *Protagoras* 320–28; Quintilian, *Inst.* 1.1.27–29.

(5) A fifth approach interprets it as a reference to the OT.[9] This is the most likely solution because Paul uses the verb γέγραπται (*gegraptai*) thirty times, excluding 4:6, to introduce citations from Scripture and never anything else.[10] To be sure, it is an unusual way to refer to Scripture. Some explain that it was possibly a slogan cautioning against any departure from Scripture and was a rabbinic adage (Robertson and Plummer 1914: 81; Ross 1970–71: 217), a phrase coined by Paul (Hooker 1963–64b: 132), or a phrase known or used by the Corinthians (Brun 1931). It could be a general reference to the spirit of the OT (Edwards 1885: 102): "that you learn by us to live according to Scripture" (RSV). But it is best to regard the saying as referring to the five quotations from the OT, all introduced by γέγραπται, cited in the first three chapters:[11]

1:19   "I will destroy the wisdom of the wise and nullify the cleverness of the clever" (Isa. 29:14).

1:31   "Let the one who boasts boast in the Lord" (Jer. 9:22–23 LXX).

2:9   "What eye has not seen and ear has not heard and what has not entered the human mind, things God has prepared for those who love him" (Isa. 64:4 LXX).

3:19   "He catches the wise in their cunning" (Job 5:13).

3:20   "The Lord knows the thoughts of the wise, that they are futile" (Ps. 93:11 LXX [94:11 MT]).

Hays (1997: 69) argues that in the case of the first two and the last two quotations "the application is explicitly spelled out: No boasting in human beings." Paul's statement in 3:21, "Let no one boast in humans," links the last two quotations to the first two.

Though Welborn (1997: 47) and Wagner (1998: 280) claim that all these passages do not apply to a commandment enjoining humility and concord, Hays's (1997: 69) conclusion about "the cumulative force" of these quotations makes the best sense of Paul's intention: "The witness of Scripture places a strict limit on human pride and calls for trust in

---

9. So Robertson and Plummer 1914: 81; Schmidt 1951; Barrett 1968: 106–7; Ruef 1977: 32; Bruce 1971: 48; Schrage 1991: 334–35; Kistemaker 1993: 135. Hooker (1963–64b: 129–32) claims that false teachers have added "human wisdom"—philosophy and rhetoric—to the gospel and have gone beyond the things that are written, since Paul understands his gospel to be the fulfillment of Scriptures. These Scriptures prophesy the destruction of human wisdom.

10. Rom. 1:17; 2:24; 3:4, 10; 4:17; 8:36; 9:13, 33; 10:15; 11:8, 26; 12:19; 14:11; 15:3, 9, 21; 1 Cor. 1:19, 31; 2:9; 3:19; 9:9; 10:7; 14:21; 15:45; 2 Cor. 8:15; 9:9; Gal. 3:10, 13; 4:22, 27.

11. So Fiore 1985: 93–94; D. Hall 1994: 147; Hays 1997: 68–69; B. Dodd 1999: 47; Soards 1999: 92.

God alone." The key passage is the quotation from Jer. 9:22–23 in 1:31 (see J. Schreiner 1974). The texts cited in 1:19; 3:19, 20 "underscore the foolishness of human wisdom before God." The text in 2:9 "highlights the mystery of God's wisdom before humans." The text in 1:31 provides a clue for how the Corinthians go beyond what is written by boasting in humans. "The citations teach that while it is the wisdom of the world to indulge in human boasting there is a simpler, more perfect kind of wisdom, that of boasting only in the Lord" (Savage 1996: 61). Instead of boasting only in the Lord, the giver of the gifts, they boast in humans, the recipients of the gifts, and create factions and dissensions.

The second purpose clause appears to be subordinate to, and to explain, the first (Linton 1930: 430; Barrett 1968: 107; Kuck 1992a: 212).[12] The Scripture teaches that they are not to be puffed up, one over against another. The verb φυσιοῦν (*physioun*, to puff up) appears predominantly in the Corinthian correspondence (4:6, 18, 19; 5:2; 8:1; 13:4; 2 Cor. 12:20; cf. Col. 2:18). Meeks (1983: 128) thinks that the image of them being "inflated" may be "wryly appropriate" since they think of themselves as πνευματικοί (*pneumatikoi*, spiritual ones), which derives from πνεῦμα (*pneuma*), which also means "wind." Dio Chrysostom (*Or.* 9.21) says that the Corinthians were infamous for being "puffed up" and assuming airs (9.8), and this disagreeable trait apparently has invaded the Corinthian church. Being "puffed up" denotes arrogance, "which results from a failure in self-knowledge" (P. Marshall 1987: 205). Since Paul reminds them that they have received everything from God, they have no reason to be puffed up about anything. Thinking too highly of oneself or others with whom one is aligned has antisocial consequences and calls for a sobering reassessment of oneself (Rom. 12:3).

4:7   Paul explains why they should not be puffed up, recognizing that the roots of their conflict lie deep in the human desire to distinguish oneself from others and to rise higher on an imagined social ladder. He punctures their inflated view of themselves with a series of questions: Who? What? Why? The first question lends itself to two possible answers. It may be interpreted negatively as referring to their presumption: "Who in the world sees anything special in you?" (Moffatt 1938: 48); "Who concedes you any superiority?" (P. Marshall 1987: 205); "Who made you so special?" (Kuck 1992a: 215).[13] The question can also be interpreted positively. They *are* special, but they forget that it was God who makes them special: Who differentiates you? Who de-

---

12. A double ἵνα (*hina*) clause also appears in Rom. 7:13; Gal. 3:14; 4:5; Eph. 5:26–27.

13. Fee (1987: 171) thinks it picks up the theme of 4:3–5 and that Paul is trying to correct their attitude toward him: "Who in the world do you think you are anyway? What kind of self-delusion is it that allows you to put yourself in a position to judge another person's servant?" (cf. also Vos 1995: 167; Winter 1997d: 198).

fines you?[14] It is God who saved them (1:18), chose them (1:27–28), and revealed to them the hidden mysteries (2:10–12), with the result that no one may boast (1:29). God is the source of their life in Christ (1:30) and activates all the spiritual gifts (12:6). God appointed the various roles in the church (12:28) and will give them the final victory over death (15:57). Everything special about them is attributable to God's calling of them.

The next question, "What do you have that you have not received?" follows this train of thought. Nothing is inherently theirs, so they cannot be arrogant and boastful (P. Marshall 1987: 205). They must learn to imitate Paul, who says, "What is Paul?"—merely a servant (3:5) who has been graced by God (3:10; cf. 15:10). Divine grace levels the ground for all and requires gratitude and humility in response. One cannot boast about being a worthy recipient of grace. The third question leads them to this proper conclusion: They are not to boast. For them to be puffed up one against another effectively denies that God is the one who has given them all things.

Using hyperbole, as he does throughout this chapter ("you have a myriad of guardians in Christ," 4:15), Paul undermines the Corinthians' misplaced boasting in themselves by juxtaposing it with the touchstone of the apostles' cruciform behavior. The apostles live according to the wisdom of the cross; the Corinthians imbibe the wisdom of this age and pass themselves off as kings.

4:8

The aorists are ingressive: "Already you have become satiated, already you have become rich, apart from us you have come to reign." Being satiated was traditionally associated with hubris (P. Marshall 1987: 208) and connected to licentiousness (R. Collins 1999: 186). The Corinthians think they are wise, and the wise person was considered to be like a king in Stoic thought (Epictetus, *Diatr.* 3.22.63, "The wise man is king"; cf. Horace, *Ep.* 1.1.106; Plutarch, *Mor.* 1058B–C). P. Marshall (1987: 209) and R. Collins (1999: 187) tie acting like kings to the slogan "All things are permitted" (6:12; 10:23), since kings could do as they pleased. Suetonius (*Caligula* 29.1; cf. *Nero* 37.3), for example, has Caligula boast to his grandmother, "Remember that I am permitted to do anything to anybody." But "king" was also the client's word for a rich patron (Highet 1973: 279, cited by D. Martin 1990: 210 n. 13) and may have a sociological connotation.[15] D. Martin (1990: 210) asks, "Were some people at Corinth styling themselves 'kings' as a claim to patronal

14. So Thiselton 2000: 356 (cf. Calvin 1960: 91). Findlay (1910: 800) admits that it "suits the verb" but finds this translation "hardly relevant." Godet (1886: 220) and Edwards (1885: 104) object that it makes this first question identical with the second, but one can argue that Paul intends to reinforce the answer to the first question to drive home its point.

15. See Juvenal, *Sat.* 5.14, 130, 137, 161; 7.45; 10.161.

position over others in the Corinthian church?" Philo's (*Virt.* 30 §§161–74) comments about pride and arrogance so closely parallel what Paul says in this unit that they suggest that Paul's intention is simply to censure the Corinthians' pride and arrogance. The proud person "considers himself superior to all in riches, estimation, beauty, strength, wisdom, temperance, justice, eloquence, knowledge; while everyone else he regards as poor, disesteemed, unhonoured, foolish, unjust, ignorant, outcast, in fact good for nothing" (Philo, *Virt.* 30 §174). Philo's conclusion also matches Paul's warnings in 3:10–17: "Naturally such a person will, as the Revealer tells us, have God for his accuser and avenger."

Some Corinthians think that they are already crowned and have undertaken their reign "apart from us." Paul does not mean that they reign without the assistance of nonentities such as Paul and Apollos (contra Weiss 1910: 108; Barrett 1968: 108). "Apart from us" means that they reign without the apostles having a share in it (Fee 1987: 173; Fitzgerald 1988: 129 n. 32; cf. Heb. 11:40). The exclamation ὄφελόν γε (*ophelon ge*) expresses an unfulfillable wish: "if you only did" (Thiselton 2000: 359). Paul may assume that they do not reign because the kingdom has not yet come (6:9–10; 15:24, 50) and also may be correcting the illusion that they can reign alone, without other Christians. But the contrast in 4:9–13 between the abased apostles on the one hand and the self-exalted Corinthian hubrists on the other is the key for understanding his point. This comparison reveals that the problem is not rooted in some mistaken "realized eschatology" (contra Thiselton 1977–78; 2000: 357). It is not that the Corinthians are "behaving as if the age to come were already consummated, as if the saints had already taken over the kingdom (Dan. vii.18)," as Barrett (1968: 109) believes (cf. Conzelmann 1975: 88; Fee 1987: 172). Kuck (1992a: 216–19) makes the vital point that Paul counters their stance with ethics, not eschatology. He does not try to correct a delusional "realized eschatology" but their worldly arrogance that prompts them to be high and mighty over against others. The problem, then, is not that they think that the judgment lies behind them but that they have not given any thought to God's judgment at all. Their pride and boasting have nothing to do with mistaken views about the end-time blessings. The Corinthians' basic blunder is that they "already see themselves as morally and spiritually perfected, without having to experience the bodily struggles which Paul sees as the sign of life in Christ" (Kuck 1992a: 216). They do not reign as kings because they are not wise according to the cross. The King reigns from the cross, which displays the only wisdom that counts with God.

Imagining oneself to be filled, rich, and reigning was a widespread fantasy in the ancient world and was not attached to any particular views about end-time blessings (Kuck 1992a: 217–18). Ideas about being accounted wealthy and reigning are found in wisdom literature without any eschatological undertone (cf. Wis. 6:20; 7:8, 11; 8:14, 18).[16] The problem is that the Corinthians think that they are wise by measuring themselves according to the world's criteria of wisdom. The "already" (ἤδη, *ēdē*) does not refer to a premature triumphalism. It means in this context "so quickly," "so easily," you are filled, are rich, and are reigning. Paul corrects this misunderstanding by presenting them with the long hard road of suffering as the only way to Christian maturity (4:9–13), embodied in the lives of the apostles (Kuck 1992a: 216–17). The Christian life is not a fast track to glory but a slow, arduous path that takes one through suffering. The suffering so visible in the lives of the apostles is not some tedious detour for an elite volunteer corps but the main highway for all Christians. By contrasting the cross-centered lifestyles of the apostles with the Corinthians' vainglory, Paul hopes to supplant their egotism with the wisdom of the cross.

It is mistaken to think that Paul is on the defensive in 4:9–13 and trying to deflect Corinthian criticism of his own destitution (cf. Hodgson 1983: 65; Fitzgerald 1988: 122). He does not describe his own personal existence but that of the apostles as a whole ("we apostles"; cf. Acts 19:29). He holds up the apostles' suffering as the life that is praiseworthy to God and as a paradigm for their own existence (Fitzgerald 1988: 148; Kuck 1992a: 219).[17] The list of hardships offers an "ironic critique" of the Corinthians' worldly mind-set (Fitzgerald 1988: 148). How can they be so exalted if they received their blessings through such lowly apostles? The hardship list also offers "a positive model for them to imitate." Paul is not defending his idiosyncratic way of living out his Christian calling but presenting the way of the cross as modeled by the apostles.[18] His argument assumes that true apostles of Christ follow the example of Christ, since everything he says about the apostles' degradation applies also to Christ. In 2 Corinthians, for example, Paul draws a direct parallel between his being "poor, yet making many rich" (2 Cor. 6:10) and the generous act of our Lord Jesus Christ, who "was rich, yet for your sakes became poor, so that by his poverty you might become

4:9

---

16. Cf. also Philo, *Alleg. Interp.* 1.13 §34; 3.56 §163; *Heir* 6 §27; *Abr.* 44 §261; *Virt.* 39 §§212–19.

17. *Diogn.* 5:12–15 understands these hardships as the lifestyle of the typical Christian, which distinguishes Christians from others.

18. Other lists of hardships appear in 2 Cor. 4:7–12; 6:4–10; 11:23–29 and become increasingly specific. Paul is not adopting a presumed rhetorical convention of a hardship catalog to vouch for his legitimacy as an ideal sage. Actual experiences of hardship from carrying out his ministry generated his listing of his afflictions. Parallels with other Greco-Roman authors who recounted their hardships, however, reveal that Paul's readers would have been familiar with such catalogs. G. Horsley (1989: 83–84) contends, "Because life was difficult for the vast majority of people in antiquity it is not surprising that the variety of adversities encountered was a common literary and philosophical preoccupation" (see Garland 1999: 224–28 for discussion and further bibliography).

rich" (2 Cor. 8:9). Apostles are first (1 Cor. 12:28), not because they out-rank others, but because they provide the model of a cruciform life.

God presents the apostles to the world as persons condemned to death. The theology of the cross expounded in 1:25–27 lies behind this description of the apostles (see Schrage 1974). Far from giving them crowns to wear, God determined that apostles should suffer like Christ and be indistinguishable from the abject poor (cf. Acts 9:16; Matt. 5:11; Luke 6:22). Being "last," then, refers to their social ranking (Fitzgerald 1988: 136 n. 58). Being "near death" and a "spectacle to the world" may draw on images from gladiatorial combats or from Roman triumphs in which the prisoners of war were dragged through the city in a parade and executed at its end (cf. 2 Cor. 2:14; Garland 1999: 140–43). The world, angels, and mortals as the bloodthirsty spectators of this macabre theater (cf. 3 Macc. 5:23–25; 4 Macc. 15:20; 17:14) underscores the cosmic significance of their suffering.

4:10 The next verses (4:10–13) fall into the following pattern (cf. R. Collins 1999: 184):

> A Three contrasts between Paul and the Corinthians (4:10)
> > B Six tribulations (4:11–12a)
> A′ Three contrasting actions (4:12b–13a)

Paul holds up the apostles as examples of those who have becomes fools for Christ's sake to discredit those who pass themselves off as powerful in Corinth. According to Philo's (*Worse Att. Bet.* 10 §34) standards, Paul's description of the apostles' destitution identifies them as lovers of virtue as opposed to pleasure seekers:

> The so-called lovers of virtue are almost without exception obscure people, looked down upon. Of mean estate, destitute of the necessities of life, not enjoying privileges of subject peoples or even of slaves, filthy, sallow, reduced to skeletons, with a hungry look from want of food, the prey of disease, in training for dying. Those, on the other hand, who take care of themselves are men of mark and wealth, holding leading positions, praised on all hands, recipients of honors, portly, healthy and robust, reveling in luxurious and riotous living, knowing nothing of labour, conversant with pleasures which carry the sweets of life to the all-welcoming soul by every channel of sense.

Witherington (1995: 143) spells out Paul's point: "In an upside-down world the truly first or wise are treated like the last or like fools."

On account of Christ, apostles appear to be foolish, weak, and dishonored because those who share in Christ's riches must share in his foolishness, weakness, and humiliation in the eyes of the world (Wagner 1998: 286). The list parallels the Beatitudes (Matt. 5:5, 10–12; Luke 6:21–26; Matt. 5:44/Luke 6:35) but, more importantly, echoes themes in 1:18–2:5 so that Paul's arguments come full circle. "Wise" versus "fools" picks up the theme of the divine foolishness versus the foolish wisdom of the world (cf. 1:18, 20, 21, 23, 25, 27). "Strong" versus "weak" picks up the theme of divine weakness versus the supposed strength of this world. Paul's understanding of the relationship between weakness (1 Cor. 9:22) and God's power emerges most clearly in 2 Cor. 11:30; 12:9; 13:4. Since Christ was crucified in weakness but lives by the power of God, those who are weak in him experience the same divine power (2 Cor. 13:4). The third antithesis, "esteemed" versus "dishonored," recalls his assertion in 1:26–28 that God chose the dishonorable to shame the honored. The apostles' spiritual status contradicts their sociological status (Schrage 1991: 343). If the Corinthians, however, are "wise," "strong," and "honored," they must be kowtowing to the world's standards, which brings into question whether they are truly Christ's.

Time references ("until the present moment," 4:11; "until this very   **4:11–13**
day," 4:13) frame a list of six hardships, three responses to abuse, and the conclusion stating how such abused persons must look to the world. The present is a time of suffering, not glory. Paul likens apostles to maltreated strangers (P. Marshall 1987: 211) and the have-nots. Their hunger and thirst (Phil 4:12) contrasts the Corinthians' satiety. Being "naked" (Rom. 8:35; 2 Cor. 11:27) is a hyperbolic reference to being "wretchedly clad" (Seneca, *De beneficiis* 5.13.3). Being "cuffed about" refers to being struck like a slave (cf. Mark 14:65; 1 Pet. 2:20); the blows are those "offered as insults . . . and accompanied by verbal abuse" (Fitzgerald 1988: 143 n. 89). Being homeless (cf. Matt. 8:20/ Luke 9:58) identifies them as wanderers. A man who works with his hands is assumed by the elite to be toiling in lowly tasks that exclude any attention to higher things (Plutarch, *Pericles* 2.1; cf. additional notes on 9:6; Hock 1978: 563). The verb κοπιᾶν (*kopian*) implies exhaustive labor.

Though apostles are reviled, persecuted, and slandered, they respond as Christ did, with blessing, endurance, and conciliation (cf. Rom. 12:14; 1 Pet. 2:23; 3:9, 15–16). Like their Lord, apostles are objects of contempt, and Paul concludes the list with two almost synonymous terms of abuse that sum up the world's opinion of apostles. Περικαθάρμα (*perikatharma*) refers to that which is removed by cleaning—the filthy residue or scum (Thiselton 2000: 364). Περίψημα (*peripsēma*) refers to the scrapings that are scrubbed off something, and Thiselton (2000: 365) translates it as "the scrapings from everyone's shoes." These are popular forms of self-deprecation (cf. Ign. *Eph.* 8:1; 18:1; Barn. 4:9), but many have noted that the words were used for human victims in rituals designed to ward off evil through an expiatory sacrifice. Worthless persons, such as condemned criminals, were chosen to be sacrificed vicariously for the purity of a city (McLean 1996: 107; cf. Lietzmann 1949: 21, 173; Hauck, *TDNT* 3:430–31; Stählin, *TDNT* 6:84–93; Barrett 1968: 112–13; Hanson 1974: 32–36; P. Marshall 1987: 213). Stählin (*TDNT* 6:90–91) offers four arguments for this connotation in this context: (1) the association of πάντων (*pantōn*, of all) with an individual or individuals perishing for a whole city; (2) the connection of the verb γίνεσθαι (*ginesthai*) to the language of the formula pronounced over the victim to transfer guilt; (3) the affinity of the image with the description of apostles being a public spectacle (4:9); and (4) the idea of the accursed conveying a blessing to their persecutors. The word picture would depict the apostles as looking like scapegoats and despised sin-offerings; but, in truth, they are bearers of reconciliation for the world and give their lives for the good of all persons. Hauck (*TDNT* 3:431) thinks that this image would suggest that they are an "expiatory offering, that which is contemptible, and that which is to be thrown out." Conzelmann (1975: 90 n. 49) argues, however, that the phrase as "near death" cancels out this interpretation, since the apostles do not die, and that Paul simply applies common terms of abuse to the apostles. Frequently, it is impossible to know exactly what associations words might have had in the minds of authors and listeners. I translate these terms simply as reproaches but allow that Paul might have intended to evoke pictures of vicarious suffering for others.

Paul's point can be clarified by his directives in Rom. 12:17–21. In 4:9–13, he presents apostles as an example of those who bless those who persecute them (Rom. 12:14) and who strive to live peaceably with all (Rom. 12:18). They embody the wisdom of the cross. If the Corinthians embodied that wisdom, they would begin to live peaceably among themselves, though they may invite the ridicule of outsiders.

Additional Note

4:6. W. Howard (1921–22) comments, "Conjectural emendation is the last resort of the harassed exegete," and ingenious interpreters have proposed several solutions to explain away the baffling phrase τὸ μὴ ὑπὲρ ἃ γέγραπται.

1. The original copyist accidentally omitted the μή and wrote it in above the α of the ἵνα. A second copyist explained it in a note in his margin: "The μή is written above the alpha." A third copyist did not understand that it was only a marginal gloss and unthinkingly incorporated these five words into the text.
2. A scribe found the μή missing in the phrase ἵνα μὴ εἷς ὑπὲρ τοῦ ἑνός (cf. D, E) and added this comment over the εἷς using α as the numerical symbol for "one" (so Héring 1962: 28–29; Legault 1971–72).
3. A marginal gloss read ἃ γέγραπται ἕνα μὴ εἷς, "the α stands in the text; read ἕνα not εἷς."

4. Hudson (1923–24) and Strugnell (1974) (cf. Murphy-O'Connor 1986: 85) think that the comment was added by a copyist who found the μή omitted in the exemplar and called attention to the fact that he had added it: "The μή is beyond what is written," that is, "Add μή to this text."

The arguments against a textual emendation are weighty (see Ross 1970–71; Kilpatrick 1981). First, there is no evidence that a gloss like this has intruded in the text elsewhere in the NT. Second, most reconstructions require multiple stages of the text being adjusted by copyists, which makes it likely that some texts would have different readings—particularly since its meaning was obscure—but none exist. Third, the wording is strange for a gloss (Ross 1970–71: 216). The glossator would have been more likely to have written ὑπὲρ τὸ α, not ὑπὲρ α. Fourth, removing the object from "learn" produces rough syntax: "in order that you learn in us in order that you not become puffed up" (Welborn 1997: 53). For my interpretation, see the comments above.

I. Appeal to Imitate Their Father Paul (4:14–21)

Paul ends this first chief division of the letter with a call to imitate him (4:16) and a warning that he will return to the Corinthian community and will challenge the obstinate. What they are to imitate is left unspecified, but it must be related to living out the foolish wisdom of the cross. As Christ's apostle, he has been sent out to proclaim and interpret the gospel to others in both words and lifestyle. As their father, he shows them how to walk in Christ and becomes, as it were, their textbook of what it means to be faithful in the Lord. Timothy has been dispatched to remind them of his ways and to clarify what he wants them to do.

The call to imitate him is based on the fact that he is their father as the founder of the church who introduced them to the gospel. He is not a lowly, slave child-minder threatening them with a rod but a father who loves them and sets an example for them to follow. His chastening of them is leavened by a father's love and a spirit of gentleness that does not seek to shame but to reform. If there is any recrimination in the tone of what he says, it springs from anger caused by his anxiety over the welfare of his children.

Exegesis and Exposition

¹⁴I do not write these things trying to shame you, but to admonish you as my beloved children. ¹⁵For you might have ten thousand caretakers in Christ, but you do not [have] many fathers. For I fathered you in Christ Jesus through the gospel. ¹⁶Therefore, I exhort you, become imitators of me. ¹⁷Because of this, I sent to you Timothy, who is my beloved and faithful child in the Lord. He will remind you of my ways which are in ⌜Christ Jesus⌝ just as I teach everywhere in every church. ¹⁸But some have become puffed up as if I were not coming to you. ¹⁹I will come to you soon, if the Lord wills, and then I will know not the talk of those who are puffed up, but their power. ²⁰For God's reign is not [based on] talk but on power. ²¹What do you want? That I should come to you with a rod, or in love and a gentle spirit?

4:14–15   Paul says that he does not write these things to shame (ἐντρέπειν, *entrepein*) the church members (cf. 2 Cor. 2:4, where he declares he did not write the letter of tears to cause them pain). "These things" could refer to the contrast in 4:6–13 between the lowliness of apostolic existence and the Corinthians' arrogance but may also refer to his entire attack on their factions, beginning in 1:10 (cf. 4:6). Shame can be good when it is the healthy desire to avoid certain actions because they bring public and divine disapproval (cf. 2 Thess. 3:14; Titus 2:8). But the shame Paul wishes to avoid causing the Corinthians is their losing face. Although he does not shy away from speaking openly about shameful behavior (cf. 5:1–13), he wants to communicate that it is their values and behavior, not their personhoods, that are unacceptable. He may intuit that their hunger for status is attributable to core feelings of shame that lead them to crave some external, compensating validation of who they are. Addressing them as "beloved" "expresses respect as much as affection" (Spicq, *TLNT* 2:550 n. 10). He wants to instill in them a sense of self-worth that comes from God's grace and power in their lives, which is able to eradicate any hunger for the mercurial, inconsequential honor bestowed by the world.

Paul stresses his unique relationship to them as the one who "fathered" (ἐγέννησα, *egennēsa*, begot) them "through the gospel."[1] Holmberg (1978: 78) finds that Paul reminds his readers of his fatherhood (or motherhood) in all his letters except Romans and that the concept "expresses the fact that he has begotten them or given them life by the transmission of the Gospel of Christ." Paul refers to "the gospel" without a qualifier, which shows that he assumes they know what he is talking about. It is shorthand for the underlying gospel narrative of God's salvific acts on behalf of humankind through Christ's cross and resurrection and assumes that the Corinthians are thoroughly familiar with it (see M. Mitchell 1994). He uses the same verb to describe his relationship to Onesimus, whom he "begot" while he was in chains (Philem. 10). It is tied to bringing them to faith (2:4–5), planting (3:6), and laying the foundation (3:10). In rabbinic literature a proselyte is likened to a "child just born" (*b. Yebam.* 22a; *b. Sanh.* 19b; see SB 3:340–41), but this concept also would have been familiar from the mystery religions. In Apuleius's novel (*Metam.* 11.25), Lucius refers to the priest who initiated him into the mysteries of Isis as "his spiritual father."

The exaggerated image of ten thousand παιδαγωγοί (*paidagōgoi*) is a gentle slam since they are to be distinguished from teachers.[2] They were trustworthy slaves charged by members of the upper class with the duty of supervising the life and morals of their boys (see N. Young 1987). The slave led the child to the schoolhouse and back home and was assigned the duty of protecting him and keeping him out of trouble. He was caricatured for his severity as a stern taskmaster. In pic-

---

1. Lassen (1991) discusses the father metaphor in the Roman context and argues that Paul resorts to this imagery to invoke his authority over them.

2. The noun μυριάς (*myrias*) literally means "ten thousand" but is more functionally equivalent to our "zillion."

tures on Greek vases, he frequently has a stick in his hand, and in Greek plays he was often portrayed as harsh and stupid. He was a comic type recognizable by his rod (Betz 1979: 177). Quintilian (*Inst.* 1.1.8) complains about the *paedagogi* who have gone a little beyond the alphabet and falsely persuade themselves that they are knowledgeable. They resist giving way to those whose job it is to teach and imperiously and sometimes brutally impose their own stupidity on their charges as though they had some claim to authority. Furthermore, Quintilian says, their foolishness harms their charges' character.

The subjunctive (ἐάν . . . ἔχητε, *ean . . . echēte*, if you . . . should have) may ease slightly the disparaging implication that they are still in a childish state and in need of a *paidagōgos*. The humorous picture of ten thousand custodians brandishing rods at their stubborn charges may also cushion the possible affront. Paul intends to draw a contrast between the *paidagōgos* and the father. Disciplinarians are likely to berate them with shaming tactics; a loving father admonishes (Eph. 6:4; cf. Wis. 11:10) to inculcate a healthy aversion to proscribed behavior. Disciplinarians come and go—their supervision is required only during the tender years of childhood, when a child's speech, dress, and manners need attention (cf. Gal. 3:24–26; 4:1–3); the relationship with a father abides. Who these caretakers are, Paul does not say. They are unlikely to be other apostles or Apollos, since that would introduce an element of competitiveness that Paul has just renounced: "You have others, but I am your founder!" (Furnish 1961: 370). Instead, they are likely to be the local leaders of the competitive factions.

4:16 The phrase παρακαλῶ . . . ὑμᾶς (*parakalō . . . hymas*, I exhort you) repeats the beginning exhortation in 1:10 and bundles 1:10–4:21 into a unit (B. Sanders 1981: 354; contra B. Dodd 1999: 64–67, who reads 4:14–21 as the introductory section to 5:1–15:58). It is natural for children to take after their fathers (D. Stanley 1959: 872), and Paul regards "his life worthy of imitation because it is defined by the 'word of the cross'" (Pickett 1997: 59). The image of pupils imitating their teacher also was widespread (Lindemann 2000: 114–15). It should be remembered that these first converts had no precedents or heritage to coach them on how to live out the radical demands of the gospel. They had only Paul's verbal instructions and what they could witness firsthand of his own behavior and attitudes. Paul's request that they imitate him, however, strikes many today as egotistical, but such criticism should dissipate when one traces what he could expect them to imitate.[3] They are to give up their hankering for high status and accept the lowliness

---

3. For a critique of Castelli (1991), who considers "imitation" to be a power strategy and accuses Paul of paternalism and authoritarianism under the masquerade of a loving father, see Witherington (1995: 144–46) and Thiselton (2000: 371–73).

that Paul models.[4] They are to welcome being regarded as fools for Christ, and as weak and dishonored. They are to return abuse with blessing, slander with conciliation, and to endure persecution (4:10–13). They are to recognize that all that they are and have comes to them as a grace-gift from God (3:10) and that they are not inherently extraordinary (4:7). They are to think of themselves as no better than menial field hands (3:5) and servants (4:1) awaiting God's judgment to determine if they were trustworthy (4:5). They are to rid themselves of all resentments and rivalries with co-workers so that they can toil together in God's field (3:5–9). They are to resist passing themselves off as wise or elite by using lofty words of wisdom or aligning themselves with those who do and to rely instead on the power of God that works through weakness, fear, and trembling (2:1–4). The ultimate aim is not to be Paul-like, but Christlike (11:1). The Corinthians are to imitate him only insofar as his behavior corresponds to the gospel (cf. 4:9–13, his suffering; 9:19, his becoming the slave of all; 2 Cor. 12:9–10, his weakness; 2 Cor. 12:12, his patience).[5]

Timothy is also identified as his beloved child in the Lord (cf. Phil. 2:22;   **4:17** 1 Tim. 1:2, 18; 2 Tim 1:2) and is on the same level with the Corinthians, who are Paul's beloved children. He is the model child who faithfully imitates his father (cf. Phil. 2:22). The verb ἔπεμψα (*epempsa*) could be translated as an epistolary aorist, "I am sending," in which the writer looks at things from the perspective of the recipients of the letter (cf. 2 Cor. 8:18, 22). By the time they receive the letter, Timothy already would have been sent. If this is correct, then Timothy could be the bearer of the letter; but the wording in 16:10, "if he comes" (ἐὰν ἔλθῃ, *ean elthē*), suggests some doubt about Timothy's arrival in Corinth and makes this rendering improbable. It is more likely that it is a true preterit: "I sent." Timothy was sent before this letter was penned. Barrett (1968: 116) suggests reasonably that Paul has not commissioned Timothy only to go to Corinth but has sent him elsewhere, to Macedonia (cf. Acts 19:22), and he expects him to arrive in Corinth after the letter. Barrett also suggests that Paul could mean that he sent word to Timothy to come to Corinth after he had set out for another destination.

Timothy will "remind them" of his ways. This statement need not mean that they have forgotten what Paul said and did (contra Edwards 1885: 117), but that Timothy will live in the same kind of way that Paul did (Lindemann 2000: 116). "My ways" are Christ's ways and reflect the soul of Christian faith: Christians live a certain way (cf. Acts 9:2; 18:25–

---

4. B. Sanders (1981: 358–60) claims that Paul never asks his churches to share his apostolic sufferings, but cf. Rom. 8:17; Phil. 1:29; 1 Thess. 3:3; 2 Tim. 3:12.

5. Paul asks the Galatians to become as he is (Gal. 4:12) as one free from the law, and asks the Philippians to imitate him (Phil. 3:17) as one who renounces advantages and privileges he once enjoyed to pursue the goal set before him in Christ.

26; 19:9, 23). Paul is interested in them learning his ways (cf. 12:31), not just his ideas or doctrines. The problem is not some theological misunderstanding of the gospel but "a failure to grasp its communal implications and its consequences for Christian conduct" (B. Sanders 1981: 363). What he asks of them and teaches them, he asks of and teaches every congregation (7:17; 11:16; 14:33). This statement underscores the interdependence of all local assemblies rather than their independence (Barrett 1968: 117).

4:18–20 Baird (1990: 131) contends, "The most common feature of the Corinthian character . . . is pride"; and Judge (1960: 60) believes that "the Corinthians . . . were dominated by a socially pretentious section of the population." It is not an open rebellion against Paul's authority. Their arrogant self-importance is like that of little children who have the house to themselves when the parents have slipped out for a minute. Fee's (1987: 190) reference to the "ringleaders" is overblown, and wrongly assumes some nefarious plot to usurp Paul's authority. Witherington (1995: 145) is correct: "1 Corinthians 1–4 is not an *apologia* or an attempt to reestablish a lost authority." Paul warns them that the father will be coming home soon (cf. 11:34; 16:3, 5–7), and he had better find everything in order.[6] The "soon" (ταχέως, *tacheōs*) must be understood in relative terms, since he says in 16:8 that he will remain in Ephesus until Pentecost. It does not indicate that these two references to his travel derive from the conclusions to different letters. It means "before long" (Moffatt 1938: 52; Belleville 1987: 32; cf. the use of ταχέως in Phil. 2:19, 24; 2 Tim. 4:9). Paul's travel plans are always conditioned upon the will of God (16:7; Rom. 1:10; 15:32; 1 Thess. 3:11; Philem. 22).

Paul implies that "the talk" (ὁ λόγος, *ho logos*) of those who are puffed up is empty wind. It will differ significantly from their power (ἡ δύναμις, *hē dynamis*), which recalls the contrast he draws between high-flown talk and divine power in 2:1–4 and the antithesis between human wisdom and the power of God in 2:5. Human pride leads persons to crow like bantam roosters, which are devoid of any power. To use a Texas idiom, Paul implies that these arrogant persons are "all hat and no cattle." He has acknowledged that they are enriched "in word" (1:5) and wants that word to be subject to the word of the cross (1:18), from which comes the true, spiritual power to transform people's lives.

The explanation "For God's reign is not in talk but in power" contains no verb in the Greek. The NIV adds "is a matter of"; the NRSV, "depends." Paul uses the phrase "the reign of God" to refer both to its

---

6. Thiselton (2000: 376) comments that "a rude shock now confronts any who were congratulating themselves that they would not need to meet Paul face to face." According to 2 Cor. 2:1–11, Paul himself met with a shock when he was rudely treated by an individual in the church on his second visit.

present effect (Rom. 14:17; Col. 1:13; 4:11; 1 Thess. 2:12) and its future reality (1 Cor. 6:9, 10; 15:24, 50; Gal. 5:20–21; Eph. 5:5; 2 Thess. 1:5). He may use it here with an eye to their boast that they "reign" (4:8). A kingdom built on a foundation of empty words (theological slogans and prescriptions) and prideful boasts will collapse in on itself.

Paul returns to the contrast between the *paidagōgos* and the father. The **4:21** "rod" was an image of severe discipline and symbolized both Jewish (2 Sam. 7:14; Prov. 10:13; 13:24; 22:15; 23:13–14; 29:15, 17; Sir. 30:12) and Greek education. A sideways glance at Philo (*Post. Cain* 28 §97), who contends that "the rod" is a symbol of discipline (παιδεία, *paideia*) and that one will not take to heart admonishment or correction without it, suggests that Paul was of a different mind. The contrast stresses that "the apostle's love is that of a father, without violence, all gentleness and serenity; it persuades rather than rails" (Spicq, *TLNT* 3:169). He avoids force, psychological and physical, because it is contrary to the nature of the cross and the way of love. He admonishes (4:14), exhorts (4:16), reminds (4:17), and is, from their perspective, perhaps too meek (2 Cor. 10:1–11). The content of his message, however, fashions not only his manner of preaching but also his manner of dealing with them. The threat of coming at them with a rod prepares for the account of disgraceful behavior in what follows.

Additional Note

4:17. "Christ Jesus" is read in $\mathfrak{P}^{46}$, ℵ, C, D[1], 33, syr[h], cop[bo], but "Christ" is read in A, B, D[2], Ψ, vg, syr[p], cop[sa], Byz; and "Lord Jesus" is read in D*, F, G. I have chosen to go with the majority of the manuscripts in reading "Christ Jesus" rather than the customary preference for the shortest reading.

IV. Incest, Lawsuits, and Prostitution (5:1–6:20)

When Paul announces his anticipated visit to Corinth in 2 Cor. 12:20–21, he expresses dismay that this spiritually boastful church not only is riddled with "quarreling, jealousy, anger, selfishness, slander, gossip, conceit, and disorder," but also still may not have repented of past "impurity, sexual immorality [πορνεία, porneia], and licentiousness." The incidents mentioned in 5:1–6:20 give us a glimpse of some of the behavior that brings moral shame on the community and causes Paul to mourn. Though the order of topics in 5:1–6:20—incest (5:1–13), lawsuits (6:1–11), and prostitution (6:12–20)—seems disjointed to some interpreters, some recurring patterns appear:

- Each passage contains an eschatological affirmation: a hope that the incestuous man's spirit might be saved on the day of the Lord (5:5); an assertion that the saints will judge the world and angels (6:2); a reminder that the body will be raised (6:14).

- Each passage contains an allusion to the opinions of outsiders and implies that the Corinthian Christians are making bad impressions on their unbelieving neighbors with their bad behavior. One has committed a sin that even the pagans find abhorrent (5:1). Brothers air their dirty linen before unbelievers in their unjust courts (6:6). The combination of the commands to flee sexual immorality (6:18) and to glorify God with their bodies (6:20) implies that unbelievers will note chaste behavior (cf. Matt. 5:16; Phil. 1:20).

- A sharp command appears in each passage: "kick out" (5:13), "set up" (6:4), "flee" (6:18).

- Passages found in the Deuteronomic code anchor Paul's response to the misconduct. Incest is specifically condemned in Deut. 22:30; 27:20. The command to purge any evil from the midst of God's people is found in Deut. 13:5 [6]; 17:7; 19:19–20a; 21:21; 24:7. Appointing judges to render just decisions when disputes arise among the people is found in Deut. 16:18–20. A connection to prostitution is declared to be abhorrent to God in Deut. 23:17–18.

- The first two passages contain a similar catalog of vices (5:9–11; 6:9–10), and both have to do with matters that may be classified as legal: expelling a church member, suing a fellow Christian.

Some spot an ABA' pattern, which is so prevalent in the letter, in which the discussions about two different kinds of sexual immorality in 5:1–13 and 6:12–20 ring the admonition against lawsuits (6:1–11; see R. Collins 1999: 225).

A The Case of Incest (5:1–13)
  B Lawsuits (6:1–11)
A' Visiting Prostitutes (6:12–20)

The center of the ABA' construction is the pivotal unit where Paul discusses the general principles applicable to the whole discussion, but it is hard to see how what is said in 6:1–11 applies in this way to either passage surrounding it. All three passages, instead, appear to be independent, self-contained units and do not form an ABA' ring construction (Pascuzzi 1997: 91).

Others attempt to identify an overarching theme linking the discussions. Each passage is said to deal with symptoms of competitive greed (Countryman 1988: 104–9; 296–314), expressions of irrational passion (Fiore 1990), confusion about purity boundaries (Meeks 1983: 129), failures to apply their faith to moral decisions (Parry 1926: 100), or the community's competence to judge (Probst 1991: 315). The three issues that Paul comments upon in this section complement the previous discussion in chapters 1–4. In these opening chapters he insinuates that the church is riven by unnecessary strife fed by unjustified spiritual pride. Threatening to come after them with a rod (4:21), however, seems a bit extreme to settle such problems. The three cases cited in 5:1–6:20 make that threat more understandable. Aside from Paul's interest in putting right these evils in the community (Forkman 1972: 139), discussing these cases at this juncture in the letter may reflect his intention to expose their carnality (3:1) and demolish their misplaced pride. He wishes to shame them (6:5) as well as admonish them (4:14). To emphasize the seriousness of a sin, Paul calls it shameful, which cuts to the quick in a shame/honor culture that is extremely sensitive to issues of reputation. R. Collins (1999: 220) notes that philosophical moralists in this era used catalogs of vices "to caricature the woeful behavior of the unlettered masses." I agree with his contention that Paul employs the vice catalogs in 5:9–11 and 6:9–10 "to confront the *hybris* of the know-it-alls in the community." In 6:9–10, he reminds them of "their shameful past before their conversion," implying that they have reverted to it (Rosner 1994: 119). How can any community afflicted with such sins be puffed up (5:2)?

In the first two cases, Paul does not reprimand the perpetrators but the entire church. The conduct of these individuals is a negative reflection on the whole church and, concomitantly, on the gospel. In 5:1–13, he does not zero in on the man who is guilty of the sin of incest but censures the church for appearing to condone it. Such immorality never can be treated as a private matter but is something so evil that it threatens the church's existence if left unpunished (Pascuzzi 1997: 147). In 6:1–11, he does not blast the disputants for suing one another in pagan courts but the church for failing to be able to resolve the disputes. The focus in these two incidents is on the failure of the church body and the dark shadow such wrongdoing casts on its reputation with outsiders. His comments in 6:12–20 about frequenting prostitutes differ from the first two sets of remarks because no specific case is mentioned. His generic remarks serve to correct any false views that they may harbor about the morality expected of Christians and Christ's lordship over their embodied existence. We can presume, however, that Paul is not worried about some imaginary wrongdoing but that some Corinthian Christians had consorted with prostitutes. The reason this passage differs from the previous two is that it serves as a hinge unit that lays the groundwork for what follows (see below on 6:12–20). Key to all three passages is Paul's concern that they do untold damage to their witness to Christ's reign by being guilty of incest, hauling fellow Christians before unbelievers to judge petty conflicts, and continuing in their former whoredom.

What has happened in Corinth demonstrates the truth of the adage "For where there is envy and selfish ambition, there is disorder and every evil practice" (James 3:16). In the opening chapters, Paul decries their envy and selfish ambition that has spawned divisions and quarrels among them (1:10). He then cites instances of every evil practice that has surfaced among church members: incest, lawsuits, prostitution. His purpose in this section is to deflate their baseless spiritual arrogance with examples of their reprehensible carnality. It reflects their ignorance of the moral claims that Christ's reign places upon his followers. The repeated question "Do you not know?" underscores this basic ignorance.[1] Paul chides them for not having one of the very things they boast about: "knowledge." They also claim to be wise, but he points out that apparently there is none wise enough in the church to settle minor disputes (6:5). The evidence presented in 5:1–6:20 testifies to the hollowness of their boasting.

---

1. Seven of the twelve occurrences of the question in Paul's letters appear in this section (5:6; 6:2, 3, 9, 15, 16, 19; elsewhere, Rom. 6:16; 11:13; 1 Cor. 3:16; 9:13, 14).

A. The Case of Incest (5:1–8)

The case of the man having his father's wife seems to be a dramatic shift from the preceding discussion, but it should not be disconnected from what precedes as something completely unrelated (Meeks 1983: 128). Paul is not moving from one topic to another. The scornful exclamation "And you are puffed up!" (5:2) recalls 4:6, 18, 19 where the verb φυσιοῦν (*physioun*) occurs (cf. 8:1; 13:4; elsewhere in the NT it appears only in Col. 2:18). The Corinthians appear to take undue pride in identifying themselves as πνευματικοί (*pneumatikoi*, spiritual ones; 2:13, 15; 3:1; 14:37). When we remember that the word πνευματικοί derives from πνεῦμα (*pneuma*), which also means "wind," the image of them being "puffed up" may be seen as a droll putdown. Paul's discussion of this case of incest is interwoven with his concern about the spiritual swaggering of the Corinthians (4:18; 5:2).

The key issue in this section is not Paul's need to reassert his authority over the community with a show of force. The root problem is their spiritual arrogance combined with moral laxity. Since Paul directs all of his commands to the church body, we can infer that he is more vexed with the congregation than he is with the culprit. The man is committing an odious sin, but they have permitted the person guilty of such sin to continue as a member in good standing without taking any disciplinary action. If they are the temple of God (3:16–17), the presence of this sin in their midst completely befouls its sanctity. Paul wants to puncture their inflated arrogance, to shake them out of their blasé attitude toward this sinful conduct, to purify the community of the contagion, and to create a situation that drives home the seriousness of the man's sin and his need for repentance.

First, Paul's concerns center on the moral stigma that such a sin, "a kind not found even among pagans," casts on the faith. This statement is not an exaggeration for rhetorical effect (contra De Vos 1998: 112). This behavior is an affront to the moral consciousness even of benighted pagans, who, as far as Jews were concerned, were the epitome of moral depravity because they did not know God (1 Thess. 4:5). Bruce (1971: 54) notes that many Gentiles were already prone to believe the worst about Christians (cf. Suetonius, *Nero* 16, "a group of people belonging to a new and malevolent fanaticism [*superstitionis*]"). Paul did not want to give unbelievers any excuse for their unbelief (10:32–33; 9:19–23; cf. Phil. 2:14–15; 1 Thess. 4:12), but this behavior would provide hostile outsiders with material evidence for their suspicions. It would also further undermine Paul's missionary efforts, which, according to Acts, were already under attack by the conservative wing of the Jerusalem church. In Galatia, the troublers appear to have maintained that Paul's gospel of grace inevitably led to outbreaks of immorality. If news of this evil arrived in Jerusalem and if it were believed that Paul in some way fostered or condoned it, his relationship with Jerusalem Christians would have eroded even further.

Second, Paul fears the dire consequences that will ensue from tolerating such wickedness. It contaminates the whole community with a moral blight that will ultimately destroy it. They cannot escape God's judgment that will fall upon the whole group if they continue to allow this corruption to remain in the community. Most Greeks would know that Oedipus's inadvertent relationship with his mother ended in tragedy. The biblical prohibition against incest, however, promises divine judgment.

Third, tolerating such evil, even if only through benign neglect, stifles the celebration of their new life in Christ (5:7). The Christian faith is to have ethical consequences and to bring about moral transformation. They are to become what they are: unleavened bread, a symbol of purity.

In his response to this egregious sin, Paul stresses his spiritual presence in the community (5:3–4). This gives him the right to speak as he does without destroying the responsibility of the congregation. He pronounces judgment on this sin, not by fiat, but with the community.[1] He gives three directives to expel the man. The first is direct: "Let the one who has done this deed be taken from your midst!" (5:2c). The second is couched in metaphorical language: "Cleanse out the old leaven!" (5:7a). The third quotes Scripture: "Purge the evil from your very midst!" (5:13b). The ambiguous command to hand over such a one to Satan (5:5) becomes clearer in this context. It means to put the man out of the church and into the world, where Satan reigns (2 Cor. 4:4): Relinquish him to Satan's sphere of influence and let Satan work him over. Satan, ironically, can become a means of his deliverance (Wink 1986: 16). The community does not determine the man's ultimate salvation or condemnation. That is left to God. But the community is to judge whether his behavior accords

---

1. Meeks's (1983: 128) suggestion that Paul may also be interested in "shaping the congregation's understanding of its responsibility for self-discipline and the relation between self-discipline and wider forms of authority" with this case may be correct. Paul seeks to create Christian communities that are mature enough to supervise themselves without someone constantly standing over them with a stick.

with the name "Christian" and is to take action against those in their number who are guilty of gross immorality.

The passage reflects the following chiastic structure:

A The prophetic identification of the heinousness of the sin that should squelch their arrogance and a call for the man's exclusion from the community (5:1–2)
B The judgment of the man's guilt and a call for the man's exclusion from the community in metaphorical language (5:3–5)
A′ A denunciation of their arrogance and a call for the man's exclusion from the community in metaphorical language (5:6–8)

Exegesis and Exposition

[1]In short, it has been reported that there is sexual immorality among you, and the sort of sexual immorality not even tolerated among the Gentiles, ⌜namely⌝, a certain one is having his father's wife. [2]How, then, can you still be puffed up? Should you not rather have mourned? Let the one who has done this deed be taken from your midst. [3]For I myself, though absent in the body but present in the spirit, have already pronounced judgment ⌜in the name of the Lord Jesus⌝, as present, on the one who has done this thing. [4]When your spirit and mine are gathered together with the power of our Lord Jesus, [5]hand over such a one to Satan for the destruction of the flesh in order that the spirit might be saved ⌜in the day of the Lord⌝. [6]Your boasting is not good. Do you not know that a little leaven leavens the whole batch. [7]Cleanse out the old leaven, in order that you might be a new batch, just as you are unleavened. For indeed Christ, our Passover, was sacrificed. [8]So then, let us keep the feast not with old leaven or with bad and evil leaven but with unleavened bread that is pure and of the truth.

Paul's indignation is prompted by an oral report from unnamed sources, perhaps Chloe's people (1:11) or Stephanas, Fortunatus, and Achaicus (16:17) or both groups. It was an awkward matter that the Corinthians were unlikely to write to Paul about in their letter (7:1) but something that those chagrined by the whole affair would leak to Paul. Boer (1994: 240) raises the question of why Paul waits until now in his letter to respond to this behavior, since it is an offense far more grave than the rise of factions, which do not call for expulsion from the church. He speculates that Paul restarted his letter at this point after hearing from Stephanas and company (cf. Bruce 1971: 53), so that chapters 1–4 and 5–16 are essentially two different letters compelled by two different circumstances. This deduction is unwarranted. The reason Paul held this serious issue in abeyance until now is tied to his rhetorical strategy. Before addressing this highly sensitive issue, he must first clear the air about the budding dissension in the church centering around different loyalties

5:1

155

and groups. Perhaps this affair contributed to the discord or was even the root of the discord. He is not present and cannot visit soon to take matters into his own hands (cf. 11:34), and so he must try to resolve things from a distance through his letter. Only after laying the theological foundation and reasserting his authority over them in chapters 1–4 can he turn his attention to this urgent matter (Jacobs 1997: 384). The dishonor that this case of incest, their lawsuits against one another, and the lechery with prostitutes brings to Christ and his church punctures any pretense for pride and boasting on their part. They may think they are "kings" and hold others in contempt, but their own contemptible behavior should strip away any veneer of arrogance.

The phrase ὅλως ἀκούεται (*holōs akouetai*) serves as a marker for this new section. The adverb ὅλως can mean "actually" (BDAG 704; cf. 15:29; T. Job 31:1; 38:1), "undoubtedly," "altogether" (cf. 6:7), or "in short" (LSJ 1218).[2] If it means "actually" (Barrett 1968: 120; Fee 1987: 199; Clarke 1993: 117 n. 33; Wolff 1996: 100), it expresses some shock that such a thing could have happened in the church. If it means "undoubtedly," "incontrovertibly" (Edwards 1885: 122; Robertson and Plummer 1914: 95), Paul asserts that he has no doubt about the truth of the report. If it means "altogether" (Lightfoot 1895: 202), he may mean "the whole story has been reported" (Kistemaker 1993: 156). If it means "in short" or "in one word" (Parry 1926: 86), it ties the discussion in chapter 5 to what Paul has just said about their haughtiness in chapter 4. The report of incest, "in short," knocks the props out from under their grandiosity (4:18). It betrays that they are not wise, that they should not be held in honor (4:10), and that he needs to come to them like an irate *paidagōgos*, rod in hand, to punish them (4:21). If this neglected meaning of the adverb is correct, then it not only makes the transition from chapter 4 to chapter 5 less abrupt, but also shows that they are interconnected.

Paul expresses shock, amazement, and horror at the report that such brazen immorality was committed by a Christian. The word πορνεία (*porneia*) is a flexible term that covers all prohibited sexual intercourse and here applies to a case of unnatural sexual vice, "incest."[3] It reappears in 6:13, 18 and 7:2 to refer to sexual relations outside of marriage (cf. 2 Cor. 12:21; Gal. 5:19; Eph. 5:3; Col. 3:5; 1 Thess. 4:3).[4] The trans-

---

2. The translation "it is universally [commonly, generally] reported" (Godet 1886: 240; Weiss 1910: 124; Héring 1962: 34; Conzelmann 1975: 94) does not fit Paul's usage of the adverb elsewhere in the letter. The spread of the report is not his concern.

3. The word πορνεία is used for Reuben's incest with his father's concubine in T. Reub. 1:6; 4:8.

4. The cognate noun πόρνος (*pornos*, fornicator) is to be differentiated from "adulterer" (μοιχός, *moichos*). Πόρνος appears in 5:9, 10, 11; 6:9 (cf. Eph. 5:5; 1 Tim. 1:10); the noun πόρνη (*pornē*, prostitute) in 6:15, 16; and the verb (πορνεύω, *porneuō*) in 6:18 (cf. 10:8).

lation "sexual immorality" seems too tame and sanitized to convey Paul's revulsion for the transgression, and the word "whoredom" may better capture his moral indignation.

Claiming that this sin is not tolerated "even among the Gentiles" serves rhetorically to heighten the Corinthians' guilt (cf. 1 Macc. 7:23) and has affinities with Amos 1–2, where the prophet decries Israel's sins as worse than those of the surrounding nations (Rosner 1994: 84; cf. Calvin 1960: 180).[5] Since Paul so disdains Gentile sexual morality (Rom. 1:18–32; 1 Thess. 4:5), their disapproval of such a sin marks it as utterly despicable.[6] The pagans' world is awash in *porneia,* but this kind of *porneia* is not even heard of (no verb is expressed in the Greek text) among them. He is not exaggerating. Incest—sexual relations with primary or adoptive kin—was regarded as a serious infraction in this culture (J. Gardner 1986: 125–27).[7]

By appealing to a universal norm of decency, Paul intends to evoke shame in the Corinthians to puncture their inflated pride and make them more amenable to change (Pascuzzi 1997: 105–9).[8] If the church tolerates sin that even pagan society condemns as deviant, it torpedoes its moral witness in the world. If its standards of sexual morality sink below those of the unconverted society around them, something is badly amiss. Their conduct in the world should bring glory and honor to God and, at the very least, respect for their faith from outsiders. If they appear to condone egregious sin, they will give offense to "Jews, Greeks, and the church of God" (10:32) and eradicate any moral boundary lines that set them apart as a holy people from their unbelieving neighbors.

Paul leaves unnamed the man guilty of this outrage, identifying him only as a "certain one." "To have his father's wife" refers to sexual intercourse (cf. 7:2), and the present infinitive "to have" (ἔχειν, *echein*) may entail marriage (cf. Mark 6:17–18, where it is synonymous with ἐγάμησεν, *egamēsen,* married) or an ongoing fling (cf. John 4:18).[9] The term

---

5. Hays (1997: 81) suggests that Paul's use of the term τὰ ἔθνη (*ta ethnē*) indicates that he no longer considers his converts to be Gentiles (cf. 12:2, 3; Gal. 3:28). They are part of the covenant people of God.

6. This reaction reflects Paul's strongly Jewish perspective regarding not only the sin of incest but also the judgment of the morality of the pagan world (see Holtz 1995: 56–57).

7. Moral outrage over incest is expressed by Cicero, *Pro Cluentio* 5.12–6.14; Martial, *Epigrams* 4.16; Tacitus, *Annales* 6.19; and Dio Cassius, *Roman History* 58.22. It is also dealt with as a grave breach in the Augustan *lex Julia de adulteriis,* which was intended to clean up moral corruption (Clarke 1993: 77–78).

8. Pascuzzi (1997: 106–9) argues that this rhetorical strategy testifies to the positive relationship Paul still has (or at least thinks he still has) with the community. Aristotle (*Rhet.* 2.6.23) observed that no one will feel shame before another "whose opinion about truth is greatly despised."

9. Hurd (1965: 278) thinks that the couple were joined in a spiritual marriage, but the language Paul uses rules out this option. He is outraged by their sexual relationship.

"father's wife" (γυνὴ τοῦ πατρός, *gynē tou patros*) does not refer to the man's biological mother. In Lev. 18:7, the prohibition against intercourse with your "mother" is juxtaposed with the same prohibition against intercourse with your "father's wife" in 18:8. The two are regarded as distinct, and the latter term is used for a stepmother (cf. Lev. 20:11; Deut. 23:1; 27:20; *m. Sanh.* 7:4; *t. Sanh.* 10:1).

As is often the case in this letter, we are hard pressed to delineate the actual circumstances that provoked this sharp denunciation. We know that Paul considers this incestuous relationship to be a sordid sin that offends even Gentile moral standards, that he intends for the church to expel the perpetrator from the community, and that he expects it to be done without delay in their assembly. We also learn why he thinks this should be done: this sinner's corruption will infect the whole church. We do not know, however, the details of the relationship between the man and the woman (see additional note). The church may be proud of him for some twisted theological reason; but if he is a rich patron, with some social standing, they are likely to have second thoughts before taking any steps to dishonor him (see Moffatt 1938: 53). If they are his clients, they dare not. Goulder (1999: 348) assumes that the man is wealthy, and he remarks, "It is easy to overlook the peccadilloes of those who contribute generously to the church funds, or open their homes for church meetings." Since Paul gives no details, we must leave open the question about the exact relationship between the man and the woman and why it came about, but the suggestion that this man possessed some social standing best explains the church's incriminating silence.

Most commentators assume that the woman is not a Christian, because Paul makes no mention of what the church should do with her. He says in 5:12–13 that he is not responsible for judging outsiders, but God will judge them; and, we might note, society will judge them as well in the case of such flagrant sin. For whatever reason, he does not address what is to be done with her.

From Paul's perspective, the man grievously transgresses God's law: "You shall not uncover the nakedness of your father, which is the nakedness of your mother; she is your mother, you shall not uncover her nakedness. You shall not uncover the nakedness of your father's wife; it is the nakedness of your father" (Lev. 18:7–8 NRSV; cf. Deut. 22:30). The penalty for breaking this law was death for the man and woman so that the evil might be purged from Israel (Lev. 20:11; cf. Deut. 22:20). The law also pronounces a curse upon the malefactor, which calls for a community "Amen" in response (Deut. 27:20).[10] The rabbis include in-

---

10. The biblical understanding of this sin as a violation of rights of the father (Deut. 22:30; 27:20; cf. Philo, *Spec. Laws* 3.3 §§20–21), whether he is living or dead, might connect this case with 2 Cor. 7:12, where Paul mentions the one who was wronged (ὁ ἀδικηθείς, *ho adikētheis*).

cest in a catalog of thirty-six offenses that required that the offender be "cut off" from the people (*m. Ker.* 1:1; cf. *m. Sanh.* 7:4–5). Jubilees 33:10–13 contains a recap of the laws against incest found in Lev. 20:11 and Deut. 22:30 and adds,

> There is no forgiveness in order to atone for a man who has done this, forever, but only to execute him and kill him and stone him and to uproot him from the midst of the people of God. For any man who does this in Israel should not have life for a single day upon the earth because he is despicable and polluted.

The phrase ἐν ὑμῖν (*en hymin,* among you) explains Paul's outrage. It could go with the verb ἀκούεται (*akouetai*) and refer to the fact that a report of the incest was circulated among them (Edwards 1885: 122; Lightfoot 1895: 202; Weiss 1910: 124). But the report has spread beyond Corinth to reach Paul in Ephesus. His problem is not that news of this sin is being noised abroad or talked about in the community (contra Robertson and Plummer 1914: 95) but that such a disgraceful deed has transpired *among* them (Schrage 1991: 371). It is better to take the phrase with the noun πορνεία. Paul directly contrasts this sin occurring "among you" with the fact that such sin does not occur "even among the Gentiles." Sexual immorality like this can never be treated as if it were only a private matter. The entire community is implicated in the sin, which explains why Paul never addresses the man directly but only the community. He regards the community no less guilty for failing to correct this infamy than the person for committing it. The unstated premise is that the community is responsible for the moral behavior of its members (Hays 1997: 82). When sinful excesses go unchecked, the church is exposed to God's vengeance.

The reference to being puffed up ties the discussion of this case to Paul's concern about their spiritual arrogance in chapter 4, where the verb φυσιοῦν appears in 4:6, 18, 19 (cf. 8:1; 13:4). The perfect periphrastic πεφυσιωμένοι ἐστέ (*pephysiōmenoi este*) indicates a continuing condition of being puffed up. From his admonitions in chapters 1–4, we can surmise that their inflated opinion of themselves sprang from an overweening sense of spiritual power, knowledge, and wisdom (Meeks 1983: 128). It expresses itself in boasting (5:6). To capture the emphatic ὑμεῖς (*hymeis*) and its connection with the previous discussion, I have translated it as a question, "How, then, can you still be puffed up?" The implication is that with such a pestilent moral virus infecting their fellowship, they of all people have no justification to be boastful.[11] In Scripture, pride, dishonorable acts, and destruction are assumed to be

5:2

---

11. Robertson and Plummer (1914: 96) translate it, "You, among whom this enormity has taken place and is notorious, you are puffed up."

somehow intertwined (2 Chron. 26:16; 32:24–25; Ps. 10:4; Prov. 8:13; 11:2; 21:4). In this case, Paul warns that the deadly combination of pride and the toleration of dishonorable acts threatens the entire community's destruction.

How does their arrogance relate to this despicable sexual transgression? Is the boasting because of the sin or in spite of the sin? Some assume that the Corinthians did not cover up this incestuous relationship with embarrassment but instead took pride in it.[12] They link such bravado to the Corinthians' theological confusion about their freedom, expressed in the slogan "All things are permitted" (6:12). As self-appointed "spiritual ones" they may have imagined that "they could break every canon of decency and yet be without sin" (Enslin 1930: 151). They may even have viewed this particular case as evidence of the man's newfound maturity and freedom in the new age (Thiselton 1977–78: 516). He may have convinced himself and others that "sexual behavior was spiritually irrelevant" (Talbert 1987: 15) and that he was now above any social taboos. He was endowed with knowledge (1:5; 8:1), reigned as one of their spiritual kings (4:8), and could judge all things but be judged by no one (2:15–16a). Such serious theological confusion may explain why Paul does not respond to this case more compassionately and encourage the Corinthians "to restore such a one in a spirit of gentleness" (Gal. 6:1). This affair was not a momentary slip sparked by passion; it was something done openly and defiantly. Fee (1987: 203) comments, "It is this lack of a sense of sin, and therefore of any ethical consequences to their life in the Spirit, that marks the Corinthian brand of spirituality as radically different from that which flows out of the gospel of Christ crucified."

This interpretation runs off the rails for four reasons. First, if this behavior had been justified by some theological pretext, we might expect Paul to rebut this error more directly and vigorously. He does not take issue with them on any theological points (De Vos 1998: 109–10). The slogan "All things are lawful" appears in a different context in 6:12, and one has to make a stretch to imagine that the man appealed to it to justify his violation of the taboo against incest (contra G. Harris 1991: 14). The slogan, in fact, may not have been the watchword of libertines to excuse their sexual excesses (see comments on 6:12).

Second, it would be a remarkable phenomenon if the whole church, or even a significant portion of it, regarded as laudable something that otherwise was so universally reckoned as forbidden. Chrysostom (*Hom. 1 Cor.* 15) comments that if they were puffed up with the sin, it

12. A. Collins 1980: 253; Minear 1983: 343–44; Fee 1987: 201–2, 215; Countryman 1988: 198; G. Harris 1991: 6–7, 11, 21; Schrage 1991: 371–72; Soards 1999: 111; Thiselton 2000: 388–89. After more reflection, I have changed my mind on this issue (Garland 1999: 121).

"would imply the want of all reason." Were their theological cogitations so bizarre that they could justify and even applaud such a sin?

Third, for Paul's remark that this sin does not exist even among the Gentiles to hit home, he must assume that they were sensitive to societal attitudes toward such a sin.

Fourth, if the church was so divided, as 1:11–12 suggests, why did none object to this behavior?[13] Is it imaginable that everyone in the church was swept away by such theological absurdity? The informers obviously were not pleased about it; otherwise they would not have reported it to Paul.

Daube (1971: 223; cf. Robertson and Plummer 1914: 97) draws upon rabbinic casuistry to offer another possible reason for their pride over this sin. The rabbis viewed the new convert to Judaism as reborn so that his or her old preconversion ties and relations no longer existed after conversion. Because of the convert's rebirth as a new creature, what once might have been regarded as an incestuous relationship would no longer be such after conversion. The Corinthians were elated over this man's conversion that then made this relationship permissible, while Paul insisted that the secular law regarding incest still applied.

This view has little to commend it.[14] How were the Corinthians instructed in the intricacies of (later) rabbinic theology? Paul does not mention "conversion" in this context (Clarke 1993: 75), and his vexation is hardly ignited by their defying civil law covering incest. He regards this sin as a blatant violation of God's law that splatters the whole community with the muck of moral defilement.

It is more likely that Paul speaks of their boasting despite the immorality rather than because of it (Clarke 1993: 76–77). This statement should be connected to his previous remarks in 4:6, 18, 19 chiding them for their "puffery." How can they boast when they have such blatant and outrageous immorality in their midst? Paul registers the irony that "a church so confident and arrogant could be guilty of tolerating incest in its midst" (Clarke 1993: 76). Godet (1886: 242) comments, "Even this fact has not suffered to disturb the proud self-satisfaction which he has

13. Deming (1996) bases his reconstruction of the storyline on the assumption that the church indeed was divided over this issue and that one faction sued the man in court over the issue and lost. Paul addresses the man's partisans in 5:1–13 and the litigants against him in 6:1–11. Deming's theory, however, is unable to explain why Paul would regard the man's sin to be so serious that it calls for him to be handed over to Satan and for the church to expunge the evil from their midst in 5:1–13 while then dismissing it as a trivial case in 6:2. If he regards the subject of the lawsuit mentioned in 6:1–11 as trivial, it is unlikely to refer to this case.

14. Tomson (1990: 100–101) critiques the conclusion of Strack and Billerbeck (SB 3:358) that the Jewish sages in this era would not have objected to a Gentile or proselyte marrying his stepmother for its historical misjudgment and misunderstanding of the spirit of the ancient halakah.

already rebuked in the Corinthians in the previous chapter, or to make them come down from the celestial heights on which they are now walking to the real state of things" (so also Weiss 1910: 125; Robertson and Plummer 1914: 96; Allo 1935: 116; Barrett 1968: 122). Findlay (1910: 807) claims that Paul bursts the Corinthians' inflated opinion of themselves "with this crushing fact, no intellectual brilliance, no religious enthusiasm, can cover this hideous blot." They are not puffed up because this man flouts taboos, but in spite of it. The problem, then, is not that they applauded this incestuous relationship but that they ignored it (Clarke 1993: 87). Paul's seeks to rid the church of this ruinous sinner and their ruinous pride alike.

As noted above, the reasons for ignoring this sin are more likely to be sociological than theological. To assume that a theological pretext lies behind every problem in Corinth is both naive and unrealistic.[15] People generally do not think through some theological rationale for an action before doing it. Greco-Roman religiosity normally did not affect moral behavior, and new converts would not have been accustomed to think through the religious implications of their conduct. It is more likely, then, that the church ignored this man's sin because of his higher social status and wealth than because of some theological stance that encouraged the absence of restraint. He also is a male. Apuleius's (*Metam.* 10.2–12) cautionary tale includes an account of the tawdry lust of a stepmother toward her stepson that probably mirrors popular attitudes toward incestuous relationships in this era. The young man escapes his stepmother's enticements, and she then vengefully plots with her slave to poison him. As fate would have it, she inadvertently poisons her natural son instead. Clarke (1993: 79) observes, "This story is interesting not only for the disgust with which incest is viewed, but also for the way in which the slave adopts a position defending the honour of his mistress, rather than upholding justice. It may be that in 1 Corinthians 5 there is a situation with some parallel where the honour of a leading figure is defended, rather than justice pursued." This fictional episode reflects a bias that sexual sin is particularly shameful when a female commits it (cf. Cicero, *Pro Cluentio* 6, "Oh! to think of the woman's sin, unbelievable, unheard of in all experience save this single instance!").[16] Men in this culture could have sexual relationships outside of marriage without shame (Witherington 1995: 157). Though that freedom did not normally apply to incest or adultery (De Vos 1998: 109), the man may have been able to get away with this deed because he was a male who

---

15. Becker (1993: 199–200) attributes some of the problems to the "differences in socialization between Paul and the church."

16. P. Watson (1995: 216–19) ascribes the wicked stepmother myth to gender bias and a reproachful view of female sexuality.

possessed clout in the community, not because he has convinced everyone that his action was theologically justified by his freedom in Christ.

Most in the church probably deemed it inexpedient or impossible to confront an influential figure on the matter of sexual immorality. Such persons are dangerous to offend, both for an individual and for a church association that has an uncertain legal status and that also may be financially dependent on them. Clarke (1993: 85–86) observes,

> To lose the favour of a key benefactor, for example, would have been unthinkable in Graeco-Roman society, and would invite hostility. It would have been more expedient for such a leading figure to be protected from criticism which might lead to his excommunication. There may be, in other words, a situation where clients have chosen to ignore the sinful actions of their benefactor rather than lose the favour of so prominent a person.

Patrons were supposed to be recipients of gratitude; and if proper gratitude was not shown by clients, it resulted in enmity. In this culture, a person who felt insulted in front of family, associates, or clients would seek revenge in an attempt to restore honor. For those on a lower or even the same rung of the social ladder, the enmity of a powerful person could have disastrous consequences.[17]

Paul is no respecter of persons and pays no regard to the man's status. He insists that they should mourn in shame rather than be swollen with pride. Rosner (1992; 1994: 71–73) maintains that the word for "mourn" (πενθεῖν, *penthein*) implies sorrow over the sins of others and confessing the sin as if it were their own, with a full awareness that it incurs deserved judgment, rather than sorrow over his spiritual death or his impending physical death (contra Findlay 1910: 808; Robertson and Plummer 1914: 97; Moffatt 1938: 55; Pfitzner 1982: 42).[18] Mourning is not "primarily a feeling" (Conzelmann 1975: 96); it entails doing something about the sin. This connotation of the verb is found in 2 Cor. 12:21. Paul voices his fear that when he returns to Corinth, he "may have to mourn over many who previously sinned and have not repented of the impurity, sexual immorality, and licentiousness that they have practiced." His mourning will lead to action, drastic measures to rid

---

17. In my interpretation of 2 Corinthians, I argue that this person did not take Paul's reproof and discipline gladly but sought to rally support within the community and to discredit Paul's authority (Garland 1999: 121–22).

18. Pascuzzi (1997: 80–84) argues that the verb "to mourn" "resonates with Stoic ideas, although in a subtle ironic way." The Stoic sage was governed by apathy and mourned over nothing; only the fool mourned. There is no hint, however, that Paul intends to be ironic here. It is far more likely that he invokes the conceptual world of Scripture, where the verb πενθεῖν occurs sixty-six times in the LXX, than that he attempts to adjust the meaning of this verb to fit a Stoic worldview.

them of these sins. The verb "to mourn" also occurs in the LXX in the context of mourning over the sins of fellow members of the covenant that will bring or worsen God's judgment on the entire nation (Exod. 33:4; Num. 14:39; Jer. 4:28; 12:4; 14:2; Dan. 10:2; Amos 8:8; 1 Macc. 2:14; Ezra 10:6; Neh. 1:4; 4 Ezra [2 Esdr.] 8:72; 9:2). For example, Jeremiah denounces the false prophets of reassurance and warns,

> For the land is full of adulterers;
> > because of the curse the land mourns,
> > and the pastures of the wilderness are dried up.
> Their course has been evil,
> > and their might is not right. (23:10)

The prophet bemoans that God has found wickedness "in my house" (Jer. 23:11). The sins ensure God's curse, not blessing. By mourning, the Corinthians acknowledge the iniquities in their midst that hazard God's crushing retribution.[19] Rather than boasting, they would recognize that they totter on the brink of destruction.

The phrase ἵνα ἀρθῇ ἐκ μέσου ὑμῶν ὁ τὸ ἔργον τοῦτο πράξας (*hina arthē ek mesou hymōn ho to ergon touto praxas*) can be taken to refer to (1) the expected consequence of their mourning—so that the man who did this work might be taken from their midst (by God); (2) the purpose of their mourning—in order that the man who did this work might be taken from their midst (by God); or (3) as an imperative (an imperatival ἵνα; see Moulton and Turner 1963: 95; cf. Cadoux 1941; A. George 1944; Morrice 1972): "Let such a man be taken from your midst," that is, expel him.[20] The last option seems best. The compound verb ἐξάρατε (*exarate*) appears in 5:13 in a quotation from Deut. 17:7 and expressly commands them to expel the evildoer. It serves as an inclusio that marks off this unit and conveys the essence of what Paul expects them to do. Their mourning is not to be passive lamentation, waiting for God to do something to the man. They are to take action against him. The γάρ (*gar*) in the next clause explains why they should take this action.

5:3–5   Paul cannot return posthaste to Corinth to deal with this matter, but he considers himself to be spiritually present with the church there through his letter. In fact, he believes that his letter, read in the gathered assembly, carries the power of the Spirit (see Fee 1987: 205). Even

---

19. A possible allusion to 5:2 appears in 1 Clem. 2:6, where the Corinthians are praised for mourning over the transgressions of their neighbors and regarding their shortcomings as their own.

20. Conzelmann (1975: 96) and Orr and Walther (1976: 185) label the ἵνα as "explicative," explaining the nature of the mourning. Barrett (1968: 122) considers it to be a Pauline ellipsis: "*Did you not rather go into mourning, and show the sincerity of your mourning by taking the necessary action in order that he that had committed this deed might be taken away?*"

his critics in Corinth regarded his letters as forceful (2 Cor. 10:10). His austere judgment on this sin and his emphasis on his presence with them serves notice to those who have become arrogant, thinking that he is not coming to them (1 Cor. 4:18). He stresses that his physical absence does not curtail his authority over them as their founder and father. He is present with them (cf. Col. 2:5), but he does not explain how. It is more than simply being with them in his thoughts. He explains in 6:17 that those united to Christ become one spirit with him. This fundamental idea may be the basis of how his spirit (cf. Rom. 1:9; 8:16; 1 Cor. 14:14–15; 2 Cor. 2:13) can be present with them. United to Christ in spirit, he is present with them through Christ's presence.

After noting his spiritual presence, he announces with an emphatic ἐγώ (*egō*; placed first in the sentence) that he has already judged the one guilty of this sin.[21] The perfect tense (κέκρικα, *kekrika*) implies that this judgment still stands when they read this letter. The "already" (ἤδη, *ēdē*) perhaps hints of impatience. As their founding apostle he takes full responsibility for their behavior even when absent, and he gives a swift, summary judgment—there can be no extenuating circumstances, and he offers no provisos. He fully expects them to confirm that judgment and to seal it with immediate and decisive action when they next assemble. Procrastination is inexcusable.

One of the many mystifying problems connected to 5:3–5 is deciding which prepositional phrase goes with which verb. Many permutations are possible, though none is without difficulties. One view connects the phrase "in the name of the Lord Jesus" with the participle "worked" and connects the phrase "with the power of our Lord Jesus" with "assembled." Murphy-O'Connor (1977a: 245) translates it "As for me, absent in body but present in spirit. I as one who is present have already judged the one who has done this thing in the name of the Lord Jesus. When you are assembled, I being with you in spirit, and empowered by our Lord Jesus, such a person should be handed over to Satan." The problem with connecting "in the name of the Lord Jesus" with their assembly is that it states the obvious. When do they assemble as a church body that is not in the name of the Lord? In the three other genitive absolutes in the letter that include a prepositional phrase (4:18; 11:18, 20), the prepositional phrase comes after the participle and pronoun. The phrases in 11:18 and 20 are almost equivalent to what Paul says here and reveal this pattern: συνερχομένων ὑμῶν ἐν ἐκκλησίᾳ (*synerchomenōn hymōn en ekklēsia*, when you come together in the assembly)

21. Conzelmann (1975: 94) translates it "I have now already resolved . . . to consign this man." Fee (1987: 205 n. 44) responds that this rendering makes "the entire action" Paul's, "with no community involvement." He translates it instead "I have already passed judgment on the one who has perpetrated this deed, that you are to hand over such a one to Satan."

and συνερχομένων . . . ὑμῶν ἐπὶ τὸ αὐτό (*synerchomenōn . . . hymōn epi to auto*, when you come together at the same place). An increasing number of interpreters opt for the possibility that Paul means to say that the man did this thing "in the name of the Lord Jesus."[22] Two arguments commend this view. It follows the literal word order of the Greek, and the phrase "in the name of the [our] Lord Jesus [Christ]" is connected to the verb it follows in 1 Cor. 6:11; Col. 3:17; 2 Thess. 3:6.

But questions immediately arise. Why and how would this man perpetrate such a thing in the name of the Lord Jesus? Translators shy away from following the natural word order of the Greek because it seems incomprehensible for this man to have done such a thing in the name of the Lord. Kistemaker (1993: 160), for example, comments that the last name this sinner would appeal to is the name of Jesus; and, had he done so, Paul would have included a scathing rebuke for this misuse of Jesus' name. A. Collins (1980: 253), however, asserts, "The hypothesis that the incestuous alliance was a bold, ideological act opens the possibility that the phrase should be taken with *katergasamenon*." Those who adopt this reading contend that the man boasted of his freedom from sexual restraints because Christ had set him free from the law and given him the authority to ignore OT taboos with impunity. Such theological chutzpah may have stoked Paul's unhesitating outrage. If this reading of the situation is correct, then this transgression was not simply a sin of passion but one justified theologically with spiritual cockiness, which may also explain why Paul cites being puffed up (5:2) and boasting (5:6) as a key problem.

I reject the view that the man's actions were based on some theological motivation. His deed stemmed from lust or greed, or both. But Paul has no interest whatsoever in why the man did what he did, and the man's theological rationale for his conduct is not in his sights. The sin warrants immediate expulsion from the covenant community regardless of the motivation. It is more likely that Paul invokes the authority of the Lord Jesus in pronouncing his judgment on this man who, presumably, carried some weight in the church. This appeal to Christ's authority finds a parallel in 2 Thess. 3:6: "Now we command you, beloved, in the name of our Lord Jesus Christ, to keep away from believers who are living in idleness" (cf. Acts 3:6; 4:7, 10; 16:18; note also 2 Kings 2:24, "He cursed them in the name of the Lord").[23]

Paul's imposition of his authority surfaces in 2 Corinthians as a sticking point in their relationship (2 Cor. 10:1–11). Some in Corinth denigrated his bodily presence as weak and humble (2 Cor. 10:1–2), and his hasty retreat following a nasty confrontation (2 Cor. 2:1–4) may

---

22. Murphy-O'Connor 1977a: 245; A. Collins 1980: 253; G. Harris 1991: 15; Snyder 1992: 60–61; Schrage 1991: 372; Hays 1997: 84; R. Horsley 1998: 79; Goulder 1999: 339.

23. See the objections to this view raised by Pascuzzi (1997: 111 n. 67).

have reinforced this impression. His bodily presence conflicted with the "bold" utterances in his "weighty" (implying severity) and "strong" letters (2 Cor. 10:10). Opponents accuse him of being only a paper apostle. He boldly asserts his authority from a safe distance through his letters but cowers in weakness when present. Paul responds to this aspersion by asserting that his authority derives from the Lord (2 Cor. 10:8), that he has formidable spiritual weapons at his disposal (2 Cor. 10:4–5), and that he is ready to punish every disobedience (2 Cor. 10:6). What he says by letter he is fully prepared to carry out when present (2 Cor. 10:11). His goal, however, is not to destroy them but to build them up. This later conflict could have stemmed from this incident, when he asserts in a letter his authority by pronouncing judgment in the name of the Lord Jesus on the one who has done this deed.

Paul insists that they are to carry out this judgment when he and they come together in spirit in their assembly. Assembling together puts them in the sphere of the Lord, which bestows on them the power to hand the man over to Satan (Murphy-O'Connor 1977a: 240). "With the power of our Lord Jesus" is equivalent to "in the name of the Lord Jesus" and refers to the authority by which they make and carry out this judgment. He judges this man under the authority of the Lord; they will judge and take action against him under the authority of the Lord. In this view, Paul makes two roughly parallel statements in 5:3–5: (1) he is present with them in spirit and pronounces judgment in the name of the Lord Jesus on the one who has done this thing (5:3–4a), (2) when they assemble together, he is present with them in spirit, and with the power of the Lord Jesus they are to hand over such a one to Satan (5:4b–5). The statements can be outlined as follows:

Statement of his presence:

as present	when your spirit and mine have gathered together

Action:

I have judged	hand over

Object of the action:

the one who has done this thing	such a one

Authority for the action:

in the name of the Lord Jesus	with the power of the Lord Jesus

Since Paul repeats three times that he is present with them, he must regard this point to be of critical importance. Murphy-O'Connor (1977a: 244) explains that he "stresses his involvement, because this gave him the right to speak without destroying their responsibility." His presence with them means that this judgment is not his alone and they do not function merely as a forum that only assents to this apostolic injunction (contra Käsemann 1969: 70–71; Conzelmann 1975: 97; Havener 1979: 338).[24] In this regard, the NASB translation of 5:3–5, "For I, on my part, though absent in body but present in spirit, have already judged him who has so committed this, as though I were present. In the name of our Lord Jesus, when you are assembled, and I with you in spirit, with the power of our Lord Jesus, *I have decided* to deliver such a one to Satan. . . ," misconstrues what Paul wishes to communicate in two ways. First, ὡς παρών (*hōs parōn*) does not mean "as though I were present." He stresses the efficacy of his real presence in their midst through his spirit. Paul has no doubt that the gathered assembly will reach the same judgment about this matter, and it will become clear to those who are puffed up by the assumption that he is not coming to them (4:18–20) that his "physical absence makes no difference" (Meeks 1983: 128). Second, the italicized insertion *"I have decided,"* while grammatically possible, implies that the church's responsibility is only to carry out his dictates. While he reasserts his authority over the community in this matter, he does not mete out a sovereign decision that makes the community's decision superfluous. They are to reach the same decision in the plenary assembly (cf. Deut. 19:20a) and then are to execute it.

The disciplinary process requires the involvement of the entire community.[25] In 5:12, he insists that "you" are the ones who make the judgments about insiders; and in 5:13, he commands that "you" (ἐξάρατε, *exarate*) are to expel the evil one from your company. By stressing his presence with them and the authority of Christ and the Spirit, he communicates that they are to reach this decision *with him* and to take ac-

---

24. Käsemann (1969: 71) maintains, "The only thing that matters is that the voice of the Spirit through prophet or apostle should somehow be heard and ratified by the community through its act of assent." Conzelmann (1975: 97) avers, "The community merely constitutes the forum; it does not share in the action." Pascuzzi (1997: 119) appropriately asks, If Paul were intending to impose his orders on them autocratically, why did he go to all the trouble of setting out his reasoning so that the community could discern what was necessary? Pascuzzi (1997:123) concludes, "When the action takes place, they and Paul with them in Spirit, will pass sentence and put it into effect, acting with the power of the Lord Jesus."

25. Paul does not appear to have made a previous, private appeal for repentance as mandated by Matt. 18:15 (cf. Titus 3:10; contra G. Lampe 1967: 346). If the textual variant in Matt. 18:15, "sins against you" (εἰς σέ, *eis se*), is to be read, then this process applies to a brother sinning against a brother (cf. "between you and him alone," and the subject of 18:21, "my brother sinning against me"). The directive need not apply when someone has committed a flagrant, conspicuous sin such as incest. If the parallels to these directives in the Qumran literature are any help, they would suggest that Jesus' teaching on this issue deals with offenses that are not witnessed by others (cf. Garland 1993: 190–93).

tion *with him*. His statement in 2 Cor. 10:6 that he is prepared "to punish every disobedience when your obedience is complete" reveals that he "does not wish to exercise his authority independently of the Corinthians but intends to act only in concert with them" (Garland 1999: 438). He does not intend to mold a spiritual community whose fitness report reads, "Works well under constant supervision." He wishes to instill in them a sense of responsibility for exercising discipline under the lordship of Christ.

The meaning of handing the man over to Satan presents the next problem to unravel. Paul identifies the culprit as a "certain one" (5:1) and as "the one who has done this deed" (5:3). Telling them to hand over "such a one" (τὸν τοιοῦτον, *ton toiouton*) instead of "this one" (τοῦτον, *touton*) to Satan suggests that this action does not apply only to this particular person but to anyone who ever does anything like this (Murphy-O'Connor 1977a: 244).

The infinitive παραδοῦναι (*paradounai*) may be an imperatival infinitive (R. Collins 1999: 212; cf. Rom. 12:15; Phil. 3:16), which would be translated "hand over." To hand the man over to Satan assumes that Satan serves in some way as God's agent for punishment (1 Tim. 1:20; 2 Cor. 12:7) and may be doubly appropriate since Satan was regarded as the cause of sexual sins (7:5; cf. T. Reub. 4:7, 11; 5:3; CD 4:15–17).[26]

How are the phrases εἰς ὄλεθρον τῆς σαρκός (*eis olethron tēs sarkos*) and ἵνα τὸ πνεῦμα σωθῇ ἐν τῇ ἡμέρᾳ τοῦ κυρίου (*hina to pneuma sōthē en tē hemeru tou kyriou*) to be understood? The εἰς in the first phrase may express purpose or result (BDAG 290). If so, then the man is to be delivered to Satan "for the destruction of the flesh." If it expresses result, then the destruction of the flesh is simply the consequence of deliverance to Satan. Fee (1987: 209) interprets the destruction of the flesh as "the anticipated result of the man's being put back into Satan's domain, while the express purpose of the action is his redemption." He notes that when Paul doubles purpose clauses elsewhere, he does so by twin clauses and not with the preposition εἰς plus a final clause (cf. Gundry Volf 1990: 118).[27] Nevertheless, the translation "for the destruction of the flesh" seems to capture best one of the intentions of handing the man over to Satan.

What do "the flesh" and its "destruction" entail? The traditional interpretation, which South (1993: 540) labels the "curse/death interpretation," understands the focus to be on what happens to the man and assumes that

---

26. First Enoch 53:3–5 refers to the chains of Satan prepared to destroy the kings and potentates.

27. Cf. ἵνα . . . ὅπως (*hina . . . hopōs*, 1 Cor. 1:28–29; 2 Cor. 8:14; 2 Thess. 1:11–12); εἰς τὸ . . . ἵνα (*eis to . . . hina*, Rom. 7:4; 15:16); ἵνα . . . ἵνα (*hina . . . hina*, 1 Cor. 4:6; 7:5). The only similar expression with εἰς . . . ἵνα (*eis . . . hina*) appears in Rom. 6:4, where the εἰς does not express purpose but means "unto death."

the flesh refers to the man's physical body.[28] Conzelmann (1975: 97) categorically asserts that "the destruction of the flesh" "can hardly mean anything else but death."[29] According to Heb. 2:14, the devil (διάβολος, *diabolos*) has death in his arsenal (cf. 1 Cor. 15:26), and turning the man over to Satan effectively signs his death warrant.[30] He either will die suddenly or will suffer the throes of a slow death. This traditional view also regards this curse somehow turning out for his eternal good. It is quite different from the ὄλεθρος αἰώνιος (*olethros aiōnios*, eternal destruction) mentioned in 2 Thess. 1:9. Either his death would expiate his sin or his lingering illness would give him time to repent, and his spirit would then be saved at the day of the Lord. If this refers to a languishing death, why he must die after repenting is left unexplained. This view understands the punishment to be remedial, to bring about the man's salvation on the day of the Lord.

Some argue in support of this view that the phrase "hand over to Satan" matches ancient magical curse formulae that turn an adversary over to a supernatural power (Deissmann 1911: 302–3; Forkman 1972: 143, 146–47; Conzelmann 1975: 97). A. Collins (1980: 255–56) identifies παραδίδωμι (*paradidōmi*) as a technical term in the magical papyri and intimates that Paul has borrowed this technical language. The Dead Sea Scrolls include curses on offenders (1QS 2:5–6, 12–18; CD 7:21–8:3). The man's death may also be akin to that of Ananias and Sapphira, who were struck dead on the spot for lying to the Holy Spirit (Acts 5:1–11), and the deaths of members of the church who abused the Lord's Supper (1 Cor. 11:30). Finally, the word ὄλεθρος (*olethros*, destruction) connotes physical death elsewhere in the LXX (Exod. 12:23; Josh. 3:10; 7:25; Jer. 2:30; cf. the destroyer [ὁ ὀλοθρευτής, *ho olothreutēs*], 1 Cor. 10:10; and the destroying one [ὁ ὀλοθρεύων, *ho olothreuōn*] Exod. 12:23; Wis. 18:25; Heb. 11:28).

This interpretation is seriously flawed for several reasons. First, Paul's blessing in 1 Thess. 5:23, "May the God of peace himself sanctify you entirely; and may your spirit and soul and body be kept sound and blameless at the coming of our Lord Jesus Christ," reveals that he does not think that one part of a person will be destroyed and another part saved.[31]

---

28. Several variations exist within this view about the effects of the handing over to Satan.

29. So also Godet 1886: 255–57; Robertson and Plummer 1914: 99–100; Bultmann, *TDNT* 1:208; Schneider, *TDNT* 5:168–69; Lietzmann 1949: 23; Barrett 1968: 126–27; Forkman 1972: 146; Conzelmann 1975: 97; Gundry 1976: 143; Havener 1979: 340–41; Goulder 1999: 340–41.

30. A parallel situation appears in the letter to the church in Thyatira in Rev. 2:20–23. Members are accused of tolerating "Jezebel," who suborns the church "to practice fornication and to eat food sacrificed to idols." She has not repented and receives the sentence of being thrown into great distress and seeing her children struck dead.

31. Gundry (1976: 142–43), however, makes a strong case for anthropological duality and the disjunction of flesh and spirit at death.

Second, the curse formulae cited are not genuine parallels. South (1993: 545–47) points out that none of the formulae have anyone hand the person over to Satan but instead appeal to the demon to hand the victim over to the supplicant. "Hand over" is not a technical term for turning offenders over to supernatural powers. The magical papyri also are not communal documents but private ones that date from a much later time. South (1993: 546) contends, "It is more likely that παραδί-δωμι found its way into the Greek magical tradition as a result of Paul's use of it in 1 Cor 5:5, understood as some sort of imprecatory formula, than the reverse." Also, if Paul understood handing the man over to Satan to be for his ultimate good as well as ridding the community of a moral contagion, that differs from the magical papyri, which target personal enemies to cause them loss and injury. The magical papyri, along with the texts from the Dead Sea Scrolls, are not relevant. In spotting parallels to the NT in the Scrolls, scholars frequently tend to ignore that the community that generated these documents was a closed one and strictly forbade the dissemination of their teachings (1QS 9:16–17). It is unlikely that Paul knew these texts firsthand, let alone was influenced by them. It is far more appropriate to try to understand this decision in light of "his Jewish Scriptures to which he alludes and from which he quotes frequently" (Shillington 1998: 32; cf. South 1993: 550–51).

Third, the references to the deaths of Ananias and Sapphira in Acts 5:1–11 and of the Corinthians in 1 Cor. 11:30 are not similar, since no action was taken by the community against them. They are neither expelled from the community nor placed under Satan's power, and their deaths come from direct divine punishment, which is not designed to bring them to salvation.[32]

Fourth, some rabbis thought that one's death, when linked to repentance, expiated sin. According to *m. Sanh.* 6:2, the criminal prays on the way to the place of his execution, "May my death be a propitiation for my transgressions." In the Talmud, a debate occurs over whether one who dies in his wickedness obtains forgiveness by his death (*b. Sanh.* 47a). A distinction is made between the one who dies a natural death and the one who is executed. The conclusion is that the one who is executed, shamefully buried, and whose flesh is completely decomposed attains forgiveness (see Forkman 1972: 145–46). But Paul shows no evidence that he shares this view. To suggest that the man's quick or slow death atones for his sins is to gut Paul's core belief that atonement comes only through Christ's death (Rom. 3:21–25; 6:3–5; 8:1–3; 1 Cor. 1:18; 2 Cor. 5:18–19). South (1993: 558) contends that this

---

32. Gundry Volf (1990: 115–16) claims that this man is a "falsely professing Christian who is yet outside the kingdom and who belongs to the world," in contrast to the Christians whom Paul mentions in 11:30.

death-as-atonement concept only "demonstrates how foreign to Paul's own thought the curse/death interpretation is and should be sufficient warning that this view does not rest on reliable exegetical ground."

Fifth, this explanation assumes that Paul's "first concern" was for "the salvation of the erring member" (Barrett 1968: 127). This interpretation may soften the harshness of Paul's response, but it is not entirely accurate. His first concern, which emerges clearly in 5:6–11, is to purify the church. This man's behavior, attitude, and influence were dangerous to their existence as God's covenant community. He needed to be purged for the survival of the community.

Another interpretation understands the handing over to Satan to mean excluding the man entirely from the fellowship and ejecting him into the realm of Satan, who is still unbound. Other parallel statements in the context are less ambiguous and lend strong support to this view. The man who did this deed is to be taken from their midst (5:2); they are to cleanse out the old leaven (5:7); they are to drive out the wicked person from among them (5:13). To preserve their sanctity as God's people (1:2; cf. 10:32; 11:22; 15:9), Paul expects them to banish this man and forbids them from associating with immoral persons like this who claim to be Christian (5:11).

This concern for their sanctity explains why Paul addresses no word to the individual but only to the church body. He metaphorically identifies them as a batch of dough (5:7), rebukes them as a group (5:2, 6), and insists that they carry out the discipline when assembled as a group (5:4).[33] Rosner (1994) shows that this concern for the church's holiness correlates well with the solicitude for the holiness of the covenant people found in Scripture. Rosner (1994: 64) interprets Paul's pronouncement to hand the man over to Satan as a curse formula comparable to two passages found in Deuteronomy. They are not to bring abhorrent things into the house but to detest them, or "you will be set apart for destruction like it" (Deut. 7:26). They are to repudiate anything devoted to destruction so that the Lord may turn from fierce anger and show compassion (Deut. 13:14–18).

According to Rosner (1994: 91, 65–68), three reasons surface in the Jewish Scriptures for excluding someone from the community. The first is covenant disloyalty. An offender who does what is evil in the sight of the Lord "is expelled to maintain Israel's obedience to the demands of the covenant" (Rosner 1994: 65).[34] This penalty served as a deterrent to

---

33. Shillington (1998: 31, 34) argues that the "individualism of twentieth-century industrial society" that tends to make "the individual central to discussions of life and death issues of human existence" has overemphasized the miscreant in the case but that a new sensitivity to group consciousness of first-century Mediterranean society now recognizes that this injunction is concerned about the body politic.

34. Rosner (1994: 65) notes that בָּעַר ($bā'ar$) is translated by ἐξαίρω ($exairō$) in the LXX of Deuteronomy.

dissuade others from committing similar sin (Deut. 13:6–11; 17:2–7, 12–13; 19:19–20; 21:18–21; cf. 1 Tim. 5:20). The second reason is grounded in the idea of corporate responsibility. Heinous sin imperiled the well-being of the entire community by incurring divine displeasure. As long as guilty parties remained in the community, the nation was implicated in their sin (Num. 16; Deut. 23:14; 29:19–21; Josh. 7:1; 22:16–18; Neh. 13:18). Purging them was the only way to forestall divine judgment from destroying the entire group (Deut. 13:5; 17:7, 12; 19:13, 19; 21:9, 21–24; 24:7; Judg. 20:13). The third reason has to do with maintaining the holiness of the community. God is holy, and God's people must also be holy. Rosner (1991; 1994: 77–80) ties this theme to 3:16–17, where Paul identifies the Corinthian church as God's temple. The declaration "If anyone destroys God's temple, God will destroy that person," Rosner claims, provides "the theological framework for understanding perhaps the most fundamental reason for the expulsion of the sinner in 5:1–13." This man's presence in the church profanes God's sanctuary and "jeopardizes its future salvation in the day of the Lord" (Shillington 1998: 44).

Putting the man outside the sphere of God's protection makes him vulnerable to satanic forces (cf. Eph. 2:12; Col. 1:13; 1 John 5:19), from which Christians have been rescued (Col. 1:13; Acts 26:18).[35] The Passover imagery in 5:6–8 presumes the audience's familiarity with the biblical account, and its overtones would color their understanding of this man's punishment. In the account, the blood of the Passover lamb protected Israel from "the destroyer" (ὁ ὀλεθρεύων, *ho olethreuōn*) who struck down the firstborn of the Egyptians (Exod. 12:12–13, 21–27). Cast out from the church, the man is "no longer inside the house (3:9, 'God's building') whose doorposts are covered by the blood of Jesus" (Hays 1997: 85). Even when Christians are sheltered within the arms of the church, they are still subject to Satan's barbed darts (2 Cor. 12:7), hindrances (1 Thess. 2:18), undercover agents (2 Cor. 11:14–15), and temptations (1 Cor. 7:5). Being cut off from the realm of Christ's salvation, however, leaves one defenseless against the malignant powers still running amok in this world. Converts to Christianity already placed themselves on the fringes of society as religious misfits. Persons expelled from the Christian community might find it difficult to be reintegrated into society. Unlike today, when an expelled member can join another church down the street, expelled Christians in this era could find themselves in social limbo—neither fish nor fowl.

What does Paul expect to be the result of this expulsion? Does he have any concern for what might happen to the man, or is he consumed

---

35. Fee (1987: 209) contends that the idea of turning him out into Satan's sphere "does not mean that Satan would not directly attack him in some way, but that is incidental to the language, not its primary intent."

only with the danger he poses to the church? One answer to this question revives Tertullian's (*De pudicitia* [*Modesty*] 13–14) view that Paul's primary concern was only for the spiritual life of the community of faith and not the individual. The Greek does not include the possessive pronoun, "his" flesh and "his" spirit, though it is often inserted in translations (cf. RSV, NRSV, NASB, NIV). Instead, it refers to "the flesh" and "the spirit." It need not refer to the man's flesh or spirit but the fleshly orientation of the church, absorbed as it is by boasting. The destruction of the flesh may mean that the church's sinful attitude will be destroyed. The Spirit to be saved on the day of the Lord would then refer to the Holy Spirit resident in the community of faith. As Shillington (1998: 35) explains it, the Spirit "is the guarantee that the community of Christ will participate in the final triumph of God over sin and death (2 Cor. 1:22; 5:5)." Defiling the Spirit with sexual immorality in their midst will cause them to be excluded from the kingdom of God (Donfried 1976: 108–9; A. Collins 1980: 260; M. Mitchell 1993: 111–16; Snyder 1992: 62; R. Collins 1999: 213). Expelling the man would preserve the Spirit in the community, who keeps them for the day of the Lord. According to this view, Paul calls for the church "to rid itself of one whose immoral life contradicts the communal life in the Spirit of Christ awaiting vindication/salvation in the day of the Lord" (Shillington 1998: 36). Although the excommunication of the man into the realm of Satan may precipitate his repentance and ultimate restoration and salvation, that is not Paul's foremost consideration. He cares only about the purity of the lump of dough, the church, not what happens to the leaven, the man, when it is discarded (5:6–8). This man's flagrant wrongdoing reveals that "he no longer belongs to the realm of those who are being saved but to the realm of those who are perishing" (1 Cor. 1:18), and the congregation should "acknowledge the obvious for the sake of the Spirit" (Donfried 1976: 110).

This view challenges interpreters' fixation on the man's fate, but it has its drawbacks. If it is correct, it is the only place where Paul talks about a need to save the Holy Spirit in the community.[36] He applies the verb "to save" (σῴζειν, *sōzein*) only to humans (particularly in this letter, which includes the most appearances of the verb, 1:18, 21; 3:15; 7:16; 9:22; 10:33; 15:2). The conclusion that Paul has no concern that this punishment might also work for the ultimate good of the offender contrasts dramatically with his solicitude for the offender in 2 Cor. 2:5–11. In 2 Corinthians he worries that their punishment might lead to irreparable spiritual harm. This is not the place to engage in the debate over whether or not this passage refers to the same incident (see Gar-

36. MacArthur (1980: 251) finds this view far-fetched and thinks (1980: 253) that the spirit refers to the man "insofar as he will exist after his death in the realm of the dead" (citing 1 Enoch 22:3–13; Luke 24:37, 39; 1 Pet. 3:19; 4 Ezra [2 Esdr.] 7:100).

land 1999: 116–23), but we can ask, Are only certain sinners worthy of compassion and restitution? Is this particular sin an unpardonable one? Paul's remarks in 2 Cor. 2:5–11 and 7:5–16 reveal his pastoral concern for both individuals and the church body, and he asserts that church discipline is intended to lead to godly sorrow and repentance. One also wonders if the Corinthians would have responded warmly to any hint of callous indifference to the ultimate fate of one of their own. They might have balked if they viewed the disciplinary action that Paul urges as having no redemptive purpose except to keep them pure.

It seems best to conclude that Paul is concerned about both the church and the man. He frets about what this sin will do to the community if it is left undisciplined but he is also solicitous for the culprit's ultimate destiny.[37] Rosner (1994) provides solid evidence from the Scriptures, which were foundational for Paul, that explains why he would have thought this action was mandatory for the sanctity and safety of the community. But it does not exclude the possibility that Paul also hoped this action would be redemptive for the individual. As with the wrath of God, which hands people over (παραδίδωμι, paradidōmi) to their own sins (Rom. 1:24, 26, 28) in the hope that their wretchedness will cause them to snap out of it, Paul hopes that the miscreant, excluded from Christ's presence in the community and exposed to dark forces, might wake up to his sin and repent (see additional note).[38] Rosner (1994: 91 n. 132) allows that this idea of repentance and restoration "may well be the distinctively Christian and 'new' element in Paul's understanding of exclusion." But he contends that it should not be overemphasized: "To state the purpose of church discipline only in terms of motivating the repentance and restoration of the sinner . . . is to miss much of Paul's (and his Bible's) teaching and seriously to truncate his ecclesiology." Rosner's point is well taken, but the best interpretation melds the two concerns. The emphasis on the community's purity emerges in 5:6–8, but in 5:3–5 the emphasis falls on the man's fate (see Roetzel 1972: 116).

If the destruction of the flesh does not refer to the man's physical death, and if Paul is concerned about the man's fate as a Christian, another view takes the destruction of the flesh to refer the eradication of his sinful orientation. The "flesh" stands for a certain orientation of life (Gal. 3:13; 5:13, 16–26; 6:8; Rom. 8:3–18; Col. 3:5). It is the sin-bent self characterized by self-sufficiency that wages war against God. Paul

37. B. Campbell's (1993: 337) statement that one would expect Paul to say something about the effect the delivery to Satan would have on the man in 5:6–8 is easily dismissed. He has already explained that in 5:5. In 5:6–8, he gives a rationale for expelling the man in terms of its effect on the church.

38. It also fits the pattern and purpose of Israel's exile when they are handed over to their enemies.

uses the adjective σαρκικός (*sarkikos*) with this meaning in 3:3. He accuses them of still being "fleshly" and driven by human inclinations. In Rom. 8:5–17 and Gal. 5:16–24, flesh and spirit "denote not two coexisting *parts* of the individual, but a contrast of tendencies and loyalties which compete for dominance as powers within each person (cf. the language of struggle in Rom 7)" (South 1993: 552). Barrett (1985a: 72–73) contends that "flesh is a positive force for evil" that seeks to take advantage of Christian freedom and to influence how it is used. He defines it as "egocentric existence" by comparing it to its opposite, love. The flesh manifests itself particularly in a devotion to self "as the focus and criterion of his own existence" (Deidun 1981: 95). In this case, this man considered his personal agenda to be more important than the mission and reputation of the church. This self has come under the control of "the Flesh," which functions like a force field and can only by counteracted and neutralized by the Spirit (Gal. 5:16–17). The "flesh" to be destroyed is not the man's fleshly body but his fleshly lusts.[39] Deidun (1981: 94) notes that the flesh is at work in the immorality of the Gentiles, the boastful wisdom of the Greeks, and the sinful self-sufficiency of the Jews. It creates estrangement from God that is broken only when persons submit in faith to the gospel and allow God's Spirit to seize control (cf. Rom. 8:9 with 7:14b). The destruction of the flesh should be interpreted in light of Gal. 5:24, "And those who belong to Christ Jesus have crucified the flesh with its passions and desires" (Fee 1987: 212; Hays 1997: 86). Only after destroying the flesh could the man be saved.

Scriptural echoes from Job imply that the man will be sifted by Satan for his spiritual betterment (South 1993: 551): "The Lord said to the devil, 'I hand him over [παραδίδωμι] to you'" (Job 2:6 LXX); and "The Lord said to Satan, 'Very well, all that he has is in your power; only do not stretch out your hand against him!'" (Job 1:12). In the case of Job, God places limits on what Satan can do. Satan may not touch "his soul" and must spare his life.[40] This echo suggests that the man will suffer both spiritually and physically at the hands of Satan but will not necessarily die. This interpretation also accords with 1 Tim. 1:19b–20, which reports that Hymenaeus and Alexander, who made a shipwreck of their faith, were disciplined: "whom I handed over to Satan [παρέδωκα τῷ Σατανᾷ, *paredōka tō Satana*] so that they may learn not to blaspheme." They are not turned over to Satan to be executed but to learn something that will cause them to correct their views and behavior (South 1993: 551). The biblical parallels contain the exact phrasing and do not take

39. Sand 1967: 144, 145; Cambier 1968–69: 228; Fee 1987: 210–14; Talbert 1987: 16; Joy 1988; South 1993: 551–52; Thiselton 2000: 400–401.

40. This phrase is interpreted in T. Job 20:3 to mean that Satan could do what he wished with respect to Job's body, but God did not give Satan authority over his soul.

us far afield from Paul's thought world.[41] They support the view that handing over to Satan is not intended to bring about death but to work some kind of positive result.

Some ask how Satan could be expected to be an agent for victory over the flesh when the god of this world normally blinds the minds of unbelievers to the truth (2 Cor. 4:4). Would not the man's sinful passions be aroused further when he is cast out into the world rather than destroyed (Godet 1886: 255; G. Lampe 1967: 351)? Schrage (1991: 376) observes correctly that it is not Satan's assignment to destroy the fleshly orientation. Satan, however, is neither omniscient nor omnipotent and often serves as an unwitting agent for good. Satan's hostility to humans can be useful to God in testing and training them (Goudge 1911: 38). In Paul's own case, he identifies the thorn in his flesh as a messenger from Satan but declares that what Satan intended for evil turned out ultimately for his own good (2 Cor. 12:8–10). It kept him from becoming boastful and taught him how totally dependent he is on God's grace. It shows how God's mercy far outpaces Satan's malevolence. Paul can hope that the shock of being banished from the church and left vulnerable to demonic powers would drive the man to change his fleshly orientation. It is a fearful thing for sinners to be delivered into the hands of an angry Satan in this life, but it need not entail spiritual annihilation. It may instead beget a spiritual awakening. As one who is cast out, the man becomes an outsider (5:12) and is to be treated differently by "insiders." He is not to be admonished, as one would a fellow Christian, but evangelized, as one would an unbeliever.

The "day of the Lord" is shorthand for the revealing of Christ (1:7) and the final judgment on the last day. In his opening thanksgiving (1:8), Paul voices his prayer that Christ will strengthen them to the end, so that they may be blameless "on the day of our Lord Jesus Christ." He cautions them not to pronounce judgment before the time, that is, before the Lord comes, when he will expose all the secrets of the heart and each one will receive commendation (or condemnation) from God (4:5). Christians are not given a bye in the judgment, and Paul does not want his boast in them (2 Cor. 1:14) to be proved vain in the day of the Lord. His concern is twofold: the church needs purging lest this deadly moral blight poison its life in Christ; the man needs to be purged lest cheap forgiveness or benign neglect lull him into thinking that all things are permissible and he ends up being banished from God's presence in the final judgment.

41. Fee (1987: 208) acidly criticizes A. Collins (1980: 258) for rejecting the Pastoral Epistles as genuine and not germane for understanding Paul yet accepting that "the remotest of parallels from pagan literature influenced him."

5:6–8 Paul continues to harp on the problem of their arrogance (5:2) and declares that their boasting is not good (on boasting, see the comments on 1:29). He has in mind the Corinthians' proclivity to exalt themselves over others and does not imply that they were boasting about this particular sin (contra Fee 1987: 215). It is inconceivable for anyone to have been tempted to boast about such perversion, given the widespread antipathy toward it; and it is incomprehensible that anyone would think that some benefit could accrue from such conduct. Why would one boast about behavior that society regards as morally reprehensible? The only way that the church's boasting might be related in any way to this man is if he was one of the leaders of the church about whom they boast (3:21), but their boast in him would be for reasons other than this sin.

The Corinthians are plagued by a penchant for self-admiration, but this scandalous case confronts them with the sobering truth that their spiritual airs are baseless. They have no reason to gloat but every reason to be ashamed. They need to quit their boasting and set their house in order. To galvanize them to take action to evict the man from the community, Paul resorts to metaphors. The metaphors are mixed. He pictures the church as the purified house from which the old leaven has been cleansed, as the new batch of dough, and as the celebrants at the feast of Passover.

Paul's first metaphor refers to the corrupting power of leaven. The image may have been suggested by a connection between leaven and conceit. In offering a symbolic explanation why leavened bread is prohibited as an offering on the altar (Lev. 2:11; 6:17), Philo (*Spec. Laws* 1.53 §293) muses that leaven produces rising, and none who approach the altar "should be uplifted or puffed up by arrogance." One is to "lay low that pestilent enemy, conceit." Leaven is also associated with sexual sin in Hos. 7:4: "They are all adulterers; they are like a heated oven, whose baker does not need to stir the fire, from the kneading of the dough until it is leavened." But the main point of comparison here is the remarkable ability of a small amount of leaven to penetrate and transform dough. Just as a little leaven can infect a whole batch of dough, so this man's one sin can infect a whole church.

Leaven, to be distinguished from yeast, was made by keeping back a piece of the previous week's dough, storing it in suitable conditions, and adding juices to promote the process of fermentation, much like sourdough (Mitton 1972–73). This moldy dough could go bad and become a contaminant, which explains why it was a fitting symbol for the infectious power of evil. This image was widely understood (cf. Matt. 16:6; Gal. 5:9). Plutarch (*Quaestiones romanae et graecae* 289F) wrote that leaven "is itself also the product of corruption, and produces corruption in the dough with which it is mixed; . . . and altogether the process of leavening seems to be one of putrefaction; at any rate if it goes too far, it completely sours and spoils the dough" (see also Pliny the Elder, *Naturalis historia* [*Natural History*] 18.26). A piece of bad leaven will pass on the taint to the next batch and so on. The only way to break the chain of baking bacteria-laden bread was to ditch the whole batch and start afresh. Applied to this case, the metaphor conveys that this man's sin brings greater harm than simply being a bad example for others or generating bad publicity; it likens his sin to a toxin that will infect and ruin the whole community.

Paul's second metaphor of old and new leaven moves from the proportional effects of a little leaven corrupting the whole to the absolute incompatibility between the old and the new (Pascuzzi 1997: 125). The command to cleanse out (ἐκκαθάρατε, *ekkatharate*) the old leaven assumes that the readers are familiar with the Jewish rituals associated with Passover. Only unleavened bread was to be eaten during Passover, and every crumb of leavened bread was removed in a ceremonial search of the dwelling on the morning when the Passover lambs were sacrificed. No leavened bread was to be found in the people's possession (Exod. 13:7; Deut. 16:4), and eating leaven during the seven-day Feast of Unleavened Bread incurred the severest penalty of being cut off from Israel (Exod. 12:15, 19).

This second metaphor shows how Paul couples the imperative to the indicative: Remove the old leaven so that you can start over as unleavened bread, because that is what you are. The imperative to cleanse out the old leaven is predicated on the indicative: they *are* unleavened. In other words, Paul tells them to be what they are, to live like Christians. Who they are is revealed in what they do. What they do comes from who they are. Turning a blind eye to such odious sin committed by one of their number betrays a shamelessness that contradicts who they are as the people of God. Their identity as those who have been "washed, sanctified, and justified in the name of the Lord Jesus Christ" (6:11), as unleavened bread, should inform their behavior. Their behavior will then inform the outsiders of their identity as God's people.

Becoming a new (νέος, *neos*; new in respect to time) batch of dough implies, however, that they were previously tainted. The singular "batch" (φύραμα, *phyrama*) "denotes the oneness of the church" (Edwards 1885: 128) and reveals Paul's corporate understanding of the church. The dough rises and falls as one mass (Pascuzzi 1997: 153). This image reinforces the danger that any contaminant in the batch will affect everything and everyone. But the word "unleavened" (ἄζυμοι, *azymoi*) is plural, which suggests that the character of each individual makes up the character of the whole.

This newness has been made possible by the sacrifice of Christ, who is identified by another metaphor as "our Passover lamb" (τὸ πάσχα ἡμῶν, *to pascha hēmōn*).[42] The passing over of the destroyer who smote the firstborn of the Egyptians began with the Jews slaughtering a lamb and smearing its blood on their doorposts. The Christian Passover began with the slaying of Christ on the cross and the pouring out of his blood. The Passover lamb was not a sacrifice in the strictest sense of the word, but it became associated with atonement (cf. Ezek. 45:18–22; Dunn 1998: 216–17). The timing of Jesus' death in the Passover season and the conviction that his death was the atoning death of "blood poured out for many" (Mark 14:24) abetted linking his atoning death to the Passover sacrifice. As God saved Israel in Egypt through the sacrifice of the Passover lamb, God now saves all people through the sacrifice of Jesus. The blood purifies and protects from the destroyer (see T. Alexander 1995: 17). After the sacrifice, the people consecrate themselves as holy in eating the Passover, which sustains and sanctifies them.

What is important to Paul in this context is that Christ's death is supposed to effect a change in their moral behavior. They should live as those who have died and risen with Christ. The present tense ἑορτάζωμεν (*heortazōmen*) may be added to the evidence from the context that Paul is not thinking in terms of the celebration of a Passover rite but metaphorically in terms of a continual celebration (Fee 1987: 218). He refers to the Christian life as a feast honoring their redemption. The noun εἰλικρινεία (*eilikrineia*, cf. 2 Cor. 1:12; 2:17; Phil. 1:10) means "purity" or "sincerity" and implies that their desires will be unmixed with impurity and there will be harmony between their words, actions, and basic convictions. In their present condition, they do not reflect the purity and truth of the gospel. If they were morally sincere and inflexibly committed to the truth, they could never have condoned this sin by a member, no matter how prominent or powerful that person might be.

Since Paul considers church discipline to be so important, and since it is little practiced in contemporary churches to good effect, it may be beneficial to attempt to distill the theological relevance of what he says in these verses.

1. Paul considers the purity of the congregation to be a serious matter, as it affects the congregation's relationship to God and its witness to the unbelieving world. The immorality of church members not only undermines any grounds for the church's boasting but also wrecks its witness of God's transforming power to change lives. Paul assumes that the church is implicated in the sins of its

---

42. The Passover metaphor says nothing about the date when this epistle was written any more than the use of Day of Atonement imagery in Rom. 3:24 fixes a date for Romans. Paul does not use the metaphor because it was Passover season, nor does its use imply that the church celebrated the Jewish rite of Passover.

individual members. There is no such thing as private morality (or immorality) for church members. The sin of one tarnishes all. Glossing over infamous sin implicates a congregation even more seriously in the sin. In many cultures, what consenting adults do in private is nobody's business. If they are Christians, however, it is very much the business of the church when it brings shame upon the believing community.

2. Infamous sin cannot be swept under the rug. The reason is that Paul understands the church body to be one lump. The moral depravity of one element affects the moral condition of the whole group. They are either leavened dough or unleavened dough. The sin must be confronted openly and decisively for the good of the individual and the good of the church body. The only way to make sinners aware of the serious plight of their dire spiritual condition is through drastic discipline—the church's complete renunciation of them. Forgiveness can come only after this discipline has been imposed and the sinner has comprehended the full gravity of the sin and genuinely repented. The church must be humbly mindful, however, that "only on the Last Day of the Lord will it become apparent what was decided on the 'previous days of the Lord'" (Baumert 1996: 155).

3. The church walks a tightrope between being a welcoming community that accepts confessed sinners and helps the lapsed get back on their feet and being a morally lax community where anything goes. The danger of carrying out disciplinary measures is that the church can become judgmental, harsh, and exclusivistic. Nevertheless, Paul assumes "that the well-being of the community is primary and cannot be compromised" (Pascuzzi 1997: 145).

Additional Notes

5:1. The ὥστε clause functions epexegetically ("namely"; cf. 2 Cor. 1:8; Phil. 1:13), explaining the nature of the πορνεία (Winter 2001: 48).

5:1. Four different options attempt to explain the circumstances behind Paul's censure:

1. The man was having an affair with his stepmother while his father is still alive and has not divorced her. Martial (*Epigrams* 4.16) condemns an amour between son and stepmother and accuses the man of never being a real stepson to his stepmother, "while she was your father's wife." Martial says that the man can never be acquitted from such an offense, even if legendary lawyers Tully and Regulus "were recalled from the nether shades" to defend him. Winter (2001: 45–49) argues that since Roman jurisprudence generally excused illicit marital unions but clamped down on adulterous incestuous affairs, the father of the Corinthian man must still be alive. Paul does not also label the offense "adultery" (μοιχεία, *moicheia*), however.

2. The woman was the former concubine of the late father and not his stepmother. A *hetaira* was sometimes treated much like a wife (see J. Davidson 1997: 131–33). An intimate re-

lationship with a late father's paramour may have raised eyebrows but would not have been illegal according to Roman law (De Vos 1998: 106; cf. Rawson 1974), and the couple appears to have escaped legal prosecution. Jewish law, however, prohibited relations between any of a father's concubines and the son and accounted such a sexual relationship as incestuous (cf. 2 Sam. 16:20–23; 1 Kings 1:1–4; 2:13–25). Pseudo-Phocylides 179–81 contains a warning against "touching" (a sexual euphemism; cf. 1 Cor. 7:1) "your stepmother" (μητρυιή, *mētruiē*) and an exhortation that one should honor her as one's own mother. It also includes a warning also against relations with the lesser loves of one's father. Amos 2:7 castigates father and son for going in to the same girl and profaning the holy name of God.

Since the description of the woman involved reflects the language of the LXX for a stepmother, it would tend to rule out a reference to a concubine. Had Paul meant his father's concubine, it would have been clearer, particularly to a Gentile audience, to have referred to her as such (ἡ παλλακὴ τοῦ πατρὸς αὐτοῦ, *hē pallakē tou patros autou*, Gen. 35:22). Also, a sexual relationship with a father's concubine could not be designated an iniquity so heinous that it was not to be found *even* among pagans. The question raised by De Vos (1998) as to why an illegal relationship was not brought to court (cf. Deming 1996, who thinks that it was) is impossible to answer. The lack of any evidence that charges were preferred against the man does not prove that the relationship was legal according to Roman law. Trials to prosecute persons for entering relationships considered to be sexually aberrant were rare and usually motivated by reasons other than moral outrage. Dixon (1992: 82) notes that marriage was very much a private affair, and the state intervened only intermittently and imposed penalties when there was some economic advantage to be gained.

3. The man was having a relationship with his divorced stepmother.

4. The man was having a relationship with his stepmother after his father has died. Cicero (*Pro Cluentio* 5.12–6.14) reports a scandalous marriage of a mother-in-law and her son-in-law and derides their mad passion that trampled modesty, scruple, and sense. In this era, stepmothers were sometimes closer in age to the children than the husband. J. Gardner (1986: 38) notes, for example, regarding girls in upper-class circles, that Cicero's daughter, Tullia, was engaged at twelve, married at sixteen, and widowed at twenty-two. If that were the case here, the son may have been old enough to enter into a relationship with her (see P. Watson 1995: 136–39, 213; Goulder 1999: 348). Chow (1992: 130–39) and Clarke (1993: 73–88) offer a sociological and economic explanation for the liaison. The man may have taken up with his stepmother to keep her dowry within the family. Clarke (1993: 80) notes that the dowry came with the bride to cover the living expenses of the household and was an important factor in arranging the marriage. She could have it repaid to her at the dissolution of the marriage, and this payment could deplete the father's inheritance. The Augustan marriage laws applied pressure for her to remarry if she were young and childless, and the inheritance, then, could pass on to another family with her remarriage (Clarke 1993: 81; cf. Chow 1992: 136–39). These Augustan marriage laws were designed to foster marriage and reverse a declining birth rate and forbade bachelors from receiving inheritances or legacies. By marrying her, the man would not have to pay the higher taxes levied on bachelors, would gain control of his share of the inheritance from the father, and would prevent the loss of family wealth. The motivation to keep the stepmother in the household for economic reasons may explain why Paul links the fornicators with the greedy predators in 5:10 (cf. the critique of this view by De Vos 1998: 110–11 and Meggitt 1998: 149–53).

5:3–4. Four readings are represented in the witnesses: (1) ἐν τῷ ὀνόματι τοῦ κυρίου Ἰησοῦ (A, Ψ, 1852); (2) ἐν τῷ ὀνόματι τοῦ κυρίου ἡμῶν Ἰησοῦ (B, D*, 1175, 1179 it^{b, d}); (3) ἐν τῷ ὀνόματι τοῦ κυρίου Ἰησοῦ Χριστοῦ (ℵ, it^{ar}, vg, geo); (4) ἐν τῷ ὀνόματι τοῦ κυρίου ἡμῶν Ἰησοῦ Χριστοῦ (𝔓^{46}, D^2, F, G, 0150, 6, 33, 104, 256, 263, 365, 424, 436, 459, 1241, 1319, 1573, 1881, 1912, 2127, 2200, 2464, and numerous church fathers). The solemnity of the pronouncement and the influence of the parallel phrase in 5:4b seems to explain best the additions to the shortest reading.

5:5. The shortest reading τῇ ἡμέρᾳ τοῦ κυρίου (𝔓^{46}, B, 1739, 2200) has again attracted solemn additions to κυρίου: τοῦ κυρίου Ἰησοῦ; τοῦ κυρίου Ἰησοῦ Χριστοῦ; and τοῦ κυρίου ἡμῶν Ἰησοῦ Χριστοῦ. The shortest reading best explains the others.

5:5. Shillington (1998: 31–32) tries to make the case that Paul "re-enacts the atonement text of Leviticus 16, in conjunction with the prohibition texts (Lev. 18:8; 20:11; Deut. 23:1; 27:20), in the texture of 1 Corinthians 5, and that at 5:5 in particular he transforms the biblical/Jewish tradition of 'handing over' the scapegoat in keeping with his vision of the new community of Christ as the holy shrine of God." He argues from this that Paul intends to purge the community of this sin to make the people right with God and that the man is doomed (Lev. 27:29): "No human beings who have been devoted to destruction can be ransomed; they shall be put to death." Handed over to Satan, the immoral man becomes a sacral victim so that the Spirit resident in the community might be saved in the day of the Lord (Shillington 1998: 37–38).

But Paul is not talking about a scapegoating ritual of an animal turned out into the desert to Azazel. The death of Christ for sinners causes him to look at fallen sinners in a different way (Gal. 6:1–2). Shillington (1998: 45) thinks that once defiled, "the community has to find recourse to save itself and gain the Lord's favour." This statement implies that the community must continue to make its own atonement by means of OT atonement rituals. If these rituals are still considered valid, it nullifies the effect of Christ's atonement and implies that we continue to need two sacrificial goats (Lev. 16:5–8). Although there is a need to purge the sin, Paul does not hint that purging the sinner atones for the community. The aim of Paul's insistence on them enforcing discipline, according to 2 Cor. 7:8–16, is not to insure the community's purity but to test its obedience and to produce godly sorrow that results in repentance.

B. Renewed Warnings about Tolerance of Sin in the Church (5:9–13)

In an earlier letter, Paul enjoined the Corinthians to avoid sexually immoral persons (πόρνοι, *pornoi*). The reference to the πόρνοι in 5:9–10 links this command to the sin of πορνεία (*porneia*) mentioned in 5:1. The previous letter may have contained a general admonition with a list of vices (cf. Gal. 5:19–21) thought to be pertinent to their situation. Their nonchalance about the man who entered into an incestuous relationship with his father's wife sadly reveals that this warning was not taken seriously. If they claimed to be confused, Paul now announces that he was not talking about unbelievers, "those outside," but moral offenders who claim to be Christian. He did not call them to separate themselves from the world but to keep the world's wickedness from infiltrating the church and extinguishing their life in the Spirit. Those claiming to be Christians who are guilty of such immorality are beyond the pale of acceptable behavior and are to be purged.

By reminding them of his prior warning about the immoral, Paul signals that he has not singled out the incestuous man for especially harsh treatment. All impenitent evildoers are to be treated the same way (South 1993: 555). He also underscores that the church, not just their apostle, has the responsibility to judge insiders and to purge itself of evil.

Exegesis and Exposition

[9]I wrote to you in my letter not to be associated with the sexually immoral, [10]not at all meaning the sexually immoral of this world, the greedy predators, or idolaters. Otherwise, you would be obligated to leave the world completely. [11]But as it stands, I wrote to you not to be associated with a person who calls himself a brother but is sexually immoral, or greedy, or an idolater, or a reviler, or a drunkard, or a swindler. Do not even eat with such a one. [12]For what business do I have judging those outside? Do you not judge those inside? [13]For God will judge those outside. "Purge the evil from your very midst!"

5:9   The verb ἔγραψα (*egrapsa*) is not an epistolary aorist, "I write," but a true preterit, "I wrote." When Paul includes the phrase ἐν τῇ ἐπιστολῇ (*en tē epistolē,* in the letter) in 2 Cor. 7:8, he clearly refers to a previous letter (see additional note). He may be directly quoting his admonition from this previous letter insisting that church members not associate with πόρνοι (*pornoi*), sexually immoral persons.

In the context of purity boundaries, the verb συναναμιγνύναι (*synanamignynai*) means more than simply "to mingle" or "to mix" with someone. Philo puts the word on the lips of the soothsayer Balaam, who describes the Hebrews as not "mixing with others" because of their distinctive customs so that they will not "depart from the ways of their fathers" (*Mos.* 1.50 §278). Christians are also set apart from others, not by distinctive customs and rituals, but by their stringent moral standards. Paul is not calling for them to be unsociable or to withdraw to their own island universe but to make unwelcome any Christians in name who flout core Christian moral values (cf. 2 Thess. 3:14; Titus 3:10–11). Those who claim the name "Christian" and act no differently than pagans have broken down fundamental boundaries. To refuse to have dealings with moral profligates testifies that such persons have no affiliation with the church and that their behavior is incompatible with the gospel (cf. 2 Thess. 3:14; John 4:9). To draw back from such persons also prevents the church from being tarnished by the moral stigma attached to such behavior so that it does not impair their evangelism efforts. It notifies both the offender and the world that the Christian's God does not tolerate such defilement and thereby safeguards God's honor and credibility so that the name of God is not blasphemed in the world because of their crimes (Rom. 2:24; cf. Isa. 52:5; Ezek. 36:20).

Paul clarifies further that his instructions did not require them to dissociate from every immoral person in the world. The phrase οὐ πάντως (*ou pantōs*) means "not absolutely" everyone (cf. Rom. 3:9). Sexual immorality was ubiquitous in the Greco-Roman world. So too were greed and idolatry. Christians could not keep from rubbing shoulders with such people in the course of daily life. Paul's need to clarify this point may suggest that the Corinthians either were playing dumb to avoid taking action against the incestuous man or were genuinely confused. He does not reprimand them for being recalcitrant or slow-witted. Possibly, they hesitated to apply the admonition to the man guilty of incest, not out of defiance, but because they did not wish to wrangle with a relatively powerful patron. Whatever was behind their failure to heed Paul's counsel, he now spells out what he meant in that warning so that they can no longer turn a blind eye to the man's sin or any other case of *porneia*.

Paul moves beyond sexual sin to include greed, idolatry, and drunkenness. One definite article governs the substantives πλεονέκται (*pleonektai*) and ἅρπαγες (*harpages*), joined together by καί (*kai*), because one cannot be rapacious without also being greedy. The πλεονέκται are those obsessed with "the unrestricted longing for possessions which sets aside the rights of others" (Delling, *TDNT* 6:269). They are the self-

5:10

aggrandizers (Findlay 1910: 811) whose aims in life are entirely directed by self-interest and the urge to gain the edge over others (Parry 1926: 92). Love of self replaces love of God (Robertson and Plummer 1914: 105) in the struggle for survival and in achieving the ambition to make it to the top. The word ἅρπαξ is used of robbers or thieves and may be distinguished from the word λῃστής, "bandits" (*lēstēs*; cf. Luke 10:30; 2 Cor. 11:26) by the translation "swindler" or "rogue" (BDAG 134). Combining the two ideas, we get the picture of those who enrich themselves unlawfully or unfairly. They are cunning, rapacious, grasping, and predatory—the greedy grabbers, the "have-mores" who want more and more. Their insatiable hankering after more causes them to disregard completely the plight of the have-nots and to trample their rights and ignore their needs.

The predominant perception in the ancient world was that the supply of goods was limited, but everyone could have the necessities of life if others did not have too much. The greedy seriously threatened the balance of society and worsened the poverty of others. They prospered only by depriving and defrauding others, who in turn became wretched and destitute (Malina 1987: 357). While the church traditionally has more readily identified and condemned those guilty of sexual sin, Paul regards greedy acquisitiveness to be no less nefarious. As far as he is concerned, the man guilty of incest and the money-grubbing mercenary are in the same boat. Both should be chastised and expelled.

Idolaters are also included in the list, which would have included nearly all the inhabitants of Corinth. In the Jewish mind, idolatry was directly related to sexual sins. In Sib. Or. 3:764–66, unlawful worship (idolatry) is to be shunned, and adultery and male intercourse with males to be avoided. Paul shares this basic assumption (Rom. 1:21–27; 1 Cor. 10:7–8; cf. Wis. 14:22–31; T. Levi 18:11). The mention of idolaters here sets up his critique in chapters 8–10 of those Christians who attend idol feasts.

If Paul were expecting them not to have any associations with these kinds of people, then (ἐπεί, *epei*, since then, for in that case; cf. 7:14; 14:16; 15:29; Rom. 3:6; 11:6, 22) they would be duty bound to leave the world. This comment reveals his bleak appraisal of pagan morality and his conviction that Christians are a distinct minority in this immoral world. Paul does not intend for them to withdraw from the world into a godly ghetto. They are to live as shining lights amid a wicked and perverse generation (Phil. 2:15) and must continue to have dealings with the world. One might wish to choose business associates and neighbors according to their morals, but one cannot. The gospel does not call Christians to retreat from the world but to witness to it. Christians are to be like salt, which does no good unless it comes into direct contact with what needs to be salted, and to be light so that others might see their good works and then see and glorify God (Matt. 5:13–16). The problem, however, is that the wicked and perverse have made inroads into this congregation. The basic premise behind Paul's statement is that the church's purity can be contaminated only from within, not from without (Kuck 1992a: 242). Bad characters abound in the world; they are not to abound in the church. Paul's grievance is that they cannot witness to an unbelieving world when one of their own members is guilty of a sin that causes even the heathens to blush.

In saying that they would otherwise have to leave the world, he reduces the whole question to an absurdity. But he might also be injecting a note of dark humor by euphemistically referring to something far more drastic than secluding oneself from the world. In 2 Clement, the phrase "to leave the world" (ἐκ τοῦ κόσμου ἐξελθεῖν, *ek tou kosmou exelthein*) is a euphemism for death (5:1, "let us not fear to go forth from this world"; 8:3, "after we have departed from this world"). Josephus (*Ant.* 1.13.1 §223; cf. 2 Bar. 14:2, 13; 48:15) also uses the verb to refer to death. Paul may be saying, "If you think that you must avoid all the sexually immoral, you will have to die and go to heaven to do so." He obviously is not calling for anything so radical. They are only to abandon the world's values and to shun those in the church who defy Christian virtues.

The verb ἔγραψα (*egrapsa*) in this verse could be rendered as a true preterit, referring to the previous letter ("I wrote," RSV) as in 5:9, with the νῦν (*nyn*) having a logical sense, "as things now stand" (BDAG 681; "But rather I wrote to you," RSV; "But actually I wrote to you," NASB). Or it could be rendered as an epistolary aorist referring to the present letter with the νῦν having a temporal sense, "but now" ("But now I am writing to you," NRSV). Findlay (1910: 812) opts for the latter and interprets it to mean, "If anyone doubted the purport of the former letter, it shall be impossible to mistake my meaning *now*" (so also Kistemaker 1993: 171; R. Collins 1999: 222; cf. Barrett 1968: 131). Robertson and Plummer (1914: 106), however, make the point that had Paul wanted to refer to the present letter, he would have written γράφω (*graphō*), as he did in 4:14. It is more likely that this verb is a true preterit as in 5:9, referring to the previous letter (Edwards 1885: 133; Weiss 1910: 138; Bruce 1971: 58; Conzelmann 1975: 102; Fee 1987: 221; Wolff 1996: 109). 5:11

After listing the works of the flesh in Gal. 5:19–21, Paul reminds the Galatians that this catalog of vices was nothing new to them. He had warned them about these things before and that those who commit them will not inherit the kingdom of God. Warnings about such wickedness are standard teaching, and it is likely that he included a list of vices in the previous letter and did not isolate the sexual immorality. Christians are identifiable by their conduct, not simply by their doctrine or verbal professions. If anyone goes by the name "Christian" and is guilty of these sins, he or she is to be ostracized.

Zaas (1988: 623) rehearses the scholarship that has assumed that in Paul's catalogs of vices he simply repeats traditional material that has no direct bearing on the situation of the church he is addressing (so, for example, Conzelmann 1975: 100–101; Scroggs 1983: 101–9). Although Paul may have utilized a conventional rhetorical form by including lists of vices, he does not parrot traditional material. Zaas (1988: 623–24) argues that the lists in 5:10–11 and 6:9–10 "are closely related to the epistolary situation of this part of the letter." One reason for this conclusion is fairly obvious. A minimal overlap occurs in the various lists of vices, which reveals that Paul did not resort to a normative, traditional list of vices that he could cut and paste into any letter (cf. Rom. 1:29–31; 13:13; 2 Cor. 12:20; Gal. 5:19–21; Eph. 4:31; 5:3–5; Col. 3:5, 8; 1 Tim. 1:9–10; 6:4–5; 2 Tim. 3:2–5; Titus 1:7; 3:3; cf. also 1 Pet. 4:15; Mark 7:22).[1] Jewish traditions also cataloged virtues commanded in the law and sins that violated God's law, and this scriptural backdrop is frequently ignored (cf. Ps. 15; Ezek. 18:5–7; Hos. 4:1–2; see Oropeza 1998–99: 9). Rather than selecting random excerpts from a canon of sins filed away in his memory, Paul more likely identifies practices that were already destroying the moral fabric of the community or were so prevalent in the surrounding culture that they threatened to encroach on the life of the church. Furnish (1968: 84) observes, "Paul was not a wandering street preacher, but an apostle and a leader of congregations, and his ethical lists reflect this function."

Zaas (1988: 626) thinks that in his previous letter Paul simply told them to avoid πόρνοι, and he now clarifies that letter by saying he was not speaking of all the fornicators but the so-called brother who is a πόρνος (5:11). Zaas (1988: 626) contends, "The catalogue of vices specifically functions to *extend* the apostle's prior prohibition of πόρνοι to include these other vicious types." Paul chose these vices because they were particularly appropriate to the situation in Corinth (so Schrage 1991: 387–88; R. Horsley 1998: 81), but it does not necessarily mean that they were rampant in the Corinthian church (R. Collins 1999: 219).[2] The vice lists serve as a kind of electrified fence that warns about the limits of admissible conduct. The key point that Paul tries to clear

---

1. Limiting his count to six vice lists appearing in the undisputed Pauline epistles, Furnish (1968: 76) tallies forty-two terms identifying thirty-nine vices.

2. Scroggs (1983: 102) thinks that Paul has a fondness for vice lists and includes one here not to forbid some particular sin but to "hit the opponent over the head or to warn the writer's own community of the penalty for evil living." The longer the list, the harder the blow. The blow, however, would not hit home unless the vices listed were germane to some actual situation.

up is that the roster of sinners to be ostracized consists of those who claim to be Christians and do these things.

The sins listed fit the epistolary situation. The πόρνος (sexually immoral, fornicator, bed-hopper) applies to the case of incest in 5:1, and the topic of concern in chapters 5–7 is immorality (6:13, 15, 16, 18; 7:2; cf. 10:8). The πλεονέκτης (*pleonektēs*) and the ἅρπαξ (*harpax*), the greedy and the swindler (racketeer), apply to the situation of Christians suing in pagan courts to gain advantage over another person in 6:1–11. The problem of idolatry is the focus of attention in chapters 8–10. Its listing here prepares for that discussion, just as the reference to sexual immorality (πορνεύω, *porneuō*) in 10:8 recalls and reinforces the exposition in chapters 5–6. The reviler (λοίδορος, *loidoros*) causes dissension, a topic dealt with in 1:18–4:21. The drunkard (μέθυσος, *methysos*) is associated with idolatrous feasts (10:7), and the problem of drunkenness emerges in the church's Lord's Supper (11:21; cf. 2 Pet. 2:13; Jude 1:12). At ancient banquets, eating and drinking to excess led to sexual debauchery afterward (see Winter 1997b: 82–84).

Murphy-O'Connor (1979a: 45) comments that the vices listed here "injure others or make one impervious to the needs of others." This statement is true, but it is too general. These vices are specifically applicable to the immediate context, which calls for the church to expel the incestuous man. Rosner (1994: 69–70) concludes that they have links with vices listed in Deuteronomy that warrant exclusion from the community (cf. Ellingworth and Hatton 1985: 105; Hays 1997. 88).

fornicator	Deut. 22:20–22, 30
idolater	Deut. 17:2–7
malicious false witness = reviler	Deut. 19:15–19
drunkard = rebellious son	Deut. 21:20–21
rapacious/thief	Deut. 24:7

These sins may also be linked together because of their connection with sexual sins. Idolatry and fornication are associated in Jewish thinking. Drunkenness and greed are associated with licentiousness in Greco-Roman thinking (Gowers 1993: 101).

Eating together connoted more than friendliness in ancient culture; it created a social bond. When Christians ate together, it reinforced and confirmed the solidarity established by their shared confession of faith in Christ. Refusing to eat with fellow Christians guilty of such acts breaks all social ties with them as well as excludes them from the Lord's Supper. This exclusion may seem harsh and intolerant, a reversion to the narrow separatism of the Pharisees, but Christians who are no different morally from unbelievers blur the clear distinctions between the church and the world and destroy their testimony to God's transforming power in their lives. Those who are blatantly immoral cannot be allowed to appear to represent what it means to be a Christian. As Godet (1886: 273) interprets the punishment, "This is the way to tear from him the mask with which he covers himself to the shame of the Church and Christ himself."

Obviously, this approach has its dangers. The church can degenerate into a defensive community that regards everyone with suspicion and deals out harsh discipline. It can lead to a vain self-righteousness, a chilly exclusivism, and a spirit of suspicion. The context, however, refers to a glaring sin that is very public and brings disgrace upon the community. There is a limit beyond which patience, toleration, and charity toward another's sin ceases to be a virtue.

5:12–13 Paul asserts that it is not his business to judge those outside. The "I" here is hortative; that is, Paul intends his readers to apply what he says to themselves (B. Dodd 1995: 47–48). He means "What do we have to do with judging outsiders?" The context implies that "to judge" (5:3) involves formally condemning someone and taking disciplinary action. It does not mean that the church should refrain from prophetic judgment of its society (cf. Rom. 1:18–32). Christians have no jurisdiction over outsiders and have no business usurping a task that belongs to God alone. Those outside are left in God's hands (Rom. 2:16; 3:6; Heb. 12:23), and the church has the responsibility to them to seek to win them over (1 Cor. 9:19–23; 14:16–17), not to nag, browbeat, or seek to control them.

The use of the term "those outside" (οἱ ἔξω, hoi exō; Mark 4:11; 1 Thess. 4:12; Col. 4:5; cf. 1 Tim. 3:7; 2 Clem. 13:1) in the NT simply "states a fact without any insinuation of censure" (Robertson and Plummer 1914: 108).[3] It refers to the host of people who are not Christians. Some members of the Corinthian church are married to "outsiders" (7:12–16), and Paul can commend these non-Christians for their willingness to maintain their marriage to their Christian spouses and forbid Christians from divorcing their non-Christian spouses on religious grounds. But he cannot command those outside not to divorce their Christian spouses. Nor does he pronounce judgment on them for doing so (7:12–16). He has no say about what unbelievers do, only about what Christians do.

Ordinary Christians, and not just apostles, also have a say in what other Christians do. The church is responsible for keeping its own moral house in order, and God will hold them accountable for it. By asking "Do you not judge those inside?" (οὐχὶ τοὺς ἔσω ὑμεῖς κρίνετε, ouchi tous esō hymeis krinete), which expects the answer yes, Paul lets

---

3. The prologue to Sirach states that the work has been translated specifically "to help the outsiders."

it be known that he alone does not have responsibility for making judgments about community discipline; they do as well. Barrett (1968: 133) comments, "Responsibility for judgment is in the hands of the whole body of believers, not of a small group of authorities." This principle of shared responsibility explains why Paul underscores his presence *with* them in 5:3–5 when they pronounce judgment and carry out the sentence against the incestuous man. It is something they do together with him in their assembly.

The final word on this issue comes from a recurring expression in Deuteronomy: "Purge the evil from your very midst." Rosner (1996: 514) cites three reasons why this is an intentional citation from the OT even though Paul does not introduce it with his customary "as it is written" (1:19, 31; 2:9; 3:19; 9:9; 10:7; 14:21; 15:45) or "for" (2:16; 10:26; 15:27, 32). It matches the wording in the LXX. The word ἐξαίρω (*exairō*) appears only here in Paul's letters. The emotionally charged tenor of his instructions explains why he omitted an introduction to the biblical quotation. It does not function as the scriptural warrant for his argument. Instead, it serves as the fundamental command at the conclusion of his discussion of the case (R. Collins 1999: 218).[4] Omitting an introductory formula for the quotation heightens its force as a command.

Various passages in Deuteronomy include this directive for the congregation to purge the evil from their midst (Deut. 13:5 [13:6 MT]; 17:7; 19:19–20a; 21:21; 24:7; cf. Judg. 20:13). Paul may have appreciated the play on words between πονηρός (*ponēros*, evil one) and πόρνος (*pornos*, sexually immoral) (so Zaas 1984: 259–60). Expelling the man rids them of a moral cancer that will spread throughout the church if left untreated, a moral stigma that repulses their society, and the impending threat of divine judgment for their toleration of evil.

Additional Note

5:9. Since the present letter is known to us as 1 Corinthians, this previous letter must no longer be extant or it may have been mortised into one of the canonical letters. The enigmatic passage in 2 Cor. 6:14–7:1 is the chief candidate as a fragment of this previous letter. A cursory reading of this passage gives the impression that it matches the description of this previous letter. Some contend that Paul works through some of the statements in this passage that the Corinthians misinterpreted in various segments of this letter. "Do not be yoked together with unbelievers" is expanded further by Paul's instructions about marriage to an unbeliever (1 Cor. 7:12–16).

4. Rosner (1994: 63) argues that this scriptural link "unveils Paul's profound indebtedness to the Scriptures but also opens up a fuller understanding of the reasons for the expulsion in 1 Corinthians 5." Paul's instruction to remove the offender derives from pentateuchal principles and directives. Tuckett's (2000: 411–16) criticism of Rosner's arguments misfires. The issue is not whether the Corinthians would have heard the echo from the OT, but whether it was the incubus for his argument.

"What agreement is there between the temple of God and idols?" is developed in more detail in the discussion of eating idol food (1 Cor. 8–10). "Come out from them and be separate" is clarified as referring to immoral Christians and not the immoral of this world (1 Cor. 5:9–11). I conclude (Garland 1999: 317), "These correlations do not prove that 2 Cor. 6:14–7:1 was originally part of the first letter Paul sent to the Corinthians. They show instead that such problems were endemic in Corinth and that Paul continually needed to address them" (for arguments that this passage originally belongs to 2 Corinthians, see Garland 1999: 315–27). The biggest problem with the view that 2 Cor. 6:14–7:1 was part of this previous letter is that the key words πορνεία or πόρνοι do not appear. The command not to be unequally yoked, for example, refers to "unbelievers" and not to immoral Christians.

If this were a portion of the previous letter, one might understand how the Corinthians may have been confused, but the most likely conclusion is that this previous letter is lost to us. If Paul published his own letters (see Trobisch 1989), he may have chosen, for whatever reason, to omit it from the collection.

C. Admonition against Lawsuits (6:1–11)

Paul now cites a second case that proves the Corinthians' boasting to be groundless. Someone in the community had the gall to haul a brother Christian to court to be judged by unbelievers. This legal action is another sign that the values of the surrounding culture were still deeply ingrained in many Corinthian Christians and that they got along quite comfortably with the heathen society. They probably viewed such things as "a part of normal everyday life," since Greeks "loved going to court" (Becker 1993: 199). As in the incest case (5:1–13), Paul focuses his attention on the church for their conspicuous failure to resolve disputes between themselves. This failure grieves him for several reasons. This lawsuit breeds enmity and factionalism and will inevitably reduce the church to an assortment of rival tribes. It undermines any claim of the church to be God's end-time community. It torpedoes their witness to outsiders of God's love. It will bar the plaintiffs from inheriting the kingdom of God if they are guilty of wronging and defrauding others.

Paul specifically says that he writes to shame them (6:5a). The Corinthians ignored the outrageous case of incest, but one Christian dares to haul a fellow Christian before pagan magistrates to settle a minor matter. The incongruity between who they are and what they are doing is underscored by the last line of the first two segments of his argument. In 6:6, Paul exclaims, "But brother takes another brother to court, and this before unbelievers!" In 6:8, he exclaims, "But instead you are the ones who wrong and defraud! And the [victims] are brothers!" These actions reveal an alarming spiritual breakdown. To bring a suit against a brother before judges who are unbelievers implies that the church has no one wise enough to settle petty disputes. Paul is not condemning them for lacking discretion, as if his only concern were that they should keep their disputes under wraps and settle them in house. It reveals a fundamental inconsistency between who they are, as defined by their future destiny with God, and what they are doing. They are "the saints" (6:1) who have been "washed, sanctified, and justified" (6:11). If they are destined to judge the world and the angels, they ought to be able to settle their own disputes without recourse to the unjust, unwashed, unsanctified, and unjustified.

Paul's argument falls into three parts. In 6:1–6, marked out by an inclusio with the repetition of κρίνω (krinō, bring to law) and ἐπί (epi, before), he makes the case that they are fully competent to judge any dispute. Even those Christians held in contempt by the world and perhaps also by other members of the church are qualified to judge. They should settle any quarrels between themselves and not bring litigation against a fellow Christian before unbelievers and entangle themselves in a judicial system that is biased toward the rich and powerful.

In 6:7–8, he plays on the word "loss" (ἥττημα, hēttēma) to chide them that no matter who might win the case in the pagan court, the only result is a disastrous moral defeat for all involved. It tarnishes the reputation of the whole church. If they truly understood the wisdom of God, they would not have such petty disputes at all but would endure being wronged and defrauded. Paul would like to exchange their relentless pursuit of honor and material advantage for sacrificial love for each other.

In the concluding segment (6:9–11), Paul reminds them that the unjust, who include the judges in these courts, will have no part in the kingdom of God. The vice list, which marks the behavior of the unjust, contains an implicit warning: Do not commit these sins lest you lose your inheritance. But Paul ends as he begins this passage, on a positive note. They are destined to judge the world and the angels (6:2) because they have been "washed, sanctified, and justified" (6:11).

Exegesis and Exposition

[1]If any of you has a legal case against another, do you dare to go to law before the unjust and not before the saints? [2]Or do you not know that the saints will judge the world? And if the world is to be judged by you, are you not competent [to judge] the most insignificant cases? [3]Or do you not know that we will judge angels, not to mention ordinary matters? [4]If you have ordinary cases, those who are disdained in the church, set them on the bench. [5]I say this to your shame. Am I to infer that there is not even one wise person among you who is able to decide between brothers? [6]But brother takes another brother to court, and this before unbelievers! [7]It is already complete loss for you that you have lawsuits against yourselves. Why not rather be wronged? Why not rather be defrauded? [8]But instead you are the ones who wrong and defraud! And the [victims] are brothers! [9]Or do you not know that the unjust will not inherit the kingdom of God? Do not be deceived; neither the sexually immoral, nor idolaters, nor adulterers, nor those males who are penetrated sexually by males, nor males who sexually penetrate males, [10]nor thieves, nor the greedy—no drunkards, no revilers, no swindlers will inherit the kingdom of God. [11]And some of you were these things. But you were washed, but you were sanctified, but you were justified in the name of ⌜the Lord Jesus⌝ and in the Spirit of our God.

This next case in Paul's litany of accusations designed to deflate the   **6:1**
Corinthians' swollen pride begins abruptly with an interrogative conveying his shock. The verb "dare" (τολμᾷ, *tolma*; cf. 2 Cor. 10:12; 11:21;
Jude 9) is placed at the beginning of the sentence to thunder his indignation over this turn of events—what gall they have! Suing one another
before pagan magistrates is something Paul considers a horrid breach
of Christian fellowship that could stem only from brazen insolence.
How dare anyone do this!

"Having a case against another" (πρᾶγμα ἔχων πρὸς τὸν ἕτερον,
pragma echōn pros ton heteron) is an idiom used for civil litigation (Epictetus, *Diatr.* 2.2.17; BDAG 859; MM 532).[1] We do not know whether
Paul refers to one case only or to their general practice (Roetzel 1972:
127). Given the relatively small numbers in the church, it is probable
that there was only one such case. The infinitive κρίνεσθαι (*krinesthai*)
has the meaning here of going to law (cf. Matt. 5:40). What makes this
action so abhorrent is that a Christian brings a fellow Christian before
the bar of the unjust. The aim of the ancient lawsuit was to prevail over
another, and that usually involved an assault on the opponent's character. Paul rejects this philosophy altogether (6:7); to try to down a fellow
Christian before, and with the aid of, those who do not worship God is
completely inimical to Christian love.

Designating the judges as οἱ ἄδικοι (*hoi adikoi*, the unrighteous) may
simply mean that they are not Christians, since the word stands in opposition to "the saints" and is synonymous with ἄπιστοι (*apistoi*, unbelievers) in 6:6.[2] Both Jews and Christians referred to themselves as οἱ
δίκαιοι (*hoi dikaioi*, the righteous; Wis. 18:20; 1 Clem. 45:4; 60:3), and
it would be natural for them to designate Gentiles or unbelievers as the
"unrighteous" or "ungodly." In a Christian context, this designation
may characterize their status before God as the "unjustified," as opposed to believers, who are "justified" (6:11). The word ἄδικος (*adikos*),
however, also means "unjust," "dishonest," "untrustworthy." It may be
used as a disparaging moral evaluation of the Corinthian courts as
crooked and biased. Lightfoot (1895: 210) contends that Paul chose it
"because of the alliteration" (ἀδίκων, *adikōn* / ἁγίων, *hagiōn*) and because "it enhances the incongruity of the whole action of seeking justice at the hands of the unjust" (an irony not lost on Chrysostom, *Hom.
1 Cor.* 16.4). Paul could have continued with the word "outsiders" from
5:12–13, but by choosing to call these judges "the unjust" he does more

---

1. R. Collins (1999: 226) notes that the governor heard more important cases: "Ordinary civil cases were heard by the duoviri, two citizens appointed to the magistrature.
Aediles heard cases pertaining to business and the agora."
2. So Edwards 1885: 137; Lietzmann 1949: 25; Dinkler 1952: 170; Barrett 1968: 135;
Conzelmann 1975: 104 n. 12; Fuller 1986: 98; Fee 1987: 232; L. Lewis 1990: 89; Schrage
1991: 406–7.

than identify them as non-Christians. In the context, which refers to these persons serving as the judges in a dispute, this term would seem to offer a moral appraisal of them.

The word ἄδικος appears only two other times in Paul's letters. In Rom. 3:5, it has a moral connotation in a context of administering legal justice: "Is God unjust [ἄδικος] to inflict wrath on us?" Paul's answer throughout Romans is that God is not unjust but righteous. His scriptural schooling would have conditioned him to expect human judges ideally to imitate God's righteousness and to be δίκαιος (dikaios, just; cf. Deut. 16:18–20; Ezra 7:25). In 1 Cor. 6:9, the word has a moral sense as the heading for the list of vices, and the verb form ἀδικεῖν (adikein) appears in 6:8 to mean "to do wrong," "to treat someone unjustly." The link between 6:1 and 6:9 is deliberate and makes clear that they are hauling brothers in Christ before the wicked, who will be barred from God's kingdom. The judicial context and the meaning of the term in Rom. 3:5 and 1 Cor. 6:9 strongly suggest that Paul intends to deprecate the moral capacity and judicial fairness of these unbelievers before whom one Christian has brought a brother Christian to be judged (see Parry 1926: 95). Those who are estranged from God and do not know the will of God (Wolff 1996: 114) could only be expected to be unjust. These pagan judges fit the description of the unjust judge (ὁ κριτὴς τῆς ἀδικίας, ho kritēs tēs adikias) in Jesus' parable (Luke 18:6), who neither feared God nor respected persons (Luke 18:2). Paul expresses disgust that someone in the church had the audacity to take a quarrel with a fellow Christian to be adjudicated by unbelievers who, if they were not outright knaves and scoundrels, were hardly paragons of impartiality and justice.

Although labeling these judges as "unjust" may be a bit of rhetorical hyperbole (Winter 1991a: 570), Paul's own run-ins with the legal system in Corinth and elsewhere may have fed his jaundiced view of it. Some point to Paul's own appeals to Roman courts (Acts 16:37–39; 25:10–12) to claim that he would not have impugned their impartiality (Fee 1987: 232). But these appeals were desperate measures in desperate circumstances. Paul's languishing in prison for two years in Caesarea because the governor Felix hoped for a bribe and wished to curry favor with the Jewish leaders presents a different picture of Roman justice (Acts 24:26–27). Paul also says that he was beaten with rods three times, a Roman punishment (2 Cor. 11:25; cf. 1 Cor. 4:9), which would not give him much reason to trust local justice. In fact, in 6:7–8 he implies that by going to law in pagan courts, the Christian litigants are implicated in defrauding others and committing injustice. The garb of law abets this injustice, which explains how Paul could regard the justices as unjust (Wengst 1987: 76).

Evidence indicates that the civil courts of this era were less than impartial and that substantial corruption did exist. They were not held in high esteem by the masses, who did not have equal access to them. Winter (1991a: 563–64) thinks that the term "unjust" specifically applies to the character of the honorary magistrates who presided and the juries who pronounced verdicts—they were open to bribery and biased toward the powerful. Dio Chrysostom (*Or.* 8.9) complains that in Corinth there were "lawyers innumerable perverting justice." Cicero (*In Verrem* 1.1.1) opens his speech to the jury (and judges) in the prosecution of Verres by citing the rumors throughout Rome and foreign lands that "the courts will never convict any man, however guilty, if only he has money." Apuleius (*Metam.* 10.33) derides judges as "gowned vultures" and claims that "all our judges nowadays sell their judgments for money."

The wealthy were able to take unfair advantage of this judicial system by exercising their prestige and influence. One's breeding, social standing, and reputation for character—one's persona—also tilted justice in favor of the elite. The poor always had the cards stacked against them in the courtroom. Pliny the Younger (*Ep.* 9.5) commends the new governor of Baetica in Spain regarding his administration of justice for "maintaining consideration for the best men." He advises him to continue to "maintain the distinctions between ranks and degrees of dignity." Social standing weighted the scales of justice; and if that did not work, bribery could tip the balance. The character Ascyltos, in Petronius's novel *Satyricon* (14), expresses fear of the perils of a lawsuit in a place where he is unknown and bemoans his situation:

> Of what avail are laws to be where money rules alone, and the poor suitor can never succeed? The very men who mock at the times by carrying the Cynic's wallet have sometimes been known to betray the truth for a price. So a lawsuit is nothing more than a public auction, and the knightly juror who sits listening to the case approves, with the record of his vote, something bought.

Cicero's remarks in his defense of Caecina (*Pro Caecina* 73) implicitly recognize how influence, power, and wealth could bend the rule of law; and he was not above using all three himself to boost the prospects of winning.[3] This background lends support to the conclusion that Paul is not simply exasperated that any Christian would take a case involving a brother to nonbelieving judges but that they would take it to those biased in favor of the rich and powerful.

---

3. Tacitus (*Annales* 1.75) specifically complains about Tiberius for disregarding "the bribes and pressure of the powerful" and thus undermining liberty.

Paul does not describe the subject of the lawsuit, which, as far as he is concerned, is immaterial—nothing could justify Christians dragging fellow Christians into court. The terms βιωτικός (biōtikos, belonging to matters of daily life) in 6:3–4 and ἀποστερεῖν (aposterein, to defraud) reveal that it was a civil matter, not a criminal one. In objecting to this action, he does not presume that Christians are somehow above being judged by secular authorities. His comments in Rom. 13:1–5 affirm that God has given the governing authorities jurisdiction to execute wrath on the wrongdoer in criminal cases. But trivial cases are a different matter.

Some contend that the litigation had to do with a sexual offense, since this passage is sandwiched between references to sexual misconduct in 5:1–13 and 6:12–20. In seeking to explain the connection between chapters 5 and 6, Bernard (1907) imagines that the incestuous man's father was still alive and was suing him in the secular courts for damages.[4] P. Richardson (1983; cf. R. Horsley 1998: 86) accepts Bernard's view and suggests three possible scenarios: (1) a father sued his son-in-law over the status of the younger man's wife; (2) two men were involved sexually or nonsexually with the same woman and one sued the other; (3) a man charged an influential "leader" in the congregation with "tampering" with his marriage (see additional note). P. Richardson argues that Paul believes that sexual misconduct should have been judged by the community, not brought out into the open. Deming (1992) goes even further by speculating that the church was divided over the man and his stepmother. Indignant hard-liners failed in their attempt to judge the matter in house and took the issue to a secular court, where they lost, leaving the church bitterly divided.

The latter view is a fanciful reconstruction (so Rosner 1998: 338–40) and goes far beyond the evidence. I argue that, in chapters 5–6, Paul cites what he regards as appalling moral failures in order to bridle the Corinthians' unwarranted boasting about their spiritual stature. This passage may be sandwiched between cases of sexual immorality, but it does not follow that the lawsuit must have something to do with sexual immorality. Paul's insistence in 6:7 that they should be willing to be wronged instead of seeking legal retribution hardly seems applicable to a case of adultery, let alone incest. Nor would he wish to imply that being cuckolded was a matter of indifference.[5] If this legal matter were re-

---

4. Some infer from the vocabulary that the law case had to do with some kind of sexual impropriety. The verbs ἐξουσιάζειν (exousiazein, to have authority over, 6:12) and ἀποστερεῖν (aposterein, to defraud, 6:8) have a sexual connotation in 7:4 and 5. The noun πλεονέκτης (pleonektēs, 5:11; 6:10) is connected to πλεονεκτεῖν (pleonektein) in 1 Thess. 4:6, which refers to sexual misconduct.

5. Paul also contends that the plaintiffs also are guilty of wronging and defrauding others, which, if one is to be consistent, would imply that they too were guilty of similar sexual violations.

lated to the case in 5:1–13, it seems highly unlikely that Paul could dismiss it as merely a minor dispute (6:2). That case was so serious that it warranted Paul's direct intervention and the whole assembly of the church to take action by handing the man over to Satan (5:5). It is unlikely that the lawsuit had anything to do with the case of incest or any other sexual transgression.[6]

Others assume that the case had something to do with disputed business dealings—a plausible scenario because Corinth was the commercial center of Greece (Edwards 1885: 142). Or perhaps it had to do with questions of dowry or inheritance. Cases related to legacies were frequent in the Roman Empire (Chow 1992: 125; cf. Luke 12:13–15), and the words βιωτικά (biōtika) and ἀποστερεῖν (aposterein) are more applicable to disputes over property (Chow 1992: 126). Possibly, the reference to the unrighteous not being able to "inherit the kingdom of God" (6:9–10) may be an ironic allusion to one who has foolishly fixed his eyes on an earthly inheritance by initiating a lawsuit.

Understanding who made use of the civil courts in the ancient world may shed more light on the matter and explain Paul's indignation. Persons of high status were prone to settle disputes through litigation. They had the upper hand in the courts because they could capitalize on their influence and wealth and could enhance their own reputation by injuring their opponent's or increase their wealth with legal conquests. The lower classes were restricted from doing so since they were unlikely to win against stacked odds. The law, for example, favored creditors over debtors and landlords over tenants (Garnsey 1974: 142). Such a suit against someone of higher rank would also show an unwelcome lack of respect for one's "betters" (Winter 1991a: 561).[7] This fact of life is reflected in Scripture: "But you have dishonored the poor. Is it not the rich who oppress you? Is it not they who drag you into court?" (James 2:6; cf. Eccles. 6:10).

In deciding to sue, one first had to calculate the cost and the chances of winning, not on the basis of the merits of the case but on the defendant's social status and powerful connections. Garnsey (1970: 217–18) maintains that suits brought by those of humble origin against men of

---

6. Winter (1991a: 561) notes that offenses such as "legal possession, breach of contract, damages, fraud and injury" were assigned to civil courts, while criminal courts handled cases of high treason, embezzlement of state property, bribery at elections, extortion in the provinces, murder by violence or poisoning, endangering public security, forgery of wills or coins, violent offenses, adultery, and seduction of reputable unmarried women (cf. Garnsey 1970: 181).

7. The elder Seneca (*Controversiae* 10.1.1–7) cites the case of a man whose father had a rich enemy, and when his father was found killed, though not robbed, the youth, dressed in mourning, began to follow the rich man about. He was unable to accuse the rich man in court because of the danger and the minimal chance of winning. His father had been killed because he tried to bring the rich man to court.

rank were unlikely to have been frequent because a person of lower rank would assume from previous experience or that of acquaintances that the decision would inevitably go against him. He would be unlikely to retain effective counsel and could be certain that the defendant would retaliate. If he did go to court, the praetor might dismiss the suit out of hand if it threatened the defendant's status.[8] Occasionally, a patron might decide to take up a client's cause and take another to court on the client's behalf. The client would then bank on the weight of the patron's persona to win the case.

This background argues for the likelihood that the plaintiff enjoyed high status (A. Mitchell 1993: 565). Either he has taken on one of his social peers or has sought to grind down a weaker member of the church who was lower in rank. People in the ancient world contended for honor in the law courts, and one gained honor by beating a rival down. The pursuit of litigation often had little to do with the pursuit of justice. Kinman (1997: 347) avers, "Lawsuits were typically initiated not merely to resolve legitimate social grievances but also to further the social status of the litigants, and this 'progress' was made only at the expense of one's opponent." The legal skirmishes usually became pitched assaults on the defendant's character. Winter (1991a: 567) comments, "Defendants could be subject to muck-raking and fabrication and this lack of legal restraint helps to explain why prosecutor and defendant could so rarely avoid *inimicitiae*." Epstein (1987: 90–100) shows how litigation was undertaken as a manifestation of enmity and that lawsuits "were perhaps the most single generator of private hostility in Rome." Such public confrontations would naturally generate factionalism in the church (see M. Mitchell 1993: 231) as the clients of these litigants would be forced to choose sides. To have members set at each other's throats would also undermine the public reputation of the church.

If the lawsuit was directed against a weaker member of the church, who would be victimized by the inequality of the court system, Paul's outrage becomes even more understandable. The Christian plaintiff has become party to inflicting injustice and fraud on a fellow Christian (6:8) who does not have equal access to justice.

Paul rejects altogether the idea of Christians initiating lawsuits against fellow Christians (6:7), but first he plays up the outrage that they have resorted to pagan courts instead of bringing their disputes "before the saints." Many Greek confraternities possessed their own jurisdiction and courts to judge disputes and crimes that took place among members (Delcor 1968: 72). Jews also were given the autonomy to settle disputes between themselves in their own courts so that they could live and be judged according to their ancestral laws (Tcherikover 1961: 301, 307;

8. Cited also by Chow 1992: 128–29.

Schürer 1986: 119–20). Josephus (*Ant.* 14.10.17 §235) mentions in an aside that the Jews of Sardis had their own courts to decide controversies with one another. According to a ruling preserved in *b. Giṭ.* 88b (a tractate on divorce settlements), a distinction is made between a divorce bill (*get*) enforced by "a heathen court" and one enforced by an Israelite court. It records that one rabbi objected to another compelling other men to give a bill of divorce: "Surely we are only laymen." Rabbi Tarfon is cited as responding, "In any place where you find heathen law courts, even though their law is the same as Israelite law, you must not resort to them since it says, 'These are the judgments which you shall bring before them,' that is to say, 'before them' and not before heathens [Exod. 21:1]."

These attitudes may also have prevailed in the time of Paul, though we see the leaders of the synagogue in Corinth handing Paul over to the governor Gallio (Acts 18:12–17). When it came to disputes that could be settled according to their own law, Jews believed that they should be resolved between themselves. For this purpose to be successful, tight discipline had to be maintained in their group. According to G. Harris (1991: 7–9), it requires (1) cohesiveness of the group, (2) authoritative leadership, (3) tension with the world or outside forces, and (4) a clear sense of the group's mission. The failure of the Corinthians to carry out such internal discipline suggests that they lacked these attributes. Some Corinthians may have resorted to these courts out of habit. They had not yet been converted from their old mentality of asserting hostility toward others and their old ways of doing things. The church was also riven by factions and appeared to lack a sense of its mission to be a witness to its world as an alternative society constrained by God's love to seek the welfare and salvation of others. Paul seeks to provide the authoritative leadership that will help them see the error of their ways. Theoretically, a church tribunal would be unbiased and never configured so as to favor the powerful, as the Roman legal system was. In fact, as baptized believers, the litigants and the judge would stand together as equals with a common destiny (L. Lewis 1990: 97).

The believers' eschatological assurance of triumph with Christ at the end of the age serves as the premise for Paul's critique of their failure to judge these matters between themselves. He argues from the fact that Christians will take part in the judgment of the world and the angels, but he does not develop precisely how "the saints" (οἱ ἅγιοι, *hoi hagioi*) will be involved. His rhetorical question "Do you not know?"—one of ten such questions in the letter—strengthens the force of his protest over their behavior. It adds ignorance to the problem of insolence plaguing the community (Findlay 1910: 814).[9] The future defines who

6:2–3

---

9. Kim (*DPL* 482) suggests that the "Do you not know that . . . ?" formula refers to teachings of Jesus that Paul had transmitted to the Corinthians when he founded the church.

they are and should determine what they do in the present. Their future status should have revealed to them how foolish it was to bring minor disputes to be settled in a court belonging to a world whose form is passing away (7:31) and destined for divine condemnation (2:6; 11:32; 15:24).

Texts from Paul's Jewish tradition, notably Dan. 7:22, contain allusions to the judgment given to the holy ones (cf. Jude 14–15),[10] and many interpreters regard them to be the source of Paul's assertion, identified as a "common motif from Jewish apocalyptic eschatology" (Fee 1987: 233). But in Dan. 7:22 it is not clear whether the "holy ones" refer to Israelites, angels, or glorified Israelites (Goldingay 1989: 178; J. Collins 1993: 317); and the scale of judgment envisioned is not so vast as to encompass the entire world. In 1 Enoch 1:9, the "holy ones" are angels, not humans. In none of the traditions do the "holy ones" make judicial decisions but instead administer God's judgment. Jesus promises the disciples that they will judge the twelve tribes of Israel (Matt. 19:28; Luke 22:30), but that judgment is limited, at least metaphorically, to the twelve tribes. Christ speaks this word about believers' authority over the nations in Rev. 2:26–27:

> To everyone who conquers and continues to do my works to
>   the end,
>   I will give authority over the nations;
> to rule them with an iron rod,
>   as when clay pots are shattered. (cf. Rev. 20:4)

Since God is the one who judges the world (Rom. 3:6), it may be best to understand the saints' judging as related to ruling (cf. Ruth 1:1; 1 Kings 15:5; Ps. 2:10; Isa. 16:5; Dan. 9:12). Lightfoot (1895: 210) comments, "Just as the faithful shall reign with Christ as kings (2 Tim. 2:12; Rev. 22:5), so they shall they sit with Him as judges of the world."

The second rhetorical question in 6:3 raises the ante from the judgment of the world to the judgment of angels (6:3). Which angels does Paul have in view? Several options have been proposed.

1. It could mean angels in general, both bad and good. The argument that God did not subject the coming world to angels but to humans (citing Ps. 8:4–6) is found in Heb. 2:5–9 (cf. 2 Bar. 51:8–12), which was composed by a member from the Pauline circle. But this text does not hint that the righteous will judge the angels.

2. Cullmann (1960: 191–210) contends that the angels refer to the patrons of the nations, the invisible angelic powers standing behind the earthly states. Barrett (1968: 136–37) allows that it might sharpen

---

10. Cf. also Wis. 3:7–8; Sir. 4:15; Jub. 24:29; 1 Enoch 1:9; 38:1, 5; 48:9; 94:10; 95:3; 96:1; 98:12; 108:12; 1QpHab 5:4–5.

Paul's point: Christians should not submit to secular courts "since these are under the authority of angels whom Christians are to judge." This interpretation would be more apparent, however, if the noun "angels" were qualified in some way to identify them as the angels of the nations; but it is not (cf. Vischer 1955: 12).

3. Several texts refer to fallen angels who constitute an imprisoned host awaiting their final punishment (cf. Isa. 24:21–23; Matt. 25:41; 2 Pet. 2:4; Jude 6; cf. 1 Enoch 10:12–14; 19:1; 21:1–10; 2 Enoch 7; 18). The angels may refer to these fallen angels who are subject to God's condemnation (see Hoskins 2001: 292–96).

4. Paul's purpose in these verses is not to articulate doctrine about the saints' role in the final judgment of the world and the angels but to point out a disturbing inconsistency between what they will be doing at the end of this age and what they are doing now. It is probable that he wishes only to remind the Corinthians of their glorious end-time destiny when they will be given dominion even over the angels. In that day, the current state of affairs will be radically reversed. For example, Paul says that now, in this present evil age, he is a spectacle both to the world and to angels (4:9). In the end time, however, things will be upended, and he will join with the saints in judging both the world and the angels. The promise of that future should control all that Christians do in the present. They should appreciate that the ἄδικοι (adikoi), to whom they are now taking their petty complaints, will be completely excluded from the kingdom of God and not crowned with glorious status.

The argument moves from the greater to the lesser. If they are destined to be participants in the celestial judgment of the world and of the angels, they ought to be able to handle mundane matters of far less consequence. If they cannot settle minor rifts between themselves, they are hardly worthy to participate in the judgment of the world, let alone of the angels.[11] The key point is not the information about their eschatological role in the judgment but the inference drawn from it. They are certainly "worthy," not ἀνάξιοι (anaxioi, unworthy, incompetent) to judge "the most minor cases" (κριτηρίων ἐλαχίστων, kritēriōn elachistōn).

The word κριτήριον usually refers to a lower-level court of justice (James 2:6; Dan. 7:10, 26), and Paul may be asking if they are incompetent to set up even the most insignificant tribunals. If this reading is correct, he is making a point about the proper venue for airing their disputes. The word κριτήριον, however, is also used to refer to the legal action (BDAG 570; Büchsel, TDNT 3:943), and he may be asking if they are incompetent to judge even the most insignificant cases (Weiss

---

11. This image does not conflict with Paul's statement in 5:12, where he claims he has no responsibility to judge outsiders. He refers there to the present. Judging the world occurs at the final judgment (cf. 4:5).

1910: 147). This meaning makes the best sense in the context. In 6:1, Paul expresses his concern that they brought their quarrels before the wrong tribunal by taking them before unjust unbelievers rather than before the saints. In 6:2–3, he identifies the nature of those cases. The phrase κριτήριοι ἐλάχιστοι is parallel to the βιωτικά (biōtika) in 6:3, which refers to the cases.[12] The βιωτικά refer to common issues pertaining to the circumstances of everyday life (cf. 2 Tim. 2:4; 1 John 2:16; 3:17). Such minor trivia pale beside the end-time judging responsibility to be placed upon the saints.

Paul makes this point to underscore the worthiness of the Christian—any Christian, even those who are regarded as inconsequential—to judge any earthly dispute. For Christians to take their legal battles to the courts of the unrighteous repudiates their end-time status and conveys that they lack the moral and intellectual capacity to settle things between themselves. By characterizing the case as ἐλάχιστος, "unimportant," "insignificant," Paul also berates the eager plaintiff who has so maltreated a brother Christian and exposed the community to shame over what amounts to nothing.

6:4 Paul moves to the issue of appointing judges. Καθίζετε (kathizete) can mean "to sit" (on the elevated bench of the magistrate, the bēma [cf. John 19:13]) or "to set up" (as judges) for these ordinary cases. The clause could be punctuated in a number of ways.

1. It could be read as a question in the indicative, "Are you appointing those who are despised by the church?" (so RSV, NRSV, NASB). The "despised" or "disdained" (οἱ ἐξουθενημένοι, hoi exouthenēmenoi) would refer to non-Christians, and the question would drip with indignation.
2. It could be a statement or an exclamation in the indicative: "You are appointing as judges these who are despised by the church!" (NJB), again expressing indignation.
3. The verb καθίζετε could be rendered as an imperative: "Appoint as judges those held in low esteem in the church" (KJV, NIV). Those held in low esteem or treated with contempt are Christians. Most ancient commentators read it as an imperative, while most modern commentators read as an indicative (Kinman 1997: 345–46).

The arguments for the indicative are as follows. In the NT, "a verb at the end of the sentence tends to be indicative rather than imperative" (Kinman 1997: 348). Rendering the sentence as a question would continue the battery of rhetorical questions in these verses.

12. Μήτιγε (mētige) is elliptical and means "not to mention" ordinary cases.

Do you dare take to court . . . ? (6:1)

Do you not know that the saints will judge the world? (6:2a)

Are you incompetent to try trivial cases? (6:2b)

Do you not know that we are to judge angels—to say nothing of ordinary matters? (6:3)

Can it be that there is no one among you wise enough to decide between one believer and another? (6:5b)

As a repetition of the reproach that Christians seek justice from unbelievers, it would fit his intention to shame them (6:5; Schrage 1991: 412).

Interpreting this sentence as a question, however, is not without problems.[13] Lightfoot (1895: 211) claims that it is awkward to have an interrogative at the end of a long sentence, and it obscures the force of μὲν οὖν (men oun, nay rather) at the beginning of the clause (Findlay 1910: 815). The Corinthians also are not empowered to "set up" secular magistrates. Fuller's (1986: 100) translation, "Are you actually appointing to adjudicate your cases the very people whom as church people you otherwise hold in contempt?" reveals the problem. They may have taken cases to secular judges, but they did not appoint them. The verb καθίζειν (kathizein) has been tweaked to make it mean "to resort to" judges already appointed by the state.[14] But the verb means "to appoint," and the Corinthian Christians are in no position to appoint judges in secular courts.[15] Finally, Paul nowhere refers to those outside the church as "the despised." Such language would reflect an attitude that is antithetical to the church's mission enterprise.

Reading the verb as an imperative gives a completely different slant to the matter: "If you have minor cases, those who are disdained in the church, set them on the bench!" Kinman (1997) musters several arguments in favor of the imperative.

1. Paul has already expressed disapproval in 6:1–3 over what they have done. Having made this protest, he instructs them in 6:4 about what they should do if such a case comes up again. He introduces it with a probable future condition ἐάν (ean, if). If it occurs again, which

---

13. The rhetorical pattern of five questions is interrupted by the statement in 6:5, but the pattern could be just as easily interrupted after four questions by an imperative followed by a statement (Kinman 1997: 350). The mere fact that Paul asks four rhetorical questions in a row does not require the next sentence to be a question.

14. Stein (1968: 89) tries to solve the problem by arguing that Paul wanted them to appoint a Jewish lay person to arbitrate the case. Fuller (1986: 100–101) contends that they were resorting to pagan neighbors, not officially appointed judges, to settle their disputes informally.

15. For this reason, Fee (1987: 236) interprets the verb to mean "to sit for a judgment or make a ruling" (cf. Dinkler 1952: 171 n. 1; Schrage 1991: 412).

he hopes it will not (6:7), appoint the despised in the church as arbiters (Kinman 1997: 353).

2. The imperatival form of the verb is the final element in several clauses in Paul's letters.[16] Paul could have put the verb last for emphasis (Kinman 1997: 349).

3. It is unlikely that Paul would characterize nonbelievers so disparagingly as "despised" by the church (Kinman 1997: 351). One of the problems in the Corinthian church is that they *do not* despise the standards of outsiders and *do not* set aside their judgments as of no account. They are too much enamored with this world and the status it can convey and are dazzled by the leverage of the high and mighty. The world, on the other hand, does not reciprocate this respect. Paul uses the term τὰ ἐξουθενημένα (*ta exouthenēmena*, the despised) in 1:28 to characterize the world's disdain for those whom God has chosen. With the exception of 1:28, which refers to the world's attitude toward Christians, Paul uses the verb elsewhere in his letters only to refer to Christians' attitudes toward fellow Christians, never toward outsiders (Rom. 14:3, 10; 1 Cor. 16:11; 2 Cor. 10:10; Gal. 4:14; cf. 1 Thess. 5:20).[17] Fuller (1986: 100; cf. Hays 1997: 94) argues, however, that if Paul refers to despised members of the church, it would fly in the face of his theme that all Christians are members of the same body and deserving of the same dignity (1 Cor. 12:4–31). But Paul's attempts to abolish these class distinctions and prejudices in this letter reveal that they already existed in the church. There were those in the church who looked down their noses at fellow members. Godet (1886: 289–90) suggests, "Paul may well apply the term with a touch of irony to designate those of whom small account is made in their assemblies. Do not go and seek your first orators to make them arbiters in such cases, but take the least among you" (so also Goudge 1911: 44; Derrett 1991: 29). It is more likely, however, from Paul's earlier reference to those chosen by God as despised by the world (1:28; cf. 4:9–13), that he alludes to secular society's evaluation of church members. He is not "trivializing the pagan courts" as having no standing within the church because of their antithetical values (contra Fee 1987: 236), since he affirms their authority in criminal matters (Rom. 13:1–5). Instead, he reminds them of the world's disdain for Christians, which was particularly evident among the unjust (6:1),

16. Cf. Rom. 12:14; 1 Cor. 4:16; 7:21; 10:31; 11:33; 14:20; 16:1, 13; Gal. 5:1; Eph. 5:11; Phil. 4:4, 8; Col. 3:15; 1 Thess. 5:22; 1 Tim. 4:11; 5:22; 6:2; Philem. 18.

17. The only other time the verb ἐξουθενέω is followed by the preposition in the NT is in Acts 4:11, where the preposition is ὑπό (*hypo*): "which was despised by the builders." It is likely that if Paul meant "those despised *by* the church" in 1 Cor. 6:4, he would have used this preposition. His use of ἐν (*en*) in the phrase τοὺς ἐξουθενημένους ἐν τῇ ἐκκλησίᾳ (*tous exouthenēmenous en tē ekklēsia*) suggests that he means "those despised *in* the church."

the very ones before whom they have made their legal appeals. To set up ostracized, lowly Christians as judges in disagreements would testify to the individual worth of all Christians and the competence of all Christians, regardless of their social status, to arbitrate disputes (cf. 2:15). It would testify to the gospel's effective reversal of the world's values. Murphy-O'Connor (1996: 285) comments,

> His point is not that the church should hide its dirty linen from the eyes of outsiders, but that they should grasp the opportunity to demonstrate the power of grace to non-believers by resolving such disputes themselves. Unless it is missionary, the church is untrue to itself. The world needs to see grace at work.

4. If the verb καθίζειν is taken literally to mean "to set up," "to appoint," rather than "to choose to put cases before," the church had only the power to appoint fellow Christians.[18] Appointing the despised in the church as arbiters would serve the purpose of undermining any intention of suing others to further one's own social-climbing agenda. Kinman (1997: 354) suggests, "The appointment of 'the despised' as arbiters might do a great deal to discourage lawsuits between the elite, for there would probably be very little to gain in the way of status if a mere 'despised one,' rather than a socially esteemed magistrate, were to be the arbiter of the dispute." By insisting that they take any future grievance over everyday affairs out of the secular arena, Paul subverts its very intent as a means to gain public honor.[19] Kinman, in my view, has the better of the argument.

"I say [this] to your shame" (cf. 15:34) contrasts with what Paul says in 4:14, where he states that he does not write to make them ashamed but to admonish them. The phrase could apply to what he has just said in 6:4 but is more likely to apply to what follows. He adopts a shaming tactic to quash their boastfulness (cf. 1:27, 29) as well as to change their contentious ways. The οὕτως (houtos) is inferential (Edwards 1885: 140), and he infers from their taking a case to the secular courts that they did not have even one wise person in the church to judge between the disputing parties. He is not directing them to select members who enjoyed a reputation for wisdom to serve as judges (contra Meeks 1983: 104; Kistemaker 1993: 182; R. Collins 1999: 233), because the word

6:5–6

---

18. A possible exception occurs in Josephus (*Ant.* 13.3.4 §75) when he records that the Jews and Samaritans in Alexandria asked King Ptolemy with his friends "to sit" (κα-θισάντα, *kathisanta*) and hear their arguments over their respective temples and to punish with death the losers.

19. Edwards (1885: 140) considers the imperative to yield "a more natural and certainly a more forcible meaning" and comments, "He is not justifying their contempt of brethren, but stating it, and, in stating it, really rebuking their pride."

"wise" (σοφός, *sophos*) is a loaded one in this letter. It has a negative connotation in every usage (1:19, 20, 25, 26, 27; 3:18, 19, 20) except 3:10. Some in the church regarded themselves as "wise" (3:18), and it is probable that they came from the ranks of those with higher status (Theissen 1982: 97). To say that apparently they do not have even one wise man capable of judging such trivial matters becomes an ironic taunt (Godet 1886: 291; Wilckens, *TDNT* 7:517; Fee 1987: 237; Pogoloff 1992: 208; Schrage 1991: 413).[20] They must not be wise enough to mediate these petty quarrels (A. Mitchell 1993: 573). The Corinthians may or may not have recognized a parallel to the philosophical ideal that the wise would rather be wronged than to wrong others (A. Mitchell 1993: 573).[21] However, the wisdom that Paul commends is not merely the wisdom of a benevolent person but *Christian wisdom*, which is bound integrally to the cross (1:18–25; 2:6–15). If they possessed this true, Christian wisdom, they would never have sunk so low as to drag a brother Christian through the mud of a public proceeding in a pagan court in the first place. He expounds on what a wise Christian would do in 6:7–8.

Schrage (1991: 414) suggests that God's decision to intervene in the judgment of the sheep in Ezek. 34 may be in the background of Paul's response. If so, the judge is not neutral but judges against the fat sheep that butted the weak animals with their horns and scattered them far and wide (Ezek. 34:17–22). To judge rightly may mean showing favor to the "lean sheep" that have been abused by the "fat" ones.

The verb διακρῖναι (*diakrinai*, 6:5) in a legal context means "to render a decision." The verb κρίνειν (*krinein*) in 6:6 in this context means "to hale before a court."[22] Godet (1886: 291) claims that the distinction between the aorist διακρῖναι and the present κρίνεται (*krinetai*) is that the decision is settled summarily "with the stroke of the pen," while the trial implies a drawn-out process. Though it is not prudent to attach too much weight to the verb tense, the context suggests that this comment may be on target. The following verses reveal that Paul is not upset simply because they aired their dirty linen before unbelievers but that they resorted to lawsuits at all. Brother Christians are pitted against brother Christians, adopting a cutthroat, adversarial relationship rather than one based on love and selflessness. The church appears to be infested with enmity between members, and he deliberately chooses an image from the family to remind them of their brotherhood. The word "brother" occurs thirty-nine times in the letter, and the choice by the

---

20. Paul is not borrowing a Jewish expression חָכָם (*ḥākām*, wise) as a title for an authorized scholar (contra Meurer 1972: 149).

21. The wise man ignores injury (cf. Seneca, *De constantia sapientis* 2.1; 4.1; 7.6; 9.3–5; 12.3; 13.5; 16.1), and Paul exemplifies this attitude in 2 Cor. 2:5–10.

22. In 11:31, a different context, the words are almost synonymous.

NRSV to render it as "believer" may cause the reader to miss this emphasis. Plutarch (*Mor.* 481B) brands siblings bringing accusations against
each other as diabolical (cited by R. Collins 1999: 234). Paul uses the
image of brothers slinging accusations against one another to shame
them for impiously violating their brotherhood.

Paul now changes tack and contends that their contests at law are a   **6:7–8**
complete loss (ἥττημα, *hēttēma*) for them. This stinging rebuke pertains
particularly to the one who initiated the court action but also to the entire church body. The word ἥττημα is used for a loss in a lawsuit (Wolff
1996: 116 n. 127), but Paul applies it to a moral loss (Edwards 1885:
141). No matter who wins or loses the lawsuit, all lose spiritually. Their
litigious spirit betrays a moral deficiency (Godet 1886: 293) and reveals
the triumph of selfishness over love—something Paul addresses in
chapter 13. The upshot is the complete loss of any sense of brotherhood
in the community. Litigation by its very nature promoted enmity from
the slander that was part and parcel of a trial and could only have fueled the church's factionalism (see additional note). Church members
who were clients of one of the parties would have to side with their patron, if they were to remain clients, over against a fellow Christian.

The image of inheriting the kingdom of God in 6:9 adds another
shade of meaning to their loss. The noun ἥττημα occurs elsewhere in
the NT only in Rom. 11:12, where Paul applies it to the stumbling of Israel that has, temporarily at least, cut them off from salvation. Paul insinuates that the plaintiff's greedy grasping for advantage in this life
may cause him to lose an eternal inheritance. If the defendant were
somehow at fault, the same principle applies.

Paul recommends an alternative to instituting legal proceedings
against a Christian brother. If such actions can result in the loss of an
eternal inheritance, why not rather be wronged? Why not rather be defrauded?[23] Even if the Christian were motivated solely by personal
gain, the option between possible minor material gain in this life versus
the certainty of a glorious legacy in the life to come should make the
decision easy. Refusing to seek redress for a wrong is not only better
than bringing charges against another Christian before pagan judges,
but also better than impaneling a jury of Christians to hear the complaint. It reveals that one understands, accepts, and lives out the wisdom of the cross.

Paul's advice springs from his ethic of refusing to repay evil for evil
but instead seeking to do good to others (Rom.12:17; 1 Thess. 5:15),
and it echoes Jesus' teaching about turning the other cheek (Matt. 5:39;
so Findlay 1910: 816; Piper 1979: 59; Fee 1987: 241). Jesus' teaching

---

23. The use of the middle voice ἀδικεῖσθε (*adikeisthe*) means "to let oneself be
wronged"; ἀποστερεῖσθε (*apostereisthe*), "to let oneself be defrauded" (Godet 1886: 294).

"stands solidly in a tradition of non-retaliatory ethics of early Judaism" (Rosner 1994: 116; cf. Zerbe 1993).[24] Others allege that Paul's advice reflects secular wisdom going back to Plato (*Gorgias* 509c) that to do wrong is the greater evil and to suffer wrong the lesser evil. A. Mitchell (1993: 573) shows that moral philosophers contend that the wise would rather "be wronged than wrong." Musonius Rufus wrestled directly with the question ("Will the Philosopher Prosecute Anyone for Personal Injury?"). He taught that the wise and sensible philosopher would never prosecute anyone for personal injury or disgrace. He should be immune to insults, malignant glances, and the jeering slap in the face and should meekly submit because "this befits one whose purpose is noble minded." "To accept injury not in a spirit of savage resentment and to show ourselves not implacable toward those who wrong us, but rather to be a source of good hope to them is characteristic of a benevolent and civilized way of life" (Lutz 1947: 76–81; cf. Epictetus, *Diatr.* 1.28.10; 2.10.24–8). From these parallels, A. Mitchell (1993: 574) claims that Paul's jab at their moral failure is even more pointed: "Having lawsuits illustrates that they lack the wisdom they claim to have." But these parallels only reveal that some unbelievers would have understood and resonated with this ethic. They need not be the source of Paul's reflections. He is not appealing to what moral philosophers thought was wise but to the very core of the gospel and the moral implications of Christ's sacrificial death for others. He sets himself up as an example for the Corinthians on how this ethic, which differs so dramatically from the ways of the world, is to be lived out: "When reviled, we bless; when persecuted, we endure; when slandered, we speak kindly" (4:12–13). This ethic finds positive expression in 9:22: "I have become all things to all persons, in order that in all circumstances I might save some of them."

In 6:8, Paul implies that the lawsuit is a "form of wronging and defrauding" (A. Mitchell 1993: 567). Those who take cases against brothers before unjust judges are themselves unjust. Instead of forbearing wrong, they are inflicting wrong. It is one thing to be a righteous victim; it is another thing to be a victimizer. It completely discredits their witness to God's love in the world. Murphy-O'Connor's (1979a: 47) remarks on this verse convey an important theological insight: "A united community in which love dominates is the existential affirmation of the truth of the gospel. A community which contains within itself the divisions which characterize the 'world' has no power to transform its environment, because the contradiction between theory and practice is too evident (Rom. 2:23–24)."

24. The rabbis also praised restraint from seeking retribution (*b. Šabb.* 88b; *b. Yoma* 23a; *b. Giṭ.* 36b).

The phrase "they will not inherit the kingdom of God" brackets the cat-   **6:9–10**
alog of sins inventoried in 6:9–10.[25] "The kingdom of God" refers to
"the future and ultimate manifestation of God as king" (R. Collins
1999: 235), and the image of "inheriting" picks up the theme of inheriting the land, which becomes a type for the blessedness to come.[26] The
image derives from Jesus' teaching (Matt. 25:34; cf. Matt. 19:29; Mark
10:17; Luke 10:25; 18:18). Paul assumes that since God's kingdom is a
kingdom of righteousness, the unrighteous can have no part in it.
God's rule brings with it moral conditions that require a radical transformation of values and behavior for believers. Those who practice
these sins cut themselves off from that rule and from any hope of a divine inheritance.

The command μὴ πλανᾶσθε (*mē planasthe*, do not be deceived, do
not go astray; cf. 15:33; Gal. 6:7) may well have a parallel in Stoic diatribe, where it serves as an exhortative slogan: "Do not err" (Braun,
TDNT 6:244–45; Barrett 1968: 140; R. Collins 1999: 235–36; for example, Epictetus, *Diatr.* 4.6.23; 2.20.7).[27] It is possible, as Godet (1886:
295) surmises, "The Corinthians seemed to imagine that their religious
knowledge and Christian talk would suffice to open heaven to them,
whatever their conduct otherwise might be." Or, as Barrett (1968: 140)
contends, humans are particularly prone to deceive themselves in such
matters by "persuading themselves that God cannot mean his moral demands seriously." The people of God frequently have trouble recognizing that injustice is as serious a sin as incest and other sexual misconduct and that it warrants the very same punishment (cf. Jer. 7:8–15).

The ten sins in this list reflect the behavior of those outside the
church, the ἄδικοι (*adikoi*) who are guilty of open rebellion against God
and destined for judgment. Paul repeats six vices from the list in 5:11,
beginning again with "fornicators" (πόρνοι, *pornoi*) and adding four
new evils: "adulterers," "males who are penetrated sexually by males,"
"males who sexually penetrate males," and "thieves." Μοιχοί (*moichoi*,
adulterers) refers to those guilty of sexual relations outside of marriage
(Exod. 20:13; Lev. 20:10; Deut. 5:18; cf. Luke 18:11). The gravity of this
sin should not be diminished simply because of its prevalence. Philo
(*Decal.* 24 §121, §131) comments that the second half of the Decalogue
begins with the command against adultery because God held it to be

25. Paul's comment accords with the rabbinic topos in *m. Sanh.* 10:1–4, where the
refrain "they have no share/portion in the world to come" is applied to those deemed
guilty of various sins.
26. The phrase "kingdom of God" appears elsewhere in Rom. 14:17; 1 Cor. 4:20;
15:50; Gal.5:21; Eph. 5:5; Col. 4:11; 2 Thess. 1:5; cf. 1 Cor. 15:24; 1 Thess. 2:12; cf. also
Acts 14:22; 19:8; 20:25; 28:23, 31.
27. The word πλανάω occurs 134 times in the LXX but never in the second person
plural imperative. Cf. T. Gad 3:1; 15:33; Gal. 6:7; Luke 21:8; James 1:16.

"the greatest of crimes." In Sir. 23:16–17, incest and adultery are treated on the same level as deserving the same divine punishment.

The meaning and significance of the words μαλακοί (*malakoi*) and ἀρσενοκοῖται (*arsenokoitai*) have been examined in recent years by those who would like to water down any condemnation in the NT of homo-erotic acts. Boswell (1980: 92, 163, 333), for example, tries to prove that the early church did not oppose homosexual acts per se. In interpreting 6:9, Boswell (1980: 338–53, 363–64) claims that no connection exists be-tween the two terms and that they do not refer to homosexual acts. He translates μαλακοί as "masturbators" (cf. Lapide 1896: 110: "those guilty of self-pollution") and ἀρσενοκοῖται as a vulgar expression for "male prostitutes," with "male" being the subject rather than the object in the compound word.[28] Scroggs (1983: 106–9) argues that Paul condemns only effeminate call boys and a specific and detested form of pederasty, not the general practice of homosexuality (so also Snyder 1992: 72–73). D. Martin (1996: 129) gibes at "heterosexist" interpreters who he thinks twist the meaning of these words to make them refer to some kind of ho-mosexual perversion. He claims that no one knows what ἀρσενοκοῖται meant, though he thinks it probable that it referred to exploiting another by means of sex. He argues that μαλακοί simply refers to those who are effeminate, which, he claims, is a malleable concept, useful for con-demning those one does not like, but too ambiguous as a "foundation for Christian ethical arguments" (1996: 130).[29] Much of this attempt to re-cast the traditional link of these words to male same-sex eroticism ap-pears to be driven by special pleading and riddled with obfuscation, but it does serve to point out the difficulty of interpreting these expressions.

The term ἀρσενοκοῖται does not appear in extant literature before Paul (cf. 1 Tim. 1:10). It seems likely, however, that it was coined in Hellenistic Judaism, or perhaps by Paul, from the Levitical prohibition against males bedding males (cf. D. Wright 1984: 129; P. Turner 1997; Dunn 1998: 122 n. 102).[30]

Lev. 18:22: "You shall not sleep with a male as with a woman, for it is an abomination" (καὶ μετὰ ἄρσενος οὐ κοιμηθήσῃ κοίτην γυναικός· βδέλυγμα γάρ ἐστιν, kai meta *arsenos* ou koimēthēsē *koitēn* gynaikos; bdelygma gar estin).

Lev. 20:13: "Whoever sleeps with a male as with a woman, both of them have committed an abomination; they are liable to be put to death" (καὶ

---

28. Boswell's conclusions about the meanings of these words have been challenged as baseless by D. Wright (1984; 1987; 1989); R. Wright (1984); Hays (1986); Petersen (1986); Malick (1993); and Winter (1997c).

29. D. Martin's (1996: 117) stated goal is "to challenge the objectivist notion that the Bible or historical criticism can provide contemporary Christians with a reliable *foundation* for ethical reflection."

30. Its rarity in the literature may be due to its coarseness (Fee 1987: 244).

ὃς ἂν κοιμηθῇ μετὰ **ἄρσενος κοίτην** γυναικός, βδέλυγμα ἐποίησαν ἀμφότεροι· θανατούσθωσαν, ἔνοχοί εἰσιν, *kai hos an koimēthē meta arsenos koitēn gynaikos, bdelygma epoiēsan amphoteroi; thanatousthōsan, enochoi eisin*).

Boswell (1980: 105) argues that Christians would not have invoked "the authority of the old to justify the morality of the new: the Levitical regulations had no hold on Christians and are manifestly irrelevant in explaining Christians' hostility to gay sexuality." This statement is easily refuted by the immediate context. Paul already has vehemently expressed his horror over the Corinthians' tolerance of incest, and the prohibition against incest appears in Lev. 18:7–8 and 20:11 in the same context in which homoerotic acts are vigorously condemned. As a Jew, he would have been no less horrified by homosexual acts than he was by incest.

Scroggs (1983: 106–8) links the two nouns together and claims that Paul condemns only pederasty (homosexual intercourse with a boy). But this interpretation collapses on itself. Had he wished to limit his critique to pederasty, he could have used the term "pederast" (παιδεράστης, *paiderastēs*). Scroggs's (1983: 117) attempt to limit Paul's censure to pederasty in Rom. 1:26–27 ignores the fact that he refers to a mutuality in the male partners' desire (ὄρεξις, *orexis*) for one another (εἰς ἀλλήλους, *eis allēlous*, 1:27). Paul also lumps this male lust together with lesbian lust, which does not involve children. Even if Paul were condemning only pederasty here, which is unlikely (cf. M. Smith 1996), one cannot conclude that he would not also condemn homoerotic acts of any kind, given his Jewish background. In the OT, lying with a male is a general concept describing "every kind of homosexual intercourse," not simply male prostitution or sexual relations with youth (G. Wenham 1990–91: 362). Though homosexual acts were generally accepted in the ancient world, Hellenistic Jewish texts are unanimous in condemning them and treat them and idolatry as the most obvious examples of Gentile moral depravity.[31] Not surprisingly, Paul shares this Jewish aversion to idolatry and homosexual acts.[32] Gagnon (2001: 306) comments, "As Rom 1:18–32 and Wisdom of Solomon 12–15 indicate, a wrong-headed view of God would invariably lead to a wrong-headed view of God's will for human behavior—particularly in the area of sex-

31. Cf. Wis. 14:26; Let. Arist. 152; Philo, *Abr.* 26–27 §§135–37; *Spec. Laws* 3.7 §§37–39; *Hypoth.* 7.1; Josephus, *Ag. Ap.* 2.25 §199; 2.38 §§273–75; 2 Enoch 10:4; 34:2; Ps.-Phoc. 3, 190–92, 213–14; T. Naph. 3:4; Sib. Or. 2:73; 3:185–88, 764; 4:33–34; 5:166–67, 386–433 (linking idolatry, homosexual acts, prostitution, and incest together), 595–600, 764; T. Jacob 7:20.

32. This pronouncement would be good news to any slaves who were subject to unwanted sexual advances from their masters.

uality where the temptation of erotic pleasure goes hand-in-hand with self-deception."

The term μαλακός (*malakos*) refers to softness (cf. Matt. 11:8 = Luke 7:25). Philo (*Dreams* 2.2 §9) associates it with the softer way of life found in the woman's quarters, which reveals its association with effeminacy. His comments in *Spec. Laws* 3.7 §§37–42 condemn pederasty (τὸ παιδεραστεῖν) as an evil overtaking the cities and refers "to passive partners [τοῖς πάσχουσιν, *tois paschousin*] who habituate themselves to endure the disease of effemination [θήλεια, *thēleia*], let both body and soul run to waste, and leave no ember of their male sex-nature to smolder." He castigates them for violating nature by transforming the male nature to the female, becoming guilty of "unmanliness" (ἀνανδρία, *anandria*) and "effeminacy" (μαλακία, *malakia*). Osiek and Balch (1997: 10–11) argue that by using the term μαλακός, "Paul assumes an aspect of contemporary Greco-Roman biology, that it is unnatural for a man to be 'soft,' like a woman, just as five chapters later, he argues that it is 'natural' for a female to cover her hair as for a male not to let his grow" (cf. Philo, *Cont. Life* 7 §§59–62). They cite Parker (1992: 98–99) on the difference between Greco-Roman and modern attitudes toward sexuality:

> Sexuality in our culture is constructed on the choice of object, heterosexual versus homosexual. Both Greek and Roman male sexuality was constructed on the division between active and passive. The active one . . . was "male," and was acting the role of a free man, whether he used as object a woman, a boy, or a man. The passive one . . . was "female," and servile, whether woman, boy, or man.

Paul considers homoeroticism to be a "dishonorable passion" and a "shameful act" because it is "against nature" (τὴν παρὰ φύσιν, *tēn para physin*; Rom. 1:26–27). According to Stegemann (1993: 164–65), the reason behind this judgment is that the partner of the same sex inverts (μετήλλαξαν, *metēllaxan*) the natural mode (φυσικὴ χρῆσις, *physikē chrēsis*). One of the males must act like a woman, and one of the women must act like a male. Or, as Philo says, the male becomes "womanish." For this reason, I have chosen to translate the μαλακοί as "those males who are penetrated sexually by males" and the ἀρσενοκοῖται as "those males who sexually penetrate males" (cf. Lietzmann 1949: 27; Barrett 1968: 140; Talbert 1987: 23; Gagnon 2001: 306–32; see additional note).[33]

---

33. D. Martin (1996: 125) argues that "all penetrated men were *malakoi,* but not all *malakoi* were penetrated men." This is certainly true, but in the context, followed as it is by the word ἀρσενοκοῖται and preceded by a reference to the sexual sins of fornication and adultery, one can reasonably infer that Paul uses it to refer to sexually penetrated men.

Gagnon (2001: 330) demonstrates that the terms μαλακοί and ἀρσε-νοκοῖται "are correctly understood in our contemporary context when they are applied to every conceivable type of same-sex intercourse."

The next vice in the list, "greed," has long since ceased to be regarded as a shameful sin that merits banishment from the kingdom of God. The greedy tend to be defined as those who have more than we do, and we tend to project on them a greater, and unacceptable, avarice. Yet, greed afflicts rich and poor. The greedy are those who treat others only as objects for their gratification. Greed is related to insatiability and can express itself in multiple ways. The greedy include those who believe that their sexuality is a right, not a responsibility, and that they can express it in any way they choose with anybody they choose. They are those who dishonor the rights and property of others by becoming the shameless revilers, larcenous sharks, and insatiable predators.

Paul continues to poke holes in the Corinthians' pride by reminding **6:11** them that before their conversion some of them were guilty of these very sins that would exclude them from the kingdom of God. The use of the neuter plural ταῦτα (tauta), "these things you once were," instead of a masculine plural pronoun, "such persons you once were," may reveal his revulsion over the filthiness of these transgressions (Robertson and Plummer 1914: 119). He insists that had they remained like these persons (or should they revert to such behavior), they would have had no share in the kingdom of God. But he most wants to emphasize the present effects of their conversion. In 5:7, he juxtaposes the indicative with the imperative, "You are . . . , now be," to make his case. Here, he juxtaposes the past and the present, "You once were . . . , but now are," to make his case. Their former life was to be just that, their former life. The repeated "but" (ἀλλά, alla) before each verb in the Greek of 6:11 adds emphasis to their break with the past and has been included in my translation even though it may sound awkward in English. The implication is that Christianity not only offers a completely new sexual ethos and a new ethos regarding material possessions but also brings about a complete transformation of individuals. God's grace does not mean that God benignly accepts humans in all their fallenness, forgives them, and then leaves them in that fallenness. God is in the business not of whitewashing sins but of transforming sinners (Fee 1993: 39).

After the list of these vices, Paul's choice of the verb ἀπελούσασθε (apelousasthe, you were washed) instead of the verb "you were baptized" is apt to refer to cleansing off the filth of these past sins (Eph. 5:26; Heb. 10:22). The compound verb stresses the removal of dirt, "washing off" (Beasley-Murray, *NIDNTT* 1:150–53). Fee (1987: 247; 1994: 130–31) thinks that Paul is primarily interested in the metaphor of "regeneration" and not the effects of baptism. The emphasis, Fee argues, is on the work of the Spirit in the Christian's life, who effects regeneration, sanctification, and justification (so also Dunn 1970: 120–23). But we need not abandon a reference to baptism—an issue that apparently was important to the Corinthians (1:13–17; 15:29)—to keep the metaphor of regeneration (cf. Titus 3:5). Baptism is not understood to effect the renewal but "is the occasion when the Spirit creatively works in the individual" (Beasley-Murray, *NIDNTT* 1:153). That is why this verb appears first, since it marks the beginning of the Christian life, when one is transferred from the sphere of darkness into the power field of the Spirit. The verb ἀπολούω (*apolouō*) occurs elsewhere in the NT only in Acts 22:16, where it is specifically connected to baptism. Baptism is also connected to the washing away of moral filth in 1 Pet. 3:21.

The verb ἀπελούσασθε is in the middle voice and may imply "that, while this washing was not their own act, it did not take place without an act of their own" (Edwards 1885: 144; cf. Godet 1886: 298; Lightfoot 1895: 213; Robertson and Plummer 1914: 119; Beasley-Murray 1962: 163; Fung 1980: 250).[34] God's action in Christ precedes their submission to baptism, but the efficacy of that action is connected to their own consent and commitment. The other two verbs, ἡγιάσθητε (*hēgiasthēte*, were sanctified) and ἐδικαιώθητε (*edikaiōthēte*, were justified), refer to what God has done alone. The difference from the command in Isa. 1:16 ("Wash yourselves, cleanse yourselves, remove the evils from your souls") is that Paul sees this cleansing as something accomplished by the power of the Spirit, not by the individual.

The order of the verbs, "sanctified," "justified," has no theological significance. Paul does not conceive of Christians being placed on a divine assembly line and having each of these things done to them in a certain order. For Paul, they are all of a piece. The same nouns appear in reverse order in 1:30: "justification, sanctification, redemption." Styler (1973: 176) makes the case that Paul's Christian assurance is based on four main points: (1) the act of God in Christ; (2) the initial response or conversion of the believer, marked by baptism; (3) the continuing Christian life, with its duties and the expectation of growth in holiness, love, and knowledge; (4) the final judgment and salvation. For Paul, these stages adhere closely together and cannot be separated from one another. They do not stand alone. Moral obligation comes as consequence of the Christian's status in Christ. Paul understands them to

---

34. Barrett (1968:141) argues that the passive form of the verb λούειν and its compounds is rare "and it is perhaps better to suppose that the middle is used for the passive." Conzelmann (1975: 107) states it is not to be rendered as a middle but as a passive "on analogy of the succeeding passives" (cf. Kistemaker 1993: 192; Fee 1994: 128 n. 158). The reason this verb is found primarily in the middle is because of the nature of the action of washing, which involves an individual's own agency. I have chosen to translate it as a passive voice because the washing away of sins is the act of God.

have been "sanctified"—claimed by God, joined to a holy people, and set apart for godly living. They were acquitted, "justified"—a legal metaphor. All this was done "in the name of the Lord Jesus Christ," which refers to the authority (1:10; 5:4) of Christ, and by the Spirit, "which accomplishes the new birth in the heart of the man baptized, and thus separates him from the pollutions of his past life" (Godet 1886: 301). "In the name of the Lord" is the objective cause and "in the Spirit of our God" is the subjective cause (Schweizer, *TDNT* 6:427). To argue that one need not be changed from a life of moral pollution disregards the objective of Christ's death. To argue that one cannot be changed from these pollutions casts doubt on the power of the Spirit. Even if Christians face temptations to continue in these past sins, the Spirit can empower them to resist (Witherington 1995: 166). Only God can untwist twisted perversions.

Additional Notes

6:1. P. Richardson (1983) offers five arguments to support the claim that 6:1–11 deals with a sexual problem: (1) the passage is bracketed by 5:1–13 and 6:12–20, which have to do with sexual issues; (2) the vocabulary can have sexual overtones; (3) the vocabulary is echoed in 7:1–7, which deals with a sexual issue; (4) the abrupt shift from 5:13 quoting Deut. 17:7 in a section that lays out ordinances, including the appointment of judges (Deut. 16:18), and then commands to purge the evil in Deut. 21:21–24 occurs in the context of family and sexual law; (5) the word πρᾶγμα appears in 1 Thess. 4:6 as a euphemism for a sexual offense. These arguments, however, are not conclusive, and the issue in the lawsuit remains undetermined.

6:5. The phrase ἀνὰ μέσον τοῦ ἀδελφοῦ αὐτοῦ is grammatically irregular. Zuntz (1953: 15) contends that it is "an unexampled and unbelievable way of speaking" that is the result of a primitive corruption of the text that omitted the completion of the phrase with "and his brother." Zuntz thinks that the emendation in the Peshitta, which includes this phrase, made the correct decision. Findlay (1910: 816) labels it a defective expression due to confusion between τῶν ἀδελφῶν and the more Hebraic expression ἀδελφοῦ καὶ ἀδελφοῦ. Rosner (1994: 105–6) argues, however, that it is a "loose reminiscence of the Septuagint of Deut. 1:16" ("I commanded your judges at that time: 'Give a hearing to your brothers and judge rightly between a man, and between a brother and between a proselyte'" (ἀνὰ μέσον ἀνδρὸς καὶ ἀνὰ μέσον ἀδελφοῦ καὶ ἀνὰ μέσον προσηλύτου αὐτοῦ). This last option may well be correct.

6:7. Lightfoot's (1895: 212) grammatical observations underscore Paul's concern about the factionalism. He contends that Paul's choice of the phrase μεθ᾽ ἑαυτῶν "differs from the reciprocal ἀλλήλων in emphasizing the idea of corporate unity." The use of "ἀλλήλων here would bring out the idea of diversity of interest, ἑαυτῶν emphasizes that of identity of interest: 'you are tearing yourselves to pieces.'"

6:9. Pederasty was the most common male homosexual act in the ancient world (Schrage 1991: 432). That is because sexual propriety was judged according to social values: "The ancients did not classify kinds of sexual desire or behaviour according to the sameness or difference of the sexes of the persons who engaged in a sexual act; rather, they evaluated sexual acts according to the degree to which such acts either violated or conformed to the norms of conduct deemed appropriate to individual sexual actors by reason of their gender, age, and social status" (Halperin, *OCD* 720; cf. Dover 1978: 277). A person's rank and status determined what was considered acceptable or unacceptable. On one side were free males; on the other side were women and slaves. A free male was free to choose women, men, or boys as sexual objects without the majority taking offense as long as he did not demean his status as a free male. A free male could not "indulge in passive acts of love like a woman or a slave" without incurring a stigma (Stegemann 1993: 164). But he could use boys, slaves, or persons of no account with impunity as long as he remained "on top." "Phallic insertion functioned as a marker of male precedence; it also expressed social domination and seniority. . . . Any sexual relation that involved the penetration of a social inferior (whether inferior in age, gender, or status) qualified as sexually normal for a male, irrespective of the penetrated person's anatomical sex, whereas to *be* sexually penetrated was always potentially shaming, especially for a free male of citizen status [e.g., Tacitus, *Annales* 11.36]" (Halperin, *OCD* 721). Homosexual acts between free males were regarded with contempt because one partner would have to take on the passive role (insertivity) suited only to women and slaves (Veyne 1987: 204). We see this cultural attitude manifested in Petronius's novel, *Satyricon* (91–100). Two close friends, Encolpius and Ascyltus, fight over the sexual favors of their slave boy, Giton; but they never engage in any homosexual act between themselves.

It should be noted also that "neither sexual desire nor sexual pleasure represented an acceptable motive for a boy's compliance with the sexual demands of his lover" (Halperin, *OCD* 721). The younger partner was not to be motivated by, or express, passionate sexual desire for his senior lover, lest he compromise his own future status as a man. As a result, sexually receptive or effeminate males were ridiculed. Society would have considered same-sex sexual acts between two men of equal standing to be shameful. What some in modern society find acceptable—male same-sex eroticism between equals in a committed relationship—would have been condemned in ancient society. Dover (1978: 104) contends that penetration was not regarded as an expression of love but "as an aggressive act demonstrating the superiority of the active to the passive partner." J. Davidson (1997: 169–82) challenges this interpretation as anachronistic but imposes his own biases on the evidence and does not win the argument. Paul differed from his society's sexual mores in condemning all same-sex sexual acts.

6:11. Three readings are represented by the witnesses: Ἰησοῦ (A, D², Ψ, 0150, 6, 424, 1241, 1852, Byz); Ἰησοῦ Χριστοῦ (𝔓[11vid], 𝔓[46], ℵ, D*, it[d]); and ἡμῶν Ἰησοῦ Χριστοῦ (B, C[vid], P, 33, 81, 104, 256, 365, 436, 459, 1175, 1319). The ἡμῶν probably was added to parallel the phrase "in the Spirit of our God." The longer reading including Christ has strong external support, but it is more likely to have been added out of piety (cf. 5:4) than accidentally omitted by a copyist (although it would have been written ΙΥΧΥ, which may have caused confusion).

D. Admonition against Visiting Prostitutes (6:12–20)

In this unit Paul takes aim at the problem of πορνεία (*porneia*, sexual immorality), which in this context refers to sex for hire, its root meaning in Greek.[1] Have some Corinthian Christians consorted with prostitutes and justified their behavior with twisted theological reasoning expressed in snappy sound bites? The majority of recent interpreters think so. They assume that the lines "All things are permissible to me" and "Food is meant for the belly and the belly for food, and God will destroy both one and the other" were Corinthian shibboleths bandied about to sanction lewd behavior with prostitutes (see Fee 1987: 251; Dautzenberg 1989: 276; Rosner 1994: 123; 1998: 337–38). Murphy-O'Connor (1978a) adds 6:18b, "Every sin that a man commits is outside the body," as another Corinthian slogan used to exonerate such conduct. Paul cites these slogans to debunk them. This approach assumes that the slogans identified in the text are the key pieces of evidence for reconstructing the situation and the positions of the Corinthian freethinkers (Stowers 1981: 59).

The problem with this view is that Paul does not specifically accuse any Corinthians of dalliances with prostitutes. This absence of any explicit allegation contrasts with 5:1, where Paul mentions a specific report about the man living with his father's wife, "in short, it is reported," and 6:1, where he mentions a specific case of someone hauling a fellow Christian to a court of unbelievers, "Does someone dare?" No such cues appear in 6:12–20 to suggest that reports of sexual misbehavior have come to Paul's ears or that anyone dares to haunt brothels or keep mistresses. Hurd (1965: 86, 90) deduces from this silence that Paul does not refer to any specific action by them and regards it instead as a transitional passage that wraps up the response to the oral reports in 1:11–6:11 and prepares the ground for his response to their written questions that follows (cf. Snyder 1992: 80; R. Collins 1999: 240).[2]

---

1. I have ruled out (above) the suggestion of Deming (1992; cf. Kempthorne 1967–68; Miguens 1975a: 46–48) that 6:12–20 offers Paul's concluding remarks about the case in 5:1–13.

2. Meeks (1983: 29) wavers on this issue: perhaps the spiritual ones patronized the local brothels, but perhaps "that is only Paul's *reductio ad absurdum* of their vaunted freedom."

Hurd's observations help us see that Paul is not simply upbraiding the Corinthians for another moral failure as he does in the previous two units (5:1–13; 6:1–11). This passage stands at the juncture of two types of material, oral reports (5:1–6:11) and written responses (7:1), and serves as a hinge unit. Paul may have chosen to discuss the topic of sexual intercourse with prostitutes at this point in his letter because it allowed him to draw to a close his previous arguments and to lay a thematic foundation for what follows.[3] It continues the moral vein of the preceding sections while setting the stage for what is to come (Hurd 1965: 87). This unit contains the seeds of many ideas that sprout and blossom in the rest of the letter (see Lightfoot 1895: 215).

- In 6:19–20, Paul reprises the theme raised in 3:16–17 that they are the temple of God and that the Holy Spirit dwells in them. Here he applies it to individual Christians.
- The maxim "All things are permissible for me," when misapplied, could be used to excuse the case of incest, the freedom to bring suit against fellow Christians, the freedom to make use of a prostitute, and particularly the freedom to eat idol food (10:23).[4] Paul cites it again in the discussion of idol food (10:23).
- Paul's argument against πορνεία primarily serves to show how grave and serious it is as a sin rather than simply to prove that it is a sin (Rosner 1994: 124). It prepares for his warnings against the danger of *porneia* in his guidance on sexuality in marriage (7:2) and his link between fornication and idolatry (10:7–8). God calls idolatry the spirit of whoredom that leads Israel astray to ask counsel from wooden idols (Hos. 4:12; cf. Jer. 2:20–24; Ezek. 23:22–30). The forceful appeal in 6:18, "Flee *porneia!*" is echoed in 10:14, "Flee idolatry!"
- What is permissible (ἔξεστι, *exesti*) relates to the issue of "authority" (ἐξουσία, *exousia*). Paul broaches this topic specifically in his discussion of idolatry (8:9; 9:4, 5, 6, 12, 18; cf. 7:37).
- The corrective that what is permissible needs to be controlled by what is beneficial prepares for his instructions about marriage (7:35), eating idol food (10:23, 35), and using spiritual gifts for the common good (12:7).

3. R. Collins (1999: 240) notes that the topos is covered in Dio Chrysostom (*Or.* 7.133–46) on banning brothel keepers.

4. R. Collins (1999: 241) suggests that the maxim "All things are permissible" forms an inclusio with 10:23, and concludes, "Within that complex the thoughts Paul develops in 6:12–20 provide a theological-anthropological basis for his response to a variety of considerations on sexual relationships in ch. 7."

- The idea that Christians are not their own but are bound exclusively to Christ (6:17, 19b–20) is the cornerstone of his argument against Christians participating in anything that smacks of idolatry. His argument expressing horror at the thought of joining a member of Christ to a prostitute (6:16) is akin to his argument against idolatry and the horror of partaking of the cup of the Lord and partaking of the cup of demons (10:16–22). Union with Christ excludes union with a prostitute and union with an idol. Both prostitutes and idol food belong to a different corporate order that is evil, and connection with either ruptures the bond with Christ.
- Ideas briefly introduced here are developed later in the letter. The issue of "food" (βρῶμα, brōma, 6:13) is central to the discussion in 8:8, 13. Being members of the body of Christ (6:15) emerges prominently in chapter 12, though with a different emphasis, and the role of the Holy Spirit (6:19) is the focus of chapters 12 and 14. The assurance of the resurrection of the body (6:14) gives us a glimpse of the major point of discussion in 15:12–58. Reference to what will be destroyed (καταργέω, katargeō) brings in an end-time note (cf. 13:8, 10, 11) that colors his discussion of marriage (7:29–31) and the resurrection (15:24, 26).

Though this unit functions as a transition point in the letter, it does not mean that Paul is not taking aim at a real problem: Christians philandering with prostitutes. That he does not censure a particular culprit may mean only that the pattern of behavior was widespread or that he had no direct report of it. For his arguments to strike home, however, the Corinthians would have had to recognize that they had something to do with actual incidents (Wire 1990: 74). We can infer from his command "Flee *porneia!*" in 6:18 that he is warning about a real, not a hypothetical, problem. The counterpart to that command in 10:14, "Flee idolatry!" occurs near the conclusion of his lengthy discussion of idolatry in chapters 8–10. He does not regard participation in idolatry to be only a hypothetical danger that the Corinthians needed to be warned against. It is a tar pit in which some already have become mired. The parallel command "Flee *porneia!*" is likely to refer to a real situation, a dangerous moral breakdown that causes Paul alarm. His threat in 2 Cor. 12:20–21 confirms that he regarded *porneia* to be a problem in the Corinthian church. He expresses fear that they have not repented of their previous "impurity, sexual immorality [πορνεία], and licentiousness."

While 6:12–20 serves as a hinge in the letter, it continues the theme, begun in 5:1, of addressing Corinthian moral failings. The difference is that Paul's rhetoric here is didactic, not polemical (Furnish 1999: 58). Most, however, read the rhetoric in this unit as a rebuttal to Corinthian theological error. Fee (1987: 251) argues, for example, that Paul does not begin by attacking their behavior as in 5:1 and 6:1 but instead "confronts the theology on which that behavior is predicated." But this approach places too much emphasis on ascertaining the Corinthians' theology by means of mirror-reading and is too confident that the theological impetus behind the Corinthians' behavior can be delineated accurately.[5] The emphasis, instead, should fall on Paul's arguments that *porneia* is a grave sin. These arguments not only provide a countercultural view of sexuality but also lay the groundwork for arguments that follow.

This perspective casts doubt on the approach of most recent interpreters that the so-called slogans, when identified and deciphered, reveal what inspired the Corinthian misbehavior. Apart from the phrase "All things are permissible to me," not all agree on what the other slogans were, let alone what they meant for the Corinthians. Some assume that the Corinthians simply knew no limits to their freedom and believed themselves free from the constraints of conventional morality (Godet 1886: 303; Robertson and Plummer 1914: 121; Orr and Walther 1976: 201–2). Their credo may be may be caricatured by the following ditty:

> Free from the law,
> O happy condition;
> I can sin as I please
> And still have remission.

Such a conviction might explain how the man living with his father's wife could do so with such boldness (see the commentary on 5:1–8 for arguments against this view). Lightfoot (1895: 213) comments that "the sin of sensuality is the scourge of the Corinthians' church," but this conclusion seems surprising in light of Paul's discussion in the next chapter. Others in the church espouse an austere asceticism and disavow sexual relations even in marriage.[6] It is unlikely that this church is so radically split between those who think that sexual license is a matter of indifference and those who argue for rigorous sexual asceticism (contra Bruce 1971: 66; Hays 1997: 118).

---

5. Witherington (1995: 231 n. 3) warns that mirror-reading becomes "especially dangerous" in this letter "where some of the arguments are meant to forestall future possible views, not presently held ones."

6. The suggestion that their desire to maintain spiritual marriages and keep their wives pure caused husbands to seek occasional sexual release with prostitutes is implausible.

Another view assumes that the Corinthians' problems with immorality began with the erroneous assumption that the body, being a material substance, has no place in the glorious destiny of the believer (cf. 15:12–19). Since the body is excluded from salvation, what is done in the body does not touch the soul. No physical act, such as eating or sexual relations, can have any moral significance. We can eat what we like and have sexual relations with whomever we like; neither has anything to do with our salvation. This idea may have arisen from a conflation of Cynic or even Stoic ethical ideas with Christian teachings. They may have reasoned, as Stowers (1981: 67) surmises, "The body is essentially separate from one's moral character. Certain virtues or vices, moral or spiritual attitudes, are important, but the body in itself is indifferent. After all, will not God destroy the body and save the soul?" The Christian has died with Christ and is now dead to the law. The Christian's body is a house that has been sold for demolition. Why should they bother with the repairs? Perhaps they also felt safe from any potential defilement from their close union with Christ, which served as a kind of prophylactic (see Barrett 1968: 146–47; Fee 1987: 253–55; Schrage 1995: 10–11, 20). The upshot of this view is "All things are permissible."

It remains a rather precarious exercise to milk a fully developed theological justification for immoral behavior from what are assumed to be Corinthians' slogans, since the reasoning behind it is, by necessity, circular. It is possible that the moral problems were simply vestiges of former pagan habits that some had not yet purged from their lives. This last option seems a more likely explanation for their behavior than one that presupposes that they promoted a bowdlerized version of Paul's teaching to excuse sexual license. Paul does not attack twisted theological reasoning that sanctions immorality, but presents arguments why sexual intercourse with prostitutes is an outrage against Christ and their own bodies.

This passage divides into an introduction and three units in which Paul presents his arguments against making use of prostitutes.[7] After the introduction in 6:12–14, each argument begins with the phrase οὐκ οἴδατε ὅτι (ouk oidate hoti, do you not know that), followed by a reference to σῶμα (sōma, body) and an inference or command (Fisk 1996: 551).

In the introduction (6:12–14), Paul makes two assertions: (1) Christians have a newfound freedom, but that freedom should orient them toward doing those things that are beneficial and away from doing those things that can ensnare them and then dominate their lives.

---

7. Burkill's (1971: 118, 120) judgment that this passage is "disjointed," "obscure," "unfinished," "imprecise," "extravagant," and "incoherent" is overstated.

(2) Christ's lordship lays claim on the Christian's body that is destined for resurrection, and Christians are not free to do with their bodies whatever they please. They are to be dedicated to the Lord. These opening declarations are buttressed by three further arguments.

The first argument (6:15) contends that the Christian's body is an organ of the body of Christ. Every relationship in life is affected by this union with Christ. To have sexual relations with a prostitute is to be guilty of what is unthinkable, to snatch away a member of Christ and join that member to one personifying rebellion against God.

The second argument (6:16–18) makes the case that all sexual relations create a one-flesh union. An unholy union with a prostitute, representing the powers of chaos and death (cf. Rev. 14:8), violates the spiritual union with Christ and is a sin against the body.

The third argument (6:19–20) makes the case that the Christian's body is the shrine of the Spirit and that Christians are not their own but have been transferred to God's ownership. Consequently, not all things are permitted. Being slaves of God, they may not do whatever they wish. The only goal of Christian existence is to bring glory to God (cf. 10:31; Rom. 3:23; 15:7; 2 Cor. 1:20; 4:15; Eph. 1:12, 14; Phil. 1:11; 2:11).

Paul's argumentation is outlined here to highlight the parallels:

1. Question: Do you not know?
   A Statement about relationship to Christ: Your bodies are members of Christ (15a).
   B Statement about sexual intercourse with a prostitute: Will you make the members of Christ as members of a prostitute?
   C Response: Never!
2. Question: Do you not know? (explaining previous response)
   B′ Statement about sexual intercourse with a prostitute: The one who joins himself to a prostitute becomes one body with her (16b). Scriptural proof: The two shall become one flesh (16c).
   A′ Statement about relationship to Christ: The one who is joined to the Lord is one spirit with him (17).
   C′ Response: Flee *porneia!*
   D Explanation: Sexual sin is an attack on the body.
3. Question: Do you not know?
   A″ Statement about relationship to Christ: Your body is a temple of the Holy Spirit, whom you have from God.
   A‴Statement about relationship to Christ: You are not your own; you were bought with a price.
   C″Response: Glorify God in your bodies!

Exegesis and Exposition

¹²All things are permissible for me, but not all things are beneficial. All things are permissible for me, but I will not be overmastered by anything. ¹³Food is for the belly and the belly is for food, and God will destroy the one and the other. But the body is not for fornication but for the Lord, and the Lord for the body. ¹⁴God both raised the Lord and ⌐will raise⌐ us through his power. ¹⁵Do you not know that your bodies are members of Christ? Shall I, then, take away the members of Christ and make them members of a prostitute? Never! ¹⁶Or do you not know that the one who is joined to a prostitute is one body [with her]. For it says, "The two shall become one flesh." ¹⁷But the one who is joined to the Lord is one spirit [with him]. ¹⁸Flee sexual immorality! Every [other] sinful act that a person commits is outside the body, but the one who is guilty of sexual immorality sins against his own body. ¹⁹Or do you not know that your body is the temple of the Holy Spirit, who is among you and whom you have from God, and that you are not your own? ²⁰For you were bought with a price. ⌐Therefore, glorify God in your bodies.⌐

The prevailing view is that the maxim "All things are permissible to me" was used by the Corinthian freethinkers to sanction their immoral behavior. The REB even adds "you say" to make this clearer. Some trace the maxim's origin to Paul's own words. He applied it originally to the irrelevancy of food restrictions, but the Corinthians did violence to it by expanding its application to matters of sexuality and idol food (Lietzmann 1949: 27; Robertson and Plummer 1914: 121; Hurd 1965: 88; Fee 1987: 255; Holtz 1995: 54; cf. Godet 1886: 304; Barrett 1968: 145).[8] Whatever its origins, many conclude that the Corinthians' *porneia* was not simply a carryover from their pagan habits but rooted in theological error. Some go so far as to label this phrase the watchword of the gnostic party in Corinth (Bultmann 1955: 341; Barrett 1968: 144; Bruce 1971: 62; Schrage 1995: 11) or the rallying cry of the libertines (Héring 1962: 45).

6:12

The following arguments are given to make the case that the Corinthians used this buzzword to justify their immorality: (1) Paul repeats it four times in the letter, twice here and twice in 10:23.[9] (2) Paul's counterstatements introduced by ἀλλά (*alla*) indicate that he introduced it with the intent of rebutting it. (3) As a slogan in vogue in Corinth, it could express in a nutshell their moral and theological positions. Carried to an extreme, this maxim would appear to legalize every

---

8. Besides 1 Cor. 6:12 and 10:23, Paul does not use ἔξεστι elsewhere in his discussions of Christian freedom, and it is assumed that it must derive from someone else (Wolff 1996: 125).

9. Weiss (1910: 158) claims that the absence of τοῦτο δέ (*touto de*) suggests that this phrase came from the Corinthians' letter: "All things are lawful, you say, but not everything is beneficial, I say."

behavior and every object and could explain the problems besetting the congregation, from the case of incest to the incidents of eating idol food. (4) The slogan reflects the sentiments of later gnostics who thought that "nothing done in the body really matters, and anything may be done" (Barrett 1968: 144–45; cf. Conzelmann 1975: 109). Some assume that this mind-set emerged much earlier among the Corinthians. Since the body is excluded from salvation as a material substance, what is done in the body does not affect salvation because what does not touch the soul is irrelevant. This logic led them to regard themselves as free from the constraints of conventional morality. Some add an "over-realized eschatology" to the mix (Thiselton 1977–78: 517), while others throw in the Corinthians' misunderstanding of their experience of the Spirit. As Fee (1987: 250–51) frames it, "Apparently, some men within the Christian community are going to prostitutes and are arguing for the right to do so. Being people of the Spirit, they imply, has moved them to a higher plane, the realm of the spirit, where they are unaffected by behavior that has merely to do with the body."

The number of those who favor the view that the Corinthians spouted this maxim to justify their licentiousness is more overwhelming than the weight of the arguments presented in favor of it.[10] It seems to offer a neat solution that sweeps away exegetical quandaries, and its weaknesses tend not to receive much attention. What is frequently ignored is that Paul does not include any indicator that he is introducing a citation here in contrast to the instances elsewhere in the letter where he introduces citations from the Corinthians, from other literature, or from a hypothetical dialogue (B. Dodd 1995: 43). Scripture citations are introduced by "it is written" (γέγραπται, gegraptai) in 1:19, 31; 2:9; 3:19; 9:9; 10:7; 14:21; 15:45, 54–55) and "it says" (φήσι, phēsi) in 6:16.[11] The Corinthians' quotes are introduced in 1:12 ("each of you says"); 3:4 ("for when one says"); 7:1 ("now concerning what you wrote"); and perhaps, 8:1, 4 ("we know that"; cf. 2 Cor. 10:10). Dialogue with a hypothetical person is introduced in 10:28 ("but if someone says to you"); 12:3 ("no one speaking by the Spirit of God ever says"); and 15:35 ("but someone will ask"). B. Dodd (1995: 44) concludes from this evidence that since Paul usually introduces his citations in 1 Corinthians, the burden of proof rests on "those who want to identify parts of his text as quotations which he does not identify as such."

---

10. Findlay 1910: 818; Hurd 1965: 86; Barrett 1968: 144; Conzelmann 1975: 108; Murphy-O'Connor 1978a; Fee 1987: 251; Talbert 1987: 29; Schrage 1995: 10, 11, 20; Witherington 1995: 167; Wolff 1996: 125; Hays 1997: 102; R. Collins 1999: 243; Thiselton 2000: 461.

11. Only three citations of Scripture (2:16; 5:13; 15:27) and the two citations of proverbial sayings (15:32, 33) do not have markers, but their absence can be explained contextually.

This catchword may well have been familiar to the Corinthians, but the key question is whether they used it to justify frequenting prostitutes (see additional note). Four considerations suggest that this was not the case. First, it seems unlikely that they could have so misconstrued or deliberately distorted Paul's teaching to proclaim such immoral conduct permissible. In his previous letter (5:9), Paul spoke out only against them associating with immoral Christians. Had someone in Corinth been promoting immoral behavior on the basis of some aberrant theological platform, why did he not vigorously denounce them? They were confused about whether following his admonition meant that they must withdraw from the world altogether, not concerned that it conflicted with their theological suppositions.

Second, it is surprising that they would have felt any need to offer a theological rationale for immoral behavior. Becker (1993: 200) notes that "going to a prostitute is culturally so natural to the Greek that such an undertaking did not first have to be introduced or maintained by a new libertine program."[12] Cicero (*Pro Caelio* 20.48), for example, wrote, "If there is anyone who thinks that youth should be forbidden affairs even with courtesans, he is doubtless austere (I cannot deny it), but his view is contrary not only to the licence of this age, but also to the custom and concessions of our ancestors. For when was this not a common practice? When was it blamed? When was it forbidden?" No shame was attached to satisfying one's passion. Plutarch (*Mor.* 140B) argues that a wife should not be angry with her husband if he is incontinent and dissolute with a paramour or maidservant: "She should reason that it is respect for her which leads him to share his debauchery, licentiousness, and wantonness with another woman."

Third, this idea was not unknown among moral philosophers. It fits the Cynic-Stoic ideal of freedom: "He is free who lives as he wills, who is subject neither to compulsion, nor hindrance, nor force, whose choices are unhampered, whose desires attain their end, whose aversions do not fall into what they would avoid" (Epictetus, *Diatr.* 4.1.1). Epictetus (*Diatr.* 4.1.4) continues, "There is no bad man who lives as he wills, and accordingly no bad man is free." Dio Chrysostom (*Or.* 14.18) defines that freedom "as the knowledge of what is allowable and what is forbidden, and slavery is ignorance of what is allowed [ἔξεστι] and what is not." His point in *Or.* 14.13–16 is that people who have the power to act as they please are free, as long as those actions are not forbidden by the laws or regarded as base and unseemly (such as keeping a brothel). Intemperance is not an expression of freedom, and it is not permissible (ἔξεστι) to do mean and unprofitable (ἀσύμφορα, *asym-*

---

12. Osiek and Balch (1997: 112) argue that such behavior should not even be labeled "libertine" because Greek males "typically, whether married or single, had sexual relationships with more than one woman."

phora) things but things that are just and profitable (συμφέροντα, *sympheronta*) and good. "The wise," he concludes (*Or.* 14.17), "are permitted [ἔξεστιν αὐτοῖς] to do anything whatsoever they wish, while the foolish attempt to do what they wish although it is not permissible" (cf. Philo, *Good Free* 9 §59). Dio argues elsewhere (*Or.* 3.10) that the king must exercise "a more rigorous self-control than he to whom all things are permissible [ἔξεστι]." It is more plausible that Paul cites a familiar notion about freedom found in the Corinthian culture and recasts it in Christian terms than that he parrots the arguments of sensualists in the church to repudiate them (B. Dodd 1995: 45–46; cf. Meeks 1983: 122).[13]

A fourth indication that Paul is not citing a Corinthian slogan is the inclusion of "for me" (μοι, *moi*) in the phrase, "all things are permissible" (Lindemann 2000: 145). When he cites it again in 10:23, the subject of the rebuttal remains the subject of the maxim, "all things." In 6:12, "for me" appears to have been included to balance the "I" in the second rebuttal, "I will not be overmastered by anything." Paul seems to be adapting this saying for his own purposes rather than quoting verbatim some Corinthian byword. B. Dodd (1995: 46–49) appeals to Paul's use of the paradigmatic "I" to make the case that the maxim reflects his characteristic persuasive style rather than a citation of a Corinthian position. The "I" statements occur "as summary transitions in the letter" (cf. 5:12; 8:13; 10:28–11:1; 12:31–13:3; 13:11–12; 14:11, 14, 18) and are employed in a hortatory sense (B. Dodd 1995: 49). Paul expects his readers to apply what he says about himself to themselves. In 6:12, Paul "portrays himself as an exemplary embodiment of the effects of the 'washing,' 'sanctification,' and 'justification' that the Corinthians presumably had experienced in baptism" mentioned in 6:11 (B. Dodd 1995: 55). He reaffirms his teaching on Christian freedom created by this "washing" but carefully qualifies it: "not all things are beneficial"; "I will not be overmastered by anything." The highest priority is to be placed on embracing what is beneficial (and what builds up, 10:23) and avoiding what enslaves. It requires "self-limitation of freedom, self-discipline and new-found ability to shun sinful behavior" (B. Dodd 1995: 55). When Paul says, "I will not allow myself to be overmastered by anything," he implies, "Neither should you."

This reading makes far better sense of Paul's response to the maxim. As Holtz (1995: 54–55) points out, Paul does not say that anything is forbidden, wrong, or harmful, only that it is not useful. If the Corinthians used this slogan to argue for complete freedom to indulge in sexual license, he would have objected far more directly and forcefully. If, on the other hand, he cites a commonplace view about freedom, then

---

13. Winter (1998: 82) contends that Paul deals with young men who had taken the *toga virilis* and followed the dictum of youth that "all things were lawful." P. Marshall (1987: 215, 284–85, 289–90) claims that the social elite used the catchphrase to justify their abuses of power and privilege.

he redefines and limits it (see Kirchhoff 1994: 73–84). Paul seeks to clarify, lest any misunderstand, that Christian freedom does not allow one to pursue pleasure wherever it leads. Christians are controlled by an entirely different ethic, a different view of freedom, and a different Lord. Freedom is freedom *from* something; but for it to be meaningful, it must be freedom *for* something. Paul emphasizes the latter. He conceives of freedom in terms of belonging to another (6:19–20; 7:22–23; 9:19; Rom. 14:8), not in terms of self-determination or self-interest. The more one seeks life's meaning in God, the freer one becomes.

Paul limits the application of this maxim with "but" (ἀλλά, *alla*). "Not all things are beneficial" (συμφέρει, *sympherei*); that is, they are not conducive to one's own advantage or that of others (cf. Sir. 37:28). In 1 Corinthians, what is beneficial primarily relates to what benefits others (Fee 1987: 252; cf. 12:7; 7:35; 10:33; cf. 2 Cor. 8:10; 12:1). Fee (1987: 252) notes that Paul turns freedom on its head: "Freedom is not to be for self but for others." It is limited by what is best for oneself, which then may be overridden by what is best for others (cf. 7:35; 10:33; 12:7).[14] Paul would seem to reject the individualism inherent in the phrase "for me." But in the context, the "me" is critical. He does not emphasize how sexual intercourse with a prostitute harms the corporate body of Christians but how it is an assault on the individual's body (6:18). Unlike 5:1–13, where he sounds the alarm about how the man's incest afflicts the whole community with a moral blight, the focus in 6:12–20 is on the effects of the sin on the individual and his relationship to Christ.

The second restriction, "but I will not be overmastered by anything," employs a play on words between ἔξεστι (*exesti*, permissible) and ἐξουσιασθήσομαι (*exousiasthēsomai*). It can be rendered "All things are in my power, but I shall not be overpowered by anything" (Edwards 1885: 145–46). People inevitably become enslaved to their sins. Paul reminds them that embodied humans easily can become hostage to their bodily appetites (cf. 2 Pet. 2:19). One can only choose the master one serves, and Paul later declares that he has chosen to become enslaved in service to Christ and others (9:16–19) and pummels his body to maintain his devotion.

The statements in 6:13–14 parallel one another (Bailey 1980: 31):   **6:13–14**

Food is for the belly.	The belly is for food.
God destroys the belly.	God destroys food.
The body is for the Lord.	The Lord is for the body.
God raised the Lord.	God will raise us (our bodies).

14. M. Mitchell (1993: 25–39) contends that this appeal to their advantage falls into the category of deliberative rhetoric, which intends to dissuade persons from a future course of action.

Again, many assume that the claim "The food is for the belly, and the belly for food" is another Corinthian slogan, and most also include "God will destroy both one and the other" as part of it.[15] Rosner (1994: 129) imagines that the Corinthians framed the question this way: "Just as food is meant for the stomach and the stomach for food, so also the body is meant for sexual activity and sexual activity for the body. Furthermore, since God will one day destroy both the stomach and the body, is not what we do with our bodies now of no moral consequence?" (see additional note). The two slogans in 6:12 and 6:13 were supposedly combined to justify the belief that Christians were free to do whatever they please in the body.

That κοιλία (*koilia*) could be used as a euphemism for sexual organs (see LXX of 2 Sam. 7:12; 16:11; Ps. 131:11; Sir. 23:6; see also Behm, *TDNT* 3:786) perhaps made it easy to draw an analogy between eating food and having sex. It is assumed that the Corinthians argued that both are natural bodily functions. One has a stomach to digest food and hunger pangs to announce when it is time to eat; the same goes for sex organs. The argument may have run thus: Sex organs exist to be used, and sexual appetites should be fulfilled, not frustrated. Just as eating food belongs wholly to our fleshly, transitory human condition (cf. Mark 7:15, 19; Col. 2:21–22) and has no effect on our soul or eternal destiny, neither do sexual relations. Just as food is broken down by digestion, the body will be dissolved at death. Such natural bodily processes have no abiding significance because the body will be destroyed.

It is more likely, however, that Paul cites these maxims to refer to the order of creation: food is for the belly and both will be destroyed; the body is for the Lord but will not be destroyed (Kirchhoff 1994: 124–29; Furnish 1999: 58). The belly may find its proper function in relation to food, and vice versa, but a person is more than a belly. Christians do not find their correlation with *porneia* but with the Lord (Miguens 1975a: 27). Consequently, Paul attaches considerable moral significance to the body. As Godet (1886: 307) spells it out, the body is "the link between our present and our future body. There exists between our body and the Lord Jesus Christ a moral relation analogous to the material and temporary relation which exists between the stomach and meats." For Paul, the body is "the place where the claim of the resurrected-crucified Lord is received, and where his lordship is to be manifested" (Furnish 1999: 57). From this premise, Paul would derive

15. Héring 1962: 46; Barrett 1968: 146; Conzelmann 1975: 110; Murphy-O'Connor 1978a: 394; Fee 1987: 255; R. Collins 1999: 245; Thiselton 2000: 462–63. Goudge (1911: 47), Jewett (1971: 93), and Beardslee (1994: 60) regard the clause "and God will destroy both" as Paul's quick response: the food and stomach have only a temporal function. Thiselton (1977–78: 517) counters that the slogan would be meaningless if it did not include this latter statement.

this moral rule: "Whatever actions respect and reflect the believer's relationship with the Lord are 'beneficial,' and therefore permissible. Whatever actions threaten to exercise their control over the believer's life are thereby subversive of this relationship, and therefore not permissible" (Furnish 1999: 57).

This rule—not some reaction to an imagined Corinthian slogan—explains why Paul says that the body is not for *porneia* but for the Lord.[16] Paul takes for granted, as one anchored in Jewish tradition, that *porneia* is a sin and sees no need to prove it. Instead, he shows what a grave sin it is. His argument is rooted in his conviction that Christ exercises his lordship over a Christian's bodily existence (cf. Rom. 6:12–13, 19; 12:1; Phil. 1:20). Godet (1886: 307) explains, "The body is *for Christ,* to belong to Him and serve Him, and Christ is *for the body,* to inhabit and glorify it." Paul does not condemn them for failing to obey the law that forbids *porneia,* nor does he command them to obey the law. He argues instead that they should live in ways congruent with who they are—those who belong to Christ and are destined to live with Christ (Furnish 1999: 58; Schrage 1995: 23–24; cf. 5:7–8; 6:11).

Paul's first argument against *porneia* is that Christ is the Lord of one's bodily existence, and we, embodied creatures that we are, are destined to be raised.[17] Styler (1973: 184) observes that "warnings of judgment provide a sanction for moral conduct, and the promises of reward an incentive." Styler (1973: 184) goes on to say, "But the future life has a deeper relevance than as supplying sanction or incentive: it is revealed as the life which we are called to live here and now. To live a life now that is out of keeping with the final resurrection-life is not merely foolish; for Paul it is unthinkable." To give oneself over to *porneia* is unthinkable because it separates one from Christ, renounces his lordship, and is irreconcilable with the resurrection life.

Paul assumes that the body is not an outer shell that the soul will slough off at death—something he develops fully in chapter 15. We cannot be ourselves as bodiless specters. The future does not promise "redemption *from* the body but the redemption *of* the body" (Schrage 1982: 218). The Christian's body is destined for resurrection.[18] Our resurrection is tied to Christ's resurrection (Rom. 8:11; 1 Cor. 15:20; Phil.

---

16. The reference to *porneia* could refer to all illicit sexual relationships or specifically to hiring prostitutes. Since Paul refers to the man having his father's wife as *porneia,* it is more likely to have a broader meaning (cf. 6:9; 7:2).

17. We might expect Paul to have written "God will raise our bodies" rather than "God will raise us." The change to the personal pronoun is more appropriate as a parallel to the personal title "Lord": "God raised the Lord"; "God will raise us." That Paul understands "us" to mean "our bodies" is clear from the use of the word σῶμα (*sōma*) before and after this verse, twice in 6:13 and once each in 6:15, 16 (Gundry 1976: 60).

18. Schnelle (1983) thinks that it is a post-Pauline gloss because of a presumed tension with 1 Cor. 15:51–52.

3:21),[19] which is the greatest demonstration of God's power (Rom. 1:4; 2 Cor. 13:4; Eph. 1:19; Phil. 3:10). The reference to God's power emphasizes that resurrection results from the miraculous intervention of God, not a natural process (Weiss 1910: 162; Schrage 1995: 24–25).

Byrne (1983: 611) thinks that "the nub of the dispute between Paul and the Corinthians concerns the value to be placed upon present bodily experience." But Paul's argument from the resurrection need not mean that he is correcting a Corinthian misconception by claiming that since the body will be raised, it is important now. The argument from the resurrection is more profound and far-reaching. Käsemann (1969: 135) asserts that Paul's view of the resurrection in 15:20–28 is not oriented toward the reanimation of the dead but toward the reign of Christ. Since Christ is to reign, Christ will not and cannot "leave his own in the grip of death." Since Christ reigns, "his own are already engaged today in delivering over to Christ by their bodily obedience the piece of world which they themselves are and in so doing they bear witness to his lordship as that of the Cosmocrator and thus anticipate the ultimate future of the reality of the Resurrection and of the untrammelled reign of Christ." This perspective determines Paul's views of immorality. Hiring a prostitute for sex essentially denies Christ's ultimate sovereignty by filching what belongs to Christ and handing it over to one who belongs to Satan.

6:15   With the question οὐκ οἴδατε (*ouk oidate*, do you not know) Paul carries on an imaginary debate with the Corinthians and presents his first argument to buttress his statements in 6:12–14. The question assumes that they should understand that the power of Christ's resurrection is active now in their lives because they have been made members of the living Christ. Union with Christ affects not only a Christian's spiritual relationship to God but also a Christian's bodily relationship to others. Paul uses the image of being a member of Christ to play up the individual's *responsibility* to Christ as his limb and organ rather than the corporate relatedness of each limb and organ to one another—something he develops in 12:12–16, 27 (cf. Rom. 12:5). The emphasis is not on many individuals becoming the one body of Christ but upon an individual's union with Christ. Christ, who lives in us (Gal. 2:20), is to have charge over how his members are to be used. Styler's (1973: 186) observations on Paul's ethics are penetrating. He writes, "The life we are to live is not just the life to which Christ points; it is the life of Christ himself." He shows how important this difference is by contrasting a rab-

---

19. The compound verb ἐξεγερεῖ (*exegerei*, raise out of) is found only here and Rom. 9:17, citing Exod. 9:16. The verb ἐγείρω (*egeirō*) appears with the phrase ἐκ [τῶν] νεκρῶν (*ek [tōn] nekrōn*, out of the dead) in Rom. 10:9; 1 Cor. 15:20; Gal. 1:1; Col. 2:12; 1 Thess. 1:10; 2 Tim. 2:8.

binic saying with Paul's perspective. Rabbi Zusya of Hannipol said, "In the coming world they will not ask me, 'Why were you not Moses?' They will ask me, 'Why were you not Zusya?'" Styler concludes, "Even with some adaptation, the Christian would not say this with reference to Christ. For Christ does not simply bid me be myself, he calls me to live in him. His Spirit is to be the source of our life, as well as the director of our path." Paul believes that Christians are to be motivated and directed by the transcendent power of Christ pulsing through their lives.

The participle ἄρας (aras) depicts one taking *away* a member from Christ's possession and giving it over to a prostitute. What Paul leaves unstated is that the prostitute represents a different cosmic body (D. Martin 1995: 176–77; Dunn 1998: 58). Käsemann (1971: 23) articulates the heart of Paul's concern: "The world is not neutral ground; it is a battlefield, and everyone is a combatant." The prostitute is not conceived here as an individual person (D. Martin 1995: 176) but as a confederate of evil, a member of the dark, death-dealing forces at war against Christ. This applies whether the prostitute was dedicated to the service of pagan gods or simply to making a profit. As far as Paul is concerned, a Christian can have no symbiosis with a prostitute (Schrage 1995: 26), since Christ cannot be made part of or subjugated to this evil. This point does not imply that Aphrodite, for example, is more potent than Christ (contra Burkill 1971: 116) but assumes that union with her is completely incompatible with union with Christ—the same argument that is made in 10:14–22 against sharing the cup and table of demons and the cup and table of the Lord.

Also left unstated throughout this discussion is Paul's assumption that a person is not a combination of incompatible parts, spirit and body, held together in an unpleasant tension. As a consequence, sex is something that involves the whole self in surrender to another (7:4). In his discussion of sexuality in marriage, Paul claims that the wife does not have authority over her own body but the husband does, and the husband does not have authority over his own body but the wife does. Is the same true for sexual relations with a prostitute? Does he wish to imply that the Christian comes under the power of the prostitute who becomes his "unlawful lord" (see Fee 1987: 253)? Sexual intercourse entails the joining together of persons with all their spiritual associations and is not simply the coupling of bodies. The prostitute indiscriminately flings herself at chance customers; but the customer, when captured by her, is also put at her disposal (cf. Philo, *Spec. Laws* 3.9 §51). No prophylactic exists that can protect this unlawful union from extending its defiling tendrils into every part of a person's being. Using a prostitute is not a victimless crime in which no one gets hurt. This sin contaminates and breaches the union with Christ. Paul does not actually say that this sin severs all ties with Christ, but only implies it, perhaps to underscore the dreadful character of the sin (Fisk 1996: 554).

The question "Shall I, then, take away the members of Christ and make them members of a prostitute?" meets with an emphatic μὴ γένοιτο (*mē genoito*, may it not be). Paul uses this phrase to repudiate a possible answer to his question that he finds appalling. The phrase μὴ γένοιτο can also mark a transition in the argument (Malherbe 1980: 232, 236, 239; Stowers 1981: 140–41). It leads to the next clause, which unpacks the reasons why such a response is so unimaginable (cf. Rom. 6:1–4; Fisk 1996: 552).

6:16–17   Paul fires off the second "Do you not know?" question to explain why sex with a prostitute is so serious a matter.[20] Sexual union creates an enduring bond. The verb κολλᾶν (*kollan*) implies that the man and the prostitute are wedded together even if there are no wedding vows (see additional note). They may regard their union as only a temporary liaison—he to gain sexual release, she to gain a living—but it is more entangling than that; neither is free from the other when they part company. Paul derives his proof for this view from Scripture.

Paul normally introduces Scripture citations with γέγραπται (*gegraptai*, it is written) and not φησί (*phēsi*). This verb could mean "he says," referring to Adam, Moses, or God in the context of Gen. 2:24; or it may have an impersonal meaning, "it is said," and serve as a citation marker. In Matt. 19:5, the citation from Gen. 2:24 is treated as an utterance of God, and this may well be Paul's intention here (Bruce 1971: 64; contra Weiss 1910: 165; Schrage 1995: 26 n. 324).

It is a bold move to apply the one-flesh union created by marriage to the seemingly casual sexual union with a prostitute (Countryman 1988: 204). The assumption is that every sexual act between a man and woman, whether licit or not, fuses the partners together into one flesh. There is no such thing as casual sex that has no enduring consequences, even when the partners have no intention of forming a mutual attachment. If a Christian joins himself to a prostitute, and if the prostitute represents forces opposed to God, this immoral act has aligned the Christian over against God. The seriousness of this transgression for Paul far outweighs other legitimate moral issues about the evils of sex for hire. He does not say anything about how such behavior violates the principle of Christian love by treating another person as a commodity that can be purchased for one's personal gratification rather than a person who is to be won to Christ (9:19–22). The primary concern is how this act violates one's relation to Christ.

---

20. The ἤ (*ē*, or) signals "his readers that he is launching another assault" (Fisk 1996: 552, citing Rom. 6:3, 16; 11:2; 1 Cor. 6:2, 9, 19; 10:19).

Paul will remind them in 6:19 that the Christian is holy as the shrine of the Holy Spirit. The argument in this verse assumes that when something holy is joined to what is unholy in an unholy union, the flesh becomes corrupted and the shrine desecrated and made unfit for the Holy Spirit. By contrast, a Christian, as one who is holy, sanctifies his or her unbelieving spouse in the marriage relationship (7:12–16) because that relationship is ordained and blessed by God.

The verb κολλᾶν is used in the LXX to refer both to sexual unions and spiritual bonds. In the latter usage, it simply means "to hold fast." In Deut. 10:20, for example, Israel is commanded to fear the Lord their God, worship him alone, and "hold fast" to him. Hezekiah is commended for "holding fast" to the Lord and keeping his commandments (2 Kings 18:6 LXX). By contrast, Solomon is chided for doing what was evil in the Lord's sight by violating the Lord's command in loving and marrying many foreign women and "clinging" to them in love. "Cleaving" to these women with their idolatrous sentiments influenced him to turn away his heart to other gods (1 Kings 11:1–8 LXX). If Paul has the meaning "hold fast" in mind when he speaks of the one who is joined to the Lord, he need not intend to conjure up the image of a nuptial relationship with Christ (contra Rosner 1994: 131–32, 134–36). The union between believers and Christ is of an altogether different kind than that created by a sexual relationship and can be expressed only in terms of the Spirit (Fee 1994: 134). The consequence of Christians cleaving exclusively to Christ is that they become one spirit with him (Rom. 8:9–11; cf. 1 Cor. 15:45; 2 Cor. 3:17). Paul does not intend to suggest that Christ unites only with the human spirit or soul. The Spirit creates the union with Christ and makes the body its temple. Christ's Spirit becomes the command center for the body, which would rule out all contact with prostitutes, because the body is to be given over in service only to its Lord.[21]

Paul's emphatic command to flee *porneia* draws the conclusion to his argument.[22] It also expresses a fundamental concern throughout these middle chapters of the letter. The man having his father's wife is guilty of a *porneia* that even pagans find revolting. Paul's initial instruction about sexual relations within marriage is governed by the fear of the danger of *porneia* (7:2, 5). His warnings about idolatry include warnings about sexual immorality (10:8). Paul shares the sentiment expressed in the Testament of the Twelve Patriarchs that "fornication is the mother of all wicked deeds; it separates from God and leads men to Beliar" (T. Sim. 5:3). It is "the pitfall of life, separating man from God

6:18

---

21. Note that one of the fruits of the Spirit is ἐγκράτεια (*enkrateia*, self-control; Gal. 5:22–23; cf. 1 Cor. 7:9), while *porneia* is one of the works of the flesh (Gal. 5:18).

22. The same command to flee *porneia* appears in T. Reub. 5:5.

and leading to idolatry" (T. Reub. 4:6).[23] Fornication and idolatry go together (1 Cor. 5:10–11; 6:9; 10:7–8) because they belong to the same evil domain that warps what can be known about God, disfigures life, and wreaks havoc in society. Anyone who finds sex with a prostitute permissible is also likely to have no qualms about idolatry.

The statement "every sin that a man commits" is a notorious crux. Many have tried to resolve the problem by turning it into "a mere Corinthian quirk" (Fisk 1996: 540–41) and dismiss it as another of their bizarre slogans.[24] This view assumes that the Corinthians' fallacious anthropology lies behind a claim that what is merely physical, such as sexual activity, is morally irrelevant because it does not touch and cannot harm the inner citadel of the soul. This view is to be rejected because Paul includes no marker to signal the presence of a quotation. The δέ (de), unlike the ἀλλά (alla) in 6:12, does not function as a contrastive particle but expresses an exception: "Every sin a man commits is outside his body with the exception of the immoral man who sins against his own body" (Rosner 1994: 144; cf. Barrett 1968: 150). If 6:18a was a slogan, the response in 6:18b is hardly an adequate refutation (Byrne 1983: 609–10). It is best, then, to regard this difficult clause as reflecting Paul's own position, in which he offers another explanation why they should flee *porneia*.

Fisk (1996) helpfully catalogs the different interpretations of this statement. The first view deduces that Paul assumes that a *quantitative* difference exists between the effects of different sins. Sexual sin is deemed particularly destructive because it causes the greatest damage to a person. As Calvin (1960: 131–32) characterizes it, "Other sins do not leave the same filthy stain on our bodies as fornication does" (cf. Barrett 1968: 150–51; Conzelmann 1975: 112).

A second view perceives that Paul refers to a *qualitative* difference between sins: "Sexual sin is different *in kind*, not just *in degree* from other sins" (Fisk 1996: 541). Bruce (1971: 65), for example, comments that other sins "consist in things which are morally neutral." Their effects can be undone by abstinence. By contrast, "the relation once es-

---

23. R. Collins (1999: 248) thinks it not improbable that Paul's references to God's indwelling in 6:19 (cf. T. Jos. 10:1–3) and the exhortation to glorify God in 6:20 (cf. T. Jos. 8:5) reveal an intertextual allusion to the biblical story of Joseph fleeing Potiphar's wife (Gen. 39). Φεύγειν (*pheugein*, flee) appears in LXX Gen. 39:12, 15, 18.

24. Miguens 1975a: 39–40; Murphy-O'Connor 1978a; Stowers 1981: 67; Talbert 1987: 33–34; Omanson 1992; Hays 1997: 105; cf. R. Horsley 1998: 92; R. Collins 1999: 248. Kempthorne (1967–68) thinks that the slogan refers to the case of the incestuous man, and the Corinthians affirm that since the stepmother is an outsider, it cannot have any affect on the church, the body. This view has little to commend it. "His own body" (6:18) can hardly refer to the church as the body of Christ (contra Schweitzer, *TDNT* 7:1070), and Paul would regard sexual impurity as an attack against the body regardless of whether or not one is a Christian.

tablished by *porneia* cannot be undone" (see also Godet 1886: 312; Kistemaker 1993: 201; and Furnish 1999: 60, who understands Paul to be using "hyperbole"). Fee (1987: 262–63) thinks that it is the unique nature of sexual sin that the man removes his body from union with Christ by putting it under the mastery of a prostitute and ruins its redemptive status "as for the Lord" (see also Robertson and Plummer 1914: 150–51; Jewett 1971: 261).

Others stress how this sin in particular distorts personal relationships. Käsemann (1964: 133) argues that the body is the instrument of intimate bodily communication between persons: "As body, man exists in relationship to others, in subjection because of the world, in the jurisdiction of the Creator, in the hope of resurrection, in the possibility of concrete obedience and self-surrender." Byrne (1983: 613) bases his view on this insight from Käsemann and contends,

> The immoral person perverts precisely that faculty within himself that is meant to be the instrument of the most intimate bodily communication between persons. He sins against his unique power of communication and in this sense sins in a particular way "against his own body." No other sin engages one's power of bodily personal communication in precisely so intimate a way. All other sins are in this respect by comparison "outside" the body—with "body" having in this verse the strong sexual overtones that appear to cling to it throughout the passage as a whole.[25]

When one has sex with a prostitute, what God intended to be a means of sharing one's life with another is dehumanized into a momentary coupling for the sole purpose of sexual release. It leaves a legacy of alienation and guilt rather than loving intimacy and mutual commitment.

Fisk (1996: 541) offers a third view, which understands sexual sin to be uniquely defiling and a sin *against the body*. Although the Greek does not include the word "other" in the phrase πᾶν ἁμάρτημα (*pan hamartēma*), it should be included in the translation: "every other sin" (Fisk 1996: 544). The word "other" is sometimes omitted in Greek and is to be understood (for example, Matt. 12:31, "people will be forgiven for every [other] sin and blasphemy, but blasphemy against the Spirit will not be forgiven"). The context and rhetorical tone suggest that Paul wants to draw out the distinctive character of sexual sin compared to every other sin a person could possibly commit. That these other sins are "outside the body" (ἐκτὸς τοῦ σώματος, *ektos tou sōmatos*) implies that they are not sins "against the body" (εἰς τὸ ἴδιον σῶμα ἁμαρτάνει, *eis to idion sōma hamartanei*), not that the body is not involved in committing them. Sexual sin, by contrast, is labeled a direct assault on the

---

25. See also Blomberg 1994: 127; Schrage 1995: 31. Byrne (1983: 614) thinks he finds in this view a high theology of sexuality but reads too much into what Paul actually says.

body (Fisk 1996: 546–47).[26] Fisk (1996: 546) shows that this view reflects the Jewish wisdom tradition that "some sins, but apparently not all, were viewed as destructive acts *against one's self,* one's ψυχή ([*psychē*] life, soul)."[27] Commentators, however, have long asked how drunkenness, gluttony, suicide, and self-mutilation do not qualify also as sins against the body. But Paul is not referring to what might physically injure the body (Jewett 1971: 261). To take one example, drunkenness does not have the capacity to make a person one flesh with alcohol. This one-flesh union is true only of the sex act. Because intercourse with a prostitute is "uniquely body joining, it is uniquely body-defiling" (Fisk 1996: 558). In the context, sex with a prostitute severs the union with Christ and sabotages its resurrection destiny.

"Body" refers not to the human self, personhood, or individuality (contra Weiss 1910: 161; Bultmann 1951: 192–203; Schweizer, *TDNT* 7:1065; Robinson 1952: 28–29; Best 1955: 74–76) but to "the corporeality of human life," its physical aspect (Käsemann 1964: 129). The body is "the locus where we experience life, death, sickness and sexuality—in short our creatureliness and our position in the realm of nature" (Schrage 1982: 219). The body is capable of becoming an instrument of wickedness or an instrument of righteousness; a slave of impurity or a slave of righteousness (Rom. 6:19); something that brings glory to God (6:20; Phil. 1:20) or something that brings shame. Paul does not view human beings as simply having a body; they are embodied, and by using the word *sōma,* he "directs attention to their bodies, not to the wholeness of their being" (Gundry 1976: 79–80). "The *sōma* is simply that part of man in and through which he performs concrete actions" (Gundry 1976: 50). "It becomes the base of operations for sin in the unbeliever, for the Holy Spirit in the believer" (Gundry 1976: 50). Fisk (1996: 548) contends that in the context, the "readers would think first of the physical frame, destined for resurrection, united with Christ, and capable of sexual intercourse."

6:19–20 Paul's third "Do you not know?" question either reminds them, if they have forgotten, or informs them, if they did not know, that their bodies are the shrine of the Holy Spirit now (Rom. 8:11). He first applied this temple imagery to the entire church (3:16–17) and now adapts it to individual Christians.[28] The Holy Spirit stamps their bodies as belonging to God and set aside for God's use, guarantees their common destiny

---

26. For the idiom "to sin against" (ἁμαρτάνειν εἰς, *hamartanein eis*), cf. Prov. 8:36; 20:2; Sir. 10:29; 19:4.

27. Josephus (*Ant.* 4.8.1 §206; 4.8.23 §245) assumes that prostitution degrades the body of the prostitute.

28. Weiss (1910: 166 n. 1) cites parallels in Philo (*Dreams* 1.23 §149; *Sobr.* 13 §§62–64; *Cher.* 2.29 §98; 2.31 §106) and analogous ideas in Epictetus (*Diatr.* 1.14.14–15; 2.8.11–12), which reveal that this idea would not have been obscure to the Corinthians.

with God (2 Cor. 1:22), and makes their bodies a sacred place of God's presence. To engage in sexual immorality not only defiles the temple of the Holy Spirit but also rejects the life God has given them. Reminding them that they received the Holy Spirit *from* God also reminds them of God's authority over their lives (cf. 1 Thess. 4:8). Reminding them that they house the Spirit means that they not only sin against their own bodies when they are guilty of sexual immorality, but they also sin against the Holy Spirit (Fisk 1996: 557; Holtz 1995: 55).

They must also recognize that they are not their own (3:23; 7:22–23). The Lord has full property rights over them.[29] The imagery derives from the slave auction, familiar to Corinthians because Corinth was a major center for slave trafficking (Harrill 1995: 74). Paying ransom for the liberation of slaves was also a familiar practice to the ancients. According to the law, those who were ransomed from enemies who had captured them in war became the property of the one who freed them (Demosthenes, *Contra Nicostratum* [*Against Nicostratus*] 53.11; see Spicq, *TLNT* 2:427). Paul does not identify to whom the price was paid, either Sin or Satan (Rom. 6:12), or the price paid, Christ's precious blood (1 Pet. 1:19). He wishes only to emphasize that they now belong entirely to Christ.

Deissmann (1911: 320–30) claims that the image evokes sacral manumission, but Bartchy (1973: 124 n. 449; see also Bartchy, *ABD* 6:72) notes that the verb most commonly used in those contexts was πρίασθαι (*priasthai*) not ἀγοράζειν (*agorazein*). Paul's image does not picture a slave being sold to a god and being set free, but being transferred by sale from one owner to another. Formerly, they were slaves of sin; now they are slaves of God (Rom. 6:16–23; 7:6). D. Martin (1990: 63) argues that since the verb ἀγοράζειν is used for an ordinary transfer of ownership, "the salvific element of the metaphor is not in the movement from slavery to freedom but in the movement from a lower level of slavery (as the slave of just anybody or the slave of sin) to a higher level of slavery (as the slave of Christ)." It portrays slave "upward mobility." God now has the title deed to their bodies. Christ's death purchased them, and they have been transferred from Satan's household to serve in Christ's household. It brings improved status, new duties, and increased accountability. G. Klein (1989: 374) sees a relation to Hos. 3, where the prophet "redeemed his wife out of a degrading life to a life bound by sexual decorum. Similarly, in 1 Corinthians 6 the audience had been redeemed out of bondage to sin (including licentiousness) to a life in which sexual sin was unconscionable."

They now must glorify God with their bodies. The sexual debauchery outlined in Rom. 1:26–27 is directly attributable to the refusal to honor

---

29. The dowry imagery (cf. Gen. 31:14; Ruth 4:5, 9–10) noted by Miguens (1975a: 40–41) hardly applies in the context of Christ as the sacrificed paschal lamb (5:7).

God as God (Rom. 1:21). The term "body" is interchangeable with δοῦλος (*doulos,* slave; cf. Rev. 18:13) and is the most common term used to describe the slave in legal texts dealing with emancipation, the transference of the slave to another owner, and property tax documents (Tomlinson 1997: 98–105). The term "bodies" recalls their slavery to God, but the context makes clear that this slavery is different. God inhabits their bodies through the Holy Spirit, and this divine presence assures their triumph over death.

Additional Notes

6:12. The old view that made Corinth almost synonymous with prostitution should be abandoned. Aristophanes (*Fragments* 354) did use "to Corinthianize" (κορινθιάζεσθαι) as a verb for dissipated living, and plays entitled *The Corinthian* (Philetaerus 13.559a; Poliochus 7.31.3c) made that name interchangeable with whoremonger. But these writers refer to Greek Corinth, destroyed in 146 B.C., not to Corinth after it had been resettled and rebuilt as a Roman colony. It is anachronistic to apply these epithets to the Corinth of Paul's day. Often cited is Strabo's (*Geogr.* 8.6.20) reference to one thousand temple prostitutes dedicated to Aphrodite: "And the temple of Aphrodite was so rich that it owned more than a thousand temple-slaves, prostitutes, whom both men and women had dedicated to the goddess. And therefore it was also on account of these women that the city was crowded and grew rich." Their prowess gave rise to many anecdotes; but, again, Strabo refers to Greek Corinth, and "the small Roman temple of Aphrodite on the Acrocorinth rules out that temple as a place for prostitution" (Winter 1997b: 78; cf. Murphy-O'Connor 1983: 55–56; Engels 1990: 97–99; Schrage 1991: 28; Oster 1995: 149; De Vos 1999: 192–93). The yarn about a thousand courtesans also appears to have been an Athenian slander maligning its rival Corinth. Aphrodite retained her significance in the city. Aelius Aristides (*For Poseidon* 23), writing in the mid–second century A.D., virtually identified Corinth with the goddess. She was not only the goddess of erotic love but also the goddess of the sea, and her importance in Corinth is related to the dependence of so many citizens on the sea for their livelihood. Aphrodite (Venus) was also hailed as ruler of Rome by Ovid (*Amores* 1.8.42) and venerated as the mother of the Roman imperial family. She did, however, shape sexual morals. Her "adultery among the gods and with mortals gave divine precedence and permission to much of the sexual conduct within Graeco-Roman society" (Garrison 1997: 38).

If the graffiti on the walls of Pompeii are any indication, prostitution was commonplace in the Greco-Roman world. Xenophon (*Mem.* 2.2.4) records this observation from an Athenian: "Of course you don't suppose that lust provokes men to beget children, when the streets and the stews are full of means to satisfy that? We obviously select for wives the women who will bear us the best children, and then marry them to raise a family." Athenaeus (*Deipnosophistae* 13.573B) cites the adage he attributes to have first been uttered by Apollodorus: "We keep mistresses for pleasure, concubines for daily concubinage, but wives in order to produce children legitimately and to have a trustworthy guardian of our domestic property" (see J. Davidson 1997: 73–77 for an interpretation of this comment as it applies to ancient Athens). Hauck and Schulz (*TDNT* 6:583) note that the Greeks were very tolerant of sexual relations with harlots.

> Only excess and overindulgence was censured. . . . On the other hand, visiting brothels was also regarded as scandalous. This ambivalence of outlook is characteristic of antiquity. Plato tries to solve the problem by compromise. Intercourse

with harlots is permissible so long as it takes place in secret and causes no offence, *Leg.* [*Laws*], VIII, 841a–c.

Besides having sex with female slaves, who could not refuse their masters, men could choose from various classes of prostitutes, depending on their status and how much money they had to spend. Often, prostitutes employed in brothels were female slaves (see Demosthenes, *In Neaeram* [*Against Neaera*] 18–20). Girls with some artistic skills plied their trade as "companions" (ἑταῖραι, *hetairai*). Rosner (1998) claims that Paul has in mind temple prostitutes. Winter (1997b: 79) argues that the context is a private banquet, the Roman *convivium,* which was marked by gluttony and drunkenness and promiscuous activities called "after-dinners," when the host brought in hired courtesans (see also J. Davidson 1997: 92–93). Paul does not identify specifically the social context and probably lumps all prostitutes together in the same class—those who sell their bodies for sex.

6:13. The assumption expressed by Rosner (1994: 129), "Certain Corinthian Christians had embraced a body/spirit dualism, involving a low view of the purpose and future of the body, which opened the door to sexual licence," need not be true. Philo assumes that the body is morally inferior, using an allegorical interpretation of "belly" passages in the OT. The belly, he claims, is "the reservoir of all the pleasures and passions" (*Alleg. Interp.* 3.47–53 §§138–59; *Migr. Abr.* 12 §§65–66; *Spec. Laws* 1.38 §206). This assumption, however, did not lead Philo to sexual permissiveness. Philo proudly exalts the sexual mores of the Hebrews: "Other nations allow their young men of 14 years of age to go to prostitutes and to other women who sell their bodies. But according to our laws, all *hetairai* are condemned to die. Until there can be legitimate relations, we do not have intercourse with a woman. Both parties enter marriage as virgins, and for us the purpose of marriage is not pleasure but the propagation of children" (*Jos.* 9 §§42–43).

6:14. The tense of the verb "raise" varies in the manuscript evidence. $\mathfrak{P}^{11}$, A, P, and uncorrected D have the present, ἐξεγείρει. The aorist, ἐξήγειρεν, appears in B, 6, 424^c, 1739, lat, Origen. $\mathfrak{P}^{46}$ had the present corrected to the future and then corrected to the aorist. The future, ἐξεγερεῖ, is found in ℵ, C, K, L, D, and the majority of minuscules and versions. The aorist reflects a baptismal understanding of the meaning of raised (cf. Eph. 2:6; Col. 2:12, 13) or is simply an unthinking duplication of the preceding "raised." The future is required by the argument, which envisions a future resurrection (cf. 2 Cor. 4:14), and the antithetical parallelism with the verb "will destroy," καταργήσει, in 6:13.

6:16. J. Miller (1980–81) claims that the verb κολλᾶν without the prefix πρός means "adhesion" and "loyalty," not sexual intercourse, and it was chosen to remove any sexual connotation from the clinging. The evidence, however, does not support this strict distinction. The compound verb προσκολλᾶν appears in Gen. 2:24; Mark 10:7; Eph. 5:31; but the verb κολλᾶν appears in Matt. 19:5 (cf. 1 Esdr. 4:20). Sirach 19:2–3 uses κολλᾶν for the man who self-destructs by joining himself to prostitutes (ὁ κολλώμενος πόρναις). The verb also has a sexual connotation in the magical papyri (Schrage 1995: 27 n. 326). S. Porter (1991) contends that the verb has an economic nuance here and implies "obligating oneself," "selling oneself," but the biblical echoes control its meaning here.

6:20. The Textus Receptus adds, at the end of the verse, καὶ ἐν τῷ πνεύματι ὑμῶν, ἅτινά ἐστιν τοῦ θεοῦ, found in later uncials and most minuscules (2464 omits ἅτινά ἐστιν τοῦ θεοῦ). The shorter reading has the strongest manuscript support from early witnesses and has a more forceful rhetorical punch. A scribe would have been more prone to add the longer reading than to drop it. This longer reading garbles Paul's point, which places emphasis on the Christian's body.

V. Instructions about Sexual Relations, Divorce, and Marriage (7:1–40)

Paul switches gears in chapter 7 by taking up specific Corinthian concerns pertaining to sexuality and marriage that were communicated to him in their letter. His response covers the gamut of issues relating to marriage: sexual relations within marriage, the choice of celibacy for the unmarried, remarriage for widows, decisions related to divorce, and the decision whether to marry or not. Paul replies to questions the Corinthians have posed and to Corinthian positions he considers to be in error.

Many conclude from Paul's answers that he is against marriage or has a low view of it, and that he has an even lower view of sexual intercourse. Calvin's (*Institutes* 2.8.41) statement that marriage is "a necessary remedy to keep us from plunging into unbridled lust" reflects a common understanding of what Paul is thought to argue in 7:2—those who marry cave in to coarse sexual cravings. Bornkamm (1971: 208), for example, claims that Paul regarded marriage to be "an emergency measure, even if sanctioned by God, in face of the overwhelming power of the sexual urge in man and as a safeguard against unchastity and the temptations of Satan." This perspective misrepresents Paul's meaning.

To understand Paul's argument, it is important to start with the recognition that he addresses specific difficulties that have developed in Corinth and is not presenting a marriage manual or his systematic thoughts on marriage. Osiek and Balch (1997: 104) correctly protest that Paul "was not a Stoic philosopher or a Christian theologian writing generally about marriage in order to shore up Greco-Roman or American urban society. We have instead his pastoral argument against some particular Corinthian Christian ascetics' rejection of their sexuality." He is not antimarriage, nor does he disparage sexuality. He knows marriage to be a divine institution in which the two become one flesh. As marriage was applied in the OT as an image for the relationship between God and Israel (Isa. 50:1; 54:6–7; Jer. 2:1–2), so Paul uses it as an image for the relationship between Christ and the church (Eph. 5:21–33). In this letter, he does not begrudge that Cephas, the apostles, and the brothers of the Lord have wives and travel with them on their mission sojourns (9:5). He too could exercise that right. In 11:7–9, he assumes that marriage is normative. Paul does not devalue marriage only as a venereal safety valve for incontinent, noncharismatic people, providing them a lawful outlet for expressing their sexual urges. Instead, he relativizes its significance "in the face of the nearness of the coming kingdom and the new estimation of the earthly life coupled with it" (Ridderbos 1975: 312; cf. 7:7, 26, 32, 40).

Some fault Paul for saying nothing here about love between husbands and wives or the "richness of family human experience in marriage and family life" (Bornkamm 1971: 207–8). Such a discussion is omitted because it is not at issue. In the opening paragraphs of this chapter, Paul is preoccupied with the sexual part of marriage because that is the problem in Corinth (Furnish 1985: 46). His statement that those who marry commit no sin (7:28) suggests that others were saying quite the opposite. This view is confirmed if the opening statement in 7:1 is not Paul's own declaration about sexuality but a citation of a Corinthian position. Paul's personal choice of celibacy is clear and would have been well known to the Corinthians. He lives out his calling in Christ as one who is celibate and thinks that it is a preferable but not superior calling (7:7, 26–28). He does not seek to make everyone conform to his own personal gifts and insists that the physical side of marriage not be curtailed by misguided spirituality (7:2–5). Celibacy is the best course only for those who have the gift of celibacy (7:8). It is not for every Christian, but the requirement of sexual purity is. Those who attempt to become celibate for utopian reasons only open the door of temptation to fornication. Paul affirms that the sexual relationship, which is integral to marriage, is fully compatible with the Christian life.

The basic principle governing his discussion is spelled out in 7:17–24: "Remain as you are." This principle emerges in 7:2, 8, 10, 11, 12–16, 26–27, 37, 40, but exceptions are allowed in each case (Fee 1987: 268–69). Paul insists in 7:2–16 that the married should remain married. In 7:2–5, he argues that married partners must remain fully married and not attempt to forgo a normal sex life to attain some sublime spiritual goal. His intention is not to argue that marriage is necessary to avoid fornication but to argue that sexual asceticism has only a limited, if any, place in the marriage relationship (Ruef 1977: 53). In 7:6–9, he commends celibacy but does not exalt it as the highest good. Those who are widowed and those who are unmarried and have sexual urges should seek marriage rather than condemn themselves to a life of racking torment trying to sublimate their desires, or, worse, acting upon them in inappropriate ways. They should not think they fail somehow by choosing marriage. In 7:10–16, he argues against divorce. Christians are forbidden to divorce and are not to divorce their pagan partners under the mistaken impression that their faith requires it. Christians should remain married to their pagan husbands or wives who are content to continue to live together with them in peace. The marriage is a prime opportunity for a Christian to save his or her spouse. Should a pagan spouse want a divorce, however, the Christian spouse is not bound by this directive.

In 7:25–40, Paul recommends that those who are unmarried remain unmarried. His reasons are purely pragmatic: the eschatological urgency of the hour and the opportunity of the single person to devote all of his or her energy to serving the Lord (7:25–35). He has no intention of shackling them with the fetters of unrealistic demands, however. Those who are engaged and desire to follow through with marriage do not sin. They do well. Those who desire to break off an engagement also do not sin. They do better (7:36–38). Widows who choose to remarry are free to do so. Those who choose to remain unmarried are more blessed, but only for practical reasons, not because singleness is a more spiritual state. One can serve God whether married or single. Satisfying one's erotic desires in marriage is not a sin. On the other hand, the erotic part of a person's life is just that, a part, and not the most important part of life. Serving God in holiness, however, is most important.

In stark contrast to the ascetic Corinthians who apparently promoted complete sexual abstinence even for married couples and dissuaded engaged couples from marrying, Paul is not doctrinaire in his advice. He walks a fine line in recommending celibacy as the preferable choice but not the only one. His own choice is not determinative for others (P. W. Gooch 1983: 66); he allows exceptions, leaving believers ethical room to make their own decisions. His appeal at the conclusion of the chapter, "I think that I also have the Spirit of God" (7:40; cf. 14:37), reveals that he understands this to be authoritative guidance. But he is not authoritarian: "He does not settle matters with any simple appeal to authority" (Stowers 1990: 262). His remarks throughout this chapter make this clear: "I say this by way of agreement, not as a command" (7:6); "I wish" (7:7, 32); "I command, not I, but the Lord" (7:10, which affirms that Jesus' teaching is more authoritative than his own); "I, not the Lord, say" (7:12); "I do not have a command of the Lord, but I give this maxim as one who has been mercied by the Lord to be faithful" (7:25); "I think" (7:26); "I am saying this for your very own benefit. I am not throwing a noose around [your neck], but [I am saying this] to promote what is seemly and constant before the Lord [that you might live] undistractedly" (7:35).

Paul's discussion about marriage and sexuality in this chapter offers the reader a unique opportunity to observe his hermeneutic at work in trying to solve practical problems that have arisen. He argues from his own spiritual insight (7:40), but a respect for the complexity of life governs his counsel. As P. W. Gooch (1983: 69) notes, "Rules and principles are to be modified in ways appropriate to the circumstances in which they are applied." Paul does not offer a one-size-fits-all guideline. He treats each person as a responsible moral agent who must learn how to please the Lord in his or her circumstances (P. W. Gooch 1983: 68). The obligation to avoid fornication and to be obedient to the word of the Lord is the only absolute. Several factors deserve consideration in choosing the right course of action: avoiding unnecessary temptation from Satan (7:5), discerning one's giftedness from God (7:7), maintaining peace in relationships (7:16), not changing one's earthly status in a futile attempt to enhance one's status with God (7:17–24), the eschatological urgency of the hour (7:29–31), freeing oneself from unnecessary anxieties that might detract from devotion to the Lord (7:32), and doing whatever promotes good order and unhindered devotion to the Lord (7:35).

In 7:1–5, Paul responds to matters raised by the Corinthians' letter about not touching a woman. He then introduces his own matters and launches each new topic with an assertion of authority: "I say" (7:6, 8); "I command" (7:10); "I say" (7:12); "I command" (7:17); "I give a maxim," "I think" (7:25–26). The following outline emerges from these markers:

A. Sexual relations within marriage (7:1–5)
B. Celibacy or marriage for the unmarried and widows (7:6–9)
C. Divorce for those married to Christians and for those married to non-Christians (7:10–16)
D. Principle underlying the discussion: Remain as you are (7:17–24)
E. The advisability of marriage for the betrothed and for widows (7:25–40)

A. Sexual Relations within Marriage (7:1–5)

Paul's mention of a letter to him complicates the task of interpretation because it obliges the interpreter to attempt some reconstruction of what in the letter prompted his response. The issue appears to be about celibacy, but we do not know whether Paul's remarks reflect an ongoing discussion with the church or whether the problem had flared up recently and they wrote to request his advice or intervention. We cannot be sure if the Corinthians asked questions or made pronouncements about whether marriage was desirable, whether sexual relations within marriage were compatible with their new life in the Spirit or were a distraction, whether divorce was advisable to ensure remaining celibate, or whether divorce was necessary for those married to unbelievers so that they would not become polluted in some way. We also do not know the precise circumstances or motivations that may have made celibacy attractive to some Corinthians. Many interpreters have advanced their different reconstructions of the situation with perhaps more confidence than is warranted by the evidence. Decisions about the situation that precipitated Paul's reply are ultimately based only on inferences from the text and judgments about the Corinthian cultural landscape. One thing is clear: Paul reacts to a particular situation at Corinth and is not offering in this chapter a compendium of his views on marriage and sexuality.

After the introduction of the topic in 7:1, Paul's argument in 7:2–5 falls into a chiastic structure, which reveals that his concern about the danger of immorality is paramount:

   A But because of fornications (7:2a)
      B Let each one have his own wife or her own husband (7:2bc)
         C Let the husband fulfill his sexual obligations to his wife (7:3a)
           D and likewise the wife to her husband (7:3b)
           D′ The wife does not have authority over her own body but her husband (7:4a)
         C′ and likewise the husband does not have authority over his own body but his wife (7:4b)
      B′ Do not deprive one another . . . (7:5ab)
   A′ because of your lack of self-control (7:5c)

D. Wright (*DPL* 873) aptly applies a saying of Jesus to spell out Paul's assumptions about sexuality: "By divine appointment marriage and sexuality go together, as do singleness and abstinence from sex; what God has joined together, humans should not separate."

Exegesis and Exposition

[1]Now concerning what you wrote, "It is good for a man not to touch a woman." [2]But because of fornications let each [husband] have his own wife and each [wife] have her own husband. [3]The husband shall fulfill his ⌜sexual obligations⌝ to his wife and likewise the wife to her husband. [4]The wife does not have authority over her own body but her husband [does], and likewise the husband does not have authority over his own body but his wife [does]. [5]Do not deprive one another, except by mutual agreement and for a limited time in order to withdraw for ⌜prayer⌝. Then, ⌜be⌝ together again so that Satan might not tempt you because of your lack of self-control.

How one understands the first verse of this section lays the foundation for understanding the rest of Paul's discussion. Two basic interpretations have emerged, with variations appearing as subsets within each option. The first interpretation assumes that Paul begins by asserting his own beliefs about what should be the ideal.[1] He thinks it good to avoid sexual relations, but the reality of the human condition and the ever present danger of *porneia* require exceptions. The adversative δέ (*de*) in 7:2 explains why concessions must be allowed: "but because of *porneia*," each one should have his own wife or her own husband. Marriage provides the only appropriate sexual outlet for those who cannot bridle their sexual urges. Paul requires those who are married to fulfill their conjugal obligations lest partners be tempted to satisfy their sexual longings by illicit means. He also insists that those who are unmarried and unable to control their sexual cravings should marry (7:7–9).[2] Human nature should not be overtaxed, because it will succumb to temptation.

The second view interprets the clause "It is good for a man not to touch a woman" as a direct quotation of a line from the Corinthians' let-

7:1

---

1. Edwards 1885: 157; Weiss 1910: 170; Robertson and Plummer 1914: 132; Baltensweiler 1967: 156; Conzelmann 1975: 115; Niederwimmer 1975: 81; Schüssler Fiorenza 1984: 223; Caragounis 1996: 552.

2. First Thessalonians 4:3–8 can be interpreted as offering parallel advice: each one should acquire a wife in holiness and honor to avoid fornication and pagan lustful passion. But the difficult phrase τὸ ἑαυτοῦ σκεῦος κτᾶσθαι (*to heautou skeuos ktasthai*) may not mean "that each one of you know how *to take a wife for himself* in holiness and honor" (RSV). It may be interpreted to mean "to gain mastery over one's body" (REB; "control your own body," NRSV; cf. "guard one's member," NAB). This latter interpretation is supported by similar wording in 1 Sam. 21:6 and 4Q416 2:21.

ter or as a summary of the gist of their argument. D. Smith (1920: 262) was perhaps the first to contend that Paul opened his discussion with a quotation from the Corinthians that he intended to contradict. A majority of recent scholars have adopted this interpretation, and it has influenced recent translations that add "you say" (REB) and/or put 7:1b in quotation marks (REB, NRSV).[3]

Several arguments can be mustered to support interpreting 7:1b as a quotation from the Corinthians' letter. The first relates to the use of the phrase περὶ δέ (*peri de,* now concerning). This phrase appears five other times in the letter, and in each instance it alerts the listener that one topic has ended and a new one is taken up: the virgins (7:25), idol food (8:1), spiritual gifts (12:1), the collection (16:1), and Apollos's return (16:12). Lightfoot (1895: 219) contends that it "is as though the Apostle were taking in detail the heads of their letter" (see also Hurd 1965: 63–64; Moiser 1983: 104–5; Fee 1987: 267). M. Mitchell (1989) argues, however, that περὶ δέ is not an answering formula in ancient letters, and it need not introduce specific items raised by the Corinthians in their letter (cf. Conzelmann 1975: 115). Paul may use it instead as a device to identify a new topic that the readers would readily identify from their common experience with the writer.[4] It is too simplistic to argue that in the rest of the letter Paul addresses sequentially issues raised in the Corinthians' letter, since he also refers to what he has heard in 11:18 and appears to react to oral reports of their beliefs about the resurrection of the dead in 15:12. But we need not dissociate the formula entirely from topics broached by the Corinthians, and this is particularly true in 7:1. Paul specifically connects the next topic he will discuss to what they wrote in their letter. It is likely that they wrote him about a number of things, and it is also likely that he would identify specifically the subject from their letter that he will discuss *before* proceeding to offer his judgment (Giblin 1969: 2841–42). In no other instance where the phrase περὶ δέ occurs does Paul follow it immediately with a pronouncement—ex cathedra, as it were—of his own views (Garland 1983: 351). He identifies the topic first. Since this is the first item taken up by Paul from their letter, it makes sense that he would clue them in on what point he is going to address rather than abruptly declare what is good. They, unlike the modern reader who has no access to their letter,

---

3. Hurd 1965: 63–68; 158–63; Barrett 1968: 154; Giblin 1969: 2842; Bruce 1971: 66; Scroggs 1972: 296; 1993: 85; Cartlidge 1975: 223; Schrage 1976: 215–16; 1995: 53–54; Murphy-O'Connor 1981b: 603; Phipps 1982: 127–28; Merklein 1983: 230–31; Wolbert 1981: 78; Yarbrough 1985: 93–94; Fee 1987: 276; Rosner 1994: 151; Deming 1995b: 110–14; Wolff 1996: 134; R. Collins 1999: 258.

4. The formula appears elsewhere in 1 Thess. 4:9 and 5:1. Paul's response in both verses, "you do not need to have anyone write to you," suggests that he is answering specific questions posed by the Thessalonians (contra M. Mitchell 1989: 253–54).

would readily recognize the use of their own language. It is reasonable to regard the περὶ δέ formula as introducing a direct quotation or paraphrase from the Corinthians' letter that serves as a subject heading for the section: sexual asceticism and marriage.[5]

Second, some argue that καλόν (*kalon*, good) is a Pauline term because it appears in 7:8 and 26. This assumption leads to the conclusion that 7:1b is Paul's own statement, not a quotation from the Corinthian letter (so Conzelmann 1975: 115 n. 10; Niederwimmer 1975: 81 n. 3). But this argument can be turned on its head. Paul could be employing the Corinthians' language in 7:8 and 26 in the same way he picked up on the Corinthian catchword "wisdom" in chapters 1–3 (Yarbrough 1985: 93–94).

The phrase καλὸν ἀνθρώπῳ (*kalon anthrōpō*) appears again in 7:26 in a very awkward sentence: "I think that this is good because of the present necessity, that it is good for a man to be thus." This cumbersome redundancy, "this is good, . . . it is good," suggests that Paul cites a Corinthian catchphrase. Deming (1995b: 111–12) contends that the first "good" may be Pauline style (cf. 7:8; 9:15; Rom. 14:21; Gal. 4:18), but the phrase "good for a man" appears to be a quotation (so Hurd 1965: 178).[6] This would mean that Paul begins the discussion in 7:26 about the virgins by repeating the Corinthian eagerness for what is "good."

Third, the principle espoused in 7:1b contradicts the practice he recommends in 7:2–5 (see Hurd 1965: 163; Wire 1990: 12–13). Why would Paul introduce a canon that scorns sexual intercourse only to refute it by insisting on full sexual relations in marriage (7:2–5)? If he truly believes it good for a man not to touch a woman, why should married couples not also try to attain that lofty ideal? Perhaps they could overcome the danger of Satan through the power of God. If, however, Paul does not espouse this principle as the ideal but instead quotes a line from

5. Paul directly cites the Corinthian position and reacts to it in 15:12: "How do some of you say there is no resurrection of the dead?" Had he used that phrasing here, the matter would be settled. In 15:12, he relies on an oral report; but in 7:1, if he repeats a line from their letter, he could only introduce it appropriately with ἐγράψατε (*egrapsate*, you wrote). Caragounis (1996: 559) argues against this view that no citation marker such as ὅτι (*hoti*) or τουτέστιν (*toutestin*) is present, which he believes makes it grammatically improbable for the clause "it is good for a man not to touch a woman" to be the content of the verb ἐγράψατε. When Paul cites Scripture with the verb γέγραπται (*gegraptai*), however, he more often than not omits ὅτι as a citation marker and never uses τουτέστιν. The presence of a citation marker is not necessary for the phrase following the verb γράφω (*graphō*) to be a direct quotation or summary of what they wrote.

6. This explanation for the clumsy phrasing seems a better alternative than to attribute it to an interpolation (Weiss 1910: 193) or to maintain that the second καλός functions as a comparative, "better" (Neuhäusler 1959: 57 n. 40).

their letter that he intends to revise, it would compare with the slogan/ retort tactic that many see elsewhere in the letter.

The pattern of citing a catchphrase and then immediately rebutting it appears in 6:12–13; 8:1–4; and 10:23. Paul's strategy in this chapter, as in chapter 8, seems to be to start his argument by quoting a Corinthian position "as if he agrees with it" and then to add "strong qualifications to its use" (Yarbrough 1985: 93).[7] He does not want to reject celibacy out of hand, since he considers remaining single the better course for unmarried Christians (7:8–9, 27, 32–35, 40). But he clarifies that it is not the only viable option for the Christian. He cites the Corinthian position only to correct its dangerous misapplication. If celibacy is chosen for the wrong reasons by those with the wrong capabilities, the results can be disastrous. For those already married, however, celibacy is not an option. It recklessly opens the door to Satan, making one vulnerable to the wanton ways of their city, and is utterly unfair to the spouse.

Fourth, the clause lays down a general principle about celibacy ("It is not good for a *man* to touch a *woman*") from a distinctively male point of view. This perspective differs markedly from Paul's response in 7:2–5. He does not address the issue of the sexual commitment incumbent on marriage partners from only the male perspective but highlights the needs and responsibilities of both husband and wife. Throughout the chapter, Paul goes out of his way to underscore that women have the same obligations and rights as their male counterparts. Eight times he painstakingly repeats in full his instructions or statements about both the male and the female—the male's relationship to the female, and the female's relationship to the male (7:2, 3, 4, 10–11, 12–13, 16, 28, 32–34). The male perspective governing this principle would seem to derive from a source other than Paul.

Fifth, Paul's other statements in this chapter (7:7–8, 27, 32–35, 40), which may seem to endorse a negative view of sexuality in line with 7:1b, emphasize instead that church members remain as they are. These statements do not exalt abstaining from sexual intercourse as a good or as especially meritorious. Yarbrough (1985: 94) notes, "Paul argues not only that those who are unmarried (whether single, widowed, or divorced) should remain unmarried, but also that those who are married should remain married." Paul prefers celibacy not only for himself but also for others (7:7, 8, 26–27, 38, 40) so that they can devote themselves entirely to serving the Lord (7:32–35); but he does not champion it as a higher good or devalue marriage as a lesser good or as incompatible with the Christian calling. The only thing he completely

---

7. Yarbrough (1985: 93 n. 14) suggests that the strategy compares with that used by Musonius Rufus when he was asked whether one must obey one's parents in all things or were there exceptions. He responds initially that it is good (καλόν) to do so but then describes situations where it is improper to do so.

rejects as evil, the opposite of "good," is *porneia,* illicit sexual encounters (7:2; cf. 5:1; 6:9, 13, 18; 2 Cor. 12:21).

Sixth, the idea that an unbelieving spouse can be consecrated or sanctified by a believing spouse and that the children of this union are holy (7:14–15) reveals that Paul essentially affirms the goodness inherent in marriage (R. Collins 1978: 13). In fact, he declares in 7:38 that the one who marries does "well" (καλῶς, *kalōs*). Elsewhere, asceticism is specifically condemned in Col. 2:20–21 and 1 Tim. 4:3, and the union between husband and wife is held up as a metaphor for the union between Christ and the church in Eph. 5:25–33. Even if these letters were not penned by Paul, as some argue, Fee (1987: 276 n. 40) correctly notes, "It is well-nigh unimaginable that later Paulinists would correct their master on this issue, since the entire history of the early church moves in another direction."

I conclude that Paul opens the discussion of marriage and sexuality by citing a line from the Corinthians' letter in 7:1b, which he intends to qualify and correct. Although Paul thinks that celibacy is advisable for some, he is not "morbidly ascetic," as some characterize his views (cf. Whiteley 1974: 215).[8] It is difficult, however, to ascertain why some Corinthians adopted this approach to sexuality. They may have been influenced by philosophical discussions, medical debates, local religious cults, theological assumptions, enthusiasm for higher spiritual experiences, practical exigencies, or a combination of all of these. The Corinthians' perception of themselves as "spiritual" beings and Paul's own example may have encouraged their ascetical bent. My interpretation of Paul's response will not hinge on choosing any one particular backdrop to explain its genesis in the community (see additional note). Suffice it to say that an ascetic attitude toward sexuality was as much part of the intellectual landscape as was licentiousness, and it was attractive to many for a variety of reasons.

The next issue to be addressed is whether to punctuate the phrase in 7:1b as a statement or a question. Fee (1987: 266–67) maintains that the letter to Paul was not "a friendly exchange" in which they asked for "spiritual advice of their mentor in the Lord." It had a certain edginess to it. As a declaration, "It is good for a man not to touch a woman" promotes the celibate life as the highest ideal. Hurd (1965: 163–65) proposes that some Corinthians had tried to impose their will on others by discouraging sexual intercourse even within marriage. They considered strict sexual abstinence mandatory for the Christian life. In their letter, they did not ask Paul to guide them or to arbitrate between competing viewpoints but hailed their choice as a higher path. Wire (1990:

---

8. Tertullian (*De monogamia* [*Monogamy*] 4.60) and Jerome (*Jov.* 1.7) assumed that if it is good for a man not to touch a woman, then it is bad to touch a woman.

80) concurs that Paul is not answering questions but questioning answers. This view explains why he might open with a principle that directly contradicts what he says in the following verses. They asserted that celibacy was the highest good, but he punctures this conceit by reminding them that marriage brings with it conjugal obligations that must be met. By trying to become celibate in the marriage relationship they are courting moral disaster.

Others presume that the Corinthians asked for Paul's consultation and think it more likely that he would cite a question rather than a statement from the Corinthians (Orr and Walther 1976: 205–6; Ellingworth and Hatton 1985: 124). Interpreting the phrase this way "alters the dynamics of the exchange from an aggressive assertion of ascetic principle to a hesitant questioning of the wisdom of the voluntary restraint being practised by some Corinthians (7:5)" (L. Alexander 1998: 238). Some Corinthians may have been distressed by the ascetic push from others in the community and asked Paul whether marriage was inadvisable or whether expressing one's sexuality even in marriage was desirable (cf. Moiser 1983: 105).

The issue is difficult to settle, and the answer affects how one interprets the thrust of the rest of the chapter. Paul's vigorous assertions that normal sexual relations within marriage are not optional but required (7:2–5) and that marriage is not a sin (7:8–9, 36, 38) suggest that someone in Corinth was demeaning marriage and prescribing sexual abstinence even for married couples. If 7:1b is a question, it may have been raised because someone in Corinth was insisting that celibacy was the only appropriate stance for Christians who had received the Spirit.

All of these questions interlock with how the word "good" (καλόν, *kalon*) is to be interpreted (see Hurd 1965: 158–60, for the various permutations of interpretations depending on how it is rendered). It appears in this opening verse and again in 7:8 and 7:26 (twice) and is a key concept in Paul's discussion. Does "good" in this context mean that celibacy is something (1) excellent; (2) valuable or useful, contributing to wholeness and order; (3) worthy; or (4) better? Paul's use of the word elsewhere in his letters makes all these options possible. He uses it to connote what is morally good—for example, righteous conduct (Rom. 7:18, 21; 2 Cor. 13:7; Gal. 6:9; 1 Thess. 5:21), what is commendable or honorable (in the plural, Rom. 12:17; 2 Cor. 8:21), what is gratifying (Gal. 4:18), and what is better (1 Cor. 9:15).

1. The majority interpret καλόν as referring to a moral good, "the highest member of a series of lesser goods," "an ethical ideal of the highest rank" (Hurd 1965: 160–61). The structure of the sentence in 7:1b compares with Rom. 14:21: "It is good not to eat [καλὸν τὸ μὴ φαγεῖν, *kalon to mē phagein*] meat . . . or drink wine or do any-

thing that makes your brother stumble." This parallel suggests that "good" would refer to what is morally good.

2. Others contend that "good" does not express a moral judgment about abstinence but instead implies that it is "expedient," "desirable," or "beneficial."[9] The expression may echo Gen. 2:18, "It is not good for a man to be alone" (cf. Tob. 8:6–7), and gives it a unique twist: it is *not* beneficial for a man to marry or to have sexual relations. The word καλόν may be synonymous with σύμφορον (*symphoron*) in 7:35, "I am saying this for your very own benefit" (cf. 6:12; 10:23, "not all things are profitable"). Paul's emphasis in this chapter on what he believes is most beneficial for them (cf. 7:26, 29, 32, 35) favors this interpretation. Celibacy is beneficial because it enhances a person's ability to concentrate on becoming holy in body and spirit (7:34) and promotes good order and unhindered devotion to the Lord (7:35).

3. Others interpret this saying to be a defense of celibacy and understand Paul to be referring to it as a "good" among several goods. Celibacy is honorable and laudable, not something unbecoming or contemptible.[10] The thrust of Paul's argument in the rest of the chapter suggests, however, that he is trying to defend marriage and sexual relations in marriage, not singleness, as unobjectionable.

4. Others read καλον as a comparative, "better" (1 Cor. 9:15; cf. Matt. 18:8–9; 26:24; Mark 9:42, 43, 45, 47; 14:21; John 2:10).[11] Translating the καλόν in 7:8 as a comparative makes sense: "It is better for them to remain as I am." It also fits 7:26: "Because of the present distress it is better for a man to remain thus." Throughout this discussion, Paul allows persons to choose different options (with the exception of choosing fornication or divorce) but expresses his judgment about what he thinks is a better choice.[12] In the opening line he may be recommending, "A man is better off having no relations with a woman" (NAB). This interpretation avoids the problem of having Paul contradict himself in what follows. It also fits his conclusion in 7:38: those who marry do well (καλῶς, *kalōs*), but those who do not marry do better (κρείσσον, *kreisson*).

---

9. Parry 1926: 69; Héring 1962: 49; Barrett 1968: 155; Fee 1987: 275; Wimbush 1987: 15 n. 11; Wolff 1996: 134.

10. Godet 1886: 321; Ramsay 1900: 381; Findlay 1910: 822; Robertson and Plummer 1914: 100.

11. Weiss 1910: 170; Conzelmann 1975: 115; Snyder 1976–77; 1992: 91; Caragounis 1996: 546.

12. He uses the comparative form κρεῖττον (*kreitton*) in 7:9 to state that it is better to marry than to burn.

If we understand this clause as a line from the Corinthian letter, either as a question or a statement, we need to distinguish between what it might have meant to the Corinthians and how Paul may have tweaked it to fit his own views. Other statements in this chapter reveal that views two, three, and four fit his perspective. Celibacy is spiritually beneficial for those who do not need to be married. It is not something aberrant but contributes order and allows for unhindered devotion to the Lord. It is the better option for those who have the gift to live it out. In light of what Paul says in 7:2–5, however, the Corinthian interpretation of celibacy as a "good" seems to have been quite different. They appear to have understood it to be a distinguishing virtue. Whether they thought that it might augment the reception of the Spirit or not, they elevated not touching a woman to a moral axiom with the result that they maligned marriage and conjugal relations. Interpreting the clause "It is good for a man not to touch a woman" requires distinguishing between what the Corinthians meant by "good" and Paul's reevaluation of it. The Corinthians understood "good" to connote a moral good, "the highest member of a series of lesser goods." Paul counteracts this view by using "good" for what is "beneficial," "honorable," and "better," given certain circumstances.

This conclusion about the interpretation of this verse assumes that the verb "to touch" is a euphemism for sexual intercourse (so Hurd 1965: 158–61; Fee 1980b; Osiek and Balch 1997: 103; Schrage 1995: 59; R. Collins 1999: 258).[13] Scripture does not use a verb that means "to have sexual intercourse" but employs euphemistic language instead. This saying, as the Corinthians applied it, casts all sexual relations in a negative light, even sexual relations within marriage (Lietzmann 1949: 29; Héring 1962: 48; Hurd 1965: 165).

Some understand the verb "to touch" (ἅπτεσθαι, haptesthai) to relate to marriage: "It is good for a man not to marry a woman" (so NIV, TEV; Godet 1886: 321; Allo 1935: 153–54; Fascher 1929: 64; Grosheide 1953: 155; Morris 1958: 105; Caragounis 1996: 547). They contend that it refers in a general way to the relationship based on sexual intercourse. But this view assumes that 7:1b reflects Paul's own position. Whenever Paul talks of marriage in this chapter, however, he does not resort to metonymy but uses the verb "marry" (γαμέω, gameō; 7:9, 28, 36, 39) and consistently refers to married persons with the participial form of the verb (7:10, 33, 34). What immediately follows in 7:2–5 reveals that he is not discussing whether Christians should get married or not but whether married partners should attempt to abstain from sexual intercourse.

13. Cf. Gen. 20:6; Prov. 6:29; T. Reub. 3:15; T. Sol. 2:3; Ps.-Phoc. 179; Plato, *Leges* [*Laws*] 8.840a; Aristotle, *Politica* [*Politics*] 7.14.12; Josephus, *Ant.* 1.7.2 §163; 4.8.23 §257; Plutarch, *Alexander* 21.9; and Marcus Aurelius, *Meditations* 1.17.6.

Paul qualifies the previous statement in 7:1b. He does not reject it **7:2** outright, since he values celibacy, but instead points out how the Corinthian maxim is untenable for those who are married. The change in vocabulary from ἄνθρωπος (*anthrōpos,* man) to ἀνήρ (*anēr,* husband) indicates that he is talking specifically about the marriage relationship. He is not offering reasons why people should marry but arguments why sexual relations in marriage are binding on spouses and why sexual abstinence in marriage is both impractical and inappropriate.

The statement "but because of fornications" (διὰ δὲ τὰς πορνείας, *dia de tas porneias*) has caused many to heap reproaches upon Paul for what appears to be an embarrassingly jaundiced view of marriage.[14] Lietzmann (1949: 29) believes that Paul regarded marriage as a necessary evil due to the weakness of the flesh. Leenhardt (1946: 22) labeled it "lawful concubinage"; Phipps (1982: 129), "a venereal safety valve"; and D. Martin (1995: 209), a "prophylaxis against *porneia*" and "against Satanic testing" for those who are "weak." Bornkamm (1971: 208) deplores the lack of "any positive appreciation of the love between the sexes or of the richness of human experience in marriage and family"; and Conzelmann (1975: 116 n. 2) declares, "This definition of the aim of marriage is unfashionable, but realistic." Cartlidge (1975: 224) avers that it is "hardly a smashing blow in favor of marital bliss." I judge these remarks to be an unfair caricature of Paul's view of marriage. He is not arguing why marriage is advisable but why it is inadvisable for married partners to withdraw from conjugal relations.[15]

As he will do in chapter 8 when discussing idol food, Paul stresses the danger involved in their current practices. Eating in an idol temple may drive a fellow Christian who has a weak conscience back into the clutches of idolatry (8:10). Trying to be celibate in a marriage relationship is a recipe for sexual misadventures that may ultimately exclude them from the kingdom of God (5:11; cf. 6:12–20). In the previous two chapters, Paul has voiced his protest against sexual misconduct. It is

14. The JB rendering of this phrase is particularly misleading: "Now for the questions about which you wrote. Yes, it is a good thing for a man not to touch a woman, but *since sex is always a danger,* let each man have his own wife and each woman her own husband" (my italics).

15. Caragounis (1996: 550) interprets πορνεία to refer to lust (cf. Matt. 5:27–28). In Tob. 8:7, Tobit professes that he does not marry Sarah out of sexual lust (οὐ διὰ πορνείαν, *ou dia porneian*). Caragounis considers the thought expressed in 7:2 to be identical with that in 7:9, though expressed with different vocabulary. He asks, If Paul was talking about maintaining sexual relations in marriage and the danger that abstinence presents, why did he not use the word for the violation of the marriage relationship, μοιχεία (*moicheia*)? But the two times that Paul alludes to the OT command against adultery (Rom. 2:22, 13:9), he uses the verb (μοιχεύειν, *moicheuein*), not the noun.

not only "detrimental to the common good" (R. Collins 1999: 256), but also will cut them off from Christ.[16] Paul takes for granted that the only rightful place for sexual intercourse is within marriage and that those who marry are sexually active. For them to attempt precipitously to suppress awakened sexual desires will only expose them to a sexual undertow that will tug them into a sea of temptation, where they will ultimately drown.

"Let each one have his own wife or her own husband" does not advise everyone to marry. The verb "to have" is used in 7:12, 13, 29 to refer to the state of being married, but that meaning does not apply here (contra Weiss 1910: 171; Robertson and Plummer 1914: 133; Yarbrough 1985: 97; Caragounis 1996: 547–48; Oster 1995: 161). Otherwise, Paul would contradict himself in 7:8–9 when he asserts that celibacy is a workable ideal for those who feel no compulsion to marry (cf. 7:38). The danger he wants to preempt is immorality, and he is fully aware that simply urging people to get married will not solve the problem of sexual sins. Married persons can violate their marriage (6:9). The state of marriage alone is not enough to guard against outbreaks of immorality.[17]

The verb "to have" was also used as a euphemism for having sexual intercourse (see the LXX of Exod. 2:1–2; Deut. 28:30; Isa. 13:16; see also Matt. 14:4; Mark 6:18; 12:33; John 4:18). The immediate context, with the reminders about what is owed in marriage, the assertion that husbands and wives have authority over one another's bodies, and the command not to deprive one another, makes clear that the phrase "let each one have his own wife or her own husband" refers to sexual relations within marriage, not getting married. Paul later discusses marriage for those who are single (7:8–10, 25–40). Here, he enjoins couples to fulfill their marital obligations to one another to avoid any danger that partners with celibacy suddenly thrust upon them might seek to satisfy their sexual urges in illicit ways.[18]

The structure of 7:3–5, with three related imperatives, shows the interconnection between the three verses. In 7:2, Paul gives the basic command: Continue to have sexual relations with one another. In 7:3, he explains why they are to do so: Marriage brings sexual obligations for both partners. In 7:4, he explains that obligation further: Each part-

16. References to πορνεία (5:1; 6:13, 18) and the "body" (6:13, 15, 16, 18, 19, 20) and the repetition of the phrase "you were bought with a price" (6:20; 7:23) establish the contact with the previous discussion (see Laughery 1997: 118).

17. That some Jewish texts connect marriage with avoiding fornication (cf. Tob. 4:12; T. Levi 9:9–10) does not mean that they have any bearing on the situation Paul addresses. Paul's ethic is grounded in the biblical injunction that husbands find sexual enjoyment only with their wives (Prov. 5:15–23).

18. A secular version of this advice appears in Catallus (*Poems* 61.147–49): "You too, O bride, be sure not to refuse what your husband claims, lest he go elsewhere to find it."

ner has given authority over his or her body to the spouse.[19] In 7:5, he demands that they no longer deprive or defraud one another of their sexual rights within marriage. Paul's repeated emphasis on the marital sexual relationship leads to the conclusion that "some of the Corinthians had apparently become celibate at their spouse's expense" (Poirier and Frankovic 1996: 2). This view best explains why he insists in 7:5 that abstinence cannot be imposed on a spouse but must be a decision reached by mutual consent for the purpose of prayer and for a limited time.

Paul's first reaction to the maxim in 7:1b reveals that he is no misogamist and that he has a realistic appraisal of human beings as sexual creatures.[20] He recognizes that the sex drive is a powerful force that can pose a great danger if it is not properly harnessed. He does not give either a positive or a negative assessment of the sexual drive. His primary concern is that Christians channel it in proper, healthful ways that do not harm the individual, the individual's salvation, the marriage, or the community. Though Paul does not explicitly say so, he may be conscious that, as Hays (1997: 118) observes, "hyperspirituality can often lead, paradoxically, to a backlash of fleshly indulgence." N. Wright's (1986: 128) comment on Col. 2:20–23 is also apropos: "The old taboos put the wild animals of lust and hatred (see [Col.] 3:5, 8) into cages: there they remain, alive and dangerous, a constant threat to their captor." Paul's initial response to the Corinthian quotation in 7:1b rejects any attempted asceticism in marriage because it is dangerous.

Although Paul may seem to imply in this verse that the only value of conjugal love is that it averts fornication, we must remember that he is reacting to a particular context in which persons are attempting to become asexual. He is not writing a theology of marriage or of sexuality. Some Corinthians may think that by renouncing worldly pleasures they will be able to rise to new spiritual heights. Paul demurs. He sees them entering territory filled with snares and traps that will only lead to their moral downfall. Obviously, his comments can be misconstrued and used to reinforce a condescending and even disparaging evaluation of marriage. John Chrysostom (*De Virginitas* 10.3) claims, "Virginity stands as far above marriage as the heavens stand above the earth." Jerome (*Jov.*

---

19. As noted above, 7:3–4 form a chiasm:
    A the husband owes the wife
      B the wife owes the husband
      B′ the wife is not lord over her body
    A′ the husband is not lord over his body

20. Deming (1995b: 3–4) asserts that Paul's perspective on marriage in this chapter "has been essentially misunderstood almost since its composition." He argues, and I agree, that Paul "was not one of Christianity's first champions of sexual asceticism." Unfortunately, this chapter has been perceived as the source of the "emergent church's obsession with sexual control and renunciation" (L. Alexander 1998: 238).

1.40) asserts, "All those who have not remained virgins, following the pattern of the pure chastity of angels and that of our Lord Jesus Christ himself, are polluted." Augustine (*De bono conjugali* [*The Good of Marriage*] 8) maintains that marriage is not a good, but it is a good in comparison with fornication. Continence, he says, is an "angelic exercise."

Before assuming that Paul would agree with these assessments because he does not expand on how conjugal relations might enhance the marriage relationship as a means of expressing love, tenderness, and commitment, we must remember that these things are not at issue here. Rather than berating Paul for what he does not say about marriage, we must hear what he does say. He basically affirms that marriage is to be a fully sexual relationship and does not hint that this state of affairs is unfortunate or regrettable. He does not lament the physical aspect of marriage but instead encourages it. He emphasizes this facet of marriage not because he thinks that the spiritual aspects of marriage, such as the joy of companionship and creating a loving environment to nurture children, were less important but because some Corinthians were repudiating their sexuality.

7:3 The principle that spouses must render to each other that which is owed fits a general perception that marriage brings certain debts. What is striking is that Paul addresses the wife as directly as the husband, contrary to the usual pattern in the ancient world of addressing men and instructing women indirectly (Stagg and Stagg 1978: 170). The verb ἀποδιδότω (*apodidotō*, let him fulfill) is a third person imperative and places a requirement on the spouses: "the husband shall fulfill, . . . and likewise the wife." "What is due" (ἡ ὀφειλή, *hē opheilē*) is another euphemism for coitus (Lietzmann 1949: 29; Schrage 1995: 63–64). His understanding that marriage incurs sexual obligations may have been influenced by the interpretation of Exod. 21:10: "If he takes another wife to himself, he shall not diminish the food, clothing, or marital rights of the first wife" (NRSV). The rabbis interpreted "marital rights" (עֹנָתָהּ, ʿwnth) to include the right to sexual intercourse (*m. Ketub.* 5:8–9; *t. Qidd.* 3:7; *Mekilta de Rabbi Ishmael*, tractate *Nezikin* 3 on Exod. 21:10; *Targum Onqelos* on Exod. 21:11).[21] His assumption that each partner is under obligation to meet the other's needs excludes spiritual unions and any unilateral attempt for a spouse to exert his or her own preference for celibacy. One cannot decide to indulge one's own private, spiritual discipline and repudiate the rights of the one to whom one belongs.

21. The LXX translates it that the husband is not "to deprive" her of association (τὴν ὁμιλίαν αὐτῆς οὐκ ἀποστερήσει, *tēn homilian autēs ouk aposterēsei*). The word ὁμιλία is also used for sexual intercourse (LSJ 1222), and Paul uses the same verb "to deprive" (ἀποστερεῖν, *aposterein*) in 7:5 to refer to withholding sexual contact.

Paul recognizes that women have sexual needs and rights as well as men, but what is also striking about Paul's remarks about marital coitus, particularly when compared to those of Philo and Josephus, is what he omits. He makes no mention of procreation. Josephus (*Ag. Ap.* 2.25 §199) states, "The Law recognizes no sexual connexions, except the natural union of man and wife, and that only for procreation of children" (cf. *J.W.* 2.8.13 §§160–61). Philo (*Spec. Laws* 3.6 §36; 3.20 §113) sneers that when married partners have intercourse for pleasure instead of for procreation, they are like "pigs and goats." In T. Iss. 2:3, we find the assertion that God blessed Rachel with two sons: "For he perceived that she wanted to lie with Jacob for the sake of children and not merely for sexual gratification." By contrast, Paul apparently believes that sexual relations within marriage are justifiable as such. He does not ask the Stoics' question "Where are the new citizens of the kingdom of God to come from?" (contrast Epictetus, *Diatr.* 3.7.19–28).[22] He assumes that God ordained marriage to include sexual relations and that sexual relations in marriage were not solely intended for the procreation of the human species.

The assertion that neither the husband nor the wife is master (ἐξου-σιάζει, *exousiazei*) of his or her own body reinforces the previous verse and explains why husbands and wives must not withhold what is due physically to their partners.[23] It assumes that they have given themselves over to each other in their marriage commitment.[24] Paul does not frame this relationship in terms of the husband's rights and the wife's duties, nor does he expect the wife to submit passively as a compliant bed partner.[25] She is an equal partner because she possesses her husband's body in the same way. Both husband and wife are to recognize that their spouse has a greater claim on them than they

7:4

22. Clement of Alexandria (*Stromata* [*Miscellanies*] 3.18.107.5) mistakenly interprets the duty in this verse to be procreation (cf. 2.163.8–12; 15.96.2; 15.97.1; 2.240.14–18, 21–24).

23. Some read more into this statement and contend that the problem was caused by wives choosing to become celibate and claiming that they have authority over their own bodies. Since it would have been unnecessary for husbands to make such a claim in this culture, they infer that Paul aims his remarks at wives: they do not have authority over their own bodies (Wire 1990: 82–83; Laughery 1997: 120–21; R. Horsley 1998: 97). This mirror-reading of the text is unwarranted and driven primarily by the thesis that the problems at Corinth stem from women prophets.

24. The passive form of the verb ἐξουσιασθήσομαι (*exousiasthēsomai*) appears in 6:12 to mean "mastered by," and ἔχειν ἐξουσίαν (*echein exousian*) appears in 7:37 and 11:10 to mean "exercise control over." The body (σῶμα, *sōma*) does not refer simply to the physical body here but to their whole physical-spiritual existence.

25. Epictetus (*Enchiridion* 40) claims that when young women soon discover that they have nothing else to do but be the bedfellows of men, they begin to concentrate on beautifying themselves and put all their hopes in that (see also *b. Ned.* 20a; *b. ʿErub.* 100a). Paul does not regard the wife's role in this light.

have on themselves.[26] Neither can claim to have authority over his or her own body and disavow further sexual relationship with the marriage partner.

Although Paul's assertions may resonate with Stoic traditions, his view is grounded in a thoroughly Christian perspective (see Schrage 1976: 230–31; Bruns 1982: 190). Love is to control all of the Christian's relationships. It does not insist on its own way (13:5), does not seek its own advantage (10:33), and always seeks to please others (7:33–34; 10:33). Caragounis (1996: 552 n. 30) correctly cautions that Paul's response is based on the Christian faith, not the legal requirements of marriage. One can extrapolate from this that Paul believes that love should govern the marriage relationship and that spouses should not treat one another as objects for sexual self-gratification. In marriage, one gives up complete self-determination and must seek to please the partner. The sexual relationship in particular requires mutual sensitivity, loyalty, care, and tenderness. Baumert (1996: 37–38) notes that Paul's statements presuppose that marriage should be free from egoism: "Marital 'surrender'" means that one "looks away from him/herself toward the other—entrusts him or herself to the other—in confidence that the other will not exploit this." It is rooted in a desire to "'belong' to their partner" (cf. Song 2:16; 6:3; 7:10).

7:5 The verb translated "deprive" (ἀποστερεῖτε, *apostereite*) also can mean "rob," "steal," "defraud" (cf. 6:7–8; Mal. 3:5; Sir. 4:1; 34:21–22; Mark 10:19; 1 Tim. 6:5) and likens abandoning conjugal relations to reneging on a debt. The force of the present imperative is generally "to *command the action as an ongoing process*" (Wallace 1996: 485, italics in original) and may imply that some are refusing sex with their spouses, and Paul commands them to stop (so Fee 1987: 274, 281; cf. Robertson 1934: 851–53).

Because abstinence is not to be the norm in marriage, Paul allows only a temporary withdrawal from sexual intercourse. The phrase πρὸς καιρόν (*pros kairon*) can imply "for a season" (cf. Luke 8:13; 1 Thess. 2:17) but may not have any time span in view and could mean "according to the situation" (Baumert 1984: 27–28). The point is that any contemplated withdrawal from sexual relations in marriage is not to be permanent. The subjunctive καὶ πάλιν ἐπὶ τὸ αὐτὸ ἦτε (*kai palin epi to auto ēte*) has the force of an imperative: "Then be together again" (BDF §98; R. Collins 1999: 260). They are not to think that they could or should go on indefinitely. They are still subject to temptation.

---

26. A similar idea is espoused by Musonius Rufus in describing how mutual love must govern the marriage relationship: "But where each looks only to his own interests and neglects the other, or, what is worse, when one is so minded and lives in the same house but fixes his attention elsewhere and is not willing to pull together with his yoke-mate nor to agree, then the union is doomed to disaster" (Lutz 1947: 88).

In Judaism, the husband had the right to absent himself from his wife for prayer or study (Jub. 1:8; *m. Yoma* 8:1) and needed only to inform the wife of his decision (for the rabbinic debate about the permissible length of withdrawal, see *m. Ketub.* 5:6; *t. Ketub.* 5:6). Paul insists that any withdrawal may occur only after husband and wife arrive at a mutual decision. Wives are not subject to a husband's vow. One spouse may not selfishly disregard the other's physical needs, no matter how lofty the goal may be. This directive defies conventions of the ancient world. Veyne (1987: 39) contends, "Lords, heads of households, settled things among themselves, dealing with each other as sovereign to sovereign. If one of them had to make an important decision, he convoked a 'council' of friends rather than discuss the matter with his wife." Paul does not regard the husband to be the lord of his wife and sovereign over their relationship.

The justification for temporary abstinence is to devote time to prayer, and Paul assumes that both partners are praying. He does not expand on why such temporary abstinence might be advisable for prayer. Perhaps he thinks that it might prevent distractions. The verb σχολάζειν (*scholazein*) is used by Philo (*Spec. Laws* 3.1 §1) to refer to his former "leisure for philosophy and contemplation of the universe" (*Spec. Laws* 1.14 §70; *Mos.* 2.39 §211). Ignatius uses the verb for diligence in unceasing prayer (Ign. *Pol.* 1:3) or for giving time to God (Ign. *Pol.* 7:3).[27]

This advice may reflect the continuing pull that Paul's Jewish tradition had on him. It enjoined abstinence during special holy days (*m. Yoma* 8:1; Joel 2:16) and to prepare for special missions (Exod. 19:15; Lev. 15:18; 1 Sam. 21:4–6; 2 Sam. 11:11–13). Poirier and Frankovic (1996) think that Paul believed that even routine prayer required withdrawal for ritual purity reasons. Prayers must be offered by supplicants who are in a pure state—a widely held Jewish view that is reflected in T. Naph. 8:8: "There is a time for having intercourse with one's wife and a time to abstain for the purpose of prayer." This view hardly commends itself, since it conflicts with the condition that Paul stipulates. They can withdraw from one another only by mutual consent. If one spouse refuses—which Paul implies he or she has a right to do—that would mean that the other spouse could not pray, since he or she would be ritually impure. That cannot be Paul's intention. Others contend that Paul is thinking of abstinence to pursue "inspiration and empowerment by the Holy Spirit" (Gundry Volf 1996: 531; see also

---

27. Deming (1995b: 112–13) thinks that the choice of the word σχολάζειν echoes Cynic traditions that objected to sexual relations because they occupied leisure time that could otherwise be devoted to philosophical studies. Paul applies it to having leisure for prayer.

1994a). Such practice was widespread in the ancient world to prepare oneself to be approachable by the divine.[28]

Both views take us far from the text. Paul does not say that sexual contact makes one impure or that it impedes spiritual activity (Schrage 1995: 68). He does not give an implied command: "In order to devote oneself to prayer, one *must* abstain from sexual intercourse" (contra Yarbrough 1985: 100). He expects married couples to maintain normal sexual relations while also expecting Christians to "pray without ceasing" (1 Thess. 5:17; cf. Rom. 12:12; Col. 4:2). Prayer and married sexual relations are not mutually exclusive, just as prayer and eating are not mutually exclusive. For various reasons, one may decide to be abstinent during a time of devoted prayer, just as one may decide to fast during a time of prayer. But neither abstinence nor fasting is a requirement for prayer. Just as occasional fasting does not denigrate eating, occasional abstinence does not denigrate sexuality. If Paul were to give any hint that the sexual relations somehow impair one's spirituality or diminish one's ability to pray, he would only play into the hands of those who may have exalted celibacy as "good" or as a means of reaching a higher spiritual plane. They could counter, "If Paul thinks that abstinence might be advantageous for such short-term spiritual inspiration, why would a permanent renunciation of coitus not optimize a deeper walk with God?" He recognizes instead that times arise when one is so overwhelmed by spiritual concern that retreat in prayer is expedient. He would surely agree with 1 Pet. 3:7 that one's prayers are hindered by mistreatment of a spouse, not by sexual activity with a spouse (cf. *m. Ber.* 2:5). The spiritual life does not cut a person off from the natural order of creation, and religious devotion is not to become a pretext for withholding sex from one's spouse.

Paul buttresses his directive that their separation is to be short-lived with a warning about Satan. The sexual drive is a powerful force, and Satan is a powerful adversary. Attempts at celibacy may cause them to fall victim to the law of unintended consequences. Abstinence may not bring them closer to God, as they intend, but may instead make them more vulnerable to Satan. Satan was believed to inflame people to commit immorality (see references to Belial/Beliar in CD 4:15–17; T. Reub. 6:3; Mart. Isa. 2:4–5). They are not free from sexuality, since God has not called them out of their somatic existence (6:17–20), nor are they free from sexual temptation. The reference to a lack of self-restraint (ἀκρασία, *akrasia*; the opposite of ἐγκράτεια, *enkrateia*; 7:9; cf. 9:25; Gal. 5:23) does not imply that the Corinthians are prone to self-indulgence any more than the reference to "fornications" in 7:2 implies that

---

28. See Ovid, *Fasti* 4.649–66; Pausanius, *Descr.* 2.24; Philo, *Mos.* 2.14 §§68–69; *Cont. Life* 2 §12; 8 §68; Plutarch, *Mor.* 438A–D; *De Iside et Osiride* 2.351F–352A; Apuleius, *Metam.* 11.19–21.

they were guilty of that sin. The noun ἀκρασία refers to the unrestrained sexual impulse (Grundmann, *TDNT* 2:342), and Paul worries that abstinence will make them particularly susceptible to sexual temptation.[29] Satan may ensnare them at a weak moment, when they lack self-control (Snyder 1992: 94).[30] They are most vulnerable if they think that they can achieve self-mastery by dint of their own willpower.

Additional Notes

7:1. Sexual asceticism was in the air during this period (R. Collins 1999: 253; L. Alexander 1998: 235). Hays (1997: 114) observes, "Sexual abstinence was widely viewed as a means to personal wholeness and religious power." Some Corinthians apparently regarded sexual asceticism to be a good and had the example of Paul, who had renounced marriage to be free for the service of the gospel. Their motivation, however, was quite different from Paul's, as he seeks to elucidate. What caused them to vaunt sexual asceticism as a good is unclear. Several options have been proposed to explain its emergence in the community:

Repudiation of the licentiousness of the culture. As those taught by the Spirit, the Corinthian Christians may have wanted to distance themselves from the vulgar expressions of sexuality in their culture and overreacted against the debauchery that beset urban environments such as Corinth by completely renouncing sexual relations (Godet 1885: 317; cf. Meeks 1983: 102).

Gnostic dualism. Many attribute the ascetic sentiments within the community to a gnostic worldview (Conzelmann 1975: 115; Schrage 1976: 217–20). A dualistic view of body and spirit may have persuaded them to conclude, "Since we are filled with the Spirit, we must accordingly abandon the things of the flesh and give up sex—including marital sex—the most obvious manifestation of the fleshly lower nature. Those who indulge their sexual urges are still fleshly (σαρκικοί) and pollute their spiritual nature." If the Corinthians had any awareness of Jesus' sayings like those found in Matt. 19:12, "Some make themselves eunuchs because of the kingdom of heaven," or Luke 20:34–36, "The sons of this age marry and are given in marriage; but those who are accounted worthy to attain that age and the resurrection from the dead neither marry nor are given in marriage," and filtered them through a world-denying hermeneutic, it may have fueled their glorification of celibacy.

Many trace a trajectory of hostility toward sexuality in later Christian writers back to the Corinthian Christians and assume that the same motivations were at work. In almost every incident in the Acts of Paul and Thecla, for example, sexual continence is hailed as the highest virtue and the center of Paul's proclamation. Paul is portrayed as pronouncing a series of beatitudes on those who "have kept their flesh pure," who are "continent," who "have wives as if they had

---

29. Theissen (1987: 172) is convinced that the temptations of Satan are "sexual fantasies that prevent concentration in prayer." Paul, however, is not simply concerned about potential interruptions of a prayerful mood, but *porneia* (7:2). Baumert (1996: 44) correctly cautions against interpreting this verse as if every sexual arousal were a temptation of Satan.

30. Baumert (1996: 43 n. 72) claims that ἀκρασία comes from κρᾶσις (*krasis,* mixing), which alludes to sexual relations. It does not imply that they are afflicted with a moral weakness, an inability to be abstinent, but that they have been practicing abstinence and become more exposed to sexual enticements. It is not that Paul thinks that they are incapable of longer abstinence; he simply does not think it wise. Cf., however, Lightfoot's comments (1895: 222–23) on the confusion between the two words.

them not," and on "the bodies of the virgins" (Acts of Paul 3.5, 6). In other apocryphal Acts, the driving aspiration of the apostles seems to be to induce people, including husbands and wives, to abstain from coitus (see Acts of Peter 33–34; Acts of Thomas 12, 14, 43, 88; 124; Acts of John 113). According to Irenaeus (*Adversus haereses* [*Against Heresies*] 1.24.2), Saturnilus taught that marriage and procreation were of Satan. Even in countering gnostic viewpoints, Tertullian (*Marc.* 1.29) argues, "We do not reject marriage, but simply refrain from it. Nor do we demand chastity, but advise it. . . ; at the same time earnestly vindicating marriage whenever hostile attacks are made against it as a polluted thing, to the disparagement of the Creator." Despite the chronological gap between Paul and these later sources, some assume that the Corinthians' attitudes toward sexuality were rooted in the same theological soil. They may have deemed their voluntary acceptance of celibacy as placing themselves at least one notch above other mortals and perhaps just below, if not equal to, the angels.

The inheritance from Judaism. Rosner (1994: 153–58) argues that Paul's own asceticism derived from his scriptural inheritance in Judaism. Some argue that this same Jewish heritage (cf. Rev. 14:4) fed their ascetic enthusiasm (for the discussion of the biblical roots of asceticism and its influence on Jewish sectarian movements, see Lindars 1984; P. Davies 1995). Philo's description of the spiritual preparation of Moses to receive oracles from God implies that asceticism was a necessary component for receiving communication from God. Moses is said first to have cleansed himself of all "the calls of mortal nature, food and drink and intercourse with women. This last he has disdained for many a day, almost from the time when, possessed by the spirit, he entered on his work as prophet, since he thought it fitting to hold himself always in readiness to receive the oracular messages" (*Mos.* 2.14 §§68–69).

Devotion to Sophia. R. Horsley (1979) draws heavily on Philo to claim that the Corinthians renounced physical marriage because they had a dualistic understanding of body and soul, aspired to ecstatic experiences, and touted spiritual marriage to divine Wisdom, Sophia.

The debate between Cynics and Stoics. Deming (1995b) thinks that Paul's discussion best fits the dynamics of the Hellenistic debate between Cynics and Stoics. The Cynics thought that marriage distracted one from pursuing philosophy with complete dedication to attain self-sufficiency, virtue, and well-being. Sexual relations took up leisure time that could be devoted to philosophical study (see Epictetus, *Diatr.* 3.22.69–72). The Stoics adopted a mediating position and emphasized that marriage was a civic duty to procreate and provide citizens for the city. They also emphasized the need to fulfill one's duties to a spouse but allowed exceptions for some in special circumstances to forgo marriage to concentrate on philosophy. Deming maintains that the Corinthians were disposed to the Cynic position, while Paul countered it with his Judeo-Christian abhorrence of fornication and with popularized Stoic notions. Deming (1995b: 49) contends that Paul drew "on a reservoir of ideas about marriage and celibacy that is neither ascetic, nor Judeo-Christian in origin, nor confluent with much of the later church's thinking, but one in which the basic anxieties of Greek culture in the Hellenistic age lay restlessly submerged" (see also L. Alexander 1998: 240–41).

Over-realized eschatology. Some attribute the catalyst for the Corinthians' sexual asceticism to the community's peculiar "over-realized eschatology" (Thiselton 1977–78). The Corinthians emphasized "the already" and underplayed "the not yet" and believed that as Christians they were already experiencing a postresurrection existence, when marriage would cease (cf. Mark 12:24–25; Luke 20:34–36; 17:26–27). Marriage belongs to this age, which is passing away, and sexual abstinence was regarded by some as a way to step out of this world and to step up to God. Not only were they speaking in the tongues of angels (13:1), but also, by renouncing marriage and conjugal relations, they were living like angels (Cartlidge 1975: 227–30). Bartchy (1973: 132) argues, "From a theological perspective, they must have claimed that their sexual freedom and their freedom from sexuality, as well as their public prophecies and their ecstatic gifts, were all signs and confirmations that they had already been called by God to an exalted and perfected existence" (see also Roetzel 1998: 144–45, 149). Paul tries to reel in these exalted Christians from the spiritual stratosphere and reacquaint them with realities of earth.

Divine men. Others attribute the impetus to renounce sexual relations to an aspiration to become "divine men" (θεῖοι ἄνδρες), perfect and wise, and to imitate the asceticism of Moses, who, according to Philo (*Mos.* 2.13 §§66–70), prepared himself to receive visions and revelations by abstaining from sexual intercourse (Balch 1971–72: 358–61; see also Bartchy 1973: 145–48).

Eschatological women. Some contend that the women were more likely to abstain from sexual intercourse so that they would be more open to the Spirit (so Beardslee 1994: 660). Scroggs (1972) first coined the phrase "eschatological women" and attributed the impetus for sexual asceticism to this "group of Christian extremists." Wire (1990) tries to make the case that some women in the church found welcome relief in being freed from having to marry, bearing an unlimited number of children, and living a life restricted to the household. Impelled by the image of the androgynous, they had taken up roles as prophets in the community and were relieved to discover a religious legitimation for suspending all sexual activity. M. MacDonald (1990b: 166) identifies them as pneumatic Corinthian women who were getting out of hand in the worship services (11:2–16). They had transcended the material world and had reached a sexless state symbolized by their removal of the veils and their abstention from sex.

Corinthian pneumatism. Gundry Volf (1996: 540) attributes the asceticism to Corinthian pneumatism. Gundry Volf claims that they viewed sexual union as sin because the body was to be consecrated to the Lord. The new creation excluded both marriage and sexual union. They were also influenced by realized eschatology and the declaration that in Christ there is neither male nor female, which connects this issue to 11:2–16 (as suggested by Wire and M. MacDonald). Moffatt (1938: 97), an early proponent of such a view, claims that their "ascetic zeal so exalted them that, defying the ordinary impulses and passions of sex, they sought to show worldly Christians what marriage ought to be—a common devotion to the Lord and yet an avoidance of intercourse, a union of two spirits, in fact, not of two bodies."

The Corinthians' cultural heritage. Oster (1992: 60–64; cf. R. Collins 1999: 253) looks to the cultural heritage of the Corinthian converts and cites the cult of Isis and other Egyptian cults prominent in Corinth, with their demands for sacral celibacy, as a possible matrix for their sexual asceticism. Apuleius (*Metam.* 11) and Plutarch (*De Iside et Osiride* 2.351Γ–352A), both devotees of the goddess Isis, describe the strict regimen of sexual abstinence that the cult required. Oster (1992: 64) claims that it is "the type of religious behavior that is transferred so easily from one religion to another."

Debates among physicians. A possible influence on the Corinthian ascetics that has been largely ignored by interpreters is the debate among ancient physicians about the healthiness of sexual relations. Soranus (*Gynecology* 1.7.32) concludes, "Permanent virginity is healthful, in males and females alike" (Temkin 1956) and contends that the emission of seed weakens both the man and the female (1.7.30) and that virginity safeguards women from the injuries caused by childbirth. Galen also thought that sexual intercourse drained away the vital spirit (Osiek and Balch 1997: 107).

Cataclysmic external circumstances. Winter (1989) musters evidence that Corinth was plagued by famine during this time. He argues that the phrase "because of this distress" in 7:26 refers to that calamity. He postulates that the Corinthians asked Paul whether it was wise to abstain from sex for the purpose of birth control and whether betrothed couples should follow through with marriage.

Since we must largely rely on guesswork via mirror-reading to identify their motivations, and since the cultural landscape of Corinth permits a mélange of influences, we must allow for a variety of factors that could have influenced their decision. Many of these views are not mutually exclusive. No one view completely explains the Corinthians' motivation. Many interpreters jump to theological conclusions about the causes and neglect the medical, cultural, and even physical circumstances that may have bred the situation. Narrowing it down to one cause or another presumes that we know more than we do. I choose to be vague about identifying the specific impulse that led to the Corinthians' attitude toward sexuality.

7:3. The Majority text and later Syriac versions have ὀφειλομένην εὔνοιαν (benevolence [or affection, kindness] that is due) instead of ὀφειλήν (duty). This reading is probably attributable to a scribe whose ascetical bent, recoiling at the implication that sexual relations in marriage were a duty, caused him to adjust the marital obligation to require only kindness. This is far more likely than Herz's (1895–96) conjecture that εὔνοια is original as a transliteration of the Hebrew עונה found in Exod. 21:11.

7:5. The omission of τῇ νηστείᾳ (fasting) is attested by the earliest and most reliable witnesses (𝔓[11vid, 46], ℵ*, A, B, C, D, G, P, Ψ, 33, 81, 104, 1739, it, vg, cop[sa, bo, fay], arm, eth). It has weak manuscript support and probably was added by later scribes because fasting was an interest of the early church (Acts 13:2; 14:23). It has been added to a reference to "prayer" in Mark 9:29 and Acts 10:30.

7:5. Συνέρχησθε (συνέρχεσθε) is read in 𝔓[46], Ψ, Byz, lat, syr instead of ἦτε. Again, it may be attributable to an ascetical inclination that sought to weaken the sexual connotations of "be together" with the idea that the couple is simply to reunite after prayer.

B. Celibacy or Marriage for the Unmarried and Widows (7:6–9)

Treating 7:6–9 as a separate unit distinct from 7:1–5 and 10–16 goes against the grain of the majority of commentaries and the printed texts but makes the best sense of the context. In each unit in this chapter after 7:1–5, Paul begins with an assertion of his authority before addressing the particular topic (cf. 7:8, 10, 12, 17, 25). In this unit, Paul backpedals a bit and cautiously agrees with the Corinthians' preference for celibacy for the unmarried, but he disagrees with any effort to coerce others to conform to what one may regard as ideal. Celibacy is good, but it is not for everyone. Celibacy is good only for those who have received this gift from God. It is not created by vows, though it might be anchored by them (Giblin 1969: 2854). Those with sexual longings would do better to marry and need not sentence themselves to unnecessary torment.

One can get the impression that Paul thinks that marriage is only a second-best choice for the "burners." That is not his intention. The issue is not what is the highest "good" but what is good for each individual Christian as he or she understands his or her endowment and calling by God. His handling of the Corinthian enthusiasm for sexual abstinence is similar to the way he will handle their enthusiasm for speaking in tongues (Bartchy 1973: 149–50; Deming 1995b: 128). In his attempt to dampen the Corinthians' enthusiasm for ecstatic speech, he diplomatically agrees with them about its value. He understands it to be a divine gift (12:10, 28; 14:1, 12) and gives thanks to God that he speaks in tongues more than all of them (14:19).[1] He says, "I wish [θέλω, thelō] that all of you spoke in tongues" (14:5), but qualifies that wish. Tongues do not benefit everyone. To some it is only a meaningless noise (14:9), and it builds up the individual rather than the church (14:4, 16). In his attempt to dampen the Corinthians' enthusiasm for celibacy, he reminds them that he is celibate. He wishes (θέλω) that all could be celibate like him but qualifies that wish. Celibacy does not benefit everyone. For some, it would only sentence them "to burn" and can lead to forni-

---

1. If any Christian in Corinth believed that one had to become celibate to receive or to facilitate spiritual gifts, Paul turns it around: one first needed the grace-gift to live the celibate life.

cation (7:2, 5, 9). Celibacy is a gift from God; but, like any grace-gift, it does not ennoble the one blessed with it. Marriage remains the best choice for those who do not have the gift of celibacy.

Exegesis and Exposition

[6] But I say this by way of ⌜agreement⌝, not as a command. [7]⌜For⌝ I wish that all were like me, but each one has his or her own grace-gift from God. One has this manner of gift, another has that. [8]But I say to the unmarried and the widows that it is good for them if they remain as I am. [9]But if they are not exercising self-control, let them marry, for it is better to marry than to burn.

7:6   Paul does not express himself as clearly as one could wish with the phrase τοῦτο δὲ λέγω (*touto de legō*). Does the demonstrative pronoun τοῦτο refer back to something he has just said or ahead to what he is about to say? What is its antecedent? What is the meaning of συγγνώμη (*syngnōmē*), usually translated "concession" (NIV, NRSV, NASB)? Most commentators understand the "this" to refer back to something that Paul wrote in 7:1–5, but they disagree on what the concession might be.

Some, who assume that 7:1b expresses Paul's own views on sexuality, understand the "this" to refer back to his statement in 7:2 (Godet 1885: 325–26; Findlay 1910: 824; Mare 1976: 229). This view contends that Paul wants to clarify that he does not command marriage but only recommends it as a concession to human sexuality. Marriage is less desirable than celibacy but better than fornication for those who lack the grace-gift of celibacy.

I have already rejected this interpretation of 7:1b and have made the case that 7:2–5 has nothing to do with the need for some to get married so that they can channel their sexuality properly within marriage. Instead, Paul gives directions to those who are already married and considering or already practicing abstinence. He reminds these couples that they are obligated by their marriage bond to maintain their sexual relationship with each other. This interpretation of 7:2–5 also rules out the possibility that the so-called concession could refer to their resumption of sexual life together after an interval of prayer.

Others understand the "this" to refer to Paul's whole response in 7:2–5 (Edwards 1885: 161; Robertson and Plummer 1914: 135; Lietzmann 1949: 30; Héring 1962: 50; Conzelmann 1975: 207; Snyder 1992: 95). But these verses contain specific commands: each husband (wife) *must* have his own wife (her own husband) (7:2); the husband/wife *must* fulfill his/her sexual obligation to the other partner (7:3); they *must* not deprive each other (7:5a). Instructing them to "be together again so that Satan might not tempt you" (7:5c) is an implicit command. In stating that he is not issuing a command but offering a concession, Paul may be backing off on a sensitive, private matter between husband and wife and trying to cushion these imperatives by saying that they are not really binding. If that were the case, however, the problem that provoked his response would remain unchanged.[2] The singular demonstrative pronoun also should refer to "a single phenomenon" (Winter 1997a: 63) and does not fit the plurality of commands (cf. the plural ταῦτα [tauta], which appears in 4:14; 9:8, 15).

Since Paul explicitly says that the "this" does not refer to something that he is commanding them, the only preceding statement that could qualify as a "concession" is his approval for a married couple not to cohabit for a period of prayer (7:5b; so Barrett 1968: 157–58; Fee 1980b: 312; 1987: 283–84; Rosner 1994: 151; R. Horsley 1998: 98). If this is the concession, he explains further that he does not require them to separate during times of prayer but only consents to it if the couple decide together that it is appropriate. But why would Paul label his permission to withdraw from sexual relations for prayer as a "concession"? Does he not allow for a couple to experience cycles of quiescence in their sexual relationship otherwise?

Since it is so difficult to identify what the concession might be in 7:1–5, a few interpreters propose that τοῦτο has a forward reference and prepares for what Paul says in 7:7–9 (Orr 1967: 12; Baumert 1984: 48–51; 1996: 46; Dungan 1971: 87; Oster 1995: 164; Winter 1997a). Unlike 7:2–5, what follows in 7:7–8 does not contain a command and could easily qualify as a concession or an agreement that meets them halfway. The τοῦτο refers to what follows in 7:26–27, which has parallel vocabulary, ἐπιταγή (epitagē, command), γνώμη (gnōmē, maxim), and καλόν (kalon, good); but it is followed by a ὅτι (hoti) clause that is absent in 7:6–7. Winter (1997a: 58) shows, however, that the neuter demonstrative pronoun, when used with verbs of saying, as in 7:6, refers to the subordinate clause introduced by an implied "that" (ὅτι), as in 7:7a.[3] Winter (1997a: 60–61) concludes, "In 7:6, it is therefore grammatically possible that the verb 'I am saying' introduces an objective clause in the following verse, and the forward place of the neuter demonstrative pronoun in the sentence is meant to give special emphasis to what is to be said."[4] The forward placement of the demonstrative pronoun sets up and adds emphasis to the statement in

2. Paul uses the same phrase, "I do not say [this] as a command" (οὐ κατ᾽ ἐπιταγὴν λέγω, ou kat' epitagēn legō), in 2 Cor. 8:8 to soften his exhortations about their contribution to the collection for the saints.

3. The neuter demonstrative τοῦτο is used as preparation for a subordinate clause in the following places: Rom. 2:3; 6:6; 13:11; 1 Cor. 1:12; 7:26, 29, 35; 15:50; 2 Cor. 5:14; 9:6; 10:7, 11; Gal. 3:17; Eph. 4:17; 5:5; Phil. 1:7, 9, 28; Col. 2:4; 1 Thess. 4:15; 2 Thess. 3:10; 1 Tim. 1:9; 2 Tim 1:5; 3:1. See BDF §290(3).

4. Schrage (1995: 71 n. 112) claims that this does not apply because in 1:12 and 7:26 the ὅτι is explicit.

7:7: "I wish that all were like me."[5] Interpreting τοῦτο as having a forward reference would mean that Paul introduces each new topic in this chapter with a verb of saying, commanding, or thinking (7:6, 8, 10, 12, 25–26).[6]

The problem with this view (vigorously rejected by Fee 1987: 283) is that in 7:35 the demonstrative pronoun in the clause "I am saying this for your very own benefit" refers to what he has said in the previous verses. It would also mean that Paul starts the new topic in 7:6 rather awkwardly, repeating λέγω (*lego*, I say) twice in verses 6 and 8 to introduce the new instructions. But when Paul interjects his own wish in 7:7 that all could be like him, he interrupts his introduction of the instructions to the unmarried and widows. Therefore, he needs to repeat the verb in 7:8.

Taking the "this" to refer to what follows makes the best sense of the word συγγνώμη (*syngnōmē*). It occurs only here in the NT and is used in secular Greek to mean "fellow-feeling," "allowance," "lenient judgment," "agreement," "forbearance," or "pardon" (LSJ 1660; Bultmann, *TDNT* 1:716). In this context, it refers to Paul's *limited agreement* with the Corinthian slogan, quoted in 7:1b, that it is good not to touch a woman. He is celibate, and he thinks it "good" if those who are unmarried remain as he is (7:8). He wants to avoid any misunderstanding that might feed an immoderate zeal for celibacy and confides that this opinion is not a command, direct or implied, by asserting that it is only a "wish." He is not bidding them to become celibate by canceling his wish with a command that those who are not able to control their sexual impulses should marry. He does not consider sexual attraction a sin. But suppressed passion to attain some misguided spiritual aspiration will inevitably lead to *porneia* and endanger the purity of the community.

The question that Paul addresses in the opening section of this chapter is whether it is good to abstain from sexual intercourse. The Corinthians assert that it is and understand "good" to be the highest virtue. Paul counters in 7:2–5 that it is absolutely not good for married couples to attempt to do so, and he vetoes any bid by the Corinthians to become celibate within marriage. On the other hand, he does agree with them to a point. He himself is celibate, quite content with this state, and able to devote himself fully to his calling in the Lord without having to worry about providing for a family. He could wish that everyone were like him, but he is wise enough not to make his own inclination the standard by which everyone else is to be compared. Whether one chooses celibacy depends entirely on how a

---

5. If the textual variant γάρ (*gar*, for) is to be counted as the original reading in 7:7, then 7:6 would refer forward to verse 7.

6. The introduction of a new topic with τοῦτο would parallel 11:17.

person has been endowed by God. He knows that implementing his wish is unrealistic and undesirable because God has gifted human beings differently. Paul does not want to force anyone into celibacy or marriage.

By saying that what follows is not a command, he takes for granted that he has authority over them as their apostle to issue commands from the Lord (7:12, 25; 14:37; cf. Philem. 8) and to clarify biblical mandates. His own example is also authoritative, and he presents his lifestyle as a model for his churches to emulate (1 Cor. 4:6; 9:24–27; 11:1; 1 Thess. 1:6; 2 Thess. 3:7–9). But his celibacy is not to be taken as a model of Christian living.

The statement "I wish that all were like me" acknowledges that all are **7:7** not like him. Paul does not mean to imply that they have somehow failed to reach his level of spiritual commitment. The issue is not about how God has gifted Paul but how God has gifted them (cf. Matt. 19:11).[7] In chapter 12, he coaxes them to see that individuals should not extol their own grace-gifts and discount others' differing gifts. His statement assumes that every Christian has a gift from God, varied as the gifts might be ("one has this manner; another has that manner," ὁ μὲν οὕτως, ὁ δὲ οὕτως, ho men houtōs, ho de houtōs), and implies that celibacy is to be included in the list of grace-gifts from God (χάρισμα ἐκ θεοῦ, charisma ek theou).[8] It is difficult to decide whether or not Paul would include marriage as a charism. Since it is a normal expression for humans, who have been created by God as sexual creatures, it probably should not be regarded as one.

Understanding celibacy as a grace-gift has three implications. First, celibate existence is not a matter of personal preference, nor is it a meritorious feat of self-mastery for which one can take credit. It comes from "the unattainable grace of God" (Schrage 1995: 72). This idea directly contrasts with Philo's view (*Spec. Laws* 1.29 §149) that "the opposite of desire [ἐπιθυμία, epithymia] is continence [ἐγκράτεια, enkrateia], the acquisition of which is a task to be practised and pressed forward by every possible means as the greatest and most perfect of blessings promoting personal and public welfare alike" (see also *Spec.*

7. Calvin (1960: 141) assumes that Paul is interpreting the words of Jesus in Matt. 19:11 here; and since he cites the Lord's command about divorce in 7:12, this inference may be correct.

8. Poirier and Frankovic (1996: 16–17) challenge the view that Paul's gift was celibacy and argue instead that his gift was prophecy and his celibacy was necessitated by his prophetic office as he regularly encountered God's presence. They contend, "Like Moses, Paul wished that all would prophesy" (Num. 11:29; 1 Cor. 14:5), but not all are prophets. The problem with this view is that Paul makes no mention of prophecy or receiving oracles or revelations in this text. Instead, he speaks of sexual urges ("to burn," πυροῦσθαι, pyrousthai) and being able to exercise control over them (ἐγκρατεύονται, enkrateuontai). He attributes that control to God's grace.

Laws 2.32 §195).[9] Paul converts ἐγκράτεια from a virtue, as promoted by moral philosophers, to a charisma bestowed by God (see Conzelmann 1975: 120). The power to control oneself comes from God, not from oneself (so also Wis. 8:21).[10]

Second, Schrage (1995: 73) points out that Paul understood gifts to be given by God for building up the body of Christ. In this case, he believes that the one who is single may be able to give more ardent service to Christ (7:34). If remaining single is driven by selfish concerns—for example, to use it as a yardstick to measure one's imagined spiritual status or to gain independence from any obligations to a spouse—it no longer can be regarded as a gift.

Third, Paul sets the example for those who may be blessed with a particular gift not to expect everyone else also to show evidence of it. His gift of celibacy is not determinative for others who have differing gifts (P. W. Gooch 1983: 62, 66). He does not want them trapped in a vow that goes against their nature and that they cannot fulfill. Whether celibacy is advisable for those who are now unmarried depends on how they honestly answer this question: How has God formed their nature?

7:8 After interjecting his own personal wish in 7:7, Paul now offers his new instructions, "but I say." He concurs with the Corinthians' high appraisal of celibacy, expressed in the maxim quoted in 7:1b, but offers a caveat that subverts it. He thinks it is good (καλόν) for the unmarried and the widows to remain as he is, unmarried and celibate (see additional note). The key distinctions between the Corinthians' position and his are that he applies this maxim only to the unmarried, not the married, and only to the unmarried who have the gift of celibacy. He does not make it a universal rule.

If Paul applies the word for the general category of the unmarried, why does he single out widows from this group? In 7:39–40, he again gives special instructions to widows, and he may have believed that widows were particularly useful to the church's ministry when they dedicated themselves completely to it and if the church could support them (cf. 1 Tim. 5:3–16; see Godet 1886: 330). On the other hand, he may have highlighted their case simply because there were more widows than widowers and they faced more serious economic problems by remaining single (Schrage 1995: 94).[11] Paul offers them spiritual encouragement to remain unmarried.

---

9. Philo (*Spec. Laws* 1.35 §173) identifies ἐγκράτεια (self-restraint) as "that most profitable of virtues, which has simplicity and frugality for its bodyguard against baleful assaults engineered by incontinence and covetousness."

10. Cf. 1 Clem. 38:2, "Let not him who is pure in the flesh be boastful, knowing that it is another who bestows on him his continence [τὴν ἐγκράτειαν]."

11. Paul may have omitted reference to "virgins" because they would have been under the control of someone else.

Some translations render the beginning of this verse, "if they are not **7:9** able to exercise self-control," but more precisely, the Greek translates as "if they are not exercising self-control" (εἰ δὲ οὐκ ἐγκρατεύονται, *ei de ouk enkrateuontai*). The verb "to be able" is not in the Greek text. Paul does not reproach them for any failure to exercise control, which, if it is acted out, implies some form of *porneia*. Since he does not censure them for this behavior, he apparently does not assume that they are guilty of sexual immorality (contra Fee 1987: 289). The clause "if they are not exercising control" probably means that they have erotic desires and are struggling with them. He offers marriage as the appropriate outlet for irresistible sexual urges rather than prescribing some morbid and futile battle to repress them. An active libido is simply a sign that celibacy is not for them.

Having sexual desires and wanting to get married is not a sin (7:36–38), but it is not the most desirable condition. Barrett (1968: 161) provides a table of what Paul values. Paul thinks most fortunate (cf. 7:40) those who are unmarried with no compunction to marry. Those who are married and express their sexual nature within marriage are in a less desirable state, not because it somehow blemishes their spirituality but because it brings fundamental obligations that make it more difficult to devote full attention to the things of the Lord. Those who are in the least desirable state are those who need marriage and attempt to do without it. This last state is to be avoided. The verb translated "let them marry" (γαμησάτωσαν, *gamēsatōsan*) is a third person plural imperative. They are to marry!

If the Corinthians are going to talk in terms of "the good" (7:1b), Paul flatly disagrees that it is good for those who are married to try to wean themselves from a sexual relationship. But it may be the case that it is "good" for the unmarried and widowed to remain unmarried. On the other hand, it is not "good" for them "to burn." If an unmarried Christian feels the need to be amorous, he or she should marry rather than simmer in a stew of unfulfilled desires or take pleasure with illicit loves. Paul recommends that they avoid frustration by getting married rather than by subjecting themselves to a regimen of hyperspiritual self-mortification, because a person cannot decide to have the gift of celibacy. It can only be bestowed by God and is not something one strives to attain.

In this context, what is "good" is relative. The ethical question is whether celibacy is "good" for the individual or something that sentences him or her to anguish. Paul affirms that it is good (καλόν, *kalon*) to remain single, but that it is better (κρεῖττον, *kreitton*) to marry than to burn. Some Latin fathers and Reformation exegetes have argued that "burning" refers to the final judgment, "to burn in hell," since nothing in the Greek says that they burn "with anything." This argument has been revived recently (Bruce 1971: 68, citing rabbinic texts that warn that lusting after women will lead to Gehenna [*m. ʾAbot* 1:5; *b. Qidd.* 81a]; Barré 1974; Snyder 1992: 97; Osiek and Balch 1997: 114). As a warning, it would recall 6:9, where Paul lists sexual sins that will prevent one from inheriting the kingdom of God. But this interpretation is unlikely because Paul never refers to the flames of hell (see Lang, *TDNT* 6:948–60), and images of the final judgment do not appear in the immediate context.

By "to burn" (πυροῦσθαι, *pyrousthai*), Paul refers to being aflame with passion. L. Alexander (1998: 252–53) notes that the unrequited state of *eros* is most characteristically described as fire that can be quenched only by its fulfillment, and asserts,

> "Burning" is one of a range of metaphors (wounding, captivity, drowning) used in the novels to describe the irresistible force of passion: and it is a sensation associated as much with the legitimate loves of hero and heroine as with the unregulated passions of the various tempters who seek to assault their chastity. Paul's metaphor of sexual desire as "burning" (7:9) is commonest in the novels and in Greek erotic poetry.[12]

The image of couples "aflame with love" (Xenophon of Ephesus, *An Ephesian Tale* 1.3.3) and lying in each other's arms "on fire" (Xenophon of Ephesus, *An Ephesian Tale* 1.9.1) is also widespread in Greco-Roman literature (L. Alexander 1998: 240; Lang, *TDNT* 6:948–50; Ward 1990: 284; cf. also Seneca, *De beneficiis* 4.14.1; Plutarch, *Mor.* 138F; 752D; 759 B–C). The image also appears in the Jewish wisdom tradition (Prov. 6:27–28; Sir. 9:8; see also T. Jos. 2:2; cf. also Philo, *Decal.* 24 §122; *Spec. Laws* 3.2 §10).

Since it was a familiar metaphor, Paul did not need to add that they burn with sexual passion.[13] What is distinctive about his use of the metaphor is his conviction that romantic passion necessitated marriage. Others in the ancient world did not think that burning required marriage. Overpowering sexual desire only necessitated having sex, not marriage (Deming 1995b: 131 n. 88, citing Epictetus, *Diatr.* 3.22.76; 4.1.147). Soranus (*Gynecology* 1.7.31) reports, for example, that some virgins "have suffered more severe sexual passion than [active] women; for the only abatement of the craving is found in the use of intercourse, not in avoidance." Achilles Tatius (*Leuc. Clit.* 5.26.2) writes, "However angry you make me, I still burn with love for you. . . . Make a truce with me at least for now; pity me. . . . A single consummation will be enough. It is a small remedy I ask for so great an illness. Quench a little of my fire." For

---

12. See L. Alexander (1998: 253 n. 48) for numerous examples.
13. The verb appears in 2 Cor. 11:29, where Paul says that he burns (πυροῦμαι, *pyroumai*), indicating either indignation or grief, when the weak are scandalized.

Paul, the fire is not to be doused by fleeting, illicit sexual encounters or by grim repression of natural sexual desire. It calls for marriage.

Additional Notes

7:6. In the prologue to Sirach (18), συγγνώμη is used to plead the reader's forbearance with the Greek translation (cf. Sir. 3:13). Philo uses the word to emphasize the merciful nature of God, "who sets pardon [συγγνώμη] before chastisement [κολάσις]." But this meaning does not apply here. Paul is not offering a pardon for marriage as if it were a veil covering the sin of sexual passion (see Calvin 1960: 140–41). Aristotle (*Eth. nic.* 6.11.1) defines συγγνώμη as "the faculty of judging correctly what is equitable." It does not refer to something grudgingly yielded, but reflects "an allowance made empathetically, out of concern, with constructive good will" (Furnish 1985: 35).

Daube (1969; followed by P. Richardson 1980: 76) claims that Paul follows a legal distinction in Jewish jurisprudence, allowing a course of action because of the majority's inability to fulfill the strictest interpretation of the law. This interpretation assumes that Paul, in giving his counsel, takes into consideration their moral weakness. But he does not consider marriage or sexual desire to be a moral weakness that requires a concession.

Caragounis (1996: 555) claims that συγγνώμη is not a natural antonym of ἐπιταγή, a binding regulation, and paraphrases it, "Pardon me for intruding. I just wanted to help. I have only given you advice, not a command." Or, "But this I am saying with your permission, not as a command." The idea of permission or allowance or pardon makes his advice in a sensitive matter more tactful and underlines that it is not binding.

7:7. The textual evidence supports two possible particles to begin the clause in 7:7, γάρ (ℵ², B, D², Ψ, 1739, 1881, Maj, vg^cl, syr) and δέ (𝔓⁴⁶, ℵ*, A, C, D*, F, G, 33^vid, 81, 326, 629, 2464, it, vg^st, Cyprian, Ambrosiaster). Both have strong external support, and the final decision hangs on the assessment of internal evidence. Most interpreters choose δέ because it is widely assumed that in 7:7 Paul changes the topic from 7:2–6. If it can be established on other grounds that the new topic begins in 7:6, then it makes γάρ more likely as the original reading. This reading ties 7:7 more closely to 7:6 and is judged to be original.

7:8. Most translations understand those addressed in this verse, τοῖς ἀγάμοις καὶ ταῖς χήραις, as "the unmarried and the widows" (NRSV). The word translated "unmarried," οἱ ἄγαμοι, appears only in this chapter in the NT. It is a masculine plural and could refer to both males and females who are single, separated, or divorced (Brown, *NIDNTT* 3:536–37; Kistemaker 1993: 217). When it is translated "unmarried," it may connote to the English ear "those who have never married," but in Greek it can also mean "de-married" and refer to those who are single again. Paul uses the word in 7:11 to refer to a wife who has separated from her husband; she is to remain de-married. In 7:32, he uses it to refer to an unmarried man who is able to concentrate on pleasing the Lord and is not saddled with the responsibility of also having to try to please a wife. In 7:34, it refers to an unmarried woman who is distinguished from a "virgin" (παρθένος) or someone never married.

One wonders, however, why Paul singles out widows (ταῖς χήραις), who also could fall into the category of the unmarried. Some note that the masculine form "widower," χῆρος, never occurs in the LXX or NT and was not used in Koine Greek, and that ἄγαμος was the word employed for widower (LSJ 5). It could have that meaning here, and Paul then would be addressing a specific category of persons who have been de-married, "widowers" and "widows," rather than a general category of persons who are unmarried (so Orr 1967: 12–13; Moiser 1983: 108;

Fee 1987: 287–88; Baumert 1996: 48; Laughery 1997: 121 n. 50; Hays 1997: 118–19; R. Collins 1999: 268). This reading would fit the other directives in the chapter that alternate between addressing men and women (7:2, 3, 4, 10–11, 12–13, 16, 27–28, 33–34, 36–38, 39–40). It would also mean that throughout 7:2–16 Paul addresses those who are presently married or have been married, and the topic of those who have never married is taken up in 7:25, "now concerning the virgins."

Possibly, then, Paul turns his attention in 7:8–9 to the case of widowers and widows whose marriages have been dissolved by the death of a spouse. Hermas *Man.* 4.4.1–4 addresses the question of whether it is a sin for a Christian (husband or wife) to remarry after the death of a spouse. Since Paul understands marriage to include a physical relationship, he would show sensitivity to the problem of how widowers and widows who have had their sexuality awakened by their marriage are abruptly deprived of the physical relationship (Orr and Walther 1976: 210–21). They do not suddenly become desexed when they become de-married and may still have desires for a sexual relationship. Should they stay unmarried or should they remarry? The danger is that they might be tempted to satisfy their desires outside of a committed marriage relationship. If they do not have the divine gift of celibacy, Paul does not expect them to repress their sexual desires and sentence themselves to a life of tortured abstinence. He encourages them instead to remarry (cf. 1 Tim. 5:14).

Although this view has much to commend it, the word ἄγαμος has a broad semantic range, as its application in this chapter to both males and females attests. It does not seem warranted to restrict its meaning here to "widowers," since it was also used to refer to "bachelors" (LSJ 5).

7:8. Was Paul ever married? If Paul is addressing those who have been de-married, "widowers and widows," his assertion "it is good for them if they remain as I am" (καλὸν αὐτοῖς ἐὰν μείνωσιν ὡς κἀγώ) may hint that he too had been married at one time. Some argue that he was a widower (Jeremias 1926; 1929; Barrett 1968: 161; Arens 1973: 1191; Moiser 1983: 108; Fee 1987: 288 n. 7; Murphy-O'Connor 1996: 62–65) or perhaps even divorced because his wife rejected his Christian faith and remained true to traditional Judaism (Bouwman 1976; Phipps 1982: 128; Kistemaker 1993: 215; for arguments against this last view, see Wili 1978).

It would have been exceptional, though not impossible, for Paul to have been as successful in Pharisaic Judaism, as he claims to have been (Gal. 1:13–14; Phil. 3:5–6), without having been married (Snyder 1992: 95). Later rabbinic tradition insists on the necessity of marriage (*m. Yebam.* 6:6), and it is plausible that this sentiment also held sway in the first century, given the biblical command to be fruitful and multiply. The Babylonian Talmud records the conviction "Any man who has no wife lives without joy, without blessing, and without goodness." The phrase "without goodness" is explained by citing Gen. 2:18, "It is not good that the man should be alone" (*b. Yebam.* 62b). Rabbi Eleazar declares, "Any man who has no wife is no proper man; for it is said, *Male and female created He them and called their name Adam* [Gen. 5:2]. Meaning only when male and female are united were they called Adam" (*b. Yebam.* 63b). Rabbi Eliezer espouses a hard-line view: "He who does not engage in the propagation of the race is as though he sheds blood . . . [and] diminishes the Divine Image" (*b. Yebam.* 63b). A similar view, attributed to Rabbi Huna, declares, "He who is twenty years old and not yet married spends all his days in sin" (*b. Qidd.* 29b). The text, however, adds, "'In sin'—can you really think so?—But say, spends all his days in sinful thoughts." The continued discussion in the *sugya* is similar to Paul's arguments in 7:32–35.

> Our Rabbis taught: If one has to study Torah and to marry a wife, he should first study and then marry. But if he cannot [live] without a wife, he should first marry and then study. Rab Judah said in Samuel's name: The halachah is with us. The

halachah is, [A man] first marries and then studies. R. Johanan said: [With] a mill-stone around his neck, shall one study Torah! Yet they do not differ: the one refers to ourselves [Babylonians]; the other to them [Palestinians].

Rashi explains that Babylonians traveled to Palestine to study Mishnah and were free of household worries, while the Palestinians studied at home and could not make progress in study if they had family responsibilities. They studied first.

Some argue from Acts 26:10, where Paul says that he received authority from the chief priests and locked up many Christians in prison and also cast his "vote against them when they were being condemned to death," that he was a member of the Sanhedrin. They then appeal to a text in *b. Sanh.* 36b, "We do not appoint as members of the Sanhedrin, an aged man, a eunuch or one who is childless," to conclude that Paul must have been married. Whether this rule about Sanhedrin members applied in the first century is doubtful, and Paul's statement in Acts 26:10 could be taken metaphorically rather than literally. Paul may only mean that he was in agreement with the Sanhedrin's decision, and his statement need not imply that he was a member of that body.

The evidence to make the case that Paul formerly was married is entirely circumstantial. Paul says nothing about it, and many argue that he was not (Edwards 1885: 164; Godet 1886: 330; Fascher 1929). We simply do not know.

C. Instructions about Divorce for Those Married to Christians and for Those Married to Non-Christians (7:10–16)

Paul turns next to the issue of divorce. In this unit, he is not intent on developing a theology of divorce and does not deal with any legal particulars—what constitutes legitimate grounds for divorce, when and if a divorced person can remarry, and so on. Given the command of the Lord, Paul permits divorce only when it is forced upon the Christian by an unbelieving spouse.

He asserts that the prohibition of divorce is not his own decree but derives from the Lord. When Jesus gave his exposition on divorce, however, he was speaking to Jewish men married to Jewish wives, who shared common religious beliefs. Paul addresses a quite different situation. Many Corinthian Christians converted from their previous worship of idols. In some cases the whole household converted. In others, only one spouse converted. It is one thing to issue commands to a Christian husband and wife committed to the same Lord, but it is another thing to address the situation of a Christian married to an unbeliever, who did not accept the authority of Christ, since this introduced new considerations.

From Paul's response in 7:12–16, it appears that the Corinthian Christians were doubting whether it was wise to continue a marriage to an unbeliever.[1] They may have been asking, "Does being married to a pagan defile me in some way as a Christian?"[2] Are they to associate with idolaters and the immoral (5:9–10)? Some may even have reached the conclusion that divorcing an unbeliever was a Christian duty (cf. Ezra 10:10–11).

A mixed marriage presents "a difficult case because it straddles the boundaries of the church body" (M. Mitchell 1993: 122). Jesus' absolute prohibition of divorce is the presupposition behind Paul's answers, but Paul applies the Lord's command to this new situation with spiritual discernment and flexibility. His arguments against di-

---

1. It is unclear whether the spouse in question is an idolater or a Jew.

2. The passage in 2 Cor. 6:14–7:1, with its command and rhetorical questions, "Do not be mismated with unbelievers. For what partnership have righteousness and iniquity? What fellowship has light with darkness?" has nothing to do with marriage or the issues raised here (see Garland 1999: 314–46).

vorcing an unbelieving spouse are twofold. First, the unbelieving spouse is "sanctified" by the Christian. Christians are not defiled by this relationship any more than the children from this union are defiled. Since the children are obviously "holy," the union is "holy." Second, they were called in peace, and he presumes that the harmony in the marriage still exists, since the unbelieving spouse consents and approves of continuing the marriage after the believer becomes a Christian. Jesus' teaching about divorce reveals that God is concerned about the permanence and well-being of marital relationships. God's purpose is that marriages be preserved and that men and women live in harmony with one another (Barrett 1968: 166). In calling persons to salvation, God did not intend to create division in a peaceful marriage by forcing believing spouses to separate from their unbelieving spouses. In some cases, such separation may be an unhappy result of answering God's call, but it is not God's purpose. Christians are not to inject needless turmoil into a relationship that formerly was characterized by peace. Simply because the spouse is not a Christian does not constitute grounds to jettison the marriage. On the contrary, the Lord's command against divorce still holds.

However, there are exceptions to this rule. Paul relaxes the prohibition against divorce when it comes to a situation not envisioned by Jesus' command: the case of the Christian joined to an unbeliever who insists on divorcing. When the decision to dissolve the marriage is out of the Christian's control, then the Christian may accept divorce (on the possibility of remarriage, see the additional note to 7:15).

The structure of Paul's argument runs as follows:

1. Command that a Christian not divorce a believer (7:10–11)
2. Command that a Christian not divorce an unbeliever (7:12–13)
3. Justification (γάρ, *gar*): For the unbelieving spouse is sanctified by Christian spouse (7:14ab)
4. Substantiation of justification (ἐπεὶ ἄρα, *epei ara*): Since otherwise the children are unclean (7:14c)
5. Exception when the decision is out of the Christian's control (7:15ab)
6. Second justification (δέ, *de*): But you are called in peace (7:15c)
7. Substantiation of second justification (γάρ, *gar*): For how can you know whether or not you will save the unbelieving spouse? (7:16)

Exegesis and Exposition

[10]To the married I command, not I, but the Lord, that the wife is not to separate from her husband. [11]If she does separate, let her remain unmarried or be reconciled to her husband. And the husband is not to divorce his wife. [12]But I, not the Lord, say to the rest, if any brother has an unbelieving wife and she consents to continue to live with him [in marriage], let him not divorce her. [13]And if any wife has an unbelieving husband and he consents to continue to live with her [in marriage], let her not divorce her husband. [14]For the unbelieving husband has been made holy in the wife, and the unbelieving wife has been made holy in the ⌜brother⌝. Otherwise, your children would be unclean, but in fact they are holy. [15]But if the unbeliever separates, let him separate. The brother or sister is not under bondage in such [cases]. But God has called ⌜you⌝ in peace. [16]For how can you know, wife, whether [or not] you will convert your husband? Or how can you know, husband, whether [or not] you will convert your wife?

7:10 Paul's tone dramatically changes. He does not "say" (7:6, 8), "wish" (7:7), or offer a concession but issues a sharp command: "I order [παραγγέλλω, parangellō] the married."[3] Plus, he declares that it is not he but the Lord who is doing the commanding. The change in tone requires some explanation.

Paul does not callously resort to the Lord's prohibition of divorce to beat down those whose marriages were in trouble and who were at wit's end as to what to do. A man "who weeps with those who are weeping" (Rom. 12:15) surely would have spoken differently to those struggling with the demise of their marriages (Baumert 1996: 53). Some think that the maxim with which Paul opens his discussion in this chapter, "It is good for a man not to touch a woman," has fomented the marital tension. They infer from his fervent repudiation of divorce that some at Corinth were arguing in favor of it. According to this view, the divorces resulted from their misguided ambition to reach a higher spiritual plateau via celibacy, rather than from the usual weaknesses of the flesh (Hurd 1965: 167; Barrett 1968: 193; Fee 1987: 296). Schrage (1995: 99) contends that the pneumatics were appealing to the direct voice of the Holy Spirit over against Jesus' ruling.

The exact situation is uncertain (see additional note). Possibly, a couple could come to no agreement about the terms of withdrawal from one another (7:5), or one of the spouses refused sexual relations on a permanent basis. Possibly, both spouses agreed to divorce, perhaps to remove the temptation to engage in sexual relations. They may have tried abstinence for awhile, but now they (or one partner) are un-

---

3. The verb παραγγέλλω occurs in 11:17; 1 Thess. 4:11; 2 Thess. 3:4, 6, 10, 12 and is used in giving specific directions to Christians on how to conduct their lives (cf. also 1 Tim. 1:3; 4:11; 6:13, 17).

able to restrain themselves and find that sleeping together as brother and sister only tempts them to sleep together again as husband and wife (Murphy-O'Connor 1981b: 604).[4]

That Paul reverses the order of male and female found in his other injunctions in the chapter (7:2–3, 4, 12–13, 14–15, 27–28, 32–34) and addresses the wives first here and the husbands almost as an afterthought in 7:11b hints, to some interpreters, that wives were the ones behind the problem. He may have become aware of a circumstance in which a woman in the church initiated a divorce against her husband or was about to do so (R. Collins 1999: 269).[5] The Corinthians' cultural environment, unlike that of Judaism (cf. Josephus, *Ant.* 15.7.10 §259; 18.5.4. §136; 20.7.2 §§141–43; *m. Yebam.* 14:1; *m. Ketub.* 7:9–10), permitted women to divorce their husbands (see Geiger 1983).

The verb in the phrase μὴ χωρισθῆναι (*mē chōristhēnai*) is passive but has a middle sense: "she is not, on her part, to separate from."[6] In the context of Greco-Roman practice, the verb means to divorce and is synonymous with the verb ἀφιέναι (*aphienai*) in 7:11b, which Paul uses to command the husband not to send away his wife. In 7:15, the passive form of the verb (χωρίζεται, *chōrizetai*) is used for the unbeliever who initiates separation, "If the unbeliever separates, let him separate" (χωριζέσθω, *chōrizesthō*); and in 7:13, the verb ἀφιέτω (*aphietō*) appears in the active voice in a command to the woman, "Let her not divorce." The verb χωριζέτω (*chōrizetō*) appears in the word of the Lord recorded in Mark 10:9: "What God has yoked together, let man not separate," which also may have influenced Paul's usage.[7] R. Collins (1999: 269) claims that if there is any distinction to be made between χωρισθῆναι and ἀφιέναι, it may be attributable to Paul's Jewish tradition that tends to use active verbs for men and passive verbs for women (but cf. 7:13).

---

4. Pesch (1975) suggests that 7:10–11 covers a case of a woman who had divorced her husband prior to becoming a Christian. He instructs her to remain unmarried because of the command of the Lord. Against this view, if this divorce transpired before her baptism, her former husband is likely to be an unbeliever. It seems improbable that Paul would encourage a Christian to seek reconciliation with an unbelieving, former husband and to return to his control. It is more probable that he addresses Christians married to Christians.

5. Whether the wife belonged to the "feminist party" (Moffatt 1938: 78), which claimed the freedom to desert or divorce a husband, or was one of the "eschatological women" (so Fee 1987: 290, 269–70; Gundry Volf 1996: 527) cannot be discerned from the text. Eusebius (*Ecclesiastical History* 5.18.3) notes that the Montanist women prophets abandoned their husbands; however, that later development does not have any relevance to the Corinthian situation.

6. The verb χωρίζειν (*chōrizein*) appears in Hellenistic legal texts related to divorce (see MM 696; Conzelmann 1975: 120 n. 18; R. Collins 1999: 269).

7. For contrasting views on the Synoptic parallels, cf. D. Allison 1982; D. Wenham 1985: 8; Neirynck 1986: 312–15.

For Paul, the whole issue of divorce among Christians is settled by the plain and uncompromising word of the Lord forbidding it. It is not a matter of simply remaining in the state in which you were called (7:17) but of obeying the command of the Lord (7:19). He introduces the word of the Lord forbidding divorce not to deter zealous ascetics from divorcing but to set up his discussion about mixed marriage and divorce.[8] The problem centers on Christians married to unbelievers—not Christians married to Christians—who were wanting to divorce for religious reasons.

Paul's distinction between what he commands as the Lord's apostle and what the Lord explicitly commanded (cf. 7:12, 25) reveals an awareness of the content of the teaching of the Lord (including Jesus' lesser-known sayings; see comments on 1 Cor. 9:14). He understands the Lord's teaching to be the norm for all Christian ethics, though he exercises the freedom to apply it to new situations. Since he felt no need to cite verbatim the full command of the Lord, he apparently assumes that the Corinthians were already familiar with it. Kim (*DPL* 474–92) challenges the view that the so-called paucity and allusive character of Paul's citations of Jesus' teaching betoken his lack of knowledge of, or interest in, the historical Jesus.[9] Dunn (1995: 101; cf. 1994) argues that the authority of Jesus' teaching is confirmed by alluding to it rather than citing it in full, because it reveals that Paul and the Corinthians shared this tradition, and thus it can be taken for granted.[10] The authority of this tradition is strengthened for those who recognize the allusion. Paul's careful distinction between his own command and that of the Lord also undercuts the assumption in modern scholarship that the early church invented sayings of Jesus as the need arose (Fee 1987: 292 n. 8). He did not declare his own commands to be the Lord's words (Schrage 1995: 97). Barrett's (1968: 162) reasoning that Paul cites the authority of the Lord here because it disagrees with the teaching found in the OT makes sense (so also Rosner 1994: 167), but Paul will then qualify Jesus' teaching in the next paragraph.

7:11 The καί (*kai*, indeed, even) in the phrase ἐὰν δὲ καὶ χωρισθῇ (*ean de kai chōristhē*, if indeed she separates) has suggested to some that the action has already occurred (Conzelmann 1975: 120). Chrysostom (*Hom. 1 Cor.* 19.4) thinks that divorces have already happened because of their attempts at abstinence. The phrase ἐὰν δὲ καὶ γαμήσῃς (*ean de kai*

---

8. It is pure speculation that the Corinthians knew the tradition recorded in Luke 18:28–30 and 20:34–36 and interpreted it through the curvature of an ascetic bias as a justification to abandon their marriages.

9. Kim (*DPL* 474–92) tabulates twenty-five certain or probable references to a saying of Jesus and forty echoes of a saying of Jesus in Paul's letters.

10. Three explicit references to the teaching of the historical Jesus appear in 7:10–11; 9:14; 11:23–25.

gamēsēs, if indeed you marry) in 7:28, however, shows that this idiom does not refer to something that has already occurred. Paul is not trying to overturn their past actions but is instructing them that Christians may not end their marriage at will.

It may seem that Paul presents the Christian wife with two options: either remain unmarried or be reconciled to her believing husband (Schrage 1995: 102). But he directs her to remain unmarried *in order to* be reconciled with her husband (R. Collins 1999: 269–70).[11] In Paul's Jewish tradition, a wife who has been divorced and has married another is forbidden to her former husband (Deut. 24:4; Herm. *Man.* 4.1.8; see also 2 Sam. 16:21–22; 20:3). If there was to be a reconciliation, she must remain unmarried. The assumption behind this instruction is the same as in the teaching of the Lord: the marriage bonds remain intact regardless of what steps spouses might take to end the marriage.

The command to be reconciled with the husband (καταλλαγήτω, *katallagētō*) assumes that the wife is the guilty party who has ruptured the relationship.[12] Paul's counsel does not think in terms of a failed marriage but of the personal failure of the married partner (N. Watson 1992: 69). Since she initiated the breakup, it is her Christian responsibility to take the initiative in healing the breach. Paul also forbids the husband to divorce his wife but does not mention the need to reconcile. R. Collins (1999: 270) contends that he mentions the husband only because of "the gender parity that characterizes Paul's entire exhortation on marriage." But his fleeting nod to the husband's responsibility may suggest instead that divorce among Christians is not at issue at all. In 7:10–11, he only lays the foundation stone for his argument in what follows: the Lord forbids Christians to divorce.

"The rest" (τοῖς δὲ λοιποῖς, *tois de loipois*), as the context later reveals, are **7:12–13** those Christians married to unbelievers, either pagans or Jews. Since Paul expects Christian widows to marry "only in the Lord," that is, to marry other Christians (7:39; cf. Deut. 7:3; Neh. 13:25), the situation presumes that one partner converted to Christianity after marriage. He extends the Lord's plain, uncompromising teaching forbidding divorce to the marriage of a Christian to an unbeliever. Corinthians married to

---

11. Paul's insistence that she remain unmarried creates problems for understanding the motivation behind the divorce as driven by a desire for celibacy or freedom. If she was motivated by either reason, why would she want to remarry? He may suspect that she might change her mind about marriage when she finds that she is unable to support herself, but this conclusion is unlikely.

12. Only Paul uses the noun "reconciliation" and the verb "to reconcile" in the NT. The noun appears four times (Rom. 5:11; 11:15; 2 Cor. 5:18, 19), and the verb six times (Rom. 5:10 [2x]; 1 Cor. 7:11; 2 Cor. 5:18, 19, 20). The verb ἀποκαταλλάσσειν (*apokatallassein*) appears in Eph. 2:16; Col. 1:20, 22.

unbelievers are to continue in that marriage so long as it depends on them. The force of the third person imperative, μὴ ἀφιέτω (*mē aphietō*), is perhaps softened when rendered "he should not divorce" (NRSV). They *must not* divorce (cf. NIV).

Intermarriage introduces a new wrinkle into the issue of divorce. When married partners dissent over basic religious commitments, the potential for that to disrupt their mutual commitment threatens their union. For a wife to adopt religious beliefs different from those of her husband flouted social mores of the ancient world. Plutarch's (*Mor.* 140D) "Advice to Bride and Groom" is often cited:

> A wife ought not to make friends of her own, but to enjoy her husband's friends in common with him. The gods are the first and most important friends. Wherefore it is becoming for a wife to worship and to know only the gods that her husband believes in, and to shut the front door tight upon all queer rituals and outlandish superstitions. For with no god do stealthy and secret rites performed by a woman find any favor.

A wife's conversion to Christianity undoubtedly would have created strife, if only as a slap at her husband's authority over her.[13] Balch (1981: 65–76) traces Roman fears about new cults emerging from the East that were regarded suspiciously as causing sedition and undermining the foundations of marriages when wives became captivated by them. On the other hand, a wife's refusal to accept Christianity after her husband's conversion also would have made things quite awkward since the Christian faith was highly intolerant of other religious beliefs and practices. The pressures on the marriage in both cases would have been enormous, but Christian wives in particular would have been subject to severe stress if their husbands frowned on their newfound faith.

Christians may have contemplated divorce as the best course to resolve the tension, and there were clear biblical warrants for divorcing pagans (cf. Ezra 10:3, 19).[14] From Paul's response in these verses that the marriage partners are "sanctified," we may infer that the Corinthians imagined that marriage with an unbeliever defiled the believing spouse in some way. This perspective is characteristically Jewish: "Whoever touches pitch gets dirty" (Sir. 13:1a). In Jos. As. 8:5–7, Joseph refuses to kiss Aseneth while she is still an idolater and responds:

> It is not fitting for a man who worships God, who will bless with his mouth the living God and eat blessed bread of life and drink a blessed

---

13. Justin Martyr (2 *Apol.* 2) gives an account of a woman who became a Christian and continued to live with her dissolute husband in hopes that he might reform. She ultimately divorced him.

14. Jews were no less concerned about mixed marriages, and later talmudic traditions regard such marriages as invalid (*b. Qidd.* 68b; *b. Yebam.* 45a).

cup of immortality . . . to kiss a strange woman who will bless with her mouth dead and dumb idols and eat from their table bread of strangulation and drink from their libation a cup of insidiousness. . . . Likewise, for a woman who worships God it is not fitting to kiss a strange man, because this is an abomination before the Lord God.

Paul's previous letter (5:9–13) warning them not to associate with immoral persons may have stoked their phobia about sexual intimacy with an unbeliever. The Corinthians may have questioned how they could allow a pagan to have power over their bodies (7:4), which belong to Christ. Religious incompatibility, however, is not grounds for divorce.

Paul again distinguishes his teaching from the Lord's ("I say, not the Lord"), but in doing so he expects them to regard his directive as no less authoritative (see Schrage 1995: 103).[15] He is not offering them "the best advice he can" on this difficult issue (contra Parry 1926: 111–12), which they can take or leave as it suits them. He too has the Spirit (7:40) in applying the Lord's command to their different situation. This explains why he uses the verb λέγω (legō), "I say," instead of παραγγέλλω (parangellō), "I command," as in 7:10. The justifications he offers for maintaining the marriage derive from his own exposition of the Lord's command.[16]

Paul begins his instruction with the situation of an unbelieving wife (γυναῖκα . . . ἄπιστον, gynaika . . . apiston).[17] He presumes that the unbelieving wife consents to live with her Christian husband. "To live with" means to live together in a marriage commitment (cf. 1 Pet. 3:7).[18] The verb "to consent" (συνευδοκεῖν, syneudokein) implies not only willingness but also some measure of approval (cf. Luke 11:48; Acts 8:1; 22:20; Rom. 1:32; 1 Macc. 1:57; 11:24; Diogn. 9:1). The verb

15. Tertullian (De exhortatione castitatis [Exhortation to Chastity] 3–4) contends with some uneasiness that Paul might be thought irreligious that in giving his advice on marriage he made a distinction between inspired commands, which are precepts, and his human counsel, which was uninspired. Thiselton (2000: 526) dismisses this as a false problem and translates "to the rest I say (not a saying of the Lord)."

16. Conzelmann (1975: 121) notes that "Paul distinguishes between the absolutely valid command of the Lord and his own exposition of it."

17. "Unbelieving" as a term to designate non-Christians occurs only in the Corinthian correspondence (1 Cor. 6:6; 10:27; 14:22–24; 2 Cor. 4:4; 6:14–15), and Christians are referred to as "brothers" and "sisters" (7:15). Deming (1995b: 144–46) argues that the terms "faithful" ("trustworthy") and "unfaithful" ("untrustworthy") derive from the Corinthians, who used them eclectically in both Stoic and Christian senses. Deming makes this claim to substantiate an argument for Stoic influence on the passage, but the use of similar terminology does not require direct influence.

18. Plutarch's (Mor. 142F) use of the verb συνοικεῖν (synoikein, to live with) to refer to a lesser union than expressed by the verb συμβιοῦν (symbioun, to live together), noted by Deming 1995b: 133 n. 93, does not apply.

also assumes that the Christian husband has not coerced his wife to become compliant. The principle of mutual agreement (7:5) as the basis for making decisions in marriage applies in this case as well. The consent presupposes that the spouse will not badger the Christian or try to stymie his or her Christian commitment.

The same principle applies in the case of the unbelieving husband whose wife has become a Christian. The non-Christian partner's willingness to continue in the marriage commitment determines whether the marriage continues. Paul does not endorse marriage to a nonbeliever, recognizing that it presents particular problems for Christians. But his intention in this unit is to allay any fear Christians might have that continuing such a marriage, with its requisite sexual intimacy (7:2–5), was somehow defiling. He wishes to quash any reason for divorcing spouses who wish to continue the marriage.

When directing Christians married to Christians in 7:10–11, he simply forbids divorce because of the Lord's command. When directing Christians married to unbelievers, he supplements the Lord's prohibition of divorce by offering two reasons why divorce in this case is unjustified. (1) To dispel any trepidation about continuing the marriage, he maintains that the Christian sanctifies the unbeliever in the marriage. (2) To discourage them from making marital changes that would create upheaval, he reminds them that they were called in peace. Their conversion does not necessitate disrupting their marriage. In between these two justifications, he inserts an exception to continuing the marriage. When an unbelieving spouse decides to divorce, the matter is out of the Christian's control. He or she can only accept the divorce.

7:14 Paul's first justification for his command that Christians should not separate from their unbelieving spouses follows a chiastic pattern:

> A A brother [Christian man] who has an unbelieving wife . . . is not to divorce (7:12)
>> B A [believing] wife who has an unbelieving husband . . . is not to divorce (7:13)
>> B′ For the unbelieving husband has been sanctified in the [believing] wife (7:14a)
> A′ And the unbelieving wife has been sanctified in the brother [Christian man] (7:14b)

The marriage of a Christian to an unbeliever should be continued because Christians have the spiritual power to make their spouses holy. Paul uses the perfect tense, "has been made holy" (ἡγίασται, hēgiastai), which implies a present condition established by some past event.[19] How this occurs, Paul does not specify, whether it is the marriage itself (Orr and Walther 1976: 212) or the Christian's baptism (R. Collins 1999: 266). The preposition ἐν (*en*) can imply that the Christian is the agent: the unbelieving spouse has been made holy "by" the Christian. Or it can have a locative sense: the unbelieving spouse has his or her holiness "in" the Christian.

What Paul means by "has been made holy" is unclear. It cannot be associated with belief in Christ, since the unbelieving partner still needs to be saved (7:16). Nor is it associated with ethical conduct (Rom. 6:19–22; 1 Thess. 3:12–13; 5:23), since that idea seems unrelated to the context. Various other options have been proposed:

1. Some apply the verb's customary biblical usage, "to be set apart for God's purposes," to the circumstance of marriage. Murphy-O'Connor (1977b: 356, 361) claims that it means to be separated from the world by divine call and argues that when non-Christians stand by their Christian spouses in their marriage commitment, their behavior exhibits a pattern of behavior that conforms to what is expected of "the holy." The unbelieving partner is holy by virtue of coming under the influence of the Christian spouse, consenting to maintain the marriage, and thereby affirming the divine intention for marriage (see also Thiselton 2000: 530). This view, however, does not comport well with the use of the perfect tense. Paul is referring to a state, not an action.

2. Laney (1982: 286–87) argues that a pagan partner is "set apart" to receive a Christian witness and influence that he or she might not otherwise have. Fee (1987: 300–301) concurs; by maintaining the marriage, they improve the potential of leading the unbeliever to salvation. Fee cites Rom. 11:16 as a parallel. Because Israel belonged to God in a special sense, Paul held out hope that Israel eventually would be converted. The part that is converted sanctifies the other part. The relationship between the patriarchs and the people of Israel, however, is hardly analogous to the relationship between partners in a mixed marriage (Wolff 1996: 144). The perfect tense of the verb also "cannot designate a hoped-for result" (Godet 1886: 338–39).

3. Others contend that Paul assumes that the unbelieving partner who is willing to continue the marriage to the Christian is somehow made a part of the Christian's covenantal status. They are consecrated by the conjugal bond that unites the couple. In this case, the spouse's membership in the church brings the unbelieving spouse into association with the church. Godet (1886: 339) argues, "By consenting to live still with his spouse, the Jewish or heathen spouse also accepts her holy consecration and participates in it." This view has some basis in Jewish

---

19. R. Horsley (1998: 100) argues from 7:34 that "holy" "was yet another term used by the Corinthian pneumatics to characterize their spiritual status, apparently in specific connection with sexual asceticism." But such speculation takes us far afield.

betrothal practices and could have informed Paul's thinking. Falk (1978: 285) notes that the betrothal ceremony had taken on the aspect of sanctification with its blessing and mention of the sanctity of Israel. Jewish marriage documents were going through a transition in this era and were altered from saying that the man acquires the woman to saying that he "sanctifies" her: "you are made holy [*qiddûšîn*] to me" (*m. Qidd.* 2:1). Money or an article given to secure the acquisition was itself called *qiddûšîn* (*m. Yebam.* 3:8). The term may also be connected with the ceremony of purification, which was part of the betrothal or marriage (*b. Zebaḥ.* 19b). Falk (1978: 285) contends, "By use of the new term, the acquisition of a wife became more and more a matter of sanctity; a man could no longer declare that the woman was his wife, or betrothed to him, but would *sanctify* her and say that she was *sanctified* to him." R. Collins (1999: 266) notes that the formula meant more than that the wife belonged to the husband; rather, she shared the groom's covenanted status: "Prior to marriage a woman participated in the covenant ('was sanctified') through her father; upon marriage she was sanctified through her husband."

4. Since Paul also identifies the children of this union as holy, the idea of "sanctification" here seems to revolve around the issues of clean and unclean (Baumert 1996: 59 n. 95). The majority of references in the OT to holiness pertain to cultic contexts (Procksch, *TDNT* 1:89–97). Paul uses the term "unclean" to contrast "holy" in Rom. 6:19 and 1 Thess. 4:7. These references imply that uncleanness is "something which belongs by its very nature to the pagan world outside the church" (Best 1990: 161). The Corinthians' worry about these marriages could stem only from some anxiety about potential defilement by intimate union with an unbeliever, particularly an idolater (Deming 1995b: 132). Paul turns this apprehension on its head by reassuring them that Christians sanctify their non-Christian spouse. The Christian united to Christ brings the non-Christian partner into a power sphere of holiness that somehow neutralizes the non-Christian's potential to contaminate the Christian (see Schrage 1995: 105–6).[20] In other words, "clean" trumps "unclean" in this relationship.

How is this sanctification effected? Paul is not thinking of some magical process. Nor does he believe that holiness can be transferred to another, as in the manner of an infectious disease. The idea hinges on the two becoming one flesh (Gen. 2:24; cited in 1 Cor. 6:16) and on God's blessing of marriage. In 6:15–17, he argues that Christians are members of Christ's body and that one who joins himself to a prostitute becomes one body with her. Here, he argues that an unbeliever joined to a Chris-

---

20. Conzelmann (1975: 122) asserts, "The decisive idea lies not in an ontological definition of the state of the non-Christian members of the family, but in the assertion that no alien power plays any part in the Christian's dealings with them."

tian spouse is made holy. What is the difference? A Christian who has relations with a prostitute cannot convey holiness, because that union is outside the will of God. Fornication is the antithesis of holiness. Marriage, on the other hand, is a divine institution that accords with God's will for man and woman. Although it is difficult to trace how Paul might have reached the conclusion that a Christian husband or wife sanctifies his or her spouse, Rosner (1994: 169–70) reasonably claims that Paul was influenced by three ideas: the holiness of the people as God's temple (cf. 3:16–17; 6:19), the transferability of that holiness to other persons (Exod. 29:37; 30:29; Lev. 6:18; contrast Num. 4:15, 20), and the concept of family solidarity and God's concern for the welfare of the whole family (see Best 1990).

Paul is not arguing for "sanctification by proxy" but making an argument against divorce (Guthrie 1981: 671). His basic argument is this: Mixed marriages have the same status as Christian marriages and should not be abandoned. Continuing the marriage accords with God's design for marriage, and it should be hallowed as "a sphere in which God's holiness and transforming power operate" (Hays 1997: 122). Contending that the Christian wife has the same power to sanctify her unbelieving husband as the Christian husband has to sanctify his unbelieving wife is quite novel. It accords with Paul's emphasis throughout the chapter on the mutuality of spouses (R. Collins 1999: 266), but it also expresses his conviction that Christians live in a new and potent field of God's holiness that works irrespective of gender.

Paul appeals to pathos to seal this argument against divorce. The phrase "since otherwise" (ἐπεὶ ἄρα, *epei ara*; cf. 5:10) introduces corroboration for his justification that mixed marriages should be continued because the Christian spouse sanctifies the unbelieving spouse: "But as it is [νῦν δέ, *nyn de*], the children from these marriages *are* holy" [ἅγιά ἐστιν, *hagia estin*]. Deming (1995b: 135) identifies it as an argument *ad absurdum* that corresponds with Paul's reasoning in 5:9–13. In this parallel passage he explains that he wrote to them not to mix together with sexually immoral persons, not at all meaning the sexually immoral of the world, "since otherwise [ἐπεὶ . . . ἄρα] you would be obligated to leave the world" (5:10); "but as it is [νῦν δέ], I was writing about immoral Christians" (5:11). It would be absurd to expect them to bid farewell to the world entirely. The assumption behind Paul's case here must be that the Corinthians also would have thought it absurd to consider the children of these mixed unions to be unholy or polluted (Godet 1886: 341). We may assume that the children in the illustration are too young to be held responsible for their own behavior. Schrage (1995: 107) assumes that they are unbaptized. How else could they possibly be regarded as unclean? The logic runs thus: if they consider their unbaptized spouse to be defiled in some way, then they must also consider their children to be so.[21]

Furnish (1985: 43) lays the argument out more clearly with two syllogisms:

> Holy children are produced by holy marriages.
> Mixed marriages produce holy children.
> Mixed marriages are therefore holy marriages.

> Holy marriages should be maintained (7:10–11).
> Mixed marriages are holy marriages.
> Mixed marriages should therefore be maintained (7:12–13).

In other words, the community did not think of expelling children who were born of mixed marriages, so neither should it encourage the breakup of those marriages. Paul leaves unsaid that, given the prevailing law at this time, wives who divorced their husbands would have to leave their children in the custody of their "unclean" husband. To leave their children under the complete influence of their unbelieving father would be lamentable.

7:15ab   The nonbeliever has no reason to acknowledge the authority of Christ or Paul, and nothing prevents the pagan from divorcing a Christian spouse. The continuance of the marriage depends entirely on the consent of the nonbeliever, since the Christian has no grounds for initiating divorce. The choice to continue the marriage may be out of the Christian's hands. If the unbeliever does not consent to live with a Christian spouse and decides to separate (that is, divorce), then the believer is not under bondage. The imperative χωριζέσθω (*chōrizesthō*), "let him separate," does not imply that the Christian resists this action by the spouse and must be commanded to let the spouse go. Instead, it is an imperative of toleration that views the act as a *fait accompli* (Wallace 1996: 488–89). Such cases lie beyond the Christian's control.

Paul chooses vivid language to describe the situation. The believer, he says, is not "enslaved," "under bondage" (δεδούλωται, *dedoulōtai*; cf. Rom. 6:18, 22; 1 Cor. 9:19; Gal. 4:3; see additional note). The verb δουλοῦν (*douloun*) is not synonymous with the verb δεῖν (*dein*, bound) that appears in 7:27 and 39 (cf. Rom. 7:2). If he had used "bound" (cf. NRSV, NIV), he could have meant that the believer is not bound by the marriage bond or the prohibition of divorce (so Lietzmann 1949: 31; Foerster, *TDNT* 2:416; Roberts 1965: 184; Conzelmann 1975: 119, 123 n. 42; Bal-

---

21. In Judaism, the children of proselytes were considered members of the covenant (*m. Qidd.* 1:2; *m. Ketub.* 4:4).

tensweiler 1967: 193, 195). Divorce in this case is tolerated. But Paul is not talking about the binding character of the marriage (Fee 1987: 303). Instead, he justifies his ruling in 7:15a by saying that the believer is not to be enslaved to a marriage relationship that an unbeliever wishes to dissolve (Murphy-O'Connor 1979a: 66; Fee 1987: 303; N. Watson 1992: 71). The slavery imagery is best understood in light of Jewish backgrounds, not Greco-Roman. Deming (1995b: 148) misuses mirror-reading to conclude that the Corinthians regarded their marriages to unbelievers as slavery. Instone-Brewer (2001: 238–39) correctly shows that the divorce deed in early rabbinic traditions (*m. Giṭ.* 1:4) is "compared to an emancipation certificate for a slave," not because they thought marriage was akin to slavery but because "the divorce legislation of Exodus 21:10–11 was based on the law of the slave wife, and they found many parallels between the release of a woman from marriage and the release from slavery." Paul deliberately chooses to use images of the slavery bond here because he wishes to communicate that "the marriage bond is to be respected and not treated lightly" (Instone-Brewer 2001: 240–41).

Three questions must be answered: (1) Who is addressed—those whose **7:15c–16** unbelieving partners want to leave, or those who may want to abandon their unbelieving partners? (2) What does "peace" connote in this context? (3) Does Paul intend to say that God called them "for peace" or that God called them "in peace" (ἐν δὲ εἰρήνῃ κέκληκεν ὑμᾶς ὁ θεός, *en de eirēnē keklēken hymas ho theos*)?

The versification of printed texts includes the clause "but God has called you in peace" in 7:15. This connection and translations that render it "for God has called us for peace" (RSV) encourage the reader to assume that the phrase is addressed to those whose partners want to divorce. If this is correct, then Paul appeals to their calling to peace to discourage them from causing strife by stubbornly clinging to a marriage that an unbeliever wants to dissolve. "Peace" means not causing conflict by disputing the decision to end the marriage. "Peace" could also refer to "peace of mind." They should not become excessively agitated by the divorce. A peaceful attitude can be present even in divorce.

This interpretation mistakenly assumes that a spouse could contest a divorce, which was not the case under the Roman law.[22] As Crook (1967: 101) states it, "Marriage was a matter of intention, if you lived together 'as' man and wife, man and wife you were." The converse also was true. Divorce was instantaneously effective whenever one party renounced the marriage (Dixon 1992: 81). Furnish's (1985: 45) comment that "marriage is not an end in and of itself that must be maintained at

---

22. This custom contrasts with Jewish law, in which a divorce was invalid without the husband's consent (*m. ʿArak.* 5:6).

any cost" is irrelevant to this situation. The partner could not maintain a marriage when a spouse wanted out. The only thing contestable was the restitution of the dowry. This interpretation also misconstrues the thrust of Paul's exhortation in this unit. He tries to discourage them from initiating divorces with the command not to divorce (7:10, 11, 12, 13), which suggests that the Corinthians were unlikely to be distraught about being divorced. His worry is not that they might cause unnecessary conflict by resisting divorce. He is barring them from causing unnecessary strife by divorcing on religious grounds unbelieving spouses who have consented to continue the marriage (7:12–13). He is not trying to comfort those who may be divorced by their unbelieving spouses.

I take the statement "but God has called you in peace" as Paul's second justification for remaining in the marriage to an unbeliever. The δέ (de) has an adversative or consecutive force ("but"), not a causal sense ("for"). It constitutes an additional argument addressed to Christians contemplating divorcing their non-Christian spouses and is intended to convince them not to do so. This conclusion requires separating this phrase from the end of verse 15 and punctuating it as the beginning of a new thought.

"Peace" in this context is the opposite of division (cf. Luke 12:51) and refers to harmony among individuals. Paul caps his argument commending order in their worship by declaring that God is not a God of discord but of peace (14:33; cf. Rom. 15:33; 2 Cor. 13:11). Peace is also something that can belong to a household (Matt. 10:34–36 = Luke 12:49–53). The phrase ἐν εἰρήνῃ (en eirēnē) need not mean that God called them "to peace," as if Paul had written εἰς εἰρήνην (eis eirēnēn; cf. 1:9, where Paul writes ἐκλήθητε εἰς κοινωνίαν, eklēthēte eis koinōnian, you were called for fellowship). It can refer to the state they were in— the harmony of their marriage—when God called them (Deming 1995b: 154). This statement is not an application of the general aphorism "Live peaceably with all, so far as it depends on you" (Rom. 12:18; contra Moffatt 1938: 84). It applies instead to the specific circumstances of their marriage when they were called by God.

Since marriages in the ancient world usually were arranged and not inspired by love between two individuals, the most that couples hoped for from marriage was that their life together would be marked by harmony. Dixon (1992: 70) writes, "The notion of *concordia*, or harmony, in marriage was frequently mentioned in literature and in epitaphs boasting that marriages, especially long marriages, had been without discord." Pliny the Younger (*Ep.* 8.5.1–2), for example, writes about how a friend was devastated by the loss of his wife of thirty-nine years and remarks that in all that time there was not "a single quarrel or bitter word between them." Whether this memory was true or not, it reveals what was valued in a marriage relationship. If peace is to be understood as something bestowed by God, and if a Christian, prior to conversion, knew peace in his or her marriage to an unbeliever, God's purpose in calling them is not to plunge them into marital turmoil (see additional note).

The idea of their calling becomes the leitmotif in the next unit 7:17–24 (see Bartchy 1973: 133), in which the verb καλεῖν (*kalein*) appears eight times (7:17, 18 [2x], 20, 21, 22 [2x], 24), and the noun κλῆσις (*klēsis*, calling) once (7:20). The phrase ἐν . . . εἰρήνῃ κέκληκεν matches the phrase ἐν ἀκροβυστίᾳ κέκληται (*en akrobystia keklētai*, was called in [the state of] circumcision) in 7:18 (Baltensweiler 1967: 192). They were not called for uncircumcision, but were uncircumcised when they were called. The point that Paul underscores three times in 7:17–24 (7:17, 20, 24) is that they should remain in the state they were in when they were called. That argument applies directly to what he counsels in 7:12–16. They were (supposedly) peacefully married before they became Christians. Their conversion to Christianity should not be used as an excuse to upset that marital harmony.

Since Paul connects peace with God's act of reconciliation, which establishes peace between God and humanity (Rom. 5:1–11; 2 Cor. 5:18–21; Eph. 2:14–17; Col. 1:20–22), he also understands that the "peace" in a marriage relationship takes on a new dimension. The Christian life is to be characterized by peace (Rom. 14:17) and requires living as peacemakers (Matt. 5:9; Rom. 12:18). To divorce not only means that they add to the chaos of a lost world, but also that they lose the opportunity to win an unbeliever. In 7:16, Paul switches to direct address and challenges the Christian spouse: "For how can you know, wife/husband, whether [or not] you will save your husband/wife?" He does not think that a spouse is able to save (σώσεις, *sōseis*) his or her partner in the way that Christ saves. "To save" is a missionary term meaning "to convert" (Weiss 1910: 183, Barrett 1968: 167). The Christian spouse becomes the avenue for the unbelieving spouse to find salvation in Christ (cf. 1 Pet. 3:1–6). Paul understands the "holiness" of unbelieving spouses (7:14) to be something different from their salvation. They may be "holy," but that does not entail salvation, because no one is "saved" by marriage (Menoud 1978: 9). Unbelieving spouses are not numbered among the "called saints" (1:2).

Again, this verse presents exegetical difficulties. Does Paul think that the prospects of converting the spouse are good or meager? Do his questions refer back to the exception noted in 7:15 and intend to dissuade the believer from trying to salvage a marriage to an unbeliever in the fond hope of eventually saving the unbelieving spouse? Those who consider Paul to be pessimistic about the chances of the spouse's conversion translate along this line: "Wife, how do you know whether you will save your husband?" (RSV, NASB, NIV). The implication would be "After all, you can never be sure" (so Foerster, *TDNT* 2:416; Kubo 1977–78; Ruef 1977: 58; Gordon 1997: 124 n. 90; Thiselton 2000: 537–40). Kubo (1977–78: 541, 544) contends that in 7:12–14, Paul first instructs those who may be uneasy about their marriage to an unbeliever and shows that the marriage relationship is legitimate and should continue. The issue is introduced in 7:12–13 and the reason is given in 7:14. According to Kubo, 7:15–16 forms another unit, in which Paul addresses those who want to remain in a relationship with an unbelieving partner who wants to separate. In this case, Paul allows the separation, amending the command of the Lord forbidding divorce, and gives his reasons for it in 7:15c–16. If the partner wants to separate, it makes the chance of conversion far less likely, if not bleak (cf. the pessimistic "who knows" in Eccles. 2:19 and 3:21). God has called them "for peace"; therefore, let the partner go. They should not desperately cling to a marriage that a partner wants to dissolve.

This interpretation mistakenly assumes that a partner could struggle to maintain a marriage that a spouse wishes to dissolve. No reason exists for Paul to coax the believer into letting go of the marriage. Contextually, the Corinthians need reassurance to maintain the marriage rather than reasons to allow a divorce. It is also uncharacteristic of Paul to be fatalistic about the hope of someone's conversion (Findlay 1910: 828). The idiom "how do you know?" (τί οἶδας, *ti oidas*) can be used in a context of optimism (cf. 2 Sam. 12:22; Esth. 4:14; Joel 2:14; Jonah 3:9; Add. Esth. 8:14; Tob. 13:8 B and A; Pseudo-Philo, *Bib. Ant.* 9:6; 25:7; 30:4; 39:3; Jos. As. 11:12; Epictetus, *Diatr.* 2.20.30). Context becomes the decisive factor in interpreting whether the phrase is optimistic or pessimistic. It is far more likely that Paul includes the prospect that the spouse might be converted, introduced by γάρ (*gar*), as a substantiation of the argument that the marriage should be continued. He argues against Christians initiating divorce: "You were called in peace, and for all you know, wife/husband, you might save your husband/wife" (cf. NRSV). Why make an unwarranted change in your marriage circumstances and lose the opportunity to convert your spouse?[23] It is worthwhile to maintain the marriage, since the Christian may be God's best instrument for bringing the unbelieving spouse to salvation (cf. 1 Pet. 3:1–2).

"To save someone" is also synonymous with "to gain someone" (κερδαίνειν, *kerdainein*), which Paul uses in 9:19–22 to appeal to his own example of doing anything to gain another for the Lord. His own missionary concern to win others at all costs is likely to color his advice about marriage. The modern idea that the purpose of marriage is to bring an

---

23. So Moffatt 1938: 84; Jeremias 1954; Burchard 1961; Barrett 1968: 167; J. Elliott 1972–73: 225; Murphy-O'Connor 1979a: 64–66; Fee 1987: 305; Rosner 1994: 171; Schrage 1995: 112; Deming 1995b: 156; Baumert 1996: 62; R. Collins 1999: 272.

individual spouse personal fulfillment and happiness was quite foreign to the ancient world. Paul gives no thought to what contributes to gaining personal gratification from the marriage relationship. Instead, he thinks only in terms of how a spouse must fulfill his or her obligations in marriage (7:3). In this situation, he would add the Christian's obligation to win another to the Lord. Lightfoot (1895: 227) captures the gist of Paul's counsel: "What he is really advising is the sacrificing of much for the possible attainment of what is a great gain though an uncertain one." Paul certainly recognizes the difficulties presented by a mixed marriage but would hardly recommend retreating from them (Barrett 1968: 167). If the partner wishes to continue in the marriage, a reasonable opportunity exists that he or she eventually will be saved. Paul's conclusion: Do not abandon the marriage; there is always the possibility that you will win your marriage partner.

Additional Notes

7:10. We should be careful not to project our own understanding of the legal ins and outs of marriage and divorce from our own culture onto the text. According to Roman marriage law, no legal or religious formalities were necessary to validate a marriage. It required only the intention of both partners to troth a lasting union. Divorce was just as easy and informal and more common among upper-class families, whose marriages were, more often than not, arranged for political and financial advantage. The marriage ended when the consent to be married was renounced by mutual agreement or when one unilaterally repudiated the marriage. It was enough for a spouse simply to leave home with the aim of ending the union. They did not need permission from some public authority and did not need to give formal notice, though it was normal to do so (Berger, Nicholas, and Treggiari, *OCD* 929; cf. Dixon 1992: 81). Extant divorce agreements from this era announce the separation of the spouses from each other, arrange financial issues, and declare it permissible for both to remarry. The young children remained with the father, not the mother; and, consequently, most families in the ancient world were blended.

Murphy O'Connor (1981b: 601–2) argues that Paul was referring to a specific situation (as in 5:1; 6:1) in which the wife was put away against her will by her husband for ascetic reasons. He bases this view on the passive voice of the verbs in 7:10, 11a, which may be translated, "A wife is not to be separated from her husband, but if she is separated . . ." (see also Orr and Walther 1976: 211; Fitzmyer 1976: 199–200). Paul protests: She is not to accept separation. If it is forced upon her, then she should not remarry but pursue reconciliation with her husband. The husband, on the other hand, is simply forbidden to divorce. The charge for the husband to remain unmarried is omitted because his reason for divorcing, to practice celibacy, precludes a desire for remarriage. The problem with this view is that the passive form of the verb is used in 7:15, where it is clear that the unbelieving spouse has initiated the separation and has not been unwillingly separated (see Roberts 1965). It also does not conform to legal realities: the wife could not refuse to accept being divorced.

7:14. The reading ἀδελφῷ has strong external support ($\mathfrak{P}^{46}$, ℵ, A, B, C, D*, F, G, P, Ψ), but the Majority texts have ἀνδρί (ℵ², D², 0150, 6, 81, 104, 256, 365, 424, 436, 459, 1241), and others add ἀνδρὶ τῷ πιστῷ (629, it[ar, b, o], vg, syr[p], Irenaeus[lat], Tertullian, Ambrosiaster). The change to "husband" from "brother" was probably made to balance "wife" in the first clause and "faithful" was added to clarify that the husband was a Christian, an idea inherent in the term "brother."

7:14. Some claim that the children are holy because they received infant baptism (O'Neill 1986: 359–61). Deming (1995b: 133 n. 95) counters, "If the children were holy by virtue of being baptized, then Paul could not prove from their holiness what he wants to prove, namely, that a Christian makes his or her unbelieving partner holy; and if the conceded point in Paul's argument was that baptism secured the holiness of the children, it is difficult to see why this whole matter surfaced in the first place, for the believing spouse was also baptized and should be in no more danger of pollution than the children."

7:15. The reading ὑμᾶς (א*, A, C, K, 0150, 81, 1175, 2127) instead of ἡμᾶς ($\mathfrak{P}^{46}$, א², B, D, F, G, Ψ) is most likely the original reading. The "you" fits Paul's style and his direct appeal in this unit. Later scribes tended, as a matter of course, to make aphoristic sayings more general (Metzger 1994: 489; R. Collins 1999: 272). Fee (1987: 297 n. 6), however, argues for ἡμᾶς on the basis of its stronger manuscript evidence and claims that scribes might tend to particularize statements. Both words would have been pronounced the same (see Caragounis 1995a), and the variations could be attributed to an unintentional mistake.

7:15. When Paul says that the Christian is not "enslaved" if the unbelieving spouse decides on a divorce, could he mean that the Christian is not bound to the mandate forbidding remarriage? Does it imply an "enslaving law" that a Christian needs to hold in a "slavish fashion" (Baumert 1996: 61)? Is the Christian who is divorced as "free" to remarry as is the widow whose husband has died (7:39)? Conzelmann (1975: 123) claims, "The Christian is not subjected to any constraint because of the pagan's behavior. He can marry again" (see also Ruef 1977: 57; Murphy-O'Connor 1979a: 66). R. Collins (1999: 272) acknowledges that the question is not addressed by Paul but thinks it a "likely possibility," given the social circumstances of his day. The slavery imagery derives from the Jewish comparison of divorce deeds to emancipation deeds (Instone-Brewer 2001: 238–39), and divorce deeds explicitly allow remarriage.

Instone-Brewer (2001: 240) argues that Greco-Roman and Jewish law "enshrined" remarriage after divorce as a right, and he concludes (2001: 241),

> When Paul says they are "no longer enslaved," any first century reader would understand him to mean that they can remarry, because they would think of the words in both Jewish and non-Jewish divorce certificates: "You are free to marry." If Paul had meant something else, he would have had to state this very clearly, in order to avoid being misunderstood by everyone who read his epistle.

Paul's primary goal in this passage is to argue against a Christian dissolving his or her marriage to an unbelieving spouse for spurious religious reasons. He disallows remarriage in the case of Christians divorcing Christians in 7:11 and argues against changing one's status in 7:17–24. But in 7:17–24, he also allows for an exception in the case of the slave obtaining freedom. In the same way, the one who has been divorced would be permitted to move from being married to being set free by divorce to being married again.

The answer to the question of divorce and remarriage need not be settled from this text alone. Other texts and other factors must weigh in, including the hermeneutical principles that Paul applies in his discussion in this chapter. He encourages the unmarried and widows to remarry if they continue to have sexual urges and "burn with passion," lest they fall victim to fornication (7:6–9). Would the same principle not also apply to the divorced to avoid unnecessary temptation from Satan (7:5)? What if they are not gifted with celibacy? Also, would Paul want the divorced woman to be sentenced to destitution because she was forbidden to remarry? Reconciliation of a divorced Christian with an unbelieving spouse, who has not experienced reconciliation with God and has little idea what reconciliation entails, is less likely than between two Christians, both of whom are committed to Christian values and principles. Can the divorced person argue that his or her remarriage would allay unnecessary anxieties (7:32) and promote better devotion to the Lord (7:35)?

7:16. M. MacDonald (1990a: 231) highlights how difficult a mixed marriage would have been, particularly for Christian wives: "The early Christians lived in a world which believed women to be inclined towards religious fanaticism and which accused unauthorized cults of leading women to behave immorally and threatening the stability of society as a whole." An unbelieving husband was not likely to welcome the wife's new faith (see 1 Clem. 6:2–3; Tertullian, *Apol.* 3). But Paul's evangelistic optimism emerges in his encouragement to continue a marriage that an unbeliever wishes to continue. We should be careful, however, in applying Paul's response to different situations in our context, when, for example, a spouse may suffer physical and emotional abuse. Different reasoning should come into play. What is important to glean from this text is not simply the answers that Paul gives, but the hermeneutical principles he employs to arrive at his answers. Christians must continually apply biblical principles to new situations.

V. Instructions about Sexual Relations, Divorce, and Marriage (7:1–40)
  C. Instructions about Divorce for Those Married to Christians and for Those Married to Non-Christians (7:10–16)
➤ D. Guiding Principle Underlying the Discussion: Remain as You Are (7:17–24)
  E. The Advisability of Marriage for the Betrothed and for Widows (7:25–40)

D. Guiding Principle Underlying the Discussion: Remain as You Are (7:17–24)

In a chapter devoted to questions about marriage and celibacy the abrupt shift to the topics of circumcision and uncircumcision and slavery and freedom may strike the casual reader as a temporary detour that rambles away from the main subject. To explain its presence, some conjecture that Paul interjects this discussion to squelch the unrest of overeager slaves who insisted on carrying their new-found freedom in Christ further and were campaigning for their manumission (Weiss 1910: 191; Moffatt 1938: 85). The letter betrays no hints that the status of slaves was of any concern in the church at Corinth, and Bartchy (1973: 130) finds no evidence of social discontent among slaves at Corinth in this period. Paul does not append this discussion to his exposition on marriage to keep slaves in their proper places. He is not concerned about slavery or circumcision (contra Braxton 2000) but chooses these topics to undergird the force of his practical instructions about marriage and celibacy with theological reasoning.

Tomson (1990: 104) labels this passage "the theological intermezzo" in a chapter filled with advice and instruction.[1] But it should not to be regarded as filler or as something independent of the two parts that precede and follow it. This passage functions as a *digressio* (*egressus, egressio*), which does not wander away from the main theme but amplifies or illustrates the main topic (see Quintilian, *Inst.* 4.3.12–15, 17). Viewed this way, "what appears at first to be something of a distraction turns out to be in fact part of the argumentation" (Dawes 1990: 683). This *digressio* supports Paul's instructions in 7:2–16 and prepares for his instructions to the unmarried in 7:25–40 (R. Collins 1999: 274). Bartchy (1973: 161–62) identifies it as the central part of an ABA' pattern or ring composition (so R. Collins 1999: 274). Like the *digressio* on love in chapter 13, sandwiched between the discussion of the use of spiritual gifts in chapters 12 and 14, it lays out the theological foundation upon which he bases his

---

1. Braxton (2000) rejects the view that this passage is a hypothetical digression intended to support Paul's advice on marriage and argues instead that it specifically addresses concrete social problems of Jews participating in the gymnasium and slaves braving the evils of slavery.

counsel. It is not an aside but the very hub of his discussion (see Baumert 1996: 63; Schrage 1995: 129–31).

What do uncircumcision and circumcision, slavery and freedom, have to do with marriage, divorce, and celibacy? They illustrate the divine principle that no earthly status, such as one's racial heritage or social standing, is incompatible with the Christian's calling by God (Dawes 1990: 697). Those who were circumcised when God called them do not advance their spiritual condition by undergoing an operation to restore their foreskin, nor do those who were uncircumcised when God called them enhance their standing with God by undergoing circumcision. Slaves are no less accepted by God than are free persons. Both belong to Christ, and their social status has no spiritual significance. Whether a Christian is circumcised or uncircumcised, slave or free, married or single is inconsequential to God. One condition is not bad and the other good, nor is one condition less good and the other better. No condition presents an obstacle to living the Christian life, since a Christian is now defined by God's call (1:9) and nothing else. As Braxton (2000: 50) summarizes it, "Change of social status is not a precondition of the call, nor is change a natural consequence of the call." What matters is keeping the commandments of God (7:19), in particular, avoiding fornication (7:2). Christians can keep the commandments of God whether circumcised or uncircumcised, slave or free, married or celibate. Thiselton (2000: 545) puts it well: "A Christian does not have to seek 'the right situation' in order to enjoy Christian freedom or to serve God's call effectively."

Consequently, Paul insists three times in this paragraph (7:17, 20, 24) that they remain in the situation in which they are called (cf. the verb "to remain" [μένειν, *menein*] in 7:8, 11): "live accordingly" (οὕτως περιπατείτω, *houtōs peripateitō*, 7:17); "in this remain" (ἐν ταύτῃ μενέτω, *en tautē menetō*, 7:20); "in this remain before God" (ἐν τούτῳ μενέτω παρὰ θεῷ, *en toutō menetō para theō*, 7:24). This reiterated principle provides the theological underpinning guiding his counsel on the practical matters of marriage and celibacy. To alter one's status in life on religious grounds gives more importance to that worldly status than it merits and denies God's calling in Christ based on grace alone. The offer of salvation came to them without requiring them to alter their ethnic, social, or domestic status. Any attempt to make changes *for religious reasons,* in effect, controverts God's grace, especially if they think that these changes—such as exchanging marriage for celibacy—boost them to a higher spiritual plateau. Such a move substitutes the call to salvation that rests upon God's grace for one that hinges on works. It substitutes a call that comes to the lowly and not to the exalted (1:26) for one that favors the (self-)exalted over the lowly.

This core principle applies to the previous instructions that correct the Corinthians' mistaken assumptions that a change in status reaps spiritual benefits—if married, better celibate; if in a mixed marriage, better divorced. Paul does not tout the status quo as if it were divinely ordained (Bartchy 1973: 153), and "stay as you are" is not to become the law of the Medes and the Persians (Dan. 6:8, 15). The point is that one *does not have to change* one's life situation as a Christian, not that one *may not change* one's life situation. Exceptions are allowed. Those who were single when called by God and those who were married and are now widowed and who have normal urges for sexual relations may marry or remarry (7:8–9, 28). Those who were married and are now widowed and those who were divorced by a non-Christian spouse (7:15) may take advantage of their new situation to become celibate.

Paul's second illustration from slavery allows him to introduce an analogous exception (Dawes 1990: 696). Change of status is unnecessary as it relates to God's call, but that does not mean that change of status is prohibited (Braxton 2000: 53). Being a slave is not an obstacle to living the Christian life, but if the opportunity for freedom comes along, a slave should seize it. This example reveals that Paul recognizes that life is complex. Simple maxims such as "Remain as you are" do not suffice in every circumstance. There are advantages to being free, just as Paul believes there are advantages to being celibate. But these advantages have nothing whatever to do with one's worth or standing with God. Dawes (1990: 697) explains, "This second example illustrates both the ultimate indifference of one's state of life (v 21a) *and* the possibility of having a preference where circumstances allow (v 21b)." In the same way that a slave may seize the opportunity for freedom, Christians may seize the opportunity for celibacy to devote themselves single-mindedly to the Lord (7:35).

Deming (1995a: 130–31) shows how this passage reflects a diatribal pattern (citing examples from Teles, *Fragments* 2.10.65–80; Philo, *Jos.* 24 §144; Seneca, *De tranquillitate animi* 4.3–4; and Epictetus, *Enchiridion* 15) in which a statement of fact is given in the form of a rhetorical question, often in the direct address of the second person singular, followed by an imperative that denies that the statement of fact has any significance in a person's life. An explanation is sometimes added to show why the statement of fact should be treated with indifference. This pattern surfaces in 7:18–19, 21–22, and 27.

Rhetorical Question	Imperative	Explanation
Were you circumcised or uncircumcised when called? (7:18)	Do not remove your circumcision or become circumcised. (7:18)	Circumcision or uncircumcision is nothing. (7:19)
Were you a slave when called? (7:21)	Do not worry. (7:21)	The slave is the Lord's freedman, and the free person is the slave of Christ. You were bought with a price; do not become a slave of humans. (7:22–23)
Are you bound to or loosed from a wife? (7:27)	Do not seek to be loosed or seek a wife. (7:27)	

The pattern is broken in 7:28, which lacks an explanation, and in 7:21cd, which includes a statement after the imperative. This break in the pattern is an important factor in trying to unpack the meaning of 7:21cd, a notorious crux.

Paul's argument in this section takes the following shape:

1. Statement of the basic principle: As the Lord has apportioned and God has called, live your life (7:17)
    a. Example: Circumcision and uncircumcision (7:18)
    b. Rationale: Circumcision and uncircumcision are nothing (7:19)
2. Restatement of the basic principle: Remain in the calling in which you were called (7:20)
    a. Example: Slavery (7:21ab)
    b. Exception: If you can gain your freedom, make use of it (7:21çd)
    c. Rationale: The slave is the Lord's freedman, and the free person is the Lord's slave (7:22–23)
3. Restatement of the basic principle: Remain before God in the calling in which you were called (7:24)

Exegesis and Exposition

[17]But, as the Lord apportioned to each one, as God called each one, live accordingly. And so I ordain in all the churches. [18]Was anyone circumcised when he was called? ⌜Let him not remove his circumcision⌝. Was anyone called in uncircumcision? Let him not be circumcised. [19]Circumcision is nothing and uncircumcision is nothing; what counts is keeping the commandments of God. [20]Let each one remain in the calling in which he or she was called. [21]Were you a slave when you were called? Do not let it bother you. But if you are able to become free, instead make use of [freedom]. [22]For whoever was a slave when called in the Lord is the Lord's freedman, and likewise whoever was a free person when called is Christ's slave. [23]You were bought for a price; do not become slaves of

humans. [24]Let each one remain before God in the [circumstances] in which he or she was called.

7:17 This *digressio* begins with εἰ μή (*ei mē*), literally, "if not," which is abrupt and somewhat confusing, since it is the only place in the NT where this expression begins a new unit. It normally has an exceptive force, introducing an exception to a preceding negative, and is translated "except" or "nevertheless." That pattern might suggest that Paul is offering an exception to 7:15b.[2] When a Christian is divorced by an unbelieving spouse, this separation is excusable; nevertheless, change is not to be the rule (so Fee 1987: 309; Dawes 1990: 686 n. 19). The εἰ μή, however, functions as an equivalent to ἀλλά (*alla*, but; Zerwick 1963: §470). In what follows, Paul spells out the guiding principle governing his counsel.

The basic principle is delineated with two "as" (ὡς, *hōs*) clauses ("as God apportioned to each"; "as God called each one") followed by two "thus" (οὕτως, *houtōs*) clauses ("live thus"; "I ordain thus in all the churches"). The verb μερίζειν (*merizein*) means to "assign," "divide," or "distribute something," as in the apportioning of the promised land to the various tribes (Num. 26:52–56; Josh. 14:5). Paul does not specify, however, what it is that the Lord has apportioned to each one (see additional note). In Rom. 12:3, he uses the verb to refer to "the measure of faith that God has assigned to each one" (ἑκάστῳ ὡς ὁ θεὸς ἐμέρισεν μέτρον πίστεως, *hekastō hōs ho theos emerisen metron pisteōs*) and then rattles off a list of gifts (12:4–8).[3] He argues in 1 Cor. 7:7 that "each one" has different gifts, and he may be thinking here of the different measures of faith, grace, or gifts they have received from Christ to live out their Christian calling (so Calvin 1960: 151; Conzelmann 1975: 126; Lang 1986: 96; Schrage 1995: 133). If the verb refers to the gifts apportioned to them by God (cf. 3:5; 12:4–11), it would underscore the assorted endowments each one has in the community. There is no one way for a Christian to live his or her calling, because each is to live in line with his or her gifts (Talbert 1987: 40). To try to become something one is not or to expect others to do so is a recipe for disaster.

---

2. Deming (1995b: 157–73) contends that 7:17–24 is "the continuation and conclusion of the argument begun in 7:15bc." The argument runs: (1) no Christian should be enslaved to his or her circumstances in life; and (2) "that undue concern for changing the circumstances of one's life disregards the efficacy of God's call, and thereby represents a form of slavery in itself." Deming contends that some Corinthians thought of marriage as "slavery" because of the control that a spouse has over their body (7:4) and were trying "to shake off the yoke of marriage slavery by divorcing a non-Christian spouse." This interpretation misses how this passage informs Paul's argument throughout this chapter.

3. In 2 Cor. 10:13, he uses the verb to refer to God's assigning him a jurisdiction in which to carry out his apostolic commission.

If Paul intended the object of the verb ἐμέρισε to be "spiritual gifts," it is perhaps surprising that he does not use the same verb when he discusses the distribution of varying gifts in chapter 12, particularly in 12:7, where he writes "to each is given [ἑκάστῳ . . . δίδοται, *hekastō . . . didotai*] the manifestation of the Spirit for the common good." Other interpreters argue that the verb's object is the individual's lot in life, which the Lord has assigned, "the circumstances . . . in which the believer was providentially placed at the time of his conversion" (Godet 1886: 353; so also Lightfoot 1895: 228; Findlay 1910: 829; Weiss 1910: 184; Holl 1928: 219; Héring 1962: 54; Barrett 1968: 168, 170; Fee 1987: 310; R. Collins 1999: 283; Thiselton 2000: 549). The philological evidence for the meaning of καλεῖν (*kalein*, to call) and κλῆσις (*klēsis*, calling, 7:20) is crucial for determining what Paul intends.

BDAG (549) gives as an alternative meaning for κλῆσις, "station in life," "position," "vocation." LSJ (960), however, does not offer this meaning as an option but suggests "religious calling" for its meaning in 7:20. Paul could have recoined the meaning of the word to apply it to one's station in life (Holl 1928: 190), but his normal usage refers to God's beckoning of persons to salvation (Rom. 11:29; Eph. 1:18; 4:1, 4; Phil. 3:14; 2 Thess. 1:11; 2 Tim. 1:9). The lack of any attestation in the NT or elsewhere that the word "calling" was used to mean "station in life" or "occupation" (Bartchy 1973: 10–25, 135–37) strongly argues against the interpretation that it applies to the condition or circumstances in which believers found themselves when God's offer of salvation reached them (contra Lightfoot 1895: 229; Moffatt 1938: 89; Barrett 1968: 168; Dawes 1990: 684). Nor does Paul have in mind two callings (Orr and Walther 1976: 216), one referring to the worldly condition when the person received God's call and another referring to God's call that eclipses that worldly condition.

The verb καλεῖν (*kalein*) is the key term in this unit, occurring eight times, along with the one appearance of the noun κλῆσις. The verb appears only four other times in the letter (1:9; 7:15; 10:27; 15:9), the noun once (1:26), and the adjective (κλητός, *klētos*, called) three times (1:1, 2, 24). Paul's usage suggests that he has in mind God's call to salvation. It transcends and transforms all external circumstances, and the perfect tense (κέκληκεν, *keklēken*) hints at the continuing effects of that call. As a consequence, he insists that they are not to make unnecessary changes in their life circumstances that their conversion and response to God's call do not require. Barth and Blanke (2000: 238) cite the forceful reasoning of Karl Barth (1960–61: 3.4.605–6) on this point: "A Christian is not called to be circumcised or uncircumcised, free or slave; he is called precisely in the state in which he is. He must always be true, not to the state, but to his calling within it, as this man with this historical background and history."

"Each one" (ἑκάστῳ, *hekastō*; ἕκαστον, *hekaston*) is placed in an emphatic position in the Greek and underscores that each is an individual and that God's call reaches the lives of those who come from different contexts, backgrounds, and niches in society. It sharpens Paul's point that, since the divine call came to each individual without regard to his or her social context, God does not esteem one particular state to be more valuable or more advantageous than another. The implication is that the only criterion of how they should live as Christians is determined by God, who called them (Baumert 1996: 65), not by humans with their faulty judgments. Paul commands them to conduct their lives (literally, "walk" [περιπατείτω, *peripateitō*]) accordingly.[4] That is, they are to walk as those called by God and in accord with God's commands and not be driven by human aims and aspirations.

Informing them that he has ordered the same thing in all the churches (in his orbit of influence) does three things. First, it reminds them of his authoritative teaching as an apostle. Second, it makes clear that he is not giving them ad hoc counsel. This principle is the rule of thumb everywhere (Tomson 1990: 271). Third, by appealing to the practices of other churches, as he does throughout the letter (cf. 4:17; 11:16; 14:33; 16:1), he notifies them that deviating from this principle makes them peculiar.

7:18 Paul's Jewish worldview that divided up humanity into the circumcised and the uncircumcised (cf. Eph. 2:11) was deep-seated, but it surfaces here in a way that is distinctively un-Jewish.[5] The Corinthian congregation included both Jews and Gentiles, an improbable fellowship, and Paul uses circumcision as an example to reinforce the principle he has just laid down: they are to remain in the condition in which they were called. Jews who responded to God's call remained Jews, and Gentiles who converted to the Christian faith remained Gentiles. They did not become Jewish proselytes by submitting to circumcision.

Most Jews felt no need to reverse the sign of their circumcision (through epispasm [see additional note]) because they became Christians, which underscores Paul's point. Winter (1994: 147–52) contends, however, that some Jewish believers may have been so tempted to hide their ethnic origins and enhance their chances for higher social status. Winter sees the search for social status as the key factor in this unit. The Galatian saga reveals, however, that Gentiles who were uncircumcised

---

4. Paul uses the verb "to walk" to refer to human behavior that is or is not in accordance with the law of God (cf. Rom. 6:4; 8:4; 13:13; 14:15; 1 Cor. 3:3; 2 Cor. 4:2; 5:7; 10:2–3; 12:18; Gal. 5:16; Eph. 2:2, 10; 4:1, 17; 5:2, 8, 15; Col. 1:10; 2:6; 3:7; 4:5; 1 Thess. 2:12; 4:1, 12; 2 Thess. 3:6, 11).

5. The noun ἀκροβυστία (*akrobystia,* foreskin) was a term that Jews used for Gentiles (Acts 11:3).

when they were converted sought circumcision not to attain social status, since circumcision was regarded by the Romans as barbaric and akin to castration (Balsdon 1979: 216, 231), but to attain religious status as bona fide sons of Abraham.[6]

To declare that circumcision is nothing (cf. Gal. 5:6; 6:15; Rom. 2:25–26) is a remarkable statement for a Jew to make, particularly one who claims to revere keeping the commandments of God, since circumcision is one of those commandments (Gen. 17:9–14; cf. Justin Martyr, *Dial.* 10). For strict Jews and Christian Judaizers, circumcision was the obligatory sign of the covenant that God established in perpetuity with Abraham and his descendants and a tangible identity marker that separated Jews from the heathen people around them. Most Jews assumed that those who were not circumcised did not belong to the sons of the covenant but to the children of destruction destined for annihilation (Jub. 8:26). The rabbis lauded it as one of the most important commands because it superseded even the Sabbath laws; that is, one could break the Sabbath to circumcise a boy on the eighth day (John 7:22; *m. Šabb.* 19:2–4). For Paul to say that circumcision and uncircumcision are nothing reveals that God's call in the crucified Christ voids all former classifications that assign worth to people based on their ethnicity.

7:19

Having accepted God's call, Christians must accept that God accepts them as they are. Their conversion requires a change in lordships, spiritual values, and moral behavior, but not a change in race, gender, or social caste. Altering their status will not make them more acceptable to the God who justifies "the uncircumcised on the ground of faith and the circumcised on the basis of the same faith" (Rom. 3:30), nor will it make them "more saved." Paul could have gone on to say, "Marriage is nothing, celibacy is nothing, neither commends us to God" (Menoud 1978: 14), but he leaves it for the Corinthians to make the application.

Remaining in the state in which one is called is not a virtue in and of itself, however. Consequently, Paul says, "Keep the commandments of God." The phrase "commandments of God" (ἐντολῶν θεοῦ, *entolōn theou*) does not appear elsewhere in Paul's letters, but he presumes that the Corinthians know what he means. The noun "commandment" (ἐντολή, *entolē*) as a reference to God's commandment appears six times in Rom. 7 (see also Rom. 13:9; Eph. 2:15; 6:2). Does Paul have in mind obedience to the Mosaic law even though he would ignore its command

---

6. Compared to Galatians, Paul's lack of passion here suggests that the circumcision controversy did not bedevil Corinth. Otherwise, he would not have chosen it as an illustration, which, he assumes, provides incontrovertible proof that one need not change one's condition.

to be circumcised?[7] Thielman (1992: 237–40) contends that the phrase "keep the commandments of God" in Jewish and Christian literature was equivalent to keeping the law of Moses (Ezra 9:4; Sir. 32:23; Matt.19:17; see also Rev. 12:17; 14:12; Wis. 6:18) and that Paul could assess the law positively in some contexts and negatively in others. Paul distinguishes between parts of the law that count and parts of the law that no longer count. Circumcision was part of the law that no longer was valid (Rom. 2:25–29) because it divided Jews from Gentiles. But the law in general was still valid, and the commandments could be summed up in "Love your neighbor as yourself" (Rom. 13:9; cf. Gal. 5:14).

Neuhäusler (1959: 46) claims that the phrase was a vestige of a pre-Pauline baptismal formula by which new Christians were exhorted to keep the commandments of God. Or, Paul may have understood keeping the commandments of God in a more general sense as equivalent to obeying the will of God (Baltensweiler 1967: 151; Barrett 1968: 169). Deming (1995b: 170–73) claims that Paul has adopted a Judeo-Christian expression and given it a Stoic twist. The Stoics used "commands," though rarely, to refer to the very essence of Stoicism, and keeping the commands was tantamount to "being a philosopher." Deming thinks that Paul adapted this turn of phrase and used it to mean "being a Christian" (so also Lindemann 2000: 171). Furnish (1999: 62) also opts for a general meaning and thinks that it means "leading one's life in accordance with God's call (v. 17a), as one who belongs to Christ (v. 22)."

Since Paul addresses Jews and Gentiles, it is plausible that the phrase "keep the commands of God" refers to the universal Noachian code that forbids unchastity, idolatry, and shedding blood (Tomson 1990: 271–72). Paul's lengthy warnings about unchastity (*porneia*) in the previous two chapters (5:1–6:18; also 7:2) and his lengthy warnings about idolatry in the next chapters (8:1–11:1) reveal that this ethical code was applicable to the Corinthian situation.

However one defines "the commandments of God," keeping them is something that Christians can do in any condition, circumcised or uncircumcised, slave or free, married or celibate. What is important is not the state that one is in, but how one lives ethically in that state. When this principle is applied to the Corinthian problem, Paul implies that the important distinction is not between those who are married and those who are celibate but between those who avoid fornication and those who fall prey to it.

---

7. E. Sanders's (1983: 161–62) claim that this was one of the most amazing sentences Paul ever wrote (see also Barrett 1968: 169; Räisänen 1983: 67–68) is overblown. The statement would not have been considered that remarkable in Hellenistic Judaism (Thielman 1992: 237; see also Tomson 1996: 263–69).

Paul reiterates the basic guiding principle: "Let each one remain in the calling in which he or she was called." They are not to alter their circumstances out of a felt need that such a change is required to better their relationship with God. When he asks them in 1:26–27 to consider their call, he reminds them that not many were wise by human standards, powerful, or of noble birth. God chose them as they were: the foolish to shame the wise, the weak to shame the strong. God's call did not hinge on their value as calculated by worldly criteria but came to them solely on the basis of God's purposes and grace. Consequently, it would discredit God's call if they were to try to become wise, powerful, and of noble birth, because that effort reveals that they regard those things as more significant than God's grace.

7:20

To change one's condition, thinking that it might spruce up one's image before God or solidify one's footing in salvation, ascribes more significance to external circumstances than they deserve. Since human categories are not ultimate, Christians may live out God's calling in the social circumstances in which God's call first reached them. This admonition does not mean they *must* remain in these circumstances but that they recognize that these circumstances do not hinder their calling to live as Christians (Fee 1987: 309). Paul adds for emphasis the phrase παρὰ θεῷ (*para theō*, before God) for his final reiteration of the guiding principle in 7:24. One can make changes in one's estate, but nothing is to be gained "before God" from any attempt to upgrade one's standing with God through these changes. Such a move implies that God's call was somehow deficient and that salvation is something they need to achieve by dint of their own powers. Paul is not sanctifying the status quo but challenging the illusions of those who think it wise to desexualize their marriage relationship, to attempt to become celibate without the gift of celibacy, to divorce their spouses, and to laud such changes as a higher calling.

In his second example, Paul shifts from ethnic status to social status. Again, this illustration would strike a chord with his readers. One third of Corinth's population were slaves, and another third were freedmen. If they were slaves when God's call reached them, Paul does not say, "Do not seek freedom," but, "Do not let it bother [μελέτω, *meletō*] you."[8] But there were plenty of things to worry about. Slaves were not legally persons, and consequently they had no legal or human rights and were classified as things and tallied as living pieces of property. Aristotle (*Politica* [*Politics*] 1.2.4) categorizes a slave as a living tool—a judgment that persisted. Varro (*De re rustica* 1.17.1) describes a slave as "an articulate implement." Slaves were constantly subject to the whip. Quintil-

7:21

8. In Paul's construction, "a pair of crisp alternative affirmatives do the work of conditional clauses" (Goodspeed 1917: 150).

ian (*Inst.* 1.3.13–14) argues against beating children by asserting that flogging is too disgraceful a mode of punishment and "fit only for slaves." Slaves were not legally permitted to marry, so Paul's discussion on marriage relationships would not apply to them. Since they lacked human worth in the world's eyes, they could easily anguish that they also lacked worth before God.

At this point, Paul breaks the diatribal pattern found in 7:18–19. He begins with the statement of fact in the form of a rhetorical question, "Were you a slave when you were called?" (7:21a), and follows it with an imperative, "Do not let it bother you!" (7:21b). But in 7:21cd, he interjects an exception before giving the explanation of why their slavery should be treated with indifference (7:22). He does not include the direct object for the phrase μᾶλλον χρῆσαι (*mallon chrēsai*, make use of), so it must be filled in: "But if you are able to become free, by all means make use of _____." Make use of what? Your "slavery" (τῇ δουλείᾳ, *tē douleia*), "freedom" (τῇ ἐλευθερίᾳ, *tē eleutheria*), or "calling" (τῇ κλήσει, *tē klēsei*)? Should μᾶλλον be rendered as "rather" or, in an elative sense, as "by all means"? The verb χρῆσθαι (*chrēsthai*) appears in 1 Cor. 7:31; 9:12, 15; 2 Cor. 1:17; 3:12; and 13:10 to mean "to make use of" or "to act." What is Paul saying? Perhaps he is encouraging slaves to be content with their slavery and not to seek freedom but rather to make use of their slavery to fulfill their Christian calling. Or perhaps he is offering an exception: Do not worry about being a slave and become consumed with a quest for freedom, but if the opportunity presents itself, by all means make use of it. The ambiguity created by this abbreviated expression continues to confound interpreters (cf. the opposing views of Schlier, *TDNT* 2:501, and Rengstorf, *TDNT* 2:272).[9]

Those who argue that Paul intends to discourage slaves from seeking their freedom translate "Even if you can gain your freedom, make the most of your present condition, your slavery, instead" (cf. NAB, NJB, NRSV).[10] Since he contends that slavery was neither shameful nor irreconcilable with Christian faith, slaves should not avail themselves of the

---

9. On the history of interpretation, see Harrill 1995: 77–108. Braxton (2000: 220–33) argues that Paul deliberately "retreated into the shadows of ambiguity" because he did not want to heighten church tension by recommending anything specific concerning manumission. Braxton refers to "the tyranny of resolution" and claims that we cannot know what Paul thought. I disagree.

10. So Chrysostom, *Hom. 1 Cor.* 19.5; Edwards 1885: 183–84; Weiss 1910: 187–88; Lietzmann 1949: 32–33; Sevenster 1961: 189–90; Héring 1962: 55; Bellen 1963; Barrett 1968: 170; Ruef 1977: 60; Conzelmann 1975: 127; Lührmann 1975: 62; Orr and Walther 1976: 215; Thiselton 2000: 553–59. Güzlow (1969: 177–81) contends that Paul has in mind slaves whose potential freedom would place them under a particularly burdensome *paramonē* contract stipulating special duties and obligations. He urges them to forgo the chance of liberation in those cases.

opportunity to gain their freedom.[11] The primary argument in favor of this interpretation is that it seems to fit the emphasis to remain in the state in which they were called (7:17, 20, 24).[12] It can also be supported by the grammar. The opening phrase ἀλλ' εἰ καί (all' ei kai) can be understood as expressing a concession, "but even if you are able to become free" (cf. 2 Cor. 4:16; 7:8a; 12:11; so Weiss 1910: 188), and would imply that they should not seek to become free. Μᾶλλον may be a contrasting comparative meaning "rather" or "instead": "Rather, make use of your slavery." The γάρ (gar) in 7:22 then could explain why they should remain in slavery: "For whoever was called in the Lord as a slave is the Lord's freedman." Paul's point: Do not regard your slavery as intolerable; endure it faithfully as a Christian.

Although this view may make sense in the context, it probably is incorrect. Rather than encouraging slaves to remain in their slavery, Paul offers an exception that encourages them to make use of any opportunity to obtain their freedom: "Though if you can gain your freedom, do so" (RSV, NIV, REB).[13] God's call does not freeze them forever in their present condition. The following arguments from syntax, literary context, historical context, and theological ramifications combine to show that this is the correct option.

First, there are arguments from syntax:

1. Many point out that when a reader needs to supply a word or phrase to complete the sense of an elliptical expression, "one would ordinarily supply a word from that sentence—in this case 'freedom'—not a word from an earlier sentence" (Fee 1987: 317). Several less controversial examples from the NT confirm this principle.[14] Since the preceding clause mentions freedom, it is logically the most likely referent: "If you can gain freedom, by all means, make use of [freedom]." If Paul had wanted to advise Christian slaves to remain in slavery, to be clear, he would have

11. Paul does not seek to quell unrest precipitated by slaves who had tried to apply their newfound religious equality to the social sphere.

12. Ignatius (Pol. 4:3) takes a similar conservative position: "Do not be haughty to slaves, either men or women; yet do not let them be puffed up, but let them rather endure slavery to the glory of God, that they may obtain a better freedom from God. Let them not desire to be set free at the Church's expense, that they be not found the slaves of lust."

13. So Godet 1886: 359–62; Lightfoot 1895: 229–30; Findlay 1910: 830; Robertson and Plummer 1914: 147–48; Trummer 1975: 352–63; Murphy-O'Connor 1979a: 67; Baumert 1984: 114–37; 315–18; 1996: 70; Fee 1987: 316–18; Talbert 1987: 42; Wolff 1996: 149–50; Horrell 1996: 162–66; Hays 1997: 125–26; R. Horsley 1998: 101–2; Lindemann 2000: 172–73.

14. John 15:4; Matt. 6:30 = Luke 12:28; Matt. 10:25; Mark 14:29; Rom. 11:12, 16; 1 Cor. 4:15; 9:2; 2 Cor. 5:13 (2x), 16; 7:12; 8:12; 11:6; Gal. 3:18; Heb. 12:25; 1 Pet. 4:11 (2x).

needed to say so explicitly: "Even if you can gain freedom, rather, make use of your slavery."

2. The choice of the aorist imperative χρῆσαι is the most suitable if Paul is referring to "taking a new opportunity rather than to the continuation in one's present state, which would really require the present tense" (Robertson and Plummer 1914: 147–48; cf. Moulton 1908: 247; Moule 1960: 21; Trummer 1975: 356–57; Fee 1987: 317; Horrell 1996: 163). Arguments from the tenses of verbs are often tenuous, and one can only argue that the aorist is more appropriate for expressing this meaning, not that it requires this meaning. The verb, however, does not mean "make the most of" or "put up with" (Barrett 1968: 170) but "make use of" (cf. 7:31; 9:12, 15; cf. 2 Cor. 1:17; 3:12; 13:10).

3. Μᾶλλον (*mallon*) may have an intensive sense that could be translated "by all means," "certainly" (cf. Rom. 5:9; Phil. 3:4; Philem. 16; see Moulton and Howard 1929: 165 n. 1). Harrill's (1995: 108–21) exhaustive philological analysis of μᾶλλον + χράομαι in the extant literature (cf. C. Dodd 1924–25) demonstrates that μᾶλλον has an adversative meaning, "instead" (or "preferably").[15]

4. The ἀλλά (*alla*, but) can have its usual adversative force, which suggests that the statement qualifies what precedes: "If you were called as a slave, don't worry about it, *but* . . ." (so Fee 1987: 317). The phrase εἰ καί need not be concessive but can have an emphatic force, as it does in 7:28 and 4:7 (cf. 7:11; 2 Cor. 4:3; 7:8b; 11:6), and can be rendered "but if indeed" (Moule 1960: 167 n. 3; Denniston 1959: 303; Thrall 1962: 81; Bartchy 1973: 178; Trummer 1975: 355–56; Harrill 1995: 119–20).

5. The γάρ clause in 7:22 need not explain why one should remain a slave but can, instead, refer back to 7:21ab and explain why the slave who can do nothing about his slavery need not be distressed about it. It does not matter to God; the slave is Christ's freedman.

Arguments from the syntax and grammar have not won the day, and arguments from the context are most important. What has gone largely unnoticed in examining the context is how this statement breaks the pattern found in 7:18–19 of rhetorical question, imperative, and explanation by adding a statement between the imperative and the explanation (Deming 1995a: 135). Horrell (1996: 164) notes that omitting this disconcerting addition in 7:21cd would not disturb the logic or smooth-

---

15. Harrill (1995: 111, 119) cites Vettius Valens (*Anthrologiae* 5.6.38–39) as the closest grammatical parallel and argues that μᾶλλον serves as an adversative to the previous apodosis, "do not worry," and not an adversative to the protasis, "if you can become free." He understands it to mean: If manumission is offered, *do be* concerned and use freedom. Avail yourself of the opportunity to become free.

ness of the thought and would match more closely the pattern evident in the previous verses: "Were you a slave when you were called? Do not let it bother you. For the one who is called in the Lord as a slave is the Lord's freedman, and likewise the one who is called as a free person is Christ's slave." He argues from this pattern that the interjection in 7:21cd would be expected by the reader to be some kind of an exception (see also Harrill 1995: 123–26).

The pattern found in 7:18–19 and 27 is broken in another, more subtle way. The imperative functions as a rebuff intended to deny that the statement of fact—circumcision or uncircumcision, marriage or singleness—has any significance for life with God. On the basis of these examples, we might expect Paul to have written, "You were called as a slave? Do not seek to become free!" What he writes instead is, "Do not let it worry you." This change cushions the force of the imperative's rebuff. Deming (1995a: 137) concludes, "This deliberate softening of the imperative . . . would seem to rule out the idea that 7:21b is somehow an attempt to heighten the imperative's impact."[16] One can infer from this alteration in the pattern that Paul encourages them to regard their slavery as a matter of indifference, but his softening of the rebuff, "do not let it bother you," implies that he does not mean they should give up any opportunity to become free.

Dawes (1990: 688) calls attention to other considerations from the use of paired illustrations elsewhere in the letter in 3:5–7 (the field and the building) and 15:35–44a (sowing and different kinds of bodies). Dawes argues that when Paul chooses to employ two different illustrations, he judges that a single illustration was inadequate to convey the point. The two images "modify and complement each other." Each has a particular purpose.

In this case, the first illustration allows no exceptions whatsoever: "Stay as you are!" The second, however, introduces the possibility of an exception to this rule. The introduction of an exception accords with Paul's instructions about the issue of marriage and celibacy throughout the chapter. Legitimate exceptions that would allow them to do something different from what he advocates lace his discussion of marriage and celibacy.

- Do not deprive one another, except (εἰ μήτι, *ei mēti*) by mutual agreement and for a limited time in order to withdraw for prayer (7:5).

16. Deming (1995a: 133) observes that Paul could not add to complete the pattern: "You were called as a freeman: don't become a slave!" Or, "You were called as a freeman: don't let it concern you!" (see also Bartchy 1973: 157; Fee 1987: 315). He also does not say, "Slavery is nothing and freedom is nothing."

- It is good for the unmarried and the widows to remain as I am, but if (εἰ δὲ οὐκ, *ei de ouk*) they are not exercising self-control, let them marry, for it is better to marry than to burn (7:8–9).
- To the married I command, not I but the Lord, that the wife is not to separate from her husband. If she has indeed (ἐὰν δὲ καί, *ean de kai*) separated, let her remain unmarried or be reconciled to her husband (7:10–11).
- Christians are not to divorce their spouses who are unbelievers. But if (εἰ δέ, *ei de*) the unbeliever separates, let him separate. The brother or sister is not under bondage in such [cases] (7:13–15).
- If you are not bound to a wife, do not seek a wife. But if indeed (ἐὰν δὲ καί, *ean de kai*) you marry, you do not sin; and if (καὶ ἐάν, *kai ean*) the virgin marries, she does not sin (7:27b–28).
- But if (ἐὰν δέ, *ean de*) anyone thinks he is acting indecently toward his virgin, if he is over the top, and so it is bound to happen, let him do what he wants, he does not sin, let them marry (7:27b, 36).
- But if (ἐὰν δέ, *ean de*) the husband dies, she is free to marry whomever she wishes, only in the Lord (7:39). I think, however, she is more blessed to remain single (7:40).

In some cases, he allows no exceptions: If you are married, you are not to become celibate—except by mutual agreement, for the purpose of prayer and for a limited time only. If you are married to a Christian, you are not to divorce. If you do divorce, remain single and seek reconciliation. In other cases, he makes exceptions: If you are married to an unbeliever, you are not to divorce the spouse. If you are divorced by the unbelieving spouse, you are no longer enslaved. If you are single, remain as you are. If you do marry, you do not sin. Widows, who may have been married when called by God, can choose to become celibate.

    The slavery analogy allows Paul to present an exception that accords with this complexity. The slave can serve God perfectly well as a slave; but if the opportunity for freedom comes, the slave should take advantage of it. The assumption is that freedom is preferable to slavery. But the analogy from slavery applies more evocatively to the question of celibacy and marriage. Paul sees a similar advantage in celibacy over marriage. He introduces the second example from slavery because it "illustrates both the ultimate indifference of one's state of life (v. 21a) *and* the possibility of having a preference where circumstances allow (v. 21b)" (Dawes 1990: 697). Paul declares his opinion in 7:32–35 that the celibate person can serve God more efficiently. That is no less true of the free person, who is not at the beck and call of a human master. One who has been "set free" (cf. 7:15, 39) from a marriage relationship can make use of this opportunity to serve the Lord with single-minded devotion. That fact does not mean that those who are married *should* make celibacy their aspiration any more than that a slave should make the prospect of manumission the center of his or her life. Just as slaves should not become absorbed in anxiety over their slavery, so those who are married should not become absorbed in anxiety over being married. Just as slaves should not force the issue of freedom by separating themselves from their masters (cf. Philem. 15, "he was separated from you for a short time"), so married persons should not force the issue by separating themselves from the spouses, either by robbing them of physical affection or by separating from them through divorce.

The third category of argument for reading this phrase as encouragement to make use of the opportunity for freedom comes from the historical context of manumission. In Roman society during this era, freedom would be offered to household slaves sooner or later, usually by the age of thirty, because the relationship between slave and master was governed by a carrot-and-stick philosophy. To keep slaves in line, masters employed draconian measures to instill fear that any offenses would meet with swift and harsh punishment. The carrot held out to the slave was the possibility of manumission as a reward for loyal service (see Garland 1998: 347).

Manumission was something initiated by a master, over which the slave had no direct control (similar to the situation of the Christian spouse who is divorced by the unbelieving spouse, 7:15). Bartchy (1973: 183) claims that the prerogative of setting a slave free belonged to the master, not to the slave, and the slave could not refuse manumission. It is mistaken, however, to say that slaves had no control whatsoever over their manumission.[17] Using δύνασαι (*dynasai*, if you are able) presumes that the slave has some choice in the matter.

A fourth argument that Paul permits slaves to seek their freedom if the chance comes up is theological in nature. Paul specifically says that he does not want to throw a noose around them when it comes to giving them advice about marriage, but he is seeking what he thinks will be most beneficial for them (7:35). Would he then want to throw a noose around slaves and fasten them ever more securely in their enslavement? If Paul were saying to slaves, "Do not avail yourself of the opportunity to gain your freedom," he would make absolute the condition in which they were called. Horrell (1996: 162) adds that Paul's injunction

---

17. Bartchy (1973:155–59) renders the verse, "But if, indeed, you become manumitted, by all means as a freedman live according to [God's calling]"—the admonition repeated three times in this unit. Bartchy bases this interpretation on evidence that the choice of remaining a slave or becoming free belonged to the master, not the slave—the slave could not refuse manumission—and on the meaning of "calling" as only God's call to salvation. Paul instructs slaves that whatever their status, they are to live according to God's calling (see also Schrage 1995: 140). For a critique of Bartchy and the historical evidence that slaves did have a choice in the matter, see Harrill 1995: 94–102.

not to become slaves of human masters (7:23) indicates that he does not regard slavery as a "desirable institution," and it should be "avoided if at all possible" (see also Trummer 1975: 364).[18] That the shame of the cross of Christ abolishes the shame of those who are enslaved does not mean that slavery can now be regarded as a desirable state. Paul's indirect appeal to Philemon on behalf of his slave Onesimus reveals that he is not an opponent of manumission (Garland 1998: 302–6).[19]

All of this evidence—grammatical, contextual, historical, and theological—adds up to the conclusion that Paul encourages the slave to take advantage of an opportunity to be granted freedom as an exception to the dictum "Remain as you are."

7:22–24   Paul's comments about slavery in the NT do not call for its abolishment but do assuage the degradation associated with it. The preceding interpretation of 7:21 assumes that the γὰρ (gar) beginning the first clause in 7:22 justifies the imperative not to worry about being a slave. It explains that in the Lord the categories of slave or free are not ultimate. God's call places the slave "in the Lord" (dative of sphere; literally, "the called-in-the-Lord slave"). Paul does not declare the Christian slave to be "free" (ἐλεύθερος, eleutheros) but a "freedman of the Lord" (ἀπελεύθερος κυρίου, apeleutheros kyriou). This metaphor reflects Roman law, in which the manumitted slave had continuing personal and legal obligations to the master (see Lyall 1970–71: 77–79; Duff 1928; Treggiari 1969; Barth and Blanke 2000: 41–53). Freed slaves were not free to do as they pleased. How true this was is reflected in Pliny the Younger's letter to a friend (Ep. 9.21) appealing on behalf of a freedman who had fled to him to request his intervention so that he might be restored to the good graces of his former master. The freedman owed the former master lifelong obsequium (eagerness to serve respectfully); a certain number of days' work per week, month, or year (operae, enforceable by civil action); gifts (munera); and moral duty (officium). In return, the master, now the slave's patron, looks after the welfare of the freedman. As Christ's freedman, the former slave takes on the name of the master, is directed by him, and owes him allegiance.

The readers would have been conscious of the social significance of being the freedman of a great patron. Freedmen took pride in their pa-

---

18. Epictetus (Diatr. 4.1.33), a former slave, wrote, "It is the slave's prayer that he be set free immediately." Does Paul intend to say, "Even though you may have yearnings for freedom, squelch them and reject any opportunity to become free"? If so, it would be akin to saying to the single person, "Even if you have sexual yearnings, squelch them and reject any opportunity to marry."

19. To argue, as Conzelmann (1975: 127) does, that civil freedom is "merely a civil affair" that is of "no value" in the church reflects the Luther's "Two Realms" view of the world, which can abet indifference to injustice. It also reflects a ruling-class viewpoint while ignoring the viewpoint of those with firsthand experience of bondage.

trons and identified themselves on their tombstones by adding that they were the *"apeleutheros* of [patron's name]" (D. Martin 1990: 64). Paul consigns honor and status to Christian slaves by designating them as the "freedmen of Christ." The slave no longer is simply the slave of so-and-so but a freedman belonging to the Lord. As D. Martin (1990: 65) explains it, "The slave's real status is determined by his or her placement in a different household entirely: the household of Christ. The slave is a freedperson of the Lord and shares in the benefits, status, and obligations that relationship brings."

Paul identifies the free person, on the other hand, as the slave of Christ (δοῦλος . . . Χριστοῦ, *doulos . . . Christou*), which includes himself (9:15–18; cf. 3:5). This assertion does not level the ground between slaves and free but actually places the free person on a lower rung on the ladder. It reverses the normal status of slave and free. D. Martin (1990: 66) comments,

> He took the highest-status person, the free man, and placed him in the lowest-status position of the household. Then he took the lowest-status person, the slave, and gave him a status above his fellow Christian, though still without making him an *eleutheros,* a free man. Paul thereby keeps both persons within the household of Christ, yet within the hierarchy of that household, he reverses their normal status positions. Freedom is not the issue here; status is.[20]

Those of lower status probably would appreciate the higher status conferred on them; those of higher status, the freeborn, would not (D. Martin 1990: 68). But Paul's intention is that Christians should now "view one another differently" (Horrell 1996: 160). This statement prepares the readers for issues that Paul will pick up in discussing the abuses surrounding the Lord's Supper. The key issue is not becoming slaves of humans. Some people did sell themselves into slavery to improve their lot. Dio Chrysostom (*Or.* 15.23) remarks, "Great numbers of men, we may suppose, who are free born sell themselves, so that they are slaves by contract, sometimes on no easy terms but the most severe imaginable." But Paul is using metaphor here. Bultmann (1956: 185) rightly contends that Paul means, "Do not make yourselves dependent on the value judgments of men" (so also Barrett 1968: 171; Deming 1995b: 164). Cultural values that venerate or stigmatize people according to their genealogy, work, wealth, or education do not affect a Christian's worth, and they should not infiltrate Christian values. Those who belong to Christ have no need to "better" themselves according to human

---

20. Comments, such as Moffatt's (1938: 87–88), that true freedom is inward (see also Deming 1995b: 157–73) are beside the point and do not capture Paul's radical tipping of the social scales.

standards. All circumstances have their advantages and drawbacks (Thiselton 2000: 559), and Christians should be content to remain as they are before God.

Additional Notes

7:17. If the verb μερίζειν refers to apportioning their lot in life, why say that it was the Lord, presumably Christ (cf. 8:6), who did it rather than God, who presides over external circumstances? This consideration apparently led the sources of the Majority text to reverse the order of the subjects of the two verbs: God apportioned and Christ called.

7:18. The command for Jews who are circumcised not to remove their circumcision (μὴ ἐπισπάσθω, mē epispasthō) refers to an operation (epispasm) that draws the loose skin on the penis over the head and stitches the wounds so that it replicates a foreskin (see Celsus, *On Medicine* 7.25.1; R. Hall 1992). The practice became an issue during a time of forced Hellenization imposed by Antiochus IV Epiphanes (175–164 B.C.). Some Jews submitted to the operation to remove the stigma of being different, especially young men wanting to fit in with Greeks when they competed in athletic events (conducted in the nude) and those not wanting to stand out when they attended the public baths (see 1 Macc. 1:15; As. Mos. 8:3; Josephus, *Ant.* 12.5.1 §241; Martial, *Epigrams* 7.35).

V. Instructions about Sexual Relations, Divorce, and Marriage (7:1–40)
    C. Instructions about Divorce for Those Married to Christians and for Those Married to Non-Christians
       (7:10–16)
    D. Guiding Principle Underlying the Discussion: Remain as You Are (7:17–24)
➤ E. The Advisability of Marriage for the Betrothed and for Widows (7:25–40)

E. The Advisability of Marriage for the Betrothed and for Widows (7:25–40)

Paul applies the principle "Remain as you are," established in 7:17–24, to a different situation regarding marriage. The topic addressed in 7:25–38 concerns those who are betrothed. Should they marry or not? The focus throughout is on the decision of the male, since in this culture males would have been the ones who took the primary initiative in such matters. An explanatory *digressio* in 7:29–35 may give the impression that Paul changes the subject, but what he says in 7:27 is so close to the more specific instructions in 7:36–38 that it must be "the same piece of advice to the same people" (Fee 1987: 332). He offers arguments as to why it is advisable for the betrothed to remain unmarried. In 7:39–40, he continues the pattern of alternating instructions to males with instructions to females in this chapter and briefly addresses the similar question of whether widows should marry or not.

Paul offers his maxim that it is best to remain as you are. Therefore, do not break a betrothal; do not seek a wife. He insists, however, that choosing marriage is no sin (7:28, 36), although he thinks it inadvisable for four reasons:

1. The death and resurrection of Christ and the giving of the Spirit mean that the new age has invaded the present. Christians can evaluate their choices in life from the perspective of the end that has come so near (7:29–31). An end-time awareness should sharpen the focus of their decisions in the mundane matters of this world.
2. Marriage brings trouble in the flesh (7:28).
3. Marriage brings responsibilities that divide a person's heart at a time when singleness of purpose is most needed (7:32–35). Preoccupation with the things of this world will result in a lack of preparedness for the world to come. The unmarried who devote themselves fully to the Lord have a practical advantage.
4. The form of this world, with its systems, values, and statuses, is passing off the stage. Everything belonging to this world is lame-duck, marriage included. Those who marry must realize

that earthly relationships will be transformed in the coming kingdom (7:29, 31).

Paul wants the Corinthians to think eschatologically, but he is not trying to stir up eschatological hysteria or dread. He mixes his eschatological orientation with practical advice. In 7:36–38, he gives the male specific directions with explicit criteria, which have nothing to do with the end time, to help him to make the decision to marry or not. It depends on whether the fiancé can keep his natural sexual impulses under control. If he cannot, he should marry. If he can, maybe he does not need to marry. In either case, the man does well.

This large section is set off by an inclusio, with the term γνώμη (*gnōmē*, maxim) appearing in the first and last verses, 7:25, 40. Paul appeals to *ethos* at the beginning and end of the unit to reinforce his argument. Before giving his directions, he reminds them that he has been mercied by the Lord to be trustworthy (7:25), and at the conclusion he reminds them that he too has the Spirit of God (7:40). The key word throughout the section is "virgin" (παρθένος, *parthenos*), which appears six times (7:25, 28, 34, 36, 37, 38).[1] Whom Paul has in mind is one of the exegetical enigmas in this section, but I identify the virgin as the woman engaged to be married. The argument runs as follows:

1. Paul's maxim concerning the unmarried (7:25–28)
2. Argument supporting the validity of the maxim: The time is compressed, with five crisp exhortations (7:29–31)
3. Practical reasons supporting his preference for celibacy (7:32–35)
4. Application of the maxim to the fiancé (7:36–38)
5. Application of the maxim to the widows (7:39–40)

Exegesis and Exposition

[25]Now concerning the virgins, I do not have a command of the Lord, but I give this maxim as one who has received mercy from the Lord to be faithful. [26]Therefore I think this to be good, because of the present distress, that it is good for a man to [remain as he is]. [27]Are you bound to a woman [by engagement]? Do not seek to be loosed. Are you loosed from a woman? Do not seek a wife. [28]But if you marry, you have not sinned, and if the virgin marries, she has not sinned. But these will have affliction in the flesh, and I would try to spare you that.

1. Elsewhere, Paul uses the term "virgin" only in 2 Cor. 11:2, "I feel a divine jealousy for you, for I promised you in marriage to one husband, to present you as a chaste virgin to Christ."

²⁹I mean this, brothers and sisters, the time has been compressed. From this point on, let those having wives be as though not having wives, ³⁰and those weeping as though not weeping, and those rejoicing as though not rejoicing, and those buying as though not possessing, ³¹and those making use of the world as though not making full use of it. For the form of this world is passing away.

³²But I want you to be without anxieties. The unmarried man is anxious about the things of the Lord, how he might please the Lord. ³³The man who is married is anxious about the things of the world, how he might please his wife. ³⁴ʳAnd he is conflicted. Likewise, the unmarried and chaste woman is anxious about the things of the Lord that she might be holy in body and spirit. But the married woman is anxious about the things of the world, how she might please her husband.⌐ ³⁵I am saying this for your very own benefit. I am not throwing a noose around [your neck] but [I am saying this] to promote what is seemly and constant before the Lord [that you might live] undistractedly.

³⁶But if anyone thinks he is acting indecently toward his virgin, if he is full of sexual passion, and so it is bound to happen, let him do what he wants. He does not sin. Let them marry. ³⁷If he stands firm in his heart, having no [sexual] necessity, and he has control over his own [sexual] impulse and has decided this in his own heart, to keep his own virgin, he does well. ³⁸So then, the one who marries his virgin does well, and the one who does not marry does better.

³⁹A wife is bound to her husband for as long as he lives. But if he passes on, she is free to marry whomever she wishes, only in the Lord. ⁴⁰But she is happier if she remains as she is, according to my maxim. And I think that I also have the Spirit of God.

Paul begins this next unit with περὶ δέ (*peri de,* now concerning), but it need not mean that he is addressing a new and different question from the Corinthians' letter to him.[2] He is still dealing with the same subject raised in 7:1 about whether it is "good" or not to touch a woman. The phrase "now concerning" serves as a topic marker denoting that he will now discuss the issue as it pertains to a specific case. "The virgins" (τῶν παρθένων, *tōn parthenōn*) serves as the subject heading. The most obvious meaning of τῶν παρθένων would be "female virgins" (Conzelmann 1975: 131), but the gender of the genitive plural has been a matter of great dispute (see Ford 1966a). To be sure, most biblical and secular usages relate the word to women, and Paul uses the noun with the feminine definite article in 7:28, 34, 36, 37, 38. But παρθένοι is also applied to men in Rev. 14:4 (see also Jos. As. 4:7) to emphasize their purity and dedication. The "virgins" may refer broadly to the unmarried of both sexes (Wolff 1996: 155; R. Collins 1999: 293), but it is unusual to apply this term to

7:25

---

2. Contra Lightfoot 1895: 231; Ellingworth and Hatton 1985: 145, who maintain that "'what you wrote' is implied in the Greek."

males.[3] Lightfoot (1895: 231) contends that Paul uses the noun in a general sense in stating his guiding principle in 7:27, applies it to both sexes in 7:28–35, and finally applies it to a special point raised by the Corinthians in 7:36–38 about fathers giving away virgin daughters in marriage. According to this view, the "virgins" in 7:25 refer to that particular subject—"marriageable virgin daughters." It is more logical, however, for the word to retain the same meaning throughout unless compelling evidence leads one to decide otherwise (Fee 1987: 323). Others venture to guess that "virgins" has a technical meaning and refers to male and female celibates who have chosen to set up house in a spiritual marriage (Hurd 1965: 169–82), or that it refers to the precursors of "ecclesiastical virgins" who consecrated themselves to service to God (Edwards 1885: 188). In 7:34, the "unmarried woman" (ἄγαμος, agamos, 7:34) is distinguished from the "virgin," so it is likely that "the virgins" refer to a special class of unmarried women, not all maidens of marriageable age (Fee 1987: 309).

The most plausible option is that "the virgins" comprise betrothed women (cf. Matt. 1:18, 23; Luke 1:27; cf. 2 Cor. 11:2).[4] Presumably, those who are engaged have misgivings about whether to go through with their marriage.[5] Paul tackles the issue under the heading "the virgins," betrothed women, but directs his specific instructions entirely to the men in 7:25–38 because males in this cultural context took the lead in contracting betrothals and marriage (Fee 1987: 327). Throughout 7:25–38, this one issue—What should the betrothed do about marriage?—is in view.[6] If someone in the community was exerting pressure on them, directly or indirectly, not to follow through with their marriage (Fee 1987: 323, 327), Paul likewise does not think that they should go through with their marriage, but he offers entirely different reasons.

3. In Matt. 19:12, those who do not marry are described as "those who have made themselves eunuchs for the sake of the kingdom," not as virgins.

4. The number of those falling into this category would be quite small, as Hurd (1965: 179) notes, but that does mean that their situation would not have posed a significant problem. The arguments for and against the various views must wait until the detailed discussion of 7:36–38, which is the crux for trying to unravel the situation. Worth mentioning in passing are the proposals that the term "virgins" refers to male celibates (M. Black 1961: 85; Bound 1984) or to young widows or that the question involves whether the deceased husband's brother should discharge his levirate obligation and marry his sister-in-law (Ford 1963–64). These interpretations stretch the meaning of the word "virgins" and assume that the Corinthian church has Jews still complying with Jewish legal customs (Fee 1987: 325 n. 13).

5. So Moiser 1983: 112; Fee 1987: 323; Wimbush 1987: 14; Hays 1997: 126; R. Horsley 1998: 104.

6. The references to married persons in 7:27a and 29 are brought up to illustrate points that he is trying to make.

Whichever of the options is chosen to explain the situation, it is clear that the Lord addressed none of them in his teaching—a father's responsibility in marrying off a daughter, or the consummation of a spiritual marriage, or the fulfillment or termination of a marriage engagement. Paul carefully distinguishes his commands from the Lord's in 7:10, 12, and here he concedes that he has no command of the Lord to interpret for them. This statement implies that *he* is the source of their knowledge of the commands of the Lord. It certainly reveals that he does not believe that having the Spirit (7:40) authorized him to invent ad hoc sayings of Jesus to meet any new circumstance the church might face (Orr and Walther 1976: 218). He will give them his γνώμη (*gnōmē*), however. Paul uses this word elsewhere to designate "purpose," "intention," or "mind": "be united in the same purpose" (1 Cor. 1:10; cf. Rev. 17:13, 17). It is used to refer to a decision he made in planning his travel itinerary (Acts 20:3). He also uses it to refer to his "advice," "opinion," or "judgment" (2 Cor. 8:10; cf. Josephus, *Ant.* 8.14.3 §379; 11.6.10 §253), and the noun is related to the wisdom with which the wise man directs others (Prov. 12:26; Wis. 7:15; Sir. 6:23). In Philem. 14, the noun refers to "previous knowledge" or "consent": "I preferred to do nothing without your consent."

The word in this context basically means "advice," but the common translation "opinion" does not adequately convey Paul's meaning. That translation may connote that when he lacks a command from the Lord, he is uncertain of his ground and only feels his way by offering an "opinion." At the end of his discussion, however, he informs them that he has the Spirit (7:40). It becomes evident in 7:29 and 31 that this "opinion" is based on his clear-sighted understanding of the end-time situation in which all now live. He speaks with his usual assurance and presents his arguments as an expert consulted for his judgment. God's mercy made him "sufficient" as a minister of the new covenant (2 Cor. 3:4–6) and certified him as "trustworthy" (πιστός, *pistos*).[7] Findlay's (1910: 831) comments offer a helpful caution against dismissing Paul's arguments in what follows as mere "opinion" that the Corinthians could take or leave: "The distinction made is not between higher and lower grades of inspiration or authority . . . but between *peremptory*

---

7. It does not mean "believer" in this context (cf. 2 Cor. 6:15) and that he simply offers his opinion "as a Christian" (contra Craig 1953: 84; Héring 1962: 57). R. Collins (1999: 289) notes that Epictetus (*Diatr.* 1.4.18, 20; 2.14.13; 2.22.26–27, 29–30; 3.20.5; 3.23.18; 4.1.133; 4.9.17; 4.13.17–24) describes the philosopher as trustworthy. Paul does not regard himself as a savant (1:18–21), however, but as a steward of God's revelation (4:1–2; cf. 1 Thess. 2:4). Dolfe (1992: 117, citing Thucydides, *History of the Peloponnesian War* 1.128.7) understands "trustworthy" to refer to Paul's fiduciary responsibility as an agent. He translates "in order to be a proxy in so far as the Lord (or because the Lord) has been and is merciful to me."

rule, and *conditional advice* requiring the concurrence of those advised. Paul's opinion, *qua* opinion, as much as his injunction, is that of the Lord's mouthpiece." The problem in this case is that Paul cannot lay down a fixed, universal rule. What should be done depends on the individual's circumstances.

Paul's use of the word γνώμη fits a more technical meaning. Ramsaran (1995: 531; cf. R. Collins 1999: 289) contends that the word has developed from "stated opinion" to "formalized maxim, a form of rhetorical proof with a concisely expressed principle or rule of conduct." It articulates a "succinct general truth or instruction" relating "to human life or the terms of human existence" (Silk, *OCD* 640). The maxim refers to the statement in 7:26 that basically restates what he propounds in 7:17, 20, and 24 and qualifies the maxim of the procelibacy faction cited in 7:1, "It is good for a man not to touch a woman." Paul agrees with it to a point (see 7:6); celibacy is the better option. He completely disagrees with their rationale and heavy-handed failure to take into consideration practical, human considerations.

Paul "underscores the authority of his maxim by appealing to his own prestige (the argument from one's personal *ethos*)" (R. Collins 1999: 289). The phrase ὡς ἠλεημένος ὑπὸ κυρίου (*hōs eleēmenos hypo kyriou*) expresses his conviction that his apostleship came through God's mercy, which he specifically says in 2 Cor. 4:1 (see also 1 Cor. 15:9–10; 1 Tim. 1:13, 16). God's mercy on him was directly tied to his call to proclaim Christ among the nations (Gal. 1:15–16). The divine confidence that bestowed this responsibility on him should inspire confidence in his instruction (cf. 2 Cor. 1:18–22).[8] This phrase could also imply that when he delivers directions to others, he is fully conscious of that mercy shown to him (Fee 1987: 328) and that his directions are, in turn, merciful (cf. Rom. 12:8). This mercy surfaces in his stated intention that he wants them to be free from anxieties (7:32), that he offers counsel for their own benefit, and that he has no intention of lassoing them (7:35). It also surfaces in his refusal to castigate as "sin" any decision to reject his advice on this particular matter (7:28, 36). He allows room for a variety of stances on how to live in obedience to God's call. One's choice, he cautions, has consequences, given the tensions that come with living during the in-between times, when the world's foundations are tottering and believers are still prey to satanic assault.

7:26   Paul echoes the Corinthians' maxim cited in 7:1: "It is good for a man not to touch a woman" (see Barrett 1968: 174; Fee 1987: 324; N. Watson 1992: 75; Deming 1995b: 110–12). This interpretation best explains the

---

8. This statement is not intended to convey some modest admission of his own "shortcomings" (contra Morris 1958: 116).

cumbersome redundancy of the repeated "good": "this to be good. . . , it is good."[9] He begins the specific discussion of the virgins by alluding to the Corinthians' catchword, with which he only partially agrees. He understands "good" to mean what is functionally beneficial, not what is the highest virtue.[10] "To be thus" (τὸ οὕτως εἶναι, *to houtōs einai*) may refer back to the previous verse and mean "it is good for a man to remain a virgin" (Godet 1886: 370). Or, it may look ahead to the next verse and essentially mean that it is good for a man not to make any dramatic changes in his life: he should remain as he is. Paul would agree with both statements, but the latter option fits best as the concrete application of the principle "Remain as you are," which he expounds in 7:17–24.

Some understand the phrase "because of the present necessity" (διὰ τὴν ἐνεστῶσαν ἀνάγκην, *dia tēn enestōsan anankēn*) to be a reference to the end-time woes that will engulf the world and are already portended in the sufferings of Christians (Barrett 1968: 175; Conzelmann 1975: 132). This rendering understands ἐνεστώς (*enestōs*) to signify "that which is about to become present" (see BDAG 337). Paul urges them to stay single in light of the imminent coming of Christ, which is preceded by a time of woe. But his use of the participle ἐνεστώς always refers to what is already present, which makes the rendering "impending" problematic (Gal. 1:4, "present evil age"; cf. Heb. 9:9, "the present time"). In Rom. 8:38 and 1 Cor. 3:22, ἐνεστῶτα (*enestōta*, things present) is an antonym of μέλλοντα (*mellonta*, things about to come). This usage of the participle suggests that he refers to something they are already experiencing. Consequently, some opt to translate the phrase as "the present difficulty," referring to the pinch of present circumstances instead of impending end-time disasters.

The word ἀνάγκη (*anankē*) has a broad range of usages. It can refer to any "necessity" or "compulsion," outer or inner, brought on by a variety of circumstances (BDAG 61). Commentators frequently cite other literature in which the word ἀνάγκη appears in connection with end-time events (Conzelmann 1975: 132 n. 13). It refers to the catastrophic events connected specifically to the destruction of Jerusalem in Luke

9. Edwards (1885: 190) labels it "redundant and incorrect"; Robertson and Plummer (1914: 152), as "irregular."

10. Lapide's comments on this passage offer a good example of the view Paul intends to counter. Lapide (1896: 163) considers the celibate to be "better off in time, better off in eternity." Virginity, Lapide argues, is a "heroic exhibition" of temperance (172), and a "mark of true religion" (175). Virgins "are more loved by Christ than others," are "the noblest part of the Church" (175), and "have in heaven a more excellent reward and crown" (176). Menoud (1978: 5), by contrast, taps the essence of Paul's view of celibacy: "The gift is not given to all, it offers no religious prerogatives, it does not enable the celibate to reach a higher level of communion with Christ."

21:23.[11] But Paul uses it to connote moral necessity (Rom. 13:5), divine compulsion (1 Cor. 9:16), duress (2 Cor. 9:7; Philem. 14), calamities or disasters (plural; 2 Cor. 6:4; 12:10), and distress (1 Thess. 3:7). In 7:37, the one who "does not have necessity" refers to one who is able to control his sexual desire without experiencing frustration (see Gager 1970: 330–33).

If ἐνεστώς means "present" and ἀνάγκη means "calamity," then Paul may have in mind something far more mundane and local than the end-time cataclysm. He may be alluding to persecution that has befallen the community (cf. 2 Cor. 1:6; Acts 18:1–17; so Grundmann, *TDNT* 1:346). Little evidence exists in the letter, however, to suggest that the Corinthians were having to cope with any open hostility from their neighbors. Winter (1991a; 1997e: 331) identifies the "present crisis" as a famine that gripped the city and caused serious economic deprivation (see also Blue 1991; Kistemaker 1993: 239). Winter translates it "the present dislocation" to describe the social unrest that the grain shortage created. Laughery (1997: 111–12) concedes that there may have been a famine but doubts that it was the genesis of the Corinthian questions. Indeed, one cannot deny the apocalyptic tenor of the whole passage, with its references to the "compressed time" (7:29) and "the form of this world passing away" (7:31). It may be that Paul uses the word "present" because he assumes that the end-time afflictions are already happening, which "portended a speedy crisis" (Findlay 1910: 831). The suggestion by Godet (1886: 371) that it refers to the "whole state of things between the first and second coming of Christ" (see also Grosheide 1953: 175) seems too amorphous. Christians are always at odds with the world because of its alien worldview and always subject to its abuse, but Paul seems to have something more definite in mind. It is most likely that he has in view a present crisis (perhaps the famine) interpreted as an end-time event. The eschatological character of this present calamity "may be deduced from the fundamentally eschatological nature of the time in which it is endured" (Schlier, *TDNT* 3:144).

Paul believes that the end of time has already broken in (cf. 10:11, "upon whom the end of the ages has come"). Affliction is inseparable from Christian life in this world (Schlier, *TDNT* 3:144; cf. 1 Thess. 3:3–

11. A textual variant in 3 Macc. 1:16 reads τῇ ἐνεστώσῃ ἀνάγκη (*tē enestōsē anankē*) to describe the desecration of the temple by Antiochus IV Epiphanes: "Then the priests in all their vestments prostrated themselves and entreated the supreme God to aid in the present situation [variant: 'the present crisis'] and to avert the violence of this evil design, and they filled the temple with cries and tears." It continues in 1:19–20: "Those women who had recently been arrayed for marriage abandoned the bridal chambers prepared for wedded union, and, neglecting proper modesty, in a disorderly rush flocked together in the city. Mothers and nurses abandoned even newborn children here and there, some in houses and some in the streets, and without a backward look they crowded together at the most high temple."

4), but he assumes that the affliction and pain, suffering and care, and sadness and fear associated with the end time will only intensify for those who are married (Schrage 1995: 159–160). Fee (1987: 329) captures the essence of Paul's argument: "In light of the troubles we are already experiencing, who needs the additional burden of marriage as well?" End-time circumstances determine his advice (see Wolff 1996: 155), but his comments in 7:33–34 reveal that he would regard the unmarried state as preferable, regardless of an imminent end, because marriage necessitates dividing one's loyalties between pleasing a spouse and serving God.

Paul clarifies what he means by "to be thus" in 7:26 with a diatribal **7:27** form in which a statement of fact about their condition is given with a rhetorical question in direct address followed by an imperative that forbids them to change that condition. The explanation of why they should not make changes follows in 7:28b–35.

The imperatives apply the principle laid out in 7:17–24, "Remain as you are," to a specific situation: "Are you bound to a woman? Do not seek to be loosed. Are you loosed from a woman? Do not seek a wife." "Do not seek to be loosed" does not refer to divorce. Such a command would be an anemic and unnecessary repetition of 7:10–16 (Schrage 1995: 157–58). Also, Paul does not use the word λύειν (*lyein*) for divorce but the words ἀφιέναι (*aphienai*, 7:11, 12, 13) and χωρισθῆναι (*chōristhēnai*, 7:10, 15).[12] Since Paul says here that he does not have a specific command of the Lord on this topic (cf. 7:10), divorce could not be in the picture. Translations that assume that he addresses a general audience of persons who are married (cf. NIV, "Are you married?") are misleading and fly in the face of his explicit statement in 7:25 that he is dealing with the "virgins" (Laney 1982: 290–91; contra Robertson and Plummer 1914: 153; Moffatt 1938: 92; Soards 1999: 160–61).

In 7:25–38, Paul deals with the same issue: persons engaged to be married. The question "Are you bound?" (δέδεσαι, *dedesai*; perfect tense) refers to having been bound by a promise or obligation, and the question "Are you loosed?" (λέλυσαι, *lelysai*; perfect tense) refers to breaking off a promise or obligation (MM 382; Fee 1987: 331–32).[13] J. Elliott (1972–73: 221) translates, "Are you engaged to a woman? Do not seek a release. Are you free from a woman? Then do not seek a woman (as wife)." The word γυνή (*gynē*), which can mean either

---

12. If Paul were referring to divorce, having already prohibited those married to Christians from remarrying after a divorce (7:11a), the command "do not seek a wife" would seem rather mild.

13. Schrage (1995: 158 n. 613) cites Aulus Gellius (*Attic Nights* 4.4) that betrothal is a binding contract. Philo (*Spec. Laws* 3.12 §72) discusses the case of seduction or rape on the eve of marriage as adultery (cf. Deut. 22:23–27) because the betrothal agreements and documents needed for marriage are equivalent to marriage.

"woman" (7:1; 11:3–15) or "wife" (5:1; 7:2–4, 10–16, 29, 33, 34, 39; 9:5), has the general meaning of "woman" in this context. With this maxim, he recommends that those who are already bound by betrothal should not break off the engagement, and those who are unmarried should remain so and not hunt for a wife (so J. Elliott 1972–73: 221–22; Fee 1987: 332; Schrage 1995: 158; Oster 1995: 178; Baumert 1996: 86; Wolff 1996: 156).

Throughout this chapter Paul carefully balances commands to males with the same commands to females. He breaks this pattern in this verse and in 7:36–38, where the subject addressed is explicitly male, with no mirror commands to females. This change in pattern is attributable to the cultural mores, which assume that males take the initiative in betrothal arrangements. But Paul continues the pattern of alternating directions to males and females in 7:39–40. These concluding remarks seem to be an afterthought only loosely connected to what precedes. But here he addresses only "widows," using similar language and motifs, "being bound," "being free," and deciding on whether or not to marry. These parallel instructions to widows about their decision to marry reinforces the conclusion that in 7:25–38 Paul addresses unmarried males faced with the decision whether to marry or not.

7:28   Paul asserts that the one who marries does not sin (7:28, 36) and does well (7:38a), and the one who does not marry, who breaks the engagement, does better (7:37, 38b). These are the same persons spoken to directly in 7:26–27. The virgin is addressed only indirectly: "and if *the* virgin [ἡ παρθένος, *hē parthenos*; not '*a* virgin'] marries, she does not sin."[14] Again, he addresses males directly because they are the ones making the proposals and the final decisions about culminating the marriage (cf. Matt. 1:19; see Schrenk, *TDNT* 3:61).[15]

Why would Paul think that he needed to absolve them from guilt for marrying? It could be that he is being generous: "Those who do not accept his advice do not in fact commit sin" (Fee 1987: 333; so also Godet 1886: 373; Kistemaker 1993: 240). Possibly, he refutes a Corinthian position. If someone in Corinth was pontificating that it is "good," in the sense of a distinguishing virtue, not to touch a woman, then they may be haranguing the affianced, saying that it is "not good" and a "sin" to marry. For Paul, marriage is not the best option, because it brings "affliction in the flesh." "Flesh" has a neutral meaning in this context and does not connote something hostile to God but something that is "lim-

---

14. The definite article is omitted in B, F, G, probably because the scribes tried to make this statement generally applicable.

15. Barrett (1968: 176) recognizes that males would take the initiative in marriage, but his argument that Paul addresses them because they "would be the primary recipients of the letter" does not stand up. If that were true, why would Paul also address females directly throughout this chapter?

ited and provisional" (Schweitzer, *TDNT* 7:126), "the physical sphere" (Barrett 1968: 176) in which our weakness and mortality are so evident (cf. 2 Cor. 4:11; 7:5; 12:7).

Paul would seem to resonate with those who had a dismal view of marriage. Diogenes Laertius (*Lives* 2.33) reports, "Someone asked [Socrates] whether he should marry or not, and received the reply, 'Whichever you do you will repent it.'" Yarbrough (1985: 106) cites others who regarded marriage as "a great struggle" (Antiphon, *On Harmony* 357.15–16), as "full of care" (Antiphon, *On Harmony* 360.1), and as "burdensome and grievous," an opinion cited and rejected by Hierocles (*On Marriage* 505.24–25). A rabbi sardonically observes, "A young man is like a colt that whinnies, he paces up and down, he grooms himself with care: this is because he is looking for a wife. But once married, he resembles an ass, quite loaded down with burdens" (*Eccles. Rab.* 1.2). Calvin (1960: 158) identifies the affliction as "the responsibilities and difficulties" that marriage brings, springing "from the affairs of the world." By contrast, Paul's reasons for assuming that marriage brings affliction in the flesh are grounded in his end-time orientation. The affliction is caused by the "present distress."

Paul does not identify the nature of the affliction. Presumably, it is related to his conviction that Christians, who are called to suffer, will have more trials than others (Fee 1987: 333 n. 44). It can also mean that through marriage they will become more deeply entangled in a world order that is passing away. That in itself can bring anguish for one who is trying to live according to the standards of God's new kingdom order. In his fatherly concern, Paul would try to spare (φείδομαι, *pheidomai*; a conative present) them any more heartache than necessary.

With a poetic rhythm, Paul discharges a fusillade of commands to show **7:29–31** how a clear-sighted end-time perspective should affect the way Christians live. Fee (1987: 337) makes a vital point that might be obscured by an emphasis on the present crisis as the key to Paul's advice not to marry: troubles do not determine the Christian's existence; Christ does. Paul does not insist that they should live as if the end is tomorrow: "Rather, in view of the 'time' and the fact that the 'form' of this present world is passing away, he calls for a radically new understanding of their *relationship to the world*" (Fee 1987: 336). Fee (1987: 337–38) correctly takes the pulse of Paul's argument in commenting that Paul wants them to rethink their existence and to live "within an *eschatological* framework as over against, presumably, their ascetic-spiritual one." Paul does not argue, "The end might come tomorrow with its terrible afflictions; therefore, do not get married." He argues instead, "The end has broken into the present, and it requires a reevaluation of all that we do in a world already on its last legs." Humans "cannot live in a vacuum even while awaiting the *eschaton*"; they need "structures and concrete rules of conduct" (Rordorf 1969: 199). Paul offers not so much concrete rules as an orientation to this earthbound life that allows them to live in this world without being hypnotized and controlled by its norms and values. The opening phrase of 7:29, τοῦτο . . . φημί (*touto . . . phēmi*), is different from τοῦτο . . . λέγω (*touto . . . legō*, 7:6, 35) in that it solemnly signals that an important declaration follows: "I mean this."[16] It makes the end-time issue the focal point for the discussion of what they should do about marriage (Winter 1997e: 330).

Paul first declares that "the time has been compressed." "Time" (καιρός, *kairos*) in this context refers to the distinctive period between the eschatological event set in motion by Christ's death and resurrection and his final revealing (cf. Rom. 8:18; 13:11; 1 Cor. 4:5; 2 Cor. 6:2; 1 Thess. 5:1). This period is not to be thought of as a lull in the action on the divine stage but a divinely ordained time marked by the giving of the Spirit, the church's task of mission to the world, and the call for decision on the part of humankind. Christians live in this "epoch of suspense" (Findlay 1910: 833), "waiting for the revealing of our Lord Jesus Christ" (cf. 1:7; 11:26).

The periphrastic participle συνεσταλμένος ἐστίν (*synestalmenos estin*) has been taken to mean that the time is "short," "shortened," or "compressed." If it means "short," then marriage is inadvisable because time is running out before Christ's imminent return. The great tribulation and the transformation of all things is at hand. If it means that the prescribed time "has been shortened" (Weiss 1910: 197), then it may reflect the divine shortening of the time until the end for the sake of the elect (cf. Mark 13:20; 2 Pet. 3:12; Barn. 4:3). The same considerations apply; the time left at our disposal for worldly endeavors is diminished. The verb συστέλλειν (*systellein*) can also mean to "compress," "contract," "make compact," "gather in," and I choose to translate the phrase "The time has been compressed." Deming (1995b: 184) translates it "Time is at a premium" or "Opportunity is tight" and takes it to mean that time for such things as marriage and the activities listed in what follows has been compressed. Deming believes that Paul emphasizes that the hardships brought on by the end will be caused "by the disruption of the world's infrastructure leading to social and economic upheaval." Rengstorf (*TDNT* 7:596–97), however, thinks that Paul may have adopted a proverbial saying (cf. *m.* ʾAbot 2:15) that does not refer to future tribulations.

Paul is not concerned about the duration of time (χρόνος, *chronos*; cf. 7:39) but the character of the time. He is talking not about how little time is left but about how Christ's death and resurrection have changed

---

16. This same phrase appears in 15:50, where it also introduces an apocalyptic communiqué (15:51–57; cf. 10:15, 19).

how Christians should look at the time that is left. He is not recommending that one should take the short-term view of life, nor is he offering an interim ethic for the impending end-time tribulation. Instead, he understands the compressing of the time to mean that the future outcome of this world has become crystal clear. The time has been "foreshortened," which means that "the event of Christ has now compressed the time in such a way that the future has been brought forward so as to be clearly visible" (Fee 1987: 339 n. 14). Fee comments (1987: 339), "Those who have a definite future and see it clearly live in the present with radically altered values as to what counts and what does not." It requires them "to rethink their existence." Paul argues that because the end is plainly in sight, Christians should see and judge more clearly what is and what is not important. Christians stand on a mountaintop, as it were, where distances are foreshortened. From this vantage point, they can see the termination of history on earth and its goal. They can discern what really matters, and they should conduct their lives accordingly.

The term τὸ λοιπόν (*to loipon*), which Lietzmann (1949: 34) characterizes as standing lost between the sentences, does not go with what precedes to mean, "from this point forward the time is short" (contra Weiss 1910: 198). This term usually begins sentences, and here it means "henceforth," "from now on." It refers to the remaining time of the *kairos* (Wimbush 1987: 27; Schrage 1995: 171 n. 679). Paul then lists five examples, beginning with marriage, in which the Christians' distinctive vision of the end should impinge on what they do henceforth in the present (see additional note).

1. *Marriage.* The one who has a wife is to live as if he did not have a wife.[17] Paul does not intend to contradict what he says in (7:2–5) and to encourage husbands to become celibate or to condone husbands neglecting their wives (cf. 7:33). Christians must be mindful that marriage is a transient arrangement and not ultimate (Schrage 1995: 174). Death breaks its bond (7:39; Rom. 7:2), which is not mended after death (Mark 12:19–25). The relationship with the Lord, by contrast, survives death. Moffatt (1938: 93) comments that this mandate "is a passionate, heroic reminder that the Christian life must never be identified with even the nearest and dearest of worldly experiences, however legitimate and appealing they may be."

2. and 3. *Weeping* and *Rejoicing.* Paul's comments on weeping and rejoicing also are not to be taken literally. He is not calling for an end to mourning or joy (Rom. 12:15). He himself weeps (Rom. 9:2; 2 Cor. 2:4; Phil. 2:25–30; 3:18) and rejoices (1 Cor. 16:17; 2 Cor. 7:4–10; Phil. 1:12–

---

17. I take the ἵνα (*hina*) as an imperatival ἵνα (BDF §387.3; Weiss 1910: 198; R. Collins 1999: 295) rather than as expressing the purpose God has for people in the compressed time (contra Fee 1987: 338 n. 10). The καί (*kai*) simply begins the series.

19; 4:10). His point is that laughter and tears are not the last word. Christians should never allow themselves "to be lost in either" (Barrett 1968: 178). This perspective not only applies to the crisis when the world is in its death throes (Ezek. 7:12 LXX), but also reflects the conviction that the end will overthrow weeping and laughter (Luke 6:21, 25; John 16:20). Christians live in a paradoxical tension "as sorrowful, yet always rejoicing; as poor, yet making many rich; as having nothing, and yet possessing everything" (2 Cor. 6:10). Paul's clear-sighted eschatological vision leads him to neutralize the sadness associated in the OT with virginity and never producing children (cf. Judg. 11:37; Gen. 19:8).

4. *Buying and not possessing.* The mandate to buy presupposes that Paul does not intend for Christians to withdraw from the world (cf. 5:10). They may continue to do business, but they must watch lest they become consumed by their consuming. It is not that buying, selling, and marriage will all end at the consummation, as some Jewish prophecies warn (Apocalypse of Elijah 2:31; Sib. Or. 2:327–29), but that these can distract people in the here and now from what is truly important. He does not expect them to quit buying but to recognize that shopping is not life and that one's so-called possessions are on temporary loan from God. The verb κατέχειν (*katechein*), "to hold firmly," "to possess," suggests that he is "forbidding that inordinate love of things which makes them possess us rather than we them" (Lapide 1896: 165). Three parables in Luke clarify the problem Paul warns against. The parable of the rich fool (Luke 12:16–21) reveals that what one thinks one owns ("my barns," "my grain," "my good things") can wind up owning the so-called owner (Luke 12:20). In Luke 14:15–24 (noted by Deming 1995b: 179), those shut out of the banquet were distracted by marrying and buying. In Luke 17:26–37, the Son of Man comes suddenly, catching off guard those distracted with marriages, buying, selling, eating, drinking, planting, and building. Overinvestment in these things results in one's ultimate insolvency at the end of the age.

5. *Making use of the world.* Paul uses the verb χρῆσθαι (*chrēsthai*) in 7:21 to encourage the slave to make use of the opportunity to gain freedom.[18] Adding the prepositional prefix κατά (*kata*) intensifies the verb χρῆσθαι so that it means "make full use of" (not "abuse," or "misuse"). It expresses another paradox: Make use of the world, but do not make full use of it or take full advantage of it. Paul presents himself as an example of this mode of existence in 9:18 when he refuses to make full use

---

18. Wimbush (1987: 28 n. 22) notes that in 2 Cor. 1:17; 3:12; 9:18, the verb occurs with the dative. For Wimbush, the accusative οἱ χρώμενοι τὸν κόσμον (*hoi chrōmenoi ton kosmon*) suggests that the phrase is non-Pauline in origin and that Paul is citing an unknown apocalyptic source. But Buttmann (1895: 181; cf. Lietzmann 1949: 34; Conzelmann 1975: 133 n. 23) explains it as influenced by the presence of καταχρῆσθαι (*katachrēsthai*).

of his rights to receive financial support as apostle because of his overriding concern about how receiving pay might affect his evangelism. His focus on pleasing God and fulfilling his calling allows him to surrender material benefits to reap spiritual ones. Paul can do this because he knows that the Christian's well-being does not depend on cleverly taking advantage of the world's opportunities and becoming "successful" according to the world's standards. Being engaged with the world is one thing; becoming enmeshed in it is another. Becoming wrapped up in the world is to become wrapped in a death shroud. One can continue to buy, sell, and marry—in sum, to use this world—but one must recognize that the things of this world are short-lived. He exhorts the Corinthians never to get so lost in the things of the world that they lose sight of this conviction (Schrage 1964: 151). The world should never be the means whereby persons attempt to create and define their lives (Doughty 1975: 72).

What, then, does Paul recommend? He does not advocate indifference to the world or flight from it (cf. 2 Thess. 3:12). He does not demonize the world as evil, since the "as nots" presuppose involvement in the world. What these "as nots" do is pose a question: What is it that molds one's life? Since the world is not the source of Christians' life or the ground of their hope, they should not allow it to cast them in the forge of its deadly furnace. He warns against the danger of "the world's power to entangle and disarm, to make one less ready for the imminent End" (Wimbush 1987: 31; cf. Fee 1987: 348). The "as nots" require Christians to detach themselves from this world's norms because an "alternative world" exists that offers a different way of living governed by a completely different set of values (Engberg-Pedersen 1987: 581). They are to live in this earthbound world, with its many gods and lords, as those who belong to another, eternal world (Phil. 3:20) and to the one God and one Lord (8:5 6). The "as nots" are a rhetorically more dashing way of saying, "Do not be conformed to this world" (Rom. 12:2).

This ethic is based on the assurance that "the form of this world is passing away" (cf. 1 John 2:17, "the world is passing away"; 2 Pet. 3:10; 4 Ezra [2 Esdr.] 4:26). The present tense of the verb παράγει (paragei) suggests that the process of this passing away has already begun and is not something that awaits in the future. Τὸ σχῆμα (to schēma) refers to the world's outward array, its arrangement, its fashion. The metaphor perhaps is drawn from the shifting scenes in a theater (Trench 1880: 266; Edwards 1885: 197), or perhaps is related to the costume and mask of an actor. "Remove the decorations, take off the masks, look what lurks behind them: you will see that all is foreign, slender, empty" (Lapide 1896: 170). Nothing in this physical world seen and experienced by our physical senses has any enduring character—including marriages, weepings, rejoicings, possessions, and business opportunities. The fabric of life is just that, a fabric, frayed and flimsy, and nothing eternal.

7:32–34   Paul explains further why he thinks that remaining single is best. He wants them to be free of pressures that will distract them from single-hearted devotion to the Lord. His argument reflects the following syllogism (Ramsaran 1995: 441, actually an enthymeme):

> Implied major premise: Less anxiety about externals increases undivided devotion to God.
>
> Minor premise: The unmarried person has less anxiety about externals.
>
> Conclusion: The unmarried person has more opportunity to give undivided devotion to God.

Paul uses words related to anxiety (ἀμέριμνος, *amerimnos*, without anxiety; and μεριμνᾶν, *merimnan*, to be anxious) in this context in a positive and a negative sense. The unmarried person is anxious to please the Lord; the married person is anxious to please the spouse. Some understand both anxieties to be negative and maintain that both persons in the illustration are unduly anxious about something: the one to please the Lord, the other to please the spouse (Barrett 1968: 179; Murphy-O'Connor 1979a: 75). Such "anxious religiosity" (desiring to win God's favor), according to this view, is out of place (Barrett 1968: 179).

This interpretation is wrong for two reasons. First, the NT admonitions not to be anxious "presuppose that every man naturally cares for himself and his life, that he is concerned about himself, that he is always intent on something and concerned about something" (Bultmann, *TDNT* 4:591). Paul does not intend to eliminate care—as if humans could achieve the state of being carefree—but to reorient that care so that a person is not torn apart by futile distress over things such as material security. The admonitions assume that one's life becomes controlled by what one cares about. This world's cares not only shorten life and make it miserable while it lasts, but also choke out the word like thorny weeds robbing cultivated plants of light and nutrients and coiling around them in a stranglehold. This futile anxiety is cast out by trust that God cares for us and knows what we truly need more than we do.

Second, in the same letter Paul can switch back and forth between using μεριμνᾶν in a good sense and in a bad sense. In Phil. 2:20, he writes that Timothy is genuinely anxious for the Philippians' welfare, but in Phil. 4:6, he exhorts them to be anxious about nothing. This means that the object of the anxiety and the context determine whether it is bad or not (Wimbush 1987: 51; Schrage 1995: 178). When the object is something that pleases the Lord, it is positive (cf. 12:25; 2 Cor. 11:28); when the object is something of the world, it is negative.

In 7:32, the anxieties are negative and refer to an "anxiety-ridden existence" (Fee 1987: 343). If one's life is determined by Christ, one should be free from anxiety about making use of the world, what to eat, drink, wear (Matt. 6:25–34), and even about whatever tribulation might come (Mark 13:11). Being anxious "for the things of the Lord" is defined as being solicitous for how to please the Lord, which is positive in Paul's letters (cf. Rom. 8:8; 2 Cor. 5:9; Col. 1:10; 1 Thess. 2:15; 4:1).[19] "To please God" is synonymous with obedience.

Paul does not intend to imply that anxiety about pleasing one's spouse is inherently negative.[20] Marriage means committing oneself in a special way to the existence of another by involving oneself with the spouse in a relationship of care and concern, and, given the Lord's teaching about divorce, it is an irrevocable commitment. Paul does not criticize the married for having these cares. He simply observes that marriage imposes demands and responsibilities that cannot be neglected. The remarks of Epictetus (*Diatr.* 3.22.70–71, 74) on the distractions of marriage that the celibate Cynic avoids are frequently cited:

> For see, he must show certain services to his father-in-law, to the rest of his wife's relatives, to his wife herself; finally, he is driven from his profession, to act as nurse in his own family and to provide for them. To make a long story short, he must get a kettle to heat water for the baby, for washing it in a bath-tub; wool for his wife when she has had a child, a cot, a cup (the vessels get more and more numerous). . . . Come, doesn't he have to get little cloaks for the children? Doesn't he have to send them off to a school teacher with their little tablets and writing-implements, and little note-books; and besides, get the little cot ready for them? For they can't be Cynics from the moment they leave the womb. And if he doesn't do this, it would have been better to expose them at birth, rather than to kill them in this fashion.[21]

19. The story of Mary and Martha illustrates well Paul's concern. Martha "was distracted by her many tasks" (Luke 10:40). Jesus gently rebukes her for being worried (με-ριμνᾶς, *merimnas*) and perturbed by many things, while Mary had chosen the better and one needful thing (Luke 10:41).

20. Baird (1964: 71) notes, "Some wag suggested that this text is proof enough that Paul had never been married—the idyllic picture of the wife scurrying about with no other interest than waiting on her spouse has little relation to reality."

21. Philo (*Hypoth.* 11.17) remarks, "For he who is either fast bound in the love lures of his wife or under the stress of nature makes his children his first care ceases to be the same to others and unconsciously has become a different man and has passed from freedom into slavery."

The problem for Paul is not marriage but the danger of becoming too distracted in trying to please a wife or a husband. The Cynics spurned marriage because they desired *freedom from obligation*. By contrast, Paul rejects marriage for himself because it gives him *freedom for service*. He takes for granted that pleasing the Lord is the paramount Christian duty. Achieving marital happiness is not. It is likely that times will arise when the demand to please God will conflict with the need to please a spouse.

That is why Paul says that the married man is divided (μεμέρισται, *memeristai*, 7:34), divided between duty to God and affection for his wife and family (Findlay 1910: 833). Being "divided" and being "anxious" derive from the same Greek root.[22] The problem of being divided is Paul's key concern. Married persons are pulled in different directions and may be torn away from the Lord. The background for this concern is not Stoicism but Paul's inheritance of the Jewish moral tradition found in the OT and the greatest commandment (Deut. 6:4–5; Josh. 22:5; Mark 12:28–30; see Rosner 1994: 164–65), cited in 1 Cor. 8:6. The Christian is to love, serve, and obey God with an undivided heart. Without saying so, Paul is thankful not to be burdened by marriage, because it allows him the practical freedom to devote himself to his apostolic calling—to endure the hardships, labors, imprisonments, floggings, scrapes with death, constant dangers, starvation, and homelessness (2 Cor. 11:23–27). Worries about supporting a family would have only compounded his worry for his churches (2 Cor. 11:27).

In 7:34b, Paul applies what he says about men in 7:32–33a to females, but with a significant difference. He specifies that the unmarried woman is also a "virgin." The Greek noun phrase ἡ γυνὴ ἡ ἄγαμος καὶ ἡ παρθένος (*hē gynē hē agamos kai hē parthenos*, literally, "the woman, the unmarried and the virgin") raises the question of whether he refers to one woman or two. It can be read in three ways (Guenther 2002: 36–37, 44): (1) as two nouns treated as a compound subject, "the unmarried woman and the virgin"; (2) as an epexegetic phrase referring to one woman, "the unmarried woman, that is, the virgin"; or (3) as a single noun conjoined by two arthrous adjectives, "the unmarried and the chaste (virgin) woman." The second and third readings are similar in describing a woman who is unmarried and chaste, but the third reading fits a common adjectival use of παρθένος in Greek literature. Guenther (2002: 37) makes the case against the majority of translations and commentators for the third reading, which best explains the use of the singular verbs μεριμνᾷ (*merimna*) and ᾖ (*ē*). Guenther (2002: 44–45) contends that this reading excludes divorcées and widows and identifies "the virgin alone as having the capacity to give herself without distrac-

---

22. A play on words occurs with the *merim* sound recurring six times in 7:32–34.

tion in serving the Lord." I agree with this reading but would not want to imply that the widowed or divorced cannot also chastely devote themselves to the Lord. Paul, however, specifies the unmarried virgin because that is the issue at hand.[23]

Instead of saying that she is anxious "how to please the Lord," he adds "in order that she may be pure in body and spirit." This statement is parallel to "how to please the Lord" in 7:32 and should be taken in a positive sense. Being holy in body does not mean that she is pure because she avoids the sexual relations that marriage imposes.[24] All Christians are to be holy in body, whether married or not (1 Thess. 5:23; cf. Rom. 6:12, 19; 12:1; 1 Cor. 6:13, 19–20; 2 Cor. 7:1; Phil. 1:20; 1 Thess. 4:4). The combination of body and spirit describes the whole person and means that she strives to be holy in every way and is totally devoted to the Lord (Schrage 1995: 180).

Paul concludes his arguments commending singleness by referring to what is "seemly." It leads into his specific advice about the virgins in 7:36–38, which begins with the concern that a man thinks he is acting in an unseemly way toward his virgin. Remaining single offers the advantage of devoting oneself entirely to the Lord. "For your very own advantage" (with an intensive αὐτῶν, *autōn*) is addressed to the betrothed. He does not insist that they remain single, because he has no intention of lassoing them (οὐχ ἵνα βρόχον ὑμῖν ἐπιβάλω, *ouch hina brochon hymin epibalō*), as if they were enemies, and dragging them about.[25] He will not ride roughshod over their freedom and decide for them how they will live out their calling. His purpose is to help them live lives that please the Lord. He thinks that celibacy promotes seemly devotion to the Lord without distraction. Εὔσχημον (*euschēmon*) refers to what is "appropriate," "proper," "seemly" (cf. 12:23–24, "unpresentable" and "presentable" parts of the human anatomy). In 1 Thess. 4:12, it refers to behavior that is orderly, belonging to proper decorum. Εὐπάρεδρον (*euparedron*) is linked to εὔσχημον by the same definite article. It literally means "good sitting beside" and may convey the idea of constant presence, hence devotion, service. According to Findlay (1910: 836), it is something that promotes "fit waiting on the Lord" (cf. Barrett 1968: 182, who thinks that the word perhaps was coined by Paul). The rare adverb ἀπερισπάστως (*aperispastōs*, undistractedly) appears at the end of the clause for emphasis.

7:35

23. Paul encourages the divorced woman to be reconciled with her husband (7:11) and addresses the concerns of the widow in 7:8–9, 39–40.
24. The phrase need not be a quotation from "the Corinthian ascetical party" (Barrett 1968: 181) or a "Corinthian buzzword used to describe a specific group of well-intentioned and zealous unmarried women in Corinth" (R. Collins 1999: 292).
25. Philo (*Mos.* 2.46 §252) uses the image of a "noose" metaphorically; Josephus (*J.W.* 7.7.4 §250) uses it literally in the context of a battle.

7:36–38   A notorious crux presents itself in 7:36–38 because of the ambiguity of "if anyone" (εἰ . . . τις, *ei . . . tis*). Moiser (1983: 114) characterizes it as "one of the most difficult and refractory passages in the entire Pauline corpus." Many commentators reject rival interpretations as "impossible," "ludicrous," or "absurd." Five exegetical questions present themselves in verse 36: (1) What is the antecedent of τις (*tis*, anyone)? (2) To what does ἀσχημονεῖν (*aschēmonein*, to act dishonorably, shamefully, indecently) apply? (3) To whom does ἡ παρθένος αὐτοῦ (*hē parthenos autou*) refer—his daughter, spiritual bride, or fiancée? (4) Does ὑπέρακμος (*hyperakmos*) refer to the girl or the man, and what does it connote? (5) What does the phrase καὶ οὕτως ὀφείλει γίνεσθαι (*kai houtōs opheilei ginesthai*), literally translated "and it ought to happen thus," mean? (See additional note.)

Major translations represent the three basic interpretations.[26]

NASB	NEB	NRSV
But if any man thinks that he is acting unbecomingly toward his virgin *daughter*, if she should be of full age, and if it must be so, let him do what he wishes, he does not sin; let her marry.	But if a man has a partner in celibacy and feels that he is not behaving properly towards her, if, that is, his instincts are too strong for him, and something must be done, he may do as he pleases; there is nothing wrong in it; let them marry.	If anyone thinks that he is not behaving properly toward his fiancée, if his passions are strong, and so it has to be, let him marry as he wishes; it is no sin. Let them marry.

The first view, represented by the NASB, understands the situation to involve a father faced with the decision of whether or not to marry off his virgin daughter.[27] It is imagined that the Corinthians asked, "What is a father's duty when he has a daughter of marriageable age?"[28] Should he allow her to marry? The "anyone" refers to a father, and "his virgin" refers to his daughter. The girl is ὑπέρακμος (*hyperakmos*), which is taken to mean that she has reached puberty or is past her bloom.[29] The father may fear that he is acting dishonorably because, according to Findlay (1910: 836, though no primary evidence is cited), society looked askance at keeping a "daughter at home, without any apparent reason, for a long period beyond adult age." The phrase καὶ οὕτως ὀφείλει γίνεσθαι is taken to refer to the father's duty and means

26. See Kümmel (1954) and Thiselton (2000: 593–602) for a summary of research.

27. So Theodore of Mopsuestia, Chrysostom, Theodoret, Augustine, Ambrosiaster; and modern scholars Edwards 1885: 200–202; Godet 1886: 388; Lightfoot 1895: 234; Findlay 1910: 836–37; Robertson and Plummer 1914: 158–60; Parry 1926: 121–24; Ketter 1947; Grosheide 1953: 184; Morris 1958: 120–22; Snyder 1992: 115–16.

28. Sirach answers the question this way: "Give a daughter in marriage, and you complete a great task; but give her to a sensible man" (7:25).

29. Tacitus (*Annales* 6.15) uses the expression "The age of the girls began to press."

"the thing ought to be done." Having ἐξουσία (*exousia*) in 7:37 is assumed to refer to the father's legal right to make arrangements for his daughter as he wishes (*patria potestas*, the father's power) and to the fact that he remains "the master of his own deliberate will" (Godet 1886: 390) to keep her unmarried.

Paul responds by saying that if the daughter has reached puberty or is getting too old and her father thinks that keeping her at home is improper, then he can marry her off without blame. If the father is without any pressure to give his daughter in marriage and he remains resolute about keeping her unmarried, his behavior is even more commendable.[30]

The strongest argument in favor of this view comes from the use of the verb γαμίζειν (*gamizein*) in 7:38. It usually means "to give in marriage." In 7:9, 10, 28, 33, 34, 36, 39, Paul uses the verb γαμεῖν (*gamein*), "to marry," and the switch in verbs seems intentional. The two verbs appear together in Matt. 22:30 = Mark 12:25 = Luke 17:27, and their meanings are distinguished: in the resurrection "they neither marry nor are given in marriage" (see also Matt. 24:38 = Luke 17:27). Robertson and Plummer (1914: 159) consider this argument to be decisive. The arguments against it, however, are substantial.

1. Nothing in 7:25–35 prepares for this reading of the situation. Since no previous mention of parental duties or relationships appears in this chapter, its emergence here seems rather jarring. If Paul describes a father's decision to give his daughter in marriage, he uses quite extraordinary language ("under no compulsion," "having authority over his own will" = "possessing sufficient willpower," "he does not sin"). This interpretation also fails to explain adequately why Paul would say in 7:28 "If the virgin marries, she does not sin," assuming that "the virgin" here is no different from "the virgin" referred to in 7:36–38.
2. The shift in 7:36 from a singular subject, "he does not sin," to a plural subject, "let them marry" (γαμείτωσαν, *gameitōsan*), rather than "let her marry," abruptly brings in a third party, the groom, who, according to this view, is not mentioned elsewhere in the passage. The NASB sidesteps this problem by choosing a weakly supported variant, γαμείτω (*gameitō*), "let her marry."
3. It is quite irregular to refer to a father's daughter as "his virgin." In Acts 21:9, Philip's four daughters are described as his "virgin *daughters*" (θυγατέρες ... παρθένοι, *thygateres ... parthenoi*; cf. Jos. As. 7:7), not his "virgins." Fee (1987: 326) notes that in such a

---

30. Orr and Walther (1976: 224) assume that the father has committed his family to absolute service to God but now finds his daughter developing an interest in a young man. He is without pressure because there is no official commitment.

discussion one might expect to find the term "father" or perhaps "guardian," but they do not appear.

4. The meaning "past marriageable age" or "overripe" for ὑπέρακμος is dubious (Winter 1998). The conclusion about the word's meaning should derive not from an analysis of its components (ὑπέρ and ἀκμή or ἀκμαῖος) but from its usage in ancient sources. The meaning "past marriageable age" also makes the question of her marriage seem rather pointless. "Having reached puberty" is a possible meaning, but it requires a sudden shift in subject from the "father" to the "daughter." Fee (1987: 351) notes, "An unexpressed subject in a dependent clause usually picks up the subject of the preceding clause." The most likely subject of the clause ἐὰν ᾖ ὑπέρακμος (ean ē hyperakmos) is therefore the male.

5. The classical distinction between -εω (-eō) and -ιζω (-izō) verb suffixes has broken down in the Koine period (Lietzmann 1949: 35–36; Moulton and Howard 1929: 410; Kümmel 1954: 289; J. Elliott 1972–73: 220). The verb γαμίζειν (gamizein) need not have a causative force and can be translated in 7:38 "the one who marries." Paul may have changed verbs for variety or because the verb γαμίζειν has a direct object, "his virgin." All uses of the verb γαμεῖν (gamein) in this chapter are intransitive, and γαμίζειν may have "carried a transitive nuance" for Paul, which explains why he chose to use it here (Fee 1987: 355).

6. Schrenk (TDNT 3:60) argues vehemently that if this passage refers to the father's authority, "Paul is justifying an unheard of tyranny, for to impose asceticism on oneself is rather different from imposing it on marriageable children." Even if they had different sentiments in their era from our own regarding such matters, Héring (1962: 63) insists that it is "grotesque to praise the unswerving constancy of the father in a decision which costs him nothing, and in which it is his daughter, who is not consulted, who bears the full weight of the sacrifice."

7. Why inform a father, who presumably is married, that marriage is good but the single life is better? It makes more sense if these words were directed to those exploring the possibility of marriage for themselves.

The second view, represented by the NEB, understands Paul to be instructing couples who are living in a "spiritual marriage." They have committed themselves to a relationship without sexual relations, but it has placed too great a strain on the sexual drive of the male. Someone has asked Paul if it is permissible for them to break the vow and consummate the marriage. Will they incur condemnation for doing so (cf.

1 Tim. 5:11–12)? Paul consents to this action if the male's sexual drive becomes too much for him to bear. They do not sin.[31]

The "anyone" and "his virgin" refer to the celibate couple who live together as brother and sister. Perhaps the woman agreed to set up house with the man to lessen the economic burdens of living the ascetic ideal alone (Delling, *TDNT* 5:836). Hurd (1965: 179) contends that this arrangement would have "the social and legal advantages of marriage, that is, they would enjoy mutual encouragement and companionship in the faith, and they would enjoy the freedom and security of a Christian household." The ὑπέρακμος refers to the man's sexual drive. It is too strong, and he is having trouble refraining from physically consummating the marriage. He thinks he has acted dishonorably because of his thoughts or actions. Paul's recommendation is that they should convert their relationship into a full, normal marriage, though it is better for them to stay as they are.

The arguments against this view also are weighty.

1. No evidence of "spiritual marriages" appears in the first-century church. The institution of *virgines subintroductae* was a much later development. In Herm. *Sim.* 9.10–11, the seer reports spending the night "as a brother, not as a husband" with twelve virgins. But this is allegory, with the virgins named after the virtues, and not evidence of the practice of spiritual marriage and certainly not evidence of the practice a century earlier in Roman Corinth.

2. It stretches the imagination to think that Paul would have countenanced "spiritual marriages," if my interpretation of 7:1–5 is correct. He understands marriage to include a physical relationship. A marriage without physical intimacy would only open the door to temptation from Satan (7:5) and to the potential of "burning" with passion (7:9) with no suitable outlet.

3. Why say, "Let them marry"? Presumably, they already are married. The verb does not mean "to consummate a marriage sexually" (Fee 1987: 352).

4. The "husband" of this spiritual marriage is given sole discretion in determining whether the relationship should be consummated, which is strange when compared to Paul's instructions in 7:2–5. He insists there that the husband cannot withdraw from his wife except by mutual agreement, but apparently the husband can consummate the marriage physically without mutual agreement if the strain is too great on him. Such inconsistency does not make sense.

31. So Achelis 1902; Weiss 1910: 206–9; Delling 1931: 86–91; *TDNT* 5:836; Moffatt 1938: 98–99; Lietzmann 1949: 35–37; Bultmann 1955: 224; Héring 1962: 62–64; Seboldt 1959; Hurd 1965: 169–82; Niederwimmer 1975: 116–20; Murphy-O'Connor 1979a: 72.

The view I adopt as the most likely is represented by the NRSV (cf. the REB). It understands Paul, throughout 7:25–38, to be addressing Christians engaged to marry.[32] R. Collins (1999: 299) considers 7:36–38 to be "a kind of commentary on v. 27." The "anyone" refers to the fiancé, and the "virgin" is his fiancée, which reveals that Paul expected chastity before marriage. The expression "his virgin" is unusual, but it may be akin to "his girl" (so Barrett 1968: 184; Baumert 1996: 82). The term may designate what is important about her. The two are bound by betrothal but wonder if they should follow through on their marriage.[33] The ὑπέρακμος refers to man's sexual desire. In helping the man make his decision, Paul proposes that if his sexual drive is strong, then it is natural for him to go ahead and marry ("it is better to marry than to burn," 7:9), particularly if he thinks he is acting dishonorably. If he has his sexual desire under control, however, he may decide not to go ahead with the marriage (7:37) in light of the present distress (7:26). It may be that the present distress led them to question whether they should follow through on their promises to marry. Paul concludes that it is fine for them to do so; it is better, because of the reasons outlined in 7:25–35, if they do not.

This view fits the preceding context and what follows in verses 39–40, where widows are told that they are free to marry if they choose but, in Paul's opinion, would be happier remaining as they are. In a setting where sexual asceticism was acclaimed as a good, the decision to marry could have easily become a moral struggle. Paul advises the fiancé who has strong sexual urges to marry. But if his desire is under control and it would not wrong his fiancée, he would do better to remain single to be devoted to the Lord.

The verb ἀσχημονεῖν (aschēmonein) may have a variety of connotations. It may mean that he is acting against social custom (R. Collins 1999: 301). But it raises the question, What custom—making a betrothal and not following through with marriage? In the context of male and female relationships, however, it has sexual connotations. The sexual innuendo of the words in the rest of the passage, ἀνάγκη (anankē, [sexual] necessity), θέλημα (thelēma, [sexual] desire) supports this view. Winter's (1998: 78–80) analysis of the verb's usage in Hellenistic literary and nonliterary sources clinches the matter. Winter (1998: 80) concludes, "The survey of literary writers and non-literary sources contains some eighty-seven occurrences of this word and its cognates and

32. So Belkin 1935; Schrenk, *TDNT* 3:61; Kümmel 1954; Chadwick 1954–55: 267; Barrett 1968: 184; Conzelmann 1975: 135–36; Baumert 1996: 120–23; J. Elliott 1972–73: 220–23; Fee 1987: 323, 327; Schrage 1995: 197–200; Wolff 1996: 161; Winter 1998; R. Collins 1999: 298–99; Thiselton 2000: 597.

33. Though betrothal was a Roman and a Jewish custom, not a Greek one, Corinth was very much a Roman city and steeped in Roman customs.

provides overwhelming evidence that, within the context of male and female relationships, the word 'to behave unseemly' has sexual connotations." The "but" beginning 7:36 contrasts this "unseemly" conduct with the goal of "seemly" (εὐσχημον, *euschēmon*) conduct extolled in 7:35. This unseemly conduct in the mind of the young man need not have been actual fornication with other women or with his betrothed, since Paul would not have tolerated that (Winter 1998: 81–82). Given the Roman view of shame, it is more likely that the man feels that his conduct and thoughts had fallen short of a personal ideal (Winter 1998: 82).

The phrase ἐὰν ᾖ ὑπέρακμος (*ean ē hyperakmos*) makes far more sense of the context if it refers to the male's sexual passions (literally, "over the top") rather than the female's sexual development (reaching puberty, or past the flower of her age, for example).[34] It keeps the male as the subject of all the verbs throughout verses 36–38. Winter's (1998: 88) exhaustive analysis of the usage of the word in literary and nonliterary contexts shows that it is used to mean "full of sexual passion."[35] Among the many sources cited (Winter 1998: 76), Hesychius, the fifth-century A.D. lexicographer, lists the verb form ὑπερακμάζειν (*hyperakmazein*) as a synonym for κατοργᾶν (*katorgan*), which refers to a heightened desire for sexual intercourse. It is synonymous with πυροῦν (*pyroun*, to burn) in 7:9 (Yarbrough 1985: 106).

This interpretation explains why the man is under compulsion. When sexual desires are inflamed, unseemly behavior can follow. Winter (1998: 84) translates καὶ οὕτως ὀφείλει γίνεσθαι (*kai houtōs opheilei ginesthai*), "and thus it is bound to happen." Paul declares that this person does not sin by marrying but will sin if he engages in sexual acts outside of marriage. Therefore, Paul advises, "Let him do what he wishes." What the man wishes is to marry and have sexual relations with his wife, and Paul is a realist about the sexual drive (R. Collins 1999: 290). The young man evidently does not have the gift of celibacy, and Paul would not lasso him and impound him in the corral of celibacy when it is clearly against his nature. Paul recommends marriage when the man's control over his sexual desire threatens to slip (Schrage 1995: 201).

Not all betrothals need end in marriage, however. A man may choose to remain single. Paul gives two criteria for making this decision. First, he must be convinced in his own heart (= mind). He is not to be a slave

---

34. Winter (1998: 79) notes that the actual word for being past one's prime is παρ-ακμή (*parakmē*), and one's understanding of the meaning of the word ὑπέρακμος should be based on its actual usage, not its components, ὑπέρ-ἀκμή. Ford's (1966b) view that it refers to "fully developed breasts" seems bizarre in the context.

35. Moffatt (1938) renders it "if his passions be strong"; Barrett (1968:182), "if he is over-sexed"; and Deming (1995b: 73), "if he is over the limit."

to the opinion of others. His decision is to come from the depths of his own being (R. Collins 1999: 302). Second, he must have "no necessity" (ἀνάγκη, *ananke*), which is exactly the opposite of being "full of sexual passion" (Schrenk, *TDNT* 3:60). Winter (1998: 85) notes that ἀνάγκη is well attested as referring to sexual need (citing Plato, *Respublica* [*Republic*] 5.7.458D; Aristophanes, *Nubes* [*Clouds*] 2.1075–76). The statement "he has authority concerning his own will" reiterates this second criterion. The noun θέλημα (*thelēma*, will) is used to refer to "sexual desire" (cf. John 1:13; so Schrenk, *TDNT* 3:60–61; Winter 1998: 85). The statement "and he has decided this in his own heart" repeats the first criterion so that the advice falls into a chiastic structure:

A   He stands firm in his own heart.

   B   He has no sexual necessity (or urges).

   B′   He has control over his sexual impulse.

A′   He has decided in his own heart.

Wanting to marry and having sexual desires are sure signs that one does not have the gift of celibacy (7:7). The phrase "to keep his own virgin" is an odd way of saying "not to marry his own virgin." It may mean to keep her "inviolate" (BDAG 1002). Conzelmann (1975: 135 n. 43) cites Achilles Tatius (*Leuc. Clit.* 8.18.2) as a source for the phrase meaning "keeping your virginity" and not touching her sexually (cf. 8.17.3).

Paul concludes that the man does well in reaching the decision either to marry or to remain single. But doing well has nothing to do with reaching idealistic spiritual heights. Fee (1987: 354 n. 28) notes that the adverb "well" (καλῶς, *kalos*) "seems to confirm that the usage 'it is good' does not carry moral overtones for Paul." "To do well" in this context means to make a careful, prayerful decision about what to do. It entails an authentic internal examination before God and then doing what is seemly and what will not detract from service to the Lord. In this case, one's service to God will be sabotaged if one sentences oneself to celibacy only to meet others' expectations.

In 7:38, Paul signals the closing of his argument with "so then" (ὥστε, *hōste*). The verb γαμίζειν can mean "to give in marriage" or "to marry," and in this context it means to enter into marriage. It summarizes 7:28, 36. D. Martin (1995: 211) spies a hierarchy of virtue in Paul's conclusions: The one who marries, due to compulsion, does not sin; but the one who does not marry, due to his self-control, does well. The one who marries does well, but the one who does not marry does better (7:38). But the context reveals why Paul thinks that the one who does not marry does better. The advantages of remaining single are purely practical (Menoud 1978: 4), and doing so is not treated as a morally superior course. Regarding one choice as better does not make the other choice bad. One can do "well" by marrying.[36] Yarbrough (1985: 122) concludes that Paul "rejects the Corinthians' attempt to make one expression of the spiritual life binding on all believers, since to claim that there is only one legitimate expression of the spirit leads to elitism, which in turn leads to divisions in the community." Paul is concerned only about what is fitting, most beneficial, and most likely to contribute to undistracted waiting on the Lord.

The final two verses of the chapter are not a postscript to 7:8–9 but continue the pattern of alternating instructions to males and females. In 7:25–38, Paul instructs single, engaged men about whether or not they should marry. In 7:39–40, he briefly instructs widows about whether or not they should marry. The latter is brief and in the third person because it is not the burning issue. The advice given to both can be only roughly parallel because of their different circumstances, but the correlations are clear. If the fiancé is bound by a betrothal, he should not breach it. The wife is bound by marriage, which she is not to breach. If a man is unattached, he is free to marry but should not seek a wife. If the married woman becomes a widow, she is free to remarry but would be happier if she did not. **7:39–40**

Stating that a wife is bound for as long as her husband lives (Rom. 7:2) is not a final word "against divorce and remarriage" (contra Edwards 1885: 203; Fee 1987: 355) but sets up the next clause. When he dies, she is then free to marry whomever she wants.[37] Paul's theological shorthand again causes confusion. The phrase μόνον ἐν κυρίῳ (*monon en kyriō*, only in the Lord) may mean that she must marry a Christian or that she must act like a Christian. Those who argue for the latter view (Edwards 1885: 204; Lightfoot 1895: 235; Barrett 1968: 186; Schrage 1995: 205–6) contend that Paul only reminds her that she is in the Lord—a Christian. She should act as a member of Christ's body and her motives must be Christian.

The first alternative, that her new marriage partner should be a Christian, best fits the context. Fee (1987: 355) claims that this is not so much a command "as good sense." Paul warns about marriage bringing affliction when Christians are married to Christians. Would he not object even more to a widow voluntarily putting herself into a more difficult situation by marrying a non-Christian who may be unsympathetic to her faith (cf. 7:15)? Thiselton (2000: 604) contends that Paul countenanced only existing mixed marriages. If Paul expects widows to marry only Christians, it would fit the endogamous mores of the OT and Jew-

---

36. For the expression "doing well," cf. Phil. 4:14; Matt. 12:12; Mark 7:37; Luke 6:27; Acts 10:33; James 2:8; 1 Pet. 1:19; 3 John 6.

37. Paul uses the euphemism κοιμᾶν (*koiman*, fall asleep) only of the Christian dead (11:30; 15:6, 18, 20, 51).

ish tradition (cf. Deut. 7:3; Josh. 23:12; Neh. 13:23–25; Tob. 4:12–13; Jos. As. 8:5–7; T. Levi 9:10; *m. Giṭ.* 9:2; *b. Qidd.* 70b), which were so much a part of his background (see also Instone-Brewer 2001: 237–38).[38] Paul had few other ways of expressing the concept "Christian" (cf. Acts 11:26; 26:28; 1 Pet. 4:16), and his greeting to "those in the Lord who belong to the family of Narcissus" (Rom. 16:11) shows that he can use the phrase ἐν κυρίῳ (*en kyriō*) to mean "Christians."

We should not be surprised, after what he says in 7:25–38, that Paul believes that the widow would be "happier" if she remained single. It accords with his maxim that the present crisis makes it good for a person to remain as he or she is (7:26). The comparative μακαριωτέρα (*makariōtera*) matches the comparative κρεῖσσον (*kreisson*, better) applied to the male in 7:38. Paul uses μακάριος (*makarios*) in the religious sense of blessed in Rom. 4:7–8 and 14:22. Some claim that he means that the widow is more blessed by remaining a widow and consecrating her life to the work of the Lord (Edwards 1885: 205; Findlay 1910: 838; Orr and Walther 1976: 225). This would fit Herm. *Man.* 4.4.1–2, which affirms that second marriages are not a sin, "but if he [the survivor] remain single he gains for himself more exceeding honour and great glory with the Lord." Paul says nothing similar, however, and many assume that the term μακαριωτέρα has no religious overtones but refers only to worldly well-being—"she is happier" (Barrett 1968: 186; Wimbush 1987: 20 n. 29; Schrage 1995: 206).

Does one have to choose between the two possibilities? In the preceding verses, Paul gives two basic reasons for remaining single. The first is mundane: it spares a person affliction in the flesh (7:28). The second is religious: it allows a person to serve the Lord undistractedly, to be holy in body and soul (7:34). We can conjecture, then, that he would assume that both were true for the widow who remains unmarried. She would be happier without the cares that marriage brings and more blessed for her devotion to the Lord. The blessedness does not make her more saintly, but being devoted to the Lord qualifies her as one of those servants identified as "blessed," "whom the master finds alert when he comes" (Luke 12:37).

Paul concludes his instructions with a second appeal to *ethos.* "I think" (δοκῶ, *dokō*) is the language of modesty, not misgiving (Findlay 1910: 838; cf. 4:9). The "I too" (κἀγώ, *ka'gō*) implies "no less than others," and we may take this as a hint that someone in Corinth also appealed to the Spirit. His conclusion may poke at the ascetic idealists who have been doctrinaire in asserting their views about celibacy: "If you think that you have the Spirit, remember that I, too, have the

---

38. Ignatius (*Pol.* 5:2) expects men and women to be united with the consent of the bishop.

Spirit" (Barrett 1968: 186). The Spirit guides his counsel, and he is not shooting from the hip. This statement also prepares for the next discussion, in which he will disagree more adamantly with the Corinthians' position on idol meat.

Additional Notes

7:29–31. What is the background of Paul's "as though not" statements? Many have spotted affinities with Stoicism (Edwards 1885: 194; Weiss 1910: 199; Braun 1967) and its concern to be free from distraction and not tied down by private duties (see Epictetus, *Diatr.* 2.14.8; 3.22.67–76; 4.1.159, 162; 4.7.5; Seneca, *Ep. morales* 9.17–18; 74.18; Diogenes Laertius, *Lives* 6.29). But the Stoic detachment from the world has nothing in common with the eschatological horizon that orients Paul's advice. The breakdown in the parallels comes from Paul's clear eschatological motivation, whereas Epictetus thought that everything remains with the boundaries of this present life and world (Conzelmann 1975: 133). The concept of the end of the world would have been incomprehensible to Epictetus. Stoic cosmology understood that the world was subject to a constant cycle of conflagrations but did not appreciate that it would come to a definitive end (Schrage 1964: 135–38, 149–52; see also Wimbush 1987: 39–43). The motivation differs significantly from Stoic detachment from the world. Kuck (1992a: 248) elaborates that for the Stoic, the tension was created by "the world's undependability and the desire for personal freedom." The Stoic could secure freedom only by detaching himself from the world. "For Paul the tension is between the demands posed by Christ and the distractions of the world." Schrage (1964: 138) judiciously claims that resemblances to Stoicism are coincidental and purely "illusory."

Others find greater affinities with Jewish apocalyptic traditions with the use of images such as "the compressed time" and "the framework of this world passing away." Schrage (1995: 168) argues that 7:29–31 derives from an apocalyptic tradition and was not formulated ad hoc, since only the first example fits in the context. He cites as a key parallel 6 Esdr. (= 2 Esdr.) 16:40–45. Other parallels can be found in Zech. 12:12–14; 6 Esdr. (= 2 Esdr.) 16:33–34; 2 Bar. 10:13–14. Some claim that Paul may be quoting from a lost apocalyptic source in 7:29–31 (Schrage 1964: 139, 153; Wimbush 1987: 44–45; Deming 1995b: 180–81). Wimbush lists as evidence the introductory formula "I mean this" (7:29), its interruption of the discussion in 7:25–40, the use of rare vocabulary and phrases: συστέλλω, τὸ λοιπόν + ἵνα, ἀγοράζειν, χρῆσθαι + κόσμος (in the accusative), and the seeming contradiction about marriage between 7:2–5 and 7:29. Deming (1995b) adds to the list that the ἵνα does not stand first, which Deming takes as the beginning of the quotation, and the expression τὸ λοιπόν, which introduces this quotation as a transitional statement. It would explain the inclusion of the seemingly irrelevant features about weeping and rejoicing, buying and using. It would also explain why these verses speak only of the passing away of the end and not also the glory and salvation of the new.

Others think that Paul integrated Stoic and apocalyptic ideas, since they need not be mutually exclusive (Deming 1995b: 186–87). Chadwick (1954–55: 268), for example, claims that this section "is set within the eschatological framework of Christian thought, fused with Stoic-Cynic ideas about the soul's detachment and ἀταραξία." Balch (1983: 430) argues that Paul accepted and used certain Stoic values that may have been in tension with his other values but "were useful in his debate with the Corinthian ascetics." Deming (1995b: 196) concludes that Paul uses apocalyptic material "to define the 'circumstances' of his (Stoic) argument against marriage." Deming contends that "the admonitions here to live 'as not' are not Paul's, but represent the authoritative voice of apocalyptic tradition describing what life in the last days, in fact, demands."

Rosner's (1994: 186) work offers a convincing array of evidence that "Paul's ethics are primarily a development of the religion of Israel, not pagan religion." The parallels do not prove dependence but only indicate that other people in the world at this time would have resonated with much of what Paul says, though they would have found his apocalyptic skyline strange. Paul is not citing an unknown written or oral apocalyptic prophecy but unfolding his own unique perspective, based on his eschatological orientation and his interpretation of his Scripture, which calls for serving God with an undivided heart (Rosner 1994: 164–65).

7:34. The textual witnesses provide eight different readings for this verse, involving transpositions of the conjunctions and of the adjective "unmarried" that affect the subject of με-μέρισται. The reading selected, found in $\mathfrak{P}^{15}$, B, 104, 181, vg, cop$^{sa, bo}$, has καὶ μεμέρισται as the conclusion of 7:33. Metzger (1994: 490) calls it "the least unsatisfactory reading," but J. Elliott (1972–73: 221) notes that it preserves the balance in 7:32–34, which contrasts the unmarried man with the married man (7:32–33) and the unmarried woman, including the virgins, with the married woman (7:34). Guenther's (2002) reading confirms this choice.

D^c, F, G, K, L, Ψ, 614, Byz omit the first καί. It leads to the KJV translation, "There is a difference between a wife and a virgin." This translation stretches the meaning of μερίζειν to try to make sense of the clause in the context. The variant can be attributed to a trick of the eye after ΓΥΝΑΙΚΙ, or it may have been a "deliberate excision" to avoid the grammatical problem of having ἡ γυνή and ἡ παρθένος as subjects of a singular verb, μεριμνᾷ.

The shift of the arthrous adjective ἡ ἄγαμος from ἡ γυνή to ἡ παρθένος (D^{gr*}, D^c, G, K, Ψ, syr^p) is difficult to explain. The addition of the adjective ἡ ἄγαμος to both ἡ γυνή and ἡ παρθένος ($\mathfrak{P}^{46}$, ℵ, A, 33, 81) is attributable to a conflation of the various readings.

7:36. Verse 36 contains two conditional sentences. The first condition is constructed with εἰ + present indicative, a real condition: "but if anyone thinks he is acting indecently." The second is constructed with ἐάν, a probable future condition: "if he is over the top." Fee (1987: 351) concludes that the first condition reflects what the Corinthians have informed Paul is happening—"as you tell me" (BDF §372.1a). The second condition interrupts the flow of thought and may be "Paul's own hypothetical contribution as to why the man may think his actions are shameful"—what Paul assumes might be the case. Winter (1998: 82–83) objects that in cases where εἰ and ἐάν follow each other they reflect a different conception of the matter. The perception of the Corinthians is found in the εἰ clause; they feel that they have acted dishonorably. Paul's understanding of what happens in such instances follows with the ἐάν clause.

VI. The Dispute over Food Sacrificed to Idols (8:1–11:1)

Interpreters divide over how to understand Paul's lengthy discussion of idol food in 8:1–11:1. The controversy over a variety of issues requires a longer introduction to the situation that Paul sought to address.

The Problem of Food Sacrificed to Idols

Paul's mission took him into a world filled with a potpourri of gods and goddesses, and temples and shrines devoted to their honor and worship (see Acts 17:16, 23). Inevitably, the new converts he made would face the vexing question of how to deal with food that had been sacrificed to idols. If they had not been converts to Judaism before becoming Christians, it would have been difficult for them to know where to draw the line (Moffatt 1938: 142). If the prohibitions against idol food in Acts 15:20, 29 and Paul's long discussion here (see also Rev. 2:14–17, 20) are any indication, the problem of idol offerings was a knotty one for the early church.[1] To avoid all contact with idolatry demanded of Christians an uncompromising devotion that unbelievers failed to comprehend and tended to disparage as antisocial behavior, if not subversive fanaticism. The pressures have not changed for new Christians today living in cultures where food is regularly offered to one god or another.

The issue that Paul addresses in chapters 8–10 involves three different types of situations (Robertson and Plummer 1914: 219; Conzelmann 1975: 177–78; Barrett 1968: 242): (1) eating food sacrificed to an idol at the temple of an idol (8:7–13; 10:1–22); (2) eating food of unknown history that is bought in the market (10:23–27); (3) eating food in the private homes of unbelievers (10:28–31).[2] Occasions for eating in connection with an idol or on the premises of an idol's temple were numerous. The celebrations of many cults were closely bound up with civic and social life because religion and politics were indivisible in ancient Hellenistic city life. If Christians took part in civic life, they would have been expected to participate in a festival's sacrificial meals in

---

1. See Cheung (1999: 165–284) for a discussion of the issue among Christians after Paul.

2. Willis (1985b: 244) oversimplifies the situation Paul is addressing by breaking it down into only two issues: (1) eating at the table of demons and becoming a partner of demons (10:14–21), which Paul absolutely forbids; and (2) eating that is permissible but qualified by consideration for others who may be offended (10:31–32).

some form or another (Smit 1996: 582).[3] The imperial cult, which frequently combined statecraft with stagecraft, was especially important to Corinthian citizens; and sacrifices were part of the Isthmian games (Broneer 1971; Engels 1990: 102; Winter 1995; 2001: 269–86). Winter (1995: 176) concludes, "Over-confident and weak Christians alike were in danger, such was the power of privilege and the importance of the imperial cult, and more so when it was established on a federal basis and celebrated in Corinth" (see also Newton 1998: 311–12).

Individuals who shared the same trades (cf. Acts 19:24–25) or a desire to worship specific gods banded together in voluntary associations (clubs, guilds), which were very popular in the Greek world.[4] Many joined them for social reasons: "a sacrifice to a god, an occasional meal, a drinking party, an exchange of different political views or a confirmation of shared ones" (Stambaugh and Balch 1986: 124).[5] In the Latin West, the poor formed funeral societies to celebrate a patron's memory and contributed to a common fund to insure that they would receive a proper burial (Fox 1986: 84). These associations "served religious, social and commercial ends" (Stambaugh and Balch 1986: 125), and some met in the dining rooms attached to major civic temples, or "their clubhouse . . . might bear the name of a divinity" (Fox 1986: 88; Stevenson and Lintott, *OCD* 352).[6] Although the social and economic facets of the associations became increasingly important, Borgen (1994: 45) notes, "Religious activities always played a role at such gatherings." This religious link explains why Philo vigorously opposed Jews joining associations: the lifestyle was characterized by gluttony and indulgence and necessitated not only breaking Jewish dietary laws but also eating idolatrous food (*Drunk.* 4 §§14–15; 6–8 §§20–29; 24 §95).[7]

Individuals might also receive private invitations to a banquet at a temple. Dining rooms, even in sumptuously large villas in Corinth, could accommodate only nine diners, and thirty to forty might squeeze into the atrium (Murphy-O'Connor 1983: 153–58). Temple banqueting rooms could be rented out for private functions (Stambaugh 1978: 583; Harding 1989: 207), like church halls today that are rented out for receptions. Several extant invitations beckon guests to attend banquets in a temple dining room commemorating a variety of rites of passage: weddings, childbirth, birthdays, coming-of-age parties, election victo-

---

3. One wonders what this expectation must have meant for someone like Erastus (Rom. 16:23), who served as a city treasurer.

4. In Roman cities they were often referred to as *collegia*.

5. Compare this to the rules dating from A.D. 176 of the Iobacchi in Athens, a hierarchical, male religious association gathered around worship of the god Dionysus (see Fox 1986: 85–88).

6. Kennedy (1987: 227–36) suggests that the meals were funerary.

7. Winter (1990: 218) cites the case of Alexandrian Jews abstaining from dining at guild meals in pagan temples even though they were members of the guild.

ries, and funerals (Kim 1975).[8] Others were more overtly cultic feasts celebrating, for example, a god's birthday.

How would such meals have been regarded? Willis claims that the focus of the meals in temples was overwhelmingly on conviviality, and any "sacramental idea" was a later construct (Willis 1985b: 8–64). Willis argues that if any sacrifice was involved, most participants would have dismissed it as a perfunctory and meaningless convention. Conzelmann (1975: 148; see also von Soden 1951; Büchsel, *TDNT* 2:379) claims that Paul "does not forbid the visiting of temple restaurants, which could be visits of a purely social kind." This conclusion imposes modern categories on the evaluation of the evidence (Cheung 1999: 28 n. 3) and should be rejected for two reasons. First, it underrates the religious overtones of such meals by overstressing conviviality. In the ancient world, people did not compartmentalize their religious, economic, and social lives, and it is anachronistic to think that they did (Sawyer 1968: 88; P. D. Gooch 1993: 33; Oropeza 1998: 65).[9] Schmitt-Pantel (1990: 200) asserts this about the Greek city: "Religion is present in all the different levels of social life, and all collective practices have a religious dimension." We cannot divide meals taking place on temple grounds into those with social purposes, which Paul would have condoned, and those with religious purposes, which Paul would have prohibited. Social meals in temples could not be purely secular or only nominally connected to idolatry, because the god or gods were honored by the meal and were considered to be present (Cheung 1999: 36). Smit (1996: 581) counters the view that dining on temple grounds did not constitute a cultic act: "Both functions, the religious and the social, are indissolubly bound together." It is inconceivable, however, that Paul would have sanctioned any participation in anything idolatrous, even if it was only "nominally" idolatrous. Paul maintains that food takes on a religious quality if a person says that it does (10:28).

Second, the suggested ambiguity of the religious status of dining rooms in temples does not mitigate the problem of participating in banquets there. Even if sacred food was not consumed, the location of the banquet would cast its idolatrous shadow on the meal. Diners could not eat in such a place without having a heightened consciousness of the gods (Cheung 1999: 28–38). P. D. Gooch (1993: 13) asks, "How could one eat in Demeter's sanctuary and not remember, or be reminded by

8. Some have claimed that the temple "was the basic 'restaurant' in antiquity, and every kind of occasion was celebrated in this fashion"—the meals included state festivals and private celebrations of various kinds (Fee 1987: 361). This is misleading. Archaeologists have uncovered in Pompeii twenty inns and 118 bars that would have served warm snack food (see Shelton 1998: 307 n. 3; Witherington 1995: 191–92).

9. Tomson (1990: 189) comments, "Religion was an integral part of ancient society at all levels and in all their relations." See Fox 1986: 64–101.

word or symbol or ritual act, that the fruit of fertile ground was her gift?"[10]

Christians might avoid overt associations with idolatry by declining to attend meals connected to idols and their shrines, but what were they to do when they were guests in someone's house and were offered meat sacrificed to an idol? Christians had friends, neighbors, relatives, and patrons who were devotees of other gods, and they would be put in socially awkward situations when invited to another's home where a religiously minded host offered them food that had been sanctified by an idol. Sacred food could be taken from the temple precincts and consumed at home, or religious rites could be performed over the food—"to fulfill a vow, to celebrate a success, to attempt to avoid 'bad luck'" (Willis 1985b: 266)—giving the meal a special character.[11] P. D. Gooch (1993: 125) points out,

> Meals involving sacrifice in private homes were not occasions focusing exclusively on high religious ritual and demanding solemn religious dedication from participants, but they also were not simple common meals bracketed by habitual, formal and essentially empty rites. Rather they seem often to be meals of some social importance. . . . They are meals where quantities are eaten, wine flows freely, and conviviality reigns— true meals and not simply ritual events. At the same time, the rites performed over the food were of significance: just as the occasions called for serious eating, they also called for authentic thanksgiving to the gods.

The Traditional View of 1 Corinthians 8–10: An Internal Squabble between the Strong and the Weak

What were the circumstances that prompted Paul's response to food sacrificed to idols? The traditional view posits an internal squabble be-

10. P. D. Gooch (1993: 80–82) conducts a survey of the archaeological and literary evidence and concludes that "the dissociation of temples and meals involving religious rites was not likely" (contra Willis 1985b). Gooch writes,

> The presence of a great number of dining rooms at the sanctuary of Demeter and Kore was not coincidental: the cult and its rites centred on the provision of food. The literary evidence shows time and again that socially significant meals involved explicit religious rites. If such meals involved rites even when held in private homes, it seems most unlikely that there would not be some cultic acts in meals celebrated in cultic settings. Finally, social events and religious events could not be separated in the Greco-roman world to the same extent as they can be in ours.

Cheung (1999: 93) concurs with this assessment.

11. Philo mentions that some people sacrificed animals to the emperor Gaius, and the worshipers took the flesh home and had a feast (*Gaius* 45 §356). Horace speaks of a private dinner and making prayers to the god Ceres and dining before his own Lar (a Roman household god) with guests (*Sat.* 2.2.120–25; 2.6.65–66; see also Plutarch, *Quaestionum convivialum libri IX* 2.10.1 [642F]).

tween the "strong" and the "weak" in Corinth, who were of different minds regarding this issue.[12] As Murphy-O'Connor (1978b: 544) puts it, "One group had no doubts about the legitimacy of eating idol-meat, the other had serious reservations." It is assumed that they argued in the name of knowledge and freedom that they had the right to continue to eat idol food because idols had no existence. The imagined "hot debate" led the Corinthians to appeal to Paul to arbitrate.[13]

Many detect the imagined propositions of the strong echoed in Paul's response:

"All of us possess gnosis" (8:1).

"An idol has no real existence" . . . because "there is no God but one" (8:4).

"Food will not bring us before God: if we do not eat, we are not lacking; and if we do, we do not excel" (8:8).

These slogans may have been combined with another, "All things are permissible" (6:12; 10:23), to reach the conclusion that eating food offered to the idols of gods who did not exist could pose no danger to Christians. What does not exist cannot contaminate them; therefore, they are free to participate in these banquets if they so wish.

The traditional view assumes that the weak Christians felt neither so free nor so bold. They were converted pagans—Jews could not be described as "until now accustomed to idols" (8:7)—and their past associations of the sacrificed food with pagan rites and shrines were simply too strong for them to eat in good conscience. They did not have the strong Christians' liberating knowledge in their emotions and sensibilities but felt pressure from the strong to imitate them and not be so squeamish or sanctimonious. Some contend that the strong labeled their more scrupulous brothers and sisters as the "weak" in their letter to Paul and sought to raise their consciousness by encouraging them to attend meals in pagan temples and to consume the idol food. They then would recognize how baseless their fears were (Hays 1997: 136). By caving in to this pressure, however, the weak violated their own consciences. They ate idol food but were not yet fully convinced that this was permissible (Schrage 1995: 256). The letter to Paul from the strong tries to enlist his support in urging the weak to get with it and "enter the world of spiritual freedom enjoyed by those who possess gnōsis" (Hays 1997: 136).

12. So Weiss 1910: 211–12; von Soden 1951; Murphy-O'Connor 1978b: 544–56; R. Horsley 1978b: 578; Willis 1985b: 92–96; Söding 1994.

13. Barrett (1982: 40–59) contends that the dispute centered around the Cephas party and Paul's about-face on the issue of idol food after the apostolic decree (see Acts 15).

The traditional view assumes that Paul agreed theologically with the strong (10:19, 25, 27), but that he introduces a catch that they failed to consider. On the one hand, Paul concurred that they were technically correct that consuming idol food per se was a matter of indifference for a Christian (Conzelmann 1975: 137; Fee 1980a: 180; Fisk 1989: 62; B. Hall 1990: 142). On the other hand, Paul reproached them for being underenlightened—they know, but not as they ought to know (8:2)—and underempathic toward the delicate consciences of the weak. They do not love and consequently they bully Christian brothers and sisters still influenced emotionally by years of conditioning regarding the temples and the gods (8:7). Paul made no attempt to controvert the slogans of those convinced of their freedom in Christ to eat anything they chose anywhere they liked. The problem for Paul was not their consumption of idol food in idol settings but their attitude toward their fellow Christians—their lack of love and consideration. Although the strong certainly were correct that eating is morally neutral and makes a person neither better nor worse spiritually, Paul insists that under certain conditions eating has a moral dimension and can become a sin against Christ (8:12).

According to the traditional view, Paul objected to the strong eating idol food, not because it constituted some inherent religious danger, but because it caused the weak to take offense or to violate their consciences. He instructs the strong to restrict their freedom because of their bonds with their fellow Christians who were weak and offended by their actions (Conzelmann 1975: 137; Horrell 1997b: 98–99). Willis (1985b: 244) concludes, "One must always forgo eating when another person is thereby endangered. At no time is eating right 'in itself,' but all eating and drinking—indeed, everything one does (10:31!), is subject to this criterion of consideration of the other person." The corollary would seem to be that as long as no one is offended, eating idol food is not sinful and is permissible. As far as Paul is concerned, the strong need only to be more sensitive and cautious and to show more Christian charity to their less progressive brothers and sisters.

This traditional view assumes that Paul made a distinction between innocuously consuming food associated with an idol (8:1–13) and participating in actual worship of an idol (10:14–22). Paul permitted idol food as long as no one was caused to stumble. Concern for the welfare of the fellow Christian becomes the hermeneutical key for deciding what is right or wrong (8:13). Brunt (1985: 115) contends that Paul does not simply give an answer to the question but shifts the focus to Christian love, "and in doing so he presents an example of principled, ethical thinking where love and respect for others transcends the rightness or wrongness of the act itself." Paul's main concern is not idolatry, but getting the Corinthians to live out the basic Christian principle "Let no one seek his own good, but the good of his neighbor" (10:24) (so Meeks 1982: 73–75). In this view, Paul tried to persuade the strong that the scruples of weaker Christians are not obstacles to the strong that stifle their freedom in Christ but opportunities to exercise their freedom. The strong are not entirely free until they are free to forgo the exercise of their freedom for the sake of others.

This view also assumes that the church's later treatment of the problem of idol food failed to grasp Paul's sophisticated hermeneutic and vision and reverted back to legalism by demanding abstinence from idol food. For example, Barrett (1982: 56) boldly maintains that the next generations "could see no way of excluding idolatry that did not include rigid abstention from heathen food and heathen dinner parties. . . . The church as a whole retreated into a narrow religious shell. Jewish Christianity (in this matter) triumphed though Jewish Christians became less important in the church." Brunt (1985: 120–22) claims that the other extant sources of Christianity speak only to the question of the rightness or wrongness of the act itself. Paul instead focused on one's responsibility to others in relationship to this issue. Brunt concludes that Paul's reflective ethical approach to the problem was rejected. Later, the "orthodox" position diverges from Paul by labeling those who ate idol food as heretics.

The Challenge to the Traditional View

Hurd (1965: 117–25, 143–48) spots the chinks in this traditional view and challenges the thesis that two groups in Corinth were knocking heads over the idol-meat issue and appealed to Paul to hold court on the matter. Hurd claims instead that the Corinthians were united on the issue of idol food and that Paul's response in these chapters was another installment in the continuing saga of his disagreement with them. The proudly enlightened Corinthians wrote to Paul, defending their belief that they could continue their practice of associating with idol food. Paul answers the vigorous objections to his prior ban on idol food. According to Hurd, the Christian with the weak conscience is only a hypothetical person conjured up by Paul to convince the Corinthians of the new policy on idol food adopted by the apostolic council, which conflicted with his earlier instructions. Hurd's challenge to the traditional view is an important corrective that has been too often ignored but still needs refinement.

The Situation behind 1 Corinthians 8–10: A Dispute between Paul and the Corinthians

The traditional view makes a basic error in assuming that chapters 8–10 constitute Paul's first word to the Corinthians on the subject of idol food. It is inconceivable that this letter would be the first time that Paul discussed this issue with the Corinthians. Idolatry would have been one of the earliest and most pressing issues confronting new converts in any place where many gods and lords existed (Tomson 1990: 190; Cheung 1999: 141 n. 82), since turning from idols was central to Christian conversion. The denunciation of idol worship was central to Paul's missionary preaching (1 Thess. 1:9–10; Gal. 4:8–9; 1 Cor. 12:2).[14] Acts presents a picture of Paul's agitation with idols in Athens (Acts 17:16; see also 14:15) and his fulminations against them sparking riots and persecution in Ephesus (Acts 19:11–40). His uncompromising attitude toward idolatry is revealed in his insistence that idolaters (among others) will not inherit the kingdom of God (1 Cor. 6:9). Such a vital issue as whether Christians may or may not eat food sacrificed to idols or eat in idol temples would not have been something that suddenly dawned on the Corinthians months later when the weak believers objected to the strong believers' exercise of their freedom. It is much more plausible that the Corinthians have been engaged in an ongoing discussion with Paul about this matter, and some of them have not welcomed his previous injunctions (Fee 1980a: 179; Comfort, *DPL* 425; Witherington 1995: 186).[15]

P. D. Gooch (1993: 136) argues that Paul's position on idol food derives from his conviction that maintaining partnership with his Lord puts limits on behavior, and that his conviction "is strongly conditioned by his religious view of the world as a Jew." He would not have jettisoned the basic covenantal demand of exclusive allegiance to the one Lord (P. D. Gooch 1993: 96–97). As one so thoroughly imbued with Scripture (see Silva, *DPL* 630–42), everything in his Jewish background would have precluded any leniency toward anything associated with pagan cults (Cheung 1999: 41; see also Holtz 1995: 60–

---

14. Grant (1986: 46) points out that every item in 1 Thess. 1:9–10 "requires amplification and proof, and presumably received it in the apostle's preaching. Why was his God living? Why real? What son? Which heavens, and why there? What resurrection? Who was Jesus? How does he deliver? What wrath? . . . Every item would raise questions and require the apostle to develop some fairly systematic thought, to move toward consistent theology in combating the worship of idols." Philo (*Virt.* 17 §102) notes that "incomers" (Jewish proselytes) have abandoned their blood relatives, their country, their customs, and the temples and images of their gods and the tributes and honors paid to them, and "they have taken the journey to a better home, from idle fables to the clear vision of the truth and the worship of the one and truly existing God."

15. Willis (1985b: 267) thinks that the Corinthians had asked Paul in their letter whether it was permissible to eat in an idol's temple. They not only asked for Paul's view, but also "gave their reasons to justify their participation," perhaps anticipating his criticism or to show off their wisdom and knowledge. Newton (1998: 264–65) suggests, "Perhaps Paul had already tackled this issue during his eighteen months in Corinth, but because of misunderstanding, rejection, disobedience, confusion or the emergence of particular circumstances such as the Isthmian Games, the conflict remained unresolved and compelled Paul to lift his pen."

62).[16] Barrett (1968: 146–47) is quite wrong in his assertion that "Paul was not a practising Jew" when it came to food sacrificed to idols. The anti-Judaism of Weiss (1910: 264) is glaringly apparent in his comments that the enlightened Paul rejects the superstition and fearfulness of Judaism regarding idol food. Paul had not become so "unjewed" that he tolerated things that overtly reeked of idolatry. The issues concerning Jewish purity and impurity laws were entirely different from the issues concerning idolatry (P. D. Gooch 1993: 135). His rejection of idol food would fully accord with his Jewish background and its "long tradition of polemic against pagan cults" (Borgen 1994: 32). We may presume that he fully expected that Christians would no longer worship in idol temples, participate in idol festivals, or dine at idol banquets. The issue is not just about meat bought in the market (contra Bruce 1971: 78) or dining in a temple (contra Fee 1980a; Witherington 1995; R. Horsley 1998: 141). It has to do with eating food conspicuously sacrificed to an idol, whether at a public feast, in a temple dining room, as a participant in an actual sacrifice, or in a private home (Cheung 1999; R. Collins 1999: 304). The Corinthians might excuse it as accommodation; Paul condemns it as religious syncretism.

The Corinthians, on the other hand, came from a quite different tradition. It is unlikely that their actions were motivated by theological bravado in which they sought to demonstrate their spiritual security and liberty by deliberately eating what had been offered to idols (Conzelmann 1975: 137–38; R. Horsley 1980–81: 48; P. Gardner 1994: 33). Cheung (1999: 120) wisely cautions that we should not confuse the justification for their eating with the motive behind their eating. They may have rationalized their eating by appealing to knowledge. That does not

---

16. Cheung (1999: 77) asserts, "In the minds of most Jews, idol food was so inextricably bound up with idolatry that they were instinctively repulsed by it. Idol food simply epitomized idol worship." Philo, living in Alexandria, took pains to explain and justify the rules for *kashrut*, often resorting to elaborate allegorical artifices. He did not explain why idolatry was forbidden and must have regarded it as self-evident from the Jew's exclusive allegiance to God. Philo (*Spec. Laws* 1.58 §§315–16) ferociously condemns any connection to idolatrous behavior by Jews:

> If anyone cloaking himself under the name and guise of a prophet and claiming to be possessed by inspiration lead us on to worship of the gods [we should not pay attention to him]. . . . And if a brother or son or daughter . . . or anyone else who seems to be kindly disposed, urges us to a like course, bidding us fraternize with the multitude, resort to temples, and join in their libations and sacrifices, we must punish him as a public and general enemy, taking little thought for the ties which bind us to him . . . and deem it a religious duty to seek his death.

Among the rabbis, idol food was absolutely banned when it was known to be such, and they debated only over ambiguous cases.

explain why they ate. The chief reason for their participation would have been social pressure from their polytheistic culture. Cheung (1999: 120) cites Niebuhr's (1951: 10) observation: "Not only pagans who have rejected Christ but believers who have accepted him find it difficult to combine his claims upon them with those of their societies." The Corinthians quite naturally did not want to give up their family and social connections, so they made compromises and justified them post hoc (Cheung 1999: 121–22).

Their responses may have ranged from brazen defiance, to petulant quibbling, to outspoken consternation. We cannot and need not map out precisely the lines of argument in any of the previous conversations, but we may guess that some bolder Corinthians countered Paul's prohibitions with clever arguments constructed from bits of his earlier teaching, wrenched out of context, with an added emphasis on how unrealistic and unreasonable his taboos were. Did he expect them to withdraw from the world completely (5:10)? They may also have justified their actions by downplaying any religious ceremony solemnizing a dinner party in a pagan temple as a bunch of religious mumbo jumbo that had no spiritual effect on them whatsoever.

Those Corinthian Christians who dreamed of social advancement faced immense difficulty in defining and maintaining boundaries.[17] The question of how far one might accommodate an idolatrous culture taxed both Jew and Christian. Rabbinic literature testifies to the lure of pagan society, with the idolaters coaxing, "Come and intermingle with us" (*Mekilta de Rabbi Ishmael*, tractate *Shirata* 3 on Exod. 15:2). Philo (*Spec. Laws* 1.5 §§28–29) complains about the attraction of idolatry even for Jews steeped in their monotheistic faith:

> But not only wealth and glory and the like are idols and unsubstantial shadows, but also all those personages which the myth-makers have invented and spread delusion therewith, building up their false imaginations into a stronghold to menace the truth, and staging as by machinery new gods, in order that the eternal and really existing God might be consigned to oblivion. And to promote the seductiveness they have fitted the falsehood into melody, metre, and rhythm, thinking to cajole their audience thereby. Further, too, they have brought in sculpture and painting to cooperate in the deception, in order that with the colours and shapes and artistic qualities wrought by their fine workmanship they may enthrall the spectators and so beguile the two leading senses, sight and hearing—sight through lifeless shapes of beauty, hearing through the charm of poetry and music—and thus make the soul unsteady and unsettled and seize it for their prey.

17. On the religious complexity in the pagan world, see Borgen 1994: 57–59.

Evidence exists of Jews compromising with polytheism and with society at large (Borgen 1994: 36). It is not surprising that newly converted Christians would have bent under this significant constraint to compromise with idolatrous practices (Oster 1995: 234), and we need not assume that they did so with theological deliberation. Yeo (1994: 308) puts it in a modern Chinese perspective: "To advise the Chinese not to offer food and not eat the food in ancestor worship may be implicitly advising them not to love their parents, not to practise love, and ultimately not to be Chinese."

Joining in meals was extremely important in the ancient world because they served as markers of socioeconomic class divisions, as opportunities to converse and build friendships, and as a means to fulfill sociopolitical obligations (P. D. Gooch 1993: 40; Newton 1998: 243–44). Smit (1996: 582) comments: "Anyone desisting from public sacrificial events was unfit for political functions." To rebuff the invitations of friends, neighbors, and patrons not only would cause one's social status to plummet but also would mark one off as "odd and repugnant" (P. D. Gooch 1993: 46).[18] Jews were considered "misanthropes" because they "did not engage in normal social intercourse, and in particular did not eat with those outside their group" (P. D. Gooch 1993: 131–32; cf. Tacitus, *Historiae* 5.1–2; Diodorus Siculus, *Library of History* 34.1.2). To shun gatherings that lubricated social and economic relations would make Christians conspicuous outcasts who held outlandish, antisocial, perverse religious beliefs. More prominent Corinthian Christians would have been understandably reluctant to draw hard-and-fast lines that would alienate such important persons in their lives and exclude them from society (see P. D. Gooch 1993: 106).[19] Willis (1985b: 266) thinks it most probable that "those who ate simply were unwilling to remove themselves from normal social life."

Hurd is correct. They were not asking, "Can we eat idol food?" but "Why can't we eat idol food?"[20] In these chapters Paul responds to the Corinthians' rebuttal (Cheung 1999: 96). He is fully aware of the intense pressure to compromise and to join in the hail-fellow-well-met conviviality, but he maintains that no temptation has overtaken them that is not common to humans (10:13). He insists that God is faithful and will not allow them to be tempted beyond what they can withstand.

---

18. Borgen (1994: 35) cites the case of the Ionians' insistence that if Jews were to be their fellows, they should worship Ionian gods.

19. Juvenal (*Sat.* 5.12–22) explains that dinner invitations from a patron were regarded as repayments for services rendered (cf. the parables of the banquets in the Gospels: Matt. 22:1–14; Luke 14:12–24).

20. Paul's "vigorous, combative" (Fee 1987: 359) response does not seem to be what one would expect if they had simply asked him to referee an internal dispute (see also Eriksson 1998: 142).

A second error of the traditional view is the assumption that there is a dispute among the "strong" and the "weak." Paul never identifies any particular group as "the strong." He does not address the weak at all and only describes them in the third person in chapters 8 and 9 as reasons for giving up what one considers a right. They do not appear in chapter 10 when Paul gives specific directions. There is no indication that the strong are trying to bend the will of the weak to see things their way. On the contrary, the weak in Paul's scenario only happen by coincidence to see the strong reclining in a temple (8:10).[21] Paul does not suggest that they recoil in pietistic horror upon observing their fellow Christians dining in an idol's shrine but instead worries that they might be drawn back into idolatry by emulating the example of those reputed to have knowledge. What Paul fears is not factionalism in the church over this issue or that the weak might act contrary to their beliefs and feel guilty; he fears that they might be reeled back into idolatry. But this is only a hypothetical example. The basic issue has to do with what Paul considers to be forbidden idolatrous behavior by those who perceive themselves as endowed with liberating knowledge.

Interpreters have read the idea that the church was split over the idol-food issue into the text from Paul's concern over factions voiced in 1 Cor. 1–4 and from his discussion of a similar kind of dispute in Rom. 14:1–15:13 (Cheung 1999: 87).[22] The parallels between Rom. 14:1–15:13 and 1 Cor. 8:1–11:1 entice one to think that the two passages are analogous rather than complementary. Both passages deal with the issue of how what one eats affects others. In both passages Paul cautions against causing another to stumble (Rom. 14:13, 15, 20–21; 1 Cor. 8:13; 10:32) and destroying another (Rom. 14:20; 1 Cor. 8:11). In both passages he mentions the weak (Rom. 14:1, 2; 15:1; 1 Cor. 8:7, 9, 10, 11, 12; 9:22). He also raises the question of your good being spoken of as evil (βλασφημεῖν, *blasphēmein*; Rom. 14:16; 1 Cor. 10:30). Paul's solution in Rom. 15:2, "Each of us must please our neighbor for the good purpose of building up the neighbor," matches his exhortation in 1 Cor. 10:24, "Let no one seek his own advantage but that of another." The appeal to the example of Christ in Rom. 15:3, "For Christ did not please himself; but, as it is written, 'The insults of those who insult you have fallen on me,'" corresponds to his conclusion in 1 Cor. 11:1, "Be imitators of me, as I am of Christ."

These parallels between the two passages, however, have misled interpreters to think that the "weak" in 1 Cor. 8 have the same problem as

21. If the division between the strong and the weak is a social one, as Theissen (1982: 137) argues, then it is only the wealthier ones who have the opportunity to join in the eating of meat at banquets. How can they encourage their poorer brethren to do so? Why would they want to be joined by poorer brethren?

22. Cranfield (1975: 691–92) lists the similarities between the chapters. See also Karris 1973.

the "weak" in Rom. 14–15. Several differences emerge from a careful reading (see Dawes 1996: 86–88).

1. In 1 Cor. 8–10, the central issue is food sacrificed to idols εἰδωλόθυτον (*eidōlothyton*; 8:1, 4, 7, 10; 10:19, 28 [ἱερόθυτον, *hierothyton*]). The issues in Rom. 14–15 concern meat or vegetables (14:2; Jewish dietary laws, according to Dunn 1988b: 799–803; T. Schreiner 1998: 730) or what days to regard as holy (14:5), not idol food.[23] Paul never mentions idol food and says nothing about the context in which the food is eaten. Questions about food being "clean" or "unclean" (Rom. 14:14, 20) are quite different from the matter of idol food, which can never be clean.

2. Commentators have adopted the terminology from Rom. 14–15 in discussing 1 Cor. 8–10 by describing it as a conflict between the "strong" (δυνατοί, *dynatoi*; mentioned in Rom. 15:1) and the "weak." But in 1 Cor. 8–10, Paul never refers to "the strong," and the weak are identified as "weak in consciousness."[24] The problem in Rom. 14–15 is a weakness in faith, not a weakness in conscience. The word "conscience" (1 Cor. 8:7, 10, 12; 10:25, 27, 28, 29) never appears in Rom. 14–15, and the word "faith" does not appear in 1 Cor. 8–10.[25]

3. In 1 Cor. 8:9 (cf. 9:4–6, 12, 18), the key word is ἐξουσία (*exousia*, authority, liberty, right). It does not appear in Rom. 14–15.

4. In Rom. 14–15, Paul sides with the strong (Rom. 14:20: "For everything is indeed clean"), and he sees no harm in their eating except for its potential effect on the weak. He warns against passing judgment (Rom. 14:1–13a) and points out that they could lead the weak to conform from their pressure and, by acting in a state of doubt, be guilty of sin in their own minds (Rom. 14:13b–23). By contrast, in 1 Cor. 8–10, Paul completely rejects eating in temples and does not agree in principle with those who have knowledge. In 10:14–22, he brands their actions as a deadly communion with demons. He only agrees—if that is the proper word—that the weak do not have "this knowledge" and does not offer any hint that their scruples are backward or unnecessary. In Rom. 14:5–6, Paul says that both the one who eats and the one who abstains give thanks to God and honor God. Can food that is known to be offered to an idol be blessed and bring

23. The problem in Rom. 14–15 may divide along lines of ethnicity—Jew versus Greek (see Walters 1993). Karris (1973), however, does not think that the strong and the weak represent ethnic communities, but individuals.

24. Paul's only mention of strength in 1 Cor. 8–10 comes in an allusion to the OT: "Are we stronger [ἰσχυρότεροι, *ischyroteroi*] than he?" (1 Cor. 10:22). In 1 Corinthians the word "strong" is more indicative of an attitude than of a specific group (1 Cor. 4:10, "We are weak, but you are strong"; so Conzelmann 1975: 174 n. 49).

25. Conzelmann (1975: 147) claims that "conscience" and "faith" are identical (see also Bultmann 1955: 220). Dunn (1998: 703), however, argues that "faith" was the appropriate criterion for an internal issue but "conscience" was more appropriate for a boundary-crossing issue.

honor to God? Paul's directive in 1 Cor. 10:28 not to eat food that one openly declares has been offered in sacrifice suggests not.

Romans 14:1–15:6 has to do with the social interaction between Jewish and Gentile Christians. First Corinthians 8:1–11:1 has to do with idol food and associations with idolatry—the interaction between Christians and idol worshipers. It does not follow that since Paul rejected Jewish food laws that erected barriers between Jews and Gentiles, he condoned the eating of idol food. Idol food was a different matter entirely that introduced the baleful influence of syncretism and polytheism. The fact that Paul and other Christians rejected narrow Jewish restrictions that separated Jewish Christians from Gentile Christians does not mean that Paul rejected restrictions involving idolatry that separated Christians, who were exclusively tied to the one true God, from idolaters, who related to many gods and lords. It is more reasonable to conclude that Rom. 14–15 is an adaptation of principles found in 1 Cor. 8–10 to a quite different situation. Consequently, Rom. 14–15 should not be read into the Corinthian context (Cheung 1999: 90). It is mistaken to assume that since Paul was in theological agreement with the strong in Rom. 14–15, he also agreed with the so-called strong in 1 Cor. 8–10 and only wanted them to be more charitable to their theologically challenged brothers and sisters.

A third error of the traditional view is the weight it places on Paul's warning about the potential harm that eating idol food might cause a Christian with a weak conscience. It assumes that this was Paul's only problem with eating idol food. The subtle nuances of Paul's lengthy argumentation may contribute to this misunderstanding. He does not start out by condemning outright the behavior, as presumably he had done in his previous discussion on this issue. Understanding chapters 8–10 as Paul's reaction to a previous protest from the Corinthians sheds light on why his arguments seem so complex and circuitous to modern readers.[26] Paul was interested in persuasion, not coercion.[27] He wants them to flee from idols (10:14), but he

26. Fee (1987: 474) notes (on 10:22) that Paul's argument may "seem terribly convoluted" for modern readers, "but it probably was not at all so for its first readers, for whom this was a response to their letter." I agree with Murphy-O'Connor (1979b: 292), who maintains that Paul's "response is so subtly argued that a correct interpretation of every verse is essential if we are to understand not only his position but that of the Corinthians."

27. Engberg-Pedersen (1987: 579) contends that in situations where the gospel requires certain behavior and is in reach of his addressees, Paul uses imperatives, "but always with the sense of reminding his addressees of things they already know and subscribe to." In situations where a certain behavior that is required by the gospel is "*not* within immediate reach of Paul's addressees," he does not use imperatives but exhorts by means of examples and "*showing* what application of the gospel in such situations *would* consist in." According to Engberg-Pedersen, 8:1–11, which is characterized as "not offending the brother," fits the first situation. I would argue that it fits the *second* case: Paul does not think that it is quite within reach because of the social complexity involved in idol food.

also wants them to see the theological implications of their behavior and the necessity of the norm of love for guiding all their behavior.

N. Wright (1992: 122) correctly recognizes that the "major issues at stake were monotheism, idolatry, election, holiness and how these issues interacted." Paul begins his counterargument in 8:1–6 by going back to first principles, "the reassertion of Jewish-style monotheism" (N. Wright 1992: 125) and something the Corinthians would readily accept. He does not draw out the full implications of what their monotheistic confession and allegiance to the one God entail until 10:1–22, however.[28]

Because the Corinthians did not yield to Paul's prior objection to idol food, he recognizes that a lengthier, more subtle approach is demanded. Yeo (1994: 310) is correct that Paul did not attempt to give an easy answer of yes or no in 1 Cor. 8 and that he did not resort "to absolute prohibitions concerning idol meat eating" (Yeo 1994: 308). But Yeo does not understand why this is the case. It was not because the situation was too complex for a simple solution. Rather, Paul adopts this tack because he intends, as he does throughout the letter, to exercise love in directing them. He wants them to flee from idols (10:14), but he also wants them to see the theological implications of their behavior and the necessity of the norm of love for guiding all their behavior. Consequently, he employs indirect means (Smit 1997b: 477). He does not condemn them at the outset and make pronouncements about idol food but instead seeks to convince them as reasonable persons to act out of love for others. First, he will appeal to their better nature, assuming that as Christians they have a loving concern for others and do not wish to lead them into sin. His first unambiguous argument against eating idol food is his assertion in 8:7–13 that their actions are not neutral but may cause others to stumble and fall.

Paul begins with an admonition against doing anything that harms the weak, and then he goes on to warn against doing anything that involves idolatry. He "builds up his arguments by stages through a series of strategic moves" (Newton 1998: 24), analyzing the different aspects of the question (see also Tomson 1990: 208; Dawes 1996: 91–92; Smit 1996: 589–91; Cheung 1999: 109, 116–17). He moves from concern for the weak and the church (8:7–13) to the example of his own behavior to do everything—including not exercising his rights as an apostle—to win others to the gospel and to do nothing that would needlessly hinder

28. Fee (1987: 363) claims that Paul's "first concern is with the incorrect ethical basis of their argument. The problem is primarily attitudinal." He prohibits their present activity only after he corrects the problem at a deeper level (Fee 1987: 391). But the problem is idolatry—behavior, not merely a bad attitude expressed in an imperious contempt for the weak. Paul must also grapple with their refusal to defer to his judgment (P. D. Gooch 1993: 83–84).

another from coming to faith (9:1–27). Only then does he develop the serious theological ramifications of their behavior from an exposition of Scripture (10:1–13). He strikes directly and hard in 10:14–22, commanding them to flee idolatry (10:14) and connecting idol food to demons. Finally, he eases up his attack by offering practical advice about food of an undetermined nature lest they think that he wants them to withdraw from the world altogether (10:23–30). He concludes the discussion with general appeals that none in Corinth would be likely to challenge (10:31–11:1).

Paul forbade eating at pagan banquets in pagan temples. He forbade eating food that was openly acknowledged to be offered to an idol. He permitted buying food in the marketplace that may or may not have been sacrificed in a pagan temple; but if its history was disclosed and it was announced to be idol food, then he forbade eating it. Paul permitted dining with friends who were worshipers of idols, but if the food was announced to be idol food, then he forbade eating it. The issue that Paul addresses is the same throughout chapters 8–10: Christians participating in any function that overtly smacks of idolatry.

Paul's argument is lengthy and may be structured as follows.[29]

> A. Introduction of the issue of idol food (8:1–6)
> B. Refutation of their practice because of its danger to fellow Christians (8:7–13)
> C. Paul's own example to undergird his counsel (9:1–27)
>   1. First example: Paul's right as an apostle to receive support (9:1–14; key word: ἐξουσία, exousia, 9:4, 5, 6, 12, 18; cf. 8:9)
>   2. Second example: Paul's freedom and his interchange with various groups (9:15–23; key word: κερδαίνειν, kerdainein, 9:19, 20, 21, 22)
>   3. Third example: The athlete's self-discipline and abstinence to win a prize (9:24–27)
> D. Refutation of their practice from the negative example of the history of Israel in the wilderness (10:1–13)
> E. Refutation of their practice from the example of the Lord's Supper (10:14–22)
> F. Practical advice for dealing with the issue of idol food in pagan settings (10:23–11:1)

---

29. R. Collins (1999: 306) identifies the structure as a three-part A-B-A′ schema, in which the final element reflects the first element. He notes that this style of writing corresponds to Aristotelian logic, which cites a major premise and a minor premise before arriving at a conclusion. Paul's argument builds up to the command in 10:14, "My beloved, flee from idolatry."

A. Introduction of the Issue of Idol Food (8:1–6)

Paul introduces the dispute over idol food by establishing common ground with the Corinthians: We Christians know that God is one and that idols have no existence despite their many adherents. This consensus allows him to introduce two key principles that will inform his argument. First, Christian love is to override knowledge that feeds arrogance. Christian love is not blind (in contrast to the popular saying about love); it is to be informed by knowledge (cf. Phil. 1:9). But knowledge without love is barren (13:2). Second, Christian monotheism defines who the people of God are as distinct from those who worship many gods and lords in their sundry guises. The confession of one God and one Lord, however, requires exclusive loyalty to God as Father and to Christ as Lord. Even a perfunctory or make-believe show of fealty to an idol compromises the loyalty owed only to God and Christ.

Exegesis and Exposition

[1]Now concerning food that has been sacrificed to an idol: We know that we all have knowledge. Knowledge puffs up, but love builds up. [2]If anyone presumes to have arrived at complete knowledge ⌜about anything⌝, this one does not yet know as it is necessary to know. [3]If anyone loves ⌜God⌝, this one is known ⌜by him⌝. [4]Therefore, concerning the eating of food that has been sacrificed to an idol: We know that an idol has no real existence and that no God exists except one. [5]For if indeed there are so-called gods, whether in heaven or upon earth, then there are in fact many gods and many lords. [6]But for us there is one God, the Father, from whom all things come and for whom we exist, and one Lord, Jesus Christ, through whom are all things and through whom we exist.

The phrase "now concerning" (περὶ δέ, *peri de*; cf. 7:1, 25; 8:4; 12:1; 16:1, 12) may signal that Paul turns his attention to another item from the Corinthians' letter (7:1): the question of "what is sacrificed to idols" (so Fee 1987: 365, 357 n. 1).[1] Some, however, question whether each περὶ δέ phrase that

8:1

---

1. Hurd (1965: 63–65) cites numerous scholars who note the significance of the repeated phrase as a structuring device. Fee (1987: 365) contends, "As in 7:1 (cf. 6:12–13) he begins by citing their letter, apparently intending, as v. 4 indicates, to set forth and qualify the *content* of their knowledge."

occurs in 1 Corinthians flags a query from the letter they wrote to Paul. The phrase need not be restricted to an answering formula or a reference to a previous letter but may simply be a topic marker (Baasland 1988; M. Mitchell 1989). Paul may only be announcing the subject that he will now address, which, in this case, abruptly switches from questions about sexuality and marriage. M. Mitchell claims that this expression does not mean that the Corinthians mentioned the topic in their letter and does not distinguish references to written information from oral information.

Although the last statement may be true, I argue that the debate over idol food between Paul and the Corinthians had been ongoing. If so, the Corinthians may have sent word back to Paul, challenging once again his position on this matter. It does seem plausible that Paul's statements "we all have knowledge" (8:1b), "an idol has no real existence," and "no God exists except one" (8:4b) are catchphrases that form the basis of the Corinthian's response, whether they carefully outlined their theological stance in their letter or not. He responds to some resistance from the Corinthians on this matter, and it is probable that they voiced their protest formally in their letter. Given the proximity of the formula περὶ δέ to 7:1, which specifically mentions what they wrote, it is likely that Paul uses it to identify items raised in the Corinthians' letter (see Eriksson 1998: 137). They apparently broached the issues of knowledge and freedom. Concerning knowledge, Paul says that it puffs up but love builds up (8:1), and that not all share this knowledge (8:7). Concerning freedom, Paul argues that one should not allow it to be used to the detriment of another.

The word τὸ εἰδωλόθυτον (to eidōlothyton; an adjective used as a substantive) literally means "something offered to images" (see also Acts 15:29; 21:25; Rev. 2:14, 20; Tyndale renders it "thinges offred unto ymages").[2] The term does not appear in papyri or literature before 1 Corinthians (Witherington 1993: 238–39; Schrage 1995: 236; Cheung 1999: 319), and idol worshipers normally used the term ἱερόθυτον (hierothyton, 10:28) to refer to something "offered in sacrifice to a deity." Τὸ εἰδωλόθυτον has a caustic, polemical edge because the word εἴδωλα (eidōla) always appears in the LXX in a negative sense to refer to forbidden false gods. The term "idol" connoted to both Jews and most Christians something detestable (Deut. 29:17), opposed to the living God (1 Thess. 1:9; 2 Cor. 6:16), lifeless and "dumb" (1 Cor. 12:2), and demonic (Rev. 9:20).[3] For Jews, idols and pagan divinities were identi-

---

2. Kennedy (1989: 20) renders it "the celebration to/for the images (with offerings)." The addition of "food" in 8:4, Kennedy thinks (1989: 21), confirms that the word does not refer to a food offering but a "'celebration' at which food was eaten."

3. Idols are reviled in the OT as mere sticks and stones, no better than scarecrows (Jer. 10:5). The psalmist mocks them not only for being the creation of human hands, but also for having human features—mouths, eyes, ears, noses, hands, feet—that do not work (Ps. 115:4–8; 135:15–18). Not only are they not divine, they are manifestly less than human.

cal, and they may have "coined a new expression out of an existing term" (Büchsel, *TDNT* 2:377; Conzelmann 1975: 139; Héring 1962: 66; Tomson 1990: 189). The phrase αἱ θυσίαι τῶν εἰδώλων αὐτῶν (*hai thysiai tōn eidōlōn autōn*, the sacrifices of their idols) appears in Num. 25:2 LXX (cf. Exod. 34:15; Lev. 17:7), and the word εἰδωλόθυτον appears in 4 Macc. 5:2; Sib. Or. 2:96; Jos. As. 12:5; and Ps.-Phoc. 31. Others believe that εἰδωλόθυτον was a contemptuous neologism fashioned in Christian, perhaps Pauline, circles (Witherington 1993: 239; P. Gardner 1994: 15–16; R. Collins 1999: 311).[4]

Sacrifice was the customary form of both public and private worship in the ancient world (Stambaugh and Balch 1986: 128). In Greek religion, sacrifice pertained to a "series of overlapping terms conveying ideas such as 'killing,' 'destroying,' 'burning,' 'cutting,' 'consecrating,' 'performing sacred acts,' 'giving,' 'presenting'" (Parker, *OCD* 1344). The sacrifice of an animal meant performing appropriate preliminary rites: killing the animal and transferring the animal by certain rites from human possession to the deity, butchering the animal and inspecting the vital organs to determine the deity's acceptance of the animal, cooking and offering the vital organs or other designated parts to the deity and cooking the rest of the victim for human consumption in honor of the deity. All sacrifices were, in principle, followed by a banquet, celebrated sometimes by the immediate participants and those with privileges in a particular sanctuary, sometimes by special sections of society (such as the elite), sometimes by larger numbers of persons with special rights to take part (such as citizens), sometimes in communal banquets under the sponsorship of benefactors (Scheid, *OCD* 1345). Leftover meat would be delivered to butchers' shops for sale, but idol food could be any kind of food consecrated to a deity in any sacred context, not just meat (P. D. Gooch 1993: 129).[5]

The term "idol offerings" tips Paul's hand that he does not regard it as something neutral (Smit 1996: 582). As far as he is concerned, Christians are never permitted to eat idol offerings that are known to be such. When

---

4. See Acts 15:29; 21:25; Rev. 2:14, 20; Did. 6:3.

5. To dispose of the problem that Paul might contradict himself in 8:1–13; 10:14–22; and 10:23–29, Fee (1987: 482–85) and Witherington (1993: 246) narrow too much the semantic range of the term εἰδωλόθυτον by claiming that it refers only to sacrificial food eaten in the presence of an idol or on the temple precincts. They think that it is opposed to ἱερόθυτον, which refers to food not eaten in the temple or used as part of temple worship. In 8:1–13, Paul forbids εἰδωλόθυτον, food eaten in the presence of an idol, while in 10:23–29, he permits eating food sold in the marketplace.

This distinction between the two terms is invalid (see Fisk 1989; Newton 1998: 268). Fisk's criticism of Fee, however, is based on the false assumption that in 8:10, Paul has in mind permissible temple attendance that involved "harmless fun and social convention," while in 10:19–22, he describes participating in cultic activity, which is forbidden. Fisk (1989: 62–63) thinks that Paul only forbade temple feasts that "had a distinctly religious focus, when participants were consciously acknowledging pagan gods." I have explained the problem of the supposed contradiction differently above.

he talks about what is purchased in the market (10:25–26), he does not call it "idol offerings," even though there was a good possibility that it might have come from an idol temple. If it is known to be "idol offerings," Paul forbids it, which is why he says to buy what is sold in the market without making extensive inquiries about its history. In these chapters, Paul is not concerned about food that may have had some past association with a sacrifice to an idol but can be bought or consumed in a context free of any idolatrous taint. Food is assumed to be innocuous and a matter of indifference *until* it is manifestly associated with some kind of idolatrous activity or setting. It becomes defiling when it is eaten in the polluted context of an idol's temple or when it is declared to be devoted to an idol.

Does Paul begin his discussion of idol offerings by citing an actual Corinthian slogan, "We all have knowledge"? Most scholars think so.[6] The saying has an aphoristic quality, which may suggest a slogan; and it makes sense that the Corinthians would have appealed to their knowledge in excusing their participation in idol feasts to Paul. They may have protested, "We possess knowledge." To which Paul responds that knowledge can feed pride (8:1a) and that they may not know as they ought to know (8:2). They may also have declared "An idol has no real existence" because "there is no God but one" (8:4). To which Paul rejoins that there still are many so-called gods and lords (8:5) that represent and serve something demonic (10:20). They may also have asserted, "Food will not bring us before God" (8:8). To which Paul responds that their eating may lead to the downfall of another member of the community and thus will bring the guilt of a sin against Christ on their own heads (8:9–13). Again, they may also have appealed to the canon "All things are permitted" (10:23a). To which Paul counters that not all things are beneficial or build up (10:23b).

Some consider the whole phrase "We know that we all possess knowledge" to be a direct quotation from the Corinthians' letter (Willis 1985b: 67–70; Parry 1926: 128). But Paul seems to have tweaked the Corinthian argument by adding the "all" in his affirmation that "we *all* have knowledge." The "we" and the "all" include himself, and this assertion does not simply reiterate a Corinthian position but reflects a basic Christian conviction (cf. Rom. 2:2). He uses the various permutations of the phrase "we know that" to cite well-known Christian doctrine or generally accepted facts.[7] Christians possess knowledge and have

6. Weiss 1910: 214; Robertson and Plummer 1914: xxv; Lietzmann 1949: 37; Hurd 1965: 279; Barrett 1968: 189; Conzelmann 1975: 140; Fee 1987: 365 n. 30; Tomson 1990: 193; P. D. Gooch 1993: 62.

7. Οἴδαμεν δὲ ὅτι (*oidamen de hoti*) appears in Rom. 2:2; 3:19; 8:28; 1 Tim. 1:8; οἴδαμεν γὰρ ὅτι (*oidamen gar hoti*) in Rom. 7:14; 8:22; 2 Cor. 5:1; τοῦτο γινώσκοντες ὅτι (*touto ginōskontes hoti*) in Rom. 6:6; and εἰδότες ὅτι (*eidotes hoti*) in Rom. 5:3; 6:9; 2 Cor. 1:7; 4:14; 5:6; Gal. 2:16; Phil. 1:16; Col. 3:24; 4:1.

moved from darkness into light (cf. Rom. 15:14; 1 Cor. 1:5; 2 Cor. 4:6; 8:7; 1 John 2:20). He begins the discussion by reminding them that they are on an equal footing in the discussion (Smit 1996: 583). All Christians have knowledge.

"Knowledge" is the key word in this chapter—five of the ten occurrences of the word in the letter appear here[8]—and possibly it was a watchword in Corinth. Paul has affirmed their knowledge in 1:5 (cf. 2 Cor. 8:7) and normally values it in Christians (Rom. 11:33; 15:14; 1 Cor. 14:6; 2 Cor. 2:14; 4:6; 6:6; 10:5; 11:6; see also Phil. 3:8). But in 8:7, he seems to contradict himself by saying that not all have knowledge. The absence of the definite article before "knowledge" in 8:1a makes it more general rather than specific (Weiss 1910: 214), while the presence of the definite article in 8:7 suggests something more specific.

The hypothesis that "knowledge" in 8:1 has something to do with some special gnostic insight is now recognized to be a red herring (Newton 1998: 22).[9] It is also unlikely that "knowledge" simply means opinion based on their personal understanding of the mechanics and dynamics of cultic occasions (contra Kennedy 1989: 20–21; Newton 1998: 275–76, 316).[10] For Paul to say, "All have opinions," would be rather banal.

A more plausible view understands the knowledge to encompass an objective, philosophical enlightenment about the gods—that there is one God and that all other so-called gods do not exist (Conzelmann 1975: 140; Schrage 1995: 228). Recognition of this fact is fundamental to conversion to both Judaism and Christianity and would have been a critical component of Paul's missionary preaching. Paul classifies idolaters as those who refuse to know that God as God has been revealed in creation, and their corruption of what can be known about God saddles them with darkened and senseless minds (Rom. 1:21–23; 1 Cor. 1:21; Gal. 4:8; 1 Thess. 4:5; 2 Thess. 1:8). The Corinthians may have ap-

---

8. See 8:1 (2x), 7, 10, 11; cf. 1:5; 12:8; 13:2, 8; 14:6.

9. Schmithals (1971: 143) argues that the expression "we all have knowledge" was a technical one in Corinth (cf. Barrett 1968: 189). Schmithals (1971: 226) claims that it was "typically Gnostic to participate in pagan cultic meals from a deliberately 'Christian stance.'" Against this view, see Arai 1972: 430–37; R. Wilson 1972–73: 65–74; Ellis 1974. R. Horsley (1980–81: 40) makes a better case by showing that ideas that Schmithals attributes to Gnosticism could be read against Hellenistic Jewish tradition found, for example, in Philo. According to Philo (*Alleg. Interp.* 3.15 §§46–48), "The wise person dwelling in *Sophia* possessed 'knowledge of God.'" See also Wis. 7:17, 21.

10. Newton (1998: 276) claims that the Corinthians had varying perspectives from varying experiences and theological sophistication and that this caused the conflict. Newton argues that Paul felt that his only option was "to shift the whole argument away from the minefield of individual interpretation and to argue from the yardstick of 'community consciousness.'"

pealed to their basic Christian knowledge that idols do not exist and rationalized that eating food dedicated to them was altogether harmless. This interpretation assumes that Paul saw the major problem to be that their knowledge translated into brash overconfidence regarding the threat of idols and callous insensitivity to fellow Christians when it came to participating in idol meals. Although this view makes sense of the context, the lack of the definite article with the noun "knowledge" in 8:1a argues against it referring to something specific, such as knowledge of God.

The best option understands "knowledge" here to refer to the revealed illumination that comes from the Spirit (Fee 1987: 366 n. 34; Borgen 1994: 40; P. Gardner 1994: 25–26). Paul would then be alluding to one of the gifts with which the Spirit has enriched the community (1:5; cf. 2 Cor. 8:7). This view is confirmed by the fact that in this verse Paul's contrast between love that builds up and knowledge that puffs up parallels his contrast between love and the gifts of the Spirit that can generate undue pride (13:2). He assumes that humans cannot know God or God's purposes apart from Christ or the Spirit that illuminates Christians. In Christ, all Christians, not just an elite few, have access to unlimited stores of truth, the deep things of God (2:10). God's mystery in Christ is no arcane puzzle that only an intellectual whiz can crack but something that has been revealed to all Christians (1:18–2:5).[11] Although the Corinthians may have vaunted their knowledge—they knew that there was nothing to idol food—Paul opens his discussion of idol food by asserting that knowledge is not their special domain. He gently reminds them that their prized knowledge of God is something that God has bestowed on them through revelation and is something all Christians share. He also reminds them that knowledge can be unhealthy when misused. All Christians possess knowledge, but not all Christians know as they are meant to know. Knowledge can be incomplete and/or misapplied. Knowledge misapplied can lead to the wrong kind of edifying (8:10) and can destroy others (8:11). Knowledge that permits one to steamroll over the scruples of others or to harm them or the church in any way is not Christian knowledge.

His statement that knowledge puffs up (φυσιοῖ, *physioi*) but love builds up (οἰκοδομεῖ, *oikodomei*) basically relativizes any claim to knowledge (Schrage 1995: 230) and discredits it as the final court of appeal to sanction eating idol food (Cheung 1999: 118). Paul is an enemy not of knowledge per se but of knowledge that is not informed by faith or directed by love, that inflates egos and wants to put itself on display

---

11. R. Collins (1999: 310) points out that in chapter 12 (12:6, 7, 11), Paul modifies the Corinthians' discussion of gifts by affirming that spiritual gifts are not accorded to an exclusive few but are given to all to build up the whole body.

and receive acclaim.[12] The verb "to puff up" occurs also in 4:6, 18, 19; 5:2; 13:4 (cf. Col. 2:8) and always has a negative connotation. What puffs up ruptures community and makes for a flimsy basis on which to build anything. By contrast, M. Mitchell (1993: 171) identifies love as "the mortar between the bricks of the Christian building, the ἐκκλησία [ekklēsia]."[13]

Paul's opening line of this section subtly indicts the Corinthians' vaunted knowledge as something objectionable rather than praiseworthy. Knowledge by itself can "edify" (οἰκοδομηθήσεται, oikodomēthēsetai) another in a detrimental way that leads to destruction (8:10–11). In this case it mis-edifies and makes liable to judgment the one who causes another to stumble (8:12). The only knowledge that counts with Paul is that which is Christ-centered and results in other-centered loving behavior.[14] Love, informed and shaped by the pattern and example of Christ (Horrell 1997b: 87), should be the norm regulating their actions.

In the overview to this section, I argue that the very manner in which Paul presents his case against idol food is itself an example of love put into practice, not some feeble compromise that tacitly affirms the social pecking order. Newton (1998: 392–93) thinks that Paul did not impose the solution "from the top" because no such solution was available. I would argue instead that he did not force his knowledge upon them by issuing mandates because of his basic love for the Corinthians. He lays out arguments for them to embrace as sensible persons who will understand the implications (10:15).

Without actually saying so, Paul raises doubts about their possession of knowledge by suggesting that it is something that one thinks to have (8:2). Paul's usage elsewhere of the verb "to think" (δοκεῖν, dokein) suggests that those who "think" or "presume" that they possess something or are something deceive themselves (cf. 3:18; 10:12; 14:37; Gal. 6:3). Boasts about one's knowledge ironically proclaim one's ignorance. In 13:4, Paul memorably articulates his position that all knowledge is incomplete and therefore flawed, and it will not be made complete until the consummation (13:12). The phrase "as it is necessary to know" (καθὼς δεῖ γνῶναι, kathōs dei gnōnai) undermines any presumption that they had perfected their knowledge.[15] It also cautions that so-called knowledge that gives one a false sense of security (10:12), allows one willfully to serve one's own inter-

8:2

---

12. Possibly, some Corinthians thought of knowledge as "lifting up," as in the Gospel of Philip 110 (cited by Conzelmann 1975: 140 n. 11).

13. Paul provides an extended commentary on love in chapter 13 and on "building up" in chapters 12 and 14.

14. Fee (1987: 367) comments, "The aim of Christian ethics is not Stoic self-sufficiency, which requires proper knowledge; rather, its aim is the benefit and advantage of the brother or sister."

15. In 15:34, Paul laments that some in Corinth who deny the resurrection in fact "have no knowledge of God" (cf. Titus 1:16).

ests and neglect the needs of another (8:7–13; 10:33), and does not create a healthy fear of the Lord (10:22) is dangerously faulty.

The term "the strong" never appears in Paul's discussion of idol food. Since so many scholars assume that a sharp division exists in Corinth between the so-called strong and the weak, the use of the former term to describe the opposition needs to be addressed. It is basically a misnomer that falsely implies that they possess a certain strength of faith or more mature insight and that Paul fully agrees with their position. Identifying the objectors as "strong" is appropriate only if we understand that term in the way Philodemus (*On Frank Criticism*), for example, used it to describe students who were disobedient and did not recognize their own sins. He categorized the dispositions of various students, and some of them fit what we know about the Corinthians to a tee: "recalcitrant," "obdurate," "puffed up," "disobedient," "irascible," and "difficult to cure." The "strong," according to Philodemus, are those "who cannot tolerate frank criticism on the part of others or who violently resist it" (Konstan et al. 1998: 11, 12):

> When rebuked, they do not think that they have sinned or that their sins will be detected. . . . When rebuked they are irritated and their sinful disposition and pretentiousness are exposed. . . . Because they think that they are perfect, they are more willing to engage in frank criticism of others than to receive it. They even resent being frankly criticized by those whom they recognize as more knowledgeable and as leaders. They thus claim to be wise and mature enough to correct others, since "those who admonish others are called 'more knowledgeable' and 'wise'"! (Konstan et al. 1998: 44)

If we understand the "strong" in this sense, the term is applicable. But Paul actually describes them here and in 8:10 as those who "presume they have knowledge." It is more accurate to identify the group as the "know alls" or, less pejoratively, as the "knowers" (Cheung 1999: 117).

8:3 Paul shifts from a more static knowledge about something, however genuine, to knowledge based on relationship. He does not say, "if one knows God" (contrast 1 John 4:6–8), but, "if one loves God." If the longer reading of this text is correct, "if anyone loves *God*, this one is known *by him*," then Paul does not assume that the Corinthian problem is simply a lack of love toward brother or sister. What is crucial is their love for God (2:9) and being known by him (cf. 13:12; Gal. 4:9). God's knowing his people refers to divine initiative in election and redemption (cf. Exod. 33:12, 17; Jer. 1:5; Amos 3:2; Bultmann, *TDNT* 1:709–10; Héring 1962: 68; R. Horsley 1980–81: 49; Schrage 1995: 5). Hays (1997: 138) comments, "The initiative in salvation comes from God, not from us. It is God who loves us first, God who elects us and delivers us from the power of sin and death. Therefore what counts is not so much our knowledge of God as God's knowledge of us." While these theological observations about *what* Paul says certainly are correct, commentators fail to explain *why* he says these things here in this particular context (see Fee 1987: 368). His reminder that their love of God means that they are known by God has direct bearing on the issue of idolatry.

Paul relates being known by God to the Galatians' conversion and turning from the weak and beggarly elemental spirits that formerly enslaved them (Gal. 4:9). Being known by God makes their turning back to the weak and beggarly elemental spirits both astonishing (Gal. 1:6) and foolish (Gal. 3:1). In 2 Tim. 2:19 (citing Num. 16:5), being known by God is related to ownership: "The Lord knows those who are his." Paul does not mean and does not say, "If someone loves God, this one should also love neighbors and refrain from offending them." He is reminding them that loving God means that they are known by God, and that draws sharp boundaries that set them apart from worshipers of false gods and delimits what they may and may not do. Those who love God and are known by God may not dally in the shrines of other gods.

After these introductory remarks, Paul broaches the specific subject. His use of the word βρῶσις (*brōsis,* eating) indicates that the problem has to do with the actual eating of idol food. His later discussion in 10:14–22 reveals his concern that eating consecrated food with idolatrous companions establishes an affiliation with whatever deities may be involved (Smit 1996: 584). Paul saves this argument until then. First, he builds his case against eating idol food by affirming their belief in the one God ("we know that") and their rejection of the reality of idols. They have not recognized the full ramifications of their confession that there is only one God, who requires absolute allegiance.

8:4

The phrase οὐδὲν εἴδωλον ἐν κόσμῳ (*ouden eidōlon en kosmō*) could be taken in a predicate sense to mean that an idol is nothing. Since this phrase parallels the next in the sentence, which has an attributive sense, "no God [exists] except one," it is more likely that it should be taken in the attributive sense to mean that no idol exists in the world. Idols purport to be images of various gods; but if the gods do not exist, then idols do not exist. Paul may be quoting a line from the Corinthians' letter (Fee 1987: 370; Hays 1997: 138). If so, they were simply parroting what they would have heard from Paul's first preaching (cf. Gal. 4:8).[16]

---

16. Newton (1998: 134, 156, 282) thinks that the ambiguity and complexity of the word εἴδωλον in the pre-Christian world and the relationship between images and divinities would have confused the former pagan who viewed idols as "an image rather than a real thing." They could assume that they were not eating a sacrificial meal. After their conversion, however, they would have become familiar with the OT abhorrence of anything associated with idols and its denunciation of these images as false gods (cf. 12:2). Newton (1998: 282) recognizes that Paul's eighteen-month stay in Corinth would have given plenty of time for this supposed "classic case of cross-cultural communications conflict" over the meaning of the word εἴδωλον to have been aired and explained.

The Jewish attitude toward idols was multifaceted. On the one hand, Jews professed that idols have no existence (Isa. 41:29; 44:9–17; Jer. 10:3–11; 16:19–20; Let. Jer. 2–73; Let. Arist. 135–37, 139; Josephus, *Ant.* 10.4.1 §50; Philo, *Spec. Laws* 1.5 §28; *Decal.* 12–17 §§52–82; *Cont. Life* 1 §§3–9). On the other hand, they recognized that idols do represent a demonic reality and that idol gods are subordinate powers (Deut. 4:19; 32:17; 1 Chron. 16:26 LXX; Ps. 106:37; Isa. 8:19; 19:3; Bar. 4:7; Jub. 1:11; 11:4–6; 22:17; 1 Enoch 19:1; 99:6–10; T. Naph. 3:3–4). It is misleading to argue that no consensus existed in rabbinic Judaism regarding the nature and significance of images (Newton 1998: 146), as if holding two apparently conflicting views at the same time were impossible, or to maintain that it is unclear "which Jewish position" Paul adopted (Newton 1998: 148), as if these views were separable and clearly differentiated (see N. Wright 1992: 124, 128 n. 20). Jews always believed both. Tomson's (1990: 155–58) discussion of the matter is more properly nuanced. Idols are nonentities, but demonic powers used idols to inveigle humans into worshiping false gods (Moffatt 1938: 139).[17]

This Jewish ambivalence toward idols is captured in a discussion from the Babylonian Talmud (*b. ʿAbod. Zar.* 55a): "[An Israelite named] Zunin said to R. Akiba: 'We both know in our heart that there is no reality in an idol; nevertheless we see men enter [the shrine] crippled and come out cured. What is the reason?'" The question refers to afflicted persons who spent a night in a healing shrine of the god Asclepius or Sarapis. The parabolic answer is that the afflictions are placed under an oath (by God) that they will not come out of a person until a set time. It is only by chance that the person went to a pagan shrine at the time the afflictions were sworn to come out. Earlier in the *sugya* (*b. ʿAbod. Zar.* 54b), philosophers ask the Jewish elders of Rome, "If your God has no desire for idolatry, why does He not abolish it?" They reply, "If it was something of which the world had no need that was worshipped, He would abolish it; but people worship the sun, moon, stars and planets; should He destroy the Universe on account of fools! The world pursues its natural course, and as for fools who act wrongly, they will have to render an account."[18]

---

17. This ambivalence toward idols emerges in Jubilees. In Jub. 12:1–5, Abraham pleads with his father, Terah, to abandon idols by arguing that they are only the work of his hands and have no spirit in them. In Jub. 22:17, however, it says that they bow down to demons (cf. 1 Enoch 19:1). See further, Elmslie (1911) and Urbach (1959).

18. The account in *m. ʿAbod. Zar.* 3:4 reveals how Jews used humor to cope with living in a world populated with idols. Rabbi Gamaliel III answers why he bathed in the bath house of the goddess Aphrodite in Acre: "I did not come to her domain, but she came into mine! They do not say, 'Let us make a bath house for Aphrodite,' but 'Let us make an Aphrodite as an adornment for the bath house.' Moreover if they would give thee much money thou wouldest not enter in before thy goddess naked or after suffering pollution, nor wouldest thou make water before her! Yet this goddess stands at the mouth of the gutter and all the people make water before her. It is written, 'Their gods' [Deut. 12:3] only; thus what is treated as a god is forbidden, but what is not treated as a god is permitted."

The creedal statement καὶ ὅτι οὐδεὶς θεὸς εἰ μὴ εἷς (*kai hoti oudeis theos ei mē heis*, that no God [exists] except one) echoes the basic Jewish confession in the Shema (Deut. 6:4; 4:35, 39; Isa. 44:8; 45:5).[19] Conzelmann (1975: 142) asserts that faith in the one God is not commitment to the thesis that there are no gods; it is a confession that overthrows the other gods. The knowledge that "an idol is nothing in the world" probably provided a theological justification for some Corinthians to think that they could attend feasts in idol temples with impunity. Idols are simply images of a deity that does not exist, except perhaps in the imaginations of their worshipers, and food sanctified to something that does not exist cannot affect Christians in any way.[20] Because of their knowledge about the one true God, they attached no religious significance to whatever rites may have been celebrated in connection with the food or whatever words of consecration were pronounced over it. The problem, however, is that their knowledge is overly simplistic. Paul agrees with the theological principle behind their behavior, but they have misapplied it. Tomson (1990: 194) claims that Paul, like the later Tannaitic sages, "while sharing the rational view that idolatry is 'nothing,' thinks it inconceivable for someone who as a member of the body of Christ is a spiritual heir of 'our fathers' in the desert (10:1–13) to participate in their cult and thus communicate with demons (10:20f)."

8:5   The γάρ (*gar*, for) beginning this clause is explanatory (Fee 1987: 371 n. 10) and introduces either a corroboration or clarification of the two statements in 8:4. It is not a continuation of the Corinthian argument (contra Findlay 1910: 841; Willis 1985b: 83–88) but Paul's explanation of what he means when he says that "idols do not exist" (8:5) and that "there is no God but one" (8:6).

Paul knows that the world is chock full of gods that are real rivals to the one God (Denaux 1996: 600), and he will not dismiss them as "nonentities." Pausanias (*Descr.* 1–5) names a plethora of deities that he found revered in Corinth: Chronos, Poseidon, the Sun, the Calm, the Sea, Aphrodite, Artemis, Isis, Dionysus, a tree, Fortune, Apollo, Hermes, Zeus, Asclepius, Bunaea, and others (R. Collins 1999: 314). Does Paul refer here to their reality only in the subjective experience of the idol worshiper (so Conzelmann 1975: 143; Fee 1987: 370, 372–73; Tomson 1990: 196, 209)? P. Gardner (1994: 39) thinks not. The dismissive

19. The καί (*kai*) can have an explicative meaning, which means, "that is to say," "namely."
20. Stowers (1990: 277) suggests a comparison with the Epicurean community, in which new converts were instructed "to give up the traditional false beliefs and superstitions about the gods, and then taught true knowledge based on reason." They were allowed to participate in the worship of traditional gods as long as they did not involve themselves in their world and understood that the rituals had no effect.

phrase "the so-called gods" (λεγόμενοι θεοί, *legomenoi theoi*; cf. 2 Thess. 2:4) defers to popular parlance that identifies them as gods, but it insinuates that it is wrong (Winter 1991b: 130–31; 1995: 174; Smit 1996: 585).[21] In 10:14–22, Paul again insists that idols are nothing, but he introduces the idea that they do represent a demonic reality that is far darker than some subjective reality in the mind of a worshiper (cf. Isa. 63:3; 65:11).[22] I adopt Smit's (1996: 585) rendering of Paul's thought: "If indeed there are so-called gods either in heaven or on earth, then in that sense there are many gods and many lords."[23] As N. Wright (1992: 128) aptly puts it, "The pagan pantheon cannot be dismissed as metaphysically nonexistent and therefore morally irrelevant. It signals an actual phenomenon within the surrounding culture that must be faced and dealt with, not simply sidestepped" (cf. Héring 1962: 68–69). In Gal. 4:8, Paul writes that the Galatians were in bondage to beings that were by nature not gods, but these "no gods" still enslave.

Paul's purpose is not to discuss the ontological existence of these gods or their existential reality—"that whatever is worshiped is indeed, for that person, a God" (Fee 1987: 372–73). Rehearsing this basic confession is intended to call to mind the command "You shall have no other gods before me" (Deut. 5:7). It fits the basic Jewish assertion that "the Lord your God is God of gods and Lord of lords" (Deut. 10:17; Ps. 82:1; 97:7; 136:3; 138:1).

The various deities worshiped in the Greco-Roman world were so diverse and numerous that it is difficult to pinpoint exactly what Paul may have meant by the reference to "many gods and many lords." The "gods" may represent the pantheon of gods, and the "lords" the figures venerated in mystery cults (so Fee 1987: 373; Hays 1997: 139). The dichotomy between gods in heaven or on earth (εἴτε ἐν οὐρανῷ εἴτε ἐπὶ γῆς, *eite en ouranō eite epi gēs*) may signify a distinction between the gods presumed to operate in the upperworld and those in the underworld. Possibly, the gods on the earth represent the deified emperors and family members given homage in the imperial cult (Winter 1990: 211–13; 1995: 175; against this, see Héring 1962: 69). The only thing that is certain is the sharp antithesis between the many gods and many lords and the one God and one Lord (8:5–6). The many only pose as

21. Jews more often referred to them as "no gods" (Gal. 4:8; 2 Chron. 13:9; Isa. 37:19; Jer. 2:11; 5:7; 16:20; Wis. 12:27; Let. Jer. 23, 29, 51–52, 64–65, 69, 72).

22. Tertullian shares this perspective. He (*De spectaculis* [*The Shows*] 10.10; 13.2; *De idololatria* [*Idolatry*] 1.5; 15.2, 4) emphasizes that idols are of no consequence in and of themselves, but they do become important when they play a role in the service of demons.

23. The εἴπερ (*eiper*) is not concessive, "even if there are. . . , but for us. . . ." Instead, it implies that the supposition agrees with the fact (cf. Rom. 3:20; 2 Thess. 1:6), and the ὥσπερ (*hōsper*) introduces the statement that the supposition is indeed a fact: "then, in that sense, there are . . ." (Smit 1996: 585 n. 27; cf. Weiss 1910: 220–21).

gods and are empty and worthless (Deut. 4:28; Ps. 115:4–8; Isa. 44:9–20; Wis. 15:15–19; Let. Jer. 3–72). Smit (1996: 580) argues that in these verses Paul gives general principles that will inform his discussion of the subject of food offered to idols: "The antitheses suggest choices that have to be made."

Paul contrasts Christians with the idolaters: "but for us. . . ." The Christian confession that there is one God and one Lord does more than simply downplay the significance of the gods; it has direct consequences on what is or is not permitted.   **8:6**

The careful parallelism connects "Jesus Christ as closely as possible with the Father" (Smit 1996: 586):

But for us
> One God, the Father
>> out of whom [come] all things and we [go] toward him and
> one Lord, Jesus Christ,
>> through whom [come] all things and we [go to the Father] through him.

Paul creatively christianizes the foundational Jewish monotheistic confession: "The Lord our God is one Lord" (Deut. 6:4; see additional note). He glosses the reference to Lord and God in that confession so that "God" refers to the Father and "the Lord" refers to Christ. N. Wright (1992: 132) labels this "christological monotheism" and applauds it as a stunning theological innovation, "one of the greatest pioneering moments in the entire history of christology" (N. Wright 1992: 136; cf. Dunn 1980: 179–83; 1991: 188–91).

Paul uses the term "Father" here to convey that God is the ultimate origin of all things (11:12) as creator and the ultimate goal of all creation (Rom. 11:36). The confession assumes the intimate relation of God and Jesus Christ, that "Jesus Christ is indissolubly involved in this activity of the Father" (Smit 1996: 586). It also asserts that Jesus Christ is the only way to the Father. Jesus Christ "fulfills an essential, mediating role: all things exist through [διά] him and 'we,' the believers, reach through [διά] him our destination" (Smit 1996: 586).

But Paul's purpose is not to reflect christologically on his monotheistic faith (cf. Rom. 3:29–30; Gal. 3:20; 1 Tim. 2:5). As N. Wright (1992: 130) puts it well, "He is going back to the foundations, and laying the claim that the people defined by *this* formula of belief form a new family with a new code of family behaviour." This confession marks out believers as having special obligations. He begins his argument by defining the nature of the people of God, who believe in one God and one Lord and who live in the midst of a pagan society where there are many gods and lords. Consorting with the many other gods and lords ruptures the relationship with the one God and one Lord. He develops this idea in 10:1–22, along with the blazing jealousy of the one God, who must be feared. This confession bars any participation in idolatry, even if it appears on the surface to be only a perfunctory and innocuous idolatry—friends gathering for convivial fellowship in an idol's temple where even the devotees do not take seriously their consecration of the food to the god or goddess.

Additional Notes

8:1–6. Theissen (1982: 138–40, 163–68) claims that an ethos of "love patriarchalism" directs Paul's advice in this section that ultimately leads to a compromise. Theissen (1982: 103) maintains, "This love patriarchalism takes social differences for granted but ameliorates them through an obligation of respect and love, an obligation imposed upon those who are socially stronger. From those who are weak are required subordination, fidelity and esteem" (cf. D. Martin 1990: 117–20, 126–29, who calls it "benevolent patriarchalism"). Theissen believes that the ones with knowledge are the socially strong, accustomed to eating relatively expensive meat at times other than festivals. The poor, on the other hand, seldom ate meat; and when they did, "it was almost exclusively as an ingredient in pagan religious celebration" (Theissen 1982: 128). According to Theissen, meat possessed, for newly converted poorer Christians, a mystical character, which made it taboo (against this reconstruction, see Meggitt 1994). To resolve the social conflict, Theissen argues, Paul tried to be realistic and practical. He allows the socially strong to continue living in the same way appropriate to their social status, but they should show consideration to their weaker brothers and sisters out of love. The weak are to display subordination, allegiance, and reverence toward the strong. The result, he hopes, will be social integration. The resulting compromise leaves the existing hierarchical structure intact.

    The fact is that Paul offers no compromise here. Engberg-Pedersen (1987: 574) critiques Theissen for reducing, in effect, the radical demand of love to merely showing "some consideration for the 'feelings' of others." Instead, "*Agape* is an attitude of radical and completely selfless concern for others, which readily can be combined with concepts like rights or fairness, both of which imply that the person has certain legitimate claims *for himself. Agape,* by contrast, requires that in his relation with others a person goes the whole way in their direction" (Engberg-Pedersen 1987: 574). In chapter 9, Paul lays out how love works itself out in renouncing legitimate rights to serve the good of others.

8:2. The omission of τι in the phrase εἴ τις δοκεῖ ἐγνωκέναι τι in 𝔓⁴⁶ and Ambrosiaster places the stress on knowing rather than on the content of what is known. Fee (1987: 367) argues for its omission so that Paul does not refer to some lack in the content of their knowledge but the lack of knowledge itself, which has to do with love (so also Zuntz 1953: 31–32). It would mean that if someone has knowledge, that person will show love. Metzger (1971: 556; not discussed in Metzger 1994) considers the textual evidence for τι as the original reading to be overwhelming and attributes the omission to an "accidental oversight" or an attempt by the one responsible for the shorter text here and in the omissions in 8:3 "to sharpen Paul's statement" that knowledge puffs up.

8:3. 𝔓⁴⁶ (also Clement) omits τὸν θεόν and ὑπ᾽ αὐτοῦ (also ℵ*, 33). Fee (1987: 367 n. 42) claims that reading the verb ἔγνωσται as passive instead of middle "led to the double addition of 'God' and 'by him'" (so also Zuntz 1953: 31–32; Yeo 1995: 187–88; Smit 1996: 580 n. 15; Cheung

1999: 118 n. 106). The text would then read, "If anyone thinks he knows, he does not yet know as he ought to know; but if anyone loves, this one knows." Fee (1987: 368) maintains that the longer text reflects Paul's theology: "That is, our love of God is predicated on God's prior knowledge of us. The problem is in finding a satisfactory reason for him to have said that here."

The only consistent witness to the shorter text is $\mathfrak{P}^{46}$. Elements of it appear in patristic witnesses but none have it exactly (R. Collins 1999: 312). Zuntz's (1953: 31) general observation that there is reason "to be particularly wary in considering omissions in $\mathfrak{P}^{46}$" seems to hold true in these cases as well, despite Zuntz's argument to the contrary. The overwhelming evidence for the longer reading cannot easily be dismissed. Fee's argument for this reading assumes that the key problem is the Corinthians' lack of loving behavior, not their flirtation with idolatry; and this interpretation is suspect. The verb ἔγνωσται as a perfect middle implies, according to Zuntz (1953: 32), that "the person who loves 'has reached the fullness of gnosis.'" Is that possible, given Paul's comments in 2:11? If the verb is passive, then one has to supply "by God." It is more likely that God fully knows than that humans fully know. A parallel to this statement appears in 13:12, where Paul confesses that now he knows only in part, but "then I will know fully [ἐπιγνώσομαι], even as I have been fully known [ἐπεγνώσθην]." The argument that the shorter text "brings Paul's point home so powerfully that it is most likely what he originally wrote" (Fee 1987: 368) begs the question. In answer to Fee's objection to the longer reading, my comments on 8:3 (above) offer a reason for Paul to say that our love of God is predicated on God's prior knowledge of us, which fits the context of his argument about idol food.

8:6. DeLacey (1982: 200) claims that Paul links Deut. 6:4 with Zech. 14:9, which was seen as the eschatological fulfillment of "the Lord is one." Such christological originality would not derive from the Corinthians, and therefore 8:4–6 could not be a reprise of the Corinthians' position (contra Willis 1985b; P. Gardner 1994: 35; cf. Fee 1987: 371 n. 10). Paul uses the appeal to "one God . . . one Lord" to insist on the Christian's exclusive allegiance (10:1–22).

Some claim that Paul uses a confessional formula. Conzelmann (1975: 114 n. 38) insists that the content "reaches far beyond the context," but I argue that it fits perfectly the context of Paul's argument. R. Horsley (1978a; 1980: 46) contends that it is "an adaptation of a traditional Hellenistic Jewish form of predication regarding the respective creative and soteriological roles of God and Sophia/Logos, which Philo or his predecessors had adapted from a Platonic philosophical formula concerning the primal principles of the universe." R. Horsley (1998: 119) points out how in Hellenistic Jewish speculation, Sophia/Logos was that "'through which/whom' all things had been created (e.g., Wis. 8:1, 6; Philo, *Det.* 54 [*Worse Att. Bet.* 16 §54]; cf. *Fuga* 190 [*Flight* 34 §190]; *Leg. All.* 3.96 [*Alleg. Interp.* 3.31 §96]) and also had a revelatory or soteriological role." See also Philo, *Sacr.* 3 §8; Wis. 7:27. R. Horsley (1998: 120) claims that Paul attempts here "to replace *Sophia,* the source of the Corinthians' *gnōsis,* with Christ."

Such speculation seems pointless. Paul uses this confession as the foundation of his argument against the Corinthians' behavior. The christological monotheism expressed here is not their justification for their participation in idol feasts. Denaux (1996: 594) cautions that it is dangerous to separate the verse from its immediate context to understand it in terms of Paul's Christology or to trace its tradition history.

B. Refutation of Their Practice because of Its Danger to Fellow Christians (8:7–13)

Paul's strict monotheism makes him rigidly opposed to any encroachment by religious syncretism, but his argument does not take the form of a raging renunciation of the actions of those who feel free to eat as they please. He chooses a more indirect route to try to convince those who have not yet been persuaded. He began his discussion by reasserting the Christian's basic confession that binds them to one God and one Lord with its distinctive obligations. Mentioning Christ recalls God's supreme act of love that made Christians a unique people. Christ died for them (8:11). This act of love that brought them into God's family requires that they respond to others in the family with love, to put others' needs and interests ahead of their own (N. Wright 1992: 133–36). It may require giving up things that one regards as a right for the sake of winning others or preventing them from falling. Hays (1997: 142) comments on 8:11, "Christ died for this person, and you can't even change your diet?" But it is more than a matter of changing their diet. Withdrawing from pagan celebrations calls for a real sacrifice that will bring inevitable ostracism and potential material loss.

Paul leaves aside, for the moment, the theological aspect of the argument and turns to the potential effect of their current behavior on a fellow believer who may not have the same level of theological sophistication to rationalize such behavior or to apprehend its theological consequences. Paul presents the hypothetical example of a fellow Christian observing another Christian, esteemed as a person of knowledge, eating food in an idol setting. The Christian who does not have the knowledge to make correct moral judgments may then be persuaded that such syncretistic practice is permissible for Christians. Paul fears that this Christian will be sucked back into the vortex of idolatry and face spiritual ruination. He concludes with a hyperbolic example of what he would do to avert such a catastrophe: he would abstain from eating meat altogether.

Exegesis and Exposition

[7]But this knowledge is not in all; some until now have been so ⌜accustomed⌝ to an idol that they eat [what is sacrificed to an idol not as ordinary food but] as

something [truly] sacrificed to an idol, and their ⌜conscience⌝, being weak, is defiled. [8]But food will not bring us before God. ⌜We are neither worse off if we do not eat nor better off if we do eat⌝. [9]But watch out, lest this authority of yours becomes a stumbling block to the weak. [10]For if someone sees you, a person having knowledge, reclining [to eat] in the place of an idol, his weak conscience will be educated [to believe it is permissible] to eat what is sacrificed to an idol.[1] [11]For the weak person—the brother for whose sake Christ died—is led to ruin by your knowledge. [12]And thus, as you sin against the brother by wounding his ⌜weak⌝ conscience, you sin against Christ. [13]For this reason, if food causes my brother to stumble, I will never eat meat forever in order that I might not cause my brother to stumble.

In 8:1, Paul affirms that all have knowledge, but in 8:7, he offers a caveat: "not all have this knowledge." In this verse Paul inserts the definite article before "knowledge" (ἡ γνῶσις, *hē gnōsis*), and so it may be translated "this knowledge." Whom does Paul have in mind when he says "not all," and what kind of knowledge do they not have?

8:7

Presumably, he refers to Christians (a brother for whom Christ died, 8:11) with weak consciences. But if they are Christians, how could they be unaware of the foundational truth that there is but one God? Some explain that in 8:1 Paul refers to head knowledge and in 8:7 he refers to heart knowledge (Parry 1926: 131; Moffatt 1938: 110; Barrett 1968: 194; Conzelmann 1975: 146; Fee 1987: 379; Murphy-O'Connor 1978b: 554; Schrage 1995: 254; Horrell 1997b: 88; Dawes 1996: 89; R. Collins 1999: 324). These Christians might give lip service to the belief that the so-called gods and lords do not exist, but their former associations with these gods have been so deeply etched in their consciousness and emotions that they would eat food sacrificed to an idol as if it were sacrificed to a true god that really exists. Their hearts have not fully absorbed the truth that the gods they once worshiped that seemed so real were nothing and that food sacrificed to them cannot be infected by their power. Their monotheism is assumed to be rather tentative.

The problem with this view is that it recasts the meaning of the word "knowledge" to denote emotional acceptance (Cheung 1999: 127–28). Also, it wrongly assumes that Paul is primarily concerned that the weak will suffer some kind of emotional turmoil (see Murphy-O'Connor 1978b: 554; Witherington 1995: 197 n. 40) or cognitive dissonance because of their qualms about idol food. What he actually says is that he fears that an individual will be drawn into idolatry again. Paul's solici-

---

1. I have forgone gender-neutral language in this translation in order to preserve the powerful dynamic of Paul's argument that is lost by resorting to the plural (as in the NRSV). The gospel's solicitude for a single struggling person emerges in this example. By harming even one individual who might see them eating in an idol sanctuary, they do irreparable harm.

tude for the weak person is not over the possibility that he or she might suffer from unnecessary pangs of conscience. His concern is explicitly expressed in 8:11: such a person may perish eternally (Cheung, 1999: 129)!

It is more likely, then, that the definite article in ἡ γνῶσις functions like a demonstrative pronoun, giving the meaning "this knowledge" (P. Gardner 1994: 40). The knowledge in 8:7 includes the knowledge alluded to in 8:1, namely, that God is one, and idols have no existence, plus the inference that this truth permits them to eat idol food as ordinary food (βρῶσις, *brōsis*), not as sanctified food (Cheung, 1999: 128). The knowers "know" that idol food is nothing but ordinary food hallowed by some empty hocus-pocus. The weak, however, regard it as idol food, sanctified and dedicated to the god.

Certain actions trigger old memories and associations. Edwards (1885: 220) asserts that the conscience (συνείδησις, *syneidēsis*) expresses the result, while "habit," "becoming accustomed" (συνήθεια, *synētheia*) refers to the process that leads up to it. The habituation forms their consciousness so that their minds have a reflex reaction when it comes to idols. Paul does not provide a direct object for the verb "they eat" and does not seem to be as concerned about *what* they eat as about their state of mind *when* they eat. It is not that they eat "idol food" but that they eat it *as* idol food (Fisk 1989: 60). For those with knowledge, the banquet may be only a social occasion, but it is not so for those with a weak conscience. Eating sanctified food had always been an act of worship that honored the god lurking behind the idol. Their minds are still infused with old conceptions that spring up involuntarily. They are not like former addicts who must fight "an inner battle" every time they come into contact with drugs, as Kistemaker (1993: 270) puts it.[2] These are not hang-ups, because Paul does not expect them to abandon them. Nor is it a matter of being half-taught, intellectually backward, overly conscientious, or hopelessly unprogressive. Paul assumes that they have been programmed to think in certain ways about sacrificed food, and he has no interest in deprogramming them. He never urges them "to get with it" and never addresses the weak at all in this section or even implies that they are mistaken.[3] In fact, his emphasis on the table

2. A better analogy might compare the weak to those today who grew up in the church but no longer practice their faith and yet occasionally participate in a Christian ritual on a holy day and still attach a certain sacredness to that act.

3. If the weak are plagued only by inadequate or incomplete knowledge, Paul makes no attempt to "edify" them. D. Martin (1995: 187) tries to explain why he does not attempt to edify the weak: "The Strong cannot simply hand over their gnosis to the Weak, as if it could be taught; rather, in Paul's rhetoric, people either have it or do not have it. Possession of gnosis is a matter of state or status, not education" (see also Horrell 1997b: 90). This explanation is based on the misjudgment that Paul believes that idol food is acceptable.

of demons in 10:14–22 would only reinforce their notions that eating idol food is not a meaningless act. It has religious significance. If the weak are stuck in the fear of demons, as Weiss (1910: 211) contends, then so is Paul. He basically dissociates himself from the knowers' knowledge in 8:9–12 by referring to *"your* authority" (8:9), someone seeing *"you,* a person having knowledge" (8:10), and the weak being destroyed "by *your* knowledge" (8:11).

What does Paul intend the adjective "weak" to connote?[4] Some claim that it repeats a disparaging epithet hurled at them by those who defended eating idol food (Parry 1926: 132; Harrisville 1987: 130; Malherbe 1994: 234; R. Horsley 1998: 121; R. Collins 1999: 321, 326). But why would Paul retain this derisive term in his discussion in Rom. 14:1–2 for those whom he calls brothers (1 Cor. 8:13; cf. 1 Thess. 5:14)? There is no evidence that the "knowers" at Corinth have labeled the scrupulous as "weak" in some condescending fashion, and no evidence that the scrupulous have objected to the actions of the knowers. Quite the contrary, Paul fears that the weak will follow suit in eating idol food; and, because they do not have the same knowledge that idols have no power, they will fall into conscious idolatry.

Others claim that "weak" refers to an overactive conscience and that Paul is afraid that they will be induced to act contrary to their consciences (Robertson and Plummer 1914: 172–73; Barrett 1968: 194–95; Jewett 1971: 422–23; Murphy-O'Connor 1978b: 554–56; Willis 1985b: 105; Stowers 1990: 278–82; Schrage 1995: 256; Dawes 1996: 84–86, 98; Newton 1998: 311).[5] Since he believes that any act contrary to conscience is sin (Rom. 14:23), their compromise will nudge them down the slippery slope to ruin.[6] They do violence to their conscience because they eat without being convinced that they may eat. This view seriously

---

4. The adjective "weak" (ἀσθενής, *asthenēs*) appears eleven times in 1 Corinthians and once in 2 Corinthians out of twenty-five occurrences in the NT (1 Cor. 1:27; 4:10; 8:7, 9, 10; 9:22 [3x]; 11:30; 12:22; 2 Cor. 10:10). Paul uses the participial form of the verb "to be weak" (ἀσθενεῖν, *asthenein*) as a substantive in 1 Cor. 8:11; Rom. 14:1, 2.

5. Robertson and Plummer (1914: 179–80) contend, "The weakness [of the weak] consists in giving moral value to things that are morally indifferent." The ghost of Baur's reconstruction of the conflict between Paul and Cephas has cast its spell on Barrett's (1982: 49) reconstruction of the problem. Barrett claims that "the problem would never have arisen in a Gentile Church like that of Corinth if the Jewish Christians (the Cephas group perhaps) has not raised it" (against this, see Conzelmann 1975: 14). They cannot have been Jewish Christians, because they would not be described as "until now accustomed to an idol" (8:7).

6. Murphy-O'Connor (1983: 164) imaginatively reconstructs a scenario in which the weak might capitulate when they receive an invitation to celebrate the marriage of a pagan family member. They could not decline by insisting that their Christian faith prohibited it, because they would know that other Christians participated in such banquets. To avoid a gratuitous insult to their family, the weak would go against their consciences and participate.

misreads the text by injecting the situation of Rom. 14–15 into this setting. It fails to take seriously that the issue here is the idolatrous context of the eating and assumes that the whole issue has to do only with innocuous marketplace food.

Theissen (1982: 70–73, 121–43) contends that the adjective "weak" describes social status (see also D. Martin 1990: 118–24; Witherington 1995: 190; Hays 1997: 136–37). The knowers, who belonged to a higher social strata, ate meat regularly and were unfazed by eating idol meat. The weak, who supposedly belonged to the lower socioeconomic group, ate meat only rarely on religious occasions. These impressionable and uninfluential members of the community were more likely to go along with the crowd or follow the lead of wealthier role models, but their previous experience of eating meat only at some public temple feast or on a holiday in the temple would weigh heavily on their minds. Meggitt (1994: 137) dismisses this interpretation as based upon "some dubious inferences from some questionable 'evidence'" regarding first-century meat consumption.[7] Paul explicitly connects weakness to their conscience, not their socioeconomic status, and his case assumes that idol food was readily accessible to the weak. D. Black (1984: 84–168, 228–46) shows that Paul uses the term "weakness" (ἀσθένεια, *astheneia*) anthropologically to refer to humanity's general powerlessness in relation to God, christologically to refer to weakness as the place where God exhibits his power, and ethically to refer to weakness as a characteristic of immature believers who must not be condemned.

It is possible that the meaning of the term "weak" was influenced by its usage among Stoic moralists, who generally applied it to those "who found it difficult to live up to the demands of the virtuous life" (Malherbe 1994: 234). The adjective characterizes the intellectually and morally immature who are "unstable in their convictions" and "easily give their assent to false judgments" (Cheung 1999: 125; cf. R. Collins 1999: 324). They do not represent a particular faction or position (Conzelmann 1975: 147; Newton 1998: 292–93; Cheung 1999: 126) and are not debate partners with the knowers.

---

7. Garnsey (1991: 100) claims that the average diet consisted of porridge, barley meal, olives, fish relish, and meat on holidays and special occasions. Blasi (1988: 61) avers "that meat was given to the poor on special holidays in honor of one god or another." Meggitt (1994: 138–39) counters that meat was expensive but consumed in considerable quantities by the nonelite in nonsacral gatherings, notably in the *popinae/ganeae* (cookshops), *tabernae* (taverns), and *cauponae* (wine shops) or from street vendors. These urban poor ate out at these cookshops; the wealthy ate in their dining rooms or private gardens. Meggitt (1994: 139) notes, "The meat from all these outlets tended to be in forms that have historically been associated with the poor: sausages or blood puddings appear to have been common, as was tripe, and various 'off-cuts' that might appear unappetizing to the modern palate." Cf. Ovid, *Metamorphoses* 8.630–34, 646–50, 664–68, 674–78.

Hurd first proposed that the person with a weak conscience may be a hypothetical construct (Hurd 1965: 125; see also Fee 1980a: 176; P. D. Gooch 1993: 66–68; N. Wright 1992: 133 n. 36; Smit 1997b: 480 n. 18). This suggestion too often has been ignored (see Schrage 1995: 214). Since Paul uses hypothetical examples (8:9, "lest in some way"; 8:10, "if someone sees you"; 8:13, "if food is a stumbling block"), it is conceivable that he did not have in mind a specific dispute but uses this example to score his point. There were members of the congregation who fit the category of those with weak consciences, and the hypothetical case about the weak had every likelihood of coming to pass. The potential danger he describes in 8:9–12 puts the knowers' participation in temple banquets in a different light and is meant to deter them (Smit 1997b: 481–82). This is where their eating will lead.

The word "conscience" (συνείδησις, *syneidēsis*) needs definition. Of the twenty times the word appears in Paul's letters, eight occur in chapters 8 and 10. Paul describes it as something that can be "defiled," "polluted" (μολύνεται, *molynetai*, 8:7), "built up," "encouraged" (οἰκοδομηθήσεται, *oikodomēthēsetai*, 8:10), or "wounded" (τύπτοντες, *typtontes*, 8:12) and connects it to raising questions (ἀνακρίνοντες, *anakrinontes*, 10:25, 27) and "judging others" (κρίνεται, *krinetai*, 10:29). The definition of conscience will have to fit something that can be defiled, built up, and wounded, and that raises questions and judges.

The word has no clear equivalent in the Hebrew OT, but its usage was widespread in Greek popular thinking (Pierce 1955: 161–62; Eckstein 1983: 65–66; Borgen 1994: 48–49).[8] It basically means knowledge shared with oneself or with someone else (cf. Rom. 9:1; 2 Cor. 4:2). The interpretation that best fits the context understands the conscience to be a moral compass. It comprises the depository of an individual's moral beliefs and principles that makes judgments about what is right and wrong (Dawes 1996: 96; cf. Edwards 1885: 221–22; Eckstein 1983: 56, 287–300; Thrall 1967–68). Paul uses the term "conscience" to refer to that faculty of moral evaluation that adjudicates whether an individual's actions are right or wrong and directs behavior according to recognized norms (I. Marshall 1999: 491). A "weak" conscience is one that is unable to make appropriate moral judgments because of a lack of proper edification. P. Gardner (1994: 43) is correct that Paul was writing at a time "when the connotation of the words relating to 'conscience' was changing" and that the meaning of the word therefore must come from "the local context" of chapters 8–10 (see also Jewett 1971: 439; Thrall 1967–68). Eriksson (1998: 143) points out that "weakness" was used in the philosophical schools for "the moral sickness suf-

---

8. For discussions of the meaning of this word, see Osborne 1931; Spicq 1938; Pierce 1955: 21–28; B. Harris 1962; Thrall 1967–68; Maurer, *TDNT* 7:898–919; Jewett 1971: 402–21; Eckstein 1983; McCaughhey 1983.

fered by those recent converts who were not yet able to make correct moral judgments" (see Epictetus, *Diatr.* 2.15.20). A "weak" conscience is prone to give assent to false judgments and to sanction actions based on faulty criteria, particularly when it has been defiled. It is untrustworthy because it does not possess the necessary knowledge (Malherbe 1994: 240). A panel from the cartoon strip *Dennis the Menace* captures this understanding of conscience. Consigned to sit in a corner as punishment for some naughtiness, Dennis reflects, "I got some bad advice from my conscience." Paul fears that the person with a weak conscience might follow the example of those presumed to have knowledge and eat idol food as truly offered to an idol, that is, as a sacrificial act. This person will be led astray in his or her moral judgment to think that such polytheistic practice is permissible for a Christian (Borgen 1994: 51; Dawes 1996: 94–95).[9] This person's conscience is then defiled (μολύνεται, *molynetai*) through idolatry (cf. Rev. 3:4). It is akin to a compass being demagnetized so that it no longer points to true north.

I have noted that Paul shows no concern to try to strengthen the person with a weak conscience. It is not that the weak one is insufficiently astute intellectually to understand all the theological intricacies of the question and so must be treated with kid gloves. The issue does not revolve around the one with a weak conscience; Paul's goal is to change the activity of the knowers, who, despite their imagined theological sophistication, are in danger of being partners with demons. His rhetorical strategy is to show those who presume to have knowledge that they also have a responsibility for the weak individual. This approach assumes that they would care about the plight of one with a weak conscience. If there were an intense debate raging between the strong and the weak over this issue, the knowers would have already shown a lack of regard for the weak. They would be likely to reject such an argument and respond that the "weak conscience" was precisely the problem. The case of the weak conscience is therefore a new wrinkle in Paul's approach to the problem. He trusts that it will carry weight because the knowers would not be callously indifferent toward the weak's situation, and they would be impressed by the grievous nature of sin against Christ (8:12) and the expected punishment for such sin. In this segment of his argument, Paul seeks to help the knowers examine their actions

9. Fee (1987: 386 n. 56) cannot understand why the weak would eat idol food unless they were pressured in some way. This impression stems from the mistaken assumption that the weak primarily faced a moral struggle about eating idol food or dining in temples and that they would act against their consciences because they were unable to counter the knower's arguments (so also P. Gardner 1994: 24; Witherington 1995: 199). The social pressure to mix in the society and not to be perceived as intolerant, aloof, or misanthropic would be sufficient motivation for them to join in the banquets. The example of the knowers would be enough to persuade their consciences that this activity was permissible.

from a new angle and see ramifications of their actions that they had not foreseen.

The verb παραστήσει (*parastēsei*) is frequently interpreted to mean that food will not "present" or "commend" us to God (cf. Rom. 6:13; 12:1; 2 Cor. 4:14; 11:2). Since Paul also uses the future tense of the verb in Rom. 14:10 with the idea of standing before God's judgment seat (cf. 2 Cor. 4:14; Acts 27:24), it may have that same connotation here. Food is an indifferent matter that will not bring us before the Judge for condemnation (Weiss 1910: 229; Bruce 1971: 81; Murphy-O'Connor 1979b: 296–97; Fee 1987: 382 n. 34).[10]

8:8

Many assume that this statement is another cornerstone in the argument of the knowers to rationalize their eating idol food, akin to 6:12–13 (Hurd 1965: 68; Jeremias 1966b: 273–74; Murphy-O'Connor 1979b; Fee 1987: 383–84; Hays 1997: 136). The knowers had seized on Paul's views about the insignificance of Jewish dietary laws and circumcision (7:19) and applied it to idol food. They may have claimed not only that idols do not exist, but also that food is morally neutral. The verbs ὑστερούμεθα (*hysteroumetha*) and περισσεύομεν (*perisseuomen*) are taken to mean "we are worse off" and "we are better off" (NRSV). These verbs occur elsewhere in the letter in connection with spiritual gifts. Paul gives thanks to God because they do not lack (ὑστερεῖσθαι, *hystereisthai*) any spiritual gifts and urges them to seek the spiritual gifts that build up the church so that they might abound (14:12, περισσεύητε, *perisseuēte*, excel [NRSV]; cf. 2 Cor. 8:7). They may have argued that their eating does neither harm nor good. It causes neither a drop nor a surge in charisms.[11]

If this was part of their argument, theoretically they are correct; eating does not affect one's relationship to God or bring God's judgment. We should not take this statement, "We do not lack if we do not eat, nor do we gain if we do eat," to hint that Paul sides with those who think that eating idol food is unobjectionable. Life is not lived in the theoretical abstract, and eating food sacrificed to idols can lead to partnership with demons (10:20). Mishandling the Lord's Supper can lead to sickness and death (11:29–30). Paul's illustrations from the OT in 10:1–13 reveal that idol food is not as harmless as they assumed. It can kill—most significantly, it kills a person's relationship to God. Kosher laws may be a matter of indifference, but idol food is not. Nothing is unclean

---

10. P. Gardner's (1994: 54) view that it means "present" in the sense of proving or demonstrating a case before God is unpersuasive.

11. Others take these verbs in a material sense (Murphy-O'Connor 1979b: 292–98; Smit 1997b: 480–81; cf. Lapide 1896: 195). Paul's argument might run thus: If you are no better off eating, then why eat? If you are not harmed by not eating, why not abstain (Cheung 1999: 135)? But the Corinthians would be harmed—at least socially—by not eating.

in itself, *unless* it is known to be idol food. Just as sexual relations are not unclean in themselves but can be perverted by human sin into *porneia*, food is not unclean in itself but can become tainted by its associations with demons and thus become something forbidden. Consuming food in an idolatrous context or food plainly associated with idolatry is not a matter of indifference but one that has deadly consequences.

Paul subtly corrects their view by pointing out that attending idol banquets can cause far greater harm than they have imagined. They might wound others eternally and harm themselves eternally. Rather than implying that neither eating nor abstaining from idol food makes any difference, this verse lays the foundation for his statement in 8:13, "I will absolutely never eat meat." Abstinence, in this case, benefits others and oneself.

8:9 Paul switches to the second person plural to warn them specifically about the consequences of their behavior on the weak. They had not thought about the damage that their participation in sacrificial meals might cause someone with a weak conscience. The word ἐξουσία (*exousia*) refers here to the "power" or "authority" to do a thing.[12] If the word is taken to be comparable to ἐλεύθερος (*eleutheros*, free) in 9:1 and ἐλευθερία (*eleutheria*, freedom, liberty) in 10:29, it might possibly be another Corinthian catchword (Willis 1985b: 98–104; Fee 1987: 384). Their knowledge leads to their liberty to act as they please (cf. 6:12; 10:23), while love, by contrast, leads to giving up rights for the sake of others. This is something that Paul will expand on at great length in the next segment of his argument in chapter 9.[13] Paul was not happy about the way they exercised this "right," but he does not directly challenge it. He may have sensed that such an approach would only cause the Corinthians to dig in their heels and more doggedly resist his direction. In-

---

12. See Foerster, *TDNT* 566; F. Jones 1987: 28–42; Vollenweider 1984: 199–201.

13. Winter (1995: 170–72) argues that ἐξουσία should not be translated as "liberty" but as "right." He understands "the right" to refer to the civic right that some Corinthian Roman citizens possessed to participate in feasts held in the temple of Poseidon in Isthmia to celebrate the games. Provincials (*incolae*) were excluded, and any Corinthian Christians who possessed these rights would naturally be reluctant to give them up "for reasons of social privilege or demonstrations of civic loyalty." Against this view, Paul uses the related words ἔξεστιν (*exestin*) and ἐξουσιασθήσομαι (*exousiasthēsomai*) in 6:12 without any connection to citizen's rights. In 9:4–6, 12, 18 ἐξουσία refers to personal "authority," "right," or "liberty" (different from his usage in Rom. 13:1–3; 1 Cor. 15:24; 2 Cor. 10:8; 13:10). R. Horsley (1998: 121) cites a parallel from Philo (*Good Free* 9 §59): the good man acts rightly and "will have the power [ἐξουσία] to do anything, and to live as he wishes, and he who has this power [ἔξεστιν] must be free [ἐλεύθερος]." Fee's view (1987: 385) that the Corinthians' captivation with their own *exousia* "has led them to question Paul's own apostleship and freedom since he does not act with the boldness of such 'authority' (which becomes the point of the defense in 9:1–23)" is unnecessary and unconvincing.

stead, he will emphasize by way of his own example the need to give up rights for the sake of the gospel.

The phrasing "this authority of yours" sounds contemptuous (cf. Luke 15:30; 18:11; Acts 2:40; 17:18; Moulton and Turner 1963: 44; BDF §290; Smit 1997b: 482). If so, it fits the sardonic tenor of 8:10, "for if someone sees you, a person having knowledge, reclining [to eat] in the place of an idol." Their so-called edification will lead instead to their demolition. The phrasing does not implicitly acknowledge their freedom to eat, as many assume. Instead, it implies that Paul himself does not share in this authority and emphasizes their guilt—their eating becomes a stumbling block (πρόσκομμα, *proskomma*) to the weak (8:9; cf. Rom. 9:32, 33; 14:13; 14:20). The word πρόσκομμα is connected to idolatry in Exod. 23:33; 34:12–13 (cf. σκάνδαλον, *skandalon*, in Rev. 2:14). It refers to something that stops people from "either being identified with or actually being the people of God" (P. Gardner 1994: 61–62). Paul is not afraid that they might offend the weak in some way but that they might cause them to fall away from their Christian faith.

The hypothetical example "if someone sees you, a person having knowledge, reclining [to eat] in the place of an idol" confronts directly those who claim to have knowledge and authority to eat idol food (see additional note). Reclining is the normal attitude at banquets (cf. Mark 14:3; Luke 5:29; 7:37; John 12:2). Paul does not clarify in what particular idol setting the one having knowledge would be visible and frames it only as a suppositional, though likely, scenario.[14] Many excavated locations in Corinth present themselves as possible places where the diners could be readily observed. P. D. Gooch (1993: 1–26) describes dining rooms found in the temple of Demeter and Kore and in the temple of Asclepius. These temples, however, were not located in the city's center, if that makes any difference. The imperial cult was vital in Corinth, and its sacrifices were part of the Isthmian games and were perhaps more visible to the public (Engels 1990: 102; Winter 1995).[15] What ac-

8:10

---

14. P. D. Gooch 1993: 67. P. Gardner (1994: 24) suggests that the ones with knowledge engaged in a "*deliberate* policy of being seen eating idol meat" (so also Weiss 1910: 228; Lietzmann 1949: 39; Schmithals 1971: 226–27). Paul frames this as a probable future condition, however, and not as something that has actually occurred. He does not attack the desire to be seen but the practice of eating in an idol's temple.

15. Winter (1995; 2001: 269–86) contends that new circumstances must have arisen that created the problem: the newly formed federal imperial cult and its links to the Isthmian games. Paul's reference to "gods on earth and in heaven" (8:5) suggests to Winter that he is alluding to the deified emperors of the imperial cult, both living and dead. Winter's discussion provides a valuable window on the pressures that the Corinthian Christians would have faced, but it still seems more likely that Paul is speaking only in hypothetical terms (Schrage 1995: 264).

tually went on at these meals or where they might have occurred, however, is not crucial for understanding this passage.[16]

Paul assumes that the intention of those who would host a gathering at an idol's shrine must be idolatrous and not benign. He also assumes that any food eaten on the precincts of an idol's shrine is contaminated by idolatry. Eating a meal there is participation in idolatry regardless of how Christian participants might have construed it in their own minds.[17] Christians should not join in these feasts. But Paul does not come right out and say so at this point in his argument. He does not give his full assessment of what it means to eat in an idol's shrine here but delays until 10:14–22 to give his final judgment about such eating (P. D. Gooch 1993: 79). His earlier prohibition (5:9) failed to convince them, for whatever reasons, and he now adopts a more subtle stratagem. He shows the potential detrimental consequences of their actions on others to persuade them to abandon such conduct. He warns them that as persons in the know, they might set a bad example for the neophyte Christian. A Christian without their sublime knowledge and with a weak conscience may be encouraged by their cavalier behavior to revert to idolatry.

The statement "his conscience, being weak, will be educated" (οἰκοδομηθήσεται, *oikodomēthēsetai*, edified) is ironic (Héring 1962: 73). Such a person will believe himself to have been edified, but edification that leads to ruin is hardly edification. This statement argues against any view that the weak person is only offended by the actions of the one with knowledge. In 8:12, Paul uses much stronger language: the weak person's conscience is "wounded," not offended. The person with the weak conscience does not object to the actions of the knowers or recoil in horror. It is not that this person might be persuaded to eat while thinking all the while that it is wrong, but that he or she will eat while thinking that it is acceptable for a Christian to do so. From this person's limited perspective, the eating is legitimized by the precedent of the knowers. The resulting syncretism opens the door to polytheism, so contrary to Christian core beliefs. The ubiquitous idolatry in this culture would exert a strong undertow that would drag the person with a weak conscience back into the dark world of demons.

16. Contra Newton (1998), who contends that his investigation into the "actual, practical, down-to-earth ground-level mechanics of temple meals" opens the door to a better understanding of the text. He shows how confusing and ambiguous things might be and contends that Paul failed to appreciate the Corinthians' legitimate rationalizations for their participation. Newton's study is helpful in describing how the Corinthians might have justified their resistance.

17. When Paul discusses permissible contexts for eating (10:23–28), Cheung (1999: 95) observes, "Temple dining is conspicuous by its absence. The apostle mentions only marketplace food and private meals, in which the link to idolatry is neither necessary nor obvious."

Paul's example also contains no hint that the knowers were egging on the weak in some way or deliberately trying to edify them by making them more knowledgeable and showing them how far they can go (contra Robertson and Plummer 1914: 171; Héring 1962: 73; Fee 1987: 381, 385, 386; P. Gardner 1994: 45; Witherington 1995: 186–87). Paul does not say, "If you keep encouraging them, you will lead them to their ruin." He also does not treat them as if they were a bloc. An individual with a weak conscience happens to see the esteemed Christian trendsetters reclining in an idol's place and will be persuaded that such conduct is harmless and allowable for Christians. If the knowers intended all along for the weak to follow their example, why does Paul warn them so severely that the weak might follow their example? The problem is that the individual will fall by following their example (R. Horsley 1998: 123; R. Collins 1999: 326).

The "for" (γάρ, *gar*) introducing this next clause elaborates what Paul **8:11** has said in 8:10 by explaining what will happen to the weak. The verb ἀπόλλυται (*apollytai*, led to ruin, perish [middle voice]) is placed first in the clause for emphasis. It connotes utter ruin, destruction, and annihilation; but some interpreters reject this extreme meaning and soften it to mean moral ruin from a lapse into paganism (D. Black 1984: 112). They interpret it to mean that the person is led to sin (Grosheide 1953: 197) or is stunted in the Christian life (Bruce 1971: 82). But Paul always uses the verb ἀπόλλυσθαι (*apollysthai*) to refer to eternal, final destruction (Barrett 1968: 196; Conzelmann 1975: 149 n. 38; Fee 1987: 387–88; Schrage 1995: 265; Cheung 1999: 129). If salvation means that God has "rescued us from the power of darkness and transferred us into the kingdom of his beloved Son" (Col. 1:13), then returning to idolatry and the regime of darkness means eternal ruin. He fears that the individual will rejoin the ranks of the perishing (1 Cor. 1:18; 10:9–10; 15:18; 2 Cor. 2:15; 4:3).

The cause of this destruction will be "your knowledge." The word σός (*sos;* second person possessive pronoun) "has more weight than the gen. σοῦ or σεαυτοῦ; it serves to emphasize or to contrast" (BAGD 759; BDAG 934). Not only does knowledge not "build up" (8:1), it also can tear down when used in a careless, insensitive, and selfish way. Their vanity in their own knowledge and their lack of consideration for others (not to mention their theological error) can lead to spiritual wreckage for others. Paul underscores the gravity of this offense by specifying that this person who might be caused to stumble is "the brother for whose sake Christ died" (cf. 15:3). The death of Christ recalls the confession in 8:6. No argument could be more convincing to a Christian than an appeal to the salvific work of Christ (see Eriksson 1998: 159–66). Christ's vicarious death for the weak of the world (cf. 1:27) made it possible for all believers to share a common destiny with him. Identifying the person with a weak conscience as a "brother" places an emphasis on community. Christ's death joined them together in a believing fellowship. In Christ, another believer cannot be ignored or sniffed at as one without knowledge and with a weak conscience but must be esteemed as a "brother" (cf. Rom. 14:15). This statement also harks back to the contrast between knowledge and love in 8:1. Christ becomes the model of love, who acts to save others. It is this behavior that the Corinthians should imitate.

8:12 The οὕτως (*houtōs*, thus) draws the consequences of the statement in 8:11. Paul labels their actions sin, not merely an offense to the brother, and makes it even more serious by branding it sin against Christ (cf. Matt. 25:45).[18] The καί (*kai*, and) before the participle τύπτοντες (*typtontes*, wounding) is epexegetical (BDF §442.9), "by wounding his conscience." The word does not mean here "causing pain to" (Wall, *ABD* 1:1129), but "striking a blow against." The weak person is not aghast at seeing a fellow Christian dining in an idol's temple; rather, the moral sensibility ("conscience") of this person is impaired (Dawes 1996: 96). Morally, the weak person does not know which way is up and is led to believe that such idolatrous actions are not wrong. Paul's strong language implies that the knowers will perish with their knowledge if they cause a weak brother to perish.

8:13 The διόπερ (*dioper*, for this reason, wherefore) marks a turning point in the argument. Paul shifts back to the first person singular and provides positive advice from an example from his own life. Given the serious nature of such sin, he personally will avoid anything that might put a weak brother at risk. He elevates the common interest above any self-interest that might cause injury to others (see M. Mitchell 1993: 144). The "common interest," however, may be determined by the needs of *one* struggling brother. The word σκανδαλίζειν (*skandalizein*) means "to cause offense," "to lead into sin." In the LXX, the noun σκάνδαλον (*skandalon*) is used as a metaphor for being trapped into sinning, especially with reference to idolatry (Judg. 2:3; Josh. 23:13; Ps. 105:36; Deut. 7:16; Willis 1985b: 108–9).

Again, he emphasizes that the person in jeopardy is "*my* brother," not merely someone with a weak conscience. "I will never eat meat forever" is hyperbole.[19] Paul does not eat meat that is known to be sacrificial meat, and he does not limit his reference to sacrificial meat but re-

---

18. Schrage (1995: 267) thinks that Paul probably has in mind "the body of Christ," but if he intended that, he could have said it (12:27; contrast 10:9). It is best to take it to mean "wounding a member of Christ wounds Christ" (Fee 1987: 389).

19. The emphatic negation οὐ μή (*ou mē*) appears only four other times in Paul's letters (Rom. 4:8; Gal. 5:16; 1 Thess. 4:15; 5:3).

fers to any kind of meat (κρέα, *krea*; cf. Rom. 14:21).[20] He adopts this extreme position—abstaining from all meat—"to underscore the heavy responsibility which a believer has toward his fellow-believers" (Newton 1998: 309).[21]

Commentators frequently have missed the radicality of Paul's argument. He wants to show what love ultimately requires from believers and how it transcends knowledge. The argument moves from the lesser to the greater. If he would do this in the case of ordinary food, how much more so in the case of something so spiritually toxic as idol food? We should not infer from this principle, however, that Paul thinks it is permissible to eat idol food as long as those with weak consciences do not observe it or if it will not cause them to stumble. Ruling out eating idol food on the basis of the "weaker brethren" principle does not affirm its appropriateness in other circumstances (Cheung 1999: 90). It is not an invitation to the "strong" to "come over and join Paul at table with the weak" (contra Hays 1997: 142). It is instead an indirect demand to withdraw from idolatry. As Augustine (*De bono conjugali* [*The Good of Marriage*] 18) observed, "It is better to die of hunger than to eat of things offered to idols."

This paradigmatic "I" in 8:13 marks a sudden shift from the indefinite third person in 8:2–3, 7, the second person plural in 8:9, 12, and the second person singular in 8:10–11. It summarizes Paul's point in 8:1–12 and introduces the seeming digression in chapter 9, in which he elaborates on his personal renunciation of rights (Jeremias 1958: 156; B. Dodd 1999: 99).

Hermeneutical Conclusions

The issue of idol food remains a burning one for many Christians (see additional note on 8:13). Since the issue of idol food is moot for most Western Christians, this passage often is ignored as irrelevant. The following principles from Paul's discussion apply to varieties of situations.

1. Paul illustrates that acting on the basis of mere propositional knowledge about God is insufficient. Believers must understand fully the broad sweep of theological implications and let their conduct be leavened with love. Presuming to possess knowledge gives one a false sense of superiority and security. Fee (1987: 363) states, "The abuse of

---

20. Hays (1997: 142) puts words into Paul's mouth: he is "willing to forego not only the specific practice of eating idol food but also the eating of meat altogether if that is necessary to protect the weak from stumbling." This misrepresents what Paul actually says.

21. Cheung (1999: 136) comments, "If Paul thought that idol food was something indifferent and if he himself had eaten idol food before, it would have been appropriate for him to say he would never eat idol food for the sake of the weak even though idol food was morally neutral."

others in the name of 'knowledge' indicates a total misunderstanding of the nature of Christian ethics, which springs not from knowledge but from love." Love deflates the vanity and arrogance that knowledge feeds and disarms it so that it is not used to hurt others.

2. Actions guided by knowledge—even seemingly correct knowledge—are not always right. Our knowledge remains partial, and knowledge frequently is used to assert freedom to do as one wills. Misleading is the comment of Robertson and Plummer (1914: 171) that the stumbling block (8:9) "is that against which the man with weak sight stumbles; it is no obstacle to the man who sees his way; but the weak sighted must be considered." Much sin can be rationalized in this way. Presuming to have an advanced level of knowledge and no misgivings about an action does not make it acceptable—particularly when it violates a clear biblical mandate.

3. Paul does not think that the freedom that the gospel bestows on Christians voids all taboos. Christianity is about freedom, but it does not grant the freedom to do whatever one likes. Brunt (1985: 115) claims that Paul's basic concern transcends the question of the "rightness or wrongness of the act [of eating] itself" (see also Talbert 1987: 58). This approach assumes that Paul's primary interest is the effect that a behavior has on another, in this case, a weaker Christian, and that he only wishes that the Corinthians would use more compassion and circumspection in dealing with such a person. It seeks to make Paul into a "nice guy" who agrees with our own enlightened views on such matters. But Paul's arguments in 8:1–11:1 assert that some things are totally irreconcilable with life in Christ and remain absolutely wrong (Fee 1987: 391, 475). Christianity breaks down the barriers that classify people by their ethnic identity, social standing, or sexual gender, but it also erects barriers that create a distinctive Christian identity (cf. 10:32). Being members of one body in Christ makes it impossible to be involved in idolatrous practices. At stake is whether allegiance to Christ will override all other attractions and attachments.

While many today may perceive a greater danger from prohibition and intolerance, Paul feared most the danger of accommodation and compromise with a pagan environment. Christianity does not require that Gentiles become Jews, but it does not allow Gentile Christians to continue to be pagans. Christian distinctiveness from a polytheistic environment cannot be compromised. Though Christianity is not about food, it does require the complete abandonment of all idolatry. Consequently, "idol-consecrated food" is a matter quite different from Jewish food laws.

P. D. Gooch (1993: 106) correctly points out, "The avoidance of idol-food in such common contexts would impose significant and extensive limitations on the social behaviour of Christians." Some claim that modern Protestantism seeks to inconvenience the believer as little as possible. It tends to avoid imposing even reasonable restrictions on a believer's behavior, let alone those that would be considered to be unreasonable. People do not like being told no. An undercurrent that courses through the interpretations contending that Paul agrees with the more "enlightened" Corinthians regarding idol food and is concerned only that they show more love for the weak is the basic assumption that Paul surely would not make such unreasonable demands as to forbid their open participation in idolatrous contexts.

4. Paul does not grant grudging permission for the Corinthians to continue eating in idol shrines. The development of his argument in 10:1–22 reveals that he adamantly objects to it for theological reasons. Rather than imperiously demanding that they cease and desist immediately, however, he employs the norm of love in leading them to make the judgment for themselves. They need to see that human knowledge is always limited and that love should dictate their actions. Acting in love often requires a radical forfeiture of what one may regard as one's rights. He appeals to their Christian charity toward others.

5. Paul's concern for the weak is not that they somehow might be offended but that they might be destroyed (8:11). This distinction becomes important for applying Paul's restriction to current situations: if food causes his fellow Christian to stumble, then he will never eat meat. It does not apply to any situation in which someone might be offended by some behavior or belief. In the context, it refers to something that would sabotage another's relationship with God (Oster 1995: 197). Paul indicts actions that "might actually jeopardize the faith and salvation of others by leading the weak to *emulate* high-risk behaviors" (Hays 1997: 145).

Additional Notes

8:7. The reading τῇ συνηθείᾳ is found in ℵ*, A, B, P, Ψ, 33, 81, 630, 1739, 1881, pc, cop, syr^[hmg]. Western and Byzantine traditions (ℵ^[c], D, G, 88, 614, minuscules, Latin Fathers) have συνειδήσει: "For some with conscience of the idol unto this hour eat [it] as a thing offered unto an idol; and their conscience, being weak, is defiled." This reading is most likely attributable to the rarity of the word συνήθεια in Paul and as an assimilation to the next συνείδησις in the sentence (so Metzger 1994: 491; Fee 1987: 376 n. 1).

8:7. The meaning of the word συνείδησις (conscience) is much debated. Some interpret it in a minimal sense to refer to a person's awareness or consciousness of the self (Maurer, *TDNT* 7:904, 907; R. Horsley 1978b: 581–82; P. W. Gooch 1987a: 244, 249; Tomson 1990: 195–96, 208–16; R. Collins 1999: 321). The ones with a weak conscience would be those who are conscious of themselves as being defiled by association with idol food. They act contrary to their moral awareness of themselves as Christians. P. Gardner (1994: 45) identifies the weak conscience as "a lack of knowledge of oneself in relation to others." Those who are weak in self-perception are likely to give in to a "much-desired group recognition" and to do "many unwise things." The weak were made to feel even worse and less secure than they did before when they acquiesced to those who arrogantly insisted that idol food was nothing (so also Kistemaker 1993: 271–72).

The problem with this view is that it reads too much into what Paul actually says. This explanation better fits Paul's analysis of the situation in Rom. 14, which concerns those who harbor doubts about whether eating is permissible but who eat nevertheless. An important difference exists. In Rom. 14, he does not say that they have a "weak conscience" that is defiled but that they do not act from faith (Rom. 14:28; Dawes 1996: 95).

A second option understands "conscience" to refer to moral consciousness or awareness of one's own actions (Murphy-O'Connor 1978b: 555–56; Fee 1987: 381; Cheung 1999: 131–33). This meaning fits well the context of Rom. 2:14–15, where "conscience" is parallel to "thoughts" (λογισμῶν, logismōn) accusing or excusing them. In Titus 1:15–16, the false teachers have defiled consciences because they behave in ways contrary to their knowledge of God. The person sins in eating idol food because of his or her consciousness that it is idol food (Osborne 1931: 178; Cheung 1999: 133).

This view is unconvincing because Paul does not say that the weak person wrestles with some wrenching moral dilemma, whether to eat or not to eat, and then caves in against his better moral judgment. Paul does not suggest that such a person might yield to peer pressure from those with knowledge, but worries that he will emulate the actions of these spiritual pacesetters. If he were to eat at an idol's temple, he would not regard the food as ordinary food but as food sacrificed to an idol. He will have reverted to his former polytheism.

A third view understands "conscience" to be an "internal witness" (P. W. Gooch 1987a: 245) that passes judgment on one's past actions. The conscience shares knowledge with the self that is either painful, recognizing that past actions were wrong (cf. Heb. 9:9, 14; 10:22), or heartening, recognizing that past actions were blameless (Acts 23:1; 24:16; 1 Cor. 4:4; 2 Cor. 1:12; 1 Tim. 1:5, 19; 3:9; 2 Tim. 1:3; Heb. 13:18; 1 Pet. 3:16, 21). It is difficult to see how this understanding fits a "weak" conscience that can be defiled.

8:8. The reading "We are neither worse off if we do not eat nor better off if we do eat" has strong external support from Alexandrian text types ($\mathfrak{P}^{46}$, B, A*, 33*, 1739, 1881, 1836, 1898, 917, 1288, vg, sah, bo, arm). The order of the clauses is reversed, "We are neither better off if we do eat nor worse off if we do not eat," in the majority of other witnesses (ℵ, A^c, D, F, G, syr, eth, Tertullian, Ambrosiaster, Augustine, Pelagius). Zuntz (1953: 161–62) guesses that an Egyptian scribe originally omitted the first clause, and it was later added in the margin of the manuscript and misplaced in a later copy, so that this second reading is superior.

A third variant, "We are neither better off if we do not eat nor worse off if we do eat," has negligible support (A^2). This variant is favored by Murphy-O'Connor (1979b: 298) as representing a Corinthian slogan related to abounding and lacking in spiritual gifts that "could be used as a tangible test of one's standing before God." The ones with knowledge sneer that eating idol food has not diminished their own spiritual gifts, while abstaining from idol food has not increased the weak's spiritual gifts. The weak showed no signs of being better off for their abstention. Murphy-O'Connor claims that this reading best explains the others, as scribes adjusted the phrasing to try to make sense of it. This interpretation basically ignores the external textual evidence to make this verse better fit an imagined Corinthian position. The reading "neither do we abound if we eat, nor do we lack if we do not eat" is the harder reading (Fee 1987: 377 n. 6) and best explains the others (see Delobel 1994: 104–7).

8:10. The term εἰδώλιον appears in the LXX (Dan. 1:2; Bel 10; 1 Esdr. 2:7; 1 Macc. 1:47; 10:83). Paul's term εἰδωλεῖον (eidōleion) may be compared to Ἀσταρτεῖον (Astarteion, 1 Sam. 31:10 LXX), a reference to the temple of Astarte, and it matches Σεραπεῖον (Serapeion, a shrine dedicated to Serapis), Ἰσιεῖον (Isieion, a shrine dedicated to Isis), and Ἀνουβιεῖον (Anoubieion, a shrine dedicated to Anubis) found in the papyri, and Καισαρεῖον (*Kaisareion,* imperial cult temple) (Kornemann 1929: 7–10). See the word study in Newton 1998: 85–86.

8:12. The adjective ἀσθενοῦσαν is absent in $\mathfrak{P}^{46}$ and Clement. Metzger (1994: 491) suggests that it was omitted to prevent a reader from thinking that wounding only one with a "weak conscience" was forbidden.

8:13. How does Paul's view on idol food compare with that of later Christians? Acts reveals that the early Christians made a distinction between food laws that served as boundary markers separating Jews from Gentiles and idol food with its connection to idolatry. Peter's vision recorded in Acts 10–11 rejects the distinctions between clean and unclean imposed by Jewish food laws. Acts depicts the apostolic council officially rejecting circumcision and other burdensome Jewish restrictions as requirements for Gentiles to be saved and accepted into Christian fellowship (Acts 15:1–29). But the leaders steadfastly retained the categorical prohibitions against idol food and any associations with idolatry ("pollutions of idols," Acts 15:20; "what has been sacrificed to idols" [εἰδωλόθυτον, *eidōlothyton*], Acts 15:29). Acts recounts that Paul railed against idolatry in Ephesus (where Paul wrote this letter to the Corinthians) even when it imperiled his life (Acts 19:23–27; see also 17:16–31).

Brunt's appraisal of this fact is curious. Brunt comments, "Luke writes in support of Paul, addresses an issue which Paul discussed, yet makes no mention of Paul's discussion, does not even show awareness of it, and appears to take an attitude which is very different from it" (Brunt 1985: 115–16). According to Brunt's interpretation of Paul's position, the principle of love transcends tradition. Luke failed to grasp that subtle hermeneutic. It is more likely, however, that Brunt has misread Paul and that Luke and Paul were in total agreement on the issue of idol food. Otherwise, chapter 8, as understood in the traditional view, is the only passage in the Bible— outside of 2 Kings 5:18–19, which records Elijah granting Naaman the Syrian an exemption to enter the house of Rimmon with his master—that shows any tolerance toward anything associated with idolatry. If Paul condoned eating idol food, he would have been not just the first but the *only* prominent early Christian to do so (F. Young 1982: 564–65; Tomson 1990: 185).

Later Christians uniformly opposed idol food and appealed to Paul to justify their prohibition. None appealed to Paul for warrant to eat idol food, and no church father felt any need to defend Paul against rumors that he advocated eating idol food or to challenge any alternative interpretation of his writings (Cheung 1999: 97). His argument that to eat idol food is to have fellowship with demons became the basic Christian argument against eating idol food. Yet some argue that these later Christians misunderstood Paul. For example, Witherington (1995: 191) contends that soon after the NT era, Paul's "ability to make nice distinctions between eating food from the temple at home and eating in the temple was misunderstood" (see also Büchsel, *TDNT* 2:379, who labels it a reemergence of Jewish legalism). Dunn's evaluation of the matter is more judicious: "If those closer to the thought world of Paul and closer to the issue of idol food show no inkling of the current interpretation, that interpretation is probably wrong" (Dunn 1998: 704).

C. Paul's Own Example to Undergird His Counsel (9:1–27)

The choppy transition from the discussion of idol food in chapter 8 to the right of an apostle to receive aid from a congregation has caused some to suspect that the section beginning in 8:13 or 9:1 represents an interpolation (Weiss 1910: xl–xliii, 212–13; Héring 1962: xii–xiv; Schmithals 1971: 92–93, 334) or an unconnected digression (Wuellner 1979: 186–88). Most now recognize that this section is integral to Paul's argument about idol food and takes it a step further (Nasuti 1988: 246). Vocabulary links reveal its direct relationship to chapters 8 and 10.[1] References to Paul's personal practice appear also in 8:13 and 11:1. The major question to answer, then, is not *whether* it fits the context, but *how* it fits. What is Paul's objective in this chapter and how does it fortify his argument about idol food?

Some think that Paul is defending himself against the winds of criticism shaking the Corinthians' confidence in his apostleship—something that he will confront head-on in 2 Corinthians. His exclamatory question "Am I not an apostle?" (9:1) sounds defensive; and his statement "This is my defense [ἀπολογία, *apologia*] to those who would examine me" (9:3, NRSV) seems plain enough to support this view.[2] The crisis of authority that Fee (1987: 393) sees behind much of this letter (cf. 4:1–5; 5–6; 14:36–37) is assumed to surface again in this section (see also Héring 1962: 75; Harrisville 1987: 143). Fee (1987: 363, 392–93) concludes from "the vigor of the rhetoric" and the "decidedly defensive nature of most of 1 Corinthians" that Paul must be defending himself against charges, and Fee claims that Paul reasserts his apostolic authority to accentuate the need for the Corinthians to heed his warnings in chapters 8 and 10. Some Corinthians have questioned whether Paul has

---

1. Ἐλεύθερος (*eleutheros*, free, 9:1, 19; 10:29); ἐξουσία (*exousia*, right, 8:9; 9:4–6, 12–18; 10:23); ἀσθενής (*asthenēs*, weak, 8:7–12; 9:22); μετέχειν (*metechein*, share, 9:10–12; 10:17, 21, 30); "obstacles" (πρόσκομμα, *proskomma*, 8:9; ἐγκοπή, *enkopē*, 9:12); and two antonyms, σκανδαλίζειν (*skandalizein*, to cause to fall, 8:13) and κερδαίνειν (*kerdainein*, to win, 9:19–23).

2. I will argue that these words alone do not make the entire argument a defense.

the proper apostolic authority to prohibit idol food.[3] This challenge to his apostolic authority is thought to stem from his refusal to accept their patronage and instead to eke out a meager living by working with his hands side by side with the lower classes (4:12; 9:6). This supposedly demeaning labor combined with his refusal to accept support is said to have fed suspicions about his character, dignity, and legitimacy as an apostle. In response to these detractors, Paul unleashes a torrent of rhetorical questions that vigorously defend his apostolic right to receive support, and then he offers his rationale for waiving that right.

Rhetorical questions, however, do not imply "heat and passion," nor do they indicate that the writer has adopted a defensive mode. They simply invite the audience to give its opinion (Lausberg 1998: §§776–79; Plett 1979: 64). They are part of Paul's style in this portion of the letter; six occur in 10:14–22 (see also 8:10; 10:30).[4] Harrisville (1987: 145) appeals to and perpetuates a perfidious caricature of Paul by referring to his supposed "vulnerability to personal pique" and "egoism"—a glaring misreading of this text that should be wholly abandoned (see the arguments against it in Jewett 1994: 3–12; Garland 1999: 109–10). Several arguments weigh in against the view that in this section Paul is circling the wagons around his apostolic authority.

First, the notion of his apostleship appears only in 9:1–2, in which he establishes his right to earn material support. These remarks are too brief for a substantive defense. The rest of his argument appeals to the everyday examples of the soldier, farmer, and shepherd (9:7), the plowman and thresher (9:10), and the priest (9:13). These illustrations simply point to "the universal norm that every person ought to profit from his labour" (Savage 1996: 94). The authority of the law (9:8–10a; Deut. 25:4), the precedent of others who already have received benefactions from the Corinthians (9:12a), and the command of Jesus (9:14) further buttress the right of an apostle who labors in the gospel to earn his living from the gospel. These arguments do not furnish any support for Paul's apostolic standing. He simply reminds them of what everybody already knows. He is not establishing (again) for the supposedly dubious Corinthians that he is a legitimate apostle but instead makes the point that apostles have the right to be supported.

3. So Weiss 1910: 233–34; Robertson and Plummer 1914: 180–81; Barrett 1968: 200–202; Conzelmann 1975: 152–53; Schmithals 1973: 270; N. Dahl 1977: 33–34; Theissen 1982: 40–46; Fee 1987: 393; P. Marshall 1987: 284; Oster 1995: 205–6; Wolff 1996: 187; R. Horsley 1998: 124. Hurd (1965: 127–28) contends that it is a defense against the charge of inconsistency concerning Paul's attitude toward idol food, showing indifference toward it in his earlier visits and now forbidding it (see also Ruef 1977: 78–79).

4. The question in 9:13, "Do you not know?" does not indicate that he is on the defense any more than do the six other similar questions in the letter (6:2, 3, 9, 15, 16, 19; see also 1 Cor. 3:16; 5:6; Rom. 6:16; 11:2).

Second, rhetorical questions that could just as easily be answered negatively would hardly win the day in a defense. Apparently, Paul did not anticipate that the Corinthians would contest the points, because he phrased the first four questions in 9:1 to expect an affirmative answer (Willis 1985a: 34; P. Gardner 1994: 69). The question "Am I not an apostle?" does not challenge any misgivings about his apostolic rank but instead establishes at the outset the premise of his discussion. He is entitled as an apostle to receive support, as they must admit, but they know he has waived those rights. He is not defensively claiming rights in this section but hammering home his renunciation of them. His statement in 9:15 that he does not write to secure his due rights for financial backing assumes that they would pay him *if* he would accept it. But why pay someone whom they suspect not to be a true apostle? These are not matters of debate, but undisputed premises. He wants them to reflect on these things as he applies his status as an apostle and his renunciation of his rights as an apostle in order to avoid putting any obstacle in the way of winning potential converts to the issue of idol food.

Third, if the Corinthians did not regard him to be a true apostle, he wastes his time describing at length his refusal to use his rights as an apostle (Horrell 1997b: 92). If they did not assume that he had those rights, the whole argument becomes pointless. As Hafemann (1986: 131) puts it, "Paul's entire argument rests on the fact that the validity of his apostleship is assumed." The key assertion comes in 9:19, where he maintains that he is free from all people (cf. 9:1), not that he is an apostle. Second Corinthians reveals that some in the church apparently have complained about Paul's refusal to accept their patronage for his upkeep (2 Cor. 11:7–12; 12:14–15). If they complained about his refusal to accept support, it is highly unlikely that they disputed his right to that support earlier. Paul's working with his hands did not cause them to question his apostolic credentials but did create a sociological problem that caused them to question his ministerial style (see Garland 1999: 474–84).[5] They objected to his humble demeanor and apparent weakness because they failed to see that it conformed to the way of the cross. But we should not read 2 Cor. 11:5–12 into this chapter after new circumstances caused their relations to deteriorate so

5. Paul makes clear in 2 Cor. 11:12 that the rival interlopers were trying to raise themselves to his same apostolic status, but he undercut their ambitions by continuing to refuse financial support. Apparently, they did not perceive that this refusal somehow invalidated his apostleship. The "superapostles" wanted to be like him! Harrisville's (1987: 143) conjecture that the Corinthians believed that "a true apostle would have accepted a salary, would have regarded remuneration for his activity as his sacred right, and not have punctured his week with tanning hides for tents" finds no support from a careful reading of the text. Accepting support does not translate automatically into having authority. Sophists and others accepted money but were still maligned.

profoundly.[6] Their objections to Paul's policy of declining their financial patronage and working with his hands to support himself have not yet fully emerged. P. Marshall (1987: 284) is probably correct that the ones who were so bold as to eat idol food and the ones from whom he refused support were one and the same. It is probable that the idol food issue continued to fester, and the wound burst when the accumulation of grievances against Paul was intensified by outside agitators who were trying to muscle in on Paul's field of work.

Fourth, Kistemaker (1993: 287) inadvertently highlights a problem with the view that Paul is on the defensive in chapter 9 with these comments: "We would have expected Paul to provide further details [about the opponents] (compare, e.g., Gal. 1:6–7; 5:10), but conclusive evidence is lacking." "We lack sufficient information about specific charges Paul's opponents are leveling against him." The most obvious reason for the paucity of details is that there were none to give. No one in Corinth was raising charges against him related to his refusal to receive support.

Fifth, the focus of this section falls on rights and the waiving of rights (ἐξουσία, exousia, 9:4, 5, 6, 12, 18; τούτων, toutōn, these things, 9:15). It develops the issue of ἐξουσία raised in 8:9. Paul's development of the theme in 9:19–23 further explains that he sets aside his own advantages for the sake of others. The argument in this section establishes his high status to set the stage for his willing acceptance of low status. D. Martin (1990: 121) comments, "Low-status persons, the weak, by definition have no exousia to surrender." The things connected with high status— rights and freedom—are the very things that those who have them recoil at surrendering. This is Paul's point. The overall argument is intended to promote a certain kind of demeanor and conduct. Having established his rights, he can then feature his refusal to profit from them.

Finally, it would be a strange defense of his apostleship for Paul to point out several respects in which he has not acted like an apostle. Why cite a command of the Lord that seems to undermine his position (i.e., those who proclaim the gospel should live from the gospel, 9:14)? If the problem is that some have disparaged him for failing to live according to the standard ordained by Jesus, Paul says nothing to offset this perception. Why also raise the possibility of being disqualified (9:27)? The best answer to these questions is that Paul is not on the defense and is not insisting on his apostolic rights. Instead, he insists that renouncing these apostolic rights is the right thing to do for one captured by Christ. He is controlled by the necessity to win others to Christ that his calling as an apostle imposes upon him, not by any selfish de-

---

6. Pascuzzi (1997: 25–46) makes the case that the situations of 1 and 2 Corinthians should be kept separate. The characterization of the situation in 1 Corinthians as one of intense enmity is not sustainable.

sire to promote his own advantage or to indulge his own fancy. He may have been aware that some in Corinth were disgruntled with his modus operandi, but his purpose here is not to defend it. Instead, he argues from his conduct (Willis 1985a: 40). His cites his own practice as an example of the attitude he wants them to adopt. The task of advancing the gospel totally dominates his life, inspiring his willingness to make any sacrifice to win others. He wishes that this attitude were more evident in their lives.

That Paul intends in this section to offer himself as a model of one who voluntarily relinquishes his rights is confirmed by the athletic metaphor that spotlights his own conduct (9:24–27) and the concluding admonition to imitate him as he imitates Christ (11:1). His personal example as an apostle who unselfishly sacrifices for others in his missionary service is particularly appropriate for those Corinthians who have demonstrated a tendency to seek personal gain. The implication is that those with knowledge should follow his example by abdicating their so-called right to eat idol food (8:9) in order to avoid any possibility of causing others without their endowment of knowledge from falling back into idolatry. The issue of food appears in 9:4, 7, 9, 10, 13 and reveals that he does not ask them to give up anything more than he himself has given up. The contrast between Paul and the "knowledgeable" Corinthians is stark. They appear to insist on a right that might cause the weak to stumble. Paul purposefully surrenders a right and adapts himself to the weak (9:22) and to others to win them. He leaves it to his readers to draw the logical inference by moving from the greater to the lesser. If Paul their apostle does this, then they, the fruit of his apostolic work, should follow suit (Smit 1997b: 489; cf. P. D. Gooch 1993: 50, 90). Knowledge (8:1), rights (8:9), and freedom (9:1) must be directed by love and concern for the spiritual well-being of others.

The function of this section is pedagogical.[7] Paul, not the Corinthians, raises the matter of his refusal to accept money for his work as an apostle, and he brings up his behavior as an example for the Corinthians to follow. He never uses autobiographical information for its own sake but to establish ethos to persuade (Lyon 1985: 226; cf.

---

7. Hock 1980: 60–61; Willis 1985a; Hafemann 1986: 127; Tomson 1990: 192; Probst 1991: 196–98; D. Martin 1990: 122; Sandnes 1991: 119–20; Witherington 1995: 203–6; Smit 1997b: 478–79; Horrell 1997b: 92; Eriksson 1998: 145–47. Some identify it as only a mock defense in the service of providing an example (M. Mitchell 1993: 243–50; Pascuzzi 1997: 34–37; R. Collins 1999: 328; B. Dodd 1999: 97–110). Also to be rejected is the idea that Paul tries "to kill two birds with one stone" (see Merklein 1984: 173)—defending his apostleship and setting forth an example to be followed—proposed by some interpreters (Hays 1997: 146–48). M. Mitchell (1993: 245) notes that no example exists from ancient literature in which a defense speech is also used as an appeal to follow one's example.

2 Thess. 3:6–10). Holladay (1990: 84) notes that using ethical paradigms was typical of Greco-Roman moralists who believed that "example was far superior to precept and logical analysis as a mean of illustrating and reinforcing appeals to pursue a particular mode of life, normally the life of ἀρετή ([*aretē*] virtue)." They would present themselves as paradigms for their audience to follow.[8] This is precisely Calvin's point (1960: 182): "A Christian teacher, above all, should discipline himself in this way, so that men may always see his teaching backed up by the example of his life." Knowledge can be taught, but love needs to be shown, especially the radical love that Christians are to live out (see Engberg-Pedersen 1987: 575). But more than providing an example of how they should show love, Paul "presents, in his own person, a summary of his gospel" (Nasuti 1988: 263).

---

8. Holladay (1990: 85–87) cites numerous examples.

1. Paul's Right as an Apostle to Receive Support (9:1–14)

In this unit, Paul is not defending his status as an apostle but establishing that as an apostle he has certain rights. These rights are framed in such a way that they tie in to the issue of food. This fact allows him to set himself up as an example to be followed (11:1). He has relinquished his right to receive support from his churches at great cost to himself so as to avoid impeding others from coming to faith. The implication is that the Corinthians should follow their apostle's example and waive any presumed right they think they have to partake of idol food so as to avoid causing others to slip from faith.

Exegesis and Exposition

¹ˈAm I not free? Am I not an apostle?ˈ Have I not seen Jesus our Lord? Are you not my work in the Lord? ²If to others I am not an apostle, I am indeed to you. For you are the seal of my apostleship in the Lord. ³My defense against those who would examine me is this. ⁴We are not without the right, are we, to [receive support so that we can] eat and drink? ⁵We are not without the right, are we, to take along a believing wife as do the rest of the apostles, and the brothers of the Lord, and Cephas? ⁶Are I and Barnabas the only ones who do not have the right not [to have] to work [to support ourselves]? ⁷Who serves as a soldier and supplies his own provisions? Who plants a vineyard and does not eat its fruit? Or who tends a flock and does not drink the milk from the flock? ⁸These are arguments from human customs, but does not the law say these things as well? ⁹For it stands written in the law of Moses, "You shall not ˈmuzzleˈ an ox [to prevent it from eating grain] while it is threshing." Oxen are not God's primary concern, are they? ¹⁰Surely, is God not speaking on our account? It was written on our account, "It is right that the one who plows plows in hope, and the one who threshes threshes in hope, that he will partake [of the crop]." ¹¹If we sowed spiritual things among you, should it cause a huge difficulty if we reap material things from you? ¹²If others partake from this right over you, should not we all the more? But we did not avail ourselves of this right but endure all things so that we might not present an obstacle to the gospel of Christ. ¹³Do you not know that those who perform sacred rites eat from the temple [sacrifices], and those who attend to the altar share from the altar? ¹⁴Thus also the Lord charged those who proclaim the gospel to live from the gospel.

Paul begins this unit with four rhetorical questions, each one beginning   **9:1**
with οὐ (*ou*), expecting the answer yes. These questions do not reveal
"the author's strong feeling in the face of the attacks which must have
been made on his apostolic authority" (Héring 1962: 75), nor do they
imply that the Corinthians have denied or held cheap his apostolic position (Moffatt 1938: 115), requiring his response. On the contrary, the
questions could be paraphrased thus: "As you well know, I certainly am
free." "As you well know, I certainly am an apostle." "As you well know,
I certainly have seen the Lord." "As you well know, you are my work in
the Lord." The questions call attention to something the Corinthians already know (P. Gardner 1994: 68–69) and establish the premise of the
illustration. He is an apostle entitled to support, but he has surrendered
that right. His rhetorical strategy is to remind them of his high station
as their apostle, to whom they are indebted for bringing to them the
gospel and whose example they are obliged to imitate (Smit 1997b:
485). Smit (1997b: 487) summarizes Paul's method: "He highlights his
right to a living by emphasizing that it is inherent in his apostolic office,
and that he is undeniably entitled to it. By increasing the weight of the
right which he voluntarily renounces, he heightens the pressure on the
Corinthians to follow his authoritative example and act likewise." Authority and imitation are two sides of the same coin.

The opening questions in 9:1, "Am I not free? Am I not an apostle?"
outline his discussion in 9:2–23. He picks them up in reverse order and
discusses the rights of his apostleship, which he has not employed, in
9:1c–18. He discusses the issue of freedom in 9:19–23.

Some manuscripts invert the order of the questions, placing the
question about his apostleship before the question about his freedom.[1]
The most likely explanation for this swap in the order is that some later
copyist mistakenly assumed that the question about apostleship should
be foremost. The question about freedom, however, picks up the central issue arising from 8:13. Because Paul limited himself by refusing to
eat something that might cause another to fall, readers might wrongly
infer that Paul's freedom was somehow curtailed. They might ask,
"Why would he limit what he eats for the sake of one who was weak?"
This seems to be a degrading and servile act for one who is supposedly
free.[2] In 9:19–23 (see also 10:29), Paul develops the point that he voluntarily makes himself a slave to all in his service of Christ (cf. 7:21–22),
and he explains that it is his freedom in the Lord that causes him to

---

1. The contention of Weiss (1910: 232) that "freedom" is a gloss reflects his misreading of the entire section.
2. Borgen (1994: 55) notes a parallel in Josephus (*Ant.* 4.6.11 §§145–49) where Zam-
brias, in his speech against the law of Moses, championed "freedom" and "self-determination" to do as he pleased. He boasts, "And woe be to any man who declares himself to
have more mastery over my actions than my own will!"

limit how he uses his freedom (P. Gardner 1994: 70). The Corinthians understand freedom in terms of the slogan "All things are lawful to me" (6:12; 10:23). Paul redefines "freedom" for them (9:1, 19; 10:29) so that it excludes the pursuit of self-interest and instead makes the well-being of the community paramount.[3] He is basically free from the way of the world, which is accustomed to persons holding the whip over others who are weaker and lording it over them as a badge of their freedom and honor.

Paul identified himself as an apostle in the greeting (1:1).[4] The next two questions simply remind them of the facts. He is a witness to Christ's resurrection and is the founder of the church at Corinth. Having seen the risen Lord is one of the criteria used to decide on the replacement of Judas (Acts 1:22; cf. Acts 2:32; 3:15; 4:33).[5] Reminding them that he has seen the Lord, however, does not mean that he must be defending his qualifications to be an apostle. In 15:8, he mentions again that he is a witness to the resurrection, with no hint of any defensiveness about his apostolic credentials.

Paul already alluded to Corinth as God's field (3:9) where he had been assigned as God's servant to work. He planted, but God gave the growth (3:6). He is careful to distinguish that they are not *his* work, about which he can boast, but his work *in the Lord,* so that his boast is in the Lord (1:30–31; 2 Cor. 10:17). The indisputable fact that they came into existence as a Christian community through his missionary preaching reveals God's grace working through his life and confirms his apostolic role (cf. 2 Cor. 3:3; 10:13–15).

9:2   If Paul is not on the defensive, why does he imply that "to others" he may not be considered an apostle? Who are the others (ἄλλοι, *alloi*)? Some would assume that he has in mind an anonymous group attacking him: outsiders from other Christian communities, such as that in Jerusalem (so P. Richardson 1994: 96); outsiders who have wormed their way into the Corinthian community, casting aspersions on his au-

---

3. P. Marshall (1987: 285–86) notes a parallel with Plato (*Respublica* [*Republic*] 557B).

4. Fee (1987: 395) claims that this is "the first direct statement in the letter that his apostleship itself is at stake in Corinthians; but such has been hinted at several times before this (1:1, 12; 4:1–5, 8–13, 14–21; 5:1–2)." P. Gardner (1994: 69–71) challenges this assertion point by point and observes that if the historical situation was indeed one of conflict over Paul's apostleship, it is strange that no "direct statement" about it appears until now.

5. Paul normally uses the name "Jesus" by itself to refer to the historical Jesus of Nazareth: cf. Rom. 3:26; 4:24; 8:11, (34); 10:9 (Lord Jesus); 14:14 (Lord Jesus); 16:20 (Lord Jesus); 1 Cor. 1:2 (Lord Jesus); 5:4 (Lord Jesus); 11:23 (Lord Jesus); 12:3; 16:23 (Lord Jesus); 2 Cor. 1:14 (Lord Jesus); 4:5, 10 (death of Jesus; life of Jesus), 11, 14; 11:4, 31; Eph. 1:15; Phil. 2:10; 1 Thess. 1:10; 2:15, 19; 3:11, 13; 4:1, 2, 14; 2 Thess. 1:7, 8, 12; Philem. 5.

thority and sufficiency; or insiders in Corinth who have grown disenchanted with Paul. It is questionable whether the Corinthians were aware of any attacks on his apostleship from other communities; and if Paul had in mind some who had infiltrated the community and sowed poisonous seeds of suspicion about him, it is more likely that he would refer to them with his usual term, τινες (*tines*, certain ones; cf. Rom. 3:8; 16:17–18; 2 Cor. 3:1; Gal. 1:7), which "damned . . . with anonymity" (Judge 1968: 41; cf. P. Marshall 1987: 341–48). The condition is hypothetical, with the emphasis falling on the fact that at least he is an apostle to them (Malherbe 1994: 239). He does not say that some are actually contending that he is not an apostle. Possibly, the word "others" refers to those who are not Christians and who make a false worldly assessment of him and treat him as an "impostor" and someone "unknown" (2 Cor. 6:8–9; cf. Garland 1999: 311–14). They are the "others" to whom he preaches and whom he wants to save (9:27). More likely, the "others" refers to churches that he did not found. The idea of apostleship here is tightly bound to the missionary work of founding churches (cf. 3:6; 2 Cor. 10:14), and he simply asserts the obvious, that "not all Christian communities are his ἔργον" (*ergon*, work; Schrage 1995: 290). The point neither calls into question his universal apostleship nor implies that others have doubts (contra Fee 1987: 396) but instead underscores that he has been sent to *them* as their apostle (R. Collins 1999: 335).[6] He may not be the apostle of other churches, but he is without question the Corinthians' apostle. Their very existence as a church is the seal of his apostleship (2 Cor. 3:2–3). The "seal" (σφραγίς, *sphragis*) is a "legally valid attestation" (Fitzer, *TDNT* 7:949) stamped by God (cf. 2 Cor. 1:22; Eph. 1:13; 4:30; Rom. 4:11), proving that his work among them was the Lord's enterprise. This authority may add force to his prohibition of idol food, but his purpose here is to establish his high status that will then accentuate the extent of his sacrifice to lower himself socially to win others. It sets up the example he expects them to follow. For the Corinthians to dissociate themselves from any event that involved eating idol food would result in a similar social lowering. It would cut them off from patrons, political allies, friends, and neighbors—something that they were loath to do.

The position of αὕτη (*hautē*) at the end of the clause indicates that the **9:3** defense refers to what follows: "my defense . . . is this."[7] The terms ἀπολογία (*apologia*) and ἀνακρίνουσιν (*anakrinousin*) can have forensic connotations (cf. 4:3–4; Acts 22:1), but that does not demand that

6. The ἀλλά γε (*alla ge*) means "yet at all events" (Edwards 1885: 227) and is emphatic (BDF §439.2).

7. Weiss 1910: 233; Héring 1962: 76; Barrett 1968: 202; Kistemaker 1993: 290; Verbrugge 1992: 124–25; cf. Zerwick 1963: 67–68; contra Robertson and Plummer 1914: 179, 174, who translate it, "There you have my answer to those who challenge my claim."

Paul is responding to Corinthian accusers. P. Gardner (1994: 76) claims that Paul puts "himself in the dock to make his example personally vivid to the readers."[8] No one is actually challenging Paul, which requires his defense, nor is he debating hypothetical adversaries who object to his manual labor (contra D. Martin 1990: 77–79; Hays 1997: 147–48). He raises the questions himself to make his case. Smit (1997b: 485) identifies it as a rhetorical figure of style, the *anticipatio* or *prokatalepsis*, which anticipates objections (Quintilian, *Inst.* 9.2.16–18). What follows are answers "to presumed questions which critical listeners might ask" in a way that makes his arguments lively and interesting (so also Sandnes 1991: 119–20; Malherbe 1994: 240; B. Dodd 1999: 102–3). Paul expected the readers to raise questions about why he would allow his freedom to be put on a short leash by someone with a weak conscience (8:13; cf. 10:29).

B. Dodd (1999: 103–5) helpfully points out that Paul casts his remarks as a fictitious defense because of the delicacy required when discussing oneself. Acceptable self-praise required following certain rules of decorum. Plutarch's essay "On Praising Oneself Inoffensively" (*Mor.* 539A–547) offers strategies to make self-praise palatable to listeners—to keep it from becoming brazen boasting or from arousing envy. Three of his recommendations are discernible in chapter 9 (see B. Dodd 1999: 105). Sounding boastful is avoided if the speaker shows that he (1) is offering a defense against charges (ἀπολογία), (2) does so because of compulsion (ἀνάγκη, *anankē*, 9:16–18), and (3) demonstrates that it is included for the good of others to admonish or instruct them (9:24–27). Paul's exposure to sociorhetorical conventions best explains why he frames the discussion of his own example as a defense.

9:4–6 Paul frames the next questions (9:4–5) to expect the answer no. "We are not without the right, are we, to eat and drink?" "We are not without the right, are we, to take along a believing wife?" "Are I and Barnabas the only ones denied the right to abstain from working to support ourselves?" (on Paul's work, see the additional notes). The first question assumes that as an apostle he obviously has the right to receive assistance for the basic necessities to survive. Phrasing it as a question about the right to eat and to drink relates it to the question at hand—eating and drinking sacrificial fare. The second question assumes that apostles also have the right to take their wives along with them and that their wives also share in the right to receive support from the churches, though this right does not explicitly appear in Jesus' command (Matt.

---

8. Barrett (1968: 201–2) interprets ἀνακρίνουσιν as a conative: "those who would like to examine me" (so also Willis 1985a: 34). Fee (1987: 401 n. 24) discredits this reading as "without grammatical warrant." Identifying the present tense verb as conative, however, emerges more from interpretation than from grammatical rules. Nevertheless, the conative indicates that an attempt is in fact being made, not that it might be made.

10:10; Luke 10:7). The third question concedes that both Barnabas and Paul work to support themselves, but it implies that they do this not because they have no right to expect support from the churches in the areas where they are preaching but because they possess the right and have waived it. What Paul is driving at in 9:4–5 becomes more explicit in 9:6. He has the right to receive support from the community so that he will not become sidetracked from his preaching task by the hardships of trying to earn a living at the same time.

Several items in these questions lead us astray from the thrust of Paul's argument but pique our interest and need attention. First, he mentions the privilege of taking along, literally, "a sister wife" (ἀδελφὴν γυναῖκα, *adelphēn gynaika*). This phrase is best translated "believing wife" (cf. Tob. 8:7), but it was read quite differently by early interpreters.[9] Tertullian (*De monogamia* [*Monogamy*] 8) claimed that it does not refer to a wife but to a female attendant who ministered to the apostles in the way that rich women ministered to Jesus (Luke 8:1–3; reversing what he said in *De exhortatione castitatis* [*Exhortation to Chastity*] 8). This opinion held sway among other church fathers (see Jerome, *Jov.* 1.26; Augustine, *De opere monachorum* [*The Work of Monks*] 5). If Paul were referring to some female member of an apostle's entourage, however, then the word γύνη (*gynē*) would be superfluous (Héring 1962: 77). "Brother" and "sister" are used in 7:12, 14, 15 to refer to male and female Christians (cf. Rom. 16:1; Philem. 2). If the apostles traveled accompanied by someone who was not their wife, it would have exposed them to unnecessary gossip and defamation of their character, to say nothing of temptation.

Clement of Alexandria (*Stromata* [*Miscellanies*] 3.53.3), who thinks that the "yokefellow" in Phil. 4:3 referred to Paul's wife, assumes that Paul had in mind being accompanied by a wife without living maritally with her—as a Christian sister rather than as a spouse—so that the apostles would not be distracted from their preaching. He believed that the apostles' wives worked as fellow ministers who spoke to the women of the household, so that the gospel could penetrate the women's quarters without causing scandal (see Calvin's [1960: 186] caustic remarks about this interpretation). Although the latter comment offers a possible window on what missionary role the apostles' wives may have played, the idea of some kind of spiritual union between husband and wife would directly contradict what Paul has insisted on in chapter 7, that marriage is to be a fully sexual relationship.

A second issue raises the question whether Paul refers to a closed circle of apostles or, rather, understands the term "apostle" in a functional

---

9. Bauer (1959: 101) claims that the verb περιάγειν (*periagein*) does not mean "to accompany on journeys," but "to have with one continually," to "be married." Appealing to such an arcane meaning for the verb is unwarranted (Fee 1987: 403 n. 33).

sense so that it included Barnabas and any traveling missionary. In 15:7, he reports that after the risen Lord appeared to James, he appeared to all the apostles. The implication is that an apostle is one who has seen the risen Lord, though he distinguishes them from the "twelve" (15:5). It is plausible that Andronicus and Junia, whom Paul identifies as prominent among the apostles (Rom. 16:7), belong to this group of apostles. If so, they are a prime example of a husband-and-wife apostle team.

Paul's tantalizing details about "the brothers of the Lord" (cf. Matt. 12:46–49; 13:55; 28:10; Mark 3:31–34; 6:3; Luke 8:19–21; John 2:12; 7:3–10; 20:17) do not divulge much about their role in the early church's mission.[10] Are they a separate category from the apostles (cf. 15:7, where James, the most famous of the Lord's brothers, is listed individually)? Does Paul cite them simply because they were known to travel with their wives and had the same privilege to receive support from the churches as apostles did? Does he envisage them touring the Greco-Roman world on missionary journeys and receiving Christian hospitality at their various stops? This brief reference does not allow any firm conclusions.

Earlier in the letter (1:12; 3:22), Paul mentions Cephas, who appears to be well known to the Corinthians. The "and Cephas" at the end of the series may mean "without forgetting Peter in particular" (Héring 1962: 77); but it does not suggest a rising order of rank—apostles, brothers of the Lord, Cephas (contra Lietzmann 1949: 41).

The reference to Barnabas reveals three things: (1) that he was known to the Corinthians, perhaps only by reputation (cf. Col. 4:10); (2) that he adopted the same modus operandi as Paul in refusing to accept financial support from the persons with whom he was ministering; and (3) that Paul and Barnabas presumably have patched up the strained relationship implied in Gal. 2:13 and Acts 15:36–41. Note that Paul uses nicknames to refer to both men: Cephas, whose given name was Simon (Mark 1:16), and Barnabas, whose given name was Joseph (Acts 4:36).

9:7 Three more rhetorical questions draw examples from typical practice in the workaday world (cf. 2 Tim. 2:4–6), where persons receive some kind of compensation for their labor. Again, the emphasis is placed upon "eating." The soldier does not have to supply his own rations when he is sent off to war. The word ὀψώνιον (opsōnion; cf. 2 Cor. 11:8) does not refer to wages or salary in this context (despite 1 Macc. 3:28; 14:32) but to food and provisions (Caragounis 1974: 51–52; Spicq, *TLNT* 2:602–3). The army supplies the soldier with the wherewithal to live, and the soldier has the bonus of enjoying any spoils of war.

---

10. The argument that these were Jesus' cousins was concocted to support the idea of Mary's perpetual virginity and has no basis in the Greek text. Paul knows the Greek word for "cousin" (ἀνεψιός, anepsios, Col. 4:10) and does not use it here. Both Paul (Gal. 1:19) and Josephus (*Ant.* 20.9.1 §200) refer to James as "the brother of Jesus."

The planter eats the fruit from his vineyard (Deut. 20:6), and the shepherd "eats" (ἐσθίει, *esthiei*; in the sense of drawing nourishment from) the milk from his flock. The analogies of army, vine, and flock have a rich heritage as imagery for God's people in the OT (Godet 1887: 10). The examples also do not refer to wages that come as something extrinsic to the work but to compensation that derives intrinsically from the work (Nasuti 1988: 250). Those who are soldiers in the army of Christ, working in God's vineyard, and shepherding God's sheep also can expect to receive upkeep from their service. These analogies refer only to maintenance for basic subsistence, and questions about wages for the work are far from Paul's mind (Heidland, *TDNT* 5:592).

Paul next shifts from human precedents to divine command. R. Collins **9:8–12a** (1999: 338) notes that rhetorically his argument comports well with "the scholarly exposition of Hellenistic rhetoric that first advances rational arguments and then an argument from authority." "The law says" is a rare expression in Paul (Rom. 3:19; 7:7; 1 Cor. 14:34) and prepares for his exegesis of the text confirming that God has authorized preachers of the gospel to receive sustenance from those to whom they preach.

The point of the analogy from Scripture is clear: If God forbids preventing an ox from enjoying benefits from its work in threshing grain, how much more is a human apostle entitled to receive benefits from his mission work (Orr and Walther 1976: 241). Those who thresh the grain, both the working beast and the human, have a divinely ordained right to be nourished from their labor (see *b. B. Meṣiʿa* 88b).

How Paul interprets the passage about not muzzling an ox (Deut. 25:4) has drawn more attention from scholars than the point he draws from it. What does he mean that God does not care for oxen (9:9)? Does he ignore Scripture's literal sense and resort to allegorizing to extract a higher, spiritual meaning from the text? Many argue yes.[11] Conzelmann (1975: 154–55) represents the extreme view that Paul's exegesis does violence to a text that contains "essentially a rule for the protection of animals" by adopting "the Hellenistic Jewish principle that God's concern is with higher things" (see also Lietzmann 1949: 41). This assessment assumes that Paul shared the same sentiments expressed in Philo (*Dreams* 1.16 §93) and Let. Arist. 144 that God does not care about "mice and weasels or suchlike creatures."[12] Trifling details

---

11. Weiss 1910: 236; Robertson and Plummer 1914: 183–84; Arndt 1932; Barrett 1968: 205; Longenecker 1975: 126–27.

12. Philo (*Virt.* 27 §§145–46) and Josephus (*Ant.* 4.8.21 §233) cite the law about muzzling the ox to show the law's humane and kindly character. Brewer (1992: 556) highlights the contrasting perspective of the later rabbis (*m. Ber.* 5:3; *m. Meg.* 4:9; *b. Ber.* 33b; *y. Ber.* 5:3) who assumed, "The Law was not given to display God's character but to be obeyed." Brewer (1992: 559) argues that Paul's exegesis of this passage reveals an affinity with the rabbinic presuppositions (see also Hanson 1974: 163–65).

in the text must point to some hidden meaning that can be unveiled only by an allegorical reading (see Philo, *Dreams* 1.3 §16). Philo spells out the basic principle: "For you will find that all this careful scrutiny of the animal is a symbol representing in a figure the reformation of your conduct, for the law does not prescribe for unreasoning creatures, but for those who have mind and reason" (*Spec. Laws* 1.48 §260). Those adopting the view that Paul allegorized the text tend to translate the πάντως (*pantōs*) in 9:10 as "altogether" (NASB) or "entirely" (NRSV), which would seem to exclude the literal meaning: "Does he not speak entirely for our sake?" Paul is understood to mean that the text does not apply to muzzling oxen but rather to paying Christian preachers.

The πάντως could also mean "surely" (NIV; Thackeray 1900: 194; BDAG 755; Fee 1987: 408), "doubtless," "assuredly" (Robertson and Plummer 1914: 184), "especially" (Kaiser 1973: 14), or "simply" (Barrett 1968: 205). This use of the term allows Paul to hold to the literal meaning of the text while emphasizing its application to humans.[13] R. Collins (1999: 339) calls it a noncontextual use of Scripture, but a few find that Paul's exegesis emerges from the tenor of the entire context of Deut. 24–25 (Godet 1887: 11; Kaiser 1973: 13–17) and does no violence to the plain meaning of the text. The context in Deuteronomy contains commands that feature the obligation of exercising due regard for the needs of others. One is to restore the poor man's garment taken in pledge (Deut. 24:10–13), to pay the laborer's wages each day (Deut. 24:14–15), to leave the corners of the field for the widows and strangers to glean (Deut. 24:19–22), and to avoid the cruel humiliation of a convicted malefactor (Deut. 25:1–3). The laws were intended to instill care for the dignity and welfare of others—from the indigent, to the wrongdoer, to the working beast. God intends for people to be magnanimous and thoughtful trustees of the benefits God has given them, which includes how they treat animals (Prov. 12:10). Paul may be affirming that the person who shows mercy to the ox in obedience to God's command benefits more than the ox does (Calvin 1960: 187–88), but he certainly understands that the law "was written not for animals, but for man to obey" (Brewer 1992: 559).

Paul's exegesis reveals his affinities with the later rabbis more than with Philo's allegorical method (Hanson 1974: 164–65).[14] The phrase ἐν

---

13. Cf. Luke 4:23; Acts (18:21); 21:22; 28:4. In 1 Cor. 9:22, πάντως (*pantōs*) may mean "at least" (BDAG 755) or "doubtless" or "assuredly" but could not mean "altogether," "entirely."

14. Brewer's (1992: 555) survey of numerous examples of exegesis prior to A.D. 70 attempts to prove that "not one used allegory or even attempted to interpret anything other than the plain meaning of the text." Witherington's (1995: 208 n. 16) questioning "whether most of Paul's audience would have recognized this hermeneutical move as something other than as allegory" ignores the more important question: How did Paul arrive at his answer? Brewer's argument that scholars too quickly assume that Paul resorted to allegorization to make the text apply merits consideration.

. . . τῷ Μωϋσέως νόμῳ γέγραπται (en . . . tō Mōyseōs nomō gegraptai) appears only here in Paul's letters, although he does refer elsewhere to what Moses "writes" and "says" (Rom. 10:5, 19), and the verb γέγραπται appears thirty-one times in his letters. Hanson (1974: 163–66) shows that the later rabbis used Deut. 25:4 as "a norm for the elucidation of other texts; it was freely applied in an analogical sense, though no rabbi suggests the literal meaning can be ignored." The laws in Scripture did not cover every conceivable instance; and some, like the command not to muzzle an ox, were used as a mold, as it were, to mint new legal decisions applicable to different circumstances (see Fee 1987: 408). Hanson (1974: 166) claims that Paul would have been more familiar with this particular text's analogical use than with its literal meaning, though he certainly would not have dismissed that literal meaning as unimportant or worthless.

The next statement (9:10) beginning with ὅτι (hoti) does not introduce some quote from an unknown noncanonical source (recitative use, so Weiss 1910: 237; Conzelmann 1975: 155; and the typeset of some Greek texts, e.g., NA²⁷). It explains instead the twice-repeated assertion that the law was written "on account of us": "because it is right that the one who plows plows in hope, and the one who threshes threshes in hope, that he will partake [of the crop]" (Calvin 1960: 188; Héring 1962: 78; Barrett 1968: 206; Kaiser 1973: 15).

Human laborers also profit from the law forbidding muzzling an ox that is harnessed to tread the grain, because they also may eat from the grain (Brewer 1992: 559). This conclusion finds a striking parallel in *m. B. Meṣiʿa* 7:2: "These may eat [of a crop in which they labour] by virtue of what is enjoined in the Law: he who labours on what is still growing after the work is finished [i.e., from ploughing to reaping], and he who labours on what is already gathered before the work is finished [i.e., threshing]" (cf. *b. B. Meṣiʿa* 87a–91b). The rabbinic argument applies the hermeneutical principle of *qal wahomer* (the light and the heavy) to conclude that if the law permits animals to eat of crops in fields that they are working, how much more may human laborers do so.[15] If God shows concern for the sustenance of working beasts, God is even more concerned for the sustenance of those who serve him. Presumably, Paul was either familiar with this traditional argument that eventually made its way into the Mishnah (R. Collins 1999: 340), or he drew the inference himself. Brewer (1992: 564) contends that this is not an allegorical reading of the text but the development of "new halakah": "This is the only occasion when Paul musters all his legal expertise to

---

15. Brewer (1992: 559) contends, "The technique of *Kal vaHomer*, unlike some other exegetical techniques, could be used to derive a new legal ruling which had all the force of the original written Law, and used properly was virtually unquestionable."

derive a new ruling using arguments that a contemporary rabbi would have been proud of."

In 9:11, Paul uses the metaphor of sowing to refer to his mission work.[16] He already has compared his ministry to agricultural laboring in 3:5–8, and in 16:15 he will describe his first converts in Achaia— Stephanas and his household—as firstfruits (ἀπαρχή, *aparchē*). The same *qal wahomer* principle is employed. If the one who sows spiritually has a right to expect a harvest of spiritual benefits, how much more does that person have a right to receive material benefits, which are far less important (Nasuti 1988: 250). This means more than "a small price to pay for the Gospel" (Barrett 1968: 206). Paul makes the case that a minister who sows spiritual things in God's field has a right to reap material things from that field. He applies this same principle to the collection for the saints in Jerusalem in writing that the Gentile churches were pleased to contribute to their needs, and indeed were bound to do so, "for if the Gentiles have come to share in their spiritual blessings, they ought also to be of service to them in material things" (Rom. 15:27, NRSV).

He underscores this point by noting that others already have partaken (μετέχειν, *metechein*, in the sense of "eating," 9:10; 10:17, 21, 30) from this right over them. The phrase τῆς ὑμῶν ἐξουσίας (*tēs hymōn exousias*) is best understood in this context as an objective genitive, "authority over you," or "claim upon you"—the right to receive material support from the Corinthians for laboring for the gospel in their midst (so Fee 1987: 410; against the subjective genitive, "authority you give," so Robertson and Plummer 1914: 185–86; Héring 1962: 79–80). Since Paul was the first to sow the seeds of the gospel in Corinth (1 Cor. 3:6; 2 Cor. 10:14), he should be the first in line to receive their financial support, even though all workers are on the same level and are to receive the same wages (1 Cor. 3:6–8).

Who were "the others" who shared in this rightful claim? Because Paul understands it as a rightful claim, they must have been persons who ministered among them. It is unlikely that Paul had in mind the rivals who make their appearance in 2 Corinthians, because there he denounces them as taking undue advantage of the church (2 Cor. 11:20). Apollos is the most likely candidate to have accepted financial assistance from them as one who "watered" (3:5).

Some translations begin a new paragraph in 9:12b (NIV, NRSV, REB), but 9:12b–14 directly links to what precedes. Paul's conclusion to his argument, "but we did not avail ourselves of this right," is extended with two additional proofs, almost as an afterthought. The result is that a command of the Lord becomes the climax of the proofs for his apos-

---

16. Paul may have been aware of the seed parables (see Riesenfeld 1970: 190–95).

tolic right to receive support. If this command was added only as a kind of postscript, then it suggests that Paul's supposed failure to live in accordance with this command was not an issue in Corinth. Otherwise, he would have addressed it more directly.

After establishing that the soldier serves at the expense of the army, the vineyard worker eats from the fruit trees, and the shepherd drinks from the milk of the flock, and after drawing a legal ruling that ministers may be compensated from the biblical command that an ox is to be allowed to eat of the grain that it is harnessed to tread, Paul declares that he does not avail himself of these rights. He compellingly establishes these rights "so that *he can make something* of his renunciation of them!" (Willis 1985a: 35). He does not glean material benefits from those to whom he preaches, so that it will not hinder reaping a spiritual harvest. The noun ἐγκοπή (*enkopē*, obstacle) recalls πρόσκομμα (*proskomma*, stumbling block) in 8:9 and σκανδαλίζειν (*skandalizein*, to cause to stumble) in 8:13. The verb form ἐγκόπτειν (*enkoptein*) is used to mean "to stop" or "to prevent" (cf. Rom. 15:22; Gal. 5:7; 1 Thess. 2:18).

How would receiving money have hampered the gospel? To whom would it have been a stumbling block? Potential converts may have shied away from converting to the gospel if they suspected that it came with strings attached: acceptance would cause them to incur financial obligations to support the one who brought them the gospel. Paul sought to avoid any impression that he was preaching only to acquire support. This policy of refusing assistance from converts caused him to endure privations. In 4:12, he lists growing weary from working with his hands as part of his hardships, and in 2 Cor. 11:9, he will remind the Corinthians that when he was with them *and in need*, he did not turn to them for help. This statement indicates that he was in need. His poverty caused the Corinthians some consternation. They did not interpret his voluntary privation as conforming to the pattern of Christ's sacrifice—"Though he was rich, yet for your sakes he became poor, so that by his poverty you might become rich" (2 Cor. 8:9). Instead, they interpreted his penury as demeaning to himself and an embarrassment to them. Paul apparently considers the Corinthians' disapproval of his choice of low social status as only a minor impediment in their relationship compared to the possible negative repercussions that accepting support would have on potential converts. His strategy of supporting himself freed him to serve all, not just his patrons. He voluntarily lowered himself from a higher status position as one supported by others to work with his hands. As a laborer, Paul could make his appeal also to the lower classes (D. Martin 1990: 124).

Most important is the principle that Paul wants the Corinthians to extrapolate from his discourse on the rights of an apostle: he gives up his rights for the sake of others out of Christian love. This ethic—being able to endure all things to benefit others (9:12), not seeking one's own advantage but the salvation of many (10:33), and imitating Christ (11:1)—is the key to his position on eating meat offered to idols (8:13). His policy is governed by the gospel and how best to win converts.

9:13 The plural τὰ ἱερά (*ta hiera*) refers to the cult in general and may be translated, "those who engage in the sacred rites" (Conzelmann 1975: 156 n. 1, citing Herodotus, *Historiae* [*Histories*] 1.1.72; 3 Macc. 3:21; Josephus, *Ant.* 14.10.18 §237; see also Fee 1987: 412; Schrage 1995: 307–8). Paul may be distinguishing between those who work in the temple precincts, such as the Levites in the Jewish temple, and priests who serve at the altar (Héring 1962: 79–70; R. Collins 1999: 342; cf. the discussion of the priests' and Levites' portions in Num. 18:8–32 and Deut. 18:1–8); or the second clause may clarify the first with more specific details: the one officiating at the altar shares with the altar a portion of the sacrifice (Robertson and Plummer 1914: 187; Fee 1987: 412 n. 86). Since Paul prefaces the illustration with the statement "you know that," he must assume that anyone familiar with pagan or Jewish sacerdotal service would understand the point, but he probably has in mind Jewish temple service.[17]

It may seem that Paul is piling up the proofs unnecessarily, and 9:13–14 appears to be affixed to the conclusion as an afterthought. But he may be shifting the argument to another level from compensation for secular work to compensation for religious service (Nasuti 1988: 251). The cultic motif, with the mention of the altar and the administrants sharing from the offerings, ties back into the central issue, food offered to idols. It also connects with the idea that those who eat the sacrifices are sharers in the altar—an idea he will develop in 10:18.

9:14 Paul raises the level of authority for this convention another notch from the law and common sacerdotal practice to the command of Jesus (cf. 1 Tim. 5:18; Did. 13:1). He gives a summary, not a direct quotation, of the instructions Jesus gave to his disciples when he sent them out on their mission to Israel (Mark 6:7–11; Matt. 10:1–15; Luke 9:1–15; 10:1–12). This citation provides evidence again (cf. 7:10) that Paul knew more of the Jesus tradition than simply the account of the passion (11:23–26) and the resurrection (15:3–7).[18] He seems to presuppose

---

17. The hapax legomenon παρεδρεύω (*paredreuō*, attend, serve) is not found in the LXX and is used by secular authors to refer to the work of pagan priests (Fee 1987: 412 n. 87; G. Horsley 1987: 34 cites an inscription using the word for "attending at the altar" in a cultic context). The word for "altar" (θυσιαστήριον, *thysiastērion*) is used in the LXX and the NT almost exclusively for the altar in the Jewish cult (Schrage 1995: 307).

18. On the issue of Paul's infrequent explicit references to Jesus' teaching (Rom. 14:14; 1 Cor. 7:10–11; 9:14–15; 11:23–25; 1 Thess. 4:15–17), see Dungan 1971: 20–21; D. Allison 1982; 1985; M. Thompson 1991: 37–76; Kim, *DPL* 475–80; Barclay, *DPL* 492–503.

that the Corinthians also were familiar with this tradition. Some suggest that this saying was transmitted to the Corinthians by someone other than Paul (Apollos, according to R. Horsley 1998: 126–27) to justify receiving support and that it was used against Paul. But he uses it as the climax to his argument about the incontestable rights of persons to receive compensation for their work. "In the same way" (οὕτως καί, *houtōs kai*, thus also) means that the Lord's command accords with reason, common practice in secular and religious occupations, and OT law.

Dungan (1971: 3, 20) claims that Paul deliberately disobeyed or set aside this explicit command of the Lord. Some try to ameliorate this problem by arguing that the command was directed to the communities that receive the missioners (Godet 1887: 23, "the dative of favor"; Barrett 1968: 208; Fee 1987: 413 n. 96; Kim, *DPL* 475). If the command was not directed to missionaries, then not availing oneself of the right would not constitute disobedience to it. The grammar suggests, however, that the command was directed toward the missionaries. The verb "to command" (διατάσσειν, *diatassein*) normally takes its direct object in the dative case (7:17; 16:1), so that the ones who preach are the direct object of the charge: "The Lord commanded those who proclaim the gospel to live from the gospel" (Horrell 1997a: 593). In the Synoptic tradition, the addressees are the disciples and not the villagers whom they might visit. The verb διατάσσειν, however, need not convey some absolute regulation or law (contra Dungan 1971: 3, 39) but may simply mean "to arrange": "the Lord arranged that those who proclaim the gospel live from the gospel" (R. Collins 1999: 342). Since Jesus considered the preaching mission to be a full-time task that prevented the missioner from earning income in a normal occupation, he established their right to be supported. The Synoptic tradition, however, portrays this instruction as a command, not as an arrangement. Jesus directed his disciples to adopt a lifestyle during their mission that trusted God to make provision for them (see Garland 1993: 112–13).

Paul did not understand himself to be disobeying a decree from the Lord but interpreted it as a right that he was free to accept or refuse. The plural pronouns "these things" (τούτων, *toutōn*, and ταῦτα, *tauta*) in the next verse connect Jesus' command with the protocol established in both the secular and the religious spheres, where the worker receives maintenance from his work. Paul does not in 9:15 say that he has disobeyed or disregarded this command but instead uses the verb χρῆσθαι (*chrēsthai*), which means he did not "make use of" or "take advantage of" (cf. 7:21) "these things." He uses the same verb in 9:12 to say "we did not avail ourselves of this right" (τῇ ἐξουσίᾳ ταύτῃ, *tē exousia tautē*). He regards "these things" in 9:15, including the Lord's command, as a "right" (cf. NRSV, NIV), not an obligation. We might imagine that preaching in pioneer areas in a pagan environment would also have required greater flexibility. Paul could hardly go to a new community and say, "The Lord commanded me to be supported by you." Jesus' words did not apply in the context of spreading the gospel in the Hellenistic world.

Theissen (1982: 43) asks the right question: "Why does he pile up the arguments on a matter about which he and the Corinthians agree? It is, after all, not his exercise of the privilege which is under debate, but his renunciation of it!" The only problem with this question is the assumption that Paul's renunciation of this right was "under debate" at this time. This interpretation reads back into this letter the later situation reflected in 2 Cor. 11:7–15 and 12:11–18. It also wrongly assumes that the renunciation of this right cast a shadow of doubt on his apostolic authority. Paul "piles up the arguments" to draw out the theological implications that his policy has for the issue at hand: the question of idol meat.[19] He surrenders an irrefutable right so that he can better win others to Christ. He enslaved himself to all (9:19; cf. 2 Cor. 11:7, he humbled himself) to fulfill his commission more effectively. He follows the paradigm set by Christ in his self-giving, self-emptying, and self-sacrifice (11:1).[20] In this section Paul has gone to great lengths to establish his rights as an apostle to receive community support in order for his renunciation of those rights to have a greater effect. Benefiting the spiritual good of others overrides insisting on divinely authorized prerogatives that he has from his service in the gospel. He lists and treats Jesus' command that those who proclaim the gospel should live from the gospel as a "right," not an obligation.

Paul may intend the phrase "to live from the gospel" (ἐκ τοῦ εὐαγγελίου ζῆν, *ek tou euangeliou zēn*) to have a double meaning (Conzelmann 1975: 157; Schrage 1995: 309; Nasuti 1988: 253). The gospel is both the preacher's message and mission (Moffatt 1938: 120). The quotation establishes that the preacher has the right to receive material sustenance from proclaiming the gospel, but Paul may further understand it to mean that the preacher also receives spiritual sustenance from the gospel. In what follows he underscores the spiritual benefits that he receives from his preaching that far outweigh any material benefit he has forfeited. Bread alone does not sustain human life. Life grounded in the gospel of Christ motivates and empowers him to endure anything

---

19. Fee (1987: 414) claims that "the whole reason for the argument is to assert that his giving up these rights does not mean that he is not entitled to them." But Paul never says that. Instead, he clarifies that he refused to use his rights so that he could win more converts. He wishes to put forward his example, not reinforce his authority.

20. If we do not think that Paul is on the defensive, we need not conclude that Paul thought that "obedient Christian discipleship (at least in the Corinthian context)—imitating Christ—required the setting aside of a specific instruction, or word, of Jesus" (Horrell 1997a: 600–601).

rather than to put obstacles in the way of others (9:12). Preachers of the gospel no longer can live to themselves, but must live for Christ (2 Cor. 5:15; cf. Phil. 1:21), which also entails doing all things for the sake of the gospel (9:23) and living for others (10:33). Paul is not simply offering himself as a model to illustrate his argument but presents himself as an apostolic standard for his churches (Hafemann 1986: 128). The one who enjoins a policy regarding idol food that would cost the Corinthians in both honor and material benefits has himself sacrificed significantly to advance the gospel. He is not blowing smoke when he says that he would not eat meat if it caused a fellow Christian to founder (8:13). He already has waived his right to eat anything supplied by the community. The lesson should be clear to the Corinthians. At great cost to himself, he renounces his legitimate and irrefutable right to eat and drink at the expense of the community, and he does so to avoid anything that may deter others from accepting the gospel. The Corinthians should follow their apostle's example and renounce their presumed right to consume idol food, which Paul regards as illegitimate and injurious, in order to avoid causing a weak brother to stumble back into idolatry. Paul's not "eating" (partaking) what the community could and should supply him as its apostle is going above and beyond the call of duty. The Corinthians' not eating idol food is simply obeying their duty as Christians.

Additional Notes

9:1. The order of two questions "Am I not free? Am I not an apostle?" is inverted in D, F, G, Ψ, Maj, syr[h], Ambrosiaster, Pelagius. Fee (1987: 394 n. 9) thinks that scribes altered the order in the interest of putting the more "important" question about Paul's apostleship first. Fee claims, however, that it misses the structure of the argument, in which Paul answers the questions in reverse order. He is an apostle (9:1–14); he is free (9:15–23). The mistake, however, is in thinking that Paul's apostleship is the more important question and that he is countering suspicions about it. The more important question is about freedom, which picks up the central question that arises from 8:13. Why would he limit what he eats for the sake of one who is weak? Is he not free? The question continues to be addressed in 9:19 and is raised again in 10:29. The statement that he has seen the Lord follows most naturally after the reference to being an apostle.

9:6. According to Acts 18:3, Paul worked in his tentmaker's trade. Pliny the Elder (*Naturalis historia* [*Natural History*] 19.23–24) notes that tentmakers made sailcloth awnings for temporary shelters, stalls, and shops in the forum area before permanent buildings were erected to provide shade. In a seaport, Paul also could have worked at making and repairing sails. Murphy-O'Connor (1983: 168) suggests that as a leather worker, Paul may have made thongs, gourds, harnesses, saddles, and shields. Stansbury (1990: 469) notes, "Although Paul's background made him socially on a par with those in the leisured classes, his sense of mission and method of support made him identify with those of relatively low social status." Three inscriptions from Rome refer to the tentmakers' association (*CIL* 6.5183b, 9053, 9053a).

Second Corinthians reveals that Paul's work caused problems in his relationship to the Corinthians. Robertson and Plummer (1914: 180) cite the Sophists' criticism of Socrates and Plato teaching for free, which declared, in effect, that their teaching was worth nothing. Antiphon said of Socrates, "If you set any value on your society, you would insist on getting the proper price for that too. It may well be that you are a just man because you do not cheat people through avarice; but wise you cannot be, since your knowledge is not worth anything" (Xenophon, *Mem.* 1.6.12; cf. Plato, *Gorgias* 520). Many interpreters assume that the Corinthians shared a similar attitude toward Paul since he did not accept any subsidy for his preaching when he was living among them. When rivals appeared later, they accepted financial support from the Corinthians and sniped at Paul, alleging that his refusal to accept a stipend betrayed his lack of apostolic status (Betz 1972: 100–117; Barrett 1973: 281–82; Georgi 1986: 238–42; R. Martin 1986: 345, 354, 438).

This hypothesis breaks down because the Corinthians know that Paul does receive support from other churches, namely, the Macedonians (2 Cor. 11:9). He also expects the Corinthians to send him on his way (προπέμπειν, *propempein*) in his missionary journeys to other communities (1 Cor. 16:6; 2 Cor. 1:16; see also Acts 15:3; Rom. 15:24; Titus 3:13; 3 John 6; Pol. *Phil.* 1:1), προπέμπειν being a technical term for providing goods (Malherbe 1983: 96 n. 11). There is no reason to assume that the Corinthians tied the amount of financial support to the legitimacy of apostleship. It is no less plausible that the competitors who arrived later on the scene contended that Paul had other congregations to whom he was more closely attached because he accepted their support. They could have promised the Corinthians, "We will commit ourselves only to you out of our special love for you." All such hypotheses about what the rivals may have argued, however, go beyond the evidence in the text and should be treated skeptically.

Understanding the social expectations that mapped out how relations worked in the Greco-Roman world is more fruitful for getting at the Corinthians' concerns. These social expectations exerted a strong influence on the Corinthians. The verb ταπεινοῦν (*tapeinoun*, to lower oneself) perhaps best expressed their misgivings about Paul: "Did I commit a sin by humbling myself in order that you might be exalted, that I proclaimed the gospel of God freely to you?" (2 Cor. 11:7; see also 1 Cor. 4:11–12). They may have considered the rigors of handwork that enabled him to preach the gospel without charge (cf. 1 Thess. 2:9) to be demeaning. Craftsmen were held in low regard by the leisured class in the ancient world (MacMullen 1974: 114–15). Cicero (*De officiis* 1.42) remarks, "Unbecoming to a gentlemen, too, and vulgar are the means of livelihood of all hired workmen whom we pay for mere manual labor, not for artistic skill; for in their case, the very wage they receive is a pledge of their slavery. . . . And all mechanics [craftsmen], too, are engaged in vulgar trades, for no workshop can have anything liberal [genteel] about it." Cicero regards working with one's hands to be a dirty business that coarsens body, soul, and manners. He calls craftsmen "the dogs of the city" (*Pro Flacco* 18). Civilized existence, he thought, required leisure. Naturally, only those belonging to the propertied upper class, having tenants and plenty of slaves to do all the work, could afford to live out this view (see de Ste. Croix 1981: 112–204). Lucian (*Somnium* [*The Dream*] 9) shares the negative estimate of workmen: you are, as a laborer, "personally inconspicuous, getting meagre and illiberal returns, humble-witted, an insignificant figure in public, neither sought by your friends nor feared by your enemies nor envied by your fellow citizens—nothing but just a labourer, one of the swarming rabble, ever cringing to the man above, . . . a man who has naught but his hands, a man who lives by his hands." The Corinthians, however, were laborers and tradespeople themselves and were probably proud of their professions (on the debate about the Corinthians' attitude toward work, see Hock 1978; Savage 1996: 84–86; P. Gardner 1994: 81–85). Nevertheless, they may have regarded such exhausting work as incongruous with Paul's status as an apostle of the glorious gospel in the same way that persons today might regard labor as laudable but be offended if their pastor refused a salary and sold vacuum cleaners door to door. They might judge such employment as incompatible with the dignity of the office. The problem for the Corinthians, however, seems to have been compounded by the fact that Paul's work apparently did not supply him with enough (2 Cor. 11:9). He was impoverished, which explains why he lists his work among his hardships (4:10–12) and speaks of "enduring anything" rather than putting obstacles in the way of the gospel by accepting support (9:12).

We can only surmise why Paul refused to accept subsidies from churches where he was preaching. His overriding concern in all that he did was whether it helped or hindered the gospel's advance (1 Cor. 9:12), and he refused to accept support at Corinth because he believed it would hinder the reception of the gospel.

1. He may have assumed that potential converts might balk at accepting a gospel that came with strings attached. Now they must provide financial support to their missionary (Barrett 1968: 207).

2. He may not have wanted to insinuate that persons had to pay to hear the message of the self-giving love of Christ, which he characterizes as a "free gift" (Rom. 5:15, 16; 6:20, 23) offered to all (Barrett 1968: 207; P. Gardner 1994: 84). Since God did not use the free-enterprise system in offering the salvation to the world—"You can have the gospel if you pay for it"—neither would Paul.

3. He wanted to become a "living paradigm" of the gospel, "offering the 'free' gospel 'free of charge'" (Fee 1987: 421). It was not simply that he did not want to profit from preaching the gospel and resonated with the pronouncement of the later rabbis, "He that makes profit out of the words of the Law removes his life from the world" (*m. ʾAbot* 3:5). He intended to present the gospel about Christ's self-sacrifice by means of his own self-sacrifice. As Christ became poor so that others might become rich (2 Cor. 8:9), so Paul depicts himself as "poor, yet enriching many" (2 Cor. 6:10).

4. On a more practical level, he did not want to become a client of the donors. Gifts brought obligations to reciprocate in some way (see Peterman 1997). Friendship in the ancient world was built around a system of unwritten accounts and debits. One had to respond in kind to gifts or benefits (Mott 1975: 60–61). Paul would not have been "free to preach the gospel with boldness if he is having to run around kissing men's hands, sending them gifts, groveling before them, and slavishly flattering them" (Garland 1999: 482). Robertson and Plummer (1914: 187) correctly identify the issue: "He must be free to rebuke, and his praise must be above the suspicion of being bought." He did not want to get trapped in the sticky web of social obligations that would hinder his freedom to preach and admonish (see Lucian's satire, *De mercede conductis* [*Salaried Posts in Great Houses*], which describes these obligations as a kind of slavery). He refused to become anyone's "kept apostle" (cf. 2 Cor. 12:14) or "house apostle" (R. Horsley 1997: 148).

5. He would have wanted to divorce himself from the variety of hucksters roaming the world with their hands always extended in hopes of getting donations (cf. Acts 20:33–35; 1 Thess. 2:3–6; and contrast Acts 16:16, 19). They taught for profit, and he castigates them as peddlers who hawk their wares and water down their goods to enhance the bottom line (2 Cor. 2:17; 4:2).

9:9. The reading φιμώσεις (to gag) has wide-ranging external support ($\mathfrak{P}^{46}$, ℵ, A, B³, C, Dᵇ·ᶜ, K, L, P, and the majority of minuscules), while κημώσεις (to muzzle) is read in B*, D*, F, G, 1739. Since κημώσεις is judged to be a more colloquial expression, and φιμώσεις a more literary term that appears in the LXX, the transcriptional probability is that the latter was introduced to assimilate it to Deut. 25:4 LXX (Metzger 1994: 492). Hanson (1974: 162) thinks that Paul's Greek version had κημώσεις and that it was not "a mistake of memory on Paul's part, nor the effort of a later scribe to smarten up Paul's Greek." The two words κημός and φιμός can be used interchangeably in translation Greek (cf. Prov. 26:3).

2. Paul's Freedom Used to Spread the Gospel (9:15–23)

Paul has argued that it is incumbent on others to pay him as an apostle sent out by Christ to preach. But he refuses support and declares that the only thing important to him is his obedience to God's calling. In 9:1–14, he musters all the arguments to establish his right to support for one purpose: to spotlight his refusal to exercise that right. Advancing the gospel in the world is the overarching reason behind his refusal to accept payment. The Corinthians have benefited from his preaching, but they also benefit from his example of self-sacrifice and self-control on behalf of others. He implies that they should imitate him in his all-consuming concern to save others.

Exegesis and Exposition

¹⁵But I have not availed myself of any of these [rights]. Nor do I write these things [now] so that it might be done in my case. For it is better for me rather to die than—⌜no one will make my boast an empty one⌝! ¹⁶For if I am preaching the gospel, it is not something about which I can boast. For necessity is laid upon me. For woe is me if I do *not* preach the gospel. ¹⁷For if I do this of my own will, I receive pay; but if [I do this] not of my own will, I am entrusted with a stewardship. ¹⁸What then is my reward? That in preaching the gospel I make the gospel free of charge so that I do not take full advantage of my right in the gospel. ¹⁹For though I am free from all, I made myself a slave to all in order that I might gain more. ²⁰And I became to the Jews as a Jew in order that I might gain Jews. To those under the law [I became] as [one] under the law, ⌜though not being under the law myself⌝, to gain those under the law. ²¹To those outside the law [I became] as [one] outside the law, though not being outside the law of God but inside the law of Christ, in order that I might gain those outside the law. ²²I became to the weak ⌜weak⌝ in order that I might gain the weak. I have become all things to all persons in order that in all circumstances I might save some of them. ²³I do all things because of the gospel in order that I might become its partner.

Paul reiterates his previous conclusion in 9:12b. Apostles have the right to receive a benefice from the community of believers among whom they work, but he has refused to avail himself of this right. The "I" is emphatic (ἐγὼ δὲ οὐ κέχρημαι οὐδενὶ τούτων, *egō de ou kechrēmai oudeni toutōn*), "I for my part"; and the verb is now changed from the

9:15

aorist in 9:12, "I did not avail myself," to the perfect tense, "I have not availed myself" (κέχρημαι), implying a settled resolve. "These things" (τούτων) refers to the right to receive support (Schrage 1995: 319) rather than the arguments substantiating this right (Weiss 1910: 239; Dungan 1971: 21 n. 2). Paul cautions that what he writes (ἔγραψα, egrapsa; referring to what he has just written in 9:3–14) should not be misconstrued as an attempt to exploit these rights now.

Paul underscores this point with the first of five clauses beginning with γάρ (gar). He starts out, "For it is better for me rather to die than," but suddenly halts in midsentence (aposiopesis) and continues with an emphatic declaration: "No one will make my boast an empty one!" Parry (1926: 140) thinks that he broke off because completing the thought might be offensive: "For it is better for me rather to die than to take anything from you" (cf. Rom. 1:11–12). But such a break often is a sign of emotion (cf. 1 Cor. 6:9; 15:1–2; Gal. 2:3–5, 6; 6:12; Phil. 2:29), and here it makes his refusal of support even more ironclad (cf. 2 Cor. 11:10). The emotion may be attributable to how closely his apostolic calling is tied to his view that he has been called both to preach the gospel and to live a cruciform lifestyle. "To die" (ἀποθανεῖν, apothanein) is parallel to the infinitive "to live" (ζῆν, zēn) in 9:14. The sentence may be completed thus: "It is better for me rather to die than to live off the gospel." Living off the gospel would mean death to his whole understanding of his prophetic calling and his reason for being. It would also entail slavery. Patterson (1982: 19) reminds us that the slave could have retained freedom by dying. By choosing to continue with physical life, the slave gives up freedom. Paul is free only as a slave of Christ (Rom. 1:1; Phil. 1:1), which necessitates that he be a slave of all.

The term "boast" (καύχημα, kauchēma) is misleading if it is interpreted in a pejorative sense of an arrogant claim that is offensive to God and humans (cf. 2 Cor. 11:1–12:13). Greek culture was ambivalent about boasting, generally encouraging persons to flaunt their wealth and wisdom to gain greater honor while condemning such behavior at the same time. But Paul is not vaunting his prowess in being able to endure greater sacrifices than other apostles endure. He does not intend to say that he is better than the others because he does not preach for pay. Nor does he imply any disapproval of legitimate apostles who receive material sustenance from preaching the gospel. Barrett (1968: 209) claims that this verse reveals the paradox of Paul's glorying in weakness. Refusing to exercise his rights and working to support himself meant that he suffered from hunger and weariness, mockery and insult; but he glories in his weakness.

The best backdrop for understanding Paul's boast is his Bible. P. Gardner (1994: 88) observes, "In the LXX, approval is given to boasting that arises out of a loving response to the gracious God." In contrast to Greek literature, the LXX has a positive understanding of a boast that stems from a person's relationship to God (P. Gardner 1994: 91; cf. Deut. 10:21; Ps. 5:12 LXX; 88:18 LXX; Jer. 9:22–23, cited in 1 Cor. 1:29, 31; 2 Cor. 10:17). In the immediate context, Paul's boast is connected to preaching the gospel, which he understands to be a divine commission laid upon him. His boast would be emptied if he stopped preaching or if he began to carry out his assignment as if it were only a job from which he received a livelihood.

Paul explains further about his boast lest it too be misunderstood. The **9:16** opening phrase ἐὰν γὰρ εὐαγγελίζωμαι (*ean gar euangelizōmai*) may be understood as concessive, "although I preach the gospel" (Kistemaker 1993: 304), and sets up his situation as an example to make a point. In this paragraph Paul gives a brief glimpse of his understanding of his calling in Christ in order to explain that his renunciation of the rights of an apostle is not some personal choice but is rooted in a pressing necessity (ἀνάγκη, *anankē*). This constraint is not a personal ethical standard that he strives to attain or an inner psychological compulsion. It is a compulsion that is laid upon him from outside by God. It is the "power of God that drives him without rest or respite like a slave through the Mediterranean" (Käsemann 1969: 228–31).[1] Munck (1959a: 20–23) connects this necessity to Acts 26:14, "It hurts you to kick against the goads," and interprets it to mean, "From now on you will have no discharge from the service that I, Christ, have now laid upon you." His expressed desire to depart to be with Christ is overruled by the necessity (ἀναγκαιότερον, *anankaioteron,* more necessary) to continue his ministry to the Philippians (Phil. 1:23–24). As a slave of Christ (Phil. 1:1), the choice is not his.

The idea of necessity evokes two themes. First, it recalls the divine conscription (cf. Gal. 1:15 and Jer. 1:5) and compulsion that drove the prophet Jeremiah (Malherbe 1994: 243).[2] Paul did not decide on his own to enlist in the apostolic ministry. To make this point, his language may deliberately echo Jer. 20:9, where the prophet speaks of his call to preach a particular message as "something like a burning fire shut up in my bones" that he could not hold in (Barrett 1968: 209; Wolff 1996: 200; Hays 1997: 153). All of the prophets felt God's hand weighing heavily upon them. It overwhelmed them, forcing them to speak God's message (Sandnes 1991: 126). Jeremiah speaks of anguish, writhing in

---

1. Friedrich (1970: 95) argues that Paul's refusal to make use of rights to which he is entitled was an act of freedom, not a constraint.

2. In Sib. Or. 3:295–99, the word ἀνάγκη is associated with divine constraint to prophesy (Sandnes 1991: 128): "When indeed my spirit ceased the inspired hymn, and I entreated the great Begetter that I might have respite from compulsion, the word of the great God rose again in my breast and bade me prophesy concerning every land and remind kings of the things that are to be."

pain, his heart beating wildly, and being unable to keep silent because God has collared him to preach in a dangerous situation. He complains bitterly about this divine force within him, since the result of his preaching brought him such suffering, and he uses the language of violent assault to describe God's overpowering his life (Jer. 20:7–8).

By contrast, Paul laments neither the overpowering nature of his calling nor the hardship that preaching the gospel of the cross free of charge creates for him. He does not preach grudgingly, because his lament has to do with *not* preaching the gospel: "For woe is me if I do *not* preach." The consequences for preaching are adversity and suffering, as they were for Jeremiah.[3] But Paul's attitude toward his suffering differs from Jeremiah's (Nasuti 1988: 258; R. Collins 1999: 348). He does not bemoan it but welcomes it as something that reveals to others the life of Christ (2 Cor. 4:7–12). Preaching the gospel brings him life, but he will not live off the gospel. Preaching the gospel brings him life but exposes him to death time and again (1 Cor. 4:9; 2 Cor. 1:8–10). Not preaching the gospel brings a fate worse than death.

The crux of the parallel with the prophet Jeremiah is that Paul can do nothing other than what God has commissioned him to do. Just as the effects of his preaching are determined entirely by God (1 Cor. 3:6), so also the initiative for his preaching comes entirely from God. Paul may resonate more with Amos's declaration:

> The lion has roared;
>   who will not fear?
> The Lord GOD has spoken;
>   who can but prophesy? (Amos 3:8 NRSV)

The second theme that the word ἀνάγκη (constraint) evokes is that of slavery, so that Paul paradoxically shifts from his opening gambit about being free (9:1).[4] He is free (9:1), but he is not free not to preach. He establishes his right to receive support as an apostle as one who was free in 9:1–15 but switches to the language of slavery in 9:16–17—ἑκών (*hekōn*, exercising free will), ἄκων (*akōn*, not exercising free will), οἰκονομίαν πεπίστευμαι (*oikonomian pepisteumai*, entrusted with the responsibility for household management)—to explain his refusal to exercise his right. He pictures himself under the yoke of slavery as one who has no rights and cannot do as he wishes (P. Marshall

3. Paul uses the same noun, ἀνάγκη, for the affliction he experiences (cf. 2 Cor. 6:4; 12:10). Kreuzer's (1985) contention that this word is a "foreign body" in Paul ignores that it (or its cognate adjective and verb) occurs often in his letters (Rom. 13:5; 1 Cor. 7:26, 37; 9:16; 12:22; 2 Cor. 9:5, 7; Gal. 2:14; 6:12; Phil. 1:24; 2:25; 1 Thess. 3:7; Philem. 14).

4. See Schreckenberg 1964: 1–54. Other slavery/constraint imagery appears in 6:20 and 7:23 (bought with a price), 2 Cor. 2:14–17 (led as a captive in God's triumph), and Phil. 3:12 (captured by Christ).

1987: 174, 292–306; D. Martin 1990: 71–74; R. Collins 1999: 345).[5] As God's slave, Paul ultimately sets himself free from others (7:22–23). Some are compelled to speak because of their need for money, which in turn means that they are compelled to preach only to those who can pay. By refusing fees, Paul was able to exercise freedom to preach to one and all.

Paul continues the slavery imagery. If he had made the choice for himself to preach from some personal ambition, he could expect payment (μισθός, *misthos*, reward, in the sense of payment for work done; cf. 3:8, 14; Rom. 4:4; 1 Tim. 5:17–18). Preaching, however, is not his choice.[6] He is not a mercenary who contracted himself out to serve God; he is Christ's prisoner and slave (cf. 2 Cor. 2:14–17) and is not to be paid for fulfilling his charge to proclaim the gospel. The conclusion to Jesus' parable of the slave in Luke 17:7–10 captures the idea: "So you also, when you have done all that you were ordered to do, say, 'We are worthless slaves; we have done only what we ought to have done!'" (NRSV). This slavery imagery also explains why Paul has a boast. He does not boast in what he is doing of his own accord as he heroically answers God's call but in what, by God's grace, he is constrained to do (P. Gardner 1994: 92). The impetus to preach does not come from himself but from the nature of the gospel as good news for all humanity.

9:17

The problem with the slavery imagery is that it might give the impression that Paul carried out his ministry only reluctantly. It might also hint at some grievance. Nothing could be further from the truth. He is talking not about his feelings concerning his calling (Héring 1962: 80) but about his status. He chooses not to receive fees from those to whom he preaches because he understands himself to be

---

5. Philo's (*Good Free* 9 §§60–61) observation that the good man is always free contains parallels in vocabulary that are instructive. The good man "cannot be compelled to do anything or prevented from doing anything, cannot be a slave. . . . Further, if one is compelled [ἀναγκάζεται, *anankazetai*] he clearly acts against his will [ἄκων, *akōn*]. . . . He does nothing unwillingly [ἄκων] and is never compelled [ἀναγκάζεται], whereas if he were a slave he would be compelled." Note also *Good Free* 3 §§21–22, the free man "obeys no orders and works no will but [his] own." D. Martin (1990: 82) points out that Paul's slavery imagery "overturns the clear categories of his contemporary readers, who assume that leaders are free, exercise authority, and do not work, whereas lower-status persons do work." In doing this, he turns "normal status indicators" upside down, as he has done throughout the letter.

6. P. Gardner (1994: 92) claims that ἑκών should not be translated "voluntarily" since Paul contrasts doing something as God's will with doing it as human will. He claims that Paul poses this contrast: preaching ἑκών, that is "intentionally"—from within himself— or preaching ἄκων, that is "under God's compulsion" (ἀνάγκη). Philo (*Unchang.* 10 §47) proposes, "Man, possessed of a spontaneous and self-determined will, whose activities for the most part rest on deliberate choice, is with reason blamed for what he does wrong with intent, praised when he acts rightly of his own will [ἑκών]."

under a commission (οἰκονομία, *oikonomia*) as Christ's slave.[7] The connection between (οἰκονομία) and slavery is clear from 4:1: "Regard us in this way, as servants [ὑπηρέτας, *hypēretas*] of Christ and stewards [οἰκονόμους, *oikonomous*] of God's mysteries."[8] Since the slave's status was embedded in that of the master, Paul has high status, particularly as a managerial slave. But his point is that stewards work to bring gain to their master, not to themselves (cf. Matt. 25:14–30). The analogy is as follows: "The royal officer or estate steward who has a commission does not get wages from the people he manages, or from the fields and laborers he supervises, but from the ruler or master he serves" (R. Horsley 1997: 130). Paul cannot receive a "reward" from the Corinthians, who are the field in which he plants. It can come only from the owner of the field, who commissioned him to plant.

9:18   What are the wages of the one commissioned? To do the work for free! Paul's reward is that he preaches freely a free gospel that sets persons free.[9] By not exercising his rightful claim to receive fees, he does nothing to hinder anyone from accepting the gospel (9:12). He is not talking about an inner satisfaction from meeting some lofty standard of "unselfish renunciation" (Fee 1987: 421 n. 42; contra Weiss 1910: 239; Preisker, *TDNT* 4:699; Grosheide 1953: 211). Nor is Paul talking about doing something extraordinary, voluntarily renouncing his rights, to accrue special merit. He is not saying that he goes over and above God's commandments and in doing so earns himself an extra bonus (see Käsemann 1969: 220–25). His reward is serving a gospel that liberates persons to serve their neighbors and moves them to love because they have been loved (Käsemann 1969: 234). This concept was fundamentally foreign to the cultural values of a place like Corinth.

---

    7. Paul is talking not about ministry in general in 9:17 (contra Witherington 1995: 211 n. 38) but about his own calling as an apostle.

    8. D. Martin (1990: 74) notes that the term οἰκονομία does not inherently imply slave status. Its primary meaning has to do "with the management of a household and, by extension, the management of business, cities, states, and governments." But D. Martin contends that in the early Roman imperial period the word "steward" "almost always points to someone of servile status." Philo (*Good Free* 6 §§35–36) offers an instructive parallel that overseers (ἐπίτροποι, *epitropoi*) may have supervision of houses, landed estates, and great properties, and may lend, purchase, collect revenues, and be much courted, but nevertheless remain slaves.

    9. P. Gardner (1994: 94) lists four reasons why "reward" should be understood "eschatologically": (1) the word "woe" has strong eschatological overtones; (2) in 3:8, 14, the word has an eschatological reward in view; (3) 3:8, 14 are the only places where the word has a metaphorical meaning in Paul, and it is likely that it retains that meaning here; and (4) in 9:24–27, Paul has in view an eschatological prize (see also Nasuti 1988: 260). Schrage (1995: 325–26) argues against this view.

The translation of καταχρήσασθαι (*katachrēsasthai*) as "to take full advantage of" assumes that the preposition κατά (*kata*) intensifies the verb χρῆσθαι (*chrēsthai*), used in 9:12 and 9:15, "to avail (oneself) of." He does not "make full use of" these rights. Fee (1987: 421) argues that the context gives the verb a negative connotation of "abuse" or "misuse." Paul's point would be that he "offers the gospel 'free of charge'; so that he will not 'misuse his authority (*exousia*) in the gospel' by 'making use of his right (*exousia*) to live by the gospel' (vv. 12b and 14)" (see also R. Horsley 1997: 130). The verb does not have this negative meaning in 7:31, however. The two verbs χρῆσθαι and καταχρῆσθαι may differ little in meaning (BDAG 530; cf. 7:31), but the Corinthians may know that Paul receives support from churches elsewhere to help him expand his mission field into new territory (2 Cor. 11:8–9; Phil. 4:15). He may be making a fine distinction that he never receives help from the people where he is preaching the gospel but does accept help from those who wish to support him when he leaves their district (see Garland 1999: 98, 475–76).

In 9:19–22, Paul affirms how he does all things for the sake of the gospel and for the purpose of gaining converts. It includes three key assertions: "Though I am free from all, I have enslaved myself to all" (9:19; cf. 9:1). "I myself am not under the law" (9:20; Rom. 7:4–6, 10:4), but he can submit to its precepts to win those who are under the law. "I am not without the law of God but under the law of Christ" (1 Cor. 9:21). The law does not determine his relationship to God, but he has not abandoned obedience to God. What drives all of his life is the goal of winning others to Christ. His comments fall into a chiastic arrangement:

    A I made myself a slave to all in order that I might gain more (v. 19).

        B I became to the Jews as a Jew, in order that I might gain Jews (v. 20a).

            C To those under the law as [one] under the law . . . to gain those under the law (v. 20b).

            C′ To those outside the law as [one] outside the law . . . to gain those outside the law (v. 21).

        B′ I became to the weak weak in order that I might gain the weak (v. 22a).

    A′ I have become all things to all persons in order that I might in all circumstances save some of them (v. 22b).

The theme of being free (ἐλεύθερος, *eleutheros*) takes up the question in 9:1, "Am I not free?" The γάρ (*gar; for* though I am free) relates back to the statement in 9:15, "But I have not availed myself of any of these [rights]."[10] Paul deals with the two questions raised in 9:1 in reverse order: "Am I not free?" in 9:15–23; "Am I not an apostle?" in 9:1–14. He first establishes his rights as an apostle to receive support before reviewing his refusal to make use of his rights. He gets sidetracked from his main assertion in 9:15, "But I have not availed myself of any of these [rights]," which begins this second segment of his argument with a concern that the battery of proofs in 9:7–14 might give the false impression that he was now soliciting their financial support. His discursive disclaimer in 9:15b–18 may be summarized in this way: "I do not write this to request your support—*for* I would rather die [than live off the gospel] and empty my boast, *for* necessity is laid upon me to preach, *for* woe is me if I do not preach, *for* I am entrusted with a stewardship and my reward comes from preaching the gospel without cost to those who receive it." In 9:19, Paul returns to the theme of freedom that he wants to expound on in this segment.

He does not avail himself of his rights as an apostle to receive support from the community where he is preaching because he chooses to enslave himself to all persons in order to gain them. He exchanges his position as a free man with high status for that of a slave (D. Martin 1990: 125). Slavery to Christ necessitates slavery to all (cf. 2 Cor. 4:5; Mark 10:42–45). Hock (1978: 558–61) interprets the phrase ἐμαυτὸν ἐδούλωσα (*emauton edoulōsa*, I enslaved myself) to refer to plying his trade, which, in the eyes of those who regarded working at a trade as slavish, betrayed his social class. This intentional self-lowering to become a manual laborer, however, was designed to make his appeal to those of low status more effective (D. Martin 1990: 139).

Two things can be noted from this assertion. First, Willis (1985a: 37) registers how "Paul takes a key dogma for Stoicism—the free man is one who does as he wishes without regard for the opinions of others—and reverses it in a paradoxical manner" (cf. Epictetus, *Diatr.* 3.24.70). Making himself a slave to all, frees him from all.[11] He need not kowtow to anyone or become their toady (cf. 7:23).

Second, the slavery imagery (steward, slave) upends the idea of the minister "as a patriarchal overlord or master" (Witherington 1995: 211). With Christ as the one Lord (8:6), there is no room for other lords.

10. Contra Fee (1987: 425 n. 18), who thinks that it connects back to 9:18: "What pay can one like myself, who did not choose this position as God's household manager, expect? Only this: that I can make the gospel 'free of charge' to all so that I not misuse my rights in the gospel. *For* being thereby free from all people [in not accepting 'pay'], I can more freely become everyone's 'slave,' so that I might 'gain' the more."

11. Being free ἐκ πάντων (*ek pantōn*) could be taken as a neuter, "from all things," instead of as a masculine, "from all men." Schrage (1995: 337) thinks it possible that the Greek reader might have thought of both and that Paul would also express his freedom from "privileges and advantages, claims to rights and dependence on others, opinions and conventions, etc."

His identity as a slave is "in harmony with the fact that his office is determined by the cross" (Conzelmann 1975: 160). D. Martin (1990: 125) argues that Paul's rhetoric "rejects the benevolent patriarchal model of aristocratic leadership" and undermines the normal status hierarchy that governed this ancient society (cf. 7:22). Paul does not lead from a secure position above others but from a position below them, incarnating the folly of the cross.

The verb κερδαίνειν (*kerdainein,* to win, to gain) appears five times in verses 19–21. It is related to conversion (1 Pet. 3:1) but can apply to winning a faltering believer (Matt. 18:15).[12] The word is also a business term related to profit (Matt. 25:16, 17, 20, 22; James 4:13), and Paul may be playing on this idea in light of his previous comment about his reward in 1 Cor. 9:17–18. The profit that he gains, his μισθός (*misthos*), comes from spreading the gospel among Jews and Gentiles. Daube (1956: 349) observes that from contexts where κερδαίνειν is used in the NT for conversion, "they all represent humility as an instrument of conversion." Courtesy toward those one hopes to win is crucial for success.

All the members of the Corinthian congregation at one time fell into one of the categories that Paul lists: the Jews, those under the law, those without the law, the weak. Seeking to gain Jews (cf. Rom. 9:1–3; 11:14) indicates that Paul did not understand the agreement outlined in Gal. 2:9 to mean that James, Cephas, and John were to go to the circumcised and he only to the Gentiles. It is surprising, however, for Paul to say that his relations with Jews reflect some kind of concession. He later will remind the Corinthians that he too is a Hebrew, an Israelite, and a descendant of Abraham (2 Cor. 11:22; cf. Rom. 9:3; Gal. 2:15; Phil. 3:5). How can he be "as a Jew"? Paul may have added the description "those under the law" to clarify for the puzzled reader what he meant by "as a Jew" (Hooker 1996: 84–85) rather than to distinguish between ethnic Jews and Gentile proselytes who came under the law (contra Robertson and Plummer 1914: 191). But what does "as a Jew" mean?

Chrysostom (*Hom. 1 Cor.* 22.5) set the tone for interpreting this passage by stating, "Paul did not become a Jew in reality but only in appearance. How could it have been otherwise, since he was so determined to convert them and deliver them from their predicament?" Many since have adopted a similar view. Barrett (1968: 211) contends that Paul's "Judaism was no longer of his very being, but a guise he could adopt or discard at will." His camouflage Judaism is assumed to have involved occasionally adopting Jewish practices, such as the accounts in Acts when he had Timothy circumcised "because of the Jews" (Acts 16:3), made a Nazirite vow (Acts 18:18), and joined four other Nazirites in

9:20

---

12. Daube (1956: 352–61) claims that the term is determined by rabbinic vocabulary for winning over a proselyte or winning back a lapsed sinner, but the evidence is sketchy.

their purification rites and paid their expenses for the sacrificial offering (Acts 21:21–26). But Paul does not mean that he occasionally obeyed Jewish customs to decoy Jews into listening to his message.

The clearest example of what Paul means by becoming "as a Jew" and as "one under the law" is his description of the thirty-nine lashes he suffered at the hands of the Jews (2 Cor. 11:24). We can only guess that the synagogue inflicted this punishment for Paul's proclaiming his faith in the crucified and risen Christ, which they presumably considered blasphemous, and his altered understanding of the hope of Israel that now included uncircumcised Gentiles in the people of God (see Garland 1999: 496–97; Kruse 1992: 260–72). Paul's motives for submitting to this discipline are a little more difficult to penetrate, but rulings from the Mishnah may help. The Mishnah lists thirty-six sins, including blasphemy, that warrant being cut off from the people without warning (*m. Ker.* 1:1). What is important to note, however, is that flogging averted both a harsher punishment at the hands of God and being cut off from the people (Lev. 18:29). The Mishnah rules, "*And thy brother seem vile unto thee* [Deut. 25:3]—when he is scourged then he is thy brother" (*m. Mak.* 3:15). This axiom clarifies what it means for Paul to become like one under the law (though he himself is not under the law). He bowed to synagogue discipline to maintain his Jewish connections (Harvey 1985: 93). Jews were given special privileges to settle their disputes in their own courts. If one wanted to stay a member of the Jewish community, one had to submit to its discipline (Harvey 1985: 80–81). Paul accepted these penalties to keep open the option of preaching the gospel message in the synagogue. For Paul to submit to this punishment *five times* testifies not only to his mettle but also to his extraordinary sense of obligation to his people. They are his kindred, for whom he has great sorrow and unceasing anguish and could wish that he were accursed and cut off from Christ if it meant their being saved (Rom. 9:2–4). His identification with Christ so controls his spirit that he would cut himself off from Christ, if he could, to save his people.

The "stripes" also may have reminded him of being under the curse of the law. If the mishnaic procedures were applicable in the first century, they stipulated that during the scourging someone read repeatedly the curse from Deut. 28:58–68: "If you do not diligently observe all the words of this law that are written in this book, fearing this glorious and awesome name, the LORD your God, then the LORD will overwhelm both you and your offspring with severe and lasting afflictions and grievous and lasting maladies" (NRSV). Coming under the law means coming under its curse. "To be under the law" means to be judged by the law (Rom. 2:12), to be under divine wrath as a violator of the law (Rom. 4:15), and under a curse (Gal. 3:10). Paul was willing to endure that judgment and punishment to win Jews. But he was not under the law when it came to relying on it as his boast before God (Rom. 2:17), being justified by it (Rom. 3:28; Gal. 2:21; 3:11), being under the power of sin (1 Cor. 15:56), or being cut off from Christ (Gal. 5:4). Robertson and Plummer (1914: 191) comment that this "parenthesis is remarkable as showing how completely St Paul had broken with Judaism." This statement is correct only if one understands "Judaism" to refer to a particular interpretation of the law. Paul understood himself to be a part of Israel but knew that in Christ there is neither Jew nor Greek (1 Cor. 12:13; Gal. 3:28; Col. 3:11).

"Those outside the law" (οἱ ἄνομοι, *hoi anomoi*) refers to Gentiles, who   **9:21** do not possess the law (Rom. 2:14; see also Wis. 17:2; 3 Macc. 6:9).[13] As the apostle to the Gentiles (Rom. 11:13; Gal. 1:16; Eph. 3:8), Paul has this task of gaining those outside the law as his fundamental calling. Conzelmann (1975: 161 n. 25) thinks that he avoids the term "the Greeks" here, as in the phrases "to the Jew first and also to the Greek" (Rom. 1:16; 2:9–10) and "neither Jew nor Greek" (Gal. 3:28; Col. 3:11; cf. Rom. 10:12), because that term might mistakenly convey the unsavory aspects of Greek life. He did not become "Greek"—that is, hedonistic in his lifestyle. On the other hand, he may have wanted simply to create a verbal parallel with "those under the law."

How did Paul become without the law? He is not simply talking about forsaking distinctively Jewish practices such as Jewish food laws or Sabbath celebrations or, as Robertson and Plummer (1914: 192) put it, behaving as a heathen to heathen.[14] The principle "When in Rome, do as the Romans do" did not regulate his actions.[15] Nor is he talking about his presentation of the gospel, using arguments that would be more persuasive in the Gentile world. Instead, he is speaking theologically about living under grace. Previously, his self-understanding as a Jew was bound up with his obedience to the law (cf. Phil. 3:6); now it is bound up with his relationship to Christ (Phil. 3:7–11). What he means by this statement is elucidated in Gal. 4:12: "Brethren, I beseech you, become as I am, because I also have become as you are." In what way did Paul become like the Galatians? He did not become a pagan sinner, but he did give up his zeal for the tradition of the fathers and

13. The term also was applied to lapsed Jews in 1 Macc. 7:5; 9:23, 58, 69; 11:25; 14:14.

14. E. Sanders (1983: 186–87) suggests that Paul is using hyperbole. He did not switch back and forth as he scurried between the two separate groups but basically lived like a Gentile wherever he went.

15. Paul would not refuse a meal offered to him by those he was trying to reach (Oropeza 1998: 57 n. 4), but he definitely would refuse food that had any manifest associations with idolatry. How else could he direct potential converts to renounce idolatry entirely? The potential awkwardness that this policy would create offers another reason why he refused support from those among whom he was ministering and why he always tried to make contact first with fellow Jews so as to avoid such situations.

righteousness earned under the law so that he might live under the grace of God (Gal. 1:13–16). In effect, he became like a Gentile, as one without heritage, without the merit of the fathers, without works of law to set him apart from others or to justify his salvation. Paul lived among the Galatians simply as a Christian, not as a Jew or a Pharisee of Pharisees (see Betz 1979: 223). He did this because God revealed to him that everything "depends on faith, in order that the promise may rest on grace and be guaranteed to all his descendants, not only to the adherents of the law but also to those who share the faith of Abraham" (Rom. 4:16; cf. Gal. 2:16).

Paul makes another clarification, as he did in the previous verse, this time using a play on words: "not being outside the law in relation to God" (μὴ ὢν ἄνομος θεοῦ, *mē ōn anomos theou*) but "inside the law of Christ" (ἔννομος Χριστοῦ, *ennomos Christou*), a phrase that appears only here in his letters. Not being under the law does not mean that he ignores the law of God (see 1 Cor. 7:19). His gospel was not lawless, and with some exasperation he declares in Rom. 3:8 that the (divine) condemnation of those who defame his gospel as encouraging sin and lawlessness will be deserved.

Paul refers to "the law of Christ" in Rom. 8:2 and Gal. 6:2. It is neither the Mosaic law code revamped and promulgated by the Messiah (contra W. Davies 1963: 109–90) nor the specific precepts given by Christ to his disciples (e.g., 1 Cor. 7:10; 9:14; contra C. Dodd 1968: 137). He may understand it to be the law "redefined and fulfilled by Christ in love" (Barclay 1988: 134). In Gal. 6:2, it is simply to bear one another's burdens. Here, it may refer to the "norm" or "principle" of Christ (Hays 1987: 276).[16] Carson (1986: 12) asserts that Paul is not simply bound by "certain teachings of Jesus but by all that Christ accomplished and represents." It could denote Christ's pattern of sacrificial living for others that has become Paul's norm (Conzelmann 1975: 161; Carson 1986: 15; Schrage 1995: 345; Hays 1997: 154). This principle is embodied in the statement in 1 Cor. 10:24: "Do not seek your own advantage, but that of the other" (cf. 11:1; Rom. 15:3–4; 2 Cor. 4:10–12; Gal. 2:19–20; Phil. 2:5–8; 3:10–11). The law of Christ compels his preaching and engenders his desire to make himself a slave to all so that he lives after the pattern of the one who gave his life as a ransom for the many (Mark 10:43–45).

9:22   In the next clause Paul breaks the pattern—"I became to the Jews *as* a Jew," "to those under the law *as* under the law," "to those outside the law *as* outside the law"—by omitting the ὡς (*hōs*): "I became to the weak weak" (ἐγενόμην τοῖς ἀσθενέσιν ἀσθενής, *egenomēn tois asthenesin asthenēs*). It is unlikely that this omission is due simply to stylistic

---

16. Räisänen (1983: 82) identifies the "law of Christ" as "the way of life characteristic of the church of Christ." Hofius (1983: 281) thinks it refers to subjection to Christ.

variation (Conzelmann 1975: 161 n. 28; Fee 1987: 431; P. Gardner 1994: 103–4; Hays 1997: 154). Paul deemed the "as" to be inappropriate. He actually became weak.[17] But what does he mean by "weak"?

Many contend that "the weak" refers to Christians who are "weak in faith" (Rom. 14:1), whom Paul tries to win to a fuller knowledge of the faith or to prevent from falling away from Christ (1 Cor. 8:10–11).[18] The verb κερδαίνειν (*kerdainein*) applies to conversion and entry into the community, but, it is argued, it also can refer to "the continuing process of winning people from inadequate ideas to a deeper Christian consciousness" (P. Gardner 1994: 99). In 10:31–33, Paul states his aim to seek the benefit of the many in order that they might be saved, and he lists three groups: Jews, Greeks, and the church of God (10:32). If the "weak" refers to Christians, the order in 9:20–22 would match that in 10:33: Jews, those without the law, and the weak (Edwards 1885: 239; P. Gardner 1994: 99). This interpretation appears to make sense in the larger context if the problem over idol food is delineated as a conflict between the strong and the weak. Paul would sacrifice his own convictions and rights to identify with weak Christians who require gentle handling to avoid sabotaging their wispy thin faith. The immediate context and the fact that Paul did not write "I became to the weak *as* weak" but "I became to the weak *weak*" argues against the view that "the weak" are Christians whose faith needs strengthening. This view mistakenly assumes that this reference mirrors the conjectured conflict between the strong and the weak in Corinth and mistakenly reads the discussion about the weak in Rom. 14:1–15:13 into this situation. In the three previous examples, the verb κερδαίνειν is used for winning non-Christians and is synonymous with "conversion." How does one "win" those who are weak in faith in the same sense that one wins Jews, those under the law and those without the law? The phrases "because of the gospel" and "becoming its partner" in 1 Cor. 9:23 suggest that Paul has in view the gospel's spread through the world. Moffatt (1938: 121) com-

17. Paul does not say that he became like the so-called strong. D. Martin (1990: 122–23) explains it this way: in 9:1–23, Paul balances a claim to high status as an apostle with self-abasement in service of others and directs his example to high-status readers (4:8–10) in hopes that they will follow it. He does not include the strong in his list of 9:19–23 because "he is directing this instruction primarily to *them*." D. Martin concludes (1990: 128) that Paul is not simply coaxing high-status persons to care for those of low status but offering his own social self-lowering as a model for them to imitate. D. Martin's view wrongly assumes that these chapters reflect a conflict between the strong and weak. Paul omits saying that he became "strong" to the "strong" because that category is an invention of scholars that is entirely foreign to the situation.

18. So Godet 1887: 39; Robertson and Plummer 1914: 192; Lietzmann 1949: 43; Barrett 1968: 215; Carson 1986: 14; Neller 1987: 136–38; P. Gardner 1994: 99; Schrage 1995: 346–47; Hays 1997: 155. Kistemaker (1993: 309) thinks that it contains "a double connotation that refers to both the weak in conscience and the economically weak."

pletely misreads Paul in commenting, "It was a struggle to adapt oneself to weaklings." Paul does not say that he adapted to them; he says, "I became weak," and does not add a qualifier, "though I myself am not weak." The "weak" in this verse represent non-Christians whom he seeks to win for the Lord (D. Black 1983).

How did Paul become weak? The term "weak" can have a social connotation as a class marker (1:27). D. Martin (1990: 123–24) takes it to mean that Paul purposely lowered himself socially by identifying with manual laborers to gain those of lower status. But "weak" may also allude to the theological condition of all humankind as ungodly—a condition that Paul discovered also included overachieving, righteous Jews: "For while we were still weak, at the right time Christ died for the ungodly" (Rom. 5:6). The gospel is the story of the Son of God taking on weakness for the sake of humankind, and Paul asserts that he follows this same divine paradigm (2 Cor. 13:4; cf. 2 Cor. 8:9; 6:10). This is why he boasts in his weakness (2 Cor. 11:30; 12:5, 9–10; 13:9), because God's power is made perfect in weakness and is more effective in winning others to the gospel of Christ's cross.

The translation "I became all things to all persons" may be misread to imply that "Paul has become everything at once to everything in turn" (Hooker 1996: 83), but he is talking only about the groups he has just mentioned. To the whole lot of them (Barrett 1968: 215), he became these different things (using a play on words: πᾶσιν . . . πάντα . . . πάντως, *pasin . . . panta . . . pantōs*). This approach, however, would seem to suggest some kind of duplicity on Paul's part and confirm a charge that he seeks human approval (Gal. 1:10). Petronius (*Satyr.* 3) lampoons the chameleon-like performance of the rhetorician who adapts himself to whatever he thinks might gain a hearing: "Like mock toadies . . . cadging after the rich man's dinners, they think first about what is calculated to please their audience." Did Paul adopt the pose of a flatterer who masquerades as something that he is not in order to ingratiate himself with potential converts? P. Richardson (1979–80: 356), for example, claims that Paul adjusted his conduct in opportunistic ways to the taste of his hearers if it helped to win some. He castigated Cephas as a hypocrite, however, for employing similar expediency in withdrawing from eating with Gentiles to avoid offending the circumcision faction (Gal. 2:11–14). Is Paul any less unprincipled?

The allegation that Paul was guilty of inconsistency is unjustified. He rebuked Cephas for acting out of fear and wilting under external pressure from the men from James. Cephas did not separate himself from the Gentiles "in order to save some of them," nor did the principle "because of the gospel" govern his actions, at least as Paul described the situation (Gal. 2:11–14). Instead, Cephas and the others went *against* the truth of the gospel (Gal. 2:14, οὐκ ὀρθοποδοῦσιν πρός, *ouk ortho-*

podousin pros). Furthermore, Paul neither outlines his mission strategy in this section (Richardson and Gooch 1978: 97; Willis 1985a: 37; Carson 1986) nor advocates an accommodation principle for mission. Carson (1986: 15) correctly reads Paul's purpose: he is "explaining how in his apostleship the principle of self-abnegation, the principle of servanthood—in short, the principle of the cross—operates in his own experience." Augustine (*Letter to Jerome* 40.4) describes such an approach as "thinking sympathetically." He writes, "A person who nurses a sick man becomes, in a sense, sick himself, not by pretending to have a fever but by thinking sympathetically how he would wish to be treated if he were sick himself."

If this reading is correct, then we can dismiss the view that some in Corinth have accused Paul of being too "wishy washy" (Moffatt 1938: 123; P. Marshall 1987: 309–17; Fee 1987: 424). It is possible that these words came back "to haunt him as his relationship with Corinth continued to deteriorate" (Willis 1985a: 37), but he is not defending himself against charges of inconsistency or a lack of integrity. Nor is he defending himself against some complaint that he himself had eaten idol food bought from a marketplace as part of his accommodation strategy to avoid antagonizing potential converts (contra Fee 1987: 393, 394 n. 11). Robertson and Plummer (1914: 193) are wrong to contend that Paul's "accommodation has no limit excepting the one just stated, he is ἔννομος Χριστοῦ [*ennomos Christou*]."

Carson (1986: 33) justly cautions that this is not granting "a licence for unlimited flexibility." Paul is flexible (Bornkamm 1966: 197), but he is "not infinitely elastic" (Carson 1986: 10–11). He does not think that fundamental and distinctive Christian demands are negotiable, depending on the circumstances. He did not eat idol food in order to become "as one without the law to those without the law." He did not tone down his assault on idolatry to avoid offending idolaters or to curry favor with them. His accommodation has nothing to do with watering down the gospel message, soft-pedaling its ethical demands, or compromising its absolute monotheism. Paul never modified the message of Christ crucified to make it less of a scandal to Jews or less foolish to Greeks. The preacher of the changeless gospel could adapt himself, however, to changing audiences in seeking their ultimate welfare, their salvation. Through his mediation of the gospel he seeks their transformation (Barton 1996: 284).

The word "interchange" is more apt than the word "accommodation" for characterizing the approach that Paul describes in these verses. Five times he says that he became what others were to win them for the gospel—that is, "As far as possible he has deliberately identified himself with those whom he has sought to win for the Gospel" (Hooker 1996: 85). This parallels what he declares that Christ did on behalf of others (Rom. 8:3–4; 2 Cor. 5:21; 8:9; Gal. 3:13; 4:4–5; Phil. 2:6–8; Col. 1:24–25). Hooker (1996: 91–92) underscores the parallel:

> Christ became what we are, he was made what we are, he was sent into our condition, *in order that* we might become what he is. Paul, in turn, became what the men and women to whom he was proclaiming the Gospel were, in order that he might gain them for the Gospel. And just as some of the statements about what Christ became needed modification— he became sin, *though he knew no sin,* and he came *in the likeness of* sinful flesh, where the word "likeness" prevents us thinking of him as sinful—so too, in the case of Paul. He came under the law, *even though he was not under the law;* he became as one without law, *even though he was not without God's law.*

The principle that Paul outlines in 9:19–23 is that he *"shares the condition of those to whom he ministers,* and so is conformed to the pattern of his Lord" (Hooker 1996: 97; cf. Garland 1999: 231–34).[19] He imitates Christ's self-emptying humiliation and suffering for others.[20]

9:23   Paul claims to do all things because of the gospel. The phrase "in order that I might become its partner" (ἵνα συγκοινωνὸς αὐτοῦ γένωμαι, *hina synkoinōnos autou genōmai*) could mean that his goal is to be a recipient of the gospel's benefits (cf. Rom. 11:17; Phil. 1:7), so that the partnership is understood in a passive sense (NIV; NRSV; NASB; Robertson and Plummer 1914: 193; Barrett 1968: 216; Kistemaker 1993: 10; Schrage 1995: 348). Against this view, one can argue that it introduces an entirely new idea at the conclusion of his argument (1 Cor. 9:1–23). Hooker (1996: 85) puts it this way: "Is it not strange that the climax of the argument should prove to be a statement that what seemed like selfless activity undertaken to win men and women for the Gospel should have as its ultimate aim his own personal salvation?" The theological implication of the ἵνα (*hina,* in order that) would be that he needs to save others if he himself is to be saved. D. Martin (1990: 132) argues that Paul "plays on the soteriological meanings of metaphorical slavery by showing that his own self-lowering will bring not only the salvation of his converts but his own eschatological salvation as well (9:23, 27)." But D. Martin forgets this point in commenting, more accurately, "Causing another person to stumble is, therefore, equivalent to placing a hindrance against the gospel itself (1 Cor. 9:12). Conversely, to aid in

---

19. The word πάντως (*pantōs*) is best interpreted as referring to the differing contexts ("in all circumstances") that Paul finds himself in while trying to reach the various groups, rather than as referring to the various means ("by all means," NRSV) he employs (Schrage 1995: 348).

20. M. Mitchell (2001) shows how Clement of Alexandria, Origen, and John Chrysostom all regard Paul's self-characterization as an example of "condescension" following the divine pattern of condescension to humans.

the salvation of another is to become a partner in the gospel (1 Cor. 9:23)."

A better option, then, is to interpret this partnership in an active sense. Paul wants to participate "in the work of the gospel" (Hooker 1996: 89; Gundry Volf 1990: 248–51). He portrays himself as a partner with the gospel in the common enterprise of winning others (9:22; cf. 2 Cor. 8:23; Phil. 1:5; Philem. 17). The NEB renders it, "All this I do for the sake of the Gospel, to bear my part in proclaiming it." The noun "gospel" (τὸ εὐαγγέλιον, *to euangelion*) without a verb denotes the preaching of the gospel (Rom. 1:1; 1 Cor. 9:14; 2 Cor. 2:12; 10:14; Gal. 2:7; Phil. 2:22; 4:15; see Hooker 1996: 87). This interpretation has ramifications for the meaning of 1 Cor. 10:18, 20. Becoming "partners with demons" means that participants join in common enterprise with the work of demons. They are not just passive participants in a pagan ritual; they contribute to spreading demonic thralldom in the world.

Additional Notes

9:15. The Majority text replaces οὐδεὶς κενώσει with ἵνα τις κενώσῃ ("I would rather die than that anyone should make this boast of mine an empty thing"). This reflects an attempt to smooth the rough syntax that reflects the intensity of Paul's feelings about this matter. Οὐδεὶς κενώσει has wide geographic representation ($\mathfrak{P}^{46}$, ℵ*, B, D*, 33, 1739, 1881, it[d, e], syr[p], arm) and is the harder reading.

9:20. Some witnesses omit the phrase μὴ ὢν αὐτὸς ὑπὸ νόμον (D[c], K, Ψ, 81, 88, 326, 330, 451, 614, 629[c], 1241, 1881, 1984, 1985, 2492, Byz, Lect, syr[p], eth, Origen, Chrysostom). Its inclusion is supported by $\mathfrak{P}^{46?}$, ℵ, A, B, C, D*, G, P, 33, 104, 181, 436, 630, 1739, 1877, 2127, 2495, it[ar, d, dem, e, f, g, x, z], vg, syr[h], cop[sa, bo], goth, arm. The four ὑπὸ νόμον phrases in a row might have led to one being accidentally omitted by a copyist.

9:22. The majority text includes ὡς before the term "weak," but it is absent in $\mathfrak{P}^{46}$, ℵ*, A, B, 1739. Scribes may have introduced it to make it parallel to "as a Jew," "as under the law," and "as without the law" in the previous clauses and perhaps to avoid the shameful insinuation that Paul was weak.

3. Paul's Self-Discipline: An Example from the World of Athletics (9:24–27)

In 9:24–27, Paul advances another example (Schrage 1995: 361–62) to undergird his admonition about idol food: the athlete's self-restraint and abstinence to win a prize and to procure honor and acclaim.[1] Living the Christian life also requires effort and the suppression of appetites and longings. This sports analogy does multiduty in clarifying three issues. First, it plays on the Corinthians' craving for honor and allows Paul to contrast the ephemeral honor bestowed on the winner of an athletic contest with the eternal prize that God will award the Christian victor in the contest against sin. Second, the prolonged, rigorous training required for success in athletic competition was a well-known image in the ancient world, and it sheds light on Paul's own voluntary restraint in his refusing to exercise his apostolic rights so that he might successfully attain his goal of saving others. Third, it warns that any who fail to exercise self-restraint when it comes to the delights of this world may be disqualified from the ultimate race directed by God. It is more than a general warning against complacency, however. It reminds Corinthians of the difficulties of living out their Christian commitment. Entry into the contest does not guarantee a prize (Yinger 1999: 252), and they cannot repose in the illusion that they are safe from failure. The athletic simile serves as a transition to the warning example of Israel in the next section (10:1–13).

In 10:23, Paul cites the catchphrase "Everything is permitted" (6:12), but in 9:24–27, he first emphasizes that everything is *not* permitted the athlete who hopes to win. Christian life "involves the limitation as well as the enjoyment of freedom" (Barrett 1968: 218). The metaphorical language may cloak how it applies to the Corinthian situation. However, it is all part of his argument that "believers should abstain from sacrificial meals" (Smit 1997b: 490). The images of an athletic competitor enduring a rigorous training regimen, running determinedly, and bruising the body to bring it under rein disclose that Paul is not asking

---

1. Pfitzner (1967: 82) notes that the interpretation of this passage "has often suffered . . . by treating the verses as a separate unit of general Pauline paraenesis." It must be read in context, which in this case is Paul's argument against idol food. Pfitzner (1967: 97–98) mistakenly reads 9:24–27 only as a defense of Paul's apostolic actions and fails to note how it also serves as an introductory transition to 10:1–13.

the Corinthian "knowers" to try to be more discreet when they join in any festivities on an idol's grounds in order to protect the weak brother. He expects them to abandon any and all such participation. The focus of Paul's argument in chapters 8–10 is the Corinthians' lethal dalliance with idolatry. Smit (1997b: 490) captures the essence of Paul's simile in 9:24–27:

> If they do not go into strict training, in other words, if they continue their participating in sacrificial meals, their faith is lost labor—aimless running, beating the air. They are then in danger of inglorious elimination. In these verses, motivation dominates again. Fear of damage and shame should induce the Corinthians to bring their practice into line with what Paul desires.

Exegesis and Exposition

[24]Do you not know that all who compete in a race run, but only one receives the prize? Run in such a way that you might capture it. [25]Every competitor exercises self-control in all things. They do so only to receive a perishable wreath, but we do it to receive an imperishable one. [26]I, for my part, do not run like one who runs haphazardly. I do not box like one flailing away at thin air. [27]But I bruise my body and enslave it lest somehow after preaching to others I myself would be disqualified.

Paul switches to the stadium for his next illustration. He uses the met-   **9:24**
aphor of "running" (τρέχοντες, *trechontes*) for the Christian life elsewhere (Gal. 5:7; Phil. 2:16) and also speaks of the victor's prize or crown
(cf. Phil. 3:12–14; 4:1; 1 Thess. 2:19; 2 Tim. 2:5; 4:8). Conzelmann
(1975: 162 n. 31; see also Pfitzner 1967: 23–37) thinks that the metaphor of the athlete was so widespread that there is no reason to think
particularly of the nearby Isthmian games. Philo uses similes and metaphors from athletics to illumine the "contest for the winning of the virtues which are divine" (*Husb.* 26 §§114–21; cf. *Alleg. Interp.* 2.26 §108;
Spec. Laws 1.7 §38; *Sacr.* 4 §17; *Migr. Abr.* 6 §§26–27; 2.24 §§133–34)
and talks about the theological athlete (*Chang. Nam.* 12 §§81–82; *Alleg.
Interp.* 3.71 §§201–2). Epictetus even more frequently uses the metaphor of the athletic contest. The training of the philosopher is arduous,
he writes, and those who say, "I wish to win an Olympic victory," must
consider the demanding task before them: "You have to submit to discipline, follow a strict diet, give up sweet-cakes, train under compulsion, at a fixed hour, in heat or in cold; you must not drink cold water,
nor wine just whenever you feel like it" (*Diatr.* 3.15.2–4). Olympic vic-
tories do not come without sweat (*Diatr.* 1.24.1–2). After one has
trained, Epictetus (*Diatr.* 4.4.30) contends, "Now God says to you,

'Come at last to the contest and show us what you have learned and how you have trained yourself. How long will you exercise alone? Now the time has come for you to discover whether you are one of the athletes who deserve victory or belong to the number of those who travel about the world and are everywhere defeated.'"

The popular use of the image would have struck a chord because Corinth sponsored the Isthmian games (cf. 2 Clem. 7:1–6), a pan-Hellenic festival celebrated every second year and featuring many of the same contestants who competed in the Olympian, and the Isthmian games "dominated the highly competitive culture of Roman Corinth" (R. Horsley 1998: 132).[2] Greek athletic festivals were intertwined with, and owed their vigor to, religion (Gardiner 1930: 22; cf. H. Harris 1976: 13; Poliakoff 1987), and the games were a prominent occasion for celebrating the patronage of the gods. The occasion may have forced the issue of eating idol food.

The metaphor of the lone athlete straining to catch at (καταλαμβάνειν, *katalambanein*) the lone prize is not adequate as a description of the Christian life. Paul does not mean that the Christian life is a competitive sport in which one seeks to outrun others who must then endure the agony of defeat. There were no team sports in the ancient world for him to draw from as examples. Identifying the "one" who wins the prize as the whole church as one body (Origen), or as Christ Jesus who has won the prize for us and shares it with others who run like him (Nasuti 1988: 263), avoids this problem but misses the point. The crux of the argument is that simply entering a race and running does not automatically qualify one as a winner (Findlay 1910: 855; Barrett 1968: 217; Oster 1995: 224). Christians not only must join the race, but also must put forth every effort to finish it well, because the laurels go only to the victor, in this case, a multitude of victors. The οὕτως (*houtōs*, thus, in such a way) means that they are to run as if winning were not guaranteed with prizes granted to every entrant. They cannot amble nonchalantly around the track and expect some kind of trophy simply for participation. They are to run as if their life depended on it. It does.

9:25 Paul appeals to a general rule: "Every competitor in the games abstains in every way." The image of "running" suggests a continuing exertion (cf. Phil. 3:12–14, with its image of the runner straining to cross the finish line), but the key is "self-control" (ἐγκρατεύεται, *enkrateuetai*). Every reader knew that winning a race or a boxing match required of the athlete hard training (expressed in the modern motto "No pain, no gain") and self-denial, particularly when it came to diet. Pausanius (*Descr.*

---

2. R. Collins (1999: 360) points out that the highest honor in Corinth was to be named *agonothete*, "leader of the games."

9.24.9) reports that athletes and their trainers participating in the Olympic games swore an oath upon slices of boar's flesh "that in nothing will they sin against the Olympic games. The athletes take this further oath also, that for ten successive months they have strictly followed the regulations for training." The idea of the athlete's rigorous diet frequently appears in the literature. Athletes who want to win cannot conform to the world and eat the same things as those who are not preparing for the rigors of competition (Epictetus, *Diatr.* 3.15.10; Philo, *Dreams* 2.2 §9; Horace, *Ars poetica* 412–14; Xenophon, *Symposium* 8.37). Tertullian (*Ad martyras* [*To the Martyrs*] 3.3) also uses the metaphor: "Athletes are set apart for more rigid training to apply themselves to the building up of their physical strength. They are kept from lavish living, from more tempting dishes, from more pleasurable drinks. They are urged on, they are subjected to tortuous toils, they are worn out. The more strenuously they have exerted themselves, the greater is their hope of victory."

Self-control is one of the fruits of the Spirit (Gal. 5:23) and refers to "vigorous control of appetite and passion" (Findlay 1910: 856). It was touted by Socrates as the fundamental virtue (Xenophon, *Mem.* 1.5.4; Schrage 1995: 366). "In all respects" (πάντα, *panta*; cf. 1 Cor. 9:23) the athlete applies self-control to every sphere of life that might affect the outcome of the race, from diet to mastering the sexual appetite (cf. 7:9). Paul pictures an athlete going through an arduous regime requiring endurance, self-denial, and abstinence, since gluttony and sensuality can bring defeat as quickly as can a skilled opponent or the enervating heat. The House of the Figured Capitals in Pompeii, named for the two capitals flanking the entrance, presents a stark contrast to this view. The figures picture the owner, naked to the waist, and his wife at a banquet along with a drunken satyr and a maenad. The self-depiction identifies the owner with the cult of Dionysus and affirms the notion of pleasure as a central value in life (Zanker 1998: 39). Paul's intention is not to commend an ascetic lifestyle but to emphasize that every victory has its price in the effort and sacrifice put forth (Schrage 1995: 367), particularly in reining in the unruly sensual appetites for food, drink, and sexual pleasure (cf. Philo, *Alleg. Interp.* 3.53 §§155–56; *Spec. Laws* 1.29 §149; 1.35 §173). He also wants to draw an ironic contrast between the athlete's great effort and the paltry prize received for it. All this discipline wins the victorious competitor only a circlet of perishable leaves (see additional note).

Greco-Roman writers generally used athletic metaphors to exhort others about what can be attained in this life by exerting oneself and accepting the discipline of hardship. Seneca (*Ep. morales* 78.16) observes that athletes endure torturous training and blows on their faces and all over their bodies only to win fame. The Stoic's reward is "not a garland or a palm or a trumpeter who calls for silence at the proclamation of our names, but rather virtue, steadfastness of soul, and a peace that is one for all time." By contrast, Paul looks to the crown that awaits the believer in the life to come beyond this passing age (7:29–31; 10:11). Christians have joined a contest that offers an imperishable crown (1 Pet. 5:4; cf. Wis. 4:2; 4 Macc. 17:11–16).

9:26–27 Paul cites himself as an example because he wants the Corinthians to follow *his* example (11:1).[3] He does not jog uncertainly, in fits and starts, or in a meandering fashion. He runs straight toward the goal (Phil. 3:14). He is not a shadow boxer who throws punches at the air in preparation for the real battle or an untrained fighter who swings wildly and never hits the mark.[4] Paul targets himself with well-aimed blows to gain self-control over cravings that weaken resolve and cause one to break training so that one crumples in the middle of the race and is disqualified. Far more is at stake here than in an athletic contest. As Philo observes (*Rewards* 1 §6), the losing athlete departs without a crown and must bear the stigma of defeat. His body is "brought low but can easily stand once more erect." For the one who fails in God's contest, it is a different matter: "Here it is whole lives that fall, which once more overthrown can hardly be raised up again."

The verb "bruise" (ὑπωπιάζειν, *hypōpiazein*) literally means "to hit under the eye," and then "to cause a black eye," and relates to the boxing imagery. Orr and Walther (1976: 240) render it, "I am beating my body black and blue." This is not a proof text for self-flagellation.[5] In the context, Paul applies subjugating his body to whatever rigors his apostolic task forces upon him. His discipline was not so much self-inflicted as "a cross laid on him by the hand of God, and borne for the Gospel's and the Church's sake" (Findlay 1910: 856). Nothing was to displace the

---

3. Contrast Dio Chrysostom (*Or.* 28.1–14), who exalted a famed, undefeated boxer as a model of training.

4. Winter (1997d: 167) thinks that this passage amounts to more than simply "an injunction to self-discipline" and claims that it packs an anti-Sophist punch. Since Philo (*Worse Att. Bet.* 1.13 §§41–42) uses the image of pugnacious but ineffectual Sophists, Paul may be alluding to them in defending his own lifestyle. Winter, however, interprets this chapter as Paul's defense rather than an expansion of his argument against idol food.

5. Some understand it to allude to some spiritual discipline. Ambroisaster (Bray 1999: 89), for example, thought that to pummel the body meant "to fast and to avoid any kind of luxury." In 2 Cor. 6:5, Paul lists "fastings" (νηστείαι, *nēsteiai*) among his hardships. Though the noun frequently means "fasting," in 2 Cor. 6:5, it is better translated as "hunger" that was involuntary since "a form of voluntary spiritual discipline would not count as an apostolic hardship" (Thrall 1994: 458–59). It is more likely that Paul went hungry (cf. 1 Cor. 4:11 and 11:27) because he refused to accept fees for his preaching, which resulted in privation (cf. 9:12).

utmost purpose of his life: proclaiming the gospel to others at whatever cost to himself (Bruce 1971: 89; Schrage 1995: 370–71).

B. Dodd (1999: 109) suggests that Paul employs this metaphor as a means of making his discussion of his own conduct more agreeable to his listeners. Dodd cites Plutarch's (*Mor.* 541B) advice:

> And so, just as we regard those who strut on a walk and hold up their chin as fatuous and vain, but when in boxing or fighting men rise to full height and hold the head erect, we applaud; so the man cast down by fortune, when he stands upright in a fighting posture like a boxer closing in, using self-glorification to pass from a humbled and piteous state to an attitude of triumph and pride, strikes us not as offensive or bold, but as great and indomitable.

According to this convention, Paul's presenting himself as a fighter battling it out in the arena helps make his presentation of himself as a paradigm that he wants the Corinthians to follow seem less egotistical and easier to accept.

The "body" is not understood as something inherently evil. It can serve God (6:20; cf. 1 Thess. 5:23; Rom. 6:17–19), be a member of Christ (1 Cor. 6:15), and be the temple of the Holy Spirit (6:19). Paul uses "body" because the metaphor of pummeling makes it the obvious object (Fee 1987: 439 n. 31; Yinger 1999: 251). But it needs to be bridled because "of its all too ready obedience to sin" so that it can be brought "into the service of God" (Barrett 1968: 218). Paul, however, is not talking about a constant battle with sin (Wendland 1972: 76; Schrage 1995: 370). He knocks out the body's desires for amenities, comfort, ease, abundance, or even small pleasures—anything that would cause him to think twice about going without or making himself a slave of all persons (9:19). He endures physical privations to win over his bodily cravings so that he can then win others over to Christ. Discipline for discipline's sake, therefore, does not drive him. He buffets his body and makes it his slave to heighten his capacity to deny himself to serve others. His point: If athletes discipline themselves with rigorous training to prepare themselves to win a perishable crown, how much more should Christians discipline themselves to win an imperishable crown. If Paul does this in his own Christian life, ought not the Corinthians follow suit?

Paul is fully aware that delivering the message of salvation does not automatically bring salvation to the messenger. He has been approved (δεδοκιμάσμεθα, *dedokimasmetha*) by God and entrusted with preaching the gospel (1 Thess. 2:4), but he does not want to become unfit (ἀδόκιμος, *adokimos*) for this task (1 Cor. 9:27). Pfitzner (1967: 96) dismisses "Practice what you preach" as too weak and general an aphorism to capture the intention of Paul's thought. To be sure, Paul's special commission as an apostle led him to renounce anything that might hinder the task of preaching to all. But he also holds himself up as an example for the Corinthians to imitate (11:1). His worry is not that they will be unfit for their task but unfit for God (cf. 2 Cor. 13:5; 2 Tim. 3:8; Titus 1:16) in spite of their professed knowledge. He uses a hypothetical lesson about himself. One may proclaim the truth and many may respond, but that same truth may not penetrate the heart and soul of the proclaimer. The warning that teachers need to conform their lives to their own teaching is captured in the aphorism in Sir. 37:19: "Some people may be clever enough to teach many, and yet be useless to themselves" (NRSV). Paul applies this principle to Jews who are instructed in the law and boast of their relation to God and are confident that they are "a guide to the blind, a light to those who are in darkness, a corrector of the foolish, a teacher of children, having in the law the embodiment of knowledge and truth." Yet they are guilty of the very same things they preach against and cause God's name to be slandered (Rom. 2:17–24). He seeks to do nothing to bring discredit to God.

Robertson and Plummer (1914: 197) suggest that Paul alludes to "a κῆρυξ [kēryx, herald] in the games who announced the coming contest and called out the competitors." But Paul is not simply a herald who announces the events from a platform and never joins in the contest. He is also a competitor. The warning in 1 Tim. 4:16 cautions Timothy, "Pay close attention to yourself and to your teaching; continue in these things, for in doing this you will save both yourself and your hearers" (NRSV). Paying close attention to what one teaches means that one will live out what one teaches and will become an example for others.

Paul's statement about being disqualified ("lest somehow after preaching to others I myself am disqualified") is rather startling because it suggests that "his conversion, his baptism, his call to apostleship, his service in the Gospel, do not guarantee his eternal salvation" (Barrett 1968: 218). Any implication that one may forfeit one's salvation may cause theological dyspepsia for some, and the Geneva Bible renders the adjective ἀδόκιμος "reproved," "lest I myself am reproved." Gundry Volf (1990: 237) contends that Paul does not mean that he might be "rejected from salvation" but instead refers to being "rejected as an apostle" (see also Pfitzner 1967: 92 n. 3, 96). Schrage (1995: 371 n. 548) notes that this view assumes that this section is primarily a defense of his apostleship and downplays its parenetic function.[6] The immortal crown to be won (9:25) is not a good job-approval rating as an apostle, but salvation. It can be won only if one exercises self-control and abstains from many things that may bring physical delight but ultimately will doom success in the contest.

6. See also Oropeza's (1999) critique.

Paul is engaged in moral exhortation and not discoursing on the security of the believer, and the word ἀδόκιμος is much stronger than "reproved." It means "proven false," as with coinage, "to be shown as counterfeit." Hebrews 6:8 contains a vivid picture of what "failing the proof" entails: "But land that produces thorns and thistles is worthless [*adokimos*] and is in danger of being cursed. In the end it will be burned." Paul fears that the Corinthians will fall short and fall by the wayside in the race as the wilderness generation did in the following example because of their contact with idolatry. The problem for many Corinthians is that they have disconnected their personal salvation from their calling to service and absolute allegiance to God. Moffatt (1938: 125–26) rings the changes in drawing the application that "to secure a share in the gospel, it is not enough to please oneself in the Church, to assert one's freedom, or to be easy-going."

Additional Note

9:25. At the Olympian and Pythian games the victor's wreath was made of laurel; at the Nemean games, celery; at the Isthmian games, originally pine, then later celery—and withered celery at that (Pindar, *Olympionikai* [*Olympian Odes*] 3.27; *Isthmionikai* [*Isthmian Odes*] 2.19d; Plutarch, *Mor.* 676C–D; Lucian, *Anacharsis* 9; see Broneer 1962; Murphy-O'Connor 1983: 17, 101; Engels 1990: 112). Garrison (1997: 97) claims that the worthlessness of the wreath underscored the honor of competing and winning itself, not the prize received, as satirized by Lucian (*Anacharsis* 10):

> My dear fellow, it is not the bare gifts we have in view! They are merely tokens of victory and marks to identify winners. But the reputation that goes with them is worth everything to the victors, and to attain it, even to be kicked, is nothing to men who seek to capture fame through hardships. Without the hardships it cannot be acquired. The man who covets it must put up with much unpleasantness in the beginning before at last he can expect the profitable and delightful outcome of his exertions.

Musonius Rufus (see Lutz 1947: 59) talks about acrobats and tightrope walkers risking their lives "for a miserably small recompense," and asks, "Shall we not be ready to endure hardship for the sake of complete happiness? For surely there is no other end in becoming good than to become happy and to live happily for the remainder of our lives." Dio Chrysostom (*Or.* 8.15) says that Diogenes spoke about the noble man as one who endured hardship "not to win a sprig of parsley as so many goats might do, nor for a bit of wild olive, or of pine, but rather to win happiness and virtue throughout all the days of his life, and not merely when the Eleans make proclamation [for Olympian games], or the Corinthians [for the Isthmian games], or the Thessalian assembly [for the Pythian games]." Diogenes (Dio Chrysostom, *Or.* 9.10–13) condemns those who wear the victor's crown of pine without ever having overcome the real battles of life against poverty, exile, disrepute, anger, pain, desire, fear, and pleasure, which he identifies as "the most redoubtable beast of all, treacherous and cowardly." Paul plays on the fact that in athletic competition, "the glory fades almost as fast as the wreath" (Edwards 1885: 241), and the point applies even in an era when champions receive gold medals and silver cups. Christians receive an immortal reward.

D. Refutation of Their Practice from the Negative Example of the History of Israel in the Wilderness (10:1–13)

This next section of Paul's argument seems so incompatible with what precedes that some claim that it must derive from a different letter.[1] If one assumes that he condoned eating idol food, the following arguments certainly do not fit. But he did not condone it, and what follows advances his arguments against it. The change in the form of his argument to extended biblical exposition also makes 10:1–13 appear to be a digression (Willis 1985b: 162), but it fits perfectly his purpose. He appeals to the OT as an authoritative source and to the history of Israel as directly applicable to Christians in Corinth. The example of "the fathers'" horrifying end highlights the peril in which the Corinthians place themselves by consorting with idols. Violating their covenant obligations and putting the Lord to the test is suicidal. Though the fathers experienced divine provisions, the presence of Christ, and a prefigurement of baptism and the Lord's Supper, they failed to enter the promised land because of their idolatry. Their fall is a direct warning to the Corinthians because the Scriptures directly apply to them. If they dally at pagan feasts, they can expect the same fate. They are not to be cravers of evil (10:6) or idolaters (10:7–8) and are not to put the Lord to the test (10:9) or grumble (10:10) if they expect their relationship to God to remain secure. They cannot grouse that being forbidden from participating in idol feasts places them in an untenable position. If they are faithful exclusively to God, they will never be in a situation too difficult for God to sustain them and to empower them to endure (10:13).

Paul's exposition of the Scriptures draws out surprising connections between the demise of the wilderness generation and the situation of the Corinthian Christians. He does not rehearse the past events to understand the past but to understand the present (R. Collins 1999: 365). Hays (1997: 159) connects the exposition to Paul's opening remarks in 8:1–6:

---

1. Hurd (1965: 43–46) discusses the groundless theories that this section stems from an earlier, more Jewish, and superstitious Paul (see additional note on 10:19–22).

Paul's use of Israel's story is crucial to his case: the God with whom we have to do, he insists, is not merely some abstract divine principle that sets us free from polytheistic superstition. The God with whom we have to do is the God of Israel, a jealous God who sternly condemns idol-worship and punishes all who dare to dabble in it.

Like Israel of old, the Corinthians have been set free from their past and have been set on a pilgrimage to an eschatological promised land. They may be derailed by an insatiable craving (a lack of self-control, 9:25) and by idolatry, as Israel of old was. The bold Corinthians may not fear the power of idols, but they should fear the wrath of God.

Exegesis and Exposition

[1]For I do not want you to be unaware, brothers and sisters, that all our ancestors were under the cloud and all passed through the sea. [2]And they all ⌜received baptism⌝ into Moses in the cloud and in the sea. [3]And they all ate the same spiritual bread. [4]And all drank the same spiritual drink. For they were drinking from the spiritual rock that was following them, and the rock was Christ. [5]But God was not pleased with most of them, for they were strewn about in the wilderness.

[6]These things happened as examples for us so that we might not become cravers of evil just as they also craved [evil]. [7]Do not become idolaters just as some of them were. As it stands written: "The people sat down to eat and drink and rose up to play." [8]Let us not commit fornication just as some of them committed fornication, and, in one day, twenty-three thousand fell. [9]Let us not sorely tempt ⌜Christ⌝ just as some of them tempted [him] and were decimated by the snakes. [10]⌜Do not grumble⌝ as some of them grumbled and were decimated by the destroyer. [11]⌜These things⌝ were happening to them as an example, and they were written for our admonishment, upon whom the end of the ages has arrived. [12]So then, let the one who presumes to stand, watch out lest he fall. [13]No testing has come upon you except that which comes [normally] to humans. God is faithful and will not allow you to be tested beyond your capacity [to endure]. But with the testing God also will provide the way out so that you are able to bear up under it.

Paul begins this next section (see additional note) with a γάρ (*gar*, for) **10:1** and thereby indicates that he now gives the grounds for his warning in 9:24–27 about the possibility of disqualification (Findlay 1910: 857; Robertson and Plummer 1914: 199; Beasley-Murray 1962: 181; Fee 1987: 443; Schrage 1995: 387–88; Wolff 1996: 214). Many commentators either ignore it (see Conzelmann 1975: 165) or downplay its significance by claiming that it connects only loosely to what precedes

(Weiss 1910: 249; Lietzmann 1949: 44; Barrett 1968: 220; Gundry Volf 1990: 239). Paul also uses the formula οὐ θέλω . . . ὑμᾶς ἀγνοεῖν, ἀδελφοί (*ou thelō . . . hymas agnoein, adelphoi*) to begin a new section or to emphasize the importance of something that follows.[2] It always indicates the phrase "brothers and sisters," last used in 7:29 (cf. Rom. 1:13; 11:25; 1 Cor. 12:1; 2 Cor. 1:8; 1 Thess. 4:13). In this instance, it marks the shift from examples from his own ministry to a theological discussion of Scripture (see Smit 1997a: 43) and underscores something he thinks the readers may know but do not fully grasp (Willis 1985b: 126). It does not mean that he is trying to correct the Corinthian "spiritual ones" on some point about which they claim full knowledge (contra R. Horsley 1998: 134). Clearly, he assumes that readers have familiarity with the OT stories he cites (Hays 1999: 398), and he highlights implications that they have missed.[3] What needed reemphasis was that nearly all Israel perished (1 Cor. 10:5) despite receiving continual tokens of God's care. This section contains the kind of "knowledge" that, when the lesson is applied, will result in their upbuilding (8:1–3).

The wilderness traditions are "retold in terms of what 'our fathers' experienced" (P. Gardner 1994: 133), and Paul may have taken the phrase "our fathers" from that tradition (P. Gardner 1994: 116). Barrett (1968: 220) thinks that it possibly indicates that he quotes "without modification, an existing Exodus midrash." I disagree that Paul draws on a preexisting exposition, but, even if he did, he clearly regards his Corinthian converts, Jews and Gentiles, to be the sons and daughters of those whom God dealt with in the OT (cf. Rom. 4:12, 16; Gal. 3:29). Gentiles may be "wild olive shoots," but they have been grafted into the scion of Israel (Rom. 11:17). His whole argument is based on the presupposition that the Corinthian Christians stand in continuity with what God has done in the past, and he affirms this point at the outset (Fee 1987: 444). He addresses them "as if they were Israelites, the covenanted and holy people of God" (R. Collins 1999: 368), and recalls the biblical axiom that the fate of the ancestors should forewarn the children.

The Gentile church, perhaps through Paul's influence, understood the biblical history to be about "*our* fathers" and not simply "the fathers of the Jews" (cf. 1 Clem. 4:8). This conviction that Gentiles are full heirs of the biblical story contrasts dramatically with the attitude toward the new convert reflected in a mishnaic tradition. The convert is instructed

---

2. The positive form, "I want you to know" (without the address "brethren"), appears in 11:3; Col. 2:1.

3. Hays (1989: 92) observes, "Israel's story, as told in Scripture, so comprehensively constitutes the symbolic universe of Paul's discourse that he can recall elements of the story for himself and his readers with the sorts of subtle gestures that pass between members of an interpretive family."

not to pray, "Our God and God of *our* fathers," because the God of the Jews was not the God of the convert's fathers. The convert ought instead to pray, "Our God and the God of *their* fathers" (*m. Bik.* 1:4).

Paul enumerates the various encounters with the divine that all the people had in the wilderness. First, he mentions that all were "under the cloud."[4] He does not mean that they literally marched out of Egypt with the cloud above them, since the narrative records that the cloud is either before them or behind them (Exod. 13:21, 22; 14:19, 23; 40:38; Ps. 78:14). Although some claim that the cloud represents the presence of God, or the Spirit connected to baptism, or even the preexistent Christ (so Origen; Goudge 1911: 84; Hanson 1965; Conzelmann 1975: 166), it is unlikely that Paul stretched the text to find such symbolic connections. It means nothing more than that from the very beginning of their journey, the cloud protected the Israelites. In Ps. 105:39, the cloud is spread as a "covering" that protected and directed the people (cf. Num. 14:14; Neh. 9:12; Wis. 10:17; 19:7). It was a symbol of their deliverance (Fee 1987: 445–46). "Through the sea" recalls the miraculous deliverance when the Lord turned the sea into dry land and divided the waters so that the Israelites crossed the sea on dry ground with the waters forming walls on both sides (Exod. 14:21–22; Ps. 78:13).

10:2 Paul moves from the experience of the Corinthian Christians to find analogous spiritual circumstances in the Scripture and interprets the exodus events in such a way that the parallels become clear and relevant (Bandstra 1971: 7; Willis 1985b: 129). He begins by claiming that the wilderness generation also received baptism; that is, the wilderness generation's deliverance compares to Christian deliverance symbolized in baptism. He does not think that they underwent some sacramental rite (cf. Titus 3:5) but imagines that the parted sea that sandwiched the people on either side and the overshadowing cloud that escorted them through the wilderness comprised their baptism into Moses. Since the people were not covered with water but miraculously crossed the sea on dry ground (Exod. 14:22)—unless Paul somehow knew the legend that the people went into the sea up to their noses before it finally parted—calling this "baptism" may seem far-fetched. A similar comparison in 1 Pet. 3:20–21, however, relates being saved from the flood in Noah's ark to baptism. The "eight souls" were saved "through water," even though they were actually saved from the deluge that consumed the world. How did Paul make the connection to baptism, and what did he understand this baptism into Moses to mean?

---

4. The word "all" is repeated five times in this unit to emphasize the unity of their experience as a people (note also the repetition of τὸ αὐτό [*to auto*, the same]). It may be that the emphasis on "all" preempts any possible counterargument that only the weak fell (P. Gardner 1994: 118–19).

The phrase "baptism into Moses" (εἰς τὸν Μωϋσῆν ἐβαπτίσθησαν, *eis ton Mōÿsēn ebaptisthēsan*) has no Jewish parallels and appears to have been coined by Paul from the Christian idiom "baptized into Christ" (Rom. 6:3; Gal. 3:27; cf. Matt. 28:19; Acts 8:16; 19:5; 1 Cor. 1:13; so Barrett 1968: 221; Willis 1985b; Schrage 1995: 390; Wolff 1996: 215). Several proposals try to explain how Christian baptism interfaces with the exodus. Possibly, Paul knew a Jewish tradition that claimed that Israel was prepared on Sinai for receiving salvation by means of immersion (*b. Ker.* 9a; 81a; *b. Yebam.* 46a). He may have been influenced by the Jewish conviction that the "latter Redeemer" would be like the first one (Barrett 1968: 221), as stated in a late rabbinic tradition (*Eccles. Rab.* 1.9):

> R. Berekiah said in the name of R. Isaac: As the first redeemer was, so shall the latter Redeemer be. What is stated of the former redeemer? "And Moses took his wife and his sons, and set them upon an ass" [Exod. 4:20]. Similarly it will be with the latter Redeemer, as it is stated, "Lowly and riding upon an ass" [Zech. 9:9]. As the former redeemer caused manna to descend, as it is stated, "Behold, I will cause to rain bread from heaven for you" [Exod. 16:4], so will the latter Redeemer cause manna to descend, as it is stated, "May he be as rich as a cornfield in the land" [Ps. 72:16]. As the former redeemer made a well to rise [Num. 21:17–18], so the latter Redeemer brings up water, as it is stated, "And a fountain shall come forth of the house of the Lord, and shall water the valley of Shittim" [Joel 4:18].

In making the association between Christ and Moses, Paul may have moved backward: as the latter Redeemer, so the first redeemer (see Jeremias, *TDNT* 6:857–63). Whether this idea entered Paul's head or not, it is likely that he read the text in light of redemption history and the revelation brought by Christ (cf. 2 Cor. 3:7–18; Gal. 3:8; 4:21–31). The exodus was understood as an act of redemption, so it was no stretch for him to associate it with the events and symbols of Christian redemption. Dunn (1970: 126–27) asserts that the Red Sea crossing, the manna, and the water were only material events of deliverance to the Israelites. They can be recognized as "baptism" or "spiritual food and drink" only from the spiritual vantage point of the new covenant brought about by Christ's death and resurrection. Dunn writes, "We can regard them as 'sacraments,' in the same way as we can regard the Israelites as 'our fathers' (v. 1), because *their* concrete experience of (literal, physical) redemption is an allegory of *our* concrete experience of (spiritual) redemption."

Baptism into Moses may mean that the people were "baptized into loyalty to Moses" (Moffatt 1938: 129; cf. Robertson and Plummer 1914: 200) or "into his leadership" (Calvin 1960: 201; Bruce 1971: 90). We may not infer too much from this reference. Paul may have used this phrase simply as shorthand for baptism "in the name of Moses" (Schrage 1995: 390) and understood the baptism to represent sharing the destiny of a leader (cf. Mark 10:38–39), which may explain why the Israelites did not need to get wet (Barrett 1968: 221). It is crucial to remember that he is not intending to formulate sacramental theology (see Beasley-Murray 1962: 182–85) but simply wants to highlight parallels between the wilderness generation and the Corinthians to make a point about idol food. In this case, he juxtaposes Israel's deliverer with the Christians' deliverer. Moses was a type of Christ who led the Israelites to freedom (Acts 7:35–36; Heb. 3:16). Paul begins with the premise that baptism marks the beginning of the Christian life, and he applies it to the beginning of Israel's existence as God's covenant people, their deliverance from Egypt, and christens that deliverance as a baptism (see Fee 1987: 444).

One can easily be diverted by Paul's mention of baptism into a debate about his view of the sacrament and lose track of the fact that he is still arguing against idol food. What is most important is what this connection means in the context of his arguments in chapters 8–10. P. Gardner (1994) contends that Paul's reference to baptism is intended to draw out the aspect of covenantal separation and the formation of the people of God. Fee (1987: 445) notes (without drawing this particular conclusion) that the Lord used the cloud to lead the Israelites by going before them (Exod. 13:21) "and then moved behind to separate them from the Egyptians" (Exod. 14:19–20). The sea marked the permanent boundary between Israel and Egypt. P. Gardner (1994: 120–21) claims that Paul has no interest in some kind of sacramental dimension of baptism but only in its significance for "*separation* and group identification" (cf. Wolff 1996: 214; Oropeza 1999: 78). Israel's deliverance through the sea marked the beginning of their separation from Egypt and their new identity as God's covenant community, and the term "baptism" fittingly represents that experience.[5]

The words τύπος (*typos*, 10:6) and τυπικῶς (*typikōs*, 10:11) show that Paul does not equate the Israelites' "baptism" with Christian baptism but that he marshals the exemplary aspects of the text. He does not understand Israel's baptism as a sacramental rite that had divine efficacy and conferred eternal blessing. Willis (1985b: 130) correctly argues that his "interest was not in the OT marks of salvation themselves, but in the danger that the people of God could void their election." In the same way that we find correlations between the disciples' experiences recorded in the Gospels and our own experiences in the church, so Paul

---

5. This interpretation offsets the need to explain "how crossing the sea on *dry* land was a 'baptism'" (P. Gardner 1994: 120).

found instructive parallels between what happened to Israel and the danger facing the Corinthians. Referring to Israel's deliverance from Egypt under the cloud and through the sea lays the foundation for his argument: All Israel experienced God's saving deliverance under Moses' direction, but they did not reach the final goal because of flagrant sin—idolatry.

Bandstra (1971: 7) attributes Paul's interpretation of Israel's experience with the cloud and the sea to a christological reading of the OT. Paul assumes that "in the historical Christ-event the pattern of God's historical dealings with Israel in the exodus is brought to fulfillment and finds its focal point." While this may be true, Paul goes back to the OT because of the Corinthians' flirtation with idolatry, which, to his mind, has placed them in mortal danger. He finds analogies in the exodus events to make his point about the Corinthians' situation. Israel was set apart to God by their baptism under the cloud and through the sea. They were divinely blessed in the time of the wilderness, but those blessings did not automatically exempt them from God's judgment when they brazenly disobeyed God's commands and veered off into idolatry. What is important for Paul is that the Corinthians are in danger of backsliding and committing the *same sin*.

Paul does not interpret the text allegorically in the way that Theodoret, for example, does. Theodoret goes so far as to identify the sea as the baptismal font, the cloud as the grace of the Spirit, Moses as the priest, his rod as the cross, and the pursuing Egyptians as the devils. Paul "does not seek a point-for-point correspondence; he is satisfied with the exemplary character of the history of Israel in one specific respect: apparently the cloud is the sign of the divine presence, and to this the Spirit in baptism corresponds" (Conzelmann 1975: 166). But the cloud and the sea also signify removal and partition from Egypt's bondage and its idolatry.

10:3–4 Paul suggests that the Israelites not only had something analogous to Christian baptism but also something analogous to the Lord's Supper. After their divine deliverance they received divine succor. The "same spiritual bread" and the "same spiritual drink" do not mean that Paul thinks that the Israelites ate the same bread or drank the same drink that Christians eat and drink in the Lord' Supper (contra Calvin 1960: 204, "The ancient people . . . shared in the same sacraments"; Edwards 1885: 245; Hanson 1965: 19). The emphasis instead is on the people's unity: they *all* received the *same* spiritual blessings (Barrett 1968: 221–22; Héring 1962: 86; Fee 1987: 446 n. 28). This affirmation prevents anyone from quibbling that some fell in the wilderness because they had somehow been left out of these privileges. All who died in the wilderness (10:5) had been recipients of God's blessings.

Paul identifies the gift of manna (Exod. 16; Ps. 78:23–29) as "spiritual bread,"[6] and the water from the rock (Exod. 17:1–7; Num. 20:2–13; Ps. 78:15–16; 105:41; 114:8; Wis. 11:4) as "spiritual drink." The term "spiritual" (πνευματικός, *pneumatikos*) appears three times: spiritual food, spiritual drink, and spiritual rock. Many assume that Paul understood "spiritual" to mean food and drink that convey the Spirit (Käsemann 1964: 113; Hanson 1965: 18; Jewett 1971: 38–39) or that effect a special relationship with God (Grosheide 1953: 220–21; Conzelmann 1975: 166 n. 23; Bandstra 1971: 10; Goppelt, *TDNT* 6:146–47; Schweitzer, *TDNT* 6:437; Schrage 1995: 392–93; Smit 1997a: 43). Barrett (1968: 222), for example, points out that the word "spiritual" "is usually employed by Paul to denote some thing (or person) that is the bearer or agent of the Holy Spirit" (9:11; 12:1; 14:1; 15:44, 46; Rom. 1:11; 7:14; 15:27). The food and drink imparted both material and spiritual sustenance. This view accords with the notion of the Eucharist found in Did. 10:3: "You, Lord Almighty, created all things for your name's sake, and gave food and drink to humans for their enjoyment, that they might give you thanks, but us you have blessed with spiritual food and drink and eternal life through your Child." This interpretation is frequently linked to the assumption that Paul wished to correct a hypersacramentalism that beguiled the Corinthians into thinking that they were immune from any dangers of falling. As Oepke (*TDNT* 1:542) articulates it, "Paul energetically combats a materialistic and superstitious estimation of baptism and the Lord's Supper which would have it that their recipients are set free from every possibility of the divine wrath." From their acquaintance with pagan mystery rites, they misinterpreted the food and drink of the Lord's Supper to be a magical means of receiving immortality that made them (*ex opere operato*) invulnerable to the power of demons or idols and made an arduous trial of obedience unnecessary. Paul is assumed to be debunking this belief in the magical power of the sacraments by interpreting the Red Sea crossing, the manna, and the water as equivalent sacraments that did not save the wilderness generation.[7]

This view is mistaken for the following reasons.[8] First, Newton (1998: 217) shows that the available evidence does not support the supposed sacramental ideas in mystery religions. Second, Paul is not at-

---

6. See 2 Cor. 8:15 for a discussion of the implications of this event in another context.

7. So Weiss 1910: 250; Lietzmann 1949: 45–46; von Soden 1951: 259–61; Héring 1962: 84–85; Käsemann 1964: 113–14; Bornkamm 1969: 128–29; Barrett 1968: 220, 224; Conzelmann 1975: 167; Bandstra 1971: 6; Fee 1980a: 180; 1987: 363, 442–43; Witherington 1995: 220 ("possibly"); Schrage 1995: 381, 385, 393, 396; Wolff 1996: 212.

8. See Malina 1968: 96–97, who calls it "a gratuitous assumption"; Sandelin 1995; Ruef 1977: 89; Perrot 1983: 445; Willis 1985b: 139–42, 154, 159–60; M. Mitchell 1993: 251–52; P. Gardner 1994: 117–19; Smit 1997a: 48.

tacking mistaken views of the Lord's Supper but is showing from the example of Israel the extreme dangers of any kind of involvement with idolatry. The problem is not their hypersacramentalism or their "sense of complacent superiority" (contra Murphy-O'Connor 1979a: 93) but their idolatry. Willis (1985b: 127, 141) is correct: Paul is not concerned to correct a Corinthian misunderstanding of the sacrament but wants to make clear the danger of idolatry. Third, Paul brings up the subject of the Lord's Supper, not because the Corinthians had a quasi-magical view of it as a rite imparting eternal security, but in order to make a comparison between it and idol meals. The Lord's Supper is analogous to the pagan meals as a rite charged with religious meaning and intention. The Lord's Supper is a sacred act that requires absolute fealty to Christ and to Christ alone, and believers cannot participate in both feasts as if they were an ancient version of a "progressive dinner" hosted by the various gods. The meals are mutually exclusive. Smit (1997a: 48) rightly sees that Paul is not interested "in the theology of the Lord's Supper for its own sake. He introduces baptism and the Lord's Supper in his exposition as a means to exclude participation in sacrificial meals for believers."

It reads too much into the text to suppose that the Corinthians thought that Christian rites gave them immunity from punishment or license to tempt God. They did not consider their actions to be potentially dangerous or punishable, and Paul must alert them ("I do not want you to be ignorant") to those dangers by boldly drawing the parallels between the wilderness generation and themselves and by casting a glaring spotlight on their wretched fate. If the Corinthians break the covenant relationship that "forms the essence of their life as Christians" (Smit 1997a: 44) by being drawn into idolatry, they too will be wiped out.

A better option understands "spiritual" as identifying the source or origin of the food and drink. They were miraculous or supernatural (cf. 15:44, "spiritual body"). This interpretation gains support from Exod. 16:4, 15. The Lord informs Moses, "I am going to rain bread from heaven for you, and each day the people shall go out and gather enough for that day" (Exod. 16:4). When the Israelites saw the manna, they asked what it was. Moses answered, "It is the bread that the LORD has given you to eat" (Exod. 16:15; cf. Ps. 78:25; Wis. 16:20; John 6:32). Ambrosiaster (cited by Bray 1999: 92) maintained, "The manna and the water that flowed from the rock are called spiritual because they were formed not according to the law of nature but by the power of God working independently of the natural elements." It was supernatural food (so Weiss 1910: 251; Lietzmann 1949: 45). This interpretation best explains the γάρ (gar) in the next clause, "for they were drinking from the spiritual rock following them." This added comment explains how the drink was a spiritual drink: It came from a spiritual rock (struck by Moses' rod). The manna from heaven did not need such an explanation, since its connection to a divine source was more obvious (Parry 1926: 145; cf. Josephus, *Ant.* 3.1.6 §26).[9]

Though the food granted Israel in the wilderness was a supernatural gift from God, by using the adjective "spiritual," Paul may also intend to say that this gift was revelatory in that it required spiritual discernment and pointed ultimately to Christ ("that which comes from God and reveals him"; Fee 1987: 447; P. Gardner 1994: 142). God's purpose in raining down bread from heaven was calculated to test the people to see if they would follow God (Exod. 16:4). Spiritual food requires a spiritual discernment to understand the spiritual realities it represents. The recipients of these redemptive gifts that kept them alive in the wilderness could look at the manna, for example, in purely material terms, asking, "What is it?" (Exod. 16:15, a play on words in Hebrew), and identifying it only as "a fine flakelike stuff" that could be ground, beaten, boiled, and made into cakes (Num. 11:8). Or, they could look at it in spiritual terms as "bread from heaven" and as proof of God's ability to provide all they need to sustain their life (cf. John 6:26). They could look at the water pouring from the rock as a hidden spring or as water provided by God to slake their thirst and silence their doubts. Those whose minds now are unveiled by the Spirit (2 Cor. 3:15–17), however, can see another "Rock" standing beside the craggy cliff at Rephidim. The meaning of the word "spiritual" need not be limited to one thing. Paul refers to "food supplied by God's special action, and food which has a spiritual or typological significance" (Orr and Walther 1976: 245). The "spiritual" food and drink contrasts what the people craved with what God actually provided.

The statement that the rock followed them is puzzling. The OT does not say anything about the rock traveling with the Israelites, from which they continued to draw their water. How did Paul extract this idea from the text? Some contend that he was influenced by extracanonical Jewish traditions about a movable well (see additional note). Enns (1996: 25) regards these traditions as incontestable evidence that the tradition of a movable well existed in the first century and that Paul is another witness to this "established exegetical tradition" (so also Edwards 1885: 245; Thackeray 1900: 195, 204–5, 211; Barrett 1968: 222; Conzelmann 1975: 196–97; Wolff 1996: 213–14; Willis 1985b: 133–42; Fee 1987: 448).[10] Others object to the hypothesis that Paul drew on Jew-

9. In Jos. As. 16:14, the manna that Aseneth ate is identified as πνεῦμα ζωῆς (*pneuma zōēs*) made from "the dew of the roses of life that are in the paradise of God," and everyone who eats it "will not die for ever (and) ever."

10. Other extracanonical Jewish traditions appear in Acts 7:53; Heb. 2:2; 2 Tim. 3:8; 2 Pet. 2:5; Jude 9.

ish legendary expansions of the text, which seems to sanction an improper, fanciful method of exegesis (Driver 1889: 17, called it a "puerile fable"; Godet 1887: 56; Bandstra 1971: 11; Ellis 1978: 211–12).[11] Even though the OT does not actually mention a rock following the Israelites through the wilderness and providing water along the way, the texts lend themselves to this inference, and it does not result from the creative embellishments of overactive and capricious imaginations (Enns 1996: 28–29). The conclusion would have stemmed from ancient readers wondering what the Israelites did for water between the two accounts of the miraculous rock, when water gushed out (Exod. 17:1–7; Num. 20:2–13). Surely, in forty years God gave them water more than twice. Someone may have noticed that the rock is described in Exod. 17:1–7 at the beginning of the wilderness wandering and again in Num. 20:1–13 at its end. The clarification of some unknown interpreter became the traditional answer: "The rock of Exodus 17 and the rock of Numbers 20 are one and the same. Hence, this rock must have accompanied the Israelites through their journey" (Enns 1996: 31).

This exegetical tradition forms the backdrop for Paul's passing comment that the rock followed them. It was not his own invention. He simply incorporated it as the "inheritor of an 'interpreted Bible,'" and he is not consciously interpreting the text (Enns 1996: 32).[12] This explanation rules out the view that Paul drew upon and adapted the concept of wisdom in Hellenistic Judaism (Barrett 1968: 223; Bandstra 1971: 12–13; Schrage 1995: 394–95; R. Horsley 1998: 137) and applied it to Christ by allegorizing the text after the manner of Philo.[13] Paul has not dehistoricized the narrative by noting that the rock followed them, but this detail has theological implications that are important for his argument.

The "following rock" implies God's continuing graciousness: these gifts recurred throughout their wanderings (P. Gardner 1994: 146). The source of this divine gift was always available to them. This idea was expressed in *Mekilta de Rabbi Ishmael*, tractate *Vayassaᶜ* 7 on Exod. 17:6: "Wherever you find the mark of man's feet, there I am before you." Wherever Israel may go, God goes with them and provides. Paul may have incorporated a traditional Jewish interpretation of the following rock, but he gives it a uniquely Christian twist: "The rock was Christ." He is not thinking of a material rock following them, or a movable well,

---

11. Contrast the views of Edwards (1885: 245), who thinks that Paul uses the legends without sanctioning them, and of Robertson and Plummer (1914: 201), who think that Paul "seems to take up this rabbinic fancy and give it a spiritual meaning."

12. Enns (1996: 33–38) also discusses the theological implications of this conclusion.

13. Philo takes the flinty rock in Deut. 8:15 as a reference to God's preexistent Wisdom, "which he marked off highest and chiefest from his powers and from which he satisfies the thirsty souls that love God" (*Alleg. Interp.* 2.21 §86; see also *Worse Att. Bet.* 31 §§115–18; *Drunk.* 29 §112).

but of the divine source of the water that journeyed with them. He understands the replenishing rock in a spiritual sense, not a physical sense.

The idea of the rock evokes a number of OT images. First, "Rock" is a title used for God in the Song of Moses (Deut. 32:4, 15, 18, 30, 31), a passage that forms the foundation for Paul's arguments against the Corinthians' participation in idolatry. The figures of "the Rock of salvation," "the Rock that begot you," "our Rock," and "my rock and my redeemer" (Ps. 19:14) all easily transfer to Christ. Israel's idolatry also spurned the Rock that had delivered and sustained them throughout their wilderness trek (Deut. 32:15). These "rock" texts may nudge the reader to remember Israel's deplorable idolatry and rejection of God, who emancipated and cared for them, and Paul would have regarded them as particularly applicable to the Corinthian situation, where they have been dallying with idols.

Second, the metaphor of the Rock emphasizes God's stability and permanence (Craigie 1976: 378) and underscores God's covenant faithfulness in choosing a covenant people (P. Gardner 1994: 125, 147). The image accentuates God's unchanging nature in contrast to the erratic, impulsive, and unreliable nature of God's covenantal people (Oropeza 1998: 62).

Third, the image of rock in the Scriptures, recalling the miraculous provision of water (Deut. 8:15; Neh. 9:15; Job 29:6; Ps. 81:16; 105:41; Isa. 48:21) or as an epithet for God (Ps. 78:35; 89:26; 92:15; 94:22; 95:1; Isa. 30:29; 44:8; Hab. 1:12), was associated with God's saving work. It harks back to God's redemptive achievement for the people of the covenant.

Paul could have made the connection that Christ was the rock from a variety of textual cues and associations. He may have made the shift from God as the Rock in the Scriptures to Christ as Rock in the same way that he applied the references to God as "Lord" in the Scriptures to Christ (Godet 1887: 57–58; Fee 1987: 449; P. Gardner 1994: 147). Since the rock was associated with God's redemptive work, it was natural to connect it to God's greatest redemptive work in Christ. Christ's death and resurrection permeated Paul's understanding of God's redemptive purposes in history, and he "saw Christ as the fulfillment of God's faithfulness and the embodiment of his grace" (P. Gardner 1994: 148). In the opening lines of this letter (1:4–7), Paul affirms that Christ is the source of every spiritual gift. He identifies Christ as the mediator of creation in 8:6, and it is only a small step to see Christ as the source of the spiritual food and water that nourished Israel in the wilderness. We need not be detained by views about whether he thinks of some manifestation of the preexistent Christ (cf. Phil. 2:6; Col. 1:15–18), as some interpreters argue (Robertson and Plummer 1914: 201; Lietzmann

1949: 44–45; Héring 1962: 85; Conzelmann 1975: 166–67; cf. Fee 1987: 449). He simply assumes, without going into any elaborate theological detail, that Christ is the source of all divine gifts and succor. Therefore, it is the same Christ, acting in saving history, who is behind both the old and the new saving events (Cullmann, *TDNT* 6:97).[14]

R. Horsley (1998: 137) helpfully reminds us that the assertion "the Rock was Christ" is a "parenthetical comment," not "a major doctrinal statement." But it serves an important purpose in the development of Paul's argument. It confirms "the continuity between Israel and the Corinthians" (Fee 1987: 449). His primary concern is to turn the Corinthians away from their reckless association with idolatry, and he wants to show how closely what they are doing parallels Israel's lunacy in spurning their Rock of salvation by mixing idolatrous practices with their worship of God. If the Corinthians do likewise, they can expect the same disastrous consequences that befell Israel. If they were to counter that their situation is different because they have received Christ's benefits, he would respond, "So did the Israelites!" He intends for them to recognize the direct parallel between Israel's situation and their own so that they might swerve from the path leading to inevitable destruction.

10:5 Deliverance from Egypt did not mean ultimate deliverance. Israel had to pass through a time of travail and testing in the desert before they could enter the promised land. In the same way, the deliverance won by Christ's death and resurrection does not mean that believers are whisked away to safety and can skip the perilous wilderness journey. They face the same dangers and temptations in their pagan wasteland that foiled the Israelites. The "but" (ἀλλά, *alla*) beginning 10:5 reveals that what eventually happened to Israel ran counter to what one might expect after they had received such divine blessings. That God was not pleased with "most of them" is an understatement since only two, Joshua and Caleb, survived and entered the promised land (Num. 14:29–32; 26:65). Moffatt (1938: 130) explains the source of God's displeasure: "Though [God] satisfied their daily needs, they did not satisfy his requirements."

The "for" (γάρ, *gar*) again justifies the previous statement, "for they were strewn about in the wilderness"—a morbid picture. If God had been pleased εὐδοκεῖν (*eudokein*) with them, they would not have perished. The verb εὐδοκεῖν is used for the sovereignty and mystery of God's choice of persons, which is inscrutable to humans (cf. Matt. 17:5; Eph. 1:4–9; 1 Cor. 1:21; Gal. 1:15; Col. 1:19; 2 Pet. 1:17). Of the terms used for election in the NT, this verb carries the strongest emotional overtones of God's love for those who are chosen (Schrenk, *TDNT*

---

14. Paul believes that the OT is the book of Christians "because it has Christ as its prime actor and final goal" (Fee 1987: 459).

2:740–41). In this case, God's displeasure refers "to the forfeiture of election" (Willis 1985b: 143; Wolff 1996: 218). God's choice is not irrevocable (Ruef 1977: 92). Despite the spiritual benefits that the Israelites enjoyed, they did not reach Canaan because their "postbaptismal" sins were so great. The lesson for the Corinthians: Failure is possible (cf. 11:30). In 10:6–10, Paul next will pinpoint the precise cause of Israel's failure.

"These things" (ταῦτα, *tauta*) refers to the events described in the preceding verses, but verse 6, which begins a new series of observations about the wilderness generation, links the divine blessings with the subsequent punishments for their disobedience (see Koet 1996: 609). In 10:7–10, Paul outlines four of Israel's transgressions that resulted from the basic sin of "craving" (Collier 1994: 71) and that broke their relationship with God: idolatry (10:7), harlotry (10:8), putting Christ to the test (10:9), and grumbling (10:10).[15] The assertion that "these things happened as examples [τύποι, *typoi*]" unfurls Paul's understanding of the Scriptures. He believes that "whatever was written in former days was written for our instruction, so that by steadfastness and by the encouragement of the scriptures we might have hope" (Rom. 15:4 NRSV; cf. 2 Tim. 3:16–17). The Scriptures do not only offer hope; they also contain warnings. The rebellious Israelites were destroyed in the wilderness as a testimony, so the Corinthians should take heed.

10:6

Justin (*Dial.* 42.4) uses τύπος (*typos*) to refer to "the prefiguration of events related to salvation history in Jesus Christ" (cf. Barn. 7:3, 7, 10, 11; 12:2, 5, 6, 10; 13:5), and some interpret it as reflecting a cause-and-effect relationship (R. Davidson 1981: 268).[16] But this meaning is unlikely here because that would entail that the Corinthians will also displease the Lord and perish, and Paul writes to *prevent* this from happening. The word τύπος is used for "a mold for producing a shape, or a wooden stamp for making an imprint in clay, the stroke of a numismatic die, the engraving of seals, a figure that juts out" (Spicq, *TLNT* 3:384; cf. Hays 1997: 162). In ethical discussion, "a *typos* is a model, hardly different from an example" (Spicq, *TLNT* 3:387). It reveals a pattern or correspondence, observed after the fact, that contains a teaching (cf. Rom. 6:17). The word clearly means "example" in Phil. 3:17; 1 Thess. 1:7; 2 Thess. 3:9; 1 Tim. 4:12; Titus 2:7. The phrase "so that we might not be" confirms that they were not types but "examples for guidance" (Robertson and Plummer 1914: 202–3; R. Collins 1999: 370; contra Goppelt 1982: 146; *TDNT* 8:251–52). Paul's high view of the church living under the new covenant in the last days emerges here. These things occurred so that they might

15. The "all," used five times in 10:1–5, is changed to "some of them" (κἀκεῖνοι, *kakeinoi*, 10:6; τινες αὐτῶν, *tines autōn*, 10:7, 8, 9, 10).

16. For a definition of typology, see Baker 1994.

be warning examples for his readers. Hays (1987: 93) argues convincingly that "Paul sees the Corinthian controversy about idol meat . . . in double exposure with Israel's wilderness idolatry." The Corinthian Christians have left the starting blocks as the elect of God and now they face the desert (Oropeza 1999: 80). An array of dangers surrounds them, as it did Israel, as they make their way. They find themselves now at a critical juncture when the choices they make mean life or death. Receiving God's spiritual blessings does not exempt them from God's judgment.

In what follows, Paul does not simply compile a conventional catalog of sins (contra Barrett 1968: 226; Willis 1985b: 147; P. Gardner 1994: 150) but lists those that specifically apply to the Corinthian situation (Bandstra 1971: 17; Cheung 1999: 145). First and foremost, the Israelites were "cravers after evil." The noun ἐπιθυμία (epithymia, desire, longing) may be a "cover term for all rebellion against God which may be manifested in many ways" (Willis 1985b: 145–46; Perrot 1983) and refers to desires of the flesh that defy God's will (Rom. 7:7; 13:8–10; Gal. 5:16, 24; cf. Rom. 1:21). But the noun ἐπιθυμητής (epithymētēs, craver), in 1 Cor. 10:6, appears in Num. 11:34 and recalls Israel's specific craving for meat (κρέα, krea; cf. 1 Cor. 8:13) in the wilderness: "The rabble among them had a strong craving; and the Israelites also wept again, and said, 'If only we had meat to eat!'" (Num. 11:4; cf. 11:13, 18, 21). They turned up their noses at the manna, the food offered by God, and longed for the fare that they enjoyed in Egypt. When quails fell in their midst, before they could swallow the meat, God struck them with a very great plague. When the "cravers" were buried, they named the place "the Graves of Craving" (Num. 11:33–34). The καί (kai) in κἀκεῖνοι (kakeinoi) may implicate the Corinthians. "They as well as you" were guilty of this sin (Robertson and Plummer 1914: 203). Paul connects the selfish craving of the wilderness rabble to the Corinthian desire to eat (meat?) in idol temples.

10:7   Paul's primary concern surfaces in the command forbidding the Corinthians to become idolaters. Of the four warnings from the wilderness experience adduced in this section, this verse contains the only explicit quotation of Scripture (Exod. 32:6b).[17] We should not go so far as to say that the other sins listed are "incidental" (Willis 1985b: 146–47; P. Gardner 1994: 150–51). They are all of a piece. Paul highlights this one verse from Exodus because it ties into the theme of eating and drinking that reverberates throughout chapters 8–10 (Hays 1997: 163). He emphasizes God's categorical intolerance of Israel's idolatry and Israel's worst sin in making the golden calf and offering sacrifice to the idol (cf. Acts 7:41). It is inter-

---

17. Paul introduces the Scripture citation with ὥσπερ (hōsper), the only time a citation is introduced this way in the NT, because the καθώς (kathōs) is used for the comparisons in 10:6, 7, 8, 9 (Koet 1996: 610 n. 16).

esting that he does not cite a verse emphasizing their worship and sacrifice before the calf, for example, Exod. 32:6a, 8, 31, 35, but chooses instead to cite their eating, drinking, and playing that *followed* their sacrifices.[18] Fee (1987: 454) points out that the text specifically indicates that the people ate in the presence of the golden calf. He infers from this that idolatry for Paul is "a matter of eating cultic meals in the idol's presence." Although Paul's concern is not limited to Christians eating in an idol setting, this connection reveals that he certainly regarded eating in the presence of an idol as idolatry.

Calvin (1960: 208) asks why Paul mentions the feast and the games rather than the worship, and gives an answer that is on target. Paul chose what best suited the Corinthian situation: "For it is not likely that they were in the habit of attending the gatherings of unbelievers in order to prostrate themselves before the idols, but they used to share in the feasts, which the unbelievers held in honour of their gods, and did not keep away from the debased rites which were the marks of idolatry." The citation scores the point that "the feasting and the playing were both aspects of the idolatry" (Calvin 1960: 207–8). With this quotation from Exod. 32:6, Paul seeks to drive home his point that willingly participating in idolatry in any way has dire consequences, if the pattern of God's dealing with the wilderness generation is any indication.

The phrase "rose up to play" (ἀνέστησαν παίζειν, *anestēsan paizein*) has sexual overtones (cf. Gen. 26:8 LXX) and may be connected metaphorically to idolatrous festivals and cultic, orgiastic dancing (Robertson and Plummer 1914: 204; Ellis 1957: 55; Barrett 1968: 225; Tomson 1990: 189–93). The NIV renders it felicitously as "indulged in pagan revelry." Paul's exhortation against immorality in 1 Cor. 10:8 may indicate that "the Corinthian idolatrous rites may have involved sexual sin" (Edwards 1885: 248; Fee 1987: 455) or that he assumes that idolatry ultimately leads to sexual debauchery (see Josephus, *Ant.* 18.3.4 §§65–80).

Paul takes the edge off any condemnation of the Corinthians with a hortatory subjunctive (πορνεύωμεν, *porneuōmen*) that includes himself in the warning, "let us not commit fornication."[19] Sexual immorality has surfaced in various forms at Corinth (5:1–13; 6:12–20; 7:2–5),[20] but he is not simply reiterating his earlier warnings. He has in mind a metaphorical harlotry (Num. 25:1–9; Rev. 2:14, 21). In the minds of most

10:8

---

18. Paul also does not refer to God's penalty for the sin as he does in 10:8–9. Koet (1996: 613) claims that he "presupposes among his audience knowledge about the dynamics of the story of the Golden Calf." His discussion of Moses' veil in 2 Cor. 3 assumes that the readers have some knowledge of this story (see Garland 1999: 183–90).

19. Conzelmann (1975: 168) thinks that "the tone is intensified by the change from the imperative of v 7 to the first person plural."

20. Someone so bold as to flaunt moral convention and have his father's wife (5:1–5) would also be likely to dare to eat in idol temples.

Jews, sexual immorality and idolatry were two sides of the same coin (Wis. 14:12; T. Reub. 4:6; Philo, *Mos.* 1.55 §302). Most assume that he alludes to Num. 25:1–9, which recounts the people having sexual relations with the women of Moab and then being invited to sacrifice to their gods: "The people ate and bowed down to their gods" (Num. 25:2). The LXX translates the "gods" in Num. 25:2 as "idols" (προσεκύνησαν τοῖς εἰδώλοις αὐτῶν, *prosekynēsan tois eidōlois autōn*) and states specifically that they ate their sacrifices. Their actions provoked God's bitter anger, and only the brutal zealotry of Phinehas, spearing an Israelite and a Midianite woman in mid-embrace, arrested a plague from destroying the people.[21] The text concludes, "Nevertheless those that died by the plague were twenty-four thousand" (Num. 25:9).

The "Case of the Missing Thousand"—the discrepancy between Paul's number, twenty-three thousand, and the twenty-four thousand mentioned in Num. 25:9—has prompted a number of solutions. Some attribute it to a lapse of memory on Paul's part (Robertson and Plummer 1914: 205; Lietzmann 1949: 47; Barrett 1968: 225) or to confusion with Num. 26:62, which gives the number of Israelite males enrolled in the census after the plague as twenty-three thousand (Conzelmann 1975: 168; Schrage 1995: 400; Wolff 1996: 219; R. Collins 1999: 371). Others attempt to harmonize the discrepancy. Fee (1987: 456) suggests that Paul may have relied on a different tradition (cf. Weiss 1910: 254), though all known sources have twenty-four thousand. Calvin (1960: 208–9) claims that the real number was 23,500 which Numbers and Paul rounded off—Paul rounding it down and Numbers rounding it up, but both being inaccurate. Morris (1958: 143) imagines that Paul makes an allowance for those slain by the judges (Num. 25:5), and Godet (1887: 62) claims that Paul attempted to avoid "the risk of exaggeration" by knocking off one thousand. Mare (1976: 249) preserves an ancient tradition that twenty-three thousand died in one day, and the other thousand died later, which Bruce (1971: 92) dismisses as "harmonistic pilpulism" (far-fetched hairsplitting argumentation used by rabbinic students).

A more promising alternative suggests that Paul deliberately mixed Num. 25:9 with Exod. 32:28, which records that three thousand died at the hands of the Levites who administered harsh punishment on the stubborn idolaters (Koet 1996). Exodus 32 forms a prominent backdrop for Paul's warnings against idolatry, and he has just quoted Exod. 32:6 in 1 Cor. 10:7. Koet (1996: 612; cf. Lapide 1896: 232–33) concludes that Paul did not make a careless mistake but intentionally combined the texts to connect the punishment in Num. 25:1–9 for having sexual

---

21. Philo (*Mos.* 1.57 §302) interprets the incident by claiming that Phinehas killed a man who was offering a sacrifice and visiting a harlot.

relations with Moabite women and joining in the sacrifices to their gods with the sin of idolatry before the golden calf. In 1 Cor. 10:8, Paul appears to have chosen Exod. 32:28 as the model for his wording, "they fell" (ἔπεσαν, *epesan*), "[in that] one day" (μιᾷ ἡμέρᾳ, *mia hēmera*), and "three thousand" (τρεῖς χιλιάδες, *treis chiliades*), and combined it with the "twenty" (εἴκοσι, *eikosi*) from the Numbers text. Since twenty-four is a much more common multiple than twenty-three in the OT, it would seem to be deliberate choice.

If Christ is to be identified as the rock that followed the Israelites (10:4), their sin could be regarded as against Christ (8:12; 10:22), and Paul connects the sin of putting God to the proof by their brazen violation of the covenant with the Corinthian situation: "Let us not sorely tempt Christ just as some of them tempted [him]." The Corinthians' participation in idol meals violates their covenant relationship with Christ. **10:9**

Moses memorialized the people's faithlessness with a play on words, calling the place where they tested God and wrangled with Moses "Massah," which means "testing, proof," and "Meribah," which means "quarreling, faultfinding" (Exod. 17:7). In the LXX version of Ps. 95:8 (94:8 LXX), these place names are not transliterated but translated into Greek as "testing" and "rebellion." The "snakes" recalls Num. 21:4–9, when the people became peevish and spoke against God and against Moses, expressing their annoyance about the menu entrées in the wilderness and the lack of water. The verb "test" (ἐκπειράζειν, *ekpeirazein*) does not appear in Num. 21, but it does in the summary of this incident in Ps. 77:18 LXX: "They tested God in their heart by demanding the food they craved" (see also Exod. 17:2; Deut. 6:16). This textual connection links the incident back to their craving (1 Cor. 10:6). God sent serpents to bite and kill many of them. With the dreaded image of vipers striking unsuspecting victims and causing painful deaths, Paul deliberately heightens the horror of the punishment that will smite those who affront God.[22]

The image of grumbling characterizes the whole wilderness experience of Israel (Num. 14:36; 16:41, 49; 17:5, 10) but is particularly associated with putting God to the test (Exod. 17:2–3). Their grumbling about food kindled God's anger against them (Num. 11:1; 14:2–4). The "destroyer" may be the destroying angel who carries out any divine sentence of punishment (Schneider, *TDNT* 5:169–70; Exod. 12:23; Wis. 18:25; Heb. 11:28; cf. 2 Sam. 24:16; 1 Chron. 21:12; 2 Chron. 32:21; Sir. 48:21; Acts **10:10**

---

22. Findlay (1910: 860–61) and Robertson and Plummer (1914: 205) may press the imperfect tense (ἀπώλλυντο, *apōllynto*) too far by suggesting that they "lay a-perishing" or perished "over several days." Paul means only to convey that disaster struck, and the aspect of the verb says nothing about the span of that disaster.

12:23), or it may refer to Satan.[23] If the destroying angel who killed the firstborn in Egypt (Exod. 12:23) is in view, it reveals a terrifying mystery that God's instrument to liberate the people can return, in boomerang fashion, to strike them dead for their disobedience.

The litany of Israel's sins in Ps. 105 LXX (106 MT and Eng.) provides the best backdrop for understanding the reference to the grumbling. Paul's exposition has noticeable vocabulary parallels with the psalm: "craving" (ἐπιθύμειν, epithymein; Ps. 105:14/1 Cor. 10:6), "putting God to the test" (πειράζειν, peirazein; Ps. 105:14/1 Cor. 10:9), "grumbling" (γογγύζειν, gongyzein; Ps. 105:25/1 Cor. 10:10), "committing fornication" as a figurative reference to idolatry (πορνεύειν, porneuein; Ps. 105:39/1 Cor. 10:7), and God's threat to destroy them ([ἐξ]ολοθρεύειν, [ex]olothreuein; Ps. 105:23/1 Cor. 10:9, 10). The psalm also lists idolatry (Ps. 105:19, 28, 36–39/1 Cor. 10:7, 14) and eating idol food (Ps. 105:28) in its condemnation of Israel's apostasy. In the psalm, their destruction (Ps. 105:23, 26) is related to their grumbling (Ps. 105:25).

Paul perhaps singles out "grumbling" because the Corinthians have been guilty of murmuring against him (so Robertson and Plummer 1914: 206; Moffatt 1938: 132; Oster 1995: 235), particularly because of his hard-line stance against their participation in idol feasts (Fee 1987: 457). As Moses protested the peoples' idolatry, so Paul has protested the Corinthians' participation in sacrificial meals. As the people of Israel grumbled against the leader appointed by God, so also Paul insinuates that the Corinthians are no less guilty of rebelliously grumbling against him and refusing to listen to his counsel.[24]

10:11 The phrase "they were recorded for our admonition" makes clear that Paul understands these accounts to serve as cautionary tales. Admonishment (νουθεσία, nouthesia) is vital for developing spiritually mature Christians (cf. Rom. 15:14; 1 Cor. 4:14; Col. 1:28; 3:16; 1 Thess. 5:12; 2 Thess. 3:15; Titus 3:10), and the string of events occurring during Israel's wilderness wanderings—God's blessings and judgments—happened "by way of example" for us.[25] They reveal to "us" both God's love and God's wrath.

This assertion implies that what is recorded in the Scriptures has meaning beyond the events themselves. The past was recorded with a view to the future. P. Gardner (1994: 114) comments, "For Paul, even

---

23. The noun "the destroyer" (ὀλοθρευτής, olothreutēs) occurs only here. The participle ὁ ὀλοθρεύων (ho olothreuōn, the destroying one), appears in Exod. 12:23; Wis. 18:25; Heb. 11:28. The noun ὄλεθρον (olethron) appears in 1 Cor. 5:5, where Paul instructs them to deliver the incestuous man to Satan for the "destruction" of his flesh.

24. Paul compares himself to Moses in 2 Cor. 3:7–18.

25. This view corresponds with the rabbinic understanding, expressed in b. Sanh. 99a and b. Ber. 34a, that all the prophets prophesied for the day of the Messiah (Wolff 1996: 221).

the writing down of these events had been overseen providentially so that people might be instructed." This axiom would have been obvious to Jews, long indoctrinated in Scripture, but Gentile Christians may have been less acquainted with it. They have blithely ignored the warning siren blaring from the biblical accounts of Israel's chronic idolatry and terrifying punishment. If the wilderness generation met such a horrifying end by spurning a concealed Christ who nurtured them throughout their journey, how much more the Corinthians will be condemned if they spurn the revealed Christ. Understanding the exodus from this particular perspective, as a morality tale that mirrors the present, reveals that God has not suddenly become more lax in punishing transgression with the shift of the ages and the transition from the "ministry of condemnation" to the new "ministry of justification" (2 Cor. 3:9).

Paul adds that the Scripture is particularly applicable for "us" "upon whom the ends of the ages has arrived." The verb καταντᾶν (*katantan*) can mean "to arrive at," "to reach," "to come to," or "to end up at" (Spicq, *TLNT* 2:269–70). In this case, it means that the ages have "reached their destination" (Robertson and Plummer 1914: 207). They have followed a long and complex divine trajectory that has now arrived at a predetermined goal, the "fullness of time" (Gal. 4:4). In another sense, it has "overtaken" (Edwards 1885: 250) those who live in this present age, encountering and confronting them with God's truth (Spicq, *TLNT* 2:270). The plural "the *ends* of the ages" may mean that "end" refers to a kind of frontier point where the old dispensation meets the new. The one reaches its completion; the other begins. The implication is that the Corinthians stand in a new age. This interpretation, however, stretches the meaning of the word "end" beyond recognition, making it also mean "beginning" or "juncture." Other options suggest that the plural "ends" derives from attraction to the plural "ages" (Bruce 1971: 93); or that it derives from a Hebraic idiom that uses plural nouns (such as "heavens," "ages"), when a singular noun is normally used in English (N. Turner 1965: 114–15), so that it should be translated "the end of the age."[26] For Paul, however, the two ages overlap (Soards 1999: 12–15, 207). It is more likely that he assumes that successive periods of God's working in the history of Israel and humankind have reached their respective ends (cf. 1 Pet. 1:20), and Christians can "reap the benefit of the experience of all these completed ages" (Robertson and Plummer 1914: 207). Only those who read the experience of the ages from the vantage point of Christ's cross and resurrection will truly be enlightened.

26. The meaning of "ends" as "spiritual revenues" (MacPherson 1943–44: 222) should be dismissed.

However we understand the term "ends," Paul believes that the Scriptures reveal the eternal purposes of God, and those purposes have been fulfilled and unveiled in Christ. Silva (*DPL* 640) points out,

> Paul's use of Scripture was guided by the conviction that God was the Lord of history. . . . And because the same God who ruled over that history inspired the biblical writers, it is inevitable that the text of Scripture would include a certain undercurrent—a "deeper meaning"?—that could only become clear after the fulfillment of the promises.

The earlier generations lived at the beginning, when God's promises were being announced. Christians stand at a point when God's promises have been fulfilled in Christ and the veil has been lifted (2 Cor. 3:14–18). Hidden realities have been revealed (1 Cor. 2:9–12, 16)—for example, that Christ was the prime mover in these events (10:4). Christians need to recognize how these realities apply to the present.

10:12 Paul clinches his argument in this segment: "So then, let the one who presumes to stand watch out lest he fall." "To fall" in the OT context meant to die (Num. 14:3) and recalls the wretched demise of the desert generation that serves as an enduring warning to the people of God in every age (Heb. 4:11). In Rom. 11:11–12, however, "stumbling" and "falling" refer to "the loss of salvation, not just occasional slips" (Willis 1985b: 157). The Corinthian "knowers" not only need to watch lest they cause others to stumble and fall (1 Cor. 8:13); they also need to watch lest they fall themselves.

The perfect infinitive ἑστάναι (*hestanai*) refers to those who think that they are standing fast now, and it may refer to a sense of covenant security (P. Gardner 1994: 153; see Jer. 7:8–15). More likely, it is shorthand for standing in the faith (1 Cor. 16:13; cf. also 15:1; 2 Cor. 1:24; Rom. 5:2; 11:20; 14:4; so Wolff 1996: 223). This false assurance does not derive from some mistaken view of the sacramental efficacy of baptism and the Lord's Supper but from self-confident trust in their own knowledge. The substantive participle ὁ δοκῶν (*ho dokōn*) recalls Paul's statement in 1 Cor. 8:2, εἴ τις δοκεῖ ἐγνωκέναι τι (*ei tis dokei egnōkenai ti*, if anyone presumes to have arrived at complete knowledge about anything). That presumed "knowledge" has led them to risk idolatrous associations and to think nothing of it. They remained oblivious to the fact that it placed them, not to mention the person with a weak conscience, in dire spiritual jeopardy. They did not sit down and cooly calculate the potential consequences of their idolatry and reach the theological conclusion that they were immune to any spiritual repercussions. They did not think that there was any danger at all—like thirsty hikers who drink from a mountain stream, unaware of the debilitating giardia that might lurk in the crystal-clear water. Paul sounds the alarm against pagan banquets that may seem to the Corinthians to be only innocuous conviviality combined with meaningless ritual. He is not addressing the question of the security of the believer but calling attention to the pitfall of being careless because of overconfidence (Robertson and Plummer 1914: 208).

Paul does not single out a particular group or indict the whole community with a broad brush. The use of the singular "let each one watch" (βλεπέτω, blepetō; sometimes translated "let those" to be gender inclusive) requires each auditor to examine his or her own life. If Paul thinks that he could fall (9:27), how much more, then, could the Corinthians fall. Their security rests on their continuing fidelity to God and God alone (cf. Rom. 11:22). Calvin's (1960: 212–13) comments are pertinent. The assurance that Paul attacks is not the assurance of faith that rests on the promises of God but the assurance that "has its roots in nonchalance." It is the assurance of swollen-headed persons who are guilty of a misplaced confidence in their own knowledge.

Because 10:13 does not seem to connect logically with what precedes, **10:13** Godet (1887: 68) labels it "undoubtedly one of the most difficult of the whole Epistle." It could have been omitted, and the imperative to flee idolatry in 10:14 would have seemed a fitting conclusion to 10:1–12 (Fee 1987: 460). The question that must be addressed is how 10:13 fits the thrust of Paul's argument.

What is the testing that Paul has in view? The best option will make sense of it in the context of the warning examples he has just enumerated and the exhortation to flee idolatry that immediately follows. M. Mitchell's (1993: 254) answer, that it refers to the temptation to split into factions, makes no sense in the context. Others argue that it is a temptation related to foolish pride. They are tempted then to flaunt their knowledge and their invincibility before idols (P. Gardner 1994: 154), and they fail to realize that they are tottering on a precipice. Still others regard it as the temptation to seize every opportunity for "good company, good food, and good fun" (Willis 1985b: 63). These interpretations assume that the πειρασμός (peirasmos) refers to some internal temptation to sin. Instead, Paul may have in mind external testing. The verb εἴληφεν (eilēphen, has come upon, befallen, or overtaken), in the perfect tense, suggests that these trials come from outside their own willful desires (Fee 1987: 460 n. 50). The verb ὑποφέρειν (hypopherein, to bear up under) appears two other times in the NT in the context of persecution (2 Tim. 3:11; 1 Pet. 2:19). The ends of the ages (1 Cor. 10:11) was assumed also to bring in its wake a time of grueling trials (Smit 1997a: 44). I conclude with Findlay (1910: 862) that the "testing" involves "both the allurements of idolatry and the persecution which its abandonment entailed."

Avoiding all overt associations with idolatry would invite hostility, especially when one was a guest at the home of a religiously minded host who offered food that had been sanctified by an idol. If the host was a patron, one's refusal to eat idol food could be taken as a grave insult to the god and the host, and such an affront could lead to financial retribution. If the host was a family member or a neighbor, the refusal could result in being cast into the outer darkness of social banishment. After her conversion and renunciation of idols and idol food, Aseneth laments being hated by her family and her people (Jos. As. 11:3–9). In the face of such pressure, Christians would be tempted to compromise and rationalize their decisions (Cheung 1999: 38). The social problems created for Christians who abandoned idolatry are described in 1 Pet. 4:3–4: former friends are surprised at the Christians' new temperance, and in their irritation they malign them and blaspheme God. Withdrawing from all idolatrous functions would scuttle any ambitions for social advancement, impair patron/client relations, fuel ostracism, and damage economic partnerships.

The pressure to compromise and to join in the hail-fellow-well-met conviviality was intense. Paul assures them, however, that any testing that comes upon Christians will be met with God's faithfulness. God will not allow them to be tempted beyond what they can withstand,[27] and God will provide a means of escape so that they can endure it. In the Corinthian situation, a refusal to participate in idol feasts will not result in any trauma that God's power cannot help them endure. Consequently, there is no excuse for any compromising involvement in idolatry (Newton 1998: 332).

Paul understands these trials to be unexceptional. Ἀνθρώπινος (anthrōpinos) indicates temptations that are common to humanity (Edwards 1885: 251; Barrett 1968: 229; Murphy-O'Connor 1979a: 96; Fee 1987: 460 n. 51; P. Gardner 1994: 154). The Corinthians do not face unique, unbearable circumstances (Oster 1995: 238). As surely as God tests, God provides a way out (see Gen. 22:1–19). That exit is not an escape hatch that allows them to evade all difficulties. God's power does not bring an end to the testing, because that would make it unnecessary to provide the means for them "to bear up under it" (τοῦ δύνασθαι ὑπενεγκεῖν, tou dynasthai hypenenkein [genitive of the articular infinitive expressing purpose or result]).

The description of God as faithful appears in Deut. 7:9 in a covenant context: "Know therefore that the LORD your God is God, the faithful God who maintains covenant loyalty with those who love him and keep his commandments, to a thousand generations." In Deut. 32:4, it is re-

---

27. Conzelmann (1975: 169) comments, "The measure of the bearable cannot be theoretically determined. It shows itself on each occasion in the measure God appoints."

lated to the epithet "rock." If the Corinthians are not faithful in their covenant obligations, if they put Christ to the test, if they compromise their loyalty and are caught in the flypaper of idolatry, they can expect no divine aid, only destruction (see Fee 1987: 460). Disporting themselves at idolatrous feasts is akin to deliberately drinking poison and then praying for miraculous healing! God cannot be blamed when recovery fails to happen. God was attested as faithful throughout the OT (Deut. 7:9; 32:4; Ps. 31:5; 69:13; 145:13; Isa. 25:1; 49:7), and yet the people who flagrantly disobeyed were destroyed or defeated and exiled. God is just as faithful to destroy the wicked as God is faithful to save the righteous.

This verse serves as both warning and encouragement (P. Gardner 1994: 155), but the emphasis lies on comfort (Robertson and Plummer 1914: 208–9; Willis 1985b: 157). After the gloomy, threatening example of Israel, Paul urges perseverance with a note of assurance. When one puts God to the test, it will inevitably result in catastrophic judgment, as it did for Israel. But when one is tested and places one's trust in God, God provides a way through the testing. Calvin (1960: 214) writes, "Therefore, once He has taken you under his own faithfulness . . . , you have no need to be afraid, so long as you depend wholly on Him." This assurance strengthens the Christian to endure unto the end (cf. Mark 13:13).

Additional Notes

10:1–13. Some argue that 10:1–13 was a carefully composed homily (possibly pre-Christian) that Paul inserts into this context (Barrett 1968: 220; Conzelmann 1975: 165; Meeks 1982: 65; R. Collins 1999: 364; Cope 1990, who claims that 10:1–22 was composed by someone other than Paul). Others assume that this list of failures during the desert period was a sustained midrash on the text of Numbers that Paul composed prior to, and therefore independent of, the Corinthian situation, and he judged it relevant for the current situation (Collier 1994: 72; Horrell 1997b: 95–96; Beardslee 1994: 92–93; P. Gardner 1994: 114 ["possibly"]). There is no valid reason to surmise that this interpretation of the wilderness story did not originate with Paul and was not composed specifically for this occasion. This does not mean that Paul had not thought or taught about these texts prior to composing this letter.

1. Using terms such as "midrash" to describe 10:1–13—even with a minimalistic definition of it ("essentially the written explanation of a written text" [R. Collins 1999: 364])—is not helpful (see Silva, *DPL* 638). Some take "midrash" to imply "a distinctive Jewish interpretation" that has a tendency to embellish the narrative, a fanciful method that employs exegetical legerdemain opposed to the grammatico-historical method. More constructive is a definition that describes midrash as exegesis that is interested in application of the text to life situations (see Neusner 1987). The term "midrash," however, casts an unwarranted aura of mystery upon what Paul is doing. On the other hand, R. Horsley (1998: 134) contends that what we have in 10:1–13 is not a midrash at all because "its point of departure is not a scriptural text, it is not set in the context of the scriptural text, and it is not presented for the sake of the scriptural text."

2. The whole question of the origin of the passage is irrelevant because Paul has made it thoroughly conform to the rhetorical situation. The warnings from the OT are selected and arranged to correspond to the situation of the Corinthians (Smit 1997a: 49–50; Oropeza 1998: 67; R. Horsley 1998: 132). Fee (1987: 442 n. 5) asks, "Why, given its perfect fit in this context with no clear 'seams' and given Paul's own rabbinic background and acknowledged genius, could he have not composed such a Christian 'midrash' ad hoc?"

3. The hapax legomena can be attributed to the exegesis of a unique passage from the OT and do not necessarily derive from some preformed source. Any parallels with Jewish exegesis can easily be explained. The wilderness tradition was so fundamental to Jewish self-understanding that Paul would not have interpreted the text in a vacuum, as if he never had heard previous interpretations of the text's meaning. The "elegant symmetry of the piece" (Meeks 1982: 71) does not require that it had been created beforehand. It may simply exhibit Paul's skill as an interpreter of the Scriptures.

10:2. The passive ἐβαπτίσθησαν should be read instead of the middle ἐβαπτίσαντο. The external evidence for the passive (ℵ, A, C, D, E, F, G, Ψ, 33, 81, 104, 365, 630, 2464, 2495, Basil, Didymus, Cyril) and the middle ($\mathfrak{P}^{46c}$, B, K, L, P, 61, 1739, 1881, + Maj, Origen) is almost equally divided. Some argue that the middle, "they accepted baptism," was changed to the passive, "they were baptized," because the latter was the more common expression for baptism (cf. 1:13; 12:13; Robertson and Plummer 1914: 200; Barrett 1968: 220–21). Paul never uses the middle for "baptize" elsewhere in his letters. Héring (1962: 86) claims that the middle corresponds to Jewish practice in which the convert baptized himself or herself, and Zuntz (1953: 234) and Fee (1987: 441 n. 2) argue that it is unlikely that a scribe would have changed the passive to the middle. In a bracketed note, Metzger and Wikgren (Metzger 1994: 493) dissent from the majority of the committee and argue that the middle form is original and was changed to the passive. However, a change from passive to middle could have been motivated by the desire to distinguish "baptism into Moses" from "baptism in Christ" (R. Collins 1999: 368).

10:4. The following texts assume a movable well (see Enns 1996: 24–25):

> He ... brought forth a well of water to follow them. ... And it [the water] followed them in the wilderness for forty years and went up the mountain with them and went down into the plains. (Pseudo-Philo, *Bib. Ant.* 10:7; 11:15)

> So the well which was with Israel in the wilderness, was like a rock, traveling with them ... and it made mighty streams. (*t. Sukkah* 3:11–12)

> Did not a brook follow them in the wilderness and provide them fat fish? (*Sipre Num.* 11:21)

> Now since it [the well] was given to them, it went down with them to the valleys. (*Targum Onqelos* on Num. 21:16–20)

> How was the well constructed? It was rock-shaped like kind of a beehive and wherever they journeyed it rolled along. ... When the standards halted ... the same rock would settle. (*Num. Rab.* 1.5 on 21:17)

10:9. Three readings are found in the witnesses: τὸν Χριστόν ($\mathfrak{P}^{46}$, D, F, G, Ψ, 1739, 1881, lat, syr, cop), κύριον (ℵ, B, C, P, 17, eth, arm), and θεόν (A, 81). "Christ" is the hardest reading because a scribe might have wondered how the wilderness generation tempted Christ instead of God and would have brought the text into line with Exod. 17:7 and Deut. 6:16 by changing it to "Lord" (Zuntz 1953: 126–27). Parry (1926: 147) argues against the reading "Christ": "Even in view of v. 4 it would not be natural to speak of the Israelites tempting Christ." This statement unintentionally articulates the reason why copyists might have been persuaded to change it. "Christ" seems to be the reading that best explains the others, unless one attributes it to an attempt to christianize the Scriptures (R. Collins 1999: 372). But Paul shows that he understands "Lord" in the OT to refer to Christ (cf. 2 Cor. 3:16), and it would not be difficult for him to interchange God and Christ to make the account directly relevant to the Corinthian situation. The external attestation and intrinsic probability point to Χριστόν as the original reading, while κύριον arose as a "theologically motivated alteration to the text" (Osburn 1981: 209).

10:10. Some witnesses read a hortatory subjunctive, γογγύζωμεν (ℵ, D, G^gr, 33, it^d, cop^bo, arm, Origen, Chrysostom, Augustine), instead of the imperative γογγύζετε (A, B, C, K, P, Ψ, 81, 104, 614, 1739, majority of minuscules, lat, syr, cop^sa, eth). The subjunctive may be attributable to intentional or unintentional assimilation to the previous clause, μηδὲ ἐκπειράζωμεν (Metzger 1971: 560; not discussed in Metzger 1994). Willis (1985b: 147) argues that the verbs in 10:7–10 form an ABB′A′ pattern:

- A second person imperative (γίνεσθε)
  - B first person subjunctive (πορνεύωμεν)
  - B′ first person subjunctive (ἐκπειράζωμεν)
- A′ second person imperative (γογγύζετε)

10:11. The majority of witnesses add πάντα, some after the ταῦτα δέ (C, K, P, Ψ, 88, 104, 326, 436, 451, 614, 629, 1241, 1877, 1984, 1985, 2127, 2492, 2495), and some before it (ℵ, D^gr, G, 81, 181). Its varying position suggests that it was a gloss, perhaps inserted to emphasize that it encompassed more than the ταῦτα δέ in 10:6.

E. Refutation of Their Practice from the Example of the Lord's Supper (10:14–22)

Paul's insistence on exclusive loyalty to a religion was something uncommon in paganism. People were accustomed to joining in the sacrificial meals of various deities, none of which required an exclusive relationship (see Walter 1978–79: 429–30; Willis 1985b: 213; Smit 1997a: 48). The Hellenistic world was a great religious melting pot, and tolerance and syncretism reflected the spirit of the times. The Greeks and, later, the Romans were very tolerant in their attitude toward the kaleidoscope of other religions and cultures. They understood that every nation had its own ancestral traditions, its own temples and gods, and that worship of these gods was a part of everyday life. For practical reasons, the Romans did not want to alienate the regional deities within the empire and did not insist that everyone worship Roman gods alone. For theoretical reasons, traditional local deities were left alone because the intellectual elite assumed that the gods of Rome, Greece, Egypt, Asia, Judea, and Persia were symbolic representatives of an ultimate ground of being. They basically said, "You may continue to worship your gods and goddesses; we will worship them as well and you can worship ours. That way, no one's gods will be slighted." This openness to other gods is reflected in the altar to an unknown god in Athens (Acts 17:23), which offered homage to whatever god the people may have neglected to honor. The relative disinterest in doctrine and the utilitarian interest in the power of individual gods to deliver a desired outcome also mitigated the potential for any theological friction.

Most people honored gods whom they thought were useful. Some believed that there was "safety in numbers" and worshiped a smorgasbord of deities. The more gods that were honored, the better their chance of success in life. Paul radically rejects all such syncretism and anything that might even hint of it. His attempt to convince the Corinthians that the Christian's fellowship with Christ restricted them from any association with other gods was not an easy task. Christian parents who have had to forbid their teenage children from attending something that the parents recognize as fundamentally opposed to Christian values may best understand the difficulty. How do they explain to the children why they may not participate when all their friends are going and they will be left out and perhaps ostracized?

Paul attempts to makes his case by arguing from the Lord's Supper. Because mention of the Lord's Supper is rare in Paul's letters, this passage has been milked for every ounce of information that it might offer about his theology and practice. It should not be forgotten that Paul brought it up only as part of his argument against idol food. He worries about the danger of "serial fellowships." The Supper of the one Lord, which unites participants to him, excludes eating idol offerings, which unites participants to idols and their demons (Smit 1997a: 48). As the Lord's Supper is a sacred meal that represents and creates a fellowship of believers in the worship of Christ, who is considered to be present, so pagan meals represent and create a fellowship of worshipers of pagan deities who also are considered to be present. Idols, however, represent the realm of the demonic. Participating in the one meal precludes participating in the other. In 10:14–17, Paul develops the theological significance of participating in the Lord's Supper (cf. 10:1–5). In 10:18–20, he develops the theological significance of participation in pagan sacrificial meals (cf. 10:6–10). He draws the conclusion in 10:21–22 that participation in the Lord's Supper bars participation in pagan sacrificial meals in any form. Believers should not fool themselves into thinking that they are strong enough to try to merge the two meals, to affiliate with Christ and demons. To attempt to do so only kindles the jealousy and judgment of God.

Exegesis and Exposition

[14]Therefore, my beloved, flee from idolatry! [15]I speak to you as sensible people. You be the judge of what I declare. [16]The cup of blessing which we bless, is it not fellowship in the blood of Christ? The bread which we break, is it not fellowship in the body of Christ? [17]Because [there is] one bread, we who are many are one body. For all partake from the one bread. [18]Consider the downfall of Israel in the wilderness. Are not those who eat the sacrifices partners in the altar? [19]What, then, do I declare? That food that has been sacrificed to an idol is anything or that an idol is anything? [20]No, [I am declaring] that ⌜what they sacrifice, they sacrifice to demons, not to God⌝. I do not want you to become partners with demons! [21]You are not able to drink the cup of the Lord and the cup of demons. You are not able to partake from the table of the Lord and the table of demons. [22]Or will we continue to provoke the jealousy of the Lord? We are not stronger than he is, are we?

Paul opens this segment of his argument against idol offerings with a direct command that is the climactic conclusion to his previous arguments.[1] The address ἀγαπητοί μου (*agapētoi mou*, my beloved; cf. 15:58; 2 Cor. 7:1; 12:19) recalls his genuine affection for the Corinthians and

10:14

---

1. Διόπερ (*dioper*, therefore, for this very reason) appears elsewhere only in 8:13.

their bond before he reloads and fires off a more direct salvo against their compromise in eating idol food. It parallels 1 Cor. 4:14, where Paul pauses after a long argument and uses "similar language to remind them that they are his dear children—despite the vigor with which he has had to argue with them" (Fee 1987: 464).

As the command in 10:12 summarizes the lesson to be learned from what happened to the wilderness generation (10:1–11), so the command in 10:14 gives the fundamental mandate from all of the arguments, beginning in 8:1. It matches the prohibition "Flee fornication" in 6:18, which follows Paul's theological castigation of sexual sins in 5:1–6:17. The two, idolatry and sexual immorality, are intertwined in Paul's mind (Rom. 1:18–32; Gal. 5:19–21; Col. 3:5; cf. 1 Pet. 4:3). The parallels with 1 Cor. 6:12–20 shed light on the thrust of Paul's argument in 10:14–11:1:

10:14: Flee from idolatry.	6:18: Flee from fornication.
10:16–17: The Lord's Supper represents that we are one body with Christ.	6:15–17: Your bodies are members of Christ; you cannot become one body with a prostitute.
10:23: All things are lawful, but not all things are helpful.	6:12: All things are lawful, but not all things are helpful.
10:31: Do all to the glory of God.	6:20: Glorify God in your body.

As a union with a prostitute is unthinkable for a Christian, so becoming a partner at the table with demons is equally unthinkable.

The preposition ἀπό (apo, from) instead of ἐκ (ek, out of) implies that Paul is not calling them out of idolatry but exhorting them to "flee away from" idolatry (Robertson and Plummer 1914: 211; Newton 1998: 334). The imperative's present tense (φεύγετε, pheugete) may imply that this must be an unremitting battle (cf. 1 John 5:21, "Guard yourselves from idols"). They are not yet bogged down in the miry swamp of idolatry and in need of being extricated, but they do need to be warned that they are walking into spiritual quicksand. The translations "shun" (RSV) or "have nothing to do with" (REB) are too weak. Paul is doing more than urging "a certain caution in the face of temptation," as Castelli (1991: 111–12) believes. Idolatry is like radioactive waste: it requires them to bolt from this area immediately to avoid contamination and certain death.

Edwards (1885: 251) claims that the command continues the metaphor from 1 Cor. 10:13 of an army caught (εἴληφεν, eilēphen) in a narrow passage between mountains and directed to flee through the mountain pass (ἔκβασις, ekbasis). Robertson and Plummer (1914: 211) also connect it to the previous verse: "Flight is the sure ἔκβασις in all such temptations, and they have it in their own power: all occasions must be shunned. . . . They must not try how near they can go, but how far they can fly." The point may be that the Corinthians cannot recklessly walk into a trap and then expect God's deliverance. They must avoid it completely.

In 10:19–20, food sacrificed to idols, εἰδωλόθυτον (eidōlothyton), and an idol, εἴδωλον (eidōlon), are in apposition. Paul considers attending idol feasts and eating idol food to be idolatry regardless of how the Corinthians may have rationalized and justified such behavior with their knowledge. The sacrificial feasts where this food was distributed did not simply border on idolatry (contra Godet 1887: 74); they *were* idolatrous. This next segment of his argument does not change the subject or broaden the topic to include actual participation in pagan sacrifices but continues the repudiation of attending gatherings of unbelievers and eating idol food. It introduces an argument from *pathos:* the ramifications of their sharing in the Lord's Supper.

The sharp command in 10:14 is balanced by persuasive argument. Some think that identifying the Corinthians as sensible people (φρόνιμοι, *phronimoi*) contains a slight touch of irony (Weiss 1910: 256; Barrett 1968: 231; P. Gardner 1994: 168; Witherington 1995: 224; probably Schrage 1995: 435 n. 314; Soards 1999: 211). Paul uses the term pejoratively in Rom. 11:25 and 12:16 in warning the readers not to claim to be wiser than they are, and he may sardonically salute "another of the Corinthians' favorite self-descriptions" (Hays 1997: 166; see also Wolff 1996: 226; Robertson and Plummer 1914: 211, "a gentle rebuke"). It is unlikely that Paul resorts to irony, as that would risk alienating his audience at this crucial stage in the argument. It would be particularly jarring just after addressing them as "my beloved" (1 Cor. 10:14). He truly believes that they are perceptive enough to see the illogic of their behavior and to discern the truth, so he presents a reasoned argument (Edwards 1885: 252; Findlay 1910: 863; Parry 1926: 150; Conzelmann 1975: 171 n. 12; Willis 1985b: 183; Fee 1987: 464–65; Smit 1997a: 49).[2] In 10:16–22, he asks seven rhetorical questions inviting their thoughtful response. He tries to persuade because it would do no good to coerce the "knowers" to stop fraternizing with idolaters in idolatrous settings—except that it might avert the weak from falling into ruin—if they do not recognize and accept in their hearts and minds how and why it is wrong. In the end, however, what counts is not just what they can understand but also their willingness to be faithful to Christ no matter the cost.

10:15

---

2. Robertson and Plummer (1914: 211) claim that the change from λέγω (*legō*) to φημί (*phēmi*) should be noted in translation, changing from "I say" to "I declare" (see Rom. 3:8).

10:16–17 Paul appeals to the Lord's Supper to make the point that sacrificial meals to idols are "similar, but opposite realities" (Smit 1997a: 51) and to admonish them to avoid any conscious contact with idolatrous rites no matter how meaningless or benign such might seem.[3] Each meal builds a bond between the participants and the deity honored in the meal (Hays 1997: 167). Willis (1985b: 193) notes, however, that verses 16–17 "frequently have been isolated from their context, and the real theme of the pericope—εἰδωλολατρία [eidōlolatria]—has been neglected." Paul is not setting forth teaching about the Lord's Supper but is using it to make an argument against reclining in idol shrines and eating food sacrificed to idols. It is misguided to try to reconstruct a Pauline doctrine of the Lord's Supper from this brief excerpt, particularly if it ignores his intention in this section.[4]

"The cup of blessing which we bless" is a Hebraic expression that may refer either to the cup that Jesus blessed at the Last Supper (Matt. 26:27; Mark 14:23; Luke 22:20; 1 Cor. 11:25; see Cohn-Sherbok 1980–81)[5] or to the church practice of pronouncing a blessing over the cup before distributing it. "Cup of blessing" is not a subjective genitive—the cup that brings a blessing (contra Karrer 1990: 212–15). The phrase "which we bless" parallels "the bread which we break" and refers to the church's celebration of the Lord's Supper. What is important for Paul is that the cup is not just any cup but the Lord's, and it recalls his action at the Last Supper when he served as host to his disciples (1 Cor. 11:25).

---

3. The order of cup then bread (cf. Luke 22:17; Did. 9:1–4) reverses the more traditional order of bread then cup found in 1 Cor. 11:23–26. Paul is not describing some form of the celebration of the Lord's Supper where the cup is distributed first, but why he alters the order is hard to determine and should not detain us. Robertson and Plummer (1914: 212–13) argue that Paul switches the order here to emphasize "the Blood-shedding, the characteristic act of Christ's sacrifice, and also to bring the eating of the bread into immediate juxtaposition with the eating at heathen sacrifices" (see also Fee 1987: 466; Hays 1997: 167). Käsemann (1964: 110) claims that Paul wants to emphasize the bread reference in 10:17 to express that the Christian community is one body.

4. The reference to "the fellowship in the body of Christ" has been misunderstood as intending to convey some sacramental view of receiving Christ (see Seesemann 1933: 51; Jourdan 1948: 111, 123–24; Bultmann 1951: 147; Robinson 1952: 65; Käsemann 1964: 111). Paul is not countering a mistaken conviction that the Lord's Supper offers invincibility over demons and immunity from retribution (contra Barrett 1968: 337). The approach of the *religionsgeschichtliche Schule* that sought to interpret passages related to the Lord's Supper from the perspective of pagan mystery religions used primary sources anachronistically, glossed over the fact that meals were not central to these cults, and made too much of a crude sacramental theophagy that was not evident in the sources (see Kane 1975; Willis 1985b: 45–63; P. Gardner 1994: 156; Newton 1998: 357–58).

5. One should exercise caution in trying to identify where this cup may have appeared in the Passover seder (contra Sigal 1983). The rituals connected to Passover that are known to us from the Mishnah developed after the destruction of the temple, when it no longer was a pilgrimage feast. Before then, the Passover practices probably were less uniform, and these later traditions may not reflect the custom in Jesus' day.

The "blood" recalls Christ's sacrifice and the benefits Christians receive from his death as an atonement for sins (Rom. 3:25; 5:9; Eph. 1:7; 2:13; Col. 1:20).

Reminding the Corinthians of their celebration of the Lord's Supper surfaces three things that directly apply to the issue of idol banquets. First and foremost is the assertion that partaking of the cup and the bread creates κοινωνία (*koinōnia*) with Christ.[6] "Fellowship" and its cognates occur four times in 1 Cor. 10:16–20. The verb μετέχειν (*metechein*, to share, partake) in 10:17, 21 is a synonym for κοινωνία (cf. 2 Cor. 6:14; Heb. 2:14; Willis 1985b: 196–97; contra Robertson and Plummer 1914: 212; Sebothema 1990).[7] Paul understands other sacral meals also to create fellowship between participants and the gods (Willis 1985b: 170–74), and the comments of Aelius Aristides (*Sarapis* 8) reveal that this idea was widespread. He says of his patron god Sarapis, "Men share in a special way the truest communion in the sacrifices to this god alone, as they invite [him] to the altar and appoint him as guest and host." Paul is leading his readers to see that they can never eat idol food as neutral participants, just as they cannot partake of the Lord's Supper as detached observers. Partaking of anything offered to a deity makes them accessories to the sacrificial act and creates solidarity with the honored deity, however tenuous their participation in the meal might be. Paul stresses that blessing the cup and partaking of the bread in the Lord's Supper forges a unique relationship between believer and Christ that excludes participation in all other sacral meals at which food is consumed in the presence of the deity (Walter 1978–79: 432–33; Fee 1987: 465, 467; Hays 1997: 167; Newton 1998: 336). Fellowship with Christ excludes all other fellowships, particularly those associated with idolatry (cf. 2 Cor. 6:14–16).

Second, Paul emphasizes that the Lord's Supper generates "partnership," "fellowship," "communion" with the fellow celebrants. The way he describes the Lord's Supper highlights its communal character (Newton 1998: 335). The cup is something *we* give thanks for, and the bread is something *we* break.[8] He draws the inference "Because there is but one loaf, the many believers who come together to the Lord's table are one body" (N. Turner 1965: 104). The Spirit, not the meal, cre-

6. Paul does not explain how this occurs, because that is not his interest.

7. R. Collins (1999: 376–77) notes, "Hos. 4:17 and 1 Enoch 104:6 speak of Ephraim being an associate (*metachos*) of idols. A second-century epigram of Serenos speaks of participation in libations and sacrifices: 'It was for libations and sacrifices that we came here [Philae], desiring to participate (*metachein*) in them' (*Sammelbuch griechischer Urkunden aus Ägypten* 8681.9)."

8. Klauck (1982: 262) thinks that Paul emphasizes an antithesis: on the table of the Lord there is bread; on the table of demons there is meat. The "breaking of bread," however, was the earliest reference to the Lord's Supper (Acts 2:42; 20:7, 11; 1 Cor. 11:23–24).

ates the unity among believers (1 Cor. 12:13), but the meal affirms and reinforces this unity in bringing them together. The disparate believers gathered around the table represent the one body of Christ—a theme that Paul will develop further in chapters 11–12.[9]

Paul's emphasis on the Corinthians' oneness with Christ and with one another is an important reminder that draws on the matrix of social assumptions connected to meals in this era. Neyrey (1991: 363) observes, "Meals-as-ceremonies replicate the group's basic social system, its values, lines, classifications, and its symbolic world." In the ancient world, people understood that meals incurred obligations. Given the ubiquitous patronage system, they also understood that one could not accept an invitation to eat with one's patron and also accept an invitation from one of that patron's bitter rivals without basically switching patrons (Smit 1997a: 53). Participating in a patron's meal displays one's solidarity with that patron. The unity with Christ and with one another in the meal has consequences for participation in any other meals that also create bonds and signal alliances. If meals embody the community (Willis 1985b: 218), then one cannot embody community with Christ and with demons. One cannot be aligned with Christ and aligned with demons.

Third, the emphasis on the blood of Christ sharpens the seriousness of the covenantal relationship to Christ. Blood seals a covenant (see Gen. 15:9–18; Exod. 24:3–8; Zech. 9:11; Heb. 9:18). The "fellowship of his blood" (1 Cor. 10:16) parallels the explanation of the cup in 11:25 as the new covenant in his blood. Willis (1985b: 218) claims, "What is decisive about the sacrifice of Jesus is that it created a new covenant between God and man (1 Cor. 11:21) and a resulting community of faith." Breaching this covenant can have only calamitous consequences.

10:18 Ἰσραὴλ κατὰ σάρκα (*Israēl kata sarka*) is frequently understood as referring to historical Israel ("the people of Israel," NIV, NRSV; Weiss 1910: 260; Robertson and Plummer 1914: 215; Barrett 1968: 235; Newton 1998: 337–39; R. Collins 1999: 380). It is more likely from the context that Paul has in mind wilderness Israel, whose sinful example (10:1–11) serves as a warning to all (Kistemaker 1993: 345–46; P. Gardner 1994: 155, 165; Schrage 1995: 442–43; Smit 1997a: 47; Cheung 1999: 148–50). The phrase κατὰ σάρκα refers, in this context, to the flesh caught in the power of sin, which leads to rebellion against God. Paul's use of the phrase in Rom. 8:5, "For those who live according to the flesh [κατὰ σάρκα] set their minds on the things of the flesh," provides the best par-

---

9. M. Mitchell (1993: 138–42, 251–56) claims that Paul focuses on the problem of factionalism and is concerned to bring about unity, and that this is the real issue behind the discussion of idol offerings. Factionalism was not the problem with the wilderness generation. It was idolatry and resistance to Moses' leadership, and that is the problem that Paul has in his sights.

allel. It also correlates with Paul's castigation of the Corinthians in 1 Cor. 3:1 for being "fleshly" (Hays 1989: 96). This interpretation makes better sense of what follows in 10:19–22, with its emphasis on idolatry and provoking the Lord to jealousy. The quotations from Deut. 32:17 in 1 Cor. 10:20 and Deut. 32:21 in 1 Cor. 10:22 apply to sinful Israel, and there is no reason to regard the next verses as representing a break in Paul's thought (cf. the gap in the NA²⁷ text).

If the phrase Ἰσραὴλ κατὰ σάρκα does not mean historical Israel over against a "spiritual Israel," then Paul is not referring to some parallel in Israel's sacrificial system. He does not bring up the sacrifices of Israel in the temple (REB, "Jewish practice") to make a transition from the Lord's Supper to pagan sacrifices in 10:19–21 (contra Godet 1887: 85–86; Goudge 1911: 90), and his point is not that Israel was bound together in their common sacrifice to God (contra Willis 1985b: 188; Fee 1987: 471).[10] There is also no need to distinguish between sacrificed food that only priests could eat (Lev. 7:6; 10:12–20; Num. 18:8–32; Deut. 18:1–8) and food that lay worshipers could share (Lev. 7:11–21; Deut. 12:5–28; 14:23, 26; 15:20; 1 Sam. 1:4; 2:19; 16:2–5). Paul has in view Israel's idolatrous sacrifices that resulted in their miserable downfall in the wilderness, and he refers to an altar dedicated to an idol, not the altar in the temple (P. Gardner 1994: 165–69; Schrage 1995: 443; Cheung 1999: 149–50). Smit (1997a: 47) claims that mentioning the altar specifically calls to mind Exod. 32:5–6, cited in 1 Cor. 10:7, which recounts Aaron building an altar in front of the golden calf. Paul's allusion to this incident makes the point that eating any food that has been consecrated on an altar binds the diner to that altar. This interpretation links 10:18 smoothly to the next verses.

Verses 19–20a do not mark a shift to a third example of a sacrificial meal that forms some sacred tie—the Lord's Supper, the sacrificial meals of Israel, and meals at the tables of pagan gods (contra Willis 1985b: 188). The question "What, then, do I declare?" qualifies 10:18 (so Bartsch 1962: 177–78; Cheung 1999: 147–49; contra Robertson and Plummer 1914: 215, who think it refers back to 10:15). Paul is conscious that his statements might seem inconsistent with what he wrote in 8:4, that "an idol has no real existence," and he is careful to avoid stumbling into some form of henotheism, a belief in one God without denying the existence of other gods. He does not concede the existence of idols but does want to introduce a new wrinkle to the problem that they have failed to see—the complication of having fellowship with demons. His two questions in 10:16 and 10:18 expect the answer yes, but this question expects the answer no. He is not implying that food sacri-

10:19–20a

---

10. "Altar" is not a reverent circumlocution for God (Willis 1985b: 185–86; contra Seesemann 1933: 52; Orr and Walther 1976: 250; Soards 1999: 212).

ficed to idols is anything or that idols are anything.[11] But how can he maintain that idols have no existence and still argue that one can be defiled and doomed for eating idol food? How can a bond be established with a god that does not exist? Paul's argument assumes that although idols are only dumb objects made from inanimate material, they still represent a reality, if only a value system, that directly competes with God. Though the deities worshiped by idolaters are unreal, the intention of the worshipers to have communion with them and the fellowship created by joining in their feasts are very real and very dangerous. Idols have no significance, but actions do. Paul assumes that idols are more than simply foolish human inventions, sordid parodies of the one true God. They represent something demonic so that any sacrifice to an idol is a sacrifice to demons. While denying the existence of pagan gods, he affirms the reality of virulent spiritual powers that are enemies of God (Hays 1997: 169). This idea accords with the view about the nature of idols in the OT (Ps. 96:5; 106:37; Isa. 65:3 LXX; 65:11 LXX; Bar. 4:7). For Paul, demons are very real and exert formidable power to defile and destroy humans.

The textual variant τὰ ἔθνη (*ta ethnē*, the Gentiles) is not the original reading but was inserted later by scribes who failed to understand the thrust of Paul's argument. There is no reason for Paul to explain what is transparently obvious, that pagan sacrifices were "not to God." But it is important for him to clarify that Israel's sacrifices in the wilderness were sacrifices to demons and not to God. Israel may have thought that they were offering sacrifices to God with the golden calf as "a festival to the LORD" (Exod. 32:5), but they were not. To support this point Paul alludes to several OT texts describing apostate Israelites sacrificing to demons.[12] The primary text is Deut. 32:17, "They sacrificed to demons, not God, to deities they had never known" (see also Lev. 17:7; Ps. 105:37; Isa. 65:11; Bar. 4:7).[13] Paul does not appeal to this text to describe pagans, but unfaithful Israel (Hays 1999: 400).

The present tense of the verb "they sacrifice" (θύουσιν, *thyousin*) may seem to present a problem for this interpretation, but Paul may have used the present tense to contemporize the language of Deut. 32:17 (Fee 1987: 472). Cheung (1999: 150) comments, "As he has done so in vv. 1–10, Paul is using the example of unfaithful Israel to warn the unfaithful Corinthians (vv. 6, 11). Like Israel, the Corinthians have their spiritual food and drink that join them to the Lord. Like Israel,

---

11. Note that idol food is set in apposition to the idol itself (Cheung 1999: 92–93).

12. References to "demons" appear only here (4x) and in 1 Tim. 4:1 in Paul's letters.

13. Other echoes from Deut. 32 in this segment are the description of God as θεὸς πιστός (*theos pistos*, Deut 32:4 = 1 Cor. 10:13) and the image of provoking the Lord to jealousy with strange gods and idols (Deut. 32:16, 21 = 1 Cor. 10:22).

they thus become partners with demons; and like Israel, unless they repent, they will face God's severe judgment."

The statement "I do not want you to become partners with demons!" is 10:20b less forceful than the command "Flee from idolatry!" but it is the key to Paul's exhortation in this section. Since idols do not exist, the Corinthians do not become partners with idols. But demons do exist, and pagan sacrifice is demonic. The Corinthians will become partners with demons if they willingly participate in pagan sacrificial feasts. Oropeza (1998: 66) expresses the view of many: "By having fellowship with idolaters in an idolatrous setting, there is always the risk of being united with them in their worship and practices." Paul's argument, however, assumes that there is more than just a "risk." They *will* become partners. There is no such thing as casual sacrifice, and Christians cannot casually join in feasts honoring these deities that epitomize demonic hostility to God. The phrase "partners of demons" (κοινωνοὺς τῶν δαιμονίων, *koinōnous tōn daimoniōn*) could refer to the thing shared: "partners in demons" (which are shared out), "partners of those who belong to demons" (Newton 1998: 360–61), or "partners of the demons." The last interpretation is the best option. Meals, particularly meals with religious associations, create partnerships (fellowship). It was assumed that the victim became the property of the deity to whom it was sacrificed, that the deity was the host of the ensuing feast, and that the diners became partners with the altar (see Philo, *Spec. Laws* 1.40 §221; Aalen 1963: 137).

The problem for Paul is not that Corinthian Christians join in camaraderie with idolaters but that they become actual partners with demons. However innocent the Christians' intentions might be, the result is that they give their assent to, collaborate with, and swell the ranks of demonic defiance of the sovereign God. They may think that they are simply joining a festive party, but in reality they are joining a party infested by Satan and forming an alliance with those who crucified the Son of God (2:8). They cannot dismiss these meals as simply a casual, meaningless social repast any more than they can dismiss a sexual relationship with a prostitute as a casual, meaningless tryst (cf. 6:15–20). If God's pattern revealed in Scripture holds true, they will provoke God to jealousy, who will turn away from them, and they will be destroyed as a perverse generation.

Drinking the cup of someone was understood as a means of entering 10:21 into a communion relationship with that person to the point that one shares that person's destiny, for good or ill (cf. Ps. 16:4–5). The anarthrous use of the nouns "Lord" and "demons" "highlights the respective qualities of the cup and table" (R. Collins 1999: 381). Drinking the cup of the Lord, which represents the binding covenant relationship, excludes drinking the cup of demons. The table of the Lord appears in the

OT to refer to the altar of the Lord, the defilement of which often brought condemnation on Israel (cf. Ezek. 39:20; 44:16; Mal. 1:7, 12). To eat food from the table of the Lord is to eat sacred food; to eat food from the table of an idol (cf. Isa. 65:11; Jos. As. 12:5) is to eat food sacred to that deity. For this reason, according to Jos. As. 8:5–7, Joseph refused to kiss Aseneth because it "is not fitting for a man who worships God, who will bless with his mouth the living God and eat blessed bread of life and drink a blessed cup of immortality . . . to kiss a strange woman who will bless with her mouth dead and dumb idols and eat from their table bread of strangulation and drink from their libation a cup of insidiousness."[14] The problem is not with the food or drink but with the different lords at the meal, demonic lords versus the Lord Christ (P. Gardner 1994: 170).

10:22   Paul's final two questions in this section again echo Scripture. The question "Will we continue [παραζηλοῦμεν, *parazēloumen*; present tense] to provoke the Lord to jealousy?" assumes that the Corinthians know that God is a jealous God who brooks no rivals. "Jealousy" is connected to God's holiness and power (Fee 1987: 474), and it is aroused by any form of idolatry by the covenant people (Exod. 20:5; 34:14; Deut. 4:24; 5:9; 6:14–15; Josh. 24:19–20; 1 Kings 14:22–23; Ps. 78:58; Ezek. 8:3; Nah. 1:2; Zeph. 1:18).

The question "Are we stronger than he?" expects an emphatic negative response. Paul does not warn against the power of the demons but about the jealousy of the Lord (Wolff 1996: 235). This is not an ironic question for the so-called strong in the church, who possessed knowledge (1 Cor. 8:1, 4, 8) and felt free to attend meals in temples (Willis 1985b: 215; Conzelmann 1969: 174; Rosner 1994: 195; contra Parry 1926: 153; Héring 1962: 1997; Barrett 1968: 238; Meeks 1982: 73). He would be more likely to address this group with a label related to knowledge (Rosner 1994: 195). The "we" instead of "you" shows that Paul addresses not one isolated group but all the Corinthians, and includes himself with them. He does not place himself above or over against them but makes his directives about idol food more palatable by implying "We are in this together." He also is one who could fall, whose feeble knowledge and strength would be demolished by the power of God. The "we" also is rooted in his understanding of the corporate responsibility and accountability for sin (cf. 5:1–13).

The question again recalls an OT motif contrasting the mighty God with frail humans (cf. Job 9:32; 37:23; Eccles. 6:10; Isa. 10:15; Ezek. 22:14), but the background that specifically connects the motif of God's strength and jealousy to idolatry is primary (Num. 14:13–35; Deut. 32).

14. Cheung (1999: 55) notes that though this passage may reflect a later Christian redaction, it would still show how such things might have been understood by Paul.

Rosner (1994: 201) notes, "All Pentateuchal references to God's jealousy have to do with idol-worship." Paul concludes his application of the OT texts to the Corinthian situation by reminding them that idols provoke God's jealousy (Deut. 6:14–15; Josh. 24:19–20; Ps. 78:58–64; Zeph. 1:18). He takes for granted that God's attitude toward idolatry has not changed with the coming of Christ. The OT paradigm reveals that association with anything idolatrous will meet with God's swift and irrevocable retribution. Rosner (1994: 202) correctly reads this climax to Paul's argument in 1 Cor. 10:1–22 as a "frightening threat of judgment upon those Corinthian Christians who provoke God to jealousy." The command to flee idolatry in 10:14 is capped off balefully with an implicit threat in 10:22: Flee idolatry—or else.

Additional Notes

10:19–22. My overview of Paul's argument finds previous scholars' notions that Paul contradicted himself or vacillated in 1 Cor. 8–10 to be groundless. They assume that Paul regarded idol food as essentially benign, a matter of indifference, and allowed participation in meals on temple grounds in 8:7–13. In 10:14–22, however, he forbids participation in cultic meals. In 8:4–6, he affirms that idols have no existence, yet he argues in 10:14–22 that idols are demons and that eating idol food is partnership with demons.

To explain these supposed contradictions, Weiss (1910: xl–xliii, 264) proposed that 10:1–22 belonged to a previous letter and that 8:1–13 and 10:23–11:1 belonged to a later letter after Paul modified his views. In the first letter, he reflected the "superstitions of Judaism"; in the second letter, he had been liberated from the Jewish fear of demons (see also von Soden 1951; Héring 1962: 11–12, 75; Schmithals 1971: 90–96; Sellin 1987: 2972–74; Richter 1996). Cope (1990) contends that 10:1–22 interrupts the flow of the argument and was composed and inserted by a later editor who sought to make Paul's views accord with the theology and practice of the later church concerning idolatry. Yeo (1995: 81–82) conjectures that Paul sent six separate letters to Corinth and that 9:24–10:22 appeared in the second letter; 8:1–13; 9:19–23; 10:23–11:1, in the third; and 9:1–18, in the fifth.

These interpolation theories collapse under careful analysis (see Hurd 1965: 131–37; Merklein 1984; Schrage 1995: 212–15). (1) Aside from the total lack of any textual evidence to support them, they ignore the practicalities that make the cutting and splicing of letters in the first century extraordinarily difficult and psychologically odd (Steward-Sykes 1996). (2) They also fail to resolve the problem. Schmithals, for example, does not doubt that Paul wrote both passages, and his advice remains inconsistent whether he gave it in one letter or two. Schmithals allows Paul to be inconsistent in two different letters—even though the time span is short—but not in one letter (Cheung 1999: 84). It is unlikely that Paul would have changed his mind in such a brief time span. (3) In 8:7, Paul seems to contradict 8:1, but no partition theory separates the two verses by putting them in separate letters (M. Mitchell 1993: 241). (4) Tensions in Paul's writing are not unusual (Horrell 1997b: 84 n. 4, noting Rom. 1:18–3:20; 9:1–11:36), which makes interpolation theories less probable as the explanations for them.

Others more reasonably attribute the apparent discrepancies to differing situations. One situation (1 Cor. 10:1–22) is presumed to deal with eating sacrificial food in cultic context; the other (8:1–13; 10:23–11:1), in a noncultic context. Newton (1998: 24) attributes the supposed disparity between the two passages to differing degrees of involvement in cultic festivals. In 8:1–13,

Paul is concerned with those who recline in an idol's temple (8:10) consuming food. In 10:1–22, he is concerned about specific acts of idolatry (10:7, 14, 20) and bans making a sacrificial offering (10:20), drinking the cup of demons (10:21a), and partaking of the table of demons (10:21b). The first situation deals with the Corinthians who attended temple feasts and ate the food, the second (10:14–22) with participation in the actual sacrificial offerings and then eating. This view assumes that Paul does not ban eating in idols' shrines outright, though he would prefer that they would not. It is not the eating of the sacrifices that makes them partners of demons but the act of sacrificing and then eating.

The imagined inconsistency in Paul's response is best attributed to the complexity of the issue and his clear-eyed theological thinking. Paul maintains that there is only one true God (8:4–6), who made all things and to whom all things belong (10:26, quoting Ps. 24:1). One can quite naturally infer from God's sovereignty and creation's goodness that all food should be permissible. But Paul concedes that other so-called gods and lords exist, though not on the same ontological level (1 Cor. 8:5). When humans worship the many gods and lords, they give that which is not god "a power over themselves, and perhaps over others, which by rights it does not have" (N. Wright 1992: 134; see also Conzelmann 1975: 145). Idolatry introduces a hitch that negates the principle that all things are lawful. It results in Paul's seemingly conflicting advice. As N. Wright (1992: 134) frames it,

> In the marketplace all is permitted: once off the idol's turf, the food reverts to the sphere of the God who made it. But to enter an idol's temple, and eat there alongside those who are actually intending to share fellowship with this non-God, this hand-made pseudo-god—this is to invite created powers to have an authority over one which they do not possess, a power which belongs only to the creator-God revealed in and through Jesus the Messiah.

Paul knows that he may sound inconsistent ("What, then, do I declare? That idol food is anything or that an idol is anything?" [10:19]), but seeming to be inconsistent does not mean that his argument is confused or unsound. He tells them, "Do not have anything to do with food known to be associated with an idol," and, "Do not consume food in a place known to be associated with an idol." But when that same food leaves the idol's domain, it is permissible to eat. N. Wright (1992: 132) concludes that for Paul to say "anything else would be to lapse into a dualism" because that would imply that "the creator has had to rule some areas of his creation permanently off limits." The one God reigns over all things, but Paul forbids Christians from doing anything that might lend credence to the worship of that which is not God.

10:20. Three basic readings are found in 10:20. Two have τὰ ἔθνη as the subject of "sacrifice," with the verb read as either a third person plural or a third person singular: ἃ θύουσιν τὰ ἔθνη, δαιμονίοις καὶ οὐ θεῷ θύουσιν ($\mathfrak{P}^{46vid}$, ℵ, A, P, C, Ψ, 33, 81, 256, 23, 365, 1175, 1241, 1319, 1573, 1739, 2127, 2200, 2464, arm, Origen[lat]; and 104, 459, 596, which insert the second θύουσιν after δαιμονίοις); ἃ θύει τὰ ἔθνη, δαιμονίοις θύει καὶ οὐ θεῷ (6, 424, 436, 1881, 1912, Byz [K (L)] Lect, it[(ar), b, f, g, s], vg, syr[p, h], geo). The third reading omits τὰ ἔθνη: ἃ θύουσιν, δαιμονίοις καὶ οὐ θεῷ θύουσιν (B, cop[sa], Eusebius), with other texts inserting the second θύουσιν after δαιμονίοις (D, F, G, it[d, (o)], Eusebius, Epiphanius, Ambrosiaster).

The first reading has strong support from Alexandrian witnesses, but scribes might have added τὰ ἔθνη to clarify the subject of the verb "to sacrifice." It fits the view expressed in Rev. 9:20 that the rest of humankind continued to worship demons and idols of gold and silver and bronze and stone and wood, which cannot see or hear or walk. It is telling, however, that this reading has a third person plural verb, θύουσιν, with the neuter plural noun τὰ ἔθνη, since a neuter plural subject often takes a singular verb (BDF §133). Later witnesses representing the second reading appear to have corrected this to a third person singular, θύει. This would lend credence to the argument that θύουσιν was original and that τὰ ἔθνη was a later addition. Omitting the subject of the verb is the hardest reading because the only subject that can be derived from the immediate context is Israel. This may have perplexed a later scribe who failed to understand that Paul was referring to "fleshly Israel" and their idolatry in the wilderness rather than referring to Israel's sacrificial system. The scribe added τὰ ἔθνη in an attempt to clarify the text. The possibility that scribes might have omitted it to harmonize with the LXX seems far less likely. In addition to being the hardest reading, the third reading is hampered by the fact that it makes no sense for Paul to explain to his readers what is transparently obvious, that pagans sacrifice to demons and not to God. It was important for him to clarify that fleshly Israel's sacrifices were sacrifices to demons and not to God, since he appealed to the wilderness generation as a warning example.

F. Practical Advice for Dealing with the Issue of Idol Food in Pagan Settings (10:23–11:1)

The question of temple dining and eating food sacrificed to idols is now left aside as Paul addresses the matter of food of questionable origins—food that may have been sacrificed to idols before it comes into the hands of a believer. To answer the question of how a Christian can act with integrity in a world brimming with idols, he moves from an absolute prohibition based on general arguments about the dangers of associating with anything idolatrous to conditional liberty based on the biblical tenet that the earth is the Lord's and everything in it (10:26; Ps. 24:1). He gives the go-ahead on everything that is beyond an idol's orbit.[1] It is not permanently poisoned.

In this section, Paul tries to insure that the Corinthians do not misconstrue what he says, as they had previously (5:9–10), and think that he is insisting that they withdraw completely from society and have nothing whatsoever to do with unbelievers. He clarifies that food is food, and it is permissible to eat *unless* it is specifically identified as idol food, which puts it in a special category that is always forbidden to Christians. As Dunn (1998: 705) observes, he does not ask them "to avoid idol food at all costs or to parade their consciences in the matter by making scrupulous enquiry beforehand." They need not abstain from all food on the chance that it may have been sacrificed to idols. He basically says, "Of course, you can buy food in the provision market" (10:25); "Of course, you can dine with friends" (10:27). His prohibition of idol food does not mean that they must retreat to the seclusion of a gloomy ghetto. Nevertheless, he anticipates potential problems presented by food that a Christian might purchase from the market or food that a Christian might eat in the home of an unbeliever who might have offered it to idols.

Many mistakenly assume that in this section Paul encourages the weak to ease up on their criticism of the so-called strong. B. Hall

---

1. Smit (1996: 591) contends that Paul's shift in 10:23–11:1 from his discussion about the idol offerings to an adjacent issue transgresses an important rhetorical rule. The transition may have made his prohibitions "easier to digest," but he does not go unpunished by the misunderstanding of his later interpreters who think that 10:23–11:1 refers to the idol offerings mentioned in 8:1. This shift has also led interpreters to suggest that Paul contradicts himself or to conjecture that the confusion is created by a later interpolation.

(1990: 143) states, "He now asks the weak to do something for the strong—namely, to begin to free themselves from their tyrannical scruples." Nowhere does Paul talk about scruples, let alone tyrannical scruples. The maxim "All things are permissible," which Paul amends with an emphasis on what is beneficial and builds up, hardly seems appropriate for launching a response to those who are weak. Hall also claims that Paul "belongs to the strong, and in his abrupt challenge to the weak he speaks not only for himself but also for those who see themselves as the strong in Corinth." But Paul has just said that he identifies with the weak (9:22), not the so-called strong. I argue that he never addresses the weak at all in chapters 8–10; they are a hypothetical construct. But even if this were incorrect, how could he encourage the weak to take a more relaxed view toward food when he expressed concern that they are extremely vulnerable to reverting to their former idolatrous practices (8:10; see Fee 1987: 477 n. 10)? This section is directed to the whole church, but if Paul were addressing a particular group, it would be the "knowers." They are most likely to seek their own advantage, be invited to a banquet in an unbeliever's home, and object to another's conscience constricting their liberty.

The section falls into the following pattern (Fee 1987: 478; Hays 1997: 174):

   A All things are permissible but seek what benefits others (10:23–24)
     B Eat whatever is sold in the market or set before you because all things belong to God (10:25–27)
   A′ Exception: abstain for the sake of another's conscience (10:28–29a)
     B′ Defense of freedom to eat (10:29b–30)
   A″ Do all things for the glory of God by seeking what benefits others (10:31–11:1)

Exegesis and Exposition

[10:23]All things are permissible, but not all things are beneficial. All things are permissible, but not all things edify. [24]Let no one seek his or her own [advantage] but that of another. [25]Eat whatever is sold in the public market without inquiring [about its history] because of conscience. [26]For "the earth is the Lord's and all its fullness." [27]If any unbeliever invites you [to dine] and you want to go, eat whatever is set before you without inquiring [about its history] because of conscience. [28]If someone should say to you, "This food is sacrificed to the gods," do not eat, out of concern for the one ⌜who informed you and because of conscience⌝. [29]By conscience, I do not mean one's own but the other's. For why is my freedom being judged by another's conscience? [30]If I partake thankfully, why am I being slandered because of what I receive with thanksgiving? [31]Therefore, whether you eat or drink or whatever you do, do all things to bring glory to God. [32]Be without blame with respect to Jews, Greeks, and the church of God, [33]just as I myself seek to please everyone in all things, not seeking my own advantage but that of the many in order that they be saved. [11:1]Become imitators of me, just as I am of Christ.

10:23 Paul returns to the issue of ἐξουσία (*exousia*) raised in 8:9. Some in the church assumed that their knowledge gave them authority to act as they saw fit (Fee 1987: 479). Their attitude could have been bolstered by the maxim "All things are permitted [ἔξεστιν, *exestin*]," an assertion first met in 6:12 (see the discussion of its meaning there). Paul has problems with this credo because it feeds the conviction that one's personal understanding of what is permitted becomes the only measuring rod of what is right and the only thing of interest. Clement of Alexandria (*Paedagogus* [*Christ the Educator*] 2.1.14) recognizes another problem with this credo: "Those who take advantage of everything that is lawful rapidly deteriorate into doing what is not lawful" (cited by Bray 1999: 100).

Paul counters this notion with two statements and an imperative: "Not all things are beneficial" (or "profitable," συμφέρει, *sympherei*); "Not all things edify"; "Act in the best interests of others, not your own" (10:24). The two statements recall the corporate dimension of Christian life (Willis 1985b: 226–27) and Paul's opening thought in 8:1 that love builds up. From his radical perspective, the only thing profitable is that which builds up the church as a whole (R. Collins 1999: 386).[2] He leaves it to the readers to infer the corollary to this principle: Anything that might destroy another becomes unlawful (cf. 8:7–13). Robertson and Plummer (1914: 219) correctly observe, "There are some things which do not build up either the character of the individual or the faith which he professes, or the society to which he belongs." But Paul also believes that there are limits beyond which Christians may not go (cf. 10:1–22). Here, however, the limits are defined by the benefit an action brings to another or the church.

10:24 Paul's command that one "not seek that which is one's own" leaves indefinite what they are not to seek.[3] We can fill in the blank with words such as "advantage," "interest," "good," "ends," "enjoyment," "needs." Instead of selfish things, they are to seek the interests of the other (τὸ τοῦ ἑτέρου, *to tou heterou*). This "other" is not restricted to the fellow

2. Paul will return to this principle in discussing the use of spiritual gifts; they are given "for the common good" (πρὸς τὸ συμφέρον, *pros to sympheron*).

3. Soards (1999: 219) is correct that the NIV rendering, "Nobody should seek," implies that Paul is simply "offering polite advice" instead of giving a direct command.

believer who might have a weak conscience, as in 8:11, but also includes the unbeliever who might offer an invitation to dinner (10:27). His concern in this section is not the effect of their behavior on other believers but its effect on nonbelievers. The overarching hermeneutical principles that govern his practical advice are these: What course of action will bring glory to God, and what course of action will be "the most effective witness to Christ?" (Ruef 1977: 103). Paul expects the Corinthians to do all things to bring glory to God (10:31) and to seek the best interests of others so that they might be saved (10:33).

Seeking the advantage of others rather than one's own runs counter to the "me first" sentiment that ruled Corinthian culture. The command that Christians act selflessly underlies the conclusion in the opening segment of Paul's argument against idol food in 8:7–13. He would do nothing that might cause a brother or sister in Christ to fall, even if it meant that he must never eat meat again. Willis (1985b: 228) comments that this principle is foundational for all Christian conduct: it "is drawn from the character of Christian love (1 Cor. 13:5), modeled upon the normative work of Christ (Phil. 2:4, 5, 20; Rom. 15:2, 3), and seen in the life of Paul himself (1 Cor. 8:13, 9; 2 Cor. 12:14)." This standard of conduct makes one's behavior distinctively Christian and brackets Paul's specific instructions in 1 Cor. 10:25–32: "Let no one seek his or her own [advantage] but that of another" (10:24); "I myself seek to please everyone in all things, not seeking my own advantage but that of the many" (10:33).

The advice that follows shows that Paul does not expect the Corinthians to give up their interests or rights entirely—only when the situation calls for it. They do not need to give up eating meat, for example (8:13), but love for others is to be the controlling factor in their choices. Food that may have an idolatrous history may be eaten unless it is specifically identified as idol food. When it is identified as idol food, however, the principle of love must overrule assumed knowledge or presumed rights. They must abstain out of concern for another's conscience as well as to avoid rousing the wrath of God for violating their covenantal obligations.

10:25 Avoiding all food that had any associations with an idol was a tall order because any food purchased in the market or served at a friend's home potentially was tainted by some idolatrous rite. That possibility does not mean that they must avoid all food on the chance that it had some past contact with an idol. Paul lays down "clear, distinct rules" (Tomson 1990: 204) about how they can live their day-to-day life in a world teeming with idolaters and markets flooded with idol food. He basically "defines what is idol food in doubtful cases"—when it is not specified as idol food (Tomson 1991: 208–9). The conscience of the weak does not determine whether it is permissible or not to buy food in the market (contra P. D. Gooch 1993: 87). As far as Paul is concerned, food outside of the idol's orbit is permitted, so he gives them leave to eat anything sold in the public market without investigating its history to certify that it is free from any idolatrous contamination. Christ has not called them to be meat inspectors. He implies "that as soon as idol food is sold at the market, it is no longer defiled" (Tomson 1990: 181). Outside of its idolatrous context, idol food becomes simply food and belongs to the one God (Rom. 14:14). This ruling is far more liberal than one found in the Mishnah: "Flesh that is entering in unto an idol is permitted, but what comes forth is forbidden" (m. ʿAbod. Zar. 2:3). Barrett's (1982: 146; cf. Fee 1987: 482) comment that "Paul is nowhere more un-Jewish" than in this statement is exaggerated. It is more accurate to say that he is nowhere more un-Pharisaic, since Pharisees spent considerable effort inquiring into the background and preparation of food. The basic premise that informs Paul's ruling (1 Cor. 10:26), "the earth is the Lord's and all its fullness" (Ps. 24:1; 50:12; 89:11), however, is Jewish to the core.

The phrase διὰ τὴν συνείδησιν (dia tēn syneidēsin) could be connected to the imperative "eat" (ἐσθίετε, esthiete) or the participial phrase "ask questions about nothing" (μηδὲν ἀνακρίνοντες, mēden anakrinontes). Also, it is unclear whose conscience Paul has in view, the purchaser's or an observer's (1 Cor. 8:7; 10:29, so R. Horsley 1978b: 587; Schrage 1995: 466–67; and P. W. Gooch 1987: 251, who translates it "their bad feelings"). If Paul were addressing the so-called strong, they would not have "bad feelings" about purchasing such food. Consequently, some conclude that he must be talking about the "bad feelings" of the weak who might spot the strong in a compromising position, and he would be saying, "In such a case, ignore the weak." Again, such interpretations mistakenly presume that a conflict exists between the so-called strong and weak. Rather, Paul gives general advice to all Christians about buying and eating food sold in the provision market and does not distinguish between the so-called strong and weak. They should buy and eat whatever they like and can afford.

Perceptions about idols are real, however. In the immediate context, Paul has raised the Corinthians' consciousness that idol food is hazardous material by linking it to demons. This new consciousness of the danger attached to idol food may encumber their decisions about purchasing food in the market that might have come from temple sacrifices, and he counsels them not to brood over that decision. Idol food is not dangerous outside of its overtly idolatrous context. To ask questions about the food's history in the open market would unnecessarily burden their consciences (Schneider, TDNT 4:372; Pierce 1955: 76). In this case, ignorance is bliss. It is not simply "What you don't know won't hurt you" (Jewett 1971: 428), but "Why worry needlessly about something that is clearly a matter of indifference?" In the same way that they need not worry that marriage to an unbeliever might somehow contaminate the believer (7:13–14), they need not worry that they will be contaminated by food that may have pagan antecedents. If God does not care, then neither should they (Fee 1987: 481).

The μάκελλον (*makellon*) was a provision market that especially sold meat and fish.[4] The eruption of Mount Vesuvius on August 24, A.D. 79, which destroyed Pompeii, froze in time a segment of everyday life during this era. Lietzmann (1949: 51) concludes that because the city's *macellum* contained a narrow chapel arrayed with statues from the imperial cult, the markets and temples were intimately connected. He argues that all or most of the meat sold in the market was idol food previously sacrificed in the temples next door. Cadbury (1934: 141) counters that the proximity of temples and meat markets in strategic locations does not mean that the two were necessarily connected. Koch (1999) confirms that the evidence from the *macellum* in Pompeii was not representative and that not all food sold in the provision market came from temple sacrifices. An excavation of a butcher shop in Pompeii revealed entire skeletons of sheep. Had those animals been slaughtered in a temple, priestly portions would have been missing. Conzelmann (1975: 176 n. 12) argues from Plutarch's (*Mor.* 729C) comment about the Pythagoreans, "If they tasted flesh it was most often that of sacrificial animals," that it implies that nonsacrificial meat must have been available. Pliny the Younger's (*Ep.* 10.96) correspondence with the emperor Trajan about the Christians in Pontus reports a resurgence in pagan observances. He exults that temples once deserted are now being thronged, sacred rites are being renewed, and "food for the sacrificial victims is once more finding a sale, whereas, up to recently, a buyer was hardly to be found." This account reveals that purchasers knew what they were buying but also that not all meat sold in the market was branded by pagan sacrifice. Tertullian's (*Apol.* 42) comment, "We [Christians] live with you [pagans], enjoy the same food. . . . We cannot dwell together in the world without the marketplace, without your butchers," is interpreted by Cheung (1999: 154–55 n. 230) to mean that nonsacrificial meat must have been available in the marketplace, because Tertullian absolutely condemns eating idol food. I assume that this also was the case in Corinth in Paul's era.[5] Paul's permission to eat

---

4. The market at Corinth has not yet been identified with certainty (see Gill 1992).

5. Willis (1985b: 230 n. 29) notes, "The macellum was not an equivalent to our supermarket, 'but rather more akin to a delicatessen, in the sense that expensive foods were for sale there that one would normally purchase only for special occasions.' This suggests that the decision about purchase of meat would not be a common issue for Christians."

whatever is sold in the market presumes that not everything offered for sale had been contaminated by idolatrous rituals.

10:26   Paul's premise for his instruction derives from Ps. 24:1 (cf. 50:12; 89:11), which in Judaism shaped the prayer to be voiced before a meal (*b. Šabb.* 119a).[6] His doctrine of creation (Willis 1985b: 235), that God is sovereign over all things (1 Cor. 8:6) and that everything created by God is good (1 Tim. 4:4), determines his judgment. Paul is not a dualist. The whole creation belongs to God, not part to God and part to idols (Maurer, *TDNT* 7:915; cf. N. Wright 1992: 126). Idol food loses its character as idol food as soon as it leaves the idol's arena and the idolater's purposes. This theology provides a ready-made answer to Celsus's mockery of Christian scruples against idols: "But when they eat food, and drink wine, and take fruits, and drink even the water itself, and breathe even the very air, are they not receiving each of these from certain daemons, among whom the administration of each of these has been divided?" (cited by P. D. Gooch 1993: 55 n. 5).

Paul does not complete the thought with a conclusion from the biblical citation, but it is implicit: "Nothing is unclean in itself" (Rom. 14:14; cf. Acts 10:15). If it can be eaten in honor of the Lord (Rom. 14:7), it is permitted. What Paul finds sinful is eating idol food in any setting that might give others the slightest hint that Christians sanctioned idolatry, no matter how attenuated the religious aspects attached to the meal or the place might be.

10:27   Paul switches to another conceivable situation in which an unbeliever invites a believer to dine. He does not clarify where they dine. It is unlikely that he is thinking about a quasi-religious social meal at a public dining facility (contra Willis 1985b: 238–39; Borgen 1994: 55–56; D. Martin 1995: 183; Schrage 1995: 461, 468–69; Horrell 1997b: 103), since most of them were related to cultic sites and he has strictly forbidden participating in any meal on an idol's turf (Fee 1987: 483). He makes no distinctions between going to a temple when cultic proceedings occur and attending social occasions that may have only a slight cultic taint (contra Conzelmann 1975: 177). He bans going to an idol's temple for any function. He must have in mind an invitation to dine in a private home from an unbeliever who apparently has no objection to including a Christian.[7] Paul would not object to this visit in principle, since food served in a private home would not necessarily have been of-

---

6. That the quotation is functioning as a premise is indicated by the addition of γάρ (*gar*) to what otherwise would be an exact quotation from Ps. 23:1 LXX (D. Watson 1989: 305 n. 24).

7. So Findlay 1910: 867; Weiss 1910: 264; Robertson and Plummer 1914: 219; Lietzmann 1949: 51; Barrett 1968: 242; Walter 1978–79: 426; Fee 1987: 482; P. Gardner 1994: 176; Wolff 1996: 238; Newton 1998: 376; Cheung 1999: 156–57.

fered to an idol. An inquiry about the nature of the food would be superfluous at a meal in an idol's temple (Wolff 1996: 238); there, one must assume the worst. Paul's advice reveals that he has no intention of cutting Christians off entirely from their pagan family, neighbors, and associates (cf. 5:9–13; cf. Luke 10:8).

The danger of getting caught up in idolatry, however, was ever present in the pagan world. The Jewish perception, reflected in *m. ʿAbod. Zar.* 5:5, was that a Gentile was always ready "to contaminate wine through idolatry, if he gets the chance" (Neusner 1988: 202), but the collection of rulings in *m. ʿAbod. Zar.* 4:9–5:10 assumes that it is permissible for a Jew to eat with a Gentile as long as precautions are taken to avoid any association with idolatry (Cheung 1999: 44).[8] Paul's approach is totally different: Christians need not, out of conscience, give their host the third degree—a highly inappropriate and unlikely event—to insure that the food is acceptable. He does not fear inadvertent contact with food offered to idols as long as it does not become an open issue. Consequently, everything depends on the Christian "wanting to go" (Fee 1987: 482; see also Tomson 1990: 233–34). Paul does not encourage Christian dinner guests to go but leaves it for them to decide. When they dine, they do not need to make a show of religious fastidiousness; they may eat everything placed before them.

In this instance, Paul makes a concession to the reality that social connections were absolutely necessary to survive in the ancient world. In his day, intrepid mavericks could not strike off on their own and expect to manage. One needed relationships with others for services and protection. Patronage bound freed slaves to former masters, plebs to patricians, tenants to landowners; and their solidarity was established by means of the exchange of honor and personal obligation (Lanci 1997: 37). Paul does not expect his readers to cut themselves off completely from the fabric of all social relationships.

Paul allows Christians to circulate in pagan society, but there are limits **10:28–29a** to what is permissible. They may not eat anything that is openly an-

---

8. Although Jub. 22:16 forbids Jews from eating with Gentiles, we find more liberal attitudes in other Jewish literature, though they vary on how rigorously to apply rules of separation. In Jos. As. 7:1, Joseph ate a meal in the house of Pentephres, the Egyptian priest of Heliopolis, at a table set apart from the others "because Joseph never ate with the Egyptians, for this was an abomination to him." In *t. ʿAbod. Zar.* 4:6 (*b. ʿAbod. Zar.* 8a), Rabbi Shimeon ben Eleazar taught, "Israelites outside the land worship idols in purity. How? If a non-Jew prepared a wedding feast for his son and sent out to invite all Jews in his town—even if they have food and drink of their own and have their own servant waiting at them, they worship idols. Thus it is said: [. . . Lest you make a covenant . . . when they sacrifice to their gods and] when one invites you, you eat of his sacrifice (Exod. 34:15)." The Letter of Aristeas 181–86, however, exhibits no qualms about eating with Gentiles as long as food laws were strictly obeyed. Ciampi (1998: 159–63) offers a helpful discussion of these issues and their relationship to Paul's argument in Gal. 2.

nounced as having been "offered in sacrifice to the gods." Paul shifts from a class-one condition (εἰ, ei) in 10:27 to a class-three probable future condition (ἐάν, ean) in 10:28. Robertson and Plummer (1914: 221) regard it as intentional (cf. Gal. 1:8–9). The first condition is likely; the second, purely hypothetical. But this conjectured situation allows Paul to remind Christians what is crucial in all eating done with unbelievers. If anyone declares that the meal has the slightest religious significance, Christians must not partake. From Paul's perspective, it becomes idol food and forbidden when someone openly proclaims it to be so. The reason should be clear from his previous arguments: "By knowingly partaking of idol food, the Christian is tacitly condoning idolatry and thus lending a hand to the transgressors" (Cheung 1999: 157; see also Tomson 1990: 217).

It is unclear how this food was sanctified. Possibly, it had been brought home from the temple (see Plutarch, *Mor.* 696E). Two other examples reveal how food might otherwise be connected to idols. Petronius (*Satyr.* 60) highlights the excesses at the dinner given by the gauche freedman Trimalchio and describes three boys in brief white tunics entering the banquet: "Two of them set down on the table the household deities, which had amulets around their necks; the other, carrying a round bowl of wine, kept shouting: 'God save all here!'" Diodorus Siculus (*Library of History* 4.3) contends, "It is the custom, they say, when unmixed wine is served during the meal to greet it with the words, 'To the Good Deity!' but when the cup is passed around after the meal diluted with water, to cry out 'To Zeus Savior!'"[9]

Paul gives only sketchy details about the informant—who it is, why he speaks, or how his conscience would be jeopardized. Is it a warning or an announcement? Several proposals are possible.[10]

First, the host may make the statement because he is sensitive to the Christians' convictions (Craig 1953: 119; Borgen 1994: 52; Witherington 1995: 227). The term ἱερόθυτον (*hierothyton*) appears only here in the Bible and is the more dignified term that a devotee of other gods and goddesses would use rather than the pejorative εἰδωλόθυτον (*eidōlothyton*) used by Christians. It means "sacrificed in a temple," "slain as sacred," or "sanctified food." This term makes it more likely that the informant is an idol worshiper than a Christian.[11]

---

9. Cf. the papyrus invitations to dinners at the table of lord Sarapis in private homes, in Blue 1991: 223 n. 11.

10. Willis (1985b: 242–43; cf. Findlay 1910: 868) does not regard 10:28 to be a continuation of 10:27, but instead contends that it begins an outline of "basic principles of conduct." Willis thinks that it functions as a "general restriction," based on 10:24, that is applicable to the situations described in 10:25 (food purchased in the market) and 10:27 (dinner invitations). Fee (1987: 483 n. 40) counters that Willis overlooks "the clear grammatical tie to v. 27" with the "but" (δέ, *de*).

11. Fee thinks that the two terms are synonymous and both mean "holy-offered."

Assuming that the host is even aware that Christians do not eat sacrificed food, the major problem with this option is that Paul uses the indefinite pronoun τις (*tis*) to refer to the host in 10:27. Why use it again to refer to the host who already has been identified? Why not use the personal pronoun αὐτός (*autos*)? Why does the host wait to make this announcement at the time of the meal? Possibly, he wants to distinguish sacrificed from nonsacrificed food on the table (Winter 1995: 175–76). This view, however, probably attributes to the host more noble motives than would be likely (P. Gardner 1994: 177), though Cheung (1999: 158 n. 240) notes that this practice is commonplace in Asian contexts. Some ascribe darker motives to the host or guest: he makes the announcement maliciously to put the Christian on the spot so as to cause embarrassment (Chrysostom, *Hom. 1 Cor.* 25). Publicly eating idol food was a test of faith and connected to apostasy during the persecutions of the Jews by Antiochus IV Epiphanes (2 Macc. 6:7; noted by Bruce 1971: 100). Thus, the person might be challenging the Christian in a ticklish situation in order to force either a compromise in faith by eating or damage to important social relations by refusing to eat.

A second alternative considers the informant to be a pagan guest (so Lietzmann 1949: 51; von Soden 1951: 250–51; N. Watson 1992: 108). Wolff (1996: 238) understands it to be an idolater referring to the food out of reverent piety, but it is unclear why the idolater would make such an announcement or how the guest knows this.

A third option identifies the informant as a Christian who is a fellow guest. Some think it difficult to see how a non-Christian's conscience could be affected and thus assume the informer to be a weak Christian who sounds the alarm on another believer.[12] The Christian might use the more dignified term ἱερόθυτον out of civility to avoid offending the host (in the same way that some today avoid using the terms "pagan" and "heathen" because others regard them to be chauvinistic and inflammatory). Or, the informer might use this term simply out of habit (Robertson and Plummer 1914: 221).

Several questions make this option unlikely. Again, how does the informant know that this is idolatrous food? Did the guest nose about the kitchen beforehand or rudely make inquiries after arriving? Why would this weaker Christian be invited to, or attend, such a banquet? Their poverty, as some have classified the "weak," or their fussy scruples, as others have pigeonholed them, would have made their presence unlikely. Unless the informer was a Christian slave required to serve the guests (see R. Collins 1999: 384), why would a weak Christian have stayed

---

12. So Edwards 1885: 264; Godet 1887: 97; Weiss 1910: 265; Robertson and Plummer 1914: 221; Pierce 1955: 75; Héring 1962: 98–99; Barrett 1968: 241–42; Maurer, *TDNT* 7:915 n. 69; Murphy-O'Connor 1979a: 101; Schrage 1995: 469–70; Hays 1997: 177; Horrell 1997b: 103.

for dinner after making this discovery (Kistemaker 1993: 355)? If the Christian were one of the so-called strong, why bother mentioning the issue at all (P. Gardner 1994: 177)? Willis (1985b: 247 n. 112) correctly contends that this view "needlessly multiplies the cast of characters."

From what follows, it is most likely that Paul envisions a pagan making the announcement. Ultimately, it makes no difference; the result is the same. Paul presents a brief case study of how a Christian should respond in pagan surroundings (see Cheung 1999: 157–60). The case is hypothetical, and there is no need to identify or to untangle the motives of the informer.[13] Most likely the host proclaims his intentions about the food, but it could be "anyone" (τις, *tis*) who makes such an announcement. The declaration makes clear that the meal's atmosphere is distinguished by an act of idolatrous piety.

Paul instructs them not to eat because of the one who makes the disclosure and because of the conscience (συνείδησις, *syneidēsis*). He clarifies in 10:29a that he refers to the conscience of the one who made the announcement, not the believer who accepted the invitation. What does the word "conscience" mean here? The discussion in 8:7 reveals that it is a slippery word whose meaning was in flux. Many assume that it must refer back to the weak conscience of the fellow believer in 8:7, 10, 12. But Paul says nothing about the conscience being weak or in danger of being wounded (8:12). It may simply refer to the person's "consciousness." The person who makes the announcement understands the food to be religiously significant.

Paul formulates another key hermeneutical principle underlying his advice. The food's history matters only when it matters to someone else who considers it sacred. Christians know that idols do not exist, that there is no God but one, and that all food belongs ultimately to God; in this sticky situation, however, it is not what the Christian knows that counts, but what others believe. His approach to this issue is very close to that of the rabbis. Tomson (1990: 214) concludes (from *t. Ḥul.* 2:18; *m. Ḥul.* 2:8; *m. Zebaḥ.* 1:1), "The Rabbinic view of idolatry is not so much concerned with material objects or actions as with the spiritual attitude with which these are approached by the gentiles. Correspondingly, the essence of idolatry is a ceremonial act of consecration, most typically expressed in slaughtering 'in the name of the deity.'" The rabbis absolutely prohibited direct or indirect contact with pagan rites, but they ruled that Jews could intermingle with Gentiles unless it became clear that the latter were engaged in some religious activity (Porton 1988: 258; Borgen 1994: 46). They assumed that individuals could discern when the Gentile was engaged in idolatrous practices. Paul takes

---

13. Conzelmann (1975: 178) goes too far in saying that the "who" should not be pressed.

a far more liberal view in doubtful cases. Christians may assume that all is well and need not become sleuths trying to detect if the food has idolatrous connections. Instead, they may depend on the pagan's own pronouncement, "This is sacred food." When Christians find themselves in this situation, they must abstain from eating that food lest they be drawn into idolatry.

Paul is not concerned here that Christians might endanger a fellow believer who has a weak conscience. Rather, their willing consumption of what has been announced as food sacrificed to idols would do three things:

1. It would compromise their confession of the one true God with a tacit recognition of the sanctity of pagan gods.
2. It would confirm rather than challenge the unbeliever's idolatrous convictions and would not lead the unbeliever away from the worship of false gods (Conzelmann 1975: 178; Ruef 1977: 102). If a Christian eats what a pagan acquaintance regards as an offering to a deity, it would signal the Christian's endorsement of idolatry.
3. It would disable the basic Christian censure of pagan gods as false gods that embody something demonic (Cheung 1999: 159) and make that censure seem hypocritical.

Paul expresses concern about the Christian's witness to the unbeliever. The announcement presents an opportunity to expound one's faith in the one God and one Lord (see Godet 1887: 97).

10:29b–30 Paul's sketchy description of the case makes it difficult to decide what the two rhetorical questions that follow in 10:29b–30 mean in the context. D. Watson (1989. 308) calls them "the major stumbling block to determining the flow of the argument in this section." Several explanations have been proposed. Some can be quickly dismissed.

The claim that these questions are a marginal gloss added by an interpolator who wondered why the scruples of others should be allowed to restrict one's freedom and may have thought that Paul had gone too far (Weiss 1910: 265–66; Zuntz 1953: 17) is pure conjecture, without any supporting evidence. The confluence of vocabulary from chapters 8–10 in these verses argues strongly against this view.[14]

Some take these questions to reflect Paul's self-defense of his own past actions, perhaps in Corinth, and claim that he anticipates some Corinthians challenging his own inconsistency in condemning them for eating idol food in temples while he ate the same idol food sold in

14. Note the recurrence of συνείδησις (syneidēsis; 8:7, 10, 12; 10:25, 27, 28, 29), ἐλεύθερος (eleutheros; 9:1, 19) and ἐλευθερία (eleutheria; 10:29), and ἀνακρίνειν (anakrinein; 9:3; 10:25, 27) and κρίνειν (krinein; 10:15, 29).

the meat market. Fee (1987: 486) stresses the language "my freedom," "being judged," and "being denounced," and thinks that it recalls Paul's defensive posture in 9:19–23. It is his "final word of defense" for eating idol foods on occasion (cf. Oropeza 1998: 57): "He is as a Gentile to Gentiles, and as a Jew to Jews. He can either eat or not eat. But if he eats, he does so in light of the benediction of v. 26, and he is not to be condemned by anyone" (Fee 1987: 487). If chapter 9 is not a defense, as I contend, then this argument is weakened. I am convinced that Paul never ate idol food that was known to be idol food and so would have no need to defend himself. Paul may have used the "I" "for the sake of vividness when a more universal application is in view" (Wallace 1996: 391; cf. BDF §28), thus presenting himself as a paradigmatic example for his readers (B. Dodd 1999: 111; cf. 8:13).

Some assume that Paul addresses the so-called weak Christians to urge them not to abuse the forbearance of the so-called strong to judge them (Grosheide 1953: 244; Héring 1962: 99; Murphy-O'Connor 1978b: 555–56, 570–71; P. Richardson 1979: 129). This view presupposes a situation in which the strong and weak are squabbling, which I already have rejected, and there is no indication in the text that Paul changes tack to address a specific and narrower audience.

A more reasonable alternative assumes that Paul suddenly adopts a diatribe style by anticipating objections raised by the Corinthians. He imagines their rejection of such a restriction to their freedom (Lietzmann 1949: 52; Pierce 1955: 78; P. D. Gooch 1993: 92; Oster 1995: 250; Witherington 1995: 228; Soards 1999: 217): "Why must the wings of our freedom be clipped by another's conscience? Cannot our thankful attitude (cf. Rom. 14:6) be the sole criterion for whether it is right to eat or not? Why should our actions be constricted by what others think who do not have knowledge?" The premise lurking behind these questions is that personal desires are the only criteria that matter (Oster 1995: 250). It assumes that one need only satisfy oneself that some action is permissible and ignores one's responsibilities to others. If this were an anticipation of some defensive response, however, one would expect an adversative particle (δέ, *de*; or ἀλλά, *alla*) to begin the clause rather than "for" (γάρ, *gar*; Barrett 1968: 243; Bruce 1971: 101; Willis 1985b: 247). This view also requires filling in something that is not in the text: "Well, then, someone asks . . ." or "You might say . . ." Paul, strangely, offers no response to this so-called objection. Consequently, this interpretation fails to convince.[15]

---

15. D. Watson (1989: 310–18) challenges the view that Paul asks questions in diatribe fashion but offers a similar conclusion from a complicated application of ancient rhetorical theory. Paul resorts to questions here to recapitulate his argument beginning in 8:1; to anticipate any objections to his argument in 10:23–29a; to add force, imagination and emotion to his argument with figures of thought; and to add the finishing touches of stylistic grandeur to his argument.

Others assume that the γάρ suggests that Paul offers further elaboration of his reasons for restricting eating by considering the reaction of the fellow believer.[16] The one who exercises restraint has not really lost any freedom of conscience and still has freedom to eat whatever can be received with thanksgiving, regardless of the judgments of others. In certain circumstances, however, one should refrain out of deference to the conscience of another. Willis (1985b: 249) paraphrases the thought in 10:29b–30 this way: "Why should I as a Christian conscious of my freedom to eat or not eat exercise freedom by eating if I know another person's awareness will lead him to condemn me?" The next question parallels it: "How can I offer grace over food, knowing that I will be blasphemed for eating that over which I have said a blessing?" If eating might cause so much misunderstanding, why eat? This argument, again, mistakenly assumes that a weak Christian will be offended by these actions and will condemn the so-called strong for eating and imposes that view on the text. When Paul specifically mentions those with a weak conscience, however, he is more concerned that they will fall into idolatry and be destroyed than that they would be offended by idolatry (8:7–13).

The best alternative takes the questions in 10:29b–30 to be responses to 10:27 after a parenthetic interruption in 10:28–29a (Craig 1953: 120; Bruce 1971: 100–101; Blomberg 1994: 203; Hays 1997: 177–78; Newton 1998: 377). Paul gives the Corinthians the latitude to attend a banquet thrown by an unbeliever without raising any question on the ground of conscience. He then interrupts this thought with a parenthetical observation. If someone announces that the food has been offered in sacrifice, they are to abstain. The conscience *does* come into play in this situation—that is, the conscience of the other. Paul then returns to the thought in 10:27 to explain why it is permissible to eat whatever is served at an unbeliever's house. If one can partake with thankfulness to the one true God, how can one be denounced for eating that over which one has said a prayer of thanksgiving?[17] When someone specifies that the food is sacrificial food, the situation is different; the Christian must not eat. In all other cases, the Christian may eat even if the food may have been sacrificed to an idol without the Christian knowing it.

The freedom in 10:29b refers to freedom "from the power of idolatry" (F. Jones 1987: 194; Tomson 1990: 216). Chrysostom (*Hom. 1 Cor.* 24.5) understands the uncleanness to reside "not in the food but in the intentions of the sacrificers and the attitude of receivers." Paul's coun-

---

16. So Edwards 1885: 265; Bultmann 1951: 217–19; Barrett 1968: 243–44; Conzelmann 1975: 178; Jewett 1971: 429–30; Maurer, *TDNT* 7:915; Willis 1985b: 247–48; Schrage 1995: 472; R. Collins 1999: 388; Cheung 1999: 161.

17. The ἱνατί (*hinati*) means "for what object," "for what purpose" (Robertson and Plummer 1914: 222; Héring 1962: 99 n. 52).

sel proposes that the Christians need worry only about their own intentions in eating food. If it is food that they can give thanks to God for, then it is permissible. He does not envision that libelous charges will be circulated by others because they ate in an unbeliever's home. He means, "Why should anyone denounce such behavior by a Christian who genuinely gives thanks for this food and has no intentional connection with idolatry?"

10:31   The οὖν (*oun*, therefore) introduces an inference from Paul's arguments in 10:23–30, particularly 10:26, but 10:31–11:1 also sums up his advice in the whole discussion of food sacrificed to idols (8:1–10:30). Whether an action brings glory to God or provokes the jealousy of God (10:22), God becomes the hermeneutical litmus test for gauging whether it is right or wrong. The ultimate aim of Christians is to please God, not themselves. The πάντα (*panta*, all things) excludes the possibility of compartmentalizing one's life so that one might reserve a segment of it to do as one pleases. It also sounds a striking counterpoint to the maxim quoted at the beginning of this unit, "All things are permissible" (10:23). Only those things that bring glory to God are permitted. As noted above, the basic structure of Paul's argument in this section against idol food matches the structure of his argument in 6:12–20 against sexual sins (πορνεία, *porneia*), which begins with the maxim "All things are permitted for me" (6:12) and ends with the imperative "Glorify God in your body" (6:20). In 10:23, Paul echoes the same maxim, and in 10:31, he begins his conclusion with a similar imperative. In the first context, glorifying God in one's body requires renouncing πορνεία. In this context, eating and drinking to God's glory requires avoiding εἰδωλόθυτα (*eidōlothyta*).

10:32–33   The translation of the command ἀπρόσκοποι γίνεσθε (*aproskopoi ginesthe*, give no offense; NRSV, NASB) may mislead the reader to think that Paul wants them only to be tactful and considerate. His other use of the adjective ἀπρόσκοπος refers to being "blameless," "void of offense" before God in the day of Christ (Phil. 1:10). In this context, "blame" would come from blocking another from coming to faith in Christ. The command summarizes his warning in 1 Cor. 8:7–13 that they should do nothing to imperil the salvation of a fellow Christian, a member of "the church of God" (see additional note). In that case, it meant never darkening the door of an idol's shrine where one might be seen by another Christian with a weak conscience who then might be persuaded from this example that participation in idolatry was permissible for Christians. If such careless sporting with idols served as a tripwire that might hurtle another back into the demonic sphere of idolatry, it would bring divine judgment on both the one who is "destroyed" (ἀπόλλυται, *apollytai*; 8:11) and the one who caused a fellow Christian to "stumble."

The certainty of God's judgment on those who cause another to trip and fall (cf. Matt. 18:6) created a healthy fear that dictated Paul's actions. He will do nothing that might cause another Christian to fall (1 Cor. 8:13) or that might unnecessarily hamper others from accepting the gospel of Christ (9:12; cf. 2 Cor. 6:3; Rom. 14:13, 20–21). He also will do anything to make an opening for others to accept the gospel of Christ (1 Cor. 9:19–22). His overriding concern as an apostle is how to gain followers for Christ. Consequently, he pays heed to how others perceive the faith and actions of Christians. One must avoid doing anything that might turn potential converts away from the gospel or that might cause Christians to betray their faith. This approach demands far more than simply trying to avoid hurt feelings. To bring glory to God, Christians must behave in ways that lead others to a saving relationship with Christ (9:19–23).

In the context of his arguments about idol food and idolatry in chapters 8–10, Paul is concerned that the Corinthians' cavalier behavior might cut the ground out from under a fellow Christian who is already wobbly in the faith or solidify the ground on which an idolater stands in resistance to the gospel's message of one God and one Lord. Being blameless with respect "to the church of God," then, means doing nothing that might cause Christians to founder in their faith by giving them license to revert to idolatrous practices. Being blameless with respect to "Greeks" means doing nothing that might validate the legitimacy of their resistance to God. Being blameless with respect to "Jews" means doing nothing that might give them the impression that Christian teaching condoned idolatry and that becoming a Christian would entail abandoning the basic confession of one God. The division between Jews, Greeks, and the church of God is thus to be explained by the fact that each has different reactions to the conduct of Christians, not that Paul thought that Christians were a third race (contra Parry 1926: 155). Paul's concern is much broader than some internal squabble in the church. The issue of food offered to idols directly affects the church's witness to the world and its ability to win converts.

Paul concludes his instructions by returning in 10:33 to his own example (cf. 9:1–27). As an apostle, he understands himself to be the norm of behavior for his churches. The verb "to please" (ἀρέσκειν, *areskein*) would seem to refer to a willingness to oblige others in all things. But Paul is not a pleaser in the sense of the flatterer who "complaisantly approves of everything and never raises an objection and thinks it is his duty to avoid giving pain to those with whom he comes in contact" (Aristotle, *Eth. nic.* 4.6.1, cited by P. Marshall 1987: 78). The verb often occurs in contexts describing slavery since "the slave's purpose [is] to please the master" (D. Martin 1990: 51–52). In Gal. 1:10, Paul clarifies that if he were pleasing humans, he could not be a slave of Christ. The term needs to be understood in the context of his rendering service to Christ. As Christ's slave, he also renders service to others regardless of the cost to himself. This statement echoes 1 Cor. 9:19, where Paul says, "I enslaved myself to all."

Seeking to please everyone in all things while not seeking one's own advantage counters the catchphrase cited in 10:23, "All things are permissible." For Paul, the individual's profit must be subordinated to what builds up the community of God and strengthens its divine mission in the world (see Weiss, *TDNT* 9:76–77). As Willis (1985b: 256) summarizes it, "What is profitable (τὸ σύμφορον [*to symphoron*]) to Paul is the salvation of others, not the exercise of one's wishes." His conclusion, "in order that the many might be saved," reiterates what he says in 9:22 and shows how this principle controls all that he does. "The many" (οἱ πολλοί, *hoi polloi*) does not refer to the church community (Barrett 1968: 157) but to the majority of people inside and outside the church. It is a Semitism for "all" (cf. Matt. 26:28; Mark 14:24).

11:1 The chapter division fails us here, for 11:1 encapsulates all that Paul wants the Corinthians to do. By relinquishing their so-called rights to act on their so-called knowledge, they follow the example of Paul and the greater example of Christ. Paul often calls on his charges to follow his example or commends them for already doing so (4:6, 16–17; 7:7; Gal. 4:12; Phil. 3:17; 4:9; 1 Thess. 1:6; 2 Thess. 3:6–9). This appeal was a common literary and hortatory motif in antiquity (B. Dodd 1999: 16–18; see also Fiore 1986: 26–163), but it takes a different twist in light of the divine command "Be holy, for I am holy" (Lev. 11:44–45; 19:2; 20:26; cf. Matt. 5:48) and Paul's assertion that he follows the example of Christ. He is to be followed only insofar as he adheres to the divine standard set forth by Christ. As the Corinthians' founding apostle, he revealed that standard to them by preaching the crucified Christ and embodying what that means. Following his example in this instance entails two things: (1) submitting to his authority (see Michaelis, *TDNT* 4:668–69) and his injunctions to dissociate themselves from anything overtly connected to idolatry; and (2) imitating his personal example by forgoing the exercise of perceived rights so that one achieves a greater benefit for others.

Castelli (1991: 111–15) rejects this rhetoric of imitation as a discourse of power that sets Paul up in the similar position of Christ over the community and implicitly functions to make sameness equal salvation and difference equal damnation. This jaundiced view of Paul understands him simply to be making a power play to gain control over the Corinthians without providing anything concrete for them to imitate (Castelli 1991: 109–10). Such a view flies in the face of the personal example he outlines in chapter 9. He does give them something to imitate. He shows himself to be a man for others, who has consciously modeled his ministry on that of Christ (Hooker 1996: 96). While it is possible to render this verse, "Become imitators of me, just as I also am of Christ," that is, "as I belong to Christ" (so B. Dodd 1999: 28–29), it seems best to interpret it to mean that he follows Christ's example: "Become imitators of me, just as I also [imitate] Christ." His summons for the Corinthians to imitate him does not issue from some attempt to put them under his thumb. It springs instead "from his conviction that the whole Christian community should reflect the love and compassion of Christ: there was no distinction here between apostle and community, except that the role of the apostle was to be a subsidiary model. The Gospel was to be proclaimed both by Paul and by the community, not simply through the preaching of the word, but in every believer's life" (Hooker 1996: 100). Paul uses the imagery that he applies to Christ's atoning work for his own mission as Christ's apostle. As Christ did not please himself (10:24) but emptied himself, taking the form of a slave even to the point of dying on the cross to save others (Phil. 2:1–8), so Paul is always given up to death and carries in his body the death of Jesus (2 Cor. 4:10–11). As Christ was rich yet made himself poor for our sakes so that by his poverty we might become rich (2 Cor. 8:9), so Paul was regarded as poor, yet making many rich (2 Cor. 6:10). As Christ loved us and gave himself up as a fragrant offering and sacrifice to God (Eph. 5:2), so Paul understands his potential martyrdom as being poured out as a libation over the sacrifice and offering of the Philippians' faith (Phil. 3:17). As Christ suffered on behalf of others, so Paul sees himself as completing what is lacking in the sufferings of Christ (Col. 1:24). As Christ did not please himself so that he might benefit others, so Paul does not please himself (1 Cor. 10:33) but endures anything (9:12) and punishes his body to enslave it (9:27) that he might save others. Christ's self-sacrifice for others becomes the norm of Christian behavior and the pattern for Christian evangelism (Ruef 1977: 106).

Were Paul's arguments in these chapters effective in persuading the Corinthians to abandon their participation in idolatrous associations? The painful visit, the letter of tears, and the continued exhortation in 2 Cor. 6:14–7:1 (see Garland 1999: 315–43) suggest not. Such complex issues that require such enormous self-sacrifice are not solved overnight.

Additional Notes

10:28. The reading τὸν μηνύσαντα καὶ τὴν συνείδησιν is omitted in $\mathfrak{P}^{46}$ but is overwhelmingly attested in the rest of the manuscripts, versions, and church fathers. Later witnesses (H^c, K, L, Ψ, 6, 104, 263, 424, 459, 1852, Byz, Lect, syr^h, geo^2, Chrysostom) add Ps. 24:1, cited in 1 Cor. 10:26, at the end of the verse. It would mean that the food is not forbidden because it is inherently contaminated and evil—all things are part of God's good creation—but only because of concern for the conscience of the other. In light of Paul's arguments against idol food, this reading makes no sense on internal grounds. It may have resulted from scribal parablepsis (R. Collins 1999: 388) when a scribe's eye returned to συνείδησιν in 10:25 preceding the citation.

10:32. The "church of God" is "the venerable title, used of Israel of old" (R. Collins 1999: 389; cf. Deut. 23:2–4, 9) that Paul appropriates and applies to the Christian community. He uses the phrase in the letter to denote the local assembly of Christians in Corinth (1 Cor. 1:2; 6:4; 11:22; cf. 2 Cor. 1:1) and also the church in general (1 Cor. 15:9; cf. Gal. 1:13). His use of the plural, "churches of God," in 1 Cor. 11:16 suggests that the singular here refers to a Christian gathering in a specific place—namely, Corinth (see Weiss 1910: 266; R. Collins 1999: 389, contra Schrage 1995: 475).

VII. Headdress in Public Worship (11:2–16)

The complexity of 11:2–16 continues to vex modern interpreters, and its comments about women rile many modern readers.[1] Because it contains one of the lengthiest discussions in the NT on the relationship between men and women, it has attracted the attention of many and the indignation of some. The danger lurks that interpreters will try to make it say what they would like it to say. Engberg-Pedersen (1991: 679) observes, "The nonscholarly interest of scholars very often influences heavily their decisions on the exegetical questions." To penetrate its meaning we need more cultural information. But which bits of cultural information apply to this situation? The most reliable clues to the passage's meaning lie in its structure.

The problem centers on head attire in worship, but interpreters cannot agree whether it has to do with some kind of head covering, hairstyles, or properly tended hair, and whether it involves both men and women or only women. Many recent interpreters assume that the problem has theological roots. Some imagine that Corinthian spiritualists attempted to blur the distinctions between the sexes to symbolize their new status in Christ. Women prophets either threw off their veils, "symbols of the inferiority and subordination which characterized their day to day living," to show that they had transcended sexual differentiation (M. MacDonald 1990b: 166) or let their hair down in a deliberate attempt "to discard a traditional marker of gender distinction" (Hays 1997: 183–84). In either case, it is assumed that the Corinthian women got carried away with their transformed spiritual status and carried things too far by breaching sexual decorum. They misapplied Paul's teaching that in Christ there is neither male nor female (Gal. 3:28) and, influenced by a "realized eschatology," sought to eradicate any con-

---

1. Walker (1975), Cope (1978), and Trompf (1980) argue that it is an interpolation (cf. Weiss [1910: 271], who thought that 11:3 might be a gloss). This view has been successfully refuted by Murphy-O'Connor (1976; 1986: 87–90) and Schrage (1995: 496–97); see also Wisse (1990).

ventional male/female distinctions (see Meeks 1974: 202).[2] Murphy-O'Connor (1980) surmises that the problem involved men as well as women and contends that it centered on hairdos. Women wore their hair in an unfeminine way, and men wore their hair in an unmasculine way. The hairstyle option has gained popularity. Dunn (1998: 590–91) claims that Paul's circuitous argument is intended primarily to support the custom of bound-up hair for women so that when they prophesy "with a 'proper' hairstyle," they will not be "distracting." Gielen (1999) modifies the hairstyle hypothesis by contending that the Corinthian women adopted a short, masculine hairstyle and that Paul argues that they should have long hair. Hjort (2001) claims that Paul argues against a form of androgyny in which the differences between the sexes are being neutralized by a kind of transvestism, in which men and particularly women are dressing and cutting their hair according to the customs of the other sex. Hjort attributes it to a carryover from some of the Corinthians' past participation in the cult of Dionysus and its transgendered revelry. All these views understand Paul's main point to be that the sexual differences between men and women are part of God's purposes in creation and that they should not be obscured in worship.

In contrast to these recent trends, I adopt the traditional way of reading this passage. Paul is concerned exclusively with the Corinthian women's behavior: their praying and prophesying without wearing the usual head covering (Delobel 1986: 387). Perriman's (1994: 621) conclusion, in my view, is correct: "The primary theme in the passage concerns the shame that attaches to a woman who prays or prophesies with her head uncovered." Why they chose to abandon the head covering—or perhaps they only carelessly neglected it—is difficult to discover from the information we have. Possibly, theological reasons inspired them to do so. I think it unlikely, however, that a burgeoning feminist movement led female prophets to assert their equality and independence so adventurously (contra Wire 1990: 130; cf. Lösch 1947: 225–30) or that a "realized eschatology" caused them to refuse to pay heed to the God-ordained differentiation between the sexes. There is no reason to infer from what Paul says in this text that Corinthian spiritualists believed themselves "to have been transformed into the image of the one who is be-

---

2. BeDuhn (1999: 316) cites Acts of Thomas 14 as evidence for this view: "But that I do not veil myself is because the veil of shame is taken from me; and I am no longer ashamed or abashed, because the work of shame and bashfulness has been removed far from me." Their gumption may have been rooted in the belief that the female gender is somehow defective and must be made male to be perfected (Gospel of Thomas 114) and that angels served as models for transcending gender identity (Mark 12:25; Luke 20:34–36).

yond gender" and consequently abandoned gender-specific hair-dressing or apparel (contra Jervis 1993: 246), no matter how many times scholars repeat it. Possibly, the women simply wanted "to overcome their traditional secondary place by behaving like men" (Delobel 1986: 387). Possibly, the fuzzy boundary between the home and the house church caused them to neglect this covering. Since they were not accustomed to wearing the covering in their home, they did not wear it when the church met in the home. Behavior acceptable in the home may not be appropriate for the church gathering in the home. We are left only with guesses as to the motivation behind this behavior.

Whatever the motivation, the structure of Paul's argument makes clear what the issue is.

11:4: Every man who prays or prophesies	11:5: Every woman who prays or prophesies
11:7a: On the one hand (μὲν γάρ, *men gar*) the man . . .	11:7b: On the other hand (δέ, *de*) the woman . . .
11:7: A man ought not (οὐκ ὀφείλει, *ouk opheilei*) . . . the head	11:10: A woman ought (ὀφείλει) . . . the head
11:11a: Neither a woman apart from the man	11:11b: Neither the man apart from the woman
11:12a: For just as the woman . . .	11:12b: Thus also the man . . .
11:13: It is shameful for a woman to pray to God uncovered	(no parallel)
11:14b: On the one hand (μέν) the man . . .	11:15: On the other hand (δέ) the woman . . .

Paul oscillates back and forth with statements about men and women, but this pattern is broken in 11:13 with a statement about the woman but none about the man. This interruption highlights the crux of the whole argument (Delobel 1986: 379–80): women are praying to God uncovered (ἀκατακάλυπτοι, *akatakalyptoi*). I agree with Delobel's conclusion that "several aspects of man's situation are mentioned as a background in contrast with which woman's situation and obligation can be more sharply described." It should also be noted that in 11:4, Paul simply states that it is shameful for a man to pray or prophesy with a head covering (literally, "having down from the head"). In 11:5, the statement that it is shameful for a woman to pray or prophesy without a head covering is supplemented by a further explanation, "for" (γάρ, *gar*; repeated, in 11:5b, 6). In 11:10, which forms the center of the argument according to the chiastic structure traced out below, Paul adds another, though highly enigmatic, explanation for why women should be covered: "because of the angels." No comparable explanation is given for why men should not be covered. The best explanation for these breaks in the pattern is that the problem that Paul wishes to correct has to do with what the women were doing with their heads. This conclusion is confirmed by the fact that the only imperative in the text, aside from the one inviting them to make a judgment on whether it is proper for a woman to be uncovered (11:13), appears in 11:6: "Let her cover herself."

It is not unusual for scholars to claim that this text lacks logical coherence (Scroggs 1993: 87) and to refer to Paul's "contorted reasoning" (Meier 1978: 218) resulting in a "theological quagmire" (Hays 1997: 186). When the issue is identified as the need for women to wear a head covering, however, Paul's argument becomes quite clear, whether or not all readers find it appealing.

He introduces the basic premise in 11:3 that everyone has a "head." Christ is the head of man, man the head of woman, and God the head of Christ. The odd sequence reveals that Paul has no interest in establishing some kind of ascending hierarchical order to show the inferiority of women, who therefore must be subordinate, or in arguing that woman are not as near to God as men are. I will argue that "head" refers to one who is preeminent and foremost and Paul plays on the anatomical and metaphorical meaning of "head." Men who participate in public worship with their physical head covered shame their metaphorical head—Christ (11:4). Likewise, women who participate in public worship with their physical head uncovered shame their metaphorical head—the man (their husband or father; 11:5). The key motif in 11:4–6 is shame, which Christians should avoid bringing on their metaphorical heads. In 11:7a Paul offers the explanation for the statement in 11:4: a man reflects the image and glory of God. In 11:7b he offers the explanation for the statements in 11:5–6: the woman (wife) reflects the glory of the man (husband). The motif of glory in these verses counterbalances the motif of shame in 11:4–6. Gundry Volf (1997: 157) captures the thrust of the main point of Paul's argument: "Man and woman are both the *glory of another* and therefore both have an obligation not to cause shame to their heads." Paul explains this assertion—primarily that the woman reflects the glory of the man—in 11:8–9 with a brief interpretation of the creation account in Gen. 2. According to Gen. 2:18–25, the woman was created for the man and out of the man. In 1 Cor. 11:10, Paul sums up the consequences of this interpretation: "Because of this" (διὰ τοῦτο, *dia touto*) a woman ought to have a symbol of authority on her head. In 11:11–12, however, he backtracks lest the Corinthians become confused and think that he implies that women are inferior to men. He is not attempting to establish a gender hierarchy that places women in a subordinate role. Since he argues from hierarchy to make his case about head coverings, he needs to caution against any misapplication of what he says. Women and men are interdependent in the Lord.

The key issue reemerges in 11:13, and Paul leaves it to their judgment to decide: Is it proper for a woman to pray to God uncovered? The answer, he assumes, is no; but he adds one more argument in 11:14–15 from the analogy of female and male hair. Nature has given women their hair as a cover, while men do not use hair as a cover. "Nature" refers to societal conventions because he contends that it is shameful (according to cultural mores) for men to have long hair. For women, however, long hair is their glory. This assertion complements his statement in 11:6 that it is shameful for women to be shorn. Women, therefore, should follow the lead of nature (and social decorum) and cover their heads. His conclusion alerts them that their practice violates his customs and those in all the churches of God (11:16).

In a hierarchically structured shame/honor society, Paul is concerned about the propriety of women's appearance in public worship. He is not worried about male Christians becoming more effeminate in appearance. Nor is he concerned that women should wear something to show that their speaking in public is permissible (contra Hooker 1963–64a). He addresses sexual propriety. When a wife converts to Christianity and learns that she is set free in Christ so that she can pray and prophesy in public, it does not mean that she can disregard social conventions. The emphasis on shame and glory reveals that to understand this text, one needs to appreciate the social clues associated with shame and honor. In this gender-divided shame/honor culture, the head of the family publicly symbolized the family's honor, and members of the family were to behave in public so as not to bring disgrace or dishonor to that person and the family's good name. A woman cannot acquire honor for the family but can only lose it (see Sir. 42:9–14). R. Williams (1997: 57) notes that "it is through the strict maintenance of her sexual purity and personal integrity that a woman contributes to her family's honour." The head covering "is a symbol of a woman's shame, worn in public to mark her off as a private person intent on guarding her purity, and so maintaining the honour of her husband and her father" (R. Williams 1997: 57–58).[3] It communicates to others in public that the woman is demure, chaste, and modest, and that she intends to

3. In Acts of Thomas 56, those hanging by the hair in the chasm of hell are identified as those who had not modesty and went about the world bareheaded.

stay that way.[4] The head covering in Paul's setting was an important piece of apparel because no male wanted his wife or a female in his charge to appear in public in a way that hints, intentionally or unintentionally, that the opposite might be true. Derrett (1977: 172) comments, "The husband is entitled to his wife's modesty in public even if their thoughts are directed towards God. For the husband's rights are not forfeited simply because their spiritual status is changed by their conversion." Derrett adds, "If ever there was a place where proprieties had to be observed and suspicions averted it was Corinth, upon which the Temple of Aphrodite looked down."

This explanation of 11:2–16 means that it forms a bookend with 14:34–35, where Paul again, in my interpretation, addresses the proper deportment of wives in public worship (see Tomson 1990: 132). The parallels with 14:33b–36 are significant:

The churches of God (11:16)	The churches of the saints (14:33b)
Allusion to Genesis 2 (11:7–12)	As the law says (14:34)
It is shameful for a woman (11:6)	It is shameful for a woman (14:35)

Several preliminary observations can be made from this text. (1) Paul takes for granted that women may pray and prophesy in the assembly as long as they have an appropriate head covering. Meier (1978: 218) thinks it an "astounding fact—astounding at least for a group rising from a Jewish synagogue—that women were free in the church to pray openly and to prophesy under charismatic inspiration." (2) The passage is not about the subordination of women, because the patriarchal order expressed in 11:3, 7–9 from creation is counterbalanced by the emphasis on the "mutual interdependence" of men and women in the Lord in 11:11–12. (3) Paul's primary concern is that they avoid doing things that might bring shame. To apply this concern to another cultural context requires one to take into account significant cultural differences related to honor and shame. This passage is "not about wearing hats to church or about proving that women are intended to be subordinate to men" (R. Williams 1997: 59). The command "let her be covered" (11:6) communicates different things in different cultures. The common denominator is that the "covering" is a sign of personal rectitude, and its absence an implication of the opposite.[5] The basic issue resolves around what is

4. One might contrast the public attire of some modern actresses and musicians who project a salacious persona because it seems to promise greater financial success in the marketplace.

5. Since Paul also mentions men, they too must conform to cultural expectations of what is appropriate dress and hairstyle. That was not at issue in the Corinthian church, however.

"proper" (11:13). Faithfulness to the teaching of the text can be maintained by female participants in the worship service by observing the proprieties of polite society.

The passage fits a chiastic pattern:

A Commendation for maintaining the traditions handed on by Paul and the assertion of the basic principle that everyone has a head (11:2–3)
  B Shame about coverings for men and women (11:4–5)
    C Social impropriety for a woman to be uncovered; theological impropriety for a man to be covered (11:6–7)
      D Theological explanation from the creation account (11:8–9)
        E Central assertion: for this reason a woman ought to have authority over her head (11:10)
      D′ Theological caveat from procreation (11:11–12)
    C′ Social impropriety for a woman to be uncovered (11:13)
  B′ Shame (and glory): lessons from nature about coverings for men and women (11:14–15)
A′ Admonition to conform to Paul's customs and those of the churches of God (11:16)

Exegesis and Exposition

[2]I salute you for continuing to remember me in every way, and you hold firm the traditions just as I handed them on to you. [3]I want you to know that the head of every man is Christ, and the head of the woman is the man, and the head of Christ is God. [4]Every man who prays or prophesies having down from the head shames his head. [5]Every woman who prays or prophesies with her head uncovered shames her head. For it is one and the same if she were completely shaven. [6]For if a woman does not cover herself, then let her have herself shaved. But since it is shameful for a woman to have herself shaven or to be shorn, let her cover herself. [7]For a man ought not to have his head covered since he is the image and glory of God, but the woman is the glory of the man. [8]For man did not come from woman but woman out of the man. [9]For, indeed, man was not created because of the woman but the woman [was created] because of the man. [10]Because of this, the woman ought to have ⌜authority⌝ over her head because of the angels. [11]Nevertheless, in the Lord, woman [cannot exist] apart from man nor man apart from woman. [12]For as the woman came from the man, so also the man comes through the woman. And all things are from God. [13]You yourselves be the judge. Is it proper for a woman to pray to God uncovered? [14]Does not even nature itself teach you that if a man wears long hair it is a dishonor to him, [15]but if a woman wears long hair it is her glory? For long hair has been given [to her] as a covering. [16]But if any is disposed to be contentious, we do not have such a custom, nor do the churches of God.

11:2   Paul begins a new section of the letter dealing with issues related to public worship by saluting (ἐπαινῶ, *epainō*, I praise) the church for keeping him (and his teaching) in mind in "all things" (πάντα, *panta*; an accusative of respect or reference).[6] He is the channel through whom they received (11:23–26; 15:3–5) the traditions (παραδόσεις, *paradoseis*). The traditions can include historical facts related to the gospel story and doctrine drawn from them (2 Thess. 2:15; 3:6; cf. Rom. 6:17; 1 Cor. 11:23; 15:3). Adherence to these traditions not only strengthens their bond to their apostle, but also connects them to the rest of God's church. Some think that the tradition he has in mind specifically has to do with the participation of men and women in worship or the equality of man and woman, but it is more likely that he refers to his teaching in general. The Corinthians' practices should be consistent with this foundational tradition.

Fee (1987: 499–500), who thinks that Paul is constantly on the defensive in this letter, is surprised by this word of praise. Findlay (1910: 870–71) presumes that Paul quotes the Corinthians' professions of loyalty made in their letter to him. Others assume that it is a response to a letter in which Paul praises them for seeking his advice on a complex matter (Hays 1997: 181–84; Thiselton 2000: 810). BeDuhn (1999: 319) goes so far as to imagine the questions they asked Paul in their letter:

> Why do we maintain distinctions between the apparel of men and women in the assembly? Why should some pray and prophesy with head covered while others do not? Have we not lost gender distinctions in the Lord? Have we not become like angels? Can you provide us with reasons for this custom? Or can we safely abandon it in light of our new identity in Christ?

Others think that the questioning was more hostile. They were at odds with Paul over this matter of head coverings (Hurd 1965: 182–86). But this tack for interpreting the passage is unpersuasive. Interpreters tend to beg the question, since the questions they imagine the Corinthians asked match the interpretation they give to Paul's answers. No formula referring to what they have written to him appears (cf. 7:1), and Terry's (1995: 43) outline of the discourse structure of the letter shows that Paul alternates between responses to oral reports (1:10–4:17/4:18–6:20; 11:2–34; 15:1–58) and responses to the Corinthian letter (7:1–40/8:1–11:1; 12:1–14:40; 16:1–12). In 11:2, Paul returns to a discussion of an oral report (cf. 11:18) and is not citing their letter. What follows is based

---

6. Thiselton (2000: 810) argues that the πάντα functions as an adverb and translates it "unfailingly" (cf. Robertson and Plummer 1914: 228; Schrage 1995: 499 n. 55), but Paul does not use πάντα with this meaning elsewhere in the letter.

on reports he has heard in which they fail to measure up to acceptable codes of behavior.

Some interpreters infer from the opening statement in this section that the Corinthians appealed to an aspect of Paul's teaching but misapplied it in this situation. They assume that his teaching on the unity of male and female in Christ contributed to a Corinthian endeavor to erase the distinctions between men and women in worship (Meier 1978: 216; Engberg-Pedersen 1991: 681; Hays 1997: 182). Jervis (1993: 238) thinks that this verse serves as "Paul's acknowledgement that he carries much of the blame for the practice that he is in the process of rebuking." There is no reason to conclude that Paul means exactly the opposite of what he says. He is not resorting to irony or giving them only a backhanded compliment, commending them for holding on to his traditions, albeit in a mistaken fashion.[7] This verse functions instead as a *captatio benevolentiae*. His affirmation of them is not ironic (contra Moffatt 1938: 149; Hurd 1965: 182–83) but designed "to placate them so that they will be receptive to critical advice" (M. Mitchell 1993: 260; cf. Conzelmann 1975: 182; Fee 1987: 500; Schrage 1995: 499). This rhetorical strategy was recognized as a sensible prelude to frank criticism (cf. Plutarch, *Mor.* 73C–74E). Though Paul begins on an encouraging note—they are to be honored—he does not praise them in 11:17, 22.

The phrase "I want you to know" (cf. Col. 2:1) is stated more positively **11:3** than the wish "I do not want you to be ignorant" (1 Cor. 10:1; 12:1) or the question "Do you not know?" (3:16; 5:6; 6:2, 3, 9, 15, 16; 9:13). It suggests that he is offering them "a new insight" (Conzelmann 1975: 183). Paul lays out an order of relationships that asserts the man's precedence over the woman. Some conclude that he is trying to reinforce the idea of the woman's inferiority and subordination. But if woman stands in a lower place, why does she stand in the middle of the sequence, and why is God mentioned last? Paul is not outlining a chain of command, since references to Christ frame the statements about man and woman.

The head of every man is *Christ*.
The head of the woman is the man.
The head of *Christ* is God.

Gundry Volf (1997: 152) contends that Paul sets up a dialectic between creation order, which created gender distinctions, and the gospel order of reciprocity and mutuality. I would argue, instead, that he establishes the premise that everyone has a head so that he can set up his argument

---

7. Edwards (1885: 268) is correct that using irony at the beginning of an argument would be "wanton."

that what individuals do to their physical head in worship reflects negatively or positively on their metaphorical head. His purpose is not to write a theology of gender but to correct an unbefitting practice in worship that will tarnish the church's reputation.

The words ἀνήρ (*anēr*) and γυνή (*gynē*) can mean "man" and "woman" or "husband" and "wife." The NRSV translates "husband" and "wife" in this verse but not in the following verses. The rendering "the husband is the head of the wife" (cf. Eph. 5:23) makes sense: as Christ is the head of the man by virtue of his faith, the man is the head of the wife by virtue of the marriage union (Findlay 1910: 871). The problem in Corinth probably centered around the impact of wives' behavior on their husbands (cf. 1 Cor. 14:34–35). The first humans in the creation account were also the first married couple, and an uncovered woman would not bring dishonor to a man who is not related to her. Winter (2001: 127) asserts, "The very mention of the word 'veil' by Paul would automatically indicate to the Corinthians that the females under discussion in this passage were married." The veil indicated the woman's marital status. But women other than wives could also pray and prophesy, and it is best to retain the generic translation, man and woman.

The meaning of κεφαλή (*kephalē*, head) is complicated. Paul uses it to refer to the anatomical head but also uses it in a metaphorical sense. Scholars have written extensively analyzing its usage. Three views commend themselves. First, "head" has been traditionally understood to designate hierarchy and to imply authoritative headship (Edwards 1885: 271–72; Robertson and Plummer 1914: 229; Schlier, *TDNT* 3:674; Grudem 1985, 1990; Kistemaker 1993: 365–67). Man as the head has authority over the woman. Grudem (1985) employs the *Thesaurus Lingua Graecae* to examine 2,336 instances of the use of the word from the eighth century B.C. to the fourth century A.D. He notes that in 2,004 occurrences, κεφαλή refers to the physical head in contrast to the rest of the body. Of the 302 metaphorical usages, 49 (which he later reduces to 41 [Grudem 1990: 71]) apply to a person who is superior in rank or to a ruler or ruling part, and none unambiguously use it to mean "source" or "origin." Fitzmyer (1989; 1993) also believes that the evidence from the LXX, Philo, and Plutarch squares with this meaning, and he thinks that Paul "could well have intended κεφαλή to mean 'head' in the sense of authority or supremacy over someone else" (1989: 510–11).

This analysis is not without its critics. First, the word "head" was rarely used to describe the relationship of one individual to another. Conzelmann (1975: 183 n. 21) notes, "Head does not denote sovereignty of one person over another, but over a community." Thiselton (2000: 815–16) goes further and maintains that κεφαλή "does *not* seem to denote a relation of 'subordination' or 'authority over.'" He cites

Chrysostom's (*Hom. 1 Cor.* 26.3) comment that if Paul had intended to convey the idea of rule and subjection, he would have used master-and-slave imagery rather than the figures of man and woman. Chrysostom, however, is primarily interested in fending off any possible heretical interpretation of the subordination of Christ to God (see additional note). Second, Perriman (1994: 602–10) argues that Grudem misinterprets the texts that he adduces as evidence.[8] Cervin (1989) is more pointed in challenging Grudem's examples and methodology (see also Fee 1987: 502 n. 42). Third, this interpretation projects anachronistic physiological notions onto the meaning of "head." Perriman (1994: 610 n. 20) notes that Plutarch's fable (*Agesilaus* 2.3) about the serpent whose tail rebels against the head and takes the lead with disastrous consequences does not illustrate the head's authority over the tail but that the head is specially equipped to go first. Finally, Perriman (1994: 620) maintains, "The question of authority is irrelevant to a discussion of the proper manner in which men and women should pray and prophesy; nor is it a valid deduction from the idea that man has authority over the woman that she should veil herself in worship, an activity directed not towards the man but towards God."

A second alternative understands κεφαλή to mean "source." Christ is the source of man's existence as the agent of creation (cf. 8:6, "through whom all things are") or as the archetypal man (15:46–49). Man is the source of woman's existence, since woman was made from man (Gen. 2:18–23; cf. 1 Cor. 11:12). God is the origin and final goal of all reality and is the source of Christ (3:23; 8:6; 11:12; 15:28). Earlier interpreters understand κεφαλή to mean "source" but with subordinationist overtones.[9] Many recent interpreters who prefer this option seek to eliminate any hint of women's subordination.[10]

The "paucity of lexicographical evidence"—no Greek lexicon offers this as an option (see Grudem 1985; 1990)—makes this meaning for "head" highly suspect. Perriman (1994: 612–14) notes that this connotation does not occur in the LXX, and the evidence adduced from extrabiblical sources is ambiguous and unpersuasive. Perriman (1994: 621) points out that nowhere "do we find anything like the idea of material origin that 'source' must imply in this context (woman created out of the body of man)." Though Paul says in 11:8–9 that woman was created from man, that statement is counterbalanced by the observa-

8. For example, Herm. *Sim.* 7.3 refers to "the head of the household," but Perriman (1994: 610) contends that it refers only to his position as sociologically defined.

9. Bedale 1954; Morris 1958: 151–52; Barrett 1968: 248–49; Bruce 1971: 103; Meier 1978: 217–18.

10. Scroggs 1993: 89, 91–92; Murphy-O'Connor 1980: 490; 1988; Fee 1987: 503; Talbert 1987: 67; Snyder 1992: 149–50; N. Watson 1992: 112; Jervis 1993: 240; R. Horsley 1998: 153.

tion that man now comes from woman. Although the idea of source may fit the account of the woman's creation from the man's rib, it does not fit God as the source of Christ and opens the door to a subordinationist Christology. Christ was not physically created from a piece taken out of God (Hurley 1981: 166), nor man out of Christ (Kistemaker 1993: 366).

The best option understands κεφαλή to mean "that which is most prominent, foremost, uppermost, pre-eminent" (Perriman 1994: 618; cf. LXX Deut. 28:44; Lam. 1:5; Isa. 7:8–9; 9:13; Jer. 38:7; Philo, *Mos.* 2.5 §30; *Rewards* 20 §125). According to Perriman (1994: 618), the noun applies to (1) "the physical top or extremity of an object, such as a mountain or river"; (2) "more abstractly, that which is first, extreme (temporarily or spatially)"; (3) "that which is prominent or outstanding"; (4) "that which is determinative or representative by virtue of its prominence."

Perriman has the best of the arguments. He shows that the meaning "ruler" or "chief" is out of place and "source" quite wrong. "To be 'head' of a group of people simply means to *occupy the position at the top or front*" (Perriman 1994: 616; cf. Cervin 1989; Thiselton 2000: 816–18; Lindemann 2000: 240).[11] The "head" denotes one who is preeminent, and though it may result in authority and leadership, that is not its basic denotation. It is not linked to ideas of obedience or submission. Delobel (1986: 378–79) notes that "in each of these relationships, there is one who has the priority as head and one who comes in second place." But second place "does not connote inferiority, since both man and Christ have a head." Paul's primary intent, then, is not to assert the supremacy of man and the subordination of woman. Instead, it is to establish that each has a head and that "what one does or doesn't put on one's physical head either honors or dishonors one's spiritual head" (Blomberg 1994: 208). It establishes the need for loyalty to the head. Perriman (1994: 621) concludes, "The point seems to be . . . that the behaviour of the woman reflects upon the man who as her head is representative of her, the prominent partner in the relationship, or that the woman's status and value is summed in the man."

11:4   The present matter concerns how the head is attired when one is praying or prophesying. Prophecy is pastoral preaching that offers guidance and instruction (see D. Hill 1979: 122–27). In 14:19, it is related to instruction: "I want to speak five words with my mind that I might instruct [κατηχήσω, *katēchēsō*] others," which explains why it builds up the church (14:5). The result of prophesying is that the hearers learn and are convicted (14:24–25).

---

11. Perriman (1994: 611–12) likens the image to a race-car driver in the pole position. That driver neither is the "source" of the other drivers nor has authority over them.

The difficulty of the phrase κατὰ κεφαλῆς ἔχων (*kata kephalēs echōn*) is normally concealed by translations. I have chosen to render it literally, "having down from the head," to highlight the problem. What is it that one has "down from the head"? Traditionally, it has been understood to refer to some kind of material covering the head. The statue from Corinth of a veiled Augustus—with his toga pulled over his head in preparation to offer a libation—may offer an important clue (Gill 1990: 246–47; Winter 2001: 121–23). The statue was a propaganda piece intended to present the emperor as a pious Roman (Zanker 1990: 301). Wearing the toga over the head at pagan sacrifices was a familiar practice (see C. Thompson 1988), and Oster (1988: 505) makes the case that such "Roman pietistic and devotional ethos" pervaded Corinth. Oster (1992: 68) claims, "The practice of men covering their heads in a context of prayer and prophecy was a common pattern of Roman piety and widespread during the late Republic and early Empire. Since Corinth was a Roman colony, there should be little doubt this aspect of Roman religious practice deserves greater attention by commentators than it has received." The toga pulled up over the head and hanging down from it fits the language "having down from the head." Plutarch (*Mor.* 200F) uses this very language in describing Scipio the Younger seeking to walk through Alexandria incognito by "having his garment down from the head" (κατὰ τῆς κεφαλῆς ἔχων τὸ ἱμάτιον, *kata tēs kephalēs echōn to himation*). In using this language, Paul is not referring to a hat or long hair. According to Paul, this action does not shame the man's anatomical head but his metaphorical head, Christ. Because of the clear association of this practice with pagan devotion, pulling the toga over the physical head in Christian worship would shame the spiritual head of the man, Christ.[12]

Weiss (1910: 271) correctly recognizes that Paul's portrayal of such a practice is only hypothetical (see also Robertson and Plummer 1914: 229; Bruce 1971: 104; Conzelmann 1975: 184 n. 35; Hurley 1981: 170). This practice was not an actual problem that Paul seeks to correct (contra Oster 1988; Gill 1990: 250–51). Instead, he argues from how shameful it would be for a man to pray or prophesy in Christian worship as one arrayed for a pagan devotional to make the case that it is no less shameful for women to pray or prophesy uncovered.

Others, however, contend that the problem involves both men and women and has to do with hairstyles (Murphy-O'Connor 1980; W. Martin

---

12. Murphy-O'Connor's (1980: 484–85) argument that Paul grew up in a tradition in which head coverings for males were not a disgrace for a Jew since priests prayed with turbans on their heads (Exod. 28:36–40; Ezek. 44:18) is not relevant. For a man to pray with something on his head does not in itself shame the head, Christ. The idolatrous connections of the headgear, however, does. Paul's example arises from his abhorrence of idol worship (C. Thompson 1988: 104).

1970: 233; Hurley 1981: 257; R. Horsley 1998: 154). Murphy-O'Connor (1980) argues from 11:14 that "having down from the head" denotes long hair hanging down. Thiselton (2000: 825) assesses Murphy-O'Connor's case as "strong" but not "conclusive" and thinks that the Roman background cited by Oster is "more probable, but not decisively so." Thiselton's translation incorporates the alternative possibility that it is a reference to hair by placing it in brackets. The argument that Paul refers to hair hanging down may sound convincing. In 11:14–15, Paul clearly refers to "long hair," and Murphy-O'Connor (1980: 484) attempts to unlock the meaning of an obscure expression, "having down from the head," with this unambiguous expression. Even though "having down from the head" is an unusual way of saying long, effeminate hair, Murphy-O'Connor infers that Paul is talking about hairstyle throughout 11:2–16. This procedure is valid, however, only if the "clear" expression has been correctly interpreted. Delobel (1986: 372) better explains the logic of 11:14–15 in relation to the head covering:

> According to Paul, men have "naturally" short hair, and they should behave in that line as far as their head is concerned. That may mean that they should keep the head uncovered like nature leaves the head uncovered. Women have "naturally" long hair, and they also should behave in that line by keeping the head covered: they need a περιβόλαιον [*peribolaion*] in line with nature's own hint.

Paul appeals to nature and hairstyles only by analogy. Nature gives a hint for what men and women should do to their heads (Conzelmann 1975: 225; cf. BeDuhn 1999: 296 n. 7). Men should be uncovered; women should be covered. The idea that Paul is referring to hair length should be rejected (see Oster 1988: 485–88), and the nonbiblical texts often cited to argue for the shameful connotations of long hair for men become irrelevant.

Shame is the governing motif in 11:4–6 (Gundry Volf 1997: 153). But the shame is not caused by long hair that conjures up images of effeminacy and sexual ambiguity (Murphy-O'Connor 1980: 487). The shame to the "head," Christ, is caused by the associations of the headdress with pagan sacrifice.

11:5–6 The parallelism with the statement about the men in 11:4 makes clear that Paul envisions both men and women praying and prophesying during the public gathering for worship (Sigountos and Shank 1983: 284; contra Holmyard 1997). Were it only some private gathering among the family or among only women, their attire would not have been an issue. Clearly, he has no problem with women taking an active part in the worship as long as they are "covered." But what constitutes a covered or uncovered (ἀκατακάλυπτος, *akatakalyptos*) head (cf. 11:13)? Does it refer to being bareheaded or to a hairstyle? Is the problem that what they do somehow blurs gender distinctions, is a symptom of disorderly behavior, has links to pagan cultic activity, disavows the authority of the husband or paterfamilias, or is a cultural sign of immodesty? Does the woman shame her anatomical head or her metaphorical head or both? How does the example of being shorn connect to the problem?

Murphy-O'Connor (1980: 488), again, represents an increasing number of scholars who think that the problem revolves around hairdos. He argues that "an uncovered head" is equivalent to disheveled hair (cf. the description of the leper's hair in Lev. 13:45 LXX), while a "covered head" is a carefully tended feminine hairdo—"to have the hair tied up on top of the head rather than hanging loose" (Hays 1997: 185).[13] The assumption is that it was shameful for women to unbind their hair in public, "a sign associated either with prostitutes or—perhaps worse from Paul's point of view—with women caught up in the ecstatic worship practices of the cults associated with Dionysius, Cybele, and Isis" (Hays 1997: 185–86). Some also suspect that it might refer to a boundary-transgressing hairstyle, since hair represents a culturally encoded symbol of female identity (Gundry Volf 1997: 153–54, 157). Murphy-O'Connor (1980: 489) interprets the long hair in 11:13 as a wrapper and understands Paul to forbid women from letting their hair down in worship. They need to keep it styled on their heads. Others think that his concern is the masculine nature of the hairstyle. If the problem centers on hair, then the root issue may be that the women were blurring lines of gender distinction or acting in a disorderly manner or both. To counter this behavior, he argues that the distinction between the sexes should be obvious and respected.

Paul's mention of hair in 11:14–15 and shaved heads in this passage, however, is only by way of illustration. It serves to bolster his argument about head coverings and is not the central problem. The syllogism runs like this:

An uncovered head for a woman is the same as being shorn.

It is shameful for a woman to be shorn.

Therefore, she should cover her head.

The issue of "hair" is a false trail that can only misdirect the interpretation of the passage.[14] The matter of concern is women's head coverings

13. So Isaksson 1963: 166; W. Martin 1970: 233–34; Hurley 1973: 199; 1981: 257; Kroeger and Kroeger 1978; Padgett 1984; Schüssler Fiorenza 1984: 227–30; Gundry Volf 1997: 153–54; Dunn 1998: 589–91; R. Collins 1999: 396–99; Lindemann 2000: 241.

14. Although those from a Western culture certainly can affirm the colorful application of this text found in Hays (1997: 186)—"Men should not come to church wearing dresses, and women shouldn't come to church topless"—it is hardly germane to Paul's issue.

(Delobel 1986: 375–76; Fitzmyer 1989: 503; Engberg-Pedersen 1991: 679; Witherington 1995: 232–35; F. Watson 2000: 534–35).

For a Hebrew woman to go out uncovered was widely regarded as a disgrace (3 Macc. 4:6; *b. Ned.* 30b) because a covered head was a sign of modesty (*b. Yoma* 47b). To go out with loose hair in public (*m. B. Qam.* 8:6) was a greater disgrace and considered grounds for divorce (*m. Ketub.* 7:6; *b. Ketub.* 72a). Paul is not imposing Palestinian customs on the Corinthians, however. The Corinthian culture also looked askance at women going out in public without a head covering. The literature suggests that it was taken for granted that respectable women would wear some kind of head covering in public (Conzelmann 1975: 185; cf. Plutarch, *Mor.* 232C, 267A). To shave one's head as part of a vow was an accepted practice for Jewish males (Acts 18:18; 21:23–24) and females (Josephus, *J.W.* 2.15.1 §313). Paul assumes, however, that his readers will regard it as shameful for a woman to have her hair sheared. Wire (1990: 119) rightly infers that this appeal to shame "shows that the women he wants to persuade are not social outcasts with no pretensions of honor but consider themselves worthy of respect in the community." The shaven head of a woman is an unnatural condition that removes nature's covering, and it must betoken some disgrace in this culture for the argument to carry any weight (cf. Aristophanes, *Thesmophoriazusae* 837; T. Job 23:7; 24:7–10).[15] According to Tacitus (*Germania* 19), the husband of an adulterous wife cuts her hair, strips her, and banishes her from the house (see also Dio Chrysostom, *Or.* 64.3; cf. Jer. 7:29; Ezek. 7:18). The shame attached to the shorn head of a woman runs deeper than that she might appear mannish. The shaved head is imposed upon the adulteress to expose her publicly (Winter 2001: 128–29). Paul resorts to hyperbole to make the point that if a woman appears bareheaded, it is as shameful as being shaven (Delobel 1986: 376). Since it is shameful, she needs to be covered. The verb κατακαλύπτεσθαι (*katakalyptesthai*) does not refer to a hairstyle in classical Greek but means "to cover up" and could also mean "to veil" (Delobel 1986: 375; LSJ 893).

Derrett (1977: 171) notes, "Greek women were usually covered in social life (as sculpture confirms), except in their, or their relations', homes." Uncovering the head in public had sexual implications. In discussing the ritual to test the suspected adulteress, Philo (*Spec. Laws* 3.10 §56) interprets the purpose of the priest's removing the woman's covering ("kerchief"; Num. 5:18) as signifying "that she may be judged with her head bared and stripped of the symbol of modesty, regularly worn by women who are wholly innocent." We can infer that, for Philo,

---

15. No evidence exists that prostitutes in Corinth shaved their heads (contra Grosheide 1953: 254).

the covering conveys that a woman is innocent, virtuous, and untouchable. Rousselle (1992: 315) contends, "Respectable women did nothing to draw attention to themselves. . . . A veil or hood constituted a warning: it signified that the wearer was a respectable woman that no man dare approach without risking . . . penalties. A woman who went out . . . unveiled forfeited the protection of Roman law against possible attackers who were entitled to plead extenuating circumstances" (cited by Thiselton 2000: 801; cf. D. Martin 1995: 229–49). Women who went uncovered in public gave nonverbal clues that they were "available." J. Davidson (1997: 312) points out that the modern liberation of women "has made it much more difficult to understand the sexual charge of female bareheadedness." Hair (exposed) is included in a list of sexual incitements in *b. Ber.* 24a. Thiselton (2000: 801–2) is on the mark in commenting, "Public worship was neither the occasion for women to become 'objects' of attraction to be 'sized up' by men; nor an occasion for women to offer cryptic 'suggestions' to men." Women are not to be ogled as sex objects during worship. Paul's primary interest in this passage is to prevent this from happening, and he argues that women should be covered.

It is not fruitful to try to guess why the women in Corinth were uncovered, since Paul offers no reasons and no real clues. Many think that it was a token of their liberation and equality, but the parallel passages adduced in support are not always germane.[16] Much of the evidence mustered by Conzelmann (1975: 185 nn. 39–40) addresses "going out in public." Fee (1987: 508 n. 70) suggests that this evidence does not apply to Christian worship, since Christian women may not have thought of themselves as going out in public when they worshiped in homes and called one another "brother" and "sister." Fee unintentionally may have identified the heart of the problem. It was not resistance to Paul's imposition of Jewish customs (contra Jaubert 1971–72), a protest statement declaring female equality and sex reversal (contra D. MacDonald 1987), or a carryover from pagan cults in which women lost control and let their hair down in a state of frenzied ecstasy (contra Kroeger and Kroeger 1978; Schüssler Fiorenza 1984: 227–28). In a worship service in a private home, the women may not have thought of themselves as being out in public (see Winter 2001: 128). Paul assumes that they should regard such a service as "going out in public," and they should be attired accordingly.

Whatever the reasons behind the absence of a covering, Paul asserts that such behavior shames the woman's head. To argue that she brings

---

16. The passage in Jos. As. 15:1, where a heavenly man instructs Aseneth to remove the veil from her head, who is then declared to be a chaste virgin whose head "is like that of a young man," is too opaque to help inform 1 Cor. 11:2–16. It does not exalt androgyny, because she dons the veil again as a bride (Jos. As. 18:6).

shame on herself (R. Collins 1999: 407) may be true but curiously makes superfluous Paul's opening gambit, in 11:3, asserting that man is the head of the woman. As "Christ" is the implied referent for "head" in 11:4, so the "man" is the most likely referent for "head" in 11:5. Hays (1997: 186) thinks that the conduct brings shame on the men in the church, whose "headship" is somehow discredited by the women's disorderly behavior. It seems more likely, however, that such behavior would reflect poorly on the particular men in the woman's life: her husband, father, or male head of the household. The husband is especially shamed when his wife uncovers her head in public.

Paul's argument ends with the only direct command in the section (other than "you yourselves be the judge," 11:13): "Let her cover herself." In this particular context, it refers to her head. In other cultures, other parts of the body may need to be covered to prevent conveying inappropriate sexual messages. Interpreters must be mindful that fashions vary and that ideas of proper decorum vary from culture to culture and among differing classes. Although Fee (1987: 512) is correct that Paul's instructions are tied to cultural norms that are relative and that literal obedience is not required to be obedient to God's word, one does need to bridge the contexts to discern what is eternally valid. Paul's concern that Christians honor sexual decorum in worship and avoid what a culture deems to be suggestive attire is a broadly applicable, though elastic, concept. He is not trying to repress women and to restrain their expression of spiritual gifts but to impress on them the need to project modesty and virtue in their dress.

11:7–9 Paul explains the basis of his previous assertions in 11:4–5 (Gundry Volf 1997: 153). The μὲν γὰρ . . . δέ (*men gar . . . de*) construction has an explanatory force. A man ought not (οὐκ ὀφείλει, *ouk ophelei*; denoting here a moral necessity) cover his head (11:4), because he is the image and glory of God. A woman, on the other hand, ought to cover her head because she is the glory of man.

Paul interprets Gen. 1:27, stating that God created man in his image, through the creation account in Gen. 2. He makes his points based on priority in creation: the man was created first (Gen. 2:7), then the woman "out of him" (Gen 2:21–23);[17] the man was not created for the woman, but the woman was created for the man (Gen. 2:22). Since the woman was created later, out of the man (Gen. 2:21–23), Paul deduces that she is not the direct image of God. Schrage (1995: 509) suggests that a Jewish exegetical tradition, which interpreted ʾādām in Gen. 1:27 as applying only to the man, may have influenced Paul. But Paul's purpose is not to establish that man, not woman, is made in the image of

---

17. The argument from priority in creation also appears in 1 Tim. 2:13: "For Adam was formed first, then Eve."

God.[18] The term "image" leads him to the term "glory" (Barrett 1968: 252), which then becomes the key term in 1 Cor. 11:7–9 and counterbalances the notion of "shame" in 11:4–6.[19] "Glory" does not appear in the Genesis narrative, but image and glory are closely associated in Jewish exegesis (Hooker 1963–64a: 411; Jervell 1960: 100–114; see also Wire 1990: 120). Paul does not mention that the woman is also created in the image of God, because he wants to stress the point that she is the glory of man (Gundry Volf 1997: 156).[20] She is to bring glory to the man because "she is the glory of man by creation." Consequently, Paul stops short of proclaiming that the woman is the image of man and argues instead that she is the glory of the man. She completes the man as well as completes creation. Paul's inference is this: As man is the reflected glory of God, so woman is the reflected glory of man.

The logic is not, "The man stands before God uncovered because of his spiritual subordination to Christ, so the woman should stand veiled because of her spiritual subordination to her husband," as Orr and Walther (1976: 263–64) contend. Instead, for Paul the key point is that the woman reflects the glory of man, not of God. His argument is this: The man stands uncovered because he reflects the glory of God; the woman must be covered because she reflects the glory of man. Ideas of obedience or submission are only ancillary (Perriman 1994: 620). The concept that the woman reflects the glory of the man appears in Prov. 11:16 LXX, in 4 Ezra (2 Esdr.) 4:13–28 (particularly 4:17, "they bring glory to man"), on a Jewish tombstone in Rome ("Lucilla, the blessed glory of Sophronius," cited by R. Collins 1999: 410), and in rabbinic lore (*y. Ketub.* 34b [11.3]). In a worship setting, where persons are to give glory only to God, Paul reasons that a woman must cover her anatomical head, which reflects man's glory, who is her metaphorical head. If a woman were to appear in worship with her head uncovered, the splendor of her tresses (11:15) would bring honor to her husband when all ought to be concerned with glorifying God alone (Hooker 1963–64a: 414–15; Wire 1990: 120–21; Hays 1997: 186). Such misplaced honor would redound only to her husband's shame before God.

Paul's purpose is not to argue for the subordination or inferiority of the woman. Verses 11–12 make this clear: in the Lord, men and women are interdependent and equal in Christ. His main point is that both man

18. Note that in 2 Cor. 4:4 and Col. 1:15, Paul identifies Christ as the image of God.

19. Getting lost in the philosophical background and meaning of the terms "image" (see Conzelmann 1975: 187–88) and "glory" will only cause one to be sidetracked and miss Paul's simple point.

20. Paul's exegesis of this text is quite different from that of Philo, who concludes, "Why, as of other animals and as man also was made, the woman was not also made out of the earth, but out of the rib of man: This was ordained in the first place, in order that the woman might not be of equal dignity with the man" (*Quest. Gen.* 1 §27).

and woman are the glory of another (Gundry Volf 1997: 157). Man, whose head is Christ and who represents the glory of God, is to be uncovered in worship. Woman, whose head is man and who represents his glory, is to be covered in worship. To do otherwise brings shame to their respective heads.

11:10 Paul draws the conclusion (διὰ τοῦτο, *dia touto*, because of this) to the argument that precedes (Fitzmyer 1974: 190), but what he concludes is far from clear. No interpretation can be held with great confidence. The first problem is the meaning of the phrase ἐξουσίαν ἔχειν ἐπὶ τῆς κεφαλῆς (*exousian echein epi tēs kephalēs*). Does it mean to have "authority on the head" or "over the head"?[21]

Those who argue that the phrase means to have authority *on* the head understand ἐξουσία to refer to the covering or veil (Edwards 1885: 276–77; Godet 1887: 122; Foerster, *TDNT* 2:574; see additional note).[22] The covering symbolizes the authority under which the woman has been placed, and wearing it signifies her acceptance of her subjection to the man. One might expect, however, that such metonymy (substituting for the name of something one of its attributes or something it suggests) would lead Paul to choose the word "subjection" (ὑποταγή, *hypotagē*; cf. 1 Tim. 3:4) rather than "authority."[23]

The chief problem with this view is that it attributes to ἐξουσία "a passive sense, which is otherwise unknown" (Fitzmyer 1974: 191). "To have authority" means that one has the right to do something, not that one submits to authority (LSJ 599; BDAG 353).[24] In every other occurrence in the NT, the phrase ἔχειν ἐξουσίαν ἐπί means "to have authority over" (cf. Mark 2:10/Luke 5:24; Rev. 11:6; 14:18; 16:9; 20:6; see also Luke 19:17). Ramsay's (1907: 203) characterization of this passive interpretation of authority as "a preposterous idea which a Greek scholar would laugh at anywhere except in the New Testament, where (as they seem to think) Greek words may mean anything that commentators choose" is often cited and deserves repeating as a humbling reminder to interpreters.

21. There is no reason to conclude, as Fee (1987: 520) does, that "authority" is a Corinthian phrase.

22. Kittel (1920: 17–34) develops the idea that the root of an Aramaic word meaning "veil" or "ornament of the head" means to "have power of dominion over," and the Greek word "authority" was taken as its equivalent either by mistranslation or by popular etymology. This idea is modified by Schwarz (1979).

23. The NAB translates it "sign of submission."

24. BeDuhn (1999: 302–3) asserts, "Paul *always* employs the term to mean authority held by the subject: the individual's right and authority to act, the individual's control over objects, persons, or situations (1 Cor. 7:37; 15:24; Rom. 9:21; 13:1–3; 2 Cor. 10:8; 13:10), and by extension as a title of individuals who exercise such authority (Rom. 13:1; Col. 1:13, 16; 2:10, 15; Eph. 1:21; 2:2; 3:10; 6:12)."

Another option understands the phrase to mean "to have a symbol of authority on her head." The head covering does not signify her subordination but her prerogative to pray and prophesy in public worship—an authority she did not formerly possess.[25] Those adopting this view reason that the woman might appear to be usurping a male role by speaking in worship and consequently needs "authority on her head" affirming her right to do so and conveying the new status of women to the angels. The symbol of authority on her head heralds that the old regime, watched over by the angels, with its strict rules for gender roles, is outmoded. Women now have authority to fulfill a role previously denied them.

This interpretation requires inserting the word "symbol" or "sign" into the text, but the meaning "symbol of authority" for ἐξουσία, though possible, is not attested elsewhere. It is telling against this view that the introductory phrase "because of this" means that Paul is drawing a conclusion from what has been argued in 11:3–9, and these verses emphasize the woman's secondary place as the glory of the man, not her authority to pray and prophesy. This view also requires the head covering to do double (and dissonant) duty as a symbol. On the one hand, it serves to efface man's glory in the presence of God; on the other hand, it serves as a symbol of the woman's authorization to pray and prophesy (Hooker 1963–64a: 415). It is more likely that the covering serves only one primary function: the cloaking of man's glory.

A third option best fits standard Greek grammar, in which "authority" means "the right to do something" or "to have control," and ἐπί plus the genitive means "over." This option takes the phrase to mean that the woman is "to have authority over her head": that is, she is to exercise control over her head or to have control of her head (Delobel 1986: 387; Padgett 1984: 71–72; Schrage 1995: 514; cf. B. Hall 1990; Thiselton 2000: 840). But what does this mean in this context and in the wider context of Roman society? Robertson and Plummer (1914: 232) tentatively wonder whether Paul meant that she "'ought to have control over her head' so as not to expose it to indignity." If she unveils her head, "every one has control over it," and she loses her dignity. Instead of shaming her head, she must control it by wearing a head covering according to custom. This suggestion makes sense of the grammar and fits the context. Wearing the head covering represents the "woman's control over her own head, by which she demonstrates her faithfulness to her husband or her acknowledgement of her status" (BeDuhn 1999: 303–4). The confession of Lucius, the main character of Apuleius's novel *Meta-*

---

25. Hooker 1964: 415–16; Barrett 1968: 255; Bruce 1971: 106; Orr and Walther 1976: 261; Scroggs 1993: 94; Kendrick 1995; see also Isaksson 1963: 181, who thinks that the covering was a document, emblem, or band that showed the woman's authority to appear as a prophetess.

morphoses (*The Golden Ass*) may shed light on Paul's concern. He states, "It has always been the prime concern of my life to observe in public the heads and tresses of beautiful women, and then to conjure up the image at home for leisurely enjoyment" (*Metam.* 2.8; trans. Lindsay 1960: 55). By wearing a head covering, the woman keeps control over her head so that males do not eye her when she is praying and prophesying. Paul wishes to curb the erotic potential of the uncovered female head in the context of worship (see F. Watson 2000: 530–32).[26]

More complicated, if not completely baffling, is Paul's explanation of why she should do this: "because of the angels."[27] He must assume that the Corinthians can fill in the blanks about what this cryptic reference means from some shared, prior knowledge—either from their own theological speculation about angels or from something he has taught them. Modern readers are left in the dark as a result, and none of the many explanations is without problems.[28]

Murphy-O'Connor (1988: 271 n. 19) claims that taking "the angels" as a reference to heavenly beings has yielded no satisfactory interpretation (cf. Luke 7:24; 9:52; Gal. 4:14). One interpretation identifies them as a figurative reference to human leaders in the church (Bornhäuser 1930; or "messengers" [Winandy 1992]).[29] This view is possible if "the angels" of the seven churches refer to their bishops or elders (Rev. 1:20; 2:1, 8, 12, 18; 3:1, 7, 14). One is hard put, however, to figure out how a reference to human leaders in the church connects in any way to what Paul says here.[30]

A venerable interpretation assumes that women are particularly vulnerable to cosmic angels who prey upon them. Tertullian (*Marc.* 5.8; *De virginibus velandis* [*The Veiling of Virgins*] 1.7) suggests that the phrase refers to the fallen angels, the "sons of God" in Gen. 6:1–4, who noticed that the daughters of humans were attractive and married them (Lietzmann 1949: 54–55 [with reservations]; Meier 1978: 220–21). Such an angelic sexual attack seems far-fetched, but this tradition continued to

26. The obscurity of Paul's language in this section may be attributable to the delicacy of the issue—that males might gaze at females in an inappropriate manner in worship—and his roundabout bid to deter that from happening.

27. The interpretation of this passage has produced tendentious and erroneous discussion of its grammar. The most egregious example is that of McGinn (1996: 98), who interprets 11:10 to mean "Owing to all these things, the woman has authority over the 'head' [i.e., the man]" and mistranslates the phrase διὰ τοὺς ἀγγέλους (*dia tous angelous*) as "through the angels."

28. Fitzmyer (1974: 190) dismisses the proposals for its emendation or claims that it is a gloss.

29. Winter (2001: 133–38) thinks that they are outsiders monitoring the Christian meeting for any unusual activities.

30. The same may be said for Winter's (2001: 133–38) proposal that they refer to information gatherers monitoring the Christian meetings for the authorities.

fascinate Jewish imaginations (see Jub. 4:22; 5:1–2; 1 Enoch 6–7; 19:1; 2 Bar. 56:10–16). According to the misogynistic tilt of T. Reub. 5:1–7, the women seduced the angels. If this tradition about the lustful sons of God was combined with the Hellenistic notion that women were particularly exposed to spirits when in an ecstatic condition, then an angelic peril to women may be Paul's meaning (Héring 1962: 106–7; Corrington 1991: 230; D. Martin 1995: 244).

Paul never uses the word "angels" with the definite article to refer to bad angels (contrast 1 Cor. 4:9 and 13:1), and good angels are not subject to sensual temptations. Many regard it as ludicrous to identify the angels with the sons of God who lusted after the daughters of humans before the flood and now haunt church buildings hoping for new opportunities to produce a new race of illegitimate giants. Would the Corinthians even have been familiar with such Jewish traditions? Would such a head covering be sufficient to ward off evil attacks or seductions from fallen angels? No evidence shows that the veil was understood to have this function. Finally, Paul says that the woman is praying and prophesying, which does not suggest that she is in an ecstatic trance, and the "weakness" and "vulnerability" of the woman in such a state is something imposed on the text.

Another view contends that Paul has in mind imitating the angels: "because the angels do so" (Edwards 1885: 278; Rösch 1932). According to Isa. 6:2, the seraphs in attendance to God covered their faces with two of their wings. As the angels veil their faces in the presence of their superior, so "a woman, when worshipping in the presence of her direct and visible superior (man), should do the same" (Robertson and Plummer 1914: 233–34). Or, it is possible that the angels model for the women those who keep their place in the order of things as ministering servants. The problem with this view is that Paul has not argued that men are women's superior.

Angels were understood to function as guardians and mediators of the law and to supervise its continuation. Some think that Paul reflects a tradition in which they serve, as it were, as God's secret agents who are God's eyes and ears in the world (Philo, *Dreams* 1.22 §140) and report all infractions (Jub. 4:6; 1 Enoch 99:3). There are angels "who watch for evil activity and restore order and harmony to the cosmic order and angels who regard all human souls, and all their deeds, and all their lives before the face of the Lord" (2 Enoch 19:4; see also 4:1–2; *b. Ned.* 20a). The women must don head covers out of deference to the angels, who are guardians of the order of creation (Brun 1913; Moffatt 1938: 152). Delobel (1986: 386) asserts, "The behaviour of women in worship has to respect the order of creation symbolised by the angels who are indeed present in worship and watching the observance of this order."

This view can fit many interpretations of the basic problem. One can argue that the angels monitor the woman's submission to the man. BeDuhn (1999: 308–19) contends, however, that the problem is rooted in the women desiring to transcend their gender identity. BeDuhn imagines that the Corinthians appealed to the angels as a model for doing so, and Paul ironically reverses their argument. BeDuhn paraphrases Paul's response thus: "Do you aspire to be like angels? It is because of the angels that you find yourselves in this differentiated condition." The angels were responsible for the woman's inferior created condition, which requires her to cover up. But this kind of mirror-reading is unwarranted, and no evidence exists that Paul attributed the creation of gendered embodiment to angels. One also wonders, since Christians have been delivered from this present evil age, why they should worry about the oppressive control of angelic powers.

A more fruitful possibility surmises that angels are participants in worship and that they function as guardians of its order (R. Collins 1999: 412). This view can take many forms. Fitzmyer (1974: 198–200) thinks that the angels denote a euphemistic way of speaking of God's presence. Fitzmyer draws on the Dead Sea Scrolls, which list strict rules for those who can enter the congregation, "for the angels of holiness are among their congre[gation]" (1QSa 2:8–9; 1QM 7:4–6). Fitzmyer (1974: 200) opines that this evidence from Qumran invites us "to understand that the unveiled head of a woman is like a bodily defect which should be excluded from such an assembly, 'because holy angels are present in their congregation.'" It means "'out of reverence for the angels,' who are present in such sacred gatherings and who should not look on such a condition." Although the use of a similar phrase is suggestive, how is an uncovered woman equivalent to someone with a bodily defect?

Evidence does exist that angels are observers of human behavior and may have been considered present in worship (see Luke 15:7, 10; 1 Tim. 5:21; Heb. 1:6; 12:22–23). If the angels are perceived as observers in Christian worship, then the woman's head covering may simply be a "symbol of womanly dignity, esp[ecially] in the presence of holy angels" (BDAG 353). Possibly, the idea is that the head covering keeps the angels from being distracted from their worship of God. Wire (1990: 121) appeals to another Jewish tradition about the angels mistakenly worshiping Adam when he is created because he reflects God's glory (see *Gen. Rab.* 8.10; *Eccles. Rab.* 6.9.1). According to the tradition in Life of Adam and Eve 13–17, God commanded the angels to worship Adam, but Satan refused, demanding that one inferior and subsequent in creation to him should worship him instead. Satan tried to incite a heavenly mutiny, so God exiled the mutineers from glory. Satan then assailed Adam's wife out of revenge. Wire (1990: 121) speculates, "If angels are to worship God, Paul may be arguing that woman must be covered to keep the heavenly host from a misplaced worship of men whose glory she reflects." This view, again, assumes that the Corinthians are aware of some version of this Jewish tradition. If the angels could be distracted from worshiping God to glorify man, how much more could human males be distracted by the woman's uncovered head. Hooker (1963–64a: 415) slyly suggests that it was indeed the men of Corinth, who would have been charmed by a woman's uncovered locks and diverted from worshiping God, whom Paul is worried about.

After examining the many different views and their permutations, I am inclined to think that Paul assumes that the angels are present in worship as observers and that their presence necessitates paying even greater heed to conventions of modesty.

Paul changes direction and introduces a caveat to his argument with **11:11–12** πλήν (*plēn*, nevertheless). What follows is not integral to his case but is inserted to offer a counterpoise to the previous emphasis on woman's secondary place in creation. He balances his earlier statement that woman was created from man by observing that man now comes from woman. Delobel (1986: 384–85) thinks that this argument serves as "a necessary complement to avoid certain negative conclusions concerning the place of women which would exceed Paul's limited goal in this pericope and indeed contradict Paul's view on women which he expounds elsewhere." Fee (1987: 517) avers that 11:11–12 is not intended to correct Paul's statements in 11:7–9, but "to qualify them so as to limit their application to the immediate argument" (see also Meier 1978: 222). In other words, what Paul says in 11:7–9 pertains only to the matter of women's head coverings.

This qualification attests that men and women are interdependent. Kürzinger (1978) argues that χωρίς (*chōris*) means "different from" ("neither the woman is *different from* the man nor the man *different from* the woman in the Lord") and that Paul asserts the equality of man and woman in Christ. It is more likely, however, that Paul attests that neither can exist χωρίς (without, apart from) the other (Gundry Volf 1997: 161). The statement that the woman came from man, suggesting the male's priority, and that she represents the glory of man is counterbalanced by the fact that males now depend upon females for their existence. This interdependence of male and female could lead to a corollary similar to the statement in 12:21: "The eye cannot say to the hand, 'I have no need of you.'"

Why does Paul qualify this state of affairs as being "in the Lord" and affirm that "all things are from God"? The stimulus for this statement may be his affirmation in 8:6, "But for us: one God, the Father, from whom all things come and we go unto him, and one Lord, Jesus Christ, through whom all things are and we [go to God] through him." It is possible, as Delobel (1986: 384) surmises, that "Christ is mentioned here as the basis of the creation order in parallel with God in v. 12. This corresponds with the roles attributed to God and Christ according to 1 Cor 8,6. When Paul speaks about creation, he gives a Christian view where Christ is involved." The source of everything is not the male or the female but God and God's saving work through Christ.

11:13–15 In 11:13, Paul circles back to the main point of his argument. "You be the judge" followed by the question "Is it proper for a woman to pray to God in public uncovered?" assumes that he has made his point so that the answer now should be self-evident (cf. 10:15). He expects them to answer, "Of course, it is not proper for a woman to pray to God uncovered." The adjective ἀκατακάλυπτος (*akatakalyptos*) does not refer to the woman's hairstyle but to a cover over the head. The issue turns on what is regarded as "fitting" (πρέπειν, *prepein*) as opposed to what is shameful and dishonorable (11:4–5, 14), and what goes against nature (11:14; cf. Rom. 1:26–27).

To clinch his case, Paul throws in a final argument by appealing to nature, which is assumed to reveal "what is fitting, honorable, and glorifying" (BeDuhn 1999: 315). That he specifically mentions hair in these verses does not mean that hair has been the topic throughout this section (contra Blomberg 1994: 213–14). It is brought up only as a final illustration as to why women should have a cover but men should not.

When Paul speaks of "nature" (ἡ φύσις, *hē physis*), he means what his society understands to be natural. Since male hair grows the same way as female hair does, he must be referring to hair that conforms to societal expectations concerning male and female hairdos. In general, it was dishonorable for men in this culture to have long hair (κομᾶν, *koman*). He may be referring to an overly elaborate coiffure, since Roman men normally kept their hair short (see Horace, *Ep.* 11.28; Juvenal, *Sat.* 2.96; Petronius, *Satyr.* 119). In a diatribe against a young student associated with Corinth "whose hair was somewhat too elaborately dressed," Epictetus (*Diatr.* 3.1.1–45) asks, "Are you a man or a woman?" and brands his hairstyle a complaint against nature. Philo rails against "the disease of effemination" among men who debase "the sterling coin of nature" and are distinguished by braiding and adorning themselves with feminine hairstyles (*Spec. Laws* 3.7 §§37–38; cf. *Cont. Life* 6 §§50–52; *Virt.* 4 §§18–21). In Ps.-Phoc. 210–12, we find this warning:

> If a child is a boy, do not let locks grow on [his] head.
> Do not braid [his] crown nor cross knots at the top of [his] head.
> Long hair is not fit for boys, but for voluptuous women.

Winter (2001: 132) points out that the only surviving statues in Corinth portraying men wearing long hair, besides male deities, are those appearing in the Facade of the Captives in the forum in Roman Corinth. Their long hair is intended to send the message that these captives were weak, soft, and effeminate. Long hair for men is unnatural for Paul because in his cultural context it conveys sexual ambiguity and hints of moral perversion.

By contrast, long hair was the norm for women (Plutarch, *Mor.* 267B). Thiselton (2000: 825) notes that κόμη (*komē*) "often denotes *hair* perceived as an ornament, while θρίξ [*thrix*] denotes *hair* in a more anatomical sense." The context suggests hair that is long, and Gill (1990: 258) contends that in Roman society long hair was a symbol of the wife's relationship to her husband.

The problem in Corinth is not hair length or its dressing. If the Corinthians, for whatever reason, deliberately rejected these conventions, calling their attention to them would hardly be a forceful argument to correct this behavior. Instead, Paul is interested in what "nature teaches" and brings up hair only by way of analogy. It serves as a type of cover. Nature has given women hair as a glorious, natural cover (see Apuleius, *Metam.* 2.8–9). Therefore, women should follow the lead of nature, as defined by social decorum, and cover their heads.[31] The περιβόλαιον (*peribolaion*) is "an article of apparel that covers much of the body" (BDAG 800), such as a cloak or a mantle (see Heb. 1:12). Men, on the other hand, do not use hair as a cover, since it is dishonorable for them to have long hair. Taking this cue from nature, men do not need a cover; women do.

Paul concludes his discussion on a negative note, warning the Corinthians not to be contentious. The etymology of the adjective "contentious" (φιλόνεικος, *philoneikos*) derives from the love of victory. Does he anticipate that the Corinthians (the women?) will not want to concede defeat but will want to wrangle with him about this issue until they win? What is the custom in the church of God? Does it refer to the custom regarding head coverings or the Corinthian custom of being quarrelsome?

11:16

Many take this final remark to be about the head coverings and find it rather peevish. Hays (1997: 189–90) comments, "Perhaps at some level he recognizes the weakness of his own rather fragmented argument." Paul resigns himself to their combativeness and the difficulty of convincing them and finally throws up his hands and insists that they should adhere to the practices of all the other churches. Others see the remark as more irenic. M. Mitchell (1993: 262) maintains that Paul is

31. Corrington (1991: 229) cites Apuleius (*Metam.* 11.10) to argue that, contrary to the custom elsewhere, female devotees of Isis in Corinth covered their hair with a light linen cloth apparently to convey that they were behaving in a seemly fashion according to Roman norms.

not warning the Corinthians that they should not resist his instructions on this matter but cautioning them about their contentiousness among themselves. M. Mitchell assumes that the Corinthians had more than one position on head attire. Paul's goal is to avoid contention in the church, "in union with the custom of the church universal" (M. Mitchell 1993: 262–63). Engberg-Pedersen (1991: 686) offers the novel thesis that "Paul is leaving the decision to the Corinthians themselves because on principle he does not want to enforce his own view of the matter in the way in which potentially contentious people do want to enforce their view. Here, then, the idea is Christians are not contentious—so *I* will not be contentious; I will not *insist*."

It is more likely, however, that the "custom" concerns head attire and that Paul is insistent about women covering their heads when they pray and prophesy. His conclusion to his argument does not signal that he has misgivings about the strength of his arguments and consequently makes a preemptive strike by attacking any who might disagree as being "contentious." Instead, his comment has the same force as that of Josephus's conclusion to an argument: "None but the most contentious of critics, I imagine, could fail to be content with the arguments already adduced" (*Ag. Ap.* 1.21 §160; see Schrage 1995: 523). Paul's concluding statement basically means that when all is said and done, they must be mindful of the universal practice in other churches. That alone should cause them to take stock and rethink their own practices.

Additional Notes

11:3. Paul's statement that God is the head of Christ was a favorite Arian text (Robertson and Plummer 1914: 229), but does not assume a subordinationist Christology. Paul refers to obedience. Christ is obedient to God, and the wife is obedient to the husband. Grudem (1990: 54–55) contends that historically in "the doctrine of the Trinity Christ's relationship to the Father has been understood to be a subordination in role but not in essence or being." Thiselton's (2000: 804) comments are edifying: "The God-Christ relation has *nothing to do with self-glory* or with affirmation of the self at the expense of the other (cf. the ethical context of Phil 2:6–11; it is *not an involuntary or imposed 'subordination,' but an example of shared love*). This shared love controls the use of freedom, and thereby each brings 'glory' to the other by assuming the distinctive roles for a common purpose."

11:10. The smattering of versions (vg, cop^bo, arm) and early fathers (Irenaeus, Hippolytus, Origen, Chrysostom, Jerome, Augustine, Bede) that occasionally read "veil" (κάλυμμα) instead of "authority" constitute an early commentary on the meaning of 11:10.

VIII. Divisions at the Lord's Supper (11:17–34)

In 11:17–34, Paul seeks to correct the Corinthian desecration of the Lord's Supper. The Lord's Supper should accent and intensify group solidarity; the Corinthians' supper accented and intensified social differences. No one ought to feel humiliated at the Lord's Supper, yet the Corinthians' manner of conducting the meal left the "have-nots" feeling that they were beneath the notice of their fellow Christians. The primary issue is their conduct surrounding the Lord's Supper, and Paul appeals to the Last Supper tradition to correct it. The problem was caused neither by the Corinthians' theological confusion about sacramental facets of the Lord's Supper nor by a conflict over eucharistic theology.[1] Bornkamm's (1969: 147) claim that the Corinthians attach all the importance to the sacrament and treat the common meal with indifference represents an earlier consensus that is flawed. The problem is simply this: when they eat the Lord's Supper, they divide along socioeconomic lines. Each one eats his or her own supper, and those who have plenty ignore those who have little or nothing. This indifference to others shows contempt for the church of God and dishonors Christ's self-giving sacrifice, which the Supper commemorates. Social questions clearly dominate the beginning (11:17–22) and the ending (11:27–34) of this section. The central part (11:23–26), which attracts so much attention because it includes the recitation of the words of institution at the Last Supper, serves to inform Paul's discussion of the social gap that their meal underscores. Commentators feel compelled to make comments about the theological meaning of the Lord's Supper. P. Lampe (1994: 36) observes, however, that Paul "presupposes a certain theological concept about the Lord's Supper that he does not develop" (cf. Engberg-Pedersen 1993: 113; contra Käsemann 1964). Attempts to dredge up hints of Paul's theology of the Eucharist frequently lead to an overinterpretation of the formulations in the text (Engberg-Pedersen 1993: 116). Paul is not trying to instruct the Corinthians on the meaning of the Lord's Supper. Instead, he is trying to correct a practice that does not

---

1. Schmithals (1971: 255) argues that the gnostics were trying to besmirch the observance of the Lord's Supper and turn it into a profane feast.

accord with what the Lord's Supper is intended to remember: Christ's sacrifice for others.

Theissen's (1982: 69–120, 145–74) argument that the church in Corinth displayed "a marked social stratification" is helpful. A meal context in which all brought their own food would only accentuate the disparity. Some enjoyed better food and greater quantities of it. Because the host of such a large gathering is likely to have been a wealthy member of the community, Murphy-O'Connor (1983: 159) pictures this scenario:

> He invited into the triclinium his closest friends among the believers, who would have been of the same social class. The rest could take their places in the atrium, where conditions were inferior. Those in the triclinium would have *reclined* . . . whereas those in the atrium were forced to sit.

The abuses that Paul reports occurring at the meal, where some members go hungry and are humiliated, were common in Greco-Roman culture and practice. J. Davidson (1997: 311) argues from Petronius's narrative of Trimalchio's feast that "in the Roman context the banquet becomes a theatre of wealth and property, of social distinction, or social-climbing." One of the problems in the Corinthian church is that it is imbued with Roman cultural values that collide with the wisdom of the cross. It is probable that the more prosperous members of the church were inured to the inequalities between the "haves" and the "have-nots," and it may have rankled some of them to have to rub elbows with the poor at one table. It goes against the human tendency to socialize with persons of one's own rank (see Barton 1986: 235–36).

Blue (1991: 232–33) questions whether this problem of eating and sharing together would not have been addressed during Paul's eighteen-month stay. Blue (1991: 234–37) attributes the problem to a famine at Corinth (cf. "the present distress," 7:26), which makes the insensitivity of the "haves" even worse. They would be gorging themselves in front of hungry brothers and sisters in the midst of a famine. But the problem of poor and wealthy members intermixing with ease at a meal is not easily corrected, and people are likely to revert to familiar and more comfortable patterns. This class division seems to be at the root of other problems at Corinth. If famine was the particular problem, why should they only share food with the "have-nots" during the Lord's Supper? Why not encourage them to set up a community soup kitchen? In his discussion of the Lord's Supper, Paul is intent on one thing: to uproot the Corinthians' meal from the poisonous soil of Greco-Roman conventions and replant it in the nourishing soil of Christ's loving sacrifice for others. His conclusion is that when they come together for the Lord's Supper, they must welcome others by sharing with them.

In Paul's discussion of the Lord's Supper, theological and ethical implications intertwine and cannot be separated. What is done at the table must take cognizance of all those who have gathered at the table—what they have and do not have, how they are treated, and how they are made to feel. Hofius (1993: 113–14) asserts, "Inconsiderateness, indifference, and lovelessness towards 'the brother for whom Christ died' [1 Cor. 8:11] are consequently nothing short of a denial of ὑπὲρ ὑμῶν ([*hyper hymōn*] 'for you'), an unheard-of disregard for Christ's saving expiatory death, and hence an inconceivable sin against Christ himself." Gaventa (1983: 385) notes that we tend to read 11:17–34 while asking, "What constitutes the right observance of the Lord's Supper? Who should be included and who excluded from it? Is the Lord's Supper to be understood as a sacrifice or as a memorial meal?" The only question that Paul raises is this: Does what is done proclaim the Lord's death or does it advertise our selfishness?

The structure of this passage is quite simple:

A Criticism of the abuses at the Lord's Supper (11:17–22)
   B Recitation of the Last Supper tradition, which should inform the Corinthian observance (11:23–26)
A′ Instructions to correct the abuses at the Lord's Supper (11:27–34)

Exegesis and Exposition

[17]But in instructing this, I do not salute you, because you do not assemble together for the better but for the worse. [18]For in the first place, I hear that when you assemble together as a church, divisions exist among you, and I believe a certain report. [19]For it is necessary that there be factions among you in order that the elite might be evident among you. [20]Therefore, when you assemble together at the same place, it is not to eat the Lord's Supper. [21]For each one devours his or her own supper during the meal, and one is hungry and another is drunk. [22]For do you not have homes in which to eat and to drink? Or do you despise the church of God and shame the "have-nots"? What shall I say? Shall I salute you? In this [matter] I will not salute you.

[23]For I received from the Lord what I also delivered to you, that the Lord Jesus, on the night in which he was handed over, took a loaf; [24]and when he gave thanks, he broke it and said, "⌜This⌝ is my body ⌜which is for you⌝. Do this unto my remembrance." [25]And in the same way [he] also [took] the cup after eating, saying, "This cup is the new covenant in my blood. Do this, as often as you drink, unto my remembrance." [26]For as often as you eat this loaf and drink the cup, you proclaim the Lord's death until he comes.

²⁷Therefore, whoever eats the loaf and drinks the cup of the Lord in an unworthy manner will be liable for the body and blood of the Lord. ²⁸But let a person examine himself or herself and in this manner eat from the loaf and drink from the cup. ^{29⌐}For the one who eats and drinks⌐, eats and drinks condemnation on himself or herself by ⌐not discerning the body⌐. ³⁰Because of this, many among you are sick and ill, and quite enough are dying. ³¹But if we were examining ourselves, we would not be judged. ³²But while being judged by the Lord, we are being disciplined in order that we may not be condemned with the world. ³³So then, my brothers and sisters, as you assemble together in order to eat, welcome one another. ³⁴If anyone is hungry, let him or her eat at home, so that you do not assemble together for your condemnation. As for the other things, I will direct you whenever I come.

11:17–18   Paul raises another, more serious issue regarding the Corinthians' assembly, and this time he begins on a reproachful note.[2] He cannot salute them (cf. 11:2) for what they are doing but instead upbraids them because of reports of serious abuses when they gather as a church. The verb "to come together" or "to assemble" (συνέρχεσθαι, *synerchesthai*) occurs five times in this section (11:17, 18, 20, 33, 34) and elsewhere in Paul's letters only in 14:23, 26 (cf. 7:5). The phrase ἐν ἐκκλησίᾳ (*en ekklēsia,* 11:18) does not mean when they assemble "in the church," as if he were thinking of a church building. Ἐκκλησία does not mean the place of meeting in the NT. He refers to them gathering "as a church," that is, "in assembly" (14:19, 28, 35), and the phrase was not unique to Christians. He understands the Christian assembly, however, to be unique in its purpose and substance. He says nothing about how frequently, when, or where they meet. We can surmise that they gathered on Sunday evenings (1 Cor. 16:2; cf. Did. 14:1), and worshipers may have stayed late into the night (cf. Acts 20:7–12). If they met in the home of a wealthier member that was large enough to accommodate the group (Acts 18:8; Rom. 16:5, 23; 1 Cor. 16:19; Col. 4:15), then space limitations, Murphy-O'Connor (1983: 158–59) claims, would have demanded discrimination between those guests who were invited to recline in the triclinium (dining room) and the others squeezed into second-class facilities in the atrium (see Osiek and Balch 1997: 201–3).

Paul's accusation is that the meal that was supposed to be a sign of their integration and unity has become a flash point highlighting their inequality and alienation. This calamitous state of affairs, which could

---

2. Τοῦτο δὲ παραγγέλλων (*touto de parangellōn*) is a nominative absolute, and the τοῦτο may refer to what precedes (Barrett 1968: 260), presumably the directives in 11:3–16. Lindemann (2000: 249) thinks that it refers both to what precedes and to what follows in 11:17–34. Its connection to the statement that they are not better off for having gathered, however, suggests that it applies entirely to what follows (see Findlay 1910: 876; Schrage 1999: 18).

only feed arrogance and nourish bitterness, makes him wish that they had no group meal at all. Their assembly is not simply a waste of time; it is downright harmful. Paul specifies the harmful effects in the third part of this section: they become liable for the body and blood of the Lord (11:27); they incur condemnation (11:29, 32); and they are beset by sickness and death (11:30).

"For in the first place" (πρῶτον μὲν γάρ, prōton men gar, first of all) becomes emphatic (R. Collins 1999: 421) since no "second" follows. Paul may have started out with other matters in mind, but by the time he concludes this unit in 11:34, he decides he will raise them when he comes in person. All other problems about their gatherings pale beside the seriousness of this distressing news. The "divisions" (σχίσματα, schismata) that he is concerned about are not theological schisms (cf. 1:10). They are rooted in the socioeconomic gulf between the "haves" and the "have-nots," as 11:22 makes clear. The rifts mentioned in 1:10 become dramatically evident when they assemble to eat the Lord's Supper. Godet (1887: 139) poignantly refers to their Lord's Supper as "a theatre of discord." Murphy-O'Connor's (1996: 273) analysis of the cause of these divisions bears repeating:

> The potential for dissension within the community is evident. Most members had in common only their Christianity. They differed widely in educational attainment, financial resources, religious background, political skills, and above all in their expectations. A number were attracted to the church because it seemed to offer them a new field of opportunity, in which the talents whose expression society frustrated could be exploited to the full. They were energetic and ambitious people, and there was little agreement among their various hidden agendas. A certain competitive spirit was part of the ethos of the church from the beginning.

Paul views these divisions as nullifying the very purpose for gathering together for worship in the name of Christ. It contradicts what the Lord's Supper proclaims as the foundation of the church: Christ's sacrificial giving of his life for others.

The phrase καὶ μέρος τι πιστεύω (kai meros ti pisteuō) may express his caution about believing rumors or appearing overly suspicious of them: "and I in part believe it." He may not want to credit such a scandalous tale, yet the persons who inform him are presumed to be credible (Godet 1887: 138–39; Robertson and Plummer 1914: 239; Barrett 1968: 261). He comments on their factionalism in the opening chapters, and such news could not have been a surprise. M. Mitchell (1993: 263–64) thinks that he expresses "mock disbelief" for rhetorical effect (cf. Witherington 1995: 247; R. Horsley 1998: 158). Hays (1997: 195) avers that he sounds a note of incredulity, "I can't believe it," to heighten the outrageousness of what they are doing. Winter (2001: 159–63) argues convincingly, however, that μέρος carries a wide range of meanings in the NT and in literary and nonliterary sources and that it refers here to a "matter" (2 Cor. 9:3) or "report" and should not be translated adverbially ("partly"). Winter contends that Paul means that he is convinced of the report he has received from Chloe's people about their factions (1 Cor. 1:10), which included tales of their fragmentation during the Lord's Supper, and thinks that the phrase should be translated, "I believe a certain report."

11:19 One finds the explanatory statement "for it is necessary that there be factions among you" (δεῖ γὰρ καὶ αἱρέσεις ἐν ὑμῖν εἶναι, *dei gar kai haireseis en hymin einai*) to be rather surprising in light of Paul's condemnation of factiousness in 1:10–17. Does he now tolerate Christ's being divided? In Gal. 5:20, the noun αἱρέσεις stands alongside διχοστασίαι (*dichostasiai*, dissensions) in the list of the works of the flesh, which suggests that the cause of such divisions is "not necessarily to be found in points of doctrine: it may simply be a matter of personal rivalries and matters of prestige and honor" (Simon 1979: 109). If that is the case, why does Paul say that these αἱρέσεις are necessary?

Some think that the factions serve some kind of divine purpose and interpret this statement from an eschatological perspective and from an *agraphon* that has Jesus predict that the end times will occasion heresies and divisions (cf. Justin Martyr, *Dial.* 35.3; Syriac *Didascalia* 6.5.2; Pseudo-Clementine, *Homilies* 2.17.4; 16.21.4; see Paulsen 1982; Schrage 1999: 21–22). If this view is correct, Paul understands that a differentiation among believers is necessary to separate the true from the false (see Horrell 1996: 150–51). This statement then sets up the theme of judgment and condemnation in 1 Cor. 11:27–32. The γάρ (*gar*, for), however, indicates that this statement provides the evidence for Paul's dismay in the previous verse. It explains *why* he cannot praise them. It is misleading to label it a slight digression (Kistemaker 1993: 387) or a "theological aside" (Fee 1987: 537). He is not describing some preliminary separation of the wheat from the chaff in preparation for the final judgment (contra Conzelmann 1975: 194; Fee 1987: 538–39). If that were the case, why would this statement not also apply to the division of Christ that he laments in 1:10–17? In the mess that Paul describes here, who is shown to be faithful and truly worshipful? The divisions at the Corinthian Lord's Supper *do not* reveal who the tried and true Christians are. Instead, they reveal a church that has failed to take to heart the message of the cross.

R. Campbell (1991: 65–67) argues that the sense of the passage must control the understanding of the words. This is sometimes a dangerous approach, but here I find it helpful. Paul is not uttering a sigh about the inevitability of such splits among church members. The divisions at the Lord's Supper are between those who are sated (though Paul uses the word "drunk," μεθύει, *methyei*, 11:21) and those who go hungry. They have chosen (the noun αἵρεσις derives from the verb "to choose") to divide themselves along socioeconomic lines, and so they stand in danger of condemnation. It is far more likely that he expresses bitter irony about these factions rather than affirming their eschatological necessity. If that is the case, he does not use the οἱ δόκιμοι (*hoi dokimoi*) in a favorable sense to mean those who will show themselves to be the "outstanding Christians" (Barrett 1968: 262). Rather, οἱ δόκιμοι denotes the "dignitaries" (R. Campbell 1991: 68; Snyder 1992: 155–56; cf. Philo, *Jos.* 34 §201). Certainly, those likely to be invited to recline in the triclinium would come from the ranks of the most dignified members of the church. R. Campbell (1991: 69–70) infers that the upper-crust Corinthians fancied themselves as οἱ δόκιμοι and concludes that Paul refers to "the requirement foisted on the Corinthian church by its well-to-do members." Campbell translates 11:19, "For there actually has to be discrimination in your meetings, so that, if you please, the elite may stand out from the rest." This reading has not been accepted by recent commentators (see, however, C. Porter 1989: 36; R. Horsley 1998: 159), but it makes the best sense of the historical context as many now reconstruct it. The splits at the Lord's Supper are imposed by prideful, insensitive humans seeking to differentiate the top-drawer members from the common rabble. The tragedy is that they impose this discrimination of persons at the observance of the Lord's Supper. In 11:28, Paul encourages them to test (δοκιμάζειν, *dokimazein*) themselves by a different measure. Those tested and approved by God (Rom. 16:10; 2 Tim. 2:15; cf. 1 Cor. 9:27) are, more often than not, quite different from the dignitaries who stand out according to worldly standards.

Gathering "at the same place" (or "for the same purpose") becomes a **11:20–21** technical term for the assembly of the church (Acts 1:15; 2:1, 44; 1 Cor. 14:23). Schweizer (1959: 400) surmises that the NT does not apply the usual terms of the cult (sacrifice, offering, worship) to the assembling of the church in order to avoid any hint that their gathering is analogous to the cults in the Jewish temple or in Greek temples. The cultic terms are used for everyday service of church members to one another or to the world (Rom. 12:1). What becomes important is that the whole church gathers together. Presumably, they assemble in a house large enough to accommodate the group. Behavior that might be acceptable in the privacy of one's own home, however, may not be appropriate in the church gathering (Blue 1991: 227). This is particularly true for the church's common meal. The Lord's Supper celebrated by the Corinthians appears to have been a full meal in which the more affluent members may have supplied the bread and wine but each member brought his or her own food.

The meaning of the verb προλαμβάνειν (*prolambanein*) in 11:21 becomes crucial for ascertaining the historical context. Many underscore the temporal force of the prefix προ- to render it "to take beforehand" (BDAG 872). The resulting picture is that each one "goes ahead without waiting for anybody else" (NIV; see Murphy-O'Connor 1983: 160–61). Those who arrived first, according to this view, began eating and drinking on their own schedule, so that they had too much by the time the late arrivals appeared. P. Lampe (1991: 198–203) explains the situation by comparing it to the Greco-Roman dinner party with dinner at "first tables," a break, and "second tables," when other guests arrived (see P. Lampe 1994: 37; Osiek and Balch 1997: 199–200). The late arrivals probably are poor freedmen getting off from work and slaves who had no control over their personal schedules. Schrage (1999: 24–26) concludes that upper-status Christians held a meal from which lower-status Christians were excluded before the Lord's Supper. Since the lower-status Christians were delayed by their work obligations, upper-status Christians seized the opportunity to enjoy a meal without them. Translating the command ἐκδέχεσθε (*ekdechesthe*) in 11:33 as "wait for one another" provides further support for this view.

As Theissen (1982: 151–55) reconstructs the scene, the wealthy not only began their private meal before the congregational meal, but also ate by themselves and had more to eat. Theissen's sociological lens is an important breakthrough for interpreting this passage, but giving the verb προλαμβάνειν a temporal meaning is a slight misstep. Winter (1978: 75–77; see also Blue 1991: 230–31; Hofius 1993: 89–91; Hays 1997: 197; Eriksson 1998: 176) argues that the verb does not refer to the consumption of food before the arrival of others; it means "to eat or drink," "to devour" (MM 542). The problem is not that some jump the gun by dining before everyone arrives and that Paul must respond by insisting that they restrain themselves and politely wait for the others to arrive. The problem is that they devour their own ample amounts of food in the presence of their fellow Christians who have little or nothing to eat. His complaint is this: During the common meal, each consumes his or her own individual food (Hofius 1993: 91). The disparity in the amounts that each one brings to consume results in one group being drunk and sated and another pinched with hunger.

The arguments for translating προλαμβάνειν as "partake" or "consume" are compelling. First, the preposition πρό need not add a temporal force to the verb but can be added to verbs to "strengthen the meaning" (Winter 1978: 76; 2001: 144). The verb προλαμβάνειν does not have a temporal meaning in Gal. 6:1 (cf. Wis. 17:16). It appears three times in an inscription (*SIG* 3.1170) on a stele in the Asclepius sanctuary at Epidaurus (second century) and clearly means "to eat." Winter (1978: 74) cites a papyrus (P. Cairo Zenon 59562, line 12) in which the verb is used for providing a substantial amount of food for the king at a festival.

Second, the temporal rendering of the verb makes no sense in the context. If Paul says that "each one" (ἕκαστος, *hekastos*) goes ahead without waiting for the others in 11:21, then "each one" must be limited to the early arrivals. But why does he immediately say that one is drunk and the other hungry? The hungry must be the late arrivals, but he does not specifically say that a later wave of guests shows up famished, to find the first arrivals already stuffed and drunk. The phrase ἐν τῷ φαγεῖν (*en tō phagein*) does not imply a private meal eaten beforehand but refers to something that takes place in the presence of all—"during the meal."[3] The unacceptable behavior occurs during the eating of the common meal, not before (Winter 1978: 77–79; 2001: 148–51; Hofius 1993: 91–93), and "each one" is a collective reference.

Third, the argument for the temporal dimension of the verb loses all its force if the verb ἐκδέχεσθαι in 11:33 does not mean "to wait." Logically, simply waiting for the "have-nots" (οἱ μὴ ἔχοντες, *hoi mē echontes*, 11:22b) would not overcome the problem of their hunger. Lexical evidence suggests that the verb ἐκδέχεσθαι means "to receive" with the idea of sharing (see below on 11:33).

"His own meal" (τὸ ἴδιον δεῖπνον, *to idion deipnon*) refers to individual persons or households bringing to the gathering their own meals prepared beforehand. The practice of "basket dinners," or *eranos* (contribution) dinner parties, in which persons make up a dinner for themselves and pack it into a basket to go to another's house to eat was well known (see Athenaeus, *Deipnosophistae* 8.365AB, and other sources in P. Lampe 1991: 192–98). The American potluck dinner is a misleading comparison because that practice assumes that each brings something to share with others. Xenophon (*Mem.* 3.14.1) reports an incident from Socrates' life that reveals that this sharing was not the norm in the ancient world. He recounts that whenever some who came together for dinner brought more meat and fish than others,

> Socrates would tell the waiter either to put the small contributions into the common stock or to portion them out equally among the diners. So the ones who brought a lot felt obliged not only to take their share of the pool, but to pool their own supplies in return; and so they put their own food also into the common stock. Thus they got no more than those who brought little with them.

This egalitarian sentiment apparently did not hold sway at the Corinthians' common meal. At their meal they divide into two groups, the

---

3. Winter (2001: 149) cites Burton's (1898: 50–51) remarks that the aorist infinitive φαγεῖν in 11:21 does not indicate action antecedent to the principal verb.

well-to-do and the "have-nots." Each partakes what he or she has brought. Since some have more than others, the upshot is that those with more gorge themselves in the presence of others who are hungry (cf. Jude 12). What Paul condemns is the callous behavior of the "haves" in front of the "have-nots," which serves only to entrench the social disparity and to remind the poor of their wretchedness. He does not encourage the wealthy to withdraw to their own private meals but admonishes them to feed the hungry during the community's shared meal (Henderson 2002).

Paul treats this state of affairs as something far more serious "than a breach of social etiquette" (Winter 1978: 73). They cannot label it the Lord's Supper, he says, when they come together and act like this. It is *their* supper, not the Lord's. It is not the Lord's dinner because the Lord's dinner is intended to convey to every participant that he or she is somebody precious to God. The Corinthians' meal communicated to some that they were worthless nobodies. It was tainted by the deadly combination of indulgence and indifference. This selfish devouring (προλαμβάνειν) of their own food contrasts with Jesus' taking bread (λαμβάνειν, 11:23). Both "take." The Corinthians "take" on their own behalf; Jesus "takes" on behalf of others. The Corinthians act selfishly; Jesus acts unselfishly in giving his life for others. The Corinthians' actions will lead to their condemnation; Jesus' action leads to the salvation of others. Each believer gets an equal share of the benefits of his sacrifice. That reality should be symbolized by what happens during the Lord's Supper. The Corinthians' observance of the Lord's Supper, in which one has more than enough and gets drunk while another has too little and goes hungry, hardly proclaims the meaning of the Lord's death for all. Call it what you will, but do not call it the Lord's Supper.

11:22   Paul clearly addresses the "haves" in 11:22 (Barton 1986: 237). In the ancient world the poor did not have kitchens in their tiny apartments and prepared their food on portable grills or ate out at a fast-food shop (*caupona, taberna,* or *thermopolium*). The privileged had the luxury of eating in their homes. Osiek (1996: 12) notes that as a result, "For the poor, a formal meal was had only for special occasions sponsored by a civic benefactor or a benefactor of some other kind; thus the regular Christian community meal would have had far greater significance than a meal would among the wealthy." Paul must be addressing those who have houses to eat in and presumably are heads of households. They also have food to consume. They possess enough status to "despise" (καταφρονεῖν, *kataphronein,* treat with contempt) and "shame" (καταισχύνειν, *kataischynein,* dishonor) the "have-nots."

Winter (1978: 81) suggests three alternatives for understanding who comprised the "have-nots": (1) the genuinely poor; (2) those who were not impoverished, but, for whatever reasons, had no food to bring to the supper; and (3) those who did not belong to a social unit (a household) or network. Most were securely attached to households (homeowners, domestic slaves, and clients), which provided some measure of security—food, clothing, and shelter. Those who were the most vulnerable to the famines and other economic problems that regularly plagued the ancient economy were persons unattached to a household and its networks. They needed their household of faith to show concern for their welfare.

Why were some Christians oblivious to the needs of their fellow Christians? The answer is that they were too much at home in a culture in which contempt for the poor was typical of the wealthier class. The well-to-do were used to having servants stand around as they ate and also would have no misgivings about feasting in the presence of others who had nothing or had only inferior fare.[4] Given the dinner conventions of the ancient world, they would have thought nothing of this inequity. Veyne (1987: 91) notes,

> Guests of different rank were served different dishes and wines of different qualities, according to their respective dignities. Symbolism reinforced the sense of hierarchy. The paterfamilias did not simply receive individual greetings from certain of his friends; he admitted into his home a slice of Roman society, respecting public rank and inequalities. Over this group he exerted moral authority, and his knowledge of proper behavior always exceeded that of his clients.

D'Arms (1990) shows that in spite of the talk of equality and social leveling among some writers—note Plutarch's (*Mor.* 644C) remark, "When each guest has his own private portion, fellowship perishes"—social hierarchy prevailed (see additional note).

The practice of serving differing portions and qualities to guests became the subject of humor (Juvenal, *Sat.* 5), but the wit also reveals the searing public humiliation it evoked. Martial (*Epigrams* 3.60) complains,

> Since I am asked to dinner, no longer, as before, a purchased guest, why is not the same dinner served to me as to you? You take oysters fattened in the Lucrina lake, I suck a mussel through a hole in the shell; you get mushrooms, I take hog funguses; you tackle turbot, but I brill. Golden with fat, a turtledove gorges you with its bloated rump; there is set before me a magpie that has died in its cage. Why do I dine without you al-

---

4. If theological conceptions come into play and some Corinthians viewed the Lord's Supper as communion only between the individual and the Lord and not as common-union between individuals and the Lord, then they may have considered it a matter of indifference who was present or not and what they had or did not have to eat.

though, Ponticus, I am dining with you? The dole has gone: let us have the benefit of that, let us eat the same fare.

Again, Martial (*Epigrams* 1.20) protests,

Tell me, what madness is this? While the throng of invited guests look on, you, Caecilianus, alone devour the mushrooms! What prayer shall I make suitable for such a belly and gorge? May you eat such a mushroom as Claudius ate![5]

Most hosts accented the inequality to maintain and demonstrate their social distance from others on a lower social level. Christian congregations, with their shared meals including masters and slaves, transcended conventional barriers. Some of the wealthier Corinthian Christians, however, seem to have wished to retain these barriers (see Passakos 1997: 198). Some of the privileged Corinthian Christians did not want their advantages to vanish when they associated with believers of lower social and economic status. In fact, they may have flaunted their affluence to notify one and all that they were members of "the elite." They had yet to be fully acculturated in the wisdom of the cross.

Paul remonstrates that they are despising and shaming God's church. The primary focus is on horizontal relationships between Christians, but he reminds them that the people they spurn belong to God, and God will not take this lightly. If the predicament is simply their need to satisfy their gluttonous hunger, then they can stay home and eat. But to ignore a brother or sister in Christ at the common meal is unconscionable. Paul understands the church to be one large extended family, and all are expected to share their resources with others (cf. 12:26). The chapter that follows, emphasizing the one body and the need to honor those who are dishonored, not only addresses the question of spiritual gifts, but also looks backward to the inequalities painfully exhibited in their Supper.

11:23   Paul abruptly cites the tradition of the institution of the Lord's Supper to reinforce his point. It is the only place in his letters in which he cites a tradition about Jesus that corresponds to a narrative in the Synoptic Gospels. Attention to the relationship between the Pauline tradition and the Synoptic tradition, questions about the original form and meaning of the words of institution, the development of the Lord's Supper from the Last Supper, and Paul's theology of the Lord's Supper are important issues, but they distract interpreters from focusing on why

---

5. Fee (1987: 544) observes that "the view 'from below' (Martial's) is that the poor should eat the same food as the rich; the view 'from above' (Pliny's [quoted in the additional note]) is that the rich should eat the same fare as others." Paul expects Christians to share with others, particularly at the common table.

Paul inserts this tradition at this point and what it means in this context.[6] The tradition is cited only by way of illustration, and excessive attention to tracing its historical particulars and theological vectors serves to eclipse the rhetorical point that Paul makes. He does not intend to teach the Corinthians something new about the Lord's Supper or to correct their theology of the Lord's Supper. He cites it only to contrast what Jesus did at the Last Supper with what they are doing at their supper.

That Paul received "from the Lord" (ἀπὸ τοῦ κυρίου, *apo tou kyriou*) distinguishes the Lord as the originator of the tradition from those who passed on the tradition.[7] It does not imply some communication from the risen Lord (contra Edwards 1885: 200–201), but it does affirm the authoritative nature of this tradition. Christ is the originator and guarantor of the tradition (Schrage 1996: 194).[8] The specific time reference, "on the night" (ἐν τῇ νυκτί, *en tē nykti*), places this occurrence in the realm of a historical event rather than in the ethereal neverland of a timeless, mythical story (Wolff 1996: 264; Lindemann 2000: 253). Most versions translate the verb παρεδίδετο (*paredideto*) to refer to Christ's "betrayal" by Judas.[9] Fee (1987: 549 n. 26) argues reasonably that since Paul cites tradition and since the Gospel accounts place the announcement of the betrayal at the Last Supper, it makes sense to conclude that he alludes to what Judas did on that night. The verb παραδιδόναι (*paradidonai*) is common in Mark's Gospel and is used to refer to this betrayal (14:10, 42, 44), but it also is used for the arrest of John the Baptist (1:14), the chief priests' handing Jesus over to Pilate (15:1), and Pilate's handing Jesus over to be crucified (15:15). Translating it "handed over" or "delivered up" instead of "betrayed" retains a measure of ambiguity that allows it to point to something beyond the treachery of wicked humans. It can be a divine passive that refers to God's plan of handing Jesus over for our salvation (Robertson and Plummer 1914: 243; Hays 1997: 198). God's hand (Rom. 4:25; 8:32; cf. Isa. 53:6–12 LXX) and Jesus' willing submission (Gal. 2:20; Eph. 5:2, 25) are ultimately behind Christ's being delivered up. Where the emphasis should lie, whether on Judas's betrayal or on God's purposes, is no longer possible to determine, according to Popkes (1967: 210). The translation should not exclude the latter alternative, particularly since it reflects Paul's perspec-

6. Among the many works on this issue, see Lietzmann 1953; Jeremias 1966a; I. Marshall 1980; Knoch 1993; Klauck 1993; Betz 2001.

7. Those who pass on the tradition are identified by the use of παρά (*para*) plus the genitive (cf. Gal. 1:12; 1 Thess. 2:13; 4:1, 2; 2 Thess. 3:6; see Hofius 1993: 76 n. 3; Wolff 1996: 264).

8. Paul does not identify how he received this tradition about the Lord's Supper (see Farmer 1993: 35–46).

9. The use of the imperfect (παρεδίδετο) as opposed to the aorist (cf. ἔλαβεν, *elaben*, took; ἔκλασεν, *eklasen*, broke; and εἶπεν, *eipen*, said) points to its duration.

tive elsewhere (see Coleman 1975–76). This "handing over" and Jesus' interpretation of what that meant in the words spoken over the bread and the cup mark this meal off from all others as something unique.

Paul's outline of the sequence of the Last Supper—bread, supper, cup—raises the historical question about the course of the celebration of the Lord's Supper in Corinth. Was the breaking of bread followed by a communal meal and then the drinking of the cup, or was the original order broken so that the sacramental meal was placed at the end after the common meal (so Bornkamm 1969: 126–28; Neuenzeit 1960: 69–76; Jeremias 1966a: 121)? We need not get sidetracked too long by this issue. Hofius (1993: 80–88) makes a convincing case that the Corinthians' Lord's Supper began with the blessing and breaking of the bread, which then was followed by the common meal. It was concluded with the drinking of the cup. Hofius (1993: 88) concludes that "the Lord's Supper *paradosis* handed on by Paul in 1 Cor 11:23b–25, presupposes, as the words μετὰ τὸ δειπνῆσαι [*meta to deipnēsai*, after the supper] clearly attest, a meal between the bread rite and the cup rite." Hofius confidently asserts, "Historically, there cannot be the slightest doubt about the existence of a Lord's Supper celebration at which a full meal took place between the bread rite and the cup rite."[10] There is no reason for Paul to cite this tradition if the Corinthians deviated from it in some way.[11] The bread rite and the cup rite frame the common meal and give it "its essential character" (Hofius 1993: 96; Eriksson [1998: 176] calls this "the new consensus").[12]

11:24–25 Paul's recounting of the words that Jesus spoke over the bread and the cup focuses on what Jesus did on behalf of believers (Winter 1978: 79). The words of institution, "This is my body which is for you," reminds them that Jesus gave his body up on behalf of others. The word order differs slightly from what is found in the Gospels (Matt. 26:26; Mark 14:22; Luke 22:19), with the μου (*mou*) placed before "my body" (τοῦτό μού ἐστιν τὸ σῶμα, *touto mou estin to sōma*). Literally, it reads, "This of mine is the body which is for you." For Paul, this formula does not represent some peculiar, sacramental alchemy. The verb "is" simply means "signifies, stands for, represents" (Engberg-Pedersen 1993:

---

10. This reconstruction fits the Jewish custom of a blessing being recited over a cup after the meal.

11. Klauck (1993: 65–66) objects that Paul's churches would not have followed this order, because those who came late would have joined only in the cup. He thinks that they had a full meal toward evening, followed by the twofold rite with bread and wine (11:23–26) and then a worship service. But Paul does not mention anyone coming late, and if the temporal aspect of προλαμβάνειν and ἐκδέχεσθαι are not stressed, this objection collapses.

12. Das (1998: 188) points out that for the Corinthians, the idea of a sacrament without a community meal would have seemed as strange to them as a fellowship meal in the midst of a worship service seems novel to us.

117).[13] It may mean that the giver is re-present in the gift. Winter (2001: 153) argues, however, that the τοῦτο, which is neuter, does not refer to the bread (ἄρτος, *artos*), which is masculine, but to Jesus' action on their behalf.[14] Paul may not be repeating the words from the institution narrative, but rather citing Jesus' sacrificial action on their behalf—"This [action of mine] is my body [given] for you"—to contrast it with their actions. This interpretation of the grammar is disputable, as Winter (2001: 154) admits, but it is clear that Paul contrasts Jesus' self-sacrifice at the Last Supper with the Corinthians' selfishness at their supper.

The ensuing words, "This cup is the new covenant in my blood," also emphasize Jesus' sacrifice (Rom. 5:9; Col. 1:20). The salvation celebrated in this meal comes at the price of his blood. The meaning of a "new covenant" and "blood" is made clear in Exod. 24:8 ("Moses took the blood and dashed it on the people, and said, 'See the blood of the covenant that the LORD has made with you in accordance with all these words'" [NRSV]) and Jer. 31:31 ("The days are surely coming, says the LORD, when I will make a new covenant with the house of Israel and the house of Judah" [NRSV]). Covenants are made through the shedding of blood. The fresh covenant relationship with God through Jesus' blood is a fulfillment of Jeremiah's prophecy (31:31–34). The two texts are combined in Heb. 9:20 and 10:16–18 to emphasize that Jesus' sacrifice replaces the ineffective blood of bulls and goats: "It is by God's will that we have been sanctified through the offering of the body of Jesus Christ once for all" (Heb. 10:10). The combination of the broken bread and the cup (which can include images of the cup of suffering) conveys the nature of Jesus' ultimate sacrifice.

Paul's citation of these words reveals a symmetry not found in the Synoptic accounts, which shows that it has been shaped by liturgical use as a confessional formula (Eriksson 1998: 100–101). The Lord's Supper was a conscious imitation of Jesus' Last Supper (Eriksson 1998:104). The command to do this εἰς τὴν ἐμὴν ἀνάμνησιν (*eis tēn emēn anamnēsin*, unto my remembrance), as Paul understands it, serves as a reminder to the church of Christ's atoning sacrifice. It does not mean that the Lord's Supper is a memorial meal for a dearly departed hero, which only cherishes the memory of Jesus. The currency of memorial feasts in Greco-Roman life reveals that this kind of meal would not have seemed unusual, but these feasts do not provide the appropriate backdrop for interpreting what Paul means. Nor is it related to any mystery rite. The memorial requires that Christians reenact ritually

---

13. Arguments about transubstantiation or consubstantiation have no substantiation in the intention of the text.

14. Winter (2001: 153) claims that the neuter demonstrative pronoun represents an action in sixteen of its seventy-four occurrences in Paul's letters.

what Christ did at his last meal to betoken his death and to explain its significance. The repeated imperative, "do this unto my remembrance," then, commands ritual remembrance of this foundational saving event (cf. Exod. 12:14; Ps. 77:11–12; 105:5).[15] It is related to Jewish liturgical remembrance that praises and proclaims the mighty acts of God. Psalm 105:5 ("Remember the wonderful deeds God has done") and Ps. 105:1 ("Tell of the wonderful deeds God has done") make clear that remembering is part and parcel of proclaiming (Hofius 1993: 105–8). The repetition of the phrase "unto my remembrance" (1 Cor. 11:24–25) stresses the integral connection between the character of what they do at the Supper and Jesus' death (Barrett 1968: 270). What is to be remembered, as far as Paul is concerned, is that "the crucified one" gave his body and sacrificed his blood in an expiatory death that brings the offer of salvation to all persons (contra Jeremias 1966a: 252). By partaking of the bread and the cup, they recall that sacrifice and symbolically share in its benefits. This conscious imitation of the Last Supper expressed in this liturgical formula allows him to make his point forcefully. They are to imitate Christ's example of self-giving. Everything they do in their meal should accord with his self-sacrifice for others. They should be prepared to give of themselves and their resources for others. Chrysostom (*Hom. 1 Cor.* 27.5) grasps the essence of Paul's admonition: "He [Christ] gave His body equally, but you do not give so much as the common bread equally."

11:26 The statement "For as often as you eat this loaf and drink the cup, the Lord's death you proclaim [καταγγέλλετε, *katangellete*; indicative mood, not imperative] until he comes" is the key for understanding why Paul recites the Last Supper tradition (Gaventa 1983: 378–79). The "for" links this statement to what precedes. Interpreters ask whether the Lord's death is proclaimed by the action (Lietzmann 1949: 58; Gaventa 1983: 381–83) or by the spoken word in a homily (Bornkamm 1969: 141; Neuenzeit 1960: 132; Jeremias 1966a: 106–7; Barrett 1968: 270; Käsemann 1964: 120–21; Fee 1987: 556). Conzelmann (1975: 201) asserts, "There is no such thing as a sacrament without accompanying proclamation." But the verbal element should not be played off against eating and drinking (Surburg 2000: 203–4). "Eating" and "drinking" are mentioned five times in 11:26–29, and this is what Paul wishes to emphasize more than the verbal repetition of the story of the Lord's death. It is not what is said during or after the meal that concerns him, but what is said in the action of eating and drinking. He is interested only in the fact that "whenever Christians eat *this* bread and drink *this* cup,

---

15. The phrase "as often as you drink" in 11:25 does not occur in the Gospel accounts, and it is repeated in 11:26. The verb "drink" does not have an object in 11:25, but from 11:26 it is clear that it refers to the cup of wine.

they are proclaiming the Lord's death" (Engberg-Pedersen 1993: 116). He believes that their *actions* in their meal do not proclaim the Lord's death, which is why he says that their meal is not the Lord's Supper (11:20).

The emphasis is on the death of the Lord, Christ crucified (1:18, 23; 2:2), which explains its forward reference in the clause (τὸν θάνατον τοῦ κυρίου καταγγέλλετε, *ton thanaton tou kyriou katangellete*). For Paul, the Lord's Supper should evoke Christ's obedience unto death, the humiliating death on a cross (Phil. 2:8). It should preach Christ crucified. Gaventa (1983: 384) comments, "That death, in Paul's view, stands diametrically opposed to the claims of social status that were at work in the Corinthian community." If they are proclaiming the Lord's death in what they do at the Lord's Supper, they will not overindulge themselves, despise others, shame them, or allow them to go hungry.

Obviously, "remembrance" does not exhaust the meaning of the Supper. Witherington's (1995: 251) observation is correct: "The Lord's Supper is . . . part of the Christian witness to the crucified, risen, and returning Lord," looking to the past, present, and future. But such affirmations are tangential to Paul's purpose in citing the liturgical tradition. His focus is *on the past*—what Jesus did on the night he was handed over. It is not his purpose to develop fully a theology of the Lord's Supper or to correct their theology. Those interpreters whose sole purpose in approaching this text is to mine it for its theological ore miss this crucial point. Their theological inferences ignore or skew Paul's particular intention in this text.[16] Jeremias (1966a: 253), for example, argues that ἄχρι(ς) οὗ ἔλθῃ (*achri[s] hou elthē*) is purposive because it is missing the particle ἄν (*an*) and refers to an eschatological goal elsewhere (cf. Rom. 11:25; 1 Cor. 15:25; Luke 21:24).[17] Jeremias translates it, "until (the goal is reached) that he comes" (so also Hofius 1967–68). Jeremias concludes that Jesus' death is proclaimed not as a past event but as an eschatological event that marks the beginning of salvation, and, thus, Christians pray for its consummation. This interpretation fails to take into account Paul's purpose in citing this tradition. He focuses on the past event—what Jesus did at his last meal on the night he was handed over—to correct what the Corinthians are doing in the present at their meal: getting drunk and treating others with contempt. The phrase "until he comes" (cf. 4:5) is a temporal reference, which is part of the liturgical tradition. It is not inserted to redress an "over-realized eschatology" (contra R. Collins 1999: 434), "to add a 'not-yet' to their eschatological 'already'" (contra Witherington 1995:

16. I do not disagree with these theological conclusions, but they are not relevant to Paul's purpose.

17. Edwards (1885: 296) comments that detecting a difference in meaning because of the omitted ἄν is an "unreal refinement."

251). Nor is it intended to deflate a sacramental enthusiasm based on an exaltation Christology (contra Conzelmann 1975: 202). Proclaiming the Lord's death is the only emphasis, and "until he comes" serves "to soften, to some extent, the harsh idea of proclaiming the Lord's death" (Engberg-Pedersen 1993: 116). Christ died horribly, but he will come again as Lord and judge.

The Lord's Supper is founded on the sacrificial death of Jesus for others, and the attitude that led him obediently to that death should pervade the Supper for Christians ever after. The way the Corinthians conducted their supper, however, gave witness to a culture of selfishness and status-mongering (Hays 1997: 200). To conduct their supper in this way and to have the temerity to call it the Lord's Supper can lead only to their condemnation.

11:27–29 Paul returns to the Corinthian problem at the Lord's Supper with an oblique warning about those who eat the loaf and drink the cup of the Lord in an unworthy manner. The adverb ἀναξίως (anaxiōs, unworthily) refers to doing something that does not square with the character or nature of something (cf. Eph. 4:1; Phil. 1:27; Col. 1:10; 1 Thess. 2:12). To eat the Lord's Supper in a manner that violates its purpose to proclaim the Lord's death makes one "liable" (ἔνοχος, enochos) for the death of the Lord. "Liable" is a judicial term (cf. Mark 14:64; 2 Macc. 13:6), which means that the Corinthians are answerable to God, the final judge, for this abuse. They become "responsible for his body and his blood" (Engberg-Pedersen 1993: 119–20)—that is, they are chargeable for his death. Paul's logic is this: The Lord's Supper proclaims the Lord's death. Those whose behavior at the Lord's Supper does not conform to what that death entails effectively shift sides. They leave the Lord's side and align themselves with the rulers of this present age who crucified the Lord (1 Cor. 2:8; cf. Heb. 6:5). This explains how they make themselves so vulnerable to God's judgment.

Paul's use of paronomasia with words related to judgment is striking and gets lost in translation: κρίμα (krima, 11:29, 34), διακρίνων (diakrinōn, 11:29), διεκρίνομεν (diekrinomen, 11:31), ἐκρινόμεθα (ekrinometha, 11:31), κρινόμενοι (krinomenoi, 11:32), κατακριθῶμεν (katakrithōmen, 11:32). The repetition of these words serves to underscore the judgment theme (see Moule 1956). As Surburg (2000: 212) notes, "Eating and drinking the Lord's body and blood has implications which no other eating and drinking ever does." They cannot treat this meal as a pleasant gathering of in-group friends (Engberg-Pedersen 1993: 115). It is fraught with spiritual peril if they treat the meal or those gathered for it in a cavalier manner. They will incur God's judgment.

The divisions in Corinth that Paul mentions in 11:19 reveal a deeper, far more serious divide. The divide is between those who incarnate the cross of Christ with their self-sacrifice and those who put Christ to death again with their self-centered feasting. He insinuates that the Corinthians violate the spirit of the meal, which remembers Christ's self-sacrifice, by eating it unworthily. Although no one is worthy of the Lord's Supper, one can eat it worthily. Paul gives three key tests to decide whether one is eating worthily.

The first test appears in 11:28. All are to examine themselves. All must remember that Christ's atoning death was necessary because of our sinfulness. Moule (1956: 470) contends that participation in the Lord's Supper entails anticipation of the Lord's judgment. Consequently, the Supper is to be eaten in an atmosphere of self-examination. They are to test (δοκιμαζέτω, *dokimazetō*) their genuineness before God does. Those who may imagine themselves to be the dignitaries and want to make sure that others recognize their higher status should check their pride at the door. They must examine themselves at this meal in light of Christ's sacrifice for all. The cross offers a different standard for who can claim to be notable. The genuine Christian recognizes that there are no class divisions at the Lord's table. No one is distinguished at this table except One, but all are honored together as his distinguished guests as the body of Christ. All are blameworthy before God, and yet all are forgiven because the sins of all have been transferred to One.

Through the negative example of the disciples, the Markan account of the Lord's Supper (Mark 14:17–21) reveals a model of what Paul intends. *Before the meal*, Jesus announces that one of his disciples will betray him. Each one asks in turn, "It is not I, is it?" Egocentricity, however, oozes from this question. Each focuses on himself and wants only reassurance that he is in the clear. Jesus gives his life for others and laments the miserable fate awaiting the betrayer. The disciples' response shows that they are concerned only about themselves. Self-examination requires focusing on more than just oneself.

A second key test is implied in 1 Cor. 11:22, and it concerns how one relates to brothers and sisters in Christ. If one partakes of the Lord's Supper with indifference to them, it is no longer the Lord's Supper. To eat the Lord's Supper worthily, one must recognize that all Christians, rich and poor, are joined together in Christ, share equally in his blessings, and should be treated worthily.

The third test requires "discerning the body" (11:29). Those who do not discern the body place themselves in dire jeopardy by "eating and drinking condemnation on themselves." Paul's meaning is unclear because the verb διακρίνειν (*diakrinein*) has a wide variety of usages in the NT. It basically means "to differentiate by separating" (BDAG 231) and then "to estimate or judge correctly." It could refer to distinguishing the holy from the unholy or having the right estimate of Christ's body. But it can also mean "to recognize" (BDAG 231 lists 11:29 under this meaning). Its use in 11:29 may be a conditional participle equivalent to a conditional clause, "if they fail to discern the body" (Burton 1898: 169; Wallace 1996: 633), or a causal clause, "by not discerning the body."

The question is, What is it that the Corinthians do not discern?

1. A venerable view going back to Justin and Augustine and reflected in some modern commentators (Godet 1887: 167; Weiss 1910: 291; Lietzmann 1949: 59; Héring 1962: 120) thinks that it refers to distinguishing the sacramental presence of Christ in the eucharistic elements from the ordinary bread on the table. But this view takes us wide of the mark of Paul's concern. He accuses the Corinthians of despising and humiliating their impoverished brothers and sisters at their supper, not profaning the elements.

2. Another view that has gained ascendancy assumes that Paul refers to the Corinthians' failure to recognize the church as the body of Christ or Christ's presence among his people.[18] Referring to the "body" and omitting any reference to the "blood" are taken as clues that he does not have in view the sacramental elements but the church as Christ's body. The Corinthians would catch this play on words from his assertion in 10:16–17 that sharing in the body of Christ by partaking of the bread means that "we, who are many, are one body" (cf. 12:26–27). The "body" to be discerned, then, is not just the piece of bread *on* the table but the body *at* the table (Keck 1982: 63–64). What they were doing accentuated the social and economic differences between the "haves" and the "have-nots" and showed a flagrant disregard for the body. Mistreating fellow members in this way at the Lord's Supper becomes an offense against Christ. As attractive as this view is, it is difficult to make it fit the basic meaning of the verb διακρίνειν, "to judge rightly."

3. Another view asserts that "body" is shorthand for both the body and the blood and refers to the corporeal stuff that one eats and drinks.[19] The meaning of "body" in 11:27, rather than in 10:16–17, should govern its interpretation here. The elements represent the crucified Lord and make this meal holy and different from any other meal. Discerning the body means recognizing this uniqueness and that the elements represent Christ's death for them

18. So Kümmel in Lietzmann 1949: 186; Bornkamm 1969: 148–49; Neuenzeit 1960: 38–39; Käsemann 1964: 130–32; Orr and Walther 1976: 274; Fee 1987: 564; C. Porter 1989: 39–40; Horrell 1996: 153; Hays 1997: 200–201; Murphy-O'Connor 1998: 123; R. Collins 1999: 439.

19. I. Marshall 1980: 114; Hofius 1993: 114; Engberg-Pedersen 1993: 121–22; Schrage 1999: 51–52; Thiselton 2000: 893–94.

(Wolff 1996: 279). A proper understanding of what these elements represent should change the Corinthians' attitude and behavior toward others. It reminds them of their dependence on Christ and their own interdependence and should cause them to share their own provisions with others at the meal who have little or nothing. Paul is arguing that when they recognize fully the meaning of the sacrifice of Christ, remembered in reenacting the Last Supper, they will act compassionately toward their brothers and sisters in Christ. Passakos (1997: 210) claims that the Lord's Supper becomes "the starting line for the transformation of the relationships and structures in the community."

"Because of this" (διὰ τοῦτο, *dia touto*) marks a shift in argument as **11:30–32** Paul applies the general truths of 11:27–29 specifically to the situation at Corinth (Surburg 2000: 204). The sick (ἀσθενεῖς, *astheneis*, literally, "weak"), ill (ἄρρωστοι, *arrōstoi*), and dying (κοιμῶνται, *koimōntai*, literally, "asleep") have been taken by one recent scholar as metaphors for those who are "weak in faith," "spiritually ill," and "spiritually asleep" (Schneider 1996). This view might appeal to those who do not like to think that sickness can be directly caused by sin or that the Lord's Supper might have numinous properties—mishandling it can lead to death. But Paul has in mind real sickness and real death (see Robertson and Plummer 1914: 253), and his words should be taken at face value (Oster 1995: 285). Real suffering in the flesh, not a decay of the spirit, is the divine warning bell that should awaken the Corinthians to the dangers of their practices. Paul probably has heard of these deaths from the same ones who told him of their divisions, and he connects these events to their improper handling of the sacred Lord's Supper and to God's judgment (cf. 10:4–5). The view of Ignatius (*Eph.* 20:2) that the Lord's Supper is "the medicine of immortality" can be reversed. When misused, it can become a mortal toxin (Lietzmann 1949: 59; cf. the image in 2 Cor. 2:14–16). Its power for wholeness can become a power of destruction (Dunn 1995: 78).

Paul does not identify who or how many have become sick or have died. The word ἱκανοί (*hikanoi*) here is often translated as "a number" (NASB) or "some" (NRSV), but it can mean "enough" (cf. 2 Cor. 2:6) in the sense of "quite enough." This translation conveys Paul's concern about the situation that he wants to remedy. For his argument to have force as a threat, one would assume that the readers could readily identify those who were sick or have died as guilty of despising and humiliating their brothers and sisters at the Lord's Supper. Another possibility, however, which is offered only tentatively, is that some have become physically weak from lack of food. The Corinthians' lack of sharing has dire repercussions for the poor in their midst. This would be particularly true if Corinth was undergoing a famine, as Winter (1989) and Blue (1991) contend. This observation about their illnesses may not be a warning threat but an appeal for them to share with the poor: "Look where your behavior has led." Hermas (*Vis.* 3.9.3–5a) uses a similar argument:

> Some are contracting illness in the flesh by too much eating and are injuring their flesh, and the flesh of the others who have nothing to eat is being injured by their not having sufficient food and their body is being destroyed. So this lack of sharing is harmful to you who are rich and do not share with the poor. Consider the judgment which is coming.

In 11:31, Paul offers a means of escape from this judgment with a contrary-to-fact condition: "But if we were examining ourselves, we would not be judged." Examining themselves (11:28) would remedy their mishandling of the Lord's Supper. It also would prevent them from being condemned in the final judgment. Joining in the Lord's Supper in the spirit of the world that put Christ to death means that they will be condemned with the world. Eating the Supper with the spirit of Christ means salvation and requires loving behavior toward others.

11:33–34   "As you assemble together" (συνερχόμενοι, *synerchomenoi*) harks back to the verb used in 11:17–18 to open this discussion and serves to bracket this unit. Paul issues the key command to correct the social discrimination: ἀλλήλους ἐκδέχεσθε (*allēlous ekdechesthe*). This phrase is usually translated "wait for one another" (cf. Acts 17:16; 1 Cor. 16:11). But this verb, when used of persons, usually means "to take or receive from another" or "to entertain" (MM 192). Orr and Walther (1976: 268) claim that the Corinthians can simply correct the situation by waiting for one another and "manifest community in taking food together." But the problem is that the "have-nots" do not have food, and it will not be solved simply by the early arrivals waiting for them to show up (Blue 1991: 231). P. Lampe (1994: 42) recognizes this point: "If everyone was to wait before unpacking his or her own food basket, it stands to reason that the contents of these would have been shared on common platters. Otherwise the waiting, which is supposed to prevent some from remaining hungry, would be senseless." In other words, even if Paul means "wait," according to Lampe, it would necessitate sharing.

Winter (2001: 151–52) argues that one should look at words within their semantic field. The other uses of this verb in the NT occur in a different social context. In the context of a dinner, the verb means "to welcome" (see 3 Macc. 5:26; Josephus, *J.W.* 2.14.7 §297; 3.2.4 §32; *Ant.* 7.14.5 §351; 11.8.6 §340; 12.3.3 §138; 13.4.5 §104; 13.5.5 §148). Hofius (1993: 94) allows that the command can be translated "Care for one another!" "Receive one another warmly!" "Grant one another table fellowship!" "Show hospitality to one another!" and cites a case in Philo (*Post. Cain* 41 §136) where it means "receive as a host."[20] Paul expects the Corinthians "to receive one another," which at a feast includes sharing food with others. Only by sharing their resources will they alleviate the acute embarrassment of the "have-nots" (Winter 1978: 79; 2001: 151–52) and capture the spirit of Jesus' sacrifice.

The final direction, "If anyone is hungry, let him eat at home," could address the problem of those who are too famished to wait for everyone to arrive at the meal. But Paul is not giving banal advice about eating at home before the worship. Instead, he is reinforcing the idea that "the community's gathering for worship . . . is not the place to satisfy one's hunger and eat one's fill" (Hofius 1993: 95). If they come only to fill their belly, then they are not there to proclaim the Lord's death—they have homes in which to do the former. Conzelmann's (1975: 203) analysis, "If they satisfy their hunger at home, they can celebrate the Supper together," misses the entire point. How can they eat the Lord's Supper with a full belly in the presence of those who are starving? He is not giving them license to indulge themselves and to ignore poor brothers and sisters so long as they do not do it in front of them at the Lord's Supper and humiliate them. Nor is he advising them that if they are worried that there might not be enough food to go around if they have to share with everyone, they should dine first at home. He does not believe that they can retreat from the demands of the gospel in their homes. This command to eat at home connects to his first warning that they are worse off for having gathered together (11:17). If they are intent only on indulging their appetites, then they should stay home. If the church's gathering is to be meaningful, it has to be an expression of real fellowship, which includes sharing.

Paul wishes to prevent the Corinthians from coming together for their condemnation (ἵνα μὴ εἰς κρίμα συνέρχησθε, *hina mē eis krima synerchēsthe*). The implication is that their gathering brings condemnation on them rather than blessing. It may also be a double entendre because κρίμα can also refer to the action of judging. M. Mitchell (1993: 265–66) thinks that he implies, "Don't come together to judge and rank one another disparagingly, because a far more serious (eschatological) judgment awaits." This provides a segue into the next chapter, which exhorts them to bestow honor on the weakest members of the body, since they are all part of one body and need one another to function properly.

We will never know what the other things are that Paul needs to instruct them about when he comes. Presumably, they are related to the

---

20. So Fee 1987: 568; Witherington 1995: 252; Hays 1997: 202–3; R. Horsley 1998: 163.

Lord's Supper as well. Winter (1978: 80) suggests that these matters are difficult and "perhaps touch the very social structures of Corinthian society." Winter guesses that this instruction serves as an interim ethic. What the "haves" need to do for the poor, he will deal with later.

Additional Notes

11:22. Pliny the Younger (*Ep.* 2.6) describes at length the convention of serving guests differing quantities and qualities of food according to their rank. In protesting this practice and his own liberality, he affirms it to be the usual custom with others:

> It would be a long story, and of no importance, were I to recount too particularly by what accident I (who am not at all fond of society) supped lately with a person, who in his own opinion lives in splendor combined with economy; but according to mine, in a sordid but expensive manner. Some very elegant dishes were served up to himself and a few more of the company; while those which were placed before the rest were cheap and paltry. He had apportioned in small flagons three different sorts of wine; but you are not to suppose it was that the guests might take their choice: on the contrary, that they might not choose at all. One was for himself and me; the next for his friends of a lower order (for, you must know, he measures out his friendship according to the degrees of quality); and the third for his own freedmen and mine. One who sat next to me took notice of this and asked me if I approved of it. "Not at all," I told him. "Pray then," said he, "what is your method on such occasions?" "Mine," I returned, "is, to give all my company the same fare; for when I make an invitation, it is to sup, not to be censored.

> "Every man who I have placed on an equality with myself by admitting him to my table, I treat as an equal in all particulars." "Even freedmen?" he asked. "Even them," I said; "for on these occasions I regard them not as freedmen but boon companions." "This must put you to great expense," says he. I assured him not at all; and on asking how that could be, I said, "Why, you must know that freedmen don't drink the same wine I do—but I drink what they do."

11:24. Two textual variants appear in 11:24. The first, represented in the Textus Receptus, adds λάβετε φάγετε before τοῦτο. These words probably were inserted from the liturgical tradition influenced by Matt. 26:26. If they were original, there would have been no reason for them to have been omitted in $\mathfrak{P}^{46}$, A, B, C*, D (Metzger 1994: 496).

Some texts bear witness to attempts to explicate the crisp expression τὸ ὑπὲρ ὑμῶν by adding participles: κλώμενον (ℵ², C³, D², F, G, Ψ, 0150, 81, 104, 256), θρυπτόμενον (D*), or διδόμενον (vg, cop^sa, bo, eth). The shortest reading best explains this assortment of readings.

11:29. Two textual variants reveal attempts to clarify the meaning of the text, but in effect, they distort it (Käsemann 1964: 123–25). The reader has to attend to the end of the sentence to catch its meaning, with its final participial phrase, μὴ διακρίνων τὸ σῶμα, explaining what made the eating and drinking inappropriate. Scribes apparently elected to clarify, before coming to the end of the sentence, that "eating and drinking" by itself does not bring condemnation but "eating and drinking" ἀναξίως does. The ἀναξίως was added from 11:27. The shorter text is found in a reliable lineup of witnesses: $\mathfrak{P}^{46}$, ℵ*, A, B, C*, 33, 1739, it°, cop^sa, bo, geo.

The participial phrase μὴ διακρίνων τὸ σῶμα also was interpreted with the addition of the phrase τοῦ κυρίου, following the pattern in 11:27. The shorter text again is found in 𝔓⁴⁶, ℵ*, A, B, C*, 6, 33, 424ᶜ, 1739, itᵒ, vgʷʷ, syrᵖᵃˡ, copˢᵃ, ᵇᵒ, geo. The shorter reading best explains the development of the longer reading. Fee (1987: 558 n. 4) notes that in liturgical texts, "addition not omission is nearly always the rule."

IX. The Use of Spiritual Gifts in Public Worship (12:1–14:40)

Paul takes up a new topic—"now concerning" (περὶ δέ, *peri de*)—that he will address in chapters 12–14. The genitive plural τῶν πνευματικῶν (*tōn pneumatikōn*) can be read as masculine, "the spiritual persons," or as neuter, "the spiritual things or gifts." The ambiguity reflects the fact that he picks up an issue raised by the Corinthians. They would understand what he means, even if we do not. In his responses to oral reports, he shares with them what he has heard and in the process informs us of what is going on (cf. 1:11–12; 5:1; 6:1; 11:17–22; 15:12). In his response to their letter, he has no need to share with them any background information. He simply quotes a line from the letter to signal the new topic (cf. 7:1; 8:1; 16:1) without going into any details (Fee 1987: 570 n. 2). This topic appears to have been something that was broached in their letter. Consequently, we are left in the dark about their specific concerns and must infer from his responses what questions he is addressing. Hurd's (1965: 186–87, 190–91, 193–95) listing of the various reconstructions shows that the task is complicated. We have seen that this exercise is a tricky business, and we easily can be misled by Paul's tactic of indirection, which is evident in chapters 7 and 8–10.

Either the Corinthians want to know, "Which spiritual gift is the highest and best?" or some are touting their own spiritual gift as "the highest and best." They regard their gift to be an official notarization from the Spirit that they are truly spiritual, and they may be insisting that others owe them esteem and deference. Competitive human ambition threatens to tarnish the expression of the gifts of the Holy Spirit in the community. The topic revolves around the issues of tongues (γλῶσσαι, *glōssai*), which is specifically mentioned twenty-one times in chapters 12–14 and nowhere else in Paul's letters, and prophecy, which is specifically mentioned twenty times (προφητεία, *prophēteia*, five of nine occurrences; προφητεύειν, *prophēteuein*, nine of eleven occurrences; προφήτης, *prophētēs*, six of fourteen occurrences). From Paul's perspective, the basic issues are, What does it mean to be spiritual? and How are Christians to exercise their spiritual gifts in the church?

The Corinthians appear to have limited the "spiritual gifts" to a handful of spectacular gifts. Apparently, they placed tongues above prophecy as a clear sign of supernatural power working in a spiritual person.[1] Gillespie (1994: 70–71) asks, If speaking in tongues was causing the problem at Corinth, why does Paul not begin straightforwardly by stating, "Now concerning speaking in tongues"? This question may reflect an impatience with beating around the bush and a penchant to get right to point. Paul first tries to help the Corinthians see that all Christians are imbued with the Spirit and broadens the spectrum of grace-gifts that manifest the Spirit. The subject is a delicate one, and Paul treads lightly. Baker (1974: 229) reasons that the Corinthians' attitude toward tongues and prophecy "is such that he has to spend two chapters setting in order their perspective before he can give a positive appraisal of them and answer their specific question in ch. 14." Paul addresses these issues obliquely, and the criticism of glossolalia is latent. He starts out by trying to find some common ground with the Corinthians. He then develops the theological implications of the issue that they have overlooked. Next, he develops what on first reading may seem to be an unrelated excursus on love, but actually presents the theological rubric that should govern their use of spiritual gifts and relationships to one another. Finally, he gives specific advice and commands on tongues and prophecy in the worship.

Paul's manner of arguing in chapters 12–14 is similar to that in chapters 8–10. While seeming to canvass a variety of issues, he actually presents a broad-ranging discussion of one particular issue. As chapters 8–10 are about the issue of eating food sacrificed to idols, chapters 12–14 are about speaking in tongues in the public assembly without an intelligible interpretation. In both cases, two factors serve as controlling concerns in his argument: (1) the need to "build up" the fellow Christian, or, negatively, to do nothing to destroy the fellow Christian (8:7–11; 10:23; 14:1b–19); and (2) the missionary effect of the Christian's conduct on unbelievers (10:23–33; 14:20–25). Since the question of tongues and prophecy was complex and evoked strong feelings on the part of some Corinthians, Paul responds delicately with an intricate argument that begins by laying the theological foundation as the basis for discussing the issue. It is followed by a *digressio* in which he uses himself as an apostolic paradigm in which the theological principles are clarified and applied. After establishing the underpinnings of his argument, he gives specific directions on the focal topic in the concluding section. The argument in chapters 12–14 follows a chiastic pattern, with an encomium to love at the center:

A Introduction of the topic of spiritual gifts (12:1–3)

   B The various allotments of the Spirit and the unity of the body (12:4–31)

---

1. Bornkamm (1969: 38) contends that the Corinthians regarded glossolalia as "an exalted form of prophecy."

In chapter 12, Paul puts in proper perspective the nature of spiritual gifts and the role of the bearers of spiritual gifts. He makes clear that there are diversities of gifts, diversities of services, and diversities of activities, but only one Spirit, who distributes them as he wills. Each gift is given to different persons for the common good. Consequently, each person is needed in the community. Inspired speech is only one among many ways the Spirit works in the body of Christ. The body cannot be all eye with no sense of smell. It cannot be all nose with no vision. No individual member should be valued as superior to another, though Paul will argue that prophecy is superior to tongues because it contributes more to building up the community. No one should feel left out in the community because he or she lacks a particular spiritual endowment. No one should feel superior because he or she possesses a particular spiritual endowment. All are gifted by God in some way, and all are encouraged to contribute their gifts in ways that will build up the community. The Spirit decides who gets what gift and apportions them according to the need in the community, not according to the value of the recipient. There is to be no spiritual elite in the church. Spiritual gifts are not indicators of one's spiritual status.

In commenting on Paul's argument for the resurrection of the dead in chapter 15, McDonald (1989: 40) identifies "radical individualism" as the chronic infection in the church that produces a variety of symptoms. McDonald claims that it "tends to substitute in its religious manifestations some kind of individual spiritual exaltation, individual hopes of being 'caught up in Paradise' (2 Cor. 12:4), in place of corporate life in Christ." The Corinthians fail to recognize that "life is a bundle of solidarities," and that "the eternal solidarity is the body of Christ."

---

2. For conclusive arguments against regarding these chapters as deriving from different letters, see Wischmeyer 1981: 16–38; Merklein 1984: 176–77.

A. Introduction of the Topic of Spiritual Gifts (12:1–3)

Casual readers who come to chapter 12 only to learn about spiritual gifts are tempted to skip over the difficult opening verses, but they are crucial for understanding Paul's intention for the entire passage. They introduce the topic and provide a thesis statement. The topic is the spiritual ones (gifts), and the thesis is that all Christians are spiritual. In this introduction, Paul contrasts the Corinthians' religious past with their spiritually transformed present as Christians and affirms that everyone who confesses that Jesus is Lord is directed by the Holy Spirit. This affirmation heads off any claim that some are more spiritual than others because they show evidence of having the more electrifying and exciting spiritual gifts (see additional note).

Exegesis and Exposition

[1]Now concerning the spiritual ones, brothers and sisters, I do not want you to be unaware. [2]You know that when [you were] pagans, you were being led off to dumb idols, whenever you were being led away. [3]Wherefore, I make known to you that no one speaking in the Spirit says, "Jesus is cursed"; and no one is able to say, "Jesus is Lord," except by the Holy Spirit.

12:1 With the phrase περὶ δέ (*peri de*, now concerning), Paul again cues the reader/auditor that he is taking up a new topic. In this case, it signals that the topic comes from the Corinthians' letter to him (cf. comments on 7:1, 25; 8:1). He alternates in his letter between oral and written reports (see Terry 1995: 43). After responding to an oral report in chapter 11, he returns to an issue raised in their letter. If the genitive plural τῶν πνευματικῶν (*tōn pneumatikōn*) is read as masculine, then the issue revolves around "the spiritual persons" and their characteristics. If it is read as neuter, then the issue concerns the nature of "the spiritual things" or "the spiritual gifts." The ambiguity reflects the fact that Paul picks up an issue raised by the Corinthians, which they would understand, even if we do not.

The adjective πνευματικός (*pneumatikos*) appears fourteen times in 1 Corinthians. Four times it refers to persons (2:13, 15; 3:1; 14:37), six times to things (2:13; 9:11; 10:3–4; 14:1), and four times to the contrast between the body animated by the Spirit and the body animated by the soul (15:44–46). Some argue from its usage in 2:15, 3:1, and 14:37 that it is masculine and refers to the spiritual people.[1] In 2:15, Paul refers to "the spiritual ones" who can discern all things but laments that because the Corinthians were not mature spiritually, he cannot refer to them as "spiritual ones" (3:1). The question "Who qualifies as 'spiritual'?" appears to be a live issue. In the immediate context, he refers only to persons: "you were" (12:2), "no one" (12:3), "each one" (12:7). At the end of this discourse, he addresses those "who think they are spiritual" (14:37), which forms an inclusio with 12:1–3 as the introduction and conclusion to the discourse. The term may be the self-designation of some of the Corinthians. Schmithals (1971: 172) contends that a group of Corinthian Christians claimed to be spiritual ("pneumatics") in a way that distinguished them from their more unassuming brothers and sisters. They defined "spirituality" according to their own inclinations toward inspired speech. The person who speaks in front of the group stands out as one who is Spirit-inspired, and the public nature of this gift puts this individual in the spotlight and makes him or her appear exceptional when compared to the gallery of listeners. This person receives the group's admiration and respect.

The majority of commentators and versions opt to read τῶν πνευμα-τικῶν as neuter, referring to "spiritual gifts," since the subject of Paul's overall argument concerns the manifestations of the Spirit in the church, not the characteristics of spiritual persons.[2] In 14:1, τὰ πνευμα-τικά (*ta pneumatika*) can mean only spiritual manifestations, not spiritual persons. The conceptual parallel between πνευματικά and χαρί-σματα (*charismata*; 12:4, 9, 28, 30, 31)—a term never applied to persons—also argues for the neuter. Elsewhere, Paul uses the substantive πνευ-ματικός to refer to persons only in Gal. 6:1. The other eight usages of the adjective outside of 1 Corinthians refer to things: "spiritual gift" (Rom. 1:11), "spiritual blessing" (Eph. 1:3), "spiritual things" (Rom. 15:27), "spiritual odes" (Eph. 5:19; Col. 3:16), and the law as spiritual (Rom. 7:14). It also is applied to the spiritual forces of evil (Eph. 6:12). Thiselton (2000: 910) tries to walk a fine line between both possibilities and comments, "The key issue which has been raised (at least in the form in which Paul wishes to address it) is this: What criteria are we to apply for specific people or gifts to be considered genuinely 'of the Holy Spirit'?" Thiselton translates τῶν πνευματικῶν as "things that come from the Spirit." This accords with Fee's (1987: 576; 1994: 153) assessment that although the term is most likely neuter and nearly inter-

1. Weiss 1910: 294; Hurd 1965: 194; Schmithals 1971: 171–72; Bruce 1971: 116–17; Wire 1990: 135; Blomberg 1994: 243.
2. Robertson and Plummer 1914: 259; Conzelmann 1975: 204; Grudem 1982: 157–60; R. Martin 1984: 8; Fee 1987: 576; 1994: 152–53; Carson 1987: 22; Gillespie 1994: 68–78; R. Collins 1999: 446–47.

changeable with χαρίσματα, the distinction between the two depends on the root word. "Spiritual" emphasizes the Spirit's role; *charisma* emphasizes the manifestation, the gift as such.

Barrett (1968: 278) thinks that the difference between the masculine and the neuter is inconsequential because a spiritual person is one who has spiritual gifts (so also Morris 1958: 163). Since gifts are incarnated in individuals, gift and bearer of the gift belong together (Schrage 1999: 118; cf. 2:13). But this view does not take into consideration that the Corinthians and Paul may have differed on how they understood the significance of this term. Schrage (1999: 118–19, anticipated by Parry 1926: 127) suggests that the masculine reflects the Corinthians' position, while the neuter refers to Paul's take on it. Paul cites the Corinthians' question about the "spiritual ones" in the announcement of the topic and then seeks to correct their misconceptions. In my opinion, they constricted its meaning to denote only those who gave evidence of the spiritual gifts prized by them—in particular, speaking in tongues. Ellis (1978: 24) offers a helpful distinction. Ellis argues from Paul's use of the term "spiritual gift" (χάρισμα πνευματικόν) in Rom. 1:11 that *charisma* can be used of any spiritual gift, but *pneumatika* applies specifically to "gifts of inspired perception, verbal proclamation and/or its interpretation." "Spiritual things," Ellis concludes, are related to speaking in the Spirit.[3] Baker (1974: 231) infers that these gifts "were thought to bestow upon the person who employed them an aura of being 'spiritual' (14:37)." Whether or not this is a correct assessment of the Corinthians' views, Paul broadens the meaning of "spiritual" to include other spiritual gifts (see Grudem 1982: 157–60). Baker's (1974: 229) reconstruction of the situation seems reasonable:

> They asked Paul about the "spiritual gifts" (πνευματικά), by which in their circumscribed understanding of the Holy Spirit they meant above all prophecy and speaking in tongues, but Paul answers their questions by referring to the many "gifts of grace" (χαρίσματα) which God gives to the Christians. Their "spiritual gifts" are only two of these, and to emphasize the point, he puts them right at the end of the list.

It is important to recognize, however, that Paul quotes from the Corinthian letter in announcing the topic. As in 7:1, he uses their language without necessarily giving it the same meaning or value that they do. In this particular case, the genitive plural is obligingly ambiguous, "the spirituals," and Paul can cite their terminology but develop his own interpretation so that it refers to gifts given by the Spirit to all Christians.

---

3. Thiselton (2000: 930) argues that the Corinthians used the term instead to refer to a wide variety of "'religious' feeling-states and observable phenomena."

I have opted to translate it "spiritual ones" for two reasons. First, to capture the rhetorical setting and the argument's flow, it is best not to impose the understanding of the term that Paul unfolds in what follows onto this announcement of the topic, which is taken from the Corinthians' letter. When he uses this term here, he quotes from the Corinthians' letter but will reinterpret what it truly means. Second, the translation "spiritual ones" matches its usage at the conclusion of the discourse in 14:37, where he refers to a Corinthian outlook—those who regard themselves as spiritual.

12:2 Paul starts his instruction by reminding the Corinthians of their pagan past, before they had experienced the Spirit's power in their lives. The noun ἔθνη (ethnē) is the Jewish term for Gentiles (the assumption is that Jews are *the* nation; the rest are simply the nations), and in the context of idols, the translation "pagans" is apropos. The sentence is terse and difficult. Literally, it reads, "You know that when pagans, you were to dumb idols, as ever you were led, being led away." The ὅτι ὅτε (*hoti hote*, that when) seems graceless, and the ὅτι clause does not have a verb unless ἦτε (ēte, you were) is repeated for ἀπαγόμενοι (apagomenoi, you were being led away [an imperfect periphrastic]). It is possible that ὅτε originally was ποτέ, "that at one time you were pagans," or that the verb dropped out. The imperfect ἤγεσθε (ēgesthe) with ἄν (an) is iterative, denoting repeated action in past time—again and again (cf. Mark 6:56).[4] My translation assumes the repetition of ἦτε: "You know that when [you were] pagans, you were being led off to dumb idols, whenever you were being led away."

The verb "being led" is frequently linked by commentators to ecstatic experiences in the Corinthians' former pagan worship (such as Dionysian revelry).[5] The Greek world had many religious groups that offered experiences of divine inspiration, and "being led" is assumed to refer to the influence of an otherworldly, demonic power (R. Martin 1984: 9; Wolff 1996: 283). This interpretation is based on the assumption that Paul cites the Corinthians' pagan religious experience in order to compare and contrast it with the spiritual gifts of tongues and prophecy that they now experience as Christians. Before, in their religious past, they had been "moved" or "led." Now, as Christians, they recognize that they had been led astray. This interpretation understands Paul to be saying that what happened before can happen again. The experience of

4. The ἄν could be the prefix to the verb ἄγειν and could mean "to lead up" (BDAG 61). It could be interpreted as being caught up by demonic powers (cf. Matt. 4:1).

5. Fee (1994: 152 n. 240) notes that the term "ecstasy" is treated rather loosely as "a synonym of 'enthusiasm' to denote any number of kinds of spiritually inspired activity or speech." Technically, it should denote being out of control, standing outside of oneself (see Callan 1985).

religious ecstasy leading to inspired speech is no criterion for the working of the Spirit (Conzelmann 1975: 206).[6]

This conventional reading of the text is questionable for the following reasons. When Paul uses the verb ἄγειν (*agein,* to lead), he never refers to the leading of demonic powers but to the leading of the Holy Spirit (Rom. 8:14; Gal. 5:18).[7] The compound verb ἀπάγειν (*apagein*) appears only here in his letters. It may suggest that they were being led away from the truth (Edwards 1985: 307; BDAG 95; cf. συναπάγειν, *synapagein,* Gal. 2:13; 2 Pet. 3:17), but its usage in the LXX, the Gospels, and Acts simply means "to lead someone from one point to another." Fee (1987: 577–78) claims that the "unusual compounding of the verbs" and the use of the passive voice, implying that they are being acted upon by others, suggest that Paul refers to their inspired utterances as pagans. This conclusion does not follow. The compounding of the verbs alone does not imply supernatural leading or some kind of ecstatic frenzy or possession. That would be true only if the context dictates this conclusion. But nothing in the immediate context justifies this inference. Grudem (1982: 162 n. 78) contends that neither verb, ἄγειν or ἀπάγειν, ever implies any religious experience by those being led. Had Paul intended to imply some ecstatic experience, he could have chosen other words, such as ἁρπάζειν (*harpazein;* 2 Cor. 12:2, 4). Had he intended to imply some kind of deception, he could have used πλανᾶν (*planan;* 1 Cor. 6:9; 15:33; Gal. 6:7), ἀπατᾶν (*apatan;* Eph. 5:6), or ἐξαπατᾶν (*exapatan;* Rom. 7:11; 1 Cor. 3:18). If the verbs hint at some kind of compulsion, it need not result from some demonic influence, but could just as well come from social pressure to participate in idol festivals (Grudem 1982: 163 n. 79).

The grammar also militates against this reading. The preposition πρός (*pros*) indicates the direction or goal of the Corinthians' movement. They were led *to* idols, not *by* idols. The agent behind their leading is left unexpressed so that the emphasis falls on the final destination of where they were being led: to idols. Being led by demons or evil spirits has to be read into what Paul actually says. The logic behind the interpretation that it refers to some ecstatic experience becomes circular. It is assumed that the problem at Corinth is their spiritual ecstasy, which is getting out of control in their worship. This ecstatic tendency is read back into their previous pagan worship to argue that they imported this frenzied abandon into their Christian worship (see, for example, R. Martin 1984: 9). Paul's language is then adjusted to fit this interpretation. While ecstatic phenomena may have been part of some

---

6. See also Weiss 1910: 294; Barrett 1968: 278–79; Baker 1974: 230; Dunn 1975: 242–43; Aune 1983: 257; R. Martin 1984: 9; Fee 1987: 577–78; Theissen 1987: 292–93; Gillespie 1994: 80–81; Wolff 1996: 283; Johnson, *ABD* 6:599–600; Schrage 1999: 119–20.

7. The NRSV translation "enticed" is completely unwarranted.

pagan cults, it was not an aspect of all idol worship. Most worshipers were not induced into frenzied trances. Since Paul does not explicitly use language that implies an ecstatic experience, this interpretation should be abandoned if an alternative can be found that fits the common meaning of the verbs, the grammar, and a familiar feature of idol worship (see Mehat 1983).

Instead of being blown about willy-nilly by various spiritual powers (so Hays 1997: 208), or being "led away captive at the will of evil spirits" (so Edwards 1885: 307), the focus is on the destination of the leading: to dumb idols. Paige (1991) shows how this phrase fits the daily life of a Hellenistic city such as Corinth (see also R. Horsley 1998: 168; R. Collins [1999: 447] translates it, "you were marched away to mute idols"). Paige (1991: 59) applies it to the *pompē*, "a cultic festival procession in which the participants normally proceeded along a sacred route." At the end of the procession, the train of adherents stood before the sanctuary images. It was "one of the most public, elaborate, expensive and exciting events in the 'liturgical year' of a sanctuary" (Paige 1991: 61). Not all, if any, Corinthian converts would have been members of ecstatic cults, but all former pagans in the church would have participated, at some time or another, in an idol pageant, since religious processions were "an extremely common feature of Greek and Roman religious practice" (Seaford, *OCD* 1250). To allow for a variety of different festival processions leading to the assortment of many idol gods, Paul inserts the phrase "whenever you were led."[8] This background suggests that he simply describes a feature of their religious past and does not insinuate that they have allowed their former pagan worship to infect their Christian worship.

Paul adopts the traditional Jewish polemic against idols as voiceless (ἄφωνα, *aphōna*; cf. 1 Kings 18:26, 29; Ps. 115:5; Hab. 2:18–19; 3 Macc. 4:16; Jos. As. 8:5; 11:8; 12:5; 13:11). "Dumb idols" means more than that they are simply mute. It connotes lifelessness and an inability to help (Wolff 1996: 283). He is not reminding them that inspired utterances ironically were part of the worship in some cults in spite of mute idols (contra Lietzmann 1949: 60–61). He simply intends to contrast their former pagan life (cf. 1 Cor. 8:7; Gal. 4:8–9; 1 Thess. 1:9) with their current Christian life in the Spirit (M. Barth 1958: 131; Aune 1983: 221). Fee (1987: 577) claims that "the difficulty of finding an adequate reason for making this point in this introductory paragraph has caused most scholars to look elsewhere for an answer," which explains why so many assume that Paul compares and contrasts their ecstatic behavior as pagans with their ecstatic behavior as Christians. This view mistakenly as-

---

8. The phrase ὡς ἄν (*hōs an*) is used in the LXX to mean "whenever" (cf. Gen. 6:4; Exod. 33:19; 1 Sam. 2:13; 2 Sam. 14:26; Job 1:5; Grudem 1982: 163 n. 79).

sumes that the problem is the ecstatic expression of gifts. It also mistakenly assumes that he broaches the topic of tongues and prophecy with this reference. I would argue instead that his point is to establish from the outset that all Christians are spiritual. The contrast is between then, when they were pagans and led to dumb idols, and now, when they confess that Jesus is Lord. Paige (1991: 62) concludes that "the *pompē* becomes a symbol for all the attractions of pagan life: the attractions of political power, religious cult, social ties and the need to belong, not to mention the enticing feast. At the same time, Paul uses the *pompē* as a symbol of the delusion involved in all of this."[9] The "dumb idols" symbolize only their former ignorance.

Paul lays down a key principle before developing his discussion of the various manifestations of the spiritual gifts. The myriad suggestions about the meaning of this verse are largely unhelpful. They start from wrong assumptions about what Paul intends to establish in this introduction. He is not providing criteria for discerning authentic inspiration (contra Gillespie 1994: 77). Gillespie's (1994: 83) perception of the logic leads us astray: **12:3**

> Premise: You know that evidence of ecstasy is an unreliable criterion of authentic divine inspiration because in your pagan past they led you to dumb idols (v. 2).
>
> Conclusion: Therefore, the genuineness of all prophetic utterances must be judged on their material content alone.

This reconstruction begs the question. Paul does not say anything about "evidences of ecstasy." He does not mention "prophetic utterances" or how to judge them. "Jesus is Lord" is the basic confession made by every Christian and is not a prophetic utterance (cf. Rom. 10:9; Phil. 2:11; Acts 16:31; 1 Cor. 5:4; 6:11; 8:6; 9:1; 11:23; 15:31, 57; 16:23). The confession is a validating sign that one is a Christian inspired by the Spirit, not a touchstone to gauge authentic prophetic speech (contra Dautzenberg 1975: 143–46; Gillespie 1994: 84; Fee 1994: 152). Grudem (1982: 167) observes that as a test of valid inspiration, it would be a poor one. Anyone could give verbal consent to this confession to gain acceptance (cf. Matt. 7:22). Paul seeks to undermine the elitism of "glossolalia-flaunting pneumatics" (Bassler 1982: 416) in the same way he seeks to thwart the elitism that surfaces at the Lord's Supper.

The pronouncement ἀνάθεμα Ἰησοῦς (*anathema Iēsous*) poses difficulties. Thiselton (2000: 918) counts twelve different explanations.

9. Later Christians used the phrase "devil's procession" (*pompa diaboli*) to express their contempt for this feature of pagan religion.

Anathema means "accursed" and derives from the LXX translation of the Hebrew *ḥērem*. The LXX uses it to refer to that which is devoted as an offering to God (cf. Lev. 27:28; 2 Macc. 2:13) and then to that which is an accursed thing (cf. Deut. 7:26; 13:16, 18 LXX) and delivered up to destruction (Josh. 6:17–7:1). It is unclear whether the imperative verb ἔστω (*estō*) should be supplied, "Let Jesus be cursed," or the indicative ἔστι (*esti*), "Jesus is cursed."[10] Most assume that the speaker pronounces a curse on Jesus. The connecting phrase, however, is "Jesus is Lord," not "Let Jesus be Lord." This suggests that the indicative should be supplied, "Jesus is cursed" (van Unnik 1973: 115–16). Was this denunciation of Jesus uttered in Christian worship?

The Corinthians must have been familiar with the construction. Otherwise, such a jarring line would have bewildered them as much as it does modern readers. Fee (1987: 579) remarks, "It is difficult for us to imagine either that anyone actually cursed Jesus in the gathered Christian assembly, or that, if he/she did, Paul would take it so casually as to speak to it only here and in this totally noncombative way." This does not stop interpreters from stretching their imaginations to argue that this cursing of Jesus did occur among the Corinthian Christians. How could such a cry arise in a Christian assembly? Some claim that it stemmed from a quasi-gnostic abhorrence of the fleshly humanity of Jesus (cf. 1 John 2:22; 4:3; 5:6). A segment of the Corinthian church is said to have made a radical distinction between the heavenly Christ and the earthly Jesus. The two could not be identified without calling into question the gnostic understanding of salvation, which extolled escape from the mortal stranglehold of the flesh. This dualistic worldview led them to confess Christ and curse Jesus (see Schmithals 1971: 124–32; Brox 1968; Dunn 1975: 234).

The habit of looking for gnostic roots behind every problem at Corinth has fallen on disfavor, and this explanation for cursing Jesus should finally be put to rest. This distinction is attested only in later sources (van Unnik 1973: 114). No evidence materializes in the Corinthian correspondence that the Corinthians ever made such a distinction, and the evidence that later gnostics pronounced a curse on Jesus is ambiguous (see Pearson 1967).

Others contend that this cry was intoned by Christians under the duress of trial and torture (cf. Mart. Pol. 9:2; 10:1; 12:1; Pliny the Younger, *Ep.* 10.96; Mark 14:71). This letter, however, evinces no signs that persecution dogged the Christians in Corinth. The texts cited to support this view come from a later time when more official and organized persecution against Christians was taking shape. It is anachronistic to read

---

10. In 1 Cor. 16:22, the imperative ἤτω (*ētō*) appears: "Let anyone who does not love the Lord be accursed" (see also Gal. 1:8–9); and in Rom. 9:3, the infinitive εἶναι (*einai*): "For I could wish that I myself were accursed from Christ in behalf of my own people."

this text in light of that later situation. More important, such a reference makes no sense in the context.

Some conjecture that it was a cry uttered by someone in an ecstatic trance during their charismatic worship (Weiss 1910: 295–97; Moffatt 1938: 179; Lietzmann 1949: 186–87; Dunn 1975: 234–35, 293).[11] The assumptions behind this view are questionable. Paul never mentions anyone going into an ecstatic trance during their worship, let alone that it resulted in them venting vile impieties. Paul assumes that the persons speaking in tongues are in complete control of their faculties. They are able to count the number of speakers, discern if someone is present to interpret, and curb the impulse to speak if necessary (14:27–28). He does not imply that a cry like this was made by a Christian under inspiration.[12] How to discern the spirits of what is said in worship is not at issue in these chapters. Consequently, he does not appeal to this pronouncement to provide a criterion by which to judge spiritual utterances but to state an obvious fact with which they would readily agree: no one could say such a blasphemous thing under the inspiration of the Spirit.

Winter (2001: 164–83) offers a fourth explanation. Winter thinks that it pertains to Christians asking Jesus to curse their enemies and consequently translates it, "Jesus [grant] a curse." Religion was popularly used in the ancient world to gain advantage over others and to hurt one's rivals or enemies. Winter cites a cache of recently discovered curse inscriptions invoking the gods to curse a person, and the formula omits the verb. This explanation assumes that Christians persisted in this pagan practice and sought to use the power of Jesus through this formula to harm their enemies. This reconstruction is quite foreign to the context. Why Paul would contrast this hex with the confession "Jesus is Lord" is difficult to explain. In none of the inscriptions cited does the word *anathema* occur.

After charting the various options, Fee (1987: 581) asks, "How could a *believer* under any circumstances say such a thing in the Christian assembly, and how is it that he or she would need such instruction? Moreover, if this were actually happening in the Corinthian assembly, one is hard pressed to explain how this introduces the rest of the argument and why Paul does not pursue such blasphemy with his usual vigor." Fee concludes that it must be hypothetical and serves to remind them that so-called inspired utterances are not all inspired by the Spirit (see also Conzelmann 1975: 204–5; Hays 1997: 209). Schrage (1999: 116–17)

---

11. Dunn (1975: 420 n. 180) cites supposed modern parallels to this phenomenon, but none suffice as evidence that this actually occurred in Corinth.

12. Efforts to explain that it was an attempt to ward off going into a trance (Barrett 1968: 280) or that the group was worried that someone speaking in tongues that they could not understand might slip in blasphemy (Grosheide 1953: 280–81) are fanciful.

thinks that it is a shocking counterpoint to the confession "Jesus is Lord." But how does it introduce what follows? Paul does not develop a contrast between inspired and uninspired utterances but instead elaborates on the diversity of the gifts of the Spirit and the unity of their source. Nowhere in these chapters does the issue of *how* to discern inspired teaching arise. Consequently, attempts to explain why Christians would say "Jesus *anathema*" are dead ends. No one was actually saying this in the Christian community, and Paul does not imagine that any Christian hypothetically would say it. Bassler (1982: 417) points out that if it were only hypothetical, it would baffle the original readers as much as it baffles the commentators.

All views that assume that the Corinthian Christians were crying out this curse fail to recognize how this introduction to the discourse functions. In an introduction, one does not immediately go on the attack. Contrast the far more brusque and straightforward conclusion in 14:37–40, with its sharp commands. Paul does not delve into the problem straightaway but instead lays the groundwork for his answers that follow. This chapter is about the allotment of spiritual gifts (12:4–7) given to individual Christians by the Spirit for the common good. He starts out by making clear that *all* who make the saving confession "Jesus is Lord" (Rom. 10:9) are led by the Spirit and qualify as spiritual ones.

Why, then, does Paul note this execration of Jesus if it was not spoken by Christians? The view that he alludes to the appraisal of Jesus as the Christ by unbelieving Jews has been too quickly dismissed by interpreters.[13] Bassler (1982: 418) thinks that Paul draws on his own past as a persecutor of the church (15:8–10; Gal. 1:13–16; Phil. 3:6), which arose from his conviction that the crucified Jesus was accursed (Gal. 3:13; Deut. 21:23). But it could also be an allusion to the Jewish rejection of the Christian confession about Jesus. Most assume that Paul compares and contrasts only the religious legacy of converted pagans, but not all Christians formerly were pagans. Some were former members of the synagogue (Acts 18:5–8). Does Paul ignore the Jewish background of these members? He cannot say "when you were Jews," as he says "when you were pagans" of the Gentiles, since Jews who became Christians did not become un-Jews. It is suggestive that it is particularly in the Jewish setting that Christ is regarded as cursed. *Anathema* language generally reflects Jewish usage, not Greek (Behm, *TDNT* 1:354; cf. Deut. 7:26). Extrabiblical use of this word in the sense of curse is found in a tablet of curses (Deissmann 1911: 95–96; Conzelmann 1975: 204

13. See Findlay 1910: 886; Robertson and Plummer 1914: 261; Moffatt 1938: 178–79; Mehat 1983: 413; Talbert 1987: 81–82; Witherington 1995: 256; and Derrett 1974–75 (in a typically creative but maverick hypothesis).

n. 9).[14] Since the following phrase requires supplying the indicative, "Jesus is Lord," not "Let Jesus be Lord," it is unlikely that this is a curse on Jesus, "Let Jesus be damned." As a statement, "Jesus is accursed," it fits perfectly the assessment of Jesus found in Jewish circles (Acts 7:54–60). They could not declare "the Christ" accursed, as pagans could, since it is the Greek term for the Messiah. They could, however, declare Jesus accursed as one who was crucified (a stumbling block to the Jews; 1 Cor. 1:23) and one whom Christians impiously claimed to be the Messiah. Justin Martyr's dialogue with Rabbi Trypho specifically mentions Jews anathematizing Christ in their synagogues (see *Dial.* 47.4; 96.2; 137.2) and cursing Christians (16.4). Some commentators suggest that this curse might have arisen in a mystery cult. If so, it uses distinctively Jewish language and breaches the instinctive pagan aversion to unnecessarily offending any god. Since the evidence reveals that this cursing of Jesus actually occurred in the synagogues, it is the most likely background.

If Paul is referring to the Jewish background of some in the church, then the statement in 12:3 should not be regarded as the development of the statement in 12:2. All three verses begin with a statement about knowledge: "I do not want you to be unaware" (ἀγνοεῖν, *agnoein*; 12:1); "you know" (οἴδατε, *oidate*; 12:2); "I make known [γνωρίζω, *gnōrizō*] to you" (12:3). Each statement addresses a different topic. Talbert (1987: 81–82) contends that in these introductory verses Paul describes three religious experiences:

1. Pagan experience: being led astray to dumb idols
2. Jewish experience: declaring Jesus is anathema
3. Christian experience in the Spirit: confessing Jesus is Lord

Paul notes these three different entities in 10:32, "Jews, Greeks, and the church of God," and in 12:13, he brings up the contrast between Jew and Greek. The Corinthians had firsthand acquaintance with Jewish obduracy (Acts 18:5–6). For them to understand the contrast in 2 Cor. 3:13–18 between Jews, whose minds are hardened, and Christians, who are enlightened, they must have been familiar with Jews who rejected their faith. Paul says that to this day the children of Israel read Moses (the Scripture that points to Christ) with a veil over their minds, but Christians have turned to the Lord and have had the veil removed so that the Spirit enables them to see the glory of the Lord (2 Cor. 3:13–

14. A gray marble gravestone discovered in the *cavea* of the Corinthian theater threatens any person opening the tomb without the owners' permission with this curse: "May the *anathema* of Annas and Caiaphas be upon him." This curse reflects later Christian tradition that imagined Annas and Caiphas to have died terrible deaths and to have been consigned to hell (see J. Elliott 1993: 224–25).

18). This contrast corresponds to the contrast in 1 Cor. 12:3: Jews call Jesus *anathema;* Christians, through the Spirit, call him Lord.

The purpose of this introduction is not to condemn the blind ignorance of pagans and Jews. The center of gravity is to be found in the last clause, "No one is able to say 'Lord Jesus' except by the Spirit."[15] This saving confession, made by every single Christian, can be made only under the inspiration of the Spirit.[16] It means that turning from their past blindness is made possible only by the reception of the Spirit. I disagree with Conzelmann's (1975: 204) assertion, "The Spirit is for him . . . a supernatural power that gives rise to 'un-normal' effects." Quite the opposite. The Spirit leads to this normal, rational, but heartfelt personal confession. For the Corinthians, the effects of the Spirit were most apparent when the Spirit manifested itself in an unusual way, such as speaking in tongues. For Paul, the Spirit of God "helps us understand the thoughts of God and his gracious acts toward us" (2:12) and results in this confession. Hays's (1997: 208) comments are pertinent: "Anyone who utters that confession (not just mouthing the words but making a self-involving confession of the lordship of Jesus) is ipso facto living in the sphere of the Holy Spirit's power." This statement "anticipates the theme of verses 12–13: All who are in Christ have entered the realm of the Spirit, and no one should be despised."[17]

This confession is not some spontaneous, ecstatic utterance that anyone could blurt out. It affirms the majesty of Jesus as the one raised from the dead to become the one universal Lord above all other so-called lords (8:6). It declares absolute allegiance to him and accepts his absolute authority over every aspect of life. Paul's purpose is to identify who qualifies as spiritual (cf. 14:37). He is not dealing with the question of how to judge inspired speech (contra Barrett 1968: 281). He counters those who think that the true mark of the spiritual person is that one engage in inspired speech. He wants to affirm from the start that all the members of the body of Christ are spiritual. He argues in Gal. 4:6 that because they cry "Abba, Father," it is proof that God sent the Spirit into their hearts and that they are "sons." In the same way, he argues here that all who confess Jesus as Lord are spiritual. Bassler (1982: 416; see also Schrage 1999: 125) gets at the truth:

15. Standaert (1983: 31) argues that this is the proposition of chapters 12–14.

16. Fee (1987: 578 n. 43) explains the phrase ἐν πνεύματι ἁγίῳ (*en pneumati hagiō*) by noting the Pauline stylistic idiosyncrasy that when πνεῦμα is in the dative, it is almost always anarthrous. It does not refer to "a" spirit. Paul uses the definite article when it refers to a person's own spirit (5:3; 7:34; 14:15).

17. Paul is not concerned that the Corinthians need to be more discriminating in their evaluations of various religious experiences, as Hays (1997: 208–9) believes. It does not take much discernment for Christians to recognize that declaring that Jesus is cursed is not of the Spirit.

Since Paul is concerned to refute those Corinthians who claim their gift of glossolalia is a special, perhaps unique, demonstration of spirit possession, he opens his response in vv 1–3 by presenting a radically different perspective. Noting the simple baptismal confession, Jesus is Lord, can only be uttered under the influence of the Holy Spirit (v 3b), Paul undermines any pneumatic elitism. All Christians make this confession, thus all Christians, not a tongue-speaking few, are πνευματικοί.

The term "spiritual" does not apply exclusively to those who, according to the Corinthians' yardstick, had this or that conspicuous speech gift, but to all Christians. This point serves to relativize "all claims to greater or lesser spiritual attainment" because a person demonstrates or lacks certain gifts (M. Mitchell 1993: 267–68). In this introduction, Paul sets the stage for his argument that "each person has his or her own individual gifts and roles to play, each of which in its own way benefits the community" (M. Mitchell 1993: 268). He seeks to correct those in the church who see themselves as a Spirit-bearing elite to be set apart from the rest of the congregation.

Additional Note

12:1–3. Commentators should not pretend that they approach 12:1–3 as completely objective observers. Those who have experienced the gift of tongues find it to be far more significant and tend to offer more sympathetic interpretations of the phenomenon than those who have not experienced it. I have not experienced publicly the gifts that many label today as "charismatic" or "Pentecostal." In many ways, then, in studying this text I feel like an outsider looking in. Natural inhibitions or social constraints may have prevented this gift from making an appearance in many churches. On the other hand, these chapters deal with a more basic phenomenon that is no respecter of denominational breeding. All will have experienced church conflict that is rooted in the hunger for status and recognition. Many will have been in communities where the more cerebral gifts have become the gifts of choice and are exalted over others. Many will have witnessed impatience with other "benighted souls," a lack of kindness, inflated self-importance, ill-mannered dismissal of fellow Christians who are judged as less gifted or wrongly gifted, and burning envy (cf. 13:4–7). Paul gives specific instructions to solve a specific problem in Corinth but calls for Christian charity as the way to prevent the conflict from arising in the first place.

IX. The Use of Spiritual Gifts in Public Worship (12:1–14:40)
  A. Introduction of the Topic of Spiritual Gifts (12:1–3)
➤ B. Variety and Unity of Spiritual Gifts (12:4–11)
  C. The Diversity and Interdependence of Members of the Body (12:12–31)

B. Variety and Unity of Spiritual Gifts (12:4–11)

Paul argues in 12:4–11 that the Spirit gives a variety of gifts to people. These gifts are not given as a sign that the recipients are especially spiritual or have received a super-sized portion of the Spirit. The Spirit distributes the gifts according to his sovereign purposes—for the common benefit of all and for the unity of the community, and certainly not to foment divisions in the church or to create a first team of select Christians and a second team of also-rans. Lowering the Corinthians' glamorized estimation of tongues, which has created division, is the ultimate target of this discussion. The key verses are 7 and 11, which speak of diversity of spiritual manifestations and the unity of the source.

The discussion fits an ABA′ arrangement (see R. Collins 1999: 451):

A Allotments of different kinds of gifts by the one Spirit (12:4–7)
  B Sample listing of gifts (12:8–10)
A′ The same Spirit allots gifts to each one (12:11)

In 12:8–10, the listing of gifts falls into a threefold division: two gifts of speech ("message of wisdom," "message of knowledge"), followed by a sampling of five gifts, concluded by two more gifts of speech ("many kinds of tongues," "interpretation of tongues").

Exegesis and Exposition

[4]Now there are allotments of grace-gifts, but the same Spirit. [5]And there are allotments of services, but the same Lord. [6]And there are allotments of workings, but the same God, who is working all things in all persons. [7]But to each one is given the manifestation of the Spirit for [mutual] benefit. [8]For to one is given through the Spirit the message of wisdom, and to another the message of knowledge, according to the same Spirit. [9]To another [is given] faith by the same Spirit, and to another grace-gifts of healings by the same Spirit, [10]and to another powers to effect miracles, and to another prophecy, and to another ability to distinguish between spirits, and to another many kinds of tongues, and to another interpretation of tongues. [11]All these things are the activity of the one and the same Spirit, distributing individually to each one just as he wills.

The force of the δέ (*de*) may be adversative and mean, "All who make the confession 'Jesus is Lord' manifest that the Spirit directs their lives, *but* that is not the only manifestation of the Spirit." Distinctions exist among those who are spiritual because they have been allotted different gifts (see Carson 1987: 31). The noun διαίρεσις (*diairesis*) occurs only here in the NT. Fee (1987: 586 n. 13) argues that it should be translated "varieties" or "differences" to fit the emphasis on the variety of gifts in the context. Most interpreters render it "allotments" or "distributions" because the cognate verb διαιρεῖν (*diairein*) clearly means "to distribute" in 12:11 (see also Jdt. 9:4).[1] This meaning becomes explicit in 1 Cor. 12:7, where Paul affirms that each one has been given a gift. The emphasis in this verse is not on the variety of the different gifts but on the one Spirit who distributes them.

Of the seventeen occurrences of χάρισμα (*charisma*) in the NT, only one appears outside of the Pauline corpus (1 Pet. 4:10), so it may be regarded as characteristically Pauline. Seven appear in this letter, and five in this chapter (12:4, 9, 28, 30, 31). The -μα (*-ma*) suffix denotes the result of an action, and in this case, *charisma* refers to the results of grace—the free gift. The word rarely appears in classical writers and in the LXX, and Dunn (1975: 206) surmises that Paul may have chosen the term "to mark off the new experience of God's grace from the OT religion of law and ritual." Grace "emphasizes the source of the gift rather than its nature" (Baker 1974: 225), and I translate *charisma* as "grace-gift." *Charisma* is defined by Dunn (1977: 191) as the experience of divine grace coming to particular expression through an individual believer in some act or word usually, but not always, for the benefit of others. Käsemann (1964: 65) defines it as "the specific part which the individual has in the lordship and glory of Christ; and this specific part which the individual has in the Lord shows itself in a specific service and a specific vocation. For there is no divine gift which does not bring with it a task, there is no grace which does not move to action." Käsemann (1964: 67) thinks that the grace-gift is validated only "by the service it renders." This definition would cast speaking in tongues, which benefits only the speaker, in a bad light. Although Paul does not denigrate tongues as a gift, he does place greater value on those gifts that lead to service to others, and he wants the Corinthians to share this same perspective. Since he believes that grace-gifts are given to individuals with a view to the mutual benefit of the community, and since the gift of tongues used without an interpreter benefits only the speaker (and otherwise tends to foster division), he relegates tongues to the bottom of the list of gifts.

---

1. Weiss 1910: 298; Barrett 1968: 283; Conzelmann 1975: 207; Wolff 1996: 288; Thiselton 2000: 929: "apportioning different gifts to differing recipients."

R. Collins (1999: 452) may be correct that Paul chooses to use the term *charisma*, rather than *pneumatikon* (12:1), to provide "a theological corrective to the popular Corinthian notion of spiritual phenomena" (cf. Schrage 1999: 137).[2] Spiritual gifts are not a "badge of spirituality," but a "mark of grace" (Fisk 2000: 75–76). The grace language accents God's generosity, which accomplishes divine purposes in the lives of humans, who do not rate any special favor.

Paul applies the word *charisma* to a wide range of phenomena. He uses it to refer to God's action in Christ to bring salvation to humans (Rom. 5:15–16; 6:23) and to his own miraculous deliverance from life-threatening danger (2 Cor. 1:11). He applies it to God's election and calling of Israel (Rom. 11:29). In this letter he uses it to characterize the absence of sexual passion that allows celibate devotion to God (7:7). The majority of uses, however, refer to the manifestations of God's working in the members of the Christian community, from which the whole community benefits (Rom. 1:11; 1 Cor. 1:4–7).

The allotment of gifts is diverse and falls into three broad categories: "grace-gifts" (χαρίσματα), "services" (διακονίαι, *diakoniai*), and "workings" (ἐνεργήματα, *energēmata*). The source of the gifts has Trinitarian overtones. These are not simply gifts of the Spirit, they are Trinitarian. The parallelism of 12:4–6 is obvious:

different distributions of grace-gifts	but the same Spirit
different distributions of services	but the same Lord
different distributions of workings	but the same God

"Services" match nicely with the Lord's ministry and with his self-sacrifice proclaimed in the Lord's Supper, which was just discussed in the previous section (11:17–34). "Workings" are appropriate to God (Gal. 2:8; Eph. 1:11; 3:20; Phil. 2:13) and imply that all things accomplished in the church are effected by God's power (Fee 1987: 588). The categories are not hard and fast, however. All these same phenomena can also be identified as "the manifestation of the Spirit" (1 Cor. 12:7) and as activated by the one and the same Spirit (12:11). "The Lord is the Spirit" (2 Cor. 3:17), and the Spirit represents the activity of God in the lives of believers, since it is God who works all things in all persons (1 Cor. 12:6) and God who places gifts in the church (12:28). Consequently, one should not infer that the three figures do different things—

2. Unconvincing is R. Martin's (1984: 8) distinction that *charismata* is "the broader term describing all the manifestations of God's grace finding particular and concrete actualization," while *pneumatika* refers to the exercise of God's gift in the public worship. I regard the term *pneumatikos* in this letter to reflect a Corinthian bias that Paul seeks to correct. They used it to apply to persons who put on exhibitions of inspired speech in public worship.

the Spirit gives only grace-gifts, the Lord only services, and God only workings. Paul approaches these spiritual phenomena from three different perspectives (Schrage 1999: 141).

One can glean three points from these statements in 12:4–6. First, Paul's intent in listing these gifts in this way seems designed to reinforce the idea of variety (cf. Rom. 12:6). God is experienced in a variety of ways, and divine gifts should be expected to be multifaceted. Second, Paul affirms that all gifts come from the same divine source. There can be no distributions without the one who distributes them (1 Cor. 12:11); there can be no workings without the one who works them (12:6). Third, Paul is intent on broadening the Corinthians' understanding of spiritual gifts to include humbler forms of expression such as everyday acts of service. He designates the collection for the saints, for example, as a διακονία (2 Cor. 8:4; 9:1, 12–13; Rom. 15:31). Although the collection may seem less spectacular than some other manifestations of the Spirit, it is no less a sign of the Spirit's working in them. All of life in the church is charismatic and has its source in God's Spirit.

Paul now gives the basic thesis for this chapter (Fee 1987: 588; Gillespie 1994: 99): "To each one is given the manifestation of the Spirit for mutual benefit." The gifts are given to individuals so that they may benefit others and serve the whole body. In 12:8–10, he develops the statement "to each one is given" by the Spirit. In 12:12–26, he develops the meaning of the phrase "for mutual benefit."[3] **12:7**

Fee (1987: 589; see also Wolff 1996: 289) seeks to limit the meaning of ἕκαστος (hekastos, each one) so that it does not include every single person in the community. But the metaphor of the bodily members (12:12–26) suggests that Paul believes that each member (cf. 3:5, 13; 7:17) in the church has been given a gift and function. One may infer from this assertion that the Corinthians identify "the work of the Spirit with a particular manifestation and . . . claim special status on this basis" (Gillespie 1994: 11). Paul directs his argument against those "who claim an exclusive privilege of being pneumatic (cf. 3:1)" (R. Collins 1999: 453). He begins by undermining the presumption that some have a monopoly on the Spirit with the comment in 12:6 that God works all things in all persons (πᾶσιν, pasin [taken as masculine]; cf. Schrage 1999: 145). His point is that the Spirit works in each member but works differently in each member (12:29–30).

The successive terms "grace-gifts," "ministries," and "workings" in the previous verses are now subsumed under the umbrella term ἡ φανέρωσις τοῦ πνεύματος (hē phanerōsis tou pneumatos, the manifestation of the Spirit), which reveals that no special significance can be attached to its

---

3. It has nothing to do with any financial or other material gain.

different expressions. "Manifestation of the Spirit" could be a subjective genitive (the manifestation that the Spirit produces as author of these things) or an objective genitive (that which manifests the Spirit's presence). Dunn (1975: 212) thinks that Paul is deliberately vague because he means both: *The Spirit reveals himself* in the charismata." "Manifestation" ("disclosure") also makes clear that grace-gifts are not "some hidden talent or latent faculty, but a particular action or utterance which can be described as manifest or open, or which makes manifest, discloses" (Dunn 1975: 212). Paul is not talking about natural propensities or the potential within a person (contra Carson 1987: 21–22). The two may be related, but "they are not one and the same thing" (Soards 1999: 256). Something is exhibited that discloses the Spirit. In that regard, Baker (1974: 232) contends that the gifts listed should not be reckoned as "permanent abilities, but possible ways in which the Spirit may choose to work at a particular time in a particular individual."

The present tense δίδοται (*didotai*, is given) underscores the Spirit's abiding presence and the believer's complete dependence on the Spirit (Parry 1926: 179). The passive voice makes clear that the source is not the individual's own talents. It implies that no gift should be construed as evidence of spiritual accomplishment (Stendahl 1977: 123), and consequently no one should boast about them or use them to show off. A corollary is that no particular manifestation of a gift is a sign of spiritual underachievement.

The phrase πρὸς τὸ συμφέρον (*pros to sympheron*, with a view to benefiting) leaves indefinite who is to benefit (cf. 10:23, 33). The context in 12:12–26 makes clear that it refers to the common advantage (M. Mitchell 1993: 146; Thiselton 2000: 936). Three things should be noted. First, if the purpose of the gifts is for the common advantage, then no member is given anything that is not given to the whole body of Christ.[4] Grace-gifts are to be exercised for the well-being of the whole body. Dominy (1983: 52) states the idea succinctly: the gifts given are "designed for ministry, not for indulgence." In chapter 14, Paul will refine "benefit" further as "edification" of the body (14:3, 12). Second, gifts are not given to promote an individual's personal status. Persons should not regard themselves as "gifted," and the manifestations of the Spirit in their lives should not be used to augment their image, prestige, or station in the community or to downgrade another's. They should recognize that the source of these gifts comes from a sovereign power outside of them, and love should govern their usage so that the persons manifesting the gifts become Christlike. Third, Murphy-O'Connor (1998: 127) makes the

---

4. This does not mean that the individual so gifted may not also receive a benefit. Those speaking in tongues, for example, speak privately to God. They claim that this experience makes them better, more prayerful persons, which in turn contributes to the welfare of the body.

important point that it is dangerous to think of the "common good" in such a way that it is assumed to be superior to the good of an individual. Paul understands the mutual benefit to represent "the success of each member."[5]

In 12:8–10, Paul gives a sampling of gifts. He alternates the pronominal adjectives, ἕτερος (*heteros*) and ἄλλος (*allos*), which may point to an ordering feature. Although the classical distinction between ἕτερος (another of a different kind) and ἄλλος (another of the same kind) does not always hold true in Koine Greek, Paul may switch adjectives to divide the gifts into a threefold structure rather than simply to create stylistic variety (contra Barrett 1968: 285).[6] The pattern can be set forth as follows: **12:8–10**

> A (ᾧ μέν) to one a message of wisdom, (ἄλλῳ δέ) to another a message of knowledge
> B¹ (ἑτέρῳ) to another faith
> B² (ἄλλῳ δέ) to another gifts of healings
> B³ (ἄλλῳ δέ) to another powers to effect miracles
> B⁴ (ἄλλῳ [δέ]) to another prophecy
> B⁵ (ἄλλῳ [δέ]) to another discernment of spirits
> A′ (ἑτέρῳ) to another tongues, (ἄλλῳ δέ) to another interpretation of tongues

Gillespie (1994: 110–11) thinks that Paul purposefully highlighted "two types of inspired speech known to have been prominent among the Corinthians" in the first and the last groups.[7] Hays (1997: 211–12) sees the breakdown as (1) speech gifts that the Corinthians prized; (2) random supernatural gifts; and (3) tongues, the particular target of the discourse. Hays (1997: 212) concludes, "By ordering the list in this way, Paul implies that the gifts on which the Corinthians are fixated are by no means the only gifts operative in the church." It does appear from this letter that the first and the third groups, mentioning wisdom,

---

5. I question Calvin's (1960: 267) assertion, "Equality is therefore in conflict with the well-being of the body, because it gives rise to confusion, which in turn leads to disaster."

6. Fee (1987: 584 n. 9) contends that ἄλλος is the normal term in such lists.

7. One should not make too much of the change in prepositions (διά, *dia*, 12:8a; κατά, *kata*, 12:8b; and ἐν, *en*, 12:9). Paul may have felt that one preposition fit better with a particular gift, but it does not mean "that he intended thereby to designate distinct operations of the Spirit" (Carson 1987: 38–39). The different prepositions suggest that the Spirit is the *means*, the *measure* (Lindemann 2000: 266), and the *sphere* in which these gifts are given.

knowledge, and tongues, are particularly prominent in Corinth. They never appear in any other catalog of gifts in the NT.

It is also worthwhile to compare the three listings of the gifts in this chapter.

12:8–10	12:28	12:29–30
	ἀπόστολοι (*apostoloi*, apostles)	ἀπόστολοι
λόγος σοφίας (*logos sophias*, message of wisdom)	προφῆται (*prophētai*, prophets)	προφῆται
λόγος γνώσεως (*logos gnōseōs*, message of knowledge)	διδάσκαλοι (*didaskaloi*, teachers)	διδάσκαλοι
πίστις (*pistis*, faith)	δυνάμεις (*dynameis*, miracles)	δυνάμεις
χαρίσματα ἰαμάτων (*charismata iamatōn*, grace-gifts of healings)	χαρίσματα ἰαμάτων	χαρίσματα ἰαμάτων
ἐνεργήματα δυνάμεων (*energēmata dynameōn*, workings of miracles)		
	ἀντιλήμψεις (*antilēmpseis*, helpful deeds)	
	κυβερνήσεις (*kybernēseis*, acts of guidance)	
προφητεία (*prophēteia*, prophecy)		
διακρίσεις πνευμάτων (*diakriseis pneumatōn*, discernment of the spirits)		
γένη γλωσσῶν (*genē glōssōn*, kinds of tongues)	γένη γλωσσῶν	γλώσσαις λαλεῖν (*glōssais lalein*, to speak in tongues)
ἑρμηνεία γλωσσῶν (*hermēneia glōssōn*, interpretation of tongues)		διερμηνεύειν (*diermēneuein*, to interpret)

It is not Paul's purpose to identify the precise nature of the gifts, but we can discern the following from these lists.[8] First, Paul assumes that "healings, miracles, and revelatory speech" are "everyday occurrences within this Spirit-endowed community" and not something abnormal (Carson 1987: 37). Second, the list is not intended to be exhaustive or complete, since it varies from the lists in Rom. 12:6–8 and Eph. 4:11. Third, the categories overlap and illuminate each other (Lietzmann 1949: 61; Dominy 1983: 52). Fourth, the list contains a "mixture of what some might label 'natural' and 'supernatural' endowments, or 'spectacular' and 'more ordinary' gifts," though Paul does not make such dis-

8. With the exception of the gifts related to tongues, these gifts were manifest in the ministry of Jesus.

tinctions (Carson 1987: 37). Gifts do not need to be spectacular to be manifestations of the Spirit. Finally, the list was created ad hoc to meet the specific situation at Corinth. These are typical gifts relevant to Corinth (Fee 1987: 585; Gillespie 1994: 105). Most are related to speech (six of the nine if discernment of the spirits is an evaluation of speech). Tongues and their interpretations are listed last, which basically subordinates them to the other gifts.[9] Carson (1987: 37) compares its placement to Judas Iscariot's coming last in every listing of the disciples and concludes, "Even if Paul does not consider tongues to be the least of the spiritual gifts on some absolute scale, it is highly likely he makes it the last entry in each list in 1 Corinthians because his readers were far too prone to exalt this one gift." A corollary is that the most important gifts are placed first (Hurd 1965: 192; Gillespie 1994: 107). The message of knowledge and of wisdom is closely related to the message delivered by apostles (2:6–7, 11–16; 2 Cor. 11:6), prophets (1 Cor. 13:2), and teachers (14:6, 26). It is this ministry of the word that most benefits the church and strengthens its mission to the world.

Wisdom and knowledge apparently are of particular interest to the Corinthians. The message of wisdom (λόγος σοφίας) differs from "the persuasive art of wisdom" (πειθοὶ σοφίας λόγοι, peithoi sophias logoi; 2:4, 13). Wisdom is the "God-given insight into the mysterious purposes and workings of God in and through Jesus Christ" (Soards 1999: 258; cf. also Schatzmann 1987: 36; Schrage 1999: 149) and, in particular, recognizes the activity of God in the crucified Christ. Dunn (1975: 221; see also Schrage 1999: 150) notes that wisdom and knowledge are not in themselves charismata. It is only the message that reveals wisdom and knowledge to others that qualifies as a charisma. The message of knowledge (λόγος γνώσεως; cf. 14:6; 15:2) may comprise such things as the affirmation that idols have no existence (8:4). It also comprises insight into what God is doing in the world (2:12–16).

Since "faith" (πίστις) is not given to everyone, it must refer to a special endowment and not saving trust that is required of all Christians.[10] In the immediate context, it appears to be related to miracles—for example, the faith to move mountains (13:2). Dunn (1977: 211) considers it to be a "mysterious surge of confidence which sometimes arises within a man in a particular situation of need or challenge and which gives him an otherly certainty and assurance that God is about to act through word or through an action (such as laying hands on someone sick)." Internal trust in God results in external results.

9. So Wendland 1972: 95; Héring 1962: 129; Barrett 1968: 286; Baker 1974: 229; Conzelmann 1975: 209; Gillespie 1994: 106.

10. Robertson and Plummer 1914: 266; Lietzmann 1949: 61; Barrett 1968: 285; Bruce 1971: 119; Conzelmann 1975: 209; Dunn 1977: 211; Fee 1987: 593; Wischmeyer 1981: 73; R. Collins 1999: 454.

It is possible that "faith" stands at the head of this next grouping of gifts because they depend especially on the power of faith (Edwards 1885: 313). Healings and miracles plainly are related to faith (Matt. 16:8; 21:21; Mark 5:34; 10:52; 11:2; Luke 17:5–6; Acts 3:16; 27:25; Heb. 11:29–30; James 5:15), and Paul says that prophecy is given "in proportion to faith" (Rom. 12:6). We may assume that discerning the spirits also takes root in faith.

"Grace-gifts of healings" (χαρίσματα ἰαμάτων) is the only item in the list specifically identified as a *charisma*, perhaps to distinguish it from cures coming from the medical arts. It does not refer to the power to heal all diseases but to instances of actual healing (Dunn 1975: 211). At various times, individuals become agents of God's healing power in another's life. Carson (1987: 40) thinks that the plurals are noteworthy and perhaps signal diversity within the gift. Carson (1987: 39) wisely cautions against the institutionalizing of gifts: "If a Christian has been granted the χάρισμα (*charisma*) to heal one particular individual of one particular disease at one time, that Christian should not presume to think that *the* gift of healing has been bestowed on him or her, prompting the founding of 'a healing ministry.'" Healing is not "an end in itself" (Schatzmann 1987: 37), and Paul does not expect them to set up a rival Asclepieum in Corinth, dedicated to Christ, to siphon business away from this flourishing healing cult. Acts records Paul healing a lame man in Lystra (14:8–10), the father of his host on the island of Malta, and then all those who had diseases and came to him to be cured (28:7–9). Acts also reports the healing powers in his work aprons and handkerchiefs (19:11–12; cf. 20:7–11). But Paul did not regard himself as a healer and apparently was not always able to cure others. He laments that Epaphroditus was at death's door (Phil. 2:27) and does not report healing him. According to 2 Tim. 4:20, he left Trophimus ill in Miletus.

"Powers to effect miracles" (ἐνεργήματα δυνάμεων) overlap with healings, but not all miracles are healings. Again, the *-ma* suffix refers to the "result of the action." It refers to the actualization of God's power in mighty deeds (cf. 2 Cor. 12:12; Gal. 3:5; Morris 1958: 166; Gillespie 1994: 101). Paul also warns that the "lawless one" will come according to the working (ἐνέργεια, *energeia*) of Satan and will work miracles (δύναμις, *dynamis*) (2 Thess. 2:9). One needs to discern whether a wondrous deed stems from God or from Satan.

The nature of "prophecy" (προφητεία) is much debated among recent scholars (see Dautzenberg 1975; D. Hill 1979; Grudem 1982; Aune 1983; Gillespie 1994; Forbes 1995), but I take it to be the declaration of God's will to the people. Origen defines prophecy as "meaningful knowledge of unseen things through speech," which is taught to others (Jenkins 1909: 36). Friedrich (*TDNT* 6:848) defines it as "the inspired speech of charismatic preachers through whom God's plan of salvation for the world and the community and His will for the life of individual Christians are made known. The prophet knows something of the divine mysteries (13:2)." The prophet declares a word of revelation, which Paul regards as the most important gift for the community worship (14:1, 5). It need not consist only of a disclosure of future events (cf. Agabus, Acts 11:28) but can also address the contemporary situation in ways that bring encouragement and comfort (1 Cor. 14:3), that bring others under conviction (14:25), and that summon them to repentance (Rev. 11:3). Thiselton (2000: 964) concludes that prophecy "combines pastoral insight into the needs of persons, communities, and situations with the ability to address these with a God-given utterance or longer discourse (whether unprompted or prepared with judgment, decision, and rational reflection) leading to challenge or comfort, judgment or consolation, but ultimately building up the addressees." Since Christians understood the prophecy of Joel 2:28–29 to have been fulfilled, Fee (1987: 595) concludes that prophecy was "potentially . . . available to all, since all now possessed the Spirit in fullness (Acts 2:17–18)." The Spirit is poured out on all, sons and daughters, young men and old men, slaves, men and women, who will prophesy.

"Discernment of the spirits" (διακρίσεις πνευμάτων) is closely related to prophecy as its auxiliary, since prophecy needs checks (Deut. 13:1–3; 1 Kings 22:19–28; Jer. 28; Matt. 24:24; 1 Thess. 5.20–21; 2 Thess. 2:1–2; 1 Tim. 4:1; 2 Pet. 2:1–2; 1 John 4:1; Did. 11:8). Dautzenberg's (1971; 1975: 122–48) view that this refers to interpreting and explaining the revelations of the Spirit has been carefully refuted by Grudem (1982: 263–88). Dunn (1975: 234) identifies it as "an evaluation, an investigating, a testing, a weighing of the prophetic utterance." The verb form διακρίνειν (*diakrinein*) appears in 1 Cor. 14:29 in connection with weighing what a prophet has said. R. Collins (1999: 455), among others, connects it to discerning true prophecy from false. This gift enables one to ascertain whether someone is preaching "another gospel" (Gal. 1:6) or "another Jesus" (2 Cor. 11:4), but with the Corinthian zeal "for spirits" (1 Cor. 14:12)—that is, manifestations of the Spirit—discernment of all kinds is necessary. "Discernment" brings out the mutual interdependence of the gifts (Dunn 1998: 556). Prophecy, in Paul's estimation, is the most valuable for building up the church, but it requires testing and evaluation, just as tongues, the least valuable gift for building up the church, requires interpretation.

The subject in question, or as Fee (1987: 591) labels it, "the problem child," is placed at the bottom of the list, in the third grouping, "many kinds of tongues" (γένη γλωσσῶν) and their interpretation (ἑρμηνεία γλωσσῶν). The nature of tongues is also much debated (see Currie 1965 and the bibliography compiled by Mills 1985). What is undeniable is that Paul considers it to be a natural part of Christian experience, though not an experience of everyone. What he says about tongues in the context of chapters 12–14 should control our conclusions.[11]

First, Paul understands it to be a language inspired by the Spirit and not a noncognitive, nonlanguage utterance. It is not simply incoherent babbling in the Spirit (Schrage 1999: 161). "Language" is the most natural meaning of the word γλῶσσα and best explains how tongues can be differentiated into various kinds (γένη). The phrase "tongues of men and of angels" in 13:1 can refer only to some kind of language. In 14:21, Paul understands Isa. 28:11–12, with its reference to "other tongues" (foreign languages), to be analogous to the tongues experience at Corinth. Tongues consist of words (λόγοι, *logoi*), which, though indecipherable, are not meaningless syllables strung together (1 Cor. 14:19).

Second, Paul understands these utterances to be addressed to God (14:2, 14, 28) and not to humans (14:2, 6, 9). It is not a language of normal human discourse, but something mysterious and "other," which may give it its appeal. It consists of "mysteries in the Spirit" that are unintelligible to humans (14:2) and that benefit only the speaker (14:4). It communicates with God through prayer and praise (14:15) in ways that analytical speech do not. Paul compares it to the indistinct sounds of a musical instrument that are garbled to the listener (14:8). The phrase "if I came to you speaking in tongues" in 14:6 recalls his description of his first preaching in Corinth (2:1, "and when I came to you"). The implication is that had he come speaking in tongues, he would have had no success as an apostle.

This rules out the view that tongues refer to the miraculous ability to speak in unlearned languages (contra Gundry 1966; Forbes 1995) or to speak in one's native language (Zerhusen 1997).[12] Corinth was a cosmopolitan seaport with a transient, multilingual population, and so if Paul came speaking in tongues, in a non-Greek or non-Latin language, he surely would have been able to communicate with someone. Since he makes reference to foreign languages, loosely quoting Isa. 28:11–12, as an analogy to explain tongues in 1 Cor. 14:10–11, he must consider it not to be identical with a foreign language but only something akin to it (Dunn 1975: 244; Fee 1987: 598). Esler (1994: 45) reminds us how odd

11. The analysis of Forbes (1995) shows that ecstatic and oracular phenomena in Hellenistic religions are inadequate parallels to understand the tongues experience of the Corinthians (see also Carson 1987: 80–81).

12. If this is someone blurting out praise or prayer to God during the worship in his or her own native language, it is hard to understand how Paul would classify it as a special grace-gift or why he would think that the individual needed to pray to God for the power to interpret (14:13). If glossolalists are unable to translate from their own native language, they are probably unable to understand anything spoken in the assembly, and one wonders why they are present. It is also hard to imagine why Paul would boast about his linguistic prowess in foreign languages by thanking God that he speaks in tongues more than all of them (14:18).

it would have been to a first-century speaker of Greek to use γλῶσσα in the sense of a language or dialect without it being modified by an adjective meaning "foreign." Esler also notes that since the interpretation of tongues is something that can be prayed for (14:13), it cannot refer to the ability to translate a foreign language, "which one obtains through instruction and practice." Paul also does not urge them to use it as a help in evangelism but expects it to arise only in their assemblies. He himself uses the gift only privately (14:18). Apparently, it offers no help to him in spreading the gospel. Best (1975: 57) labels it an "idiolect" (a language peculiar to one person, as opposed to a dialect), and D. Martin (1991: 548) labels it "esoteric speech acts."

Third, because of the reference to "the tongues of angels" in 13:1, many think that it is something like an angelic language.[13] The Testament of Job (an Egyptian Jewish text dating from the first century B.C. or first century A.D.) offers a reasonable parallel. Job bequeaths to his daughters a miraculous belt that had cured him. When they put it on, they took on a new heart and spoke in a heavenly language that is described as an "angelic dialect" (48:2), "the dialect of the archons" (49:2), "the dialect of those on high" (50:1), "the dialect of the cherubim" (50:2), and a "distinctive dialect" (52:7). Tertullian (*De anima* [*The Soul*] 9) refers to a woman who receives ecstatic visions and converses with angels. Later rabbinic tradition also attributes to Johanan ben Zakkai the ability to understand the language of angels because of his great learning and piety (see *b. B. Bat.* 134a; *b. Sukkah* 28a). The evidence that tongues was understood by the Corinthians as some kind of angelic speech remains inconclusive, but if it was such, then speaking in tongues would be a sign of participation in higher spiritual realms (cf. 2 Cor. 12:4).

Fourth, the rational mind is not engaged (1 Cor. 14:14), but that does not necessitate that this speech is irrational or that the person has lost control (see the discussion on 14:14). Nowhere does Paul refer to the mental state of the speaker, and he does not use a Greek word that implies some ecstatic state or trance. It is an expression of profound emotion from the deepest recesses of the soul that can be vocalized in prayer (14:2, 14, 28), singing, praise, and perhaps the "sighs too deep for words" (Rom. 8:26). Paul says that a stranger who wandered into the assembly and found everyone speaking in tongues might think that they all were crazy, but that does not necessarily mean that all are in a frenzy (contra Theissen 1987: 281; see comments on 1 Cor. 14:20–25). The instructions for regulating tongues in 14:28–29 assume that glos-

---

13. Barrett 1968: 299–300; Dautzenberg 1971; Dunn 1975: 244; Ellis 1978: 70–71; Fee 1987: 598–99; D. Martin 1991: 574; Witherington 1995: 258; Wolff 1996: 293–94; Hays 1997: 212; R. Collins 1999: 456; Schrage 1999: 159. Thiselton (2000: 973) considers this the least plausible view; see also Grudem 1982: 120–29.

solalists are in control of their faculties. Forbes (1995) shows that referring to tongues as "ecstatic utterance" is misleading (cf. Thiselton 2000: 980).

Fifth, speaking in tongues appears to have been a high-status indicator for the Corinthians. D. Martin (1991: 547–50) asks how speaking in tongues relates to other status issues at Corinth and makes the case that we should not read the marginal status of contemporary glossolalia back into the first-century church and assume that the Corinthian glossolalists were the lower-status church members. D. Martin (1991: 561) contends that in Corinth glossolalia bestowed high status on the speaker, since "esoteric speech seems almost always to be the property of leaders within the group." Only in "modern 'scientific' cultures" does the status of the one speaking in tongues become questionable (D. Martin 1991: 558). The problem with tongues, then, is not only its unintelligibility but also its contribution to the conflict between those of higher and of lower status in the church. This social divide is intensified if glossolalia is also perceived as a sign of superior spirituality. Paul again encourages those of higher status to act out of love and alter their behavior for the sake of the members of lower status so as to maintain unity (D. Martin 1991: 579).

Sixth, if one "kind" of tongue applies to the unspeakable groanings—sighs too deep for words—in which the Spirit intercedes in Rom. 8:26–27 (Stendahl 1977: 111; cf. Macchia 1992), it offers new insights into Paul's understanding of this phenomenon. Käsemann (1971: 134) contends that far from being a "sign that the Christian community has been translated with Christ into heavenly existence (the view taken by the Corinthian enthusiasts), the apostle (Paul) hears in these things the groans of those who, though called to liberty, still lie tempted and dying and cry to be born again with the new creation." Tongues, from this perspective, are a sign of weakness, not spiritual superiority. We do not know how to pray except with unspeakable groans, and the Spirit comes to our aid. As a token of our weakness, it explains why tongues will end (1 Cor. 13:8). Dunn (1988a: 493) thinks it unlikely that Paul has glossolalia in mind when he speaks of inarticulate groaning, but comments that if glossolalia was "recognized as something undignifying, something beneath man's self-respect as a rational being (cf. 1 Cor. 14:20)," then it would "be of a similar order to the wordless groaning," expressing "human helplessness, ignorance, and inarticulateness."

The "interpretation of tongues" is a necessary companion to tongues, as discerning the spirits is to prophecy. It is not a word-for-word translation but more likely an interpretation of the meaning of what was said, the "mysteries" spoken to God, or an explanation of the experience. Thiselton (1979; 2000: 976) argues that it means to put into articulate speech, not to translate. It could simply "amount to nothing more than the first utterance in the vernacular which followed an utterance in a tongue" (Dunn 1975: 248). According to T. Job 51:3–4, Nereus, Job's brother, wrote out the magnificent things of God that he heard as Job conversed with an angel.

Paul recapitulates the main point from verse 7, repeating the same words, "work" (ἐνεργεῖ, *energei*; cf. 12:6), "distributing" (διαιροῦν, *diairoun*; cf. 12:4), "to each one" (ἑκάστῳ, *hekastō*; cf. 12:7), and "the same Spirit" (τὸ αὐτὸ πνεῦμα, *to auto pneuma*; cf. 12:4), which brackets this unit. We can deduce the following conclusions from this summary statement:

12:11

1. The Spirit is sovereign in distributing the gifts (cf. Heb. 2:4).
2. The credit for these gifts belongs solely to the Spirit (the two definite articles, "*the* one and *the* same," are emphatic). Christians do not possess anything that they are not given.
3. No single person has all these gifts. No one can be venerated as an ideal Christian, and no gift makes one more spiritual than another. Doughty (1975: 90) identifies "the fundamental fallacy of the Corinthians" as "their audacious assumption that the spirit is a possession which one individual can appropriate to exalt himself against his neighbor."
4. The Spirit works in every Christian in the community (to each one his or her own [ἰδίᾳ, *idia*] gift).
5. The Spirit ensures that there will be a diversity of gifts. M. Mitchell (1993: 268) comments, "The differences between members are not only natural, but have in fact been divinely ordained and sanctioned."

C. The Diversity and Interdependence of Members of the Body (12:12–31)

Paul now develops the second point of his statement in 12:7, "the manifestation of the Spirit is given *for mutual benefit* [πρὸς τὸ συμφέρον, *pros to sympheron*]" by enlisting the analogy of the human body. Paul previously has referred to the Corinthian church as a field (3:5–9) and a building (3:9–15) in dealing with their division, and now he draws on a familiar and easily understood metaphor about the body with its many limbs and organs to address the problem of "the narrowness and uniformity of the Corinthians' view of the operation of the Spirit" (Hurd 1965: 191). His main concern is how their distorted view of spiritual gifts contributes to their lack of social cohesion. The elitist regard for some of the manifestations of the Spirit has exacerbated their disunity. To rebut this notion, he insists that all have been immersed in the one Spirit into the body of Christ, which he likens to a complex, living organism. The first three verses (12:12–14) give the theological basis for the body imagery that is developed in the rest of the section. This body is not an agglomeration of autonomous body parts but a symbiotic whole. Snyder (1992: 169–70) summarizes the point: "Each part of the body takes its meaning from being a functional body member. A collection of arms, legs, and torsos does not create a body." In 12:15–19, Paul develops the analogy that the body is made up of many different parts, not one. In 12:20–26, he emphasizes that although the body has many parts, it is nonetheless one body. Diversity is necessary for a body to function, but the body is unified as each member is interrelated and interdependent. In 12:27–30, he concludes with a list of functions in the church and a series of rhetorical questions expecting the answer no: "Not all are apostles, are they?" and so on. He confirms the need for diversity (as opposed to hierarchy) for the body to function properly.

Paul is not articulating his doctrine of the church but addressing a specific problem of disunity in a particular community (see M. Mitchell 1993: 161). It is a mistake to think that he finishes dealing with the problem of factions in chapters 1–4 and then moves on to other topics. Mitchell shows that he addresses the scourge of factionalism throughout the entire letter. Here he seeks to correct the elite's overemphasis on certain conspicuous gifts that they felt set them apart and above the rest of the members. It deepened their disunity. Carson (1987: 41–42) concludes that Paul seeks

> to prevent them from making any one gift the sine qua non, the sign without which one might legitimately call in question whether the Holy Spirit was present and active. Christians may pursue what is best of the χαρίσματα (*charismata*); but they have no right to any particular one, and must ultimately trust the wisdom of their heavenly Father's gracious distribution through the mediation of his Holy Spirit.

The body metaphor was readily understandable as a common motif in political oratory and useful to underscore the folly of the Corinthians' fragmentation as a community. The argument emphasizes the interrelationships of bodily members to ridicule these rifts. Paul seeks to impress upon them the need for solidarity and to persuade them to show loving concern for the less honored members. He also emphasizes that diversity in the body is something divinely implanted and therefore necessary. If any think that they are so gifted that they can do without others, he calls them back to a renewed sense of community. One person alone, no matter how gifted, cannot play a Beethoven symphony, act a Shakespearian tragedy, or compete against another team. The same is true in the church. It can never be a solo performance.

The structure of this unit follows an ABB′A′ pattern:

A The body as one but with many members (12:12–14)
   B The inescapable diversity of members within the body (12:15 20)
   B′ The inescapable interdependence of members of the body (12:21–26)
A′ The differing functions within the body (12:27–31)

Exegesis and Exposition

[12]For just as the body is one and has many members and all the members of the body, though many, are [part of] one body, so also is Christ. [13]For indeed, we were all baptized in one Spirit into one body, whether Jews or Greeks, whether slaves or free, and all were given one Spirit to drink. [14]For indeed, the body is not one member but many.

[15]If the foot says, "Because I am not a hand, I am not [part of] the body," it is not for this reason not [a part] of the body. [16]And if the ear says, "Because I am not an eye, I am not [part of] the body," it is not for this reason not [a part] of the body. [17]For if the whole body were an eye, where would be the [faculty of] hearing? Where would be the sense of smell? [18]But as a matter of fact, God

arranged the members, every single one of them, in the body just as he pleased. [19]But if they are all one member, where is the body? [20]But as a matter of fact, there are many members and one body.

[21]The eye is not able to say to the hand, "I have no need of you!" Or again, the head [is not able to say] to the feet, "I have no need of you!" [22]But the parts of the body that seem to be much weaker are all the more necessary. [23]And what we think to be the less honorable [members of the body], these we invest with the greater honor, and our unpresentable parts receive greater presentability. [24]Our presentable [members of the body] do not have [this] need. But God composed the body giving greater honor to the lacking members [25]in order that there might not be division in the body but that the members might have the same concern for one another. [26]And if one member suffers, all the members suffer with it. If one member is glorified, all the members rejoice together with it.

[27]But you are [the] body of Christ and members each as a part. [28]And God placed these in the church: first apostles, second prophets, third teachers, then miraculous deeds, then grace-gifts of healings, helpful deeds, acts of guidance, kinds of tongues. [29]All are not apostles, are they? All are not prophets, are they? All are not teachers, are they? All are not miracle [workers], are they? [30]All do not have grace-gifts of healings, do they? All do not speak in tongues, do they? All do not interpret [tongues], do they?

[31]But eagerly desire the greater grace-gifts. And moreover, I will show you an incomparable way.

12:12–14 Paul introduces the body metaphor by reference to the Corinthians' baptism and their immersion in the Spirit. The clause "so also is Christ" is awkward only because "Christ" is shorthand for the church as the body of Christ (12:28). He leaves it to the reader to complete the thought: Just as the body has many limbs and organs and despite their number and differences make up one body, so Christ's body has many limbs and organs and despite their number and differences make up one body. The mention of Christ in this context recalls his first question in the letter, "Is Christ divided?" (1:13). This section continues his argument against the Corinthians' damaging factionalism (M. Mitchell 1993: 157–64). He pictures the church not as a body of Christians but as the body of Christ. There is unity in plurality, but not uniformity. Individual integrity remains. Soards (1999: 263) observes that Paul's point is not unity in diversity and diversity in unity, as many have it, but rather "unity dominates diversity and makes diversity genuinely meaningful and constructive."

In 12:13, Paul explains how "we" (he includes himself) as many different individuals are all part of this one body of Christ. We were all baptized in the one Spirit into one body and were all given one Spirit to drink (cf. Gal. 3:26–28). The "all" is repeated for emphasis, and the basis of their unity is their common experience of the one Spirit. Baptism recalls, again, one of his opening questions about their disunity, "Were you baptized into the name of Paul?" (1 Cor. 1:13). What he means by baptism here is not clear. He could have in mind "water baptism," which took place at conversion, or a figurative Spirit baptism, which occurred when the new convert is immersed in the Spirit. If he refers to water baptism, then the phrase ἐν ἑνὶ πνεύματι (*en heni pneumati*) is instrumental, "by one Spirit."[1] If he refers to a Spirit baptism, then they were baptized in the sphere of the Spirit. The two views are not mutually exclusive. The point is that every Christian has been made a part of one body and immersed in (or by) the Spirit.

The meaning of the phrase all "were given to drink one Spirit" (ἒν πνεῦμα ἐποτίσθημεν, *hen pneuma epotisthēmen*) is even more difficult.[2] Paul uses this verb to mean "to give to drink" in 3:2. Because of the language of "drinking," some contend that it is an allusion to the Lord's Supper (cf. 10:1–4, and the reference to "spiritual drink"; Calvin 1960: 265–66; possibly Conzelmann 1975: 212 n. 17). Nowhere in the NT is it assumed, however, that one "drinks" the Holy Spirit at the Lord's Supper. Fee (1987: 604–5) proposes that 12:13 is a piece of Semitic parallelism whereby both clauses about the Spirit make the same point. Others connect it to OT prophecies of the Spirit's being poured out on the people (Isa. 29:10; Ezek. 36:25–27; Joel 2:28), since Paul uses the image of the love of God being poured out on believers through the Holy Spirit (Rom. 5:5). John's Gospel draws on this imagery and uses "water" as a symbol for the Spirit (John 4:10, 14; 7:37–39). The verb ποτίζειν (*potizein*) can also mean "to water" (1 Cor. 3:6).[3] Carson (1987: 46) renders it, "'We were all drenched' or 'we were all flooded' in one Spirit." Hays (1997: 214) notes that "the metaphor of 'being baptized in the Holy Spirit' elsewhere in early Christian tradition (Matt. 3:11; Mark 1:8; Luke 3:16; John 1:33; Acts 1:5) suggests that it should be distinguished from water baptism rather than simply identified with it." The problem with this view is that ἐν πνεῦμα is not in the dative case, which one would expect if this view were correct (cf. Isa 29:10 LXX). Whatever the specifics of Paul's analogy, the point is that the Spirit saturates the church body and that all Christians are imbued with the same Spirit. It occurs at their conversion when they confess Jesus as Lord and are placed by the Spirit in Christ's body, in which they become interdependent limbs and organs.

---

1. Many think that the reference to Jews and Greeks, and slaves and free, reflects a vestigial baptismal confession (Gal. 3:28; Col. 3:10–11; see Bouttier 1976–77).

2. Cottle (1974) contends that the first clause refers to a water baptism at conversion and the second clause to a Spirit baptism at a later time, but Paul understands the experience of the Spirit to mark the beginning of the Christian life (Gal. 3:2–3).

3. Cuming (1980–81) argues that the phrase refers to baptism by "affusion," which was practiced at Corinth. It was viewed as conveying the gift of the Holy Spirit. This view is successfully challenged by Rogers (1983).

The question raised by interpreters, "Is the church constituted by this accumulation of believers, or is the church a divinely constituted entity, i.e. the Body of Christ, before anyone ever believes?" (Ruef 1977: 134), is tangential to Paul's concerns. His image implies that baptism incorporates people into the body of Christ; it does not create it (Carson 1987: 44). He also is not making a statement about a "mystical truth" but making a simple comparison with a physical body (contra Lietzmann 1949: 62). Fee (1987: 602 n. 13) perceptively comments, "Much of the theological discussion of the metaphor, as to whether Paul is concerned with some 'mystical' truth of the church as a living organism, is quite irrelevant. For Paul it is a metaphor pure and simple, whose point is not the nature of the church per se but the need for it to experience its proper diversity in unity" (see also Yorke 1991: 29–50; Kirchhoff 1994: 154–56).

The purpose of this experience of the Spirit is to form the Corinthians into one body (Fee 1987: 606). The εἰς ἓν σῶμα (eis hen sōma, into one body) represents the goal (Findlay 1910: 890; Robertson and Plummer 1914: 272; Lindemann 2000: 271). Baptism washes away the ethnic and sociological barricades that previously separated and alienated them. It may seem surprising in a discussion of the diversity of gifts that Paul brings up the issue of their social diversity, but this is not simply a vestige of a baptismal confession, because their social stratification is a contributing factor in their division. Racial prejudice and social stereotypes are supposed to be submerged and put to death in baptism, but all too frequently these evils survive the experience, dry themselves off, and form cankers on the body.

Many note the absence of the pair "male and female" from the formula (cf. Gal. 3:28), and some scholars think that Paul omitted them deliberately because he did not want to feed the Corinthians' attempts to transcend sex and gender distinctions that some commentators perceive behind some of the problems in the church (Wolff 1996: 298–99; Hays 1997: 214; R. Horsley 1998: 172). It is more likely that "male and female" are omitted (cf. 1 Cor. 7:21) because the primary division in the church was sociological. Paul affirms that in Christ—and only in Christ—are these ethnic and sociological differences negated. What may polarize the world does not or should not divide the church. The segmentation of the Corinthian congregation into cliques is the by-product of human depravity that spurs individuals to treat their differing spiritual experiences as a pretext for reinstating class divisions—now employing spiritual classifications—so as to elevate themselves over others.

The body analogy was familiar in Stoic philosophy, in which the unity of the cosmos was likened to a body. It also appears in ancient political theory, which compared the city-state to a body. M. Mitchell

(1993: 268–69) argues that the image is an "exact correlative of its Greco-Roman counterparts not only in its details, but especially its application: to demonstrate the interrelatedness of all members in one body politic in order to urge concord and end factionalism."[4] A. Hill (1980) and Murphy-O'Connor (1983: 165, 167) question whether Paul's metaphor of the church as a body derives from the Greek philosophical reflections on the body politic and suggest instead that it was provoked by Paul's reaction to one of the striking features of the temples dedicated to the healing god, Asclepius, widely scattered across the Mediterranean world. Murphy-O'Connor notes the discovery in Corinth of "a huge number of terracotta ex-votos, representing heads, hands and feet, arms and legs, breasts and genitals, eyes and ears"—afflicted members that the god was entreated to heal. Murphy-O'Connor (1983: 167) concludes, "Against this background Paul would have seen the dismembered limbs displayed in the Asclepion as symbols of everything that Christians should *not* be: 'dead,' divided, unloving and unloved." These disconnected body parts were useless and dead apart from the body to which they belonged. The sight of sundered clay pieces encouraged him to view Christian life as one of shared existence in a living body.

This background is interesting but reveals only that the image of the body may have evoked a variety of associations in his hearers. If Paul adopted it from his culture, he has adjusted it to fit his own purposes and theology (see M. Barth 1958). He is not interested in the cosmos or the city-state, but a local congregation. Since Calvin (1960: 264), many cite the memorable fable in a speech delivered by Menenius Agrippa in 494 B.C. (Livy, *History of Rome* 2.32.9–12), which compares the state to the human body.[5] He uses the analogy to exhort the plebs to stop their sedition and submit to the rule of the patricians:[6]

> In the days when man's members did not all agree amongst themselves, as is now the case, but each had its own ideas and a voice of its own, the other parts thought it unfair that they should have the worry and the trouble and the labour of providing for the belly, . . . they therefore conspired together that the hands should carry no food to the mouth, nor the mouth accept anything that was given it, nor the teeth grind up what was received. While they sought this in an angry spirit to starve the belly into submission, the members themselves and the whole body were reduced

4. See Seneca, *Ep. morales* 95.52; Epictetus, *Diatr.* 2.10.3–4; Dio Chrysostom, *Or.* 34.22–23; 39.5–8; 41.1–3; 50.3–4; Marcus Aurelius, *Meditations* 2.1; 7.13.

5. It is probably more familiar to commentators than it was to the original recipients of the letter.

6. The illustration is also found in Xenophon, *Mem.* 2.13.18; Cicero, *De officiis* 3.5.22; Plutarch, *Marcius Coriolanus* 6; Dionysius of Halicarnassus, *Antiquitates romanae* 6.86 [6.83.2].

to utmost weakness. Hence it had become clear that even the belly had no idle task to perform, and was no more nourished than it nourished the rest. . . . Drawing a parallel from this to show how like was the internal dissension of the bodily members to the anger of the plebs against the Fathers, he prevailed upon the minds of his hearers.

The plebs' rebellion does not damage the belly but the whole body. The speech worked, and the city returned to harmony. Comparison with this fable puts Paul's point in sharp relief. He is not fearful that the inferior members might rise up in revolt but is concerned about the pride of the so-called superior members (Héring 1962: 130). His use of the body metaphor turns things upside down. Rather than urging the weak to stop their unruly behavior and to give due honor and respect to the strong, "Paul urges the strong (probably the well-to-do) to give more honor and respect to the weak, and so cease their fractious behavior" (Witherington 1995: 253–54; Hays 1997: 213).

12:15–20 In 12:15–20, Paul fancifully addresses the envy or the disdain that one member of the body might have for another. A foot says, "Because I am not a hand, I am not a part of the body," or an ear says, "Because I am not an eye, I am not a part of the body." The response οὐ παρὰ τοῦτο (*ou para touto*, literally, "not along this") is an idiom meaning "not for that reason" (Moule 1960: 51). The "this" may refer to what the member says, but Paul is not interested in the personal feelings of the dejected member. He is concerned with the facts of the matter (Ruef 1977: 135). The double negative (οὐ παρὰ τοῦτο οὐκ ἔστιν, *ou para touto ouk estin*) strengthens the affirmative: "not for that reason any the less." No matter what ears and feet might say if they could talk, they are integrally part of the body. Note that the ear does not say that it wants to be an eye, and the foot does not say that it wants to become a hand. Both assume that they are unimportant in comparison, but both have their assigned position in the body. Grace sets a limit on what a Christian may aspire to attain (Käsemann 1964: 76–77).

The fablelike conversation has clear allegorical features. Paul shows sensitivity to those who were made to feel that they had received no special spiritual gift. He encourages the "'unglorious members' that they are not any less part of the body than the glorious" (M. Mitchell 1993: 269). For example, ears that constantly hear someone say how beautiful the eyes are can easily get the idea that they are inconsequential, and the eyes can easily get the idea that they are all-important. But both eyes and ears, hands and feet, have their assigned function in the body, without which the body becomes disabled. The failure of one little valve can shut down the whole bodily system. The implication is that there is no unimportant gift or person in the body of Christ.

In 12:17, Paul carries the whimsy further. What if the whole body were an eye? This freakish object would have no sense of smell, no faculty of hearing, no way to perambulate except to roll around, no way to feed itself or to digest. A well-functioning body requires a multiplicity of members with a multiplicity of functions. The application may or not have been obvious to the Corinthians. A church full of only glossolalists would be no less freakish. It would quickly shrivel up and die from the loss of its other senses and its lack of nourishment. Stendahl (1977: 128) makes a contemporary application: "The fullness of the church cannot be better ridiculed than by the habit, long established, according to which every denomination or sect takes its gift of the Spirit and builds a special little chapel around it."

The νυνὶ δέ in 12:18 (cf. 12:20) introduces the real situation after an unreal conditional clause: "but as a matter of fact," God made the body with its intricately interconnected parts so that it could perform at its optimum in this world. The diversity is not only necessary for the body to function; it is the will of God. The conclusion is obvious that no single body part can claim to be the essence of the body, and no single bodily function can be considered the only legitimate manifestation of the body's life. The application may not be so obvious. Members of the body should accept humbly their gifts without pretentiously flaunting them, belittling another's, or envying another's. As Baker (1974: 232) puts it, "Just as not every member of the human body is expected to have the gift of hearing, so not every member of the body of Christ is expected to have the gifts of prophecy and speaking in tongues."

12:21–26 Paul continues with the fancy of speaking body parts to illustrate how foolish it would be for the eye to say to the hand, or the head to the feet, "I have no need of you." This verbalizes the actual attitude of some Corinthians toward their brothers and sisters that Paul seeks to change (R. Horsley 1998: 172). "Eye" and "head" are transparent metaphors for those in leadership roles, who are likely to be more affluent and better educated. The "hands" and "feet" represent the laboring class or slaves. "Eyes" and "heads" in the church always get special treatment and then begin to think that they are special. A sense of superiority can breed notions of self-sufficiency (Oster 1995: 304), since those who think that they are all-important can imagine that the minor players are superfluous and dispensable.

It is obvious in a body that no part is autonomous, but Paul uses the body analogy to turn self-centered vanity upside down. It is, in fact, the unpresentable parts that are the most necessary for the body to live, and they receive special treatment (12:22–23). Paul refers euphemistically to the genitalia.[7] The weaker and superior members are only ap-

---

7. See Artemidorus Daldianus, *Onirocritica* 1.45, 79, 80, for the use of the expression "the necessary member" for the male organ.

parently or seemingly so (τὰ δοκοῦντα, *ta dokounta*; 12:22), and appearances are deceiving. Fee (1987: 613) notes that "such apparent weakness has no relationship to their real value and necessity to the body." A body can survive without eyes, ears, hands, and feet, but it cannot survive without the function of these unpresentable parts. Genitalia appear to be honorless, are regarded as "unpresentable," and are shown a special modesty. Their function is not public, and they are kept hidden, but they are essential to the body's survival. In the same manner, the persons with deceptively ordinary and unprestigious gifts are as necessary for the proper functioning of the community as those who put on a more glittery display. All are of equal value; but if there is to be any overcompensation, it is to be for the less favored. The church is not to be like its surrounding society, which always honors those who are already honored. It is to be countercultural and bestow the greatest honor on those who seem to be negligible.

The description of them as the "seemingly" weaker parts of the body may recall to mind God's choice of what is weak in the world (1:27; cf. 4:10; 9:22).[8] Are the weaker ones in the allegory the coarse and common members? If so, Paul would discomfit their smug opposites by arguing that the ones who appear "to occupy positions of lower status are actually more essential than those of higher status and therefore should be accorded more honor" (D. Martin 1991: 568–69). He continues the analogy in 12:23 by noting the special attention paid to these necessary members. D. Martin's (1991: 567) comments are edifying: "The genitals may *seem* to be the most shameful part of the body, but our very attention to them—our constant care to cover them and shield them from trivializing and vulgarizing public exposure—demonstrates that they are actually the most necessary of the body's members, those with the *highest* status." Verse 24 affirms that this is God's very intention (cf. 12:18). God "composed" (συνεκέρασεν, *synekerasen*), implying mixing and blending, deliberately so. Parry (1926: 185) comments that "the instincts of decency and self-respect were implanted by God" (cf. Gen. 3:7, 10, 21), and it causes us to pay special attention to private parts by clothing them. This figure results in the lower being made higher and vice versa (D. Martin 1991: 569; Horrell 1996: 181)—a divine reversal prefigured by the cross. Paul employs the body analogy to undermine

8. Smit (1993a: 224–25) argues that the weak, dishonorable, and indecent represent the apostles, who are the most indispensable (cf. the depreciation of the apostles in 4:6–13). Smit thinks that Paul uses irony to rank the services about the gifts. But Paul is talking, instead, about how the Corinthians should relate to one another and is defending the weak over against the more respectable members with their higher status and income (Witherington 1995: 254 n. 4). They assume that they could get along well without the weak. The only connection with this description and the apostles is that Paul compassionately identifies himself with the weak.

the hierarchy of values that habitually honors those already honored and humiliates those already humbled in society. The so-called gifted and glorious members should share their glory with the unglorious (M. Mitchell 1993: 269) and invest them with honor instead of flaunting their gifts or gloating over their illusory superiority. Luther captures the essence of Paul's sentiments in a meditation (cited by Bainton 1962: 29). One should frankly admit one's gifts:

> The sun does not say that it is black. The tree does not say, "I bear no apples, pears, or grapes." That is not humility, but if you have gifts you should say, "These gifts are from God; I did not confer them upon myself. One should not be puffed up on their account. If someone else does not have the gifts I have, then he has others. If I exalt my gifts and despise another's, that is pride." The sun does not vaunt himself, though more fair than the earth and the trees, but says, "Although tree, you do not shine, I will not despise you, for you are green and I will help you to be green."

The conclusion in 12:25–26 expresses the purpose of this ordering of the body: "in order that there might not be division in the body but that the members might have the same concern for one another." The opposite of division (σχίσμα, *schisma*) is showing care for one another (Ruef 1977: 136). Evidence of callous indifference to the plight of the "have-nots" at the Lord's Supper (11:17–34) reveals a bodily breakdown. Their behavior at their Lord's Supper disclosed their prejudice: these members could go missing with no great loss to the church. All have experienced, at one time or another, how the whole physical body suffers when one member hurts. The same is true for the body of Christ. As one attends to physical ailments in the body, so Paul expects the church to attend to those members who are suffering. The principle of love embodied in the cross mandates that one should always seek honor for others, which stands in absolute antithesis to the dominant value that seeks honor only for oneself in a preening self-indulgence. Thiselton (2000: 1009) affirms Moltmann's (1992) suggestion that the gift of the weaker, unpresentable members to the church is that they give others a concrete opportunity to practice love and patience.

One can understand how an ache or malfunction of one part of the body brings stress to the rest of the body. It is harder to understand what Paul means in the companion image: when one part of the body is glorified, the whole body rejoices with it. Does he refer to some kind of adulation or some special treatment, or the satisfaction of some special need? Here, the allegory would seem to break down. But M. Mitchell (1993: 162) contends that the themes of co-suffering and co-rejoicing in the body are topoi of political unity and standard definitions of solidarity. M. Mitchell cites Isocrates' (*Or.* 4.168) description of a major symptom of factionalism in the Greek city-state: "They are so far from feeling pity that they even rejoice more in each other's sorrows than in their own blessings." The same problem can emerge in the church body, where some might find it harder to rejoice than to succumb to jealousy when another member is glorified. Suffering *and* rejoicing together (cf. 13:5–6) are a sign of unity in which each one truly seeks the advantage of the other. Plato (*Respublica* [*Republic*] 5.10.462C–D) uses a similar analogy:

> When one of us has a wounded finger, the body and soul of that person and their inter-relationship are affected, and we say *the man* feels pain in his finger. Even so with every other part of the body—when one part suffers there is pain, and there is joy when one part is restored to health.

12:27–30 Paul returns to the opening affirmation about the body of Christ. In case the Corinthians have not realized it, he clarifies that he is talking about them. They are Christ's body, but only as they live as Christ's body (M. Barth 1958: 147). Everybody relates to Christ and to one another as a part (ἐκ μέρους, *ek merous,* part by part, individually) of his body. As "parts," each has his or her own function that contributes to the body's welfare. Again, Paul focuses on God as the one who orchestrates the gifts in the church (12:6, 18, 24) in the same way that God arranged the intricacies of the body. "In the church" could refer to the church universal, but since apostles are the founders of local communities of faith, it could also refer to a local community.

Paul lists a sampling of members that God has placed in the church body. From the use of the ordinal series—"first . . . second . . . third . . ."—they appear to be ranked in order of importance. Apostles appear first as the founders of church communities, but it is difficult to see how prophets and teachers rank differently. "Miraculous deeds" and "grace-gifts of healings" (12:28) appear in reverse order in 12:9–10, suggesting that one should not impose any strict chain of preeminence on the items in the list. But the ordinal numbers do suggest some hierarchical valuation. Apostles, prophets, and teachers, with their threefold ministry of the word, are essential for both the founding and the continued edification of the church. The others in the list following "then" may be regarded as of roughly equal importance. Tongues, notably, are listed last again. This hierarchy would seem to undercut Paul's whole argument against the ranking of spiritual gifts (Soards 1999: 266), but his discussion in chapter 14 reveals that he does think that some gifts are more important than others for the proper function of the church. He clearly ranks prophecy above speaking in tongues for its value in edifying the church and its missionary effect. The criterion for appraising the value of gifts is their utility (Smit 1993a: 224)—what benefits others

(14:6). In the context of the group gathered to worship, prophecy has "more communicative power to convey the message of God to the congregation" (van Unnik 1993: 143). Knox (1950: 22) notes that this hierarchy of gifts was something that the Corinthians would not have expected: "The apostles come first, then the prophets, then (without any claim to miraculous powers) those engaged in teaching" (cited by Thiselton 2000: 1095–96). It should also be noted that this "first . . . second . . . third . . ." order does not reflect the evaluation of the surrounding culture. The ranking of apostles as first and tongues as last is a reversal of the world's appraisal of apostles as society's scum (4:9–13). Paul understands apostles as first in importance but not first in status. Chevallier (1966: 148–50) notes that Paul lists functions, not supergifted persons, that God has appointed to build up the body and that it makes no difference who serves in these roles.

It may be pressing too much to attempt to discern some order from this listing, but Paul seems deliberately to mix into an amalgam a diverse sampling of ministries, supernatural grace-gifts, and services. The point would be to illustrate briefly the broad spectrum of spiritual manifestations in the church (Fee 1987: 619). "Apostles" refers to the witnesses of the resurrection who were especially called out by God and appear to be a closed circle. Anyone can potentially become a "prophet," but some functioned regularly in this way in the assembly and became known as prophets. Christian prophets appear in Acts, predicting the future (11:28; 21:10) but also serving as teachers and encouragers (13:1; 15:32; 21:9). "Teachers" appear in Rom. 12:7 and Eph. 4:11.

"Miraculous deeds" (here it implies "miracle workers") and "grace-gifts of healings" appear in each listing in this chapter. "Helpful deeds" (ἀντιλήμψεις, antilēmpseis) is a new addition to the list and appears only here in the NT. It may be a "general term for all kinds of assistance" (Carson 1987: 41), but in Acts 20:35, the verb form (ἀντιλαμβάνεσθαι, antilambanesthai) appears in Paul's speech to the Ephesian elders, in which he connects it specifically to helping the weak. He buttresses it by words of the Lord Jesus: "It is more blessed to give than to receive." It may be linked to assisting the socially disadvantaged (cf. Sir. 11:12; 51:7) and would be similar to the items listed in Rom. 12:8: "service, giving to the needs of others, and doing acts of mercy" (Fee 1987: 621).

"Acts of guidance" (κυβερνήσεις, kybernēseis), a translation proposed by Fee (1987: 622), is also new to the lists. It is a term used for piloting a ship (Acts 27:11; Rev. 18:17)—an appropriate metaphor for use in a maritime community such as Corinth. The helmsman was a popular image for one who leads and pilots the ship steadily through the waves of dissension (see M. Mitchell 1993: 163–64). It refers to the gift of setting the direction and guiding a community, not just employing "administrative skills." Thiselton (2000: 1021–22) interprets it as formulating church strategy so that it heads in the right direction.

"Tongues" comes last and appears in no other list outside of 1 Corinthians because, according to M. Mitchell (1993: 270), it is "the spiritual gift which has caused the most friction in the group, due to its public and separatist nature." Fee (1987: 572) rejects this reasoning and argues that tongues is listed last only because it is at the heart of Paul's argument and the Corinthian problem. Fee contends, "It is listed last not because it is 'least,' but because it is the problem." In chapter 14, Paul gives specific instructions correcting the problem of too many tongues being spoken at one time and left uninterpreted. But their disruption of orderly worship is not the only problem he has with tongues. They also disrupt the unity of the body because they erect linguistic barriers. Those in the community who prized tongues have also sown seeds of division by exalting their gift as the all-important manifestation of the Spirit.

Each one of the battery of rhetorical questions in 12:29–30 expects the answer no and reinforces the need for diversity in the body. All the parts do not have the same function. It is interesting to contrast this listing with a similar one in 1 Clem. 37:1–5. Clement first uses military terminology, "not all are prefects, nor tribunes, nor centurions, nor in charge of fifty men," to describe those who must obey the orders of those above them. He then uses the body metaphor to argue for a "common subjection to preserve the whole body." The emphasis in Clement is on order, the great and the small, and obedience of the small to the great. This interest in which person has authority over whom is absent from Paul's use of the metaphor. He is more interested in redressing the balance of power toward those with seemingly meager gifts than establishing a well-oiled hierarchy (see Kirchhoff 1994: 153–54).

12:31 The options for interpreting 12:31 are almost as diverse as the members in the body that Paul has just described. Modern printed editions of the Greek text and most modern translations split the verse into two halves, so that 12:31a concludes the unit beginning in 12:12, and 12:31b begins the unit on love in chapter 13. Smit (1993b: 253) reads it as "an ironic exhortation" that opens a demonstrative excursus on love and forms an inclusio with 13:13 and the adjective μείζων (meizōn) (cf. Carson 1987: 51–58). I treat the verse as a whole, believing that it serves as a transition from the discussion of the diversity and unity of the body to the discussion of the incomparable way of love. It serves as an announcement of Paul's excursus on love (Lambrecht 1994: 85).

The verb ζηλοῦν (zēloun), when used in a positive sense, means to devote oneself to something with fervor and is coupled with the verb "to pursue" in 14:1. Ζηλοῦτε (zēloute) can be read as an indicative, "You eagerly desire the greater grace-gifts," which would conform with the statement in 14:12 that the Corinthians are "zealots" for spiritual gifts (so Iber 1963; Chevallier 1966: 158–63; R. Martin 1984: 35; Louw 1988; Wolff 1996: 308). If it is an indicative that describes what they are doing, then Paul offers an alternative in 12:31b of a more excellent way. Some read the indicative as sardonic: "So, you eagerly desire the greater grace-gifts, but I will show you a more excellent way." The major problem with taking ζηλοῦτε as indicative here is that it clearly is imperative in 14:1. For the same reason, we also can dismiss reading the verb as an interrogative, "Are you eagerly desiring the greater grace-gifts?"

Most interpreters take the verb as an imperative: "Eagerly desire the greater grace-gifts."[9] But there are variations of how to interpret its meaning. Baker (1974: 227; cf. Chevallier 1966: 158–63) claims that Paul cites a Corinthian watchword. Baker's argument is based on the fact that each time the verb occurs, Paul qualifies it:

> "Eagerly desire the greater gifts, but I will show you a more excellent way." (12:31)
>
> "Eagerly desire the spiritual gifts, but especially that you may prophesy." (14:1)
>
> "Eagerly desire to prophesy, . . . but do everything in decency and order." (14:39–40)

Baker (1974: 227–28) claims that Paul takes up the Corinthian word "strive" or "eagerly desire" and tries to readjust what they strive for. Paul also substitutes χαρίσματα (charismata) for πνευματικά (pneumatika) "to remind them of the many possible manifestations of the Spirit," and "adds 'greater' to direct their attention to the more useful gifts" (Baker 1974: 232). This interpretation is unconvincing because no signal that Paul is quoting a Corinthian phrase appears (see Grudem 1982: 162).

Smit (1993b: 247–55) draws on classical rhetorical canons to classify 12:31a as an ironic *permissio:* "Continue to strive for the greater gifts! It will be to your ruin!" In 12:31b, Paul continues with hyperbole, an ironical exaggeration: "Yes, I will show you a more extraordinary way." This introduces the discourse on love, which Paul uses to ridicule the Corinthians' overvaluation of the *charismata* (Smit 1993b: 246). But surely Paul would not introduce a discussion of love with mockery. The rhetorical canons are a questionable guide here. Robertson and Plummer (1914: 282) stress the aspect of the present tense and translate,

---

9. Edwards 1885: 336; Findlay 1910: 896; Barrett 1968: 296; Orr and Walther 1976: 288; Conzelmann 1975: 215; Fee 1987: 623; R. Collins 1999: 471; Schrage 1999: 240.

"continue to desire earnestly the greater gifts." It expresses Paul's sincere desire for them. No irony, no double entendre, and no antagonism should be read into this appeal.

But how does one strive for or eagerly desire something that can only be given? Does Paul expect them to try to attain gifts that they do not have? In 12:11, he asserts that the Spirit apportions to each one as he wills; and in 1:7, he assures them that they are not lacking in any spiritual gift. Is this command similar to the injunction in Phil. 2:12–13 for believers themselves to work out what God is working in them? Some argue that it is an admonishment to prayer (Godet 1887: 232; Robertson and Plummer 1914: 282; Barrett 1968: 296). He does not tell them to pray for these greater gifts, however. Van Unnik (1993: 154) argues that those who "have received the various gifts of the Spirit should be zealous in them, that is to say: zealously practise them, and that not in an ordinary way, but as much as they can, even to the highest degree (καθ' ὑπερβολήν [*kath' hyperbolēn*])." This interpretation depends on van Unnik's idiosyncratic interpretation of the phrase καθ' ὑπερβολήν, which will be dealt with below, but van Unnik (1993: 156–57) offers keen spiritual insight that is overlooked by others: "The gifts of God's grace do not work automatically; they are not in the state of permanent activity." These gifts are not permanent possessions of individuals that are at their disposal. They cannot be referred to as "my" gift (see Dunn 1975: 221), and they need not be continually active. They also can be neglected or quenched (1 Thess. 5:19). The reminder "Rekindle the gift of God that is within you" (2 Tim. 1:6) and the command "Do not neglect the gift that is in you" (1 Tim. 4:14) warn that gifts can fall into disuse and may need reviving. Paul never exhorts his charges to practice what today are called "spiritual disciplines," which can leave the impression that growing in grace in the Christian life is something that happens spontaneously and almost unintentionally. But the encouragement to devote oneself eagerly to these gifts of grace, rather than waiting for some divine automatic pilot to kick in, may be commensurate with the idea that practicing spiritual discipline is necessary to the Christian life.

Some think that the "greater grace-gifts" (τὰ χαρίσματα τὰ μείζονα, *ta charismata ta meizona*) refers sarcastically to the greater gifts as the Corinthians ranked them. From their perspective, the greater gifts were the most eye-catching and personally gratifying and those that bestowed the highest status. But Paul does not resort to irony or sarcasm here. He does have a gradation of gifts in mind. The gradation is calibrated according to how each gift contributes to building up the body of Christ. Thiselton (2000: 1024) thinks that Paul must redefine what "greatest" really means in what follows. The greater gifts are those that edify, encourage, and comfort others. No gift is worth anything, however, if its use is not motivated by love. Love is *not* a greater gift or a substitute for gifts. It is a fruit of the Spirit, and love must accompany the gifts, not replace them. Paul does not confuse gifts with virtues (Godet 1887: 231). Love is the framework in which all gifts, greater and lesser, must be used.

The phrase καὶ ἔτι καθ᾽ ὑπερβολὴν ὁδόν (*kai eti kath' hyperbolēn hodon*) is problematic.

1. The ἔτι can be linked with different parts of the sentence:
   a. It can qualify καθ᾽ ὑπερβολήν and mean "a still more excellent way" (NRSV), "even better" (REB), or "the best way of all" (NJB).
   b. It can go with the verb δείκνυμι (*deiknymi*) and mean "to show in a superlative sense."
   c. It can go with the καί (*kai,* and) and mean "moreover" (Godet 1887: 233; Robertson and Plummer 1914: 283).
2. The phrase "I will show you a way" (ὁδὸν ὑμῖν δείκνυμι, *hodon hymin deiknymi*) can be metaphorical in the sense of teach, to give a didactic explanation (see Epictetus, *Diatr.* 1.4.29; 10.32). Or, it may have a demonstrative force: "display," "point out," or "demonstrate." Holladay (1990: 87–88) maintains that the verb has its normal NT sense of "demonstrate" and argues that it is "less a didactic explanation than it is a paradigmatic exhibition." The two functions are not so easily disconnected, but the point is well taken (B. Dodd 1999: 118). "Showing a way" is a biblical expression (1 Sam. 12:23; Ps. 32:8; Isa. 40:14; 48:17; Mic. 4:2; cf. 4 Ezra [= 2 Esdr.] 4:3; Jdt. 10:13).[10] The implication is that the way they are headed will destroy community. Paul talks about "my ways" in 1 Cor. 4:17 and "God's ways" in Rom. 11:33. He does not intend to expound on the wondrous qualities of love but to show from his own life as an apostle how all that he does would be for naught without love.
3. The phrase καθ᾽ ὑπερβολήν means "extremely," "to the highest degree" (literally, "according to excess").
   a. Normally, it has an adverbial sense (Rom. 7:13; 2 Cor. 1:8; Gal. 1:13), and van Unnik (1993: 147–48) claims that it never appears as an adjective (including 4 Macc. 3:18). Van Unnik (1993: 149) thinks that it goes with the verb "to seek." They should seek "to the highest degree," that is, zealously practice the greater gifts and even do so excessively. Its distance (six words) from the verb "to desire eagerly" makes this option unlikely.

---

10. Scripture speaks of "the way of the Lord" (Judg. 2:22; Ps. 37:34; Prov. 10:29), "the way of faithfulness" (Ps. 119:30), "the way of wisdom" (Prov. 4:11), "the way of righteousness" (Prov. 8:20), "the way of life" (Jer. 21:8); cf. also "the way of truth" (Wis. 5:6). Unconvincing is Sandnes's (1991: 100–102) argument that Paul uses this prophetic expression to introduce a revelatory criterion that trumps the Corinthians' pursuit of spiritual wisdom.

b. Michaelis (*TDNT* 5:85 n. 151) claims that it refers to "surpassing force and *élan*" and should be linked to the verb "to show": "Now in superlative fashion I will show you a way." Holladay (1990: 88) takes it as a rhetorical term—a way expressed in hyperbole. Thurén (2001: 104) argues that Paul warns his readers that he is going to speak with exaggeration, "by means of hyperbole," to protect them from misunderstanding theologically what he says in chapter 13. For example, his celebration of love does not discount the significance of faith, in spite of what he says (13:2, 13).

c. Most interpreters give it an attributive function that modifies the noun "way": "a way beyond what I have said" (Barrett 1968: 297), "an extraordinary way" (R. Collins 1999: 474–75), "a way beyond comparison."[11] Conzelmann (1975: 216) is, I think, right: "Paul does not promise a way that leads to the πνευμα-τικά, 'spiritual gifts,' but one that leads beyond them; nor is it the way that leads to love, but love *is* the way, at the same time also the goal of the διώκειν [*diōkein*] and ζηλοῦν [*zēloun*], the 'pursuing' and the 'striving for.'" Love is *not* a spiritual gift (contra Lietzmann 1949: 64; M. Mitchell 1993: 270). As a consequence, love is a way that *everyone* can travel. All can display love that is able to transform what otherwise would be selfish, competitive, and divisive into something that builds up (8:1). What Paul is talking about is "an entire way of life" that far surpasses the claims attached to this or that grace-gift (Carson 1987: 56–57). Christianity is not about gifts but about a way of life, which turns out to be the way of love. An emphasis on gifts can veer off into an emphasis on status and promoting oneself. Only when the exercise of gifts is controlled by love will they keep on track, moving toward serving others and building up the community.

---

11. Cf. 2 Cor. 4:17, "an eternal weight of glory beyond all comparison."

D. Love: A More Excellent Way (13:1–13)

After the discussion of spiritual gifts in 12:1–30, we might expect Paul to tackle the next question. Instead, he waxes eloquent on the superiority of the way of love. By placing before them a completely different issue, Paul seeks to defuse the Corinthians' competitive notions about gifts, which appear to have engendered conflict among those who deem their particular gift more crucial than another's. The question is not, Which gift is the most beneficial, stimulating, or spiritual? It is, instead, Is love radiated in exercising their gifts? This chapter is not a digression—a charming, self-contained hymn on love that Paul drew from his files to serve as a pleasant diversion or to give people something to read at weddings. It comprises an essential link in the flow of argumentation from chapter 12 to chapter 14. He again employs a *digressio* (*egressus, egressio*), which does not wander away from the main theme but amplifies or illustrates it (see Quintilian, *Inst.* 4.3.12, 15, 17). He previously used this technique in 7:17–24 and 9:1–10:22.

M. Mitchell (1993: 165–71, 273–77) demonstrates how love plays a fundamental role in combating factionalism and strife in the Greco-Roman world and Hellenistic Judaism and assumes that this background influenced Paul's appeal to love as the solution to factionalism in the church.[1] M. Mitchell (1993: 171) describes love as "the mortar between the bricks of the Christian building." To be sure, Paul considers love to be the panacea for their factionalism, but he does not appeal to it simply because of its utilitarian benefit to bring about concord. Bornkamm (1969: 188) connects it to the grace-gifts:

> "Love" is related to the multiplicity of the "gifts of grace"; as Christ is to the many members of his body . . . ; indeed, we may not speak of an analogy at all, but must understand the relationship between Christ and love as being still closer: love is the new aeon already present now; that is, the presence of Christ himself in the congregation.

---

1. Words have usages and not meanings, and the word ἀγάπη (*agapē*) is not a magical word, as Joly (1968) and Barr (1987) make perfectly clear. The verb ἀγαπᾶν (*agapan*), for example, is used in the LXX for Amnon's illicit love for Tamar (2 Sam. 13:1–4) and in the NT for Demas's love for the world (2 Tim. 4:10). We may assume, however, that Paul deliberately exalts *agapē* over *eros*, which was associated with immorality (Garrison 1997: 35).

In this context, "love means concern for the community and is the check on the exercise of the gifts for personal gratification or the gratification of some rather than all" (Stendahl 1977: 124). Though God and Christ are not mentioned, the cross of Christ as the manifestation of God's love for the world (cf. Rom. 5:8; 8:37; Gal. 2:20; Eph. 5:2) is the central defining reality for Paul's understanding of ἀγάπη (agapē). He is speaking not about some human virtue but about love that is rooted in God's love in Christ.

Much attention has been paid to the genre of this chapter, with no consensus emerging.[2] Smit (1993b: 246) identifies this chapter as depreciatory speech, in which Paul "successively demonstrates how useless, devoid of virtue and limited these gifts are compared to love." M. Mitchell (1993: 273) classifies it as "deliberative" rhetoric designed to persuade the Corinthians to take a particular course of action. Sigountos (1994) argues that the encomium is the simplest and closest example.[3] Standaert (1983) identifies the chapter as an elegy to love, which puts spiritual gifts in proper perspective and disposes the readers to react favorably to Paul's arguments that follow in chapter 14.[4] Sigountos (1994: 248) notes that though encomia are usually written about people, they also were used to praise other subjects and especially virtues. An encomium included five elements: prologue, birth and upbringing, acts, comparison, and epilogue. The second would be omitted as irrelevant to a virtue. Sigountos (1994: 248) concludes, "The two major elements in an encomium of a virtue would then be acts and comparison. The acts are deeds done with the assistance of the virtue which are praiseworthy. The σύγκρισις [synkrisis] compares the subject with other entities so as to praise the subject." Anderson (1999: 254) counters that this passage is too short for an encomium and thinks that it is better viewed as a simple comparison (σύγκρισις). Sigountos's analysis, however, does seem to fit the structure of the chapter:

Prologue (13:1–3)
Acts (13:4–7)
Comparison (13:8–12)
Epilogue (13:13–14:1a)

---

2. Wischmeyer (1981: 205) lists eleven proposed genres (encomium, ekphrasis, priamel, hymn, aretology, psalm, series of creedal formulas, sermon, instruction, diatribe, didactic psalm) and adds that of "religious ethical λόγος (logos)."

3. Cf. Penna (1996: 195–96), who cites the praise of wisdom (Wis. 7:7–8:1), the praise of truth (1 Esdr. 4:33–41), and the praise of hard labor (Philo, Sacr. 6–9 §§35–41).

4. Lambrecht's (1994: 81) critique of Standaert (1983) applies to most rhetorical assessments: "We hesitate to ascribe a too conscious use of rhetorical structures to Paul" (see also Anderson 1999: 253–54).

This analysis leads to three corollaries.

1. It means that the passage is a "unified entity," not "a collection of disjointed units" (Sigountos 1994: 251; contra Conzelmann 1975: 217).[5]

2. Rules for constructing an encomium (and for a comparison) were found in handbooks as preliminary exercises in the *progymnasmata*. It is quite possible that Paul practiced composing such speeches as a student, and "his ability to create such a passage extemporaneously demonstrates nothing more than the emphasis on rote learning in ancient education and should not surprise us" (Sigountos 1994: 256). This chapter, then, need not have been a piece written at an earlier time and inserted in its present place (so also Smit 1993b: 246; Lambrecht 1994: 86). Anderson (1999: 254 n. 21) notes that "it forms an important link in the chain of argumentation from chapters twelve to fourteen," and Paul "could have applied a particular kind of method, commonly practiced in school exercises, to a portion of his argumentation." The prologue (13:1–3) directly relates to the context, with a reference to tongues of humans and of angels, prophecy, and knowledge. The acts in 13:4–7 "are particularly appropriate to the Corinthian situation" (Sigountos 1994: 256). Hays (1997: 228) notes that love is mentioned only at the beginning, but the intervening material (13:8–12) "highlights the temporary status of spiritual gifts, especially, tongues, prophecy, and knowledge." Such material would be unlikely to appear in a generic paean to love.[6]

3. An encomium is praise in form but exhortation in function. In praising love, Paul indicts the church for its lack of love, which he judges to lie at the bottom of the Corinthians' problems, and the recognition of which to be the beginning of their solution. Sigountos (1994: 256) concludes,

Since virtually every behavioural problem at Corinth is mentioned in vv. 4–7, Paul seems to say that the real prob-

---

5. Those who contend that this chapter did not originally occupy this place in the letter and is not integral to Paul's argument (Weiss 1910: 309–16; Héring 1962: 134 [inserted by an "unknown interpolator"]; J. Sanders 1966: 181–83; Schmithals 1971: 90–96; Conzelmann 1975: 217; and Titus 1959 [who thinks that it was not written by Paul]) have been refuted by Hurd 1965: 189; M. Mitchell 1993: 270.

6. Romans 12 constitutes an interesting parallel. In Rom. 12:3–8, Paul discusses the church as the body of Christ and the different gifts according to the grace given to each member; he includes a list of gifts followed immediately by the call to love fellow members (Rom. 12:9–10) and then to treat those outside the church, including persecutors, in a loving manner (Rom. 12:14–21).

lem is their lack of love, for love does not behave in the way they do. The section becomes quite ironic, because while Paul is praising love, he is at the same time blaming the Corinthians.

Far from being a displaced hymn singing the praise of love as a virtue, chapter 13 is a call to a way of life that addresses real problems in the church. The purpose is to debunk "self-centered spirituality" (Thiselton 2000: 1028) and to exhort the Corinthians to pursue love (Spicq 1965: 141). If any extol their own particular gift(s) as the highest and best, Paul demonstrates how devoid of value these gifts are without love. To seek personal distinction by showing off one's spiritual prowess in some way is a self-defeating exercise that destroys community. Godet (1887: 237) eloquently gets at the heart of the matter: "Experience proves that a man, after opening his heart with faith to the joy of salvation, may soon cease to walk in the way of sanctification, shrink from complete self-surrender, and, while making progress in mystical feeling, become more full of self and devoid of love than he ever was." Paul reminds the Corinthians that love, not spiritual gifts, is the marrow of their Christian existence.

Exegesis and Exposition

[1]If I should speak in the tongues of humans and of angels, but I do not have love, I have become a clanking chunk of bronze or a clamorous cymbal. [2]And if I should have [the gift of] prophecy and know all the mysteries and [have] all knowledge, and if I should have all faith to remove mountains, but I do not have love, I am nothing. [3]And if I should dole out all my property and if I hand my body over ⌜to be burned⌝, but I do not have love, I profit myself nothing.

[4]Love is patient; love is kind; love is not filled with jealousy. It is not vainglorious; it is not puffed up. [5]It does not behave indecently; it does not seek its own [advantage]; it is not cantankerous; it does not keep a score of wrongs. [6]It does not rejoice over injustice; it does rejoice with the truth. [7]It bears all things, believes all things, hopes all things, endures all things.

[8]Love never falls, but [as for] prophecies, they shall be abolished; or tongues, they shall cease; or knowledge, it shall be abolished. [9]For we know partially and prophesy partially. [10]But whenever the perfect comes, what is partial shall come to an end. [11]When I was a child, I was speaking like a child, I was thinking like a child, I was reckoning like a child. But when I became an adult, I put an end to childish ways. [12]For now we see through a mirror indirectly; then [we will see] face to face. Now I know in part; then I will know just as I am known. [13]So now abide faith, hope, love, these three. But the greatest of these is love.

The opening verses (13:1–3) serve as a prologue that recalls the gifts **13:1** from chapter 12: tongues, knowledge, and prophecy. Smit (1993b: 246) contends that Paul seeks to demonstrate "how useless, devoid of virtue and limited these gifts are compared to love." Actually, Paul intends to show "how useless, devoid of virtue and limited these gifts" are *without love*. Only when they are exercised with love do they become useful in building up the church. Otherwise, they are meaningless, no matter how sublime and admirable they may seem to be.

Tongues were mentioned last in the three lists in chapter 12 but now are mentioned first. Some in the Corinthian congregation seem to have championed tongues as evidence of their spirituality. It is almost as if Paul allows the glossolalists to enjoy the spotlight for a fleeting moment before he yanks them back down to earth with the phrase "but have not love." Long (1989: 124) comments, "In terms of rhetorical effect, Paul has summoned forth the tongue speakers, given them an instant of glorious recognition, and then suddenly pulled the carpet out from under them by calling into question the adequacy of their gift." The letter form, Long (1989: 124) notes, creates the safety of distance:

> If Paul had been present in the flesh, pointing his finger at the Corinthians as they worshiped, the moment may well have proved too intense. There probably would have been more shame than growth. The freedom of the letter form protected the Corinthians from the full glare of Paul's presence and gave them at least the possibility of receiving what was to come next.

Paul's shift to the first person singular is also rhetorically significant. It keeps this speech from the appearance that he is scolding them for their deplorable failure to love one another. He says he will "show" (δείκνυμι, *deiknymi*) them a more excellent way (12:31), and he intends to illustrate love from his own apostolic life rather than offer platitudes about it. Van Unnik (1993: 142–43) observes that Paul does not approach the focal subject of tongues as "the outsider or objective judge" who dispenses regulations on glossolalia and prophecy. He approaches them as one who shares these experiences. He "is involved here in a very existential way and not just as a teacher of his fellow-Christians who must be corrected in their wrong views and excessive behaviour" (van Unnik 1993: 143). He speaks in tongues more than all of them and gives sincere thanks to God for this grace (14:18), and he has the gift of prophecy.

These verses are not normally thought to refer to Paul's own apostolic experiences (Lambrecht 1994: 88–89). Holladay (1990: 98), however, takes seriously "the self-referential language and its parenetic function" and makes a convincing case that it is "a typical Pauline move" to adduce "himself or certain aspects of his behavior either to illustrate his teaching or to buttress his paraenetic appeals" (1990: 82–83; citing Fiore 1986: 164–90). Wischmeyer (1981: 90–91) contends that the "I" is more generalizing as he sets himself up as an example through a hypothetical persona (cf. M. Mitchell 1993: 58). B. Dodd (1999: 120) agrees: "His 'I' is a caricature, based on the problems he confronts." Holladay's (1990: 88–94) insistence that the "I" is not general or typical but autobiographical assumes that the audience admires him (Witherington 1995: 266–67), and this fits my interpretation of the personal reflection of 9:1–27. In both sections, chapters 8–10 and 12–14, "there is a conspicuous shift midway in the discussion from the use of imperatives to the use of examples that illustrate the appeal" (Holladay 1990: 83) and then a return to the imperative. It is not unreasonable to think that Paul returns to this strategy and presents his apostolic behavior and experiences—with some allowance for hyperbole to make the point—as a paradigm for the Corinthians to follow. He puts before them his own way of life *to show them the way* (12:31) rather than to toss out heartwarming sound bites about love (R. Collins 1999: 474).

The mysteries of God have been revealed to Paul (2:1, 9–10; 15:51), and he regards himself as a "steward of God's mysteries" (4:1). He claims (along with them) to know the mind of Christ (2:16) and to have knowledge (8:1), and he imparts his knowledge to them throughout the letter. Paul has faith and has performed miracles (2 Cor. 12:12; Rom. 15:19). He voluntarily gave up his rights as an apostle to receive support so that he could carry out his ministry more effectively (1 Cor. 9:1–23). The hardship catalogs (4:11–12; 2 Cor. 4:7–12; 6:3–10; 11:7–11) reveal the toll that this service has taken on him. He also understands that he is being given up to death for Jesus' sake and for others (2 Cor. 4:11; Col. 1:24). But love rules his apostolic work (cf. 1 Cor. 16:24; 2 Cor. 2:4; 11:11; 12:15). If he did not do all in love, it would all be for naught. Saying that he is nothing without love in spite of the wondrous possibility of receiving extraordinary gifts makes it easier for the Corinthians to accept the exhortation to assess their spiritual gifts more humbly.

Each verse in 13:1–3 begins with a conditional clause (ἐάν, *ean*) highlighting a spiritual proficiency: speaking in tongues (13:1), prophecy and knowledge (13:2), giving away all one's goods (13:3). In 13:2–3, a second condition is appended with ἐάν that escalates the glory quotient of the gift: faith to move mountains and giving over one's body to be burned.[7] The conditions are linked to the negative condition of not having love (ἀγάπην δὲ μὴ ἔχω, *agapēn de mē echō*). One can put on a show of love without having love, but one who truly has love cannot help but show it. Consequently, Paul emphasizes having love. Each verse con-

---

7. Since the second ἐάν does not appear in 13:1, speaking in the tongues of angels may not be an exaggeration of speaking in the tongues of humans (see Petzer 1989: 240).

cludes with a negative consequence. The last two use the word "nothing": "I am nothing [οὐθέν, *outhen*]"; "I profit myself nothing [οὐδέν, *ouden*]." This does more than invalidate the gift; it touches a person's very being.

The nature of speaking in tongues has been dealt with in the discussion of 12:8–10. The question arises here whether the "tongues of angels" are an expansion of human tongues or hyperbole. Petzer (1989: 239–40) thinks that the phrase's emphatic position after the verb ("if in the tongues of humans I speak *and of angels*") means that "the tongues of angels" are not simply an extension of human tongues. The two are not linked. Petzer takes Paul to mean: even if speaking in human tongues "could be perfected to such an extent that it would be comparable to the angelic tongues. . . ." Petzer assumes that Paul exaggerates (Petzer's term is "defamiliarizes") by putting glossolalia out of the reach of ordinary humans (see also Sigountos 1994: 252–53). These are tongues beyond any ever known by humans. The parallel with 13:2, "having prophecy and knowing all mysteries," suggests that the two items listed are distinct and that the last element is hyperbole.

I have presented evidence earlier, however, that speaking in the tongues of angels would not have been regarded as unattainable (see comments on 12:8–10). Paul's rapture into the third heaven, into paradise, where he heard things that a human may not speak, assumes that he heard things in some heavenly tongue (2 Cor. 12:1–4). It is more likely that he poses a realistic possibility that some may indeed believe that they speak in a celestial language (cf. the combination of humans and angels in 1 Cor. 4:9 [so Spicq 1965: 145; Conzelmann 1975: 221 n. 27]). In fact, to identify as hyperbole the second element in the next verses is misleading. Faith to move mountains does not refer literally to moving mountains but is an idiom for doing what is impossible. Giving one's body is also not an exaggeration, because many Christians had done so. The ascending scale in the dazzle factor of the gifts described is not correlated to their impossibility but to their potential to accrue greater glory for the individual.

Paul's strategy is to place in center stage the gift that the Corinthians prized the most and that was causing the greatest disruption in their assembly and then to bring it down several notches by showing its emptiness without love. It becomes a hollow performance that falls flat. Those who speak in tongues without love become something other than what they intended. Carson (1987: 59) contends that the perfect tense γέγονα (*gegona*) may suggest that "it has left a permanent effect on me that has diminished my value and transformed me into something I should not be." The problem is identifying what Paul means by χαλκὸς ἠχῶν (*chalkos ēchōn*, sounding brass). The noun χαλκός is never used for a musical instrument. The verb ἠχεῖν (*ēchein*) appears in some manuscripts of Luke 21:25 to describe the roar of the sea (in other manuscripts, the noun ἦχος). Some think that this reference is intended to be reminiscent of the liturgical practice of pagan cults and basically means to become like a pagan.[8] Others think that it connects to the description in philosophical traditions of empty-headed sophists. Spicq (1965: 146) asserts, "After Plato . . . the description of an 'empty' sophist or rhetor as a gong, lyre, cymbal, or trumpet became a commonplace of literature and philosophy."[9] But the term "sounding brass" does not appear in these texts, and Paul describes something quite different from witless buffoons trying to wax eloquent.

A more promising option argues that the "sounding brass" refers to acoustical sounding-vases, not a musical instrument. W. Harris (1981; 1982) proposes that Paul has in mind the acoustic amplification or resonance system to project sound found in stone amphitheaters (see Vitruvius, *On Architecture* 5.5.1, 7–8). Harris points out that they were called "sounders" (*ēcheia*) and generally were made from bronze. A bronze sounder suggests endless reverberations of sound (see also W. Klein 1986; Murphy-O'Connor [1983: 75–77] offers a critique). Hays (1997: 223) combines the views so that the glossolalist is compared to "the empty echo of an actor's speech or the noise of frenzied pagan worship." But this reads too much into what Paul actually says. T. Sanders (1990: 614) objects that this is a "particularly exotic usage of χαλκός." How would an "echoer" be negative, particularly if the glossolalist thinks that he or she is echoing some divine utterance? Echoes also are passive, and Paul appears to be referring to something that is active (Schrage 1999: 285 n. 44).

T. Sanders makes the case that Paul contrasts a clanking chunk of brass with the delicate sounds of a ringing cymbal, a tuned musical instrument. The difference between them is not the material but the sound they produce: one clanks, the other chimes. T. Sanders (1990: 614, 616) argues against the disjunctive rendering of ἤ (*ē*) in the phrase ἤ κύμβαλον ἀλαλάζον (*ē kymbalon alalazon*) as "or" and renders it as a comparative, "than." The "cymbal" is singular, so we should not think of modern orchestral cymbals clashed together. Our image of cymbals as only shrill and thunderous may be misleading.

The verb ἀλαλάζειν (*alalazein*) could have the negative connotation of a loud clashing, but T. Sanders (1990: 616) raises doubts that a cymbal would have been unpleasing to the ancient ear or that it would have evoked the image of "discordant cacophony." To claim that it is a "soul-

---

8. Lietzmann 1949: 65; Moffatt 1938: 192; Barrett 1968: 300; Conzelmann 1975: 221; Fee 1987: 632; Carson 1987: 59; Wolff 1996: 314–15; possibly, Spicq 1965: 145; Héring 1962: 136.

9. See Plato, *Protagoras* 329A; Dio Chrysostom, *Or.* 8.2; Pliny the Elder, *Naturalis historia* (*Natural History*) preface.25; Tertullian, *De pallio* (*The Pallium*) 4.

less instrument" (Robertson and Plummer 1914: 289) or that it makes a "tom-tom noise" (Moffatt 1938: 192) is a chauvinistic judgment reflecting modern musical tastes. T. Sanders (1990: 615) notes that "cymbals continued to be important in the religious and social life of the ancients." They were used by street musicians, as part of the cultic worship of Dionysus and Cybele, and in joyous celebrations and worship in the OT (see 1 Sam. 18:6; 2 Sam. 6:5; 1 Chron. 13:8; 15:16, 19, 28; 16:5; 2 Chron. 5:12–13; Ps. 150:5; Josephus, *J.W.* 5.3.5 §§384–85). T. Sanders also argues that the verb ἀλαλάζειν is used in the LXX for enthusiastic outbursts and that such expressions are encouraged in the worship of God (see LXX Ps. 46:2; 65:1; 80:2; 97:4, 6; 99:1; 94:1–2). It can connote a loud sound that is joyous and exciting. T. Sanders (1990: 617) translates, "If I speak in the tongues of men and angels, but do not have love, I am a dinging piece of bronze rather than a joyfully sounding cymbal."[10]

This creative theory makes it unnecessary to look for an obscure meaning for χαλκός (raw metal) that is not substantiated in ancient literature. Thiselton (2000: 1038) objects, however, that speaking in tongues would not be likened by the glossolalist to the clash of a cymbal, but this objection assumes that the image conjures up an unpleasant din. The contrast is between raw material that makes clangor and a finished musical instrument that makes music. The contrast between a lump of bronze that makes a dull clank when hit and a cymbal that makes a joyous ring when hit is an attractive option (see also R. Horsley 1998: 176; R. Collins 1999: 475). However, the verbs ἠχεῖν and ἀλαλάζειν together suggest a clamorous noise. The noise they make is something that thunders. Paul seems to be saying that glossolalists who show no love are no more than a bunch of loud clangers.

Paul employs hyperbole in referring to knowing all mysteries, though Enoch claimed to have seen "all the secrets of heaven" (1 Enoch 41:1; 52:1; 61:5; 63:3; 71:4). He understands some mysteries (Rom. 11:25; 1 Cor. 15:51), particularly the mystery of God revealed in the cross (1 Cor. 2:1, 7; 4:1), but he does not fathom all mysteries (cf. Rom. 11:33–35) or have all knowledge, since he concedes that "we know only in part and prophesy only in part" (1 Cor. 13:9). But even if Paul were to have this prize knowledge revealed to him by God, it becomes meaningless information without love (cf. 8:1–3). Only love can understand the wisdom of the cross. Fellowship with God does not come through knowing everything there is to know (Thiselton 2000: 1040). This omniscience is topped off by faith to move mountains, which has become

13:2

---

10. Weiss (1910: 313) argues that the comparison is between something that makes an inarticulate noise, the brass and the cymbal, and something that makes a melody, such as a flute.

a proverbial expression for accomplishing something impossible in a miraculous way (see Matt. 17:19–20; 21:21; Mark 11:22–24; Luke 17:6; *b. Ber.* 64a; *b. Sanh.* 24a). Paul's crisp response, "I am nothing," sums it all up (see 2 Cor. 12:11 for a different rhetorical use of this phrase). Spiritual gifts minus love equal zero.

For Paul, one is "'something' or 'nothing' only in relation to God" (Furnish 1999: 100). Penna (1996: 199) interprets him to mean, "Loving is equal to being, the one who loves *is*." One could alter Descartes's famous axiom to read, "I love, therefore I am" (cf. 1 John 3:14). Since love is concerned not with itself but with the other and creates communion with others, Penna further modifies the axiom: "I love, therefore we are." Love is not something achieved by isolated moral giants but by those in a community of love (O'Brien 1975–76: 143).

13:3 Paul now cites examples of extreme self-denial and again discounts anything that is not motivated by love. Such costly self-sacrifice probably was not what the Corinthians had in mind whenever they thought of *charisma*. He first introduces philanthropy. The verb ψωμίζειν (*psōmizein*) means "to eat" or "to give others morsels to eat" (Rom. 12:20), so the word picture is one of doling out one's substance to give food to others. Stansbury (1990: 467) objects to supplying the word "poor" or "those in need" because care for the poor was not a motivation in Greco-Roman giving. But the biblical context permeates Paul's thinking, and he is not offering a critique of the Greco-Roman cultural hunger for prestige and honor. He probably has in mind the biblical concern to feed and care for the poor and needy since giving others something to eat is a core Christian value (Acts 4:32–37). There is a catch, however. If the rich man had followed Jesus' directive to a tee and sold all his goods to give to the poor (Mark 12:17–22), but did so selfishly, solely to possess an inheritance in the kingdom of God, then it would have been for naught. Feeding the poor is not enough. It must be driven by love for the poor, which is motivated by love for Christ, who has identified himself with the poor. If the wealthier Corinthians gave sops to the "have-nots" gathered around the Lord's table, or more than sops, the best portions of their food, but did it only as a palliative to avoid getting weak and ill (1 Cor. 11:30), then it would be for nothing. They would still be under God's judgment. Paul has impoverished himself for the cause of his apostolic ministry, but if it were not because the love of Christ constrains him to do so, then it would all be for nothing.

The self-sacrifice of giving away all one's possessions is intensified by the extreme self-denial of "giving my body." A notorious textual variant requires deciding whether Paul gives his body (παραδῶ τὸ σῶμά μου, *paradō to sōma mou*) "to boast" (καυχήσωμαι, *kauchēsōmai*) or whether he gives his body "to be burned" (καυθήσωμαι, *kauthēsōmai*).

It is possible that Paul thinks of giving his body to boast, but this makes the qualifier "and have not love" superfluous. All unworthy motives are subsumed under the category of "not having love." Can one boast lovingly about giving up one's possessions and one's body? Hardly. Paul believes that he will have a boast at the end-time judgment, but it is a boast in his churches, not of his great sacrifices, and it is a boast he can have only "in Christ Jesus our Lord" (15:31). This reading is also vague: Give his body over for what? Clement reports that believers had given themselves over to captivity as a ransom for others, and many more gave themselves over to slavery and used the money to provide others with food (1 Clem. 55:2). But the language of giving over the "body" does not appear in Clement. The reading "to be burned" best fits the context (see additional note).

The wording agrees closely with Dan. 3:95 Theodotion: παρέδωκαν τὰ σώματα αὐτῶν εἰς πῦρ (ἐμπυρισμόν in Old Greek), *paredōkan ta sōmata autōn eis pyr* (*empyrismon*). The account of the obedience of Shadrach, Meshach, and Abednego that led to their death sentence in the blazing furnace may form the backdrop for this image (cf. Heb. 11:34). The story of the seven brothers who gave themselves up to a fiery death rather than compromise their faith (2 Macc. 7; 4 Macc. 9:16–25; 10:13–14; 16:1–4, 18–25) was also well-known and read in light of Dan. 3. One brother says to his torturers, "You do not have a fire hot enough to make me play the coward" (4 Macc. 10:14). Their sacrifice is interpreted as a vicarious atonement in 4 Macc. 17:20–22: they became, "as it were, a ransom for the sin of our nation." We can also compare Josephus's account of Eleazar's rousing speech to the besieged rebel holdouts at Masada, which holds up the example of the self-immolation of the Asiatic Indians, who long for the immortal state and hand their bodies over to the fire (πυρὶ τὸ σῶμα παραδόντες, *pyri to sōma paradontes* [*J.W.* 7.8.7 §355]).[11] Paul gives as his climactic example "the most painful death which anyone can voluntarily suffer" (Robertson and Plummer 1914: 291).

Paul has had more than one near-death experience in carrying out his apostolic mission, and he reports in 1 Cor. 15:32 that he has fought with beasts in Ephesus. Giving his body over to the flames epitomizes the most extreme form of self-sacrifice, but this ultimate sacrifice is meaningless if done without love. Paul's model for self-sacrifice is Christ, "who loved me and gave himself for me" (Gal. 2:20; cf. Rom. 5:6–8; 2 Cor. 8:9; Gal. 1:4). Martyrdom for loveless reasons is ultimately meaningless: "Love accepts only what is inspired by love" (Godet 1887: 243).

---

11. Lucian (*De morte Peregrini* [*The Passing of Peregrinus*] 21–37) describes the self-immolation of Peregrinus. He had visions of attaining posthumous glory from this deed, but it resulted only in ridicule.

The language of the apodosis changes from "I am nothing" (1 Cor. 13:2) to "I profit myself nothing" (οὐδὲν ὠφελοῦμαι, *ouden ōpheloumai*; 13:3), presumably, before God. The "totality of the gift" contrasts dramatically with "the nothingness of the result" (Spicq 1965: 149). Paul may be echoing a saying of Jesus: "What will it profit [ὠφελεῖ, *ōphelei*] a person to gain the whole world and lose his or her life?" (Mark 8:36/ Matt. 16:26/Luke 9:25). Paul would turn it around: "If I give up the whole world and even give my life over to fiery death, it profits me nothing if it is done without love." Robertson and Plummer (1914: 291) observe the different result in each apodosis: in the first, "I produce nothing of value" (1 Cor. 13:1); in the second, "I am of no value" (13:2); in the third, "I gain nothing of value" (13:3). Persons with the attributes listed in these verses may seem on the surface to be invaluable to the church, but God, who inspects beneath the surface, sees the lovelessness, which makes all these glorious endowments worthless.

13:4–7 Paul now personifies love to show its superior acts. Three things are noteworthy. First, many observe that he does not use adjectives to describe love but verbs, fifteen of them in three verses. Love is dynamic and active, not something static. He is not talking about some inner feeling or emotion. Love is not conveyed by words; it has to be shown. It can be defined only by what it does and does not do. Spicq (*TLNT* 1:12) notes, "Unlike other loves, which can remain hidden in the heart, it is essential to charity to manifest itself, to demonstrate itself, to provide proofs, to put itself on display, so much so that in the NT it would be necessary to translate *agapē* as 'demonstration of love.'" Each thing that love does is something in which the ego does not dominate; each thing that love does not do is something in which the ego does dominate. A wealth of English synonyms can be chosen to translate the Greek verbs, and their different nuances create a kaleidoscopic effect for the meaning of love, revealing its boundless capacities that can never be captured in a word or two.

Second, this is not a hymn to love. It is an integral part of Paul's exhortation to the Corinthians, and the list of things that love does and does not do is "aimed at the special faults of the Corinthians" (Robertson and Plummer 1914: 292). Hurd (1965: 112) suggests that omitting the negatives in each clause leaves us with a good description of the Corinthians' behavior. They are impatient and unkind, filled with jealousy, vainglorious, and puffed up. They insist on their own way, are cantankerous and resentful, and rejoice in wrong rather than right. Sigountos (1994: 257) writes, "Such specific repetition of catchwords and phrases cannot be accidental: Paul intends to praise love by choosing acts that blame the Corinthians." This section becomes quite ironic. While praising love, Paul is blaming the Corinthians at the same time (Sigountos 1994: 256–57). The upshot is that although the gifts of the

Spirit are conspicuous in their assembly, their lack of love is even more conspicuous (Holladay 1990: 98). Rather than being a hymn glorifying how wonderful love is, this text becomes a subtle commentary on what is rotten in Corinth. "The stark message here is that while love stands the test of life, the Corinthian Christians have failed it miserably" (Sigountos 1994: 257). As it relates to the focal issue of glossolalia in the public gathering, Paul implies that when this gift is exercised apart from love, it becomes "a boastful, arrogant, rude, selfish and irritating expression of insensitivity to the community" (Robeck, *DPL* 941).

Third, the list of things that love does and does not do corresponds to the Christian's experience of "God's own gracious, saving activity" (Furnish 1999: 100). God is patient (forbearing; Rom. 2:4; 9:22; 11:22) and kind (Rom. 2:4; 11:22; Titus 3:4) toward humans. God does not tolerate unrighteousness (Rom. 1:18; 2:8). God does not reckon sins against us (Rom. 4:7–8; 2 Cor. 5:19). Christ's sacrifice seeks the advantage of others and not his own (Rom. 15:1–6; Phil. 2:4–8). It becomes clear that Paul is describing a particular demonstration of love: God's love in Christ. Paul imitates Christ (1 Cor. 11:1), and he has demonstrated this same love toward the Corinthians as their founding father.

The present tense of the verbs describing what love does and does not do expresses "habitual as well as present actions" (O'Brien 1975–76: 143). Love is patient (μακροθυμεῖ, *makrothymei*). This can apply to a variety of situations. It "performs the positive act of waiting" (O'Brien 1975–76: 143). Love is patient in suffering (Rom. 12:12; Col. 1:11). It endures injuries without seeking retaliation (Carson 1987: 62). Suffering injustice with goodwill (1 Cor. 6:7) requires loving patience (see Matt. 18:26, 29). Love is also patient with individuals. The exhortation "to admonish the idlers, encourage the fainthearted, help the weak" is capped off with the exhortation "to be patient with all of them" (1 Thess. 5:14). Paul claims that he has carried out his mission with patience (2 Cor. 6:6; 12:12; cf. 2 Tim. 3:10). It reflects a willingness to "live the situation out to the full in the belief that something hidden there will manifest itself to us" (Nouwen 1987: 9).

Love is kind (χρηστεύεται, *chrēsteuetai*). It responds to others with the same tender heart and forgiveness that God has shown to us in Christ (Eph. 4:32). Kindness recognizes that everyone carries a heavy load. The kindness of Christians in the second century so surprised their pagan counterparts that, according to Tertullian (*Apol.* 3.39), they called Christians *chrestiani*, "made up of mildness or kindness," rather than *christiani*.

Love is not filled with jealousy (ζηλοῖ, *zēloi*). This verb can have a positive or a negative sense. It can refer to "intense negative feelings over another's achievements or success" (BDAG 427), which becomes envy. Envy is behind much of the party strife in the Corinthian church, and Paul says as much in 1 Cor. 3:3. This word can also have a positive meaning and refer to "intense positive interest in something" (BDAG 427; cf. 12:31; 14:1). The Corinthians' zeal for spiritual gifts (14:12) may contribute to the envy. Wischmeyer (1981: 92) thinks that Paul implicitly criticizes their zeal for anything that does not build up the community.

Love is not vainglorious (περπερεύεται, *perpereuetai*). The verb περπερεύεσθαι (*perpereuesthai*) is extremely rare (see Braun, *TDNT* 6:93–94) and may refer to "ostentatious rhetorical boasting" (Sigountos 1994: 257) that lacks any sense of proportion and wounds others (Braun, *TDNT* 6:94). It is used to describe the pompous windbag and may allude to the rhetorically sophisticated speech (1:17; 2:1) that so enamors the Corinthians and fosters boasting.

Love is not puffed up (φυσιοῦται, *physioutai*). Arrogance is one of the particular faults in Corinth. Six of the seven occurrences of this verb in the NT appear in this letter (4:6, 18, 19; 5:2; 8:1). Judge (1984: 23) claims that Paul's clashes with the Corinthians stimulate "his reflection on constructive as opposed to destructive relations." Love is constructive. It builds up the building (8:1). The puffed-up spirit blows up the building.

Love does not behave indecently (ἀσχημονεῖ, *aschēmonei*). "To act indecently" may have sexual overtones (cf. 7:36; Cranfield 1975: 126) or refer to shameful behavior in general. If so, this may be an allusion to the gross impropriety of the man living with his father's wife (5:1–2).

Love does not seek its own advantage (ζητεῖ τὰ ἑαυτῆς, *zētei ta heautēs*; cf. Rom. 15:3; Phil. 2:4). This love differs from *eros*, which always seeks its own interests (Thiselton 2000: 1051), and from *philia*, which "denotes devotion to one's own, whether self, or family, chosen friend, or lover" (O'Brien 1975–76: 144). Paul's exhortation in 1 Cor. 10:24, "Let no one seek his or her own [advantage] but that of another," may indicate that self-seeking is another major problem at Corinth (cf. Phil. 2:4, 21). At the end of his discourse in 1 Cor. 8–10, Paul invites the Corinthians to imitate him as he does Christ: "just as I myself seek to please everyone in all things, not seeking my own advantage, but that of the many, in order that they may be saved" (10:33).

Love is not cantankerous (παροξύνεται, *paroxynetai*). The verb refers to an inward state of arousal and can have a positive sense, "to stimulate," or a negative sense, "to irritate." As a passive verb, it means to be irritated. Love does not go into paroxysms (fits) of anger, nor does it provoke anger in others with its irritability (LSJ 1342–43). Where tensions arise in a community, one may assume that the disputants engaged in irascible responses (see Seesemann, *TDNT* 5:857).

Love does not keep books on evil (λογίζεται τὸ κακόν, *logizetai to kakon*). The image is of keeping records of wrongs with a view to paying back injury. Paul uses the verb in referring to God's not counting our sins against us (R. Martin 1984: 50; Fee 1987: 639). It ties in with his question raised in 6:7, "Why not suffer wrong?" Love is painfully aware of evil and does not ignore it, but love tries to overcome it with good and does not keep a record to return evil for evil. Paul embodies this attitude in 2 Cor. 2:5–11 in forgiving the one who offended him. When Jesus tells his disciples that they must forgive seventy-seven times (or seventy times seven), "One has learned nothing if one keeps a tally of the number of times one has forgiven another so that when the magic number is reached, one can stop forgiving and mete out punishment" (Garland 1993: 194). On the one hand, keeping tabs on wrongs done to us presumes that we are the ones who get to repay the wrongs. Love absorbs evil without calculating how to retaliate. On the other hand, keeping count of wrongs allows us to take advantage of another's guilt (Bornkamm 1969: 183). Spicq (1965: 157) describes it as "absolute forgetfulness, as if the marks of the stylus vanished from the wax tablet."

Love does not rejoice over injustice (χαίρει ἐπὶ τῇ ἀδικίᾳ, *chairei epi tē adikia*). Some think that this may be a reference to 1 Cor. 5:2 (so Sigountos 1994: 258), but my interpretation of 5:2 makes this highly unlikely. Since the word "injustice" occurs in Paul's remarks on lawsuits, it is probable that he has in mind the matter of Christians defrauding other Christians in pagan courts (so Holladay 1990: 95).

Love rejoices with the truth (συγχαίρει δὲ τῇ ἀληθείᾳ, *synchairei de tē alētheia*). The verb means "to rejoice together" (cf. 12:26; Phil. 2:17–18). Love does not suppress the truth (Rom. 1:18), exchange it for a lie (Rom. 1:25), do anything against the truth (2 Cor. 13:8), or become upset when faced with the truth, no matter how uncomfortable it is (Gal. 4.16).

In 1 Cor. 13:7, the key word is πάντα (*panta*), which may be translated adverbially as "always" (BDAG 783; BDF §154; R. Martin 1984: 51; Carson 1987: 63; Lambrecht 1994: 91). This is what love continually does. Thiselton (2000: 1056) notes that it basically means that love has no limits, and he argues that a negation best captures the idea: "Love never tires of support, never loses faith, never exhausts hope, never gives up." This translation avoids the impression that love is gullible—for example, in believing "all things." But "all things" has a certain chiming quality that I have kept in my translation. Verse 7 follows a ring arrangement:

bears all things
    believes all things
    hopes all things
endures all things

The two verbs in the center, "believes" and "hopes," are joined with love in 13:13 to form the abiding triad. Love never loses faith and never loses hope. Hope can refer to the Christian hope in the eternal blessings of the future resurrection (15:19) and is sometimes equivalent to trust in God's care and protection (2 Cor. 1:10). Paul also uses it as an expression of confidence in others (2 Cor. 1:7; 10:15). Schrage (1999: 302) comments, "For love there is no hopeless case," but Lindemann (2000: 288) thinks that it applies only to the Christian hope and not to profane hopes. But Paul also uses hope language to express optimism about his churches. As the relationship with Corinth gets rockier, Paul keeps firing off letters to the Corinthians because he does not believe that they are a hopeless case. He is confident in God that they will reform.

The verbs at the beginning and the end of this ring construction are nearly synonymous. "Bears all things" (πάντα στέγει, *panta stegei*) means that love puts up with anything (Oster 1995: 319). The verb does not have its classical sense here, "to keep hidden," and does not refer to discretion and keeping things confidential (contra Kasch, *TDNT* 7:587; Spicq, *TLNT* 3:290). It recalls Paul's affirmation in 9:12, "But we did not avail ourselves of this right but endure all things so that we might not introduce an obstacle [in the way of] the gospel of Christ" (cf. Wischmeyer 1981: 105).[12] "Endures all things" (πάντα ὑπομένει, *panta hypomenei*) refers to love's ability to hold out during trouble and affliction (cf. 2 Cor. 6:4; 12:12; 2 Tim. 2:10).

13:8–12   In the concluding paragraph, Paul attests to the permanence of love in comparison with spiritual gifts so prominent in Corinth—prophecy, knowledge, and tongues. The unit is bounded by the affirmation that "love never fails" (13:8) and that "love abides" along with faith and hope (13:13). The spiritual gifts are valid until the end, but they are imperfect and will come to an end. Since love endures forever, it is superior to these imperfect gifts no matter how impressive they might seem in this present age. Holladay (1990: 97) comments that these verses underscore "the partial quality of human existence" and adds "especially existence 'in Christ,'" but I would alter this to say "*even* Spirit-filled existence in Christ." In 2 Corinthians, Paul reminds his readers that their experience of the Spirit's power is only the beginning of what is still to be attained. The real transformation of the Christian into the glory of Christ does not take place until the resurrection and the new creation. The Spirit received in this life is only a guarantee of this future transformation, not the actual transformation itself (2 Cor. 1:22; 5:5). Holladay (1990: 97) observes,

12. By contrast, when Clement writes that "love covers a multitude of sins" (1 Clem. 49:5), he uses the verb καλύπτει (*kalyptei*).

The Corinthians have erred because they have reversed this fundamental eschatological truth. For them, essentially partial gifts possess finality, and these gifts are worth making ultimate claims about, when in fact ἀγάπη alone can be seen to possess such finality. It alone reveals the interior of the Christ-event that turned the ages. The quintessential eschatological reality, then, is ἀγάπη, and it is the only such reality to have invaded the now in any absolute sense. For this reason, it alone can be called the earmark of existence "in Christ" (ἐν Χριστῷ [*en Christō*]).

"Love never falls" (οὐδέποτε πίπτει, *oudepote piptei*). There are different types of falls. Paul may mean that love never collapses in defeat, is never destroyed (cf. Luke 6:49), never falls apart, never falls short, or never fails to have an effect. The verb "fall" calls to mind the warning in 1 Cor. 10:12, "See that you do not fall." But Paul is introducing an eschatological perspective on love and spiritual gifts. "To fall" is synonymous with καταργηθήσεται (*katargēthēsetai*, be abolished) in 13:8, 10, 11 and with παύσονται (*pausontai*, cease) in 13:8; and the statement that love *never* falls is synonymous with the conclusion in 13:13 that "it abides" (μένει, *menei*). It means that love "never ceases to exist, even in heaven" (Spicq, *TLNT* 3:107) and usually is translated as love "never fails" or "never ends." The present tense (πίπτει) has a future nuance and accords with the verbs in the future tenses that follow (Schrage 1999: 304; contra Michaelis, *TDNT* 6:165–66).

In contrast to love, the spiritual gifts have a built-in obsolescence. They are not permanent and do not get perfected. Prophecy and knowledge will be brought to an end. These gifts are only partial and must give way to something beyond themselves. The verb καταργηθήσεται means "to be abolished," "to pass away," or "to be rendered inoperative." The verb is used in 1:28 for God's reducing to nothing "the things that are"; in 6:13, for the destruction awaiting "food and the belly"; in 2:6, for the doom awaiting the rulers of this age; in 15:24, for the dethroning of "every ruler and every authority and power"; and in 15:26, for the destruction of "the last enemy, death." The verb makes clear that these gifts do not flow into something new, like a ramp feeding onto a superhighway; they reach a dead end. On the day of the Lord their assignment will be finished and they will be scrapped as functionless.

Paul's choice of which gifts to contrast with love is directly relevant to the situation in Corinth. The Corinthians treasure tongues and knowledge. Paul adds what he considers to be the most beneficial for building up the church: prophecy. All three are transitory and suitable only for "between the times"—between the inauguration of the end, through the death and resurrection of Jesus, and the consummation of all things, when God will be "all in all" (15:20–28; Fee 1987: 643). Since these gifts relate to what Christians do in this world, "they must give way to a more perfect state" (Lund 1931: 274). When that state arrives, these gifts will disappear.

Paul varies the verb in describing the destiny of tongues: tongues cease (γλῶσσαι παύσονται, *glōssai pausontai*).[13] This fact probably surprised the Corinthians if they considered this gift to be a sign of the presence of the heavenly world. If tongues come to an end and have no part in the next world, they cannot be "the appearing of the eternal in time" (Conzelmann 1975: 225). The implication is that these gifts (and any others) are not to be understood as either the indispensable criterion of the Christian life or its goal.

The reason why prophecy and knowledge will come to an end is twofold and is explained in 13:9–10. In 13:9, Paul clarifies, "For we know partially [ἐκ μέρους, *ek merous*] and prophesy partially." Parry (1926: 195) christens this an example of "Christian agnosticism," which defines as "the recognition of present limitation, combined with the confidence in the coming of full truth." In 13:10, Paul explains that whenever the perfect comes, what is partial will come to an end. Some interpret the "perfect" or "what is complete" (τὸ τέλειον, *to teleion*) as a process that leads to maturity in this life and does not refer to the parousia and the ultimate consummation. He contrasts today with the immediate future, tomorrow. Miguens (1975b: 87) contends that Paul presents three contrasts—partial/complete, infancy/adulthood, now/then—which refer to the gradual development of the Christian life (see also Standaert 1983: 140; Thomas 1999: 78–80). This view would translate τὸ τέλειον as "the maturity"—"when maturity arrives."[14] It assumes that he wants these gifts to pass away in their lives because they are obstructing love. This last argument clearly is wrong. Although these gifts are neither essential for, nor indicative of, Christian maturity in an individual, the variety of gifts is necessary for the functioning of the body. Paul's discussion of love is not intended to persuade the Corinthians to abandon their prized spiritual gifts but is meant to convince them to employ the gifts with love. Unless they are governed by love, they are spiritually barren.

"The perfect" refers to the state of affairs brought about by the parousia (Robertson and Plummer 1914: 287, 299–300; Lietzmann 1949: 66, 189; Fee 1987: 646; Schrage 1999: 307–8). Paul uses the verb ἐλθεῖν (*elthein*) in Gal. 4:4 to refer to the coming of the fullness of time. Here, the battery of future tenses, the disappearance of the par-

---

13. Some contend that the change in verbs is deliberate and meaningful, but it is more likely that the alteration is only a stylistic variation. The verb does not mean that it stops of its own accord (see Carson 1987: 66–67; Fee 1987: 643 n. 17).

14. The view that maintains that "the perfect" refers to the closure of the NT canon is driven more by an intent to limit the validity of tongues to the apostolic age than by any credible historical analysis.

tial replaced by the complete, and the reference to knowing as God knows us, all point to the end time. He contrasts the present age with the age to come. The "perfect" is shorthand for the consummation of all things, the intended goal of creation; and its arrival will naturally displace the partial that we experience in the present age. Human gifts shine gloriously in this world but will fade to nothing in the presence of what is perfect. But they also will have served their purpose of helping to build up the church during the wait and to take it to the threshold of the end. When the anticipated end arrives, they will no longer be necessary.

Using a common example contrasting infancy with adulthood (cf. Eph. 4:13–14), Paul explains in 13:11, why tongues will cease. The illustration of the child and childish ways punctuates Paul's conviction that the gifts belong to an order that will come to an end. The verb καταργεῖν (katargein) reappears: "When I became a man, I put an end to [κατήργηκα, katērgēka] childish ways."[15] The point of comparison is not between a babbling infant and an articulate adult. He does not intend to imply that speaking in tongues is infantile and that one should hope to grow out of this immature stage soon (see Findlay 1910: 900; Johansson 1963–64: 389–90; Bruce 1971: 128; Holladay 1990: 174). Johnson (*ABD* 6:600) misinterprets Paul in asserting that tongues may be "an optional mode of prayer, but one which may need to be outgrown." Fee (1987: 644 n. 23) offers a devastating theological critique of those who would consider "mature" a "totally cerebral and domesticated—but bland—brand of faith, with the concomitant absence of the Spirit in terms of his supernatural gifts!" (see also W. Richardson 1986: 148). Paul does not denigrate tongues as a sign of immaturity. Instead, his point is this: There is an age appropriate to certain activities, but there comes a time when those activities are no longer appropriate. Speaking in tongues is not a sign of perfection. It is something "suited to the time between the times" (Hays 1997: 229), and only for this period. Paul looks at prophecy, knowledge, and tongues from an eschatological perspective. When the end of time comes, speaking in tongues will no longer be appropriate or necessary (see Bertram, *TDNT* 4:919).

Paul progressively narrows the list of gifts from three in verse 8, to two in verse 9, to one in verse 12. He returns to the issue of partial knowledge and illustrates it with another common metaphor, seeing through a mirror: "Just now [ἄρτι, arti] we see through a mirror in a puzzle [δι᾽ ἐσόπτρου ἐν αἰνίγματι, di' esoptrou en ainigmati]." The image

---

15. The perfect tense instead of a preterite perhaps is used for vividness.

of seeing through a mirror had three possible connotations (Conzelmann 1975: 227).[16]

1. The phrase was used to exemplify seeing with clarity. Philo, for example, interprets Num. 12:7–8 to mean that Moses received a clear vision of God's form as through a mirror (*Alleg. Interp.* 3.33 §§100–101). For Philo, mirrors produce "clear reflections of the original" (*Abr.* 29 §153).[17] "Wisdom" is touted as a "reflection of eternal light, a spotless mirror of the working of God, and an image of his goodness" (Wis. 7:26). The rabbis never refer to the mirror as giving an indistinct image but use it as a metaphor for receiving prophetic revelation and clear knowledge (Kittel, *TDNT* 2:696–97).
2. Seeing in a mirror was also used as a metaphor for self-knowledge through which one catches glimpses of one's true character (James 1:23; Philo, *Migr. Abr.* 34 §190; *Jos.* 16 §87; *Mos.* 2.27 §139).
3. The phrase was also used to refer to the indirectness of vision. One does not see the thing itself but its mirror image through an intermediary.

By adding the phrase ἐν αἰνίγματι (in a puzzle, riddle, or enigma), Paul clearly understands this image negatively to imply imperfect knowledge, and therefore he must have the third option in mind (cf. 2 Cor. 3:18; Fee 1994: 317). Robertson and Plummer (1914: 298) contend that concave and convex mirrors led to distortions and that mirrors could also become tarnished. But Paul does not seem to imply that mirrors provide only dim, dark, or distorted images. They could be polished to remove the scale and rust (Sir. 12:11), and Hugedé (1957: 97–100) notes that the ancients took great pride in their mirrors and did not regard them as a medium that produced only hazy images. The phrase ἐν αἰνίγματι occurs only here in the NT and echoes Num. 12:6–8, where the Lord chides Aaron and Miriam:

> Hear my words: When there are prophets among you, I the LORD make myself known to them in visions; I speak to them in dreams. Not so with my servant Moses; he is entrusted with all my house. With him I speak face to face [literally, "mouth to mouth"]—clearly, not in riddles [LXX: δι' αἰνιγμάτων, *di' ainigmatōn*]; and he beholds the form of the LORD. Why then were you not afraid to speak against my servant Moses? (NRSV)

16. Cf. Hugedé 1957. Downing (1983–84) claims that the image derives from "pious philosophical agnosticism" about the possibilities of comprehending deity. Seaford (1984) contends that it derives from the initiation in which the initiate is stimulated prior to the final revelation. Fishbane (1986) thinks that it derives from a midrash on Num. 12:8 and a play between vision and mirror in the Hebrew. All three views seem unlikely and irrelevant.

17. See also Philo, *Creat.* 24 §76; *Flight* 38 §213; *Dreams* 2.31 §206; *Decal.* 21 §105; *Spec. Laws* 1.39 §219; *Cont. Life* 9 §78.

"Face to face," "mouth to mouth," and "eye to eye" are OT idioms (see Gen. 32:30; Exod. 33:11; Num. 14:14; Deut. 5:4; 34:10; Judg. 6:22; Isa. 52:8; Ezek. 20:35) that imply that something comes directly, not through an intermediary or medium, such as a vision or dream. Paul contrasts the limitations imposed by seeing in a mirror with seeing God directly. What one gets in a mirror is only a reflection of reality, not the reality itself (Hugedé 1957: 145–50; cf. Spicq, *TLNT* 2:75). Fee (1987: 648) aptly converts the image to a modern analogy by comparing it to the difference "between seeing a photograph and seeing someone in person." Spicq (1965: 165) makes the application to the Corinthian situation:

> The charismatic phenomena at Corinth were like the prophetic revelations of the Old Testament. They were imperfect, nocturnal, and—according to the metaphor of the mirror—made through some intervening object. St. Paul recognizes that *gnōsis* and prophecy have a miraculous role in the Church and that they also have an essential imperfection—they are only obscure reflections.

This image is followed up with knowing (ἐπιγνώσομαι, *epignōsomai*, I will know through and through) as we are known by God (cf. 1 Cor. 8:3; Gal. 4:9). Being known by God is far more important than our infinitesimal knowledge of God in this world. In this world we "only touch the hem of the garment in regard to understanding the mind of God" (Oster 1995: 320). Holladay (1990: 98) comments, "Ultimate knowledge is beyond the reach of this age," and maintains that Paul's "maturity" helps him appraise "knowledge for what it is: excessively inflating and incurably partial." At the consummation, our fragmentary knowledge will be replaced. Our notions, illusions, and misconceptions about ourselves, the world, and God will be dispelled and clarified. Paul's point is that we will know God fully only after the parousia. In the meantime, all our knowing is indirect and incomplete.

The triad of faith, hope, and love appears elsewhere in Paul's letters (see Rom. 5:1–5; Gal. 5:5–6; Col. 1:4–5; 1 Thess. 1:3; 5:8; Eph. 4:2–5; Titus 2:2) and in Heb. 6:10–12; 10:22–24; and 1 Pet. 1:3–9 (see also Barn. 1:4; 11:8; Pol. *Phil.* 3:2–3). They are well known as essential Christian virtues. Paul probably added faith and hope to love here to allow the familiar combination to balance the triad of prophecy, knowledge, and tongues. The inclusion of faith and hope also allows Paul to magnify love even more. Not only is love superior to spiritual gifts that are partial and will come to an end, but also it is superior to virtues that are absolutely essential to being a Christian. **13:13**

The exegetical questions concern the meaning of νυνὶ δέ (*nyni de*) and whether the verb μένει (*menei*, abides) applies to the present or the future. One option takes νυνί as a temporal adverb: "now," "at the present time." It would mean that for the moment, during this age, these three virtues remain. "Faith, hope, and love are the enduring character marks of the Christian life in the present time, in this anomalous interval between the cross and the *parousia*" (Hays 1997: 230–31). Some argue that faith and hope are not eschatologically permanent (cf. 2 Cor. 5:7; Rom. 8:24–25). Love is singled out as the greatest "because it alone never fails and will in fact carry on into the next life" (Witherington 1995: 272). When the perfect comes, faith becomes sight, and hope is finally realized, but love is "the one attribute to bridge this age and the eschatological reality" (Witherington 1995: 272). Love is the greatest because of its "pre-eminent, irreplaceable role in Christian life on earth," but mostly because of "its unique eschatological nature, its eternal permanence" (Lambrecht 1994: 100).

The problem with this view is that Paul does not hint that spiritual gifts will not also endure until the parousia. They too remain in the present time, though they will not continue beyond the end. If Paul is saying that faith, hope, and love abide only in the present epoch, then the contrast that he has set up between their duration and that of tongues, prophecy, and knowledge has been wiped away (Godet 1887: 259).

Another option takes νυνὶ δέ as the logical conclusion to the argument: "so now," "therefore" (Godet 1887: 259; Barrett 1968: 308; Conzelmann 1975: 230; Carson 1987: 73; Schrage 1999: 316). Parry (1926: 197) paraphrases it, "as things are," "taking all into account." The verb μένει would mean "abides eternally."[18] In the two other occurrences of νυνὶ δέ in the epistle (12:18; 15:20), it has a logical function. Paul contrasts the triad of prophecy, knowledge, and tongues, which are transitory, with the triad of faith, hope, and love, which last eternally. These three virtues remain both in time and in eternity (Kistemaker 1993: 470–71; Schrage 1999: 318). Since they will remain when the others come to an end, they should also be regarded as the most important in the present. Paul feels no compunction to explain why love is the greatest. Perhaps he takes it as self-evident because it undergirds all things. It is God's love revealed in Christ that creates the possibility of faith and hope. It also reveals that God is love (cf. 1 John 4:7–8, 16). As an essential reflection of God's character, love can never end and is elevated to the highest good.

Gifts are dispensable for the Christian's life because Christians need not be graced with any of the particular gifts listed in chapter 12 in order to be Christian and spiritual. What is absolutely indispensable for the Christian life is the presence of faith, hope, and love. As Brunner (1956: 61) well puts it, "Faith has to do with the basis, the ground on

---

18. Cf. 1 Esdr. 4:38: "But truth abides [μένει] and is strong forever, and lives and prevails forever and ever."

which we stand. Hope is reaching out for something to come. Love is just being there and acting." The situation at Corinth demands love, and Paul concludes with the appeal to pursue love (14:1a).[19]

Additional Note

13:3. Four readings are attested for the verb following ἵνα:

καυχήσωμαι—$\mathfrak{P}^{46}$, ℵ, A, B, (048 καυχήσομαι), 33, 69, 1739*, cop$^{sa, bo}$, goth^{mg}, Clement, Origen, Jerome

καυθήσομαι—C, D, F, G, L, 81, 88^{vid}, 104, 436, 630, 1881*, 1985

καυθήσωμαι—K, Ψ, 181, 326, 451, 614, 629, 1739^c, 1881^c, 1962, 1984, and a majority of patristic writers

καυθῇ—2127, *l* 1443, Chrysostom$^{1/3}$

The problem arose either from a confusion between the θ and the χ or from a scribe's making a deliberate change. The external evidence supporting καυχήσωμαι (boast) as the reading is strong and is adopted by most recent textual editions and many recent commentators. The argument, however, turns on the evaluation of intrinsic probability. Those who defend this reading commend it as the most difficult and the one that supposedly best explains the others. If the original text had "burn," it is argued, why would a scribe change it to "boast"? One can easily imagine how a pious scribe might change "boast" to "burn," regarding "martyrdom as virtuous and boasting as vicious" (Holladay 1990: 91). Boasting appears to be at odds with Paul's theological critique of it, but defenders of this reading claim that it refers to some kind of legitimate boast. Metzger (1994: 498) contends that "'glorying' is not invariably reprehensible; sometimes [Paul] regards it as justified (2 Cor 8.24; Php 2.16; 1 Th 2.19; 2 Th 1.4)." Fee (1987: 634–35) concedes that if boasting has a pejorative meaning, then we would have to assume that Paul wrote "burned"; but Fee thinks that boasting has "eschatological overtones" and refers to boasting on the day of the Lord. Fee cites 2 Cor. 11:23–29 and 12:10 as examples of bodily sufferings of which Paul boasts. The first example (2 Cor. 11:23–29) is inadmissible because Paul specifically identifies it as foolish boasting. The second example (12:10) makes no reference to boasting and refers to Paul's sufferings only as contributing to his weakness, which leads him to trust more In the grace of God. It, too, is inapplicable as an example to illumine what boasting might mean in this context. Boasting has a negative connotation in 1 Cor. 1:29; 3:21; 4:7.

Petzer (1989) appeals to semiotic principles to argue for "boast." These principles assume that parallel structures create parallel meaning; parallel structures create advance in meaning (a climactic effect); defamiliarization transposes something familiar into something strange and unfamiliar (exaggerated) to cause the reader to rethink. Petzer (1989: 242, 247) contends that the phrase "giving my body" alludes to the Lord's Supper passage (Luke 22:19) and that Paul refers to giving up one's body in the same way that Jesus did, as a sacrifice for others. Petzer (1989: 241) paraphrases: "even when your willingness to prove your piety through your deeds be perfected to such an extent as giving up not only your own belongings, but even your own body, with the result that you may be able to legitimately boast about it."

The strongest argument for "boast" is that feeding people would seem to be related to the motivation to bask in honor. The phrase "so that I might boast" governs the reason for giving to

---

19. Sigountos (1994: 259) argues that a hortatory appeal is a "constitutive part" of epilogues of encomia.

others and for handing over one's body. The motivation to gain prestige vitiates the religious value of any self-sacrifice.

Petzer (1989: 246–47) offers, and tries to refute all the objections to, "boast" but is unsuccessful. (1) Citing boasting as the reason for giving over one's body makes the addition of "and not have love" superfluous (Godet 1887: 241–43; J. Elliott 1971: 298). Boasting by its very nature evinces self-love. (2) No references to unworthy motives such as boasting occur elsewhere in the context because all unworthy motives are subsumed under the category of "not having love." Caragounis (1995b: 125) also argues that the verb παραδῶ requires a complement expressing purpose, not motivation. (3) "If I give my body" hangs in the air with the reading "in order to boast" (Barrett 1968: 302–3; J. Elliott 1971: 298). An allusion to the Lord's Supper and Jesus' giving his body (Petzer 1989: 246) is hardly convincing. (4) Petzer is right that the sequence in each verse builds to a climactic conclusion: tongues of humans and of angels, having prophecy, knowing all mysteries, moving mountains. But "boasting" is hardly the rhetorical climax that one would expect to appear after the reference to giving up one's possessions. Giving oneself over to be burned, however, is a notable climax and a powerful image. (5) It is possible that scribes changed "burn" to "boast," since the latter verb is far more frequent in Paul's writings (thirty-five times), and since tradition does not record his being burned (J. Elliott 1971: 298).

The reading καυθήσομαι (to be burned) is defended in special studies by Zuntz 1953: 35–37; J. Elliott 1971; Kieffer 1975–76; Riesenfeld 1978; Sigountos 1994: 253; Caragounis 1995b (see also Godet 1887: 241–43; Weiss 1910: 314–15; Lietzmann 1949: 65; Robertson and Plummer 1914: 290–91; Barrett 1968: 302–3; Bruce 1971: 124; Conzelmann 1975: 217 n. 1; R. Collins 1999: 476; Lindemann 2000: 283–84). Zuntz (1953) discounts the external evidence for καυχήσωμαι as stemming entirely from Egypt and claims that the error originated in Egypt in the second century. Caragounis (1995b) argues that the variant readings based on καίομαι go back to one reading and should be taken in their totality as attempted grammatical corrections of καυθήσομαι. The external evidence for this reading, then, becomes geographically extensive and substantial.

E. The Comparison between Tongues and Prophecy (14:1–19)

Paul turns now to the focal topic of his discussion: the problem of un-interpreted tongues in public worship (on the nature of the tongues, see the commentary on 12:8–10). Wedderburn (1975: 371) describes the issue of glossolalia as "puzzling, troublesome, divisive; for some it is of the essence of the Christian faith, to others it is incomprehensible and repellent." Speaking in tongues is a euphoric experience that causes the speaker to emit a pattern of sounds that have no meaning to those who do not have the gift of interpretation. Without articulate interpretation, glossolalia cannot edify, encourage, or exhort others. Instead, it cloaks the truth of the gospel in a veil of incoherence. It creates estrangement for those who are mystified by what is happening and can potentially alienate the speaker from fellow members because they no longer speak a common language.

In this section, Paul presents a judicious critique of glossolalia by comparing its effects to those of prophecy. Beare (1964: 244; see also Hurd 1965: 188) says:

> There can no doubt, then, that the main purpose of Paul is to discourage the practice of speaking with tongues among Christians. He does not suggest that it is an evil; for him, it is in its own way a manifestation of the Spirit; but he certainly directs his readers to seek other manifestations, and especially to seek gifts that will be helpful to the church at large.

This statement needs to be qualified. Paul does not wish that the Corinthians would abandon the practice altogether, since he regards it as a gift of the Spirit and one way to commune directly with God in praise and prayer. He himself speaks in tongues more than all of them (14:19). The problem is not with tongues per se but with uninterpreted tongues in the public assembly. Van Unnik (1993: 143) better grasps Paul's intent: "The point is that Paul is not speaking here of what happens in the life of an individual Christian to whom special gifts are given, but of glossolalia and prophecy *within the context of the church that has gathered together in a particular place,* where even unbelievers attend." Johanson (1978–79: 202) is quite wrong to claim that "a partisan struggle for authoritative status came to a head between two groups distinguished by prophecy and glossolalia respectively" and to assert that the glossolalists "are the major offenders, challenging the authoritative status which fell more naturally to the prophets." Fee (1987: 662) correctly reads the situation: "The real issue is not tongues and prophecy as such, but tongues and intelligibility, for which prophecy serves as the representative gift."

Paul does not want to suppress their spiritual experiences but does want to curb uninterpreted tongues in the assembly. He limits the expression of tongues to two or three speakers and only if an interpretation accompanies it. He also wants to adjust the Corinthians' attitudes toward it in relation to the gift of prophecy. Since they understand tongues to be a sign of divine inspiration, those speaking in tongues would be accorded some prestige. The problem seems to be that they are accorded too much prestige at the expense of other gifts, and Paul holds up what contributes most to "building up" the church (14:3, 4, 5, 12, 17, 26) as the touchstone for ranking the relative value of gifts, particularly for public worship. Those speech gifts that are intelligible to all, including outsiders, are the most fruitful and should be the most valued. Unlike tongues, prophecy is intelligible even to unbelievers and can lead them to repent and to recognize God's presence among them (14:24–25). Tongues only confuse. The believer does not know how to respond with the "Amen" (14:16); the unbeliever becomes convinced that glossolalists are insane (14:23). Paul's goal is to make the Corinthians sensitive to the needs of the unbeliever and to have them do all things in the assembly according to decency and order.

Chapter 14 can be subdivided by Paul's use of the vocative "brothers and sisters" (14:6, 20, 26). Each occurrence of this phrase marks a new train of thought. The structure of 14:1–19 falls into three units:

1. The criterion of edification (14:1–5)
2. The criterion of intelligibility (14:6–12)
3. The application of the criteria to speech in public worship (14:13–19)

Exegesis and Exposition

[1]Pursue love and eagerly desire the spiritual gifts, but especially that you might prophesy. [2]For the one who speaks in a tongue does not speak to humans but to God. For no one hears [with understanding], but he or she speaks mysteries by the Spirit. [3]The one who prophesies speaks words to others that edify, exhort, and comfort. [4]The one speaking in a tongue builds up himself or herself. The one who prophesies builds up the church. [5]I wish for all of you to speak in tongues, but even more that you prophesy. The one who prophesies

is greater than the one speaking in tongues, unless one interprets so that the church receives edification.

⁶Suppose, brothers and sisters, that I come to you speaking in tongues; how shall I benefit you unless I speak to you either with a revelation, or with knowledge, or with prophecy, or with teaching? ⁷Likewise, lifeless instruments give a sound, whether a flute or a harp. Unless it emits a distinction in the tones, how will it be known what [tune] is being played on the flute or the harp? ⁸For also if a bugle gives an indistinct sound, who will prepare themselves for battle? ⁹And so it is with you; unless you give a clear word through the tongue, how will it be known what is being said? For you will be speaking into the air. ¹⁰There are so many kinds of languages in the world, whatever their number, and none without meaning. ¹¹Therefore, unless I know the force of the sound, I will be a barbarian to the one speaking, and the one speaking will be a barbarian to me. ¹²And so it is with you; since you are so eager [to possess] spiritual powers, seek to abound in [those] that build up the church. ¹³Therefore, let the one speaking in a tongue pray [for the power] to interpret [what is said]. ¹⁴[For] if I should pray in a tongue, my spirit prays but my mind is unfruitful. ¹⁵What does this mean? I will pray with [my] spirit, but I will also pray with [my] mind. I will sing with [my] spirit, and I will sing with [my] mind. ¹⁶For if you give a blessing in the spirit, how will the one who is uninitiated say the "Amen" to your prayer of thanksgiving, since he or she does not know what you are saying? ¹⁷For indeed, you give thanks well enough, but it does not edify the other. ¹⁸I give thanks to God that I speak in tongues more than all of you. ¹⁹But in the assembly, I would rather speak five words with my mind, that I might instruct others, than ten thousand words in a tongue.

Like 12:31, so also 14:1 serves as a transitional verse. "Pursue [διώκετε, **14:1** *diōkete*] love"—the kind of love just described—completes the *digressio* in chapter 13 and recalls the "incomparable way" in 12:31. Paul frequently applies the verb "to pursue" as a metaphor for spiritual effort (cf. Rom. 9:30, 31; 12:13; 14:19; Phil. 3:12, 14; 1 Thess. 5:15; 1 Tim. 6:11; 2 Tim. 2:22). "Eagerly desire the spiritual gifts" (ζηλοῦτε τὰ πνευματικά, *zēloute ta pneumatika*) picks up another phrase from 1 Cor. 12:31 ("eagerly desire [ζηλοῦτε] the greater grace-gifts") and prepares for the conclusion of his argument, which now addresses specifically the expression of tongues in the assembly.

What is to be pursued is clearly superior to what is merely to be desired. The δέ (*de*) may be an adversative, "but": "Pursue love but nevertheless eagerly desire the spiritual gifts"—as if to say that his exaltation of love is not intended to diminish the value of the spiritual gifts (so Chrysostom, *Hom. 1 Cor.* 35.1; Edwards 1885: 357; Barrett 1968: 312; Thiselton 2000: 1083). Or, it may be resumptive and so translated "and" (so Fee 1987: 235; Kistemaker 1993: 476; Hays 1997: 235; Lindemann 2000: 297). This last seems the best option. Love is to be yoked to the Corinthians' zeal for spiritual gifts. With love as their aim, it will prevent them from being zealous only for those gifts that will enable them to steal the show and outshine others.

Paul returns to the Spirit-language (τὰ πνευματικά, *ta pneumatika*) with which he opened this discourse in 12:1, rather than continuing with the grace-gift language he took up in 12:4 and used in 12:9, 28, 30, 31. I agree with the distinction that Ellis (1978: 24) makes that τὰ πνευματικά applies specifically to "gifts of inspired perception, verbal proclamation and/or its interpretation." It is related to speaking in the Spirit (see the discussion on 12:1). Thiselton (2000: 1083) thinks that the term refers to "the gifts of the Spirit for utterance" within the context of worship (though Thiselton gives the term a completely different meaning in 12:1 [see 2000: 930]). The predominance of the verb "to speak" (λαλεῖν, *lalein*), twenty-four times in chapter 14, makes clear that Paul has in mind gifts of speech: glossolalia and prophecy.

"Prophecy" is not an "incomparable way," but it is unquestionably the gift to be preferred over tongues. The μᾶλλον δέ (*mallon de*, but rather, especially) makes this clear, and in what follows, Paul clarifies why he favors prophecy. The Corinthians have not asked which of the two is to be preferred (contra Findlay 1910: 902). After laying the groundwork for his argument in chapters 12–13, his purpose, to temper their uninhibited zest for tongues in the assembly, becomes more explicit. Prophecy is to predominate in the worship. "To prophesy" means to proclaim a divine revelation (see further the comments on 12:8–10) or, more simply, "to speak on behalf of God" (R. Collins 1999: 491). Thiselton (2000: 1084) labels it even more simply as "healthy preaching" (cf. D. Hill 1979: 123, "pastoral preaching"). Prophecy is not individualistic in focus (Friedrich, *TDNT* 6:854) but is meant to communicate to others in rational, intelligible language. It builds up the community (14:4, 5) through exhortation and consolation (14:3, 31) and its didactic function (14:19, 31). It convicts unbelievers and leads them to repentance and worship of the one true God (14:25). The prophet is inspired by revelation but is not regarded as infallible, since the word spoken is to be weighed and sifted (14:29). Since Paul encourages all the addressees to desire eagerly to prophesy, he does not envision it as a spiritual activity limited only to persons holding a particular office. In principle, any person might be gifted by God to prophesy (Grudem 1982: 231–39; Schrage 1999: 384; so also Wolff 1996: 328; Lindemann 2000: 297). Implicit in this exhortation is the conviction that the Spirit is free "to choose any Christian through whom to speak" (Forbes 1995: 258). In 14:24, Paul does not think it out of the question that all could prophesy so that an unbeliever is convicted "by all." In 14:31, he again emphasizes the "all" by asserting that they *all* are able to prophesy in turn so that *all* may learn and *all* be instructed. If he were referring only to a limited circle of prophets, there would be no need to retain the "all" (Forbes 1995: 259). Some may have the gift of prophecy in greater measure, but Paul believes that all the Lord's people can be prophets (cf. Num. 11:29).

Some interpreters argue that prophecy is something that is only spontaneous and excludes some previously prepared sermon (Dunn 1975: 228; Fee 1987: 660; Forbes 1995: 229, 236). Why otherwise, it is asked, would the first prophet need to stop when another receives a revelation (1 Cor. 14:30)? Thiselton (2000: 1091–92) insists, however, that prophecy should not be equated with oracular forms of prophecy in the surrounding culture, which did tend to be spontaneous. Thiselton contends that prophecy can "involve sustained reflection" (cf. Lindemann 2000: 299). The moment of revelation should not be restricted to flashes that come only during worship. Revelation can come at other times, allowing the individual to ponder it and share it later, in the next worship.

Paul explains why he prefers prophecy over tongues. Tongues consti- **14:2** tute communion with God, not communication with others. The one who speaks in tongues utters mysteries πνεύματι (*pneumati*), which could mean "with the human spirit" (as opposed to "with the mind," 14:14–15; so Godet 1887: 266; Parry 1926: 200; Morris 1958: 191; Héring 1962: 146) or "by the Holy Spirit." Fee (1987: 656 n. 22) argues for the latter because in 12:7–11 tongues are one of the "manifestations of the Spirit of God." Kistemaker (1993: 478) also points out that it is the Holy Spirit who reveals mysteries. According to Talbert (1987: 90–91), tongues are Christian because of their *source,* the Holy Spirit; the *location,* in a confessing community; and the *results,* thanksgiving to God (14:4). What Paul emphasizes, however, is that they are spoken to God alone. Glossolalia is a holy soliloquy that others, hearing only amorphous sounds, do not comprehend. Consequently, there is no such thing as a "message in tongues" (Fee 1987: 656). If the mysteries uttered are "revealed truths," they are not revealed to anyone else, and there is no "stewardship" of the mysteries (2:7; 4:1). Some may be impressed by the display of mumbo jumbo, but no one is enlightened. Glossolalia is revelatory only if it is interpreted into understandable language. Therefore, Paul contends that the one who communicates intelligibly is greater than the one who speaks in tongues. Perhaps the Corinthians believed that the opposite was true: the one who spoke in tongues had graduated "with high honors into the category of the truly spiritual" (Stendahl 1976: 111). If so, Paul inverts their pyramid of values.

Edification (οἰκοδομή, *oikodomē,* 8:1; 10:23; 1 Thess. 5:11) is the bench- **14:3–4** mark by which to measure what goes on in the public worship. It refers primarily to the qualitative growth of the church but can also apply to its quantitative growth. Paul wants nothing done in worship that will unnecessarily drive unbelievers away. Παράκλησις (*paraklēsis*) has a broad range of meanings, all of which have a pastoral dimension (Thiselton 2000: 1088–89). It can refer to exhortation (Phil. 2:1), consolation (2 Cor. 1:3–7), assurance (Luke 2:25), and encouragement (Rom. 15:4–5). The description of the activity of Judas and Silas in Acts 15:32 epitomizes what Paul means by prophecy. They are identified as prophets who said much to encourage and strengthen the believers (regarding the apostolic decree). Παραμυθία (paramythia) appears only here in the NT and is nearly synonymous with paraklēsis. It refers to "that which serves as encouragement to one who is depressed or in grief" (BDAG 769). The prophets' words connect to the hearers' lives. They convey to others God's comfort, which "strengthens weak knees and jacks up sagging spirits so that one faces the troubles of life with unbending resolve and unending assurance" (Garland 1999: 60).

Those who speak in tongues "edify" or "build up" only themselves. Paul does not mean this in a derogatory way. Speaking in tongues does offer a benefit, but only to the individual. Theissen (1987: 304–15) speculates how: It affords access to the unconscious dimensions of the soul and allows repressed impulses access to the consciousness. It enters into an inner space dissociated from the everyday realities surrounding them and it may result in a feeling of peace and even euphoria (Esler 1994: 41–42). At best, it serves the corporate good only indirectly because it is meaningful only to the individual who experiences it. But the verb "build up" can have a double meaning in the context, which reveals the danger with tongues. It can be used to meet one's own ego needs rather than the needs of the church, particularly if speaking in tongues was a status-conferring activity, as D. Martin (1991: 556) argues. Its practice can slip into self-assertion, and only love would check such self-display.

The use of the word "church" (ἐκκλησία, ekklēsia) refers to the context—the gathering of the church community. Since worship is a corporate experience, Paul promotes what strengthens the entire group. Prophecy, he insists, serves all who gather.

14:5 Héring (1962: 146) attempts to downplay Paul's wish (θέλω, thelō) that all the Corinthians speak in tongues by claiming that it is a "concession in the form of a wish that is unlikely to be fulfilled." But it is no less a serious wish than those found in 7:7, 32; 10:20. Paul approves of speaking in tongues, but if he limits its public expression to only two or three speakers, then he must assume that the majority will speak privately. This wish that "all" speak basically democratizes the gift. It need not belong to an "elitist monopoly." Kistemaker (1993: 481) ties this wish to Moses' response to Joshua, who has implored him to muzzle the prophesying of Eldad and Medad before they became serious rivals. Moses responds that he wishes for all the Lord's people to become prophets and experience the Spirit (Num. 11:29). Kistemaker argues that Paul follows Moses' example in wishing that "the Holy Spirit might come upon God's people in full measure." Thiselton (2000: 1097) agrees and understands this wish to be a rejection of the "individualism and elitism of any exclusive bestowal of the Spirit." Spiritual gifts must not be the cause of competitive jealousy.

Paul's preference (μᾶλλον δέ, *mallon de*), however, is for the Corinthians to prophesy. Prophecy is greater than tongues unless someone interprets the tongues, which then produces something of value for upbuilding the community.[1] I agree with Thiselton's (1979; 2000: 1098–99) assessment that "interpret" means to put into articulate intelligible speech what is difficult to express or almost beyond human expression. In other words, glossolalia is transformed into prophecy (Godet 1887: 269). Who interprets is not specified, though the command in 1 Cor. 14:13 that the one speaking in tongues should pray to be able to interpret suggests that the subject could be the glossolalist. This statement clarifies the problem for Paul: it is not "speaking in tongues per se but speaking in tongues without interpretation—which from the context seems very likely what the Corinthians were doing" (Fee 1987: 659).

The address "brothers and sisters" marks a shift in Paul's argument throughout this chapter. The νῦν δέ (*nyn de*) has a logical sense, as in 12:20 (cf. νυνὶ δε ⌊*nyni de*⌋ in 12.18, 13.13; 15:20). It means something like "let us look at the facts" (Héring 1962: 147), "but as it is" (Fee 1987: 661 n. 5), or "suppose" (REB). The issue concerns what benefits, and Paul provides an illustration that assumes the obvious. No one benefits from something that he or she cannot understand. Paul uses the rhetorical "I" to help his critique of tongues go down easier. He could come and speak to them only in tongues, but it would have no positive effect. Only if he communicates with a revelation, prophecy, or teaching could they possibly benefit. A babbling apostle is a contradiction in terms.

14:6

Paul uses "revelation" (ἀποκάλυψις, *apokalypsis*) to refer to the revelation of the gospel to him (Gal. 1:12), a revelation about what to do (Gal. 2:2), and a visionary experience (2 Cor. 12:1, 7), though he never shared the content of this particular revelation, since it was prohibited for him to do so and it would serve only to build up himself. Knowledge, prophecy, and teaching were listed earlier (1 Cor. 12:8–10, 28, 29–30; 13:1–2, 8). How the terms differ from one another is open to speculation (see Fee 1987: 663). Conzelmann (1975: 235 n. 20) claims that revelation and knowledge are gifts that express themselves in prophecy and teaching. Schrage (1999: 390) notes that there can be no prophecy without revelation, or teaching without knowledge. Paul's point is that

---

1. The phrase ἐκτὸς εἰ μή (*ektos ei mē*) is normally explained as a Pauline pleonasm, "except if, unless."

there would be no positive results and no enrichment if he did not communicate with them through intelligible speech.

14:7–9   Paul makes his case for forbidding uninterpreted tongues in the assembly with three analogies. The first compares the indistinct tones played on musical instruments, a flute and a harp (or zither). They are described as τὰ ἄψυχα (*ta apsycha*, lifeless instruments). If they are plucked or piped without giving a distinct pitch, they will simply make noise and no discernible tune. The word φθόγγοι (*phthongoi*) should be rendered "tones" or "notes" and refers to a recognizable melody (Gale 1964: 130). Only when these instruments are directed by the mind does a melody come forth. Paul's logic is this: if lifeless things require "distinctness, and harmony, and appropriateness," how much more so this is true of humans (Chrysostom, *Hom. 1 Cor.* 35.3).

His second analogy appeals to a bugle that is intended to give out a signal rather than music (cf. Matt. 24:31; 1 Cor. 15:52; 1 Thess. 4:16; Rev. 1:10; 4:1; 8:6–13; 9:1, 13; 10:7; 11:15).[2] If it makes only a garbled sound that falls dead on the ear, it will fail to produce the appropriate action. It serves no purpose but instead defeats its purpose.

Paul connects the illustrations to their situation. If the Corinthians do not speak in clear, distinct, recognizable words with their tongue, they will be speaking into the air. Trying to decipher what they mean when they speak in tongues is like trying to translate the sounds that the wind makes. The implication from this description of tongues as indistinct sounds is that the Corinthian tongues are not xenoglossolalia—speaking an unlearned foreign language—but the utterance of inarticulate noises and syllables (Schrage 1999: 394–96). No earthly lexicon could decipher their meaning.

In drawing the comparison, Paul treats the "tongue" as the organ of speech, which is like the other sound-producing instruments. To avoid confusing this organ of speech with speaking in tongues, Paul includes the definite article (τῆς γλώσσης, *tēs glōssēs*) and the preposition διά (*dia*). The tongue also can make indistinct sounds, which no one understands, or articulate sounds, which communicate. The glossolalists probably imagined themselves as glowing with a certain spiritual aura and probably relished basking in the admiration of others. He puts their performance in a completely different light with the implication that the indistinct sounds made on the flute, harp, and bugle are made by inexpert players—mere novices. Perhaps to some extraterrestrial creature it may be music, but to the human ear it is only screeches and

---

2. The trumpet (σάλπιγξ, *salpinx*) can be a musical instrument (Rev. 18:22), but in 1 Corinthians refers to a military bugle. It sounded the alarm of a coming attack (Jer. 4:19; 6:1, 17; Ezek. 33:3–6; Hos. 5:8; Joel 2:1), the beginning of an attack (Judg. 3:27; Jer. 51:27), and the end of an attack (2 Sam. 20:1).

squawks. The same is true of tongues, which communicate nothing to others. Garbled speech is the stuff of comedy. In Apuleius's novel *Metamorphoses* (*The Golden Ass*), Lucius turns into a donkey after drinking a magic potion. He tries to free himself from a band of thieves who had commandeered him by invoking the name of the emperor when Roman troops approached. He brayed "O" with sonorous fluency, but he could not enunciate the word "Caesar" (*Metam.* 3.29). The resulting discordant donkey braying caused him to be flayed. The analogies leave the Corinthians to draw the inherent contrast between the glossolalists, who utter incoherent sounds, and the prophets, who utter intelligible sounds.

14:10–11 Paul introduces a third example related to "sound" from the many different languages in the world—something that would have been very familiar in the melting pot that was Corinth (see additional note). The word φωνή (*phōnē*, sound) is also used for "language" or "dialect" (Gen. 11:1, 7; 4 Macc. 12:7). He uses this word for "languages" because the term "tongues" is used for glossolalia (Betz, *TDNT* 9:273, 289). It also permits a play on words that is impossible to capture in English: "There are many sounds in the world and none without sound [ἄφωνον, *aphōnon*]"; that is, the sounds in the different languages are not without meaning to someone who speaks the language. But if one does not understand the meaning of the sounds—literally, "the power of the sound" (the "force of the word")—then its meaning is lost. The different speakers speaking different languages only baffle each other—literally, they become "barbarians" to each other. The word βάρβαρος (*barbaros*) is an onomatopoetic term in Greek because foreign speech sounded to the Greek ear like "bar, bar, bar." Persons speaking different languages cannot communicate with each other. Like foreign languages, tongues require some kind of interpretation to become meaningful. Since Paul exhorts the Corinthians to pray to be able to interpret (14:13), even the glossolalists appear to be clueless about what is being said.

The picture is of "two intelligent persons" who are "unintelligible to one another" (Robertson and Plummer 1914: 310). Anyone who has lived in or visited a country whose language was different knows the frustration created by the inability to understand or to communicate except by a primitive sign language. Paul's critique of tongues implies that it does more than simply create frustration; it erects barriers of alienation—the sick feeling that one does not belong. What is worse, these feelings are awakened in a place where one is supposed to feel at home: the community of believers. Unintelligible tongues also foster cliques. M. Mitchell (1993: 172) points out that a "common language is needed for concord." Paul's fear is this: if persons chattering in tongues without interpretation dominate the worship, then the church will become a Babel-ground of competing gibberish.

14:12 Paul testifies to the Corinthians' eagerness for spiritual phenomena, which explains why the command in 14:1 to be zealous for spiritual gifts needed to be qualified by the preference for prophecy. They are zealots for spiritual endowments—literally, "spirits" (πνευμάτων, *pneumatōn*; cf. 12:1). Oster (1995: 335) thinks that the peculiar wording reflects an "animistic perspective . . . which leads them to associate the supernatural spiritual gifts with the activity of various spirits." But Paul's statement is not intended to be ironic, sarcastic, or a mild rebuke (contra Robertson and Plummer 1914: 311; Oster 1995: 335), because he says much the same thing in 2 Cor. 8:7. In encouraging them to renew their commitment to the collection, he praises them for excelling in faith, speech, knowledge, and zeal.[3] Most think that he refers to spiritual gifts by metonymy by referring to the Spirit. Thiselton (2000: 1107) interprets "spirits" as meaning the "powers of the Spirit." Paul's concern is that their ambition for spiritual powers or phenomena needs some constraint, without putting the brakes on it entirely. He would redirect their zeal to those things that contribute to the edification of the entire church: "If you are eager for spiritual powers, strive to excel in those that build up the church." That rules out speaking in tongues, since it builds up only the individual who speaks (1 Cor. 14:4). This command amends the opening injunction to strive for spiritual gifts. The most important spiritual gifts are those that edify others.

14:13–15 The key issue for Paul emerges in the command that the one speaking in a tongue should pray to interpret.[4] What is spoken in the assembly should be understandable; and if it is not, it must be interpreted into comprehensible language. Glossolalists are to pray to God, who apportions gifts (12:28), for the additional gift to interpret their incoherent speech into coherent speech. This prayer would occur during the worship service when the person is moved to speak in tongues (Schrage 1999: 397).

This command leaves the clear impression that verbalized tongues are deficient without intelligible interpretation. As a wise pastor, however, Paul identifies with those whom he wishes to correct (Chadwick 1954–55: 268–69) and switches to the first person in verse 14: "[for] if I should pray in a tongue." Speaking in tongues, he argues, causes the mind to lie fallow. It is "fruitless" (ἄκαρπος, *akarpos*), which also applies to the effect of the prayer on the listeners, who understand nary a word. Many assume that Paul reflects a common view about inspiration in his time (Conzelmann 1975: 237). Plato (*Ion* 534E) said, "To be filled by God entails relinquishing one's own thoughts to make room

---

3. It seems that the Corinthians are not yet zealots in doing good (cf. 1 Pet. 3:13).

4. The present subjunctive after the ἵνα (*hina*) can be equivalent to the infinitive. The phrase ἵνα διερμηνεύῃ (*hina diermēneuē*) can be translated "to interpret."

for God" (cited by Thiselton 2000: 984; cf. the texts listed by Theissen 1987: 285–86). Philo (*Heir* 52–53 §§263–65) adopted this notion and argued that when the divine light enters the mind, "naturally ecstasy and divine possession and madness fall upon us. For when the light of God shines, the human light sets; when the divine light sets, the human dawns and rises." He concludes, "The mind is evicted at the arrival of the divine Spirit, but when that departs, the mind returns to its tenancy" (see also *Spec. Laws* 1.11 §65; 4.8 §49). D. Martin (1991: 574) contends that the mind/Spirit dichotomy has nothing to do with the rational/irrational dichotomy. According to ancient authors (Plato, Philo, Iamblichus), "the pneumatic realm of discourse *is* a language in itself; it has its own form of rationality hidden from the 'common.'" D. Martin (1991: 575) proposes that "pneuma is the agent of higher status and authority" and that "the *nous* is the lower member of the dichotomy." The mind becomes inactive in order to give "full play" to the higher, divine element.

This interpretation is probably closer to how the Corinthians understood things than how Paul did. Thiselton (2000: 1112) insists, "Platonic or Idealist notions of the human spirit as a point of 'divine contact' are alien to Paul and plainly alien to the explicit thrust of 1 Cor. 2:10–12." To assume that Paul thinks that the Spirit evicts the mind is "to fall into the very trap to which the Corinthians and many today fall prey, namely, of associating the operation of the Holy Spirit more closely with noncognitive 'spontaneous' phenomena than with a self-critical reflection upon the word of God as that which addresses the understanding and thereby transforms the heart (cf. 14:23–25)" (Thiselton 2000: 1112–13). The question, then, turns on what Paul means by "my spirit."

Barrett (1968: 320) lays out three options: (1) "My spirit" may refer to the nonrational part of a person's psychological makeup that serves as the counterpart of the mind. (2) "My spirit" could refer to the spiritual gift entrusted to Paul (cf. 14:12). (3) "My spirit" could refer to the Holy Spirit given to Paul. The last option can be excluded. Paul is not talking about *the Spirit* when he calls it "my spirit."[5] As a divine power, the Holy Spirit can never become "my Spirit," though the Spirit does dwell in Christians (Rom. 8:11, 15; Gal. 4:6). Barrett opts for the spirit as the spiritual gift, but I am inclined to think that in the context "my spirit" refers instead to Paul's "innermost deepest depths" (cf. 1 Cor. 16:18; 2 Cor. 2:13; Rom. 1:9). "My spirit" parallels "my mind," which indicates that he is thinking in anthropological terms (Gillespie 1994: 154). R. Collins (1999: 502) explains Paul's reasoning: "The spirit is the

---

5. Thiselton (2000: 1112–13) challenges Fee's judgment (1987: 670) in translating it "my S/spirit prays" as the Holy Spirit gives utterance, because it connects the Spirit with "noncognitive 'spontaneous' phenomena."

faculty by which one is in communion with the deity. The mind is an organ of thought that allows for ordinary communication among human beings." The spirit may be in prayerful communion with God without the reason formulating the thoughts and feelings into comprehensible language. R. Martin (1984: 69) describes the experience this way: "It suggests an enraptured fellowship with God when the human spirit is in such deep, hidden communion with the divine Spirit that 'words'— at best broken utterances of our secret selves—are formed by a spiritual upsurge requiring no mental effort." Irrationality, however, is not a sign of the abundance of the Holy Spirit. The mind, too, can be in communion with the deity, and the use of the mind is important for Paul. He wants them to be of "the same mind" (1 Cor. 1:10), not the same spirit. He says that he has "the mind of Christ" (2:16), not the Spirit of Christ. He expects Christians to "be transformed by the renewing of your minds, so that you may discern what is the will of God" (Rom. 12:2). When one speaks rationally with the mind, it does not necessarily mean that the spirit lies fallow or that the Spirit does not inspire.

Paul sums things up in 1 Cor. 14:15: "What is the conclusion, then?" The phrase τί οὖν ἐστιν (ti oun estin) is similar to "What, then, shall we say?" (Rom. 4:1; 6:1; 7:7; 8:31; 9:14, 30). Does his argument lead him to exclude speaking in tongues altogether? Not at all. Thiselton (2000: 1113) unpacks Paul's reasoning: "If only the mind is active, everything remains at a theoretical level; if only the heart is active, the door lies open to self-deception and credulity. If both are open to the Holy Spirit, the result can build up the community and bear fruit (v. 14a) of love for the other." Paul's conclusion is that he will do both: he will pray and sing with spiritual ecstasy, and pray and sing in full possession of his mental faculties. That implies that the spiritual ecstasy will be complemented by rational interpretation that communicates to others and produces fruit. His specific instructions regarding tongues in 1 Cor. 14:27–28 reveal that he does not mean that he will vocalize this spiritual rapture with abandon. If none are present to interpret, he will remain silent and pray privately to God in the Spirit. The principle of love aimed at serving the best interests of others (cf. 8:13; 9:19–23)—in this case, their edification in public worship—curtails how he will express his spiritual experiences publicly. He makes the case for the intelligibility of worship (see Thiselton 2000: 1113)—a principle that has wide-ranging implications for contemporary worship. An idle mind produces the same result as blowing indiscriminately into a lifeless instrument. For a melody to be played, the mind must be active.

14:16–19 Giving a blessing (εὐλογεῖν, eulogein) is "virtually synonymous with offering thanksgiving in this context" (Thiselton 2000: 1114; Lindemann 2000: 305). It reflects the language of Jewish benedictions (Tomson 1990: 140). The blessing cannot evoke the proper response if no one knows what is said. The question "How will the one . . . say 'Amen'?" assumes that no one will be able to answer. The one who is supposed to chime in with the "Amen" to the blessing is identified as ὁ ἀναπληρῶν τὸν τόπον τοῦ ἰδιώτου (*ho anaplērōn ton topon tou idiōtou*), which reads literally, "the one who fills the place of the uninitiated." "Place" could be understood in a literal or metaphorical sense. Some assume that Paul distinguishes believers, outsiders, and unbelievers, and this phrase refers to outsiders. The term ἰδιώτης (*idiōtēs*) is attested in inscriptions for those who are not members of an association (Weiss 1910: 329–31), but it is unlikely that in a house church they reserved special seats for outsiders (Robertson and Plummer 1914: 313). Outsiders who are unbelievers also are not likely to join in the "Amen" in response to prayers. Theissen (1987: 296) identifies the person as "the outsider . . . who already belongs to the community but has not yet delivered proof of possession of the Spirit—a proof that some understand as speaking in tongues." Héring (1962: 151) broadens it to include "sympathizers who are not yet baptized, or quite simply 'ordinary Christians' who do not possess any gifts of inspiration." Héring thinks that Paul's concern is that they will be "repelled by unintelligible . . . speech." Tomson (1990: 143–44) believes that it reflects synagogue practice and a technical Hebrew phrase referring to the "representative of the community" who prays aloud in front of the congregation for those unable to pray. But why would this particular person be the one to respond with the "Amen"? Edwards (1885: 368–69) anticipates this view but thinks that the term refers to the person who occupies the position of hearer as opposed to the officiating minister.

It is far more likely that this phrase is metaphorical and open-ended and refers to all those who find themselves in the role of the novice when someone prays in a tongue. In this case, it describes all members of the community who do not understand what is said (Godet 1887: 282–83; Lietzmann 1949: 71–72; Robertson and Plummer 1914: 313; Conzelmann 1975: 239; Fee 1987: 673; Wolff 1996: 333; Schrage 1999: 401–2). The term refers to the nonexpert and is used for the layperson in contrast to a philosopher, a doctor, or a rhetorically trained speaker (2 Cor. 11:6; cf. Acts 4:13). The NIV aptly translates it "those who do not understand," which is more accurate than "ungifted" (NASB), "outsider" (NRSV), or "inquirers" (NIV margin). Someone speaking in tongues makes everyone else a neophyte since no one except an interpreter knows what the speech means. Paul basically assumes that the "neophyte" is the most important person in the worship (cf. 1 Cor. 14:23), because if this one cannot understand what is said, then what is said—no matter how miraculous—is all for nothing (Schweizer 1959: 405).

Again, Paul underscores the failure of tongues to edify the church. No one will say the "Amen" at the appropriate place but will sit in dumbfounded silence. The "Amen," a transliteration of the Hebrew אָמֵן (*ʾāmēn*), is a solemn assent made by the whole assembly to prayers (cf. 2 Cor. 1:20), which has been taken over from Jewish synagogue worship (along with psalm singing and prayers).[6] Paul assumes that it is customary in Christian worship, and Justin Martyr (*1 Apol.* 65) attests that it has become a fixture in Christian worship in noting that the whole congregation assents with "Amen" when he finishes prayers and thanksgiving.

It should be clarified that Paul does not think that praying in a tongue is completely inappropriate in worship. Quite the contrary: it gives fitting thanks. He does not intend to cast any doubt that the glossolalist is genuinely giving thanks, which makes a subjunctive translation, "You may be giving thanks well enough," unwarranted (Barrett 1968: 321; Fee 1987: 674). The glossolalist does well, and Paul is not intending to be ironic (cf. Mark 7:9; contra Robertson and Plummer 1914: 314, who see "touches of irony" throughout this section; and Oster 1995: 339). His problem is simply that no one else is edified by an outpouring of unfathomable utterances. The congregation is only disconcerted, disoriented, and distracted from their worship of God. Worshipers should strive to give thanks in such a way that everyone will know that they are giving thanks, know what they are giving thanks for, and know when to respond suitably with the "Amen."

Paul gives genuine thanks that he speaks in tongues more than all of them and does not resort to irony. He has identified tongues as a gift of the Spirit and is not on the defensive (contra Fee 1987: 675, who interprets him to be saying, "Despite what you may think, I too speak in tongues—more than all of you"). Paul always seeks to find common ground with those whom he must correct (Johnson, *ABD* 6:599), and he wishes to make clear that his criticism of the use of this gift in the public assembly is not rooted in any lack of understanding or appreciation for this particular gift on his part. He understands, appreciates, and experiences this gift more intensely—in a qualitative sense, rather than quantitative—than do all of them. His own experience with speaking in tongues gives him authority to argue that tongues are less than beneficial for communal worship.

For this reason, he would rather speak five words with his mind in the assembled congregation than ten thousand words in a tongue. The number "five" is a round number meaning "a few" (cf. Isa. 30:17; Edwards 1885: 371; Conzelmann 1975: 240; Thiselton 2000: 1118). The hyperbole of speaking ten thousand (μυρίους, *myrious*; the largest number in Greek [cf. 1 Cor. 4:15]) words in a tongue drives home the point

6. 1 Chron. 16:36; Neh. 5:13; 8:6; Tob. 8:8; Num. 5:22; Deut. 27:15; Rom. 1:25; 11:36; 15:33; Gal. 1:5; Eph. 3:21; Phil. 4:20; 2 Tim. 4:18; 1 Pet. 5:11; Rev. 1:6.

that mindless, incomprehensible jabber instructs no one (though tongues may speak meaningfully to God if led by the Spirit). A fruitful mind, by contrast, instructs others and leads to fruitful results. It too must be led by the Spirit to have the right results. The criterion governing Paul's conclusion is what will do the most good for the community (9:19–22; R. Collins 1999: 504). Public worship is for mutual edification, not private enrichment. Paul may also believe that Christ came to make the word intelligible and accessible at the human level. Tongues are discarnational rather than incarnational (Stagg 1973: 55–56) and make the word unintelligible and inaccessible. Tongues can do more harm than good in the public worship (Thiselton 2000: 1117). Paul's criterion is rooted in the principle of exercising love for others. As one richly endowed with this gift, he refrains from using it because it does not benefit others and may even harm them (cf. 8:13). Hays (1997: 238) is one of the few to recognize that Paul sets himself up here as an example to be imitated (as he does so many other times in the letter). He portrays himself renouncing "spiritual glory and status" and "rights and privileges" to benefit others in the church.

Additional Note

14:10. Paul uses the protasis of a fourth-class conditional sentence, εἰ plus the optative τύχοι (second aorist) from τυγχάνειν. I adopt Edwards's (1885: 363) translation: "There are so many—whatever the number may be." It implies a large number, but the exact number does not matter (Robertson and Plummer 1914: 310).

F. The Preference for Prophecy (14:20–25)

Verses 20–25 constitute Paul's final argument to persuade the Corinthians to put the emphasis on prophecy instead of tongues in their public worship (Sandnes 1996: 1). Not only do tongues not edify believers, but also they are a sign of the alienation of unbelievers that cements their unbelief. Tongues, being unintelligible, cannot convince outsiders of the truth of the gospel. Only prophecy, which is understandable, can do that. The outline of the structure of the passage is adapted from Fee (1987: 677):

1. Exhortation (14:20)
2. OT text: other tongues are a sign of God's retribution (14:21)
3. Application (14:22)
    a. Tongues are a sign not for believers but unbelievers
    b. Prophecy is a sign not for unbelievers but believers
4. Illustrations (14:23–25)
    a. The negative effect of tongues on unbelievers
    b. The positive effect of prophecy on unbelievers

Exegesis and Exposition

[20]Brothers and sisters, do not become children in your understanding but be as children in wickedness. Become mature in your understanding. [21]It stands written in the law: "In strange tongues and by the lips of foreigners I will speak to this people and not even then will they obey me," says the Lord. [22]So, then, tongues are a sign not to believers but to unbelievers, and prophecy is [a sign] not for unbelievers but believers. [23]Therefore, if the whole church comes together at the same place and all speak in tongues, and an uninitiated person or an unbeliever enters, will he or she not say, "You are mad"? [24]But if all prophesy and an unbeliever or uninitiated person enters, he or she is convicted by all [that is said], and is called to account by all [that is said]. [25]The secrets of the heart become open, and so he or she will fall on his or her face and worship God, proclaiming, "Certainly God is among you."

14:20   Paul says in 3:1 that he cannot address the Corinthians as "spiritual ones" but only as "babes [νήπιοι, nēpioi] in Christ." In 13:11, he uses the image of childishness—speaking, thinking, reckoning as a child (νήπιος)—as a contrast to reaching maturity, to illustrate the superiority of love over spiritual gifts that eventually will come to an end. Now he exhorts them not to be children (παιδία, *paidia*), that is, "childish," in their understanding but to be as babes (νηπιάζετε, *nēpiazete*) in regard to wickedness and to become mature in their understanding.[1]

The first child image in 14:20 calls to mind the natural tendency of children to be self-centered and vain, to call attention to themselves, and to be enthralled by what is showy—"to prefer the amusing to the useful, the brilliant to the solid" (Godet 1887: 287). The second child image calls to mind childish innocence, a naivete that is unspoiled by the wicked ways of the world. When it comes to villainy, they are to be like those "born yesterday" (Thiselton 2000: 1119; cf. Rom. 16:19). "Wickedness" may be an allusion to the ethical lapses in the congregation (cf. 5:8) but may also refer to wicked attitudes that create division.

Although Paul deftly avoids accusing the Corinthians of being childish by saying do not "become [γίνεσθε, *ginesthe*] childish" rather than do not "be childish" (Edwards 1885: 371), he does imply that they are not mature in their thinking in telling them that they need to become (γίνεσθε) mature. This admonition is tied to his negative appraisal of their use of tongues in their worship. He has just said that tongues bypass the mind (14:14). The implication is that the Corinthians' fondness for tongues, at the expense of other gifts that use the mind, will result in their church degenerating into an unthinking, incoherent cult, "more interested in entertainment than education" (Kistemaker 1993: 498). They are to use their intelligence to develop an enlightened maturity, and they need to be weaned from an overemphasis on tongues. Gillespie (1994: 159) writes, "What separates the children from the adults in this instance is their respective attitudes toward the value of ecstatic speech."

Paul weighs in with Scripture (Isa. 28:11–12), which he cites as "the law" (cf. 1 Cor. 9:8, 9, 20; 14:34), to lay the basis of his crowning argument against uninterpreted tongues in worship. In Isaiah's context, the prophet pronounces a judgment against Israel. Since Israel refused to heed what God spoke to them in understandable language through the prophet, God will now approach them by means of the foreign language of the conquering Assyrians. Isaiah clashes with priests and prophets who have mocked his prophetic declarations as simplistic nonsense lessons for small children (Isa. 28:9–10, 13), which, in the Hebrew, they seem to mimic as baby talk.[2] These critics are dismissed as reeling drunks, overconfident in their own twisted judgments (Isa. 28:7). God's judgment for rejecting the prophet's simple, straightfor-

14:21

---

1. The word "understandings" is plural (φρένες, *phrenes*) and refers to the seat (originally the midriff) of the mental faculties.
2. The Hebrew is obscure and strikes many as an approximation of glossolalia: ṣaw lāṣāw, ṣaw lāṣāw, qaw lāqāw, qaw lāqāw, zĕʿêr šām, zĕʿêr šām.

ward message will be that the word of the Lord will now come to them "as sounds without meaning, as alphabet letters in a language in which they yet understand no words" (Grudem 1979: 383). Since they will not be able to understand this message, it assures their unbelief and becomes a sign of God's judgment.

Paul's citation of Isa. 28:11–12 does not match the LXX or the MT, and the differences are numerous.[3]

1. Paul's text inverts the order of "other tongues" and "stammering lips" so that "other tongues" comes first.
2. Paul's text substitutes "other lips" for "stammering lips" with the result that it is synonymous with "other tongues" and correlates more closely to the Corinthian situation.
3. Paul's text uses the first person, "I will speak," which is closer to the MT, where the Lord is the speaker, than the LXX, "for they [the Assyrian invaders] will speak to this people." This difference could be attributable to Paul's deliberate alteration or could be text based (C. Stanley 1992: 201–2).
4. Paul's text omits "To whom he said, 'This is rest, give rest to the weary, and this is repose,'" which does not apply to the Corinthian situation. The result is that the quotation is no longer "a reference to past stubbornness but to a future refusal to hear speech in foreign tongues" (Grudem 1979: 386).
5. Paul's text has οὐδ᾽ οὕτως (*oud' houtōs*, not even thus) instead of οὐκ (*ouk*, not). This substitution "bridges the gap" created by the previous omission (C. Stanley 1992: 203) and makes the text more pointed. Not even when God's communication takes this unusual form of expression will they listen.
6. Paul's text uses the compound verb εἰσακούειν (*eisakouein*), which implies hearing and giving heed, instead of ἀκούειν (*akouein*), which need only imply hearing.
7. Paul's text has the future tense, "they will not hear and respond," instead of the infinitive and omits the idea that they will not want to hear. The future tense lays out the consequences if they persist in not responding. The result is that the judgment theme is altered. Johanson (1978–79: 182) comments, "The MT would indicate that since the people refuse to listen to God's intelligible message previously given, they will now be spoken to by men of 'strange tongues.'" In Paul's version, they are not blamed for their refusal to believe when they hear these other tongues; they simply

---

3. C. Stanley (1992: 198) claims that determining the relationship between Paul's wording and the LXX "is one of the greatest challenges in the entire corpus of Pauline citations." The text is used in 1QH 4:16 to refer to false prophets who speak to God's people in an alien tongue.

cannot understand. This change makes sense in the context, since Paul is urging the Corinthians to address outsiders in understandable language (Sandnes 1996: 8). In Isaiah, God speaks to Israel through a foreign tongue as retribution, and the consequence is that they will not understand. The Corinthians are speaking in tongues to outsiders who cannot understand, not who refuse to understand. The results are the same, however. Both Israel and the outsider fail to obey the message, which leads to judgment.

8. Paul's text adds οὐδ᾽ οὕτως, which means "not even thus" or "not even then" will they hear and respond. In Paul's context, this means that "other tongues" will be useless in causing them to hear and to respond to the Lord.

9. Finally, Paul adds the phrase "says the Lord" to add punch to the quotation (cf. Rom. 12:19).

C. Stanley (1992: 198–201) concludes that it is difficult to determine whether the difference is attributable to a revision of the LXX tradition or to a different translation entirely. Lietzmann (1949: 73; see also Moffatt 1938: 224; Héring 1962: 152 n. 14; Conzelmann 1975: 242 n. 17) attaches credence to Origen's statement (*Philocalia* 9.2) that he found a similar reading in Aquila's rendering of the OT and that Paul followed a similar translation. The nine differences from the LXX and the MT fit Paul's purposes so well, however, that it seems more likely that 14:21 represents an interpretive paraphrase of the text that he adapts to this context.

The two passages seem to connect only in the reference to "speaking in other tongues." Sandnes (1996: 8) contends that the point of comparison is this: "God once approached Israel with tongues, and the result was that their disbelief was confirmed. Now the Corinthians are speaking in tongues while outsiders are present, which causes the latter to abandon the Christian fellowship as being mad." As it applies to the Corinthian situation, Paul insinuates that "speaking in tongues is not able to convey adequate understanding of God's message. On the contrary, it confirms disbelief" (Sandnes 1996: 8–9). While Smit (1994: 186) thinks that the original context and meaning "are entirely irrelevant here," Thiselton (2000: 1121) maintains that the two contexts "match well":

> Those who are "wise" and "gifted" in their own eyes dismiss the plain message as "childish," when in reality it is the supposedly wise who think and act like children. Divine judgment, as so often occurs in life, has a dimension of "internal grammar," i.e., God permits the seeds of its own fall to operate. The disdain of plain speech comes home with a vengeance: if they want something other than intelligible speech, they can have it; however, it will serve as an uncomfortable judgment, for it will

place many of God's own people from whom they ought to care in the position of *aliens and outsiders.*

Thiselton (2000: 1122) also maintains that *"Paul is simultaneously quoting and applying the passage,"* which accounts for the similarities and divergences. Paul applies this passage to the effect of tongues on unbelievers in the Corinthian situation (Fee 1987: 677, 680). Thiselton (2000: 1121–22) broadens this to include the effect of tongues on both unbelievers and fellow Christians. Thiselton thinks that the application of this passage makes two points:

> (i) tongue-speaking in public worship is inappropriate in the first place because *it places many of God's own people in the situation of feeling like foreigners in a foreign land and "not at home" in their own home;* (ii) second, tongue-speaking, contrary to some mistaken assumptions about "spirituality" in Hellenism, *will not bring the message of the gospel of Christ home to unbelievers.*

This reading makes good sense of what follows. When God speaks intelligibly, it is to reveal. When God speaks unintelligibly, it is to judge. In the Corinthian context, speaking in "other tongues" will fail to convey any meaningful message or bring repentance, just as it failed to do in Isaiah's day. The citation from Isaiah makes clear that tongues are not a saving sign but a sign of retribution. They do not stimulate belief but instead seal unbelief. In jeering at the simple message of the cross, the unbelievers in the Corinthian setting are like Isaiah's nemeses. They find the message of Christ crucified to be utter foolishness. Nevertheless, this simple message is the only message that will bring about their repentance.

14:22   Paul draws out the implications from the Isaiah citation in parallel statements:

> tongues are a sign
> > not to believers
> > > but to the unbelievers
> and prophecy [is a sign (an ellipsis)]
> > not to unbelievers
> > but to believers

This assertion presents another knotty problem. Paul says that tongues are a sign to unbelievers while prophecy is not, but the illustrations in 14:23–35 seem to contradict this statement. They depict the negative effect of tongues upon unbelievers and the positive effect of prophecy not on believers but on unbelievers (Johanson 1978–79: 180; cf. Héring

1962: 152). If tongues are a sign for unbelievers, why does he encourage them to use prophecy instead when unbelievers are present? The role of the believer is also puzzling (Sandnes 1996: 2). Tongues are not a sign for believers while prophecy is, yet he describes the positive effect of prophecy on unbelievers, not believers. The solution to this problem hinges on what Paul means by "sign." This statement also needs to be read in light of the interpretation of the Isaiah citation and in light of the illustrations that follow.

Paul uses the word "sign" infrequently but with a variety of meanings that make it difficult to pinpoint what connotation he intends here. He uses it to refer to an "outward token" (Rom. 4:11), "miracles" ("signs and wonders," positive: Rom. 15:19; 2 Cor. 12:12; cf. Heb. 2:4; negative: 2 Thess. 2:9), evidence of God's confirmation or approval (1 Cor. 1:22), and a distinguishing handwriting mark (2 Thess. 3:17). None of these usages applies in this context. It is clear from what follows that he is concerned about the effect of speaking in tongues on the church's missionary witness on unbelievers. How does he understand tongues to be a sign for unbelievers that, from the example that follows, only establishes them ever more firmly in their unbelief? Several explanations have been proposed.

Johanson 1978–79 (see also Talbert 1987: 87–88) tries to solve the problem by postulating that 1 Cor. 14:21–22 constitutes a Corinthian assertion and not Paul's own conviction. Paul responds to a rhetorical question posed by the Corinthians. They imagined that speaking in tongues was a sign that God was among them (Johanson 1978–79: 200) and claimed that it had apologetic value, which prophecy did not.[4] Paul counters this assertion by arguing that unbelievers will not be convicted by witnessing tongues but will think it incoherent lunacy instead. Prophecy is the only speech that will convict unbelievers that God is among them.

This interpretation founders because the text contains no signals that Paul cites a Corinthian position, and he does not state his own counterconviction. It fails to take into account the οὖν (oun) in 14:23, which serves to point out the consequences of the statement in 14:22 rather than to contradict it (see Smit 1994: 177). Interpreters should refrain from resorting to Corinthian slogans or quotations to solve exegetical riddles unless there is clear textual evidence that Paul is citing another's position.

---

4. Thiselton (2000: 1125), who disagrees with this view, notes that in the contemporary Pentecostal movement, tongues are understood to be a bond of love, the fullness of divine power, and something that awakens faith like a bell. It is precarious, however, to read this text in light of modern Pentecostal practices and assume that they would also hold true for the Corinthians.

Another view assumes that a sign is ambivalent. It leaves room for various interpretations, while prophecy is something that plainly reveals the truth. Smit (1994: 182) claims that Paul depicts glossolalia as a sign, "which inexpert outsiders do not interpret as a gift from God but as a μανία [*mania*] coming from the idols. Prophesying, however, he depicts as a 'refutation,' which irresistibly reveals the truth to critical hearers and unmistakably confronts them with God, who addresses them through believers." Glossolalia conjures up for the unbeliever previous religious experiences of ecstatic phenomena in pagan worship (Smit 1994: 183, 187, 189). Since Smit thinks that speaking in tongues is so similar to pagan mania, the unbeliever's misinterpretation of the "sign" is understandable. Smit (1994: 185) translates this verse, "The tongues are proper not to believers but to unbelievers; the prophecy, however, is proper not to the unbelievers but to the believers."

To be sure, signs are not always understood (see Exod. 10:1–2; Luke 11:30–32), but Smit's (1994: 187) view is based on the erroneous assumption that 1 Cor. 12:2 refers to the Corinthians' previous pagan ecstatic experiences in which they supposedly were "swept away." Smit's (1994: 188) conclusion that they leave the impression that they are still heathen by continuing these enthusiastic utterances in Christian worship directly contradicts Paul's perspective on tongues. Paul understands tongues to be a gift of the Spirit, not an unfortunate spiritual residue from the Corinthians' pagan past, and he assures them that he speaks in tongues more than all of them.[5] His own tongue-speaking experience is certainly not a pagan vestige.

In my view, "sign" has a double meaning in this context that is both negative and positive (cf. Grudem 1979; Fee 1987: 683). Glossolalia as a sign is to be taken in a negative sense with regard to unbelievers because it hardens them in their unbelief, as it did Israel in Isa. 28 (Rengstorf, *TDNT* 8:259; Sweet 1966–67: 244–45; Dunn 1975: 230–32; Grudem 1979: 390–91). It is a sign of alienation that will lead to judgment. On the other hand, glossolalia cannot be a negative sign for believers, because they are already believers. To Christians, speaking in tongues is a manifestation of the Spirit, though they may not understand what is said. Thiselton (2000: 1125) objects that tongues seem to have a negative effect on uninitiated Christians as well as on unbelievers. But

5. R. Collins (1999: 508) thinks that Paul is talking about pagan assumptions concerning tongues and prophecy: "In the Hellenistic world 'prophecy' connoted ecstatic utterance, sounds expressed by someone in a trance. In the biblical tradition the prophet . . . spoke an intelligible utterance." Collins concludes, "Nonbelievers may be impressed by those who utter unintelligible sounds, but believers are edified by those who prophesy." But this is not what Paul says; on the contrary, nonbelievers are not impressed. In fact, the question in 14:23, expecting the Corinthians to give the answer yes, assumes that they will recognize this reality. Paul appeals to the Corinthians' pride: they do not want to gain a reputation in the community as those who are mad (Sandnes 1996: 6).

Paul does not say that believers are driven away or hardened in their disobedience by witnessing someone speaking in tongues, only that they do not understand and consequently are not edified—a more neutral result.

By contrast, Paul does not specifically say that prophecy is a "sign." It certainly is not a sign of the unbelievers' exclusion, but something that can lead them to obedience. In fact, it is the only means of reaching outsiders because it lays open their souls and prepares the way for repentance (see Sandnes 1996: 14–15). Prophecy delivers the greatest good for unbelievers and Christians alike since it communicates, enlightens, and convicts. For Christians, the conversion of unbelievers through their prophecy is another sign of God's presence among them. Paul indirectly reproaches the Corinthians for the negative effect that speaking in tongues has on unbelievers. The church owes them more than a sign of estrangement and retribution (Rowe 1990: 57); the church must offer a coherent proclamation of the gospel by which they might be saved. Prophecy thereby becomes a means of grace (Thiselton 2000: 1126).

Paul's first illustration to corroborate his point envisions the whole church speaking in tongues. The image of all speaking in tongues "is impressionist rather than numerical" (Thiselton 2000: 1127). The effect that this outpouring of tongues will have on an unbeliever who happens to witness it will not be positive but will be like what happened in Isaiah's day. There will be no positive response from the untutored unbeliever. Those who are uninitiated (cf. 14:16), or as Findlay (1910: 910) aptly renders it, "unacquainted with Christianity," do not belong to a different category from the unbeliever, though the two nouns are listed separately (Schrage 1999: 411). The two terms supplement each other in describing the visitor as an "unbelieving outsider" (Barrett 1968: 324). They are not undecided Christians or seekers, but unbelievers who are ignorant of Christianity. These persons could include the non-Christian spouse (7:12–15), unconverted slaves, invited guests, or possibly the curious who might wander in. They will not be impressed by this spiritual outburst but will conclude that these Christians are stark raving mad. This example illustrates how the OT quotation would be fulfilled: the unbeliever will not repent and obey but will be repulsed and continue in disobedience to God. Paul's concern for the possible effects that their worship practices might have on unbelievers is consistent with his concern about the effect that the Corinthians' eating idol food might have on unbelievers (10:23–33).

The verb μαίνεσθαι (*mainesthai*) means "to be mad" or "out of one's mind." Thiselton (2000: 1126 n. 243) notes that the word "frequently combines *insanity* or *mind* with *raving* or *wild speech*." Many interpreters see an association with the mantic frenzy in mystery religions (Con-

14:23

zelmann 1975: 243 n. 26; Smit 1994: 183–84; Hays 1997: 238; R. Horsley 1998: 186) and conclude that the visitor will regard these goings-on as a typical mystery celebration. To be sure, uncontrolled ranting was part of some mystery rites. Livy (*History of Rome* 39.8–19) records the crackdown on Bacchic rites in Italy in 186 B.C. and describes them as a cacophony of noise resounding with shrieks, chanting, cymbals clashing, drums beating, and cries. He contends that the worshipers thought that they hit the height of religious achievement when they could regard nothing as forbidden: "Men, apparently out of their wits, would utter prophecies with frenzied bodily convulsions, matrons, attired as Bacchantes, with their hair disheveled. . . ." Achilles Tatius (*Leuc. Clit.* 2.3) speaks of Cupid and Dionysus as violent gods who can "grasp the soul and drive it so far towards madness that it loses all restraint" (see also Catullus, *Poem* 63.20–24). Thiselton (2000: 1127), however, cautions against defining too restrictively how the outsider would have responded. This one verb does not warrant reading some association with mystery rites into the unbeliever's reaction, because the same verb occurs elsewhere in the NT and simply means "crazy" (John 10:20; Acts 12:15; 26:24–25; see also Wis. 14:28; 4 Macc. 7:5; 8:5; 10:13).[6] Celsus provides a good example of an unbeliever's reaction to unintelligible speech in Christian worship:

> Having brandished these threats they then go on to add incomprehensible, incoherent, and utterly obscure utterances, the meaning of which no intelligent person could discover, for they are meaningless and nonsensical, and give a chance for any fool or sorcerer to take the words in whatever sense he likes. (Origen, *Cels.* 7.10)

Paul's point is simply that the unbeliever who witnesses everyone speaking in tongues will think that they have gone berserk or are possessed (Schrage 1999: 407–8) and will make for the exits as soon as possible.

14:24–25 Prophecy, by contrast, has the potential to penetrate the innermost sanctum of an unbeliever's soul with the laser light of divine judgment. It presents evidence that causes the individual to be scrutinized, exposed, and convicted of sin or of the truth (ἐλέγχεται, *elenchetai*; cf. John 8:46; 16:8; Acts 6:10; Titus 2:15). It calls the individual to account (ἀνακρίνεται, *anakrinetai*). In this case, prophecy must be gospel proclamation (so D. Hill 1979: 124–25; Gillespie 1994: 157). The phrase "by all" (ὑπὸ πάντων, *hypo pantōn*) does not imply gang evangelism, but that an unbeliever is probed and convicted "by all that is said" (Thiselton 2000: 1129). Alcibiades claimed that Socrates had this effect on him

---

6. One can speak rationally and still be thought to be crazy (John 10:20; Acts 26:24).

(Plato, *Symposium* 215–16), and Epictetus (*Diatr.* 3.23.29) writes that Musonius Rufus (the "Roman Socrates") so effectively grasped what humans did and revealed each person's particular weaknesses that they fancied that someone had informed him of their faults. The difference is that Paul says that Christian prophecy causes unbelievers to experience an overwhelming sense that they are in the presence of God (Moffatt 1938: 224). This happens in a house church, not a grand temple, and it happens through the instrument of simple people articulating God's power and love in simple language without pomp and circumstance or spiritual fireworks.

What are exposed are the secrets that are buried like splinters in the hidden recesses of the heart and that one hopes no one else will discover. Prophecy lays open these secrets and heals them, though it might be a painful process. In a society concerned about external appearances, the message rips away the camouflage used to hide who one really is. It unmasks secrets but also reveals the one who loves and accepts them even when they are fully exposed. This prophetic scrutiny of inner thoughts, conscious and unconscious, leads to the recognition of God's presence (Kuck 1992a: 208).[7]

Prophets know the secrets in a person's heart (see Luke 7:36–50); but, against Theissen's (1987: 78) proposal, there is no indication that the prophets speaking knew the innermost depths of the visitors. The prophet does not know to whom the words he or she speaks apply, except as one might generally understand the human condition and its alienation and depravity. The unbeliever comes to recognize, "These Christians know things that could only have been revealed to them by God" (Grudem 1979: 395). "Struck by this light, he casts himself in the dust, not before man, but before God" (Godet 1887: 296–97), as Paul had done on the road to Damascus (Acts 9:4). Falling on one's face is an attitude of worship (Gen. 17:3; Rev. 7:11; 11:16) and an acknowledgment of unworthiness. The experience leads an unbeliever to recognize the truth of the Christian faith and the divine inspiration of the speakers. It leads to confession and to worship of the one true God. It is the confession of the vanquished in Isa. 45:14 (see also 1 Kings 18:39; Dan. 2:47; Zech. 8:23), but in this case they are vanquished by the word. The positive sign that God is present among them and that they are moved by the Spirit is the conversion and the confession of the outsider.

The purpose of worship, as Chrysostom (*Hom. 1 Cor.* 36.2–3) recognizes, is not to astonish but to bring people to a sense of wonder. It should expose them to the divine presence so that they confess, "I ought

---

7. Barrett (1968: 324) cannily remarks, "The Corinthians tend to shut their ears to prophecy because they gain more satisfaction from listening to tongues than from hearing their faults exposed and their duties pointed out in plain rational language."

not to live as I do but must change and allow this God to effect that change." Judge (1984: 6) offers a shrewd observation:

> His [Paul's] only use of a technical term of worship in connection with the church-meeting is to describe the reaction of the hypothetical unbeliever who is stunned to discover, contrary to what would have seemed obvious, that God was actually present there (1 Cor. 14:25). In that scene of lively social intercourse there was neither solitude nor mystery, no shrine, no statue, no cult, no ceremony, no offering to ensure that all was well between gods and men. Instead there was talk and argument, disturbing questions about belief and behaviour (two matters of little or no concern to religion in antiquity), conscious changes to accepted ways, and the expectation of a more drastic transformation soon to come. The purpose of classical religion was to secure what was already there against just such an upheaval.

The upshot of Paul's long argument to this point is that prophecy is superior to tongues because it bears fruit in producing illumination, conviction, confession, and worship. Glossolalia does not do this and must be restricted in public worship. Tongues must be uttered by one speaker at a time, limited to no more than three speakers, and accompanied by articulate speech that is comprehensible. Bornkamm (1969: 177 n. 4) correctly recognizes that Paul attacks "all irresponsible speaking in worship that does not concern itself with those on the fringe and those outside, and that with self-satisfied will makes use of an esoteric language or even a Christian 'jargon'" that makes the stranger "feel hopelessly on the outside."

IX. The Use of Spiritual Gifts in Public Worship (12:1–14:40)
    E. The Comparison between Tongues and Prophecy (14:1–19)
    F. The Preference for Prophecy (14:20–25)
➤ G. Regulations for Worship and Concluding Instructions on Spiritual Gifts (14:26–40)

G. Regulations for Worship and Concluding Instructions on Spiritual Gifts (14:26–40)

In the final unit of chapters 12–14, Paul issues regulations for worship. Gatherings in which each person could make a contribution under the guidance of the Holy Spirit need some ground rules. Openness to the Spirit and to individual expression of spiritual gifts is not to become a pretext for chaos. Paul does not see tongues or prophecy as a solo performance. The glossolalist requires an interpreter; the prophet requires reviewers who assess what is said (Friedrich, *TDNT* 6:852). He offers three criteria to control what is done. First, edifying others becomes the touchstone to determine the fitness of everything that is done in the Corinthians' worship. Contributions to the church's worship are not to become an ego trip or an exercise in "unbridled individualism" (Talbert 1987: 93). Second, they are to speak one at a time (14:27, 30, 31) and may be limited to no more than three speaking at any given gathering (14:27, 29). Third, they are to do nothing that is shameful (14:35); wives are to refrain from speaking in any way that brings shame or shows insubordination.

In developing his argumentation, Paul states an overarching principle in 14:26. He then gives a rule regarding tongues, followed by a condition (14:27–28). In 14:29–33, he follows the same pattern of giving a rule followed by a condition regarding prophets but adds an explanation in 14:31–33a. In 14:33b–36, he follows this pattern regarding the conduct of wives: rule (14:33b–34a), condition (14:35a), explanation (14:34b, 35b), with a double rhetorical question added in 14:36 to underline the point. His discussion can be outlined as follows:

1. Restraints concerning speaking in tongues (14:27–28)
2. Restraints concerning prophecy and discernment (14:29–36)
   a. Restraints on the number of prophets speaking and others discerning (14:29)
   b. Restraints on a prophet speaking (14:30–33a)
   c. Restraints on wives in discerning (14:33b–36)
3. Injunction (14:37–38)
4. Encouragement of prophecy and tongues (14:39)

      5. Concluding statement of general principles for worship gatherings: all things must be done in decency and order (14:40)

This unit is similar to the conclusion of Paul's long discussion of the issues related to idol food in 10:23–11:1 in that it gives specific instructions about what should be done in concrete situations. The pattern for his instructions in both passages is comparable:

Statement of general principles
- All things are to be done for the edification of others (10:23–24/14:26)

Specific instructions for one situation
- Eating whatever is sold in the public market (10:25)
- Speaking in tongues (14:27–28)

Theological rationale
- The earth is the Lord's (10:26)

Specific instructions for a second, correlative situation
- Eating in an unbeliever's home (10:27)
- Prophecy (14:29–32)

Theological rationale
- God is not a God of disorder but of peace (14:33a)

Exception applicable to the second situation
- If someone points out that it is idol food (10:28–29a)
- Wives joining in the evaluation of prophecy (14:33b–35)[1]

General principle stated as a question
- Partaking thankfully (10:29b–30)
- The word of God not reaching the Corinthians alone (14:36)

Concluding statement of general principles
- Do all to the glory of God (10:31–11:1)
- Do all things properly and in good order (14:37–40)

Exegesis and Exposition

[26]What, then, does this mean, brothers and sisters? Whenever you come together, each one has a song, has a teaching, has a revelation, has a tongue, has an interpretation. Let all things be [done] for edification. [27]If anyone speaks in a tongue—two or at the most three [may speak], and each in turn—and let one interpret. [28]But if there is no interpreter, let the [speaker] be silent in the assembly and speak to himself or herself and to God.

---

1. I agree with Grudem (1982: 245–47) that 14:33b–35 is not a third topic on the prohibition of women speaking in the assembly. Instead, it offers more instructions about prophecy—in this case, the process of evaluating the prophecies.

²⁹But let two or three prophets speak, and let the others discern. ³⁰And if a revelation comes to a seated [listener], let the first [speaker] be silent. ³¹For you are all able to prophesy in turn so that all may learn and all may be encouraged. ³²And the spirits of the prophets are subject to the prophets. ³³For God is not a God of disorder but of peace.

As in all the churches of the saints, ⌐³⁴let the wives keep silent in the assemblies. For it is not permitted for them to speak; but let them be subject, just as the law says. ³⁵But if there is anything they wish to learn, let them ask their own husbands at home, for it is shameful for a wife to speak in the assembly.¬ ³⁶Or did the word of God go out from you, or has it reached you alone?

³⁷If someone presumes to be a prophet or spiritual, let him or her understand that what I am writing to you is a command of the Lord. ³⁸But if anyone disregards [this], ⌐that one is disregarded¬ [by God]. ³⁹So then, my brothers and sisters, seek to prophesy and do not hinder speaking in tongues. ⁴⁰Let all things be done properly and in good order.

Paul now sums up the implications of his discussion for what the Corinthians should do in their gatherings (τί οὖν ἐστιν; *ti oun estin?* What, then, does this mean? cf. 14:15). "Whenever you come together" (11:18, 20, 33–34; 14:23) presumably refers to the time after the meal. The terse syntax, repeating "he/she has" (ἔχει, *echei*) a "song," a "teaching," a "revelation," a "tongue," an "interpretation," may give the impression that their worship has become a competitive sport. Each one waits impatiently to go on stage to show off his or her gift. But Paul does not mean that every single worshiper has one of these gifts in the ready and is eager to exercise it. As in 7:2 and 11:21, "each one" does not mean every single individual. Though Corinth is a church "rich in speech" (1:5), not all in the congregation have speech gifts. Paul presents a hypothetical scenario, "suppose that when you assemble," rather than a real description of what is happening (Thiselton 2000: 1133; Lindemann 2000: 312). He imagines that when they gather, one has this gift, another has that.

Each gift listed has been mentioned previously in the chapter—psalm (14:15), teaching (14:6), revelation (14:6), tongue (14:2, 4, 5, 6, 9, 13, 14, 18, 19, 22, 23), and interpretation (14:5, 13). This should not be regarded as exhaustive or as an outline of the order of worship (contra Findlay 1910: 912). Paul's wording suggests a "superabundance" of gifts (Conzelmann 1975: 244), the allocation of these gifts among a wide variety of persons, and a gathering buzzing with excitement. These elements can threaten orderliness, however, and he aims to regulate what happens so that the expression of their spiritual gifts contributes to the overall good of the body.

We do not know whether the "song" (ψαλμός, *psalmos*; cf. 14:15; Eph. 5:19; Col. 3:16) is a prayer or a sacred song of praise. If it is the latter, we do not know whether it is a fresh composition or a known

14:26

composition (from the Psalms); something for all to sing or for only one; something accompanied by an instrument or unaccompanied; or a vehicle to exhort, instruct, or uplift others. Some conclude that Paul has the Psalter in view (Lindemann 2000: 313); others assume a Christian composition (see Col. 1:15–20; 1 Tim. 3:16; Rev. 4:11; 5:9; Moffatt 1938: 227; Wolff 1996: 338–39; R. Collins 1999: 518). We can only conclude with certainty that hymnody was an important feature of early Christian worship.

"Teaching" would appear to require "sustained biblical reflection" (Thiselton 2000: 1135; cf. 1 Cor. 4:17) rather than something spontaneous. "Revelation" refers to something divinely disclosed and presented in comprehensible language. The revelation could occur prior to or during the worship (cf. 2 Cor. 12:1–7; Gal. 1:12, 16; 2:2). The "tongue" is spontaneous, as is the "interpretation" of what it means. The purpose of all these manifestations of the Spirit is to build up the community. "Building up" others becomes the litmus test for determining the relative value of gifts, and Paul underscores its importance throughout this chapter (1 Cor. 14:3, 4, 5, 12, 17; see also 8:1; 10:23). The thrust of this chapter makes clear that he wishes to thwart those expressions of spiritual gifts that build up only the individual (14:4) and to encourage those gifts that edify the entire community. The controlling factors are to be order, self-control, and concern for others (Fee 1987: 688).

14:27–28   Paul imposes limitations on the use of tongues in the gathering: only two or three speakers, only one at a time, and only if an interpreter is present who can make sense of it in intelligible language.[2] Fee (1987: 691) allows that verse 27 could mean no more than two or three tongues before an interpretation. But "at most" (τὸ πλεῖστον, to pleiston) suggests no more than two or three at any one worship service. R. Collins (1999: 518) interprets this restriction to mean that many "were eager to demonstrate their charismatic prowess in the midst of the assembly."[3] The insistence that each one speak in turn also suggests that many were chiming in at the same time. This rule eliminates the bedlam pictured in 14:23, with "all" speaking in tongues, and also prevents tongues from dominating the worship.

Paul grants that speaking in tongues is a way of communicating with God (14:2) but now insists that it should become public only when someone is present to interpret what it means in plain language. The key phrase is "in the assembly" (ἐν ἐκκλησίᾳ, en ekklēsia). The glossola-

---

2. Edwards (1885: 378–79) interprets κατὰ δύο ἢ τὸ πλεῖστον τρεῖς (kata dyo ē to pleiston treis) to mean "two or at the most three together," and ἀνὰ μέρος (ana meros) to mean that they may speak antiphonally. However, the ensuing babble of sound is precisely what Paul intends to check.

3. Fee (1987: 691 n. 15) notes that constraints of time would not have been a factor motivating this limitation.

lists may speak in tongues privately to themselves, but in public it must be made intelligible or it must be restrained. Consequently, Paul insists, if no one is present to interpret, the glossolalist is to keep silent: Keep it to yourself; it is to remain private between you and God.

It is unclear whether Paul understands the εἷς (heis, one) who interprets to be one individual interpreting all of the tongues (so R. Martin 1984: 78) or one who interprets after each tongue. He also does not specify how a glossolalist can determine in advance of speaking whether or not another is present to interpret.[4] Perhaps certain believers were known to have the gift of interpretation; and if they are not there ("but if no interpreter is present"), then those who speak in tongues should keep silent (Lietzmann 1949: 74). Some contend, however, that the speaker and the interpreter are one and the same person. Weiss (1910: 340) renders the εἷς, "but if he is not an interpreter," he should keep silent. This interpretation can be supported from 14:5: "The one who prophesies is greater than the one speaking in tongues, unless he interprets." If τις (tis, someone) is not added to the text (as it is in only a handful of minuscules), then Paul seems to refer to the same person as speaking in tongues and interpreting. It would also explain why he urges that "the one who speaks in a tongue should pray for the power to interpret" (14:13). Thiselton (2000: 1137–39) argues that the εἷς functions here as a pronoun (so also R. Collins 1999: 518).

Others contend that the interpreter is not one of the glossolalists (Lindemann 2000: 313). In 1 Cor. 12:10, Paul pictures speaking in tongues and interpretation as different gifts bestowed on different persons: "to another the working of miracles, to another prophecy, to another the discernment of spirits, to another various kinds of tongues, to another the interpretation of tongues." Paul's question in 12:30 ("Do all speak in tongues or all interpret?") also suggests different persons. Nevertheless, we cannot exclude the possibility that the person who speaks in a tongue may also be able to interpret what it means in plain language.

Paul clearly believes that persons inspired by the Spirit remain in control of themselves (Conzelmann 1975: 244).[5] They are not "carried away" so that they are not fully responsible for what they say or do, but rather can hold their tongues. By contrast, the Greek world had many religious groups that claimed to have experiences of divine inbreathing, which were likened to playing a flute: the flute plays what is

---

4. "Interpretation" is not translation of another language, such as Aramaic, nor is it a word-for-word translation of what was said. Rather, it interprets the significance of the utterance.

5. This contrasts with Mart. Pol. 7:3, which describes Polycarp filled with the grace of God and praying so that he could not be (μὴ δύνασθαι, mē dynasthai) silent for two hours (see also Herm. Man. 11.8).

breathed into it, no more, no less. The enthusiast is compelled to speak and has no control over it. Philo (*Plant.* 9 §39) shares such a view in describing the psalmist, who cries, "Delight in the Lord" (Ps. 36:4 LXX), as moved to an ecstasy of heavenly and divine love, and whose "whole mind" was snatched up "in holy frenzy [οἴστρῳ, *oistrō*] by a divine possession." The noun οἶστρος is a term for a tormenting insect and is used metaphorically to describe "insane passion" or "madness," such as the Maenads caught up in a Dionysian frenzy (Euripides, *Bacchae* [*Bacchanals*] 665). By contrast, Paul does not view tongues as an uncontrollable emotional experience that overpowers an individual. The promptings of the Spirit do not contribute to confusion or unbridled outbursts. In fact, Paul lists "self-control" as one of the fruits of the Spirit (Gal. 5:23). If tongues are of the Holy Spirit, then one should be able to hold one's peace to maintain order in the worship so that things do not get out of hand. Fee (1987: 692) comments, "It is indeed the Spirit who speaks, but he speaks through the controlled instrumentality of the believer's own mind and tongue. In this regard it is no different from the inspired utterances of the OT prophets, which were spoken at the appropriate times and settings."

14:29–32   Though Paul prizes prophecy over tongues because of its greater usefulness for building up the community (14:5) and convicting unbelievers (14:20–25), it too needs to be regulated. Héring (1962: 153) describes it as a need to "dam the floods of eloquence." Paul limits the number of prophets speaking, instructs the one speaking to be silent whenever a fresh revelation comes to another, and expects the assembly to appraise all that is said.

    In offering these guidelines, Paul may not be concerned simply to promote good "order." He also may wish to check any selfish monopoly of prophecy by those who may esteem themselves as belonging to a select circle of prophets (12:28; 14:37; Rom. 12:6) and who are used to taking center stage during the worship. He does not limit the power of the Holy Spirit from enabling anyone in the congregation to prophesy, which best explains the repetition of "all" (πάντες, *pantes*) in 1 Cor. 14:31: "For you are *all* able to prophesy in turn so that *all* may learn and *all* may be encouraged." It makes sense in the context of chapter 14 if the "all" refers to every person in the church without distinction (social status, gender, race) rather than to every person without exception (Grudem 1982: 235–36). Some, however, understand the "all" in this statement to refer only to all those "who are able to prophesy"—that is, specialists in mediating divine revelation (Conzelmann 1975: 245; Aune 1983: 198, 402 n. 36). Advocates of this view ask, How could Paul expect "all" to prophesy (14:31) if only two or three prophets may speak in the assembly? On the other hand, Paul may assume that all potentially can prophesy (Fee 1994: 253). They must do it in turns and not all at the same meeting. Others can prophesy at other meetings (so Robertson and Plummer 1914: 322). He does not include the phrase "at most" (τὸ πλεῖστον) as he did in regulating the glossolalists, and a larger number of prophets speaking may be allowable (Schrage 1999: 449). Possibly, he intends for two or three prophets to speak before the others weigh what they have said, and then another two or three can speak (Fee 1987: 693). Smit (1993a: 221) argues that Paul's hierarchy of spiritual gifts in 12:27–30 lies behind his instructions. He contends that Paul believes tongues to be incidental and consequently he permits them in the worship only under strict limitations. Prophecy, however, is an essential part of the meetings and requires a minimum of two to three speakers. No limits are placed on the number, since all can prophesy.

According to Paul, the prophetic Spirit is not limited to a few men and women; it can be imparted to all. Barrett (1968: 329) contends, "It is not any human decision that makes a man a prophet, or prevents him from being a prophet. The decision lies wholly within the freedom of the Holy Spirit, and prophecy is a function rather than an office." For this reason, Paul can exhort the whole church to seek earnestly to prophesy (14:1, 39).[6] He also concludes that if "all prophesy" (rather than speak in tongues), an unbeliever may be led to faith in God (14:24–25). Forbes (1995: 260) thinks it likely that those who reckoned themselves to be wise and spiritually gifted dominated the assembly, competed with one another for air time, and discouraged others from evaluating their statements: "There may have been too many prophets wishing to speak, or there may have been a few individuals 'holding the floor' for long periods" (Forbes 1995: 262). Paul seeks both to ensure order in their speaking and to quash any elitist tendencies in the assembly. A revelation might come to "another" (ἄλλῳ, *allō*), and that could be anyone, a learned or a simple person, an eloquent or an unpolished speaker. God is able to use them as they are.

As the glossolalist is able to control when to speak and when to keep silent, the prophet is able to restrain the prophetic spirit and determine when to speak and when to keep silent (R. Martin 1984: 82). The "spirits of the prophets" (14:32; cf. Rev. 22:6) refers to the impulses of the Spirit at work in the prophets (Godet 1887: 307) or to the manifestations of the Spirit's work (Robertson and Plummer 1914: 323; Grudem 1982: 126–27).[7] The urge to prophesy is subject (ὑποτάσσεται, *hypotassetai*) to the prophet. The impulse to speak may still be present, but the speaker can restrain those impulses and must yield the floor to another who receives

---

6. In the same way, he can wish that they "all" (πάντες, *pantes*) speak in tongues (14:5).

7. Herm. *Man.* 11.9 refers to the angel of the prophetic spirit resting upon the prophet (cf. 1 Cor. 13:1), but Paul never employs this idea. Nor does 14:32 refer to the human spirits of the prophets (cf. 14:14).

a revelation.[8] Presumably, the speaker is standing and is signaled to stop when another stands to speak after receiving a revelation.

"Revelations" are insights from a divine perspective, and all prophecy is based on revelation. The passive voice of ἀποκαλυφθῇ (*apokalyphthē*, is revealed) suggests that God's Spirit reveals something to an individual during the worship or before it (cf. Phil. 3:15). Previous speakers may also need to be silent after a third prophet has spoken, but the point of this instruction is to prevent anyone from dominating the worship.[9] One may also infer, since prophecy is based on receiving a revelation, that someone known to be a prophet may not always have a revelation. Believers do not own their spiritual gifts "in the sense of expecting to reproduce them at will in some future gathering of the congregation" (Koenig 1978: 108).

A church plagued by the commotion of competing prophets vying for attention and dominated by conceited members who refuse to listen to what others have been given to say does not testify to the presence of God (14:25). Paul's instruction to be silent makes reciprocity the rule in the congregation (Thiselton 2000: 1145). The directive prevents any prophet from filibustering or hogging the spotlight by claiming to be compelled by the Spirit to continue speaking.

After a prophet speaks, "the others" are to discern what is said. The verb διακρίνειν (*diakrinein*) has a wide range of meanings in Paul's writings (cf. 4:7; 6:5; 11:29, 31), but here it means "to evaluate carefully" (Grudem 1982: 64). The assumption is that the prophets do not speak with unquestionable divine authority. The congregation is not to accept everything that is said just because a person claims to speak under the influence of the Spirit. The prophet's words invite appraisal and discussion (Grudem 1982: 66–67). This is quite different from ascertaining whether the individual is a true or a false prophet. Presumably, the speakers reside in their midst, and the congregation would not need to examine them week after week, but they do need to evaluate what they say (Grudem 1982: 63). Paul himself invites the Corinthians to judge whether what he is writes in this letter is true (10:15; 11:13; cf. 7:25–26, 35, 40). Prophets must allow the content of their revelation to be tested in the community and may need reminding that their "prophecy" is only partial and temporary (13:9–10).

This principle does not entail that the majority is always right, and it may pose the danger that the listeners will become hypercritical rather than responding with the obedience of faith (Rom. 1:5). But Paul's in-

---

8. Herm. *Man.* 11.8 assumes that the true prophet never speaks on demand, but only when "God wishes him to speak."

9. Interruptions of prophets may have been a problem in the church, as the Didache labels testing or examining (διακρινεῖτε, *diakrineite*) any prophet who is speaking in the Spirit as an unforgivable sin (Did. 11:7).

tention seems to be to bring prophets down a notch to the level of the community. They are not to regard themselves as infallible and unanswerable to the church body.

This interpretation assumes that "the others" (οἱ ἄλλοι, *hoi alloi*) in 1 Cor. 14:29 who discern what has been said refers to the congregation as a whole.[10] Some, however, identify them as "other prophets." This view assumes that those with the gift of prophecy are best qualified to scrutinize what other prophets have said.[11] The sentence lends itself to this interpretation: "two or three prophets . . . the others." The parallels between the regulations concerning tongues and prophecy may suggest that as tongues are interpreted by one who has that gift, so prophecy is to be evaluated by those with that gift (Gillespie 1994: 163). But Paul does not say that the interpreter of tongues also has the gift of tongues.[12] The two phenomena, tongues and prophecy, are too dissimilar to draw such conclusions. Several arguments support the view that Paul believes that the prophet's message, which is for all the people, is to be examined by all the people and not by a special circle of prophets alone.[13] (1) Paul assigns the responsibility to evaluate the words of the prophets to "everyone" in 1 Thess. 5:20–21: "Do not despise the words of prophets, but test everything; hold fast to what is good." (2) According to 1 Cor. 2:12–16, all Christians receive the Spirit from God so that they might know the things that have been freely given to them by God and can examine all things.[14] (3) At the beginning of this section in chapter 12, Paul undermines the basis for anyone to think that he or she belongs to a spiritual caste that ranks above the rest of the congregation. It is unlikely that Paul would undo what he has said earlier and validate such a hierarchy. By placing the stress on "all," he makes no one special over others. (4) In 14:37–38, Paul expects those who consider themselves to be prophets or spiritual to be the most likely to object to what he says. His instructions would prevent the "specialists" from dominating and monopolizing the worship (see Forbes 1995: 269).

10. So Lietzmann 1949: 74; Barrett 1968: 328; Grudem 1982: 60–62; Fee 1987: 694; Carson 1987: 120; Wolff 1996: 340; Forbes 1995: 265–68; Schrage 1999: 451–52.

11. So Calvin 1960: 302; Findlay 1910: 913; Robertson and Plummer 1914: 322; Friedrich, *TDNT* 6:851; Conzelmann 1975: 244–45; D. Hill 1979: 133; Aune 1983: 220–22; Gillespie 1994: 163.

12. By this logic, if no other prophet is present to examine what a prophet says, the prophet should remain silent. But certainly Paul would not think that to be necessary, because it is intelligible to the congregation and all could discern what is said.

13. In 14:19, "the others" refers to the members of the congregation. If Paul were referring to other prophets, one might have expected him to write οἱ λοιποί (*hoi loipoi*; 9:5).

14. Gillespie (1994: 165) contends that Christian prophecy is the "unlabeled subject matter."

Paul does not list any criteria for gauging what a prophet says, but we can infer some norms from his discussions in this letter. (1) Does what is said accord with the tradition of Jesus (7:10; 9:14; 11:23; 12:3; 15:3; cf. 2 Thess. 2:15–3:6) and with the preaching of Christ crucified (1 Cor. 1:18–25)? (2) Does it accord with the Scripture as it is properly interpreted through Christ (1:19, 31; 4:6)? (3) Does it accord with what their apostle has handed on to them and taught them (2:1–5; 7:25; 11:2; 15:3)? (4) Does it accord with sacrificial love for others (13:1–13; 8:1)? (5) Does it promote the community's good (14:3–5, 12, 17, 26; cf. 12:7)? (6) Does it not cause another Christian to stumble in the faith (8:7–13)? (7) Does it lead outsiders to come to faith by reproving, convicting, and convincing them that God is present in their midst (14:20–25)?[15]

14:33a The statement "For God is not a God of chaos [ἀκαταστασίας, akatastasias] but of peace" (cf. 1:3; 7:15) sums up the basic hermeneutical principle that governs Paul's instructions about the use of the spiritual gifts in the gathering. Christian worship is to reflect the character of God. The Holy Spirit is not like a Ping-Pong ball careening from one person to another and creating mass confusion. The disorder in Corinth is not attributable to the workings of the Holy Spirit but to narcissistic exhibitionism, disdain for others with "lesser" gifts, and disregard for the common good. James 3:16–17 provides a fitting commentary on what is happening in Corinth: "For where there is envy and selfish ambition, there will also be disorder and wickedness of every kind. But the wisdom from above is first pure, then peaceable, gentle, willing to yield, full of mercy and good fruits, without a trace of partiality or hypocrisy" (NRSV). The pandemonium of their worship mirrors the fractures in the church.

14:33b–35 The command for women to keep silent in the churches has become particularly problematic to "gender-sensitive ears" (Jervis 1995: 69). This text is validated by some as establishing the universal norm for women's role in public worship and vilified by others as deplorably oppressive. It seems to say, "If you want peace rather than disorder in the assembly, do not permit women to speak." It also seems to prohibit women from actively trying to learn in the assembly. If they want to learn anything, they are to ask "their own men" at home. This restriction raises several questions. Why single out women? Were they more prone to disrupt the worship or to interrupt speakers than were the men? Or does Paul think, as Lapide (1896: 360) claims, that since man is "endowed with better judge-

---

15. Herm. *Man.* 11 offers good advice for discerning false prophets: "Test the man who has the divine Spirit by his life" (11.7). The false prophet "exalts himself and wishes to have first place, and he is instantly impudent and shameless and talkative, and lives in great luxury and in many other deceits, and accepts rewards for his prophecy, and if he does not receive them he does not prophesy" (11.12).

ment, reason, discursive power, and discretion than woman," women naturally should remain silent in public gatherings? Does Paul enjoin absolute silence on all women at all times in the churches, or does this directive apply only to a particular circumstance?

The command to silence is further complicated by its apparent contradiction of 11:5, where Paul affirms that it is quite permissible for women to pray or prophesy as long as they attend to their head covering. It also appears to contradict 14:31, where he affirms that "all" (πάντες, *pantes*) are able to prophesy in turn.[16] The demand that women are to keep silent in the churches comes as a surprise in this letter. If tongues and prophecy are spiritual gifts, and if each individual is allotted gifts as the Spirit chooses (12:11)—presumably without regard to gender, social status, or race—why should women with these gifts be silent in the assembly? Does Paul countermand Joel's prophecy that the Spirit will be poured out on both men and women so that they will prophesy (Joel 2:28; Acts 2:18; cf. 21:9)? Bassler (1992: 327–28; cf. Rowe 1990: 43) asks more pointedly,

> How can women like Euodia and Syntyche (Phil. 4:2–3), Prisca (Rom. 16:3; 1 Cor. 16:19), Mary (Rom. 16:6), Junia (Rom. 16:7) and Tryphaena and Tryphosa (Rom. 16:12) function as co-workers in the churches if they cannot speak in those churches? How can Phoebe fulfill her role of deacon (Rom. 16:1–2) if she cannot speak out in the assembly? How can a woman like Nympha, who is influential enough to host a house church (Col. 4:15), have been required to remain silent in her own home (cf. also Prisca, the wife of Aquila, 16:19)?

Three interpretations explaining this controversial text merit attention.

An interpolation. In recent years, an increasing number of scholars judge 14:34–35 (sometimes including v. 36) to be written by someone other than Paul and inserted into the text.[17] The NRSV, for example, puts 14:33b–35 in parentheses to suggest its textual uncertainty. Chagrin over the idea that women should be silent as a sign of their subordination to men perhaps leads many interpreters to give greater weight to the handful of texts that place 14:34–35 after 14:40. They infer from this

16. Paul is not withdrawing his earlier permission for them to speak in 11:5, as Edwards (1885: 381) supposes, or now expressing his real opinion, as Lietzmann (1949: 75) infers. Nor does he envision a small, informal gathering in 11:2–16 as opposed to the assembly of the entire church in 14:33b–36. Both refer to the meetings of the entire church.

17. So Weiss 1910: xli, 342; Zuntz 1953: 17; Fitzer 1963; Conzelmann 1975: 246; Dautzenberg 1975: 257–73; Walker 1975: 109; Munro 1983: 67–69; 1988: 28–29; Murphy-O'Connor 1986: 90–92; Sellin 1987: 2984–85; Fee 1987: 699–711; 1994: 272–83; Trompf 1980: 215; Snyder 1992: 184–85; Scroggs 1993: 71; Horrell 1996: 186–89; Beardslee 1994: 140; Payne 1995; 1998; Osiek and Balch 1997: 117; Hays 1997: 247–48; R. Horsley 1998: 188–89; Schrage 1999: 481–87; Lindemann 2000: 317–21; cautiously, Barrett 1968: 333.

displacement that 14:34–35 was not original to Paul but stems from an early marginal gloss written by someone wishing to impose the views expressed in 1 Tim. 2:11–15 on church gatherings. Later copyists inserted the gloss into the text at these different places. Conzelmann (1975: 246) states it boldly: "In this regulation we have a reflection of the bourgeois consolidation of the church, roughly on the level of the Pastoral Epistles: it binds itself to the general custom."

Intrinsic evidence weighs heavily in making this textual judgment. In addition to questioning how Paul would contradict himself so quickly in the same letter about the role of women in worship, many note that these instructions in 1 Cor. 14:34–35 interrupt the flow of Paul's thought dealing with tongues and prophecy. Omitting them does not disturb the sense of the paragraph. Some of the phrases that appear in these verses also seem anomalous in Paul. A few spot a rabbinic formula in the phrase "it is not permitted" (οὐ ἐπιτρέπεται, *ou epitrepetai*; an un-Pauline term) and attribute the insistence on silence, subjection, and the appeal to the law to a conservative Jewish bias.[18] The appeal to the law in general, "as the law says," also seems to be out of character for Paul (see Fee 1994: 279–81; Lindemann 2000: 319–21).

Treating 14:34–35 as a later addition to the text may expunge a difficult passage, but it does not erase the fact that no ancient manuscript lacks it, which raises a canonical issue.[19] What status does a text have that may not be original but is represented in every extant manuscript? Identifying 14:34–35 as an interpolation seems driven more by the difficulty of finding a "viable solution" to the meaning of these verses (see Fee 1994: 281) than by the weight of the textual evidence.[20] The external evidence is too weak to support this theory (see additional note). Arguments claiming that it "interrupts the theme of prophecy and spoils the flow of thought" (Conzelmann 1975: 246) are also insubstantial and ignore evidence that points to its close ties to the context.

A Corinthian quotation. Others seek to solve the problem by identifying 14:34–35 as Paul's summary of an authoritarian Corinthian pronouncement on the part of some male traditionalists who wanted to bar women from speaking in the church.[21] Paul rejects this view

18. Crüsemann (2000: 28–36) vigorously critiques those who attribute this command to a misogynistic Judaism.

19. Crüsemann (2000: 35–36) offers the radical solution of adding a footnote to any translation explaining that whether this portion of the text was written by Paul or another, it is a hurtful attempt "to exclude de facto one half of the Christian people from public church life in teaching and preaching," which should be rejected.

20. R. Martin (1984: 84) comments, "We should strive to excel in the gift of interpreting the text as it stands before we embrace these devices."

21. So Flanagan and Hunter 1981; Odell-Scott 1983; 1987; 2000; Talbert 1987: 92–93; and Arichea 1995: 111, who thinks it "worth considering and pursuing further."

with a sarcastic rebuttal in 14:36.[22] He cites their opinion in 14:34–35 only to repudiate it with two rhetorical questions. This argument assumes that Paul regularly cites Corinthian assertions throughout the letter to rebut them (Flanagan and Hunter [1981: 11], for example, cite 1:12; 2:15; 6:12/10:23; 6:13; 7:1; 8:1, 4, 8; 11:2; 15:12). Paul's response, "Are you the only ones [μόνους, *monous*; accusative masculine] the word of God has reached?" is also interpreted as referring to the males who wished to silence the women because their participation in worship proved threatening. The linchpin of this interpretation is the assumption that the particle ἤ (*ē*) in 14:36 functions as an exclamation expressing disapproval (an option listed in LSJ 761). It is rendered, "What! Did the word of God originate with you [males], or are you the only ones [masculine] it reached?" (Odell-Scott 2000: 69).

Hays (1997: 248) rightly dismisses this view as "farfetched in the extreme." Compared with other so-called quotations of Corinthian positions, this one is overly long, and Paul does not clearly counter it. I have not found as many Corinthian slogans and positions cited in this letter as other scholars have found, but no evidence exists elsewhere in this letter that the Corinthians held this view or that a significant Jewish element was imposing conservative synagogue traditions on the church's gatherings. In fact, the letter suggests the opposite. Paul seeks to curb the Corinthians' unruly and wayward expressions of freedom rather than to encourage them.

Concern for accord in husband and wife relationships. These instructions apply to how wives are to relate to their husbands in the church's public assemblies. Paul is not laying down rules for women in general or for women prophets (contra Wire 1990: 156; Jervis 1995: 51 n. 3). The noun αἱ γυναῖκες (*hai gynaikes*) can mean "women" or "wives." When Paul pairs it with the noun ὁ ἀνήρ (*ho anēr*) elsewhere in this letter, he refers to wives and husbands (7:2–5; 11:3). The instruction in 14:35 that they should ask their questions at home strongly suggests that Paul has wives in mind who are to ask their own husbands, the most obvious meaning of ὁ ἴδιος ἀνήρ (*ho idios anēr,* one's own man; cf. 7:2; Eph. 5:22; 1 Pet. 3:1).[23] The reminder that they are to "be subject" (ὑποτασσέσθωσαν, *hypotassesthōsan*) is most appropriate to the hus-

22. R. Allison (1988: 43–53) thinks that 14:34–36 is a fragment from a different letter to the Corinthians that an editor of 1 Corinthians interpolated into the text. Its original setting was Paul's defense of eschatological freedom against the attempt of a spiritual group to establish an exclusively male leadership that followed a synagogue model. Paul's rejection of this position is contained in verse 36. The editor introduced the phrase "as in all the churches of the saints" in 14:33b "to smooth the connection with the preceding context."

23. That Paul has in mind only married women here is further supported by the lack of any reference to what widows should do.

band-and-wife relationship.[24] Women are not called to be subject to every man in the church any more than slaves are called to obey every master (Rowe 1990: 59). They are expected to be submissive to their husbands (cf. Eph. 5:21–24; Col. 3:18; 1 Tim. 2:11–15; Titus 2:5; 1 Pet. 3:1–6).[25] The wife's silence, then, would be a sign of her willing submission to her husband.

It is crucial to note that Paul does not label the disallowed behavior as disorderly (1 Cor. 14:33a) but as "shameful" or "disgraceful" (αἰσχρόν, aischron, 14:35). Shame, in this context, pertains to what society views as inappropriate behavior and is relative to a given culture. The word occurs in 11:6 and is related to a wife's shaming her spouse. A marriage contract from Alexandria in 92 B.C. (Tebtunis Papyrus 104.24) reflects a typical view; it stipulates that the wife "is not to bring shame upon [her husband] in whatever causes a husband shame." In this culture, "the female who tested or broke the limits of narrowly defined roles could bring irreparable shame to spouse, family, or group" (Stansbury 1990: 443). Juvenal (*Sat.* 6.449–56), for example, castigates the intellectual woman who shows up her husband or other men at a dinner party. Plutarch (*Mor.* 142D) counsels that a wife should not speak in public and should do her talking to her husband or through her husband, "and she should not feel aggrieved, if like the flute player, she makes a more impressive sound through a tongue not her own." Forbes (1995: 275) cites the fulminations of Cato (Livy, *History of Rome* 34.2.9) over women publicly protesting a law restricting the amount of jewelry they could own: "Could you not have asked your husband the same thing at home?" Aristophanes treats the women taking over the Athens assembly as high comedy in his *Ecclesiazusae* (cited by Barrett 1968: 331).

The situation that best fits the adjective "shameful" is one in which wives defy convention by publicly embarrassing their husbands through their speaking. In the context, it is likely that Paul imagines a wife joining in the process of weighing what is being said during the congregational scrutiny of prophecy (14:29). They either raise questions or contradict their husbands or other senior male relatives. By doing so, they compromise their husband's authority over them and appear to undermine the good order of the household (Dunn 1998: 592). The problem, then, concerns how wives are to

24. This attitude is reflected in Clement's opening word of praise of the Corinthians: "And to the women [γυναιξίν, *gynaixin*] you gave instruction that they should do all things with a blameless and seemly pure conscience, yielding a dutiful attention to their husbands. And you taught them to remain in the rule of obedience [ὑποταγῆς, *hypotagēs*] and to manage their households with seemliness, in all circumspection" (1 Clem. 1:3).

25. In Rom. 7:2, Paul uses the phrase "the under-a-man woman" (ἡ ὕπανδρος γυνή, *hē hypandros gynē*), and in 1 Cor. 11:3, he identifies the husband as the head of his wife.

comport themselves in the public sphere in the context of examining prophecies and has nothing to do with the public ministry of women, as many suppose (Ellis 1981: 217). Paul does not contradict what he says in 11:5 but imposes silence on wives in matters other than praying and prophesying.[26]

It should also be noted that the distinction between home and church, so clear to persons accustomed to worshiping in buildings dedicated to worship, would have been fuzzier for those worshiping in house churches. Barton (1986) claims that the ambivalence created by the church meeting in a home may have caused some of the problems. Women may have felt more comfortable in a home setting and were more expressive. Certain behaviors permissible at home, however, were out of place in the church. Dunn (1998: 592) clarifies the key questions involved:

> Could she behave in church as she did in the privacy of the home, where she could exercise a certain amount of authority over other members of the household? Or alternatively, once home had become church, was she in effect in a new (Christian) family structure, with old structures of authority relativized? The tensions would be twofold: for the married woman who was both prophet and wife, and yet had to function as prophet in a space which was both church and home. If this is the correct setting for 1 Cor. 14:33b–36, then we have to conclude that in this case Paul's instruction was not only mindful of social convention but also socially conservative in character, since he instructs wives to act as wives while in church and to show by their conduct in church that they respect the authority of their husbands.

This perspective best explains other difficult elements in the text. First, the statement "as in all the churches of the saints" does not conclude 14:33a (contra Hays 1997: 244) but introduces the new thought that follows in 14:34–35.[27] The phrase ἐκκλησίαι τῶν ἁγίων (*ekklēsiai tōn hagiōn*) occurs only here.[28] Normally, Paul identifies churches by their region (Rom. 16:1, 4; 1 Cor. 16:1, 19; 2 Cor. 8:1), or as belonging to God (1 Cor. 1:2; 10:32; 11:16, 22; 15:9; 2 Cor. 1:1) or to Christ (Rom. 16:16). The repetition of ἐκκλησίαι seems clumsy, but it is easier to understand how church custom applies to a wife's silence than it does to

---

26. So Thrall 1965: 102; Orr and Walther 1976: 312–13; Ellis 1981: 217; Schüssler Fiorenza 1984: 230–33; Rowe 1990: 58; Blomberg 1994: 282; Dunn 1998: 592–93. Grudem (1982: 239–55) objects that allowing immature single women to challenge male prophets would be no less shameful and concludes that it applies to women generally. One could argue, however, that it is only wives who are causing the problem in this situation (see also Liefeld 1986: 150; Carson 1987: 129–31).

27. In 4:18, ὡς (*hōs*) starts a new clause.

28. It is remotely possible that Paul has reference to Jewish churches, since the saints are connected to the Jerusalem church in 16:1 (cf. Rom. 15:25–26, 31; 2 Cor. 8:4, 9:1).

the statement that God is a God of peace and not disorder. The second ἐκκλησίαι is better rendered "assemblies." In the Greek world, it represented the body politic assembled to conduct affairs of state (see Acts 19:39). The question was raised more than once by the Greeks, "What have women to do with a public assembly?" The answer: "If old-established custom is preserved, nothing" (Thucydides, *History of the Peloponnesian War* 2.45.2). Philo (*Spec. Laws* 3.31 §§169–75) reaffirms this basic fact of ancient life:

> Market-places and council-halls and law-courts and gatherings and meetings where a large number of people are assembled, and open-air life with full scope for discussion and action—all these are suitable to men both in war and in peace. The women are best suited to the indoor life which never strays from the house, within which the middle door is taken by the maidens as their boundary, and the outer door by those who have reached full womanhood.

Paul's command to the "brothers" in general in 1 Thess. 5:14 assumes that each member has the responsibility to admonish other members when they are in the wrong. Such a practice may have sparked tension if members from the lower strata of society took it upon themselves to admonish those with higher status. Plutarch (*Mor.* 42F) complained that those "who lead the speaker to digress to other topics and interject questions, and raise new difficulties, are not pleasant or agreeable company at a lecture; they get no benefit from it, and they confuse both speaker and his speech." In the early church, the mixed participation of women and men gathered together probably created delicate problems affecting relationships between the genders. Sevenster (1961: 198) is on the right track: "Paul is probably alluding in the first place to a passion for discussion which could give rise to heated argument between a wife and husband." It would be particularly embarrassing to a husband for his wife to transgress social boundaries and question him in public. This behavior still makes persons uncomfortable in cultures that have an unwritten rule between spouses that one does not shame or embarrass the other in public.

The problem centers on the type of speaking that wives might engage in rather than the possibility that they might speak (Jervis 1995: 52). Many identify the speaking that Paul interdicts as something unspiritual, such as idle chatter or jabbering that disrupts the worship (Moffatt 1938: 233; Barrett 1968: 332; Wolff 1996; R. Collins 1999: 513–14). But why forbid all women from speaking and not just the guilty parties? Men can be just as guilty of idle chatter. Why not ban all chitchat in the worship? In the context of chapter 14, the verb λαλεῖν (*lalein*) does not imply prattling or yammering, and there is no indication in the text that this was a problem needing correction.[29]

Stansbury (1990: 442) notes, "Religion had long been the realm in which women were sometimes allowed to break out of their domestic roles, mingle with men, and even take on important status." We need not surmise, however, that the women's newfound freedom in Christ made them so bold as to lose control in the assembly. Paul does not hint that the wives became "clamorous," "shrill," or "excessive," as Orr and Walther (1976: 313) imagine. Speculation about some carryover from the orgiastic practices in Hellenistic cults causing them to become unruly is also unfruitful. To contend that Paul refers to a frenzied outburst of tongues (Kroeger and Kroeger 1978) ignores the context. Paul has moved on from his specific instructions about tongues in 14:27–28 and is now giving guidelines about prophecy and its testing (see the outline of the structure above). Again, if the abuse of tongues were the problem, he would be more likely to impose silence on the guilty parties rather than imposing it on all women. Since the immediate context refers to sifting what has been said, "Let two or three prophets speak, and let the others discern what is said" (14:29), it is more credible that the wives are asking questions or challenging what has been said. This scenario best explains why Paul tells them "to ask" (ἐπερωτᾶν, eperōtan) their questions of their own men (husbands) at home (14.35). He does not mean: if they have something to contribute in the assembly, they should wait and tell their husbands later at home (see additional note). The key phrase is "if they want to learn [μαθεῖν, mathein] something," which implies a situation in which they are reacting to prophecy (Wolff 1996: 346). It also implies that they do not understand and have no positive contributions to make on the topic at hand (Forbes 1995: 276; see also Hasitschka 1997: 51). Paul disallows speech in the assembly that would suggest that a wife is being insubordinate toward her husband, whether it is an interruption or a challenge to a prophetic utterance. The delicate relationship between husband and wife is imperiled by the wife's public questioning, correcting, or challenging.

Second, "silence" in the context is a temporary renunciation of speech (14:28, 30).[30] It refers to "holding one's tongue." There are times

---

29. The verb λαλεῖν (lalein) is used for speaking in tongues, utterances that are unintelligible to others (14:2 [3x], 4, 5 [2x], 6, 9, 11, 13, 18, 21, 23, 27), for speaking to oneself silently (14:28), for speaking a revelation (14:6), intelligible speaking with the mind (14:6, 29), and for both speaking in tongues and with the mind (14:19). If Paul refers only to some kind of prattle, why did he not use a word like κενοφωνία (kenophōnia, empty talk; 1 Tim. 6:20; 2 Tim. 2:16) or ματαιολογία (mataiologia, idle talk; 1 Tim. 1:6; Titus 1:10) to convey the point more clearly?

30. The NIV obscures the fact that the verb σιγᾶν (sigan) occurs three times in a row by translating it "keep quiet" in 14:28, "should stop" in 14:30, and "remain silent" in 14:34.

when spiritual contributions are not valuable and are unwelcome. Some speech must be suppressed momentarily for the good order of the community.[31] This command does not permanently and absolutely enjoin women's silence in every circumstance, requiring them to learn only at home (contra R. Allison 1988: 36–42). "All" are to learn in the assembly (14:31). They are asked to hold their speech for the moment to avoid any embarrassment.[32]

Third, the reminder that the wives are to be "subject" does not imply inferiority (cf. 16:15–16). It assumes a temptation to do just the opposite and requires them "to recognize that the other person has greater claims upon oneself than one's own interests" (Rowe 1990: 65–66). Jervis (1995: 66–67) suggests that it means that they should submit "to the cause of the good functioning of the Christian assembly" (cf. Thiselton 2000: 1155). Jervis thinks that the concern is for the interruption of the assembly's exercise of prophecy. But why apply this directive only to wives and not to all persons in worship? Elsewhere, Paul uses the same verb ὑποτάσσειν (*hypotassein*) to refer to persons being subject to other persons (Lindemann 2000: 315). The command to be subject introduced by ἀλλά (*alla*) implies that their speech was somehow insubordinate.[33] Their submission is a token of their Christian love for their husbands.

Fourth, "as the law says" does not refer to secular law restricting women's actions in the public arena but to the OT law.[34] Paul's presumed impatience with the law is exaggerated. He appeals to it in the context in 14:21 and also in 7:19 and 9:8–10 (cf. Rom. 3:19; 7:7). The problem is that he does not cite a text from the law, and no OT passage instructs women to be silent. Perhaps he refers to a general assumption that the law calls for the wife's submission to her husband. Others pinpoint Gen. 3:16, "Your desire shall be for your husband, and he shall rule over you," as the backdrop. Oster (1995: 356) maintains that since Paul alludes to the Genesis creation narrative in 1 Cor. 11:3, 8–10, which lays the scriptural foundation for the wife's submission, he saw no need to cite these texts again. The problem with this view is that Gen. 3:16 is predictive, not prescriptive, and Jewish exegetes did not ground the subordination of women in the creation narrative (Rowe 1990: 66).

---

31. The application of the command to silence is contextual (Grudem 1982: 242–44). In the context, it applies to a particular mode of speech in the case of the glossolalist's remaining silent when no one can interpret and keeping quiet when another is speaking. It does not assume permanent silence.

32. Paul assumes that marital obligations override any spiritual inclinations (7:3–4), and that the wife's pleasing the husband (and vice versa) is vital (7:33–34).

33. I do not think that Paul is espousing the same view found in Sir. 26:14: "A silent wife is a gift from the Lord, and nothing is so precious as her self-discipline."

34. The expression ὁ νόμος λέγει (*ho nomos legei*) appears in Rom. 3:19 and 1 Cor. 9:8.

Liefeld (1986: 149–50) suggests that Paul alludes to the patriarchal perspective in Num. 12:1–15, which records Miriam's punishment for questioning Moses' authority. This passage fits the context of discerning, which may involve questioning, what the one prophesying has said. On the other hand, it may be best to see the reference to the "law" functioning in this case as another reference point beside cultural rules ("the common feeling of humankind" [Barrett 1968: 331]), the practice of all the churches, and the command of the Lord (1 Cor. 14:37; cf. the same pattern in 9:7–14, noted by Baumert 1996: 196–97). Citing the support of the law is "incidental to Paul's argument rather than foundational" (Rowe 1990: 680). He assumes that they know what he is alluding to in the law, and it confirms that the universal consensus concerning this custom is correct.

I conclude that Paul's instructions are conditioned by the social realities of his age and a desire to prevent a serious breach in decorum. The negative effect that wives publicly interrupting or contradicting their husbands might have on outsiders (let alone the bruising it would cause to sensitive male egos) could not be far from his mind. Paul may fear that the Christian community would be "mistaken for one of the orgiastic, secret, oriental cults that undermined public order and decency" (Schüssler Fiorenza 1984: 232), in which women exercised more prominent roles. To forestall this impression, he presents the practice of the Palestinian communities as a model to be imitated (see Nadeau 1994).

14:36 Paul often uses ἤ (ē) to introduce a rhetorical question in the letter (1:13; 6:2–3, 9, 16, 19; 9:6; 10:22; 11:22; 2 Cor. 3:1; 11:7). It does not introduce a sarcastic rebuttal of a Corinthian decree of silence, but basically means, "Can it be that. . . ?" (R. Collins 1999: 522). As in 1 Cor. 12:29–30, he ends the discussion with rhetorical questions (Witherington 1995: 288) and apparently anticipates some opposition to his rulings (Schüssler Fiorenza 1984: 233). He addresses the whole church, not just the males, and with two questions attacks their maverick practices that differ from other churches.

"The word of God" refers to the gospel (cf. 2 Cor. 4:2–3). Since the gospel did not originate in Corinth, and since it did not come to them alone, who are they to act as if they are the only Christians who matter in the world and can do as they please? "Unto you alone" (εἰς ὑμᾶς μόνους, eis hymas monous) is the counterpoint to "in all the churches of the saints" in 1 Cor. 14:33b and resumes the thought of 14:33. The Corinthians' worship is to conform to the character of God and to be in tune with the rest of God's churches (Fee 1987: 698).

14:37–40 Smit (1993a: 215–16) identifies 14:37–40 as the *peroratio* of the speech that began in 12:1–3. The *peroratio* "closes the discussion on the subject and exerts pressure on the audience to take the intended decision." If this conclusion is correct, it means that the phrase "what I am writing to you" does not refer to the immediate context (14:25–36) but to the entire passage beginning in 12:1. The *peroratio* emphatically drives home the point, with no beating around the bush. It is short and not necessarily sweet. The polite speech with which Paul begins in chapter 12 is now put aside for direct, blunt speech. An imperative appears in each verse. First, he asserts that he speaks with the authority of the Lord: "It is the Lord's command." He uses a phrase that he has used previously in the letter, "if someone presumes" (εἴ τις δοκεῖ, *ei tis dokei*; 3:18, ". . . to be wise"; 8:2, ". . . to have knowledge"; cf. 11:16). Fee's (1987: 11) observation that it is "probably no accident that the statement . . . is found in each of the three major sections of the letter (chaps. 1–4; 8–10; 12–14)" is fruitful. It highlights the Corinthians' perception of themselves as wise, knowing, and spiritual. Paul reminds them that perception is a subjective evaluation (Grudem 1982: 232), and the objective proof comes from their obedience to the Lord and their recognition of the truth. A spiritual person is not simply one who speaks under the inspiration of the Spirit. A spiritual person also discerns that what Paul writes is a command of the Lord (cf. 7:12, 25, where he distinguishes his own command from the Lord's). He began this discourse (12:1) by saying that he did not want them to be ignorant (ἀγνοεῖν, *agnoein*). If they do not recognize his instructions as valid, then they are invalidated as prophets and as spiritual persons. Barrett (1968: 334) translates εἰ δέ τις ἀγνοεῖ, ἀγνοεῖται (*ei de tis agnoei, agnoeitai*), "If anyone does not recognize this, he is not recognized." Barrett takes it to mean that Paul does not recognize the dissenting opinion as inspired. But these words contain a far more serious threat. The person who disregards these instructions will be disregarded. The implication of the passive voice is that such a person will not be acknowledged by God (BDAG 13; cf. 8:3, "Anyone who loves God is known by him"). As a covert allusion to God's judgment (Edwards 1885: 384), it becomes a strong denunciation (Fee 1987: 712; Kistemaker 1993: 516; Hays 1997: 244). It means that the Lord will say to such persons, "I do not know you" (Matt. 7:22–23).

Second, in 1 Cor. 14:39, Paul repeats the key charge, "Seek to prophesy and do not hinder speaking in tongues," which recalls 14:1 (cf. 1 Thess. 5:19–20). The hierarchy between the two gifts is clear: prophecy is to be eagerly sought; tongues are not to be hindered.

Third, Paul states the overarching principle that should govern the expression of spiritual phenomena in worship. Everything must be done in an orderly manner. The Spirit of ardor is also the Spirit of order. It expresses Paul's concern that their ardor for spiritual manifestations has destroyed the order of their assembly. Order alone, however, does not build up the body either (see additional note). Hays's (1997:

245) comment is apt: "Order is necessary only to constrain self-indul-
gent abuses and to create an atmosphere in which the gifts of all can
work together to build up the community in love." Carson (1987: 121)
concludes that "wise and biblically informed Christian worship" will
not pursue "freedom at the expense of order, or unrestrained spontane-
ity at the expense of reverence."

Additional Notes

14:34–35. Three Greek-Latin bilingual manuscripts, Claromontanus (D, 5th cent.), Augiensis (F,
9th cent.), and Boernerianus (G, 9th cent.), place 14:34–35 after 14:40 so that 14:36 immediately
follows 14:33. So also do two other Old Latin manuscripts (a, b); a single Vulgate manuscript,
Codex Fuldensis, copied for Bishop Victor at Capua A.D. 541–46 and corrected by him; and two
Latin Fathers, Ambrosiaster (4th cent.) and Sedulius Scotus (9th cent.). The first hand of MS 88
(12th-cent. minuscule) inserts a double slash before writing verses 34–35 and a smaller double
slash above the last letter of 14:33, which indicates that the scribe intended the verse to be read
after 14:33. Payne (1998) interprets this as evidence that the manuscript was copied from a
Greek manuscript that omitted 14:34–35. Fee (1994: 273–75) argues for the value of this evidence for the Western text as pre-Vulgate. Payne (1995) also claims that a bar umlaut in Vatica-
nus (B) at 14:33 was included to note a textual problem: that a comparison text lacked 14:34–35.

This textual evidence offers rather slim support for the interpolation theory. It need not mean
that the text did not originally belong and was added later at two different places. It could indicate that a scribe moved it to what he thought was a better place that did not interrupt the perceived context. Fee (1994: 275–79), however, questions the transcriptional probability of moving
the text as a *"radical rewriting of Paul's argument"* and not a simple transposition. Fee also contends that there is no historical precedent for this in Paul's letters and thinks that one must explain why this arrangement would have occurred if it were simply a moving of the text.

The intrinsic evidence for the original absence of 14:34–35 from the text is a bit stronger. Removing these verses from the text solves the problem of its apparent contradiction with 11:5. The
topic of women's silence in the church also does not seem to fit the context, which refers to controlling manifestations of the Spirit in worship. Fee (1994: 280) argues that verses 34–35 have
nothing to do with tongues, prophecy, or the Spirit and simply demand of women unqualified
silence in the churches. Fee thinks that they were inserted here because of their catchword relation to silence. Fee (1994: 279) also claims that these verses contain linguistic aberrations: the
use of the plural "in the churches"; the appeal to the law in the absolute sense without quoting
or referring to a specific passage; and the appeal to shame as a general cultural matter (as opposed to shaming the spouse [11:5]). Others posit that the language reflects that of 1 Tim. 2:11–
12, which is assumed to derive from a later time and not from Paul. They conclude that someone
sharing the views expressed in 1 Timothy added these words to ban women's participation in
mixed assemblies.

Fee's (1994: 281) confident assertion that "this passage is almost certainly not by Paul, nor
does it belong to his argument," however, is a curious oxymoron. "Almost certainly" is not certain. Niccum (1997: 254) musters compelling external evidence that "argues for the authenticity
of 1 Cor 14:34–5 in its traditional location" (see also Ross 1992: 155–56). No extant manuscript
lacks the passage, and Ross (1992: 155) contends that the interpolation would have had to occur
very early to explain this phenomenon. Witherington (1995: 288) also argues, "Displacement is
no argument for interpolation." Fee's appeal to J. A. Bengel's rule—preference for the reading
that best explains the others—does not apply to emendations of the text (Niccum 1997: 243).

The manuscripts that displace the text are few and do not represent a widespread tradition (see Wire 1990: 149–52; Niccum 1997: 244–52). The "transposition occurs in only a few, closely related MSS from northern Italy spread abroad in the Middle Ages by Irish monastics" (Niccum 1997: 254). Manuscripts D*, F, and G also move other texts to make a passage seem less disjointed: Rom. 16:20b is placed after Rom. 16:24; Rom. 16:5a is placed after Rom. 16:3; and Rom. 16:16b is placed after Rom. 16:21—presumably to improve style. Wire (1990: 252) also notes a tendency in these manuscripts to alter the meaning of other verses in the context. Manuscripts D, F, and G add ὑμῶν after γυναῖκες (also K and Old Syriac), perhaps to make sure that this rule applies only to Corinth and/or only to wives. Niccum (1997: 244–45) contends that the bar umlaut in B postdates the fourteenth century, and that its significance is misinterpreted by Payne. Wire (1990: 151) attributes the displacement in 88 to a scribe's following one format and noting that the other is the correct way to read the text.

Petzer (1993) argues that the internal evidence and external evidence point to different stages in the development of the text. The external evidence reveals that the text had become "a fixed part of the tradition when a textus receptus of this epistle came into being" (Petzer 1993: 136). The internal evidence discloses the original autograph, which Petzer claims omitted these words, and should have the upper hand if the purpose is to reconstruct the author's original text. But the internal evidence does not rule out its original inclusion in the text. The passage contains words from the context (see Osburn 1993) and not just the catchword "be silent" (14:28, 30). The verbs μανθάνειν (14:31), ὑποτάσσειν (14:32), and λαλεῖν (14:27, 28, 29) appear in the immediate context, and the noun ἐκκλησία appears in 14:28, 33a. Payne (1995: 246–47) contends that these words are appropriated by the glossator and are used in quite different ways. I regard the differences as slight and attribute them to the different situation that Paul attempts to regulate: the sensitive relationship between men and women in public settings. Wire (1990: 231) points out that the extension of the interpolation theory from 14:34–35 to include 14:33b (Weiss 1910) and 14:36 and 14:37–38 (Dautzenberg 1975: 253–57) may "indicate that the two verses are more tightly welded to their context than at first appears." If only 14:34–35 were removed, the resulting text still reads roughly. It would make better sense if 14:33b and 14:36 were removed as well (Ross 1992: 155). The context refers specifically to anything that causes *disorder*. The women's speaking in this situation may be assumed to be causing some kind of disorder. I also suggest that these brief instructions in 14:33b–36 about what is inappropriate for women to do in the church and 11:2–16 serve as bookends that bracket Paul's discussion of public worship. Both passages refer to what is αἰσχρόν (11:6), to the relationship between men and women (11:3, 7), and to a woman's (wife's) submission (11:10), and include a supporting reference to Scripture (11:8–12).

Finally, if this were a gloss, one wonders why the scribe neglected to gloss 11:2–16 as well (see Jervis 1995: 540–41). The motivation for adjusting this particular text is unknown (see the suggestions in Wire 1990: 151–52). If the change was intentional, Metzger (1994: 499) guesses that it was an attempt to find a "more appropriate location in the context" for the directive concerning women. Ross (1992: 156) conjectures that these words were removed by an early copyist because they seemed to contradict 11:5, "but the omission was preserved (perhaps in the margin) and a later copyist restored them to the text, but in the wrong place." Odell-Scott (2000: 70) thinks that this portion of the text was removed to ensure that 14:36 would not be construed as Paul's negative critique of the silencing and subordination of women in the church. Ellis (1981: 219–20; see also Moffatt 1938: 230–33; Barton 1986: 229–31) suggests that the transposition was attributable to a marginal note added by Paul after reading through a draft of the letter by the amanuensis. This view would explain the differing order and why no manuscript omits it. It could also explain its supposedly rough fit in the context if it were a marginal note added later by Paul. Ellis, however, errs regarding a key piece of evidence in claiming that the Latin Codex Fuldensis (perhaps following Metzger 1971: 565; cf. Metzger 1994: 499–500) places 14:34–35 after 14:40 and also in the margin after 14:33.

14:35. Oster (1995: 358–59) makes this important observation: "The Roman world was anything but homogeneous in regard to its attitudes toward women. Not only were there differing attitudes among individuals toward women in the Greco-Roman setting, but the views vary depending whether the women were being characterized from the perspectives of Roman law, ancient medicine and gynecology, Greco-Roman religious mores, ancient social institutions, etc." Oster cites Cornelius Nepos, who prefaces his work on the great generals by noting how customs and values vary in different cultures: "Not all peoples look upon the same acts as honourable or base, but . . . they judge them all in the light of the usage of their forefathers" (*De viris illustribus* preface.3). He writes,

> Many actions are seemly according to our [Roman] code which the Greeks look upon as shameful. For instance, what Roman would blush to take his wife to a dinner-party? What matron does not frequent the front rooms of her dwelling and show herself in public? But it is very different in Greece; for there a woman is not admitted to a dinner-party, unless relatives only are present, and she keeps to the more retired part of the house called "the women's apartment," to which no man has access who is not near of kin. (Cornelius Nepos, *De viris illustribus* preface.7)

14:35. In this first-century culture, women tended to marry at a young age. If they did not come from a wealthy family, they had few formal educational opportunities. They would be instructed only in areas regarded as suitable to their future role of managing a household. It is unlikely that many women in the Corinthian church were educated.

Keener (1992: 84) gives this a positive spin by claiming that Paul takes a progressive view. The husband is not to dismiss the wife's desire to learn but is to take responsibility for teaching her at home. They are to discuss spiritual and intellectual issues at home. This differs from the extremely restrictive view of Rabbi Eliezer, who thought that giving a daughter knowledge of the law was akin to teaching her lechery (*m. Soṭah* 3:4).

14:38. The present passive ἀγνοεῖται has weaker manuscript support (ℵ*, A*[vid], [F, G, ἠγνοεῖται], 33, 1739, it[b, d], syr[pal], cop) than the present imperative ἀγνοείτω, "let him continue in his ignorance" (𝔓[46], ℵ[2], B, D[2], K, Ψ, 81), but it matches the syntax of 8:3, with an indicative followed by a passive. The reading ἀγνοεῖτε in D[gr] is explained by the fact that it would have been pronounced exactly the same as the passive. Zuntz (1953: 108) argues for the imperative and compares the syntax to 7:15. Zuntz thinks that the passive creates problems: "is ignored" by whom? "By men" does not fit the context; "by God" is "too far-fetched" and "credits Paul with unbelievable recklessness in cursing his adversaries." But this argument makes the case that the passive is the hardest reading, and explains why a scribe might change it to the imperative.

14:40. Seemliness and order were valued by members of other cults. Meyer (1987: 54) notes the Rule of the Andanian Mysteries of Messenia from 92–91 B.C.: "Regarding those who are disorderly. When the sacrifices and the mysteries are celebrated, all are to be still and attend to the orders that are given. The sacred men are to scourge anyone who is disobedient or who behaves improperly toward what is holy and exclude such a one from the mysteries."

X. The Resurrection (15:1–58)

In chapter 15, Paul moves on from the problem of "their disorderly worship, which required correction (14.40), to their disordered belief, which was equally in need of being set right" (McDonald 1989: 38). Unlike the other issues he has addressed in the letter, this is not a case of inadmissible behavior, but the ethical admonitions in this discourse betray his conviction that errant belief inevitably leads to inadmissible behavior. Also, unlike his handling of every other issue raised in the letter, he does not explain at the outset what precipitates this lengthy deliberation on the resurrection. Not until 15:12 does he note that some are claiming that there is no resurrection of the dead. He mentions no oral report or written query that informs how he knows this. But this discussion falls structurally in the section of oral reports. How he came to know about this problem is unknown. His only concern is to correct this misinformed opinion about the possibility and nature of the resurrection of the dead.

The Corinthians do not deny the futurity of the resurrection by assuming that it has already occurred and is past (cf. 2 Tim. 2:18) but have come to believe that there is "life after death without a resurrection of the dead" (Soards 1999: 315). Paul is not trying to prove the resurrection of Jesus but to argue from it that Christians will be resurrected (Sellin 1986: 235–36; Fee 1987: 718). As Christ was resurrected from the dead, so those who are in Christ and pattern their lives after him can hope to be resurrected by God.

The Corinthians' error is not rooted in some deliberate doctrinal rebellion but in honest confusion, given their Greek worldview. They fail to comprehend how an earthly body that is physical and perishable can be made suitable for a heavenly realm that is spiritual and imperishable. The question "With what kind of body are the dead raised?" (1 Cor. 15:35) is not sarcastic, as Sider (1977: 131) suggests, but states the heart of the enigma for them. Earthly bodies and heavenly existence are altogether incompatible, as different as chalk from cheese. The Corinthians fail to understand, then, how the resurrection of the dead makes sense, given this inherent polarity between the earthly and the heavenly spheres. J. Wilson (1968: 94) is correct that Paul is "not dealing with a rebellion of the Corinthians against previous, clearly spelled out teachings of his. He is making explicit, probably for the first time, a new line of thought on the basis of his Jewish presuppositions but contrary to their Hellenistic presuppositions." Paul's argument in this chapter combines history, the church's preaching, and logical argument to make the case for the resurrection of the dead.

The argument divides into two distinct sections. The first section, 15:1–34, makes the case for the reality of the resurrection. The second section, 15:35–58, explains how the resurrection is possible. The first section has a tripartite structure. In 15:1–11, Paul gives a prolonged recitation of the facts that provide the essential background for the discussion of the issue. This opening unit is set off by an emphasis on what was and is preached by Paul and others (εὐηγγελισάμην, *euēngelisamēn* [15:1], and κηρύσσομεν, *kēryssomen* [15:11]) and by what the Corinthians believed (ἐπιστεύσατε, *episteusate* [15:2, 11]). In this introductory segment he establishes the resurrection's connection to the essence of the gospel that has been preached from the very beginning and does not attempt to prove that the resurrection of Christ actually happened (Barrett 1968: 341; Conzelmann 1975: 250; cf. Fee 1987: 737). By reiterating the tradition, he establishes the uniform apostolic witness to its truth and the continuity of that witness. The resurrection is and always has been the foundation of all preaching about Christ. Without it, the gospel dwindles into an inspiring story of a wise teacher who suffered heroically as a victim of human perfidy. Paul hints that if they deviate from this belief, it brings their salvation into question.

In 15:12, Paul states the issue that prompts his discussion, and in 15:13–28, he lays out his arguments for the resurrection of the dead. He contends that because Christ was raised, the dead also must be raised. Christ as the firstfruits implies that there will be a harvest of others at the end. In 15:29–34, he draws out the implications of no resurrection of the dead and the ethical consequences of belief in the resurrection.

The second section of the chapter (15:35–58) begins by presenting the issue in question form (15:35): How are the dead raised? What kind of body will they have? It is followed by arguments for the possibility of resurrection (15:36–57) and a concluding brief exhortation (15:58). Paul begins with the diatribe form, answering the imagined objections of a slow-witted student, by which he can explain how so counterintuitive a thing as the resurrection could possibly occur and even must occur. The resurrection of the dead does not mean the resuscitation of mortal human bodies. The argument proceeds, using illustrations from agriculture (15:36–38), with the example of the seed that dies and is transformed and comes to life. One could not imagine from merely looking at the seed of a watermelon what a watermelon will look like.

In 15:39–41, Paul appeals to biology and cosmology—the example of the many different kinds of bodies in animal life and the different kinds of heavenly bodies—to prove that the resurrection body can be a different kind of body from anything experienced on earth. Since God has provided earthly creatures and celestial bodies with flesh or glory suitable for their environment and purpose, God can provide a glorious body for the dead in the resurrection.

In 15:42–44, Paul appeals to anthropology. The natural (physical), perishable body is sown as a body suitable for its earthly habitation. The dead are raised and given a spiritual, imperishable body suitable for its heavenly habitation.

Christology comes to the fore in 15:45–49. Paul contrasts the first man, Adam, with the last Adam, Christ. The first Adam became a living soul; the last Adam is a life-giving spirit. The first Adam was a man of the dust of the earth, who began the sequence of life for those who also are of the dust of the earth; the last Adam is the man of heaven, and his resurrection marks the inauguration of life for those who will be raised in him. Just as they bore the earthly image of the first Adam, so those who are raised from the dead will bear the heavenly image of the last Adam.

In 15:50–57, Paul concludes with a description of how what is mortal will put on immortality and how God will conquer all the opposing powers and, finally, death itself. The essence of his argument is based on the polarity between the resurrection body and the earthly body. Those who are resurrected will be transformed and clothed with immortality and incorruptibility. Scripture will be fulfilled (15:54–55; Isa. 25:7; Hos. 13:14), and thanks will redound to God's glory (1 Cor. 15:57). Paul concludes with an ethical exhortation to be steadfast and excel in the work of the Lord (15:58). Jesus' resurrection means that we are saved from our sins (15:14, 17), and the Corinthians must come to their right minds and sin no more (15:34). The chapter can be outlined as follows:

A. Prologue: preaching and belief about the resurrection of Christ (15:1–11)
B. The consequences if the resurrection of the dead is not true (15:12–19)
C. The consequences since the resurrection of the dead is true (15:20–28)
D. The consequences if the resurrection of the dead were not true (15:29–34)
E. The bodily character of the resurrection (15:35–49)
F. All will be changed (15:50–58)

A. Prologue: Preaching and Belief about the Resurrection of Christ (15:1–11)

Paul begins with a prologue about what has been preached from the beginning about Christ's being raised from the dead. His purpose is not to argue that Christ's resurrection was real—he assumes as much—but to remind the Corinthians of "the consensus of preaching and testimony that he shares with the apostles and other resurrection witnesses" (Sloan 1983: 73). He chooses to start with a matter on which there is complete unanimity among the Corinthians—Christ was raised from the dead—and then argue from that the necessary consequences of Christ's resurrection for believers.[1] His strategy is to work from where they are—asserting twice that they believed the preaching about his resurrection—to get them to move to where he wants them to be. Eriksson (1998: 7) correctly observes that throughout the letter Paul deliberately begins his argumentation from Corinthian premises, but here he begins with the basic kerygma, which they believed, but whose eschatological implications they have not fully apprehended. He wants them to understand that all Christians will be raised from the dead (or changed if they are alive at Christ's coming), which means that the victory of sin and death is only temporary. God will defeat the last enemy. While graveyards may remind one of the brevity of life, the resurrection ensures the brevity of death.

Exegesis and Exposition

[1]I make known to you, brothers and sisters, the gospel, which I preached to you, which you also received, in which you also stand, [2]and through which you are being saved, with what message I preached to you, if you hold fast, unless you believed to no avail. [3]For I delivered to you among the first things what I also received, that Christ died on behalf of our sins, according to the Scriptures. [4]And that he was buried and that he has been raised on the third day, according to the Scriptures. [5]And that he appeared to Cephas, then to ⌜the Twelve⌝. [6]Then he appeared to more than five hundred brothers and sisters at one time, many of whom remain alive until now, but some have passed away. [7]Then he appeared to James and then to all the apostles. [8]And last of all, as to an aborted

---

1. Paul's discussion of the resurrection in 2 Cor. 5 is not relevant to the issues he addresses in this situation (Tuckett 1996: 248).

fetus, he appeared also to me. ⁹For I am the least of the apostles and not fit to be called an apostle, because I persecuted the church of God. ¹⁰By the grace of God, however, I am what I am, and his grace toward me has not been in vain. Indeed, I have labored harder than all of them, yet not I, but ⌜the grace of God with me⌝. ¹¹Whether I or they, thus we preach and thus you believed.

15:1–2 The introduction to the first section on the resurrection is abrupt and launched by the address "brothers and sisters" (ἀδελφοί, *adelphoi*). The phrase "I make known to you" (cf. 12:3; Gal. 1:11; 2 Cor. 8:1) solemnly heralds the initial subject—the gospel Paul preached (cf. 1 Cor. 1:17)— and indicates Paul's intention to teach and persuade (S. Lewis 1998: 30). He wants the Corinthians to know what they should already know since they believed the gospel that he preached to them. The language of "handing on" and "receiving" was used in 11:23 to refer to his transmission of the tradition of the Lord's Supper. In both instances, the reminders of the tradition he passed on to them imply that they have veered off course. He does not question their loyalty to the gospel, however, but seeks to establish at the outset their common ground. They are not willfully perverting what he preached but are confused about a central tenet. The difficult syntax of 15:1–2 can be clarified when it is recognized that Paul correlates his preaching of the gospel with their response.[2]

The Announcement of God's Act in Christ	The Believers' Response
the gospel I preached	which you received (past)
	in which you stand (present)
	through which you are saved (present/future)
with what word I preached	if you hold fast
	unless you believed to no avail

The first reference to Paul's preaching is followed by an affirmation of the Corinthians' positive response. The second reference to his preaching is followed by a caveat implicitly warning them not to deviate from that gospel. The phrase "with what word [τίνι λόγῳ, *tini logō*] I proclaimed the gospel" does not refer to the reasoning he used or the form of his speech (Barrett 1968: 336) but to the content of his message: "the substance of the gospel I proclaimed to you" (Thiselton 2000: 1185). In 15:3–5, he reminds them of the gospel's basic content he preached to them but introduces the possibility that they could have believed the

2. Héring (1962: 157) claims that "the text is certainly not in correct order."

gospel in vain if they fail to hold it fast (cf. 11:2). According to S. Lewis (1998: 29), this tactic subtly appeals to the audience's emotions "by provoking doubt and anxiety about their existential condition." The implication is that they may be departing from it (Sider 1977: 130), whether they accepted it in a hasty fashion without due deliberation of the facts or now decide to question it. Thiselton (2000: 1186) contends that Paul refers to a lack of a coherent grasp of the gospel (cf. Robertson and Plummer 1914: 332, "without consideration"; BDAG 281, "without careful thought"; Morris 1958: 205, "belief on an inadequate basis").

The Corinthians' belief is confused, which suggests that they accepted the gospel without fully understanding the facts that lie at its foundation. We cannot exclude the possibility that Paul also has in mind the ultimate outcome of such a truncated faith (cf. Rom. 13:4; Gal. 3:4; 4:11), since it has an impact on their salvation. The gospel is the power of God for salvation (Rom. 1:16), and they owe their new existence as Christians to Paul's preaching of this gospel. He uses the present tense "you are being saved" (σῴζεσθε, sōzesthe), which refers to both a present process (cf. 1 Cor. 1:18) and a future reality (Findlay 1910: 918; Robertson and Plummer 1914: 331). If they do not hold firmly to what has been preached about the resurrection, they jeopardize their future with God. If they do not have faith that holds out, they believed in vain (cf. 15:58; 16:13). If they have faith in something that is untrue, they believed in vain (15:14). The resurrection is the keystone that integrates the incarnation and Christ's atoning death. If it is removed, the whole gospel will collapse. If there is no resurrection of the dead (15:12), humans remain under the tyranny of sin and death, and their bouts of doubt and despair are fully justified.

15:3–5 Before citing the content of the tradition of faith he preached, Paul establishes that it was something he received and passed on to them like a baton. He stresses the continuity of tradition. "Among the first things" means "the most important things," or "things of first importance." What was first in importance was also probably spoken first. The statement that he received the gospel from others is only an apparent contradiction of his declaration in Gal. 1:11–12 that he did not receive the gospel that he preached "from a man," nor was he taught it, but he received it through a revelation of Jesus Christ. The same verb (παραλαμβάνειν, paralambanein), a technical term for receiving tradition, appears in both passages. In 1 Cor. 15:3–5, however, Paul is speaking only about the facts surrounding Jesus' death and resurrection. Many agree that he was not an eyewitness to Jesus' ministry, and these facts were passed on to him by the tradition.[3] In Gal. 1:11–12, he does

---

3. His early mission partners, Barnabas and Silas/Silvanus, came from the Jerusalem church, and Paul also spent time, however brief, with Peter (see Gal. 1:18).

not have in view the historical details on which the gospel is based but the interpretation of what those facts mean. The gospel is not simply a litany of facts, but something much more. It is the message that by grace God has acted decisively to save all humans, Jews and Gentiles, through Jesus Christ alone, apart from the law and human performance. Paul asserts in Gal. 1:11–12 that he came to understand the theological ramifications of Christ's death and resurrection through a revelation from Christ and did not receive it from another's interpretation, which his limited contact with the other apostles proves (Gal. 1:15–2:21). Schütz (1975: 111–12) clarifies: "The tradition cannot by itself be substituted for 'the gospel' and hence agreement on the tradition does not guarantee that the word is rightly heard and understood." The Corinthians heard and accepted the tradition about Christ's death and resurrection, but they did not rightly understand it.

Most understand Paul to be taking over a compressed account of the facts expressed in creedal form, though they disagree on its extent and Paul's redaction of it (see Conzelmann 1975: 251–54). Wilckens's (1963) attempt to extract the different traditions supposedly inlaid in 1 Cor. 15:3–7 is intriguing (see also Kloppenborg 1978; Murphy-O'Connor 1981c), but I concur with Lambrecht (1991: 661) that Paul himself probably articulated this traditional formula, which summarizes the historical basis of the gospel in a nutshell. It offers a theological snapshot of the gospel, reminding the Corinthians of basic facts that do not need any amplification because the story had already been narrated and interpreted for them (Hengel 2000: 147; cf. 11:23–26). The key verbs underscore Christ's atoning death and resurrection and are punctuated by the assertion that it was in accord with the Scriptures:

> Christ died for our sins
>> according to the Scriptures
> and that he was buried
> and that he was raised on the third day
>> according to the Scriptures
> and that he appeared to Cephas and the Twelve

That Christ died and that he was resurrected on the third day are facts, but their meaning is interpreted by the Scriptures.

Christ's atoning death is a central tenet of the faith (Rom. 5:6, 8; 8:32; 1 Cor. 8:11; 2 Cor. 5:14–15; Eph. 5:2; Titus 2:14; cf. Gal. 1:4). This death was not a sad misadventure but something God destined for him because of (or "with reference to," "concerning"; Barrett 1968: 338) the sins of humankind. Thiselton (2000: 1191) contends that since Paul rarely uses the plural "sins," it suggests that he is citing tradition. However, Paul uses the plural "sins" in 1 Cor. 15:17 and is not citing tradition there (see additional note). Fee (1987: 724) observes that since "Christ" refers here to the Messiah, though it functions like a proper name, and since Judaism did not connect an atoning death to the works of the Messiah, whoever made this connection is "the founder of Christianity." I would agree with Fee that this interpretation goes back to Jesus himself (cf. 11:23–25). Paul faithfully passed on this tradition, which presumes that the sins of humankind made Christ's death necessary. Hengel (1981: 37) states that Christ's vicarious death for others and his resurrection is "the most frequent and most important confessional statement in the Pauline Epistles."

The idea of dying for others was not unique, since its expression can be found in a wide variety of secular writers who laud those who died to save others from enemies or defeat. As Origen notes (*Cels.* 1.30.31), Celsus affirmed that a life laid down for others could and did remove evils that have fallen upon cities and countries, but he denied any value to Christ's death because his manner of dying was so inglorious and shameful in comparison with that of the Greco-Roman heroes. In answer to the objections of a Celsus, Christ's death is unique because of

1. the manner of his death, which is so foolish and scandalous to the world;
2. the purpose of his death as an atonement that expiates human sins and extricates them from the tentacles of sin and death;
3. the universal consequences of his death for all who will trust, not just for a particular city, nation, or group;
4. the conformity of his death to God's purposes revealed in the Scriptures; and
5. his being raised by God to life after death.

The phrase "according to the Scriptures" (see Matt. 21:42; Mark 12:24; Luke 24:32; Rom. 1:2; 15:4) affirms in shorthand that Christ's death was "according to the definite plan and foreknowledge of God" (Acts 2:23). It continued the story of God's saving activity, but it uniquely accomplished God's purposes established before the foundation of the world and fulfilled God's promises of old. Paul does not necessarily have in mind a particular passage, such as Isa. 52:13–53:12 (cf. Rom. 4:25; 1 Pet. 2:22–25). The allusions to the psalms of the righteous sufferer in Mark's passion narrative, for example, reveal how Christians found scriptural antecedents and associations with Jesus' death in a broad range of Scripture.[4] Godet

4. Cf. Mark 14:1/Ps.10:7–8; Mark 14:18/Ps. 41:9; Mark 14:34/Ps. 42:5, 11; 43:5; Mark 14:41/Ps. 140:8; Mark 14:55/Ps. 37:32; 54:3; Mark 14:57/Ps. 27:12; 35:11; Mark 14:61/Ps. 38:13–15; 39:9; Mark 15:24/Ps. 22:18; Mark 15:27/Ps. 22:16; Mark 15:29/Ps. 22:7; Mark 15:30–31/Ps. 22:8; Mark 15:32/Ps. 22:6; Mark 15:34/Ps. 22:1 (11, 19–21); Mark 15:36/Ps. 69:21; Mark 15:40/Ps. 38:11.

(1887: 331) notes that Paul ranks the testimony of the Scriptures *before* all the apostolic testimonies that follow.

The brief notice that "he was buried" is connected primarily to Jesus' death, not his resurrection (Conzelmann 1975: 255). Death and burial are interconnected in Scripture.[5] This detail verifies the reality and finality of Christ's death (Calvin 1960: 314; J. Wilson 1968: 92; Bruce 1971: 139; Fee 1987: 725; Schrage 2001: 37). It could be used to combat docetic ideas that deny that Christ died, but that is not Paul's primary purpose. Instead, this fact serves to corroborate the statement about the "resurrection from the dead" (15:12; Wolff 1996: 363). Paul does not mention Jesus' burial to highlight the empty tomb (Lindemann 2000: 331; Schrage 2001: 35–37). An empty tomb allows for different explanations (cf. Matt. 28:13; John 20:2, 13, 15). The mention of the burial functions "as the bridge between cross and resurrection" (Lambrecht 1991: 664).

Paul shifts from using the aorist tense to describe Christ's death and burial to the perfect tense (ἐγήγερται, *egēgertai*) to describe Christ's resurrection (see additional note). It is not something that belongs to the past, but something that has an effect on present reality (Schrage 2001: 38). Holleman (1996: 45) contends that he uses the perfect tense (see also 15:12, 13, 14, 16, 17, 20) in its classical sense and not as a simple past, because he believes that "Jesus' resurrection is the new situation which, by necessity, must come to its completion in the eschatological resurrection." The use of the passive voice, "has been raised," assumes that he was raised by God, because it is unthinkable that anyone—even Christ—could raise himself (see M. Dahl 1962: 96–100). "The third day" refers to the next day plus one (Luke 13:32) and is an expression most prominent in Luke-Acts (Luke 9:22; 18:33; 24:7, 21, 46; Acts 10:40). Paul rehearses the bare facts from the tradition, and "the third day" is a historical reminiscence that goes back to the discovery of the empty tomb on the third day (Héring 1962: 160; Wolff 1996: 365).

"According to the Scriptures" may apply only to the resurrection (see Ps. 16:9b–10; 56:13; 116:8) rather than to resurrection on the third day. Hays (1997: 256) cites 1 Macc. 7:16 as reflecting similar syntax, in which the reference to what is written refers to the deed and not the timing of the deed. Hays suggests the translation "and that he was raised in accordance with Scriptures, on the third day." Thiselton (2000: 1195) contends that Paul has no specific text in Scriptures in mind, but the phrase ties Jesus' resurrection to patterns of promise and grace in the OT. It is more likely, however, that just as the phrase "according to the Scrip-

---

5. See for example, Gen. 35:8, 19, 29; 48:7; Num. 20:1; Deut. 10:6; Judg. 8:32; 10:2, 5; 12:7, 10, 12, 15; 1 Sam. 28:3; 2 Sam. 17:23; 1 Kings 2:10, 34; 11:43; 14:31; 15:8, 24; 16:6, 28; 22:37, 50; 2 Kings 8:24; 10:35; 12:21; 13:9, 13, 20; 14:16; 15:7, 38; 16:20; 21:18; 23:30; Matt. 14:12; Luke 16:22; Acts 2:29; 5:6, 10; 8:1–2; 13:29.

tures" applies to the entire statement "he died on behalf of our sins," so also it applies to the entire statement "he was raised on the third day." Hosea 6:2, which speaks of the national revival of Israel, is thought by many to be an obvious allusion:

> After two days he will revive us;
> on the third day he will raise us up,
> that we may live before him. (NRSV)[6]

This text is never cited elsewhere in the NT, however. Christensen (1990) contends that Christ's rising on the third day is connected to the third day of creation (Gen. 1:11–13) and the new creation in Christ (2 Cor. 5:17; Gal. 6:15). The scriptural connection possibly derives from a slew of texts that link "the third day" with the day of salvation and divine manifestation (Gen. 22:4; 42:18; Exod. 19:11, 16; Josh. 3:2; Hos. 6:2; Jon. 1:17 [2:1 MT]).

As Christ's burial follows his death and confirms its reality, the account of his appearances to others after death confirms the reality of resurrection. The verb ὤφθη (*ōphthē*) can mean "was seen" or "appeared." The usage of the verb in the LXX, in which it became a technical term for the appearance of God or God's messengers (cf. Gen. 12:7; 26:24; 35:1, 9; Exod. 3:14–16; see Bartsch 1979–80: 184–89; see also the comments of Philo, *Abr.* 17 §77, §80), suggests that Jesus took the initiative in the appearances. Given this scriptural backdrop, the use of this term in the tradition would imply that the Lord made himself visible or showed himself (Lorenzen 1995: 131; cf. Michaelis, *TDNT* 5:358), and it should be translated "he appeared." The chiastic structure of active and passive verbs (noted by Schrage 2001: 48) supports this interpretation:

He died
  He was buried
  He was raised
He appeared

The common view that Jesus appeared to persons who really saw him has been challenged by Michaelis (*TDNT* 5:358–59), who argues that the visual aspect is never stressed when the verb is used in the LXX for encounters with God. Michaelis concludes that when it is used in the NT to denote the resurrection appearances, "there is no primary

---

6. Rabbinic exegesis connected the third day to the time of God's deliverance, and this text was applied to the resurrection (*b. Sanh.* 97a; *Gen. Rab.* 56.1; *Deut. Rab.* 7.6; *Esth. Rab.* 9.2).

emphasis on seeing as sensual or mental perception" (*TDNT* 5:358). Rengstorf (1967: 119) argues just the opposite, that the verb ὤφθη refers to seeing with the eyes. Lorenzen (1965: 133) concludes that the verb connotes an actual experience in which these persons encountered Jesus—in this case, a unique event. The appearances of Christ to these persons cannot be limited to visual perception, but must also include hearing him. They comprise presenting "himself to them as living by many convincing proofs" (Acts 1:3). Lorenzen (1995: 133–34), while acknowledging that all analogies and similarities break down when comparing Christ's resurrection to OT appearance narratives, draws three important conclusions that may help give some context for understanding Christ's appearances. (1) Persons see God only when God makes special provision for it. (2) This sovereign God "step[s] out of his elusive mystery and reveals himself in a real and perceptible way to people." Lorenzen (1995: 134) notes, "God or his messengers 'appear' and 'speak,' and the people 'see' and 'hear.'" (3) The appearance often results in a radical call to a divine task. Lambrecht (1991: 664) argues that the appearance does more than verify the facticity of the resurrection; for Paul, it also implied "conversion, vocation, sending." The emphasis in 1 Cor. 15:5–8, however, falls on the appearances that attest to Christ's actual resurrection (Wolff 1996: 369). The eyewitnesses did not glimpse a mirage or hologram; rather, Christ encountered them as the one raised from the dead. Paul does not bother to identify the circumstances, timing, or nature of these appearances, because he is only rehearsing something already familiar to the Corinthians and wishes to keep things brief.

Paul normally uses the Aramaic name "Cephas" for Peter (1:12; 3:22; 9:5; Gal. 1:18; 2:9, 11, 14). Luke 24:34 and perhaps Mark 16:7 support this personal appearance to Peter, but the Gospels do not develop this tradition. This is the only place where Paul mentions "the Twelve," which suggests that he is drawing from the tradition. "The Twelve" refers to the disciples of Jesus, and the continued use of this number, even after Judas's defection, shows its important pre-Easter symbolic significance to the disciples (but contrast Matt. 28:16).[7]

15:6–7 Paul continues a tally of the resurrection appearances: to five hundred brothers and sisters, to James, and to all the apostles. If he is adding a supplement to the basic tradition, as many assume (Conzelmann 1975: 257), why does he do so?

---

7. Paul never could qualify for membership in the Twelve according to the criteria laid out in Acts 1:21–25. The one who would replace Judas as an apostle was required to have been with Jesus from the beginning as well as to have been a witness to the resurrection and chosen for the purpose by Christ (in this last case, through lots). Paul was not a witness of the historical ministry of Jesus and did not receive a commission from the earthly Jesus.

1. One reason would be to confirm the tradition's veracity (Fee 1987: 729). An array of witnesses can testify to Jesus' resurrection, which is inferred by his appearance to them. Sider (1977: 128) asserts against K. Barth (1933: 150, 154–58) and others that "it is altogether more satisfactory to admit, however much some deplore the fact, that in 6b Paul intends to guarantee the historicity of the resurrection by suggesting that doubters may check with the many eyewitnesses who are still living." Paul did not necessarily assume, however, that some in Corinth had come to doubt this teaching (contra Sider 1977: 132). Again, he provides no details—when, where, how—about this appearance to the five hundred. Presumably, this conclave was not simply a continuation of their pre-Easter gatherings but was precipitated by reports of Jesus' resurrection (Schrage 2001: 55). The adverb ἐφάπαξ (*ephapax*, at the same time, at once) emphasizes that this was not a spiritual vision that each experienced over the course of time; it was an event that all witnessed together. Murphy-O'Connor (1981c: 586) argues that adding this adverb underlines "the objectivity of the experience." If it were only a small group, they could be accused of collusion in trying to deceive others or of suffering from a self-deception.

2. A second reason for mentioning these witnesses is to form a chain from Cephas to the Twelve, to the five hundred, to James, to the apostles, to Paul himself. It establishes a continuity in the message that he passed on to them that goes back to the very beginning. It also reveals a pattern in which Jesus appeared both to larger groups and to individuals. Christ's appearance to Paul was not something unusual, but comparable to the appearances to Peter and James.

3. The chain of witnesses leads to the conclusion in 15:11: "Whether I or they, thus *we* [together] preach and thus you believed." In other words, Peter, the Twelve, James, Paul, and all the other apostles are unified on the basic fact of Christ's resurrection and its meaning. There are not several conflicting versions. Had there been, the movement would have collapsed in on itself.

4. Noting that many of these witnesses are alive while some have died may imply that many are still around to be consulted, if any should want to investigate this account. But Paul provides no names. How are they to check out the facts if they entertain doubts? The emphasis must fall instead on the fact that *some have died*. Paul uses a euphemism, ἐκοιμήθησαν (*ekoimēthēsan*, fallen asleep; cf. 7:39; 11:30; 15:18, 51; 1 Thess. 4:13, 14, 15). Thiselton (2000: 1220) observes that the notion of sleep "carries with it *the expectation of awaking to a new dawn in a new day*." Paul may wish

to convey that even encountering the risen Lord does not preserve one from death. It is more likely, however, that he broaches the subject of these Christians' deaths as preparation for his argument that the dead are raised (Lindemann 2000: 333). Their deaths are nothing alarming. Death precedes resurrection, and using the figure of sleep for death implies that it is not a permanent condition but one of waiting.

Paul presumes that the readers know who James is, and this casual mention also testifies to his importance. He does not identify him as the brother of the Lord. No record of this resurrection appearance to James occurs elsewhere in the NT, but Jerome cites a fictional account of it from the Gospel of the Hebrews.

The third group to which Christ appeared, "the apostles," comprises a larger group than "the Twelve" (cf. 1 Cor. 9:5; 12:28; Gal. 1:17, 19; Rom. 16:7), though it can also be inclusive of the Twelve.

15:8 Paul confidently includes the risen Christ's appearance to him in the roll call of eyewitnesses even though it occurred at some distance in time from the other appearances and no one else could corroborate his account. Schütz (1975: 105–6) takes the phrase "last of all" in a nontemporal sense to mean "the least significant." Schütz (1975: 106–7) contends that Paul is last because apostles generally are last (4:9) and are "the living exemplification of the truth of the kerygma" in which the power of the resurrection is accompanied by the "weakness and ignominy of death." Though this statement is true, it is not Paul's point. "Last" (ἔσχατον, eschaton) in 15:8 is not synonymous with "least" (ἐλάχιστος, elachistos) in 15:9. After four occurrences of "then" (εἶτα, eita; ἔπειτα, epeita), the phrase "last of all" (ἔσχατον δὲ πάντων, eschaton de pantōn) must have a temporal connotation (cf. 15:26, "last enemy"; Mark 12:22, "last of all"). Paul is listing the resurrection appearances in a chronological sequence (Lietzmann 1949: 77) in which Christ appeared to him last of all (cf. Acts 26:16). He declares two things: he is last in time (1 Cor. 15:8) and least in dignity (15:9; P. Jones 1985: 13). As the last one, he represents the closing of a series "so that from the time of this 'last' there can be no similar or equivalent events" (P. Jones 1985: 16).[8] He writes in a culture and environment in which visions, dreams, and ecstatic experiences were not unusual, and identifying Christ's resurrection appearance to him as the "last" restricts the appearances to a certain period of time and makes clear that others should not expect to experience such an event (Lorenzen 1995: 135).

---

8. P. Jones (1985: 30) concludes that the notion "of a unique apostolic ministry limited to the time of the incarnation carries within it the idea of completed revelation as norm or canon for the church."

Others may have visions of Christ, but they are not on the same level as the appearances of the resurrected Christ to the apostles.

Paul is not trying to legitimize his apostolic authority in this section (contra Wilckens 1963: 62–69; 1968: 73) or to make the case that he stands on the same level with Peter and the Twelve as an apostle. Instead, he seeks to authenticate the gospel he preached (Plevnik 1988), which assumes the facticity of the resurrection (Sider 1977: 131; Lambrecht 1991: 669–70). He is responding to those Corinthians who say that there is no resurrection of the dead, not to those who say that Paul is no apostle. He argues more for "the equivalence of the appearances" than for the equality of the witnesses (Schrage 2001: 66). Schütz (1975: 99) points out that Paul does not ground his sufficiency as an apostle in the resurrection appearance given him, "but in the surpassing 'grace' of God manifested in his missionary labors" (cf. 2 Cor. 3:1–6). Paul is not on the defense here (contra Schmithals 1969: 73–80) and is not taking their criticism of him a step further (contra Fee 1987: 734). We must not take everything he says about his apostleship as a defensive remark. Schütz (1975: 101) is correct that Paul identifies himself "with a wider apostolic circle," but he is interested not in "the size of the circle" but in the "nature and function of the apostle." Insisting that he qualifies as an apostle has nothing to do with the issue at hand and would not persuade the Corinthians that his view about the resurrection was right (Schütz 1975: 109).

In Paul's mind, the nature of the appearance to him differed from that granted to Cephas and the rest of the Twelve in only one detail: he was not yet a follower of Jesus when it occurred (perhaps that was also true of James); he was instead a persecutor of Jesus' followers. This fact occasions his use of the term ἔκτρωμα (ektrōma). The term appears in the LXX of Num. 12:12; Job 3:16; and Eccles. 6:3; and in Ps. 57:9 (58:8 MT) in the Greek versions of Aquila, Theodotion, and Symmachus for a dead fetus or stillborn child. What Paul intends by the point of comparison is much debated. Many assume that the word reflects some anti-Pauline sentiment, an abusive epithet that he appropriates and bends to his own ends (so Weiss 1910: 351–52; Parry 1926: 218; Fridrichsen 1932; Björk 1938; Boman 1964; Schneider, TDNT 2:466–67; Fee 1987: 733). Neyrey (1986: 168) takes it to mean that he is the "runt of the litter." But there is no evidence that this term was used as an epithet against Paul or any evidence in this letter that the Corinthians viewed his apostleship as somehow abortive, monstrous, or demonic. The simplest explanation is that it is Paul's own description of his calling as an apostle (see Nickelsburg 1986: 205; Lambrecht 1991: 120; and Schrage [2001: 64–65], who compares it with 1 Cor. 4:13). The ὡσπερεί (hōsperei, as if) softens the harshness of the expression (Schrage 2001: 65).

The metaphor is often thought to refer to the timing of Paul's call, "as to one untimely born" (NRSV, NASB). The point of comparison of not being born at the right time would be that he was not privileged to be a disciple during Jesus' earthly ministry (Schneider, *TDNT* 2:466). The resurrection appearance came to him "out of due time." The timing of this appearance, however, is not Paul's concern, and this view is ruled out because an ἔκτρωμα is always born prematurely, never late. It refers to a fetus expelled from the womb before being fully formed, whether it lives or not (Schneider, *TDNT* 2:465).

Calvin (1960: 315) thinks that the metaphor refers to Paul's being "pushed out from the womb, before the living spirit had scarcely had time to be properly conceived in him." Barrett (1968: 344) follows this line of reasoning by interpreting it to mean that Paul "was hurried into the world before his time." Compared with the "other apostles who had accompanied Jesus during his ministry, he had been born without a due period of gestation." The REB captures this idea with the translation "it was like a sudden, abnormal birth." But Barrett concedes that this is an odd term to use to make this point.

Others connect the image to what follows and take it to refer to the odious fact that Paul persecuted the witnesses of the resurrection (Fridrichsen 1932; Björk 1938). The NEB renders it "though this birth of mine was monstrous."

Munck (1959b: 190–91) suggests that the term refers to "something embryonic" and needing to be formed. Munck thinks that Paul refers to his experience in Judaism as embryonic and that he became fully formed only when he became a Christian. Boman (1964: 49) agrees with this line of reasoning but thinks that Paul means that he had hardly been born as a Christian when Christ appeared to him. The accounts of his Damascus experience in Acts suggest, however, that he was not a Christian when Christ appeared to him. He had no rudimentary faith. Nickelsburg (1986: 200–205) modifies this approach by connecting it to Paul's statement in Gal. 1:15: alluding to Isa. 49:1, 5, 6, Paul reflects on his call and affirms that he had been set apart by God in his mother's womb. In 1 Cor. 15:10, he alludes to Isa. 49:4 ("I have labored in vain") in affirming that God's grace toward him was not in vain, because he has labored more abundantly than all. Nickelsburg concludes from this connection that Paul understands himself to be an ἔκτρωμα "with respect to the purpose for which he was appointed from the womb." His persecution of the church meant that God's purpose for him, established in the womb, had "miscarried or been aborted" (Nickelsburg 1986: 204). The appearance of Christ to Paul made him what God intended him to be. Nickelsburg's proposal assumes that the Corinthians were aware of Paul's divine appointment in the womb, to which the term ἔκτρωμα alludes, whether it was his own coinage or that of opponents. As attractive as this connection to Gal. 1:15 is, this assumption remains rather speculative.[9]

A simpler interpretation of this term would allow the readers to understand the point of comparison from the context without some previous insight into Paul's calling. Sellin (1986: 250) is correct that Paul refers to his pre-Christian existence (contra Tuckett 1996: 268, who thinks that it refers to the context in which "resurrection faith is created, preached, and handed on"). He was tantamount to an ἔκτρωμα *when* Christ appeared to him, not afterward. If he means by this that he was something embryonic and unfit for life, then his life could be sustained only by divine intervention (Schütz 1975: 104–5). If he means that he was an aborted fetus or a stillborn child, which is more likely, then he is referring to his state of wretchedness as an unbeliever and persecutor of the church. Hollander and van der Hout (1996: 230–32) contend that Paul draws on Jewish usage of the term to stress that the person in question is in a "deplorable position," whose life is "miserable and worthless" and "cannot sink lower." Hollander and van der Hout (1996: 234–36) contend that the figure fits the traditional prophetic motif of sufficiency in spite of insufficiency. Paul was unfit for the task God called him to do. God's grace does not remove this obstacle but overcomes it so that it is clear that God, not the messenger, "is responsible for the message." Hollander and van der Hout (1996: 227–28) point out that the fundamental idea of the word in classical and Hellenistic non-Jewish texts is that of miscarriage implying death. Though it tended to be used literally in this background, it does not exclude the possibility that Paul could apply this meaning in a figurative sense. Before his call and conversion he was dead, but he was miraculously given life through God's grace. God made him sufficient to be a minister of a new covenant, "not of letter but of spirit; for the letter kills, but the Spirit gives life" (2 Cor. 3:6). His sufficiency as an apostle is tied to resurrection imagery of being given life. The appearance of the risen Christ to him was a kind of resurrection from the dead (Sellin 1986: 250). This image fits the theme running through the chapter of God's power giving life to the dead. Both his unworthiness and his lifelessness are overcome by God's power.

15:9–10 Paul's self-abasement is sincere. He regards himself as the least of the apostles (cf. Eph. 3:8), primarily because of his past record of persecuting the church. As a persecutor, Paul acted out of zeal for the law and faithfulness to a vision of what he thought the nation of Israel should

9. The same criticism applies to Schaefer's (1994) view that the term refers to the description in Hos. 13:13 of Ephraim as the foolish child who does not want to leave the mother's womb—that is, he will not heed God's call. Paul applied it to his activity as a persecutor of Christianity who also did not heed God's call. This view also fails to convince, as the word in question does not even occur in Hosea.

be (Gal. 1:13; Phil. 3:6; see also Acts 9:1–5; 22:7–8; 26:14–15). He believed that those who were not properly obedient were a contagion needing to be eradicated. Doing what he thought was well pleasing to God became the cause of his greatest guilt because it was directed, he later discovers, against the church of God (cf. 1 Cor. 1:2; Gal. 1:2). This ignoble past means that he is an apostle by God's choice (cf. John 15:16) and God's grace (Rom. 1:5) alone. Christ's appearance to him and his call reveal God's extraordinary power to create change in people. Fee (1987: 734) contends that Paul's encounter with the risen Christ formed the basis of his theology of grace: "Since God was gracious to him, God's enemy, in this way, he came eventually to realize that this is the way God is toward all, Jew and Gentile alike, making no distinctions." He was not worthy (ἱκανός, *hikanos*; cf. 2 Cor. 2:16; 3:5–6), but grace takes persons who are not worthy or sufficient and makes them fit.[10] Grace does not so much require response as it enkindles response. It empowers and equips. Paul hints at his success as a successful missionary by asserting that the grace shown to him was not without its intended effect (cf. 2 Cor. 6:1). Its goal is being accomplished as he successfully spreads the gospel through his labor (contrast Isa. 49:4, where the prophet laments that he has labored in vain; cf. 1 Thess. 2:1; 3:5). Paul does not believe, however, that he is repaying the divine grace shown to him with hard work. Robertson and Plummer (1914: 342) compare it to the child who joyfully gives the parent a birthday present after having spent the parent's own money to buy it.

Fee (1987: 735) notes that Paul is not comparing himself to the others, "as if to say, 'I am better than they because I worked harder.'" Schütz (1975: 103) avers,

> The apostle's sufficiency comes solely from God's grace, not from the apostle's own resources. His *calling and authority* are not the product of his own natural gifts, but are attributable only to God. Thus if Paul did labor harder than all of the others, it was still "not I, but the grace of God which is with me."

Paul's boast is in the Lord (1 Cor. 1:31), and he testifies that his work is evidence of a continuing abundance of divine grace that produces abundant results. God's grace, which brought this stillborn child to life, continues to work itself out in his life. It changed him from zealous persecutor of Christ to zealous laborer for Christ. The greater (περισσότερον, *perissoteron*) laboring may be a reference to his hardships suf-

---

10. P. Jones (1985: 24) observes, "If Paul is an unnatural, apparently illegitimate member of the apostolate through whom God shows his grace (1 Cor. 15:10–11), the same can be said of the Gentiles, who against all normal expectations, become the means for the salvation of Israel, the 'natural' people of God."

fered in the course of carrying the gospel to the world beyond Palestine (cf. 2 Cor. 11:23–29) and its fruitfulness (Rom. 15:18–19; Phil. 1:22). His intention is not to set himself on a par with other apostles or on a level above them. He sets an example for the Corinthians, and at the conclusion of this discourse he admonishes them also to abound (περισσεύοντες, *perisseuontes*) in the work of the Lord because "you know that your labor is not in vain in the Lord" (1 Cor. 15:58).

Paul reprises the opening verse (15:1) in 15:11. "Thus we preach" (κηρύσσομεν, *kēryssomen*) includes all of the apostles, and the present tense conveys that it continues to be their message. Christ's resurrection is the common denominator on which all are in accord. It is non-negotiable and cannot be jettisoned without gutting the Christian faith. The Corinthians received this word from the least of all the apostles so that the same grace that had made him a most improbable apostle worked also to make them believers (15:2), though they were, according to the world's criteria, a foolish, insignificant, and weak lot (1:26–31). The word that he preached and that they believed is not merely a digest of historical facts; it is a living and powerful word that transforms lives and conveys the power of God (2:4). This statement declares that the proclaimers of the gospel were not riddled by confused diversity of opinion on this matter.

15:11

Additional Notes

15:3. De Saeger (2001) concludes from his analysis of the phrase ὑπὲρ τῶν ἁμαρτιῶν ἡμῶν in 15:3 and Gal. 1:4 that the context in 1 Cor. 15:3 is the future eschatological judgment. Christ's death delivers believers from the penalty for their sins. In Gal. 1:4, the phrase refers to liberation in the present.

15:4. The use of the perfect tense in the death-and-resurrection formula in the NT is without parallel (cf. Rom. 4:25; 8:34; 14:9; 2 Cor. 5:15; 1 Thess. 4:14). Holleman (1996: 44–45) argues that it is not a postclassical perfect, which would function as an aorist. Few examples of such usage of the perfect occur in the NT. The emphasis here is on the abiding results of the event.

15:5. Some texts (D*, F, G, 330, 464*) change "the Twelve" to read ἕνδεκα (eleven) out of an overly fastidious interest in accuracy, since Judas could not have been included (cf. Matt 28:16; Luke 24:9, 33; Acts 1:26). They fail to realize that "the Twelve" is being used as a title for a particular group of disciples.

15:10. The majority of the texts read ἡ σὺν ἐμοί, but 𝔓46 reads ἡ εἰς ἐμέ. This reading seems to be a mistaken repetition or deliberate assimilation of that phrase in the first part of the verse. Some texts (ℵ*, B, D*, F, G, 0243, 0270*, 6, 1739) read σὺν ἐμοί, omitting the definite article. The lack of ἡ could be an accidental omission, or its presence could be insertion following the pattern of the previous phrase.

B. The Consequences If the Resurrection of the Dead Is Not True (15:12–19)

In 15:12, Paul announces the topic and what has precipitated his long discussion of the resurrection. Some of the Corinthians are saying that there is no resurrection of the dead in spite of believing the apostolic proclamation that Christ has been raised. I agree with Asher (2000: 2, 30–90) that Paul is not countering opponents in this section, as so many assume, but dealing with the Corinthians as students who need further instruction. His tone and style are didactic throughout. The Corinthians' cosmological categories made the resurrection of the dead in which a terrestrial body ascends to the celestial world seem inconceivable. Paul will show that their denial of the resurrection of the dead is theologically untenable (15:12–19) and how the resurrection is not only possible but also can fit into their cosmological thinking (15:35–58). The polarity between earth and heaven exists. A body fit to inhabit this world therefore must be changed by the power of God before it is fit to inhabit the heavenly world.

In 15:12–19, Paul correlates the tenet that Christ has been raised with the Corinthians' denial of the resurrection of the dead to expose the logical implications of this denial. He sets up, as it were, theological dominoes that fall, one after another, when the first domino—if Christ is not raised—is knocked over. McDonald (1989: 38) perceptively comments, "The nub of the issue is precisely the connection which Paul has taken as self-evident, namely, that the raising of Christ cannot be neatly extracted from its eschatological setting, which includes the resurrection of the dead (15:13)." Christ's resurrection entails the resurrection of the dead.

Paul argues his case from a syllogism that omits the middle term:

There is no resurrection of the dead
[Christ died, 15:3–4a]
Therefore, Christ has not been raised from the dead.

He restates this conclusion as another false premise, which leads to further logical consequences. The false premise—if Christ is not raised—is repeated again in 15:16, followed by a list of more repercussions:

Premise (false): if there is no resurrection of the dead (15:13a)
Conclusion: then Christ is not raised (15:13b)
Premise (false): if Christ is not raised (15:14a)
Conclusions: our preaching is null and void (15:14b)
your faith is null and void (15:14c)
we are false witnesses (15:15)
Premise (false): if the dead are not raised (15:16a)
Conclusion: then Christ is not raised (15:16b)
Premise (false): if Christ is not raised (15:17a)
Conclusions: your faith is futile (15:17b)
you are still in your sins (15:17c)
the Christian dead have perished (15:18)
we are the most pitiable of humans (15:19)

This is the first section of 15:12–34, whose structure follows an ABA′ pattern:

A The consequences if the resurrection of the dead is not true (15:12–19)
B The consequences since the resurrection of the dead is true (15:20–28)
A′ The consequences if the resurrection of the dead were not true (15:29–34)

Exegesis and Exposition

¹²But if Christ is being preached as raised from the dead, how do some among you say that there is no resurrection of the dead? ¹³And if there is no resurrection from the dead, then neither has Christ been raised. ¹⁴But if Christ has not been raised, then our preaching is null and void, and so is ⌜your⌝ faith. ¹⁵And we are found also [to be] false witnesses about God because we bear witness about God that he raised Christ, whom he did not raise if indeed the dead are not [really] raised. ¹⁶For if the dead are not raised, then neither has Christ been raised. ¹⁷If Christ has not been raised, then your faith is futile and you are still in your sins. ¹⁸Then those who have fallen asleep in Christ have perished. ¹⁹If in this life we have hoped in Christ—that and nothing more—we are the most pitiable of all human beings.

15:12 Paul's question "How do some among you say. . . ?" expresses astonishment (cf. Gal. 4:9; Lindemann 2000: 337). He has established that all apostolic preaching is unified in proclaiming that Christ has been raised from the dead, and he has confirmed that the Corinthians believed this preaching (1 Cor. 15:1, 11). If they did not deny that Jesus was raised from the dead, what is it that they denied about the resurrection of the dead (cf. 2 Clem. 9:1; Pol. *Phil.* 7:1)? How many are the "some among you" (ἐν ὑμῖν τινες, *en hymin tines*)? Was their influence in the community dominant (Fee 1987: 713), or were they only a faction (M. Mitchell 1993: 176–77)? The wording suggests the latter. Paul addresses a conviction held by some of the community's members.

We can reconstruct what they denied about the resurrection and the reasons behind this denial only by making inferences from Paul's reply. Obviously, this method is fraught with difficulties that can result in a serious misreading of the text, and proposals about what the Corinthians denied about the resurrection differ.

Based on Paul's response in 15:17–19, 22–34, some argue that the Corinthians denied any postmortal life (Schweitzer 1931: 93–94; Spörlein 1971: 190–91). The Epicurean position that the soul can no longer exist after the dissolution of the body appears to have been prevalent (Acts 17:18–21, 32). Lattimore (1942: 342) concludes from his study of Latin epitaphs, "The belief of the ancients, both Greek and Roman, in immortality, was not widespread, nor clear, nor strong." One tombstone inscription, *non fui, fui, non sum, non desidero* ("I was not. I was. I am not. I am free from wishes" [*CIL* 8.3463]), was so common that it was abbreviated *nffnsnd[uro]* (like R.I.P., *requiescat in pace*, "may he/she rest in peace").[1] In the dialogue with Socrates about the immortality of the soul, Cebes points out that most are prone not to believe in it: "They fear that when the soul leaves the body it no longer exists anywhere, and that on the day when the man dies it is destroyed and perishes, and when it leaves the body and departs from it, straightway it flies away and is no longer anywhere, scattering like a breath or smoke" (Plato, *Phaedo* 70A). Aeschylus (*Eumenides* 645–48) has Apollo lament that Zeus could undo the fetters of death, but when the dust has drunk a person's blood, "once he is dead, there is no resurrection [ἀνάστασις, *anastasis*]."

Such fatalism led people to want to live life now to the fullest: "Eat, drink, and be merry" (cf. 1 Cor. 15:32). Concern was primarily for blessing in *this* life, not a life to come, which seemed unlikely to come. Trimalchio, at his gluttonous feast, says, "Well, well, if we know we must die, why should we not live?" (Petronius, *Satyr.* 72; see also 32). People yearned for "salvation" but not the salvation that entails "deliverance from this world and safe passage to the next" (Savage 1996: 27). Salvation had to do with matters of this life and present benefits: health, wealth, protection, sustenance. The use of the "I" in the inscriptions, however, might suggest that individuals really did want to continue after they were dead. Christianity offered the promise of resurrection, a promise not truly offered elsewhere. Since the Corinthians baptized for

---

1. Cf. οὐκ ἤμην, ἐγενόμην, οὐκ εἰμί, οὐ μέλει μοι (*ouk ēmēn, egenomēn, ouk eimi, ou melei moi*, "I was not. I was. I am not. I do not care" [G. Horsley 1987: 43]).

the dead (15:29), it seems highly unlikely that they did not hold out a hope for life with God beyond death.

A handful of interpreters assume that Paul misunderstood the Corinthians' position and mistakenly thought that they denied any hope in the life hereafter (Bultmann 1951: 169; Schmithals 1971: 156). Not only does this misread what Paul says, but also, as Holleman (1996: 36) responds, "If one supposes that Paul misrepresents the Corinthian opinion it becomes impossible to know the Corinthian point of view at all."

Others surmise that some Corinthians, influenced by an "over-realized eschatology," believed that they had already experienced resurrection (cf. 2 Tim. 2:16–18).[2] They understood Jesus' being raised as exaltation to heaven, not as bodily resurrection, and concluded that they were exalted with Jesus through the sacraments (cf. Rom. 6:4). These Corinthians would be the theological forerunners of the second-century gnostics who appear to adapt and rebut Pauline statements. The Nag Hammadi *Treatise on the Resurrection* alludes to a spiritual resurrection: Christ swallowed up death, gave us the way of our immortality, and we suffered with him, rose with him, and went to heaven with him (45.25–28; 49.15–16). The Gospel of Philip declares, "Those who assert: 'One dies first and is then raised,' are wrong. If the resurrection is not received first, while still alive, there is nothing to be received upon death" (73.1–5; see also Irenaeus, *Adversus haereses* [*Against Heresies*] 1.23.5; 2.31.2; Tertullian, *De anima* [*The Soul*] 50.2).

This interpretation might explain why Paul emphasizes the futurity of the resurrection, but the wording of 1 Cor. 15:12 militates against it. He does not say, as he does in 2 Tim. 2:18, that the Corinthians claim that the resurrection has already happened, but says, instead, that they claim that "there is no resurrection of the dead" (Wedderburn 1981: 231; Boer 1988: 105). Wedderburn (1987: 164–295) offers a lengthy refutation of the view that the Corinthians believed that a resurrection had already happened to them. Kuck (1992a: 16–25) persuasively critiques those who appeal to realized eschatology to explain various problems that have arisen in Corinth (see also Asher 2000: 39–41).

It is most likely that the Corinthians rejected a materialistic aspect to the resurrection.[3] Seneca (*Ep. morales* 24.18) outlines the two alternatives about what happens at death that were considered to be the most reasonable—immortality of the soul or annihilation: "Death either annihilates us or strips us bare. If we are then released, there re-

2. So von Soden 1951: 259; Bultmann 1951: 169; Schniewind 1952; Barrett 1968: 348; J. Wilson 1968: 95; Käsemann 1969: 126; Talbert 1987: 98; Kistemaker 1993: 540; Tuckett 1996; Lindemann 2000: 339.

3. So Robertson and Plummer 1914: 329; Lietzmann 1949: 79; Sandelin 1995: 149–53; Sider 1977; R. Horsley 1978c: 231; Sellin 1986: 79–189; Fee 1987: 741; D. Martin 1995: 107–8, 122–23; Holleman 1996: 37–40; Hays 1997: 259–60; Schrage 2001: 111–19.

mains the better part, after the burden has been withdrawn; if we are annihilated, nothing remains; good and bad are alike removed." The Corinthians apparently believed in an afterlife but retained the dualistic anthropology that was the legacy of their Hellenistic environment. According to this view, humans are composed of two inharmonious parts, body and soul, that are of unequal value. At death, the mortal body is shed like a snake's skin, and the immortal soul continues in a purely spiritual existence. In Homer, the vital breath or psyche of a person leaves the body at death and exists merely as a specter separated from the world of the living by an impassable barrier. In Plato's *Phaedo* 73A, Socrates assumes that the soul is immortal and that death is a release from the body (see also *Phaedo* 66E–67A). The "soul" is "entirely fastened and welded to the body and is compelled to regard realities through the body as through prison bars" (Plato, *Phaedo* 82D–E), but death is the separation of the soul from the body (Plato, *Phaedo* 67D). Winter (2001: 96) contends that "evidence abounds for the concept of the immortality of the soul," as can be seen in this inscription: "[Friend, this] tomb Attica did win. But Italy [kept my body], and my soul went up on high" (SEG 37 [1987], no. 198). Josephus (*J.W.* 7.8.7 §344) reflects this view in his report of the speech of the Zealot chieftain Eleazar, who sought to rouse those trapped on Masada to kill themselves rather than to die at the hands of the Romans or to become their slaves: "For it is death which gives liberty to the soul and permits it to depart to its own pure abode, there to be free from all calamity; but so long as it is imprisoned in a mortal body and tainted with all its miseries, it is, in sober truth, dead, for association with what is mortal, ill befits that which is divine." Justin Martyr (*Dial.* 80) derides false Christians who say that there is no resurrection of the dead but that their souls are received up into heaven at death.[4] The Corinthians may have assumed the inherent immortality of the spirit or some kind of assumption into glory at death in much the same way that Paul was whisked up to the third heaven (2 Cor. 12:2–3), which from this perspective would have been "outside of the body."[5] Their absorption with wisdom may have augmented this view since, according to Wis. 8:17, immortality comes from kinship with wisdom. D. Martin (1995: 122) also shows how natural it would have been for them to think about "the resurrection of the dead" in terms of the popular tales of the resuscitation of corpses. The less educated might think of the resurrection in terms of magical spells;

4. In contrast to Justin's dismissal of these persons as not being Christians, we should note that Paul treats the doubters rather gently as those who need to be instructed and not as heretics (see Robertson and Plummer 1914: 347).

5. A complementary idea of the separation of the spirit from the body is found in Eccles. 12:7 and in Jub. 23:31: "And their bones will rest in the earth, and their spirits will increase joy."

others, educated in the assumptions of philosophers, would tend to think of this as unsophisticated or ludicrous. For the latter, the spirit needs no transformation or body to enter eternity.

That some in Corinth questioned how a terrestrial body could be raised up to live in a celestial realm makes the best sense of Paul's explanation of the nature of the resurrection body.[6] He rejects any idea of the existence of the soul/spirit without a body. It is possible that the Corinthians may have thought of the resurrection of the dead in literal terms of a reanimation of decayed corpses. They may have been mystified as to how a body that perishes and rots could be resurrected, or they may have found the whole idea repulsive.[7] Paul's argument in 15:35–41 that God can give a different body to each creature as it suits its environment may correct this mistaken impression. This view also makes sense of his argument that spiritual immortality is not received upon death and that death is not destroyed until the end. It clarifies why he argues that a radical discontinuity exists between mortal existence and life after death, a discontinuity that can be bridged only by the resurrection. Holleman (1996: 38) comments, "Resurrection will therefore be another act of creation, this time resulting in a spiritualized body."

In 15:13–19, Paul argues ad absurdum to show how futile the Christian **15:13–19** faith would be if there were no resurrection of the dead. If there is no resurrection of the dead, then how can Christ be raised from the dead? If Christ is not raised from the dead, then everything based on that belief collapses in a heap of broken dreams.

The first thing to fall is the content of the gospel, which he summarized in 15:3–5. The preaching that led the Corinthians to faith would be empty (κενός, *kenos*), devoid of any spiritual value (15:14). It makes no difference whether it was delivered with a persuasive, rhetorical flourish or not (2:1–4); if it is bogus, it is worthless. Everything stands or falls on the truth of the assertion that God raised Christ from the dead.

The second thing to fall is their faith. If this core belief proves to be a delusion, then everything else they believed from this preaching of the

---

6. Other views should be mentioned in passing. Schweitzer (1931: 93) claims that the Corinthians believed that only those who survived until the return of Jesus would enter the kingdom of God. The situation would be identical to that in 1 Thess. 4:13–18, but Paul responds quite differently there. Schütz (1975: 87–92) contends that what Paul writes in 1 Cor. 15:12–19 reflects entirely the argument of the Corinthians (cf. Tuckett 1996: 264–69). Gundry (1976: 170) counters that it is far too lengthy a quotation of his opponents' argument. Tuckett's (1996: 268) rejoinder that it is not impossible does not mean that it is probable.

7. There is no reason to think that the Corinthians were sarcastic or mocking in expressing their puzzlement (contra J. Wilson 1968: 90; Sider 1977: 131).

gospel is discredited. The gospel is not good news but a hoax that has no real power to change lives or to do anything else except to deceive.

Third, the trustworthiness of all the apostles who proclaimed that Christ is risen (15:15) is thrown into question. They are perjurers conspiring to make false statements by announcing that God raised Christ, when in fact, God does not raise the dead.[8] They speak in God's name what they know to be untrue. God is not, as they claim, the one who raises the dead.

Fourth, the Christian assertion that Christ died on behalf of humankind's sins is to be discounted. If Christ was not raised, then they are still damned in their sins and will not inherit the kingdom of God (6:9–11). Death's stinger (15:56) still spears its victims; its shroud will forever bind them. Sin's wages must be paid (Rom. 6:23), and redemption has been foiled by the last enemy. Paul asserts in Romans that Jesus was raised "for our justification" (Rom. 4:25), which enables us "to walk in newness of life" (Rom. 6:4–5). He visualizes the resurrected Christ at the right hand of God, interceding for us against all who would condemn us (Rom. 8:34). But if Christ has not been raised, none of this is true.

Fifth, those believers who have died (cf. 1 Cor. 11:30; 15:6) remain in the clutches of death. They have perished (15:18). The ἄρα (*ara*, then) goes back to the εἰ (*ei*, if) in 15:17a. If Christ has not been raised, then there will be no resurrection of Christians either. "In Christ" governs those who have fallen asleep (cf. 1 Thess. 4:16). If Christ has not been raised, then those who "fall asleep in Christ" are no different from unbelievers, who are consigned to doom and ruin (1 Cor. 1:18). The human terror of death as a gloomy portal leading to oblivion and divine condemnation would be justified, for God abandons to perdition even those who have been faithful. This statement packs a punch because, as Goulder (2001: 181) trenchantly states it, "No one wants to think that their relatives have kidded themselves in this life and are now rotting or, worse, frying."

Sixth, all hope is dashed (15:19).[9] Paul uses a perfect periphrastic (ἠλπικότες ἐσμέν, *ēlpikotes esmen*), "we have set our hope and continue to hope." The word "only" (μόνον, *monon*) occurs at the end of the clause and could apply to "this life" ("if only for this life we have hope in Christ," NIV) or to "setting one's hope" ("if in this life we have set our

---

8. The phrase ψευδομάρτυρες τοῦ θεοῦ (*pseudomartyres tou theou*) is an objective genitive, "false witnesses against God"; that is, they bear false witness to what God did. The next clause explains why they are false witnesses.

9. The lament in 2 Bar. 21:13, "For if only this life exists which everyone possesses here, nothing could be more bitter than this," is only a superficial parallel, as Hays (1997: 261–62) shows. Paul is not talking about human mortality in general but the hopelessness of Christians in the face of death.

hope only in Christ"). Since "only" appears at the end of the clause, it is more likely that it applies to the whole clause: "if in this life we have hoped in Christ—that and nothing more" (Edwards 1885: 407; Morris 1958: 212; Barrett 1968: 350). The Corinthians have nothing more than "a mere wistful, faint trust in some larger hope, which rests on nothing," and they "face life with nothing better than a Christ of their own devotional dreams or speculative insight" (Moffatt 1938: 242, 244). Hope then becomes only wishful thinking. "This life" may contrast with "eternal life" (cf. Rom. 2:7; 5:21; Wolff 1996: 380), but Paul does not say so. Instead, he seems to be saying that if Christ is not raised, then the relationship with Christ and any hope based on that relationship cannot continue beyond the grave. "In Christ" refers to the source of this hope that "if we have been united together in the likeness of his death, then we shall certainly be united in the likeness of his resurrection" (Rom. 6:5). But if Christ is not raised, then our hope is nothing more than whistling in the dark. Christians become pathetic dupes, taken in by a colossal fraud. Their transformation and glorious spiritual experiences in this life are all make-believe. They are the most pitiable (ἐλε-εινότεροι, eleeinoteroi) of all human beings because they have embraced Christ's death and suffering in this life for nothing. Christianity would be an ineffective religion that is detrimental to one's health since it bestows only suffering on its followers. Suffering the loss of all things because of Christ and sharing his sufferings by becoming like him in his death with the hope of attaining the resurrection (Phil. 3:7–11) turn out to be foolish. The world would be right: the cross is utter folly (1 Cor. 1:23). The joy that characterizes the basic orientation of Christian life is based on the confidence that Christ will return, the dead will be raised, and all wrongs will be made right. If that is not true, then joy is replaced by despair.

Additional Note

15:14. The reading ἡμῶν ("our" faith) is found in B, D^gr*, 0243, 6, 33, 81, 1241, 1739, 1881 instead of the ὑμῶν ("your" faith) found in the majority of texts. Both words would have been pronounced the same, but the ἡμῶν is probably an unthinking assimilation to the previous ἡμῶν ("our" preaching). The thought would seem to anticipate "your faith" as the response to "our preaching."

C. The Consequences Since the Resurrection of the Dead Is True (15:20–28)

In 15:20–28, Paul argues that Jesus is the first to be raised and his resurrection will be followed by others. He introduces the idea of corporate existence and a contrast between Adam and Christ. All humans are included in Adam with respect to sin and death; all Christians are included in Christ with respect to the future resurrection. Christ's resurrection cannot be viewed in isolation from that of others (McDonald 1989: 39). Jesus is the representative of others who also will be raised, and the eschatological resurrection "is the necessary sequel to Jesus' resurrection" (Holleman 1996: 44).[1] A chronological order exists between the resurrection of Christ and the eschatological resurrection, and Paul emphasizes that Christ reigns from the time of his resurrection until all enemies are subjugated (S. Lewis 1998: 63). The two "when" clauses in 15:24 describe what happens at the Lord's parousia: the kingdom is handed over to God when every ruler, authority, and power has been destroyed. In 15:25, Paul explains why this is so: Christ must reign until he puts all enemies under his feet. This leads to the key statement that death is the last enemy to be eliminated, which demands the resurrection of the dead. He explains why this is so in 15:27: God has put all things, including death, under Christ's feet. When this last enemy is annihilated, then Christ submits himself in obedience to God.

This unit unveils why Paul so adamantly defends the resurrection of the dead. If there is no resurrection of the dead, then death remains unconquered and still holds sway beyond the end as a power set over against God. This circumstance, obviously, is theologically untenable. Therefore, because God is sovereign and omnipotent, death must be vanquished in the end, which demands the resurrection of the dead.

---

1. Holleman (1996: 93) notes, "The Christian expectation that there will be a resurrection at the end of time is the natural continuation of the Jewish tradition concerning the eschatological resurrection."

Exegesis and Exposition

²⁰But now [as a matter of fact] Christ has been raised from the dead, the firstfruits of those who have fallen asleep. ²¹For since through a human death [came], so also through a human [comes] the resurrection from the dead. ²²For just as in Adam all die, so also in Christ all will be made alive. ²³Each one in his own rank: Christ the firstfruits, then those who belong to Christ at his parousia. ²⁴Then [comes] the end, when he hands over the kingdom to God the Father, when he will have dethroned every ruler, every authority and power. ²⁵For it is necessary for him to continue to reign until that time when he sets all his enemies under his feet. ²⁶Death is the last enemy to be abolished. ²⁷"For he subjected all things under his feet." But when it says, "All things have been made subject," clearly that excludes the one who made all things subject to him. ²⁸And when he subjects all things to him, then the Son himself will be made subject to the one who made all things subject to him, in order that God might be all in all.

Paul begins the next phase of his argument with a new premise that is true. Barrett (1985b: 102) notes that elsewhere when Paul uses the expression νυνὶ δέ (*nyni de*, but now), it is followed by "profound statements of the gospel" (cf. Rom. 3:21; 6:22; 7:6; 1 Cor. 12:18; 13:13). A resurrection from the dead *has already occurred*. Christ has been raised from the dead (15:4), and Paul identifies him as "the firstfruits [ἀπαρχή, *aparchē*] of those who have fallen asleep." "Firstfruits" is a cultic term that Jews used for the first sheaf of the grain harvest (Lev. 23:10–11) that on the sixteenth of Nisan was consecrated to God in the temple. In the LXX, the concept of firstfruits applies to "offerings" (Exod. 23:16; 34:22), "taxes" (Exod. 25:2–3; Num. 18:8, 11; Ezek. 45:13), and "children" (Gen. 49:3). The custom of offering the firstfruits of the harvest was common in the Greco-Roman world as well (Spicq, *TLNT* 1:145–47). Firstfruits of any kind "were holy to the divinity and were consecrated before the rest could be put to secular use" (BDAG 98), but it is assumed that this original meaning "is greatly weakened" so that it becomes almost equivalent to "first" (BDAG 98.1.b.α).[2] Spicq (*TLNT* 1:152) notes that in Philo and the NT, what is emphasized is the link between the firstfruits and the whole of the harvest rather than the offering to God. Paul uses the term in Rom. 8:23 and 11:16 to refer to the "first and representative part," and in 1 Cor. 16:15 and Rom. 16:5 to refer to the first converts of a region—the household of Stephanas in Corinth and Epaenetus in Asia.

The term "firstfruits" does not simply signify Christ's chronological precedence as the first one raised from the dead, however. It conveys

15:20

2. The phrase "firstborn from the dead" appears in Col. 1:18 and Rev. 1:5, and that expression refers not only to chronological precedence but also to Christ's rank.

that his resurrection is the "first of a kind, involving the rest in its character or destiny" (Parry 1926: 223). That is why Paul says that Christ is "the firstfruits of those who have fallen asleep," not "of the resurrected." His resurrection was not simply God's miraculous intervention that rescued him from death, but was "the beginning of God's renewal of all things" (Perkins 1984: 318; cf. Schrage 2001: 160). The concept of firstfruits expects that "the rest *must* follow" (Weiss 1910: 356). Holleman (1996: 204) contends that by choosing this term, "Paul presents Jesus' resurrection as the beginning of the eschatological resurrection." As the firstfruits, Christ's resurrection is a pledge of the full harvest of resurrection to come: "The resurrection bodies . . . of the redeemed . . . are to correspond to and flow from Christ's in the same way that the harvest corresponds to and flows from its first fruits" (Kreitzer, *DPL* 11).[3] The imagery expresses that the resurrection of Jesus and the resurrection of believers are integrally related and that they are two decisive moments "comprising the total event of the resurrection" (Sloan 1983: 77). The imagery conveys this point: "Christ risen is to the multitude of believers who shall arise again at His Advent what a first ripe ear, gathered by hand, is to the whole harvest" (Godet 1887: 351).[4]

15:21–22 Paul explains how Christ's resurrection was not merely an isolated occurrence (Dykstra 1969: 211) but one that has consequences for others who follow by comparing it to Adam's sin (C. Hill 1988: 304). He presents the comparison through a double parallelism:

> For since through a man death [came],
>   so also through a man [comes] the resurrection from the dead.
> For just as in Adam all die,
>   so also in Christ all will be made alive.

Paul is not interested in making the point that Adam's sin brought death (cf. Rom. 5:12–21), but in showing how Adam's sin had a universal effect on all who came after. The same applies to Christ's resurrection. As physical death came inevitably from Adam's sin, so physical resurrection comes inevitably from Christ's resurrection. He underscores the incarnation with the phrase "through a man." This detail prevents anyone from arguing that Christ was some divine figure whom death could not really touch. It also foils the argument that his resurrection was of a different order because he was divine (Fee 1987: 751).

3. Describing Christ's resurrection as the firstfruits evokes the harvest metaphor used to describe the end of the age (Matt. 13:30, 39; Gal. 6:9; Rev. 14:15).

4. Godet (1887: 351) also notes that the image might recollect that Jesus died on the afternoon of Nisan 14 and was raised on morning of Nisan 16, the day when firstfruits are to be offered (see also Findlay 1910: 925; Barrett 1985b: 103).

Christ's death was the death of a man, and his resurrection was the resurrection of a man (cf. Heb. 2:14–15).

The analogy assumes human solidarity with those at the beginning of a line who then become the representatives of those who follow. Adam leads the way and represents the old order; Christ leads the way and represents the new order. Paul assumes that the representative determines the fate of the group. All those bound to Adam share his banishment from Eden, his alienation, and his fate of death so that death becomes the common lot of his posterity (see additional note). All those bound to Christ receive reconciliation and will share his resurrection and heavenly blessings. Not all humans are in Christ, however. Holleman (1996: 53) comments, "Since only Christians are united with Christ, only Christians will be made alive through Christ." Christ's death and resurrection will finally drive sin and death from the field at the very end, but the effects of these salvific events benefit only those who believe in him and become in him a new humanity.

Edwards (1885: 412) explains the difference in this way: humans "are in Adam by nature, in Christ by faith." But this view needs to be refined. If Paul modeled the phrase "in Adam" after the phrase "in Christ," "it will involve more than the necessary hereditary relationship; an element of choice, or decision, will be included" (Barrett 1985b: 108). According to Barrett, "in Adam" would imply that humans "have taken Adam's side, they have joined the revolt against God, and for that reason die" (cf. Rom. 5:12). Not all have chosen Christ's side, however. Only those who are so united with him such that they die with him (Rom. 6:8) will be those who also rise with him. In this section, then, Paul speaks only about the Christian dead, not about a general resurrection (Conzelmann 1975: 264–65; Fee 1987: 749 n. 19), and the phrase "all will be made alive" refers only to those who have fallen asleep in Christ (cf. 1 Thess. 4:16; contra Boer 1988: 112–13; Lindemann 2000: 344; Schrage 2001: 163–66). Paul affirms throughout the letter that those who are not in Christ ultimately will perish (1 Cor. 1:18; 3:17; 5:13; 6:9–10; 9:27; cf. 2 Thess. 1:9).[5] Death's power is broken, however, for those who are in Christ. The verb ζῳοποιηθήσονται (zō-opoiēthēsontai, will be made alive) implies a new creation (cf. Rom. 4:17), and Paul applies the verb only to believers, not unbelievers (Kistemaker 1993: 550; cf. Rom. 4:17; 8:11; 1 Cor. 15:45). He uses the term here for those who will be made alive to enter into eternal life—namely, Christians.

The imagery of "firstfruits" implies that Christ's resurrection sets in **15:23–24** motion a series of events that will culminate at his parousia. Paul is not answering the question "Why is the resurrection in the future and not

---

5. For the general resurrection, see Acts 24:15.

now?" (contra J. Wilson 1968: 95), but he does affirm that it lies in the future. He describes a divinely ordained chronology of events related to the resurrection but makes no attempt to elaborate on all that will happen. Robertson and Plummer (1914: 355) contend that the wisest course in interpreting these verses is not to attempt to ferret out the details of the consummation but "to adopt a reverent reticence and reserve." Paul's main argument is this: The resurrection of the dead follows a certain sequence ("each one in his own rank"): first, Christ is raised as the firstfruits; then, at his parousia, all those who belong to Christ will be raised (cf. Rom. 8:11); and then comes the end.

The noun τάγμα (*tagma*) refers to something placed in its proper order, and the text can be translated "each in his own proper rank (or order)." The word was used in a military context for a body of soldiers (a regiment; 2 Sam. 23:13 LXX; Ign. *Rom.* 5:1; Josephus, *J.W.* 1.9.1 §183), but it was used also for the order or rank assigned to individuals (see 1 Clem. 37:3; 41:1). If the military image predominates, it pictures Christ as the leader (captain; Heb. 2:10) rising first, then his sleeping army rising when the last trumpet sounds (1 Cor. 15:52; Findlay 1910: 926). It may imply a third order rising after the resurrection of Christians. If the image of ranking predominates (so Carrez 1985: 129), the picture is similar to the image of firstfruits and harvest. The sequence of the resurrection occurs according to the rank: first, the resurrection of Christ as the one who ranks highest; then, the resurrection of the host who belong to Christ. This last view best fits Paul's conviction that Jesus' resurrection inaugurates the eschatological resurrection (Holleman 1996: 51), which has two stages and two categories: Christ, who already has been raised, and those who belong to Christ, who will be raised at his parousia (cf. 1 Thess. 4:16–17). It means also that the resurrection of Christians "is not merely an arbitrary, isolated occurrence but is grounded in the cosmic victory of Christ over the power of death itself (v. 26)" (Doughty 1975: 81).

The term παρουσία (*parousia*) means "to be present" or "to become present." It was used in this latter sense for the arrival of a potentate in a formal visit to a place as well as for the epiphany of a deity (Oepke, *TDNT* 5:859–61; Spicq, *TLNT* 3:53–55). As inhabitants of a Roman colony, the Corinthians would have been fully aware of the pomp and circumstance associated with imperial visits in which sovereigns were honored as gods.[6] Paul subverts imperial ideology by applying this term to Christ's glorious arrival at the end (cf. 1 Thess. 2:19; 3:13; 4:15; 5:23; 2 Thess. 2:1).[7] Fee (1987: 752–53) grasps the point of this outline of the

---

6. Corinth struck an advent coin to commemorate Nero's visit in A.D. 66 with the inscription *Adventus Aug*[*usti*] *Cor*[*inthi*] (see Deissmann 1911: 371–73).

7. Paul also uses παρουσία (and the verb παρεῖναι, *pareinai*; 5:3) for his own arrival or presence in 2 Cor. 10:10; Phil. 1:26; 2:12; for the arrival of friends in 1 Cor. 16:17; 2 Cor. 7:6–7; and for the coming of the lawless one in 2 Thess. 2:8–9.

events leading up to the end. Paul has not lost the focus of his argument against those who say that there is no resurrection of the dead. He is arguing that the final events marking the end, with the final defeat of all other dominions, including death (15:54–55), are all integrally linked to the resurrection of Christ and the resurrection of the dead. The significance of Christ's resurrection from the dead extends not only to the resurrection of those belonging to Christ, but also to the destruction of every ruler, authority, and power, and to the final enemy, death.

Christ's parousia and the resurrection whistle the close of world history: εἶτα τὸ τέλος (*eita to telos*, then the end). Some, however, take the "then" (εἶτα) in 15:24 to refer to a third stage of resurrections: the raising of non-Christians (so Weiss 1910: 358; Lietzmann 1949: 80–81, who is corrected by Kümmel [see Lietzmann 1949: 193]). The argument for this view assumes that 15:22–23 refers to Christians and that τὸ τέλος in 15:24 refers to "the rest" or "the last" of those to be raised—all the unbelievers. From the parallelism in 15:22–23, it is assumed that since all humans die in Adam, all humans must also be made alive in Christ. This conclusion is untenable. (1) The first "all" in 15:22 refers to those related to Adam; the second "all" refers only to those related to Christ, which does not include all humans. (2) Paul's purpose is to convince the Corinthians that Christians will experience a bodily resurrection. A reference to the resurrection of non-Christians would only confuse matters. He mentions only those things that are germane to his argument (Holleman 1996: 54). Barrett (1968: 355) concludes, "Nothing is said about the future life of those who are not Christians, and with this silence we must be content." (3) No evidence exists that the word τέλος was ever used to mean "the rest" (Héring 1962: 166; Delling, *TDNT* 8:49–59; C. Hill 1988: 309; Wolff 1996: 386), but it is used in the NT to mean "the end of all things" (see Matt. 24:6, 14; Mark 13:7; Luke 21:9). Fee (1987: 754 n. 39) observes that Paul "is perfectly capable of saying οἱ λοιποί [*hoi loipoi*, the rest] when that is what he intends." In the context, τέλος could balance ἀπαρχή (*aparchē*, firstfruits; Robertson and Plummer 1914: 354). (4) His statement in Phil. 3:11, "if I might somehow attain the resurrection of the dead," suggests that he does not understand this event to include every single person. (5) The sequence "Christ . . . those who belong to Christ . . . the end" indicates only that the handing over of the kingdom of God will take place after the resurrection of Christians. (6) The noun τέλος is tied directly to two ὅταν (*hotan*, when) clauses, which clearly give it a temporal stamp (Lambrecht 1994: 130 n. 16). Those clauses—"when he will hand over the kingdom to God the Father" and "when he will have dethroned every ruler, every authority and power"—describe events completely unrelated to the resurrection of the unrighteous. The noun must refer to the end of human history as well as God's goal for history (Schrage 2001: 169–71).

Since an interval exists between the first order of the resurrected and the second, some interpreters assume that another interval exists between Christ's parousia and the final handing over of the kingdom to God (Godet 1887: 359–60; Lietzmann 1949: 81; Barrett 1968: 357; W. Wallis 1975; Kreitzer 1987: 142–45). Some assume that this verse alludes in passing to the millennial kingdom (cf. Rev. 20:4–6). C. Hill (1988: 312–20) argues against this view and contends that the kingdom refers to Christ's present, cosmic reign exercised from heaven until the end. The next verse, affirming the necessity of Christ's continuing reign until every enemy is neutralized, would seem to support this view. Christ's reign does not wait until the parousia, but rather begins at his resurrection (Rom. 8:34; Eph. 1:20–23; Col. 1:13; 1 Pet. 3:22).[8] Plevnik (1997: 129, 142) argues that a reign of Christ after the resurrection of the dead would transfer the climax from the resurrection of the dead—the theme of the entire chapter—to a subsequent act of Christ, but in 1 Cor. 15:54–55 the ultimate act of Christ is the eradication of death. If this eradication does not occur at the resurrection of the dead, then what could it be? I favor this second view, but S. Lewis (1998: 55) offers a balanced judgment: "There is no conclusive argument preventing one from holding that Paul believed in an intermediate kingdom between the parousia and the final resurrection, but if he did, he failed to develop it in any of his works." In this passage, Paul mentions only what is pertinent: the resurrection of the dead and the handing over of the kingdom, which symbolize "the final and full sovereignty of God" (S. Lewis 1998: 55).

"Every ruler" (ἀρχή, archē; cf. 2:6, 8), "every authority" (ἐξουσία, exousia) and "power" (δύναμις, dynamis; cf. Rom. 8:38) could refer to cosmological powers or earthly rulers.[9] Forbes (2001: 68–69) notes Paul's "characteristic clustering of abstract, impersonal terms where names or types of spiritual beings might have been expected," and since death is named as the last of these powers, it is likely that he has in mind powers from the spirit world.[10] These enemies and archenemies of God all take the side of death, the last and greatest of the opponents to be defeated. They all challenge the lordship of Christ and must be overcome (Wengst 1987: 78–79). The verb καταργεῖν (katargein) means "to render ineffective" (see the discussion on 2:6). It is best to translate it here as

---

8. Witherington (1995: 295–98) and Hays (1997: 265) consider this statement to be "a frontal challenge to the ideology of imperial Rome," but that is not Paul's central purpose.

9. Calvin (1960: 324) judges them to be "the legitimate powers, which have been ordained by God," secular and religious, instead of hostile powers.

10. Forbes (2002) argues against the view that Paul borrows the terminology for the spiritual world from Jewish apocalyptic and attempts to show that he derives it instead from a creative interaction between the angelology and demonology of his Jewish heritage and ideas found in popular Platonism.

"dethrone," "abolish," or "overthrow," rather than "destroy." This allows for the possibility of Christ's reconciling all things (Col. 1:20). Paul does not precisely lay out when Christ will make these powers impotent. Presumably, the dethronement of the powers occurs before the handing over of the kingdom, so the aorist subjunctive καταργήσῃ (*katargēsē*) functions like a future perfect (R. Collins 1999: 553). The handing over the kingdom occurs after the destruction of every rule, authority, and power. Paul's only intent is to show that Christ's resurrection will culminate in the dethronement of all the malignant powers. Faith in Christ's resurrection embraces the conviction that the oppressors will not ultimately triumph over their victims (Lorenzen 1995: 274). The victory belongs to the God who raises the dead. Paul has no interest, however, in delineating any end-time battles.

Barrett (1968: 358) aptly translates the present infinitive βασιλεύειν **15:25–28** (*basileuein*) in 15:25 as "to continue to reign." Christ reigns from the time of his resurrection until he subjugates every enemy at the end. Paul draws the imagery of every enemy being set under "his feet" from the concluding words of Ps. 110:1 (109:1 LXX).[11] The subject of the verb θῇ (*thē*, he sets) is debated. If he quotes from Ps. 110:1 and in 1 Cor. 15:27 quotes from Ps. 8:6 (8:7 LXX), then, it is assumed, the subject in both statements must be the same. This verse would anticipate 1 Cor. 15:27, where the subject is assumed to be God's putting all things under Christ's feet (so Maier 1932; Heil 1993: 28–29; Boer 1988: 116–17; S. Lewis 1998: 66). In the psalm the messianic figure reigns passively while God crushes the enemies (S. Lewis 1998: 65). God is the agent and source of power, and Christ is the one to whom all things are subjected.

Psalm 110:1 is not cited exactly in 1 Cor. 15:25, but Paul appears to paraphrase and adapt it to his context (Plevnik 1997: 131–32; see additional note for the differences). The context suggests that the subject is Christ (Edwards 1885: 416; Robertson and Plummer 1914: 356; Conzelmann 1975: 273; Fee 1987: 755–56). Beginning in 15:23, Christ is the referent: "his parousia," "he hands over the kingdom," "he dethrones," "it is necessary for him to continue to reign." To shift to God as the subject of "he sets" without injecting the noun "God" only confuses the reader. Paul may have deliberately replaced the first person, "I set" (θῶ, *thō*), which clearly refers to God, with the third person, "he sets," to allow for Christ to be the one who sets all his enemies under his feet. This subjection of the enemies would also explain why "it is necessary" (δεῖ, *dei*) for Christ to continue to reign. He does not reign passively from

11. Psalm 110:1 (109:1 LXX) is the most frequently cited OT passage in the NT (Matt. 22:44/Mark 12:36/Luke 20:42–43; Matt. 26:64/Mark 14:62/Luke 22:69; Acts 2:34–35; Heb. 1:13; see also Eph. 1:20–21; 1 Pet. 3:22).

afar, having completed his assignment, but remains actively engaged in vanquishing all the powers hostile to God until the end, when they are all finally subdued. To be sure, "although it is Jesus who actually destroys every rule, authority, and power, it is God who acts through Jesus" (Holleman 1996: 60). It is impossible for Paul to think of Christ's acting independently of God, or of God's acting independently of Christ, or of one doing all the work while the other does nothing.

No conjunction or particle connects 15:26 to what precedes; consequently, it stands out from its surrounding context. Since death has the definite article (ὁ θάνατος, *ho thanatos*), it should be treated as the subject of the verb, with ἔσχατος ἐχθρός (*eschatos echthros*, last enemy) placed first for emphasis. S. Lewis (1998: 58) comments, "By separating it and drawing special attention to it, emphasis is placed on the fact that the reign of Christ is not complete until death is conquered; everything is still in process."

This last enemy is vividly represented by the psalmist as strangling with cords (Ps. 18:4–5). Fear of it causes anguish and distress (Ps. 116:3; cf. Heb. 2:14–15). Paul personifies death as "a cosmic power which entered into the world through Adam and reigns over everyone" (Holleman 1996: 65) and continued its dominion even after the giving of the law (Rom. 5:14). The verb καταργεῖται (*katargeitai*, it is rendered inoperative) is repeated from 1 Cor. 15:24. The present tense is the present of certainty (Robertson and Plummer 1914: 356). This certainty explains why Paul assumes that not even death can separate believers from God's love (Rom. 8:38–39) and that the Christian dead belong to the Christ (Rom. 14:7–9). Death's eradication serves as a metaphor for the resurrection of the dead (Plevnik 1997: 126, 128). Death will be rendered impotent by the very raising of the dead (Fee 1987: 756). The process began with Jesus' resurrection; it will be completed with the resurrection of Christians at the end. Robbed of its victims, death's threatening menace is neutralized.[12] Paul's purpose here is not to describe the end-time events but to explain the logical and salvific necessity of the resurrection of the dead. The relevance of this point to his larger argument is this: if there is no resurrection of the dead, then death will still hold sway beyond the end as a power set over against God. These verses (1 Cor. 15:24–28) are not intended to reveal why the resurrection has not yet taken place (contra Plevnik 1997: 124–25) but to make clear that if the dead are not raised, then death remains unconquered.

In 15:27, Paul explains why death is to be conquered: God has subjected all things under his feet. The subject from 15:25, "he sets" (θῇ,

12. Cf. Pseudo-Philo, *Bib. Ant.* 3.10, with its images of hell paying back its debt, returning its deposit, and shutting its mouth.

thē), shifts from Christ to God, "he subjected" (ὑπέταξεν, *hypetaxen*), because Paul understands God to be the one who raises the dead. Therefore, God is the one who defeats this last foe. The exegetical principle of *gezerah shawah* (comparing similar expressions) leads Paul to Ps. 8:6 (8:7 LXX): "And you set him over the works of your hands, having put all things under his feet."[13] Paul interprets this psalm as applying to the Messiah, not to Adam or human beings in general. The key word he finds in this psalm is πάντα (*panta*, all things), which he inserts in the allusion to Ps. 110:1 in 1 Cor. 15:25. He interprets "all things" to include death.

"When it says" (ὅταν . . . εἴπῃ, *hotan . . . eipē*) refers to what the Scripture says that needs special interpretation, not to Christ's making an announcement or to God's speaking in Scripture. Paul wishes to avert any mistaken impression that somehow God becomes subject to Christ or that Christ's reign infringes on God's absolute sovereignty. We need not speculate whether the Corinthians held some fanciful notion that God would become subject to Christ. Paul holds fast to his monotheism, which creates a tension. All things have been placed in subjection to Christ, but that does not include God. It refers only to creation and the hostile powers that have provoked and abetted creation's fall, not to the Creator. The ultimate power belongs to God at the beginning and at the end. He explains, "When it says, 'All things have been made subject' [by God], clearly that excludes the one [God] who made all things subject to him [Christ]."

Paul sums up his argument in 15:28. The powers had rebelled against God; the Son subjects himself to God in obedience. "But when he [God] subjects all things [through the raising of the dead] to him [Christ], the Son himself will become subject [God as agent] to the one [God] who subjected all things to him [Christ]." This is the only place in Paul's letters where the absolute use of the title "the Son" appears (which corresponds to the absolute use of God the Father in 15:24 [Lindemann 2000: 348]). It connotes submission to the Father. This is "the Son" who prays to his Father, "Not my will but yours be done" (Mark 14:36/Matt. 26:10). The title refers to the subjection of his will to God's will and does not imply the inferiority of his person. Schweizer (1970: 283) explains,

> "Son of God" (see [Mark] 15:39) is an expression of majesty, in contrast to "son of a human father." But whenever "the Son" is used absolutely, it calls to mind the contrast to "the Father" and at the same time it describes a subordinate position in relation to the Father. In the same way, 1 Corinthians 15:28 uses this expression in an eschatological context to

---

13. The principle assumes that when the same words ("his feet") appear in two separate cases, the same considerations apply to both verses. Psalm 110:1 helps clarify who is referred to in Ps. 8:6.

warn against the misunderstanding of Christ the Lord of the end-time as a second God alongside the Father. The strong emphasis upon the exaltation of Jesus as the Son of God who reigns in heaven (Rom 1:4) must have compelled the church, which had its roots in the Old Testament, to stress that Jesus was not a second God, but that in him the one God turned his attention to the world.

Calvin (1960: 327) comments, "Of course we acknowledge that God is the Ruler, but His rule is actualized in the man Christ. But Christ will then hand back the Kingdom which He has received, so that we may cleave completely to God."

The affirmation "God will be all things in all" refers to "the unchallenged reign of God alone," not some metaphysical absorption (Barrett 1968: 361; so also Fee 1987: 759–60).[14] It applies to the pacification and redemption of the created order and is similar to saying that God is over all (Rom. 9:5; see also Rom. 11:36; 1 Cor. 8:6; Sir. 43:27–28). It affirms God's undivided and total power over the enemies (S. Lewis 1998: 68). According to Boer (1988: 126), all things "constitute the *totality* of the world experienced by human beings." It means that humans will no longer be subject to the destructive forces of the powers. Therefore, whoever denies the resurrection of the dead basically denies God's power over death and that God will reign over all things unchallenged (Lindemann 2000: 349).

Additional Notes

15:22. "In Adam" is a Jewish idea rooted in Gen. 3:19 (cf. 4 Ezra [2 Esdr.] 3:7, 21; 4:30–31; 2 Bar. 17:2–3; 19:8; 23:4; 48:42–43; 54:15, 19; 56:6; Sir. 25:24 attaches the blame to Eve). It is fully expressed in 4 Ezra (2 Esdr.) 7:116–26: "O Adam, what have you done? For though it was you who sinned, the fall was not yours alone, but ours also who are your descendants" (7:118).

15:25. Comparing Ps. 110:1 (109:1 LXX) with Paul's citation of it reveals the following differences:

ἄχρι οὗ θῇ πάντας τοὺς ἐχθροὺς ὑπὸ τοὺς πόδας αὐτοῦ (1 Cor. 15:25)
ἕως ἂν θῶ τοὺς ἐχθρούς σου ὑποπόδιον τῶν ποδῶν σου (Ps. 109:1)

Paul changes direct speech, with the verb θῶ (first person), to indirect speech, with the verb θῇ (third person). He inserts the word πάντας and changes references to the second person, "your enemies" and "your feet," to "every enemy" and "his feet." He omits the word "footstool."

---

14. Cf. Col. 3:11, which refers to Christ as "all in all" to emphasize the equality of those who are in Christ.

D. The Consequences If the Resurrection of the Dead Were Not True (15:29–34)

Paul's argument in 15:29–34 parallels 15:13–19 in bringing to light the negative consequences if there were no resurrection (S. Lewis 1998: 70). He appeals to *pathos* with two examples, one from the practice of baptism on behalf of the dead and the other from his own personal brushes with danger. These examples are punctuated with rhetorical questions that show baptism and personal sacrifice to be meaningless if there is no resurrection of the dead. The two examples are separate from one another and not part of a continuous argument, so attempts by some interpreters to make 15:29 somehow fit what follows are unnecessary. The examples intersect only in showing the foolishness of both activities if there is no resurrection from the dead.

Paul's argument moves from the third person: what those do who are baptized on behalf of the dead (15:29); to the first person: his own experiences of suffering as an apostle (15:30–32); and culminates in second person plural imperatives for the Corinthians to come to their senses and stop sinning (15:33–34). For Paul, Christian belief in the resurrection clearly impinges on ethical living (cf. 6:12–14), and he draws a close connection between moral decadence—one of the dangers facing the church—and the failure to believe in the resurrection. If there were no resurrection of the dead, then hedonistic self-indulgence and overindulgence (cf. 11:21) would be legitimate options because the ethical prohibitions no longer would have their foundation in a legitimate faith. The resurrection of the dead is true, which imposes on believers the need for moral rectitude in this life.

Exegesis and Exposition

^{29}Otherwise, what will those do who are being baptized on behalf of the dead? If the dead are not raised at all, why indeed are they being baptized on behalf of them? ^{30}And why do we also face peril every hour? ^{31}Every day I die, truly, ⌜brothers and sisters⌝, by my boast about you, which I have in Christ Jesus our Lord. ^{32}If with only human aspirations I fought with wild beasts in Ephesus, what does it profit me? If the dead are not raised, "Let us eat and drink, for tomorrow we die." ^{33}Do not be deceived: "Bad company ruins reputable behavior." [34]Wake up from your stupor, as you ought, and do not go on sinning, for certain ones have no knowledge of God. I say this to put you to shame.

15:29 What Paul means by the phrase "those who are being baptized on behalf of the dead" (οἱ βαπτιζόμενοι ὑπὲρ τῶν νεκρῶν, *hoi baptizomenoi hyper tōn nekrōn*) presents the interpreter with a major conundrum. The gist of his argument is clear, but its specifics are not. The ritual of a baptism for the dead assumes that there will be a future resurrection of the dead. He cites this practice to highlight the absurdity of baptizing on behalf of the dead while denying the resurrection of the dead. The future tense of ποιήσουσιν (*poiēsousin*, what will they do?), however, is unusual. Does it mean, "What will they achieve?" "What will they do?" or "What are they doing?"[1] The parallel in 15:32, "What does it profit me?" suggests that it implies "What good will it do them?" If there is no resurrection of the dead, nothing could possibly accrue from that rite. They will be shown to be fools.

Conzelmann (1975: 276) asserts that the "the ingenuity of the exegetes has run riot" in trying to explain the baptism of the dead, but some throw up their hands in despair at ever being able to understand its meaning (Kistemaker 1993: 560). Many different interpretations have been proposed, but I will discuss only the three most defensible options (see additional note for a listing of other, less plausible options).[2]

The majority of commentators today think that Paul refers to some kind of vicarious baptism for dead persons: "in the place of the dead."[3] This view offers the most natural interpretation of the phrase "on behalf of the dead." DeMaris (1995a, 1995b) demonstrates the existence of a preoccupation with the underworld in Corinth, and the Corinthian Christians may have shared the interests of their surrounding culture (R. Collins 1999: 556). They may have pioneered this ritual in response to these interests: to claim a place for the deceased in the world of the dead (DeMaris 1995a: 679), to ward off the threat from hostile cosmic principalities and powers to their nonbaptized dead (Downey 1985), to assure an early resurrection for the deceased to participate in the messianic kingdom (Schweitzer 1931: 279, 285), or generally to impart the

---

1. Edwards (1885: 421) explains from other Greek writers: "When an opinion concerning a future act is expressed, the pres[ent] is used; and when an opinion concerning a present act is expressed, the fut[ure] is used."

2. For a history of research, see Foschini 1950; 1951; Rissi 1962; Beasley-Murray 1962: 185–92; Thiselton 2000: 1242–49.

3. Weiss 1910: 363; Lietzmann 1949: 82; Parry 1926: 228–29; Conzelmann 1975: 275; Wolff 1996: 396–97; Hays 1997: 267; R. Horsley 1998: 207; R. Collins 1999: 556; Schrage 2001: 239.

benefits of their spirituality or their salvation to the dead (cf. 2 Macc. 12:43–45 in the additional note).

Evidence exists that in pagan cults persons underwent rites in the place of others (BDAG 165), but three problems cause this particular interpretation to founder.

First, although DeMaris's study (1995a) demonstrates that an interest in the underworld existed in Corinth, it can provide no trace of evidence that anyone baptized on behalf of the dead. Tertullian (*Marc.* 5.10; *De resurrectione carnis* [*Resurrection of the Flesh*] 48) and Chrysostom (*Hom. 1 Cor.* 40.1) refer to the Marcionites practicing this rite in the second century. Epiphanius (*Panarion* [*Refutation of All Heresies*] 28.6) refers to a similar practice among the Cerenthians, and Philaster (*Heresies* 49) refers to the Montanists. None of these writers believes that Paul has this practice in mind, however.

Second, it seems unlikely that Paul would pass over, without comment, a practice that "smacks of a 'magical' view of sacramentalism of the worst kind" (Fee 1987: 764). Such a ritual is not theologically benign, since it completely bypasses the necessity for an individual to express his or her own faith to receive the benefits of Christ's death. Conzelmann (1975: 275) explains Paul's failure to criticize this practice by contending that he only wishes to make use of it for the sake of his argument (cf. Oepke, *TDNT* 1:542, "the argument is purely tactical"; and Schrage 2001: 240). Paul intends only to highlight the inconsistencies between their belief and their practice. But would he tacitly sanction (through silence) such a practice simply to score a point for his argument about the resurrection?[4] To win one argument, he opens a Pandora's box of new theological problems. Edwards (1885: 424–25) accounts for it by attributing it to the nature of an ad hominem argument. One risks appearing to approve of, in this case, a superstitious custom. If this view is correct, however, one can understand why Paul might confuse his charges and must constantly have to write letters to put out theological backfires arising from that confusion.

Third, the use of the third person—"What will *they* do?" "Why are *they* being baptized?"—rather than the second person (cf. 15:12, "some among you") is puzzling. It could suggest that the practice of vicarious baptism was not widespread among the Corinthians. If it was not widespread among them, then how could Paul expect the argument to carry any weight?

Another view explains the term "dead" (οἱ νεκροί, *hoi nekroi*) as a metaphor for the condition of believers who receive baptism. The re-

---

4. If Paul were treating such a ritual as benign, however, it would have implications for the toleration of the continuation of practices by recent converts that might be viewed as sub-Christian, such as the veneration of ancestors.

cipients are, in effect, dead bodies when they are baptized (Oliver 1937; K. Thompson 1964; R. Martin 1984: 120–21; Talbert 1987: 99). O'Neill (1979–80) understands "on behalf of the dead" to refer not to some third party but to the subject, "those who are being baptized," and paraphrases it "Otherwise what do those hope to achieve who are baptized for their dying bodies? If the completely dead are not raised, why then are they baptized for themselves as corpses?"

This view has several advantages.

First, it was the unanimous view of the Greek fathers, who argue that the dead are the bodies "because of which we are baptized" (Staab 1963). Chrysostom (*Hom. 1 Cor.* 40.2) contends that the wording recalls a baptismal confession.

Second, it explains the use of the third person. Paul uses the third person because he is referring grammatically to those who are being baptized.

Third, it is compatible with Pauline theology. Paul interprets baptism as a symbol of death and resurrection, and "the dead" either characterizes the individual's prebaptismal state or refers to the individual's soon-to-be dead body (cf. Rom. 6:3–14; Eph. 2:1, 5; Col. 2:13). Paul's specific statement in Rom. 8:10 that "the body is dead because of sin" gives further credibility to this interpretation.[5] If this view is correct, then he uses a theological shorthand, familiar to his readers, to refer to Christian baptism.

Fourth, it fits the context. If, as I argue, the problem is that the Corinthians assumed the inherent immortality of the soul or some kind of assumption into glory at death (1 Cor. 15:12, 36), then the issue addressed here is "death as a presupposition of resurrection" (R. Martin 1984: 121). Baptism connotes sharing Christ's death to share his resurrection (cf. Rom. 6:3–14, which uses the image of dying and rising in baptism differently to convey the necessity of ethical living).

A third view contends that the preposition ὑπέρ (*hyper*) need not mean "in place of" or "for the benefit of" but can mean that they are being baptized "with a view toward" or "for the sake of." Some interpreters imagine that they are being baptized with the view toward being reunited with their departed loved ones in heaven (Findlay 1910: 931; Robertson and Plummer 1914: 359–60; Raeder 1955: 260; J. Howard 1965: 140–41; Thiselton 2000: 1248–49). This interpretation, however, places too great a burden on the meaning of the preposition. One also has to assume that a dying mother, for example, appeals to an unbelieving child, "Meet me in heaven," and the child responds by becoming a Christian (so Findlay 1910: 931). Nothing in the context suggests such

5. It also accords with Jesus' wry characterization of bodily human existence, "Let the dead bury the dead" (Matt. 8:22; Luke 9:60).

a touching scene as the backdrop. If Paul had this idea in view, he could have expressed himself more clearly.

The view that bests suits the context is the second one (for still others, see additional note). Paul refers to "the common Christian experience of baptism" (Talbert 1987: 99). Baptism assumes death and resurrection. If there is no resurrection of the dead, then baptism becomes a pointless rite that falsely represents something that will not happen. The dead will not rise.

15:30–32 Paul next appeals to his own life to reveal an inconsistency between the motivation behind his apostolic travail—the hope of the resurrection—and the reality if there is no resurrection of the dead. His hardships testify that death remains a dark, menacing foe (J. Wilson 1968: 95). He tallies in 2 Cor. 11:23–27 the many times and ways that carrying out his commission endangered his life and brought him to the brink of death. If there were no resurrection of the dead, he would be foolishly risking his life for nothing. If he places his trust in something that is completely false, he would be well advised to give up the fight since the fight results in his dying "every day."

The verb ἀποθνῄσκω (apothnēskō) implies real death in 1 Cor. 8:11; 9:15; 15:3, 22, 32, 36 and probably alludes here to the mortal danger he faces in the course of his ministry (R. Collins 1999: 539). Thiselton (2000: 1250) renders it "From day to day I court fatality." It means that he not only faces death (cf. 2 Cor. 1:8–9), but also lives in willing "identification with the death of Christ" and accepts "the vulnerability and fragility of life" that Christian service brings (Thiselton 2000: 1250). He does not have in mind the martyr's death but refers to "the concrete consequence of a life of service as a disciple and apostle of the crucified and risen Christ" (Lorenzen 1995: 216–17). This death encompasses the sleepless nights, the hunger and thirst, the ceaseless labor, and being ill-clad, buffeted, reviled, persecuted, afflicted, beaten, imprisoned, and homeless (see 1 Cor. 4:8–13; 2 Cor. 1:3–7; 4:8–10; 6:1–10; 11:23–29; Gal. 6:17). It entails willing identification with the death of Christ. His dying can be seen as an allusion to Christian baptism in 1 Cor. 15:29 (as I interpret it) and would explain the καὶ ἡμεῖς (kai hēmeis, we also) at the beginning of 15:30.

Paul punctuates this statement that he dies every day with a strong asseveration, "truly, by my boast in you." The νή (nē, as surely) serves as a marker for a strong affirmation or oath followed by the accusative of the person or thing affirmed or sworn by. It is found only here in the NT (cf. Gen. 42:15–16).[6] The phrase τὴν ὑμετέραν καύχησιν (tēn hymeteran kauchēsin) functions like an objective genitive and means "his

---

6. Other affirmations of the truth of Paul's statements appear in 2 Cor. 1:23; 2:17; 11:10; 12:19.

boast over them," not "their boast over him" (contra Parry 1926: 229–30). His boast is that the Corinthians are the fruit of his apostolic labor and suffering (1 Cor. 9:1–2). It is not a self-serving boast, but rather confirms that Christ has worked in and through him as his apostle; and this work is distinguished by "always carrying in his body the dying of Jesus, so that the life of Jesus may also be made visible in our bodies" (2 Cor. 4:10), so that death's mortal coil entwines Paul as life takes hold in those he serves (2 Cor. 4:12). Edwards (1885: 425–26) interprets this affirmation to mean "In proof of his declaration that his life was a constant dying unto himself and the world, he calls to witness the glorious results of his ministry at Corinth, self-sacrifice being a necessary condition and infallible guarantee of ministerial power." Thiselton (2000: 1251) notes that people swear by something "of *ultimate importance* to them." Fee (1987: 770) affirms this by commenting that Paul "swears by that which is dearest to him, their own existence in Christ, which also came about by labors that had exposed him to such dangers." In his boast over them, he never forgets that he is but a lowly servant through whose "foolish" preaching they came to believe (1 Cor. 3:5). He was only the sower, and the Lord gave the harvest, but he was a sower who has laid his life on the line to scatter the seeds of the gospel. Barrett (1968: 365) interprets Paul's statement to mean that winning the Corinthian believers to the Lord is worth many deaths to him. This sentiment reveals his deep attachment to this troubled church. He trusts that he will receive his recompense from the Lord in the resurrection (3:10–15), and in 2 Cor. 4:16–5:10, he affirms that his body, weighed down and wasting away, will be transformed in the resurrection. If there is no resurrection, all is for naught.

Paul does everything in expectation of the future resurrection. If there is no resurrection of the dead, why not eat, drink, and be merry, since life is so short? Why fight with beasts? Why not join those who try to drown out death's relentless knell with ceaseless reveling? Fighting wild beasts (θηριομαχεῖν, *thēriomachein*) in Ephesus is unlikely to refer to a gladiatorial struggle with beasts in the arena. How would he have survived such an encounter except by some miraculous Daniel-like deliverance? Why would Acts not mention something so dramatic? Why is it absent from his list of travails in 2 Cor. 11:23–29? Many cite the Roman law (see Justinian, *Digest* 28.1.8.4) that those condemned to the beasts lose their civil rights. Paul, however, can still appeal to his citizenship in Acts 22:25–29 and 23:27 (Lietzmann 1949: 83). Weiss (1910: 365–66) and Héring (1962: 171–72) think that it expresses an unreal condition: "Had I fought with beasts in Ephesus with only human hopes (which I did not) . . ." (cf. 1 Cor. 13:3). But one would expect Paul to try to make his case with an example of something that really happened, not some imaginary event.

Malherbe (1968) provides evidence that the expression "fighting with beasts" was used metaphorically in Cynic-Stoic diatribe as a euphemism for struggling with human passions so as to become virtuous (cf. 9:24–27). Human passions are described as "wild beasts" as early as Plato, and this view may tie into the ethical admonition in 15:34. But it is more likely that Paul speaks metaphorically about great danger that threatens his life (cf. 2 Tim. 4:16–17). If he is writing this letter from Ephesus, he speaks of an open door of opportunity but many adversaries (1 Cor. 16:8–9). The "wild beasts" plausibly are bloodthirsty human antagonists who would eagerly tear him to pieces.[7] His Roman citizenship did not provide him protection from mob violence, but only the right to certain formal procedures. Ignatius (*Rom.* 5:1) uses the verb θηριομαχεῖν metaphorically in referring to the guards escorting him from Syria to Rome as "ten leopards" but also mentions the literal beasts that await him when he arrives, and he expresses his hope that they will devour him promptly. He also uses the verb in a literal sense to refer to "the privilege of fighting wild beasts in Rome" (*Eph.* 1:2). Paul draws on the image of the arena to describe the deadly peril he faces in his mission. In Jewish legend, the willingness to sacrifice one's life in the arena for God is evidence of faith in the resurrection (see 2 Macc. 7, which records the story of the brothers who proclaimed their belief in the resurrection in the face of roasting, scalping, and dismemberment).

The phrase κατὰ ἄνθρωπον (*kata anthrōpon*) can be rendered variously, depending on the context. It can mean "from human motives" (NASB)—that is, from human sentiments and not those implanted by God's Spirit (Edwards 1885: 427). If that is its meaning here, then Paul could be saying, "If I did this looking for some kind of payoff from God, it will prove entirely unprofitable." In the context, it is more likely that it means "'from a human viewpoint,' with a horizon limited by earthly humanity, that is, without hope of the resurrection" (Héring 1962: 171; see also Fee 1987: 771; NRSV; REB). If there is nothing more than life on this earth, why suffer voluntarily? Why not pursue sensual pleasure instead?

Resurrection means endless hope, but no resurrection means a hopeless end—and hopelessness breeds dissipation. Barrett (1968: 362) comments, "Take away the resurrection and moral standards collapse." A cynical fatalism toward life encourages people to try "to go for the gusto," to have it all now, to amuse themselves endlessly. If life ends at death, why not live it up? Paul quotes Isa. 22:13 (cf. 56:12; Wis. 2:6–9), "Let us eat and drink, for tomorrow we die," but the sentiment was

---

7. Paul uses the image of biting and devouring one another to describe the Galatians' infighting (Gal. 5:15).

widespread (Luke 12:19–20). Herodotus (*Historiae* [*Histories*] 2.78.1) reports, "After rich men's repasts, a man carries around an image in a coffin, painted and carved in exact imitation of a corpse two or four feet long. This he shows to each of the company, saying 'While you drink and enjoy, look on this; for to this state you must come when you die.'" If the Christian hope is taken away, not only will any motive for a person to endure suffering for Christ be crushed, but also any moral standards will be crumpled (Barrett 1968: 366–67).

15:33–34 Paul has warned the Corinthians before about being deceived (3:18; 6:9). He may be trying to prevent anyone from taking what he says in 15:32 seriously. Do not be misled, he warns: bad company (ὁμιλίαι, *homiliai*; here referring to "company," "social intercourse," not "conversations" or "speeches") destroys or corrupts (like leaven; 5:6) reputable behavior. This may be a quotation from Menander's (died 292 B.C.) lost comedy, *Thais* (fragment 187 [218]), but one cannot assume that Paul was familiar with Menander any more than one can assume that a person who cites a famous line from a Shakespeare play has read Shakespeare. It had become a cliché, perhaps even before Menander. Paul does not specify whom they are to shun, but one may presume that it includes those who deny the reality of death, who do not share the Christian hope of resurrection, and who behave disreputably.

The command to come out of their drunken stupor and to stop sinning caps his argument in this unit. The stupor would refer to a benighted worldliness and a lack of spiritual awareness. Philo (*Drunk.* 38 §154) defines drunkenness in the soul as "ignorance of things of which we should naturally have acquired knowledge." Similarly, Paul insists that the Corinthians come to their senses: "Wake right [δικαίως, *dikaiōs*] up" (Moffatt 1938: 257), "Snap out of it, as you ought." The root of the problem is their ignorance of God. He does not itemize all the things about God they do not know, but this sweeping accusation is a sharp jab, particularly if it is directed at those in the church who claim to have special spiritual knowledge (so Barrett 1968: 368). In a similar vein, Jesus accused the Sadducees of being deceived and knowing neither the Scriptures nor the power of God because of their disavowal of the resurrection (Mark 12:24). Jews also took for granted that ignorance of God led inevitably to immorality (Rom. 1:18–32; 1 Thess. 4:5).

Paul eschews shaming other Christians (1 Cor. 4:14), and he vigorously objects to the "haves" shaming the "have-nots" at the Lord's Supper, and those with more conspicuous spiritual gifts shaming those with less noticeable gifts. Treating other Christians in a shabby way serves only to nudge them away from the community and "back into the bosom of society to no good purpose" (DeSilva 2000: 77). It is a different matter, however, when it comes to core values and beliefs. Shaming is one way to enforce these values and beliefs to prevent persons from behaving and believing inappropriately (6:5; 2 Thess. 3:6, 14–15; 1 Tim. 5:20). This deviance is not to be tolerated. It can corrupt the whole group.

Additional Notes

15:29. Other options for interpreting "those who are being baptized on behalf of the dead" explain it by tweaking the meaning of the verb "baptize," the preposition ὑπέρ, or the noun "the dead."

1. The term "baptism" is explained as a metaphorical reference to martyrdom. It refers to a baptism in blood or being drowned in suffering (cf. Mark 10:38–39; Luke 12:50) rather than water baptism. The Corinthians were being baptized into the ranks of the dead (Godet 1887: 389–90). Murphy-O'Connor (1981a) adapts this view by claiming that the phrase originated with the Corinthians as a gibe at Paul. "Baptism" refers to his apostolic suffering (see also J. R. White 1997), and "the dead" are the unspiritual who are not worth bothering about. Murphy-O'Connor paraphrases it "Supposing that there is no resurrection from the dead, will they continue to work, those who are being destroyed on account of an inferior class of believers who are dead to true Wisdom?"
2. The term "baptism" is redefined as a reference to the ritual washing of the dead body before burial (Beza).
3. The preposition ὑπέρ is interpreted in a localized sense to mean that the Corinthians are being baptized "over" the graves of the dead (Luther; Grosheide 1953: 373).
4. The preposition ὑπέρ is interpreted to mean that the Corinthians are being baptized "because of" the influence of deceased Christians on their lives (Reaume 1995) or because of the heroic behavior of Christian martyrs (John Edwards [1692], cited by Edwards 1885: 422).
5. The term "dead" is explained as referring to people "nearing death" (Calvin 1960: 330–31). It may refer to recent converts or those on the way to becoming converts who died before receiving baptism (see Rissi 1962: 85–92; Fee 1987: 768; N. Watson 1992: 172). The baptism functions as a sign of the person's union with Christ rather than as a magical rite that effects that union. Though Chrysostom (*Hom. 1 Cor.* 40.1) does not think that this is what Paul meant, he mockingly describes the practice among the Marcionites when an unbaptized catechumen dies. Someone approaches the corpse and asks if the corpse wants to be baptized, and a living person, hidden beneath the couch on which the corpse lies, answers yes and is baptized in the corpse's stead.
6. Paul's use of the third person leads Oster (1995: 388) to suggest that he refers to a pagan practice that formed the matrix of the Corinthians' understanding of baptism. The other two occurrences of the third person plural of ποιεῖν in Paul's letters refer to what Gentiles do (Rom. 1:32; 2:14). It would be odd, however, for Paul to allude to some pagan practice to try to buttress the Corinthians' belief in the resurrection.

15:29. Second Macc. 12:43–45 offers an interesting parallel to 1 Cor. 15:29:

> He also took up a collection, man by man, to the amount of two thousand drachmas of silver, and sent it to Jerusalem to provide for a sin offering. In doing this he acted very well and honorably, taking account of the resurrection. For if he were not expecting that those who had fallen would rise again, it would have been superfluous and foolish to pray for the dead. But if he was looking to the splendid reward that is laid up for those who fall asleep in godliness, it was a

holy and pious thought. Therefore he made atonement for the dead, so that they might be delivered from their sin. (NRSV)

Fee (1987: 767 n. 32) contends that this passage does not depict a vicarious sacrifice for the dead but makes "an appeal to God to have mercy on the circumcised Jews who at the time of their death were wearing expressions of idolatry."

15:31. Important witnesses ($\mathfrak{P}^{46}$, D, F, G, Ψ, 075, 0243, 6, 424, 1739, 1852, 1881, 2200, Byz, Lect, it[b, d, f, g, o]) omit ἀδελφοί from the text. Zuntz (1953: 175–76) argues that had it been original, its omission by these witnesses would be "inexplicable." The vocative occurs nineteen other times in the letter and may have been inserted as a natural complement to Paul's solemn affirmation.

E. The Bodily Character of the Resurrection (15:35–49)

In the next segment of his argument, Paul corrects those who deny the possibility of the resurrection because they assume that earthly embodied existence is completely incompatible with heavenly spiritual existence. He corrects them indirectly by adopting the guise of chiding a foolish student who espouses this view. He grants that the principle of polarity between heaven and earth is valid, but the student fails to understand that transformation can occur. As in nature the bare seed that is sown is not the plant that miraculously sprouts from the ground, so in the resurrection the earthly body that is sown is not the spiritual body that is miraculously raised. As God chooses to give the seed a different body (15:37), so God will give humans, sown with a natural body, a spiritual body in the resurrection (15:42–44a).

Any observer can also note that different kinds of earthly flesh and different kinds of heavenly glories exist. "Flesh" represents earthly bodily existence; "glory" represents the heavenly bodily existence. The varieties reveal that God is not restricted in what kind of body he can give to any creation. The body's present fleshly mortality, then, does not prohibit the possibility of resurrection to glory, because the body fit for our earthly habitation is not the body that will be raised. For Paul, resurrection is not the resuscitation of the corpse. What is mortal will be changed by the power of God so that those who are raised will be given a body that is consistent with its new celestial habitat. The polarity between earthly and heavenly existence will be bridged by the power of God, who will not raise mortal "flesh" but will give those who are resurrected a new, glorious, spiritual body. Lorenzen (1995: 289) comments, "While the present life is lived within the parameters of time and space, and is delimited by death, the resurrection of Christ has revealed the foundation for a new reality: He 'will never die again; death no longer has dominion over him' (Rom 6:9)."

The argument begins with the question of an objector. Paul delineates various principles before presenting the solution that explains how the resurrection of the dead is possible:

    1. A skeptical question setting up the issue of how bodily resurrection is possible (15:35)

2. The principle of change from the example of botanical processes (15:36–38)
3. The principle of different types of bodies and glories from the example of terrestrial bodies and celestial glories (15:39–41)
4. The radical difference between the risen body and its earthly counterpart (15:42–44a)
5. The explanation of how the polarity between the earthly and heavenly will be bridged through Christ (15:44b–49)

Exegesis and Exposition

[35]But someone will ask, "How are the dead raised? With what kind of body do they come?" [36]Fool! What you sow is not brought to life unless it dies. [37]As for what you sow, you do not sow the body that the seed will become, but the bare grain, whether it be wheat or of some other kind, [38]but God gives to it a body just as he willed and to each one of the seeds its own body.

[39]Not all flesh is the same flesh, but there is a different kind for human beings, a different kind of flesh for animals, a different kind of flesh for birds, and a different kind for fish. [40]And there are heavenly bodies and earthly bodies, but the glory of the heavenly [body] is of a different order than the glory of the earthly [body]. [41]There is a different kind of glory for the sun, a different kind of glory for the moon, and a different kind of glory for the stars. For glory differs from star to star.

[42]Thus also the resurrection of the dead. It is sown in a state of corruptibility, it is raised in a state of incorruptibility. [43]It is sown in dishonor, it is raised in glory. It is sown in weakness, it is raised in power. [44]It is sown a natural body, it is raised a spiritual body.

If there is a natural body, then there is also a spiritual one. [45]Thus it stands written: "The first man, Adam, became a living soul." The last Adam [became] a life-giving Spirit. [46]But the spiritual [body] does not [come] first but the natural [body], then the spiritual [body]. [47]The first human [came] from the earth [and was] made of dust; the second ⌜human⌝ [will come] from heaven. [48]As [was] the one made of dust, so also [are] the others made of dust, and as [is] the heavenly one, so also [are] the heavenly ones. [49]And just as we have borne the image of the [one] made of dust, so also ⌜we will bear⌝ the image of the heavenly [one].

15:35–38   The objector's question (cf. James 2:18; Rom. 9:19; 11:19) may be a serious inquiry, "How is it possible that the dead are raised?" or a mocking question that presents a grotesque conundrum, "How can the dead come with a body?" (cf. Mark 12:23). Will the body not rot in the grave and become nothing more than dust? For the first time the word "body" appears in the discussion of the resurrection. Many assume that the objectors cannot imagine how a new body, fit for the glorious spiritual experience of the next world, could arise from a carcass (Findlay 1910: 934). Because the Corinthians could not fathom *how* this was possible, they had abandoned any trust *that* it was possible (Fee 1987: 779). Though many think that the problem of "how?" is tied to Paul's insistence that the body is raised (see Müller 1985: 171–76), it is more likely that he takes the objection "There is no resurrection of the dead" (15:12) and turns it into a leading question to teach rather than to answer some specific objection (Asher 2000: 67–68).[1] Jeremias (1955–56; so also Sider 1974–75; Soards 1999: 342) errs in arguing that Paul deals with two questions and takes them up in reverse order: (1) What kind of body will the resurrected believer assume (15:36–44 plus an addendum in 45–49)? (2) How are the dead raised (15:50–57)? Both questions ask the same thing, but the second is more specific. It clarifies the issue involved in the question of the resurrection of the dead (Conzelmann 1975: 280; Fee 1987: 780; Wolff 1996: 402). The first question is a "'leading question' designed to limit possible alternatives." Paul introduces "body" as a philosophically neutral term that moves the discussion in the direction he wishes it to go (Asher 2000: 71–77). It allows him to present evidence for the resurrection of the dead that the Corinthians had not considered. For Paul, life after death is unthinkable without some kind of bodily existence, and the objecting question "With what kind of body?" allows him to show how a resurrection body is possible (see additional note). He does not offer answers to the questions immediately, however. Only at the conclusion of this section do the answers to the questions become clear (Boer 1988: 128). The dead are raised incorruptible (15:52), and they are raised with a spiritual body (15:44a).

Placing a leading question in the mouth of a conjectural objector allows Paul to rebuke the questioner as a "fool" (Asher 2000: 77) without directly insulting the Corinthians as foolish students. The "fool" (ἄφρων, *aphrōn*) is the opposite of the "wise" (φρόνιμος, *phronimos*; 4:10; 10:15). In this segment Paul sets himself up as the wise teacher correcting the dull-witted student and is not directly disputing argumentative Corinthians. The objector is undiscerning, because everyone knows that a seed's life springs from its death. The harsh epithet "fool" has deeper biblical roots, however.[2] It is the fool who says in his or her heart, "There is no God" (Ps. 14:1; 53:1). The fool does not simply suffer from an intellectual deficiency but fails to take God into account (Barrett 1968: 370; Fee 1987: 780; Schrage 2001: 280–81; cf. Rom. 1:21–22). In particular, this fool fails to take into account the creative power of God.

---

1. Among recent works analyzing this chapter rhetorically, Asher 2000 is the most convincing (cf. Saw 1995; Eriksson 1998: 232–78).

2. Asher (2000: 78) notes that the appellative ἄφρων differs from μωρέ (*mōre*), generally used by Epictetus in his diatribes (*Diatr.* 3.22.83–85; 3.23.16–17; 4.10.33–34).

Paul's first example argues by analogy from the known world of seeds to the unknown world of the resurrection (Bonneau 1993: 79). The illustration contains three points (Asher 2000: 79):

1. The seed is not made alive unless it dies.
2. The seed planted is not the body that will come up from the ground.
3. God effects the transition between the seed and the plant.

The resurrection remains a mystery, but its mystery does not tell against its reality (Findlay 1910: 934). The same mystery shrouds the germination of seeds. Moderns, influenced by a scientific understanding of germination as a natural process of development (Boer 1988: 130), may misunderstand what Paul says. He is not talking about a natural development but thinks in terms of God's transforming a bare grain and making it into something different. He understands God to give the growth in physical and spiritual harvests (1 Cor. 3:6–7). The farmer does not know how the seed grows in the earth (Mark 4:27) but only trusts that God is active and will bring it to pass. What is true in the case of seeds planted in the earth provides a lesson that can help the objector appreciate the possibility that a human corpse buried in the earth can also be transformed into something new. Paul has no intention of explaining how the resurrection happens but wishes only to make the case that it can happen. The assertion that the seed does not live unless it dies is not intended to underline a pattern of dissolution and new life or to underscore the necessity of death (contra Godet 1887: 403; Riesenfeld 1970: 174; cf. John 12:24), since Paul specifically argues in 1 Cor. 15:51–54 that not all will die. Nor is the purpose of the analogy to reveal that "dissolution and continuity are not incompatible" (contra Robertson and Plummer 1914: 369). He intends only to underscore *the change* between the naked seed sown in the ground and what will be harvested.[3] The farmer plants a bare seed, and "God miraculously clothes it with a new body, green and thriving" (Goulder 2001: 191). In the same way, the body that dies is not the same body that God raises (see additional note).

Asher (2000: 80) observes that by introducing the notion of the body in his leading question, Paul is able to chide the imaginary objector "for not considering that bodies change," as "exemplified in botanical processes." Paul explains the discontinuity in 15:37: the body sown is not the body that will be (γενησόμενον, *genēsomenon*).[4] Findlay (1910: 934)

---

3. Greeks tend to say that seeds spring to life, not die, but Paul's point requires using the metaphor of death.

4. The "bare grain" is literally the "naked seed" or "kernel" (γυμνὸς κόκκος, *gymnos kokkos*; cf. 2 Cor. 5:3).

catches Paul's point: "The grain of wheat gives to the eye no more promise of the body to spring from it than a grain of sand." A bare seed is
sown, dies, is made alive, and is given a new body as it is transformed
through God's creative power into "a plant luxuriantly clad in leaves"
(Edwards 1885: 434). The same is true of humans. The eye sees nothing
in a mortal, perishing body that promises any hope of a resurrection to
come, but God will transform it into a body clothed with glory through
the same creative power that gives life to seeds. As humans were dressed
at birth in the clothing of the "man of dust," so Christians will put on the
clothing of the "heavenly man" in the resurrection (15:47–49).

In 15:38, the emphasis once again is on the dramatic contrast between before and after. The seed buried in the ground is subject to
forces outside of its control. The phrase "God gives to it a body just as
he willed [ἠθέλησεν, *ethelēsen*; aorist tense]" refers to the apparent laws
established for plants in creation (Gen. 1:11–12; Godet 1887: 405; Findlay 1910: 934; Müller 1985: 196–97). The key concepts are "God gives"
and "God wills." Divine agency must be accounted for in life and in
death and in what comes after, or else one is to be accounted a fool.[5]
Paul assumes that plants do not rise of their own volition or by chance,
but as God has determined (Morris 1958: 225). Likewise, the resurrection of the dead is something willed by God and realized by God's
power. God wills to raise the dead and transform the body committed
to the grave into one fitted for glory, and God has the power to do so.
This point is especially emphasized by Asher (2001: 104, 108), who
claims that 1 Cor. 15:36–38 is "merely an illustration of how God's creative power effects the transition between a seed and a plant."

To fit his argument about the resurrection of the dead, Paul uses the
term "body" to describe the sprouting of the seed and partially answers the question "With what body?" by saying "With its own body"—
one that is proper to it, but one that has been transformed. The body
raised is not the body that inhabits the earth or that lies moldering in
the grave, but one that has been utterly transformed (cf. 2 Cor. 3:18;
Phil. 3:21). Edwards (1885: 435) comments that Paul "introduces here
the conception of identity of kind. If the seed is rye, the plant is rye."
The assumption that some kind of somatic continuity exists lies behind the earlier argument that a Christian may not use the body for
fornication as if it were something disconnected from the future resurrected life (1 Cor. 6:13).

Paul expands on the statement that each seed has its own body, but he **15:39–41**
takes the argument in a new direction by shifting the imagery from agricultural realities to different kinds of terrestrial flesh and different

---

5. This divine agency is also implied in the use of the passive verb ζῳοποιεῖται (*zō-opoieitai*, is made alive, is given life) in 15:36.

kinds of brilliance among celestial bodies. Bonneau (1993) demonstrates that the examples given in 15:39–41 do not reiterate the point in 15:36–38 (see Burchard 1984: 234 n. 6 for a list of scholars who think that it is redundant), but make a new point (see also Asher 2000: 100 n. 22). The problem that must be resolved to the Corinthians' satisfaction is how the polarity between the earthly sphere and the heavenly sphere is to be bridged. How can an earthly body be made fit for heavenly habitation, since what is perishable cannot inherit imperishability (15:50)? Asher (2000: 82; see also 91–145) cites many ancient philosophers who contended "that it is metaphysically impossible for a terrestrial body to ascend to the celestial realm."[6] The Corinthians appear to have shared this presupposition. In 15:39–41, Paul acknowledges its validity but introduces the principle of transformation in 15:42–44, 50–57 to show that it is not an insurmountable problem for belief in the resurrection of the dead.

Fee (1987: 783) discerns a chiastic structure in 15:39–41:

A Not all flesh is the same flesh.
  B There is a different kind for human beings,
        a different kind of flesh for animals,
        a different kind of flesh for birds,
        a different kind for fish.
    C There are heavenly bodies and earthly bodies.
       The glory of the heavenly is different from the glory of the earthly.
  B′ There is a different kind of glory for the sun,
        a different kind of glory for the moon,
        a different kind of glory for the stars,
A′ For glory differs from star to star.

The key words—σάρξ (*sarx*) in 15:39 and δόξα (*doxa*) in 15:41—are preceded by the adjective ἄλλη (*allē*, another). The items in 15:39 are listed in descending order of complexity: humans, animals, birds, and fish (cf. Gen. 1:20–27). The list also reveals a different kind of flesh for their different domains: earth, sky, and sea. The items in 15:41 are listed in descending order of their radiance: the blazing of the sun, the soft glow of the moon, the twinkling of the stars. The statement in 15:40 that the glory of heavenly bodies is different in kind from that of earthly bodies serves as "the pivot" between 15:39 and 15:41 (Bonneau 1993: 84). It introduces the term "glory," which, in this context, means "radiance," but can also apply to what is heavenly (cf. 1 Thess. 2:12). All of the examples

---

6. This problem applies not only to the resurrection, but also to the incarnation.

in 15:39 and 15:41 contribute in different ways to Paul's case for the feasibility of the resurrection of the dead.

Bonneau (1993: 85) notes that in 15:36–38, Paul highlights the distinction that exists between the seed before it is sown and after it is sown. In 15:39–41, he highlights the distinction that exists between below and above. The "below" is characterized by the use of the term "flesh"; the "above" is characterized by the use of the term "glory." This creates a hierarchy of opposites: "earthly/below/lesser" and "heavenly/above/greater." "Flesh" is used in a nonpejorative way to refer to the physicality of earthly bodies—their creatureliness, weakness, and transitoriness (Schrage 2001: 290). The substance of heavenly beings is "glory" (Lietzmann 1949: 84), which is one reason why it is so reprehensible for humans to exchange the glory of the immortal God for images of mortal humans, birds, four-footed animals, or reptiles (Rom. 1:23). Since the stars have a resplendence unlike anything on earth, one can expect the resurrected body, fit for a heavenly existence, to be unlike anything known on earth (Bonneau 1993: 85). Paul wants to disabuse the Corinthians of the mistaken impression that all bodies are the same so that they can begin to appreciate that the resurrection body is not identical with the familiar, earthly body—a mistake that is reinforced in the modern era by cartoons, commercials, and movies that portray heavenly scenes with characters taking on accustomed, earthly characteristics.

Paul notes that God's creation includes a differentiation of various kinds of flesh. Just as the flesh given to humans is not one that is appropriate for animals, birds, or fish, so also the resurrection body will not be the same as the one that is buried and returned to dust. The Corinthians' familiarity with "the infinite variety that reigns in the world which God created" (Bruce 1971: 151) should lead them to expect that the human body experienced in this life is not the only kind of body possible. Even heavenly bodies emit different levels of brightness. The body that is raised will be transformed into something entirely different from what is known on earth and something appropriate for heavenly existence. The Corinthians should also recognize that heavenly bodies differ from earthly bodies.[7] It would be foolish to think that an earthly body is appropriate for a heavenly existence. Mentioning the stars might be intended to bring to mind the glorious state of those resurrected from the dead, who are likened to astral bodies (Dan. 12:2–3; Matt. 13:43; Wis. 3:7; 2 Bar. 51:10; so D. Martin

---

7. Some argue that the term "heavenly bodies" (σώματα ἐπουράνια, *sōmata epourania*) refers to living, heavenly beings (Findlay 1910: 935–36; Parry 1926: 235–36; Morris 1958: 225), so that heavenly bodies refers to spiritual bodies fit for the spiritual sphere. But this verse serves as the hinge between 15:39, referring to terrestrial bodies, and 15:41, referring to the stars (cf. Sir. 43:9).

1995: 118–20).[8] Paul's point is that the resurrection body is not a reanimated corpse but something of a completely different order that is appropriate to celestial existence. Since the Corinthians recognize that heavenly bodies differ from earthly bodies, they should not expect the resurrected body to be a recycled earthly body.

Bonneau (1993: 85–86) contends that the two examples lead to the following question: "Can God transform (before/after) an earthly body into a heavenly body (below/above)?" This question is addressed in the next units. God, who provides appropriate bodies for cows and fish and appropriate glory for the sun and moon, certainly can be trusted to provide an appropriate celestial body for those who are raised. What this body will be and the nature of its glory are beyond imagining since it is beyond earthly experience, but it is not an absurd notion to think that the risen will exist in an altogether different body.

15:42–44a "Thus [is] the resurrection of the dead" serves as the conclusion of Paul's preceding argument and the heading for its next step. He does not specify the subject of the verbs σπείρεται (*speiretai*, it is sown) and ἐγείρεται (*egeiretai*, it is raised), but "whatever 'it' is, it represents a measure of continuity between the two orders" (Sloan 1983: 81). Yet Paul wants to emphasize that the body that will be raised is radically different from its earthly counterpart. This difference is underscored by four antitheses in which he contrasts what is sown with what is raised. Elsewhere, he uses the verb "to sow" figuratively to refer to his mission work (9:11), to charitable giving (2 Cor. 9:6, 10), and to moral/immoral living (Gal. 6:7–8). Its figurative meaning in this context is not clear. Several options are possible; here, I focus on two.

"Sowing" could refer to the burial of a human being (Chrysostom, *Hom. 1 Cor.* 41.5; Weiss 1910: 371; Robertson and Plummer 1914: 371–72). Since Paul introduces the topic as "the resurrection of the dead," it seems reasonable to infer that the subject of the verb is "one of the dead": "One is buried in corruptibility, raised in incorruptibility." It also comports well with the expectation that what is sowed will be harvested (2 Cor. 9:6; Gal. 6:7–8). This interpretation has several problems, however. "In dishonor" and "in weakness" do not seem applicable descriptions of interment, though some interpret them as references to the foulness and immobility of the corpse. But "weakness" applies to a lack of power, not to its complete absence (Asher 2001: 110). It hardly seems fitting to refer to a corpse as "animated by the soul" (σῶμα ψυχικόν, *sōma psychikon*; 15:44). This phrase is difficult to translate, and the renderings "natural body" or "physical body" do not adequately

---

8. The gradation of the splendors of heavenly bodies should not be taken to mean that differences of rank will exist among the risen (contra Tertullian, *De resurrectione carnis* [*Resurrection of the Flesh*] 52; Chrysostom, *Hom. 1 Cor.* 41; Robertson and Plummer 1914: 371–72).

convey its meaning. It means a "soulish body" (Edwards 1885: 440), which suggests a "body formed by and for a soul" (Godet 1887: 413) as its instrument to carry out its wishes. A dead body, however, is soulless. Therefore, it is improbable that "sowing" refers to burial.[9]

The verb "to sow" can be used for the procreation of humans (see Gen. 9:19; 4 Macc. 10:2), and many assume that it applies to human existence in general ("the present state from birth to death" [Edwards 1885: 438–39]).[10] This view makes the best sense of the passage, but Asher (2001: 102) refines it by arguing that "sowing" is "an anthropogenic metaphor describing the creation of the first human being, Adam." It refers to "the state of humanity upon its creation in the person of Adam" (Asher 2001: 110). Asher contends that the examples from 1 Cor. 15:36–41 are intended to illustrate the creative power of God in the generation of life, but that the divine passive, "it is raised," repeated three times, makes it difficult to assume that humans are the agents of the "sowing." "Sowing" was used as a metaphor in the Greco-Roman world for human origins (Asher 2001: 112–21), and Paul's first readers could have understood it in this sense. The advantage of this interpretation is that it draws on the contrast between those in Adam and those in Christ articulated earlier, in 15:21–22, and anticipates the contrast between Adam and Christ in 15:45–49. Humankind bears all the hallmarks of the first human, made of the same corruptible dust. This interpretation means that throughout these verses Paul refers to one-time events: Adam's creation, Christ's resurrection (15:45–48), and the believers' resurrection (15:49, 51–52).

The Corinthians have trouble conceiving of the resurrection of the dead because they know the terrestrial body to be

1. Susceptible to corruption—the condition of fallen creation (Rom. 8:21; Gal. 6:8; Col. 2:22; see also 2 Bar. 44:9)
2. Dishonored—the condition of being subject to shame and shameful treatment (1 Cor. 4:11–13; 2 Cor. 6:8)
3. Weak—the condition of being embodied in something that is subject to physical infirmities and deformities (2 Cor. 12:9–10) and that wastes away (2 Cor. 4:16)

Paul's point is that the resurrection body is not a spruced-up version of the physical body. The two bodies are totally different:

9. In 1 Enoch 62:8, the image of sowing is used for the resurrection of the congregation of the holy ones.

10. So also Calvin 1960: 337; Godet 1887: 410–12; Findlay 1910: 937; Bruce 1971: 152; Ruef 1977: 172; Conzelmann 1975: 283; Fee 1987: 784; Wolff 1996: 406; Hays 1997: 272; Schrage 2001: 294. Moffatt (1938: 259) interprets it as a reference to human birth.

The physical body is sown . . .	The resurrection body is raised . . .
in a state of corruptibility	in a state of incorruptibility
in dishonor	in glory
in weakness	in power
a natural body	a spiritual body

What Paul is talking about becomes clear in 15:44a. "The body kindled by the soul [σῶμα ψυχικόν]" and "the body kindled by the Spirit [σῶμα πνευματικόν, *sōma pneumatikon*]" are poles apart. The first term characterizes earthly life; the second, heavenly life (see additional note). In 2 Cor. 5:1, Paul likens this earthly body to a tent that is to be folded up and replaced by an eternal building waiting in the heavens. Those who are raised will be given spiritual bodies, ones animated by the Spirit of God (Barrett 1968: 372) and bearing the image of the heavenly person. The spiritual body is a body "that eye has not seen and ear has not heard and has not entered the human mind" (1 Cor. 2:9), that is transformed into the likeness of Christ (Phil. 3:21), and that is fitted for the new age. All of this is possible only by the power of God.

15:44b–49 Boer (1988: 129) notes with many that the comparison with the first Adam and the last Adam in 15:45–49 seems to break the flow of the argument begun in 15:35 (cf. Fee 1987: 787). But that is not the case if the sowing in 15:42–44a is understood to be a reference to the creation of the first human being, Adam. Only when one fails to grasp the logic of Paul's reasoning and the nature of the Corinthians' objections to the resurrection do these verses seem to break the flow of the argument.[11] The argument contains five steps (Asher 2000: 113):

1. The statement in 15:44a introduces the principle that an opposite presupposes its counterpart: "If there is a natural body, then there is also a spiritual one." The contrast assumes a polarity between the locations where these bodies are suitable—the terrestrial and the celestial. The οὕτως (*houtōs*, thus) in 15:45 draws the conclusion from this principle.

2. Paul argues in 15:45–46 that these opposites are temporally successive. He cites Gen. 2:7 as proof and adds "first" and "Adam" to that text. There is a first and a last. The last has the sense of being the ultimate. Adam received life as an embodied soul in a natural body (see

11. Asher (2000: 110) calls 15:45–49 "one of the most controversial passages in the New Testament." The only apparent consensus is the impression among scholars that these verses contain Corinthian terminology that can lead us back to the roots of the Corinthian error. Asher (2000: 111) argues convincingly, however, "There is no need to pose elaborate theories about the source of Paul's language and ideas and no need to attribute this language to the Corinthians."

also Wis. 15:11). Christ gives life as a life-giving Spirit (1 Cor. 15:22; cf. 1 Thess. 4:14). "Giving life" is synonymous with raising the dead (Rom. 4:17; 8:11; 2 Cor. 3:6). The point is this: If there is a natural body represented by the first Adam in a sown body, then there must be a spiritual body represented by the last Adam, the risen Christ. The first is appropriate for existence in creation; the second will be appropriate for existence in the world to come.

In 1 Cor. 15:46, the adjectival nouns τὸ πνευματικόν (*to pneumatikon*, the spiritual) and τὸ ψυχικόν (*to psychikon*, the natural) are neuter, so it is clear that Paul is talking about the bodies in 15:44 and not Adam or Christ (15:45, 47–49). He is not arguing against hypothetical dissenters in Corinth who supposedly "assumed that they had already entered into the totality of pneumatic existence while they were still in their *psychikos* body," as Fee (1987: 791) would have it (see also Kistemaker 1993: 577; Soards 1999: 350). Oster (1995: 401) strongly rejects this view as "ill-founded exegetically" and "flawed historically." Paul's argument in this passage has nothing to do with the Corinthians' self-centered spirituality but with their bewilderment over how a terrestrial body can be raised as a celestial body. We cannot be certain whether the Corinthians did or did not use the terms ψυχικός and πνευματικός (contra Dunn 1973: 129; R. Horsley 1976), and so we should be careful before constructing theories based on the assumption that they did. We do know, however, that one of these terms, ψυχικός, appears in the scriptural proof cited in 15:45 (Gen. 2:7). The use of the other term, πνευματικός, would follow from the principle enunciated in 1 Cor. 15:44b that the one thing, the natural body, demands an opposite counterpart, the spiritual body.[12] Asher (2000: 111) concludes, "Paul uses this terminology for the sole purpose of moving his argument from a discussion of the relationship between the resurrection and locative polarity to a discussion of the relationship between the eschatological resurrection and locative polarity." Oster (1995: 402) maintains,

> For Paul, in light of Adamic influence, the natural body is annihilated at the return of Christ and the End. The spiritual body, on the other hand, does not refer to the condition and state of the believer following his personal death, but rather to the body at, and only at, the time of Christ's return and the End.

The Corinthians are not trying to assume their "heavenly body" now (contra Fee 1987: 795), but rather fail to understand that in the resurrection their earthly bodies will be completely transformed into spiri-

---

12. These terms are used in an entirely different way in 2:14–15 to refer to the natural person and spiritual person, not to the body. They coexist and refer to two types of humans (Asher 2000: 113 n. 49). Paul's usage differs here.

tual bodies. Paul argues that they will not become spirit vapors at death. The inherent incompatibility between earthly and heavenly bodies is remedied by the transformative power of God.

3. The first two points of locative polarity and temporal succession are combined in 15:47. The natural or sown body and the spiritual or heavenly body are appropriate to different cosmic spheres that are polar opposites, and they are also temporally successive and not coexistent opposites.

Paul does not use verbs in 15:47, and so they must be supplied. He is talking not about the substance of the first and the last Adams but about their origin and character. The first human (ὁ πρῶτος ἄνθρωπος, *ho prōtos anthrōpos*) "came" from dust from the earth, and the second human (ὁ δεύτερος ἄνθρωπος, *ho deuteros anthrōpos*) "will come" from heaven.[13] A past tense verb is the obvious choice to refer to Adam. The future tense is more suited for Christ's coming (Barrett 1968: 375). The removal of the Adamic condition occurs only at the resurrection.

The prepositional phrase ἐξ οὐρανοῦ (*ex ouranou*, from heaven) does not mean that Christ is made of heavenly stuff as Adam was made from dust. Paul is talking about how the polarity between heaven and earth is to be bridged. The backdrop for understanding this conclusion is not, as some propose, Philo's (*Alleg. Interp.* 1.12 §31) exegesis of Gen. 2:7:

> There are two types of persons; the one a heavenly person, the other an earthly. The heavenly person, being made after the image of God, is altogether without part or lot in corruptible and terrestrial substance; but the earthly one was compacted out of the matter scattered here and there, which Moses calls "clay." For this reason he says the heavenly person was not molded, but was stamped with the image of God; while the earthly is a molded work of the Artificer, but not of his offspring.

Philo interprets Adam's becoming a living soul to mean that God breathed into his corruptible (φθαρτός, *phthartos*), earthlike mind the power of real life. Paul's emphasis is totally different. It is christological and eschatological and picks up the contrast between above and below in 15:40–41, the earthly flesh and the heavenly glory. The second person is the resurrected Christ, and "from heaven" identifies him as coming from the divine and eternal realm at the parousia (see Robertson and Plummer 1914: 374; Schweizer, *TDNT* 9:478; contra Lincoln 1981: 45–46). Paul writes elsewhere that we await God's Son "from heaven" (ἐκ τῶν οὐρανῶν, *ek tōn ouranōn*; 1 Thess. 1:10), that Christ will come down "from heaven" (ἀπ᾽ οὐρανοῦ, *ap' ouranou*) at the parousia (1 Thess.

---

13. Paul may have coined the adjective χοϊκός (*choikos*, dusty; from χοῦς, *chous*) to convey how closely related the sown body is to its earthly environment and to contrast it with adjective ἐπουράνιος (*epouranios*, heavenly).

4:16–17), that he will be revealed "from heaven" (ἀπ' οὐρανοῦ) with his mighty angels (2 Thess. 1:7), and that "our citizenship is in heaven, from which [ἐξ οὗ, *ex hou*] we also eagerly await a Savior, the Lord Jesus Christ, who will transform our body of humiliation into conformity with the body of his glory" (Phil. 3:20–21; cf. Dan. 7:13; Mark 13:26; 14:62).[14] These parallels make clear that the one from heaven is the one who appears at the end, when the dead will be raised.

4. Paul treats Adam and Christ as representatives, not simply individuals (Barrett 1968: 376). The first Adam influences humans, all of whom are sown with a natural body in this terrestrial habitat. The principle of antithetical counterparts laid out in 1 Cor. 15:44b leads to this conclusion: If humans take the shape of the first Adam sown with a body made from dust that goes back to dust, then Christians will take the shape of Christ in their heavenly existence, who is from heaven and has a spiritual body. The last Adam, then, sets the pattern for all who will be resurrected and given a spiritual body for their new celestial habitat.

5. In 15:49, Paul makes clear that this transformation has not yet occurred. It lies in the future at the resurrection. Until then, humans bear the image of the person of dust, Adam. In the resurrection, Christians will bear the image of the heavenly person, who has dominion and uses it properly in complete obedience to God. Cosmic polarity, therefore, is not an insurmountable problem. In the same way that those in Adam bear Adam's characteristics in their home on earth, those in Christ will be made like Christ, with spiritual bodies appropriate for their new heavenly existence.

Additional Notes

15:35. When Baruch asks God how the dead will be raised ("In which shape will the living live in your day?" [2 Bar. 49:1–3]), he receives the answer that they will be raised in the exact same form in which they were buried (50:1–4). This facilitates the recognition of persons for the judgment, after which the righteous will be transformed into a state appropriate to eternal glory (51:10). The debate in *b. Sanh.* 90b about the nature of the resurrection is much closer to Paul's form of argument. An emperor asks Rabbi Gamaliel how the dead, who have turned to dust, can come to life. The rabbi's daughter intervenes with a clever parable that argues for the case from the greater to the lesser:

> "In our town there are two potters; one fashions [his products] from water, and the other from clay: who is the most praiseworthy?" "He who fashions them from water," he replied. "If he can fashion [man] from water [semen], surely he can do so from clay [the dust to which he returns]!"

Morissette (1972a) contends that Paul's argument follows the same pattern: an objecting question (1 Cor. 15:35), examples from everyday life (15:36–41), and concluding application (15:42–

---

14. The prepositions ἐκ and ἀπό are synonymous for Paul (cf. Gal. 1:18).

49). Bonneau (1993: 86–89) limits the application to 15:42–44a, rightly pointing out that 15:44b begins another argument.

15:37. An argument for the resurrection in rabbinic literature that is attributed to Rabbi Meir uses the imagery of the naked seed, but the question prompting the response and the application is completely different from Paul's. The question is "Will the dead rise nude or clothed?" The naked seed is used to argue from lesser to the greater: "The seed is sown naked and it comes up clothed. How much more will the dead, which depart clothed (in shrouds) come up clothed" (*Eccles. Rab.* 5.10.1; see also *b. Sanh.* 90b; *b. Ketub.* 111b).

15:44a. Christians have been given "the firstfruits of the Spirit" (Rom. 8:23; or "first install-ment" [2 Cor. 1:22; 5:5]) in anticipation of the spiritual body but still groan inwardly as they await the redemption of their earthly bodies. In the meantime, they are being transformed by the Spirit into the image of the glory of the Lord by degrees (2 Cor. 3:18). The total transformation awaits the resurrection.

15:47. The reading ἄνθρωπος after "second" has strong textual support from a broad geo-graphical range (א*, B, C, D*, F, G, 33, 1739*, it^{ar, b, d, f, g, o}, vg, cop^{bo}). It is the shortest reading and best explains the others, ὁ κύριος (1912), ἄνθρωπος ὁ κύριος (א², A, D¹, Ψ, 81), and ἄνθρωπος πνευματικός (𝔓⁴⁶), which appear to be attempts to bring the wording into line with the spiritual one (15:46) or the heavenly one (15:48).

15:49. The future indicative φορέσομεν has weaker attestation (B, I, 6, 630, 945^{vid}, 1881) than the aorist subjunctive φορέσωμεν (𝔓⁴⁶, א, A, C, D, F, G, Ψ, 075, 0243, 33, 1739), but a hortatory subjunctive, "let us bear," is impossible if Paul is arguing that bearing the image of the heavenly person awaits the future resurrection. This mode of existence is possible only at the end. Until the end, Christians bear all the hallmarks of Adamic existence. Only Christ has been granted this mode of existence. It cannot have an ethical thrust in which Paul exhorts the readers to look to Christ "as source and hope of transformation, rather than looking to their own wisdom or to some primal divine image within" (contra Hays 1997: 273–74; cf. Héring 1962: 179; Sider 1974–75: 434; Lincoln 1981: 50–51; Fee 1987: 787 n. 5, 794–95; Eriksson 1998: 271). Robertson and Plummer (1914: 375) recognize that the subjunctive implies that "the attaining to the glorified body depends upon on our own effort." Nothing could be more wrong. Internal evidence must outweigh the external evidence. The context is neither polemical nor hortatory, but didactic. Paul is teaching the Corinthians how "a body, conditioned by ψυχή, derived from Adam, will be transformed into a body conditioned by πνεῦμα, derived from Christ" (Robertson and Plummer 1914: 374). The variation in the readings probably arose from the identical pronunciation of the two verbs (see Caragounis 1995a) or from a mistaken desire, repeated by some modern commen-tators, to turn Paul's argument about bodies into an ethical discourse.

X. The Resurrection (15:1–58)
    D. The Consequences If the Resurrection of the Dead Were Not True (15:29–34)
    E. The Bodily Character of the Resurrection (15:35–49)
➤ F. All Will Be Changed (15:50–58)

F. All Will Be Changed (15:50–58)

Deciding how the concluding remarks of Paul's resurrection discourse link with what precedes is key for interpreting them. A majority of scholars assume that 15:50 introduces a new issue (Weiss 1910: 377; Jeremias 1955–56: 154–55; Thiselton 2000: 1290–91). Jeremias (1955–56) interprets 15:50–57 as providing the answer to the question raised in 15:35, "How are the dead raised?" Only a few scholars (Gillman 1982: 332; Fee 1987: 798; Asher 2000: 147–57) posit any connection to what immediately precedes. As in 7:29, the phrase τοῦτο δέ φημι, ἀδελφοί (*touto de phēmi, adephoi*) solemnly signals that an important declaration follows: "I mean this, brothers and sisters." Asher (2000: 151) contends that here this phrase introduces a principle "that summarizes what [Paul] has previously said" and guides the subsequent discussion. With this solemn introductory formula, Paul authoritatively states an enduring fact. As Gillman (1988: 443) expounds it,

> An absolute opposition is drawn between earthly entities and heavenly entities, such that the former cannot inherit the latter. This faith conviction upon which Paul stands firm is given first in more Semitic, concrete terms "flesh and blood," "kingdom of God," then in more Hellenistic, abstract terms, "perishable," "imperishable." The Hellenistic terms give the logical basis for the exclusion principle: the condition of flesh and blood, because it is perishable, is inappropriate for the kingdom of God because it is imperishable. The new body must be compatible with its new environment. The force of v 50 conclusively sets forth the opposition between two incompatible conditions.

What few have recognized is that this principle summarizes the Corinthians' basic objections to the resurrection: a human body is unfit for a heavenly abode. Paul continues his rhetorical strategy, evidenced throughout the letter, of accommodating the Corinthian view by stating "as a principle what has been assumed all along" (Asher 2000: 154). The Corinthians are indeed right that the earthly sphere and the heavenly kingdom of God represent extreme opposites. The phrase "flesh and blood" underscores that physical polarity even more. In Jewish parlance, "flesh and blood" generally denotes the frailty of human creatures. The Corinthians' inferences about life after death based on this polarity, however, are wrong. Paul draws his argument for the resurrection of the dead to a close by emphasizing in this unit that this polarity will be overcome when both the living and the dead are changed.

In 15:50–57, Paul expands on his previous argument by introducing the tenet of change that resolves the problem of how it is possible for the dead to be raised. As J. Wilson (1968: 96) summarizes these verses, "Every Christian must undergo a future transformation. No one, living or dead, can enter the kingdom of God without radical change." Paul hammers home this concept in 15:51–53:

> Not everyone will die before the parousia, but everyone will be changed (15:51).
> The dead will be changed, and those still alive will be changed at the parousia (15:52).
> Whether one has died or survived until the parousia, the corruptible and mortal will be clothed with what is incorruptible and immortal (15:53).

A divinely wrought transformation occurring at the parousia will make what is earthly become fit for heavenly existence. God then will claim the final victory over death, which is vanquished by the resurrection.

Exegesis and Exposition

[50]But I mean this, brothers and sisters, that flesh and blood cannot inherit the kingdom of God, nor can what is corruptible inherit what is incorruptible. [51]Behold, I tell you a mystery. ⌜We will not all sleep, but all will be changed⌝, [52]in a flash, in the blink of an eye, at the last trumpet. For the trumpet will sound, and the dead will be raised incorruptible, and we will be changed. [53]For this corruptible [body] must put on incorruption, and this mortal [body] must put on immortality. [54]But ⌜when this corruptible [body] puts on incorruptibility⌝, and this mortal [body] puts on immortality, then the word that stands written will come to pass, "Death has been swallowed up in victory." [55]Where, O death, is your victory? Where, O death, is your sting? [56]The sting of death is sin, and the power of sin is the law. [57]Thanks be to God, who gives to us the victory through our Lord Jesus Christ. [58]So then, my beloved brothers and sisters, be firm, immovable, abounding in the work of the Lord always, knowing that your labor is not in vain in the Lord.

15:50 Jeremias (1955–56: 153–54) has convinced many interpreters that Paul contrasts the living with the dead in 15:50–53. In 15:50, Jeremias maintains that "flesh and blood" refers to the living (cf. Gal. 1:16; Matt.

16:17; Eph. 6:12; Heb. 2:14; Sir. 14:18; 17:31) and that "corruption" (ἡ φθορά, *hē phthora*) refers to corpses in the state of decomposition. "Flesh and blood" (15:50), the living (15:52), and "that which is mortal" (τὸ θνητόν, *to thnēton*; 15:53) will be changed and put on immortality. "Corruption" (15:50), "the dead" (15:52), and "that which is corruptible" (τὸ φθαρτόν, *to phtharton*; 15:53) will be raised incorruptible and put on incorruption. In other words, "the dead experience what happened to the Lord in the resurrection, the living experience what happened to the Lord in the transfiguration" (Jeremias 1955–56: 154).

Jeremias misinterprets Paul's train of thought. Paul is not using synthetic parallelism that introduces a further thought ("flesh and blood" = the living; "corruptible" = the dead), but synonymous parallelism ("flesh and blood" = "corruptible") to refer to the condition of physical human existence.[1] The first assertion, that flesh and blood cannot inherit the kingdom of God, is explained by the second in ways that any Greek reader could understand. "Flesh and blood" represents what is corruptible, and what is corruptible cannot stake a claim on what is incorruptible. In 15:42, the word φθορά (corruption) applies to the living, not the corpse buried in the ground (see also Rom. 8:21). "Flesh and blood," a Semitic expression, recalls the many kinds of flesh confined to the earth in contrast to the different glories of the heavenly bodies (1 Cor. 15:40–41).[2] Its meaning cannot be confined to the living (Gillman 1982: 316; cf. Sir. 14:17–18, which refers to "the generations of flesh and blood: one dies and another is born"). Paul is not making a distinction between the living and the dead, and his concern here is not that of 1 Thess. 4:13–18: Will the living precede the dead at the parousia (contra Jeremias 1955–56: 159)? He has made no previous reference to any contrast between the living and the dead in this chapter. Instead, he simply concedes the point that this earthly dress is unfit for heavenly habitation. The emphasis falls on the necessity that the living and the dead be changed, because in their earthly physicality they cannot inherit the kingdom of God.

In 1 Cor. 15:50–57, Paul continues to address the same problem that has driven the entire discussion: the metaphysical incompatibility between the heavenly order, which is spiritual and imperishable, and the earthly, organic order, which is fleshly and perishable. The polarity between the terrestrial and the celestial prohibits the ascent "of a terrestrial human form or substance to the celestial region" (Asher 2000:

---

1. So Morissette 1974: 46–48; Conzelmann 1975: 290 n. 10; Fee 1987: 798; Witherington 1995: 310; Wolff 1996: 414; R. Collins 1999: 579; Asher 2000: 153–54; Schrage 2001: 366; contra Godet 1887: 434; Jeremias 1955–56: 152.
2. In 1 Enoch 15:4, the renegade angels who took wives from the earth are described as "spiritual living ones, [possessing] eternal life," while their progeny are described as "flesh and blood."

153). Older commentators get it right: "Our present bodies, whether living or dead, are absolutely unfitted for the Kingdom" (Robertson and Plummer 1914: 376; cf. Godet 1887: 434; Edwards 1885: 449; contra Thiselton 2000: 1291). What is raised is not flesh and blood. The earthly frame will be utterly changed into a heavenly body of glory. Barrett (1968: 379) missteps in saying that Paul does not intend "to teach a direct incompatibility between flesh and the kingdom of God." He does not need to teach it, because the Corinthian dissenters already take it for granted. Paul only concedes it. What he wishes to teach, however, is that this inherent incompatibility is overcome by change. His view differs significantly from 2 Bar. 50:2, which has God telling Baruch that the earth gives back the dead as it received them, "not changing anything in their form." For Paul, change is *absolutely necessary* to make what was flesh and blood and perishable fit for what is imperishable and immortal.

"Inheriting the kingdom of God" is a Jewish turn of phrase. Jewish texts speak of inheriting ("to come into possession," or "to acquire") "the earth" (1 Enoch 5:7; Jub. 32:19), the coming "time" (2 Bar. 44:13), or "what is to come" (4 Ezra [2 Esdr.] 7:96); but "inheriting the kingdom of God" is found only in the NT (Foerster, *TDNT* 3:782). The expression appears in a context of moral exhortation in Matt. 25:34; 1 Cor. 6:9–10; and Gal. 5:21. Witherington (1995: 310) assumes that it is a moral exhortation in this context: "One must not be so satisfied with one's present spiritual life as to mistake the part for the whole of Christian existence." But spiritual pride is not the problem that Paul is addressing in this section, and it should not be imported into the discussion. In 1 Cor. 15:50, he merely acknowledges the Corinthians' point that this terrestrial body cannot simply relocate from this world to the heavenly realm. He headlines this metaphysical roadblock to set up its solution. All will undergo transformation, allowing both the living and dead to rise to a new, celestial existence (Perriman 1989: 515; Asher 2000: 157).

15:51–53 If "flesh and blood" cannot inherit "the kingdom of God" and if "what is susceptible to corruption" cannot inherit "incorruption," it certainly would seem that the resurrection of the dead is impossible and that life after death should be conceived in purely immaterial terms. "Behold" (ἰδού, *idou*) injects a solemn accent into Paul's unveiling of an eschatological mystery that reveals how the impossible will happen (cf. Rev. 17:7 for similar wording). "Mystery" refers to something that was formerly hidden and undiscoverable by human methods but now has been divinely revealed (Rom. 11:25; cf. 1 Cor. 2:1, 7; 13:2).

Paul does not intend to hint that he and the Corinthians belong to the last generation with the assertion "we will not all sleep" (cf. 11:30; 15:6). Those who interpret this verse to mean that he assumed that he would survive until the parousia must reckon with what he says in 1 Cor. 6:14, "God both raised the Lord and will raise us through his power." This statement could be interpreted to mean that he expected death for himself and the Corinthians, but the identity of the "us" in 6:14 is as indeterminate as the "we" in 15:51. "We will not all sleep" anticipates only that the parousia will break into human history and directly affect those who are alive at that time (cf. 1 Thess. 4:15). When that event will occur is unknown and not at issue. The "all" refers generically to Christians who happen to be alive at the parousia. Since it can happen at any time, and since he is still among the living, Paul can include himself and the Corinthians in the first group: "We will not all sleep."

The second "all" ("all will be changed"), however, must include both the dead and the living, since the only way that the barrier presented by the polarity between an earthly body and a celestial body can be overcome is through a dramatic change. The Corinthians considered this barrier to be insuperable, which caused them to question the possibility of the resurrection of the dead. It is the only issue that Paul addresses. Paul's answer, as Asher (2000) explains, is that the polarity is overcome by the change that will occur at the end. The verb ἀλλαγησόμεθα (allagēsometha) is repeated twice in 1 Cor. 15:51–52 and is aptly translated "undergo transformation" (Thiselton 2000: 1258).[3] The mystery is not that the living and the dead will be on a par with one another at the parousia but that both the living and the dead will undergo the prerequisite transformation so that they can attain incorruptibility and immortality. This "mystery" that all will be changed is a revealed truth, but it also connotes that this transformation will be effected by God's mysterious power—a power that only the "foolish" fail to appreciate.

Paul has no intention of outlining the events of the parousia. The final judgment, for example, is omitted, though it is clearly assumed in other parts of the letter (3:8, 13–15; 5:5; 6:2–3; 9:27). He intends to argue only that the change will occur at a certain moment in time—on the last day, when this world is brought to an end. The word ἄτομος (atomos) refers to what is indivisible (the "atom" was considered to be a particle too small to split). In the context of time, it refers to the smallest conceivable instant (BDAG 149). The image of "the blink of an eye" reinforces the instantaneous nature of the change—it all happens in a flash. According to Gillman (1988: 443), the imagery emphasizes the equality of the living and the dead, refutes any view of a gradual trans-

---

3. M. Dahl (1962: 103–5) argues that ἀλλάσσειν (allassein) is "the *weakest* word" Paul could have used (cf. Phil. 3:21) and that his choice of verbs can be explained by the assumption that this change will not alter or destroy our identity. The continuity of identity may be underscored by the fourfold repetition of τοῦτο (touto) in 15:53–54 (Sider 1974–75: 437).

formation of the resurrected (cf., for example, 2 Bar. 50:1–51:10), and "highlights the miraculous, supraterrestrial and ineffable nature of the transformation event." The image of the blasting trumpet is a traditional eschatological motif (see Matt. 24:31; 1 Thess. 4:16; Joel 2:1; Zeph. 1:14–16; Zech. 9:14; 4 Ezra [2 Esdr.] 6:23; Sib. Or. 4:173–75) and is associated with manifestations of God's presence (Exod. 19:13, 16, 19; 20:18; Zech. 9:14).[4] The "last" trumpet is not the last in a series (Rev. 8:2–13; 11:15–19) but is the trumpet that signals the end (Fee 1987: 802).

The clothing imagery in 1 Cor. 15:53–54 provides a concrete picture of the transformation mystery by which a mortal, corruptible body changes to an immortal, incorruptible body.[5] "Putting on" is equivalent to bearing the image of the heavenly one (15:49) and affirms that the new existence will be corporeal. The demonstrative τοῦτο in 15:53 refers to the bodies of all believers, living and dead. "It is necessary" (δεῖ, *dei*) may refer to "the compulsion of divine authority" (Gillman 1988: 444), but it is also self-evident that this investiture is necessary for something that is perishable to be made fit for imperishable existence.

Gillman notes that Paul does not say that the old, earthly body is to be stripped off so that the (immortal) soul may escape—an idea found in Philo (*Alleg. Interp.* 2.15 §§54–59; 2.19 §80; *Dreams* 1.8 §43) and in the *Corpus Hermeticum* (1.24–26; 10.18; 13.3, 14). Instead, Paul's clothing imagery conveys the idea that the transformation to an immortal body is accomplished by adding a new garment to the mortal body. In 2 Cor. 5:2 and 5:4, he uses the doubly compounded verb ἐπενδύσασθαι (*ep + en + dysasthai*), meaning "to put on over," to stress continuity in the process of moving from an earthly tent to a heavenly dwelling (M. Harris 1971: 44). Therefore, "one does not have to slip off the earthly body before being garbed in the heavenly one" (Garland 1999: 258). Though Paul never attempts to explain "the nexus between the present physical frame and the spiritual body" (Moffatt 1938: 265), he understands the change as something that occurs within the same genus, like the seed miraculously changing into the plant.

15:54–55 Paul repeats the clothing terminology in 15:53, but the δέ in 15:54 introduces "a subtle, though significant, advance in thought" (Gillman 1988: 444). He moves from what "must" take place (15:53) to what will take place "when this corruptible [body] puts on incorruptibility and this mortal [body] puts on immortality."[6] The prophecy from Scripture seals its certainty and draws out the theological implications. The cita-

---

4. The "trumpet" refers to both the instrument and its sound (Conzelmann 1975: 291 n. 19).

5. Putting on garments of glory as a metaphor for eternal life is familiar in Jewish apocalyptic tradition (see 1 Enoch 62:15–16; 1QS 4:7–8).

6. Ὅταν (*hotan*) plus the aorist subjunctive indicates future eventuality (cf. 15:28).

tion combines Isa. 25:8 LXX (25:7 MT) with Hos. 13:14 (see C. Stanley 1992: 209–15). From Isa. 25:8, Paul gleans that death will be "swallowed up." The LXX version, however, reads that death, "being strong," has swallowed up the nations. He adopts the verb καταπίνειν (katapinein, to gulp down), suggesting "hostile destruction" (Goppelt, *TDNT* 6:159), but follows the Hebrew textual tradition in which God will destroy death forever (cf. Rev. 21:4, citing the same tradition). He treats the realm of death as a "power in its own right" that destroys earthly life and looms as an unremitting threat (Gillman 1988: 445). Death, for him, is not a blessed release but "the annihilation of the human person by an alien, inimical power" (Boer 1988: 184).

Where Paul came up with the phrase εἰς νῖκος (*eis nikos*, in victory) is difficult to discern. He may have altered δίκη (*dikē*, plague), found in Hos. 13:14 LXX, to νῖκος (*nikos*, victory) and inserted it in his quotation to create a word link (Hays 1997: 276), or utilized a "pre-Theodotion" version of the LXX (Gillman 1988: 444; see also the text of Aquila), or drawn upon an idiom connected to the cognate Aramaic verb of the Hebrew adverb לָנֶצַח (*lāneṣaḥ*, forever) in Isa. 25:8 that means "to overcome, prevail over" (Caird 1969: 34; Morissette 1972b: 168–70; Fee 1987: 803). This last option best explains the variations in the different Greek renderings of the Hebrew text. What is clear is that the ultimate destruction of death requires the resurrection of the dead.

The rhetorical questions "Where, O death, is your victory? Where, O death, is your sting?" derive from Hos. 13:14, though the text is so different that Calvin (1960: 344–46) thinks that Paul does not cite the prophet but adapts his words according to his own purposes. Barrett (1968: 383) surmises that he is "writing freely, in scriptural language, of the ultimate victory over death." In Hosea's context, death and Sheol serve to punish the iniquity of Ephraim and are summoned to inflict due punishment. Paul's citation turns "plague" or "penalty" (δίκη) into "victory" (νῖκος), replaces the reference to "Sheol" (or "Hades" in the LXX) with "death," and interprets the passage from the perspective of Christ's resurrection by turning it into a taunt. The rhetorical questions now sneer defiantly at death's impotence before the power and mercy of God, who wills to forgive sins (1 Cor. 15:3, 17) and to raise the dead.

The noun κέντρον (*kentron*) can refer to a goad that drives on or wounds (Acts 26:14; Prov. 26:3; Sir. 38:25; Ps. Sol. 16:4), or to a stinger (Rev. 9:10 [of scorpions]; 4 Macc. 14:19 [of insects]). Does Paul picture death wielding a goad in its hand to rule over humans and torture them? Or does it puncture the flesh with its poison-filled stinger? Here it must refer to something that harms far more seriously than either a goad or a stinger, and it must be synonymous with "power" in 1 Cor. 15:56 (Schmid, *TDNT* 3:668; Schrage 2001: 381). It enables death to exercise its dominion over the entire world, but its venom has been absorbed by Christ and drained of its potency so that the victory over death now belongs to God and to God's people, who benefit from it.

15:56 Paul adds a theological aside that identifies "the sting of death" as "sin," and "the power of sin" as "the law." The relationship between sin and the law is developed in Romans (5:12–14; 7:7–13), which most believe was written in Corinth, but not in this passage. One should not assume, however, that Paul had not yet fully thought through this connection until he finally worked it out in Romans. The letter to the Romans is written to a community he had never visited. Presumably, what he writes to them he had taught others before. Here, he must assume that the Corinthians would understand this theological shorthand. He did not need to provide an in-depth explanation on the connection between sin and the law, because he had articulated this idea previously, and the law as a delusive basis of salvation is not at issue (see additional note).

From its mysterious laboratory where death distills its poisons, it unleashes the power of sin (adapting a metaphor from Godet 1887: 445). Death gains its power over humans through sin because sin demands capital punishment as its moral penalty (Rom. 6:23). The law, not only unable to arrest sin, spurs it on and pronounces death as its sentence. Paul assumes that his readers understand that through Adam came sin and death (1 Cor. 15:21–22). Through Moses came the law. The law brings awareness of sinfulness (Rom. 4:15; 5:13, 20; 7:7; Gal. 3:19), provokes impulses to sin, which then become deliberate transgressions, with the result that death tightens its stranglehold. The law cannot give life or impart righteousness (Gal. 3:21) but brings only condemnation (2 Cor. 3:6). Through Christ alone come the gracious forgiveness of sins, redemption from the law, and the resurrection from the dead. It is this last element, the resurrection of the dead, that is at issue and that the Corinthians fail to grasp. The resurrection does not simply overturn death's destructive forces of decay but prevails over sin's deadly poison (see Fee 1987: 806). Christ's death for the forgiveness of sins causes death to lose its ultimacy, because "when sin is overcome, death is robbed of its power" (Schmid, *TDNT* 3:668). Christ's death and resurrection signify that Christians are delivered from the fallen world under the tyranny of the triumvirate of sin, law, and death and await only the final manifestation of Christ, which will inaugurate their final transformation.

15:57–58 In 15:57–58, argument gives way to praise as Paul offers thanks to God (cf. Rom. 6:17; 7:25) for the victory won through Christ (1 Cor. 15:57) and the salvific benefits of the resurrection. The Corinthians would have been familiar with the songs of victory celebrating the feats of athletes at the Isthmian games. But Paul does not celebrate the victory of Christians over death (Moffatt 1938: 268). It is God's victory—but a victory in which all believers are graciously allowed to share. The present participle in "God, who gives [τῷ διδόντι, *tō didonti*] to us" reveals that Paul understands the victory over death to be certain because of the resurrection of Christ, who is now a "life-giving spirit" (15:45) and redeems us from sins (15:3). Christians will not be the most pitiable of human beings (15:19), because their hope is assured. But the present tense also indicates that Christians experience forgiveness of sins now and can celebrate this victory proleptically in their daily lives (cf. 2 Cor. 3:18).

Paul concludes this second stage of his argument on the resurrection with a moral word to the wise, just as he did the first stage in 1 Cor. 15:34. The affectionate address "my beloved brothers and sisters" reveals that he is not engaging in hot polemic. He has been teaching them. The exhortation consists of three parts. The first part, "be firm, immovable," interlocks with his opening admonition in 15:1–2. There, he reminds them about the gospel he preached to them, "in which you stand" and "through which you are being saved," with a significant proviso: "if you hold fast, unless you believed to no avail." They should not allow anything to knock them loose from the moorings of the testimony about Christ (15:3–5) that has been established among them (1:6; cf. Col. 1:23). If they lose their grip on the foundational truth that Christ was raised as the firstfruits of the dead and move away from it, they will have believed to no avail.

The second part, "abounding in the work of the Lord always," recalls his earlier language describing the Corinthians as the work of God because of the labors of God's servants (1 Cor. 3:5–15; 9:1; 15:10; cf. 16:10). The exhortation "to abound" or "to excel" (περισσεύειν, *perisseuein*) also appears in 14:12 and is connected to building up the church.[7] Putting these two pieces together may shed light on the meaning of the ambiguous phrase "abounding in the work of the Lord." It would be related to whatever contributes to building up the church.

The third part, "knowing that your labor is not in vain [κενός, *kenos*] in the Lord," recalls the statement in 15:14: "If Christ has not been raised, then our preaching is null and void [κενός] and your faith is null and void [κενός]." Paul connects the adjective κενός to his own labor in 15:10. "God's grace to me," he says, "was not in vain, because I labored harder than all of them." Convinced of the resurrection of the dead, the Corinthians also know that their labor for Christ (3:8; cf. 2 Cor. 6:5; 11:23, 27; 1 Thess. 1:3), which may lead them into life-threatening peril, is not in vain (cf. 1 Cor. 15:29–33). God will use it to give growth (3:6) and will give the laborer the due reward in the end (3:8). Until the end, the present is marked by struggle and labor. It is "an existence un-

---

7. The verb περισσεύειν pictures something flowing over the edges on all sides (Godet 1887: 448).

der the cross, sustained by the hope which is based on the resurrection of Jesus Christ" (Lorenzen 1995: 274). The reality of the future colors the reality of the present, which is why Paul uses the present tense, "your labor is not in vain," rather than the future tense, "your labor will not be in vain."

Additional Notes

15:51. The textual tradition preserves five readings for 15:51.

1. πάντες οὐ κοιμηθησόμεθα, πάντες δὲ ἀλλαγησόμεθα (B, D^c, K, Ψ, 075, 0243, 1881, syr^{p, h}, cop^{sa, bo}, Maj) surely is correct. Other readings appear to be attempts to correct perceived theological problems with this reading.

2. πάντες [μὲν] κοιμηθησόμεθα, οὐ πάντες δὲ ἀλλαγησόμεθα (ℵ, C, 0243*, 33, 1739) may be attributable to a scribe's recognizing that Paul and the Corinthians had already died and seeking to remove any hint of error by transferring the "not" from the first clause to the second to express that all humans will die, but not all will transformed as believers will be.

3. πάντες οὐ κοιμηθησόμεθα, οὐ πάντες δὲ ἀλλαγησόμεθα (𝔓⁴⁶, A^c, Origen) appears to conflate readings 1 and 2. A scribe either carelessly repeated the negative in the second clause (Barrett 1968: 380) or assumed that "change" could apply only to those who were alive at the time of the parousia.

4. οἱ πάντες μὲν κοιμηθησόμεθα, οἱ πάντες δὲ ἀλλαγησόμεθα (A*) removes the οὐ and replaces it with the οἱ in both clauses.

5. πάντες ἀναστησόμεθα, οὐ πάντες δὲ ἀλλαγησόμεθα (D*, Marcion, Tertullian, Ambrosiaster) introduces an extraneous issue: the fate of the unrighteous. It assumes that all will be raised in the last day, but the unrighteous will not be changed as the righteous will be.

In the best reading, πάντες οὐ κοιμηθησόμεθα does not mean that all will not die. Paul negates the verb even though it is the "all" that he intends to negate (cf. 2 Cor. 7:3; Edwards 1885: 452–53; Barrett 1968: 380). He transposes the negative particle to create a parallelism with the next clause (Robertson and Plummer 1914: 158; Schrage 2001: 370). He means that some Christians will be alive at the parousia.

15:54. The general rule that the shorter reading is to be preferred does not apply to the reading represented by 𝔓⁴⁶, ℵ*, 088, 0121, 0243, 1175, 1739*, 1852, 1912, 2200, which omits the clause "when this corruptible [body] puts on incorruptibility." The omission probably is attributable to a trick of the eye caused by the similar beginning or similar ending of both clauses. Apparently, this same type of visual error explains the omission of the entire verse in F, G, 6, 365, because of the similar ending in 15:53. Metzger (1994: 502–3) attributes the reading found in A, 326, cop^{sams}, arm, which reverses the order of the clauses, to an errant attempt to correct the oversight in manuscripts that omit the one clause: the missing clause was restored, but in the wrong order.

15:56. Why does Paul insert a short aside on death, sin, and the law into an argument about the resurrection of the dead in which the law has not figured at all? This is difficult to answer. Some suggest that 15:56 was an interpretive gloss that slipped into the text or was added by a later editor (Weiss 1910: 380; Moffatt 1938: 268; Horn 1991: 104–5; R. Horsley 1998: 215). Horn (1991) notes that this idea was first proposed in 1865 by J. W. Straatmann and reviews the subsequent history of research. Using various methodologies, Horn concludes that it could be a gloss. Without question, however, it expresses Paul's theology. Thielman (1992: 249) concludes, "Paul can make compressed statements about the law which have underneath them a coherent—albeit unexpressed—foundation." Weima (1990) challenges Räisänen's contention that Paul's treatment of the law and sin was muddleheaded, and understands the different passages as expressing one of three interrelated functions: (1) cognitive—the law reveals a person's true sinful condition (Rom. 3:20; 7:7; Gal. 3:19); (2) converting—the law transforms sin into more clearly defined and serious acts of transgression (Rom. 5:13; 4:15); and (3) causative—the law provokes or stimulates sin (Rom. 7:5, 8–11; 5:20; 1 Cor. 15:56). Fee (1987: 806) concludes that this statement on death, sin, and the law expresses matters theologically essential to Paul apart from the Judaizing controversy that forced him to discuss them in a more thoroughgoing way in Galatians and Romans. Hollander and Holleman (1993) contend that the connections between death and sin and between sin and law should be understood against the background of popular Hellenistic notions of the degeneration of humanity and the Cynic view that regarded laws as a contributing factor to that degeneration. This view sheds more light on how such a declaration could have been understood by Paul's auditors than it does on where he derived the idea or why he included it here (see Wolff 1996: 419 n. 421).

XI. Instructions for the Collection and Travel Itineraries (16:1–12)

Paul's next-to-last section contains obscure instructions that remind us that this letter was written to specific people (Hays 1997: 283). Paul appears to be responding to the Corinthians' questions about how to organize the offering for the saints in Jerusalem. He offers no explanation about why this collection is necessary or what significance he attaches to it. A long motivational speech encouraging them to follow through with their original zeal for the collection appears in 2 Cor. 8–9. Here, he takes that zeal for granted.

He also outlines his tentative travel plans. This issue will also emerge as a problem that he must address in 2 Corinthians, because his plans appear to have gone awry, and he changed them. In the later letter, he defends himself against apparent charges that he makes his plans willy-nilly and does not follow through. Here, he briefly mentions mission opportunities and many adversaries—perhaps an ominous foreshadowing of the extreme hardships that brought him what he thought was the sentence of death. He writes about this experience with relief in 2 Cor. 1:8–11.

Two brief notices about Timothy and Apollos conclude this section. Timothy will be visiting them soon before returning to Paul; Apollos will not. The story behind the text regarding both of these men is murky and offers material for imaginative yarn-spinning but little hard data.

The unit may be outlined as follows:

1. Instructions for the collection for the saints (16:1–4)
2. Paul's travel itinerary (16:5–9)
3. Notice about Timothy (16:10–11)
4. Notice about Apollos (16:12)

Exegesis and Exposition

[1]Now concerning the collection, which is for the saints: As I directed the churches of Galatia, so you also should do. [2]On the first day of every week, let each one of you set aside [money] individually to save up whatever he or she has been prospered, so that no collections might take place when I come. [3]As soon as I arrive, whomever you have approved, I will send these persons with

letters to carry your gift to Jerusalem. ⁴If it is advisable that I should go also, they will go with me.

⁵I will come to you after I pass through Macedonia—for I intend to pass through Macedonia—⁶and perhaps I will stay with you awhile or even spend the winter in order that you can send me on my way wherever I go next. ⁷For I do not want to see you just in passing, for I hope to remain with you for some time, if the Lord permits. ⁸I will remain in Ephesus until Pentecost, ⁹for a wide and effective door stands opened to me, and there are many adversaries.

¹⁰Now when Timothy arrives, see that he be fearless among you, for he is doing the work of the Lord just as I am. ¹¹Therefore, let no one disdain him. Send him on his way in peace in order that he might come to me; for I expect him along with the brothers.

¹²Now concerning Apollos, our brother: I have urged him strongly to come to you with the brothers, and it was simply not the will that he come now. He will come when a good opportunity presents itself.

For the sixth time in the letter Paul introduces a new section with the phrase περὶ δέ (*peri de*; 7:1, 25; 8:1, [4]; 12:1; cf. 16:12), here followed by the subject τῆς λογείας τῆς εἰς τοὺς ἁγίους (*tēs logeias tēs eis tous hagious*, the collection that is for the saints). If the pattern holds true from the other occurrences of περὶ δέ in the letter, this transition suggests that he is responding to another issue raised by the Corinthians in their letter to him. But what was their question? Did they get wind of the collection that Paul was organizing among the Galatian churches and ask to play a part so that they too could become benefactors (Barrett 1968: 385; Witherington 1995: 313)? Or had Paul previously solicited them to participate, and they only inquired about the best way to make this collection? The latter is more likely for four reasons.

16:1

1. The word λογ(ε)ία is used in the papyri for financial contributions (Deissmann 1903: 142–44; 1911: 104–5; MM 377) and especially for engaging in a collection for sacred purposes (BDAG 597; cf. Kittel, *TDNT* 4:282). Paul never uses this word in any other discussion of this "collection," which makes it conceivable that he picks up the Corinthians' language from their letter (see additional note).[1] Since he gives instructions only for "the actual 'collecting' of the money" (Fee 1987: 812), they appear to have asked him how they should manage its implementation.[2]

2. Paul does not identify the intended recipients except as "the saints." The Corinthians are also saints "with all those who in every

---

1. Kittel (*TDNT* 4:282–83) argues that the choice of the word has no relation to any imposed tax but refers to a gift being gathered (see Thiselton 2000: 1318). For Paul, the λογ(ε)ία is a εὐλογία (*eulogia*, blessing, generous gift [2 Cor. 9:5]).

2. Conzelmann (1975: 296; see also Schrage 2001: 429) thinks that these instructions suggest that the early Christians did not have an "organized system of finance." On the other hand, they may have given in a more or less organized fashion and wanted clarification only on how to handle this special offering.

place call upon the name of the Lord" (1:2; cf. 6:1–2). Only in 16:3 does he mention that the fund will be delivered to Jerusalem. He says nothing of the recipients' poverty (cf. 2 Cor. 9:12), their persecution (1 Thess. 2:14), or the Corinthians' indebtedness to the mother church (Rom. 15:27), which suggests that he has informed them previously of the plight of the Jewish Christians in Jerusalem.

3. For Paul, the collection is far more than a relief offering, but he does not explain anything about its objective—what implications this project has for his ministry or why the Corinthians should be involved. Consequently, discussions about its purpose belong more properly to commentaries on 2 Cor. 8–9 (see Garland 1999: 386–90) and Rom. 15:25–32 (see T. Schreiner 1998: 776–78). We know that the "pillar apostles" asked him to remember the poor and that he was eager to do so before being asked (Gal. 2:10), but he says nothing about that here. We know from 2 Corinthians and Romans that he hoped that the gift would cement the bond between the Gentile and the Jewish Christian communities and that it would demonstrate that Christian unity transcended ethnic barriers and did not require Gentile Christians to become Jewish proselytes. He also insists in those letters that Gentile churches should not forget their roots or the privation of their Jewish brothers and sisters. Since he evinces no need to explain the purpose of the collection here, presumably the Corinthians already have learned of its nature from him and not from hearsay.

4. Jewish piety mandated generosity toward the poor out of compassion for their plight and obedience to God's commands. Generally, in Greco-Roman society, charity toward strangers was not regarded as a virtuous act or as something to be divinely rewarded (Peterman 1997: 156). Giving to others displayed one's personal virtue and social power, not one's compassion. Saller (1982: 126) states, "The most basic premise from which the Romans started was that honour and prestige derived from the power to give to others what they needed or wanted." Peterman (1997: 149) notes, "In the Greco-Roman world the only non-material return that givers could expect would be the honour the receiver(s) pay to the giver." Peterman points to the convictions of Aristotle (*Eth. nic.* 8.14.2), "Honor is the due reward for virtue and beneficence," and Plutarch (*Mor.* 808D), "Rulers should show philanthropy to their friends and the friends should shower them with love and honor." Charitable works normally were done to bring praise to oneself. Those who were poor and socially inferior and could not repay benefits in some material way could repay only by giving honor to the benefactor. In this cultural context, people gave to others who were capable of giving them something in return, either through repayment in kind or through the bestowal of honor by lauding them publicly. This worldview assumes that it is most blessed to receive honor from others, and that is what moti-

vated giving. By contrast, Paul expects the Corinthians to do good works for people they have never met so as to bring praise to God and not to themselves. But he says nothing here about how their generosity will redound to God's praise, or how God will reward them, or how the saints will give thanks for them. One must assume either that the Gentile Corinthians are unusually altruistic or that he has previously convinced them to contribute.

Paul has directed the Galatians on how to carry out the collection, and here he instructs the Corinthians to follow the same routine. He refers to the Roman province of Galatia and the churches founded during his first missionary journey, described in Acts 13–14 (Antioch of Pisidia, Iconium, Lystra, and Derbe). Their mention may be intended to suggest how many others are involved in the enterprise (Robertson and Plummer 1914: 384) and how their examples (cf. 1 Cor. 9:14; 11:16; 14:33b) should be followed (R. Collins 1999: 588). Paul does not mention the Macedonians, probably because he had not asked them to contribute; they became involved only after pleading with him to be allowed to contribute to the project (2 Cor. 8:4).[3] The verb διατάσσειν (*diatassein*) can mean "command," "make arrangements," "direct" (see 1 Cor. 7:17). According to R. Collins (1999: 588), Paul ordered them: "the verb connotes authority." However, Paul is not issuing orders, but only making arrangements that will help the process.

Fee (1987: 817) finds Paul's matter-of-fact discussion of how to manage the collecting of the money to be noteworthy: "No pressure, no gimmicks, no emotion. A need had to be met, and the Corinthians were capable of playing a role in it." Soards (1999: 357) and Talbert (1987: 105) identify principles that undergird Paul's instructions for the collection. It is to be done regularly ("on the first day of every week"), universally ("let each one of you"), systematically ("set aside," "save up"), proportionately ("as one has been prospered"), and freely ("so that no collections might take place when I come"). **16:2**

1. On the "the first day of the week" (κατὰ μίαν σαββάτου, *kata mian sabbatou*) refers to the Christians' day of worship in commemoration of the resurrection.[4] Paul appears to avoid the heathen term "Sunday." On the "first day" Christians gather for the breaking of bread to honor the Lord (Acts 20:7) and to remember the sacrifice of their Lord. Paul would have them also remember the poor among the saints, and regularly setting a portion aside each week makes it easier to give a larger amount.

---

3. Paul does not say that the Macedonians *also* (i.e., along with the Corinthians) pleaded to become involved, which argues against the view that the Corinthians had volunteered to join the project.

4. Here Paul uses the Greek cardinal number instead of the ordinal (see BDF §247). "Sabbath . . . lent its name to the whole week . . . and every day is named in reference to the day which consecrated all" (Edwards 1885: 463).

2. Fee (1987: 813) claims that the phrase παρ᾿ ἑαυτῷ (*par heautō*, by himself) means "at home" and suggests that each person stores up his or her own money privately. Llewelyn (2001: 209) argues that it means "individually." Paul does not expect offering plates to be passed in church or for the collection to be kept in a central fund. He fully expects every member to take part in the project, which differs significantly from the picture that Justin Martyr (*1 Apol.* 67) gives of collections in the church: each well-to-do member deposits what he thinks fit with the presiding minister. Chow (1992: 185–86) notes Paul's concern throughout the letter to build up horizontal relationships among the Corinthians and thinks that his expectation that everyone will take part in this project on a voluntary basis fosters this goal. If a few patrons were to give all the money, they would gain all the honor and divide the "haves" from the "have-nots" even more. If free artisans, small traders, and slaves also give, then the gift will represent the entire body, not just a few wealthy donors. The storing up (θησαυρίζων, *thēsaurizōn*) is understood in a positive sense as the purpose of setting aside the money. Since they are saving money for others, this hoard will be come a heavenly treasure (Matt. 6:19–21; Luke 12:21; Robertson and Plummer 1914: 384).

3. Paul is not soliciting a tithe but is asking all to give as they are able (cf. 2 Cor. 8:11–12). This collection is not an oppressive dunning of the churches and, unlike the temple tax (Matt. 17:24–27), does not require rich and poor alike to give the same amount. The verb "prosper" can be read as a present passive subjunctive, εὐοδῶται (*euodōtai*), a perfect passive indicative (εὐόδωται), or a very rare perfect middle subjunctive (εὐοδῶται); most texts choose the first option. The word originally was related to a prosperous journey, but then it came to have a more general meaning connoting success in something. Rather than translating the verb in an active sense, "save up whatever profit he makes" (Barrett 1968: 387), we should retain the passive voice. It reminds the givers that God is the one who prospers them. This phrase does not refer to "income," as the NIV has it, but to "whatever success or prosperity may have come their way this week" (Fee 1987: 814). Since many lived at subsistence levels, their gift is to come out of their surplus (Witherington 1995: 315 n. 7). Paul asks them to give out of their abundance, not sacrificially (contrast the giving of the Macedonians in 2 Cor. 8:2–3). It might be less than a tithe; it might be far more than a tithe.

4. Several reasons may lie behind Paul's wish that no collections take place after he arrives. His use of the noun "grace" in 1 Cor. 16:3 to describe the gift suggests that he considers it to be a freewill offering that is a response to God's grace in their lives. By taking up the collection in advance, they are completely free in what they give, and he will not know who contributed what. Possibly, he wanted to avoid being per-

ceived as twisting arms to get money by asking in person (cf. 2 Cor. 9:5), or he did not want to take time from other labors to try to raise money (Barrett 1968: 387). Since he intended to spend the winter with the Corinthians, he may have "anticipated sending the delegation (v. 3) to Jerusalem almost immediately upon his arrival in Corinth" (R. Collins 1999: 589) in the late summer or in early autumn. In addition, he may fear that the sum would be meager if collected belatedly, and he wishes to avoid a last-minute scraping for funds (Thiselton 2000: 1325). He has no desire "to go round begging" (Robertson and Plummer 1914: 385). He also may be sensitive to possible accusations of chicanery (cf. 2 Cor. 8:20; 12:14–18). He may have been aware of an event that made a collection of money for Jerusalem a touchy issue. Josephus (*Ant.* 18.3.5 §81) reports that a Palestinian Jew and three cohorts induced one of their notable Roman converts, Fulvia, to send valuables for the temple in Jerusalem. Rather than conveying the goods to Jerusalem, they absconded with them. When their scam was discovered, it created such a clamor that the emperor Tiberius ordered all Jews to be banished from Rome.

The clause "as soon as I arrive" marks the third reference to Paul's coming to Corinth (cf. 4:19; 11:34).[5] Paul's sense of preeminence emerges in his wording: "I will send them" and "they will go with me." It is his special project, but he does not infringe on the church's autonomy in choosing their representatives. As each individual decides how much to give, the church decides whom they will entrust to represent them in this mission (cf. 2 Cor. 8:19). The "letters" accompanying them may be written by Paul ("I will give letters of introduction to persons approved by you," NEB) or by the Corinthians ("I will send those whom you accredit by letter," RSV). The latter option seems less likely. Why would Paul require the Corinthians to accredit with letters those whom they chose? Why would they write the letter to Jerusalem when it is Paul who has the relationship, however tenuous, with the apostles there? Paul is the one who will provide the letters of commendation (cf. Acts 15:23–29; Rom. 16:1–2; 1 Cor. 16:10–11; 2 Cor. 3:1–3; 8:16–24), and the phrase "with letters" is placed before the verb "I will send" for emphasis. If he is the author of the letters, this detail indicates that at this time he does not yet intend to go with the emissaries and believes that his letters of commendation would be well received in Jerusalem.

16:3–4

The phrase ἐὰν δὲ ἄξιον ᾖ (*ean de axion ē*) reveals Paul's current uncertainty about traveling with the emissaries. Many interpret the word "worthy" (cf. 2 Thess. 1:3) to refer to the amount collected. Robertson and Plummer (1914: 387) comment, "He could not abandon other work

---

5. The aorist subjunctive (ὅταν . . . παραγένωμαι, *hotan . . . paragenōmai*) reflects anticipation (Conzelmann 1975: 296 n. 24).

in order to present a paltry sum; and an Apostle could not take the lead in so unworthy a mission."[6] If he implies, "I will not go if you are stingy and do not raise a suitable amount of money," would it not rankle the Corinthians? Why would a paltry sum not scuttle the whole mission, since it would be an insult that might only worsen the fracture between Jewish and Gentile Christians? Would it be any less embarrassing if a negligible amount were delivered by only the delegates from the Gentile churches? Although Paul may well be concerned that the amount of the gift accord with the abundance of blessings they have received from the gospel, other factors will determine whether or not he should go to Jerusalem. It is best to translate ἄξιον as "advisable." It reflects "his own concerns about his ministry in the West and perhaps his reception in Jerusalem" (Fee 1987: 816). Soards (1999: 358) sagely comments that "advisability" has nothing to with "prudence." The evidence from Rom. 15:30–32; Acts 20:22–24; and 21:10–13 suggests that it was extremely imprudent for Paul to go to Jerusalem, but something developed that compelled him to go.

Personal representation from the Gentile churches makes the gesture of unity concrete. By sending messengers from Gentile churches to Jerusalem, he devises a strategy whereby Gentile converts from across the world will come face-to-face with Jewish Christians in the mother church. It is similar to his gambit to bring along Titus to the first conference in Jerusalem to confront head-on the Jew/Gentile issue (Gal. 2:1–5). Titus's presence was intentionally provocative, designed to prompt a positive decision from the Jerusalem apostles about their acceptance of uncircumcised Gentile believers. In the same manner, the tangible evidence of the faith of Gentiles and their gratitude represented by the collection probably was intended by Paul to provoke the acceptance of Gentile believers by the Jerusalem saints. He hopes that the gift will alleviate their suffering, but also that it will drive home the point that in Christ there is neither Jew nor Greek.

If a large amount were collected, a larger number of couriers would be required to transport it. The security of the funds would have been a major issue, and Paul assumes that there is safety in numbers. He could not hire an armored chariot to transfer the funds! Murphy-O'Connor (1996: 345–46) notes that the money would have to be converted to the smallest volume to transport it. Pack animals would have invited the unwanted attention of bandits who controlled the countryside in many areas. More inconspicuous means would have been chosen to convey the money. Murphy-O'Connor imagines that the couriers would carry the funds in a money belt or in a bag suspended from the neck and also

6. So also Godet 1887: 457; Findlay 1910: 946; Parry 1926: 246; Moffatt 1938: 272; Lietzmann 1949: 88; Morris 1958: 239; Blomberg 1994: 325; Wolff 1996: 430; Schrage 2001: 432.

would have sewed gold coins into their garments in such a way that they would not clink or misshape the clothing.

Paul promises to come to the Corinthians after he passes through Macedonia, the Roman province that includes the cities of Philippi, Thessalonica, and Berea. He will "pass through" (διέρχεσθαι, *dierchesthai*) Macedonia, but he hopes to "remain" (παραμένειν, *paramenein*) in Corinth (see additional note). Our modern, compressed sense of time, however, should not limit the span of "passing through" to an overnight stay (cf. the use of the verb in Acts 8:4, 40; 11:19; 13:6, 14; 14:24; 15:3, 41; 16:6; 18:23, 27; 19:1, 21; 2 Cor. 1:16). It simply implies that he will not linger in Macedonia for an extensive visit. Corinth was an important seaport, but Paul makes clear that he does not regard the congregation there as merely a convenient stopover while in transit to somewhere else.[7] "With you" is placed before the verb "to stay" for emphasis. The τυχόν (*tychon*, perhaps) may not reflect uncertainty about his future plans so much as a polite desire "not to seem to be forcing himself upon them" (Parry 1926: 247). If he is there when winter sets in, he will stay with them because sea travel essentially shut down in mid-September (Pliny the Elder, *Naturalis historia* [*Natural History*] 2.47)—not only because of the hazard of storms, but also because overcast skies and longer nights made navigation uncertain (Riesner 1998: 308). We learn from 2 Corinthians that these initial plans changed, and he made an emergency voyage to Corinth that proved to be disastrous and disheartening. A nasty confrontation with an unknown individual caused him to beat a hasty retreat and to fire off the letter of tears (2 Cor. 2:1–4). But he appears to have followed the route proposed here at a later date when he traveled to Macedonia and then to Corinth (2 Cor. 2:12–13; 7:5; 8:1; 9:4; Acts 19:21; 20:1–3; see also Rom. 15:26; 16:1).

16:5–9

The emerging problems at Corinth dictate that he remain with them for a longer period to help correct them, but he politely states that the purpose behind a protracted stay is that they can send him on his way wherever he ventures next. The verb προπέμπειν (*propempein*) is used in the NT for sending departing travelers on their way and can entail providing them with all the resources—such as money, supplies, and companions—necessary for the journey (see 2 Cor. 1:16; see also Acts 15:3; Rom. 15:24; Titus 3:13; 3 John 6; 1 Macc. 12:4). Although Paul did not receive support from a congregation while he was working among them, he did allow them to equip him for his travel to his next mission point.

---

7. The phrase ἄρτι ἐν παρόδῳ (*arti en parodō*) literally means "now in a passage" and is best translated idiomatically as "just in passing." It does not allude to an earlier short visit.

Paul qualifies his plans with an important proviso: "if the Lord permits" (cf. James 4:15; Acts 18:21; Heb. 6:3; Josephus, *Ant.* 20.11.2 §267). The Lord's will directs his plans (cf. 1 Cor. 4:19; Rom. 1:10; 15:32). This condition should have forestalled any criticism that he makes his plans capriciously, but apparently it did not (see 2 Cor. 1:17).

Paul states his present intention to stay in Ephesus until Pentecost. The reference to Pentecost indicates that he assumes his readers' knowledge of the Jewish calendar, but it does not narrow down the exact time when this letter was written. "Pentecost" is the Greek name applied to the Feast of Weeks, the forty-nine days after Passover (cf. Lev. 23:15; Deut. 16:9; see also Acts 20:16; Tob. 2:1; 2 Macc. 12:31–32; Josephus, *J.W.* 6.5.3 §299; Philo, *Decal.* 30 §160; *Spec. Laws* 2.30 §176), and it applies to its closing on the fiftieth day (Josephus, *Ant.* 3.10.6 §252). "Pentecost" is probably a reference to a season (much like modern "Christmas") rather than to the actual feast, and its "significance as a season may lie at least in part in that it is a favorable time for travel" (Thiselton 2000: 1329–30). This note means that Paul intends to start his travels when summer arrives. An "open door" that presents itself impels him to stay in Ephesus until then.

The "open door" image refers to receptivity to Paul's preaching (cf. 2 Cor. 2:12; Col. 4:3; Acts 14:27), which explains how the seemingly odd adjective "effective" (ἐνεργής, *energēs*, actively at work) is added to the adjective "great" (μεγάλη, *megalē*, wide) to describe the door (a great and effective door). The gospel always meets with resistance because it topples all persons from their thrones, great and small (Phil. 1:28; 1 Thess. 2:2), and it is no surprise that many adversaries rise up in resistance (cf. 1 Cor. 15:32). Paul may be experiencing resistance that later will erupt into the uproar sparked by the artisans of the silver shrines of Artemis because of the sharp drop-off in their business (Acts 19:23–20:1). Hostility, however, is no hindrance to the spread of the gospel (Phil. 1:12–14): "Evangelism flourishes under fierce opposition" (Findlay 1910: 948).

16:10–11 Paul mentioned Timothy's trip to Corinth in 1 Cor. 4:17 and now refers to it again. He uses ἐάν (*ean*), which could produce the translation "if he comes," but he is not expressing doubt about Timothy's showing up. The ἐάν is close to ὅταν (*hotan*; 16:3, 5) and means "whenever he comes" (Moulton and Turner 1963: 114; Conzelmann 1975: 297; Fee 1987: 821; Lindemann 2000: 380). The vagaries of travel in the ancient world may have caused Paul to express himself in this way, since he cannot predict the timing of his arrival (Fee 1987: 821). Belleville (1987: 32) points to Paul's normal language expressing contingency to refer to his travel plans ("I hope" [Rom. 15:24; Phil. 2:19, 23; 1 Tim. 3:14; Philem. 22]; "if the Lord permits" [1 Cor. 16:7]; "I trust in the Lord that" [Phil. 2:24]; "if the Lord wills"

[1 Cor. 4:19]).[8] Paul specifies the purpose of Timothy's visit in 4:17–21: he is to remind them of Paul's ways in Christ Jesus, which he teaches in every church. In 16:10–11, he focuses on how Timothy should be received and issues three directives: "see to it," "let no one disdain him," and "send him on his way (with provisions) in peace."

The clause ἀφόβως γένηται πρὸς ὑμᾶς (aphobōs genētai pros hymas, [that] he be fearless among you) could refer to Timothy's coming in fear or, more likely, to his state subsequent to his arrival (cf. ἐγενόμην πρὸς ὑμᾶς, egenomēn pros hymas, I was among you [2:3]). What circumstances would cause Timothy to fear?

1. Many assume that it refers to the possibility of a negative reception by the Corinthians. Barrett (1968: 391) notes that the Corinthians could be "a very unpleasant and threatening society" (citing 2 Cor. 10:10; 11:6, 7, 29; 12:11, 16, 21), and Paul speaks forthrightly about their arrogance in 1 Cor. 4:18–19 in connection with Timothy's commission to represent him. Fee (1987: 821–22) contends that Paul worries that the community's negative sentiment toward him would spill over to Timothy. He will become "a victim of transference" (R. Collins 1999: 596). People in this society conventionally expressed their enmity toward others by mistreating their associates. But if their contempt is directed toward Paul, how would the assurance that Timothy is engaged in the very same work diminish that contempt?

2. It is possible that Timothy had a previous awkward encounter with the Corinthians (R. Collins 1999: 595). But why would Paul not recall such an incident and warn them not to let it happen again?

3. Some suggest that Timothy's youth (1 Tim. 4:12) or his timid disposition may be a factor (Morris 1958: 241–42; note the rendering of the RSV, "see that you put him at ease among you"). Paul's statements in 2 Tim. 1:7; 2:1; and 2:3 have been mirror-read to infer that Timothy was shy, cowardly, or reticent. Hutson (1997: 58–59) refutes attempts to develop a psychological profile of Timothy from the merest scraps of evidence and "to read this profile into everything that is said about him." Hutson shows that the presumption that Timothy was timid is baseless. Nothing in Paul's letters or in Acts reflects negatively on Timothy's temperament or suggests that he was "anything but a strong, dependable, and self-sacrificing evangelist" (Hutson 1997: 65). Hutson (1997: 64) argues convincingly that βλέπετε (blepete, see to it) in 16:10, in conjunction with the commands γρηγορεῖτε (grēgoreite, watch) and στήκετε (stēkete, stand firm) in 16:13, "is not an exhortation for the Corinthians to 'look after' sensitive, inexperienced Timothy; rather, it is an admonition for them to 'recognize' the coming of an agent of the Lord." Paul

8. The statements regarding Timothy's arrival in 4:17 and 16:10 do not contradict one another and should not be interpreted as indications that they originally belonged to separate letters.

does not fear that they will not take seriously this young "greenhorn," but rather warns that they will incur God's judgment for failing to heed the Lord's agent.

4. Barrett's (1968: 391) conclusion, "We are bound simply to admit our ignorance," may be the safest course rather than spinning theories from gossamer-thin evidence. Hutson (1997: 65), however, offers a new twist by claiming that Paul emphasizes Timothy's fearlessness. Hutson renders 16:10 as "If Timothy comes, recognize that he is fearless toward you; for he is doing the work of the Lord, as I am."[9] This interpretation may be correct, since the adverb ἀφόβως (aphobōs) appears in Phil. 1:14 to describe the preaching of the word without fear. The verb ἐξουθενεῖν (exouthenein, disdain, despise) belongs to the rhetoric of status in 1 Cor. 1:28 and 6:4 (cf. Rom. 14:3, 10), but in 2 Cor. 10:10 and 1 Thess. 5:20, it is used for holding in contempt what is preached (cf. Gal. 4:14). The key phrase, then, is the reminder that Timothy is engaged in the same work of the Lord that Paul is doing (cf. 1 Cor. 9:1; 15:58; Rom. 14:20; 16:3; 2 Cor. 6:1; Gal. 4:11; Phil. 1:22; 2:22, 30; 4:3). That work requires spiritual fortitude, which the Corinthians themselves cannot instill in Timothy. It comes instead from a reliance on God's power (2 Tim. 1:8), and Paul is unlikely to send an envoy who lacks this fortitude on important missions. That work, which may include rebuking and admonishing others, must be recognized by them lest they harm themselves (see Chrysostom, *Hom. 1 Cor.* 44.1) because he speaks God's word to them.

Who delivers this letter to the Corinthians is unclear. It may be Timothy, or it may be Stephanas, Fortunatus, and Achaicus (16:17–18). If the latter carry it, which is the more likely option, then their sea voyage will bring them to Corinth ahead of Timothy, who is wending his way through Macedonia. In either case, Paul expects this letter to be in their hands when Timothy arrives. Their reception of him will reflect on how they receive and respond to Paul's rebukes and guidance in this letter. Hays (1997: 287) understands that this letter could serve only to heighten the tension for Timothy: "He has sternly castigated powerful members of the church and called for basic changes in their behavior, including their sex lives, social contacts, forms of worship, and legal dealings." M. Mitchell (1993: 293) points out that "one shows one's acceptance of the message of a letter by the way in which one treats the sender's envoy." Paul stresses Timothy's authority as his envoy (Hutson 1997: 62 n. 18) and his authority as one who does the Lord's work ("an agent of the Lord" [Hutson 1997: 63]). To command, "Let no one disdain him,"

---

9. Hutson (1997: 62) suggests that the ἵνα (hina) after βλέπετε may reflect the tendency in Koine Greek to use it in place of the epexegetical infinitive or of ὅτι (hoti, that; cf. Robertson 1934: 993).

is to say that no one should disdain the message he brings from Paul or how he interprets what Paul means in this letter.

"Sending him on in peace" is a traditional formula (see Exod. 4:18; 1 Sam. 20:42; 2 Kings 5:19; Acts 15:33; 16:36; James 2:16; 1 Clem. 65:1), and it does not refer to a reconciliation between Paul and the community. If anything, it refers to a reconciliation among themselves. Most commentators concentrate on the supposed conflict between Paul and the community and ignore the actual conflict that has arisen among the members of the community themselves, which is the central concern of this letter. Timothy has the role of a reconciler in the community, and intervening in altercations can be a dangerous job.

Are "the brothers" traveling with Timothy, or are they waiting with Paul? In Acts 19:22, only Erastus is mentioned as traveling with Timothy. But it was too dangerous to travel alone, and Timothy may have been traveling with more than one companion. On the other hand, "the brothers" may be the same people mentioned in 1 Cor. 16:12 and the three Corinthians mentioned in 16:17. The text is unclear as to who is meant, but it likely refers to the companions of Timothy. Also unclear is where Paul expects to receive Timothy—in Ephesus or somewhere else.

The final περὶ δέ (peri de) clause in this letter is also thought to be a response to an item in the Corinthians' letter. Against M. Mitchell (1989; see also Furnish 1999: 14 n. 25), who thinks that the phrase simply marks the next topic to be addressed, Ker (2000: 94 n. 71) contends that Paul would have no reason to raise the issue of Apollos's return had not the Corinthians raised it themselves (so also Fee 1987: 824). Ker (2000: 94) conjectures that they have asked that Apollos visit them again and considers it significant that Paul postpones dealing with this request until the end of the letter, with a fleeting rebuff. Ker thinks that the return of Apollos ranks high on their agenda, but "Paul takes the whole of his letter to outline his own theological position, and makes his plans to visit clear, before replying." Many assume that the Corinthians "were enamored with the rhetoric of Apollos and wanted him back" (Witherington 1995: 313).

16:12

If Apollos was so prominent in the minds of the Corinthians and semi-independent of Paul, one wonders, why did they not write directly to Apollos instead of to Paul? It may be the case that they made no inquiry about Apollos in their letter, and Paul simply anticipates their disappointment that Apollos had not returned and averts any suspicion that somehow he had prevented him from returning (Calvin 1960: 354; cf. Schrage 2001: 446). The περὶ δέ clause would simply introduce the shift to this final topic in the letter and need not be a reference to something they wrote (M. Mitchell 1989).

Ker (2000: 95) also claims that the description of Apollos as "the brother," when compared to the description of the household of

Stephanas in 16:15–17, comes off as rather "stark." But Paul uses the appellation "the brother" following the proper name to refer to Sosthenes (1:1), Timothy (2 Cor. 1:1; Col. 1:1; Philem. 1), and Titus (2 Cor. 2:13). There is nothing stark about the designation "the brother," since Paul also uses it twice in the immediate context (1 Cor. 16:11, 12) and refers to Timothy without *any* designation.

Apollos appears to be independent of Paul, but Paul affirms that he has urged Apollos to return to Corinth. Πολλά (*polla*) used adverbially could mean "many times," "repeatedly" (R. Collins 1999: 598), but it is more likely in the context to mean "strongly" or "earnestly" (Thiselton 2000: 1333; cf. 16:19). Since no adjective modifies the noun "will" (contrast 7:37), it is unclear whose "will" prevents Apollos from returning.[10] Most ancient commentators assume that it refers to God's will (Schrage 2001: 446), and some modern interpreters regard it as "a reverential, absolute use of the term" (Moffatt 1938: 275; cf. Rom. 2:18; Matt. 18:14; 1 Macc. 3:60).[11] If this view is correct, the Corinthians must bow to God's will in this matter. Others argue that the context requires that it must refer to the will of Apollos because he is the subject of the final clause.[12] Paul may be deliberately ambiguous to avoid hurting feelings.

There is no lack of guesses as to why Apollos cannot go back to Corinth at this time. Witherington (1995: 87, 317) claims that he realized that he was "the unwilling catalyst" of some of the difficulties and feared exacerbating the division—adding "fuel to the fire of Corinthian party spirit" (cf. Thiselton 2000: 33). Godet (1887: 463) claims that he was disgusted that some had used him as a rallying point in the factions, and Robertson and Plummer (1914: 393) confidently assert that he will not come "while there is an Apollos party in opposition to the Apostle." Moffatt (1938: 275) surmises that he may not have wished to abandon Paul in the moment of evangelistic opportunity and trial. The reasons why he did not come remain unknown, but we need not assume with Ker (2000: 96) that Paul offers no clear explanation as part of a stratagem to heighten their disappointment and to redirect their criticism from himself to Apollos.

The statement that Apollos will come when he has opportunity is vague, but this promise should not be characterized as an "unhelpful fudge" (contra Ker 2000: 96). The bottom line is this: Apollos is unlikely to return in the near future. Paul does not add any greeting from Apollos and does not mention him in 2 Corinthians. Since there is so little evidence to go on, caution is advised before giving free rein to the imagination.

10. Πάντως (*pantōs*) means "at all," "simply."
11. So also Weiss 1910: 385; Schrenk, *TDNT* 3:59; Héring 1962: 185; Barrett 1968: 391; Bruce 1971: 160.
12. Godet 1887: 463; Robertson and Plummer 1914: 392; Parry 1926: 248; Fee 1987: 824; R. Collins 1999: 598; Ker 2000: 95–96; Lindemann 2000: 382; Schrage 2001: 447.

Additional Notes

16:1. Elsewhere, Paul couches references to the gift for the saints in Jerusalem in theological language to portray it as something far more than simply a collection of money:

χάρις (grace; 1 Cor. 16:3; 2 Cor. 8:4, 6, 7, 19; 9:14)

κοινωνία (partnership, sharing; 2 Cor. 8:4; Rom. 15:26)

διακονία (service; 2 Cor. 8:4; 9:1, 12, 13; Rom. 15:31)

σπουδή (earnestness; 2 Cor. 8:8)

ἀγάπη (love; 2 Cor. 8:7, 8, 24)

προθυμία (willingness; 2 Cor. 8:11, 12, 19; 9:2)

ἁπλότης (generosity; 2 Cor. 8:2; 9:11, 13)

περίσσευμα (abundance; 2 Cor. 8:14)

ἁδρότης (liberal gift; 2 Cor. 8:20)

ὑπόστασις (undertaking; 2 Cor. 9:4)

εὐλογία (blessing; 2 Cor. 9:5)

ἔργον ἀγαθόν (good work; 2 Cor. 9:8)

τὰ γενήματα τῆς δικαιοσύνης ὑμῶν (the yield of your righteousness; 2 Cor. 9:10)

λειτουργία (service; 2 Cor. 9:12)

16:4. The collection in Corinth stalls after a good beginning, and in 2 Cor. 8–9 Paul must coax the Corinthians to revive their zeal for it. No mention is made of any representatives from Achaia in the list of Paul's travel companions to Jerusalem in Acts 20:4. No mention is made of Galatia in Rom. 15:26. Both passages are only a partial listing of the participants (Fee 1987: 815 n. 34; cf. Schrage 2001: 431).

16.5. The use of the present tense διέρχομαι does not mean that Paul is currently passing through Macedonia and writing "from Philippi," as surmised in the letter's postscript found in D², 075, 1739, 1881, and Maj. Instead, it expresses his firm intention for the future (Barrett 1968: 389).

XII. Letter Closing (16:13–24)

The letter closing consists of 16:13–24. Eriksson (1998: 284, 289) thinks that it gives important clues to the purpose of the whole letter and "recapitulates the main points of the argumentation." But those who argue that the closing highlights the central concerns of the letter tend to read those central concerns into what Paul actually says. This section is most susceptible to interpretive abuse because it does not contain a sustained argument but a smattering of different exhortations and greetings. They can become like a Rorschach test—interpreters see what they want to see, namely, confirmations of what they have predetermined to be key emphases in the letter. Hays (1997: 289) alone spots the close parallel between 16:13 and 16:22 with Ps. 31:23–24:

> Love the LORD, all you his saints.
>> The LORD preserves the faithful,
>> but abundantly repays the one who acts haughtily.
> Be strong, and let your heart take courage,
>> all you who wait for the LORD. (NRSV)

The scriptural echo may be only coincidental, but if not, it brackets the closing before the final greeting. Those who hear the echo may recognize that "strength and courage are rooted in love for God and set in opposition to boasting and arrogance" (Hays 1997: 289). It is clearer how "love" frames this letter's closing: "Let all things you do be done in love" (16:14); "My love be with all you in Christ Jesus" (16:24). Love is the remedy for many of the ills that afflict the Corinthian church community, and Paul makes clear that his many remonstrances throughout the letter were minted in his love for them.

The closing may be outlined as follows:

1. Moral exhortations (16:13–14)
2. Commendation of Stephanas, Fortunatus, and Achaicus (16:15–18)
3. Greetings from the churches of Asia and the house church of Aquila and Prisca (16:19–20)
4. Salutation from Paul's own hand with final admonition, grace benediction, and assurance of his love (16:21–24)

Exegesis and Exposition

[13]Be on your guard; stand fast in the faith; be courageous; be strong. [14]Let all things you do be done in love.

[15]I exhort you, brothers and sisters—you know that the household of Stephanas was the firstfruits of Achaia, and they have devoted themselves to the service of the saints—[16]that you also be subject to such ones as these and to everyone working together with [them] and laboring. [17]I delight in the arrival of Stephanas, Fortunatus, and Achaicus because these make up for your absence, [18]for they have refreshed my spirit and yours. Therefore, acknowledge fully such persons as these.

[19]The churches of Asia greet you. Aquila and Prisca, along with the church in their house, greet you ardently. [20]All the brothers and sisters greet you. Greet one another with a holy kiss.

[21]This greeting is in my own hand—Paul. [22]If anyone does not love the Lord, let that one be accursed. *Maranatha.* [23]The grace of the Lord Jesus be with you. [24]My love be with all of you in Christ Jesus.

A sudden fusillade of commands often appears at the conclusion of **16:13–14** Paul's letters (a similar battery of five imperatives appears in 2 Cor. 13:11). The first command, γρηγορεῖτε (*grēgoreite*), may sound an eschatological note of "watch" (Mark 13:34–35/Matt. 24:42–43; Matt. 25:13; Luke 12:37; 1 Thess. 5:6, 10; Rev. 3:3).[1] Throughout the letter, Paul reminds the Corinthians about the coming eschatological judgment, which should shape how they live their lives (1 Cor. 1:8; 3:13; 5:5; perhaps 7:26). Hays (1997: 288) concludes that this command "should certainly be understood as a call for them to look intently for the coming of the Lord and to conduct themselves in a way appropriate to that hope."

Another option interprets the verb γρηγορεῖτε in connection with the subsequent imperative to stand in the faith. It would mean "be on your guard," which entails a vigilance against worldly threats to the faith. Fee (1987: 827) argues that Paul enjoins the Corinthians "to watch out for corrosive influences and the enemy." Seen in this light, the command assumes that they live in an age of prevailing night, a time of temptation and danger. They must remain awake, align their lives in accordance with the approaching day of Christ (Lövestam 1963: 45), and lay aside the deeds of darkness (cf. Rom. 13:11–14). This interpretation accords with other usages of the verb in the NT (Acts 20:31; Col. 4:2; 1 Pet. 5:8; Rev. 3:3). The verb may have an eschatological nuance.

---

1. See also Mark 14:34, 37, 38 = Matt. 26:38, 40, 41. Thiselton's (2000: 1336) belief that it refers to "alert, coherent reflection" is unconvincing. This conclusion is more applicable to 1 Cor. 15:34, where Paul exhorts them to "wake up from your stupor" (ἐκνήψατε, *eknēpsate*).

Being on guard against the pressures, enchantments, and habits of their society will also prepare them for the ensuing judgment at the Lord's coming (cf. Rev. 3:2–3).

"Stand fast in the faith" (στήκετε ἐν τῇ πίστει, *stēkete en tē pistei*) refers to the traditions that are the foundation of the community and that Paul passed on to them.[2] The definite article before a noun may sometimes be rendered as a personal pronoun, "stand firm in your faith" (NRSV; Soards 1999: 362), but "your faith" does not fit the context. Hays (1997: 289) challenges this rendering and asserts, "We stand in the proclaimed word, not in our own subjectivity." Paul's statement in 2 Cor. 1:24 that he does not "lord it over your [ὑμῶν, *hymōn*] faith" because "you stand fast in the faith" (τῇ πίστει ἑστήκατε, *tē pistei hestēkate*) makes it clear that "faith" can refer to the content of what is believed as well as the act of trusting (Fee 1987: 828). "Stand fast in the faith" is shorthand for what Paul exhorts in 2 Thess. 2:15: "Stand fast and hold firmly the traditions that you were taught by us, either by word of mouth or by our letter." In the immediate context, "faith" refers to the traditions about Christ's death and resurrection that Paul delivered to the Corinthians (1 Cor. 15:3–5; cf. 15:14, 17), but it also applies to the belief in one God over all the earth, a jealous God (8:4–6), who prohibits all forms of idolatry and sexual immorality. It is not a "building" metaphor to encourage concord (contra Eriksson 1998: 289), but a military image that urges them "to hold their ground" and not retreat before an enemy (Lövestam 1963: 59). They are to "contend for the faith" entrusted to them (cf. Jude 3). The theme is more developed in Eph. 6:10–17.

Eriksson (1998: 289) misreads the call to "be courageous" (ἀνδρίζεσθε, *andrizesthe*, literally, "be manly") and "strong" (κραταιοῦσθε, *krataiousthe*) as solely "masculine virtues" and consequently "an exhortation to the men in the church to assume a leadership role against the women tongue speakers, thereby picking up the theme of charismatic giftedness." This interpretation stems from the assumption that this section recapitulates all the key themes of the letter—an assumption that motivates the interpreter to discover these themes in Paul's closing remarks, whether they are obvious or not. Thiselton (2000: 1336) argues that ἀνδρίζεσθε does not simply stand in contrast with supposedly "feminine" qualities but also "with *childish ways.*" The imperative may be calling for "maturity and courage" as opposed to childishness (cf. 3:1; 13:10–11; 14:20).[3] It is more likely, however, that the OT influences Paul's language (Schrage 2001: 451). The dual commands to be coura-

2. The verb στήκετε (stand fast) appears in Gal. 5:1 (in freedom); Phil. 1:27 (in one spirit); 4:1 (in the Lord); 1 Thess. 3:8 (in the Lord); see also 2 Thess. 2:15.

3. Cf. Luke 1:80; 2:40, where the verb κραταιοῦσθαι (*krataiousthai*) is used for a child's growing and becoming strong.

geous and strong appear frequently in the LXX.[4] This scriptural echo calls for the Corinthians to be valorous and not cowardly and reflects Paul's conviction that Christians, who are set apart to be holy (1:2; 6:11), must stand over against the extraordinary pressures of their pagan society. Acting out the convictions of their faith will lead inevitably to severe testing (cf. 10:13). Moffatt (1938: 276) comments, "The Corinthians have been tolerant when they should have been strict, and intolerant or uncharitable when they should have been manly enough to make allowances for those who were less robust; they had not always been alive to their risks and to their responsibilities." But the military nature of the metaphors (cf. 1QM 15:7–8) suggests a situation of danger that requires them to be vigilant, strong, and valiant to withstand the attacks of the power of darkness (Lövestam 1963: 60).

In 16:14, Paul reiterates the emphasis on love (cf. 16:22, 24) that runs throughout the letter and reaches its apex in chapter 13. Love will pour balm into the wounds of their schism, their lawsuits, and their mistreatment of the "have-nots" at the Lord's Supper. It should superintend the exercise of their spiritual gifts and should override any selfish desires to eat idol food, since such an action could destroy fellow Christians and fails to witness to unbelievers that there is only one God.

Paul's exhortation (παρακαλῶ, parakalō; cf. 1:10; 4:16) about Stephanas and his household introduces a request on the basis of their friendship (see Bjerkelund 1967: 35–111, 141–48, 188–90; Thiselton 2000: 1337). He briefly mentioned the baptism of Stephanas's household in 1:16, and here he identifies them as the firstfruits (ἀπαρχή, aparchē) of Achaia—that is, their conversion marked the starting point of the church there (cf. Rom. 16:5). "Achaia" was the name given to the Roman province in Greece.[5] Paul may use "Achaia" to refer to a more limited area around Corinth rather than the whole province comprising the southern half of Greece, since Acts 17:34 mentions some becoming believers in Athens, including Dionysius the Areopagite and a woman named Damaris, before Paul traveled to Corinth. The term "firstfruits" attaches particular honor to them, since it appears in 1 Cor. 15:20 to refer to Christ as the "firstfruits of the dead" and is used in the OT to apply to what is the best. Using cultic language to refer to his converts suggests that Paul regards them as offerings to God (cf. Rom. 15:16). As the

16:15–18

---

4. The verb ἀνδρίζεσθαι (andrizesthai) appears with ἰσχύειν (ischyein, to be strong) in Deut. 31:6, 7, 23; Josh. 1:6, 7, 9, 18; 10:25; 1 Chron. 22:13; 28:20; 2 Chron. 32:7; Dan. 10:19; 1 Macc. 2:64; with ἐνισχύειν (enischyein) in 1 Chron. 19:13; Dan. 11:1 (see also Mart. Pol. 9:1); and with κραταιοῦσθαι (krataiousthai) in 2 Sam. 10:12; Ps. 26:14 (27:14 MT); 30:25 (31:24 MT); see also 1 Sam. 4:9.

5. The name commemorated the Roman defeat of the Achaean Confederacy in 146 B.C.

firstfruits offered to God, they are "the harbinger" of more to come (R. Collins 1999: 604).[6]

It is probable that Stephanas, Achaicus, and Fortunatus brought the Corinthians' letter to Paul, and that he mentions them here because they are the carriers of his letter to them (see Gamble 1977: 81). The command "acknowledge fully [or 'give recognition to'] such persons as these" (16:18) implies that they were present in Corinth when this letter was read. Fee (1987: 831) regards the commendation of Stephanas as "one more attempt on Paul's part to urge the Corinthians not only to accept him and his own ministry, but also to extend that acceptance to those who are his colaborers." Eriksson (1998: 290) thinks that "it functions to specify the authority of the church leadership as against the factionalism of some Corinthians." But Paul normally includes a note of commendation for the carriers of his letters (Rom. 16:1–2; 2 Cor. 8:16–24; Phil. 2:25–30; Col. 4:7–9) because they "would verify the contents of the letter, deliver oral messages, and answer questions after its reading" (Belleville 1987: 34). He is not lobbying for these three men to receive special authority in the church, since he also adds a commendation for *all* who labor like them. What is notable about them is their selfless service, which he hopes others will imitate. He bids the Corinthians to be subject to those who are dedicated to serving others.[7] Recognition should be based on function, not status (Clarke 1993: 126), so that authority derives from selfless service and hard toil for others (cf. 1 Cor. 15:10). The image of co-workers also presents a picture of *"mutuality* and *complementarity"* (Thiselton 2000: 1339), not an over/under relationship.

The unusual phraseology of "they devoted [or 'appointed'] themselves for service to the saints" (εἰς διακονίαν τοῖς ἁγίοις ἔταξαν ἑαυτούς, *eis diakonian tois hagiois etaxan heautous*) does not refer to the role of Stephanas, Achaicus, and Fortunatus as leaders. Otherwise, as Thiselton (2000: 1339) observes, it would manifest "the very self-centered forwardness that troubles Paul." Instead, it refers to a "self-imposed duty" (Robertson and Plummer 1914: 395) and means that they set themselves aside for service to other Christians (cf. Rom. 16:1).[8] Barrett (1968: 394) comments, "They were appointed directly by God, who pointed out to them the opportunity of service and (we may suppose)

6. Clement's claim that the apostles "appointed their first converts [τὰς ἀπαρχὰς αὐτῶν, *tas aparchas autōn*], testing them by the Spirit, to be bishops and deacons of the future believers" (1 Clem. 42:4) is not supportable by the evidence.

7. Paul deliberately plays on forms of the verb τάσσειν when he says that "they devoted themselves" (ἔταξαν ἑαυτούς, *etaxan heautous*) and that the Corinthians are to be subject (ὑποτάσσησθε, *hypotassēsthe*) to such persons.

8. The idiom is found in Xenophon, *Mem.* 2.1.11, and Plato, *Respublica* (*Republic*) 2.12.371C.

equipped them to fulfill it. It is now for the church to recognize this ministry, as Paul does." But their appointment is not at issue. Paul simply holds them up as examples of those who make it their business to serve others. Clarke's (1996: 299) comments on this passage are apropos: "Where participation in pagan cults was largely self-seeking in motivation, Paul's phrase draws attention to what is distinctive in this new religion—all of one's actions should be directed to the benefit of others." Winter (1989) calls attention to the famines that afflicted Corinth after Paul left, and it is possible that the service of Stephanas to the saints involved the distribution of food.

Winter (2001: 184–205) makes the case that this service turns ideas of patronage and its ranking system upside down. The Stephanas household was "there to serve others—others were not there for them, which was the traditional role of clients" (Winter 2001: 184). Winter (2001: 193) claims that "Paul was seeking to wrest the community from the grasp of patrons, who sought to exercise control over other Christians," which was at the root of their factions and power struggles. The persons to be honored are the servants and the laborers. Their behavior shows that others are not to be treated as stepping-stones to increase one's personal status, to build a power base, or to fashion an impressive entourage. Paul strives to root out the patronage system that served only to bolster tribalism in the church. The household of Stephanas becomes a model of what Paul indirectly enjoins in 13:5 with the statement that love "does not seek its own [advantage]." They emulate his own example: "For though I am free from all, I made myself a slave to all in order that I might gain more" (9:19).

Paul rejoices over the arrival of Stephanas and company because, literally, "these filled up your lack."[9] The English translation of this clause may give the false impression that he imputes some failing to the Corinthians. Delling (*TDNT* 6:306), for example, claims that Paul's choice of words implies that they helped settle the tensions between Paul and the Corinthians. It is, instead, *the arrival* or *presence* (παρουσία, *parousia*) of the three that makes up for what is lacking. He does not reproach them for some failure. This statement expresses his affection for them because what he regards as "lacking" is their physical presence (cf. Phil. 2:30). The clause can be translated idiomatically as "They make up for your absence." By choosing the word ὑστέρημα (*hysterēma*) instead of the normal word for "absence," ἀπουσία (*apousia* [Phil. 2:12]; cf. ἀπεῖναι, *apeinai* [1 Cor. 5:3; 2 Cor. 10:1, 11; 13:2, 10; Phil. 1:27; Col. 2:5]), Paul implies "need" or "want" (R. Collins 1999: 606) and conveys that their absence from him left a gap in his life (Fee 1987: 832; cf. Parry

---

9. Thiselton (2000: 1339) convincingly argues that χαίρω (*chairō*) should be translated "I am delighted."

1926: 250). As the incarnation of the Corinthian church, these three men filled that gap and refreshed Paul's spirit. The full phrase ἀνα-παύειν τὸ πνεῦμα (*anapauein to pneuma,* to refresh the spirit; cf. 2 Cor. 7:13; Philem. 7, 20) is not found in other Greek writers (Clarke 1996: 277–86). It literally means "to put the spirit at rest." The phrase may or may not imply that prior to the action Paul's spirit was in tumult, but it does communicate the salutary effects that their action had on his spirit.

Following Fee's assumption that this closing reveals hints of the growing tension between Paul and the church, Weima (1994: 204) interprets Paul's expression of joy over these members rather than over the church as evidence of an underlying conflict. Expressing delight over the arrival of the visitors rather than over the whole church, however, is to be expected. They, rather than the church, came to visit him; and Paul interprets their presence as the representation of the entire church. Fee exaggerates the supposed division between Paul and the church. To assume that these three men bore bad news about what was happening in Corinth does not require this recognition of them to be ironic (contra Fee 1987: 832). Paul rejoices in them because they have refreshed *both* "my spirit and yours."[10] This statement assumes that the Corinthians will be cheered to learn that their visit had so comforted him (Findlay 1910: 951) and presumes a positive relationship with the church.

We need not interpret this visit to be some kind of special delegation to Ephesus. The three travelers may have arrived on business and naturally made contact with their apostle. Since Stephanas (short for Stephanophoros) bears a Greek name, he may have been an indigenous Greek or an immigrant. The mention of his household suggests that he was a man of means. Achaicus and Fortunatus may be slaves, freedmen, Stephanas's fellow artisans, or, less likely, his sons or brothers.[11] "Achaicus" ("man of Achaia") is a Latin name, and Murphy-O'Connor (1996: 272) reasons that he must have been given the name outside of Achaia (like the American nicknames "Tex" and "Okie"). The Latin form suggests that it was given to him in the West, and it is likely that he had been a slave (Meeks 1983: 56). "Fortunatus" also is a Latin name, meaning "lucky" or "blessed," and is not an uncommon name for a slave. Meeks (1983: 56) identifies them as freedmen whose families belonged "to the original stock of colonists." Meeks surmises that

10. Paul uses the verb "to refresh" (ἀναπαύειν, *anapauein*) in Philem. 7 to refer to Philemon's past benevolence to fellow Christians, which emboldens Paul to make his audacious request about Onesimus.
11. Edwards (1885: 472) thinks that all three were "the slaves of Chloe" (1:11), but the status accorded Stephanas would rule this out.

the family of Achaicus lived in Italy and moved to Corinth as one of the colonists.

Paul sends greetings from the churches in Asia, the Roman province in **16:19–20** the western part of Asia Minor of which Ephesus served as the economic and administrative hub (see Rom. 16:5; 2 Cor. 1:8; cf. Strabo, *Geogr.* 14.1.24). This is the only place in his letters where he sends greetings from all the churches in a province. How many churches from how many cities are to be included in this greeting is unspecified, which tends to confirm Fee's (1987: 835 n. 7) suggestion that this global greeting serves as another reminder that the Corinthians belong to a much larger family of Christians (cf. 1 Cor. 1:2; 4:17; 11:16; 14:33, 36; 16:1).

Paul adds the personal greetings of Aquila and Prisca and their house church to those of the churches in Asia. The cameo appearances of this husband and wife team in the NT (Acts 18:2, 18, 26; Rom. 16:3; 2 Tim. 4:19) reveal that they were well traveled. Their Latin names may suggest that they were the freed slaves of the same distinguished Roman family (Murphy-O'Connor 1992: 43–44). They were forced to leave Rome when the emperor Claudius expelled all the Jews in A.D. 49 (Acts 18:2; Suetonius, *Divus Claudius* 25.4), and they settled in Corinth, probably because of its promising job prospects with its Isthmian games, which explains why they asked to have their personal greetings added to the letter.[12] The couple shared Paul's Christian faith and his occupation as a tentmaker (Acts 18:3), and they collaborated in that trade and in the work of the gospel (see additional note). Murphy-O'Connor (1996: 263) imagines that Prisca and Aquila made their home in Corinth in the loft of their shop, "while Paul slept below amid the tool-strewn work-benches and the rolls of leather and canvas."[13] Chrysostom (*Hom. Rom.* 30) describes the vocation of tentmaking as dishonorable, but he quickly adds that "their virtue covered all this [the shame], and made them more conspicuous than the sun." When Paul greets or mentions Prisca, she is never characterized as Aquila's wife. Instead, she stands on her own. In his homily on Romans, Chrysostom entitles her "noble" and declares that her gender did not hinder her from a virtuous life. He goes on to say,

> What is greater or so great, as to have been a succorer of Paul? at her own peril to have saved the teacher of the world? . . . The width that the sun

12. The church in their house may refer to "a church that assembles in their house or their household as a church" (Conzelmann 1975: 299; cf. Rom. 16:5, 23; Philem. 2; Col. 4:15).

13. Their house could not have been large, since Paul avails himself of Titius Justus's house instead of theirs to carry on his preaching when he was blocked from returning to the synagogue (Acts 18:7; Murphy-O'Connor 1992: 49).

sees over, is no more of the world than what the glory of this woman runs unto. . . . [For Paul] does not feel ashamed to call a woman his helper but even finds an honor in doing so. (*Hom. Rom.* 30)

By contrast, Paul completely ignores the issue of her gender.

The couple has since moved to Ephesus, and presumably they will later return to Rome (Rom. 16:3) and then back to Ephesus (2 Tim. 4:19). Murphy-O'Connor (1992: 50–51) conjectures that they relocated in Ephesus at Paul's bidding rather than because of some business slump. They became part of his missionary strategy in helping to establish a base in Ephesus for him and disregarded the personal financial loss that this move might incur for them.

In 1 Cor. 16:20, Paul adds greetings from all the brothers and sisters, and it is not clear how they differ from the churches in Asia, since he does not specify that they are the believers with him (cf. Phil. 4:21; Titus 3:15). If it serves as a kind of inclusio with 1 Cor. 1:2 ("all those who call upon the name of our Lord Jesus Christ in every place"), as Schrage (2001: 468) suggests, then it would include the broad array of believers.

The "holy kiss" (Rom. 16:16; 1 Cor. 16:20; 2 Cor. 13:12; 1 Thess. 5:26) or the "kiss of love" (1 Pet. 5:14) is an outward act that affirms a common bond among Christians.[14] Some think that the kiss was a prelude to the Lord's Supper (see Stählin, *TDNT* 9:140). Justin Martyr (*1 Apol.* 65) describes the process of initiation and mentions exchanging a kiss after intercessory prayers and then describes the Lord's Supper, but it is unclear whether this was the practice in the time of Paul (Lindemann 2000: 387). Klassen (1993: 132) argues that the kiss "is to be seen in a living context of people who are building a new sociological reality rather than in restrictive eucharistic or liturgical terms." Klassen thinks that it is "the kiss which 'saints' give each other when they meet." Gamble (1977: 76) regards it as a greeting "extended in a formal and tangible way as a communal act," which becomes "a concrete actualization of greeting given in the letter, as a sign of fellowship with the community, of the community with the Apostle, and indeed of one community with others." This kiss is more than an extension of social custom, since it is identified as "holy." It was a distinctive practice that served as "a sign of mutual fellowship among persons of mixed social background, nationality, race, and gender who are joined together as a new family in

14. In Scripture, the kiss was given to a close relation (Gen. 27:26; 29:13; 31:28, 55; 33:4; 45:15; 48:10; 50:1; Exod. 4:27; 18:7; Ruth 1:14; 2 Sam. 14:33; 1 Kings 19:20; Tob. 5:17; 10:12), to close friends (1 Sam. 20:41), and as a token of honor (1 Sam. 10:1; 2 Sam. 15:5), which is why the kiss in an act of betrayal is so villainous (2 Sam. 20:9; Mark 14:44; Matt. 26:48; Luke 22:47; cf. Prov. 27:6). A kiss appears in the NT as a greeting (Luke 7:45), as a sign of love and reverence (Luke 7:38, 45), as a sign of reconciliation (Luke 15:20), and as a parting gesture of love (Acts 20:37).

Christ. For those who came from differing ethnic and national backgrounds it was means to express their unity" (Garland 1999: 554–55).[15] The holy kiss becomes a token of the joy, love, reconciliation, peace, and communion that all Christians (slave and free, Jew and Gentile, Greek and Roman, patron and client) have in Christ and with one another. Ambrosiaster regards the kiss as a sign of peace that does away with discord (Thiselton 2000: 1345), which would be particularly important here in light of the evidence of fractured relationships in Corinth (cf. Chrysostom, *Hom. 1 Cor.* 44.4).

Paul takes up the pen to sign off on the letter. We do not have an auto- **16:21–24** graph to detect the second hand in the letter, but letters written by a secretary customarily included an autographic conclusion (see Richards 1991: 172–75). Stowers (1986: 61) likens it to "adding a signature to a typed letter." The closing is unusually sharp-edged in pronouncing a curse (ἀνάθεμα, *anathema*; cf. 12:3; Rom. 9:3; Gal. 1:8–9) upon those who do not love the Lord (contrast the promises to those who do love the Lord in Rom. 8:28; 1 Cor. 2:9; 8:3; Eph. 6:24).[16] The malediction is probably intended to apply to any headstrong provocateurs within the church. A ban formula is found in the conclusion to 2 Thess. 3:14 ("If anyone does not obey our instruction in this letter, note them, do not associate with them [cf. 1 Cor. 5:9], in order that they be put to shame") and in Titus 3:10–11 ("After a first and second admonition, shun a factious person, because you know that such a person perverts and sins, being self-condemned"). By contrast, a positive formula appears in Gal. 6:16 ("For those who will follow this rule—peace be upon them, and mercy") and in Eph. 6:24 ("Grace be with all who love our Lord Jesus Christ in incorruption").

The Aramaic *Maranatha* formula occurs only here in Scripture and has three possible renderings: (1) "Our Lord has come!" (a confession); (2) "Our Lord is coming!" or "Our Lord is now present!" (a confession); and (3) "Our Lord, come!" (an imperative petitioning the parousia; cf. Rev. 22:20).[17] Many connect its setting in the church to the celebration of the Lord's Supper, when it was uttered as an invocation or affirmation of the Lord's presence and as a plea for his return (see Did. 10:6), and they infer from this supposed setting that Paul meant his letter to be read as a lead-in to the Lord's

---

15. We can infer from the anxiety of later writers about the potential impropriety of the kiss that it was extended to male and female alike. Athenagoras (*Legatio pro Christianis* 32) quotes a lost apocryphal text asserting that if one kisses with the slightest ulterior motive, it excludes one from eternal life.

16. The verb φιλεῖν (*philein*, to love) appears only in 1 Cor. 16:22 and Titus 3:15 in Paul's letters.

17. Fitzmyer (1981: 226) lists five more meanings given to the phrase (see also additional note).

Supper.[18] Gamble (1977: 82), however, considers it "ill-advised to regard 1 Cor 16:20b–23 as a fixed and unitary liturgical sequence, or as serving a peculiarly liturgical function in the conclusion of the letter."[19] M. Black (1973: 196) compares the formula with Jude 14–15 and 1 Enoch 1:9 and concludes that it means "the Lord *will* (soon, surely) come (i.e., at the *parousia*)." Black attributes the popularity of the formula to its "ambiguity and hence flexibility: it could be fitted into different contexts, in the eucharist, as an imprecation, or as a confession ('the Lord has come')." In this context, it serves to reinforce the curse ban (Moule 1959–60; Eriksson 1998: 292). The Lord's return brings blessings for some (2 Tim. 4:8) and condemnation for others.[20]

According to Eriksson (1998: 298; see also Thiselton 2000: 1351), loving the Lord is part of covenant loyalty. The covenant brings curses to those who do not love and obey and bestows blessings on those who do (cf. 1 Cor. 2:9). These blessings and curses will be meted out at the parousia, when the Lord returns. Eriksson (1998: 298) contends that Paul means that anyone who does not love the Lord is accursed at the Lord's coming.[21] The unstated premise is that God requires love (Deut. 6:4–6), and those who do not love the Lord can expect only condemnation.

It is well known that the concluding grace wish in Paul's letters contrasts starkly with other Hellenistic letters, which normally closed with a simple "farewell." Paul frames his letters "with a greeting and benediction informed by the congregation's relation to Jesus Christ" (Roetzel 1998: 91). The additional note—"My love be with all of you in Christ Jesus"—after the grace wish is peculiar to this letter. Only in this benediction does Paul assert his own love for a community (cf. 2 Cor. 13:14 and Eph. 6:23, which refer to God's love). Weima (1994: 204) claims that "a careful reading of the letter's epistolary conventions, as well as its contents, reveals the fact of a growing conflict between Paul and the Corinthians." The problem with this "careful reading" is that it is weighted by the presumption that conflict is the key for understanding

18. See Lietzmann 1949: 186; Robinson 1953; Kuhn, *TDNT* 4:466–72; Bornkamm 1969: 169–79; Cuming 1975–76; Wu, *DPL* 559–60. Fitzmyer (1981: 228–29) contends that it originally was a liturgical acclamation in a eucharistic setting but hesitates to see a similar eucharistic context for the ending of the letter.

19. Van Unnik (1959: 272) warns against "pan-liturgism," which "sees everywhere in the Pauline epistles the background of the liturgy whenever a simple parallel in wording between them and the *much later* liturgies is found."

20. Eriksson (1998: 295) overreaches in claiming that "this stress on the future coming of the Lord at the end of Paul's argument is an indication that the problem throughout 1 Corinthians has been an over-emphasis on the present benefits of salvation."

21. Eriksson (1998: 294–95), drawing on P. Marshall (1987: 341–48), claims that Paul uses the rhetorical figure of non-naming to impugn well-known persons with this charge and concludes that the targets were of "higher social standing," making it "dangerous to criticize them outright."

this epistolary conclusion. Weima (1994: 204–8) reads a strained relationship between Paul and the church into every detail in this letter closing. Pascuzzi (1997: 38–39) objects that Weima's assertions about the epistolary conclusion "rely heavily on the disputable positions of others" and contends that Weima's evidence for the strained relationship based, for example, on omissions in the thanksgiving section has "the potential to prove everything or prove nothing." I am not convinced that this added love salutation is a sign of the conflict and animosity between Paul and the congregation rather than a genuine token of affection. This concluding assurance of his love harks back to his role as their father (1 Cor. 4:15) and his desire to come to them in a gentle spirit rather than with a rod (4:21). His fatherly role requires him to censure them when they go wrong, but this concluding sentiment shows that he intends his reproofs to be read in light of his love for them.

"Love" frames this letter's closing: "Let all things you do be done in love" (16:14); "My love be with all you in Christ Jesus." "In Christ Jesus" frames the entire letter with the greeting to those "sanctified in Christ Jesus" (1:2). Their experience of God's grace (1:4), their present life (1:30), and the hope of the resurrection (15:22) all spring from their relationship in Christ.

Additional Notes

16:19. Priscilla (diminutive of "Prisca") is named before Aquila in Acts 18:18, 26; Rom. 16:3; and 2 Tim. 4:19, which reverses the normal pattern of listing the husband first. It may be an indication that she outranks her husband on the social scale as one of noble birth. If that was the case, however, why does she engage in manual labor alongside her husband (Acts 18:3)? Murphy-O'Connor (1992: 42) believes that it is more likely that she is listed first because she was converted first and that it reveals the radical egalitarian nature of Pauline communities.

The trade of tentmaking probably involved making awnings from stout sailcloth for the retailers in the forum (see Pliny the Elder, *Naturalis historia* [*Natural History*] 19.23–24) and for private homes; making tents for sheltering visitors to the athletic games, for the military, and for wealthy travelers; and perhaps making sails for merchant ships (Engels 1990: 112; Murphy-O'Connor 1992: 44).

16:22. Since uncial manuscripts did not separate the letters between words, pointing the Aramaic represented by the Greek transliteration ΜΑΡΑΝΑΘΑ is uncertain. It could be pointed מָרַנָא תָא ("Our Lord, come") or מָרַן אֲתָא ("Our Lord has come"). The presence of Aramaic in the letter suggests that the Corinthian church was familiar with traditions derived from Aramaic-speaking Christian circles, which, presumably, were quite early (cf. Ἀββά [Rom. 8:15; Gal. 4:6]; Ἀμήν [1 Cor. 14:16]). It reveals that this tradition was eschatological at its core and ascribed the title "Lord" to Jesus early on.

Works Cited

Aalen, S.
1963   "Das Abendmahl als Opfermahl im Neuen Testament." *Novum Testamentum* 6:128–52.

ABD   *The Anchor Bible Dictionary.* Edited by D. N. Freedman et al. 6 vols. New York: Doubleday, 1992.

Achelis, H.
1902   *Virgines Subintroductae: Ein Beitrag zum VII. Kapitel des I Korintherbriefs.* Leipzig: Hinrichs.

Agnew, F. H.
1986   "The Origin of the New Testament Apostle Concept: A Review of Research." *Journal of Biblical Literature* 105:75–86.

Alexander, L.
1989   "Hellenistic Letter-Forms and the Structure of Philippians." *Journal for the Study of the New Testament* 37:87–101.

1998   "'Better to Marry Than to Burn': St. Paul and the Greek Novel." Pp. 235–56 in *Ancient Fiction and Early Christian Narrative.* Edited by R. F. Hock, J. B. Chance, and J. Perkins. Atlanta: Scholars Press.

Alexander, T. D.
1995   "The Passover Sacrifice." Pp. 1–24 in *Sacrifice in the Bible.* Edited by R. T. Beckwith and M. Selmon. Carlisle: Paternoster/Grand Rapids: Baker.

Allison, D. C., Jr.
1982   "The Pauline Epistles and the Synoptic Gospels: The Pattern of the Parallels." *New Testament Studies* 28:1–32.
1985   "Paul and the Missionary Discourse." *Ephemerides theologicae lovanienses* 61:369–75.

Allison, R. W.
1988   "Let Women Be Silent in the Churches (1 Cor. 14:33b–36): What Did Paul Really Say, and What Did It Mean?" *Journal for the Study of the New Testament* 32:27–60.

Allo, E.-B.
1935   *Saint Paul: Première épître aux Corinthiens.* Études bibliques. Paris: Gabalda.

Anderson, R. D., Jr.
1999   *Ancient Rhetorical Theory and Paul.* Biblical Exegesis and Theology 18. Revised edition. Leuven: Peeters.

Angus, S.
1925   *The Mystery-Religions and Christianity: A Study in the Religious Background of Early Christianity.* London: Murray.

Arai, S.
1972–73   "Die Gegner des Paulus im I. Korintherbrief und das Problem der Gnosis." *New Testament Studies* 19:430–37.

Arens, E.
1973   "Was St. Paul Married?" *Bible Today* 66:1188–91.

Arichea, D. C., Jr.
1995   "The Silence of Women in the Church: Theology and Translation in 1 Corinthians 14.33b–36." *Bible Translator* 46:101–12.

Arndt, W.
1932   "The Meaning of 1 Cor. 9,9.10." *Concordia Theological Monthly* 3:329–35.

Asher, J. R.
2000   *Polarity and Change in 1 Corinthians 15: A Study of Metaphysics, Rhetoric, and Resurrection.* Hermeneutische Untersuchungen zur Theologie 42. Tübingen: Mohr.
2001   "Σπείρεται: Paul's Anthropogenic Metaphor in 1 Corinthians 15:42–44." *Journal of Biblical Literature* 120:101–22.

Aune, D. E.
1983   *Prophecy in Early Christianity and the Ancient Mediterranean World.* Grand Rapids: Eerdmans.

Baasland, E.
1988   "Die *peri*-Formel und die Argumentation (situation) des Paulus." *Studia theologica* 42:69–87.

BAGD *A Greek-English Lexicon of the New Testament and Other Early Christian Literature.* By W. Bauer, W. F. Arndt, F. W. Gingrich, and F. W. Danker. 2d edition. Chicago: University of Chicago Press, 1979.

Bailey, K. E.
1975 "Recovering the Poetic Structure of 1 Cor i 17–ii 2." *Novum Testamentum* 17:265–96.

1980 "Paul's Theological Foundation for Human Sexuality: I Cor. 6:9–20 in the Light of Rhetorical Criticism." *Near East School of Theology Theological Review* 3:27–41.

Bainton, R. H.
1962 *Luther's Meditations on the Gospels.* Philadelphia: Westminster.

Baird, W.
1964 *The Corinthian Church: A Biblical Approach to Urban Culture.* Nashville: Abingdon.

1990 "'One against the Other': Intra-Church Conflict in 1 Corinthians." Pp. 116–36 in *The Conversation Continues: Studies in Paul and John in Honor of J. Louis Martyn.* Edited by R. T. Fortna and B. R. Gaventa. Nashville: Abingdon.

Baker, D. L.
1974 "The Interpretation of 1 Corinthians 12–14." *Evangelical Quarterly* 46:224–34.

1994 "Typology and the Christian Use of the Old Testament." Pp. 313–30 in *The Right Doctrine from the Wrong Texts?* Edited by G. K. Beale. Grand Rapids: Baker.

Balch, D. L.
1971–72 "Backgrounds of I Cor. vii: Sayings of the Lord in Q; Moses as an Ascetic Θεῖος Ἀνήρ in II Cor. iii." *New Testament Studies* 18:351–64.

1981 *Let Wives Be Submissive: The Domestic Code in I Peter.* Society of Biblical Literature Monograph Series 26. Atlanta: Scholars Press.

1983 "1 Cor 7:32–35 and Stoic Debates about Marriage, Anxiety, and Distraction." *Journal of Biblical Literature* 102:429–39.

Balsdon, J. P. V. D.
1979 *Romans and Aliens.* London: Duckworth.

Baltensweiler, H.
1967 *Die Ehe im Neuen Testament: Exegetische Untersuchungen über Ehe, Ehelösigkeit und Ehescheidung.* Abhandlungen zur Theologie des Alten und Neuen Testaments 52. Zurich/Stuttgart: Zwingli.

Bandstra, A. J.
1971 "Interpretation in 1 Cor 10:1–11." *Calvin Theological Journal* 6:5–21.

Barbour, R. S.
1979 "Wisdom and the Cross in 1 Corinthians 1 and 2." Pp. 52–72 in *Theologica Crucis–Signum Crucis: Festschrift für Erich Dinkler zum 70. Geburtstag.* Edited by C. Andresen and G. Klein. Tübingen: Mohr.

Barclay, J. M. G.
1987 "Mirror-Reading a Polemical Letter: Galatians as a Test Case." *Journal for the Study of the New Testament* 31:73–93.

1988 *Obeying the Truth: Paul's Ethics in Galatians.* Minneapolis: Fortress.

1992 "Thessalonica and Corinth: Social Contrasts in Pauline Christianity." *Journal for the Study of the New Testament* 47:49–74.

Barr, J.
1987 "Words for Love in Biblical Greek." Pp. 3–18 in *The Glory of Christ in the New Testament: Studies in Christology in Memory of George Bradford Caird.* Edited by N. T. Wright and L. D. Hurst. Oxford: Oxford University Press.

Barré, M. L.
1974 "To Marry or to Burn: Purousthai in 1 Cor. 7:9." *Catholic Biblical Quarterly* 36:193–202.

Barrett, C. K.
1968 *The First Epistle to the Corinthians.* Harper's New Testament Commentaries. New York: Harper & Row.

1973 *The Second Epistle to the Corinthians.* Harper's New Testament Commentaries. New York: Harper & Row.

1982 *Essays on Paul.* Philadelphia: Westminster.

1985a *Freedom and Obligation: A Study of the Epistle to the Galatians.* Philadelphia: Westminster.

1985b "The Significance of the Adam-Christ Typology for the Resurrection of the Dead: 1 Cor 15,20–22.45–49." Pp. 99–126 in *Resurrection du Christ et des Chrétiens (1 Co 15)*. Edited by J.-N. Aletti, S. Agourides, and L. De Lorenzi. Monographic Series of "Benedictina": Biblical-Ecumenical Section 8. Rome: St. Paul's Abbey.

Bartchy, S. S.
1973   *Μᾶλλον Χρῆσαι: First-Century Slavery and the Interpretation of 1 Corinthians 7*. Society of Biblical Literature Dissertation Series 11. Missoula, Mont.: Society of Biblical Literature.

Barth, K.
1933   *The Resurrection of the Dead*. Translated by H. J. Stenning. London: Hodder & Stoughton.
1960–61   *Church Dogmatics*. Translated by G. T. Thomson et al. Edited by G. W. Bromiley and T. F. Torrance. Edinburgh: Clark.

Barth, M.
1958   "A Chapter on the Church—the Body of Christ." *Interpretation* 12:131–56.

Barth, M., and H. Blanke
2000   *The Letter to Philemon*. Eerdmans Critical Commentary. Grand Rapids: Eerdmans.

Barton, S. C.
1986   "Paul's Sense of Place: An Anthropological Approach to Community Formation in Corinth." *New Testament Studies* 32:225–46.
1996   "'All Things to All People': Paul and the Law in the Light of 1 Corinthians 9:19–23." Pp. 271–85 in *Paul and the Mosaic Law*. Edited by J. D. G. Dunn. Wissenschaftliche Untersuchungen zum Neuen Testament 89. Tübingen: Mohr.

Bartsch, H. W.
1962   "Der korinthische Missbrauch des Abendmahls: Zur Situation und Struktur von 1. Korinther 8–11." Pp. 168–83 in *Entmythologisierende Auslegung*. Theologische Forschung 26. Hamburg-Bergstedt: Reich.
1979–80   "Inhalt und Funktion des urchristlichen Osterglaubens." *New Testament Studies* 26:180–96.

Bassler, J. M.
1982   "1 Cor 12:3—Curse and Confession in Context." *Journal of Biblical Literature* 103:415–18.
1990   "1 Corinthians 4:1–5." *Interpretation* 44:179–83.

1992   "1 Corinthians." Pp. 411–19 in *The Women's Bible Commentary*. Edited by C. A. Newson and S. H. Ringe. Louisville: Westminster/John Knox.

Bauer, J. B.
1959   "Uxores circumducere (1 Kor 9,5)." *Biblische Zeitschrift* 3:94–102.

Baumann, R.
1968   *Mitte und Norm des Christlichen: Eine Auslegung von 1 Korinther 1,1–3,4*. Neutestamentliche Abhandlungen 5. Münster: Aschendorff.

Baumert, N.
1984   *Ehelosigkeit und Ehe in Herrn: Eine Neuinterpretation von 1 Kor 7*. Forschung zur Bibel 47. Würzburg: Echter.
1996   *Woman and Man in Paul: Overcoming a Misunderstanding*. Translated by P. Madigan and L. M. Maloney. Collegeville, Minn.: Liturgical Press.

Baur, F. C.
1831   "Die Christuspartei in der korinthischen Gemeinde der Gegensatz des petrinischen und paulinischen Christentums in der ältesten Kirche." *Tübinger Zeitschrift* 4:61–206.

BDAG   *A Greek-English Lexicon of the New Testament and Other Early Christian Literature*. By W. Bauer, F. W. Danker, W. F. Arndt, and F. W. Gingrich. 3d edition. Chicago: University of Chicago Press, 2000.

BDF   *A Greek Grammar of the New Testament and Other Early Christian Literature*. By F. Blass, A. Debrunner, and R. W. Funk. Chicago: University of Chicago Press, 1961.

Beacham, R. C.
1999   *Spectacle Entertainments of Early Imperial Rome*. New Haven/London: Yale University Press.

Beardslee, W. A.
1994   *First Corinthians: A Commentary for Today*. St. Louis: Chalice.

Beare, F. W.
1964   "Speaking with Tongues: A Critical Survey of the New Testament Evidence." *Journal of Biblical Literature* 83:229–46.

Beasley-Murray, G. R.
1962   *Baptism in the New Testament*. London: Macmillan. Reprinted Grand Rapids: Eerdmans, 1973.

Becker, J.
1993   *Paul: Apostle to the Gentiles.* Translated by O. C. Dean Jr. Louisville: Westminster/John Knox.

Bedale, S.
1954   "The Meaning of Κεφαλή in the Pauline Epistles." *Journal of Theological Studies,* n.s., 5:211–15.

BeDuhn, J. D.
1999   "'Because of the Angels': Unveiling Paul's Anthropology in 1 Corinthians 11." *Journal of Biblical Literature* 118:295–320.

Beker, J. C.
1980   *Paul the Apostle: The Triumph of God in Life and Thought.* Philadelphia: Fortress.

Belkin, S.
1935   "The Problem of Paul's Background: III, Marrying One's Virgin." *Journal of Biblical Literature* 54:49–52.

Bellen, H.
1963   "Μᾶλλον Χρῆσαι (1 Cor. 7,21): Verzicht auf Freilassung als asketische Leistung?" *Jahrbuch für Antike und Christentum* 6:177–80.

Belleville, L. L.
1987   "Continuity or Discontinuity: A Fresh Look at 1 Corinthians in the Light of First-Century Epistolary Forms and Conventions." *Evangelical Quarterly* 59:15–37.

Berger, K.
1974   "Apostelbrief und apostolische Rede: Zum Formular frühchristlicher Briefe." *Zeitschrift für die neutestamentliche Wissenschaft* 65:191–207.
1977–78 Zur Diskussion über die Herkunft von I Kor. ii.9." *New Testament Studies* 24:270–83.

Bernard, J. H.
1907   "The Connexion between the Fifth and Sixth Chapters of I Corinthians." *Expositor,* 7th series, 3:433–43.

Best, E.
1955   *One Body in Christ.* London: SPCK.
1975   "The Interpretation of Tongues." *Scottish Journal of Theology* 28:45–62.
1990   "1 Corinthians 7:14 and Children in the Church." *Irish Biblical Studies* 12:158–66.

Betz, H. D.
1972   *Der Apostel Paulus und die sokratische Tradition: Eine exegetische Untersuchung zu seiner "Apolo-*

gie" 2 Korinther 10–13. Beiträge zur historischen Theologie. 45. Tübingen: Mohr.
1979   *Galatians.* Hermeneia. Philadelphia: Fortress.
1985   *2 Corinthians 8 and 9: A Commentary on Two Administrative Letters of the Apostle Paul.* Hermeneia. Philadelphia: Fortress.
1986   "The Problem of Rhetoric and Theology according to the Apostle Paul." Pp. 16–48 in *L'Apôtre Paul: Personnalité, style et conception du ministère.* Edited by A. Vanhoye. Bibliotheca ephemeridum theologicarum lovaniensium 73. Leuven: Leuven University Press/Peeters.
2001   "Gemeinschaft des Glaubens und Herrenmahl: Überlegungen zu 1 Kor 11,17–34." *Zeitschrift für Theologie und Kirche* 98:401–21.

BGU   *Aegyptische Urkunden aus den Königlichen Staatlichen Museen zu Berlin, Griechische Urkunden.* 15 vols. Berlin, 1895–1983.

Bjerkelund, C. J.
1967   *Παρακαλῶ: Form, Funktion, und Sinn der Παρακαλῶ-Sätze in den paulinischen Briefen.* Oslo: Universitetsforlaget.

Björk, G.
1938   "Nochmals Paulus Abortivus." *Coniectanea Neotestamentica* 3:3–8.

Black, C. C.
1996   "Christ Crucified in Paul and Mark: Reflections on an Intracanonical Conversation." Pp. 184–206 in *Theology and Ethics in Paul and His Interpreters: Essays in Honor of Victor Paul Furnish.* Edited by E. H. Lovering Jr. and J. L. Sumney. Nashville: Abingdon.

Black, D. A.
1983   "A Note on 'the Weak' in 1 Corinthians 9:22." *Biblica* 64:240–42.
1984   *Paul, Apostle of Weakness: Astheneia and Its Cognates in the Pauline Literature.* American University Studies. New York: Lang.

Black, M.
1961   *The Scrolls and Christian Origins: Studies in the Jewish Background of the New Testament.* New York: Nelson.
1973   "The Maranatha Invocation and Jude 14, 15 (1 Enoch 1:9)." Pp. 189–

98 in *Christ and Spirit in the New Testament: Studies in Honour of Charles Francis Digby Moule*. Edited by B. Lindars and S. S. Smalley. Cambridge: Cambridge University Press.

Blasi, A. J.
1988   *Early Christianity as a Social Movement*. New York: Lang.

Blomberg, C.
1994   *1 Corinthians*. NIV Application Commentary. Grand Rapids: Zondervan.

Blue, B. B.
1991   "The House Church at Corinth and the Lord's Supper: Famine, Food Supply, and the *Present Distress*." *Criswell Theological Review* 5:221–39.

Boer, M. C. de
1988   *The Defeat of Death: Apocalyptic Eschatology in 1 Corinthians 15 and Romans 5*. Journal for the Study of the New Testament: Supplement Series 22. Sheffield: JSOT Press.

1994   "The Composition of 1 Corinthians." *New Testament Studies* 40:229–45.

Boman, T.
1964   "Paulus abortivus (1 Kor. 15:8)." *Studia theologica* 18:46–50.

Bonneau, N.
1993   "The Logic of Paul's Argument on the Resurrection Body in 1 Cor 15:35–44a." *Science et esprit* 45:79–92.

Borgen, P.
1994   "'Yes,' 'No,' 'How Far?': The Participation of Jews and Christians in Pagan Cults." Pp. 30–59 in *Paul and His Hellenistic Context*. Edited by T. Engberg-Pedersen. Edinburgh: Clark.

Bornhäuser, D.
1930   "'Um der Engel willen,' 1 Kor 11,10." *Neue kirchliche Zeitschrift* 41:475–88.

Bornkamm, G.
1966   "The Missionary Stance of Paul in Acts and His Letters." Pp. 194–207 in *Studies in Luke-Acts*. Edited by L. Keck and J. L. Martyn. Nashville: Abingdon.

1969   *Early Christian Experience*. Translated by P. L. Hammer. New York: Harper & Row.

1971   *Paul*. Translated by D. M. G. Stalker. New York: Harper & Row.

Boswell, J.
1980   *Christianity, Social Tolerance, and Homosexuality: Gay People in Western Europe from the Beginning of the Christian Era to the Fourteenth Century*. Chicago: University of Chicago Press.

Bound, J. F.
1984   "Who Are the 'Virgins' Discussed in 1 Corinthians 7:25–38?" *Evangelical Journal* 2:3–15.

Bouttier, M.
1976–77   "*Complexio Oppositorum*: sur les Formules de I Cor. xii.13; Gal. iii.26–8; Col. iii.10, 11." *New Testament Studies* 23:1–19.

Bouwman, G.
1976   "Paulus en het celibaat." *Bijdragen* 37:379–90.

Branick, V. P.
1982   "Source and Redaction Analysis of 1 Corinthians 1–3." *Journal of Biblical Literature* 101:251–69.

Braun, H.
1967   "Die Indifferenz gegenüber der Welt bei Paulus und bei Epiktet." Pp. 156–67 and 343–44 in *Gesammelte Studien zum Neuen Testament und seiner Umwelt*. 2d edition. Tübingen: Mohr.

Braxton, B. R.
2000   *The Tyranny of Resolution: 1 Corinthians 7:17–24*. Society of Biblical Literature Monograph Series 181. Atlanta: Society of Biblical Literature.

Bray, G.
1999   *1–2 Corinthians*. Ancient Christian Commentary on Scripture: New Testament 7. Downers Grove, Ill.: InterVarsity.

Brewer, D. I.
1992   "1 Corinthians 9:9–11: A Literal Interpretation of 'Do Not Muzzle the Ox.'" *New Testament Studies* 38:554–65.

Broneer, O.
1962   "The Isthmian Victory Crown." *American Journal of Archaeology* 66:259–63.

1971   "Paul and the Pagan Cults at Isthmia." *Harvard Theological Review* 64:169–87.

Brown, A. R.
1995   *The Cross and Human Transforma-tion: Paul's Apocalyptic Word in 1 Corinthians.* Minneapolis: Fortress.

Brox, N.
1968   "Ἀνάθεμα Ἰησοῦς (I Kor. 12.3)." *Biblische Zeitschrift* 12:103–11.

Bruce, F. F.
1971   *I and II Corinthians.* New Century Bible. Grand Rapids: Eerdmans.

Brun, L.
1913   "'Um der Engel willen' 1 Kor 11,10." *Zeitschrift für die neutestamentliche Wissenschaft* 14:303–8.

1931   "Noch einmal die Schriftnorm 1 Kor. 4,6." *Theologische Studien und Kritiken* 103:453–56.

Brunner, E.
1956   *Faith, Hope, and Love.* Philadelphia: Westminster.

Bruns, B.
1982   "'Die Frau hat über ihren Leib nicht die Verfügungsgewalt, sondern der Mann . . .': Zur Herkunft und Bedeutung der Formulierung in 1 Kor 7,4." *Münchner theologische Zeitschrift* 33:177–94.

Brunt, J. C.
1985   "Rejected, Ignored, or Misunderstood? The Fate of Paul's Approach to the Problem of Food Offered to Idols in Early Christianity." *New Testament Studies* 31:113–24.

Bultmann, R.
1951   *Theology of the New Testament,* vol. 1. Translated by K. Grobel. New York: Scribner.

1955   *Theology of the New Testament,* vol. 2. Translated by K. Grobel. New York: Scribner.

1956   *Primitive Christianity in Its Contemporary Setting.* Translated by R. Fuller. Cleveland: World/New York: Meridian.

Burchard, C.
1961   "*Ei* nach einem Ausdrücke des Wissens oder Nichtwissens Joh. 9,25; Act. 29,12; 1 Kor. 1,16; 7,16." *Zeitschrift für die neutestamentliche Wissenschaft* 52:73–82.

1984   "1 Korinther 15:39–41." *Zeitschrift für die neutestamentliche Wissenschaft* 75:233–58.

Burford, A.
1969   *Greek Temple Builders at Epidauros.* Liverpool: Liverpool University Press.

Burkill, T. A.
1971   "Two into One: The Notion of Carnal Union in Mark 10:8; 1 Kor. 6:16; Eph. 5:31." *Zeitschrift für die neutestamentliche Wissenschaft* 62:115–20.

Burton, E. DeW.
1898   *Syntax of the Moods and Tenses in New Testament Greek.* 3d edition. Edinburgh: Clark.

Buttmann, A.
1895   *A Grammar of the New Testament Greek.* Translated by J. H. Thayer. Andover: Draper.

Byrne, B.
1983   "Sinning against One's Own Body: Paul's Understanding of the Sexual Relationship in 1 Corinthians 6:18." *Catholic Biblical Quarterly* 45:608–16.

1987   "Ministry and Maturity in 1 Corinthians 3." *Australian Biblical Review* 35:83–87.

Cadbury, H. J.
1931   "Erastus of Corinth." *Journal of Biblical Literature* 50:42–58.

1934   "The *Macellum* of Corinth." *Journal of Biblical Literature* 53:134–41.

Cadoux, C. J.
1941   "The Imperatival Use of Ἵνα in the New Testament." *Journal of Theological Studies* 42:165–73.

Caird, G. B.
1956   *Principalities and Powers: A Study in Pauline Theology.* Oxford: Clarendon.

1969   "Towards a Lexicon of the Septuagint, II." *Journal of Theological Studies,* n.s., 20:21–40.

Callan, T.
1985   "Prophecy and Ecstasy in Greco-Roman Religion and 1 Corinthians." *Novum Testamentum* 27:125–40.

Calvin, J.
1960   *The First Epistle of Paul the Apostle to the Corinthians.* Calvin's New Testament Commentaries 9. Translated by J. W. Fraser. Edited by D. W. Torrance and T. F. Torrance. Grand Rapids: Eerdmans.

Cambier, J.
1968–69   "La Chair et l'Esprit en I Cor. v.5." *New Testament Studies* 15:221–32.

Campbell, B.

1993   "Flesh and Spirit in 1 Cor 5:5: An Exercise in Rhetorical Criticism of the NT." *Journal of the Evangelical Theological Society* 36:331–42.

Campbell, R. A.

1991   "Does Paul Acquiesce in Divisions at the Lord's Supper?" *Novum Testamentum* 33:61–70.

Caragounis, C.

1974   "Ὀψώνιον: A Reconsideration of Its Meaning." *Novum Testamentum* 16:35–57.

1995a   "The Error of Erasmus and Un-Greek Pronunciation of Greek." *Filologia Neotestamentica* 8:151–85.

1995b   "'To Boast' or 'To Be Burned'? The Crux of 1 Cor 13:3." *Svensk exegetisk årsbok* 60:115–27.

1996   "'Fornication' and 'Concession'? Interpreting 1 Cor 7,1–7." Pp. 543–59 in *The Corinthian Correspondence.* Edited by R. Bieringer. Bibliotheca ephemeridum theologicarum lovaniensium 125. Leuven: Peeters.

Carr, A. W.

1976–77   "The Rulers of This Age—I Corinthians ii.6–8." *New Testament Studies* 23:20–35.

Carrez, M.

1985   "Résurrection et seigneurie du Christ: 1Co 15,23–28." Pp. 127–69 in *Resurrection du Christ et des Chrétiens (1 Co 15).* Edited by J.-N. Aletti, S. Agourides, and L. De Lorenzi. Monographic Series of "Benedictina": Biblical-Ecumenical Section 8. Rome: St. Paul's Abbey.

Carson, D. A.

1986   "Pauline Inconsistency: Reflections on I Corinthians 9.19–23 and Galatians 2.11–14." *Churchman* 100:6–45.

1987   *Showing the Spirit: A Theological Exposition of 1 Corinthians 12–14.* Grand Rapids: Baker.

Carter, T. L.

1997   "'Big Men' in Corinth." *Journal for the Study of the New Testament* 66:45–71.

Cartlidge, D.

1975   "1 Corinthians 7 as a Foundation for the Christian Sex Ethic." *Journal of Religion* 55:220–34.

Castelli, E. A.

1991   *Imitating Paul: A Discourse of Power.* Louisville: Westminster/John Knox.

Cerfaux, L.

1931   "Vestige d'un florilège dans 1 Cor 1,18–3,23?" *Revue d'histoire ecclésiastique* 27:521–34.

Cervin, R. S.

1989   "Does Κεφαλή Mean 'Source' or 'Authority over' in Greek Literature? A Rebuttal." *Trinity Journal* 10:85–112.

Chadwick, H.

1954–55   "'All Things to All Men' (I Cor ix.22)." *New Testament Studies* 1:261–75.

Cheung, A. T.

1999   *Idol Food in Corinth: Jewish Background and Pauline Legacy.* Journal for the Study of the New Testament: Supplement Series 176. Sheffield: Sheffield Academic Press.

Chevallier, M.-A.

1966   *Esprit de Dieu, paroles d'hommes.* Neuchâtel: Delachaux.

Chow, J. K.

1992   *Patronage and Power: A Study of Social Networks in Corinth.* Journal for the Study of the New Testament: Supplement Series 75. Sheffield: JSOT Press.

Christensen, J.

1990   "And That He Rose on the Third Day according to the Scriptures." *Scandinavian Journal of Old Testament* 2:101–13.

Ciampi, R. E.

1998   *The Presence and Function of Scripture in Galatians 1 and 2.* Wissenschaftliche Untersuchungen zum Neuen Testament 2/102. Tübingen: Mohr.

Clarke, A. D.

1993   *Secular and Christian Leadership in Corinth: A Socio-Historical and Exegetical Study of 1 Corinthians 1–6.* Arbeiten zur Geschichte des antiken Judentums und des Urchristentums 18. Leiden: Brill.

1996   "'Refresh the Hearts of the Saints': A Unique Pauline Context." *Tyndale Bulletin* 47:275–300.

2000   *Serve the Community of the Church: Christians as Leaders and Ministers.* First-Century Christians in the Graeco-Roman World. Grand Rapids: Eerdmans.

Cohn-Sherbok, D.
1980–81 "A Jewish Note on Τὸ Ποτήριον τῆς Εὐλογίας." *New Testament Studies* 27:704–9.

Coleman, P.
1975–76 "The Translation of Παρεδίδοτο in 1 Co 11:23." *Expository Times* 87:375.

Collier, G. D.
1994 "'That We Might Not Crave Evil': The Structure and Argument of 1 Cor. 10:1–13." *Journal for the Study of the New Testament* 55:55–75.

Collins, A. Y.
1980 "The Function of 'Excommunication' in Paul." *Harvard Theological Review* 73:251–63.

Collins, J. J.
1993 *Daniel.* Hermeneia. Minneapolis: Fortress.

Collins, R. F.
1978 "The Bible and Sexuality, II." *Biblical Theology Bulletin* 8:3–18.
1999 *First Corinthians.* Sacra Pagina 7. Collegeville, Minn.: Liturgical Press.

Colson, F. N.
1916 "Μετεσχημάτισα in 1 Cor. iv. 6." *Journal for Theological Studies* 17:379–83.

Conzelmann, H.
1975 *1 Corinthians.* Translated by J. W. Leitch. Hermeneia. Philadelphia: Fortress.

Cope, L.
1978 "1 Cor 11:2–16: One Step Further." *Journal of Biblical Literature* 97:435–36.
1990 "First Corinthians 8–10: Continuity or Contradiction?" *Anglican Theological Review,* Supplement, 11:114–23.

Corrington, G. P.
1991 "The 'Headless Woman': Paul and the Language of the Body in 1 Cor. 11:2–16." *Perspectives in Religious Studies* 18:223–31.

Cottle, R. E.
1974 "All Were Baptized." *Journal of the Evangelical Theological Society* 17:75–80.

Countryman, L. W.
1988 *Dirt, Greed, and Sex: Sexual Ethics in the New Testament and Their Implications for Today.* Philadelphia: Fortress.

Craig, C. T.
1953 "The First Epistle to the Corinthians (Exegesis)." Vol. 10 / pp. 1–262 in *The Interpreter's Bible.* Edited by G. A. Buttrick. Nashville: Abingdon.

Craigie, P. C.
1976 *The Book of Deuteronomy.* New International Commentary on the Old Testament. Grand Rapids: Eerdmans.

Cranfield, C. E. B.
1975 *A Critical and Exegetical Commentary on the Epistle to the Romans.* International Critical Commentary. 2 volumes. Edinburgh: Clark.

Crook, J. A.
1967 *Law and Life of Rome.* London: Thames & Hudson.

Crüsemann, M.
2000 "Irredeemably Hostile to Women: Anti-Jewish Elements in the Exegesis of the Dispute about Women's Right to Speak (1 Cor. 14.34–35)." *Journal for the Study of the New Testament* 79:19–36.

Cullmann, O.
1960 *Christ and Time: The Primitive Christian Conception of Time and History.* Translated by F. V. Filson. Philadelphia: Westminster.
1964 "All Who Call on the Name of the Lord Jesus Christ." *Journal of Ecumenical Studies* 1:1–21.

Cuming, G. J.
1975–76 "Service-Endings in the Epistles." *New Testament Studies* 22:110–13.
1980–81 "'Εποτίσθημεν (I Corinthians 12.13)." *New Testament Studies* 27:283–85.

Currie, S. D.
1965 "Speaking in Tongues: Early Evidence outside the New Testament Bearing on 'Glōssais Lalein.'" *Interpretation* 19:274–94.

Dahl, M. E.
1962 *The Resurrection of the Body: A Study of 1 Corinthians 15.* Studies in Biblical Theology 36. Naperville, Ill.: Allenson.

Dahl, N. A.
1977 *Studies in Paul: Theology for the Early Christian Mission.* Minneapolis: Augsburg.

Danker, F. W.
1989 *II Corinthians.* Augsburg Commentary on the New Testament. Minneapolis: Augsburg.

D'Arms, J.
1990   "The Roman *Convivium* and the Idea of Equality." Pp. 308–20 in *Sympotica: A Symposium on the Symposium*. Edited O. Murray. Oxford: Clarendon.

Das, A. A.
1998   "1 Corinthians 11:17–34 Revisited." *Concordia Theological Review* 62:187–208.

Daube, D.
1956   *The New Testament and Rabbinic Judaism*. London: Athlone.
1969   "Concessions to Sinfulness in Jewish Law." *Journal of Jewish Studies* 10:1–13.
1971   "Pauline Contributions to a Pluralistic Culture: Re-creation and Beyond." Vol. 2 / pp. 223–45 in *Jesus and Man's Hope*. Edited by D. G. Miller and D. Y. Hadidian. Pittsburgh: Pickwick.

Dautzenberg, G.
1971   "Zum religionsgeschichtlichen Hintergrund der Διάκρισις Πνευμάτων (1 Kor 12,10)." *Biblische Zeitschrift* 15:93–104.
1975   *Urchristliche Prophetie: Ihre Erforschung, ihre Voraussetzungen im Judentum und ihre Struktur im ersten Korintherbrief*. Beiträge zur Wissenschaft vom Alten (und Neuen) Testament 6/4. Stuttgart: Kohlhammer.
1989   "Φεύγετε τὴν Πορνείαν (1 Kor. 6,18): Eine Fallstudie zur paulinischen Sexualethik in ihrem Verhältnis zur Sexualethik des Frühjudentums." Pp. 271–98 in *Neues Testament und Ethik: Für Rudolf Schnackenburg*. Edited by H. Merklein. Freiburg: Herder.

Davidson, J. N.
1997   *Courtesans and Fishcakes: The Consuming Passions of Classical Athens*. New York: St. Martin's Press.

Davidson, R. M.
1981   *Typology in Scripture: A Study of Hermeneutical Τύπος Structures*. Andrews University Seminary Studies 2. Berrien Springs, Mich.: Andrews University Press

Davies, P. R.
1995   "Who Can Join the 'Damascus Covenant'?" *Journal for Jewish Studies* 46:134–42.

Davies, W. D.
1963   *The Setting of the Sermon on the Mount*. Cambridge: Cambridge University Press.

Davis, J. A.
1984   *Wisdom and Spirit: An Investigation of 1 Cor. 1:18–3:20 against the Background of Jewish Sapiential Traditions in the Greco-Roman Period*. Lanham, Md.: University Press of America.

Dawes, G. W.
1990   "'But If You Can Gain Your Freedom' (1 Corinthians 7:17–24)." *Catholic Biblical Quarterly* 52:681–97.
1996   "The Danger of Idolatry: First Corinthians 8:7–13." *Catholic Biblical Quarterly* 58:82–98.

DBSup   *Dictionnaire de la Bible: Supplément*. Edited by L. Pirot and A. Robert. Paris: Letouzey et Ané, 1928–.

Deidun, T.
1981   *New Covenant Morality in Paul*. Analecta biblica 89. Rome: Pontifical Biblical Institute Press.

Deissmann, A.
1903   *Bible Studies*. 2d edition. Translated by A. Grieve. Edinburgh: Clark.
1911   *Light from the Ancient East*. Translated by L. R. M. Strachan. London: Hodder & Stoughton. Reprinted Grand Rapids: Baker, 1964.

DeLacey, D. R.
1982   "One Lord in Pauline Christology." Pp. 191–203 in *Christ the Lord: Studies in Christology: Festschrift for D. Guthrie*. Edited by H. H. Rowdon. Leicester: Paternoster.

Delcor, M.
1968   "The Courts of the Church in Corinth and the Courts of Qumran." Pp. 69–84 in *Paul and Qumran: Studies in New Testament Exegesis*. Edited by J. Murphy-O'Connor. London: Chapman. Reprinted New York: Crossroad, 1990.

Delling, G.
1931   *Paulus' Stellung zu Frau und Ehe*. Beiträge zur Wissenschaft vom Alten und Neuen Testament 4/5. Stuttgart: Kohlhammer.

Delobel, J.
1986   "1 Cor 11:2–16: Towards a Coherent Explanation." Pp. 369–89 in *L'Apôtre Paul: Personnalité, style et conception du ministère*. Edited by A. Vanhoye.

Bibliotheca ephemeridum theologicarum lovaniensium 73. Leuven: Leuven University Press/Peeters.

1994   "Textual Criticism and Exegesis: Siamese Twins?" Pp. 98–117 in *New Testament Textual Criticism, Exegesis, and Church History: A Discussion of Methods*. Edited by B. Aland and J. Delobel. Contributions to Biblical Exegesis and Theology 7. Kampen: Kok Pharos.

DeMaris, R. E.
1995a   "Corinthian Religion and Baptism for the Dead (1 Corinthians 15:29): Insights from Archaeology and Anthropology." *Journal for Biblical Literature* 114:661–82.

1995b   "Demeter in Roman Corinth: Local Development in a Mediterranean Religion." *Numen* 42:105–117.

Deming, W.
1992   "The Unity of 1 Corinthians 5–6." *Journal of Biblical Literature* 115:289–312.

1995a   "A Diatribe Pattern in 1 Cor 7:21–22: A New Perspective on Paul's Directions to Slaves." *Novum Testamentum* 37:130–37.

1995b   *Paul on Marriage and Celibacy: The Hellenistic Background of 1 Corinthians 7*. Society of New Testament Studies Monograph Series 83. Cambridge: Cambridge University Press.

1996   "The Unity of 1 Corinthians 5–6." *Journal of Biblical Literature* 115:289–312.

Denaux, A.
1996   "Theology and Christology in 1 Cor 8,4–6." Pp. 593–606 in *The Corinthian Correspondence*. Edited by R. Bieringer. Bibliotheca ephemeridum theologicarum lovaniensium 125. Leuven: Peeters.

Denniston, J. D.
1959   *The Greek Particles*. Oxford: Oxford University Press.

Derrett, J. D. M.
1974–75   "Cursing Jesus (I Cor. xii.3): The Jews as Religious 'Persecutors.'" *New Testament Studies* 21:544–54.

1977   *Studies in the New Testament*, vol. 1: *Glimpses of the Legal and Social Presuppositions of the Authors*. Leiden: Brill.

1991   "Judgement and 1 Corinthians 6." *New Testament Studies* 37:22–36.

1997   "Paul as Master-Builder." *Evangelical Quarterly* 69:129–37.

De Saeger, L.
2001   "'Für unsere Sünden': 1 Kor 15,3b und Gal 1,4a im exegetischen Vergleich." *Ephemerides theologicae lovanienses* 77:169–91.

DeSilva, D. A.
2000   *Honor, Patronage, Kinship, and Purity: Unlocking New Testament Culture*. Downers Grove, Ill.: InterVarsity.

de Ste. Croix, G. E. M.
1981   *The Class Struggle in the Ancient Greek World*. Ithaca: Cornell University Press.

De Vos, C. S.
1998   "Stepmothers, Concubines, and the Case of Πορνεία in I Corinthians 5." *New Testament Studies* 44:104–14.

1999   *Church and Community Conflicts: The Relationships of the Thessalonian, Corinthian, and Philippian Churches with Their Wider Civic Communities*. Society of Biblical Literature Dissertation Series 168. Atlanta: Scholars Press.

Dinkler, E.
1952   "Zum Problem der Ethik bei Paulus: Rechtsnahme und Rechtsverzicht, I Kor. 6,1–11." *Zeitschrift für Theologie und Kirche* 49:167–200.

Dixon, S.
1992   *The Roman Family*. Baltimore: Johns Hopkins University Press.

Dodd, B.
1995   "Paul's Paradigmatic 'I' and 1 Corinthians 6.12." *Journal for the Study of the New Testament* 59:39–58.

1999   *Paul's Paradigmatic "I": Personal Example as Literary Strategy*. Journal for the Study of the New Testament: Supplement Series 177. Sheffield: Sheffield Academic Press.

Dodd, C. H.
1924–25   "Notes from Papyri." *Journal of Theological Studies* 26:77.

1968   *More New Testament Studies*. Manchester: University of Manchester Press.

Dolfe, K. G. E.
1992   "1 Cor. 7,25 Reconsidered (Paul a Supposed Adviser)." *Zeitschrift für die neutestamentliche Wissenschaft* 83:115–18.

Dominy, B.
1983   "Paul and Spiritual Gifts: Reflections on I Corinthians 12–14." *Southwestern Journal of Theology* 26:46–68.

Donfried, K. P.
1976   "Justification and Last Judgment in Paul." *Zeitschrift für die neutestamentliche Wissenschaft* 67:90–110.

Doughty, D. J.
1975   "The Presence and Future of Salvation in Corinth." *Zeitschrift für die neutestamentliche Wissenschaft* 66:61–90.

Dover, K. J.
1978   *Greek Homosexuality*. London: Duckworth.

Downey, J.
1985   "1 Cor 15.29 and the Theology of Baptism." *Euntes Docete* 38:23–25.

Downing, F. G.
1983–84   "Reflecting the First Century: 1 Corinthians 13:12." *Expository Times* 95:176–77.

DPL   *Dictionary of Paul and His Letters*. Edited by G. F. Hawthorne and R. P. Martin. Downers Grove, Ill.: InterVarsity, 1993.

Driver, S. R.
1889   "Notes on Three Passages in St. Paul's Epistles." *Expositor*, 3d series, 9:15–23.

Duff, A. M.
1928   *Freedmen in the Early Roman Empire*. Oxford: Oxford University Press. Reprinted Cambridge: Heffer, 1958.

Dungan, D. L.
1971   *The Sayings of Jesus in the Churches of Paul: The Use of the Synoptic Tradition in the Regulation of Early Church Life*. Philadelphia: Fortress.

Dunn, J. D. G.
1970   *Baptism in the Holy Spirit*. Philadelphia: Westminster.
1973   "1 Corinthians 15:45—Last Adam, Life-Giving Spirit." Pp. 113–26 in *Christ and Spirit in the New Testament: Studies in Honour of Charles Francis Digby Moule*. Edited by B. Lindars and S. S. Smalley. Cambridge: Cambridge University Press.
1975   *Jesus and the Spirit: A Study of the Religious and Charismatic Experience of Jesus and the First Christians as Reflected in the New Testament*. Philadelphia: Westminster.
1977   *Unity and Diversity in the New Testament*. Philadelphia: Westminster.
1980   *Christology in the Making*. Philadelphia: Westminster.
1988a   *Romans 1–8*. Word Biblical Commentary 38A. Dallas: Word.
1988b   *Romans 9–16*. Word Biblical Commentary 38B. Dallas: Word.
1991   *The Partings of the Ways between Christianity and Judaism and Their Significance for the Character of Christianity*. Philadelphia: Trinity.
1994   "Jesus Tradition in Paul." Pp. 155–78 in *Studying the Historical Jesus: Evaluations of the State of the Current Research*. Edited by B. Chilton and C. A. Evans. Leiden: Brill.
1995   *1 Corinthians*. New Testament Guides. Sheffield: Sheffield Academic Press.
1998   *The Theology of Paul the Apostle*. Grand Rapids: Eerdmans.

du Plessis, P. J.
1959   *Τέλειος: The Idea of Perfection in the New Testament*. Kampen: Kok.

Dykstra, W.
1969   "1 Corinthians 15:20–28: An Essential Part of Paul's Argument against Those Who Deny the Resurrection." *Calvin Theological Journal* 4:195–211.

Ebner, M.
1991   *Leidenlisten und Apostelbrief: Untersuchungen zu Form, Motivik und Funktion der Peristasenkataloge bei Paulus*. Forschung zur Bibel 66. Würzburg: Echter.

Eckstein, H.-J.
1983   *Der Begriff Syneidesis bei Paulus*. Wissenschaftliche Untersuchungen zum Neuen Testament 2/10. Tübingen: Mohr.

Edwards, T. C.
1885   *A Commentary on the First Epistle to the Corinthians*. 2d edition. London: Hodder & Stoughton.

Ellingworth, P., and H. Hatton
1985   *A Translator's Handbook on Paul's First Letter to the Corinthians*. London/New York/Stuttgart: United Bible Societies.

Elliott, J. K.
1971   "In Favour of Καυθήσομαι at 1 Cor. 13:3." *Zeitschrift für die neutestamentliche Wissenschaft* 62:297–98.

1972–73   "Paul's Teaching on Marriage in 1 Corinthians: Some Problems Considered." *New Testament Studies* 19:219–25.

Elliott, J. K. (ed.)

1993   *The Apocryphal New Testament: A Collection of Apocryphal Christian Literature in an English Translation.* Oxford: Clarendon.

Elliott, N.

1997   "The Anti-Imperial Message of the Cross." Pp. 167–83 in *Paul and Empire: Religion and Power in Roman Imperial Society.* Edited by R. A. Horsley. Harrisburg, Pa.: Trinity.

Ellis, E. E.

1957   *Paul's Use of the Old Testament.* Grand Rapids: Eerdmans.

1974   "'Wisdom' and 'Knowledge' in 1 Corinthians." *Tyndale Bulletin* 25:82–98.

1978   *Prophecy and Hermeneutic in Early Christianity.* Grand Rapids: Eerdmans.

1981   "The Silenced Wives of Corinth (1 Cor 14:34–35)." Pp. 213–20 in *New Testament Textual Criticism and Its Significance for Exegesis: Essays in Honour of Bruce M. Metzger.* Edited by E. J. Epp and G. D. Fee. Oxford: Clarendon.

Elmslie, W. A. L.

1911   *The Mishnah on Idolatry.* Translated by J. A. Robinson. Text and Studies 8.2. Cambridge: Cambridge University Press.

Engberg-Pedersen, T.

1987   "The Gospel and Social Practice according to 1 Corinthians." *New Testament Studies* 33:557–84.

1991   "1 Corinthians 11:16 and the Character of Pauline Exhortation." *Journal of Biblical Literature* 110:679–89.

1993   "Proclaiming the Lord's Death: 1 Corinthians 11:17–34 and the Forms of Paul's Theological Argument." Pp. 103–32 in *Pauline Theology,* vol. 2: *1 and 2 Corinthians.* Edited by D. M. Hay. Minneapolis: Fortress.

Engels, D.

1990   *Roman Corinth: An Alternative Model for the Classical City.* Chicago: University of Chicago Press.

Enns, P. E.

1996   "The 'Moveable Well' in 1 Cor 10:4: An Extrabiblical Tradition in an Apostolic Text." *Bulletin of Biblical Research* 6:23–38.

Enslin, M. S.

1930   *The Ethics of Paul.* New York: Harper.

Epstein, D. F.

1987   *Personal Enmity in Roman Politics, 214–43 B.C.* London: Croom Helm.

Eriksson, A.

1998   *Traditions as Rhetorical Proof: Pauline Argumentation in 1 Corinthians.* Coniectanea biblica: New Testament Series 29. Stockholm: Almqvist & Wiksell.

Esler, P. F.

1994   *The First Christians in Their Social Worlds: Social-Scientific Approaches to New Testament Interpretation.* London/New York: Routledge.

Evans, C. A.

1982   "The Colossian Mystics." *Biblica* 63:188–205.

Evans, O. E.

1974–75   "New Wine in Old Wineskins: XIII. The Saints." *Expository Times* 86:196–200.

Exler, F. X. J.

1923   *The Form of the Ancient Greek Letter of the Epistolary Papyri.* Washington, D.C.: Catholic University of America. Reprinted Chicago: University of Chicago Press, 1976.

Falk, Z. W.

1978   *Introduction to Jewish Law of the Second Commonwealth.* Arbeit zur Geschichte des antiken Judentums und des Urchristentums 11. Leiden: Brill.

Fanning, B. M.

1990   *Verbal Aspect in New Testament Greek.* Oxford: Clarendon.

Farmer, W. R.

1993   "Peter and Paul, and the Tradition concerning 'The Lord's Supper' in 1 Cor 11:23–26." Pp. 35–55 in *One Loaf, One Cup: Ecumenical Studies of 1 Cor 11 and Other Eucharistic Texts.* Edited by B. F. Meyer. New Gospel Studies 6. Macon, Ga.: Mercer University Press.

Fascher, E.

1929   "Zur Witwerschaft des Paulus und der Auslegung von 1 Cor 7." *Zeitschrift für die neutestamentliche Wissenschaft* 8:62–69.

Fee, G. D.

1980a   "Εἰδωλόθυτα Once Again: An Interpretation of 1 Corinthians 8–10." *Biblica* 61:172–97.

1980b   "1 Corinthians 7:1 in the *NIV*." *Journal of the Evangelical Theological Society* 23:307–14.

1987   *The First Epistle to the Corinthians.* New International Commentary on the New Testament. Grand Rapids: Eerdmans.

1993   "The Bishop and the Bible." *Crux* 29:34–39.

1994   *God's Empowering Presence: The Holy Spirit in the Letters of Paul.* Peabody, Mass.: Hendrickson.

Feldman, L. H.

1982   "Josephus' Portrait of Saul." *Hebrew Union College Annual* 53:45–99.

Feuillet, A.

1963   "L'énigme de 1 Cor. ii,9: Contribution à l'étude des sources de la christologie paulinienne." *Revue biblique* 70:52–74.

Filson, F. V.

1939   "The Significance of the Early House Churches." *Journal of Biblical Literature* 58:105–12.

Findlay, G. G.

1910   "St. Paul's First Epistle to the Corinthians." Pp. 728–953 in *The Expositor's Greek Testament.* Edited by W. R. Nicoll. Reprinted Grand Rapids: Eerdmans, 1979.

Fiore, B.

1985   "'Covert Allusion' in 1 Corinthians 1–4." *Catholic Biblical Quarterly* 47:85–102.

1986   *The Function of Personal Example in the Socratic and Pastoral Epistles.* Analecta biblica 105. Rome: Pontifical Biblical Institute Press.

1990   "Passion in Paul and Plutarch: 1 Corinthians 5–6 and the Polemic against Epicureans." Pp. 135–43 in *Greeks, Romans, and Christians: Essays in Honor of Abraham J. Malherbe.* Edited by D. L. Balch, E. Ferguson, and W. A. Meeks. Philadelphia: Fortress.

Fishbane, M.

1986   "Through the Looking Glass: Reflections on Ezek 43:3, Num 12:8 and 1 Cor 13:[12]." *Hebrew Annual Review* 10:63–75.

Fishburne, C. W.

1970–71   "1 Corinthians iii.10–15 and the Testament of Abraham." *New Testament Studies* 17:109–15.

Fisk, B. N.

1989   "Eating Meat Offered to Idols: Corinthian Behavior and Pauline Response in 1 Corinthians 8–10 (A Response to Gordon Fee)." *Trinity Journal* 10:49–70.

1996   "Πορνεύειν as Body Violation: The Unique Nature of the Sexual Sin in 1 Corinthians 6:18." *New Testament Studies* 42:540–58.

2000   *First Corinthians.* Interpretation Bible Studies. Louisville: Geneva.

Fitch, W. O.

1971   "Paul, Apollos, Christ: [1 Cor 1:12]." *Theology* 74:18–24.

Fitzer, G.

1963   *"Das Weib schweige in der Gemeinde": Über den unpaulinischen Charakter der mulier-taceat-Verse in 1. Korinther 14.* Theologische Existenz Heute, n.f., 110. Munich: Kaiser.

Fitzgerald, J. T.

1988   *Cracks in an Earthen Vessel: An Examination of the Catalogues of Hardships in the Corinthian Correspondence.* Society of Biblical Literature Dissertation Series 99. Atlanta: Scholars Press.

Fitzmyer, J. A.

1974   "A Feature of Qumran Angelology and the Angels of 1 Cor 11:10." Pp. 187–204 in *Essays on the Semitic Background of the New Testament.* Sources for Biblical Study 5. Missoula, Mont.: Scholars Press.

1976   "The Matthean Divorce Texts and Some New Palestinian Evidence." *Theological Studies* 37:199–226.

1981   "Kyrios and Maranatha and Their Aramaic Background." Pp. 218–35 in *To Advance the Gospel.* New York: Crossroad.

1989   "Another Look at Κεφαλή in 1 Corinthians 11:3." *New Testament Studies* 35:503–11.

1993   *"Kephalē* in 1 Cor. 11:3." *Interpretation* 47:32–59.

Flanagan, N. M., and E. S. Hunter

1981   "Did Paul Put Down Women in 1 Cor 14:34–36?" *Biblical Theological Bulletin* 11:10–12.

789

Forbes, C.
1995   *Prophecy and Inspired Speech in Early Christianity and Its Hellenistic Environment.* Wissenschaftliche Untersuchungen zum Neuen Testament 2/75. Tübingen: Mohr.
2001   "Paul's Principalities and Powers: Demythologizing Apocalyptic?" *Journal for the Study of the New Testament* 82:61–88.
2002   "Pauline Demonology and/or Cosmology? Principalities, Powers and the Elements of the World in Their Hellenistic Context." *Journal for the Study of the New Testament* 85:51–73.

Ford, J. M.
1963–64   "Levirate Marriage in St Paul (I Cor. vii)." *New Testament Studies* 10:361–65.
1966a   "The Meaning of 'Virgin.'" *New Testament Studies* 12:293–99.
1966b   "The Rabbinic Background of St. Paul's Use of Ὑπέρακμος." *Journal of Jewish Studies* 17:89–91.

Forkman, G.
1972   *The Limits of Religious Community: Expulsion from the Religious Community within the Qumran Sect, within Rabbinic Judaism, and within Primitive Christianity.* Translated by P. Sjolander. Coniectanea biblica: New Testament Series 5. Lund: Gleerup.

Foschini, B. M.
1950   "'Those Who Are Baptized for the Dead,' 1 Cor. 15:29: An Exegetical Historical Dissertation." *Catholic Biblical Quarterly* 12:260–76, 379–88.
1951   "'Those Who Are Baptized for the Dead,' 1 Cor. 15:29: An Exegetical Historical Dissertation." *Catholic Biblical Quarterly* 13:46–78, 172–98, 276–83.

Fox, R. L.
1986   *Pagans and Christians.* San Francisco: HarperCollins.

Francis, J.
1980   "As Babes in Christ—Some Proposals regarding 1 Cor. 3:1–3." *Journal for the Study of the New Testament* 7:41–60.

Frid, B.
1985   "The Enigmatic *Alla* in 1 Corinthians 2.9." *New Testament Studies* 31:603–11.

Fridrichsen, A.
1932   "Paulus abortivus: Zu 1 Kor. 15,8." Pp. 78–85 in *Symbolae philologicae O. A. Danielsson octogenario dicatae.* Uppsala: Lundequist.

Friedrich, G.
1956   "Lohmeyer's These über das paulinische Briefpräskript kritisch beleuchtet." *Theologische Literaturzeitung* 81:343–46.
1970   "Freiheit und Liebe im ersten Korintherbrief." *Theologische Zeitschrift* 26:81–98.

Fuller, R. H.
1986   "First Corinthians 6:1–11—an Exegetical Paper." *Ex auditu* 2:96–104.

Fung, R. Y. K.
1980   "Justification by Faith in 1 and 2 Corinthians." Pp. 246–61 in *Pauline Studies: Essays Presented to Professor F. F. Bruce on His Seventieth Birthday.* Edited by D. A. Hagner and M. J. Harris. Grand Rapids: Eerdmans.

Funk, R. W.
1966   *Language, Hermeneutic, and Word of God: The Problem of Language in the New Testament and Contemporary Theology.* New York: Harper.

Furnish, V. P.
1961   "Fellow Workers in God's Service." *Journal of Biblical Literature* 80:364–70.
1968   *Theology and Ethics in Paul.* Nashville: Abingdon.
1985   *The Moral Teaching of Paul.* 2d edition. Nashville: Abingdon.
1999   *The Theology of the First Letter to the Corinthians.* New Testament Theology. Cambridge: Cambridge University Press.

Gaffin, R. B.
1995   "Some Epistological Reflection on 1 Cor 2:6–16." *Westminster Theological Journal* 57:103–24.

Gager, J. G., Jr.
1970   "Functional Diversity in Paul's Use of End-Time Language." *Journal of Biblical Literature* 89:325–37.

Gagnon, R. A. J.
2001   *The Bible and Homosexual Practice: Texts and Hermeneutics.* Nashville: Abingdon.

Gale, H. M.
1964   *The Use of Analogy in the Letters of Paul.* Philadelphia: Westminster.

Gamble, H., Jr.

1977   *The Textual History of the Letter to the Romans.* Studies and Documents 42. Grand Rapids: Eerdmans.

Gardiner, E. N.

1930   *Athletics of the Ancient World.* Oxford: Clarendon. Reprinted Chicago: Ares, 1980.

Gardner, J. F.

1986   *Women in Roman Law and Society.* Bloomington/Indianapolis: Indiana University Press.

Gardner, P. D.

1994   *The Gifts of God and the Authentication of a Christian: An Exegetical Study of 1 Corinthians 8:1–11:1.* Lanham, Md.: University Press of America.

Garland, D. E.

1983   "The Christian's Posture toward Marriage and Celibacy: 1 Corinthians 7." *Review and Expositor* 80:351–62.

1993   *Reading Matthew: A Literary and Theological Commentary on the First Gospel.* New York: Crossroad.

1998   *Colossians/Philemon.* NIV Application Commentary. Grand Rapids: Zondervan.

1999   *2 Corinthians.* New American Commentary. Nashville: Broadman & Holman.

Garnsey, P.

1970   *Social Status and Legal Privilege in the Roman Empire.* Oxford: Clarendon.

1974   "Legal Privilege in the Roman Empire." Pp. 141–65 in *Studies in Ancient Society.* Edited by M. I. Finley. London/Boston: Routledge & Kegan Paul.

1991   "Mass Diet and Nutrition in the City of Rome." Pp. 90–112 in *Nourir la plebe.* Edited by A. Giovanni. Basel: Herder.

Garrison, R.

1997   *The Graeco-Roman Context of Early Christian Literature.* Journal for the Study of the New Testament: Supplement Series 137. Sheffield: Sheffield Academic Press.

Gärtner, B. E.

1965   *The Temple in the Community in Qumran and the New Testament: A Comparative Study in the Temple Symbolism of the Qumran Texts and the New Testament.* Society for New Testament Studies Monograph Series 1. Cambridge: Cambridge University Press.

1967–68   "The Pauline and Johannine Idea of 'to Know God' against the Hellenistic Background: The Greek Philosophical Principle 'Like by Like' in Paul and John." *New Testament Studies* 14:209–31.

Gaventa, B. R.

1983   "'You Proclaim the Lord's Death': 1 Corinthians 11:26 and Paul's Understanding of Worship." *Review and Expositor* 80:377–87.

1996   "Mother's Milk and Ministry in 1 Corinthians 3." Pp. 101–13 in *Theology and Ethics in Paul and His Interpreters: Essays in Honor of Victor Paul Furnish.* Edited by E. H. Lovering Jr. and J. L. Sumney. Nashville: Abingdon.

Gebhard, E. R.

1993   "The Isthmian Games and the Sanctuary of Poseidon in the Early Empire." Pp. 78–94 in *The Corinthia in the Roman Period.* Edited by T. E. Gregory. Journal of Roman Archaeology, Supplementary Series 8. Ann Arbor, Mich.: Journal of Roman Archaeology.

Geddert, T. J.

1989   *Watchwords: Mark 13 in Markan Eschatology.* Journal for the Study of the New Testament: Supplement Series 26. Sheffield: JSOT Press.

Geiger, R.

1983   "Die Stellung der geschiedenen Frau in der Umwelt des Neuen Testaments." Pp. 134–57 in *Die Frau im Urchristentum.* By J. Blank et al. Edited by G. Dautzenberg et al. Quaestiones disputatae 95. Freiburg: Herder.

George, A. R.

1944   "The Imperatival Use of ῞Ινα in the New Testament." *Journal of Theological Studies* 42:56–60.

George, T.

1988   *The Theology of the Reformers.* Nashville: Broadman.

Georgi, D.

1986   *The Opponents of Paul in Second Corinthians.* Philadelphia: Fortress.

Giblin, C. H.
1969 "A Negative Theology of Marriage and Celibacy?" *Bible Today* 41:2839–55.

Gibson, J. B.
1990 "Jesus' Refusal to Produce a 'Sign' (Mark 8.11–13)." *Journal for the Study of the New Testament* 38:37–66.

Gielen, M.
1999 "Beten und Prophezeien mit unverhülltem Kopf? Die Kontroverse zwischen Paulus und der korinthischen Gemeinde um die Wahrung der Geschlechtsrollensymbolik in 1 Kor 11,2–16." *Zeitschrift für die neutestamentliche Wissenschaft* 90:220–49.

Gill, D. W. J.
1989 "Erastus the Aedile." *Tyndale Bulletin* 40:293–301.
1990 "The Importance of Roman Portraiture for Head-Coverings in 1 Corinthians 11:2–16." *Tyndale Bulletin* 41:245–60.
1992 "The Meat-Market at Corinth (1 Corinthians 10:25)." *Tyndale Bulletin* 43:389–93.
1993 "Corinth: A Roman Colony in Achaea." *Biblische Zeitschrift* 37:259–64.

Gillespie, T. W.
1994 *The First Theologians: A Study in Early Christian Prophecy.* Grand Rapids: Eerdmans.

Gillman, J.
1982 "Transformation in 1 Cor 15,50–53." *Ephemerides theologicae lovanienses* 58:309–33.
1988 "A Thematic Comparison: 1 Cor 15:50–57 and 2 Cor 5:1–5." *Journal of Biblical Literature* 107:439–54.

Godet, F. L.
1886 *Commentary on the First Epistle of St. Paul to the Corinthians,* vol.1: *Chapters 1–8.* Translated by A. Cusin. Edinburgh: Clark.
1887 *Commentary on the First Epistle of St. Paul to the Corinthian,* vol. 2: *Chapters 9–16.* Translated by A. Cusin. Edinburgh: Clark.

Goldingay, J. E.
1989 *Daniel.* Word Biblical Commentary 30. Dallas: Word.

Gooch, P. D.
1993 *Dangerous Food: 1 Corinthians 8–10 in Its Context.* Studies in Christianity and Judaism 5. Waterloo, Ont.: Wilfred Laurier University Press.

Gooch, P. W.
1983 "Authority and Justification in Theological Ethics: A Study in 1 Corinthians 7." *Journal of Religious Ethics* 11:62–74.
1987a "'Conscience' in 1 Corinthians 8 and 10." *New Testament Studies* 33:244–54.
1987b *Partial Knowledge: Philosophical Studies in Paul.* Notre Dame: University of Notre Dame Press.

Goodspeed, E. J.
1917 "A Patristic Parallel to 1 Cor. 7:18, 21." *Journal of Biblical Literature* 36:150.
1950 "Gaius Titius Justus." *Journal of Biblical Literature* 69:382–83.

Goppelt, L.
1982 *Typos: The Typological Interpretation of the Old Testament in the New.* Translated by D. H. Madvig. Grand Rapids: Eerdmans.

Gordon, J. D.
1997 *Sister or Wife? 1 Corinthians 7 and Cultural Anthropology.* Journal for the Study of the New Testament: Supplement Series 149. Sheffield: Sheffield Academic Press.

Goudge, H. L.
1911 *The First Epistle to the Corinthians.* 3d edition. Westminster Commentaries. London: Methuen.

Goulder, M. D.
1991 "Σοφία in 1 Corinthians." *New Testament Studies* 37:516–34.
1994 *St. Paul versus St. Peter: A Tale of Two Missions.* Louisville: Westminster/John Knox.
1999 "Libertines? (1 Cor. 5–6)." *Novum Testamentum* 41:334–48.
2001 *Paul and the Competing Mission in Corinth.* Peabody, Mass.: Hendrickson.

Gowers, E.
1993 *The Loaded Table: Representations of Food in Roman Literature.* Oxford: Clarendon.

Grant, R. M.
1986 *Gods and the One God.* Library of Early Christianity. Philadelphia: Westminster.

Grindheim, S.
2002 "Wisdom for the Perfect: Paul's Challenge to the Corinthian Church

(1 Corinthians 2:6–16)." *Journal of Biblical Literature* 121:689–709.

Grosheide, F. W.
1953   *Commentary on the First Epistle to the Corinthians.* New International Commentary on the New Testament. Grand Rapids: Eerdmans.

Grudem, W. A.
1979   "1 Corinthians 14:20–25: Prophecy and Tongues as Signs of God's Attitude." *Westminster Theological Journal* 41:381–96.
1982   *The Gift of Prophecy in 1 Corinthians.* Lanham, Md.: University Press of America.
1985   "Does *Kephalē* (Head) Mean 'Source' or 'Authority over' in Greek Literature? A Survey of 2,336 Examples." *Trinity Journal* 6:38–59.
1990   "The Meaning of Κεφαλή: A Response to Recent Studies." *Trinity Journal* 11:3–72.

Guenther, A. R.
2002   "One Woman or Two? 1 Corinthians 7:34." *Bulletin of Biblical Research* 12:33–45.

Gundry, R. H.
1966   "'Ecstatic Utterance' (N.E.B.)?" *Journal for Theological Studies* 17:299–307.
1976   *Sōma in Biblical Theology with Emphasis on Pauline Anthropology.* Society for New Testament Studies Monograph Series 29. Cambridge: Cambridge University Press.

Gundry Volf, J. M.
1990   *Paul and Perseverance: Staying in and Falling Away.* Wissenschaftliche Untersuchungen zum Neuen Testament 2/37. Tübingen: Mohr. Reprinted Louisville: Westminster/John Knox, 1990.
1996   "Controlling the Bodies: A Theological Profile of the Corinthian Sexual Ascetics (1 Cor 7)." Pp. 519–41 in *The Corinthian Correspondence.* Edited by R. Bieringer. Bibliotheca ephemeridum theologicarum lovaniensium 125. Leuven: Peeters.
1997   "Gender and Creation in 1 Corinthians 11:2–6: A Study in Paul's Theological Method." Pp. 151–71 in *Evangelium Schriftauslegung Kirche: Festschrift für Peter Stuhlmacher zum 65. Geburtstag.* Edited by J. Ådna, S. J. Hafemann, and O.

Hofius. Göttingen: Vandenhoeck & Ruprecht.

Guthrie, D.
1981   *New Testament Theology.* Downers Grove, Ill.: InterVarsity.

Güzlow, H.
1969   *Christentum und Sklaverei in den ersten drei Jahrhunderten.* Bonn: Habelt.

Hafemann, S. J.
1986   *Suffering and Ministry in the Spirit: Paul's Defense of His Ministry in II Corinthians 2:14–3:3.* Wissenschaftliche Untersuchungen zum Neuen Testament 2/19. Tübingen: Mohr. Reprinted Grand Rapids: Eerdmans, 1990.
1996a   *Paul, Moses, and the History of Israel: The Letter/Spirit Contrast and the Argument from Scripture in 2 Corinthians 3.* Peabody, Mass.: Hendrickson.
1996b   "Paul's Argument from the Old Testament and Christology in 2 Cor 1–9." Pp. 277–303 in *The Corinthian Correspondence.* Edited by R. Bieringer. Bibliotheca ephemeridum theologicarum lovaniensium 125. Leuven: Peeters.

Hall, B.
1990   "All Things to All People: A Study of 1 Corinthians 9:19–23." Pp. 137–57 in *The Conversation Continues: Studies in Paul and John in Honor of J. Louis Martyn.* Edited by R. T. Fortna and B. R. Gaventa. Nashville: Abingdon.

Hall, D. R.
1994   "A Disguise for the Wise: Μετασχηματισμός in 1 Corinthians 4.6." *New Testament Studies* 40:143–49.

Hall, R. G.
1992   "Epispasm: Circumcision in Reverse." *Bible Review* 8.4:52–57.

Hanges, J. C.
1998   "1 Corinthians 4:6 and the Possibility of Written Bylaws in the Corinthian Church." *Journal of Biblical Literature* 117:275–98.

Hanson, A. T.
1965   *Jesus Christ in the Old Testament.* London: SPCK.
1974   *Studies in Paul's Technique and Theology.* Grand Rapids: Eerdmans.

Harding, M.
1989 "Church and Gentile Cults in Corinth." *Grace Theological Journal* 10:203–23.

Harrill, J. A.
1995 *The Manumission of Slaves in Early Christianity.* Hermeneutische Untersuchungen zur Theologie 32. Tübingen: Mohr.

Harris, B. F.
1962 "Συνείδησις (Conscience) in the Pauline Writings." *Westminster Theological Journal* 24:173–86.

Harris, G.
1991 "The Beginnings of Church Discipline: 1 Corinthians 5." *New Testament Studies* 37:1–21.

Harris, H. A.
1976 *Greek Athletics and the Jews.* Cardiff: University of Wales Press.

Harris, M. J.
1971 "2 Corinthians 5:1–10: A Watershed in Paul's Theology?" *Tyndale Bulletin* 22:32–57.

Harris, W.
1981 "Echoing Bronze." *Journal of the Acoustical Society of America* 70:1184–85.
1982 "'Sounding Brass' and Hellenistic Terminology." *Biblical Archaeology Review* 8:38–41.

Harrisville, R. A.
1987 *1 Corinthians.* Augsburg Commentary on the New Testament. Minneapolis: Augsburg.

Hartman, L.
1974 "Some Remarks on 1 Cor. 2:1–5." *Svensk exegetisk årsbok* 39:109–20.

Harvey, A. E.
1985 "Forty Strokes Save One: Social Aspects of Judaizing and Apostasy." Pp. 79–96 in *Alternative Approaches to New Testament Study.* Edited by A. E. Harvey. London: SPCK.

Hasitschka, M.
1997 "'Die Frauen in den Gemeinden sollen schweigen': 1 Kor 14,33b–36—Anweisung des Paulus zur rechten Ordnung im Gottesdienst." *Studium zum Neuen Testaments und seiner Umwelt* 22:47–56.

Havener, I.
1979 "A Curse for Salvation—1 Corinthians 5:1–5." Pp. 333–44 in *Sin, Salvation, and the Spirit.* Edited by D. Durken. Collegeville, Minn.: Liturgical Press.

Hays, R. B.
1986 "Relations Natural and Unnatural: A Response to John Boswell's Exegesis of Romans 1." *Journal of Religious Ethics* 14:184–215.
1987 "Christology and Ethics in Galatians: The Law of Christ." *Catholic Biblical Quarterly* 49:268–90.
1989 *Echoes of Scripture in the Letters of Paul.* New Haven: Yale University Press.
1997 *First Corinthians.* Interpretation. Louisville: John Knox.
1999 "The Conversion of the Imagination: Scripture and Eschatology in 1 Corinthians." *New Testament Studies* 45:391–412.

Heil, U.
1993 "Theo-logische Interpretation von 1 Kor 15,23–28." *Zeitschrift für die neutestamentliche Wissenschaft* 84:27–35.

Henderson, S. W.
2002 "'If Anyone Hungers . . .': An Integrated Reading of 1 Cor 11.17–34." *New Testament Studies* 48:195–208.

Hengel, M.
1977 *Crucifixion in the Ancient World and the Folly of the Message of the Cross.* Translated by J. Bowden. Philadelphia: Fortress.
1981 *The Atonement: The Origins of the Doctrine in the New Testament.* Translated by J. Bowden. Philadelphia: Fortress.
1991 *The Pre-Christian Paul.* Translated by J. Bowden. Philadelphia: Trinity.
2000 *The Four Gospels and the One Gospel of Jesus Christ.* Translated by J. Bowden. Harrisburg, Pa.: Trinity.

Héring, J.
1962 *The First Epistle of Saint Paul to the Corinthians.* Translated by A. W. Heathcote and P. J. Allcock. London: Epworth.

Herz, N.
1895–96 "A Hebrew Word in Greek Disguise: I Cor. vii.3." *Expository Times* 7:48.

Highet, G.
1973 "Libertino patre natus." *American Journal of Philology* 94:268–81.

Hill, A. E.
1980 "The Temple of Asclepius: An Alternative Source for Paul's Body Theol-

ogy." *Journal of Biblical Literature* 99:437–39.

Hill, C. E.
1988   "Paul's Understanding of Christ's Kingdom in I Corinthians 15:20–28." *Novum Testamentum* 30:297–320.

Hill, D.
1979   *New Testament Prophecy.* Atlanta: John Knox.

Hjort, B. G.
2001   "Gender Hierarchy or Religious Androgyny? Male-Female Interaction in the Corinthian Community—A Reading of 1 Cor. 11,2–16." *Studia theologica* 55:58–80.

Hock, R. F.
1978   "Paul's Tentmaking and the Problem of His Social Class." *Journal of Biblical Literature* 97:555–64.

1980   *The Social Context of Paul's Ministry: Tentmaking and Apostleship.* Philadelphia: Fortress.

Hodgson, R.
1983   "Paul the Apostle and First Century Tribulation Lists." *Zeitschrift für die neutestamentliche Wissenschaft* 74:59–80.

Hofius, O.
1967–68   "'Bis dass er kommt' I. Kor. xi.26." *New Testament Studies* 14:439–41.

1975   "Das Zitat 1 Kor 2:9 und das koptische Testament des Jakob." *Zeitschrift für die neutestamentliche Wissenschaft* 66:140–42.

1983   "Das Gesetz des Mose und das Gesetz Christi." *Zeitschrift für Theologie und Kirche* 80:262–86.

1993   "The Lord's Supper and the Lord's Supper Tradition: Reflections on 1 Corinthians 11:23b–25." Pp. 75–115 in *One Loaf, One Cup: Ecumenical Studies of 1 Cor 11 and Other Eucharistic Texts.* Edited by B. F. Meyer. New Gospel Studies 6. Macon, Ga.: Mercer University Press.

Holl, K.
1928   "Die Geschichte des Wortes Beruf." Vol. 3 / pp. 189–219 in *Gesammelte Aufsätze zur Kirchengeschichte.* Tübingen: Mohr.

Holladay, C. R.
1990   "1 Corinthians 13: Paul as Apostolic Paradigm." Pp. 80–98 in *Greeks, Romans, and Christians: Essays in Honor of Abraham J. Malherbe.* Ed-

ited by D. L. Balch, E. Ferguson, and W. A. Meeks. Philadelphia: Fortress.

Hollander, H. W.
1994   "The Testing by Fire of the Builders' Works: 1 Corinthians 3.10–15." *New Testament Studies* 40:89–104.

Hollander, H. W., and J. Holleman
1993   "The Relationship of Death, Sin, and Law in 1 Cor 15:56." *Novum Testamentum* 35:270–91.

Hollander, H. W., and G. E. van der Hout
1996   "The Apostle Paul Calling Himself an Abortion: 1 Cor. 15:8 within the Context of 1 Cor. 15:8–10." *Novum Testamentum* 38:224–36.

Holleman, J.
1996   *Resurrection and Parousia: A Traditio-Historical Study of Paul's Eschatology in 1 Corinthians 15.* Supplements to Novum Testamentum 84. Leiden: Brill.

Holmberg, B.
1978   *Paul and Power: The Structure of Authority in the Primitive Church as Reflected in the Pauline Epistles.* Philadelphia: Fortress.

Holmyard, H. R., III
1997   "Does 1 Corinthians 11:2–6 Refer to Women Praying and Prophesying in Church?" *Bibliotheca Sacra* 154:461–72.

Holtz, T.
1995   "The Question of the Content of Paul's Instructions." Pp. 51–71 in *Understanding Paul's Ethics: Twentieth Century Approaches.* Translated by G. S. Rosner and B. S. Rosner. Edited by B. S. Rosner. Grand Rapids: Eerdmans.

Hooker, M. D.
1963–64a   "Authority on Her Head: An Examination of I Corinthians 11.10." *New Testament Studies* 10:410–16.

1963–64b   "'Beyond the Things Which Are Written'? An Examination of I Corinthians 4.6." *New Testament Studies* 10:127–32.

1966   "Hard Sayings: 1 Cor. 3:2." *Theology* 69:19–22.

1996   "A Partner in the Gospel: Paul's Understanding of Ministry." Pp. 83–100 in *Theology and Ethics in Paul and His Interpreters: Essays in Honor of Victor Paul Furnish.* Edited by E. H. Lovering Jr. and J. L. Sumney. Nashville: Abingdon.

Hopkins, K.
1978   *Conquerors and Slaves*. Sociological Studies in Roman History 1. Cambridge: Cambridge University Press.

Horn, F. W.
1991   "1 Korinther 15,56—ein exegetischer Stachel." *Zeitschrift für die neutestamentliche Wissenschaft* 82:88–105.

Horrell, D. G.
1996   *The Social Ethos of the Corinthian Correspondence: Interests and Ideology from 1 Corinthians to 1 Clement.* Studies of the New Testament and Its World. Edinburgh: Clark.
1997a   "'The Lord Commanded . . . but I Have Not Used . . .' Exegetical and Hermeneutical Reflections on 1 Cor 9.14–15." *New Testament Studies* 43:587–603.
1997b   "Theological Principle or Christological Praxis? Pauline Ethics in 1 Corinthians 8.1–11.1." *Journal for the Study of the New Testament* 67:83–114.

Horsley, G. H. R.
1987   *New Documents Illustrating Early Christianity*, vol. 4. North Ryde, N.S.W.: Macquarie University.
1989   "Review of Fitzgerald's *Cracks in an Earthen Vessel*." *Australian Biblical Review* 37:83–84.

Horsley, R. A.
1976   "Pneumatikos vs. Psychikos: Distinctions of Spiritual Status among the Corinthians." *Harvard Theological Review* 69:269–88.
1977   "Wisdom of Word and Words of Wisdom in Corinth." *Catholic Biblical Quarterly* 39:223–39.
1978a   "The Background of the Confessional Formula in 1 Cor 8:6." *Zeitschrift für die neutestamentliche Wissenschaft* 69:130–35.
1978b   "Consciousness and Freedom among the Corinthians." *Catholic Biblical Quarterly* 40:574–89.
1978c   "'How Can Some of You Say That There Is No Resurrection of the Dead?': Spiritual Elitism in Corinth." *Novum Testamentum* 20:203–31.
1979   "Spiritual Marriage with Sophia." *Vigiliae christianae* 33:46–51.
1980–81 "Gnosis in Corinth: I Corinthians 8.1–6." *New Testament Studies* 27:32–51.

1998   *1 Corinthians*. Abingdon New Testament Commentary. Nashville: Abingdon.

Hoskins, P. M.
2001   "The Use of Biblical and Extrabiblical Parallels in the Interpretation of First Corinthians 6:2–3." *Catholic Biblical Quarterly* 63:287–97.

Howard, J. K.
1965   "Baptism for the Dead: A Study of 1 Corinthians 15.29." *Evangelical Quarterly* 37:137–41.

Howard, W. F.
1921–22 "1 Corinthians iv.6 (Exegesis or Emendation?)." *Expository Times* 33:479–80.

Hudson, J. T.
1923–24 "1 Cor. iv.6." *Expository Times* 35:332.

Hugedé, N.
1957   *La métaphore du miroir dans les épîtres de Saint Paul aux Corinthiens.* Neuchâtel: Delachaux & Niestlé.

Hurd, J. C., Jr.
1965   *The Origin of 1 Corinthians*. New York: Seabury.

Hurley, J. B.
1973   "Did Paul Require Veils or the Silence of Women? A Consideration of 1 Cor 11,2–16 and 1 Cor 14,33b–36." *Westminster Theological Journal* 35:190–220.
1981   *Man and Woman in Biblical Perspective*. Grand Rapids: Zondervan.

Hutson, C. R.
1997   "Was Timothy Timid? On the Rhetoric of Fearlessness (1 Cor. 16:10–11) and Cowardice (2 Tim 1:7)." *Biblical Research* 42:58–73.

Iber, G.
1963   "Zum Verständnis von 1 Cor 12,31." *Zeitschrift für die neutestamentliche Wissenschaft* 54:43–53.

IG   *Inscriptiones graecae*. Editio minor. Berlin: de Gruyter, 1924–.

IGR   *Inscriptiones Graecae ad res Romanas pertinentes*. Edited by R. Cagnat et al. Rome: L'Erma, 1964.

Instone-Brewer, D.
2001   "1 Corinthians 7 in the Light of the Jewish Greek and Aramaic Marriage and Divorce Papyri." *Tyndale Bulletin* 52:225–43.

Isaksson, A.
1963   *Marriage and Ministry in the New
        Temple: A Study with Special Refer-
        ence to Mt 19.3–12 and 1 Cor 11.3–16.*
        Acta seminarii neotestamentici up-
        saliensis 24. Lund: Gleerup.

Jacobs, L. D.
1997   "Establishing a New Value System in
        Corinth: 1 Corinthians 5–6 as Per-
        suasive Argument." Pp. 374–87 in
        *The Rhetorical Analysis of Scripture:
        Essays from the 1995 London Confer-
        ence.* Edited by S. E. Porter and T. H.
        Olbricht. Journal for the Study of the
        New Testament: Supplement Series
        146. Sheffield: Sheffield Academic
        Press.

Jaubert, A.
1971–72 "Le voile des femmes (I Cor. xi.2–
        16)." *New Testament Studies* 18:419–
        30.

Jenkins, C.
1909   "Origen on I Corinthians." *Journal of
        Theological Studies* 10:29–51.

Jeremias, J.
1926   "War Paulus Witwer?" *Zeitschrift für
        die neutestamentliche Wissenschaft*
        25:310–12.
1929   "Nochmals: War Paulus Witwer?"
        *Zeitschrift für die neutestamentliche
        Wissenschaft* 29:321–23.
1954   "Die missionarische Aufgabe in der
        Mischehe (1 Cor 7.16)." Pp. 255–60
        in *Neutestamentliche Studien für Ru-
        dolf Bultmann zu seinem siebzigsten
        Geburtstag.* Edited by W. Eltester.
        Beihefte zur Zeitschrift für die neu-
        testamentliche Wissenschaft 21.
        Berlin: Töpelmann.
1955–56 "Flesh and Blood Cannot Inherit the
        Kingdom of God." *New Testament
        Studies* 2:151–59.
1958   "Chiasmus in den Paulusbriefen."
        *Zeitschrift für die neutestamentliche
        Wissenschaft* 49:145–56.
1966a   *The Eucharistic Words of Jesus.*
        Translated by N. Perrin. London:
        SCM.
1966b   "Zur Gedankenführung in den pauli-
        nischen Briefen: (3) Die Briefzitaten
        in 1 Kor 8:1–13." Pp. 273–76 in *Abba.*
        Göttingen: Vandenhoeck & Ru-
        precht.

Jervell, J.
1960   *Imago Dei: Gen 1,26f. im Spätjuden-
        tum, in der Gnosis und in den pauli-*
        nischen Briefen. Forschungen zur
        Religion und Literatur des Alten und
        Neuen Testaments 58. Göttingen:
        Vandenhoeck & Ruprecht.

Jervis, L. A.
1993   "'But I Want You to Know . . .': Paul's
        Midrashic Intertextual Response to
        the Corinthian Worshipers (1 Cor
        11:2–16)." *Journal of Biblical Litera-
        ture* 112:231–46.
1995   "1 Corinthians 14:34–35: A Recon-
        sideration of Paul's Limitation of the
        Free Speech of Some Corinthian
        Women." *Journal for the Study of the
        New Testament* 58:51–74.

Jewett, R.
1971   *Paul's Anthropological Terms: A
        Study of Their Use in Conflict Set-
        tings.* Arbeiten zur Geschichte des
        antiken Judentums und des Urchris-
        tentums 10. Leiden: Brill.
1994   *Paul the Apostle to America: Cultural
        Trends and Pauline Scholarship.* Lou-
        isville: Westminster/John Knox.

Johanson, B. C.
1978–79 "Tongues, a Sign for Unbelievers? A
        Structural and Exegetical Study of
        I Corinthians xiv.20–25." *New Testa-
        ment Studies* 25:180–203.

Johansson, N.
1963–64 "I Cor. xiii and I Cor xiv." *New Testa-
        ment Studies* 10:383–92.

Joly, R.
1968   *Le vocabulaire chrétien de l'amour
        est-il original?* Brussels: University of
        Brussels Press.

Jones, F. S.
1987   *"Freiheit" in den Briefen des Apostels
        Paulus: Eine historische, exegetische
        und religionsgeschichtliche Studie.*
        Göttinger theologicshe Arbeiten 34.
        Göttingen: Vandenhoeck & Ru-
        precht.

Jones, P. R.
1985   "1 Corinthians 15:8: Paul the Last
        Apostle." *Tyndale Bulletin* 36:3–34.

Jourdan, G. V.
1948   "Κοινωνία in 1 Corinthians 10:16."
        Journal of Biblical Literature 67:111–
        24.

Joy, N. G.
1988   "Is the Body to Be Destroyed?
        (1 Corinthians 5:5)." *Bible Translator*
        39:429–36.

Judge, E. A.

1960   *The Social Pattern of Christian Groups in the First Century.* London: Tyndale.

1968   "Paul's Boasting in Relation to Contemporary Professional Practice." *Australian Biblical Review* 16:37–50.

1974   "St. Paul as a Radical Critic of Society." *Interchange* 16:119–203.

1983   "The Reaction against Classical Education in the New Testament." *Journal of Christian Education* 77:7–14.

1984   "Cultural Conformity and Innovation in Paul: Some Clues from Contemporary Documents." *Tyndale Bulletin* 35:5–23.

Kaiser, W. C., Jr.

1973   "The Current Crisis in Exegesis and the Apostolic Use of Deuteronomy 25:4 in 1 Corinthians 9:8–10." *Journal of the Evangelical Theological Society* 21:3–18.

1981   "A Neglected Text in Bibliology Discussion: 1 Corinthians 2:6–16." *Westminster Theological Journal* 43:301–18.

Kane, J. P.

1975   "The Mithraic Cult Meal in Its Greek and Roman Environment." Vol. 2 / pp. 313–51 in *Mithraic Studies.* Edited by J. R Hinnels. Manchester: Manchester University Press.

Karrer, M.

1990   "Der Kelch des neuen Bundes: Erwägungen zum Verständnis des Herrenmahls nach 1 Kor 11,23b–25." *Biblische Zeitschrift* 34:198–221.

Karris, R. J.

1973   "Rom 14:1–15:3 and the Occasion of Romans." *Catholic Biblical Quarterly* 35:155–78.

Käsemann, E.

1964   *Essays on New Testament Themes.* Translated by W. J. Montague. Studies in Biblical Theology 1. London: SCM.

1969   *New Testament Questions of Today.* Translated by W. J. Montague. Philadelphia: Fortress.

1971   *Perspectives on Paul.* Translated by M. Kohl. Philadelphia: Fortress.

Keck, L. E.

1982   *Paul and His Letters.* Philadelphia: Fortress.

Keener, C. S.

1992   *Paul, Women, and Wives.* Peabody, Mass.: Hendrickson.

Kempthorne, R.

1967–68 "Incest and the Body of Christ: A Study of I Corinthians vi.12–20." *New Testament Studies* 14:568–74.

Kendrick, W. G.

1995   "Authority, Women, and Angels: Translating 1 Corinthians 11:10." *Bible Translator* 46:336–43.

Kennedy, C. A.

1987   "The Cult of the Dead in Corinth." Pp. 227–36 in *Love and Death in the Ancient Near East: Essays in Honor of Marvin H. Pope.* Edited by J. H. Marks and R. M. Good. Guilford, Conn.: Four Quarters.

1989   "I Cor. 8 as a Mishnaic List." Pp. 17–24 in *Religious Writings and Religious Systems*, vol. 2: *Christianity.* Edited by J. Neusner. Brown Studies in Religion 2. Atlanta: Scholars Press.

Kent, J. H.

1966   *The Inscriptions, 1926–1950.* Corinth 8.3. Princeton, N.J.: American School of Classical Studies at Athens.

Ker, D. P.

2000   "Paul and Apollos—Colleagues or Rivals?" *Journal for the Study of the New Testament* 77:75–97.

Ketter, P.

1947   "Syneisakten in Korinth? Zu 1 Cor. 7,36–38." *Trierertheologische Zeitschrift* 16:175–82.

Kieffer, R.

1975–76 "'Afin que je sois brûlé' ou bien 'Afin que j'en tire orgueil'? (I Cor. xiii.3)." *New Testament Studies* 22:95–97.

Kilpatrick, G. D.

1981   "Conjectural Emendation in the New Testament." Pp. 349–60 in *New Testament Textual Criticism: Essays in Honor of Bruce M. Metzger.* Edited by E. J. Epp and G. D. Fee. Oxford: Clarendon.

Kim, C.-H.

1975   "The Papyrus Invitation." *Journal of Biblical Literature* 94:391–402.

Kinman, B.

1997   "'Appoint the Despised as Judges!' (1 Corinthians 6:4)." *Tyndale Bulletin* 48:345–54.

Kirchhoff, R.

1994   *Die Sünde gegen den eigenen Leib: Studien zu Πόρνη und Πορνεία in 1 Kor 6,12–20 und dem sozio-kulturellen Kontext der paulinischen Adressaten.* Studien zur Umwelt des Neuen Testaments 18. Göttingen: Vandenhoeck & Ruprecht.

Kistemaker, S. J.

1993   *1 Corinthians.* New Testament Commentary. Grand Rapids: Baker.

Kittel, G.

1920   *Rabbinica.* Arbeiten zur Religionsgeschichte des Urchristentums 1/3. Leipzig: Hinrichs.

Klassen, W.

1993   "The Sacred Kiss in the NT: An Example of Social Boundary Lines." *New Testament Studies* 39:122–35.

Klauck, H.-J.

1981   *Hausgemeinde und Hauskirche in frühen Christentum.* Stuttgarter Bibelstudien 103. Stuttgart: Katholisches Bibelwerk.

1982   *Herrenmahl und hellenistischer Kult: Eine religionsgeschichtliche Untersuchung zum ersten Korintherbrief.* Münster: Aschendorff.

1993   "Present in the Lord's Supper: 1 Corinthians 11:23–26 in the Context of Hellenistic Religious History." Pp. 57–74 in *One Loaf, One Cup: Ecumenical Studies of 1 Cor 11 and Other Eucharistic Texts.* Edited by B. F. Meyer. New Gospel Studies 6. Macon, Ga.: Mercer University Press.

Klein, G. L.

1989   "Hos 3:1–3—Background to 1 Cor 6:19–20?" *Criswell Theological Review* 3:373–75.

Klein, W. W.

1986   "Noisy Gong or Acoustic Vase? A Note on 1 Corinthians 13.1." *New Testament Studies* 32:286–89.

Kloppenborg, J.

1978   "An Analysis of the Pre-Pauline Formula 1 Cor 15:3b–5 in Light of Some Recent Literature." *Catholic Biblical Quarterly* 40:351–67.

Knoch, O.

1993   "'Do This in Memory of Me!' (Luke 22:20; 1 Cor 11:24–25): The Celebration of the Eucharist in the Primitive Christian Communities." Pp. 1–10 in *One Loaf, One Cup: Ecumenical Studies of 1 Cor 11 and Other Eucha-ristic Texts.* Edited by B. F. Meyer. New Gospel Studies 6. Macon, Ga.: Mercer University Press.

Knox, R. A.

1950   *Enthusiasm: A Chapter in the History of Religion.* Oxford: Clarendon.

Koch, D.-A.

1999   "'Alles was ἐν Μακέλλῳ verkauft wird, esst. . . .': Die *Macella* von Pompeji, Gerasa und Korinth und ihre Bedeutung für die Auslegung von 1 Kor 10,25." *Zeitschrift für die neutestamentliche Wissenschaft* 90:194–219.

Koenig, J.

1978   *Charismata: God's Gifts for God's People.* Philadelphia: Westminster.

Koester, H.

1971   "*Gnomai Diaphorai:* The Origin and Nature of Diversification in the History of Early Christianity." Pp. 114–57 in *Trajectories through Early Christianity.* Edited by J. M. Robinson and H. Koester. Philadelphia: Fortress.

Koet, B. J.

1996   "The Old Testament Background to 1 Cor 10,7–8." Pp. 607–15 in *The Corinthian Correspondence.* Edited by R. Bieringer. Bibliotheca ephemeridum theologicarum lovaniensium 125. Leuven: Peeters.

Konstan, D., D. Clay, C. E. Glad, J. C. Thom, and J. Ware

1998   *Philodemus on Frank Criticism: Introduction, Translation, and Notes.* Society of Biblical Literature Texts and Translations. Atlanta: Scholars Press.

Kornemann, E.

1929   *Neue Dokumente zum lakonischen Kaiserkult.* Breslau: Marcus.

Kreitzer, L. J.

1987   *Jesus and God in Paul's Eschatology.* Journal for the Study of the New Testament: Supplement Series 19. Sheffield: JSOT Press.

Kreuzer, S.

1985   "Der Zwang des Boten—Beobachtungen zu Lk. 14.23 und 1 Kor. 9.16." *Zeitschrift für die neutestamentliche Wissenschaft* 76:123–28.

Kroeger, R. C., and C. C. Kroeger

1978   "An Inquiry into Evidence of Maenadism in the Corinthian Congregation." Vol. 2 / pp. 331–38 in

Society of Biblical Literature Seminar Papers. Edited by P. J. Achtemeier. Missoula, Mont.: Scholars Press.

Kruse, C. G.
1992 "The Price Paid for a Ministry among Gentiles: Paul's Persecution at the Hands of Jews." Pp. 260–72 in *Worship, Theology, and Ministry in the Early Church: Essays in Honor of Ralph P. Martin.* Edited by M. J. Wilkens and T. Paige. Journal for the Study of the New Testament: Supplement Series 87. Sheffield: JSOT Press.

Kubo, S.
1977–78 "I Corinthians vii.16: Optimistic or Pessimistic?" *New Testament Studies* 24:539–44.

Kuck, D. W.
1992a *Judgment and Community Conflict: Paul's Use of Apocalyptic Judgment Language in 1 Corinthians 3:5–4:5.* Supplements to Novum Testamentum 66. Leiden: Brill.
1992b "Paul and Pastoral Ambition: A Reflection on 1 Corinthians 3–4." *Currents in Mission and Theology* 19:174–83.

Kümmel, W. G.
1954 "Verlobung und Heirat bei Paulus (1 Cor 7,36–38)." Pp. 275–95 in *Neutestamentliche Studien für Rudolf Bultmann zu seinem siebzigsten Geburtstag.* Edited by W. Eltester. Beihefte zur Zeitschrift für die neutestamentliche Wissenschaft 21. Berlin: Töpelmann.

Kürzinger, J.
1978 "Frau und Mann nach 1 Kor 11,11f." *Biblische Zeitschrift* 22:270–75.

Lake, K.
1914 *The Earlier Epistles of St. Paul: Their Motive and Origin.* 2d edition. London: Rivingtons.

Lambrecht, J.
1991 "Line of Thought in 1 Cor 15,1–11." *Gregorianum* 72:655–70.
1994 *Pauline Studies: Collected Essays.* Bibliotheca ephemeridum theologicarum lovaniensium 115. Leuven: Peeters.

Lampe, G. W. H.
1967 "Church Discipline and the Interpretation of the Epistles to the Corinthians." Pp. 337–61 in *Christian History and Interpretation: Studies*

Presented to John Knox. Edited by W. R. Farmer, C. F. D. Moule, and R. R. Niebuhr. Cambridge: Cambridge University Press.

Lampe, P.
1990 "Theological Wisdom and the 'Word about the Cross': The Rhetorical Scheme in 1 Corinthians 1–4." *Interpretation* 44:117–31.
1991 "Das korinthische Herrenmahl im Schnittpunkt hellenistisch Mahlpraxis und paulinischer Theologia Crucis (1 Kor 11,17–34)." *Zeitschrift für die neutestamentliche Wissenschaft* 82:183–213.
1994 "The Eucharist: Identifying with Christ on the Cross." *Interpretation* 48:36–49.

Lanci, J. R.
1997 *The New Temple for Corinth: Rhetorical and Archaeological Approaches to Pauline Imagery.* Studies in Biblical Literature 1. New York: Lang.

Laney, J. C.
1982 "Paul and the Permanence of Marriage in 1 Corinthians 7." *Journal of the Evangelical Theological Society* 25:283–94.

Lang, F.
1986 *Die Briefe an die Korinther.* Das Neue Testament Deutsch 7. Göttingen: Vandenhoeck & Ruprecht.

Lapide, C.
1896 *The Great Commentary of Cornelius à Lapide: I Corinthians and Galatians.* Translated and edited by W. F. Cobb. London: John Hodges.

Lassen, E. M.
1991 "The Use of the Father Image in Imperial Propaganda and 1 Cor 4:14–21." *Tyndale Bulletin* 42:127–36.

Lattimore, R.
1942 *Themes in Greek and Latin Epitaphs.* Urbana: University of Illinois Press.

Laughery, G. J.
1997 "Paul: Anti-marriage? Anti-sex? Ascetic? A Dialogue with 1 Corinthians 7:1–40." *Evangelical Quarterly* 69:109–28.

Lausberg, H.
1998 *Handbook of Literary Rhetoric: A Foundation for Literary Study.* Translated by M. T. Bliss, A. Jansen, and D. E. Orton. Edited by D. E. Orton and R. D. Anderson. Leiden: Brill.

Lautenschlager, M.
1992   "Abschied von Disputier: Zur Bedeutung von συζητητής in 1 Kor 1,20." *Zeitschrift für die neutestamentliche Wissenschaft* 83:276–85.

Leenhardt, F.
1946   *Le marriage chrétien.* Neuchâtel: Delachaux & Niestlé.

Legault, A.
1971–72   "'Beyond the Things Which Are Written' (I Cor. iv.6)." *New Testament Studies* 18:227–31.

Le Goff, J.
1984   *The Birth of Purgatory.* Translated by A. Goldhammer. Chicago: University of Chicago Press.

Lewis, L. A.
1990   "The Law Courts in Corinth: An Experiment in the Power of Baptism." *Anglican Theological Review Supplement* 11:88–98.

Lewis, S. M.
1998   *"So That God May Be All in All": The Apocalyptic Message of 1 Corinthians 15,12–34.* Tesi Gregoriana Serie Teologia 42. Rome: Pontifical Gregorian University Press.

Liefeld, W. L.
1986   "Women, Submission and Ministry in 1 Corinthians." Pp. 134–54 in *Women, Authority, and the Bible.* Edited by A. Mickelsen. Downers Grove, Ill.: InterVarsity.

Lietzmann, H.
1949   *Die Briefe des Apostels Paulus. An die Korinther I, II.* Edited by W. G. Kümmel. 5th edition. Handbuch zum neuen Testament 9. Tübingen: Mohr.

1953   *Mass and Lord's Supper: A Study in the History of the Liturgy.* Translated by D. H. G. Reeve. Leiden: Brill.

Lightfoot, J. B.
1895   *Notes on the Epistles of St. Paul.* London: Macmillan. Reprinted Winona Lake, Ind.: Alpha, n.d.

Lim, T. H.
1987   "Not in Persuasive Words of Wisdom but in Demonstrations of the Spirit and Power." *Novum Testamentum* 29:137–49.

Lincoln, A. T.
1981   *Paradise Now and Not Yet: Studies in the Role of the Heavenly Dimension in Paul's Thought with Special Reference to His Eschatology.* Society of New Testament Studies Monograph Series 43. Cambridge: Cambridge University Press.

Lindars, B.
1984   "The Bible and the Call: The Biblical Roots of the Monastic Life in History and Today." *Bulletin of the John Rylands University Library* 66:228–45.

Lindemann, A.
2000   *Der erste Korintherbrief.* Handbuch zum Neuen Testament 9/1. Tübingen: Mohr.

Lindsay, J. (trans.)
1960   *Apuleius: The Golden Ass.* Bloomington: Indiana University Press.

Linton, O.
1930   "'Nicht über das hinaus, was geschrieben ist' (1 Kor. 4,6)." *Theologische Studien und Kritiken* 102:425–56.

Litfin, D.
1994   *St. Paul's Theology of Proclamation: 1 Corinthians 1–4 and Greco-Roman Rhetoric.* Society of New Testament Studies Monograph Series 83. Cambridge: Cambridge University Press.

Llewelyn, S. R.
2001   "The Use of Sunday for Meetings of Believers in the New Testament." *Novum Testamentum* 43:205–33.

Lohmeyer, E.
1927   "Probleme paulinischer Theologie: I. Briefliche Grussüberschriften." *Zeitschrift für die neutestamentliche Wissenschaft* 26:158–73.

Long, T. G.
1989   *Preaching and the Literary Forms of the Bible.* Philadelphia: Fortress.

Longenecker, R.
1975   *Biblical Exegesis in the Apostolic Period.* Grand Rapids: Eerdmans.

Lorenzen, T.
1995   *Resurrection and Discipleship: Interpretive Models, Biblical Reflections, Theological Consequences.* Maryknoll, N.Y.: Orbis.

Lösch, S.
1947   "Christliche Frauen in Corinth (1 Kor 11,2–16): Ein neuer Lösungsversuch." *Theologische Quartalschrift* 127:216–61.

Louw, J. P.
1988   "The Function of Discourse in a Sociosemiotic Theory of Translation Illustrated by the Translation of

Zēloute in 1 Corinthians 12:31." *Bible Translator* 39:329–35.

Lövestam, E.
1963   *Spiritual Wakefulness in the New Testament.* Translated by W. F. Salisbury. Lund universitets årsskrift 55/3. Lund: Gleerup.

LSJ   *A Greek-English Lexicon.* By H. G. Liddell, R. Scott, and H. S. Jones. 9th edition. Oxford: Clarendon, 1968.

Lührmann, D.
1975   "Wo man nicht mehr Sklave oder Freier ist: Überlegungen zur Struktur frühchristlicher Gemeinden." *Wort und Dienst* 13:53–83.

Lund, N. W.
1931   "The Literary Structure of Paul's Hymn to Love." *Journal of Biblical Literature* 50:266–76.

Lutz, C. E.
1947   *Musonius Rufus: "The Roman Socrates."* New Haven: Yale University Press.

Lyall, F.
1970–71   "Roman Law in the Writings of Paul—The Slave and the Freedman." *New Testament Studies* 17:73–79.

Lyons, G.
1985   *Pauline Autobiography: Toward a New Understanding.* Society of Biblical Literature Dissertation Series 73. Atlanta: Scholars Press.

MacArthur, S. D.
1980   "'Spirit' in Pauline Usage: 1 Corinthians 5:5." Pp. 249–56 in *Studia Biblica, 1978.* Edited by E. A. Livingstone. Journal for the Study of the New Testament: Supplement Series 3. Sheffield: JSOT Press.

Macchia, F. D.
1992   "Sighs Too Deep for Words: Toward a Theology of Glossolalia." *Journal of Pentecostal Theology* 1:47–73.

MacDonald, D. R.
1987   *There Is No Male and Female: The Fate of a Dominical Saying in Paul and Gnosticism.* Harvard Dissertations in Religion 20. Philadelphia: Fortress.

MacDonald, M. Y.
1990a   "Early Christian Women Married to Unbelievers." *Studies in Religion* 19:221–34.
1990b   "Women Holy in Body and Spirit: The Social Setting of 1 Corinthians 7." *New Testament Studies* 36:161–81.

MacMullen, R.
1974   *Roman Social Relations, 50 B.C. to A.D. 284.* New Haven: Yale University Press.

MacPherson, P.
1943–44   "Τὰ τέλη τῶν αἰώνων: 1 Corinthians x.11." *Expository Times* 55:222.

Maier, F. W.
1932   "Ps. 110.1 (LXX 109.1) in Zussamenhang von 1 Kor 15.24–27." *Biblische Zeitschrift* 20:139–56.

Malherbe, A. J.
1968   "The Beasts at Ephesus." *Journal of Biblical Literature* 87:71–80.
1980   "Μὴ Γένοιτο in the Diatribe and Paul." *Harvard Theological Review* 73:231–40.
1983   *Social Aspects of Early Christianity.* 2d edition. Philadelphia: Fortress.
1988   *Ancient Literary Theorists.* Society of Biblical Literature Sources for Biblical Study 19. Atlanta: Scholars Press.
1990   "Did the Thessalonians Write to Paul?" Pp. 246–57 in *The Conversation Continues: Studies in Paul and John in Honor of J. Louis Martyn.* Edited by R. T. Fortna and B. R. Gaventa. Nashville: Abingdon.
1994   "Determinism and Free Will in Paul: The Argument of 1 Corinthians 8 and 9." Pp. 231–55 in *Paul in His Hellenistic Context.* Edited by T. Engberg-Pedersen. Edinburgh: Clark.

Malick, D. E.
1993   "The Condemnation of Homosexuality in 1 Corinthians 6:9." *Bibliotheca Sacra* 150:479–92.

Malina, B. J.
1968   *The Palestinian Manna Tradition: The Manna Tradition in the Palestinian Targums and Its Relationship to the New Testament Writings.* Arbeiten zur Literatur und Geschichte des antiken Judentums und des Urchristentums 7. Leiden: Brill.
1987   "Wealth and Poverty in the New Testament." *Interpretation* 41:354–67.

Manson, T. W.
1962   "The Corinthian Correspondence (1)." Pp. 190–209 in *Studies in the Gospels and Epistles.* Edited by M. Black. Manchester: Manchester University Press.

Mare, W. H.
1976 "1 Corinthians." Vol. 10 / pp. 173–297 in *The Expositor's Bible Commentary*. Edited by F. E. Gaebelein. Grand Rapids: Zondervan.

Marshall, I. H.
1980 *Last Supper and Lord's Supper*. Grand Rapids: Eerdmans.
1999 *The Pastoral Epistles*. International Critical Commentary. Edinburgh: Clark.

Marshall, P.
1987 *Enmity in Corinth: Social Conventions in Paul's Relation with the Corinthians*. Wissenschaftliche Untersuchungen zum Neuen Testament 2/23. Tübingen: Mohr.

Martin, D. B.
1990 *Slavery as Salvation: The Metaphor of Slavery in Pauline Christianity*. New Haven: Yale University Press.
1991 "Tongues of Angels and Other Status Indicators." *Journal of the American Academy of Religion* 59:547–89.
1995 *The Corinthian Body*. New Haven: Yale University Press.
1996 "*Arsenokoitēs* and *Malakos*: Meanings and Consequences." Pp. 117–36 in *Biblical Ethics and Homosexuality: Listening to Scripture*. Edited by R. L. Brawley. Louisville: Westminster/John Knox.
2001 "Review Essay: Justin J. Meggitt, *Paul, Poverty, and Survival*." *Journal for the Study of the New Testament* 84:51–64.

Martin, R. P.
1984 *The Spirit and the Congregation: Studies in 1 Corinthians 12–15*. Grand Rapids: Zondervan.
1986 *2 Corinthians*. Word Biblical Commentary 40. Waco, Tex.: Word.

Martin, W. J.
1970 "I Corinthians 11:2–16: An Interpretation." Pp. 231–41 in *Apostolic History and the Gospel: Biblical and Historical Essays Presented to F. F. Bruce*. Edited by W. W. Gasque and R. P. Martin. Grand Rapids: Eerdmans.

McCaughhey, T.
1983 "Conscience and Decision Making in Some Early Christian Communities." *Irish Biblical Studies* 5:115–31.

McCready, W. O.
1996 "Ekklēsia and Voluntary Associations." Pp. 59–73 in *Voluntary Associations in the Graeco-Roman World*. Edited by J. S. Kloppenborg and S. G. Wilson. London/New York: Routledge.

McDonald, J. I. H.
1989 *The Resurrection: Narrative and Belief*. London: SPCK.

McGinn, S. E.
1996 "Ἐξουσίαν Ἔχειν ἐπὶ τῆς Κεφαλῆς: 1 Cor 11:10 and the Ecclesial Authority of Women." *Listening* 31:91–104.

McLean, B. H
1996 *The Cursed Christ: Mediterranean Expulsion Rituals and Pauline Soteriology*. Journal for the Study of the New Testament: Supplement Series 126. Sheffield: Sheffield Academic Press.

Meeks, W. A.
1974 "The Image of the Androgyne: Some Uses of a Symbol in Earliest Christianity." *History of Religions* 13:165–208.
1982 "'And Rose Up to Play': Midrash and Paranaesis in 1 Corinthians 10:1–22." *Journal for the Study of the New Testament* 16:64–78.
1983 *The First Urban Christians: The Social World of the Apostle Paul*. New Haven: Yale University Press.

Meggitt, J. J.
1994 "Meat Consumption and Social Conflict in Corinth." *Journal of Theological Studies*, n.s., 45:137–41.
1998 *Paul, Poverty, and Survival*. Studies of the New Testament and Its World. Edinburgh: Clark.

Mehat, A.
1983 "L'enseignement sur 'Les choses de l'Esprit' (1 Corinthiens 12,1–3)." *Revue d'histoire et de philosophie religieuses* 63:395–415.

Meier, J. P.
1978 "On the Veiling of Hermeneutics (1 Cor 11:2–16)." *Catholic Biblical Quarterly* 40:212–26.

Menoud, P. H.
1978 "Marriage and Celibacy according to Saint Paul." Pp. 1–18 in *Jesus Christ and the Faith: A Collection of Studies*. Translated by E. M. Paul. Pittsburgh Theological Monograph Series 18. Pittsburgh: Pickwick.

Merklein, H.
1983 "'Es ist gut für den Menschen, eine Frau nicht anzufassen': Paulus und die Sexualität." Pp. 225–53 in *Die*

Frau im Urchristentum. By J. Blank et al. Edited by G. Dautzenberg et al. Quaestiones disputatae 95. Freiburg: Herder.

1984 "Das Einheitlichkeit des ersten Korintherbriefes." *Zeitschrift für die neutestamentliche Wissenschaft* 75:153–83.

Metzger, B. M.

1971 *A Textual Commentary on the Greek New Testament.* New York: United Bible Societies.

1994 *A Textual Commentary on the Greek New Testament.* 2d edition. Stuttgart: Deutsche Bibelgesellschaft.

Meurer, S.

1972 *Das Recht in Dienst der Versöhnung und des Friedens: Studie zur Frage der Rechts nach dem Neuen Testament.* Abhandlungen zur Theologie des Alten und Neuen Testaments 63. Zurich: Theologischer Verlag.

Meyer, M. W.

1987 *The Ancient Mysteries: A Sourcebook: Sacred Texts of the Mystery Religions of the Ancient Mediterranean World.* San Francisco: Harper & Row.

Miguens, M.

1975a "Christ's 'Member' and Sex." *Thomist* 39:24–48.

1975b "1 Cor 13:8–13 Reconsidered." *Catholic Biblical Quarterly* 37:76–97.

Miller, G.

1972 "Ἀρχόντων τοῦ Αἰῶνος Τούτου—A New Look at 1 Corinthians 2:6–8." *Journal of Biblical Literature* 91:522–28.

Miller, J. I.

1980–81 "A Fresh Look at I Corinthians 6.16f." *New Testament Studies* 27:125–27.

Mills, W. E.

1985 *Glossolalia: A Bibliography.* Studies in the Bible and Early Christianity 6. New York: Mellen.

Minear, P.

1983 "Christ and the Congregation: 1 Corinthians 5–6." *Review and Expositor* 80:341–50.

Mitchell, A. C.

1993 "Rich and Poor in the Courts of Corinth: Litigiousness and Status in 1 Corinthians." *New Testament Studies* 39:562–86.

Mitchell, M. M.

1989 "Concerning Περὶ δέ in 1 Corinthians." *Novum Testamentum* 31:229–56.

1993 *Paul and the Rhetoric of Reconciliation: An Exegetical Investigation of the Language and Composition of 1 Corinthians.* Louisville: Westminster/John Knox.

1994 "Rhetorical Shorthand in Pauline Argumentation: The Functions of 'the Gospel' in the Corinthian Correspondence." Pp. 63–88 in *Gospel in Paul: Studies on Corinthians, Galatians, and Romans for Richard N. Longenecker.* Edited by L. A. Jervis and P. Richardson. Journal for the Study of the New Testament: Supplement Series 108. Sheffield: Sheffield Academic Press.

2001 "Pauline Accommodation and 'Condescension' (Συγκατάβασις): 1 Cor 9:19–23 and the History of Influence." Pp. 197–214 in *Paul beyond the Judaism/Hellenism Divide.* Edited by T. Engberg-Pedersen. Louisville: Westminster/John Knox.

Mitchell, S.

1993 *Anatolia: Land, Men, and Gods in Asia Minor,* vol. 2. Oxford: Clarendon.

Mitton, C. L.

1972–73 "New Wine in Old Wine Skins: IV. Leaven." *Expository Times* 84:339–43.

MM *The Vocabulary of the Greek Testament: Illustrated from the Papyri and Other Non-literary Sources.* By J. H. Moulton and G. Milligan. Reprinted Grand Rapids: Eerdmans, 1976.

Moffatt, J.

1938 *The First Epistle of Paul to the Corinthians.* Moffatt New Testament Commentary 7. London: Hodder & Stoughton.

Moiser, J.

1983 "A Reassessment of Paul's View of Marriage with Reference to 1 Cor. 7." *Journal for the Study of the New Testament* 18:103–22.

Moltmann, J.

1967 *Theology of Hope.* Translated by J. W. Leitch. New York: Harper & Row.

1992 *The Spirit of Life: A Universal Affirmation.* Translated by M. Kohl. London: SCM.

Morissette, R.

1972a   "La condition de ressuscité: 1 Corinthiens15:39–49: Structure littéraire de la péricope." *Biblica* 53:208–28.

1972b   "Un midrash sur la mort (1 Cor. xv,54c à 57)." *Revue biblique* 79:161–88.

1974   "'La chair et le sang ne peuvent hériter du Règne de Dieu' (1 Cor. xv,50)." *Science et esprit* 26:39–67.

Morrice, W. G.

1972   "The Imperatival Ἵνα." *Bible Translator* 23:326–30.

Morris, L.

1958   *The First Epistle of Paul to the Corinthians.* Tyndale New Testament Commentaries. Grand Rapids: Eerdmans.

Mott, S. C.

1975   "The Power of Giving and Receiving: Reciprocity in Hellenistic Benevolence." Pp. 60–72 in *Current Issues in Biblical and Patristic Interpretation: Studies in Honor of Merrill C. Tenney.* Edited by G. F. Hawthorne. Grand Rapids: Eerdmans.

Moule, C. F. D.

1956   "The Judgment Theme in the Sacraments." Pp. 464–81 in *The Background of the New Testament and Its Eschatology: In Honour of C. H. Dodd.* Edited by W. D. Davies and D. Daube. Cambridge: Cambridge University Press.

1959–60   "A Reconsideration of the Context of Maranatha." *New Testament Studies* 6:307–10.

1960   *An Idiom Book of New Testament Greek.* 2d edition. Cambridge: Cambridge University Press.

Moulton, J. H.

1908   *A Grammar of New Testament Greek,* vol. 1: *Prolegomena.* 3d edition. Edinburgh: Clark.

Moulton, J. H., and W. F. Howard

1929   *A Grammar of New Testament Greek,* vol. 2: *Accidence and Word Formation.* Edinburgh: Clark.

Moulton, J. H., and N. Turner

1963   *A Grammar of New Testament Greek,* vol. 3: *Syntax.* Edinburgh: Clark.

Müller, K.

1985   "Die Leiblichkeit des Heils 1 Kor 15,35–58." Pp. 171–281 in *Résurrection du Christ et des Chrétiens (1 Co 15).* Edited by J.-N. Aletti, S. Agourides, and L. De Lorenzi. Monographic Series of "Benedictina": Biblical-Ecumenical Section 8. Rome: St. Paul's Abbey.

Munck, J.

1959a   *Paul and the Salvation of Mankind.* Translated by F. Clarke. Richmond: John Knox.

1959b   "Paulus Tanquam Abortivus (1 Cor. 15:8)." Pp. 180–93 in *New Testament Essays: Studies in Memory of Thomas Walter Manson, 1893–1958.* Edited by A. J. B. Higgins. Manchester: Manchester University Press.

Munro, W.

1983   *Authority in Paul and Peter: The Identification of a Pastoral Stratum in the Pauline Corpus and 1 Peter.* Society of New Testament Studies Monograph Series 45. Cambridge: Cambridge University Press.

1988   "Women, Text, and the Canon: The Strange Case of 1 Corinthians 14:33–35." *Biblical Theological Bulletin* 18:26–31.

Murphy-O'Connor, J.

1976   "The Non-Pauline Character of 1 Corinthians 11:2–16?" *Journal of Biblical Literature* 95:615–21.

1977a   "I Corinthians v,3–5." *Revue biblique* 84:239–45.

1977b   "Works without Faith in 1 Cor. vii,14." *Revue biblique* 84:349–61.

1978a   "Corinthian Slogans in 1 Cor. 6:12–20." *Catholic Biblical Quarterly* 40:391–96.

1978b   "Freedom or the Ghetto (I Cor. viii,1–13; x,23–xi,1)." *Revue biblique* 85:543–74.

1979a   *1 Corinthians.* New Testament Message 10. Wilmington, Del.: Glazier.

1979b   "Food and Spiritual Gifts in 1 Cor 8:8." *Catholic Biblical Quarterly* 41:292–98.

1980   "Sex and Logic." *Catholic Biblical Quarterly* 42:482–99.

1981a   "'Baptized for the Dead' (1 Cor. xv,29): A Corinthian Slogan." *Revue biblique* 88:532–43.

1981b   "The Divorced Woman in 1 Cor 7:10–11." *Journal of Biblical Literature* 100:601–6.

1981c   "Tradition and Redaction in 1 Cor 15:3–7." *Catholic Biblical Quarterly* 43:582–89.

1983   *St. Paul's Corinth: Texts and Archae-
        ology.* Good News Studies 6. Wil-
        mington, Del.: Glazier.
1984   "The Corinth That Saint Paul Saw."
        Biblical Archaeologist 47:147–59.
1986   "Interpolations in 1 Corinthians."
        Catholic Biblical Quarterly 48:81–94.
1988   "1 Cor 11:2–16 Once Again." *Catholic
        Biblical Quarterly* 50:265–74.
1992   "Prisca and Aquila: Travelling Tent-
        makers and Church Builders." *Bible
        Review* 8.6:40–51, 62.
1993   "Co-authorship in the Corinthian
        Correspondence." *Revue biblique*
        100:562–79.
1996   *Paul: A Critical Life.* Oxford: Claren-
        don.
1998   *1 Corinthians.* Doubleday Bible
        Commentaries. New York: Double-
        day.

Myrou, A.
1999   "Sosthenes: The Former Crispus(?)."
        Greek Orthodox Theological Review
        44:207–12.

NA²⁷   *Novum Testamentum Graece.* 27th
        revised edition. Edited by [E. and E.
        Nestle,] B. Aland, K. Aland, J.
        Karavidopoulos, C. M. Martini, and
        B. M. Metzger. Stuttgart: Deutsche
        Bibelgesellschaft, 1993.

Nadeau, D. J.
1994   "Le problème des femmes en 1 Co
        14.33b–35." *Etudes théologiques et re-
        ligieuses* 69:63–65.

Nasuti, H. P.
1988   "The Woes of the Prophets and the
        Rights of the Apostle: The Internal
        Dynamics of 1 Corinthians 9." *Cath-
        olic Biblical Quarterly* 50:246–64.

Neirynck, F.
1986   "Paul and the Sayings of Jesus." Pp.
        265–321 in *L'Apôtre Paul: Personna-
        lité, style et conception du ministère.*
        Edited by A. Vanhoye. Bibliotheca
        ephemeridum theologicarum lo-
        vaniensium 73. Leuven: Leuven Uni-
        versity Press/Peeters.

Neller, K. V.
1987   "1 Corinthians 9:19–23: A Model for
        Those Who Seek to Win Souls." *Res-
        toration Quarterly* 29:129–42.

Neuenzeit, P.
1960   *Das Herrenmahl: Studien zur pauli-
        nischen Eucharistieauffassung.* Mu-
        nich: Kösel.

Neuhäusler, E.
1959   "Ruf Gottes und Stand des Christen:
        Bemerkungen zu 1 Kor 7." *Biblische
        Zeitschrift* 3:43–60.

Neusner, J.
1987   *What Is Midrash?* Guides to Biblical
        Scholarship. Philadelphia: Fortress.
1988   *Judaism: The Evidence of the Mish-
        nah.* Atlanta: Scholars Press.

Newton, D.
1998   *Deity and Diet: The Dilemma of Sacri-
        ficial Food at Corinth.* Journal for the
        Study of the New Testament: Supple-
        ment Series 169. Sheffield: Sheffield
        Academic Press.

Neyrey, J. H.
1986   "Witchcraft Accusations in 2 Cor 10–
        13: Paul in Social Science Perspec-
        tive." *Listening* 21:160–70.
1991   "Ceremonies in Luke-Acts: The Case
        of Meals and Table Fellowship." Pp.
        361–87 in *The Social World of Luke-
        Acts: Models for Interpretation.* Ed-
        ited by J. H. Neyrey. Peabody, Mass.:
        Hendrickson.

Niccum, C.
1997   "The Voice of the Manuscripts on the
        Silence of Woman: The External Evi-
        dence for 1 Cor 14.34–5." *New Testa-
        ment Studies* 43:242–55.

Nickelsburg, G. W. E.
1986   "An Ἔκτρωμα, Though Appointed
        from the Womb: Paul's Apostolic
        Self-Description in 1 Corinthians
        15 and Galatians 1." Pp. 198–205 in
        *Christians among Jews and Gen-
        tiles: Essays in Honor of Krister
        Stendahl on His Sixty-Fifth Birth-
        day.* Edited by G. W. E. Nickelsburg
        and G. W. MacRae. Philadelphia:
        Fortress.

NIDNTT   *The New International Dictionary of
        New Testament Theology.* Edited by
        L. Coenen, E. Beyreuther, and H.
        Bietenhard. English translation
        edited by C. Brown. 4 vols. Grand
        Rapids: Zondervan, 1975–86.

Niebuhr, H. R.
1951   *Christ and Culture.* New York:
        Harper.

Niederwimmer, K.
1975   *Askese und Mysterium: Über Ehe,
        Ehescheidung und Eheverzicht in den
        Anfangen des christlichen Glaubens.*
        Göttingen: Vandenhoeck & Ru-
        precht.

Nordheim, E. von
1974 "Das Zitat des Paulus in 1 Kor 2:9 und seine Beziehung zum koptischen Testament Jakobs." *Zeitschrift für die neutestamentliche Wissenschaft* 65:112–20.

Nouwen, H. J. M.
1987 "A Spirituality of Waiting: Being Alert to God's Presence in Our Lives." *Weavings* 2:6–17.

O'Brien, J.
1975–76 "Sophocles' Ode on Man and Paul's Hymn on Love: A Comparative Study." *Classical Journal* 71:138–51.

OCD *Oxford Classical Dictionary.* Edited by S. Hornblower and A. Spawforth. 3d edition. Oxford: Oxford University Press, 1996.

O'Day, G. R.
1990 "Jeremiah 9:22–23 and 1 Corinthians 1:26–31: A Study in Intertextuality." *Journal of Biblical Literature* 109:259–67.

Odell-Scott, D. W.
1983 "Let the Women Speak in Church: An Egalitarian Interpretation of 1 Cor 14:33b–36." *Biblical Theology Bulletin* 13:90–93.

1987 "In Defense of an Egalitarian Interpretation of 1 Cor 14:34–36: A Reply to Murphy-O'Connor's Critique." *Biblical Theology Bulletin* 17:100–103.

2000 "Editorial Dilemma: The Interpolation of 1 Cor 14:34–35 in the Western Manuscripts of D, G, and 88." *Biblical Theology Bulletin* 30:68–74.

Oliver, A. B.
1937 "Why Are They Baptized for the Dead? A Study of I Cor. 15.29." *Review and Expositor* 34:48–53.

Omanson, R.
1992 "Acknowledging Paul's Quotation." *Bible Today* 43:201–13.

O'Neill, J. C.
1979–80 "1 Corinthians 15:29." *Expository Times* 91:310–11.

1986 "1 Corinthians 7:14 and Infant Baptism." Pp. 357–61 in *L'Apôtre Paul: Personnalité, style et conception du ministère.* Edited by A. Vanhoye. Bibliotheca ephemeridum theologicarum lovaniensium 73. Leuven: Leuven University Press/Peeters.

Oropeza, B. J.
1998 "Laying to Rest the Midrash: Paul's Message on Meat Sacrificed to Idols in Light of the Deuteronomic Tradition." *Biblica* 79:57–68.

1998–99 "Situational Immorality: Paul's 'Vice Lists' at Corinth." *Expository Times* 110:9–10.

1999 "Apostasy in the Wilderness: Paul's Message to the Corinthians in a State of Eschatological Liminality." *Journal for the Study of the New Testament* 75:69–86.

Orr, W. F.
1967 "Paul's Treatment of Marriage in 1 Corinthians 7." *Pittsburgh Perspective* 8:5–22.

Orr, W. F., and J. A. Walther
1976 *1 Corinthians: A New Translation and Commentary.* Anchor Bible 32. Garden City, N.Y.: Doubleday.

Osborne, H.
1931 "Συνείδησις." *Journal of Theological Studies* 32:167–79.

Osburn, C. D.
1981 "The Text of I Corinthians 10:9." Pp. 201–12 in *New Testament Textual Criticism, Its Significance for Exegesis: Essays in Honor of Bruce M. Metzger.* Edited by E. J. Epp and G. D. Fee. Oxford: Clarendon.

1993 "The Interpretation of 1 Cor. 14:34–35." Pp. 219–42 in *Essays on Women in Earliest Christianity.* Edited by C. D. Osburn. Joplin, Mo.: College Press.

Osiek, C.
1996 "The Family in Early Christianity: 'Family Values Revisited.'" *Catholic Biblical Quarterly* 58:1–24.

Osiek, C., and D. L. Balch
1997 *Families in the New Testament World: Household and House Churches.* Louisville: Westminster/John Knox.

Oster, R. E., Jr.
1988 "When Men Wore Veils to Worship: The Historical Context of 1 Corinthians 11:4." *New Testament Studies* 34:481–505.

1992 "Use, Misuse, and Neglect of Archaeological Evidence in Some Modern Works on 1 Corinthians (1 Cor 7:1–5; 8:10; 11:2–16; 12:14–26)." *Zeitschrift für die neutestamentliche Wissenschaft* 83:52–73.

1995   *1 Corinthians.* College Press NIV
        Commentary. Joplin, Mo.: College
        Press.
OTP   *The Old Testament Pseudepigrapha.*
        Edited by J. H. Charlesworth. 2 vols.
        Garden City, N.Y.: Doubleday, 1983–
        85.

Padgett, A.
1984   "Paul on Women in the Church:
        The Contradictions of Coiffure in
        1 Corinthians 11:3–16 and Its Con-
        text." *Journal for the Study of the New
        Testament* 20:69–86.

Paige, T.
1991   "1 Corinthians 12:2: A Pagan
        Pompe?" *Journal for the Study of the
        New Testament* 44:57–65.
1992   "Stoicism, Ἐλευθερία, and Commu-
        nity at Corinth." Pp. 180–93 in *Wor-
        ship, Theology, and Ministry in the
        Early Church: Essays in Honor of
        Ralph P. Martin.* Edited by M. J.
        Wilkins and T. Paige. Journal for the
        Study of the New Testament: Supple-
        ment Series 87. Sheffield: Sheffield
        Academic Press.

Parker, H. N.
1992   "Love's Body Anatomized: The An-
        cient Erotic Handbooks and the
        Rhetoric of Sexuality." Pp. 90–107 in
        *Pornography and Representation in
        Greece and Rome.* Edited by A. Rich-
        lin. New York: Oxford University
        Press.

Parry, R. St. J.
1926   *The First Epistle of Paul the Apostle to
        the Corinthians.* 2d edition. Cam-
        bridge Greek Testament. Cambridge:
        Cambridge University Press.

Pascuzzi, M.
1997   *Ethics, Ecclesiology, and Church Dis-
        cipline: A Rhetorical Analysis of
        1 Corinthians 5.* Tesi Gregoriana
        Serie Teologia 32. Rome: Pontifical
        Gregorian University Press.

Passakos, D. C.
1997   "Eucharist in First Corinthians: A
        Sociological Study." *Revue biblique*
        104:192–210.

Pate, C. M.
2000   *The Reverse of the Curse.* Wissen-
        schaftliche Untersuchungen zum
        Neuen Testament 2/114. Tübingen:
        Mohr.

Patterson, O.
1982   *Slavery and Social Death: A Compara-
        tive Study.* Cambridge: Harvard Uni-
        versity Press.

Paulsen, H.
1982   "Schisma und Häresie: Unter-
        suchungen zu 1 Kor 11,18.19."
        Zeitschrift für Theologie und Kirche
        79:180–211.

Payne, P. B.
1995   "Fuldensis, Sigla for Variants in Vat-
        icanus, and 1 Cor. 14:34–35." *New
        Testament Studies* 41:240–62.
1998   "MS. 88 as Evidence for a Text with-
        out 1 Cor 14:34–5." *New Testament
        Studies* 44:152–58.

Pearson, B. A.
1967   "Did the Gnostics Curse Jesus?"
        Journal of Biblical Literature 86:301–
        5.
1973   *The Pneumatikos-Psychikos Termi-
        nology in 1 Corinthians: A Study in
        the Theology of the Corinthian Oppo-
        nents of Paul and Its Relation to
        Gnosticism.* Society of Biblical Liter-
        ature Dissertation Series 12. Mis-
        soula, Mont.: Scholars Press.
1975   "Hellenistic-Jewish Wisdom Specu-
        lation and Paul." Pp. 43–66 in *Aspects
        of Wisdom and Judaism and Early
        Christianity.* Edited by R. L. Wilken.
        Notre Dame: University of Notre
        Dame Press.

Penna, R.
1996   *Paul the Apostle: A Theological and
        Exegetical Study,* vol. 1: *Jew and
        Greek Alike.* Translated by T. P.
        Wahl. Collegeville, Minn.: Liturgical
        Press.

Perdelwitz, R.
1911   "Die sogenannte Christuspartei in
        Korinth." *Theologische Studien und
        Kritiken* 84:180–93.

Perkins, P.
1984   *Resurrection: New Testament Witness
        and Contemporary Reflection.* New
        York: Doubleday.

Perriman, A. C.
1989   "Paul and the Parousia: 1 Corin-
        thians 15:50–7 and 2 Corinthians
        5:1–5." *New Testament Studies*
        35:512–21.
1994   "The Head of a Woman: The Mean-
        ing of Κεφαλή in 1 Cor. 11:3." *Journal
        of Theological Studies,* n.s., 45:602–
        22.

Perrot, C.
1983   "Les exemples du désert (1 Co. 10.6–11)." *New Testament Studies* 29:437–52.

Pesch, R.
1975   "Paulinische Kasuistik: Zum Verständnis von 1 Kor 7,10–11." Pp. 433–42 in *Homenaje a Juan Prado: Miscelánea de estudios bíblicos y hebráicos.* Edited by L. A. Verdes and E. J. A. Hernandez. Madrid: Consejo Superior de Investigaciones Científicas.

Peterman, G. W.
1997   *Paul's Gift from Philippi: Conventions of Gift Exchange and Christian Giving.* Society for New Testament Studies Monograph Series 92. Cambridge: Cambridge University Press.

Petersen, W. L.
1986   "Can Ἀρσενοκοῖται Be Translated by 'Homosexual'? (1 Cor. 6:9; 1 Tim. 1:10)." *Vigiliae christianae* 40:187–91.

Peterson, B. K.
1998   *Eloquence and the Proclamation of the Gospel in Corinth.* Society of Biblical Literature Dissertation Series 163. Atlanta: Scholars Press.

Peterson, E.
1951   "1 Kor 1,18f und die Thematik des jüdischen Busstages." *Biblica* 32:29–103.

Petzer, J. H.
1989   "Contextual Evidence in Favor of Καυχήσωμαι in 1 Corinthians 13.3." *New Testament Studies* 35:229–53.

1993   "Reconsidering the Silent Women of Corinth—A Note on 1 Corinthians 14:34–35." *Theologia Evangelica* 26:132–38.

Pfitzner, V. C.
1967   *Paul and the Agon Motif.* Supplements to Novum Testamentum 16. Leiden: Brill.

1982   "Purified Community–Purified Sinner: Expulsion from the Community according to Matthew 18:15–18 and I Corinthians 5:1–5." *Australian Biblical Review* 30:34–55.

Phipps, W. E.
1982   "Is Paul's Attitude toward Sexual Relations Contained in 1 Cor. 7.1?" *New Testament Studies* 28:125–31.

Pickett, R.
1997   *The Cross in Corinth: The Social Significance of the Death of Jesus.* Journal for the Study of the New Testament: Supplement Series 143. Sheffield: Sheffield Academic Press.

Pierce, C. A.
1955   *Conscience in the New Testament: A Study of Syneidesis in the New Testament.* Studies in Biblical Theology 15. London: SCM.

Piper, J.
1979   *"Love Your Enemies": Jesus' Love Command in the Synoptic Gospels and in the Early Christian Paraenesis: A History of the Tradition and Interpretation of Its Uses.* Society for New Testament Studies Monograph Series 38. Cambridge: Cambridge University Press.

Plett, H. F.
1979   *Einführung in die rhetorische Textanalyse.* 4th edition. Hamburg: Buske.

Plevnik, J.
1988   "Paul's Appeals to His Damascus Experience and 1 Cor. 15:5–7: Are They Legitimations?" *Toronto Journal of Theology* 4:101–11.

1997   *Paul and the Parousia: An Exegetical and Theological Investigation.* Peabody, Mass.: Hendrickson.

Pogoloff, S. M.
1992   *Logos and Sophia: The Rhetorical Structure of 1 Corinthians.* Society of Biblical Literature Dissertation Series 134. Atlanta: Scholars Press.

Poirier, J. C., and J. Frankovic
1996   "Celibacy and Charism in 1 Cor. 7:5–7." *Harvard Theological Review* 89:1–18.

Polhill, J. B.
1983   "The Wisdom of God and Factionalism: 1 Corinthians 1–4." *Review and Expositor* 80:325–39.

Poliakoff, M. B.
1987   *Combat Sports in the Ancient World.* New Haven: Yale University Press.

Ponsot, H.
1983   "D'Isaie 64:3 a la 1 Corinthiens 2,9." *Revue biblique* 90:229–42.

Popkes, W.
1968   *Christus traditus: Eine Untersuchung zum Begriff der Dahingabe im Neuen Testament.* Abhandlungen zur Theo-

logie des Alten und Neuen Testaments 49. Zürich/Stuttgart: Zwingli.

Porter, C. L.
1989 "An Interpretation of Paul's Lord's Supper Texts: 1 Corinthians 10:14–22 and 11:17–34." *Encounter* 50:29–45.

Porter, S. E.
1991 "How Should Κολλώμενος in 1 Cor 6,16.17 Be Translated?" *Ephemerides theologicae lovanienses* 67:105–6.

Porton, G. G.
1988 *Goyim: Gentiles and Israelites in the Mishnah-Tosefta.* Brown Judaic Studies 155. Atlanta: Scholars Press.

Price, S. R. F.
1984 *Rituals and Power: The Imperial Cult and Asia Minor.* Cambridge: Cambridge University Press.

Prigent, P.
1958 "Ce que l'aeil n'a pas vue, 1 Kor 2,9." *Theologische Zeitschrift* 14:416–29.

Prior, M.
1989 *Paul the Letter-Writer.* Journal for the Study of the New Testament: Supplement Series 23. Sheffield: JSOT Press.

Probst, H.
1991 *Paulus und der Brief: Die Rhetorik des antiken Briefes als Form der paulinischen Korintherkorrespondenz (1 Kor 8–10).* Wissenschaftliche Untersuchungen zum Neuen Testament 2/45. Tübingen: Mohr.

Raeder, M.
1955 "Vikariatstaufe in 1 Kor. 15.29?" *Zeitschrift für die neutestamentliche Wissenschaft* 46:258–60.

Räisänen, H.
1983 *Paul and the Law.* Wissenschaftliche Untersuchungen zum Neuen Testament 29. Tübingen: Mohr.

Ramsaran, R. A.
1995 "More Than an Opinion: Paul's Rhetorical Maxim in First Corinthians 7:25–26." *Catholic Biblical Quarterly* 57:531–41.

Ramsay, W. M.
1900 "Historical Commentary on the Epistles to the Corinthians." *Expositor,* 6th series, 1:380–87.
1907 *The Cities of St. Paul: Their Influence on His Life and Thought.* London: Hodder & Stoughton. Reprinted Grand Rapids: Baker, 1960.

Rawson, B.
1974 "Roman Concubinage and Other de Facto Marriages." *Transactions of the American Philological Association* 104:279–305.

Reaume, J. D.
1995 "Another Look at 1 Corinthians 15:29, 'Baptized for the Dead.'" *Bibliotheca Sacra* 152:457–75.

Reiling, J.
1988 "Wisdom and the Spirit: An Exegesis of 1 Corinthians 2,6–16." Pp. 200–211 in *Text and Testimony: Essays in Honor of A. F. J. Klijn.* Edited by T. Baarda. Kampen: Kok.

Rengstorf, K. H.
1967 *Die Auferstehung Jesu: Form, Art und Sinn der urchristlichen Osterbotschaft.* 5th edition. Witten/Ruhr: Luther.

Reumann, J.
1958 "'Stewards of God': Pre-Christian Religious Application of *Oikonomos* in Greek." *Journal of Biblical Literature* 77:339–49.

Richards, E. R.
1991 *The Secretary in the Letters of Paul.* Wissenschaftliche Untersuchungen zum Neuen Testament 2/42. Tübingen: Mohr.

Richardson, P.
1979 *Paul's Ethic of Freedom.* Philadelphia: Westminster.
1979–80 "Pauline Inconsistency: I Corinthians 9:19–23 and Galatians 2:11–14." *New Testament Studies* 26:347–62.
1980 "'I Say, Not the Lord': Personal Opinion, Apostolic Authority, and the Development of Christian Halakah." *Tyndale Bulletin* 31:65–86.
1983 "Judgment in Sexual Matters in 1 Corinthians 6:1–11." *Novum Testamentum* 25:37–58.
1994 "Temples, Altars, and Living from the Gospel (1 Cor. 9.12b–18)." Pp. 89–110 in *Gospel in Paul: Studies on Corinthians, Galatians, and Romans for Richard N. Longenecker.* Edited by L. A. Jervis and P. Richardson. Journal for the Study of the New Testament: Supplement Series 108. Sheffield: Sheffield Academic Press.

Richardson, P., and P. W. Gooch
1978 "Accommodation Ethics." *Tyndale Bulletin* 29:89–142.

Richardson, W.
1986   "Liturgical Order and Glossolalia in
        1 Corinthians 14:26c–33a." *New Tes-
        tament Studies* 32:144–53.

Richter, H.-F.
1996   "Anstössige Freiheit in Korinth: Zur
        Literarkritik der Korintherbriefe."
        Pp. 561–75 in *The Corinthian Corre-
        spondence.* Edited by R. Bieringer.
        Bibliotheca ephemeridum theologi-
        carum lovaniensium 125. Leuven:
        Peeters.

Ridderbos, H.
1975   *Paul: An Outline of His Theology.*
        Translated by J. R. De Witt. Grand
        Rapids: Eerdmans.

Riesenfeld, H.
1970   *The Gospel Tradition.* Translated by
        M. Rowley and R. Kraft. Philadel-
        phia: Fortress.
1978   "Vorbildliches Martyrium: Zur Frage
        der Lesarten in 1 Kor 13:3." Pp. 210–
        14 in *Donum Gentilicum: Festschrift
        for David Daube.* Edited by C. K. Bar-
        rett, E. Bammel, and W. D. Davies.
        Oxford: Oxford University Press.

Riesner, R.
1998   *Paul's Early Period: Chronology, Mis-
        sion Strategy, Theology.* Translated
        by D. Stott. Grand Rapids: Eerd-
        mans.

Rissi, M.
1962   *Die Taufe für die Toten.* Abhandlun-
        gen zur Theologie des Alten und
        Neuen Testaments 42. Zurich/Stutt-
        gart: Zwingli.

Roberts, R. L.
1965   "The Meaning of *Chorizō* and *Douloō*
        in 1 Corinthians 7:10–17." *Restora-
        tion Quarterly* 8:179–84.

Robertson, A., and A. Plummer
1914   *A Critical and Exegetical Commentary
        on the First Epistle of St. Paul to the
        Corinthians.* International Critical
        Commentary. Edinburgh: Clark.

Robertson, A. T.
1934   *A Grammar of the Greek New Testa-
        ment in the Light of Historical Re-
        search.* Nashville: Broadman.

Robinson, J. A. T.
1952   *The Body: A Study in Pauline Theol-
        ogy.* Studies in Biblical Theology 5.
        London: SCM.
1953   "Traces of a Liturgical Sequence in
        1 Cor 16:20–24." *Journal of Theologi-
        cal Studies,* n.s., 4:38–41.

Roetzel, C. J.
1972   *Judgment in the Community: A Study
        of the Relationship between Eschatol-
        ogy and Ecclesiology in Paul.* Leiden:
        Brill.
1998   *Paul: The Man and the Myth.* Colum-
        bia: University of South Carolina
        Press.

Rogers, E. R.
1983   "Ἐποτίσθημεν Again." *New Testa-
        ment Studies* 29:139–42.

Romano, D. G.
1993   "Post-146 B.C. Land Use in Corinth
        and Planning of the Roman Colony."
        Pp. 9–30 in *The Corinthia in the
        Roman Period.* Edited by T. E.
        Gregory. Journal of Roman Archae-
        ology, Supplementary Series 8. Ann
        Arbor, Mich.: Journal of Roman
        Archaeology.

Rordorf, W.
1969   "Marriage in the New Testament and
        in the Early Church." *Journal of Ec-
        clesiastical History* 20:193–210.

Rösch, K.
1932   "'Um der Engel willen' (1 Kor
        11:10)." *Theologie und Glaube*
        24:363–65.

Rosner, B. S.
1991   "Temple and Holiness in 1 Corin-
        thians 5." *Tyndale Bulletin* 42:137–
        45.
1992   "'Οὐχὶ Μᾶλλον Ἐπενθήσατε': Corpo-
        rate Responsibility in 1 Corinthians
        5." *New Testament Studies* 38:470–
        73.
1994   *Paul, Scripture, and Ethics: A Study
        of 1 Corinthians 5–7.* Arbeiten zur
        Geschichte des antiken Judentums
        und des Urchristentums. Leiden:
        Brill. Reprinted Grand Rapids:
        Baker, 1999.
1996   "The Function of Scripture in 1 Cor
        5,13b and 6,16." Pp. 513–18 in *The
        Corinthian Correspondence.* Edited
        by R. Bieringer. Bibliotheca ephe-
        meridum theologicarum lovanien-
        sium 125. Leuven: Peeters.
1998   "Temple Prostitution in 1 Corin-
        thians 6:12–20." *Novum Testamen-
        tum* 60:336–51.

Ross, J. M.
1970–71 "Not above What Is Written: A Note
        on 1 Cor 4:6." *Expository Times*
        82:215–17.

1992 "Floating Words: Their Significance for Textual Criticism." *New Testament Studies* 38:153–56.

Rousselle, A.

1992 "Body Politics in Ancient Rome." Pp. 229–37 in *A History of Women in the West,* vol. 1: *From Ancient Goddesses to Christian Saints.* Edited by G. Duby and M. Perot. Cambridge: Harvard University Press.

Rowe, A.

1990 "Silence and the Christian Women of Corinth." *Communio viatorum* 33:41–73.

Rowland, C. C.

1982 *The Open Heaven: A Study of Apocalyptic in Judaism and Early Christianity.* New York: Crossroad.

Ruef, J.

1977 *Paul's First Letter to Corinth.* Westminster Pelican Commentaries. Philadelphia: Westminster.

Saller, R. P.

1982 *Personal Patronage under the Early Empire.* Cambridge: Cambridge University Press.

Sand, A.

1967 *Der Begriff "Fleisch" in dem paulinischen Hauptbriefen.* Regensburg: Pustet.

Sandelin, K.-G.

1995 "Does Paul Argue against Sacramentalism and Over-Confidence in 1 Cor. 10:1–14?" Pp. 165–82 in *The New Testament and Hellenistic Judaism.* Edited by P. Borgen and S. Giverson. Aarhus: Aarhus University Press.

Sanders, B.

1981 "Imitating Paul: 1 Cor 4:16." *Harvard Theological Review* 74:353–63.

Sanders, E. P.

1983 *Paul, the Law, and the Jewish People.* Philadelphia: Fortress.

Sanders, J. T.

1966 "First Corinthians 13: Its Interpretation since the First World War." *Interpretation* 20:159–87.

Sanders, T. K.

1990 "A New Approach to 1 Corinthians 13.1." *New Testament Studies* 36:614–18.

Sandnes, K. O.

1991 *Paul—One of the Prophets?* Wissenschaftliche Untersuchungen zum Neuen Testament 2/43. Tübingen: Mohr.

1996 "Prophecy—A Sign for Believers (1 Cor 14,20–25)." *Biblica* 77:1–15.

Sänger, D.

1985 "Die dynatoi in 1 Kor 1:26." *Zeitschrift für die neutestamentliche Wissenschaft* 76:285–91.

Savage, T. B.

1996 *Power through Weakness: Paul's Understanding of the Christian Ministry in 2 Corinthians.* Society for New Testament Studies Monograph Series 86. Cambridge: Cambridge University Press.

Saw, I.

1995 *Paul's Rhetoric in 1 Corinthians 15: An Analysis Utilizing the Theories of Classical Rhetoric.* Lewiston, N.Y.: Mellen.

Sawyer, W. T.

1968 "The Problem of Meat Sacrificed to Idols in the Corinthian Church." Th.D. diss., Southern Baptist Theological Seminary.

SB *Kommentar zum Neuen Testament aus Talmud und Midrasch.* By H. L. Strack and P. Billerbeck. 6 vols. Munich: Beck, 1922–61.

Schaefer, M.

1994 "Paulus, 'Fehlgeburt' oder 'unvernünftiges Kind'? Ein Interpretationsvorschlag zu 1 Kor 15,8." *Zeitschrift für die neutestamentliche Wissenschaft* 85:207–17.

Schatzmann, S.

1987 *A Pauline Theology of Charismata.* Peabody, Mass.: Hendrickson.

Schmidt, K. L.

1951 "Nicht über das hinaus, was geschrieben steht! (1. Kor. 4,6)." Pp. 101–9 in *In Memoriam Ernst Lohmeyer.* Edited by W. Schmauch. Stuttgart: Evangelisches Verlag.

Schmithals, W.

1969 *The Office of Apostle in the Early Church.* Translated by J. E. Steely. Nashville: Abingdon.

1971 *Gnosticism in Corinth: An Investigation of the Letters to the Corinthians.* 2d edition. Nashville: Abingdon.

1973 "Die Korintherbriefe als Briefsammlung." *Zeitschrift für die neutestamentliche Wissenschaft* 64:263–88.

Schmitt-Pantel, P.

1990 "Collective Activities and the Political in the Greek City." Pp. 199–213 in *The Greek City from Homer to Alexander*. Edited by O. Murray and S. R. F. Price. Oxford: Clarendon.

Schneider, S.

1996 "Glaubensmängel in Korinth: Eine neue Deutung der 'Schwachen, Kranken, Schlafenden' in 1 Kor 11:30." *Filogia Neotestamentaria* 9:3–19.

Schnelle, U.

1983 "1 Kor. 6:14—eine nachpaulinische Glosse." *Novum Testamentum* 25:217–19.

Schniewind, J.

1952 "Die Leugner der Auferstehung in Korinth." Pp. 110–39 in *Nachgelassene Reden und Aufsätze*. Edited by E. Kähler. Berlin: Töpelmann.

Schrage, W.

1964 "Die Stellung zur Welt bei Paulus, Epiktet und in der Apokalyptik." *Zeitschrift für Theologie und Kirche* 61:125–54.

1974 "Leid, Kreuz und Eschaton: Die Peristasenkataloge als Merkmale paulinischer theologia crucis und Eschatologie." *Evangelische Theologie* 34:141–75.

1976 "Zur Frontestellung der paulinischen Ehebewertung in 1 Kor 7,1–7." *Zeitschrift für die neutestamentliche Wissenschaft* 67:214–34.

1982 *The Ethics of the New Testament*. Translated by D. E. Green. Philadelphia: Fortress.

1991 *Der erste Brief an die Korinther (1 Kor 1,1–6,11)*. Evangelisch-katholischer Kommentar zum Neuen Testament 7/1. Zurich: Benziger/Neukirchen-Vluyn: Neukirchener Verlag.

1995 *Der erste Brief an die Korinther (1 Kor 6,12–11,16)*. Evangelisch-katholischer Kommentar zum Neuen Testament 7/2. Zurich: Benziger/Neukirchen-Vluyn: Neukirchener Verlag.

1996 "Einige Hauptprobleme der Diskussion des Herrenmahls im 1. Korintherbrief." Pp. 191–98 in *The Corinthian Correspondence*. Edited by R. Bieringer. Bibliotheca ephemeridum theologicarum lovaniensium 125. Leuven: Peeters.

1999 *Der erste Brief an die Korinther (1 Kor 11,17–14,40)*. Evangelisch-katholischer Kommentar zum Neuen Testament 7/3. Zurich: Benziger/Neukirchen-Vluyn: Neukirchener Verlag.

2001 *Der erste Brief an die Korinther (1 Kor 15,1–16,24)*. Evangelisch-katholischer Kommentar zum Neuen Testament 7/4. Zurich: Benziger/Neukirchen-Vluyn: Neukirchener Verlag.

Schreckenberg, H.

1964 *Ananke: Untersuchungen zur Geschichte des Wortgebrauchs*. Zetemata 36. Munich: Beck.

Schreiner, J.

1974 "Jeremia 9,22.23 als Hintergrund des paulinischen 'Sich-Rühmens.'" Pp. 530–42 in *Neues Testament und Kirche: Für Rudolf Schnackenburg*. Edited by J. Gnilka. Freiburg: Herder.

Schreiner, T. R.

1998 *Romans*. Baker Exegetical Commentary on the New Testament 6. Grand Rapids: Baker.

Schubert, P.

1939 *Form and Function of Pauline Thanksgiving*. Beihefte zur Zeitschrift für die neutestamentliche Wissenschaft 20. Berlin: Töpelman.

Schürer, E.

1986 *The History of the Jewish People in the Age of Jesus Christ*, vol. 3.1. Revised and edited by G. Vermes, F. Millar, and M. Goodman. Edinburgh: Clark.

Schüssler Fiorenza, E.

1984 *In Memory of Her: A Feminist Theological Reconstruction of Christian Origins*. New York: Crossroad.

Schütz, J. H.

1975 *Paul and the Anatomy of Apostolic Authority*. Society for New Testament Studies Monograph Series 26. Cambridge: Cambridge University Press.

Schwarz, G.

1979 "Ἐξουσίαν Ἔχειν ἐπὶ τῆς Κεφαλῆς? (1. Korinther 11:10)." *Zeitschrift für die neutestamentliche Wissenschaft* 70:249.

Schweitzer, A.

1931 *The Mysticism of the Apostle Paul*. Translated by W. Montgomery. London: Black. Reprinted New York: Seabury, 1968.

Schweizer, E.
1959 "The Service of Worship: An Exposition of 1 Corinthians 14." *Interpretation* 13:400–408.
1970 *The Good News according to Mark.* Richmond: John Knox.

Scroggs, R.
1967–68 "Paul: Σοφός and Πνευματικός." *New Testament Studies* 14:33–55.
1972 "Paul and the Eschatological Woman." *Journal of the American Academy of Religion* 40:283–303.
1983 *The New Testament and Homosexuality: Contextual Background for Contemporary Debate.* Philadelphia: Fortress.
1993 "Paul and the Eschatological Woman." Pp. 69–95 in *The Text and the Times: New Testament Essays for Today.* Minneapolis: Fortress.

Seaford, R.
1984 "1 Corinthians xiii.12." *Journal of Theological Studies,* n.s., 35:117–20.

Seboldt, R. H. A.
1959 "Spiritual Marriage in the Early Church: A Suggested Interpretation of 1 Cor. 7:36–38." *Concordia Theological Monthly* 30:103–19, 176–89.

Sebothema, W. A.
1990 "Κοινωνία in 1 Corinthians 10:16." *Neotestamentica* 24:63–69.

Seesemann, H.
1933 *Der Begriff Koinōnia im Neuen Testament.* Beihefte zur Zeitschrift für die neutestamentliche Wissenschaft 14. Berlin: de Gruyter.

Selby, G. S.
1997 "Paul, the Seer: Rhetorical Persona in 1 Corinthians 2.1–16." Pp. 351–73 in *The Rhetorical Analysis of Scripture: Essays from the 1995 London Conference.* Edited by S. E. Porter and T. H. Olbricht. Journal for the Study of the New Testament: Supplement Series 146. Sheffield: Sheffield Academic Press.

Sellin, G.
1982 "Das 'Geheimnis' der Weisheit und das Rätsel der 'Christuspartei' (zu 1 Kor 1–4)." *Zeitschrift für die neutestamentliche Wissenschaft* 73:69–96.
1986 *Der Streit um die Auferstehung der Toten.* Forschungen zur Religion und Literatur des Alten und Neuen Testaments 138. Göttingen: Vandenhoeck & Ruprecht.
1987 "Hauptprobleme der ersten Korintherbriefes." Pp. 2940–3044 in *Aufstieg und Niedergang der römischen Welt,* part 2: *Principat,* vol. 25.4: *Religion.* Edited by W. Haase and H. Temporini. Berlin/New York: de Gruyter.
1991 "1 Korinther 5–6 und der 'Vorbrief' nach Korinth: Indizien für eine Mehrsichtigkeit von Kommunikationsakten im ersten Korintherbrief." *New Testament Studies* 37:535–58.

Senft, C.
1979 *La première épître de saint Paul aux Corinthiens.* Commentaire du Nouveau Testament. Neuchâtel: Delachaux & Niestlé.

Sevenster, J. N.
1961 *Paul and Seneca.* Supplements to Novum Testamentum 4. Leiden: Brill.

Shanor, J.
1988 "Paul as Master Builder: Construction Terms in First Corinthians." *New Testament Studies* 34:461–71.

Shelton, J.-A.
1998 *As the Romans Did: A Sourcebook in Roman Social History.* 2d edition. Oxford: Oxford University Press.

Shillington, V. G.
1998 "Atonement Texture in 1 Corinthians 5.5." *Journal for the Study of the New Testament* 71:29–50.

Sider, R. J.
1974–75 "The Pauline Conception of the Resurrection Body in I Corinthians xv.35–54." *New Testament Studies* 21:428–39.
1977 "St. Paul's Understanding of the Nature and Significance of the Resurrection in 1 Cor 15:1–19." *Novum Testamentum* 19:124–41.

SIG *Sylloge inscriptionum graecarum.* Edited by W. Dittenberger. 3d edition. 4 vols. Leipzig: Hirzelium, 1915–24.

Sigal, P.
1983 "Another Note to 1 Corinthians 10.16." *New Testament Studies* 29:134–39.

Sigountos, J. G.
1994 "The Genre of 1 Corinthians 13." *New Testament Studies* 40:246–60.

Sigountos, J. G., and M. Shank

1983   "Public Roles for Women in the Pauline Church: A Reappraisal of the Evidence." *Journal of the Evangelical Theological Society* 26:283–95.

Simon, M.

1979   "From Greek *Hairesis* to Christian Heresy." Pp. 101–16 in *Early Christian Literature and the Classical Intellectual Tradition: In Honorem Robert M. Grant.* Edited by W. Schoedel and R. L. Wilken. Théologie Historique 53. Paris: Beauchesne.

Sloan, R. B.

1983   "Resurrection in 1 Corinthians." *Southwestern Journal of Theology* 26:69–91.

Smit, J. F. M.

1991   "The Genre of 1 Corinthians 13 in the Light of Classical Rhetoric." *Novum Testamentum* 33:193–216.

1993a   "Argument and Genre of 1 Corinthians 12–14." Pp. 211–30 in *Rhetoric and the New Testament: Essays from the 1992 Heidelberg Conference.* Edited by S. E. Porter and T. H. Olbricht. Journal for the Study of the New Testament: Supplement Series 90. Sheffield: Sheffield Academic Press.

1993b   "Two Puzzles: 1 Corinthians 12.31 and 13.3: A Rhetorical Solution." *New Testament Studies* 39:246–64.

1994   "Tongues and Prophecy: Deciphering 1 Cor 14,22." *Biblica* 75:175–90.

1996   "1 Corinthians 8,1–6, a Rhetorical Partitio: A Contribution to the Coherence of 1 Cor 8,1–11,1." Pp. 577–91 in *The Corinthian Correspondence.* Edited by R. Bieringer. Bibliotheca ephemeridum theologicarum lovaniensium 125. Leuven: Peeters.

1997a   "'Do Not Be Idolaters': Paul's Rhetoric in First Corinthians 10:1–22." *Novum Testamentum* 39:40–53.

1997b   "The Rhetorical Disposition of First Corinthians 8:7–9:27." *Catholic Biblical Quarterly* 59:476–91.

Smith, D.

1920   *The Life and Letters of St. Paul.* New York: Harper & Row.

Smith, M. D.

1996   "Ancient Bisexuality and the Interpretation of Romans 1:26–27." *Journal of the American Academy of Religion* 64:223–56.

Snyder, G. F.

1976–77   "The *Tobspruch* in the New Testament." *New Testament Studies* 23:117–20.

1992   *First Corinthians: A Faith Community Commentary.* Atlanta: Mercer University Press.

Soards, M. L.

1999   *1 Corinthians.* New International Biblical Commentary. Peabody, Mass.: Hendrickson.

Soden, H. F. von

1951   "Sakrament und Ethik bei Paulus: Zur Frage der literarischen und theologischen Einheitlichkeit von 1 Kor. 8–10." Pp. 239–75 in *Urchristentum und Geschichte: Gesammelte Aufsätze und Vorträge,* vol. 1. Edited by H. von Campenhausen. Tübingen: Mohr.

Söding, T.

1994   "Starke und Schwache: Der Götzenopferstreit in 1 Kor. 8–10 als Paradigma paulinischer Ethik." *Zeitschrift für die neutestamentliche Wissenschaft* 85:69–92.

South, J. T.

1992   *Disciplinary Practices in Pauline Texts.* Lewiston, N.Y.: Mellen.

1993   "A Critique of the 'Curse/Death' Interpretation of 1 Corinthians 5.1–8." *New Testament Studies* 39:539–61.

Sparks, H. F. D.

1976   "1 Kor 2:9 a Quotation from the Coptic Testament of Jacob?" *Zeitschrift für die neutestamentliche Wissenschaft* 67:269–76.

Spawforth, A. J. S.

1994   "Corinth, Argos, and the Imperial Cult: *Pseudo-Julian, Letters 198.*" *Hesperia* 63:211–32.

Spicq, C.

1938   "La conscience dans le NT." *Revue biblique* 47:50–80.

1965   *Agape in the New Testament,* vol. 2. Translated by M. A. McNamara and M. H. Richter. St. Louis/London: Herder.

Spörlein, B.

1971   *Die Leugnung der Auferstehung: Eine historisch-kritische Untersuchung zu 1 Kor. 15.* Biblische Untersuchungen 7. Regensburg: Pustet.

Staab, K.

1963   "1 Kor 15,29 im Lichte der Exegese der griechischen Kirche." Pp. 443–50 in *Studiorum Paulinorum Congressus Internationalis Catholicus 1961*, vol. 1. Analecta biblica 17. Rome: Pontifical Biblical Institute Press.

Stagg, E., and F. Stagg
1978   *Woman in the World of Jesus.* Philadelphia: Westminster.

Stagg, F.
1973   *The Holy Spirit Today.* Nashville: Broadman.

Stambaugh, J. E.
1978   "The Functions of Roman Temples." Pp. 554–608 in *Aufstieg und Niedergang der römischen Welt*, part 2: *Principat*, vol. 16.1: *Religion*. Edited by W. Haase. Berlin: de Gruyter.

Stambaugh, J. E., and D. L. Balch
1986   *The New Testament in Its Social Environment.* Philadelphia: Westminster.

Standaert, B.
1983   "Analyse rhetorique des chap. 12 à 14 de 1 Cor." Pp. 23–50 in *Charisma und Agape (1 Ko 12–14)*. Edited by L. De Lorenzi. Monographic Series of "Benedictina": Biblical-Ecumenical Section 7. Rome: St. Paul's Abbey.

Stanley, C. D.
1992   *Paul and the Language of Scripture: Citation Techniques in the Pauline Epistles and Contemporary Literature.* Society for New Testament Studies Monograph Series 69. Cambridge: Cambridge University Press.

Stanley, D. M.
1959   "Become Imitators of Me." *Biblica* 40:859–79.

Stansbury, H. A.
1990   "Corinthian Honor, Corinthian Conflict: A Social History of Early Roman Corinth and Its Pauline Community." Ph.D. diss., University of California, Irvine.

Stegemann, W.
1993   "Paul and the Sexual Mentality of His World." *Biblical Theology Bulletin* 23:161–68.

Stein, A.
1968   "Wo trugen die korinthischen Christen ihre Rechtshandel aus?" *Zeitschrift für die neutestamentliche Wissenschaft* 59:86–90.

Stendahl, K.
1976   *Paul among Jews and Gentiles.* Philadelphia: Fortress.

1977   "Glossolalia and the Charismatic Movement." Pp. 122–31 in *God's Christ and His People: Studies in Honour of Nils Alstrup Dahl*. Edited by J. Jervell and W. A. Meeks. Oslo: Universitetsforlaget.

Steward-Sykes, A.
1996   "Ancient Editors and Copyists and Modern Partition Theories: The Case of the Corinthian Correspondence." *Journal for the Study of the New Testament* 61:53–64.

Stowers, S. K.
1981   "A 'Debate' over Freedom: 1 Cor 6:12–20." Pp. 59–71 in *Christian Teaching: Studies in Honor of LeMoine G. Lewis*. Edited by E. Ferguson. Abilene, Tex.: Abilene Christian University Press.

1984   "Social Status, Public Speaking, and Private Teaching: The Circumstances of Paul's Preaching Activity." *Novum Testamentum* 26:59–82.

1990   "Paul on the Use and Abuse of Reason." Pp. 253–86 in *Greeks, Romans, and Christians*. Edited by D. L. Balch, E. Ferguson, and W. A. Meeks. Minneapolis: Fortress.

Strugnell, J.
1974   "A Plea for Conjectural Emendation in the New Testament, with a Coda on 1 Cor 4:6." *Catholic Biblical Quarterly* 36:543–58.

Styler, G. M.
1973   "The Basis of Obligation in Paul's Christology and Ethics." Pp. 175–87 in *Christ and Spirit in the New Testament: Studies in Honour of Charles Francis Digby Moule*. Edited by B. Lindars and S. S. Smalley. Cambridge: Cambridge University Press.

Surburg, M. P.
2000   "Structural and Lexical Features in 1 Corinthians 11:27–32." *Concordia Journal* 26:200–217.

Sweet, J. P. M.
1966–67 "A Sign for Unbelievers: Paul's Attitude to Glossolalia." *New Testament Studies* 13:240–57.

Talbert, C. H.
1987   *Reading Corinthians: A Literary and Theological Commentary on 1 and 2 Corinthians.* New York: Crossroad.

Tcherikover, V.
1961   *Hellenistic Civilization and the Jews.* Philadelphia: Jewish Publication Society.

TDNT   *Theological Dictionary of the New Testament.* Edited by G. Kittel and G. Friedrich. Translated and edited by G. W. Bromiley. 10 vols. Grand Rapids: Eerdmans, 1964–76.

Temkin, O.
1956   *Soranus' Gynecology.* Baltimore: Johns Hopkins University Press.

Terry, R. B.
1995   *A Discourse Analysis of First Corinthians.* Dallas: Summer Institute of Linguistics/Arlington: University of Texas Press.

Thackeray, H. St. J.
1900   *The Relation of St. Paul to Contemporary Jewish Thought.* London/New York: Macmillan.

Theissen, G.
1982   *The Social Setting of Pauline Christianity: Essays on Corinth.* Translated by J. H. Schütz. Philadelphia: Fortress.

1987   *Psychological Aspects of Pauline Theology.* Translated by J. P. Galvin. Edinburgh: Clark.

Thielman, F.
1992   "The Coherence of Paul's View of the Law: The Evidence of First Corinthians." *New Testament Studies* 38:235–53.

Thiselton, A. C.
1977–78   "Realized Eschatology at Corinth." *New Testament Studies* 24:510–26.

1979   "The Interpretation of Tongues: A New Suggestion in Light of Greek Usage in Philo and Josephus." *Journal of Theological Studies,* n.s., 30:15–36.

2000   *The First Epistle to the Corinthians: A Commentary on the Greek Text.* New International Greek Testament Commentary. Grand Rapids: Eerdmans/Carlisle: Paternoster.

Thomas, R. L.
1999   *Understanding Spiritual Gifts: A Verse by Verse Study of 1 Cor 12–14.* Revised edition. Grand Rapids: Kregel.

Thompson, C. L.
1988   "Hairstyles, Head-Coverings, and St. Paul: Portraits from Roman Corinth." *Biblical Archaeologist* 51:99–115.

Thompson, K. C.
1964   "1 Corinthians 15,29 and Baptism for the Dead." Vol. 2 / pp. 649–57 in *Studia Evangelica.* Edited by F. L. Cross. Texte und Untersuchungen 87. Berlin: Akademie.

Thompson, M. B.
1991   *Clothed with Christ: The Example and Teaching of Jesus in Romans 12.1–15.13.* Journal for the Study of the New Testament: Supplement Series 59. Sheffield: JSOT Press.

Thrall, M. E.
1962   *Greek Particles in the New Testament: Linguistic and Exegetical Studies.* Grand Rapids: Eerdmans.

1965   *I and II Corinthians.* Cambridge: Cambridge University Press.

1967–68   "The Pauline Use of Συνείδησις." *New Testament Studies* 14:118–25.

1994   *A Critical and Exegetical Commentary on the Second Epistle to the Corinthians,* vol. 1. International Critical Commentary. Edinburgh: Clark.

Thurén, L.
2001   "'By Means of Hyperbole' (1 Cor 12:31b)." Pp. 97–113 in *Paul and Pathos.* Edited by J. L. Sumney. Symposium Series 16. Atlanta: Society of Biblical Literature.

Titus, E. L.
1959   "Did Paul Write 1 Corinthians 13?" *Journal of Bible and Religion* 27:299–302.

TLNT   *Theological Lexicon of the New Testament.* By C. Spicq. Translated and edited by J. D. Ernest. 3 vols. Peabody, Mass.: Hendrickson, 1994.

Tomlinson, F. A.
1997   "Sacral Manumission Formulae and Romans 6." Ph.D. diss., Southern Baptist Theological Seminary.

Tomson, P. J.
1990   *Paul and the Jewish Law: Halakha in the Letters of the Apostle to the Gentiles.* Compendia rerum iudaicarum ad Novum Testamentum 3/1. Assen/Maastricht: Van Gorcum/Minneapolis: Fortress.

1996   "Paul's Jewish Background in View of His Law Teaching in 1 Cor 7." Pp. 251–70 in *Paul and the Mosaic Law.* Edited by J. D. G. Dunn. Wissenschaftliche Untersuchungen zum Neuen Testament 89. Tübingen: Mohr.

Trebilco, P. R.
1991   *Jewish Communities in Asia Minor.* Society for New Testament Studies Monograph Series 96. Cambridge: Cambridge University Press.

Treggiari, S.
1969   *Roman Freedmen during the Late Republic.* Oxford: Clarendon.

Trench, R. C.
1880   *Synonyms of the New Testament.* London: Macmillan.

Trobisch, D.
1989   *Die Entstehung der Paulusbriefsammlung: Studien zu den Anfängen christlicher Publizistik.* Göttingen: Vandenhoeck & Ruprecht.

Trompf, G. W.
1980   "On Attitudes toward Women and Paul and Paulinist Literature: 1 Corinthians 11:3–16 and Its Context." *Catholic Biblical Quarterly* 42:196–215.

Trummer, P.
1975   "Die Chance der Freiheit: Zur Interpretation des Μᾶλλον Χρῆσαι in 1 Kor 7,21." *Biblica* 56:344–68.

Tuckett, C. M.
1996   "The Corinthians Who Say 'There Is No Resurrection of the Dead' (1 Cor 15,12)." Pp. 247–75 in *The Corinthian Correspondence.* Edited by R. Bieringer. Bibliotheca ephemeridum theologicarum lovaniensium 125. Leuven: Peeters.
2000   "Paul, Scripture, and Ethics: Some Reflections." *New Testament Studies* 46:403–24.

Turner, N.
1965   *Grammatical Insights into the New Testament.* Edinburgh: Clark.

Turner, P. D. M.
1997   "Biblical Texts Relevant to Homosexual Orientation and Practice: Notes on Philology and Interpretation." *Christian Scholar's Review* 26:435–45.

Tyler, R. L.
1998   "First Corinthians 4:6 and Hellenistic Pedagogy." *Catholic Biblical Quarterly* 60:97–103.

UBS⁴   *The Greek New Testament.* 4th revised edition. Edited by B. Aland, K. Aland, J. Karavidopoulos, C. M. Martini, and B. M. Metzger. Stuttgart: Deutsche Bibelgesellschaft/United Bible Societies, 1993.

Unnik, W. C. van
1959   "*Dominus Vobiscum:* The Background of a Liturgical Formula." Pp. 270–305 in *New Testament Essays: Studies in Memory of Thomas Walter Manson, 1893–1958.* Edited by A. J. B. Higgins. Manchester: Manchester University Press.
1973   "Jesus: Anathema or Kyrios (1 Cor. 12:3)." Pp. 113–26 in *Christ and Spirit in the New Testament: Studies in Honour of Charles Francis Digby Moule.* Edited by B. Lindars and S. S. Smalley. Cambridge: Cambridge University Press.
1993   "The Meaning of 1 Corinthians 12:31." *Novum Testamentum* 35:142–59.

Urbach, E. E.
1959   "The Rabbinical Laws of Idolatry in the Second and Third Centuries in the Light of the Archaeological and Historical Fact." *Israel Exploration Journal* 9:149–65.

Verbrugge, V. D.
1992   *Paul's Style of Church Leadership Illustrated by His Instructions to the Corinthians on the Collection.* San Francisco: Mellen Research University Press.

Verheyden, J.
1996   "Origen on the Origin of 1 Cor 2,9." Pp. 491–511 in *The Corinthian Correspondence.* Edited by R. Bieringer. Bibliotheca ephemeridum theologicarum lovaniensium 125. Leuven: Peeters.

Veyne, P.
1987   *A History of Private Life,* vol. 1: *From Pagan Rome to Byzantium.* Translated by A. Goldhammer. Cambridge: Harvard University Press.

Vischer, L.
1955   *Die Auslegungsgeschichte von 1. Korinther 6,1–11.* Beiträge zur Geschichte der neutestamentlichen Exegese 1. Tübingen: Mohr.

Vollenweider, S.
1984   *Freiheit als neue Schöpfung: Eine Untersuchung zur Eleutheria bei Paulus und in seiner Umwelt.* Forschungen zur Religion und Literatur des Alten und Neuen Testaments 147. Göttingen: Vandenhoeck & Ruprecht.

Vos, J. S.
1995 "Der Μετασχηματισμός in 1 Kor 4,6." *Zeitschrift für die neutestamentliche Wissenschaft* 86:154–72.
1996 "Die Argumentation des Paulus in 1 Kor 1,10–3,4." Pp. 87–119 in *The Corinthian Correspondence*. Edited by R. Bieringer. Bibliotheca ephemeridum theologicarum lovaniensium 125. Leuven: Peeters.

Wagner, J. R.
1998 "'Not beyond the Things Which Are Written': A Call to Boast Only in the Lord (1 Cor 4.6)." *New Testament Studies* 44:279–87.

Walker, W. O.
1975 "1 Corinthians 11:2–16 and Paul's View regarding Women." *Journal of Biblical Literature* 94:94–110.
1992 "1 Cor. 2:6–16: A Non-Pauline Interpolation?" *Journal for the Study of the New Testament* 47:75–94.

Wallace, D. B.
1996 *Greek Grammar beyond the Basics: An Exegetical Syntax of the New Testament*. Grand Rapids: Zondervan.

Wallis, P.
1950 "Ein neuer Auslegungsgeschichte der Stelle I. Kor. 4,6." *Theologische Literaturzeitung* 75:506–8.

Wallis, W. B.
1975 "The Problem of an Intermediate Kingdom in 1 Corinthians 15:20–28." *Journal of the Evangelical Theological Society* 18:229–42.

Walter, N.
1978–79 "Christusglaube und Heidnische Religiosität in Paulinischen Gemeinden." *New Testament Studies* 25:422–42.

Walters, J.
1993 *Ethnic Issues in Paul's Letter to the Romans: Changing Self-Definitions in Earliest Roman Christianity*. Valley Forge, Pa.: Trinity.

Ward, R. B.
1990 "Musonius and Paul on Marriage." *New Testament Studies* 36:281–89.

Watson, D. F.
1989 "1 Corinthians 10:23–11:1 in the Light of Greco-Roman Rhetoric: The Role of Rhetorical Questions." *Journal of Biblical Literature* 108:301–18.

Watson, F.
2000 "The Authority of the Voice: A Theological Reading of 1 Cor 11.2–16." *New Testament Studies* 46:520–36.

Watson, N.
1983 "'. . . To Make Us Rely Not on Ourselves but God Who Raises the Dead': 2 Cor. 1,9b as the Heart of Paul's Theology." Pp. 384–98 in *Die Mitte des Neuen Testaments*. Edited by U. Luz and H. Weder. Göttingen: Vandenhoeck & Ruprecht.
1992 *The First Epistle to the Corinthians*. Epworth Commentaries. London: Epworth.

Watson, P. A.
1995 *Ancient Stepmothers: Myth, Misogyny, and Reality*. Supplements to Mnemosyne 143. Leiden: Brill.

Weber, H.-R.
1979 *The Cross: Tradition and Interpretation*. Translated by E. Jessett. Grand Rapids: Eerdmans.

Wedderburn, A. J. M.
1973 "Ἐν τῇ Σοφίᾳ τοῦ Θεοῦ—1 Kor 1:21." *Zeitschrift für die neutestamentliche Wissenschaft* 64:132–34.
1975 "Romans 8:26—Toward a Theology of Glossolalia?" *Scottish Journal of Theology* 28:369–77.
1981 "The Problem of the Denial of the Resurrection in I Corinthians xv." *Novum Testamentum* 23:229–41.
1987 *Baptism and Resurrection: Studies in Pauline Theology against Its Graeco-Roman Background*. Wissenschaftliche Untersuchungen zum Neuen Testament 44. Tübingen: Mohr.

Weima, J. A. D.
1990 "The Function of the Law in Relation to Sin: An Evaluation of the View of H. Räisänen." *Novum Testamentum* 32:219–35.
1994 *Neglected Endings: The Significance of the Pauline Letter Closings*. Journal for the Study of the New Testament: Supplement Series 101. Sheffield: Sheffield Academic Press.

Weiss, J.
1910 *Der erste Korintherbrief*. Kritisch-exegetischer Kommentar über das Neue Testament. 9th edition. Göttingen: Vandenhoeck & Ruprecht.

Welborn, L. L.
1997 *Politics and Rhetoric in the Corinthian Epistles*. Macon, Ga.: Mercer University Press.

Wendland, H.-D.
1972 *Die Briefe an die Korinther*. 13th edition. Das Neue Testament Deutsch 7.

Göttingen: Vandenhoeck & Ruprecht.

Wengst, K.

1987   *Pax Romana and the Peace of Jesus Christ.* Translated by J. Bowden. London: SCM.

Wenham, D.

1985   "Paul's Use of the Jesus Tradition: Three Samples." Pp. 7–37 in *The Jesus Tradition outside the Gospels.* Gospel Perspectives 5. Edited by D. Wenham. Sheffield: JSOT Press.

Wenham, G. J.

1990–91   "The Old Testament Attitude to Homosexuality." *Expository Times* 102:359–63.

White, J. L.

1986   *Light from Ancient Letters.* Foundations and Facets: New Testament. Philadelphia: Fortress.

White, J. R.

1997   "Baptized on Account of the Dead": The Meaning of 1 Corinthians 15:29 in Its Context." *Journal of Biblical Literature* 116:487–99.

Whiteley, D. E. H.

1974   *The Theology of St. Paul.* 2d edition. Oxford: Blackwell.

Widmann, M.

1979   "1 Kor 2:6–16: Ein Einspruch gegen Paulus." *Zeitschrift für die neutestamentliche Wissenschaft* 70:44–53.

Wilckens, U.

1959   *Weisheit und Torheit: Eine exegetisch-religionsgeschichtliche Untersuchung zu 1 Kor 1 und 2.* Beiträge zur historischen Theologie 26. Tübingen: Mohr.

1963   "Der Ursprung der Überlieferung der Erscheinungen des Auferstandenen." Pp. 56–95 in *Dogma und Denkstrukturen.* Edited by W. Joest and W. Pannenberg. Göttingen: Vandenhoeck & Ruprecht.

1968   "The Tradition-History of the Resurrection of Jesus." Pp. 51–76 in *The Significance of the Message of the Resurrection for Faith in Jesus Christ.* By W. Marxsen et al. Edited by C. F. D. Moule. Studies in Biblical Theology, 2d series, 8. London: SCM.

1980   "Das Kreuz Christi als die Tiefe der Weisheit Gottes." Pp. 43–81 in *Paolo a una chiesa divisa (1 Co 1–4).* Edited by L. De Lorenzi. Monographic Series of "Benedictina": Biblical-Ecumenical Section 5. Rome: St. Paul's Abbey.

Wili, H.-U.

1978   "Das Privilegium Paulinum (1 Kor 7,15f)—Pauli eigene Lebenserinnerung? (Rechtshistorische Anmerkungen zu einer neueren Hypothese)." *Biblische Zeitschrift* 22:100–108.

Wilk, F.

1998   *Die Bedeutung des Jesajabuches für Paulus.* Forschung zur Religion und Literatur des Alten und Neuen Testaments 179. Göttingen: Vandenhoeck & Ruprecht.

Williams, C. K., II

1987   "The Refounding of Corinth: Some Roman Religious Attitudes." Pp. 26–37 in *Roman Architecture in the Greek World.* Society of Antiquaries of London Occasional Papers, n.s., 10. Edited by S. Macready and F. H. Thompson. London: Society of Antiquaries of London.

1989   "A Re-evaluation of Temple E and the West End of the Forum of Corinth." Pp. 156–62 in *The Greek Renaissance in the Roman Empire.* Edited by S. Walker and A. Cameron. Bulletin of the Institute of Classical Studies Supplement 55. London: University of London Press.

1993   "Roman Corinth as a Commercial Center." Pp. 31–46 in *The Corinthia in the Roman Period.* Edited by T. E. Gregory. Journal of Roman Archaeology, Supplementary Series 8. Ann Arbor, Mich.: Journal of Roman Archaeology.

Williams, R.

1997   "Lifting the Veil: A Social-Science Interpretation of 1 Corinthians 11:2–16." *Consensus* 23:53–60.

Willis, W. L.

1985a   "An Apostolic Apologia? The Form and Function of 1 Corinthians 9." *Journal for the Study of the New Testament* 24:33–48.

1985b   *Idol Meat in Corinth: The Pauline Argument in 1 Corinthians 8 and 10.* Society of Biblical Literature Dissertation Series 68. Chico, Calif.: Scholars Press.

1989   "The 'Mind of Christ' in 1 Corinthians 2,16." *Biblica* 70:110–22.

1991 "Corinthusne deletus ist?" *Biblische Zeitschrift* 35:233–41.

Wilson, J. H.
1968 "The Corinthians Who Say There Is No Resurrection of the Dead." *Zeitschrift für die neutestamentliche Wissenschaft* 59:90–107.

Wilson, R. M.
1972–73 "How Gnostic Were the Corinthians?" *New Testament Studies* 19:65–74.

1982 "Gnosis at Corinth." Pp. 102–14 in *Paul and Paulinism: Essays in Honour of C. K. Barrett.* Edited by M. D. Hooker and S. G. Wilson. London: SPCK.

Wimbush, V. L.
1987 *Paul the Worldly Ascetic: Response to the World and Self-Understanding according to 1 Corinthians 7.* Macon, Ga.: Mercer University Press.

Winandy, J.
1992 "Un curieux *casus pendens:* 1 Corinthiens 11.10 et son interprétation." *New Testament Studies* 38:621–29.

Winer, G. B.
1877 *A Treatise on the Grammar of New Testament Greek.* 2d edition. Translated by W. F. Moulton. Edinburgh: Clark.

Wink, W.
1984 *Naming the Powers: The Language of Power in the New Testament.* Philadelphia: Fortress.

1986 *Unmasking the Powers: The Invisible Forces That Determine Human Existence.* Philadelphia: Fortress.

1992 *Engaging the Powers: Discernment and Resistance in a World of Domination.* Minneapolis: Fortress.

Winter, B. W.
1978 "The Lord's Supper at Corinth: An Alternative Reconstruction." *Reformed Theological Review* 37:73–82.

1989 "Secular and Christian Response to Corinthian Famines." *Tyndale Bulletin* 40:86–106.

1990 "Theological and Ethical Responses to Religious Pluralism—1 Corinthians 8–10." *Tyndale Bulletin* 41:209–26.

1991a "Civil Litigation in Secular Corinth and the Church: The Forensic Background to 1 Corinthians 6.1–8." *New Testament Studies* 37:559–72.

1991b "In Public and in Private: Early Christians and Religious Pluralism." Pp. 112–34 in *One God, One Lord: Christianity in a World of Religious Pluralism.* Edited by A. D. Clarke and B. W. Winter. Cambridge: Tyndale House.

1994 *Seek the Welfare of the City: Christians as Benefactors and Citizens.* Grand Rapids: Eerdmans/Carlisle: Paternoster.

1995 "The Achaean Federal Imperial Cult, II: The Corinthian Church." *Tyndale Bulletin* 46:169–78.

1997a "1 Corinthians 7:6–7: A Caveat and a Framework for 'the Sayings' in 7:8–24." *Tyndale Bulletin* 49:57–65.

1997b "Gluttony and Immorality at Elitist Banquets: The Background to 1 Corinthians 6:12–20." *Jian Dao* 7:77–90.

1997c "Homosexual Terminology in 1 Corinthians 6:9: The Roman Context and the Greek Loan-Word." Pp. 275–79 in *Interpreting the Bible: Essays in Honour of David Wright.* Edited by A. N. R. Lane. Leicester: Inter-Varsity.

1997d *Philo and Paul among the Sophists.* Society for New Testament Studies Monograph Series 96. Cambridge: Cambridge University Press.

1997e "'The Seasons' of This Life and Eschatology in 1 Corinthians 7:29–31." Pp. 323–34 in *"The Reader Must Understand": Eschatology in Bible and Theology.* Edited by K. E. Brower and M. W. Elliott. Leicester: Apollos.

1998 "Puberty or Passion? The Referent of Ὑπέρακμος in 1 Corinthians 7:36." *Tyndale Bulletin* 49:71–89.

1999 "Gallio's Ruling on the Legal Status of Early Christianity." *Tyndale Bulletin* 50:213–24.

2001 *After Paul Left Corinth: The Influence of Secular Ethics and Social Change.* Grand Rapids: Eerdmans.

Wire, A. C.
1990 *The Corinthian Women Prophets: A Reconstruction through Paul's Rhetoric.* Minneapolis: Fortress.

Wischmeyer, O.
1981 *Der höchste Weg: Das 13. Kapitel des 1. Korintherbriefes.* Studium zum Neuen Testament 13. Gütersloh: Mohn.

Wiseman, J.
1979 "Corinth and Rome, I: 228 B.C.–A.D. 267." Pp. 438–548 in *Aufstieg und Niedergang der römischen Welt*, part 2: *Principat*, vol. 7.1: *Politische Geschichte*. Edited by H. Temporini. Berlin: de Gruyter.

Wisse, F. W.
1990 "Traditional Limits to Redactional Theory in the Pauline Corpus." Pp. 167–78 in *Gospel Origins and Christian Beginnings*. Edited by J. E. Goehring et al. Sonoma, Calif.: Polebridge.

Witherington, B., III
1993 "Not So Idle Thoughts about *Eidolothuton*." *Tyndale Bulletin* 44:237–54.

1995 *Conflict and Community in Corinth: A Socio-Rhetorical Commentary on 1 and 2 Corinthians*. Grand Rapids: Eerdmans.

Wolbert, W.
1981 *Ethische Argumentation und Paränese in 1 Kor 7*. Moraltheogische Studien, Systematische Abteilung 8. Düsseldorf: Patmos.

Wolff, C.
1996 *Der erste Brief des Paulus an die Korinther*. Theologischer Handkommentar zum Neuen Testament 7. Berlin: Evangelische Verlagsanstalt.

Wright, D. F.
1984 "Homosexuals or Prostitutes? The Meaning of Ἀρσενοκοῖται (1 Cor. 6:9; 1 Tim. 1:10)." *Vigiliae christianae* 38:125–53.

1987 "Translating Ἀρσενοκοῖται (1 Cor. 6:9; 1 Tim. 1:10)." *Vigiliae christianae* 41:396–98.

1989 "Homosexuality: The Relevance of the Bible." *Evangelical Quarterly* 61:291–300.

Wright, N. T.
1986 *Colossians and Philemon*. Tyndale New Testament Commentaries. Grand Rapids: Eerdmans.

1992 *The Climax of the Covenant: Christ and Law in Pauline Theology*. Minneapolis: Fortress.

Wright, R. J.
1984 "Boswell on Homosexuality: A Case Undemonstrated." *Anglican Theological Review Supplement* 66:79–94.

Wuellner, W.
1970 "Haggadic Homily Genre in 1 Cor 1–3." *Journal of Biblical Literature* 89:199–204.

1973 "The Sociological Implications of I Corinthians 1:26–28 Reconsidered." Pp. 666–73 in *Studia Evangelica*, vol. 6. Edited by E. A. Livingstone. Texte und Untersuchungen 112. Berlin: Akademie Verlag.

1979 "Greek Rhetoric and Pauline Argumentation." Pp. 177–88 in *Early Christian Literature and the Classical Intellectual Tradition: In Honorem Robert M. Grant*. Edited by W. R. Schoedel and R. L. Wilken. Paris: Beauchesne.

Yarbrough, O. L.
1985 *Not like the Gentiles: Marriage Rules in the Letters of Paul*. Society of Biblical Literature Dissertation Series 80. Atlanta: Scholars Press.

Yeo, K.-K.
1994 "The Rhetorical Hermeneutic of 1 Corinthians 8 and Chinese Ancestor Worship." *Biblical Interpretation* 3:294–311.

1995 *Rhetorical Interaction in 1 Corinthians 8 and 10: A Formal Analysis with Preliminary Suggestions for a Chinese, Cross-Cultural Hermeneutic*. Biblical Interpretation Series 9. Leiden: Brill.

Yinger, K. I.
1999 *Paul, Judaism, and Judgment according to Deeds*. Society of New Testament Studies Monograph Series 105. Cambridge: Cambridge University Press.

Yorke, G. L. O. R.
1991 *The Church as the Body of Christ in the Pauline Corpus: A Re-examination*. Lanham, Md.: University Press of America.

Young, F. M.
1982 "Notes on the Corinthian Correspondence." Pp. 563–66 in *Studia Evangelica*, vol. 7. Edited by E. A. Livingstone. Texte und Untersuchungen 126. Berlin: Akademie Verlag.

Young, N. H.
1987 "*Paidagōgos:* The Social Setting of a Pauline Metaphor." *Novum Testamentum* 29:150–76.

Zaas, P.
1984   "'Cast Out the Evil Man from Your Midst.'" *Journal of Biblical Literature* 103:259–61.

1988   "Catalogues and Context: 1 Corinthians 5 and 6." *New Testament Studies* 34:622–29.

Zanker, P.
1990   *The Power of Images in the Age of Augustus.* Translated by A. Shapiro. Ann Arbor: University of Michigan Press.

1998   *Pompeii: Public and Private Life.* Translated by D. L. Schneider. Revealing Antiquity 11. Cambridge: Harvard University Press.

Zerbe, G.
1993   *Non-retaliation in Early Jewish and New Testament Texts.* Journal for the Study of the Pseudepigrapha: Supplement Series 13. Sheffield: Sheffield Academic Press.

Zerhusen, R.
1997   "The Problem of Tongues in 1 Corinthians: A Reexamination." *Biblical Theology Bulletin* 27:139–52.

Zerwick, M.
1963   *Biblical Greek.* Translated by J. Smith. Rome: Pontifical Biblical Institute Press.

Zuntz, G.
1953   *The Text of the Epistles: A Disquisition upon the Corpus Paulinum.* Schweich Lectures 1946. London: Oxford University Press for the British Academy.

Index of Subjects

Index of Authors

Index of Greek Words

Index of Scripture and Other Ancient Writings

Old Testament

New Testament

Romans

Old Testament Apocrypha

Old Testament Pseudepigrapha

New Testament Apocrypha

Nag Hammadi

Rabbinic Writings

Qumran / Dead Sea Scrolls

Papyri

P. Cairo Zenon

59562 line 12 541

P. Oxyrhynchus

1766 [18] 9
2190 42

Tebtunis Papyrus

104.24 668

Josephus

Against Apion

1.21 §160 532
2.25 §199 213 n. 31,
    259
2.38 §§273–75 213
    n. 31

Jewish Antiquities

1.7.2 §163 254 n. 13
1.13.1 §223 187
3.1.6 §26 455
3.10.6 §252 758
4.6.11 §§145–49 403
    n. 2
4.8.1 §206 238 n. 27
4.8.21 §233 409 n. 12

4.8.23 §245 238 n. 27
4.8.23 §257 254 n. 13
7.14.5 §351 554
8.2.9–3.9 §§58–98 114
    n. 12
8.14.3 §379 321
10.2.1 §§28–29 69
    n. 14
10.4.1 §50 372
11.6.10 §253 321
11.8.6 §340 554
12.3.3 §138 554
12.5.1 §241 316
13.3.4 §75 207 n. 18
13.4.5 §104 554
13.5.5 §148 554
14.10.17 §235 201

14.10.18 §237 414
15.7.10 §259 281
18.3.4 §§65–80 461
18.3.5 §81 755
18.5.4 §136 281
20.7.2 §§141–43 281
20.8.6 §§167–70 69
    n. 14
20.9.1 §200 408 n. 10
20.11.2 §267 758

Jewish War

1.9.1 §183 708
1.17.4 §§331–32 69
    n. 14
2.8.13 §§160–61 259

2.14.7 §297 554
2.15.1 §813 520
3.2.4 §32 554
5.3.5 §§384–85 613
6.5.2 §285 69 n. 14
6.5.2 §295 69 n. 14
6.5.3 §299 758
7.7.4 §250 335 n. 25
7.8.7 §344 700
7.8.7 §355 615

Philo

**Allegorical
Interpretation**

1.12 §31 736
1.13 §34 139 n. 16
1.15 §48 114
2.19 §80 744
2.21 §86 456 n. 13
2.25 §§54–59 744
2.26 §108 439
3.15 §§46–48 367 n. 9
3.31 §96 377
3.33 §§100–101 624
3.47–53 §§138–59 241
3.53 §§155–56 441
3.56 §163 139 n. 16
3.71 §§201–2 439

**Every Good Per-
son Is Free**

3 §§21–22 425 n. 5
6 §§35–36 426 n. 8
9 §59 228, 386 n. 13
9 §§60–61 425 n. 5

Hypothetica

7.1 213 n. 31
11.17 333 n. 21

On Abraham

17 §77 687
17 §80 687
26–27 §§135–37 213
    n. 31
29 §153 624
44 §261 139 n. 16

On Dreams

1.3 §16 410
1.8 §43 744
1.16 §93 409
1.22 §140 527
1.23 §149 238 n. 28
2 §§10–11 107
2.2 §8 115
2.2 §9 214, 441
2.31 §206 624 n. 17

On Drunkenness

4 §§14–15 348
6–8 §§20–29 348
24 §95 348
29 §112 456 n. 13
38 §154 722

**On Flight and
Finding**

34 §190 377
38 §213 624 n. 17

On Husbandry

2 §§8–9 107
26 §§114–21 439

On Joseph

9 §§42–43 241
16 §87 624
24 §144 300
34 §201 539

**On Noah's Work
as a Planter**

9 §39 660

**On Rewards and
Punishments**

1 §6 442
20 §125 516

On Sobriety

2–3 §§9–10 107
13 §§62–64 238 n. 28

**On the Change of
Names**

12 §§81–82 439

On the Cherubim

2.29 §98 238 n. 28
2.31 §106 238 n. 28

**On the Contem-
plative Life**

1 §§3–9 372
2 §12 262 n. 28
6 §§50–52 530
7 §§59–62 214
8 §68 262 n. 28
9 §69 73
9 §78 624 n. 17
10 §75 89

On the Creation

24 §76 624 n. 17

On the Decalogue

12–17 §§52–82 372
21 §105 624 n. 17
24 §121 211
24 §122 274

Classical Writers

Church Fathers